Police Law

Thirteenth Edition

Richard Card LLB LLM HON LLD FRSA
Emeritus Professor of Law
De Montfort University, Leicester

The late **Jack English** OBE QPM MA
Ex-Assistant Chief Constable, Northumbria Police
Ex-Director of the Central Planning, Instructor Training and
Police Promotion Examinations Unit
Ex-Chief Examiner to the Police Promotions Examinations Board

OXFORD
UNIVERSITY PRESS

OXFORD
UNIVERSITY PRESS

Great Clarendon Street, Oxford, OX2 6DP,
United Kingdom

Oxford University Press is a department of the University of Oxford.
It furthers the University's objective of excellence in research, scholarship,
and education by publishing worldwide. Oxford is a registered trade mark of
Oxford University Press in the UK and in certain other countries

Thirteenth Edition published in 2013

Impression: 1

British Library Cataloguing in Publication Data

Data available

ISBN 978-0-19-966550-1

Printed in Great Britain by
Clays Ltd, St Ives plc

Preface

When Jack English and I wrote the first edition of this book nearly thirty years ago, our aims were to cover comprehensively, and in terms easily understood by those who had received no legal training, those areas of the law and legal procedure with which all police officers are concerned. The material included in *Police Law* and its appendices has been prepared in a way which recognises the ordinary needs of police officers, of those in legal advice agencies, and of members of the public who wish to refer to a legal text. Now in its 13th edition, the work remains true to its original aims.

This is the second edition of this book which I have prepared on my own following Jack English's untimely death in January 2010.

Jack was born in 1931. He became a police cadet at the age of 16, and subsequently became a constable in the Northumberland constabulary. The early 60s saw his first period in the area of police training. Jack spent two years in Yorkshire training new recruits, something that would become his passion and vocation. He rose steadily through the ranks, achieving the highest-ever mark in his Inspectors' promotion examination, and was promoted into the training department in 1965. 1968 saw another promotion, this time to Chief Inspector at Whitley Bay, the place at which he would settle and stay for the remainder of his life. In 1971 Jack was seconded to the regional training centre at Dishforth in North Yorkshire and on completion of that secondment he took up the position of head of the Examinations Unit at Ryton on Dunsmore, near Coventry, which included promotion to Superintendent. A few years later the unit moved to Harrogate and the newly-formed Central Planning Unit was established with Jack as its head. Following regular success at the Central Planning Unit, Jack finally reached the rank of Assistant Chief Constable and in 1984 he was awarded the Queen's Police Medal for services to the police. Jack retired from the police service in 1985, in which year he was awarded the OBE. Jack enjoyed 57 happy years of marriage to Jeanne and was a strong family man.

For 25 years Jack and I worked closely together producing new editions of *Police Law*. Jack's imprint can be found throughout this edition. He was an utterly reliable colleague in every respect. Always entertaining, he was a joy to work with.

The law is stated as it was on 1 August 2012. The previous edition, published in 2011, has been extensively amended in consequence of the large amount of subsequent legislation. I have indicated within the text, for example by using the word 'prospectively', those provisions which are not yet in force.

As a result of the large amount of legislation which continues to be made, the increasing size of *Police Law* edition by edition has become a concern. A further increase in size is not sustainable. It has been necessary to exclude from the body of the book, and to place in on-line appendices, some topics previously contained in chapters which reader feedback has shown are of less importance to most police officers. In this respect, I would like to thank a range of readers at all levels and with varying interests for their advice about the contents of this book. In particular, a significant debt is owed to the Chief Constable of Norfolk, Mr Phil Gormley, for finding the time to give me the benefit of his considerable wisdom and experience. The topics, revised as necessary, which now appear as appendices to *Police Law* on the companion website are:

Appendix 1 Public Service Vehicles
Appendix 2 Goods Vehicles
Appendix 3 Aliens
Appendix 4 Animals, Birds and Plants
Appendix 5 Game, Deer and Fish.

The companion website also contains regular updates to the chapters contained in the book. It can be found at <http://www.oup.com/>.

1 August 2012   Richard Card

Contents

Table of Primary Legislation

The European Convention on Human Rights is tabled under Sch 1 of the Human Rights Act 1998

Table of Secondary Legislation

European Secondary Legislation

DIRECTIVES

Abbreviations

AA 1967	Abortion Act 1967
ACPO	Association of Chief Police Officers
ADBA	American Dog Breeders' Association
AETR	European agreement concerning the work of crews of vehicles engaged in international transport
AHA 1981	Animal Health Act 1981
Arrest Code	PACE Code G: Code of Practice for the Statutory Power to Arrest by Police Officers
A-sBA 2003	Anti-social Behaviour Act 2003
ASBO	Anti-social behaviour order
Audio Recording Code	PACE Code E: Code of Practice on Audio Recording Interviews with Suspects
AWA 2006	Animal Welfare Act 2006
BA 1976	Bail Act 1976
BA 2010	Bribery Act 2010
BNA 1981	British Nationality Act 1981
BTP	British Transport Police
CA 2003	Communications Act 2003
CAA 1981	Criminal Attempts Act 1981
CAA 1984	Child Abduction Act 1984
CA(YP)A 1997	Confiscation of Alcohol (Young Persons) Act 1997
CBL	children's barred list
CDA 1971	Criminal Damage Act 1971
CDA 1998	Crime and Disorder Act 1998
CDHR	Community Drivers' Hours Regulations (EC) 561/2006
C(IC)A 2003	Crime (International Co-operation) Act 2003
CJA 1967	Criminal Justice Act 1967
CJA 1988	Criminal Justice Act 1988
CJA 2003	Criminal Justice Act 2003
C&JA 2009	Coroners and Justice Act 2009
CJIA 2008	Criminal Justice and Immigration Act 2008
CJPA 2001	Criminal Justice and Police Act 2001
CJPOA 1994	Criminal Justice and Public Order Act 1994
CLA 1967	Criminal Law Act 1967
CLA 1977	Criminal Law Act 1977
CMA 1990	Computer Misuse Act 1990
CMCHA 2007	Corporate Manslaughter and Corporate Homicide Act 2007
CNEA 2005	Clean Neighbourhoods and Environment Act 2005
CPC	Certificate of Professional Competence
CPIA 1996	Criminal Procedure and Investigations Act 1996

CPM	Commissioner of Police of the Metropolis
CPS	Crown Prosecution Service
CRER	Community Recording Equipment Regulations (EEC) 5821/85
CSO	community support officer
C-TA 2008	Counter-Terrorism Act 2008
CYPA 1933	Children and Young Persons Act 1933
CYPA 1969	Children and Young Persons Act 1969
CYP(HP)A 1955	Children and Young Persons (Harmful Publications) Act 1955
DA 1991	Deer Act 1991
DA 2005	Drugs Act 2005
DBS	Disclosure and Barring Service
DDA 1991	Dangerous Dogs Act 1991
D(FL)A 1996	Dogs (Fouling of Land) Act 1996
Detention Code	PACE Code C: Code of Practice for the Detention, Treatment and Questioning of Persons by Police Officers
DPA 1998	Data Protection Act 1998
DPP	Director of Public Prosecutions
DSCC	Defence Solicitor Call Centre
DVLA	Driver and Vehicle Licensing Agency
EA	Environment Agency
EA 1875	Explosives Act 1875
EC	European Community
ECE	European Community Equipment
ECHR	European Convention on Human Rights
EEA	European Economic Area
ELPB	Elected Local Policing Body
EPA 1990	Environmental Protection Act 1990
ESA 1883	Explosive Substances Act 1883
EU	European Union
FA 2006	Fraud Act 2006
FCA 1981	Forgery and Counterfeiting Act 1981
FiA 1968	Firearms Act 1968
FLA 1996	Family Law Act 1996
F(O)A 1991	Football (Offences) Act 1991
FSA 1989	Football Spectators Act 1989
GCHQ	Government Communications Headquarters
GV(LO)A 1995	Goods Vehicles (Licensing of Operators) Act 1995
HA 1980	Highways Act 1980
HA 2004	Hunting Act 2004
HRA 1998	Human Rights Act 1998
IA 1971	Immigration Act 1971
IAA 1999	Immigration and Asylum Act 1999
IDA 2010	Identity Documents Act 2010
ID(C)A 1981	Indecent Displays (Control) Act 1981

Identification Code	PACE Code D: the Code of Practice for the Identification of Persons by Police Officers
IPCC	Independent Police Complaints Commission
KA 1997	Knives Act 1997
LA 1872	Licensing Act 1872
LA 2003	Licensing Act 2003
LGV	large goods vehicle
MCA 1980	Magistrates' Courts Act 1980
MDA 1861	Malicious Damage Act 1861
MDA 1971	Misuse of Drugs Act 1971
MOPC	Mayor's Office for Policing and Crime
MV(DL)R 1999	Motor Vehicles (Driving Licences) Regulations 1999
MV(IR)R 2011	Motor Vehicles (Insurance Requirements) Regulations 2011
MV(IR)(I, R and D)R 2011	Motor Vehicles (Insurance Requirements) (Immobilisation, Removal and Disposal) Regulations 2011
NHS	National Health Service
NPIA	National Policing Improvement Agency
NSPCC	National Society for Prevention of Cruelty to Children
OAPA 1861	Offences against the Person Act 1861
OPA 1959	Obscene Publications Act 1959
PA 1871	Pedlars Act 1871
PA 1911	Perjury Act 1911
PA 1996	Police Act 1996
PACE	Police and Criminal Evidence Act 1984
PATR 2008	Police Appeals Tribunal Rules 2008
PBA 1992	Protection of Badgers Act 1992
PCA 1953	Prevention of Crime Act 1953
PCA 1978	Protection of Children Act 1978
PCA 2002	Proceeds of Crime Act 2002
P&CA 2009	Policing and Crime Act 2009
PCC	Police and Crime Commissioner
P(C)R 2008	Police (Conduct) Regulations 2008
P(CM)R 2012	Police (Complaints and Misconduct) Regulations 2012
PCV	passenger-carrying vehicle
PEA 1977	Protection from Eviction Act 1977
PFA 2012	Protection of Freedoms Act 2012
PHA 1997	Protection from Harassment Act 1997
PII	public interest immunity
PNC	Police National Computer
POA 1936	Public Order Act 1936
POA 1986	Public Order Act 1986
P(P)R 2008	Police (Performance) Regulations 2008
PPVA 1981	Public Passenger Vehicles Act 1981
PRA 2002	Police Reform Act 2002

PRSRA 2011	Police Reform and Social Responsibility Act 2011
RD(A)A 1978	Refuse Disposal (Amenity) Act 1978
RDVR 1986	Removal and Disposal of Vehicles Regulations 1986
RIPA 2000	Regulation of Investigatory Powers Act 2000
RNLI	Royal National Lifeboat Institution
RSA 2006	Road Safety Act 2006
RSPB	Royal Society for the Protection of Birds
RTA 1988	Road Traffic Act 1988
RTOA 1988	Road Traffic Offenders Act 1988
RTRA 1984	Road Traffic Regulation Act 1984
RTSA 2003	Railway and Transport Safety Act 2003
RV(C&U)R 1986	Road Vehicles (Construction and Use) Regulations 1986
RV(DRM)R 2001	Road Vehicles (Display of Registration Marks) Regulations 2001
RV(R&L)R 2002	Road Vehicles (Registration and Licensing) Regulations 2002
SCA 2007	Serious Crime Act 2007
SE(CA)A 1985	Sporting Events (Control of Alcohol etc) Act 1985
Searching of Premises Code	PACE Code B: Code of Practice for Search of Premises by Police Officers and the Seizure of Property Found by Police on Persons or Premises
SI	statutory instrument
SOA 1956	Sexual Offences Act 1956
SOA 2003	Sexual Offences Act 2003
SOCA	Serious Organised Crime Agency
SOCPA 2005	Serious Organised Crime and Police Act 2005
SOPO	sexual offences prevention order
StOA 1959	Street Offences Act 1959
Stop and Search Code	PACE Code A: Code of Practice for the Exercise by Police Officers of Statutory Powers of Stop and Search
SVGA 2006	Safeguarding of Vulnerable Groups Act 2006
TA 1968	Theft Act 1968
TA 1978	Theft Act 1978
TA 1985	Transport Act 1985
TA 2000	Terrorism Act 2000
TA 2006	Terrorism Act 2006
TfL	Transport for London
TMA 2004	Traffic Management Act 2004
TPIMA 2011	Terrorism Prevention and Investigation Measures Act 2011
TULR(C)A 1992	Trade Union and Labour Relations (Consolidation) Act 1992
TWA 1992	Transport and Works Act 1992
UKBA	UK Border Agency
UKBA 2007	UK Borders Act 2007
VA 1824	Vagrancy Act 1824
V(C)A 2001	Vehicles (Crime) Act 2001

VCRA 2006	Violent Crime Reduction Act 2006
VERA 1994	Vehicle Excise and Registration Act 1994
Visual Recording Code	PACE Code F: Code of Practice on Visual Recording with Sound of Interviews with Suspects
WM(P)A 1996	Wild Mammals (Protection) Act 1996
YJCEA 1999	Youth Justice and Criminal Evidence Act 1999

CHAPTER 1
General Principles

This book deals with those branches of the law of England and Wales of particular relevance to police officers.

SOURCES OF ENGLISH LAW

There are two principal sources of English law: common law and legislation.

Common law

Common law is that part of English law which is not the result of legislation, ie it is the law which has been developed by the decisions and rulings of the judges.

In modern times legislation has played a preponderant part in the branches of the law dealt with in this book. As will be seen, very few offences are now governed and defined by the common law (ie the rulings of the judges). Moreover, the judges do not now have the capacity to extend the criminal law, by creating new offences or widening existing ones. Examples of common law offences are murder, manslaughter, and conspiracy to defraud.

Although most offences are now governed by legislation, most of the general principles of criminal liability are derived from the common law. For example, most of the general defences to crime and most of the rules concerning accomplices to crime are to be found in the rulings of the judges, and not in legislation.

The common law has been built up on the basis of the doctrine of precedent, under which the reported decisions of certain courts are more than just authoritative legal statements whose effect is persuasive, since they can be binding (ie must be applied) in subsequent cases. In the context of courts with criminal jurisdiction, it is the following which have binding effect: decisions of the Supreme Court (and of the House of Lords, which was the supreme court of appeal until 2009), the Court of Appeal (Criminal Division), a divisional court of the Queen's Bench Division of the High Court, and a judge sitting in the Administrative Court of that Division. Each of these courts has a criminal jurisdiction limited to appeals. Whether or not one of their decisions is binding in a particular case depends on the relative standing of the court which made the decision and the court in which that decision is subsequently cited. The reason is that the doctrine of precedent depends on the principle that the courts form a hierarchy which, in the case of courts with criminal jurisdiction, is in the following descending order: *Supreme Court (House of Lords), Court of Appeal (Criminal Division), divisional court, judge in the Administrative Court,* Crown Court and magistrates' courts. The basic rule is that a decision by one of the courts italicised is binding on those courts below that in which it was given and, save in exceptional circumstances, will be followed by a court of equal status. A decision which is not binding under the above rules is nevertheless of persuasive authority, and may be cited to a court in a subsequent case.

Legislation

Statute

'Statute' has traditionally meant an Act of the UK Parliament. Except for the very few common law offences, all serious offences are defined by statute, as are many minor offences.

Since 2011, the National Assembly for Wales has had power to enact its own Acts, which only apply in relation to Wales, on any matter within its legislative competence, which is limited to 20 devolved areas. The devolved areas do not include criminal justice and the impact of the Acts of the Assembly on Police Law will be marginal.

Subordinate legislation

A statute may give power to some body, such as the Queen in Council, a minister, or a local authority or other public body, to make Orders in Council, regulations, or by-laws (respectively), and prescribe for their breach. This method of creating criminal offences is of increasing importance in the present day, although it is not new. A good example is the power of the Secretary of State for Transport under the Road Traffic Act 1988 to make regulations concerning the construction and use of motor vehicles. Prosecutions for breach of these regulations are regularly instituted. Subordinate legislation made at central government level is normally required to be made by way of 'statutory instrument' (SI).

European Union law

This has a limited impact on our criminal law, although that impact is growing. In order for breach of EU legislation to be an offence in English law, an Act of Parliament or subordinate legislation to this effect is required. An example of a piece of European legislation which is of major importance to our law is the Community Drivers' Hours Regulation (EC) 561/2006 (which is concerned with the driving hours of drivers of goods vehicles); breach of the Regulation is an offence by statute.

European Convention on Human Rights and the Human Rights Act 1998

The European Convention on Human Rights (ECHR), taken together with the Human Rights Act 1998 (HRA 1998), is of major importance. The provisions of the Act referred to below have great influence over the interpretation and development of the law by the judges and over new legislation.

Impact of HRA 1998

There has for a considerable time been a right of individual petition to the European Court of Human Rights in Strasbourg against a breach by the UK of a right under the ECHR. The importance of HRA 1998 is that it 'brings home' the Convention rights set out in its Sch 1 (the Convention rights). Essentially what this means is that remedies are available in the courts of England and Wales in respect of breach of the Convention rights. This has not been achieved by the incorporation of the Convention rights into English law. Unlike the directly effective legislation of the European Union (EU), the Convention does not automatically take priority over English law. Our courts have not been given a power to disapply an inconsistent Act of Parliament (primary legislation), but the effect of the main provisions in the Act comes close to permitting disapplication. On the other hand, subordinate legislation incompatible with a Convention right can sometimes be quashed.

The Convention rights The Convention rights specified in HRA 1998, Sch 1 include:

(a) the right to life (ECHR, art 2);
(b) the right not to be deprived of liberty save in specified cases, eg after conviction or lawful arrest, and in accordance with a procedure prescribed by law (ECHR, art 5);
(c) the right to a fair trial (including the presumption of innocence) (ECHR, art 6);
(d) the right to respect for private and family life (ECHR, art 8);
(e) the right to freedom of thought, conscience and religion (ECHR, art 9);
(f) the freedom of expression (ECHR, art 10); and
(g) the freedom of assembly and association (ECHR, art 11).

The exercise of the last four rights or freedoms mentioned may be restricted by the law on specified grounds if this is necessary in a democratic society (for example in the interests of national security, for the prevention of disorder or crime, for the protection of health or morals or for the protection of the rights and freedoms of others).

By ECHR, art 14 the enjoyment of the Convention rights must be secured without discrimination on any ground such as sex, race, opinion, national or social origin or other status.

The implications of HRA 1998 are dealt with at appropriate points in this book.

Statutory interpretation Acts of Parliament and other legislation must, *so far as possible*, be read and given effect to in a way which is compatible with the Convention rights. The courts, where necessary, will prefer a strained but possible interpretation which is consistent with Convention rights to one more consistent with the statutory words themselves. In the rare case where the mismatch between Convention rights and the statute is so great that a court cannot interpret the statute so as to be compatible, the court may make a declaration of incompatibility.

Declaration of incompatibility If a court is unable to interpret a statutory provision compatibly with a Convention right, it will have to proceed as normal. The issue of incompatibility can be raised on appeal. As far as criminal cases are concerned, if satisfied that a provision of primary legislation (Act of Parliament) is incompatible with a Convention right, a judge of the Administrative Court, a divisional court, the Court of Appeal or the Supreme Court may then make a declaration of incompatibility. The court may also make such a declaration in respect of a provision of other legislation which is so incompatible if satisfied that (disregarding the possibility of revocation) the primary legislation prevents removal of that incompatibility.

If a declaration of incompatibility is made, the government and Parliament are not required to take remedial action. There is a fast-track route for doing so via a ministerial order.

Unlawful acts It is unlawful for a 'public authority', a term which includes a police officer, to act in a way incompatible with a Convention right, unless:

(a) as a result of one or more provisions of primary legislation, the authority could not have acted differently; or
(b) in the case of one or more provisions of, or made under, primary legislation which cannot be read or given effect in a way which is compatible with the Convention rights, the authority was acting so as to give effect to or enforce those provisions.

This provides some protection for police officers who act in accordance with the law as it stands at the moment in question.

A person who is a victim of such an unlawful act, but not anyone else (such as a civil liberties group), may bring civil legal proceedings against a public authority in respect of any act by that authority. A court may grant such relief or remedy (including compensatory damages) or make an order as it considers appropriate within the terms of HRA 1998. A chief constable, for example, has been held vicariously liable for breaching a person's rights to life and to family life, when one of his officers failed to respond to the intimidation of a prosecution witness and to protect him, which led to that person's death.

GENERAL PRINCIPLES OF CRIMINAL LIABILITY

Criminal liability

There are two elements of criminal liability:

(a) the outward conduct which must always be proved against the defendant (hereafter 'D') (which is customarily known as the actus reus, 'the legally blameworthy act'); and

(b) the state of mind which, apart from in exceptional offences, it must be proved that D had at the time of the relevant conduct (customarily known as the mens rea, the 'legally blameworthy state of mind').

Of course, the definition of these two things varies from offence to offence, but if the relevant conduct and state of mind can be proved by the prosecution D is guilty unless he can rely successfully on a defence.

Actus reus

It would be wrong to think that proof of the relevant conduct required for an offence is limited to proof of an act on the part of D. There are two reasons.

First, some offences can be committed (and, indeed, some can only be committed) by a failure to do a particular act on the part of a person who was under a legal duty to do that act; an example of such an offence is that of failing to provide a specimen of breath for analysis, without reasonable excuse, when required to do so under the Road Traffic Act 1988, s 7. It should also be noted that there are some offences whose definitions require neither an act nor an omission but simply the existence of a state of affairs on the part of D; an example is the offence of being found drunk in a public place, contrary to the Licensing Act 1872, s 12.

The second reason why more than an act on D's part must be proved is that rarely, if ever, is a mere act (or omission or state of affairs) sufficient for criminal liability for a substantive offence. The definitions of offences often specify surrounding circumstances, such as time and place, which are essential to render the act, etc criminal. Sometimes the definition requires a consequence to result from the act or omission, such as the consequence in murder cases that another human being dies unlawfully. The need to prove that a requisite consequence resulted from D's act or omission is known as the requirement of causation. The legal rules about causation are dealt with on pp 715–16 in relation to homicide offences, but the principles described there are also generally applicable to the other offences in this book with a causation requirement. The specified circumstances and/or consequences of an offence are part of its actus reus.

Mens rea

Mens rea is not concerned with whether D had an evil mind or knowledge of the wrongfulness of the act. D's ignorance of the criminal law is no defence, nor generally is the fact that D did not personally regard his conduct as immoral or know that it was so regarded by the bulk of society.

The expression mens rea refers to the state of mind expressly or impliedly required by the definition of the offence charged. This varies from offence to offence, but typical instances are intention, recklessness, knowledge and belief.

Intention

A number of offences require D to have acted with a particular intention: in murder D must have acted with intent unlawfully to kill, or cause grievous bodily harm to, another person; in theft D must have dishonestly appropriated another's property with intent permanently to deprive him of it. Generally speaking, 'intention' refers to a state of mind in relation to a potential consequence of one's act. In some crimes, that consequence must actually result in order for there to be criminal liability; in others, such as theft, it is not necessary that the intended consequence should occur.

In law, a person 'intends' a consequence of his conduct if he has decided to bring it about, in so far as it lies within his power, no matter whether he desires that consequence or not, ie if achieving that consequence is his aim or purpose. A person who has not decided to bring about a particular consequence may nevertheless be found by a jury or magistrates' court to have intended that consequence if it is proved that it was virtually certain to result from his conduct and he foresaw that it was virtually certain to result.

Recklessness

In some offences 'recklessness', either as to the consequence required for the actus reus, or as to a requisite circumstance of it or as to some other risk, suffices for criminal liability as an alternative to some other mental state such as intention or knowledge.

A person acts recklessly with respect to:

(a) a circumstance when he is aware of a risk that it exists, or will exist;
(b) a consequence when he is aware of a risk that it will occur,

and it is, in the circumstances known to him, unreasonable to take the risk.

Transferred malice

Provided that D intends the specified consequence to occur, or (where recklessness suffices) is reckless as to that consequence occurring, it is irrelevant that the actual object of that consequence is not the person or property whom D intends to harm, or is reckless as to harming. Thus, if D fires a gun intending to kill X, it is irrelevant that the person killed is Y. D will have intended to kill another human being, and will therefore have acted with mens rea for murder. This is called the doctrine of transferred malice.

Knowledge

Many offences require 'knowledge' as to the material circumstances (ie the circumstances by virtue of which an act, omission, or state of affairs is criminal). Generally speaking, where 'knowledge' is required as to a circumstance it suffices that D actually knew of the existence of the circumstance or was wilfully blind as to it (ie D realised the risk that it might exist but deliberately refrained from making inquiries).

Belief

In some offences 'belief' as to the material circumstances is required. A person believes that a circumstance exists if he is virtually certain that it does.

Statutory expressions

In some statutes the mens rea requirement, in whole or part, is denoted by adverbs such as 'wilfully', 'maliciously', or 'dishonestly'. These terms have acquired special meanings in law; see further pp 663, 681, and 945.

Effect of inadvertence or mistake

If D lacks the requisite intention, recklessness or other state of mind because he did not think about the matter in issue or made a mistake which prevented him having that state of mind, D is not guilty of the offence, however unreasonable his inadvertence or mistake. Of course, the more unreasonable an allegation of inadvertence or mistake is, the less likely it is that the allegation will be accepted by the jury or magistrates.

Proof of a state of mind

In proving whether D had a requisite state of mind, regard must be had:

(a) to the statements of D; and
(b) to the conduct and circumstances of D, and the presence of any motive, since these *may* give rise to the inference that he had the necessary state of mind.

Certain acts are known to be likely to produce certain consequences which are frequently spoken of as the 'natural and probable' consequences of those acts. The Criminal Justice Act 1967, s 8 provides that a court or jury in determining whether a person has committed an offence:

(a) is *not bound* in law to infer that he intended or foresaw a result of his actions by reason only of its being a natural and probable consequence of those actions, but
(b) must decide whether he did intend or foresee that result by reference to all the evidence, drawing such inferences from the evidence *as appear proper* in the circumstances.

Strict liability

In the case of some offences, the courts have held that a person can be convicted of a particular offence despite having no type of mens rea as to a particular element of the actus reus (or sometimes even though he had no type of mens rea as to any element of the actus reus). These offences are known as offences of 'strict liability'. Most strict liability offences are minor in nature, but this is not always so; for example, a person can be convicted of the offence of raping a girl under 13 despite the fact that he did not know that she was under 13 and reasonably believed that she was over that age.

The overwhelming majority of strict liability offences are statutory offences. Clearly, an offence is not one of strict liability if the statutory definition expressly uses a word such as 'intentionally', 'recklessly' or 'knowingly'. The fact that a statutory definition does not use any word importing the concept of mens rea does not necessarily mean that the offence is one of strict liability; it depends on whether or not the courts are prepared to imply a requirement of mens rea into the definition. The basic rule is that, where a statute is silent on the point, it is presumed that Parliament intended a requirement to prove mens rea (so that the offence is not one of strict liability), unless this is rebutted by clear evidence that Parliament intended the contrary. Such evidence includes the wording of the definition of the offence and of other offences in the statute, the subject matter of the offence, its aim, and the maximum punishment. Thus, if other offences in the statute contain a word like 'knowingly' and/or if the offence in question concerns something which is not 'truly criminal' and only punishable with a fine, the presumption that it is required that mens rea must be proved is liable to be rebutted. By way of example, many offences in the Road Traffic Acts have been interpreted as being of strict liability.

JUSTIFICATIONS

An offence is not committed if D has a legal justification such as the use of reasonable force in the prevention of crime, effecting a lawful arrest, self-defence or defence of property (see Chapter 23) which renders the conduct lawful. Police officers are often empowered to do something which would otherwise be an offence. Such powers are another example of a legal justification.

GENERAL DEFENCES

Infancy

A child under 10 is irrebuttably presumed not to be guilty of an offence.

Insanity

Everyone is presumed sane until the contrary is proved. The mere fact that a person is medically insane is no defence, but a person proved to be legally insane has a defence. The test of insanity for the purposes of legal responsibility is provided by the *M'Naghten Rules*, which comprise three elements which must be proved by D (unless it is the prosecution which alleges insanity). At the time of the conduct in question:

(a) *D must have been suffering from a 'disease of the mind'*, ie an impairment of the mental faculties of reason, memory and understanding due to a disease (whether organic or functional, and whether permanent or transient) as opposed to some external factor like a blow on the head;

(b) *D must have been suffering a 'defect of reason' due to disease of the mind*, ie a deprivation of reasoning power (as opposed to momentary confusion or absent-mindedness); and

(c) *as a result, D must not have known the physical nature and quality of his act or, if he did know this, not have known he was doing 'a legal wrong'*. The mere fact that, because of a defect of reason due to a disease of the mind, D acted under an irresistible impulse is not enough.

It has been held by a divisional court that the defence of insanity is not available where the offence charged is an offence of strict liability as to every element of the actus reus, ie one where no mens rea is required.

Defendants found not guilty by reason of insanity in the Crown Court are made subject to any of a number of orders, one of which is indefinite detention in hospital until this is no longer necessary for the protection of the public.

Automatism

Generally, it is a defence that D was in a state of automatism at the time of the act in question. An act is done in a state of automatism if it is done by the muscles without any control of the mind (eg a reflex action, or a spasmodic or convulsive act) or if it is done during a state involving lost consciousness (eg concussion, or a hypoglycaemic coma resulting from insulin taken by a diabetic).

It should be noted that, if the alleged cause of automatism in a case in the Crown Court is ruled by the trial judge to be a disease of the mind, he will direct the jury to consider only the defence of insanity, so that an acquittal on the ground of the defence of (non-insane) automatism will not be possible.

D does not have to prove the defence of (non-insane) automatism. Instead he simply has the burden of adducing sufficient evidence to raise the issue; D's evidence will very rarely be sufficient unless it is supported by medical evidence. If D adduces sufficient evidence, he must be acquitted unless the prosecution disproves the alleged automatism.

Sometimes, non-insane automatism is self-induced in that it results from something done or not done by D (as where a diabetic becomes an automaton as a result of taking insulin, or, having taken insulin, failing to eat sufficiently thereafter). In such a case, D cannot be convicted of an 'offence of specific intent' (which is defined below). Nor can he be convicted of an offence which does not require a specific intent *unless* either automatism was caused by his voluntary intoxication *or,* before becoming an automaton, D was aware that something done or not done was likely to make him aggressive, unpredictable or uncontrollable (as opposed simply to becoming unconscious), and he deliberately disregarded the risk.

Intoxication

The rules relating to the effect of intoxication in criminal liability are the same whether the intoxication was caused by drink or drugs. Intoxication is not in itself a defence. It is no excuse that because of intoxication D's power to judge between right and wrong, or to exercise self-control, was impaired.

Voluntary intoxication

In most cases a person's intoxication is regarded as 'voluntary'. Intoxication is voluntary if it results from knowingly taking alcohol or some other drug. There are two exceptions: intoxication is not voluntary where it is caused by something taken under and in accordance with medical advice, or where it is caused by a non-dangerous drug (ie a sedative or soporific drug), provided that D is not aware of the risk of becoming unpredictable, or aggressive when taking it. These cases of involuntary intoxication are dealt with below.

Where D was voluntarily intoxicated, D may rely on the intoxication as evidence that he lacked mens rea if, but only if, the offence requires proof of a specific intent. Even if an offence is one of specific intent, an intoxicated, mistaken belief that he is acting in self-defence or the like will not excuse D. Where an offence is one of basic intent, ie does not require a specific intent, D may be convicted of it if he was voluntarily intoxicated at the time of his conduct, even though because of his intoxication he did not have the mens rea required for that offence, and even though he was then in a state of automatism, provided that he would have been aware of the risk in question had he been sober. However, the fact that an offence is one of basic intent does not prevent D relying on evidence of his voluntary intoxication as evidence that his act (as opposed to its consequences) was an 'accident', such as where he stumbles into someone in an intoxicated state.

The following have been held to be offences of specific intent in this context: murder; wounding or causing grievous bodily harm with intent contrary to the Offences Against the Person Act 1861, s 18; theft; robbery; burglary with intent to steal; the common law offences of kidnapping and false imprisonment; and attempt to commit an offence.

Conversely, the following have been held *not* to be offences of specific intent: manslaughter; maliciously wounding or inflicting grievous bodily harm contrary to the Offences Against the Person Act 1861, s 20; assault occasioning actual bodily harm; assault on a constable in the execution of his duty; rape; sexual assault; taking a conveyance without lawful authority; and offences against the Criminal Damage Act 1971, s 1(1) or (2) (unless only an intentional offence is alleged).

Involuntary intoxication

The situation is different where a person is involuntarily intoxicated. Intoxication is involuntary in the two exceptional cases outlined four paragraphs above, and also where it is not self-induced (as where a person's glasses of lemonade have been laced with vodka or where he has been secretly drugged).

Where he was involuntarily intoxicated, D can use evidence of this intoxication as evidence that he lacked the mens rea for the offence in question (whether or not it is an offence of specific intent). However, if it can be proved that D had the necessary mens rea when the offence was committed, it is no defence that involuntary intoxication led him to commit an offence which he would not have committed when sober, and this is so even though, because of the intoxication, he acted under an irresistible impulse.

Duress

The defences of duress by threats and duress of circumstances are restricted to cases where D was impelled to act as he did because, on the facts as he reasonably believed them to be, he had good cause to believe that he or someone for whom he felt responsible was subject to a threat of imminent death or serious physical injury unless he acted as he did to avoid the threatened harm. The defence of duress by threats deals with the case where the threat comes from another person and, expressly or impliedly, is in the form of an order to do a particular, nominated act or suffer the harm; the defence of duress of circumstances deals with the case where the threat of death or serious physical injury is of any other type (as where the threat comes from the surrounding circumstances).

The threat must be such that an ordinary, sober person of reasonable firmness sharing D's characteristics would have responded as D did. Because this 'ordinary person' is someone of reasonable firmness he is not invested with a characteristic of D which did not make D less able to resist the threat than an ordinary person of reasonable firmness. In addition, the ordinary person of reasonable firmness is not invested with a characteristic of D, such as pliancy, vulnerability to pressure or timidity, since it would be a contradiction in terms to invest an ordinary person with these. On the other hand, if D is in a category of persons who might be less able to resist pressure than people outside that category, the characteristic which puts him in that category may be a relevant one. Obvious examples are age (a young person may not be as robust as a mature person); pregnancy (added fear for the unborn child); serious physical disability (may inhibit self-protection); and a recognised mental illness or psychiatric condition (may make the person more susceptible to pressure).

The defences of duress by threats and duress of circumstances are not applicable in respect of conduct committed after a threat has ceased to be operative or if D could have neutralised the threat by seeking police protection. With a few exceptions, the defences are generally available in respect of offences, including road traffic offences. The principal exceptions are murder and attempted murder.

The defence of duress by threats is not available to a person who foresaw or ought to have foreseen that voluntary association with other people involved a risk of being subjected to any compulsion by threat of violence. Thus, the defence is not available to a person who joins a criminal gang, knowing that other members might bring pressure to bear on him to rob someone, and who is subsequently put under such pressure.

Coercion

This is an alternative defence to duress by threats, which is available to married women in the following circumstances. It is a defence on a charge of any offence, other than murder or treason, for a wife to prove that she committed the alleged offence in the presence of, and under the coercion of, her husband. It will be noted that the defendant wife has the burden of proving this defence. In contrast, D does not have to prove the defence of duress; D merely has to adduce evidence that D is covered by that defence, whereupon it is for the prosecution to prove that D is not (otherwise D must be acquitted). The defence of coercion can apply where the threat is of something less than death or serious bodily harm, although there must be some (as yet undetermined) limit on the type of threat that can suffice.

PARTIES TO A CRIME

There are a number of ways in which people may participate in an offence.

Perpetrators

A perpetrator is otherwise known as the principal. Normally, it is clear who is the perpetrator; this is the person who, with the relevant mens rea, fires the fatal shot in murder, or has intercourse in rape, and so on. Of course, there can be more than one perpetrator, as where a group of men enter a building as trespassers in order to steal therein; in such a case there are said to be joint perpetrators of the offence.

A person who makes use of an innocent agent in order to procure the commission of an offence is the perpetrator of the offence, even though he is not present at the scene of the offence and does nothing with his own hands. Thus, a person who kills another by posting a time bomb to him which is delivered by an innocent postman, or who employs a child under ten (the age of criminal responsibility) or a trained dog to remove goods from a shop, may be convicted of murder or theft, as the case may be, if he acts with the appropriate mens rea.

Accomplices

A person who aids, abets, counsels or procures the commission of an offence (an accomplice) is liable to be tried and punished for that offence as a principal offender.

Aiding, abetting, counselling, and procuring

The terms 'aiding' and 'abetting' are often used together, but they refer to different things; 'aid' describes the activity of a person who assists the perpetrator to commit the principal offence, and 'abet' describes the activity of a person who encourages the perpetrator to commit it, whether or not in either case present at the time of commission. 'Counsel', which means 'encourage', does not add anything strictly but is used to describe encouragement before the commission of the principal offence. A person 'procures' the commission of an offence where he sets out to see that it is committed and takes appropriate steps to produce its commission.

It can be seen from the above that basically there must be some assistance or encouragement by a person in the commission of an offence by another before he can be convicted as an accomplice to it. That assistance or encouragement must be given before, or at the time of, the commission of the offence. Someone who assists the perpetrator after the commission of an offence is not liable as a party to it, but one who assists the perpetrator to escape detection or arrest may be guilty of the statutory offence of assisting offenders, dealt with in Chapter 38.

The assistance or encouragement of the perpetrator which must be proved against an alleged accomplice may take a variety of forms. Examples are: holding a woman down while she is raped; keeping watch; shouting words of encouragement; providing a jemmy to a burglar; and buying paper for use by a forger. A person who merely stands by when it is committed and does nothing to prevent its commission is not an accomplice to an offence, but if he was deliberately present at the scene of the crime and it can be proved that his presence encouraged the perpetrator, as he intended it should, he can be convicted as an accomplice.

Mens rea

The mens rea required of an accomplice is, first, an intention to assist or encourage the commission of the offence. This is proved by proving that the act of aiding, abetting, etc was done intentionally, in the sense that it was done deliberately (and not accidentally), knowing that this conduct was capable of assisting or encouraging the commission of the principal offence. D need not be proved to have acted with the aim or purpose that the principal offence be committed. Thus, for example, someone who deliberately sells someone else a gun to be used for murdering V can be convicted as an accomplice to the subsequent murder, even if he was only interested in making money and was indifferent about whether or not V was killed.

Second, it must be proved that D had knowledge (or recklessness) as to any facts essential to constitute the offence (including the perpetrator's mens rea) (although, of course, D need not know that those facts constitute an offence, nor need he know any more details). Where the assistance or encouragement is given before the time of the principal offence, it is more appropriate to speak in terms of whether D was aware that facts essential to the commission of the principal offence would, or might as a real possibility, exist or occur at the material time.

The above requirements apply even though the offence in question is one of strict liability.

Liability as accomplice for another offence committed by perpetrator in course of joint criminal enterprise

If, in the course of a joint criminal enterprise with D, a person (E) *accidentally* commits the actus reus of an offence of a different type from that intended, neither he nor D will be guilty of that offence unless they have the necessary mens rea required for it. If the have, D is guilty as an accomplice to that offence. D and E might have that mens rea where the offence concerned is of a type which does not require foresight of the necessary consequence. Examples of such cases are manslaughter and unlawfully wounding or inflicting grievous bodily harm contrary to the Offences Against the Person Act 1861, s 20. A person is guilty of manslaughter if death results from the commission by him of an unlawful act likely to harm another, even though he did not foresee that death or grievous bodily harm was likely to result. If D encourages E to assault V with fists, and V unexpectedly dies in consequence of the blows received, they are each guilty of manslaughter, D as an accomplice.

It is different where a party (E) to a joint criminal enterprise *intentionally* perpetrates an offence which is not the common object of the venture. In such a case, another party to the venture (D) is liable for that offence if D contemplates as a real possibility that any other party to the venture may, in the course of carrying out the venture, do an act, with the requisite mens rea, constituting that offence, unless the act done by the perpetrator was fundamentally different from that foreseen by D. Suppose that a person (D) encourages a second person (E) to commit burglary and to use a jemmy to frighten off anyone who might come upon them and E, disturbed in the course of the burglary, strikes the householder with the jemmy and kills him, both parties are guilty of burglary, D as accomplice and E as perpetrator: but is D guilty of murder? The House of Lords has held that someone like D can be convicted of the further offence if it is proved that he contemplated as a real possibility that another party to the joint criminal enterprise might commit it but still participated in the enterprise. In some cases someone like D will have agreed to or authorised the commission of the further offence but this is not necessary. If it was proved that in the circumstances set out above he had contemplated as a real possibility that the jemmy might be used intentionally to kill or do grievous bodily harm to someone in such circumstances, D could be convicted as an accomplice to murder even without proof that he had agreed to its use for that purpose, and even though he had forbidden the use of violence.

In the case above, D contemplated as a real possibility the act carried out by the perpetrator. But what if he did not contemplate the act? The House of Lords has held that, even if D intended or foresaw that the perpetrator would or might act with the mens rea for the principal offence which was committed, he cannot be convicted as a party to that offence (except, in the case of murder, where he intended the perpetrator intentionally to kill) if the perpetrator's act is fundamentally different from the act intended or foreseen by D (such as where the act done is done by a more dangerous weapon (perhaps a gun) of which D, who thought that a club would be used, was unaware). On the other hand, if the perpetrator's act, though different, is as dangerous as that foreseen as a 'real possibility' by D, such as where the actual act was stabbing with a knife and that foreseen as a real possibility was shooting to kill, D cannot escape liability for the offence.

Miscellaneous points

A person who cannot in law perpetrate a particular offence may nevertheless be convicted as an accomplice to it. For example, a woman can be convicted of rape as an accomplice where she has encouraged or assisted a man to rape another woman.

Where D is alleged to be an accomplice to an offence, the charge may allege that he aided, abetted, counselled, or procured it, and he will be convicted if he is proved to have participated in one or more of these four ways.

Vicarious liability

Vicarious liability means liability for the acts of another person which D has not authorised and of which he was ignorant.

Vicarious *criminal* liability is exceptional; it is imposed only on employers and, in some cases, certain other people with a similar status. It arises in three ways:

(1) Where a statute expressly states that a specified person is vicariously liable for the prohibited act of another. This is rare.
(2) Where a statutory strict liability offence uses a word like 'use' or 'sell' which connotes an activity which can be performed by an employee on behalf of his employer, an employer can be vicariously liable for a prohibited 'using', etc by the employee in the course of his employment.
(3) Certain statutes impose duties on someone who is a licensee and make it an offence for someone with that status knowingly to contravene them. If a licensee completely delegates his statutory responsibilities to someone else such as an employee, and the delegate knowingly contravenes one of these duties, the conduct and the state of mind of the delegate are imputed to the person with the specified status, who is consequently vicariously liable for the offence in question. If this were not so, licensees could easily escape their statutory responsibilities by delegating their responsibilities.

CORPORATE LIABILITY

A company or other corporate body may be criminally liable:

(a) on the basis of vicarious liability (above); or
(b) for breach of a duty imposed on it as an 'occupier' of premises or as an employer, etc,

in the same way as a natural person. The offences to which these principles apply are essentially ones of strict liability.

A company or other corporate body may also be liable for most offences (murder is a notable exception) requiring proof of mens rea where the acts and state of mind of an individual who physically committed the offence can be attributed to it. In the case of a *common law offence*, such as conspiracy to defraud, such attribution is only possible in respect of a person who is a 'controlling officer', ie someone who represents the 'directing mind and will' of the corporation (such as a director). Whether or not the conduct of a particular employee of a corporation can be attributed to the corporation for the purposes of criminal liability for a *statutory offence* depends on the proper construction of the particular rule of law concerned; a particular statute may be interpreted so that the act and state of mind of someone lower down the company or other corporate body's hierarchy can be attributed to it.

EXEMPTION FROM CRIMINAL LIABILITY

The Diplomatic Privileges Act 1964 provides that ambassadors and Commonwealth High Commissioners, members of their families, and their administrative and technical staff and their families are immune from arrest and criminal proceedings whilst in the UK in that capacity. There is no immunity for a member of the family who is a UK national. Members of the service staff also have immunity but only in respect of acts in the course of their duties. A report should be sent to the Diplomatic Protection Group of the

Metropolitan Police where a person dealt with for an offence claims diplomatic immunity; a copy will be forwarded to the Foreign and Commonwealth Office for advice as to whether the offender has immunity.

The Consular Relations Act 1968 grants immunity from criminal proceedings to career consular officers and members of their administrative or technical staff in the exercise of consular functions. As well as this, career consular officers may not be arrested or detained pending trial unless the offence is grave and the detention is authorised by a competent judicial authority. Honorary consular officers are not immune from the jurisdiction of our criminal courts nor from arrest or detention.

The provisions of the Road Traffic Act 1988, ss 6–11, which are concerned with drink/driving, apply to consular personnel (but not to Ambassadors, etc). However, if a preliminary test is positive there can be no arrest of a career consular officer and the procedure must end there unless the officer is happy for the next steps to be taken. Such a person would be liable if he failed to co-operate with a preliminary test.

CHAPTER 2

Elements of Criminal Procedure

INSTITUTION OF CRIMINAL PROCEEDINGS

Responsibility for prosecutions

Prosecutions (criminal proceedings) are normally instituted on behalf of:

(a) a police force;
(b) the Director of Public Prosecutions (DPP); or
(c) a governmental or quasi-governmental organisation, such as the Serious Fraud Office, the Department for Work and Pensions or a local authority.

Where prosecutions are instituted on behalf of a police force (whether by a police officer or other person) the DPP is obliged to take over their conduct (with the exception of various minor traffic offences, and even then only where the defendant fails to appear before a magistrates' court and the court proceeds in his absence, or where the 'pleading guilty by post' procedure (described on p 22) is adopted).

The DPP is the head of the Crown Prosecution Service. The DPP is under the general supervision of the Attorney General. The DPP's functions are discharged on his behalf and under his direction by Crown Prosecutors working in the Crown Prosecution Service (CPS).

There is generally nothing to prevent a private individual or an organisation which is not governmental or quasi-governmental from instituting and conducting criminal proceedings, and such 'private' prosecutions are occasionally instituted. The DPP may take over a private prosecution even if his purpose is to offer no evidence against the defendant in the public interest and thereby to abort those proceedings.

An exception to the general rule that a police officer, a private individual or an official of a public or private body may institute criminal proceedings is that there are numerous offences where the leave of the Attorney General or of the DPP is required. For example, proceedings for one of the offences relating to racial or religious hatred under the Public Order Act 1986 may only be instituted by or with the consent of the Attorney General, and proceedings for over 50 offences may only be instituted by or with the consent of the Director. In the latter case, the DPP's functions can, of course, be exercised by a Crown Prosecutor on his behalf. Where proceedings for an offence may only be instituted by or with the consent of the Attorney General or of the Director, this is indicated at the appropriate point in this book.

Alternatives to prosecutions

Traditionally, the criminal process involved prosecution, trial (if the defendant (D) pleaded not guilty), and sentence. In modern times these are not the only ways of disposal of a case.

Where a person admits his guilt he may alternatively be dealt with by a caution in an appropriate case: see Chapter 5. In addition, many road traffic offences can be dealt with by the issue (and satisfaction) of a fixed penalty notice, and so may a score or so of offences involving disorderly behaviour. The former are dealt with in Chapter 11, and the latter at the end of this chapter. (There are also other offences in respect of which penalty notices may be issued by officials not associated with the police.) Mention may also be made of restorative justice processes which give victims of crime the chance to tell offenders the impact of their crimes, to get answers to their questions, and an apology and amends.

Ways of instituting criminal proceedings

Criminal proceedings may be instituted in one of three ways:

(a) a public prosecutor may institute criminal proceedings against a person by issuing a document (a written charge) which charges the person with an offence and then securing D's presence by issuing a requisition and, if necessary, by an arrest under a warrant;

(b) a person who is not a public prosecutor (eg a private person) may institute criminal proceedings by laying an information alleging that D has, or is suspected of having, committed an offence and then securing D's presence before a magistrates' court by a summons or by an arrest under a warrant. At present this method is available as an alternative to (a) for public prosecutors; or

(c) by an arrest without warrant, followed by a charge.

Public prosecutors

A 'public prosecutor' is:

(a) a police force;
(b) the DPP;
(c) the Attorney General;
(d) the Director of the Serious Fraud Office;
(e) the Director of Revenue and Customs Prosecutions;
(f) the Director General of the Serious Organised Crime Agency,
or, in each case above, a person authorised by such a body or person to institute criminal proceedings;
(g) a Secretary of State or a person authorised by a Secretary of State:
    (i) to conduct and appear in proceedings under the Vehicle Excise and Registration Act 1994; or
    (ii) to institute criminal proceedings on behalf of the Vehicle and Operator Services Agency;
(h) the Secretary of State for Work and Pensions or the Secretary of State for Health or the Secretary of State for Business, Innovation and Skills or a person authorised by such a Secretary of State where the proceedings are instituted by such a Secretary of State; and
(j) any person specified in an order made by the Secretary of State for this purpose or anyone authorised by such a person to institute criminal proceedings. Transport for London has been so specified.

Written charge or information

A written charge or information must contain:

(a) a statement of the offence which describes the offence 'in ordinary language' and (if the offence is created by statute) identifies the legislation that creates it; and

(b) sufficient particulars of the conduct constituting the commission of the offence to make clear what the prosecutor alleges against the defendant.

Where a number of incidents, taken together, amount to a course of conduct (having regard to the time, place, or purpose of commission), those incidents may be included in the allegation. Moreover, a single document may contain more than one charge.

A public prosecutor may institute criminal proceedings by issuing a written charge charging the person concerned with an offence. The prosecutor must at the same time issue another document, a 'requisition', which requires a person to appear before a magistrates' court to answer the written charge. Both documents must be served on the person concerned and a copy must be served on the court named in the requisition.

In view of these powers being available to them, public prosecutors will prospectively no longer be empowered to lay an information for the purpose of obtaining a summons.

A public prosecutor may still apply for an arrest warrant by laying an information. Where a written charge and requisition have previously been issued a warrant may be issued by a magistrate before whom a copy of the written charge is laid.

A summons is a written order issued by a justice of the peace or by a justices' clerk (or authorised assistant) on behalf of a justice. It is directed to the person named in the information and requires him to appear before a magistrates' court to answer the charge against him.

A requisition or summons must contain a notice setting out when and where the defendant must attend the court, and must specify each offence in respect of which it has been issued. Additionally, a summons must identify the issuing court, and a requisition must identify the person under whose authority it is issued.

Time limits

By the Magistrates' Courts Act 1980, s 127, a written charge or information relating to an offence triable only summarily cannot generally be tried unless it has been laid within six months from the time when the offence was committed. An example of an exception to this general rule is provided by the Vehicle Excise and Registration Act 1994, which permits an information (or written charge) to be laid in respect of offences of using or keeping a vehicle without an excise licence up to three years after the commission of the offence. The general rule does not apply to an information (or written charge) relating to an offence which is triable on indictment. There is no set time limit in the case of such an offence, unless its parent statute expressly provides one.

Arrest without warrant, followed by charge

This is dealt with later in Chapters 3 and 5.

Other types of summonses

These are mentioned here for convenience.

Summonses for a breach of the peace   A summons may also be issued as a result of a complaint. A complaint is a written or verbal allegation made before a justice in respect of anything which is within the civil jurisdiction of a magistrates' court to make an order. Of particular importance to a police officer is the fact that a complaint may be made to the effect that a person has committed a breach of the peace. Breach of the peace is *not in itself a criminal offence*. If the complaint is proved, that person may be bound over to keep the peace. A magistrates' court has jurisdiction to hear any complaint.

Summonses in respect of a witness   Where a justice of the peace or justices' clerk (or authorised assistant) is satisfied that any person in England or Wales, or outside the British Isles, is likely to be able to give material evidence, or to produce any document or thing likely to be material evidence, at the summary trial of a written charge or information or the hearing of a complaint by a magistrates' court, and it is in the interests of justice to issue a summons to secure the attendance of that person to give evidence or produce the document or thing, the justice may issue a summons requiring that person to attend before the court to give evidence or produce the thing or document. Unlike other summonses, such a summons may not be served by post. A justice may refuse to issue a witness summons if he is not satisfied that the application was made as soon as reasonably practicable after the defendant pleaded not guilty. Crown Courts are also empowered to issue witness summonses in prescribed circumstances.

Service of requisitions or summonses

A requisition or summons may be served on an individual:

(a) by handing it to him (except that if he is under 18, it must be handed to a parent, guardian, or other appropriate adult if such a person is readily available);

(b) by leaving it at the appropriate address for service (ie an address in England and Wales where it is reasonably believed that he will receive it); or

(c) by sending it to that address by first class post or by the equivalent of first class post;

and may be served on a corporation:

(i) by handing it to a person holding a senior position in that corporation;

(ii) by leaving it at the appropriate address for service (ie the corporation's principal office in England and Wales, and if there is no readily identifiable principal office then any place in England and Wales where it carries on its activities or business); or

(iii) by sending it to that address by first class post or the equivalent of first class post.

Lawful service of such a document may therefore be effected and proved by sending the document for a summary offence, by post, to the appropriate address. Service is deemed to be effected when a pre-paid, properly addressed letter, which contains the document which is to be served, is posted. Unless the contrary is proved, service is deemed to be effected at the time at which the letter would be delivered in the ordinary course of post.

Proof of service is usually by means of a certificate of service signed by the person who effected the service, or who posted the document. Such a certificate contains details of the place, date and time of posting or of service by delivery.

A requisition or summons may be served, in accordance with rules of court, in Scotland or Northern Ireland. The same is true vice versa in respect of a Northern Irish summons. A Scottish citation may be served in England and Wales in the same way as may be done in Scotland.

Special provision is made as to service on a person outside the UK by the Crime (International Co-operation) Act 2003 and the Criminal Procedure Rules 2012, and as to service on an overseas company by the Companies Act 2006, s 1139.

Warrants of arrest

A justice of the peace (but not the justices' clerk or anyone else) may issue a warrant to arrest when information is laid before him to the effect that a person has, or is suspected of having, committed an offence.

Where a person who is not a public prosecutor lays an information in respect of:

(a) a 'qualifying offence' alleged to have been committed outside the UK or
(b) an offence of attempting, conspiring or encouraging or assisting the commission, of such an offence where it is alleged that the qualifying offence was, or would have been, committed outside the UK,

no arrest warrant may be issued without the consent of the DPP. A 'qualifying offence' means an offence under the Criminal Justice Act 1988, s 134 (torture: see p 697), the Aviation Security Act 1982, s 1, 2, or 6 (hijacking, etc), or the Aviation and Maritime Security Act 1990, s 1 (endangering safety at aerodromes) or 9 to 14 (hijacking ships, etc) or certain other offences (eg grave breaches of Geneva Conventions and offences relating to nuclear material) over which the UK has asserted jurisdiction regardless of where in the world the offence is committed and regardless of the nationality of the defendant or the victim. These provisions are designed to make it more difficult to arrest in this country foreign ministers and officials who are suspected by groups such as Amnesty of being war criminals.

An arrest warrant may be executed anywhere in England and Wales by any constable for the police area in which the warrant is issued. Alternatively, it may be executed by a constable for another police area within his police area. It may also be executed by a civilian enforcement officer or an approved enforcement agency.

An arrest warrant remains in force until executed or withdrawn. If the original is lost a justice may issue a replacement. However, an arrest warrant must not be issued in the first instance unless the offence to which it relates is either triable on indictment or punishable with imprisonment, or the defendant's address is not sufficiently established for a requisition or summons to be served on him. An arrest warrant may be endorsed with a direction that on arrest the person to be arrested shall be released on bail, with or without sureties. This is known as 'backing for bail'.

Arrest warrants issued by judicial authorities in some EU countries may be executed in the UK.

Other warrants

For the sake of completeness, mention is made of some other warrants which may be issued by a justice or magistrates' court on an information being laid.

Warrant to arrest a witness   Such a warrant may be issued by a justice, under the Magistrates' Courts Act 1980, s 97(2), who is satisfied that a person who could give material evidence, etc is unlikely to attend court voluntarily. Such a warrant will only be issued where a summons would be ineffective.

Warrants for distress or commitment   The Magistrates' Courts Act 1980, s 76 authorises a magistrates' court to issue a warrant of distress or of commitment where a person is in default of payment of a sum adjudged to be paid by a conviction or order of a magistrates' court. 'Warrant of distress' is prospectively renamed 'warrant of control'.

'A warrant of distress for the purpose of levying the sum which is unpaid' is usually executed by a civilian enforcement officer or an approved enforcement agency but it may be executed by a constable in his police area. It requires that goods be seized; this is done initially by labelling the goods, after which they are in legal custody. No electrical plant, line, or meter belonging to a public electrical supplier can be seized, nor can wearing apparel or bedding, nor tools or implements of the person's trade. It is an offence under the Magistrates' Courts Act 1980, s 78(4) for any person to remove the goods, or the marks placed on them to signify seizure.

A warrant of commitment orders the defaulter to be arrested and committed to prison. It may be issued *either* where it appears on the return to a warrant of distress that the defaulter's assets are insufficient to satisfy the sum adjudged *or* instead of a warrant of distress. If the magistrates' court considers this expedient, it may fix a term of imprisonment and suspend the issue of the warrant until such time and on such conditions as it thinks fit. A receipt must be obtained for the defaulter when he is handed over to a prison pursuant to a warrant of commitment.

Search warrant   This type of warrant is discussed in Chapter 3.

Execution of warrants

A warrant of arrest, or of distress, or of commitment, or a search warrant, may be executed anywhere in England and Wales by any constable for the police area in which the warrant is issued. Alternatively, it may be executed by a constable acting in his police area.

In addition, by the Criminal Justice and Public Order Act 1994, s 136 a warrant issued in England, Wales or Northern Ireland for the arrest or commitment of a person (or a like warrant issued in Scotland) may, without endorsement, be executed in one of the other home countries by a constable of a police force of the country of issue or of the country of execution or by a British Transport Police constable, as well as by any other persons within the directions of the warrant. As in the case of other arrest warrants, a constable who arrests the person named in the warrant is not liable for false imprisonment if that person is in fact innocent of the offence, unless there is malice on the part of the constable.

A warrant may not be executed by a constable who does not have it in his possession at the time. Exceptions are:

(a) warrants to arrest a person in connection with an offence;
(b) warrants under the armed forces legislation (desertion, etc);
(c) warrants relating to the non-appearance of a defendant, warrants of distress (or control), warrants of commitment and warrants issued to arrest a potentially unwilling witness in respect of a forthcoming summary trial or trial on indictment (under the Magistrates' Courts Act 1980, ss 55, 76, 93, 97, and 97A and the Crime and Disorder Act 1998, Sch 3);
(d) warrants under the Family Law Act 1996, s 47(8) (failure to comply with occupation order or non-molestation order); and
(e) warrants under the Youth Justice and Criminal Evidence Act 1999 Sch 1, para 3(2) (offender referred to court by youth offender panel).

However, such a warrant must, on the demand of the person concerned, be shown to him as soon as practicable (Magistrates' Courts Act 1980, s 125D).

Entry to execute warrants   The Police and Criminal Evidence Act 1984 (PACE), s 17 permits a constable to enter and search premises, including any vehicle, vessel, aircraft or tent, in specified circumstances for the purpose of executing a warrant of arrest issued in connection with or arising out of criminal proceedings, or a warrant of commitment issued under the Magistrates' Courts Act 1980, s 76. See p 67.

CLASSIFICATION OF OFFENCES BY METHOD OF TRIAL

Offences can be classified as indictable offences or summary offences, according to their mode of trial.

'Indictable offence' means an offence which, if committed by an adult, is triable in the Crown Court, whether it is exclusively so triable (eg murder or robbery) or triable either way, ie in the Crown Court or a magistrates' court (eg unlawful wounding or theft).

'Summary offence' means an offence which, if committed by an adult, is triable only in a magistrates' court (eg most driving offences).

The vast majority of offences are summary ones. *Where an offence is indictable (whether triable only on indictment or triable either way) this will be stated at an appropriate point in the text. Otherwise, it should be assumed that the offence is only summary.*

COURTS OF CRIMINAL JURISDICTION

There are two methods of trying persons accused of criminal offences. One is by judge and (almost invariably) jury in the Crown Court; the other is summarily by a magistrates' court without a jury. With a few exceptions, all criminal proceedings in the Crown Court begin in a magistrates' court since a defendant (D) tried in the Crown Court must normally have been sent for trial there by a magistrates' court.

Magistrates' courts

A magistrates' court is normally composed of two or three justices of the peace, unless a special exception applies. The normal sittings of a magistrates' court take place in a properly appointed courthouse on appointed days of the week. On other occasions, or in other places, a court may sit as an occasional court but with quite limited powers. A District Judge (Magistrates' Courts), a legally qualified, salaried magistrate, may sit alone and has all the powers of two lay justices.

The court is advised by a legally qualified justices' clerk. Some matters authorised to be done by, to or before a single justice may be done before a justices' clerk or an assistant clerk.

A magistrates' court has jurisdiction in relation to a range of civil matters, including preventative orders such as sexual offences prevention orders and foreign travel orders on an application by complaint.

In criminal matters a magistrates' court has jurisdiction in relation to the following matters.

Offences triable summarily only

A magistrates' court has jurisdiction to try any summary offence alleged to have been committed by a person who appears or is brought before the court.

A person appearing before a magistrates' court does so either in answer to a requisition or summons, or under arrest.

Guilty plea   A person (D) who appears before the court will have the charge read over to him and will be asked if he pleads guilty or not guilty. If D pleads guilty the court must be satisfied that it is a clear and unequivocal plea. On a plea of guilty being entered, the court may convict without hearing evidence. In practice, however, the facts of the case are outlined by the prosecution, and D or his legal representative is at liberty to dispute those facts should he wish to do so and may also put before the court any mitigating facts which he feels that the court should consider before passing sentence. Usually the court will also hear any evidence by the prosecutor of any previous recorded convictions of D and of his general character in order to enable it to decide the appropriate penalty. D may also ask the court to take into consideration, when passing sentence, other offences which he has committed.

Pleading guilty by post   In the case of many offences triable summarily only, the Magistrates' Courts Act 1980 permits pleas of guilty to be entered at a magistrates' court (or where D is 16 or 17 when the summons or requisition is issued, at a youth court) without the necessity for D to attend the proceedings, or for any witnesses to be called. There are certain conditions which must be met in respect of the offence:

(a) the proceedings must be by way of requisition or summons;
(b) it is not an offence specified by the Secretary of State;
(c) the designated officer for the court must have been notified by the prosecutor that D, when served with the requisition or summons for the offence, was also served with:
  (i)   a notice explaining the prescribed procedure;
  (ii) *either* a concise statement of the facts of the case which will be put before the court in the event of his pleading guilty without appearing before the court *or* a copy of such signed written statement or statements complying with the Criminal Justice Act 1967, s 9(2)(b) ((a) on p 242) and (3) (p 242) (proof by written statement) as will be so placed in those circumstances; and
  (iii) if any information relating to D will, or may in the circumstances, be placed before the court by or on behalf of the prosecutor, a notice containing or describing the information; and
(d) D or his solicitor must have notified the designated officer that he wishes to plead guilty. On receipt of this notification, the officer will inform the prosecutor.

Where D does not appear and proof of service of the documents referred to in (c) is given, the court may hear and dispose of the case in the absence of D, the prosecutor or both. The documents are read to a court before a conviction is registered.

Should D appear even though the notification referred to in (d) has been received, the court may, with his consent, proceed as just described but D may make oral submissions with a view to mitigation of sentence, in place of any written submission which he may have sent.

Not guilty plea   If D pleads not guilty the court must hear the evidence and, at the request of either party, the court will order all witnesses out of court so that evidence may be presented independently. The proceedings will be opened by the prosecution outlining the facts of the case and calling its witnesses one by one to give evidence to the court. Each witness will either take the oath or affirm, and will give evidence during *examination-in-chief*. After the prosecution has asked questions to introduce and identify the witness, it may not ask *leading questions* in relation to the facts in issue. Leading questions are those which may usually be answered 'yes' or 'no'. For example, a prosecutor may not ask, 'Did you see the defendant standing outside the premises at 2 East Street?' but instead should ask, 'Where was the defendant when you saw him?'

When a witness has given evidence for the prosecution he may be *cross-examined* by the defence upon any aspect of the evidence which he has given. Leading questions may be asked. Questions put in cross-examination (a) must be calculated to elicit answers which are directly relevant to an issue in the case, or (b) must be calcu-lated to test the credibility of the evidence or to diminish its value. In respect of (a), cross-examination is not limited to matters arising during the examination-in-chief; it may relate to anything relevant to an issue in the case. Questions may be asked in respect of new facts unexpectedly introduced in the witness's testimony which do not form part of the cross-examining side's case and could not reasonably have been anticipated.

At the conclusion of the cross-examination the prosecution has a right to *re-examine* the witness upon *any new facts* which have come to light, or to clear up ambiguities which might have arisen, during cross-examination. Leading questions may not be put, nor may new evidence be introduced.

D or his legal representative may then address the court, whether or not he calls wit-nesses. PACE 1984, s 79, which also applies to trials in the Crown Court, requires that, if the defence intends to call two or more witnesses to the facts of the case and those witnesses include D, D must be called before the other witness or witnesses unless the court in its discretion otherwise directs. Such a direction is likely where, for instance, a witness is to speak of an occurrence before the matters about which D is to give evidence.

When a witness for the defence, including D, has given his evidence, he may be cross-examined by the prosecution and may then be re-examined by the defence on any new facts or ambiguities which have arisen during the cross-examination.

When the prosecution and defence have finished calling their evidence, each side has a right to address the court (except that the prosecution does not have the right if D has not called witnesses and is not legally represented), the prosecution's closing speech coming before that of the defence.

The court may adjourn to consider its verdict and may seek the advice of its clerk by specific request. If it decides to convict, its pronouncement of this verdict will usually be followed by evidence by the prosecutor of any previous recorded convictions of D and of his general character in order to enable the court to decide on the appropriate penalty. A plea in mitigation may be made by D or his legal representative. D may also take the opportunity to ask the court to take into consideration, when passing sentence, other offences which he has committed.

Before beginning to try an offence, or at any time during such proceedings, a magis-trates' court may adjourn the proceedings to a time which it fixes. It may remand D, either in custody or on bail. If the remand is in custody, the remand will be for a maxi-mum of eight clear days; if D is allowed bail, the remand may be for longer with the consent of both parties. Remands may be for longer periods after conviction where the proceedings are adjourned for a medical report or for other enquiries to be undertaken.

Offences triable either way: where to be tried

An offence which is triable either way may be tried either on indictment in the Crown Court or summarily in a magistrates' court. Where it is tried depends on the follow-ing rules.

The procedure which is being superseded   Unless a notice of transfer to the Crown Court has been given in cases of serious or complex fraud or certain cases involving child witnesses, where D appears or is brought before a magistrates' court charged with an either-way offence, the court must cause the charge to be written down, if this has not already been done, and to be read to D. The court must explain to D that he may indicate whether (if the offence were to proceed to trial) he would plead guilty or not guilty; and explain that if he indicates that he would plead guilty:

(a) the court must proceed as if the proceedings constituted from the beginning the summary trial of the offence, and the court had asked whether he pleaded guilty or not guilty; and

(b) he may be committed for sentence to Crown Court if the court is of the opinion that certain grounds exist.

The court must then ask D whether (if the offence were to proceed to trial) he would plead guilty or not guilty. If he indicates that he would plead guilty the court must proceed as if the proceedings constituted from the beginning the summary trial of the offence and D had pleaded guilty. If the court is of the opinion that one of the specified grounds exists the court may commit D in custody or on bail to the Crown Court for sentence.

If D indicates that he would plead not guilty, or fails to indicate how he would plead, the court must decide whether the offence appears to be more suitable for summary trial or for trial on indictment. Before making that decision it must afford first the prosecutor and then D an opportunity to make representations as to which mode of trial would be more suitable. The court must consider the nature of the case; whether the circumstances make the offence one of a serious character; whether the punishment which a magistrates' court could inflict would be adequate; and any other relevant circumstances. Unless it would be contrary to the interests of justice to do so, in determining the mode of trial the court must follow the guideline that, in general, either way offences should be tried summarily unless it is likely that the court's sentencing powers will be insufficient.

If, having considered these issues, the magistrates' court decides that trial on indictment is more suitable, it will commence to hold committal proceedings in respect of the offence to determine whether there is evidence on which a reasonable jury properly directed could convict of the offence. If there is, it will commit D to the Crown Court for trial. On the other hand, if the court decides that summary trial is more suitable, it must explain to D that the offence appears more suitable for summary trial and that he can either consent to such trial or, if he wishes, be tried on indictment. He must also be warned that, if tried summarily and convicted, he may be committed for sentence by the Crown Court if the court considers that a ground for this is satisfied. If D consents to summary trial, the magistrates' court will proceed to this (in the same way as described above in relation to offences triable summarily only); if he does not so consent, committal proceedings will be held, just as the court would do if it had decided that trial on indictment was more suitable.

The procedure which is being rolled out   A new procedure under the Criminal Justice Act 2003 is being rolled out to replace the above. At the time of writing, it is only in force in the following local justice areas: Bath and Wansdyke, Berkshire, Bristol, Liverpool and Knowsley, North Avon, North Hampshire, North Somerset, Ormskirk, Sefton, St Helens, Wigan and Leigh, and Wirral. The new procedure is as follows.

Unless a notice has been given under the Crime and Disorder Act 1998 (CDA 1998), s 51B or s 51C (below), where D appears or is brought before a magistrates' court charged with an either-way offence, the court must cause the charge to be written down, if this has not already been done, and to be read to D. The court must explain to D that he may indicate whether (if the offence were to proceed to trial) he would plead guilty or not guilty; and explain that if he indicates that he would plead guilty:

(a) the court must proceed as if the proceedings constituted from the beginning the summary trial of the offence, and the court had asked whether he pleaded guilty or not guilty; and

(b) he may be committed for sentence to the Crown Court if the court is of the opinion that a Crown Court sentence should be available.

The court must then ask D whether (if the offence were to proceed to trial) he would plead guilty or not guilty. If he indicates that he would plead guilty the court must proceed as if the proceedings constituted from the beginning the summary trial of the offence and D had pleaded guilty. If the court is of the opinion that one of the specified grounds exists the court may commit D in custody or on bail to the Crown Court for sentence.

If D indicates that he would plead not guilty, or fails to indicate how he would plead, the court must go on to the next stage.

The next stage is that the court must decide in 'allocation of trial proceedings' whether the offence appears to be more suitable for summary trial or for trial on indictment. Before making a decision the court must give the prosecutor an opportunity to disclose any previous convictions (including, prospectively, convictions under a foreign law for an offence corresponding to an offence under English law), and both parties must be given an opportunity to make representations about the mode of trial. The court must consider whether the sentencing powers of a magistrates' court would be adequate for the offence(s), together with the representations made by both parties and the guideline referred to on p 24.

Where a summary trial appears to be more suitable the court must explain to D that summary trial appears to be more suitable and that he can either consent to be so tried or, if he wishes, be tried on indictment and that, if tried summarily and convicted, he may be committed to a Crown Court for sentence. At this stage, D may request an indication of whether a custodial or a non-custodial sentence would be more likely to be imposed if he were to be tried summarily and plead guilty. The court may or may not give such an indication. If it does, it must ask D whether, on the basis of the indication, he wishes to change his plea. If D indicates that he would plead guilty the court must proceed to summary trial. Where the court does not give an indication as to sentence, or D does not indicate that he would plead guilty, the court must ask D whether he consents to summary trial or wishes to be tried on indictment. If he consents, the court must proceed to summary trial. In a case where a court has indicated whether or not a custodial sentence would be imposed no court may impose such a sentence unless that possibility was indicated. There is only one exception; it relates to the second type of committal for sentence described on p 28.

If D does not consent to summary trial, or the court decides that the offence appears to be more suitable for trial on indictment, or the prosecution requests that the offence be tried on indictment, the court must proceed to send D to the Crown Court for trial.

In the case of a child or young person (ie someone under 18) brought before a magistrates' court charged with an indictable offence (with certain exceptions), the procedure to be followed is similar. However, special provisions are made in the case of such a person who, by reason of disorderly conduct before the court, makes it impracticable to proceed in that manner. In such a case, a court may proceed in D's absence but in the presence of his legal representative who may make the choices in relation to mode of trial.

If a notice is served on a magistrates' court under CDA 1998, s 51B or s 51C, the effect is that the magistrates must forthwith send D to the Crown Court for trial; they cannot allocate the case for summary trial if the offence is an either-way one. By s 51B, in *serious or complex fraud cases* a notice may be given by a designated authority (the Director of Public Prosecutions or of the Serious Fraud Office or of Revenue and Customs Prosecutions, or the Secretary of State) in respect of an indictable offence where the authority is satisfied that there is sufficient evidence for the person charged to be put on trial and that a case of fraud of such seriousness or complexity is revealed making it appropriate that the management of the case should, without delay, be taken over by the Crown Court. By s 51C, in *certain offences involving child witnesses*, the DPP may give such a notice if he is of the opinion that the evidence is sufficient for the person to be put on trial for the offence; that a child would be called as a witness at the trial; and that, for the purpose of avoiding prejudice to the welfare of the child, the case should be taken over by the Crown Court and proceed without delay. The offences are sexual offences; those which involve an assault on, or injury or a threat of injury to, a person; cruelty to a person under 16; making etc indecent photograph etc of a child; kidnapping, false imprisonment or abduction, or encouragement or assistance, attempt or conspiracy to commit, aiding, abetting, counselling, procuring, or inciting such offences. For these purposes a child is a person who is under the age of 17, or a person of whom a video recording was made when he was under the age of 17 with a view to its admission as evidence-in-chief in the trial.

Sending cases to Crown Court for trial

The following describes the procedure which will apply when the relevant provisions of the Criminal Justice Act 2003, which are already in force in the local justice areas listed in the penultimate paragraph on p 24, are fully brought into force.

Where an *adult* (D) appears or is brought before a magistrates' court charged with an offence which is triable on indictment only, or where (under the above provisions) an offence triable either way is not to be tried by a magistrates' court, or where a notice under CDA 1998, s 51B or s 51C has been given, the court must send him forthwith to the Crown Court for trial. It may at the same time send D for trial for any related either-way offence, and for a related summary offence if it satisfies the 'requisite conditions', namely is punishable with imprisonment or involves obligatory or discretionary disqualification from driving. Other adult persons who are jointly charged with D with an either-way offence for which D is sent for trial must be sent for trial if they appear before the magistrates' court on the same occasion as D (and may be so sent if they appear later). If another such adult is so sent in respect of an either-way offence with which he is jointly charged with D, he must also be sent for trial in respect of any either-way offence, or any summary offences which meet the requisite conditions, related to that offence. In addition, where a court sends an adult for trial in this way, it may also send for trial a child or young person who is jointly charged with the adult with an indictable offence for which the adult is sent for trial, or an indictable offence related to that offence. If it does, it may also send the child or young person for trial for any related either-way offence or any related summary offence which meets the 'requisite conditions', if it considers it necessary to do so in the interests of justice.

Generally, *children and young persons* (ie persons under 18) have to be tried summarily in a youth court (or sometimes a magistrates' court other than a youth court);

see below. However, in the following cases a person under 18 may be sent to the Crown Court for trial. The first, mentioned above, is where such a person is charged jointly with an adult with an indictable offence for which the adult is sent for trial, or an indictable offence related to that offence. The second is where a child or young person appears or is brought before a magistrates' court charged with an offence for which any of the following conditions is satisfied:

(a) the offence is one of homicide, or one of a number of particular types of offence of possessing a prohibited weapon and the accused young person was aged 16 or 17 when he committed it;

(b) the offence is one in respect of which a long period of detention may be ordered and the court considers that such a sentence ought to be possible;

(c) a notice has been served under CDA 1998, s 51B or s 51C in respect of the child or young person; or

(d) the offence is a 'specified offence', namely one of a range of violent or sexual offences, and it appears to the magistrates' court that if the defendant child or young person is found guilty of the offence the criteria for the imposition of detention for public protection (prospectively abolished) or an extended sentence would be met.

If one of the conditions (a)–(d) is satisfied, the magistrates' court must send the child or young person for trial. In such a case, it may also send the child for trial for any related indictable offence or a any relevant summary offence which meets the 'requisite conditions'.

Where a court sends a child or young person for trial in such a case it may also send for trial an adult person who is jointly charged with an either-way offence or a related either-way offence or a related summary offence which meets the 'requisite conditions'.

The court is required to give notice of the offence or offences for which a person is sent for trial and the place at which the trial is to take place. A copy of this notice must be served on D and given to the Crown Court.

Live television links at certain preliminary hearings

Under CDA 1998, s 57B a magistrates' court may direct a live link hearing where D is in 'custody' (a term which does not include police detention but does include secure juvenile accommodation), and, by s 57C, it may direct a live link hearing where D is at a police station.

A magistrates' court may only make a live link direction under s 57C:

(a) where D is in police detention at a police station in connection with the offence and appears likely to remain there until the beginning of the preliminary hearing; or

(b) where D is at a police station in answer to live link bail (see p 158) in connection with the offence.

A live link direction may not be given under s 57C unless the court is satisfied that it is not contrary to the interests of justice to give the direction.

A direction given in relation to a defendant to whom (a) above applies has no effect if he does not remain in police detention at a police station until the beginning of the preliminary hearing. A defendant who answers 'live link bail' is to be treated as if he has surrendered to the custody of the court.

Committal for sentence

Where on the summary trial of an either-way offence a person aged 18 or over is convicted of the offence (but only after an indication of a guilty plea in the areas listed on p 14) and the magistrates' court considers that the offence, or the combination of the offence and one or more offences associated with it, was so serious that the Crown Court should have the power to deal with him, the court may commit him, in custody or on bail, to the Crown Court for sentence for that offence and any related either-way offences to which he has also pleaded guilty. Similar provisions are made in respect of children and young persons.

There are special provisions in respect of dangerous adult offenders who have been convicted on a summary trial of an offence triable either way. If it appears to the court that the criteria would be met for the imposition of a sentence under the CJA 2003, ss 225(3) or 227(2) (imprisonment for public protection for serious offences and extended sentences for certain violent or sexual offences) (prospectively replaced by s 226A (extended sentences for certain violent or sexual offences)), the court must commit the offender in custody or on bail to the Crown Court for sentence. Similar provision is made in respect of dangerous young offenders in relation to offences covered by CJA 2003, ss 226(3) or 228(2) (prospectively replaced by s 226B) which deal with corresponding sentences for such offenders.

In all cases, the Crown Court must inquire into the circumstances of the case and may deal with the offender in any way in which it could have dealt with him had he been tried and convicted before that court.

Youth courts

A youth court is a summary court (ie a magistrates' court) and is composed of justices who are specially appointed because of their qualifications. It sits for the purpose of hearing any charge against a child or young person or to exercise any other jurisdiction conferred on youth courts by the Courts Act 2003 or any other enactment.

The general public do not have a right of access to proceedings in a youth court.

A magistrates' court before which a person under 18 (hereafter described as a 'juvenile') appears charged with an offence which, in the case of an adult, is triable only on indictment or triable either way must deal with it *summarily* unless:

(a) the charge is one of homicide, or one of a number of particular types of offence of possessing a prohibited weapon and the young person was aged 16 or 17 when he committed it;

(b) the offence is so grave that, if found guilty, under specific statutory powers he may be sentenced to be detained for a long period;

(c) the offence charged is one of serious or complex fraud or one of certain offences involving child witnesses and a notice requiring trial on indictment has been served; or

(d) he is charged jointly with an adult (ie a person who has attained 18) and the court considers it necessary in the interests of justice to commit the case for trial.

With certain exceptions, no charge against a person under 18 may be heard summarily by a magistrates' court other than a youth court. The exceptions, which allow trial by an 'adult' magistrates' court, are:

(a) where the juvenile is charged jointly with an adult;

(b) where an adult is charged with aiding, abetting, counselling, procuring, allowing, or permitting an offence with which a juvenile is charged;

(c) where a juvenile is charged with aiding, etc an offence committed by an adult;

(d) where the fact that the person is a juvenile is discovered in the course of proceedings in a magistrates' court; and

(e) where the charge against a juvenile arises out of circumstances which are the same as, or are connected with, those which give rise to an offence by an adult (eg a theft by a youth and a handling by an adult).

The law recognises the specialist nature of youth courts by requiring a Crown Court or adult magistrates' court which finds a juvenile guilty of an offence other than homicide to send the case to a youth court for sentencing as if that juvenile had been found guilty by that court, unless satisfied that it would be undesirable to do so. In effect, subject to that exception, they must send the case to the youth court for sentence to be passed.

On occasions problems are caused in respect of the hearing of indictable offences where the person charged is a juvenile at the time of the commission of the offence but is an adult when it finally comes to trial. In such circumstances the appropriate date at which to determine whether a defendant has turned 18 for the purpose of the above procedures is the date of his appearance before the court when it determines which mode of trial is to be adopted, which is not necessarily his first appearance.

The 'pleading guilty by post' provisions described on p 22 do not generally apply to proceedings in a youth court. The only exception is where D is aged 16 or 17 when the summons or requisition is issued.

The sentencing powers of courts generally are limited in relation to children and young persons.

Crown Court

For convenience the locations of the Crown Court are grouped in six circuits. The towns on the list of Crown Court locations are divided into three tiers. In the first, sittings of the High Court are held for civil cases as well as of the Crown Court for criminal cases (and such civil matters as are within its jurisdiction). On the other hand, in second- and third-tier locations only sittings of the Crown Court are held.

The Crown Court has jurisdiction over all offences which are triable only on indictment and also over offences triable either way in respect of which D has been committed, or sent, for trial on indictment. Trials on indictment are heard with a jury who determine the issue of guilt after a direction on the relevant law by the judge. A trial can be without a jury where there is a risk of jury tampering.

Indictable offences are divided into three classes for the purposes of trial in the Crown Court; these classes depend on the seriousness of the offence. When committing, or sending, a person to a Crown Court, magistrates' courts will commit him to the appropriate tier of the Crown Court according to this classification.

A person who has been convicted by a magistrates' court may appeal to the Crown Court against sentence if he pleaded guilty, or against conviction or sentence if he pleaded not guilty. Appeals are heard by a court consisting of a judge and no more than four justices of the peace. The Crown Court also deals with people convicted in a magistrates' court who have been committed to it for sentence. These cases are determined by a judge sitting alone.

The Central Criminal Court in London is a Crown Court.

Queen's Bench Division of the High Court

One function of the High Court is to hear appeals on points of law from magistrates' courts or from the Crown Court in respect of appeals from magistrates' courts to the Crown Court. Such an appeal is known as appeal by case stated, since the magistrates' court or Crown Court is asked to 'state a case', that is set out its reasons for its finding on the basis of its interpretation of the law in relation to the facts found by it. The High Court is not concerned with any form of retrial.

Cases of the above type are dealt with by the Administrative Court, which is part of the Queen's Bench Division. They are heard by a divisional court or a single judge. A divisional court consists of two (or sometimes three) judges.

Judicial review

Judges in the Administrative Court also deal with the *judicial review* of the decisions of an inferior court or other body. In such cases the court will examine whether there was authority or power by which the decision made could have been properly reached; whether the procedure followed the rules of natural justice; or whether the exercise of discretion on the part of the decision-making body was lawful. Thus the court is not examining the correctness of the decision but whether it was lawfully, reasonably and proportionately reached.

Court of Appeal (Criminal Division)

Appeals to this division are normally heard by a court consisting of three judges.

If convicted of an offence on indictment before the Crown Court, a person may appeal to this court against *conviction* with the leave of the Court of Appeal or the trial judge. On an appeal against conviction, the Court of Appeal can dismiss the appeal, allow it and quash the conviction, or substitute a conviction for another offence if it appears that D should have been convicted of that offence, rather than the one of which he was actually convicted. If fresh evidence has come to light, the court may order a new trial. It may also do so in any other case where the interests of justice so require.

A person convicted on indictment before the Crown Court may appeal against *sentence* with the leave of the Court of Appeal, and so may a person who has been sentenced by the Crown Court on committal for sentence. On *appeal* against sentence, the Court of Appeal may vary a sentence but cannot increase it. However, the Attorney General may (in certain cases) refer a sentence to the Court of Appeal with its leave if it appears to him to be unduly lenient. On such a reference, the court may impose a more severe sentence.

CJA 2003, Part 9 permits a prosecutor to appeal to the Court of Appeal in relation to any ruling made by the judge within a trial on indictment, other than a ruling that a jury be discharged. Following notice, proceedings may be adjourned and the judge's ruling has no effect within the period of adjournment. Such an appeal may only be made against one ruling but in the case of a submission of 'no case to answer' other rulings may be specified which are related to that submission.

Supreme Court

The Supreme Court took over the House of Lords' judicial functions on 1 October 2009.

The Supreme Court is the highest court in the land and hears criminal appeals from the Court of Appeal or the Queen's Bench Division, but only where:

(a) the court has certified that a question of law of general public importance is involved; *and*

(b) the court or the Supreme Court is satisfied that the point of law is one which ought to be considered by the Supreme Court; *and*

(c) leave to appeal to the Supreme Court has been given by the court or the Supreme Court itself.

JURISDICTION OF ARMED SERVICE AUTHORITIES TO DEAL WITH CRIMINAL OFFENCES

The Acts relating to armed service personnel make provisions for concurrent jurisdiction in respect of civil and service courts. As a result, arrangements have been made between civilian and military prosecuting and investigating authorities governing how they will work together, decide issues of jurisdiction and, where necessary, decide how an allegation will be investigated.

PENALTY NOTICES FOR 'DISORDERLY BEHAVIOUR'

The Criminal Justice and Police Act 2001 (CJPA 2001), s 2, which is prospectively amended by the Legal Aid, Sentencing and Punishment of Offenders Act 2012, provides that a constable who has reason to believe that someone aged 10 (prospectively, 18) or over has committed a 'penalty offence' *may* issue a 'penalty notice for disorder' (PND). Until a day to be appointed, with the following exception, the constable must be in uniform. Until a day to be appointed, a penalty notice may only be given at a police station by a constable authorised by the chief officer of police; in such a case the officer need not be in uniform.

Prospectively, if the penalty offence is a 'relevant penalty offence', ie a penalty offence in relation to which there is an approved educational course, the constable may issue a penalty notice with an education option. Chief constables are prospectively given the power to set up within their area a scheme which will permit this to be done. An educational course run as part of the scheme will be an approved educational course. The scheme will give recipients of a penalty notice with an education option the opportunity to discharge their liability to be convicted of the penalty offence by paying for and completing an educational course related to the offence for which notice was given. An educational course might, for example, be aimed at making individuals aware of the social and health implications of their conduct and would be designed to reduce the risk of re-offending.

Until a day to be appointed, if a child under 16 is given a penalty notice, the chief officer of police must within 28 days notify in writing such parent or guardian of the child as he thinks fit, either by first class post or by delivery to the parent or guardian personally, of the giving of the penalty notice. The chief officer is given power to cancel the original notification within 21 days of its service if it is discovered that the person on whom the notification was served was not the parent or guardian of the child, or if it is desired that the notification should have been served on another parent or guardian of the child (in which case the parent or guardian served with the original notification must be informed in writing of the cancellation). If the chief officer cancels the original notification, he must notify such other person who is a parent or guardian of the child of the giving of the penalty notice.

Penalty offences

'Penalty offences' under CJPA 2001 fall into two groups:

Offence creating provision	Description of offence
First group:	
Explosives Act 1875, s 80	Throwing fireworks in a thoroughfare
Criminal Law Act 1967, s 5(2)	Wasting police time or giving false report
Criminal Justice Act 1967, s 91	Disorderly behaviour while drunk in a public place
Theft Act 1968, s 1	Theft
Criminal Damage Act 1971, s 1(1)	Destroying or damaging property
Misuse of Drugs Act 1971, s 5(2)	Possession of various forms of cannabis and cannabis derivatives, etc
Public Order Act 1986, s 5	Behaviour likely to cause harassment, alarm, or distress
Licensing Act 2003, s 141	Sale of alcohol to person who is drunk
Licensing Act 2003, s 146(1), (3)	Sale of alcohol to person under 18
Licensing Act 2003, s 149(3), (4)	Purchase of alcohol on behalf of person under 18, etc
Licensing Act 2003, s 151	Delivery of alcohol to person under 18 or allowing such delivery
Communications Act 2003, s 127(2)	Using a public electronic communications network in order to cause annoyance, inconvenience, or needless anxiety
Fireworks Act 2003, s 11	Contravention of a prohibition or failure to comply with a requirement imposed by or under fireworks regulations or making false statements
Fire and Rescue Services Act 2004, s 49	Knowingly giving a false alarm to person acting on behalf of a fire and rescue authority
Second group:	
Licensing Act 1872, s 12	Being drunk in a highway, other public place or licensed premises

Parks Regulation (Amendment) Act 1926, s 2(1) so far as it creates an offence against Parks Regulation Act 1872 relating to Royal Parks and Other Open Spaces Regulations 1997:	Failing to comply with, or contravening those Regulations by:
(a) reg 3(3)	littering
(b) reg 3(4)	cycling except on Park road or designated area
(c) reg 3(6)	dog fouling
British Transport Commission Act 1949, s 55	Trespassing on a railway
British Transport Commission Act 1949, s 56	Throwing stones, etc at trains or other things on railways
Environmental Protection Act 1990, s 87	Depositing and leaving litter
Criminal Justice and Police Act 2001, s 12	Consumption of alcohol in designated public place
Licensing Act 2003, s 149(1)	Purchase of alcohol by person under 18 on relevant premises
Licensing Act 2003, s 150	Consumption of alcohol by a person under 18 on relevant premises or allowing such consumption

Amount of penalty

The Penalties for Disorderly Behaviour (Amount of Penalty) Order 2002 prescribes penalties of £80 (£40 where notice given to child under 16) for the first group of offences, and £50 (£30 where notice given to child under 16) for the second group.

Payment of the penalty does not constitute an admission of the offence or any proof that it has been committed by the person to whom the notice was issued.

Effect of penalty notice

CJPA 2001, s 4 provides that, if a penalty notice is given to a person (A) under s 2, and A asks to be tried for the alleged offence in the specified manner before the end of the suspended enforcement period (21 days beginning with the date the notice was given), proceedings may be brought against him. If, in the case of a penalty notice that is not a penalty notice with an education option, by the end of the suspended enforcement period the penalty has not been paid, and A has not made a request to be tried, a sum equal to one and a half times the amount of the penalty may be registered under s 8 for enforcement against A as a fine. Prospectively, in the case of a penalty notice with an education option, a sum equal to one and a half times the amount of the penalty may be registered under s 8 for enforcement against A as a fine if, by the end of the suspended enforcement period, A does not:

(a) (i) ask to attend an approved educational course relating to the offence to which the notice relates,

(ii)   pay the penalty, or

(iii)   request to be tried; or

(b)   (i)   A has asked to attend an approved education course, and

(ii)   A does not, in accordance with regulations, pay the course fee, start such a course, or complete such a course.

General restrictions on proceedings

The relevant provisions are in CJPA 2001, s 5.

Proceedings for the offence to which a penalty notice relates may not be brought during the suspended enforcement period. If the penalty is paid before the end of the suspended enforcement period, no proceedings may be brought for the offence.

Prospectively, proceedings for an offence to which a penalty notice with an education option relates may not be brought against a person who has, by the end of the suspended enforcement period, asked to attend an approved educational course relating to the offence, unless (b) above applies. If the person to whom a penalty notice with an education option is given:

(a)   completes, in accordance with regulations, an approved educational course relating to the offence to which the notice relates, and

(b)   pays the course fee in accordance with those regulations,

no proceedings may be brought for the offence.

Miscellaneous points

The provisions in respect of registration of penalties and sums payable in default, and enforcement, are the same as those provided in relation to the more widely available fixed penalties for road traffic offences; see Chapter 11.

It is not intended that a penalty notice should always be issued in respect of the specified cases; the constable has discretion. Penalty notices are designed for minor and straightforward cases. More serious cases should be dealt with by using the traditional criminal process.

Community support officers and accredited persons may issue penalty notices under CJPA 2001, except they may not issue a notice in respect of theft or of depositing and leaving litter, and in addition an accredited person may not issue a notice in respect of criminal damage.

The issue of a fixed penalty notice for a specified offence (eg an offence under the Public Order Act 1986, s 5) and the payment of the penalty under it is only a bar to proceedings. It does not constitute an admission of the offence or any proof that it has been committed by A, in respect of the offence specified in the notice. It does not prevent proceedings against A for another, more serious offence (eg unlawfully inflicting grievous bodily harm, contrary to the Offences Against the Person Act 1861, s 20), which it subsequently becomes apparent was committed in the course of the same incident.

CHAPTER 3

Police Powers

Throughout this book, but particularly in this and the next four chapters, references are made to the Police and Criminal Evidence Act 1984, hereafter PACE.

Conduct in breach or in excess of a relevant statutory or common law power may constitute a breach of a 'Convention right' under the Human Rights Act 1998 and may cause the police officer concerned to be liable in civil law or in criminal law. It may also render inadmissible evidence obtained as a result.

The Equality Act 2010 makes it unlawful for police officers to discriminate against, harass, or victimise any person on the grounds of the 'protected characteristics' of age, disability, gender re-assignment, race, religion or belief, sex and sexual orientation, marriage and civil partnership, pregnancy, and maternity when using their powers. When police forces are carrying out their functions they also have a duty to have regard to the need to eliminate unlawful discrimination, harassment, and victimisation and to take steps to foster good relations.

CODES OF PRACTICE UNDER PACE

PACE, s 66 requires the Secretary of State to issue Codes of Practice, approved by both Houses of Parliament, to provide, within the terms of the Act, strengthened safeguards for the suspect and workable guidelines for the police. The Secretary of State may at any time revise a Code of Practice then in force. Such a revision does not require the approval of the Houses of Parliament, although it may be submitted for approval, but it must at least be laid before Parliament.

Eight Codes of Practice have been issued under PACE and apply throughout England and Wales. They are: Code A (stop and search); Code B (search and seizure); Code C (detention, treatment and questioning of persons); Code D (identification); Code E (audio recording of interviews); Code F (visual recording of interviews); Code G (arrest); and Code H (detention, treatment, and questioning of persons detained under the Terrorism Act 2000, s 41 and Sch 8).

The powers covered by the PACE Codes must be used fairly, responsibly, with respect for people suspected of committing offences, and without unlawful discrimination.

Apart from the PACE Codes of Practice, there are a number of codes under other statutes which are referred to at the appropriate points.

Compliance with PACE Codes

A police officer may be liable to disciplinary proceedings for a failure to comply with any provision in one of the Codes if that failure indicates that his conduct has not met the appropriate standards of behaviour, but such a failure does not of itself render him liable to civil or criminal proceedings (although it is admissible in such proceedings where a case is founded on some other ground). Evidence obtained in a way which involves a breach of a Code is not automatically inadmissible at the trial stage but the magistrates or judge may rule that it is inadmissible on the grounds (in the case of a confession) that it was obtained by oppression or is unreliable (p 245) or (in the case of any evidence) that it poses a threat to the fairness of the proceedings (p 260).

Any person with police powers conferred by a designation or accreditation under the Police Reform Act 2002 (see p 282) must have regard to relevant provisions of a Code in the exercise of powers and duties.

Wherever the PACE Codes of Practice require the prior authority or agreement of an officer of at least inspector or superintendent rank, a sergeant is treated as holding the rank of inspector, and a chief inspector as holding the rank of superintendent, if he has been authorised by a superintendent to perform the functions of the higher rank (PACE, s 107).

Police powers described in this chapter

Police powers are dealt with in the following order in this chapter:

(a) powers to stop and search;
(b) powers to conduct a road check;
(c) powers to arrest;
(d) powers of entry and search in relation to an arrest;
(e) powers to search under a search warrant;
(f)   general provisions on entry, search, seizure, access and retention;
(g) interception of communications, surveillance and the conduct and use of 'covert human intelligence sources'; and
(h) authorisation of action in respect of property.

A judge in the Administrative Court has held that, where a police officer effects a stop, search, or arrest under a power to do so, which the officer is justified in using, there is no requirement at common law for him to be aware of the legal origin of that power in order for its exercise to be lawful. The judge went on to express the point as follows:

> A legally accurate identification of the precise legal power under which a police officer acts is not, in the absence of specific provision to that effect, a requirement of its lawful exercise. There is no requirement to call the statutory provision or the correct section or subsection to mind at the moment a police officer exercises any power of stop, arrest or search in order for its exercise to be lawful. An act is not unlawful because a police officer does not ask himself or forgets which power he had, provided that he had the power to do what he did with knowledge and belief which he had.

Gender-related issues

All searches and procedures should be carried out with courtesy, consideration, and respect for the person concerned.

Certain provisions of the PACE Codes explicitly state that searches and other procedures may only be carried out by, or in the presence of, persons of the same sex as the person subject to the search or other procedure.

Annexes to Codes A, C, and H contain general provisions dealing with the implications of this in respect of transgender individuals (including transsexuals) and transvestites. The latest guidance is in Codes C and H. Police officers should show particular sensitivity when dealing with such persons. While there is no agreed definition of *'transgender'* (or 'trans'), it is generally used as an umbrella term to describe people whose gender identity (self-identification as being a woman, man, neither, or both) differs from the sex they were registered as at birth. The term includes, but is not limited to, transsexual people. *'Transsexual'* means a person who is proposing to undergo, is undergoing, or has undergone a process (or part of a process) for the purpose of gender re-assignment which is a protected characteristic under the Equality Act 2010 (see p 35) by changing physiological or other attributes of that person's sex. This includes aspects of gender such as dress and title. '*Transvestite*' means a person of one gender who dresses in the clothes of a person of the opposite gender; a transvestite does not live permanently in the gender opposite to that person's birth sex.

Legally, the *gender* (and, accordingly, the sex) of an individual (P) is P's gender as registered at birth unless P possesses a gender recognition certificate (GRC), in which case P's gender is the acquired gender.

When establishing whether someone should be treated as being male or female the following approach, designed to minimise embarrassment and secure the person's co-operation, should be followed:

(1) The person (P) must not be asked whether P has a GRC.
(2) If there is no doubt as to whether P should be treated as being male or female, P should be dealt with as being of that sex.
(3) If at any time (including during the search or carrying out the procedure) there is doubt as to whether P should be treated or continue to be treated as being male or female:
    (a) P should be asked what gender P considers P to be. If P expresses a preference to be dealt with as a particular gender, P should be asked to indicate and confirm a preference by signing the custody record or, if a custody record has not been opened, the search record or the officer's notebook. Subject to (b) below, P should be treated according to that preference;
    (b) if there are grounds to doubt that the preference in (a) accurately reflects P's predominant lifestyle, eg if P asks to be treated as a woman but documents and other information make it clear that P lives predominantly as a man, P should be treated according to what appears to be P's predominant lifestyle;
    (c) if P is unwilling to express a preference, efforts should be made to determine P's predominant lifestyle and P should be treated as such;
    (d) if none of the above apply, P should be dealt with according to what reasonably appears to have been P's sex as registered at birth.

Once a decision has been made about which gender P is to be treated as having, each officer responsible for the search or procedure should where possible be advised before the search or procedure of any doubt as to P's gender and P informed the doubts have been disclosed. This is important so as to maintain the dignity of the officer concerned.

Where the gender of P is established under the above procedures, the decision should be recorded either on the search record, in the officer's notebook, or, if applicable, in P's custody record. Where P elects which gender P considers P to be but is not treated in accordance with that preference, the reason must be recorded.

Information relating to a person's application for a GRC or to a successful applicant's gender before it became their acquired gender is 'protected information' and must not be disclosed by a police officer or police staff to any other person in contravention of the Gender Recognition Act 2004. Disclosure includes making a record of 'protected information' which is read by others.

POWERS TO STOP AND SEARCH

PACE, s 1 gives *every* constable (p 282), with reasonable grounds for suspicion, a power to stop and search for stolen goods, articles for use in certain property offences, offensive weapons, bladed or pointed articles, or fireworks.

Various statutes give *every* constable the power on reasonable suspicion to stop and search for particular articles, for example, controlled drugs, firearms, and game or poaching equipment.

PACE Code A: the Code of Practice for the Exercise by Police Officers of Statutory Powers of Stop and Search (hereafter referred to as the Stop and Search Code) applies to the following powers of stop and search:

(a) powers requiring reasonable grounds for suspicion that articles unlawfully obtained or possessed are being carried (or under the Terrorism Act 2000, s 43 (p 807) that a person is a terrorist);

(b) powers under the Criminal Justice and Public Order Act 1994, s 60 (see p 42); and

(c) powers to search a person who has not been arrested in the exercise of a power to search premises.

On the other hand, Code A does not apply to the powers of stop and search under PACE, s 6 (powers of constables employed by statutory undertakers (bodies authorised by statute to carry out any railway, road transport, inland navigation, or harbour undertaking) on premises of statutory undertaker), or under the Aviation Security Act 1982, s 27 (hijacking), or to searches carried out for the purposes of examination under the Terrorism Act 2000, Sch 7 (port and border controls) and to which the Code of Practice for Examining Officers issued under that Act applies.

Power under PACE, s 1 to stop and search

PACE, s 1(2) states that a constable:

(a) may search any person or vehicle ('vehicle' includes vessels, aircraft, and hovercraft), *and* anything which is in or on a vehicle, for stolen or prohibited articles or an article to which PACE, s 1(8A) applies or any firework to which subsection 1(8B) applies; and

(b) may detain persons or vehicles for the purpose of such a search.

PACE, s 1(3) provides that a constable only has this power to search if he has *reasonable grounds for suspecting* (see further p 40) that he will find stolen or prohibited articles or an article to which PACE, s 1(8A) applies or any firework to which PACE, s 1(8B) applies; he must of course have such grounds *before* carrying out a search. Reasonable force may be used in the exercise of these powers, but every effort should be made to persuade a person to co-operate and force should only be used as a last resort. A compulsory search may only be made if it is established that the person is unwilling to co-operate.

The courts have held that the test of lawfulness of a search under s 1 is:

(a) whether the searching constable suspected that he would find stolen or prohibited articles or anything to which s 1(8A) or (8B) applies;

(b) assuming that that constable had the necessary suspicion, whether there was reasonable cause for that suspicion; and

(c) if the answer to (a) and (b) is 'yes', whether that constable exercised his discretion to make a search in accordance with the general principles for the exercise of executive discretion, ie the decision to search must have been made taking into account relevant matters and excluding irrelevant ones, it must have been made for a proper purpose, and it must not have been one that no reasonable constable (taking account of the relevant matters) could have made.

It is not necessarily essential that the searching constable reasonably suspects each and every individual member of a group to be carrying a prohibited article etc before he can search the individual members of the group. A divisional court has held that, if (a) and (b) above have been satisfied in respect of the group, the issue in relation to searching the individual members goes to (c), namely whether the constable's decision to search the individuals, given his suspicion, reasonably held, went beyond the bounds of decision open to him under (c) in the circumstances in question.

Where a police officer has reasonable grounds to suspect that a person is in innocent possession of a specified article, the power to stop and search exists notwithstanding that there would be no power of arrest. However, every effort should be made to secure the voluntary production of the article before the power is resorted to.

A '*prohibited article*' is defined by PACE, s 1(8) as:

(a) an offensive weapon (which, by PACE, s 1(9), means any article made or adapted for use for causing injury to persons, or intended by the person having it with him for such use by him or by some other person); or
(b) an article made or adapted for use in the course of or in connection with an offence of burglary, theft, taking a conveyance without authority, fraud, or destroying or damaging property, or intended by the person having it with him for such use by him or by some other person.

An *article to which PACE, s 1(8A) applies* is any article with a blade or point in relation to which a person has committed, or is committing or is going to commit, an offence under the Criminal Justice Act 1988, s 139 or (prospectively) s 139AA.

An *article to which s 1(8B) applies* is any firework which a person possesses in contravention of a prohibition imposed by fireworks regulations. The term '*firework*' has the same meaning as in the Fireworks Act 2003, s 1(1) (ie devices which are fireworks for the purposes of the relevant British Standard specification or which would be if intended as a form of entertainment) and 'fireworks regulations' means the Fireworks Regulations 2004 referred to on p 651.

Places in which powers to search can be exercised

PACE, s 1(1) states that a constable may exercise any powers under s 1:

(a) in any place to which at the time when he proposes to exercise the power the public or any section of the public has access, on payment or otherwise, as of right or by virtue of express or implied permission; or
(b) in any other place to which people have ready access at the time when he proposes to exercise the power but which is not a dwelling.

Persons have a right to use streets and highways; they have express permission to access cinemas, theatres, or football grounds subject to paying an entry fee. There is an implied permission for persons to enter buildings to carry out business transactions with the owners, and even to use a footpath to a dwelling house for the purpose of paying a *lawful call* upon the householder.

'Place to which people have ready access' in (b) is wide in meaning. It extends the power of search to any place (other than a dwelling) to which the public have access in fact, whether lawfully or not; for example, a private field or grounds into which people regularly gain access as trespassers.

PACE, s 1(4) states that, if a person is in a garden or yard occupied with, and used for, the purposes of a dwelling or on other land so occupied and used, a constable may not search him under s 1 unless the constable has reasonable grounds for believing that:

(a) he does not reside in the dwelling; and

(b) he is not in the place in question with the express or implied permission of a person who resides in the dwelling.

Similar restrictions apply to the search of a vehicle (or anything in or on it) in a garden, yard, or land occupied with and used for the purpose of a dwelling. By PACE, s 1(5), a constable may not search it unless he has reasonable grounds for believing that:

(a) the person in charge of the vehicle does not reside in the dwelling; and

(b) the vehicle is not in the place in question with the express or implied permission of a person who resides in the dwelling.

In effect, the only places in which a constable cannot exercise s 1 powers are dwelling houses, the curtilage of dwelling houses if the person or vehicle is there lawfully, or any other place which is secure and does not permit ready access.

Seizure of articles

PACE, s 1(6) provides that suspected stolen or prohibited articles, or an article suspected to be one to which s 1(8A) or (1(8B) applies, found in a search may be seized.

Reasonable suspicion

The Stop and Search Code gives the following guidance on what may be 'reasonable suspicion' for the purposes of statutory powers of stop and search which require a reasonable suspicion. 'Reasonable suspicion' requires (a) that the officer suspects that the relevant matter is satisfied, and (b) that there are reasonable grounds for that suspicion.

'Suspicion' exists where a person thinks that there is a possibility, which is more than fanciful, that the relevant matter is satisfied. It can be contrasted with 'belief' which requires more than mere suspicion, since belief refers to having no substantial doubt about the matter in question.

Whether reasonable grounds for suspicion exist will depend on the circumstances in each case, but there must be some objective basis for it based on facts, information, and/or intelligence which are relevant to the likelihood of finding an article of a certain kind. Reasonable suspicion can never be supported on the basis of personal factors alone. It must rely on intelligence or information about, or some specific behaviour by, the person concerned. For example, unless the police have a description of a suspect, a person's physical appearance (including any of the 'protected characteristics' set out in the Equality Act 2010 (see p 35), or the fact that the person is known to have a previous conviction, cannot be used alone or in combination with each other, or in combination with any other factor, as the reason for searching that person. Reasonable suspicion cannot be based on generalisations or stereotypical images of certain groups or categories of people as more likely to be involved in criminal activity.

Reasonable suspicion can sometimes exist without specific information or intelligence and on the basis of the behaviour of a person. For example, if an officer encounters someone on the street at night who is obviously trying to hide something, the officer may (depending on the other surrounding circumstances) base such suspicion on the fact that this kind of behaviour is often linked to stolen or prohibited articles being carried.

However, reasonable suspicion should normally be linked to accurate and current intelligence or information, such as information describing an article being carried, a suspected offender, or a person who has been seen carrying a type of article known to have been stolen recently from premises within the area. This, however, does not prevent stop and search powers being exercised in other locations where such powers may be exercised and reasonable suspicion exists.

Where there is reliable information or intelligence that members of a group or gang habitually carry knives unlawfully or weapons or controlled drugs, and wear a distinctive item of clothing or other means of identification to indicate their membership of the group or gang, that distinctive item of clothing or other means of identification may provide reasonable grounds to stop and search a person. Other means of identification might include jewellery, insignias, tattoos, or other features which are known to identify members of the particular gang or group.

A police officer may have reasonable grounds to suspect that a person is in innocent possession of a stolen or prohibited article or other item for which he or she is empowered to search. In that case the officer may stop and search the person even though there would be no power of arrest.

An officer who has reasonable grounds for suspicion may detain the person concerned for the purpose of carrying out a search. Before doing so he may ask questions about the person's behaviour or presence in circumstances which gave rise to suspicion. As a result of questioning the detained person, the reasonable grounds for suspicion necessary to detain that person may be confirmed or, because of a satisfactory explanation, be eliminated. Questioning may also reveal reasonable grounds to suspect the possession of a different kind of unlawful article from that originally suspected. Reasonable grounds for suspicion, however, cannot be provided retrospectively by such questioning during a person's detention or by refusal to answer any questions put.

If, as a result of questioning before a search, or other circumstances which come to the attention of the officer, there cease to be reasonable grounds for suspecting that an article which is being carried is of a kind for which there is a power to stop and search, no search may take place. In the absence of any other lawful power to detain, the person is free to leave at will and must be so informed.

There is no power to stop and detain in order to find grounds for a search. Police officers have many encounters with members of the public which do not involve detaining people against their will. If reasonable grounds for suspicion emerge during such an encounter, the officer may search the person, even though no grounds existed when the encounter began. If an officer is detaining someone for the purpose of a search, he should inform the person as soon as the detention begins.

Whether or not an officer has reasonable suspicion will be judged objectively in the light of the knowledge which was available to the police officer when he made his decision. This might be a description of a person suspected of offences given to the officer when briefed for duty. However, such a general description of a person would not allow a search by itself; the officer would have to apply his mind to the circumstances surrounding the particular person under observation. The fact that such person appeared to be seeking an opportunity to commit a similar type of crime might reinforce suspicion sufficiently to satisfy the objective test.

Although information received from a member of the public may constitute a basis for reasonable suspicion, whether it actually does so depends on the content and nature of the information as well as the credibility of the informant. If the manager of a filling station tells a police officer that a man, of whom he gives a description, stole two cartons of cigarettes from the kiosk before driving off in a green Golf which was damaged on the front offside wing, the issue is fairly clear. If the officer sees a Golf of that description, driven by a man of the description given by the station manager, he may accept that the information which he was given was clear and that it was given by a reliable witness. He may reasonably act upon that information since it provides him with the necessary reasonable suspicion.

The Stop and Search Code does not affect the ability of an officer to speak to or question a person in the ordinary course of his duties (and in the absence of reasonable suspicion) without detaining him or exercising any element of compulsion. It is not the purpose of the Code to prohibit such encounters between the police and the community with the co-operation of the person concerned and neither does it affect the principle that all citizens have a duty to help police officers to prevent crime and discover offenders.

Authorisation of stop and search in anticipation of violence or after violence

The Criminal Justice and Public Order Act 1994 (CJPOA 1994), s 60 provides further powers to stop and search. Section 60(1) provides that where a police officer of the rank of inspector or above reasonably *believes* (p 54):

(a) that incidents involving serious violence may take place in any locality in his police area, and that it is expedient to give an authorisation under s 60 to prevent their occurrence; or

(b) that
    (i) an incident involving serious violence has taken place in England and Wales in his police area;
    (ii) a dangerous instrument or offensive weapon used in the incident is being carried in any locality in his police area by a person; and
    (iii) it is expedient to give an authorisation under s 60 to find the instrument or weapon; or

(c) that persons are carrying dangerous instruments or offensive weapons in any locality in his police area without good reason,

he may give an authorisation that the powers conferred by the section are to be exercised at any place within that locality for a specified period not exceeding 24 hours. 'Offensive weapon' in (b) is extended in the case of an incident of the kind mentioned in (b) to include 'any article used in the incident to cause or threaten injury to any person or otherwise to intimidate'.

'Locality' is intentionally not defined, as the extent of a 'locality' will differ in relation to the nature of the incident. An anticipated serious disorder at a pub would be in a small 'locality' while one within a housing estate would be in an extensive 'locality'. Provided that thought has been given to defining the locality, and this can be proved, a court is unlikely to rule that the authorisation was invalid. The authorising officer should not set a geographical area which is wider than that he believes necessary for the purpose of preventing anticipated violence or the carrying of knives or offensive weapons or for the purpose of finding dangerous instruments or weapons that have been used.

Whether or not it is expedient to give an authorisation may involve consideration of the effectiveness of other powers, and the resources available to deal with the type of incidents which might arise. Provided that such judgements are made in good faith, a court is unlikely to interfere.

The period during which these powers may be exercised must be the minimum considered necessary to deal with the risk of violence or the carrying of knives or offensive weapons.

The area within which these powers may be exercised must be carefully specified and officers must be aware of the geographical area enclosed. If the powers are to be used in response to a threat or incident which straddles police force areas, an officer from each of the forces affected must give an authorisation.

Where an inspector gives such an authorisation he must, as soon as it is reasonably practicable to do so, cause an officer of or above the rank of superintendent to be informed.

The authorisation may be extended once only for a further 24 hours on the authority of an officer of or above the rank of superintendent, where expedient, having regard to offences committed, or reasonably suspected to have been committed, in connection with an activity falling within the authorisation. Thereafter further use of the powers requires a new authorisation.

Police powers

Stop and search   Where an authorisation is in force under CJPOA 1994, s 60 a constable in uniform is empowered:

(a) to stop any pedestrian and search him and anything carried by him, for offensive weapons or dangerous instruments; and

(b) to stop any vehicle and search the vehicle, its driver, and any passenger for offensive weapons or dangerous instruments.

A driver of a vehicle which has been stopped is entitled to obtain a written statement to that effect, if he applies within 12 months. The same rights apply to pedestrians or a person in a vehicle.

These stops and searches may be carried out *whether or not* the *constable in question* has any grounds for suspecting that the person or vehicle is carrying weapons or articles of the specified kind. A constable may seize any dangerous instrument or any article which he has reasonable grounds for suspecting to be an offensive weapon. A 'dangerous instrument' is one which has a blade or is sharply pointed; a vehicle includes a 'caravan'; and an 'offensive weapon' is as defined by PACE, s 1(9) (see p 39). A person carries a dangerous instrument or an offensive weapon if he has it in his possession.

The selection of persons and vehicles under s 60 to be stopped and, if appropriate, searched should reflect an objective assessment of the nature of the incident or weapon in question and the individuals and vehicles thought likely to be associated with that incident or those weapons. The powers under s 60 must not be used to stop and search persons and vehicles for reasons unconnected with the purpose of the authorisation. When selecting persons and vehicles to be stopped in response to a specific threat or incident, officers must take care not to discriminate unlawfully against anyone on the grounds of any of the protected characteristics set out in the Equality Act 2010 (see p 35).

Require removal of marks etc   In addition, where an authorisation under CJPOA 1994, s 60 is in force in relation to any locality, by s 60AA(2) a constable in uniform is given the power in that locality:

(a) to require any person to remove any item (eg a face mask) which the constable reasonably believes that person is wearing wholly or mainly for the purpose of concealing his identity; and

(b) to seize any item which the constable reasonably believes any person intends to wear wholly or mainly for that purpose.

An authorisation may also be given for the exercise of the powers under CJPOA 1994, s 60AA(2) in a case where an authorisation under s 60 is not in force in relation to a locality if an officer of or above the rank of inspector reasonably believes that activities may take place in any locality in his police area that are likely (if they take place) to involve the commission of offences, and that it is expedient, in order to prevent or control the activities to give the following authorisation. In such a case that officer may authorise under s 60AA(3) that the powers under s 60AA(2) shall be exercisable at any place within that locality for a specified period not exceeding 24 hours. Where it then appears to a superintendent that, in view of offences which have been, or are reasonably suspected to have been, committed in connection with the activities to which the authorisation relates, he may direct that the authorisation continues in force for a further 24 hours. Where an inspector gives the initial authorisation under s 60AA(3), as soon as practicable he must inform a superintendent (or above).

Further points

In the case of the British Transport Police references to a 'locality' or to 'a locality in his police area' are references to any locality in or in the vicinity of any policed premises, or to the whole or any part of such premises.

An authorisation under s 60 or s 60AA must be in writing and signed and must specify the grounds for it, the locality and the period during which the powers are exercisable. There is one exception: an authorisation under s 60(1)(aa) need not be given in writing where it is not practicable to do so but any oral authorisation must state the matters which otherwise would have to be specified in respect of an authorisation under s 60 and must be recorded in writing as soon as practicable. It is for the authorising officer to determine the period of time during which he proposes to exercise these powers. It should be the minimum period he considers necessary to deal with the risk of violence or the carrying of knives or offensive weapons or to find dangerous instruments or weapons that have been used.

An extension of the initial 24-hour period must be signed by the superintendent (or above) making it, or where that is not practicable, recorded in writing as soon as practicable.

As indicated above, an officer exercising the power to require the removal of a face covering must reasonably believe that someone is wearing the item wholly or mainly for the purpose of concealing his identity. There is no power to stop and search for a face covering. However, a face covering may be seized if it is discovered when searching for something else, or is seen to be carried in circumstances in which an officer reasonably believes it is intended to be used for the purpose of concealing identity.

A person who fails to stop or (as the case may be) to stop his vehicle when required to do so by a constable exercising these powers commits an offence (s 60(8)). Failure to remove an item when required is an offence (s 60AA(7)).

Authorisation of stop and search for the prevention of terrorism

This is dealt with in Chapter 28 (see p 809).

Power to stop and search at aerodromes

The Aviation Security Act 1982, s 24B permits a constable to search without warrant any person, vehicle, or aircraft in an aerodrome, or anything which is in or on such a vehicle or aircraft, for stolen or prohibited articles, provided that he has reasonable grounds for suspecting that he will find such articles. For the purposes of carrying out such a search, a constable may enter any part of an aerodrome; detain a person, vehicle, or aircraft; and board any vehicle or aircraft. He may seize any article which he has reasonable grounds for suspecting to be a stolen or prohibited article.

For these purposes, a 'prohibited article' is an article:

(a) made or adapted for use in the course of or in connection with criminal conduct; or
(b) intended by the person having it with him for such use by him or some other person.

'Criminal conduct' means conduct which constitutes an offence in the part of the UK in which the aerodrome is situated, or would constitute an offence in that part of the UK if it occurred there.

Section 24B does not authorise entry into a dwelling.

Searches where no power to search

An officer must not search a person, even with his consent, where no power to search is applicable. The Stop and Search Code specifies, as a sole exception, that an officer does not require a specific power to search persons with their consent given as a condition of entry to sports grounds or other premises. See, further, p 787.

Factors to be considered before carrying out a search

PACE, s 2(1) provides that, if a constable detains a person or vehicle in the exercise of the power under s 1 or any similar power to stop and search, he need not subsequently carry out that search if it appears to him that no search is required or that a search is impracticable. These circumstances will frequently arise: a person will often be detained on valid grounds for the purpose of a search and then satisfy the constable of his bona fides by answering his questions, or because of other circumstances which come to the attention of the officer. In such a case it is unnecessary to search and the detention will not be unlawful merely because the search was not carried out.

Procedure before carrying out a search

The following procedure is provided by the Stop and Search Code. Before any search of a detained person or attended vehicle takes place the officer must take reasonable steps, if not in uniform, to show his warrant card to the person to be searched or in charge of the vehicle to be searched, and whether or not in uniform, to give that person the following information:

(a) that he is being detained for the purposes of a search;
(b) the officer's name (except in the case of enquiries linked to the investigation of terrorism, or otherwise where the officer reasonably believes that giving his name might put him in danger, in which case a warrant or other identification number must be given and the name of the police station to which the officer is attached);
(c) the legal search power which is being exercised; and
(d) a clear explanation of the object of the search in terms of the article or articles for which there is a power to search; and in the case of:

    (i)   the power under the Criminal Justice and Public Order Act 1994, s 60, the nature of the power, the authorisation and the fact that it has been given;

    (ii) all other powers requiring reasonable suspicion, the grounds for that suspicion;

(e) that he is entitled to a copy of the record of the search if one is made if he asks within three months from the date of the search and:

    (i)   if he is not arrested and taken to a police station as a result of the search and it is practicable to make the record on the spot, that immediately after the search is completed he will be given, if he requests, either a copy of the record, or a receipt which explains how he can obtain a copy of the full record or access to an electronic copy of the record, or

    (ii) if he is arrested and taken to a police station as a result of the search, that the record will be made at the station as part of his custody record and he will be given, if he requests, a copy of his custody record which includes a record of the search as soon as practicable whilst he is at the station.

A divisional court has held that a failure to take the above reasonable steps renders a search unlawful.

The above requirements apply even if the police officer reasonably believes that the suspect is about to dispose of the item in question. The Court of Appeal has suggested that they can be satisfied by simply saying, eg 'Jones, Central; drug search; spit it out'.

Because non-compliance with the requirements renders a search unlawful, a suspect who obstructs the search or resists it will not be guilty of assaulting or obstructing a police officer in the execution of his duty.

The person should also be given information about police powers to stop and search and the individual's rights in these circumstances.

If the person to be searched, or in charge of a vehicle to be searched, does not understand what is being said, or there is any doubt about his ability to understand English, the officer must take reasonable steps to bring to that person's attention his rights and any relevant provisions of the Stop and Search Code. If that person is deaf or cannot understand English and has someone with him, the officer must establish whether that person can interpret or otherwise help him to give the required information.

A constable asking a person to remove a mask pursuant to the CJPOA, s 60AA is not performing a search, so the above requirements do not apply.

Conduct of search

Every reasonable effort must be made to minimise the embarrassment that a person being searched may experience. By PACE, s 2(8) a person may be detained for a search for such time as is reasonably required to permit a search to be carried out either at the place where the person or vehicle was first detained or nearby.

The co-operation of the person to be searched must always be sought, even if he initially objects to being searched. A forcible search may be made only if it has been established that the person is unwilling to co-operate (eg by opening a bag) or resists. A judge in the Administrative Court has held that a pat-down search does not constitute a forcible search, and that neither does placing a hand on a person's body without applying pressure. Reasonable force may be used as a last resort, but only if this is necessary to detain the person or to search him. The length of time for which a person or vehicle may be detained will depend on the circumstances, but it must be reasonable and not extend beyond the time taken for the search.

The Stop and Search Code advises that, where the exercise of the power requires reasonable suspicion, the extent of the search will be related to the nature of the article sought and the circumstances. If a person is seen to put an offensive weapon into a particular pocket, then, unless there are grounds for suspecting that it has been moved elsewhere, the search must be confined to that pocket; whereas, if the article sought may easily be concealed anywhere on the person, the search may have to be more thorough.

The term 'nearby' in PACE, s 2(8) is not defined but it is submitted that it should be interpreted quite narrowly. To move a vehicle from a congested spot into a side street, or a person from the public gaze into an alley, would be a reasonable action to take and would not prevent the search from being 'nearby'.

An officer who is not in uniform may not stop a vehicle for the purpose of a search.

Removal of clothing

The Stop and Search Code restricts searches in public to a 'superficial examination of outer clothing'. A constable is not authorised under PACE, s 1, or under any other power of stop and search, to *require* a person to remove any of his clothing in public other than an outer coat, jacket, or gloves, or under CJPOA 1994, s 60AA (see p 43: power to require the removal of any item worn to conceal identity). Where there might be religious sensitivities about asking someone to remove a face covering, as in the case of a Muslim woman, the police officer should permit the item to be removed out of public view (for example, in a police van or police station if there is one nearby). Where practicable, the item should be removed in the presence of an officer of the same sex and out of sight of anyone of the opposite sex. A search in public of clothing which has not been removed must be restricted to a superficial examination of outer garments. This does not prevent an officer placing his hands inside the pockets of outer clothing, or feeling around the inside of collars, socks, and shoes if this is reasonably necessary. Subject to the restrictions upon removal of headgear, a person's hair may be searched in public.

If, on reasonable grounds, a more extensive search than a superficial examination of outer clothing is considered necessary (eg by requiring a person to take off a T-shirt or headgear) it must be done out of view of the public, for example in a police van or a police station if there is one nearby. Any search involving more than the removal of an outer coat, jacket or gloves, headgear or footwear, or any other item concealing identity, may only be made by an officer of the same sex as the person searched and may not be made in the presence of anyone of the opposite sex (see p 36) unless the person being searched specifically requests it.

Searches which involve exposure of intimate parts of the body must not be conducted as a routine extension of a less thorough search simply because nothing is found in the course of the initial search. Searches involving such exposure may be carried out only at a nearby police station or other nearby location which is out of the public view.

A search in a street itself should be regarded as being in public, even though the street is empty at the time the search begins. As a search of a person in public should be a superficial examination of outer clothing, such searches should be completed as soon as possible.

Recording requirements

Searches which do not result in an arrest

A record of the search must be made, electronically or on paper, unless there are exceptional circumstances making this wholly impracticable (eg in situations involving public disorder or when the recording officer's presence is urgently required elsewhere). If a record is to be made, the officer carrying out the search must make the record on the spot unless this is not practicable, in which case, the officer must make the record as soon as practicable after the search is completed.

If the record is made at the time, the person searched or in charge of the vehicle searched must be asked if he wants a copy; if he does, he must be given immediately (a) a copy of the record, or (b) a receipt which explains how he can obtain a copy of a full record or access to an electronic copy of the record.

An officer is not required to provide a copy of the full record or a receipt at the time if he is called to an incident of higher priority. In such a situation, the officer should consider giving the person details of the station which he may attend for a copy of the record. A receipt may take the form of a simple business card which includes sufficient information to locate the record should the person ask for a copy, for example, the date and place of the search, a reference number, or the name of the officer who carried out the search (unless the exception below in the case of terrorism investigations applied).

Searches which result in an arrest

If a search results in a person being arrested and taken to a police station, the officer carrying out the search must ensure that a record of the search is made as part of the custody record. The custody officer must then ensure that the person is asked if he wants a copy of the record, and if he does, that he is given a copy as soon as practicable.

The requirement to make the record of the search as part of the person's custody record does not apply if the person is granted 'street bail' after arrest (p 62) to attend a police station and is not taken in custody to the police station. An arrested person's entitlement to a copy of the search record which is made as part of his custody record does not affect his entitlement to a copy of his custody record or any other provisions of PACE Code C (Detention Code) about custody records.

Record of search

The record of a search must always include the following information:

(1) *A note of the self-defined ethnicity, and, if different, the ethnicity as perceived by the officer making the search, of the person searched or of the person in charge of the vehicle searched (as the case may be).*

Officers should record the self-defined ethnicity of every person stopped according to the categories used in the 2001 census question listed in Annex B. The person should be asked to select one of the five main categories representing broad ethnic groups and then a more specific cultural background from within this group. The ethnic classification should be coded for recording purposes using the coding system in Annex B. An additional 'Not stated' box is available but should not be offered to respondents explicitly. Officers should be aware and explain to members of the public, especially where concerns are raised, that this information is required to obtain a true picture of stop and search activity and to help improve ethnic monitoring, tackle discriminatory practice, and promote effective use of the powers. If the person gives what appears to the officer to be an 'incorrect' answer (eg a person who appears to be white states that he is black), the officer should record the response that has been given and then record his own perception of the person's ethnic background by using the PNC classification system. If the 'Not stated' category is used the reason for this must be recorded on the form.

(2) *The date, time and place the person or vehicle was searched.*

(3) *The object of the search in terms of the article or articles for which there is a power to search.*

(4) *In the case of:*

   (a) *the power under the Criminal Justice and Public Order Act 1994, s 60, the nature of the power, the authorisation, and the fact that it has been given;*

   (b) *all other powers requiring reasonable suspicion, the grounds for that suspicion.*

(5) *Subject to one exception, the identity of the officer carrying out the search.*

   Where a stop and search is carried out by more than one person the identity of all the officers must be recorded in the record. The exception referred to is that the names of police officers are not required to be shown on the search record or any other record required to be made under the Stop and Search Code in the case of enquiries linked to the investigation of terrorism or otherwise where an officer reasonably believes that recording names might endanger the officers. In such cases the record must show the officers' warrant or other identification number and duty station.

For the purposes of completing the search record, there is no requirement to record the name, address, and date of birth of the person searched or the person in charge of a vehicle which is searched and the person is under no obligation to provide this information.

A record is required for each person and each vehicle searched. However, only one record is required where a person who is in a vehicle is searched in addition to the vehicle, and the object and grounds of the search are the same. Where only a vehicle is searched, the self-defined ethnic background of the person in charge of the vehicle must be recorded, unless the vehicle is unattended.

The record of the grounds for making a search must, briefly but informatively, explain the reason for suspecting the person concerned, by reference to the person's behaviour and/or other circumstance.

Where officers detain an individual with a view to performing a search, but the need to search is eliminated as a result of questioning the person detained, a search should not be carried out (see p 41) and a record is not required. A guidance note states that, where there are concerns which make it necessary to monitor any local disproportionality, forces have discretion to direct officers to record the self-defined ethnicity of persons whom they detain with a view to searching but do not search. Guidance should be provided locally and efforts made to minimise the bureaucracy involved. Records should be closely monitored and supervised in line with the monitoring provisions below and forces can suspend or reinstate recording of these encounters as appropriate.

Encounters not governed by statutory powers

The revised Stop and Search Code does not contain the national recording requirement (and associated provisions) in respect of such encounters (request in public place to account) which used to be specified. Reversing the previous position, it provides that there is no national requirement for an officer who requests a person in a public place to account for himself, ie his actions, behaviour, presence in an area, or possession of anything, to make any record of the encounter or to give the person a receipt. The guidance note referred to in the previous paragraph applies equally where there are concerns which make it necessary to monitor any local disproportionality; forces have discretion to direct officers to record the self-defined ethnicity of persons whom they request to account for themselves in a public place. A person who is asked to account for himself should, if he requests, be given information about how he can report his dissatisfaction about how he has been treated.

Unattended vehicles

If an unattended vehicle, or anything in or on it, is searched the constable is required to leave a notice:

(a) stating that he has searched it;
(b) giving the name of the police station to which he is attached;
(c) stating that any application for compensation for any damage caused by the search may be made to that police station; and
(d) stating that the person in charge of the vehicle may obtain a copy of the record of the search (if there is one) if he asks for it within three months.

The notice should explain how (if applicable) an electronic copy of the record may be accessed. The notice must be left inside the vehicle (or on it, if things have been searched without opening it). A vehicle which has been searched must, if practicable, be left secure.

Monitoring and supervising the use of stop and search powers

Supervising officers must monitor the use of stop and search powers and should consider whether there is evidence of such powers being exercised on the basis of stereotyped images or inappropriate generalisations and should satisfy themselves that officers are acting in accordance with the Stop and Search Code. They must also examine whether the records reveal any trends or patterns which give cause for concern, and, if they recognise such trends, take appropriate action. Senior officers with area or force-wide responsibilities must also monitor such matters on a broader basis. Disproportionate use in relation to particular sections of the community should be investigated. Arrangements must be made, in consultation with local policing bodies, for records to be scrutinised by community representatives. Such scrutiny must take account of an individual's right to confidentiality.

Search and seizure powers of community support officers

If their designation so provides, community support officers may exercise specified powers to search and seize. All references to 'officers' in the provisions about records and related matters include community support officers so designated.

POWERS TO CONDUCT A ROAD CHECK

Statutory power

PACE, s 4 governs the conduct of road checks by police officers for the purpose of ascertaining whether a vehicle is carrying:

(a) a person who has committed an offence other than a road traffic offence or a vehicle excise offence;
(b) a person who is a witness to such an offence;

(c) a person intending to commit such an offence; or

(d) a person unlawfully at large.

For these purposes, a 'road check' consists of the exercise in a locality of the power conferred by RTA 1988, s 163 (power of a constable in uniform to stop a mechanically propelled vehicle or pedal cycle on a road) in such a way as to stop all vehicles or vehicles selected by any criterion.

PACE, s 4 is mainly concerned with setting up road checks to arrest actual or intending criminals or escaping prisoners. The purpose of the check will be to stop all vehicles or selected vehicles. It may be that the person the officers are seeking to arrest is known to be in a black Volkswagen Golf car and therefore only vehicles similar to that description will be stopped. Section 4 does not in any way affect an officer's powers to deal with road traffic matters and he may stop as many vehicles as he thinks necessary for that purpose. An officer who wishes to stop a single vehicle, which he reasonably suspects may be carrying a person who has committed or intends to commit an offence, etc, may do so under the powers given by RTA 1988, s 163, which are unaffected in such circumstances.

Authorisation of road checks

A road check must be authorised in writing. Normally, the authorisation must be given by an officer of the rank of superintendent or above. PACE, s 4 limits the instances in which authorisation may be given. An officer may only authorise a road check under s 4:

(a) for the purpose specified in (a) above, if he has reasonable grounds:–
   (i) for believing that the offence is an indictable offence; and
   (ii) for suspecting that the person is, or is about to be, in that locality in which vehicles would be stopped if the road check were authorised;

(b) for the purpose specified in (b) above, if he has reasonable grounds for believing that the offence is an indictable offence;

(c) for the purpose specified in (c) above, if he has reasonable grounds:–
   (i) for believing that the offence is an indictable offence; and
   (ii) for suspecting that the person is, or is about to be, in that locality in which vehicles would be stopped if the road check were authorised;

(d) for the purpose specified in (d) above, if he has reasonable grounds for suspecting that the person is, or is about to be, in that locality.

PACE, s 4 recognises that there will be emergencies rendering it impracticable to obtain the authorisation of a superintendent in sufficient time for a road check to be effective. In such circumstances, authorisation may be given by an officer below the rank of superintendent, but that officer must, as soon as practicable:

(a) make a written record of the time of authorisation; and

(b) cause a superintendent (or above) to be informed.

The superintendent (or above) may then authorise, in writing, the road check to continue. If he decides it should not continue, he must record the fact that it took place, and its purpose (including the relevant indictable offence).

Time limits, records and searches

The maximum period for which a road check may be authorised is seven days, but written authorisation may be given for a further period not exceeding seven days if a superintendent (or above) believes that a road check ought to continue.

The authorisation may be for a road check to be carried out throughout the 24 hours of each day, or may be limited to specified times.

The record (ie written authorisation) which must be kept of a road check must show:

(a) the period during which the road check is authorised to continue;
(b) the name of the officer who authorised it;
(c) the purpose of the road check (including any relevant indictable offence); and
(d) the locality in which vehicles are to be stopped.

The person in charge of a vehicle stopped in a road check is entitled to obtain a written statement *of the purpose* of the road check if he applies for it within 12 months.

PACE does not give direct powers to a constable to search a vehicle stopped in a road check. However, he is empowered to do so:

(a) if he has reasonable grounds for suspecting that it contains stolen or prohibited articles (PACE, s 1); or
(b) for the purpose of arresting someone for an offence or certain other offences if he has reasonable grounds to suspect that the person is there (PACE, s 17); or
(c) under powers granted by any other statute, eg the Firearms Act 1968.

Common law powers

The power under PACE, s 4 does not affect or replace the existing common law power to set up road checks where an imminent breach of the peace is reasonably apprehended.

Having stopped the vehicle under this power, the police may also search it thereunder. Anyone who insists on continuing his journey is liable to arrest under the common law power to arrest for an apprehended breach of the peace (see p 57).

Clearly, where the imminent breach of the peace would involve the commission of an indictable offence a road check can be operated either under PACE, s 4 or under the common law power. The procedural safeguards laid down for s 4 road checks do not, of course, apply to those under the common law power.

Prevention of terrorism: police cordons and prohibitions or restrictions on parking

TA 2000, ss 33 to 36 and 48 to 52 provide powers to impose a police cordon and to prohibit or restrict parking for the purposes of a 'terrorist investigation' (as defined by TA 2000, s 32). These provisions are discussed in Chapter 28 (see pp 805 and 821).

POWERS TO ARREST

An arrest may be authorised by a warrant or be lawfully made without warrant. The law relating to the issue and execution of warrants of arrest issued by a justice of the peace was explained in Chapter 2. The law relating to arrest without warrant is as follows.

ARREST WITHOUT WARRANT: CONSTABLES

PACE, s 24, supplemented by PACE Code G: the Code of Practice for the Statutory Power to Arrest by Police Officers, hereafter 'the Arrest Code', deals with this.

A lawful arrest under PACE, s 24 requires two elements:

(a) a person's involvement, or attempted involvement, or suspected involvement, in the commission of a criminal offence; and
(b) reasonable grounds for believing that the person's arrest is necessary for one of a number of specified reasons.

The Court of Appeal has held that, if elements (a) and (b) are satisfied, it is immaterial to the lawfulness of an arrest that the arresting constable erroneously believes that another constable has begun the process of arresting the person concerned.

Involvement or suspected involvement in the commission of an offence

By PACE, s 24(1) to (3):

(1) A constable may arrest without warrant:
    (a) anyone who is *about to* commit an offence;
    (b) anyone who *is in* the act of committing an offence;
    (c) anyone whom *he has reasonable grounds for suspecting to be about* to commit an offence;
    (d) anyone whom *he has reasonable grounds for suspecting to be* committing an offence.
(2) If a constable has *reasonable grounds for suspecting* that an offence *has been* committed he may arrest without warrant anyone whom *he has reasonable grounds* to suspect of being guilty of it.
(3) If an offence *has been committed*, a constable may arrest without warrant:
    (a) anyone who *is* guilty of the offence;
    (b) anyone whom *he has reasonable grounds for suspecting to be* guilty of it.

'Suspicion' exists where a person thinks that there is a possibility, which must be more than fanciful, that the relevant matter is satisfied.

There must be some reasonable, objective grounds for the suspicion, based on known facts or information which are relevant to the likelihood that the offence has been committed and to the fact that the person to be questioned committed it. There may be grounds for arresting a suspect on the sole basis of the word of an informant but any police officer should treat that information with considerable reserve.

As in the case of most other police powers where phrases like 'reasonable grounds for suspecting' are used, it is not enough that such reasonable grounds for suspicion exist; the constable must actually suspect the matter in question. The Court of Appeal has emphasised that whether a police officer has reasonable grounds for suspicion depends on the information which he has, and that an officer instructed to arrest a person but without being given reasonable grounds to suspect that person's guilt cannot assume that his superior who instructed him must have other information providing reasonable grounds which has not been disclosed to him. The Court of Appeal has held that, when an arresting officer's suspicion is formed on the basis of a Police National Computer entry, that entry is likely to provide him with a reasonable suspicion.

The necessity criteria

By s 24(4), the power of arrest without warrant conferred by s 24(1) to (3) is only exercisable if the constable has *reasonable grounds for believing* that it is *necessary* for specified reasons (the 'necessity criteria' set out in s 24(5)) to arrest the person. 'Belief' is more than 'suspicion'; it refers to having no substantial doubt about the relevant matter.

Noting that PACE, s 24(4) requires the arresting constable to have had reasonable grounds for believing that it was necessary to arrest the person in question, a High Court judge has held that the constable's own reasons for that belief were material to the consideration of whether s 24(4) had been satisfied. The grounds on which the constable formed the belief would be tested against objective criteria to determine the reasonableness of the belief, and a court would only interfere with the operational discretion given to a constable if his belief was so unreasonable that no reasonable person could have come to it. If there were no reasonable grounds at the time of the arrest, which is the crucial time, that defect cannot be cured subsequently by the custody officer considering that there were reasonable grounds when the arrested person was presented before him.

The Court of Appeal has held that an arresting officer is not required actively to consider all possible courses of action alternative to arrest. The effect of PACE, s 24(4), it held, is that (a) the officer must believe arrest to be necessary for one of the reasons specified in s 24(5); and (b) that belief must be objectively reasonable; there is not a third requirement actively to consider all possible courses of action alternative to arrest.

The specified reasons   are set out in s 24(5) as follows:

(a) to enable the name of the person in question to be ascertained (in the case where the constable does not know, and cannot readily ascertain, the person's name, or has reasonable grounds for doubting whether a name given by the person as his name is his real name);

(b) correspondingly as regards the person's address;

(c) to prevent the person in question:
   (i)   causing physical injury to himself or any other person;
   (ii)   suffering physical injury
   (iii) causing loss of or damage to property;
   (iv)   committing an offence against public decency (but only where members of the public going about their normal business cannot reasonably be expected to avoid the person in question); or
   (v)   causing an unlawful obstruction on the highway;

(d) to protect a child or other vulnerable person from the person in question;

(e) to prevent any prosecution for the offence from being hindered by the disappearance of the person in question, as where there are reasonable grounds for believing that if the person is not arrested he will not attend court, or that street bail after arrest would be insufficient to deter the suspect from trying to evade prosecution;

(f) to allow the prompt and effective investigation of the offence or of the conduct of the person in question.

As the Arrest Code points out, head (f) may include cases such as:

(a) where there are reasonable grounds to believe that the person concerned:
   (i)   has made false statements;
   (ii)   has made statements which cannot readily be verified;
   (iii) has presented false evidence;
   (iv)   may steal or destroy evidence;
   (v)   may make contact with co-suspects or conspirators;
   (vi)   may intimidate or threaten or make contact with witnesses; or
   (vii) may have information which may be obtained by questioning; or

(b) when considering arrest in connection with an indictable offence there is a need
to:
(i)   enter and search any premises occupied or controlled by a person;
(ii) search the person;
(iii) prevent contact with others; or
(iv) take fingerprints, footwear impressions, samples, or photographs of the sus-
      pect; or
(c) to ensure compliance with statutory drug testing requirements.

The Arrest Code adds the following points. An arrest interferes with the right to liberty recognised by the European Convention on Human Rights, art 5. The power must
be used fairly, responsibly, with respect for the suspect, and without unlawful discrimination. It remains an operational decision at the discretion of the arresting officer as to:

(a) which one or more of the necessity criteria (if any) applies to the individual; and
(b) *if any of the criteria do apply*, whether to arrest, grant street bail after arrest, report
    for summons or for charging by post, issue a penalty notice, or take any other
    action that is open to the officer.

In applying the criteria, the arresting officer has to be satisfied that at least one of the
reasons supporting the need for arrest is satisfied.

Applying the necessity criteria requires the constable to examine and justify the reason or reasons why a person needs to be arrested or (as the case may be) further
arrested.

The criteria in PACE, s 24 are exhaustive. However, the circumstances that may satisfy those criteria remain a matter for the operational discretion of individual officers.
In considering the individual circumstances, the constable must take into account the
situation of the victim, the nature of the offence, the circumstances of the suspect, and
the needs of the investigative process.

A police officer must consider carefully the necessity to arrest when deciding whether
or not to do so. For example, not every refusal to provide a name and address at the officer's
first request necessitates an arrest. Such a refusal should be followed by an explanation of
the consequences of a continued refusal to provide an identity and an address which the
officer believes to be true, and only if there is a continued refusal to provide such an identity and address should the arrest be made. However, a divisional court has accepted that
where a person, whose name was unknown to a constable, was reasonably suspected by
the constable of having committed an offence, these requirements were satisfied by the
questions, 'What is your name?' and 'What is your address?' followed by a refusal to answer.
In the event of refusal to answer, the offender should be told that he is being arrested in
relation to the particular offence *and* for refusing to give his name and address. If an arrest
is made, PACE, s 30 requires that a person arrested by a constable at a place other than a
police station must be released without bail if a constable is satisfied, before the person
arrested reaches a police station, that there are no grounds for keeping him under arrest or
releasing him on bail. It follows that, should an arrest be made on the grounds that a satisfactory name and address have not been provided but they are subsequently provided (or
the person is identified in some other way), the arrested person must be instantly released.
A record of such a release must be made as soon as practicable after the release.

Action to be taken in relation to an arrest

See p 59 below.

Limits on powers resulting from arrest

The powers available to an officer as a result of an arrest—for example, entry and search of premises (with exceptions), holding a person incommunicado, setting up road checks—are only available in respect of an indictable offence.

ARREST WITHOUT WARRANT: OTHER PERSONS

PACE, s 24A provides that:

(1) A person other than a constable may arrest without warrant:
    (a) anyone who is in the act of committing an indictable offence;
    (b) anyone whom he has reasonable grounds for suspecting to be committing an indictable offence.
(2) Where an indictable offence has been committed, a person other than a constable may arrest without warrant:
    (a) anyone who is guilty of that offence;
    (b) anyone whom he has reasonable grounds for suspecting to be guilty of it.
(3) The power of arrest conferred by (1) and (2) is only exercisable if:
    (a) the person making the arrest has reasonable grounds for believing that for any of the reasons mentioned in (4) it is necessary to arrest the person in question; and
    (b) it appears to the person making the arrest that it is not reasonably practicable for a constable to make it instead.
(4) The reasons are to prevent the person in question:
    (a) causing physical injury to himself or any other person;
    (b) suffering physical injury;
    (c) causing loss of or damage to property; or
    (d) making off before a constable can assume responsibility for him.

The above provisions do not apply in relation to an offence under the Public Order Act 1986, Parts III or IIIA (racial etc hatred offences). Nor do they apply to the arrest inside a polling station of a person who has committed or is suspected of committing an offence of personation.

Thus, the conditions under which an arrest can be made by some 'other person' are more limited than in the case of a constable. The reason in (4)(d) is included because of the power given to community support officers to detain persons with a view to handing them over to a constable.

OTHER POWERS OF ARREST WITHOUT WARRANT

Specific statutory power of arrest without warrant

PACE, s 26 repealed all previous statutory powers for a constable to arrest without warrant (including those provided by local Acts) with the following exceptions listed in Sch 2:

(a) the arrest of absentees and deserters from Visiting Forces;
(b) the arrest of persons who are absent from places of detention or who have broken bail;
(c) the arrest of persons under certain powers under the Immigration Act 1971;
(d) the arrest of persons under the provisions of the Mental Health Act 1983.

Power to arrest at common law

At common law a police officer or anyone else has power to arrest without warrant in certain circumstances, and this power is not affected by PACE. The common law power exists:

(a) where a breach of the peace is committed by the person arrested in the presence of the person making the arrest; or
(b) where no breach of the peace has occurred in the presence of the person making the arrest, but he reasonably believes that such a breach by the person arrested is actually imminent.

'Breach of the peace' is defined on p 730.

These common law powers of arrest are important to police officers. They are in no way restricted by the nature of the place in which the breach of the peace occurs or is anticipated. The arrest within the above terms is a preventive measure and should be effected wherever it is necessary to preserve the peace; even on private premises and even if no member of the public is present. If two men are fighting, that is a breach of the peace regardless of all other considerations and an arrest by anyone who sees it occur is justified. It might be that the stage at which a fight actually occurs has not been reached but a constable reasonably believes that it will occur in the immediate future; in such a case he may arrest those in dispute. Likewise, where an actual fight might have been discontinued but a constable reasonably believes that the argument is not at an end and that the fight is likely to be resumed, and a breach of the peace occur, an arrest is justified.

Once a constable reasonably foresees a breach of the peace, he is entitled to remain on premises in which, until that time, he has been a trespasser.

Since a breach of the peace does not necessarily require anyone to be acting, or threatening to act, unlawfully, the power to arrest for breach of the peace is not limited to cases where unlawful conduct occurs, is suspected or anticipated. By way of a limit on the arrest of those who are not acting unlawfully, the Court of Appeal has set out four factors to be considered in such a case.

(1) There must be a real and present threat to the peace justifying depriving a citizen, not at the time acting unlawfully, of his liberty.
(2) The threat must come from the person arrested.
(3) The conduct must clearly interfere with the rights of others and its natural consequence must be 'not wholly unreasonable violence' from a third party.
(4) The conduct of the person to be arrested must be unreasonable.

Cross-border powers of arrest

CJPOA 1994, s 137 provides that, where it appears to a constable that it would have been lawful for him to have exercised the power had the suspected person been in England or Wales, a constable of an English or Welsh police force, who has reasonable grounds for suspecting that an offence has been committed or attempted in England and Wales and that the suspected person is in Scotland or Northern Ireland, may arrest without warrant the suspected person wherever he is in Scotland or Northern Ireland. Scottish officers and those of the Northern Ireland Police Service have similar powers of arrest within England and Wales in respect of offences committed or attempted in Scotland or Northern Ireland respectively. This power may be exercised in England and

Wales and Scotland (but not Northern Ireland) by a British Transport Police officer. Thus, for example, such an officer can arrest someone in Scotland for an offence committed in England or Wales.

Where a person is arrested in Scotland or Northern Ireland under this power, he must be taken to the nearest convenient designated police station in England or Wales or to a designated police station in a police area where the offence is being investigated. This must be done as soon as reasonably practicable.

Arrest of service personnel—absentees without leave and deserters

Under the Armed Forces Act 2006, s 314, a constable who is a member of a police force or of the Ministry of Defence police has power to arrest without warrant any person whom he has reasonable cause to suspect of being a person subject to service law who has deserted or is absent without leave. Warrants authorising such arrests may also be issued by justices of the peace. Whether or not a person so arrested admits to being an absentee or deserter he *must* be brought before a court as soon as practicable. Where a court is satisfied that such a person is a deserter or absentee, it will remand him in custody to await a service escort unless he is also in custody for some other reason.

Immediately such an arrest has been effected, the appropriate service authority must be informed and provided with all particulars of the case, stating whether the identity of the person arrested is disputed and whether his behaviour is refractory (non-compliant). Details of escort arrangements should be noted. Where an escort arrives before the court rises the person concerned can be handed over immediately, thereby avoiding his committal to prison or to other civil custody. Where the escort is likely to arrive quite soon, the court will usually commit such a person to police custody. The court must provide a certificate giving details of the serviceman's arrest (or surrender, see below).

Absentees frequently surrender to the police, having simply overstayed their leave. Such persons need not be taken before a magistrates' court but they may be if this is desirable for any reason. In such a case the court will remand the person in custody to await a service escort, subject to the same rules as just set out. Where an absentee serviceman is not taken before a court, a certificate must be made out by the police officer who causes the serviceman to be handed over to the escort. Care must be taken in completing this certificate. If it is incorrectly completed or is not signed by the officer in charge of the police station, it is inadmissible in evidence at a subsequent court martial.

In all such cases of arrest or surrender the appropriate authority to be informed is as follows:

(a) in the case of a naval rating or Royal Marine, the Commodore, HMS *Nelson*, Portsmouth PO1 3HH (Metropolitan Police report to Naval Provost Marshal, London);

(b) in the case of a soldier, the Central Criminal Record and Intelligence Office, Royal Military Police; and

(c) in the case of an airman, the HQ RAF Provost and Security Services (UK).

On occasions the service authorities may issue a warrant to arrest a serviceman. In such a case, the serviceman should be arrested and handed to a service escort. He need not be placed before a court unless he is to be dealt with for some other reason. The appropriate certificate must be handed over to the escort.

OTHER POINTS ABOUT ARREST

The nature of an arrest

An arrest involves deprivation of a person's liberty to go where one pleases as an initial stage of the criminal process. Some recent decisions have said that there cannot be an arrest unless the person depriving the other of liberty intends to arrest him and tells him that he is under arrest and informs him of the offence for which he is being arrested. In terms of the last two points, this is clearly wrong because PACE states that these factors are necessary for an arrest to be lawful (as opposed to being necessary for an arrest). A police officer who restrains someone but does not at that time intend or purport to arrest him, eg because he simply wants to detain him temporarily to establish his identity, commits an assault, even if he would have been justified in arresting that person; there is no power to detain someone short of an arrest.

An arrest is normally effected by the seizing or the touching of a person's body with a view to his detention. It is possible, however, to effect an arrest merely by words if they bring to the person's notice that he is under restraint and will be compelled to remain, and he submits to that compulsion. Where unreasonable force is used to effect an arrest the arrest is unlawful.

If the arrest occurs outside, it is probable that some form of physical restraint will be applied as the constable will be anxious to ensure that his prisoner does not escape. However, if the person arrested is a quiet, elderly person who is not physically capable of such escape, physical restraint would be unnecessary and undesirable. In the same way, persons already in custody who are arrested for other offences do not require a show of restraint, nor would it serve any purpose.

Information to be given on arrest

PACE, s 28 provides that where a person is arrested, otherwise than by being informed that he is under arrest, the arrest is not lawful unless, as soon as practicable after his arrest, the person arrested is informed that he is under arrest. This is so whether or not the fact of his arrest is obvious. In addition, no arrest is lawful unless the person arrested is informed of the ground for arrest at the time of arrest, or as soon as practicable thereafter. This is a separate requirement from that set out above. It applies regardless of whether the ground for arrest is obvious. Hence, an arrested person must be told two things: that he is under arrest; and the ground which exists for the arrest. An arrested person must be given sufficient information to enable him to understand that he has been deprived of his liberty and the reason for his arrest, eg when a person is arrested on suspicion of committing an offence, he must be informed of the suspected offence's nature and when and where it was committed. He must also be informed of the reason or reasons why arrest is considered necessary. The constable should outline the facts, information, and other circumstances which provide the grounds for believing that the arrest is necessary and which he considers satisfy one or more of the necessity criteria. When determining whether a person has been informed of the grounds for his arrest, the question is whether, in all the circumstances, he was told, in simple, non-technical language that he could understand, the essential legal and factual grounds. Vague or technical language should be avoided. The adequacy of the information must be judged objectively having regard to the information reasonably available to the arresting officer.

While it is preferable that the person arrested is informed of the precise offence for which he is being arrested, for example: 'I am arresting you for an offence of burglary which I have seen you commit', this is not essential (although the ground given must be a valid one). It suffices if, by the use of commonplace language, he is informed of the type of offence for which he is being arrested, so that he has the opportunity to give information which would avoid the arrest. Thus, where a constable making an arrest reasonably suspected that the offence was theft, handling, or taking a conveyance (a car), her statement that she was arresting the suspect for unlawful possession of a car was held to be sufficient. The Court of Appeal has held that the requirements of s 28 are satisfied where a suspect is arrested by one officer, but informed by another of the reason for his arrest.

PACE, s 28 exempts an officer from the necessity to give either item of information if it was not reasonably practicable to do so by reason of the person's escape before the information could be given.

Caution

The Arrest Code requires that a person must be cautioned upon arrest for an offence unless:

(a) it is impracticable to do so by reason of his condition or behaviour at the time; or
(b) he has already been cautioned immediately prior to arrest and before questions, or further questions, were put to him under PACE Code C: the Code of Practice for the Detention, Treatment and Questioning of Persons by Police Officers (hereafter referred to as the Detention Code) (p 105) as a person suspected of an offence.

The caution must be in the following terms:

> 'You do not have to say anything. But it may harm your defence if you do not mention when questioned something which you later rely on in court. Anything you do say may be given in evidence.'

Records of arrest

A police officer who makes an arrest must record in his pocket book or by any other method used for recording information:

(a) the nature and circumstances of the offence leading to arrest;
(b) the reason or reasons why arrest was necessary;
(c) the giving of the caution; and
(d) anything said by the person at the time of arrest.

The record should be made at the time of the arrest unless impracticable to do so. If not made at the time, it must be completed as soon as possible thereafter.

On arrival at the police station, or after being arrested at a police station, the arrested person must be brought before the custody officer as soon as practicable. The custody officer must open a custody record and the information given by the arresting officer on the circumstances and reason or reasons for arrest must be recorded as part of the custody record. As an alternative, a copy of the entry made by the officer (as required above) may be attached to the custody record. The custody record stands as a record of the arrest.

Juveniles

The Detention Code states that a juvenile should not be arrested at school unless this is unavoidable. In the event of this happening, the head teacher or his nominee must be informed.

Arrest elsewhere than at a police station

PACE, s 30(1) and (1A) requires that, where a person is arrested by a constable for an offence (or is taken into custody by a constable having been arrested for an offence by someone other than a constable) at any place other than a police station, he must be taken to a police station as soon as practicable. The policy of s 30 is to bring the arrested person within the protective rules of the Detention Code as soon as practicable. A deliberate breach of s 30(1) and (1A) may render inadmissible evidence obtained during that breach. Section 30(1) and (1A) is subject to the rules below concerning release on street bail or without bail. The inclusion of 'as soon as practicable' allows for the circumstances in which it would be unrealistic to take such a person directly to a police station. This is expressly recognised by s 30(10) and (10A) which provides that a constable may delay taking an arrested person to a police station (or releasing him on bail) if that person's presence elsewhere is necessary in order to carry out such investigations as it is reasonable to carry out immediately; in such a case any questions put to the arrested person should be confined to those investigations. Thus, where a person is arrested for a theft which he was seen to commit but the property was not in his possession when arrested after a chase, a constable carrying out one of the duties of his office, to protect property, could quite properly retrace the route of the chase with his prisoner in order to recover the stolen property as soon as possible. However, in circumstances where the property is not in imminent danger of being lost in consequence of any delay in effecting its recovery, the prisoner should be taken immediately to a police station unless it is essential that he indicates the precise place in which the property has been hidden or the place at which it was disposed of.

If there is any delay in taking an arrested person to a police station, the reason must be recorded on first arrival there or, as the case may be, when he is released on bail. With certain exceptions, the police station to which the person arrested must be taken under s 30 must be a '*designated police station*' (s 30(2)). This term is explained in Chapter 5, but in essence it refers to a police station approved for the purpose of detention of prisoners. In exceptional circumstances, a person arrested may be taken to *any police station*. These circumstances are where:

(a) the constable is working in a locality covered by a police station which is not a designated police station; or
(b) he is a constable belonging to a police force maintained by an authority other than a local policing body (eg the British Transport Police) (s 30(4)).

The exception at (a) recognises that a 'designated police station' may be many miles from the place at which an arrest is made. If a person is arrested for an offence in respect of which he is likely to be released on bail more or less immediately, it would be unrealistic to require him to be taken to a designated police station many miles from the scene of the arrest. Neither exception applies if it appears to the constable that it may be necessary to keep the arrested person in police detention for more than six hours. In that case the person arrested must be taken to a *designated* police station (s 30(3)).

In addition, by s 30(5), any constable may take an arrested person to *any* police station if:

(a) the constable has arrested him without the assistance of any other constable and no other constable is available to assist him; or

(b) the constable has taken him into custody from a person other than a constable without the assistance of any other constable and no other constable is available to assist him,

and (in either case) it appears to the constable that he will be unable to take the arrested person to a designated police station *without the arrested person injuring himself, the constable or some other person.*

When the person is arrested and taken to a non-designated police station, and there is no officer present at that police station to act as a custody officer, the inspector at that designated police station to which that person would have been taken must be informed. If the first police station to which an arrested person is taken is not a designated police station, he must be taken to a designated police station within six hours unless he is previously released (s 30(6)).

A separate custody record must be opened as soon as practicable for each person who is brought to a police station under arrest. Custody records are discussed in the next chapter.

A person arrested by a constable at a place other than a police station may be released without bail if a constable is satisfied before that person reaches a police station that there are no grounds for keeping him under arrest or releasing him from bail under s 30A (s 30(7) and (7A)). The constable must record the fact of the release as soon as practicable (s 30(8) and (9)).

Bail elsewhere than at a police station

PACE, s 30A provides that a constable may release on bail ('street bail') a person who has been arrested for an offence by a constable, or taken into custody after arrest by someone other than a constable, at any time before he arrives at a police station. Such a person must be required to attend at a police station. Where a constable releases such a person (A) on bail:

(a) no recognisance for A's surrender to custody may be taken from him;

(b) no security for A's surrender to custody may be taken from him or from anyone else on his behalf;

(c) A may not be required to provide a surety or sureties for his surrender to custody; and

(d) no requirement to reside in a bail hostel may be imposed as a condition of bail (s 30A(3A)).

Subject to (a)–(d) above, a constable may impose, as conditions of bail, requirements which he considers to be necessary:

(a) to secure that A surrenders to custody;

(b) to secure that A does not commit an offence while on bail;

(c) to secure that A does not interfere with witnesses or otherwise obstruct the course of justice, whether in relation to himself or any other person;

(d) for A's own protection or, if A is under the age of 17, for A's own welfare or in A's own interests (s 30A(3B)).

No other requirements may be imposed as a condition of bail.

Where conditions are applied to street bail under s 30A, the person released on bail (A) has the right to apply for variation of the conditions to a custody officer or to a magistrates' court (ss 30CA, 30CB).

By s 30B, a notice in writing must be given to A by the constable granting bail. The notice must state the offence for which A was arrested and the ground on which he was arrested. The notice *must* inform A that he is required to attend a police station. It *may* also specify the police station at which A is required to attend, and the time of attendance. Where bail has been granted subject to conditions under s 30A, the above notice must specify the requirements imposed by those conditions; must explain the provisions relating to variation of conditions; and, if it does not specify the police station at which A is required to attend, must specify a police station at which A may request a variation by a custody officer. (If the police station and time of attendance are not stated in the notice referred to above, a further written notice containing that information must be sent later. An amended notice may be sent requiring attendance at a different police station or at a different time.)

Section 30C provides that the requirement to attend a police station may be cancelled by written notice and that, if A is required to attend a non-designated police station, he must be released or taken to a designated police station not more than six hours after his arrival. Nothing in the Bail Act 1976 applies to bail under s 30A, nor do the provisions of PACE prevent re-arrest without warrant of a person released on bail under s 30A if new evidence justifying a further arrest has come to light since his release.

By s 30D, a constable may arrest without warrant a person who has been released on bail under s 30A but:

(a) fails to attend the specified police station at the appointed time; or
(b) is reasonably suspected by the constable to have broken a condition of bail.

A person so arrested must be taken to any police station as soon as practicable after the arrest. An arrest under s 30D is treated as an arrest for the purposes of PACE, s 30 (above) and s 31 (below).

Arrest for a further offence

Where a person is under arrest at a police station for an offence and it appears that, if released, he would be liable to arrest for some other offence, PACE, s 31 requires that he be arrested for that other offence. The usual procedures to be followed after an arrest must be carried out; the person must be told that he is being arrested for that other offence and what the reasons are for that arrest, and he must be cautioned. This must be done whether or not it is intended to release him at that time.

POWERS OF ENTRY AND SEARCH IN RELATION TO AN ARREST

Search and seizure on arrest for an offence

Search

PACE, s 32(1) provides that, where a person has been arrested elsewhere than at a police station, a constable may search him if the constable has reasonable grounds for believing that the arrested person may present a danger to himself or others.

PACE, s 32(2) goes further and also empowers a constable in such a case:

(a) to *search* the *arrested person* for anything which he might use to assist him to escape from lawful custody or which might be evidence relating to an offence (s 32(2)(a)); *and*

(b) if the offence for which he has been arrested is an indictable offence, to *enter and search* any *premises* in which he was when arrested or immediately before he was arrested for evidence relating to the offence (s 32(2)(b)).

This power to search only extends to a search which is reasonably required for the purpose of discovering any such thing or any such evidence. A constable may not search a person under (a) unless he has reasonable grounds for believing that the person may have concealed on him anything for which a search is permitted under (a) (s 32(5)). Similarly, a constable may not search premises under (b) unless he has reasonable grounds for believing that there is evidence for which a search is permitted under (b) on the premises (s 32(6)).

(a) gives statutory authority to 'on the spot' searches at the time of an arrest. That search may be for weapons or dangerous articles, for things which might assist escape, or for things which might be evidence of an offence. The power to search for evidence is particularly important since, if such property is not recovered at the time of such arrest, it is likely to be disposed of by the arrested person if an opportunity presents itself.

'Premises' in (b) and elsewhere in the PACE provisions in this chapter includes any place and, in particular, includes any vehicle, vessel, aircraft, or hovercraft, any renewable energy installation, any offshore installation, and any tent or movable structure. If a police officer is seen approaching the premises in which a thief is lodged, it is likely that the thief will conceal the property within those premises. If he leaves and is arrested outside, it is reasonable that the constable should be empowered to examine the premises which he has immediately vacated.

PACE, s 32(7) deals with the problem in relation to (b) of communal occupation (including bedsit premises) by stating that where there are two or more separate dwellings, the search must be limited to the dwelling in which the arrest took place or in which the arrested person was immediately before his arrest *and* any part of the premises which the occupier of the dwelling uses in common with the other occupiers of other dwellings comprised in the premises. In the case of a bedsit, therefore, the constable would be able to search the room in which the arrested person was found and the common kitchen and lounge area used by all of the residents. It may be that a thief occupying one room, on seeing the approach of a constable, might enter the room of his neighbour and hand over property to the neighbour to conceal on his behalf. If the constable knows that the thief was in that room immediately before arrest he is empowered to search it. A divisional court has stated that there is no decisive test to determine when a place of occupation is to be treated as divided into separate dwellings and that each case must be decided on its own facts. In the case in question, the bedrooms which homeless people had a licence to occupy for a day in a local authority hostel, each of which had a lock, were separate dwellings, because each licensee had a sufficient degree of exclusive possession.

The powers under PACE, s 32 do not authorise the removal of clothing in a public place other than an outer coat, jacket, or gloves, but they do authorise a search of a person's mouth (s 32(4)).

PACE, s 32 does not provide any general powers of search either of persons or premises when an arrest is made. The particular circumstances described in s 32 must exist. If a man is arrested for a sexual assault and is known to be of a non-violent disposition, there are no grounds for an 'on the spot' search; nor would there be, in most circumstances, reason to search premises unless articles had been used in the commission of the offence.

Seizure from a person

A constable searching under s 32(1) may seize and retain anything which he has reasonable grounds for believing that the person searched might use to cause physical injury to himself or another (s 32(8)).

A constable searching a person under PACE, s 32(2)(a) may seize and retain anything, other than an item subject to legal privilege (see p 71), if he has reasonable grounds for believing that the person might use it to escape from lawful custody or that it is evidence of an offence or has been obtained in consequence of the commission of an offence (s 32(9)).

The Criminal Justice and Police Act 2001 (CJPA 2001), s 51 provides additional powers of seizure from the person which apply to the power of seizure under PACE, s 32. Section 51 deals with the case where a person carrying out a lawful search of another person finds something which he reasonably believes may be, or may contain, something for which he is authorised to search and to seize. It provides that if, in the circumstances, it is not reasonably practicable for it to be determined whether what he has found (or its contents) is (or are) something which he is entitled to seize, his powers of seizure include seizing so much of what he has found as is necessary to remove from the place of the search to enable that to be determined. The details of this power, and the circumstances in which it applies, are set out below (s 50(2)) in relation to the power of seizure of property on premises. The powers are the same, with the modifications necessary to recognise that CJPA 2001, s 51 applies to a search of a person.

Where a person exercises this power of seizure under CJPA 2001, s 51, he must give written notice to the person from whom such property is seized:

(a) specifying what has been seized;
(b) specifying the grounds under which the power was exercised;
(c) setting out the effect of CJPA 2001, ss 59–61 (remedies and safeguards);
(d) specifying the name and address of the person to whom any application for the return of the seized property must be made; and
(e) specifying the name and address of the person to whom an application may be made to be allowed to attend the initial examination of the seized property which must be held to determine how much of it is property for which the person seizing had a power to search (s 52(4)).

A divisional court has held that compliance with the provisions of s 52 is not a precondition of a lawful seizure.

Any person with a relevant interest in the seized property may apply to a judge for its return on the grounds that there was no power of seizure, or that the seized material contains matter subject to legal privilege or contains excluded or special procedure material, as defined on p 71 (CJPA 2001, s 59). Section 59 also applies to property seized under s 50 below.

CJPA 2001, s 51 also applies to a number of other powers of seizure from the person listed in CJPA 2001, Sch 1, Part 2, some of which are referred to later in this book.

Seizure from premises

The powers of seizure under PACE, s 19 (p 83) apply to a search of premises under PACE, s 32(2)(b).

In addition, the CJPA 2001, s 50(1) deals with situations where a person who is lawfully on any premises finds objects on those premises which he reasonably believes to contain something for which he is authorised to search and in respect of which there would be a power of seizure under s 32 or under one of the more than 70 other statutory provisions to which s 50 applies. CJPA 2001, s 50(1) provides that where it is not reasonably practicable *to establish the nature of the contents on the premises, or the extent to which the contents comprise something which there is power to seize,* the power of seizure includes power to seize so much of that which has been found as it is necessary to remove from the premises to enable its nature to be determined.

CJPA 2001, s 50(2) provides a power of seizure where a person lawfully on any premises finds anything on those premises ('the seizable property') which he would be entitled to seize but for its being comprised in something else that he has (apart from s 50(2)) no power to seize. CJPA 2001, s 50(2) provides that where:

(a) the power under which that person would have power to seize the seizable property is a power to which s 50 applies; and
(b) in all the circumstances it is not reasonably practicable *for the seizable property to be separated in those premises from that in which it is comprised,*

that person's power of seizure includes power to seize both the seizable property and that from which it is not reasonably practicable to separate it.

CJPA 2001, s 50(3) states that the factors to be taken into account in considering whether it is reasonably practicable to achieve one of the things italicised in s 50(1) or (2) are confined to:

(a) how long it would take to carry out the determination or separation on those premises;
(b) the number of persons who would be required to carry out that determination or separation on those premises within a reasonable period;
(c) whether the determination or separation would (or would if carried out on those premises) involve damage to property;
(d) the apparatus or equipment that it would be necessary or appropriate to use for the carrying out of the determination or separation; and
(e) in the case of separation, whether the separation:
    (i)   would be likely, or
    (ii) if carried out by the only means that are reasonably practicable on those premises, would be likely,
    to prejudice the use of some or all of the separated seizable property for the purpose for which something seized under the power in question is capable of being used.

Where a power of seizure under s 50 has been exercised, written notice containing the same information as under s 52(4) must be given to the occupier, or some other person on the premises who is in charge (s 52(1) and (2)). Where there is no person on the premises a notice must be attached, in a prominent place, to the premises (s 52(3)).

Examination and return of property seized under s 50 or 51

CJPA 2001, s 53 requires that at a subsequent initial examination, which must take place as soon as reasonably practicable, property seized under s 50 or 51 which does *not* fall within (a) to (c) below must be separated from the rest of the seized property and returned as soon as reasonably practicable. Property does not have to be returned if:

(a) it is property for which there was a power of search and it is not an item subject to legal privilege;
(b) there are reasonable grounds for believing that it is property obtained in consequence of an offence, or evidence in relation to any offence, and that it is necessary for it to be retained in order to prevent its concealment, loss, alteration, or destruction; or
(c) it is property which cannot be reasonably practically separated from that in (a) or (b).

Property which is excluded or special procedure material must be returned unless its retention is authorised by the grounds set out in (b) or, where comprised in something else, it cannot reasonably practicably be separated from other property whose return is not required or which satisfies (b).

Seizure: general

Officers should be aware of the need for confidentiality in relation to the contents of any documents and property must be returned as soon as possible. Delay is only justified where there are clear and compelling reasons, eg that the person to whom the material is to be returned is unavailable or where it is necessary to make arrangements for the return of a large quantity of material.

Anything seized in accordance with the above provisions may be retained for as long as is necessary for:

(a) use as evidence at a trial for an offence;
(b) facilitating the use in an investigation or proceedings of anything to which it is inextricably linked (eg on a computer disk) without damaging evidential integrity;
(c) forensic examination or other investigation in connection with an offence;
(d) establishing its lawful owner when there are reasonable grounds for believing it has been stolen or obtained by commission of an offence.

On request, the person who had custody or control of such property immediately before seizure must be provided with a list or description of the property within a reasonable time, and he or his representative must be allowed supervised access to examine the property or have it photographed or copied (or must be provided with a photograph or copy) within a reasonable time and at his own expense, unless the officer in charge of the investigation has reasonable grounds for believing that this would prejudice the investigation of the offence or criminal proceedings, or lead to the commission of an offence by providing access to unlawful material such as pornography. A record of such grounds must be made if access is denied.

Entry to premises to effect an arrest, etc

PACE abolished all the common law rules which gave a constable power to enter premises without a warrant, except that the power still exists at common law to enter premises to deal with a breach of the peace or to prevent it (p 731).

PACE, s 17 provides that, without prejudice to any other enactment, a constable may enter and search any premises (as defined on p 64) for the purpose:

(a) of executing a warrant of arrest issued in connection with or arising out of criminal proceedings, or a warrant of commitment issued under the Magistrates' Courts Act 1980, s 76;
(b) of arresting someone for an indictable offence;
(c) of arresting someone for an offence under the Public Order Act 1936, s 1 (prohibited uniforms), the Public Order Act 1986, s 4 (fear or provocation of violence), RTA 1988, s 4 (driving, etc under the influence of drink or drugs) or s 163 (failure to stop when required to do so by a police constable in uniform), the Transport and Works Act 1992, s 27 (drink or drugs on public guided transport systems), or the Animal Welfare Act 2006, ss 4, 5, 6(1) or (2), 7, and 8(1) or (2) (unnecessary suffering, mutilation, docking of tails, administering poisons, and animal fighting);

(d) of arresting someone for an offence under CJPOA 1994, s 76 (failure to comply with an interim possession order), the Criminal Law Act 1977, ss 6 to 8, or 10 (offences of entering and remaining on property), or the Legal Aid, Sentencing and Punishment of Offenders Act 2012, s 144 (squatting in a residential building)—in these cases the arresting constable must be in uniform;

(e) of arresting, in pursuance of the Children and Young Persons Act 1969, s 32(1A), any child or young person who has been *remanded or committed to local authority accommodation* (prospectively the words italicised are replaced by *remanded to local authority accommodation or youth detention accommodation*);

(f) of arresting someone for an offence to which the Animal Health Act 1981, s 61 applies (powers of entry and search in relation to rabies offences);

(g) of recapturing someone who is, or is deemed for any purpose to be, unlawfully at large while liable to be detained:
(i) in a prison, remand centre, young offender institution, or secure training centre; or
(ii) in pursuance of the Powers of Criminal Courts (Sentencing) Act 2000, s 92 (dealing with children and young persons guilty of grave crimes), in any other place;

(h) of recapturing someone unlawfully at large whom he is pursuing (ie chasing); or

(i) of saving life or limb or preventing serious damage to property. A divisional court has held that the words 'life or limb' are wide enough to cover saving someone from himself as well as saving someone from a third party.

Except in the case of (i), the powers of entry and search under PACE, s 17: (a) are only exercisable where a constable has reasonable grounds for believing that the person whom he is seeking is on the premises, and (b) are limited in respect of premises consisting of two or more dwellings in the same way as with the powers to search under s 32 described on p 64.

A search under s 17 may only be made to the extent reasonably required for the purpose for which the power of entry is required. The courts have ruled that, when exercising his right of entry by force under s 17, a police officer must give any occupant present the reason why he is seeking entry even if that reason is apparent in the circumstances. Otherwise the forcible entry will be unlawful, unless circumstances make giving reasons impossible, impracticable, or undesirable. If the real reason is to arrest a person inside for an offence, for instance, it is insufficient to tell the occupants that the officer wishes to 'speak to' that person about the offence.

Entry, search, and seizure after an arrest

Entry and search

PACE, s 18(1) empowers a constable to enter and search any premises (as defined on p 64) which *are* occupied or controlled by a person under arrest for an indictable offence before that person is taken to a police station or released on street bail, if he has reasonable grounds for suspecting that there is on the premises evidence, other than items subject to legal privilege (p 71), which relates to that offence or to another indictable offence connected with or similar to that offence (eg, if the person has been arrested for burglary, the proceeds of other burglaries or large-scale theft, but not drugs). A search under s 18 is only permitted to the extent reasonably required for the purpose of discovering such evidence (s 18(3)). Because the power under s 18 only applies to premises occupied or controlled by the arrested person, a search of premises not so occupied or controlled is unlawful—even if they are reasonably believed to be so occupied or controlled (eg because the arrested person has given a false name and address).

A search under PACE, s 18 may not be made without the written authorisation of an officer of the rank of inspector or above, unless it is carried out before a person is taken to a police station or released on street bail in accordance with s 30A in circumstances where the presence of that person elsewhere is necessary for the effective investigation of the offence (s 18(4)–(5A)). In such a case, the constable who conducts the search must notify an inspector (or above) of it as soon as practicable. PACE Code B: the Code of Practice for Searches of Premises by Police Officers and the Seizure of Property Found by Police Officers on Persons or Premises (hereafter the Searching of Premises Code) provides that if possible the authorising officer should record the authority on the Notice of Powers and Rights (which should be given or left as explained on pp 80–1). The record of the grounds for the search and the nature of the evidence sought should be made in:

(a) the custody record if there is one, otherwise
(b) the officer's pocket book, or
(c) the search record.

If the person in occupation or control of the premises is in police custody at the time that the search is carried out, the record must be made in the custody record.

An officer who proposes to enter and search premises under a written authorisation under s 18 must explain to the occupier, in so far as it is practicable to do so, the reason why he intends so to act. Failure to do so will render his subsequent conduct unlawful. A divisional court has held that simply offering to show the warrant at a window to an occupier who refused to come to the window was insufficient; the reason must be stated.

The effect of PACE, s 18 is that, if a television retailer is arrested in the living quarters above his shop premises on a charge of theft of television sets, the constable would be empowered to search not only his living quarters but also the shop premises after arrest as they are premises 'occupied or controlled' by that person. If the constable searches the shop premises before taking the retailer to a police station, he must inform an officer of the rank of inspector or above that he has done so as soon as practicable.

A search of any person who has not been arrested, which is carried out during a search of premises, must be carried out in accordance with the Stop and Search Code.

Seizure

A constable may seize and retain anything on the premises for which he may search under the above power. (Although a vehicle, vessel, or tent is 'premises' for the purpose of PACE, this does not prevent the seizure of the vehicle, vessel or tent itself.) The additional powers of seizure under CJPA 2001, s 50 (see p 65) apply to this power of seizure.

POWERS TO SEARCH UNDER A SEARCH WARRANT

Power to issue warrant

Many statutes provide *particular* powers to enter and search premises under the authority of a warrant. An example is provided by the Terrorism Act 2000, Sch 5 referred to on p 74.

Search warrants under PACE, s 8

In addition, PACE, s 8 provides justices with a *general* power to issue warrants to enter and search premises (as defined on p 64).

A person authorised to accompany police officers or designated persons in the execution of a search warrant and the search and seizure of anything related to the warrant has the same powers as a police officer. An officer of the rank of inspector or above may direct a designated investigating officer not to wear a uniform for the purpose of a specific operation.

Requirement for issue of search warrant under s 8

PACE, s 8(1) provides that if, on an application made by a constable, a justice is satisfied that there are reasonable grounds for believing:

(a) that an indictable offence (or a 'relevant offence' under the Immigration Act 1971) has been committed; and

(b) that there is material on premises mentioned in s 8(1A) (below) which is likely to be of substantial value (whether by itself or with other material) to the investigation of the offence; and

(c) that the material is likely to be relevant (ie admissible) evidence; and

(d) that it does not consist of or include items subject to legal privilege, excluded material or special procedure material (described on p 71); and

(e) that *any* of the conditions specified in PACE, s 8(3) below applies, in relation to each set of premises specified in the application;

he may issue a warrant authorising a constable to enter and search the premises.

PACE, s 8(1A), provides that the 'premises' mentioned in (b) above are:

(a) one or more sets of premises specified in the application (in which case the application is for a 'specific premises warrant'); or

(b) any premises occupied or controlled by a person specified in the application, including such sets of premises as are so specified (in which case the application is for an 'all-premises warrant').

PACE, s 8(1B) provides that, if the application is for an all-premises warrant, the justice of the peace must also be satisfied:

(a) that, because of the particulars of the offence referred to in s 8(1)(a) above, there are reasonable grounds for believing that it is necessary to search premises occupied or controlled by the person in question which are not specified in the application in order to find the material referred in s 8(1)(b) above; and

(b) that it is not reasonably practicable to specify in the application all the premises which he occupies or controls and which might need to be searched.

These additional provisions assist in the investigation of serious organised crime. Crime syndicates may occupy or control many sets of premises and the search of one might lead to the discovery of other premises upon which the material being sought is situated. Provided that the search continues within buildings which are within the syndicate's control, it will be authorised by an 'all-premises warrant'.

It is vital to remember that the justice must be satisfied that all the requirements in s 8(1)(a) to (d) above are satisfied. If that is so, then it is necessary for him to be satisfied of the existence of any one of the conditions set out in PACE, s 8(3) referred to in s 8(1)(e) above, namely:

(a) that it is not practicable to communicate with any person entitled to grant entry to the premises;

(b) that it is practicable to communicate with a person entitled to grant entry to the premises but it is not practicable to communicate with any person entitled to grant access to the evidence;

(c) that entry to the premises will not be granted unless a warrant is produced; or

(d) that the purpose of the search may be frustrated or seriously prejudiced unless a constable arriving at the premises can secure immediate entry to them.

If the application for the warrant does not identify which of these conditions is being relied on, the issue of the warrant will be unlawful.

Condition (a) would apply if there was no one occupying the premises at the time; (b) would apply if, for example, there was a caretaker to a block of flats who had master keys and who could therefore allow access but would have no right to grant access to the material; (c) would apply in the usual circumstances in which a warrant is sought; and (d) in circumstances in which the nature of the evidence is such that it could be easily disposed of if the occupier was aware of police interest. 'Practicable' in (a) and (b) does not simply mean feasible or physically possible. The circumstances must also be considered, eg the nature of the inquiries and the persons subject to them.

Items for which a search warrant under s 8 should not be sought

A constable should never apply for a search warrant under s 8 where the material in question may consist of or include items prima facie subject to legal privilege, excluded material or special procedure material. In such a case application should be made to a judge under the provisions of PACE, Sch 1 described on pp 72–4.

Various terms included in PACE, s 8(1) require explanation.

Items subject to legal privilege   These are defined as communications between lawyer and client, the broad purpose of which is the giving and receiving of legal advice, and items enclosed with or referred to in such communications. A solicitor's record of appointments and attendances, therefore, is not subject to legal privilege. The exemption relating to items subject to legal privilege only applies if the material is in the possession of a person entitled to possess it. Items held with the intention of furthering a criminal purpose are specifically excluded from being subject to legal privilege, even though that intention does not exist on the part of the holder (eg a solicitor) but does on the part of another (eg a solicitor's client). The High Court has held that the retention of a small amount of legally privileged material inadvertently seized during a search does not render the execution of the search warrant unlawful.

Excluded material   This means:

(a) personal records (ie documentary and other records relating to the health of an individual or counselling given to him) acquired or created by a person in the course of a trade, business, etc or for the purpose of any paid or unpaid office and held in confidence by him;

(b) human tissue or tissue fluid taken for diagnosis or medical treatment and held in confidence; or

(c) journalistic material (ie material acquired or created for the purpose of journalism and held by the person acquiring or creating it for that purpose) consisting of documents or other records and held in confidence.

Special procedure material   This means:

(a) journalistic material, other than excluded material, and

(b) material, other than items subject to legal privilege and excluded material, held in confidence and acquired or created in the course of any trade, business, etc.

Production orders and search warrants under Sch 1

Although a justice may not issue a search warrant under PACE, s 8 in respect of material of any of the three types set out above, PACE, s 9 recognises that there may be occasions in which it is necessary to enter premises and search for excluded material or special procedure material by providing that a constable may obtain access to such material by making an application under PACE, Sch 1. PACE, s 9 does not provide for access to items subject to legal privilege.

At the time of writing the powers to make a production order or issue a warrant under PACE, Sch 1 are exercisable only by a Circuit judge but when amendments are brought into force the powers will also be exercisable by a judge of the High Court, Recorder, a Qualifying Judge Advocate or a District Judge (Magistrates' Courts). For convenience, 'judge' is used hereafter to cover the existing and future positions.

Under Sch 1, a judge may make a 'production order' or, in certain cases, issue a search warrant in respect of excluded material or special procedure material.

These provisions are intended to protect the confidence of the maker or holder of the record, etc, and not that of the suspect. Consequently, it is open to the maker or holder voluntarily to disclose the material. It is only where there is no consent on his part to do so that the special provisions of s 9 and Sch 1 come into play.

Production order

The basic order which a judge may issue under PACE, Sch 1 is a 'production order'. An application for such an order must be made by a constable. The person who has custody of the material must be notified of the application (and of the material sought) and allowed to attend the hearing of the application and make representations. Unless he is in custody of the material, there is no need to give notification to a suspected person.

A production order requires the person apparently in possession of the material in question *either* to produce it to the constable for him to take away *or* to give the constable access to it not later (*in either case*) than the end of a seven-day period from the date of the order or the end of such longer period as the order may specify. Where the material consists of information stored in electronic form, an order to produce has effect as an order to produce the material in a form in which it can be taken away and in which it is visible and legible, and an order to give access has effect as an order to give a constable access to the material in a form in which it is visible and legible.

The making of a production order depends on one or other of two sets of 'access conditions' being fulfilled.

The two sets of access conditions   The first set of access conditions is fulfilled if:

(a) there are reasonable grounds for believing that:
   (i)   an indictable offence has been committed;
   (ii)   there is material which consists of special procedure material or includes special procedure material and does not also include excluded material on premises specified in the application, or on premises occupied or controlled by a person specified in the application (including all such premises on which there are reasonable grounds for believing that there is such material as it is reasonably practicable so to specify);
   (iii) the material is likely to be of substantial value (whether by itself or together with other material) to the investigation in connection with which the application is made; and
   (iv)   the material is likely to be relevant evidence;

(b) other methods of obtaining the material:
    (i)   have been tried without success; or
    (ii) have not been tried because it appeared that they were bound to fail; and
(c) it is in the public interest having regard:
    (i)   to the benefit likely to accrue to the investigation if the material is obtained; and
    (ii) to the circumstances under which the person in possession of the material holds it, that the material should be produced or that access to it should be given.

The second set of access conditions is met if:

(a) there are reasonable grounds for believing that there is material which consists of or includes special procedure material or excluded material on premises specified in the application or on premises occupied or controlled by a person specified in the application (including all such premises on which there are reasonable grounds for believing that there is such material as it is reasonably practicable so to specify);
(b) prior to the enactment of PACE, s 9, a search of such premises for that material could have been authorised by the issue of a warrant to a constable under an enactment other than Sch 1; and
(c) the issue of such a warrant would have been appropriate.

It will be noted that the second set of access conditions is not limited to cases where it is reasonably believed that an indictable offence has been committed. A production order can be made even if it infringes or might infringe the privilege against self-incrimination of the person ordered to make production.

A divisional court has held that, before granting the application, the judge must be satisfied that it is substantially the last resort, ie that other practicable methods of obtaining the material have been exhausted without success.

Search warrant

The requirement of notice, together with the seven (or more) days' grace referred to above, gives a person time to dispose of incriminating material.

Sch 1 provides that a judge, on application by a constable, may issue a specific premises or all-premises search warrant in two types of case.

First a judge may do so if satisfied that:

(a) either set of access conditions is met; and
(b) any of the further conditions is also met in relation to each set of premises specified in the application:
    (i)   that it is not practicable to communicate with any person entitled to grant entry to the premises;
    (ii) that it is practicable to communicate with a person entitled to grant entry to the premises but it is not practicable to communicate with any person entitled to grant access to the material;
    (iii) that the material contains information which is subject to a statutory restriction on disclosure or obligation of secrecy and is likely to be disclosed in breach of it if a warrant is not issued;
    (iv) that service of notice of an application for a production order may seriously prejudice the investigation.

A search warrant (as opposed to a production order) will not be granted in practice in respect of a solicitor's office, unless proceeding by way of production order might seriously prejudice the investigation.

Second, a judge may also issue a search warrant under Sch 1 if satisfied that:

(a) the second set of access conditions is met; and
(b) a production order relating to the material has not been complied with.

The judge may not issue an all-premises warrant under Sch 1 unless he is satisfied:

(a) that there are reasonable grounds for believing that it is necessary to search premises occupied or controlled by the person in question which are not specified in the application, as well as those which are, in order to find the material in question; and
(b) that it is not reasonably practicable to specify all of the premises which he occupies or controls which might need to be searched.

The issue of a search warrant under the above provisions is a major infringement of individual liberty; consequently, the reason for authorising it must be made clear.

The Searching of Premises Code requires that an inspector or above be present and in charge of a search under a warrant issued under PACE, Sch 1 or TA 2000, Sch 5. The Code also contains further provisions concerning such a search.

Search warrants under Terrorism Act 2000

By TA 2000, Sch 5, a constable may apply to a justice of the peace for the issue of a warrant for the purposes of a terrorist investigation authorising a constable to enter specified premises, to search those premises and persons found there, and to seize and retain relevant material. The 'premises' may be one or more sets of premises specified in the application (in which case the application is for a specific premises warrant); or any premises occupied or controlled by a person specified in the application, including such sets of premises as are so specified (in which case the application is for an 'all-premises' warrant). A search warrant under the present provision does not authorise the seizure and retention of items subject to legal privilege.

The Stop and Search Code points out that, although the power to search persons found on premises to which a search warrant issued under TA 2000, Sch 5 applies does not require prior specific grounds to suspect that the person to be searched is in possession of an item for which there is an existing power to search, it is still necessary to ensure that the selection and treatment of those searched under these powers is based upon objective factors connected with the search of the premises, and not upon personal prejudice.

TA 2000, Sch 5 also provides for production orders and search warrants in respect of excluded or special procedure material for the purposes of a terrorist investigation.

Procedure before application is made for a search warrant or a production order

The relevant provisions are contained in the Searching of Premises Code. Where information is received appearing to justify an application for *any* search warrant or for a production order, the officer concerned must take reasonable steps to check that the information is accurate, recent, and not provided maliciously or irresponsibly. An application is not permitted on the basis of information from an anonymous source where corroboration has not been sought. The nature of the articles and their location must be established as specifically as possible.

The officer must also make reasonable inquiries to establish what, if anything, is known about the likely occupier of the premises and the nature of the premises themselves, and whether they have previously been searched (and, if so, how recently); he must also obtain any other information relevant to the application.

An application to a justice of the peace for a search warrant or to a judge for a search warrant or production order may not be made without the signed written authority of an officer of at least the rank of inspector or, in a case of urgency where no officer of this rank is readily available, the senior officer on duty. Where the application is made to a judge under TA 2000, Sch 5 it must be supported by a signed written authority from a superintendent. In addition, other than in a case of urgency, the community relations officer must be consulted before a search takes place which might have an adverse effect on police/community relations. In urgent cases, the local police community liaison officer should be informed of the search as soon as possible after it has been made.

The making of an application

Between them, PACE, s 15 and the Searching of Premises Code provide the following rules for *all* search warrants. An application for a search warrant must be supported by information in writing, specifying:

(a) the enactment under which the application is made;
(b) (i) whether the warrant is to authorise entry and search of:
    (*a*) one set of premises, or
    (*b*) if the application is under PACE s 8, or Sch 1, more than one set of specified premises or all premises occupied or controlled by a specified person;
  (ii) the premises to be searched;
(c) the object of the search;
(d) the grounds on which the application is made (including, when the purpose of the search is to find evidence of an alleged offence, an indication of how the evidence relates to the investigation);
(e) where the application is under PACE, s 8 or Sch 1, for a single warrant to enter and search:
  (i) more than one set of specified premises, the officer must specify each set of premises which it is desired to enter and search;
  (ii) all premises occupied or controlled by a specified person, the officer must specify:
    (*a*) as many sets of premises which it is desired to enter and search as it is reasonably practicable to specify,
    (*b*) the person who is in occupation or control of those premises and any others which it is desired to search,
    (*c*) why it is necessary to search more premises than those which can be specified, and
    (*d*) why it is not reasonably practicable to specify all the premises which it is desired to enter and search;
(f) whether an application under PACE, s 8 is for a warrant authorising entry and search on more than one occasion; if so, the officer must state the grounds for this and whether the desired number of entries authorised is unlimited or a specified maximum;
(g) that there are no reasonable grounds for believing that material to be sought:

(i)   consists of or includes items subject to legal privilege (when applying to a justice of the peace or a judge); or

(ii)   consists of or includes excluded material or special procedure material (when applying to a justice of the peace);

however, this does not affect the additional powers of seizure in the Criminal Justice and Police Act 2002, Part 2 (material to be sifted and examined elsewhere—see pp 65–6);

(h)   if applicable, a request for the warrant to authorise a person or persons to accompany the officer who executes the warrant.

Although the identity of an informant need not be disclosed, the officer must be prepared to deal with questions about the accuracy of previous information provided by that source or other related matters. An application for a search warrant under PACE, Sch 1 must, where appropriate, indicate why it is believed that service of notice of an application for a production order may seriously prejudice the investigation. An application under TA 2000, Sch 5 must indicate why a production order would be inappropriate.

The constable must answer on oath any question asked by the justice or judge. If an application is refused, no further application may be made for a warrant to search those premises unless supported by additional grounds.

A divisional court has emphasised that the obtaining of a search warrant is never to be treated as a formality. All of the material necessary to justify the grant of a warrant should be accurately contained in the information provided on the application form.

The search warrant

PACE, s 8(1C) provides that a warrant may authorise entry to and search of premises on more than one occasion if, on the application, the justice of the peace is satisfied that it is necessary to authorise multiple entries in order to achieve the purpose for which he issues the warrant. PACE, s 8(1D) provides that, if multiple entries are so authorised, the number of entries authorised may be unlimited, or limited to a maximum.

PACE, s 8(2) authorises a constable to seize and retain anything for which a search has been authorised.

Although PACE distinguishes between a 'specific premises warrant' and an 'all-premises warrant', a single warrant may include both types provided that the relevant information is given in the application.

By s 15(6), a warrant (which term includes a schedule to the warrant):

(a)   must specify:

(i)   the name of the person who applies for it (it is not enough to state, for example, that that applicant is 'the paedophile intelligence unit'),

(ii)   the date on which it is issued,

(iii)   the enactment under which it is issued, and

(iv)   each set of premises to be searched, or (in the case of an all-premises warrant) the person who is in occupation or control of premises to be searched, together with any premises under his occupation or control which can be specified and which are to be searched; and

(b)   must identify, so far as is practicable, the articles or persons to be sought.

Section 15(7) provides that there must be two copies of a specific premises warrant which specifies only one set of premises and does not authorise multiple entries. In the case of any other warrant, as many copies as are reasonably required may be made. Where a warrant authorises multiple entries it must specify whether the number of entries authorised is unlimited, or limited to a specified maximum.

A divisional court has held that 'a copy' of a search warrant means a full copy, and that therefore a copy which omitted the premises to be searched and left that information to be filled in by hand in respect of particular premises by the officer executing the warrant on those premises was not a valid copy of the warrant.

Execution of a search warrant

An entry on or search of premises under a warrant is unlawful unless PACE, ss 15 (above) and 16 are complied with. PACE, s 16 sets out the following provisions which apply to all search warrants.

A warrant may be executed by any constable. It may authorise other persons to accompany any constable executing it; a person so authorised has the same powers as a constable in relation to the execution of the warrant and the seizure of anything to which it relates. Entry and search must be within three calendar months of issue and must be at a reasonable hour unless this would frustrate the purpose of the search. However, this does not apply to warrants issued under TA 2000, Sch 5 which are exercisable only within 24 hours of issue. PACE, s 16(3A) covers the execution of all-premises warrants. It provides that in the case of an all-premises warrant, no premises which are not specified in the warrant may be entered or searched unless a police officer of at least the rank of inspector has in writing authorised them to be entered. Section 16(3B) provides that no premises may be entered or searched for the second or any subsequent time under a warrant which authorises multiple entries unless a police officer of at least the rank of inspector has authorised that entry in writing. The Searching of Premises Code provides that the officer of at least the rank of inspector referred to in s 16(3A) and (3B) must not be involved in the investigation.

A divisional court has held that, where a search warrant authorises entry 'on one occasion' to search for specified goods, the word 'occasion' does not equal one day, or require the search to be completed in one calendar day. Thus, it is not a breach of such a warrant for the police to occupy the premises for a number of days while the search is carried out.

Where the occupier of the premises is present, the constable must, when seeking to execute a search warrant:

(a) identify himself (by warrant or other identification number in the case of terrorism inquiries) and, if not in uniform, show his warrant card (but in so doing in the case of terrorism inquiries, he need not reveal his name);

(b) produce the warrant to the occupier; and

(c) supply him with a copy of it.

The constable must act likewise in relation to a person apparently in charge of the premises in the absence of the occupier. A divisional court has held that requirements (a) to (c) existed so that the occupier of premises might know that those who executed a search warrant had lawful authority to do so and could see before the search began what property might be seized under the search warrant. It held that a failure by a constable executing a search warrant to hand over a copy of it until after the search had been completed was in breach of the requirements.

In any other case, the constable must leave a copy of the warrant in a prominent place on the premises.

The premises may only be searched to the extent required for the purpose for which the warrant was issued.

Save in exceptional circumstances the media should not be invited to be present when a search warrant (or any other investigative procedure) is being executed, nor should they be invited to police briefings prior to the execution of a warrant, because reports emanating from such involvement are liable to prejudice a fair trial.

SEIZURE

A constable who is searching any person or premises under any statutory power or with the consent of the occupier may seize anything, other than a legally privileged item, which:

(a) is covered by a warrant;
(b) the officer has reasonable grounds for believing is evidence of an offence or has been obtained in consequence of the commission of an offence but only if seizure is necessary to prevent the items being concealed, lost, disposed of, or tampered with;
(c) is covered by the powers in CJPA 2001 allowing an officer to seize property and retain it for sifting or examination elsewhere.

GENERAL PROVISIONS ON ENTRY, SEARCH, SEIZURE, ACCESS AND RETENTION

In addition to the specific rules already described, the Searching of Premises Code lays down a number of rules which apply to searches of premises (as defined on p 64), whether those of the suspect or anyone else including the victim:

(a) undertaken for the purposes of an investigation into an alleged offence, with the occupier's consent, other than searches made in the following circumstances:
  (i) routine scenes-of-crime searches;
  (ii) calls to a fire or burglary made by or on behalf of an occupier or searches following the activation of fire or burglar alarms;
  (iii) searches where it is unnecessary to seek consent because in the circumstances this would cause disproportionate inconvenience to the person concerned;
  (iv) bomb threat calls;
(b) under powers conferred by PACE, ss 17 (entry to arrest/search), 18 (entry and search after arrest) and 32 (search on arrest);
(c) undertaken in pursuance of a search warrant issued in accordance with PACE, s 15 or under PACE, Sch 1 or under TA 2000; or
(d) under any other police power to enter premises with or without a search warrant for any purpose connected with the investigation into an alleged or suspected offence.

The exception for routine scenes-of-crime searches ceases to apply if the search develops into more than just a routine scenes-of-crime search. At that point, at the latest, the Searching of Premises Code applies.

On the other hand, the Searching of Premises Code does not apply to the exercise of a statutory power to enter premises or to inspect goods, equipment or procedures if the exercise of that power is not dependent on the existence of grounds for suspecting that an offence may have been committed and the person exercising the power has no reasonable grounds for such suspicion. This exception excludes from the Code inspections, etc by local authority inspectors under health and safety provisions.

Entry other than with consent

The officer in charge must first attempt to communicate with the occupier or any other person entitled to grant access to the premises by explaining the authority under which he seeks entry to the premises and ask the occupier to allow him to do so, unless:

(a)   the premises are unoccupied;
(b)   the occupier and any other person entitled to grant access are absent; or
(c)   there are reasonable grounds to believe that to alert the occupier or any other person entitled to grant access by attempting to communicate with him would frustrate the object of the search or endanger the officers concerned or other persons.

The circumstances in (c) might exist where there are known to be a number of persons on the premises all of whom are suspected of being involved in the offence, any of whom could dispose of the evidence whilst these procedures are being followed; or, in the case of entry to search for an armed criminal, where danger might arise if he was warned of imminent arrest. Although, in the circumstances in (c), an officer need not comply with the requirements as to identification, production of his warrant card (if not in uniform) and search warrant (if any) before effecting entry, he must do so before conducting the search (except that if the search is under a search warrant it is enough if he gives a copy of the search warrant at the first reasonable opportunity).

Unless (c) applies, where the premises are occupied, the officer in charge of the search must before the search begins:

(i)   identify himself (by warrant or other identification number in a terrorist investigation) and, if not in uniform, show his warrant card (although he may do so without revealing his name in a terrorist investigation);
(ii)   state the purpose of the search and the grounds for undertaking it; and
(iii) identify and introduce any person accompanying the officer on the search (such persons should carry identification for production on request) and briefly describe that person's role in the process.

If a search warrant includes a schedule of documents to be searched for and the schedule has been detached when a copy of the warrant is given to the occupier of the premises, the search is unlawful and there is no right to retain anything seized. This is so even if an uncertified photocopy of the schedule is attached to the rest of the warrant.

Searches with consent

The Searching of Premises Code provides that, if it is proposed to search premises with the consent of a person (X) entitled to grant entry, the consent must, if practicable, be in writing. Before seeking such consent the officer in charge must state the purpose of the search and its extent. This information must be as specific as possible, particularly regarding the articles or persons sought and the parts of the premises to be searched. X must be clearly informed that he is not obliged to consent, that any consent may be withdrawn at any time, including before the search starts or while it is underway, and that anything seized may be produced in evidence. If, at the time, X is not suspected of an offence the officer must tell him so when stating the purpose of the search. An officer cannot enter and search premises or continue to search premises if consent has been given under duress or is withdrawn before the search is completed.

In the case of a lodging house or other similar accommodation, a search should not be made on the basis solely of the landlord's consent.

It is unnecessary to seek consent where this would cause disproportionate inconvenience to the person concerned; for example, where it is reasonable to assume that innocent occupiers would agree to, and expect that, police would take the proposed action. Examples are where a suspect has fled from the scene of the crime and it is necessary quickly to check surrounding gardens and the like to see whether he is hiding; or where police have arrested someone in the night after a pursuit and it is necessary to make a brief check of gardens along the route of the pursuit to see whether stolen or incriminating articles have been found.

Use of force

Where the police are acting under a warrant or under one of the above statutory powers, reasonable and proportionate force may be used if necessary in the following cases if the officer in charge is satisfied that the premises are those specified in the warrant:

(a) where the occupier or another person entitled to grant access has refused to allow entry;
(b) where it is impossible to communicate with such a person;
(c) where the premises are known to be unoccupied or the occupier, etc is known to be absent; or
(d) where there are reasonable grounds to believe that to do so would frustrate the object of the search or endanger someone.

It is permissible to restrict the movement of occupants to one room while another room is being searched.

Designated persons

A designated person in this context refers to a person, other than a police officer, designated under the Police Reform Act 2002, Part 4 who has specified powers and duties of police officers conferred or imposed upon him. If a power conferred on a designated person:

(a) allows reasonable force to be used when exercised by a police officer, a designated person exercising that power has the same entitlement to use force; and
(b) includes power to use force to enter premises, that power is not exercisable by that designated person except:
   (i)   in the company and under the supervision of a police officer; or
   (ii) for the purpose of:
       • saving life or limb; or
       • preventing serious damage to property.

Notice of Powers and Rights

An officer conducting a search of premises under a search warrant issued under PACE or TA 2000 or under a power given by PACE (see (a) below), or with the occupier's consent, must, unless it is impracticable to do so, provide the occupier with a copy of a notice in a standard format:

(a) specifying whether the search is made under warrant, or with consent, or in the exercise of powers under PACE, ss 17, 18, or 32;

(b) summarising the extent of the powers of search and seizure conferred in PACE and other relevant legislation as appropriate;

(c) explaining the rights of the occupier and of the owner of property seized;

(d) explaining that compensation may be payable in appropriate cases for damage caused in entering and searching premises, and giving the address to which an application should be directed; and

(e) stating that a copy of the Searching of Premises Code is available for consultation at any police station.

If the occupier is present, copies of the notice, and of the warrant (if the search is made under warrant), should if practicable be given to him before the search begins, unless the officer in charge of the search reasonably believes that to do so would frustrate the object of the search or endanger the officers concerned or other persons. If the occupier is not present, copies of the notice, and of the warrant where appropriate, should be left in a prominent place on the premises or appropriate part of the premises and should be endorsed with the names of the officer in charge of the search and of his police station and the date and time of the search. The officer's warrant number, not his name, should be given in the case of a terrorism investigation. The warrant itself should be endorsed to show that this has been done.

Conduct of searches

Premises may be searched only to the extent necessary to achieve the object of the search, having regard to the size and nature of what is sought. This means that a search cannot be made in places where the articles specified in the warrant could not possibly be found or for longer than necessary to find those articles. For example, a warrant to search for television sets would not authorise the examination of the contents of small drawers.

A search may not continue under the authority of the warrant once everything specified in it has been found, or the officer in charge is satisfied that things specified are not on the premises.

The search must be conducted with due consideration for the property and privacy of the occupier, and with no more disturbance than necessary. Reasonable force may only be used to conduct the search where it is necessary because the co-operation of the occupier cannot be obtained or is insufficient for the purpose. An occupier must not be discouraged or prevented from securing the services of a friend, neighbour, or other person to witness the search, unless the officer in charge has reasonable grounds to believe that this would seriously hinder the investigation or endanger the officers concerned or other people. A search need not be unreasonably delayed for this purpose. If the premises have been entered by force the officer in charge must satisfy himself, before leaving, that they are secured either by arranging for the occupier or his agent to be present or by any other appropriate means.

The Counter-Terrorism Act 2008, s 1 prospectively empowers a constable, for the purpose of ascertaining whether a document is one that may be seized under the provisions of TA 2000, Sch 5 (terrorist investigations) to remove a document to another place for examination. See further p 808.

A person need not be cautioned before being asked questions solely concerned with the proper and effective conduct of a search; for example, to locate the key to a locked drawer or otherwise to seek co-operation during the search. If questioning goes beyond this point it may amount to an interview and would require the associated safeguards.

In determining when to make a search, the officer in charge must always give regard to the time of day at which the occupier is likely to be present, and should not search at a time when the occupier or any other person on the premises is likely to be asleep unless this is unavoidable. If the wrong premises are mistakenly searched, everything possible should be done to allay any sense of grievance. In appropriate cases assistance should be given to obtain compensation.

The local police/community consultative group or its equivalent should be informed as soon as practicable after a search where there is reason to believe that it might have had an adverse effect on relations between the police and the community.

Records of searches

The Searching of Premises Code requires that, if premises have been searched, a record of the search must be made. That record must be made by or on behalf of the officer in charge of the search, on his return to the police station. The record must include:

(a) the address of the premises;

(b) the date, time, and duration of the search;

(c) the authority for it (including a copy of the warrant and the written authority to apply for it, or the written consent where the search was made thereunder);

(d) the names of officer(s) in charge of, and of the other officers conducting, the search (except in the case of inquiries linked to the investigation of terrorism, or where it is reasonably believed that disclosing their names might endanger the officers, where the record must state the warrant or other identification number and duty station of each officer);

(e) the names of any persons on the premises (if known);

(f) any grounds for refusing the occupier's request to have someone present during the search;

(g) a list of articles seized (or a note of its location) and, if not covered by a warrant, the reason for seizure;

(h) whether force was used and, if so, the reason;

(i) a list of any damage caused, and the circumstances in which it was caused;

(j) if applicable, the reason it was not practicable to give the occupier a copy of the 'Notice of Powers and Rights'; and

(k) when the occupier was not present, the place where copies of the Notice of Powers and Rights and search warrant were left on the premises.

Search registers must be maintained at each sub-divisional or equivalent police station and the above record must be made, copied, or referred to in the register.

On each occasion when premises are searched under a warrant, the warrant must be endorsed to show:

(a) whether any articles specified in the warrant were found and the address where found;

(b) whether any other articles were seized;

(c) the date and time at which it was executed and, if present, the name and address of the occupier, or if he was not present, the name of the person in charge of the premises;

(d) the names of the officers who executed it and any authorised persons who accompanied them (except in the case of inquiries linked to the investigation of terrorism, in which case the warrant or other identification number and duty station of each officer concerned, and any identification number of police staff, should be given); and

(e) whether a copy, together with a copy of the Notice of Powers and Rights, was handed to the occupier; or whether it was endorsed as required (see p 81).

A warrant must be returned to the appropriate person within three months from issue or sooner on completion of the search(es) authorised by it. The appropriate person is:

(a) if the warrant was issued by a justice of the peace, the designated officer for the local justice area; or

(b) if it was issued by a judge, the appropriate officer of the court from which he issued it.

General powers of seizure

PACE, s 19 gives the police wide powers of seizure in addition to those otherwise provided by the Act or elsewhere. It provides that a constable lawfully on any premises (as defined on p 64) (eg with the occupier's consent) may seize anything on the premises if he has reasonable grounds for believing that:

(a) it has been obtained in consequence of the commission of an offence; or

(b) it is evidence in relation to an offence which he is investigating or any other offence; *and* (in either case)

(c) it is necessary to seize it in order to prevent it from being concealed, lost, altered or destroyed.

Although a vehicle, vessel, or tent is premises for the purpose of PACE, the reference to anything 'on the premises' does not prevent the seizure of a vehicle, vessel, or tent as a whole.

In the same circumstances (ie (a) to (c)), a constable may require any information stored in any electronic form and accessible from the premises to be produced in a form in which it can be taken away and in which it is legible or from which it can readily be produced in such a form.

PACE, s 19 also provides that no relevant statutory power of seizure authorises the seizure of an item which the constable has reasonable grounds for believing to be subject to legal privilege as defined on p 71. Generally, a constable will have to examine an item to test a claim to legal privilege and, if no claim is made, the constable will not have reasonable grounds for believing it to be privileged until he has examined it. If the constable later obtains reasonable grounds, the item must be returned forthwith, but the seizure does not become unlawful.

A divisional court has held that, where property has been obtained by an unlawful search and is stored at a police station, PACE, s 19 cannot be relied on to enable a constable to seize it there and thereby to convert unlawful possession into lawful possession.

Additional powers of seizure

The additional powers of seizure under CJPA 2001, s 50 and related provisions (see p 65) apply where there is a right of seizure under a search warrant or under PACE, s 19.

Record of seizure and access

PACE, s 21 provides that a constable who seizes anything *under any statutory power* must, on request, provide within a reasonable time the occupier of premises where it was seized or a person who had custody or control of the thing immediately before seizure with a record of what he seized.

Section 21 also provides for access to a thing which has been seized, and for the photographing or copying of it, by a person who had custody or control of it immediately before seizure.

Retention

PACE, s 22 provides that anything seized or taken away under s 19 may be retained so long as is necessary in all the circumstances. 'So long as necessary' in PACE, s 22 means so long as necessary for carrying out the purposes for which the powers of seizure (referred to on p 83) are conferred. In particular, anything seized under s 19 for the purposes of a criminal investigation may be retained (unless a photograph or copy would suffice) for use as evidence at a trial for an offence, or for forensic examination or investigation in connection with an offence. Moreover, anything may be retained to establish its owner, where there are reasonable grounds for believing that it has been obtained in consequence of the commission of an offence.

Nothing seized on the grounds that it may be used:

(a)   to cause physical injury;
(b)   to damage property;
(c)   to interfere with evidence; or
(d)   to assist in escape from police detention or lawful custody,

may be retained after the person from whom it was seized has been freed from detention or custody or has been bailed.

There is no power to retain seized property for any purpose other than that for which it was originally seized.

Any person who had custody or control of property prior to its seizure must, if it is retained, be provided on request within a reasonable time with a list or description of the property. A person claiming property seized by the police may apply for its possession to a magistrates' court under the Police (Property) Act 1897 and should, where appropriate, be advised of this procedure. The Court of Appeal has ruled that the police may retain seized property so long as necessary in all the circumstances after the CPS has decided not to prosecute but a private prosecution is being contemplated or taking place.

INTERCEPTION OF COMMUNICATIONS, SURVEILLANCE, AND CONDUCT AND USE OF 'COVERT HUMAN INTELLIGENCE SOURCES'

Interception of communications and public postal services

The Regulation of Investigatory Powers Act 2000 (RIPA 2000), Part I, Chapter 1 (ss 1–21) deals with the interception of telecommunications and public postal services.

Most of the provisions of RIPA 2000 are aimed at protecting the confidentiality of public postal services and telecommunications systems, and some private systems which are attached to a public system. It is an indictable (either way) offence under RIPA, s 1(1) (public systems) and s 1(2) (private systems) intentionally and without lawful authority to intercept a communication in the course of its transmission by one of these means. However, in the case of a private system, an interceptor does not commit an offence if he is a person with a right to control the operation or use of the system, which means the right to authorise or forbid the operation or use of the system, *or* if he has the express or implied consent of such a person to make the interception. In the case of the interception of a communication made by means of a public telecommunications system, a sanction has been provided to deal with cases of interceptions without lawful authority which do not constitute the above offence.

The recording by a covert listening device in a motor car of one person's voice speaking on a telephone is not an interception. Nor is the audio recording by an undercover police officer of a telephone conversation with a suspect, although it does amount to surveillance (dealt with below).

RIPA 2000 makes special provisions for the issue of *interception warrants* and provides for lawful interception without an interception warrant where one or more of the parties has consented (for example, calls received from kidnappers). Such an interception will be authorised as surveillance, rather than by means of an interception warrant.

The Regulation of Investigatory Powers (Interception of Communications: Code of Practice) Order 2002 implemented a code of practice relating to the interception of communications, to which anyone exercising or performing a power or duty to which the Code applies must have regard.

Surveillance and the conduct and use of 'covert human intelligence sources'

RIPA 2000, Part II deals with these matters, which are of most direct concern to the police. It creates a regulatory framework for three types of activity: directed surveillance; the use of covert human intelligence sources; and intrusive surveillance. A fundamental feature of each of these is that it is 'covert'.

Each of the three types of activity involves a different authorisation procedure. RIPA 2000, s 27 provides that conduct falling within one of these three types is lawful if it is authorised and carried out in accordance with the authorisation. No civil liability will be incurred in respect of conduct 'incidental' to such lawful conduct, which is not in itself conduct in respect of which an authorisation or warrant is capable of being granted under a relevant enactment and might reasonably have been expected to be sought. A 'relevant enactment' means the RIPA 2000; the Intelligence Services Act 1994, s 5 (warrants for the intelligence services); or an enactment contained in the Police Act 1997 (PA 1997), Part III (powers of covert entry and interference with property by the police).

Directed surveillance

Surveillance is directed if it is *covert*, but *not intrusive*, and is undertaken:

(a) for the purpose of a specific investigation or a specific operation;
(b) in such a manner as is likely to result in the obtaining of *private information* about a person (whether or not one specifically identified for the purposes of the investigation or operation); and

(c) otherwise than by way of an immediate response to events or circumstances the nature of which is such that it would not be reasonably practicable for an authorisation under RIPA 2000, Part II to be sought for the carrying out of the surveillance.

Surveillance is *covert* if it is carried out in a manner that is calculated to ensure that the persons who are subject to the surveillance are unaware that it is or may be taking place. Surveillance is *intrusive* if, and only if, it is covert surveillance that is carried out in relation to anything taking place on any residential premises or in any private vehicle and involves the presence of an individual on the premises or in the vehicle or is carried out by means of a surveillance device. However, there are qualifications to this. Surveillance is *not intrusive* if it involves no more than the placing of a vehicle location device, or it is surveillance involving the interception of a communication which is sent by, or intended for, a person who has consented to the interception. In addition, it is *not intrusive* if it is carried out by a device which is not present upon the residential premises or private vehicle concerned, unless the device is such that it consistently provides information of the same quality and detail as might be expected to be obtained from a device which was actually present on the premises or in the vehicle. Lastly, surveillance by devices designed to catch TV licence dodgers is neither directed nor intrusive. '*Private information*' includes any information relating to a person's private or family life.

By RIPA 2000, s 28, a 'designated person' may grant an authorisation for the carrying out of directed surveillance if he believes it is necessary on specified grounds, including national security, the prevention or detection of crime, and the prevention of disorder. The designated person must believe that the authorised surveillance is proportionate to what is sought to be achieved by it.

Among the persons designated for the purposes of s 28 (and s 29, below) are police officers of the rank of superintendent (inspector in urgent cases). For the purposes of the grant of an authorisation that combines an authorisation under ss 28 or 29 and an authorisation for carrying out intrusive surveillance (see below), the Secretary of State is the person designated for the purpose.

A written authorisation has effect for three months. Urgent oral authorisations or written authorisations granted by a person who is entitled to act only in urgent cases only have effect for 72 hours, unless renewed.

Code of practice

The Regulation of Investigatory Powers (Covert Surveillance and Property Interference: Code of Practice) Order 2010 brought into force a revised code of practice relating to covert surveillance which applies to directed surveillance.

Use of a covert human intelligence source

A person is a covert human intelligence source if:

(a) he establishes or maintains a personal or other relationship with a person, for the covert purpose of facilitating:
  (i)   the covert obtaining of information or the provision of access to information to another person; or
  (ii) the covert disclosure of information obtained by the use of such a relationship or in consequence of such a relationship;
(b) he covertly uses such a relationship to obtain information or to provide such access; or

(c) he covertly discloses information obtained by the use of such a relationship, or as a consequence of the existence of such a relationship.

The 'use of a covert human intelligence source' refers to inducing, asking or assisting a person to engage in the conduct of such a source, or to obtain information by means of such a source.

A purpose is covert in relation to the establishment or maintenance of a personal or other relationship only if the relationship is conducted in a manner that is calculated to ensure that one of the parties to the relationship is unaware of the purpose. A relationship is used covertly, and information obtained is disclosed covertly, only if it is used or disclosed in a manner that is calculated to ensure that one of the parties to the relationship is unaware of the use or disclosure in question.

RIPA 2000, s 29 governs the authorisation of a covert human intelligence source. An authorisation is generally valid for 12 months. It may be granted by a designated person (see above).

The criteria which apply to the grant of an authorisation for directed surveillance also apply to covert surveillance. However, there are additional requirements concerning satisfactory arrangements for the supervision of the source depending on whether or not a source is a source of a relevant collaborative unit, and there are further requirements where matters subject to legal privilege are involved, and also about records relating to the use of the source.

The Regulation of Investigatory Powers (Covert Human Intelligence Sources: Matter Subject to Legal Privilege) Order 2010 applies where any conduct that is, or is to be, authorised in an authorisation under s 29 consists in any activities involving conduct or a source, or the use of a source to:

(a) obtain matters,
(b) provide access to another person to any matters, or
(c) disclose matters,

subject to legal privilege (as defined on p 71).

An authorisation for such conduct must not be granted or renewed unless it satisfies the additional requirements set out below. Such conduct is referred to hereafter as 'specified conduct'.

Where a single authorisation under s 29 authorises conduct to which the 2010 Order applies and other conduct falling within RIPA 2000, Part II, the additional requirements only apply in relation to those parts of the combined authorisation which authorise obtaining, giving access to, or disclosing, matters subject to legal privilege.

The additional requirements where matters subject to legal privilege are involved are as follows in relation to police operations.

Before a person grants or renews an authorisation for specified conduct, he must in accordance with arrangements made by an ordinary Surveillance Commissioner (ie a Commissioner appointed by the Prime Minister under PA 1997, Part III), give or transmit electronically written notice to the Commissioner. The notice must state that the requisite approval is sought and include the specified matters.

An authorisation for conduct to which the 2010 Order applies must not be granted or renewed until it has been approved by the Commissioner, and written notice of the Commissioner's decision to approve the grant or renewal of the authorisation has been given or transmitted electronically.

The Commissioner must give his approval to the grant or renewal of the authorisation if, and only if, satisfied that there are reasonable grounds for believing that the authorisation is necessary and the requirements of proportionality and satisfactory arrangements which apply to authorisations are met.

Where an authorisation authorises conduct to which the 2010 Order applies, it has effect for three months.

An authorisation will specify the conduct which is authorised and require that it is carried out in accordance with the authorisation. In the case of informants the authorisation will be specific to the individual and the particular investigation.

The Regulation of Investigatory Powers (Covert Human Intelligence Sources: Code of Practice) Order 2010 brought into force a revised code of practice which must be observed by a person exercising or performing a power or duty to which the code applies.

Intrusive surveillance

As already stated, surveillance is *intrusive* if, but only if, it is *covert* surveillance (see above) carried out in relation to anything taking place on any residential premises or in any private vehicle and involves the presence of an individual on the premises or in the vehicle or is carried out by means of a surveillance device.

Directed surveillance that is carried out in relation to anything taking place on so much of a police station, court building, lawyer's business premises, or a prison or similar place as is, at any time during the surveillance, used for the purpose of legal consultations is treated for the purposes of RIPA 2000, Part II as intrusive surveillance.

RIPA 2000, s 32 states that intrusive surveillance authorisations may be granted by the Secretary of State (valid for six months) and senior authorising officers (chief constables and equivalents, plus assistant commissioners of the Metropolitan Police) (three months). Such authorisations will only be granted where it is believed that this is necessary in the interests of national security or of the economic well-being of the UK, or for the purpose of preventing or detecting serious crime, *and* that the authorised surveillance is proportionate to what is sought to be achieved.

Authorisations valid for 72 hours for intrusive surveillance may be granted under s 34, by the appropriate deputy chief constable or an assistant chief constable who is designated to act, or their equivalents (specified as a commander in the metropolitan police force) in urgent cases where it is not reasonably practicable for the senior authorising officer to do so.

When an authorisation for intrusive surveillance is granted or cancelled, notice must be given to an ordinary Surveillance Commissioner (ie a Commissioner appointed by the Prime Minister under PA 1997, Part III).

Except in cases of urgency, the approval of an ordinary Surveillance Commissioner is needed before an authorisation for intrusive surveillance, other than one made by the Secretary of State, may take effect.

The Regulation of Investigatory Powers (Covert Surveillance and Property Interference: Code of Practice) Order 2010 brought into force a revised code of practice relating to covert surveillance which applies to intrusive surveillance.

Corresponding powers of Independent Police Complaints Commission

The Independent Police Complaints Commission (Investigatory Powers) Order 2004 and the Regulation of Investigatory Powers (Direct Surveillance and Covert Human

Intelligence Sources) Order 2010 provide powers, equivalent to those exercised by the police under RIPA 2000, Part II, in respect of the Independent Police Complaints Commission.

AUTHORISATION OF ACTION IN RESPECT OF PROPERTY

PA 1997, Part III introduced a system whereby authorisations may be given in respect of entry on or interference with property or with wireless telegraphy. No act carried out in accordance with an authorisation is unlawful. Although authorisations may be given by 'authorising officers' (which term includes, among others, a chief constable, the Commissioner or an Assistant Commissioner of Police of the Metropolis, and the Commissioner of the City of London Police) they are subject in some cases to approval by the Chief Commissioner or a Commissioner appointed under PA 1997, Part III by the Prime Minister.

The law is as follows where the authorising officer is a chief constable, or the Commissioner or an Assistant Commissioner of the Metropolitan Police, or the Commissioner of the City of London Police. Where an authorising officer believes:

(a) that it is necessary for the action specified to be taken to prevent or detect serious crime; and

(b) that that action is proportionate to what the action seeks to achieve,

he may authorise:

(i)   the taking of such action, in respect of such property in his police area (or area specified in a collaboration agreement with another force), as he may specify;

(ii) the taking of such action in respect of property outside that area for the purpose of maintaining or retrieving any equipment, apparatus or device the placing of which in the relevant area has been authorised under PA 1997, Part III or RIPA 2000, Part II (above); or

(iii) the taking of such action in that area as he may specify, in respect of wireless telegraphy.

Provision is made for authorisations to be given by specified senior officers (assistant chief constables or commander in the case of police forces) where it is not reasonably practicable for an authorising officer or his designated deputy to consider an application for an authorisation.

Authorisations must be in writing, although in urgent cases they may be given orally. Unless renewed, they cease to have effect after 72 hours if given orally, or by someone other than the actual authorising officer or his designated deputy. In any other case an authorisation may last for three months. An authorisation may be renewed for a further three months by the authorising officer.

The Regulation of Investigatory Powers (Covert Surveillance and Property Interference: Code of Practice) Order 2010 provides guidance on entry on or interference with property or with wireless telegraphy by public authorities under PA 1997, Part III.

As soon as is reasonably practicable, the giving, renewal or cancellation of an authorisation must be notified to a Commissioner appointed under PA 1997.

Where the person who gives an authorisation believes that any of the property specified in it is used wholly or mainly as a dwelling or as a bedroom in a hotel, or constitutes office premises, or that the action authorised is likely to result in someone acquiring knowledge of legally privileged matters (p 71), confidential personal information, or confidential journalistic material, the authorisation is ineffective until approved by a Commissioner and the person who gave the authorisation has been notified of that approval. However, this does not apply in a case of urgency.

Confidential personal information is (a) personal information which a person has acquired or created in the course of any trade, business, profession or other occupation, or for the purpose of any paid or unpaid office, and which he holds in confidence, and (b) communications as a result of which personal information is so acquired or created and is held in confidence.

Confidential journalistic material is (a) material acquired or created for the purposes of journalism which is in the possession of persons who acquired or created it for those purposes, is held in confidence and has been continuously held (by one or more persons) subject to such an undertaking, restriction or obligation since it was first acquired or created for those purposes; and (b) communications as a result of which information is acquired for those purposes and so held.

Similar provision for the making of authorisations under PA 1997, Part III is made in respect of the Independent Police Complaints Commission by the Independent Police Complaints Commission (Investigatory Powers) Order 2004.

TAKING PHOTOGRAPHS OF DEMONSTRATORS OR ACTIVISTS, ETC

Where the police take and retain photographs of persons such as demonstrators or activists, etc who are not committing or suspected of committing any offence this may involve an infringement of the European Convention on Human Rights, art 8. Whether or not it does so depends on the facts of the case and whether the measures taken are proportionate to any legitimate aims that the police may be pursuing.

INVESTIGATION ANONYMITY ORDER

An investigation anonymity order (IAO) is an order, made by a justice of the peace, which prohibits the disclosure of information identifying or potentially capable of identifying the person specified in the order as a person who is or was able or willing to assist a specified criminal investigation into a gun- or knife-killing. IAOs were introduced by the Coroners and Justice Act 2009 (C&JA 2009), Part 3, Ch 1. The purpose of an IAO is to prevent disclosure of information relating to the identity of someone like an informant and thus to protect him from harm and to provide a reluctant informant with reassurance that his identity will be protected.

An IAO can only be made in respect of a criminal investigation conducted by a local police force, the British Transport Police, or SOCA, wholly or partly to ascertain whether a person should be charged with a 'qualifying offence', or whether a person charged with such an offence is guilty of it. 'Qualifying offence' means murder and manslaughter, where the death was caused by being shot with a firearm, and/or by being injured with a knife.

Only a chief officer of police, the Director General of SOCA, the DPP, or the Director of Revenue and Customs Prosecutions (or, in each case, his delegate) may apply for an IAO. No notice of the application need be given. The justice of the peace may make an IAO if satisfied that there are reasonable grounds for believing that:

(a) a qualifying offence has been committed;
(b) the person likely to have committed it (X) was at least 11 but under 30 at the time of the offence;

(c) X is likely to have been a member of a group of the following type when the offence was committed, namely a group:
   (i) which it is possible to identify from the criminal activities that its members appear to be engaged in, and
   (ii) it appears that the majority of the members of the group are at least 11 but under 30;
(d) the person who would be specified in the order (P) has reasonable grounds to fear intimidation or harm if identified as a person who is or was able or willing to assist in the investigation into the homicide at issue; and
(e) (i) P is able to provide information that would assist the qualifying criminal investigation, and
   (ii) P is more likely than not to provide the information if the order were made.

By C&JA 2009, s 76(10), disclosing information in contravention of an investigation anonymity order is an indictable (either way) offence. However, by s 76(2)–(9), an IAO is not contravened where the discloser does not know and has no reason to suspect that an IAO is in force, or that the information might enable the specified person to be so identified, or where disclosure is required by any enactment or rule of law, or where required by a court order, or in certain other cases.

CHAPTER 4

Police Questioning and the Rights of Suspects

INTRODUCTION

The Detention Code

In this and the following chapter, frequent reference is made to PACE Code C: the Code of Practice for the Detention, Treatment and Questioning of Persons by Police Officers (hereafter the Detention Code). This Code applies to persons in custody at police stations, whether or not they have been arrested, and (except for its provisions as to reviews and extensions of detention) to those who have been removed to a police station as a place of safety under the Mental Health Act 1983, ss 135 and 136. (A police station should only be so used as a last resort.) Persons who are voluntarily at police stations must be treated with no less consideration.

The Detention Code does not apply to the following persons in custody:

(a) persons arrested on warrants issued in Scotland by police officers under the Criminal Justice and Public Order Act 1994 (CJPOA 1994), s 136, or arrested or detained without warrant by officers from a police force in Scotland under s 137. In these cases, police powers and duties and the person's rights and entitlements whilst at a police station in England and Wales are the same as those in Scotland;

(b) persons arrested for the purpose of fingerprinting under the Immigration and Asylum Act 1999, s 142;

(c) persons whose detention is authorised by an immigration officer under the Immigration Act 1971;

(d) persons who are convicted or remanded prisoners held in police cells on behalf of the prison service; and

(e) persons detained for searches under stop and search powers except as required by the Stop and Search Code.

No part of the Detention Code applies to a detained person:

(a) to whom PACE Code H (p 35) applies because:
   (i) he is detained following arrest under the Terrorism Act 2000 (TA 2000), s 41 and not charged, or
   (ii) an authorisation has been given for post-charge questioning of him as a terrorist suspect; matters dealt with in Chapter 28;

(b) to whom the Code of Practice for Examining Officers applies because he is detained for examination under TA 2000, Sch 7.

Nothing in the Detention Code requires the identity of officers or other police staff to be recorded or disclosed if the persons concerned reasonably believe that recording or disclosing their names might put them in danger. In such cases they must use their warrant or other identification number and the name of their police station.

Where the Detention Code requires the prior authority or agreement of an officer of at least inspector or superintendent rank, that authority may be given by a sergeant or chief inspector, respectively, authorised to perform the functions of the higher rank by a superintendent (or above).

Evidence obtained in breach of the procedures set out below is liable to be excluded in any subsequent court proceedings. In addition, a failure to comply with the Detention Code may lead to a disciplinary offence.

Custody officer

The Detention Code makes frequent reference to 'the custody officer'; such references include any police officer performing the functions of a custody officer. References in the Code to a police officer include a 'designated person' (ie a person designated under the Police Reform Act 2002, (p 282)) acting in the exercise or performance of the powers and duties conferred or imposed by their designation. Nothing in the Code prevents a custody officer from allowing civilian support staff who are not designated persons to carry out individual procedures or tasks at the police station if the law allows. However, the officer remains responsible for making sure the procedures and tasks are carried out correctly in accordance with the Codes of Practice. Any such civilian must be a person employed by a police force and under the direction and control of the Chief Officer, or employed by a person with whom a force has a contract for the provision of services relating to persons arrested or otherwise in custody.

A custody officer must perform the functions in the Detention Code as soon as practicable. A custody officer will not be in breach of the Code if delay is justifiable and reasonable steps are taken to prevent unnecessary delay. The custody record must show when a delay has occurred and the reason. Examples of where delays would be justifiable would be where a large number of suspects are brought to a police station simultaneously to be placed in custody, or interview rooms are all in use, or where there are difficulties in contacting the appropriate adult, solicitor, or interpreter.

VOLUNTARY ATTENDANCE AT POLICE STATION

PACE, s 29 provides that where, for the purpose of assisting with an investigation, a person attends voluntarily at a police station or at any other place where a constable is present, or accompanies a constable to a police station or any other place without having been arrested, he is entitled to leave at will unless he is placed under arrest. If the interview is at 'any other place' where the interview requires the person's informed consent to remain (eg that person's home) 'entitled to leave' means 'require the interviewer to leave'. If, during an interview, it is decided that it is necessary to arrest him, he must be informed at once that he is under arrest and the grounds and reasons (see p 59), and be brought before the custody officer at that police station or one to which he is then taken. The same rules apply thereafter as in the case of other detainees.

The Detention Code goes further, requiring that, at any stage at which a person voluntarily attending is cautioned, the officer must tell him that he is not under arrest and is free to leave and must remind him of his right to free, independent legal advice. The police should assist a 'volunteer' who asks how he should go about obtaining such advice. The person must also be given a copy of the notice explaining the arrangements for obtaining legal advice and told that the right to legal advice includes the right to speak with a solicitor on the telephone and be asked if he wants advice. If advice is requested, the interviewer is responsible for securing its provision without delay by contacting the Defence Solicitor Call Centre (DSCC) and for ensuring that the provisions of the Detention Code, and those of the PACE Codes concerning the conduct and audio or visual recording of interviews of suspects, are followed insofar as they can be applied to suspects who are not under arrest.

DOCUMENTATION

The Detention Code provides as follows.

When a person is brought to a police station under arrest, or is arrested at a police station having attended there voluntarily, or attends a police station in answer to bail, he must be brought before the custody officer as soon as practicable after arrival, or following arrest at the police station. This equally applies to designated and non-designated police stations. Such a person is 'at a police station' if he is anywhere upon the premises or enclosed yards forming part of the premises.

As stated in Chapter 3, a separate custody record must be opened as soon as practicable for each person who is brought to a police station under arrest or who is arrested at the police station, having attended there voluntarily.

Where the arresting officer is not physically present when a detainee is brought to the police station, the arresting officer's account must be made available to the custody officer remotely or by a third party on the arresting officer's behalf. All information which is required to be recorded under the Detention Code must be recorded as soon as practicable in the custody record unless otherwise specified. Any audio or visual recording made in the custody area is not part of the custody record. It is a matter for the custody officer to determine whether a record should be made of the property a detained person has with him or had taken from him on arrest. Any record made is not required to be kept as part of the custody record but the custody record should be noted as to where such a record exists. Whenever a record is made the detainee must be allowed to check and sign it as correct. Any refusal to sign must be recorded.

Where a person is answering street bail, the custody officer should link any documentation held in relation to the arrest with the custody record and any further action must be recorded in accordance with the Code.

In the case of any action requiring the authority of an officer of a specified rank, his name and rank must be recorded in the custody record, *except where the person is detained under TA 2000, or where there are reasonable grounds to believe that naming him would endanger him (in which case the record must state the officer's warrant or other identification number and duty station).*

All entries in the custody record must be timed and signed by the maker. In the case of a record held on a computer, this should be timed and contain the operator's identification. Warrant or other identification numbers and the name of the duty station should be used rather than names in the cases italicised above where the special rule applies.

If a person is arrested and taken to a police station as a result of a search in the exercise of any stop and search power to which the Stop and Search Code or the 'search powers code' issued under TA 2000 applies, the officer carrying out the search is responsible for ensuring that the record of the stop and search is made as part of the person's custody record. The custody officer must then ensure that the person is asked if he wants a copy of the search record and, if he does, that he is given a copy as soon as practicable.

The custody officer is responsible for the accuracy and completeness of the custody record and for ensuring that the record (or a copy) accompanies a detained person if he is transferred to another police station. The record must show the time of, and reason for, a transfer and the time a person is released from detention. As soon as practicable after his arrival at the police station, a solicitor or appropriate adult must be permitted to consult the custody record of a person detained. When a person leaves police detention or is taken before a court, he or his legal representative or his appropriate adult must be supplied on request with a copy of the custody record as soon as practicable. This entitlement lasts for 12 months after his release.

The fact and time of any refusal by a person to sign a custody record when asked to do so in accordance with the Detention Code must be recorded.

INITIAL ACTION

When a person is brought to a police station under arrest or arrested at the station having gone there voluntarily, the custody officer must make sure that the person is told clearly about the following continuing rights which may be exercised at any stage during the period in custody:

(a) the right to have someone informed of his arrest;
(b) the right to consult privately with a solicitor and that free independent legal advice is available;
(c) the right to consult the PACE codes of practice.

The detainee must also be given:

(a) a written notice setting out:
  • the three rights;
  • the arrangements for obtaining legal advice;
  • the right to a copy of the custody record;
  • the caution in the terms set out on p 107;
(b) an additional written notice briefly setting out his entitlements while in custody. An audio version of the notice of entitlement should be available, and also translations into the main ethnic and European languages if likely to be helpful.

The detainee must be asked to sign the custody record to acknowledge receipt of these notices. Any refusal must be recorded on the custody record.

A citizen of an independent Commonwealth country or a national of a foreign country, including the Republic of Ireland, must be informed as soon as practicable about his rights of communication with his High Commission, Embassy or Consulate: see pp 107–9.

The custody officer must:

(a) record on the custody record the offence(s) that the detainee has been arrested for and the reason(s) for the arrest;
(b) note on the custody record any comment the detainee makes in relation to the arresting officer's account but may not invite comment. If the arresting officer is not physically present when the detainee is brought to a police station, the arresting officer's account must be made available to the custody officer remotely or by a third party on the arresting officer's behalf. If the custody officer authorises a person's detention, he must record the grounds for detention in the detainee's presence and, at the same time, inform the detainee of them unless he is incapable

of understanding, or is (or may become) violent, or in urgent need of medical attention. In such a case, the information must be given as soon as practicable. The detainee must be informed of the grounds for his detention before he is questioned about any offence;

(c) note any comment the detainee makes in respect of the decision to detain him but shall not invite comment;

(d) not put specific questions to the detainee regarding his involvement in any offence, nor in respect of any comments he may make in response to the arresting officer's account or the decision to place him in detention. Such an exchange is likely to constitute an interview and require the associated safeguards set out on pp 111–15.

The custody officer or other custody staff as directed by him must:

(a) ask the detainee whether at this time he would like legal advice, or wants someone informed of his detention;

(b) ask the detainee to sign the custody record to confirm his decisions in respect of (a);

(c) determine whether the detainee is, or might be, in need of medical treatment or attention, or requires an appropriate adult, help to check documentation, or an interpreter; and

(d) record the decision in respect of (c).

Where any of these duties have been carried out by custody staff, the outcomes must, as soon as practicable, be reported to the custody officer.

When these needs are determined, the custody officer is responsible for initiating an assessment to consider whether the detainee is likely to present specific risks to custody staff or himself. This should always include a Police National Computer (PNC) check. It may be necessary for him to consult and involve others, eg the arresting officer or an appropriate healthcare professional. Risk assessments must follow a structured process which clearly defines the categories of risk to be considered and the results must be incorporated in the detainee's custody record. The custody officer must ensure those responsible for the detainee's custody are appropriately briefed about the risks. The content of any risk assessment and any resulting analysis need not be shown to the detainee or any person acting on his behalf. But information should not be withheld from anyone acting on his behalf, if to do so might put that person at risk. The custody officer is responsible for implementing the response to any specific risk assessment.

As to detainees who are at risk because of their youth, mental vulnerability, deafness, or language skills, see pp 124–8.

RIGHT NOT TO BE HELD INCOMMUNICADO

Notification of detention

A detainee has a right under PACE, s 56 to have someone informed at public expense and as soon as practicable of his detention. However, this extends only to one friend, relative, or other person who is known to him or is likely to take an interest in his welfare. If the person cannot be contacted, the detainee may choose up to two alternates. If they cannot be contacted the custody officer may allow further attempts. If a person is moved from one police station to another, the right to have someone informed of his whereabouts arises again.

Delay

PACE, s 56, together with Annex B to the Detention Code, provides that a delay in informing someone may be authorised by an inspector (or above) where the person is in police detention for an indictable offence and has not been charged with it. In such circumstances, the authorisation may only be given in two types of case. The first is where the inspector has reasonable grounds for believing that telling the person named of the arrest:

(a) will lead to interference with, or harm to, evidence connected with an indictable offence or interference with or physical harm to other persons; or

(b) will lead to the alerting of other persons suspected of having committed such an offence but not yet arrested for it; or

(c) will hinder the recovery of any property obtained as a result of such an offence.

The second type of case is that an inspector (or above) may authorise delay where he has reasonable grounds for believing that the person detained for an indictable offence has benefited from his criminal conduct (decided in accordance with Part 2 of the Proceeds of Crime Act 2002) and that the recovery of the value of the property constituting that benefit will be hindered by telling the named person of the arrest.

There are similar, but not identical, grounds for delay where a person is detained under TA 2000, s 41 or Sch 7 (p 823). In such a case delay can only be authorised by a superintendent (or above) who has reasonable grounds to believe the necessary things.

If a delay is authorised, then, as soon as possible, the detainee must be informed of the reason for it and the reason must be noted on his custody record. If given orally, the authorisation must be confirmed in writing as soon as practicable. When the reasons for delay have been removed, for example by the arrest of other persons, the request to communicate must be granted. The right to communicate cannot be delayed for more than 36 hours.

Where a person has been detained under TA 2000, s 41 communication to a friend, etc may be delayed up to 48 hours.

Any delay authorised under the above provisions should be proportionate and last no longer than necessary.

Visits, letters, and phone calls

If a person in detention agrees, he may, at the discretion of the custody officer, receive visits from friends, family, or others likely to take an interest in his welfare, or in whose welfare the detainee has an interest. Where inquiries by interested persons are received concerning his whereabouts, the information must be given if the detainee agrees and an inspector (or above) has not authorised delay in the release of such information. The custody officer must exercise his discretion as to visits in the light of the availability of sufficient manpower to supervise a visit and any possible hindrance to the investigation.

The detainee must also be supplied on request with writing material. Letters and messages must be sent (at his expense) as soon as practicable, but all letters, other than those to his solicitor, may be read. The detainee may speak for a reasonable time to one person on the telephone. Whether or not the call can be made at police expense is a matter for the custody officer's discretion. Unless the call is to a solicitor, a police officer may listen to the call and may terminate it if it is being abused. The detainee must be cautioned that what he says in a letter, call, or message (other than to his solicitor) may be read or listened to and may be given in evidence. An interpreter may make a call on behalf of a detainee. Where an inspector (or above) considers that the sending of a letter or the making of a telephone call might result in any of the consequences referred to in the list referred to on p 97, and the person is detained in connection with an indictable offence or under TA 2000, s 41 or Sch 7, that officer can deny or delay the exercise of either or both these privileges.

Any delay or denial of these rights should be proportionate and should last no longer than necessary.

Prisoners

Where a prisoner has been transferred to police custody for specific purposes and periods under the Crime (Sentences) Act 1997, Sch 1, the exercise of the above rights is subject to any additional conditions specified in the transfer direction for the purpose of regulating his contact and communication with others whilst in police custody.

Documentation

A record must be kept:

(a) of any request made in relation to matters of communication and of the action taken in consequence of that request;
(b) of letters or messages sent, calls made, or visits received; and
(c) of any refusal by the prisoner to have information about himself or his whereabouts given to an outside inquirer.

The prisoner must be asked to countersign the record accordingly and any refusal to do so should be recorded.

Juveniles under 17

Where someone under 17 is in police detention, the Children and Young Persons Act 1933 (CYPA 1933), s 34 requires that his parent or guardian must be informed as soon as practicable that he has been arrested; why he has been arrested; and where he is being detained. If a supervision order is in force in respect of the juvenile, reasonable steps must be taken to notify the person responsible for his supervision as soon as practicable. If the juvenile is in care, the care authority or voluntary organisation must be informed in place of the parent or guardian. Such steps as are practicable must be taken to identify the person responsible for the juvenile's welfare.

Aliens, etc

The Detention Code provides that a detainee who is a citizen of an independent Commonwealth country or a foreign national is entitled on request to communicate at any time with his High Commission, Embassy, or Consulate. Such a person must be informed as soon as practicable of this right and asked if he wants his High Commission etc told of his whereabouts and the grounds for his detention. Such a request should be acted on as soon as practicable.

A detainee who is a national of a country with which a consular treaty is in force requiring notification of arrest (for the list of countries, see http:///www.fco.gov.uk/en/publications-and-documents/treaties/treaty-texts/prisoner-transfer-agreements) must also be informed that, with the following qualification, notification of his arrest will be sent to his High Commission etc as soon as practicable, whether or not he requests it. The qualification is that, if the detainee claims that he is a refugee or has applied or intends to apply for asylum, the custody officer must ensure that the UK Border Agency (UKBA) is informed as soon as practicable of the claim. UKBA will then determine whether compliance with relevant international obligations requires notification of the arrest to be sent and will inform the custody officer as to what action police need to take.

Consular officers may visit to advise such persons and those visits must take place out of the hearing of a police officer.

A record must be made:

(a) when a detainee is informed of the above rights and of any requirement to notify under a consular treaty;
(b) of any communications with a High Commission, etc, and
(c) of any communications with UKBA about a detainee's claim to be a refugee or to be seeking asylum and the resulting action taken by police.

LEGAL ADVICE

By PACE, s 58 a person arrested and held in police custody is entitled, if he so requests, to consult a solicitor privately at any time. This is a fundamental right. The Detention Code provides that the consultation may be in person, in writing, or by telephone, and that free independent legal advice is available.

A detainee has a right to free legal advice and to be represented by a solicitor. What follows explains the arrangements which enable detainees to obtain legal advice. The arrangements also apply, with appropriate modifications, to persons attending a police station or other location voluntarily who are cautioned prior to being interviewed.

When a detainee asks for free legal advice, the Defence Solicitor Call Centre (DSCC) must be informed of the request.

Free legal advice will be limited to telephone advice provided by CDS Direct if a detainee is:

(a) detained for a non-imprisonable offence;
(b) arrested on a bench warrant for failing to appear and being held for production at court (except where the solicitor has clear documentary evidence available that would result in the client being released from custody);
(c) arrested for drink-driving (driving/in charge with excess alcohol, failing to produce a specimen, driving/in charge whilst unfit through drink); or
(d) detained in relation to breach of police or court bail conditions,

unless one or more exceptions apply, in which case the DSCC should arrange for advice to be given by a solicitor at the police station.

Examples of exceptions are:

(a) the police want to interview the detainee or carry out an eye-witness identification parade;

(b) the detainee needs an appropriate adult, is unable to communicate over the telephone, or alleges serious maltreatment by the police;

(c) the investigation includes another offence not included in the list;

(d) the solicitor to be assigned is already at the police station.

When free advice is not limited to telephone advice, a detainee can ask for free advice from a solicitor he knows or, if he does not know a solicitor or the solicitor he knows cannot be contacted, from the duty solicitor.

To arrange free legal advice, the police should telephone the DSCC. The call centre will decide whether legal advice should be limited to telephone advice from CDS Direct, or whether a solicitor known to the detainee or the duty solicitor should speak to the detainee.

When a detainee wants to pay for legal advice himself:

(a) the DSCC will contact a solicitor of his choice on his behalf;

(b) he may, when free advice is only available by telephone from CDS Direct, still speak to a solicitor of his choice on the telephone for advice but the solicitor would not be paid by legal aid and may ask the person to pay for the advice;

(c) he should be given an opportunity to consult a specific solicitor or another solicitor from that solicitor's firm. If this solicitor is not available, he may choose up to two alternatives. If these alternatives are not available, the custody officer has discretion to allow further attempts until a solicitor has been contacted and agreed to provide advice;

(d) he is entitled to a private consultation with his chosen solicitor on the telephone or the solicitor may decide to come to the police station;

(e) if his chosen solicitor cannot be contacted, the DSCC may still be called to arrange free legal advice.

Apart from carrying out duties necessary to implement these arrangements, an officer must not advise the suspect about any particular firm of solicitors.

In the case of a juvenile or mentally disordered or otherwise mentally vulnerable person, an appropriate adult (pp 124–5) should consider whether legal advice from a solicitor is required. If a juvenile, etc indicates that legal advice is not required the appropriate adult has the right to ask for a solicitor to attend if this would be in the best interests of the person. However, the juvenile, etc cannot be forced to see the solicitor if he is adamant that he does not wish to do so.

A detainee who requests legal advice must be permitted to consult a solicitor as soon as practicable, except to the extent that delay is permitted (see p 101). Whenever legal advice is requested (and unless delay is so permitted), the custody officer must act without delay to secure the provision of such advice. If the detainee declines to exercise his right to speak to a solicitor in person, the officer should point out that the right to legal advice includes the right to speak with a solicitor on the telephone. If the detainee continues to waive his right, or a detainee whose right to free legal advice is limited to telephone advice from CDS Direct declines to exercise that right, the officer should ask him why. Any reasons must be recorded on the custody record or the interview record as appropriate. Once it is clear that a person neither wishes to speak to a solicitor in person, nor by telephone, he should cease to be asked his reasons.

Except as allowed in the case of persons arrested under TA 2000, s 41 (see p 821), if the requirement for privacy of consultation is compromised because what is said or written by the detainee or the solicitor for the purpose of the giving or receiving of legal advice is overheard, listened to, or read by others without the informed consent of the detainee, the right will effectively have been denied. Where a detainee speaks to a solicitor on the telephone, he should be allowed to do so in private unless this is impractical because of the design and layout of the custody area or the location of the telephones. However, the normal expectation should be that facilities will be available, unless they are being used, at all police stations to enable such private communications to be made.

Delay

The right of access to legal advice may be delayed if the person is in police detention for an indictable offence, has not yet been charged, and an officer of the rank of superintendent (or above) authorises the delay. If such authorisation is given orally it must be confirmed in writing as soon as practicable. Delay may only be authorised under this power in two types of case specified in Annex B to the Detention Code.

The first is where the superintendent (or above) has reasonable grounds for believing that access to a solicitor at a time when the detainee wishes to have access will:

(a) lead to interference with or harm to evidence connected with an indictable offence or interference with or physical injury to other persons; or

(b) lead to the alerting of other persons suspected of having committed such an offence but not yet arrested for it; or

(c) hinder the recovery of any property obtained as a result of such an offence.

Superintendents should authorise such delays only after careful consideration of these issues. The Court of Appeal has ruled that such an authorisation can only be justified by reference to specific circumstances, including evidence as to the person detained or the *actual solicitor* sought to be consulted. Thus, if it is believed that a particular solicitor may bring about one of the consequences at (a) to (c) above, that belief would only be relevant to that particular solicitor and would not apply to others selected by the detainee. The court stated that a solicitor who deliberately did something, knowing that it would result in consequence (a), (b), or (c), would commit a serious criminal offence. A superintendent must believe that, accident apart, the solicitor in question would do so.

The second type of case is that a superintendent may authorise delay where he has reasonable grounds to believe that:

(a) the person detained for an indictable offence has benefited from his criminal conduct (decided in accordance with the Proceeds of Crime Act 2002, Part 2); and

(b) the recovery of the value of the property constituting that benefit will be hindered by the exercise of the right to consult a solicitor privately.

Access to a solicitor may not be delayed on the ground that he might advise the detainee not to answer any questions or that he was initially asked to attend by someone other than the detainee, provided the detainee wishes to see him. In the latter case the detainee must be told that the solicitor has come to the police station at another person's request, and must be asked to sign the custody record to signify whether or not he wishes to see the solicitor.

If delay is authorised the detainee must be told the reason and the reason must be noted in his custody record as soon as practicable. Once the reason for delay ceases, no further delay in permitting access to a solicitor is permissible. *In any case* the detainee must be permitted to consult a solicitor within 36 hours from the 'relevant time' (a term defined on p 149).

There are similar, but not identical, provisions about delaying access to legal advice when a person is detained under TA 2000, s 41 or Sch 7 (p 823).

Where a delay has been authorised under Annex B and an interview takes place during it, a court or jury may not draw adverse inferences from a suspect's silence.

Arrival of solicitor at police station

Unless Annex B applies, when a solicitor arrives at a police station to see a particular person, that person must be informed of his arrival whether or not he is being interviewed, and asked if he wishes to see the solicitor. This applies even if the detainee has declined legal advice or, having requested it, subsequently agreed to be interviewed without receiving advice. The attendance and the detainee's decision must be recorded. Where a consultation is permitted, a solicitor is entitled to be present whilst the detainee is interviewed if the detainee so wishes.

Accredited or probationary representatives

For the purposes of the Code a 'solicitor' is a person who holds a current practising certificate, or an accredited or probationary representative included on the register of representatives maintained by the Criminal Defence Service.

An accredited or probationary representative sent to provide advice on a solicitor's behalf must be admitted to the police station for this purpose unless an officer of the rank of inspector (or above) considers that such a visit will hinder the investigation of crime and directs otherwise. (Giving proper legal advice to a detained person may not be regarded as hindering the investigation of crime.)

In exercising his discretion as to admittance to such a person, an inspector must take into account in particular whether the identity or status of the accredited or probationary representative has been satisfactorily established; whether he is of suitable character to provide legal advice (a person with a criminal record is unlikely to be suitable unless the conviction was for a minor offence and is not of recent date); and any other matters in any written letters of authorisation provided. The Court of Appeal has held that a chief constable is not entitled to make a blanket order banning a particular solicitor's probationary representative from all police stations in his area. He may advise his officers that a particular representative is likely to hinder an investigation but the officer dealing with the case must decide whether, in the particular circumstances, the representative should be excluded.

If an inspector (or above) refuses access to an accredited or probationary representative or a decision is taken that such a person shall not be permitted to remain at an interview, he must forthwith notify the solicitor on whose behalf that person was to have acted, or was acting, and give him an opportunity of making other arrangements. The detainee must also be informed and the custody record noted. If an inspector (or above) considers that a particular firm of solicitors is persistently sending probationary representatives who are unsuited to provide legal advice, he should inform a superintendent (or above), who may wish to take the matter up with the Solicitors Regulation Authority (SRA).

Removal of solicitor

A solicitor (or his representative, etc) may only be required to leave if his conduct is such that the investigating officer is unable properly to put questions to the suspect.

The solicitor's only role in the police station is to protect and advance the legal rights of his client. On occasions this may require the solicitor to give advice which has the effect of avoiding his client giving evidence which strengthens a prosecution case. The solicitor may intervene to seek clarification or to challenge an improper question to his client or the manner in which it is put, or to advise his client not to reply to particular questions, or if he wishes to give his client further legal advice. He may only be required to leave if his approach or conduct prevents or unreasonably obstructs proper questions being put to the detainee or his response being recorded, as where a solicitor answers on his client's behalf or provides written replies for his client to quote. If the investigating officer considers that a solicitor is acting in such a way, he will stop the interview and consult an officer not below the rank of superintendent, if one is readily available, and otherwise an officer not below the rank of inspector who is not concerned with the investigation. After speaking to the solicitor the officer who has been consulted will decide whether or not the interview should continue in the presence of the solicitor. If he decides that it should not, the detainee will be given an opportunity to consult another solicitor before the interview continues and that solicitor will be given an opportunity to be present.

The Detention Code points out that the removal of a solicitor from an interview is a serious step and, if it occurs, the officer of superintendent rank (or above) who took the decision will consider whether the incident should be reported to the SRA (and to the Legal Services Commission in the case of a duty solicitor). If the decision was taken by an officer below the rank of superintendent, a superintendent (or above) must consider whether to make such a report. A note of guidance in the Code points out that where an officer takes the decision to exclude a solicitor, he must be in a position to satisfy the court that the decision was properly made. In order to do this, he may need to witness what is happening himself.

Other points

In the absence of compelling reasons, delaying access to a solicitor is likely to amount to a breach of the right to a fair trial under the European Convention on Human Rights, art 6(1) and (3)(c) (below).

Any request for legal advice, and the action taken on it, must be recorded in the custody record. If a person has asked for legal advice and an interview has commenced in the absence of his solicitor, etc (or the solicitor, etc is required to leave) a record must be made in the interview record.

A detainee who wants legal advice *may not be interviewed or continue to be interviewed* until he has received it unless:

(a) a delay has been authorised in accordance with the provisions in Annex B to the Detention Code set out above (see p 101), in which case the restriction on drawing adverse inferences from silence (see p 107) will apply because the detainee is not allowed an opportunity to consult a solicitor; or

(b) a superintendent (or above) has reasonable grounds to believe that:

(i) the consequent delay might lead to interference with, or harm to, evidence connected with an offence; lead to interference with, or harm to, other people; lead to serious loss of, or damage to, property; lead to alerting other people suspected of having committed an offence but not yet arrested for it; or hinder the recovery of property obtained in consequence of the commission of the offence; or

(ii) when a solicitor, including a duty solicitor, has been contacted and has agreed to attend, awaiting his arrival would cause unreasonable delay to the process of investigation;

in which instances the restriction upon drawing adverse inferences from silence (p 107) will apply; or (c)　the solicitor nominated or selected from a list by the detainee cannot be contacted, has previously indicated that he does not wish to be contacted, or having been contacted has declined to attend, and the detainee has been advised of the Duty Solicitor Scheme but has declined to ask for the duty solicitor; in which instances the restriction upon drawing inferences from silence will not apply because the detainee has been allowed an opportunity to consult a solicitor; or

(d)　the detainee changes his mind about wanting legal advice or (as the case may be) no longer wishes to speak to a solicitor present at the interview. In these circumstances the interview may be started or continued without delay provided that:

　(i)　an inspector (or above) speaks to the detainee to enquire about the reasons for the change of mind, and makes reasonable efforts to ascertain the solicitor's expected time of arrival and to inform the solicitor that the suspect has stated that he wishes to change his mind and the reason (if given);

　(ii)　the detainee's reason for his change of mind (if given) and the outcome of the action in (i) are recorded in the custody record;

　(iii)　the detainee after being informed of the outcome of the action in (i) confirms in writing that he wants the interview to proceed without speaking or further speaking to a solicitor or (as the case may be) without a solicitor being present and does not wish to wait for a solicitor by signing an entry to this effect in the custody record;

　(iv)　an inspector (or above) is satisfied that it is proper for the interview to proceed in these circumstances, and

　　(a)　gives authority in writing for the interview to proceed; if the authority is not recorded in the custody record, the officer must ensure that the custody record shows the date and time of the authority and where it is recorded, and

　　(b)　takes or directs the taking of reasonable steps to inform the solicitor that the authority has been given and the time when the interview is expected to commence, and records or causes to be recorded the outcome of this action in the custody record;

　(v)　when the interview starts and the interviewer reminds the suspect of his right to legal advice, the interviewer must ensure that the following is recorded in the written interview record or the interview record made in accordance with the PACE Codes concerning the conduct of audio or visual recording of interviews with suspects:

　　(a)　confirmation that the detainee has changed his mind about wanting legal advice or (as the case may be) about wanting a solicitor present and the reasons for it if given;

　　(b)　the fact that authority for the interview to proceed has been given and, with the usual exception, the name of the authorising officer;

　　(c)　that, if the solicitor arrives at the station before the interview is completed, the detainee will be so informed without delay and a break will be taken to allow him to speak to the solicitor if he wishes, unless (b) above applies;

　　(d)　that, at any time during the interview, the detainee may again ask for legal advice and that, if he does, a break will be taken to allow him to speak to the solicitor, unless (a), (b), or (c) applies.

　　In these circumstances there will be no restriction on drawing adverse inferences from silence because the detainee is allowed an opportunity to consult a solicitor if he wishes.

If (a) applies, where the reason for authorising the delay ceases to apply, there may be no further delay in permitting the exercise of the right in the absence of a further authorisation unless (b), (c), or (d) applies. Where (b)(i) applies, once sufficient information has been obtained to avert the risk, questioning must cease until the detainee has received legal advice unless (a), (b)(ii), (c), or (d) applies. Where (c) applies, the interview may be started or continued without further delay provided that an inspector (or above) has agreed. Where (d) applies, the interview may be started or continued without further delay provided that the detainee has given an agreement in writing, or on recording media, to being interviewed without receiving legal advice and that an inspector (or above), having inquired into the detainee's reasons for his change of mind, has given authority for the interview to proceed. Confirmation of the detainee's agreement, his change of mind, his reasons where given, and the name of the authorising officer, except where it might endanger the officer to do so, must be recorded in writing or in the interview record made in accordance with the relevant Recording Code, at the beginning or recommencement of the interview. It is permissible for such authorisation to be given over the telephone, if the authorising officer is able to satisfy himself as to the reason for the detainee's change of mind and is satisfied that it is proper to continue the interview in those circumstances.

In considering whether awaiting the arrival of a solicitor would cause unreasonable delay (see (b) above), the superintendent should, where practicable, ask the solicitor for an estimate of the time he is likely to take in coming to the station, and relate this to the time for which detention is permitted, to whether a required period of rest is imminent, and to the requirements of other investigations in progress. If the solicitor says that he is on his way or that he will set off immediately, it will not normally be appropriate to begin an interview before he arrives. If it appears that it will be necessary to begin an interview before the solicitor's arrival he should be given an indication of how long the police could wait so that he has the opportunity to make arrangements for someone else to provide legal advice.

A breach of the requirement that detainees should generally be allowed access to a solicitor does not necessarily justify exclusion of evidence obtained at the interview. Where a challenge is made, the court must establish whether a request was made and whether it had been refused. If this is so it must then consider whether a delay in compliance with such a request was permissible under PACE, s 58. If it was not, the court must then consider whether the evidence obtained at the interview should be excluded under PACE, s 76 (confessions) or s 78 (unfairly obtained evidence (pp 245 and 260)) or by any rule of common law.

The Supreme Court has decided that the effect of art 6 of the European Convention on Human Rights is that legal advice must be available not only to a person in custody but also to anyone else who has been 'charged' for the purposes of art 6, which occurs where the person's situation has been substantially affected. This situation is likely to occur where questions are addressed to a person which the police have reason to think may well elicit an incriminating response, ie when he has ceased to be a potential witness and become a suspect. However, even if someone not in police custody has been 'charged' in this sense, this did not necessarily mean that he has been deprived of a fair trial contrary to art 6; it would simply be a circumstance to be taken into account when considering whether he has been so deprived.

CAUTIONS

The Detention Code provides as follows.

A person whom there are grounds to suspect of an offence must be cautioned before any questions about an offence, or further questions if the answers provide the grounds for suspicion, are put to him if either his answer or silence (ie failure or refusal to answer or answer satisfactorily) may be given in evidence to a court in a prosecution. The grounds for suspicion referred to must be reasonable grounds, based on known facts or relevant information. Cautions may be given in the Welsh language where use of the Welsh language is appropriate.

Statements made under caution may be used only for the purposes for which they are provided. To use them for an extraneous purpose, for example to leak to the press, whether or not for reward, is legally actionable as a breach of confidence.

Where no arrest has been made

Where a person has not been arrested but there are grounds to suspect him of an offence, he must be cautioned before any questions about it (or further questions, if it is his answers to previous questions that provide grounds for suspicion) are put regarding his involvement or suspected involvement in that offence if his answers or his silence may be given in evidence to a court in a prosecution. The Court of Appeal has held that 'grounds to suspect' means 'reasonable grounds to suspect'.

A person need not be cautioned if questions are put to him for other purposes, for example solely:

(a) to establish his identity or his ownership of any vehicle; or
(b) to obtain information in accordance with any relevant statutory requirement or in furtherance of the proper and effective conduct of a search (for example, to determine the need to search in the exercise of powers to stop and search or to seek co-operation while carrying out a search); or
(c) to seek verification of a written record; or
(d) when examining persons in accordance with TA 2000, Sch 7 (port and border controls) and the Code of Practice for Examining Officers issued under that Act.

Assistance is provided by a case where a suspect was being interviewed concerning burglaries and said he was wanted for 'something bad'. The police officer asked what it was, to which the suspect replied, 'I'm ashamed, I done a rape'. It was held that the officer, at the stage of asking his question, was merely trying to find out what was disturbing the suspect and that there had been no breach of the Detention Code by a failure to caution.

Whenever a person not under arrest is initially cautioned, or is reminded that he is still under caution after a break, he must at the same time be told that he is not under arrest, and be informed about how (see p 99) he may obtain legal advice. The officer must point out that the right to legal advice includes the right to speak with a solicitor over the telephone. The officer must ask the person whether he wishes to do so. A person who is arrested, or further arrested, must be informed that he is under arrest and given the grounds for that arrest.

Since the Detention Code obliges police officers to administer a caution if the answer to a question may be offered in evidence in criminal proceedings, it is necessary to caution motorists when pointing out to them that they have committed an offence as their reply is almost certainly going to be relevant to the proceedings. Indeed, although there is no direct requirement to caution when informing a person that he will be reported for an offence, the admissibility of his reply in evidence may depend upon whether or not he has been cautioned at some stage. Practice may still require that such a reply is included in an officer's report and, if this is so, the offender should be cautioned at some stage before he makes it.

The caution prescribed by the Detention Code is:

'You do not have to say anything. But it may harm your defence if you do not mention when questioned something which you later rely on in court. Anything you do say may be given in evidence.'

Minor deviations do not constitute a breach of this requirement provided that the sense of the caution is preserved.

Other forms of caution are prescribed by Annex C to the Code for use where the restriction on drawing adverse inferences from silence applies (see below).

On arrest

A person must be cautioned on arrest for an offence unless:

(a) this is impracticable by reason of his condition or behaviour at the time; or
(b) he has already been cautioned prior to arrest as described above.

After arrest

Following the arrest of a person, a police officer must caution him (or cause him to be cautioned or remind him that he remains under caution):

(a) before putting to him any questions or further questions to obtain evidence which may be given to a court in a prosecution (unless the questioning immediately follows the arrest);
(b) when arresting him for any further offence in accordance with PACE, s 31 (dealt with on p 63);
(c) when charging him with an offence (or informing him that he may be prosecuted for it); or
(d) when bringing to his notice a written statement or questioning him as permitted by the Detention Code.

Special cautions when the restriction on drawing adverse inferences from silence applies

When a suspect who is interviewed at a police station or authorised place of detention after arrest fails or refuses to answer certain questions, or to answer them satisfactorily, after due warning, a court or jury may draw such inferences as appear proper under CJPOA 1994, ss 34, 36, and 37 (pp 248–53). This applies when:

(a) it was reasonable to expect the arrested person to have mentioned a fact on which he later relies;
(b) a suspect is arrested by a constable and there is found on his person, or in or on his clothing or footwear, or otherwise in his possession, or in the place where he is arrested, any objects, marks, or substances, or marks on such objects, and the-person fails or refuses to account for the objects, marks, or substances found; or
(c) an arrested person was found by a constable at a place at or about the time the offence for which he was arrested is alleged to have been committed, and the person fails or refuses to account for his presence at that place.

These provisions are subject to an overriding *restriction* on the ability of a court or jury to draw inferences from a person's silence. This restriction applies:

(a) to any detainee at a police station who, before being interviewed, or being charged or informed that he may be prosecuted, has:

    (i) asked for legal advice;

    (ii) not been allowed an opportunity to consult a solicitor, including the duty solicitor, as in the Detention Code; and

    (iii) not changed his mind about wanting legal advice;

    (Note that the condition in (ii) will apply when a detainee who has asked for legal advice is interviewed before speaking to a solicitor, but will not apply if the detained person declines to ask for the duty solicitor.)

(b) to any person charged with, or informed that he may be prosecuted for, an offence who:

    (i) has had brought to his notice a written statement made by another person or the content of an interview with another person which relates to that offence;

    (ii) is interviewed about that offence; or

    (iii) makes a written statement about that offence.

Where a requirement to caution arises at a time when the restriction on drawing adverse inferences from silence applies, the caution must be:

'You do not have to say anything, but anything you do say may be given in evidence.'

Whenever the restriction begins or ceases to apply after a caution has been given, the person must be re-cautioned in the appropriate terms. The changed position in relation to inferences and the fact that the previous caution no longer applies must be explained to the detainee in ordinary language.

The Detention Code suggests, in a note for guidance, that where the restriction on drawing adverse inferences begins to apply it should be explained that the caution previously given no longer applies because after caution the detainee asked to speak to a solicitor but has not yet had an opportunity to do so (restriction (a)); or because the detainee has been charged with or informed that he will be prosecuted for the offence (restriction (b)). He should be informed that this means that, from now on, adverse inferences cannot be drawn at court and his defence will not be harmed just because he chooses to say nothing. He should be asked to note that the new caution does not say anything about his defence being harmed.

Where any such restriction ceases to apply before or at the time the person is charged or informed that he may be prosecuted, the detainee should be told that the caution previously given no longer applies. This is because after that caution he has been allowed an opportunity to speak to a solicitor. He should be told to listen carefully as the caution now being given explains how his defence at court may be affected by his choosing to say nothing. The important factor is that where legal advice has been requested all bets are off in relation to silence until the detainee has had an opportunity to speak to a solicitor.

General

It is important that the appropriate caution is given; if an inappropriate one is chosen the court is liable to exclude evidence subsequently obtained.

Where there is a break in questioning under caution the officer in charge must ensure that the person being questioned is aware that he remains under caution; if there is any doubt the caution should be given again in full when the interview resumes. This is important because the officer may have to satisfy a court that the person understood that he was still under caution when the interview resumed.

If it appears that a person does not understand what the caution means, the officer who has given it should go on to explain it in his own words.

The Detention Code also requires that, if a person is not under arrest when an initial caution is given at a police station (or other premises), the officer must tell him that he is not under arrest and is not obliged to remain with the officer. The officer must also tell him that he is free to leave if he wishes *and remind him that he may obtain free legal advice* if he wishes and that the right to legal advice includes the right to speak to a solicitor on the telephone, and ask him if he wishes to do so.

Documentation

A record must be made when a caution is given, either in the officer's pocket book (or by other methods used for recording information) or in the interview record as appropriate.

Written statements under caution

All written statements made at police stations after caution must be written on the forms provided for the purpose and be taken in accordance with the rules in Annex D to the Detention Code. Before a person makes a written statement under caution at a police station he must be reminded about the right to legal advice. It is not normally necessary to ask for a written statement if the interview was recorded in writing, and the record signed, or audibly or visually recorded in accordance with PACE Code E: the Code of Practice on Audio Recording Interviews with Suspects or PACE Code F: the Code of Practice on Visual Recording with Sound of Interviews with Suspects.

Written by a person under caution

(1) A person must always be invited to write down himself what he wants to say.

(2) A person who has not been charged with, or informed that he may be prosecuted for, any offence to which the statement relates, must, unless the statement is made at a time when the restriction on drawing adverse inferences from silence applies, be asked to write out and sign the following before writing what he wants to say:

> **'I make this statement of my own free will. I understand that I do not have to say anything but that it may harm my defence if I do not mention when questioned something which I later rely on in court. This statement may be given in evidence.'**

If the statement is made at a time when the restriction on drawing adverse inferences from silence applies, he must be asked to write out and sign the following before writing what he wants to say:

> *'I make this statement of my own free will. I understand that I do not have to say anything. This statement may be given in evidence.'*

(3) When a person, on the occasion of being charged with, or informed that, he may be prosecuted for any offence, asks to make a statement which relates to any such offence and wants to write it he must, unless the restriction on drawing adverse inferences from silence applied when he was so charged or informed that he might be prosecuted, be asked to write out the words in bold above and sign them before

writing what he wants to say. If the restriction on drawing adverse inferences from silence applied when the person was so charged or informed that he would be prosecuted, he must be asked to write out the words italicised above and sign them before writing what he wants to say.

(4)   Where a person, who has already been charged with or informed that he may be prosecuted for any offence, asks to make a statement which relates to any such offence and wants to write it, he must be asked to write out and sign the words italicized above before writing what he wants to say.

(5)   Any person writing his own statement must be allowed to do so without any prompting except that a police officer or civilian interviewer may indicate to him which matters are material or question any ambiguity in the statement.

Written by a police officer or other police staff

(6)   If a person says that he would like someone to write it for him, a police officer or other police staff must write the statement.

(7)   If the person has not been charged with, or informed that he may be prosecuted for, any offence to which the statement he wants to make relates, he must, before starting, be asked to sign or make his mark, to the appropriate one of the following endorsements.

(a)   Unless the statement is made at a time when the restriction on drawing adverse inferences from silence applies, the endorsement is:

'I, …, wish to make a statement. I want someone to write down what I say. I understand that I do not have to say anything but that it may harm my defence if I do not mention when questioned something which I later rely on in court. This statement may be given in evidence.'

(b)   If the statement is made at a time when the restriction on drawing adverse inferences from silence applies, the endorsement is:

'I, …, wish to make a statement. I want someone to write down what I say. I understand that I do not have to say anything. This statement may be given in evidence.'

(8)   If, on the occasion of being charged with or informed that he may be prosecuted for any offence, the person asks to make a statement which relates to any such offence, he must before starting be asked to sign, or make his mark to, the following as appropriate. Unless the restriction on drawing adverse inferences from silence applied when he was so charged or informed that he may be prosecuted, the words are the same as in (7)(a). If the restriction on drawing adverse inferences from silence applied when he was so charged or informed that he may be prosecuted, the words are the same as in (7)(b).

(9)   If, having already been charged with or informed that he may be prosecuted for any offence, a person asks to make a statement which relates to such an offence, he must, before starting, be asked to sign or make his mark to the form of words in (7)(b).

(10)   The person writing the statement must take down the exact words spoken by the person making it and he must not edit or paraphrase it. Any questions that are necessary (eg to make it more intelligible) and the answers given must be recorded contemporaneously on the statement form.

(11)   When the writing of a statement is finished the person making it must be asked to read it and to make any corrections, alterations or additions he wishes. When

he has finished reading it he must be asked to write and sign or make his mark on the following certificate at the end of the statement:

> 'I have read the above statement, and I have been able to correct, alter or add anything I wish. This statement is true. I have made it of my own free will.'

(12) If the person making the statement cannot read, or refuses to read it, or to write the above-mentioned certificate at the end of it or to sign it, the person taking the statement must read it over to him and ask him whether he would like to correct, alter or add anything and put his signature or make his mark at the end. The person taking the statement must then certify on the statement itself what has occurred.

INTERVIEWS

General provisions concerning interviews

What is an 'interview'?

The Detention Code defines an interview as 'the questioning of a person regarding his involvement or suspected involvement in a criminal offence or offences which, by virtue of the Code, is required to be carried out under caution'. For example, where, after arresting a man for possessing an offensive weapon, police officers asked him in the police car why he had the knife and he told them there had been some trouble and that he had it for his own protection, it was held that this amounted to an interview for the purposes of the Code, so that a record should have been made of it. Whenever a person is interviewed he must be informed of the nature of the offence, or further offence. Procedures undertaken under the Road Traffic Act 1988, s 7 or the corresponding provisions under the Transport and Works Act 1992 (both dealt with in Chapter 15) do not constitute interviews for the purposes of the Code. Nor is an informal conversation at or near the scene of a crime an 'interview', but it will be if it descends into detailed questioning.

Thus, we are considering an 'interview' which takes place under caution, or which should have taken place under caution. Some decisions of the Court of Appeal continue to be helpful in establishing a divide.

In one case, police officers attended the house of a suspect to arrest him for handling stolen furniture and taking a lorry without consent. The officers put to him that they had seen him some days previously driving the stolen lorry. One of them said, 'What have you got to say about this?' He later said to him, 'But you are not doubting that we saw you last Thursday . . . in the lorry?' It was held by the Court of Appeal that these questions, asked without caution, were for purposes other than establishing identity as the officers already knew the name of the suspect. They were put for the purpose of obtaining evidence and therefore constituted an interview, and should not have been asked until arrival at the police station when the suspect had been informed of his right to legal advice.

In another case, an officer escorting a suspect to the custody office saw the suspect drop a packet containing four ecstasy tablets. She said to him 'I have just seen you drop this. Things are looking a bit more serious now.' The suspect replied 'Yeah.' The officer asked 'Are these ecstasy tablets?' and the suspect replied 'Yes.' The Court of Appeal held that this was clearly an interview. Even one question regarding a suspect's involvement or suspected involvement in an offence can be sufficient in appropriate circumstances.

On the other hand, the Court held, a conversation in which the suspect asked 'What will I get for this?', the officer replied 'What do you mean?', the suspect said 'At court for sup-plying drugs, what will I get?' and the officer replied 'That's not for me to say', did not amount to an interview. Clearly, the officer's question did not relate to the suspect's involvement in an offence. This conversation was simply an unsolicited comment which had to be recorded.

Action

Following a decision to arrest a suspect he must not be interviewed about the relevant offence except at a police station (or other authorised place of detention) unless the consequent delay would be likely:

(a) to lead to interference with or harm to evidence connected with an offence, or interference with or physical harm to other persons, or serious loss of, or damage to, property; or

(b) to lead to the alerting of other persons suspected of having committed an offence but not yet arrested for it; or

(c) to hinder the recovery of property obtained in consequence of the commission of an offence.

Interviewing in any of these exceptions should cease once the relevant risk has been averted or the necessary questions have been put in order to attempt to avert that risk.

Immediately prior to the commencement or recommencement of any interview at a police station (or other authorised place of detention), the interviewing officer must remind the suspect of his entitlement to free legal advice and that the interview can be delayed for him to obtain legal advice (unless one of the exceptions where delay is per-mitted applies (see p 101)).

At the beginning of an interview carried out in a police station, the interviewing officer, after cautioning the suspect, must put to him any significant statement or silence which occurred in the presence and hearing of a police officer or civilian interviewer before the start of the interview and which has not been put to the sus-pect in the course of a previous interview, and must ask him whether he confirms or denies that earlier statement or silence and whether he wishes to add anything. This does not prevent an interviewer from putting significant statements and silences to a suspect again at a later stage of a further interview. A 'significant statement' is one which appears capable of being used in evidence against the suspect, in particular a direct admission of guilt. A 'significant silence' is a failure or refusal to answer a ques-tion or answer satisfactorily when under caution which might, allowing for the restriction on drawing adverse inferences from silence, give rise to an inference under CJPOA 1994. The interviewing officer must ensure that all such reminders are noted in the record of the interview.

No interviewer may try to obtain answers to questions or to elicit a statement by the use of oppression. Except as provided by the Detention Code, no police officer may indicate, except in answer to a direct question, what action will be taken on the part of the police if the interviewee answers questions, makes a statement, or refuses to do either. If the interviewee asks the officer directly what action will be taken in the event of his answering questions, making a statement or refusing to do either, the officer may inform him what action the police propose to take in that event provided that the action is itself proper and warranted.

An interview concerning an offence with which the interviewee has not been charged or for which he has not been informed that he may be prosecuted must cease when:

(a) the officer in charge of the investigation is satisfied that all relevant questions to obtain accurate and reliable information about the offence have been put to the interviewee, including giving an opportunity for an innocent explanation to be put forward and asking any questions to test the accuracy or reliability of such explanation (eg to clear up ambiguities);

(b) the officer in charge of the investigation has taken account of any other available evidence; and

(c) the officer in charge of the investigation, or (in the case of a detained suspect) the custody officer, reasonably believes that there is sufficient evidence to provide a realistic prospect of conviction for that offence if the interviewee was prosecuted.

This does not, however, prevent officers in revenue cases or acting under the money laundering confiscation provisions from inviting suspects to complete a formal question and answer record after the interview is concluded.

In addition, according to the Court of Appeal, provided the officer has an open mind and is prepared not to charge (or not to refer to another officer responsible for charging) if the suspect produces a convincing account, the interviewer may proceed in order to see whether the suspect can produce an explanation.

Interview records

An accurate record must be made of each interview with a person suspected of an offence, whether or not the interview takes place at a police station. The record must state the place of the interview, the time it begins and ends, the time the record is made (if different), any breaks in it, and the names of those present. The requirement to record names of those present is subject to the special rule on p 92.

An interview record:

(a) enables the prosecutor to make informed decisions;

(b) is capable of being exhibited to an officer's witness statement and used pursuant to the Criminal Justice Act 1967, s 9 (see p 241);

(c) enables the prosecutor to comply with advance disclosure rules; and

(d) where the record is accepted by the defence, facilitates the conduct of the case by the prosecution, the defence and the court.

Such a record must, therefore, comprise a balanced account of the interview including points in mitigation and/or defence made by the suspect. Where an admission is made, the question as well as the answer containing the admission must be recorded verbatim in the record. Matters which might be considered to be prejudicial or inadmissible by a court should be brought to the attention of the prosecutor by means of a covering report.

The record must be made on the forms provided or in the interviewer's pocket book or in accordance with PACE Code E: the Code of Practice on Audio Recording Interviews with Suspects (hereafter the 'Audio Recording Code') or PACE Code F: the Code of Practice on Visual Recording with Sound of Interviews with Suspects (hereafter the 'Visual Recording Code').

The Audio Recording Code states that, with the exceptions mentioned below, audio recording must normally be used at a police station for any interview:

(a) with a person who has been cautioned in accordance with the Detention Code (on grounds of suspicion of his committing an offence) in respect of an indictable offence;

(b) which take place as a result of a police officer exceptionally putting further questions to a suspect about an offence described in (a) after he has been charged with, or informed that he may be prosecuted for, that offence; or

(c) in which a police officer wishes to bring to the notice of a person, after he has been charged with, or informed he may be prosecuted for, an indictable offence, any written statement made by another person, or the content of an interview with another person, which may be done by playing an audio recording.

There is no requirement visually to record interviews, but the Visual Recording Code suggests that it might be appropriate to choose to do so in the above three cases and also when the interview is with, or in the presence of, a deaf, deaf/blind or speech-impaired person who uses sign language to communicate, or where the presence of the appropriate adult is required, or where the suspect or his representative requests it.

The custody officer may authorise the interviewing officer not to audibly record or visually record the interview in three cases:

(a) where it is not reasonably practicable to do so, because of failure of the equipment or the non-availability of a suitable interview room or recording equipment, and the custody officer considers on reasonable grounds that the interview should not be delayed. In such cases, he may authorise the interviewing officer not to so record the interview;

(b) where a person refuses to go into or remain in a suitable interview room for such recording and the custody officer considers, on reasonable grounds, that the interview should not be delayed. In such cases the interview may be conducted, at the custody officer's discretion, in a cell using portable audio recording equipment or, if none is available, recorded in writing;

(c) where it is clear from the outset that no prosecution will ensue.

TA 2000 makes separate provision for the visual recording of interviews of persons arrested under TA 2000, s 41 (suspected terrorists) (see p 822) and neither the above provisions nor any other part of the two Recording Codes apply to such interviews.

If an interview is not audibly or visually recorded it must be recorded in writing. The custody officer must record in the custody record the reasons for not taking an audio or visual record, as the case may be.

Written interview records must be signed and timed by the maker.

Any written record must be made during the interview, unless in the investigating officer's view this would not be practicable or would interfere with the conduct of the interview, and must constitute either a verbatim record or, failing this, an account of the interview which adequately and accurately summarises it. If the record is not made during the interview, it must be made as soon as practicable thereafter and the reason must be recorded in the officer's pocket book (or by other methods used for recording information) or the official book issued to a member of police staff.

The whole of an audibly or visually recorded interview must be so recorded, including the taking and reading back of any statement. If, during the course of any audibly or visually recorded interview, it becomes apparent that the interview should be conducted under one of the terrorism codes for video recording of interviews, the interview should continue in accordance with the relevant code.

The recording of interviews must be carried out openly but unobtrusively, and it must be made clear to the suspect that there is no opportunity to interfere with the equipment or recording media. Where the recording is not by secure digital network, the 'master recording' will be sealed before it leaves the presence of the suspect. A master recording may be either one of two recording media used in a twin deck/drive machine or the only medium used in a single deck/drive machine. A second medium will be used as a working copy and it may be either the other medium in the case of a twin deck/drive machine, or a copy of the master used in a single deck/drive machine. Such a copy must be made in the presence of the suspect and without the master recording leaving his sight.

It must be borne in mind that CJPOA 1994, ss 34, 36, and 37 describe the conditions under which adverse inferences may be drawn from a person's failure or refusal to say anything about his involvement in the offence, when interviewed, after being charged or informed that he may be prosecuted. In effect, in the case of such a detainee at a police station who has asked for legal advice but has not yet been allowed an opportunity to consult a solicitor, adverse inferences may not be drawn from his failure to say anything concerning his involvement in an offence. It would therefore be wrong to use the normal caution which includes the words 'but it may harm your defence if you do not mention when questioned something which you later rely on in court' as that simply would not be true. It has been held that no adverse inferences may be drawn where a person who has asked for legal advice has not received it. In such circumstances the words in inverted commas above are omitted from the caution. However, it must be remembered that, when legal advice becomes available to the detainee, the full caution must then be given as any failure to respond may create circumstances which will permit adverse inferences to be drawn.

Checking the interview record

Unless it is impracticable, the person interviewed must be given the opportunity to read the interview record and to sign it as correct or to indicate the respects in which he considers it inaccurate. When a suspect agrees to read records of interviews and of other comments and to sign them as correct, he should be asked to endorse the record with words such as 'I agree that this is a correct record of what was said' and add his signature. Where the suspect does not agree with the record, the officer should record the details of any disagreement and then ask the suspect to read these details and then sign them to the effect that they accurately reflect his disagreement.

If the person concerned cannot read, or refuses to read the record or to sign it, the senior police officer present must read it over to him and ask him whether he would like to sign it as correct or to indicate the respects in which he considers it inaccurate. The police officer must then certify on the interview record itself what has occurred.

If the interview is audibly or visually recorded the arrangements set out in the Audio Recording Code or Visual Recording Code apply.

Records of comments outside interview

A written record must be made of any comments made by a suspected person, including unsolicited comments, which are outside the context of an interview but which might be relevant to the offence. Any such record must be timed and signed by the maker. Where practicable the person must be given the opportunity to read that record and to sign it as correct or to indicate the respects in which he considers it inaccurate. Any refusal to sign must be recorded.

Interviews in police stations

The Detention Code provides that if a police officer wishes to interview a detained person, or to conduct inquiries which require the presence of a detained person, it is the custody officer who must decide whether to deliver his prisoner into that officer's custody. An investigating officer who is given custody of a detainee takes over responsibility for the detainee's care and safe custody until he returns the detainee to the custody officer when he must report the manner in which he complied with the Code whilst having custody of the detainee.

In any period of 24 hours a detained person must be allowed a continuous period of at least eight hours' rest, free from questioning, travel or any interruption by police officers in connection with the investigation concerned. This period should normally be at night or other appropriate time which takes account of when the detainee last slept or rested. If a detainee is arrested at a police station after going there voluntarily, the 24-hour period runs from the time of arrival at the police station. The period of rest may not be interrupted or delayed except:

(a) when there are reasonable grounds for believing that not delaying or interrupting that period would:
    (i)   involve a risk of harm to people or serious loss of, or damage to, property;
    (ii)   delay unnecessarily the detainee's release from custody;
    (iii) otherwise prejudice the outcome of the investigation;
(b) at the request of the detainee, his appropriate adult, or his legal representative;
(c) when a delay or interruption is necessary in order to comply with the legal obligations and duties under the Detention Code relating to reviews and extensions of detention or as to the care and treatment of detained persons who are intoxicated or in need of clinical treatment and attention.

If such a period of rest is interrupted in accordance with (a), a fresh period must be allowed. Interruptions under (b) and (c) do not require that a fresh period be allowed.

As far as practicable, an interview must take place in a properly heated, lit, and ventilated interview room. The detained person must not be required to stand.

A suspect whose detention without charge has been authorised under PACE, because his detention is necessary so that he may be interviewed with a view to obtaining evidence of the offence for which he was arrested, may choose not to answer questions. However, the police do not require a suspect's consent to interview him for this purpose. If a suspect takes steps to prevent an interview, such as refusing to leave his cell, or trying to leave the interview room, he must be cautioned and be told that refusal to co-operate could lead to the interview taking place in the cell and that such failure to co-operate may be given in evidence. A further invitation should then be given to co-operate by going to the interview room.

Before the start of an interview, each interviewing officer must identify himself and any other officers present to the prisoner by name and rank, except in the case of persons detained under TA 2000 when each officer must identify himself by his warrant or other identification number and rank rather than his name.

In all interviews, there must be breaks at the recognised meal times and there must also be short breaks for refreshment at intervals of approximately two hours, subject to the interviewing officer's discretion to delay a break if there are reasonable grounds for believing that it would:

(a) involve a risk of harm to persons or serious loss of, or damage to, property; or
(b) delay unnecessarily the person's release from custody; or
(c) otherwise prejudice the investigation.

Meal breaks should normally last at least 45 minutes and shorter breaks after two hours should last at least 15 minutes. If a break is delayed as permitted by the Detention Code and prolongs the interview, a longer break should then be provided. If there is a short interview, and a subsequent short interview is contemplated, the length of the break may be reduced if there are reasonable grounds to believe that this is necessary to avoid any of the consequences set out at (a)–(c) above.

A record must be made of times during which a detainee was not in the custody of the custody officer, and why; of any reason for refusal to deliver the detainee out of that custody; of any reason why it was not practicable to use an interview room; and of any action taken in consequence of a refusal to be interviewed.

Audio recorded interviews

The Audio Recording Code provides as follows.

Recording and sealing master recordings

Recording of interviews must be carried out openly to instil confidence in its reliability as an impartial and accurate record of the interview.

One recording, the master recording, will be sealed in the suspect's presence. A second recording will be used as a working copy. The master recording is either of the two recordings used in a twin deck/drive machine or the only recording in a single deck/drive machine. The working copy is either the second/third recording used in a twin/triple deck/drive machine or a copy of the master recording made by a single deck/drive machine. *This paragraph does not apply to interviews recorded using a secure digital network (SDN) (see below).*

The identity of officers or police staff conducting interviews need not be recorded or disclosed in the case of enquiries linked to the investigation of terrorism, or if the interviewer reasonably believes recording or disclosing their name might put them in danger. In these cases interviewers should use warrant or other identification numbers and the name of their police station.

A sign or indicator which is visible to the suspect must show when the recording equipment is recording.

Commencement of interview

When the suspect is brought into the interview room the interviewer must, without delay, but in sight of the suspect, load the audio recorder with new recording media and set it to record. 'Recording media' means any removable, physical audio-recording medium (such as magnetic tape, optical disc, or solid state memory) which can be played or copied. The recording media must be unwrapped or opened in the suspect's presence. *This paragraph does not apply to interviews recorded using a SDN.*

The interviewer must then:

(a) explain that the interview is being audibly recorded and point out the sign or indicator which shows that the recording equipment is activated and recording;
(b) give his name and rank and the name and rank of any other interviewer present, except in the case of inquiries linked to the investigation of terrorism, or where it is reasonably believed that this may endanger the individual concerned, where warrant or other identification numbers and the name of his police station must be stated;
(c) ask the suspect and any other person present (eg a solicitor) to identify themselves;

(d) state the date, time of commencement, and place of the interview; and

(e) *except where the recording uses a SDN*, state that the suspect will be given a notice about what will happen to the copies of the recording.

The interviewer must then caution the suspect in the appropriate form (see p 105). He must remind the suspect of his right to free and independent legal advice and that he can speak to a solicitor on the telephone in accordance with the provisions of the Detention Code.

The interviewer must then put to the suspect any significant statement or silence (ie a failure or refusal to answer a question or to answer it satisfactorily) which occurred before the start of the audibly recorded interview, and must ask him whether he confirms or denies that earlier statement or silence or whether he wishes to add anything. A 'significant' statement or silence means a statement which appears capable of being used in evidence against the suspect, in particular a direct admission of guilt, or failure or refusal to answer a question or to answer it satisfactorily, which might give rise to an inference under CJPOA 1994, s 34 (see p 248), s 36 or s 37 (see p 252).

The reader is reminded that a special warning must be given before inferences can be drawn under CJPOA 1994, ss 36 or 37 and of the fact that adverse inferences cannot be drawn where legal advice has been requested but has not yet been received.

Objections

If the suspect raises objections to the interview being audibly recorded at the outset, or during the interview, or during a break in the interview, the interviewer must explain that the interview is being audibly recorded and that the provisions of the Audio Recording Code require the suspect's objections to be recorded on the audio recording. The suspect's objections must be noted. When any objections have been recorded or the suspect has refused to have his objections recorded, the interviewer may turn off the recorder. In this eventuality, he must say that he is turning off the recorder and give his reasons for doing so and then turn it off. The interviewer must then make a written record of the interview in accordance with the Detention Code. If, however, the interviewer reasonably considers that he may proceed to put questions to the suspect with the audio recorder still on, he may do so. He should bear in mind that a decision to continue recording against the wishes of the suspect may be the subject of comment in court.

If a suspect indicates that he wishes to tell an interviewer about matters not directly connected with the offence of which he is suspected and that he is unwilling for these matters to be recorded, he must be given the opportunity to tell the police officer about these matters after the conclusion of the formal interview.

Changing recording media

Where recording media are coming to an end, the interviewer must inform the suspect and round off that part of the interview. If the interviewer leaves the room for a second set of recording media, the suspect should not be left unattended. The interviewer will remove the recording media and insert new ones which must be unwrapped or otherwise opened in the suspect's presence. Recording media must be marked with an identification number immediately they are removed from the recorder.

The above paragraph does not apply to a recording using a SDN as this does not use removable media; nor do the paragraphs below relating to breaks in interview, equipment failure, removing recording media, the conclusion of the interview, after the interview, and media security.

Breaks in interview

When a break is taken, that fact must be recorded on the audio recording together with the reason for it and the time it was taken. If the interview room is vacated by the suspect, the recording media must be removed from the recorder and dealt with in the same manner as if the interview had been concluded (see below).

When a break is a short one and both the suspect and the interviewer remain in the interview room, the recording may be stopped. There is no need to remove the recording media. The time of recommencement of the interview must be recorded.

Whenever there has been a break in questioning under caution the interviewer must ensure that the person being questioned is aware that he remains under caution. If there is a doubt, the caution must be renewed. The interviewer must bear in mind that he may have to satisfy a court that the person realised that the caution still applied. He may also have to show that nothing occurred during a break in an interview or between interviews which influenced the suspect's recorded evidence. In view of this, he should consider, at recommencement or at a subsequent interview, summarising on recording media the reason for the break and confirming this with the suspect. As to lengths of breaks, see p 116.

Equipment failure

In the event of an equipment failure which can be rectified quickly, eg by inserting new recording media, this must be done following the prescribed procedures about the changing of recording media. When the recording is resumed, the interviewer must record the reason and the time the interview recommences. Where the further use of the audio recorder is impossible and no alternative is readily available, the interview may continue without being audibly recorded but the authority of the custody officer must first be obtained.

Where the media or recording equipment fail during the interview the interviewer should stop the interview immediately. Where part of the interview is unaffected by the error and is still accessible on the media, those media must be copied and sealed in the suspect's presence and the interview recommenced using new equipment/media as required. Where the content of the interview has been lost in its entirety the media should be sealed in the suspect's presence and the interview begun again.

Removing recording media

When recording media are removed from the recorder during the interview, they must be retained and the procedures which apply to them at the conclusion of the interview (below) followed.

Conclusion of the interview

At the conclusion of the interview, the suspect must be offered the opportunity to clarify anything he has said and asked if there is anything he wishes to add. At the conclusion of the interview, including the taking and reading back of any written statement, the time must be recorded and the audio recorder stopped.

The 'master' recording must then be sealed with a master recording label and treated as an exhibit. The interviewer must sign the label and ask the suspect and any third party to sign it also. If either, or both, refuse to sign the label, an officer of at least the rank of inspector, or if one is not available the custody officer, must be called in to the interview room and asked to sign it.

The suspect must be handed a notice explaining the use which will be made of the audio recording and the arrangements for access to it and explaining that a copy of the audio recording will be supplied as soon as practicable (or as otherwise agreed with him or on the order of a court) if he is charged or informed that he will be prosecuted.

After the interview

The interviewer must make a note in his pocket book of the fact that the interview has taken place, was audibly recorded, of its time, duration, and date and of the identification number of the master recording. Where no proceedings follow in respect of the person whose interview was recorded the recording media must nevertheless be kept securely as required by the Audio Recording Code. Where proceedings follow, the interviewer must prepare a written record of the interview and sign it. Any such record should be made in accordance with the national guidelines approved by the Secretary of State and with regard to the advice contained in the Manual of Guidance for the preparation, processing, and submission of prosecution files. Before preparing it the interviewer may refresh his memory by listening to the working copy of the recording media to check its accuracy. The interview record must be exhibited to any written statement prepared by the interviewer. If the interviewer's evidence of the interview is accepted by the defence, the evidence must refer to the fact that the interview was audio recorded and may be presented to the court in the form of the interview record. Where the interviewer's evidence is not accepted by the defence, the interviewer must refer to the fact that the interview was audibly recorded and produce the master recording medium of the whole interview, as an exhibit, informing the court of any transcription which has been made of which he is aware.

Media security

The security of master recordings is the responsibility of the officer in charge of each police station. A police officer must not break the seal on a master recording required for criminal trial or appeal proceedings, except in the presence of a representative of the CPS. In such a case, the defendant, or his legal adviser, must be informed and be given a reasonable opportunity to be present. If either is present, he must be invited to reseal and sign the master recording. If not present, or in the event of refusal, this will be done by the representative of the CPS. If the recording has been delivered to the Crown Court following sending for trial, the Crown Prosecutor will apply to the Chief Clerk of the Crown Court for the release of the media for unsealing by the Crown Prosecutor.

Recording interviews by secure digital network (SDN)

Initially piloted in Lancashire, the relevant provisions, as amended in 2010, were extended to all police forces on a 'rolling out' basis. The pilot highlighted significant reductions in police bureaucracy saving officers' time, reducing interview length, and providing easier access to interview records.

The term 'secure digital network' means a computer network system which enables an original interview recording to be stored, as a digital multimedia file or a series of such files, on a secure file server which is accredited by the National Accreditor for Police Information Systems in NPIA in accordance with the UK Government Protective Marking Scheme.

The Audio Recording Code applies to such recordings with exceptions. The differences in procedure are described below:

Commencement of interview

When the suspect is brought into the interview room, the interviewer must, without delay and in the sight of the suspect, switch on the recording equipment and enter the information accessory to log on to the secure network and set it to record. The interviewer must then inform the suspect that the interview is being recorded using a SDN and that recording has commenced. In addition to explaining that the interview is being audibly recorded and saying the other things required by the Audio Recording Code at the commencement of an interview (see p 117), the interviewer must also inform the person that:

(a) he will be given access to the recording of the interview in the event that he is charged or informed that he will be prosecuted, but if he is not charged or informed that he will be prosecuted he will only be given access as agreed with the police or on the order of a court;

(b) he will be given a written notice at the end of the interview setting out his rights to access the recording and what will happen to the recording.

Taking a break during interview

When a break is taken, the fact that a break is to be taken, the reason for it, and the time must be recorded on the audio recording. The recording must be stopped and the procedures for the conclusion of an interview followed. When the interview recommences the above procedures for commencing a SDN recorded interview must be followed to create a new file to record the continuation of the interview. The time the interview recommences must be recorded on the audio recording.

Failure of recording equipment

Where there is an equipment failure which can be rectified quickly, eg by commencing a new SDN recording, the procedure laid down in the previous paragraphs must be followed. On resumption, the interviewer must explain what has happened and record the time of recommencement. Where it is not possible to continue on the SDN the interview should be recorded on removable audio-recording media as on p 117, unless the necessary equipment is not available. In the event of such unavailability, the interview may continue without being audibly recorded and the consent of the custody officer should be sought.

Conclusion of the interview

At the conclusion of the interview, the suspect must be given the opportunity to clarify anything he has said and asked if there is anything that he wants to add.

In addition, at the conclusion of the interview, including after the taking and reading back of any written statement:

(a) the time must be orally recorded;

(b) the suspect must be handed a notice which explains: how the audio recording will be used; the arrangements for access to it; and that if he is charged or informed that he will be prosecuted, he will be given access to the recording of the interview either electronically or by being given a copy on removable recording media, but if he is not charged or informed that he will be prosecuted, he will only be given access as agreed with the police or on the order of a court;

(c) the suspect must be asked to confirm that he has received a copy of the notice and, should he fail to acknowledge receipt, the interviewer will state for the recording that a copy of the notice has been provided to the suspect and that he has refused to accept it or has refused to acknowledge receipt; and

(d) the time must be recorded and the interviewer must inform the suspect that the recording is being saved to the secure network; the saving of the recording must be done in the presence of the suspect who should be told that the interview is terminated.

The notice referred to in (b) should provide a brief explanation of the SDN and how access is strictly limited to the recording. The notice should also explain the access rights of the suspect, his legal representative, the police and the prosecutor to the recording of the interview. Space should be provided on the form to insert the date and the file reference number for the interview.

After the interview

The interviewer must make a note in his pocket book that the interview has taken place, was audibly recorded, its time, duration, and date and the original recording's identification number. If no proceedings follow in respect of the person whose interview was recorded, the recordings must be kept securely as set out below. Any written record should be made in accordance with the national guidelines and the advice referred to on p 120.

Security of SDN interview records

Interview record files are stored in read-only format on non-removable storage devices, for example, hard disk drives, to ensure their integrity. The recordings are first saved locally to a secure non-removable device before being transferred to the remote network device. If for any reason the network connection fails, the recording remains on the local device and will be transferred when the network connections are restored.

Access to interview recordings, including copying to removable media, must be strictly controlled and monitored to ensure that access is restricted to persons who have been given specific permission to access them for specified purposes when this is necessary. Such persons may, for example, be police officers and CPS lawyers involved in the preparation of any prosecution case, and persons interviewed if they have been charged or informed they may be prosecuted and their legal representatives.

Visual recording of interviews

Police officers may choose to visually record, with sound, interviews with suspects (see p 114); if they do, they must have regard to the terms of the Visual Recording Code.

Where an interviewing officer wishes to make a visual recording on removable media, the rules which govern the conduct of visually recorded interviews largely follow those applicable to audibly recorded interviews which do not involve a SDN. The recording must be carried out openly to instil confidence in its reliability as an impartial and accurate record of the interview. The cameras should be placed in the interview room so as to ensure coverage of as much of the room as possible. The 'certified recording medium' must be previously unused and the correct date and time in hours, minutes, and seconds will be superimposed automatically and be recorded throughout the filming process. The master copy must be sealed before leaving the presence of the suspect. A second copy will be used as a working copy. The usual safeguards apply to identification of officers in terrorism cases or where it is reasonably believed that identification might endanger the officers. Such officers will be seated with their backs to the camera and must use their warrant number and the name of the police station to which they are attached.

The procedure concerning the explanation and identification of persons present is the same as that which applies to audio recording. Similar provisions also apply to objections.

Should the recording media run out before the interview is concluded further certified recording media will be used. As recording media near completion, a suspect should be warned and allowed to wind up that part of the interview. A suspect must not be left alone in the room while further recording media are sought. Care must be taken when a number of recording media have been used to ensure that they are properly identified.

When a break is taken, provided that the suspect and the police officer do not leave the room, it is sufficient that the break, time, and reasons are recorded and the equipment may be switched off. If the room is to be vacated, the same facts must be recorded, the equipment must be switched off, the recording media removed, and the procedure for concluding an interview must be adopted.

At the conclusion of the interview, the master must be sealed with a label and treated as an exhibit. The label should be signed by the interviewer who should ask the suspect and any other person present to sign also. If no other such person will sign, an officer of at least inspector rank should be asked to do so and, if no such officer is available, the custody officer should sign the label. In addition, the suspect will be given a notice which explains the use to which the recording will be put and the arrangements for access to it. The notice will also advise the suspect that a copy of the recording will be supplied as soon as practicable if the person is charged or informed that he will be prosecuted.

The same procedures apply in relation to the security of the master copy and the breaking of the seal on a master copy which is required for criminal trial or appeal procedures, as apply in the case of audio-recording media.

Where an officer wishes to make a visual recording with sound of an interview using a SDN which does not use removable media, the above provisions will not apply to the SDN recording. Instead, the requirement and provisions for the audio recording of interviews using a SDN set out in the Audio Recording Code should be applied to the visual recording of interviews as if references to audio recordings of interviews included references to visual recordings with sound.

Where a person raises objections to an interview being visually recorded the interviewer must explain that the objection must be recorded on the visual recording. When any objections have been visually recorded, or the person refuses to have his objections so recorded, the interviewer must say that he is turning off the recorder, giving his reasons for doing so. If a separate audio recording is being made, the interviewer must ask the person to record the reasons for refusal to agree to visual recording. If the person objects to audio recording, the provisions of the Audio Recording Code relating to objections by suspects will apply.

Complaints

If, at any stage, the detained person makes a complaint concerning a matter covered by the Detention Code, the Audio Recording Code or the Visual Recording Code, it must be recorded in the interview record and the interviewing officer must inform the custody officer who must deal with it in accordance with the Detention Code (see p 136).

(These obligations also apply if it comes to the interviewer's notice that the interviewee may have been treated improperly.) Where the interview is being audibly recorded, the recording should be left running until the custody officer has entered the room and has spoken to the interviewee. Continuation or termination of the interview should be at the discretion of the interviewing officer pending action by an inspector.

Where, during the course of an interview which is being recorded, a complaint is made about a matter not connected with the Detention Code, the Audio Recording Code or the Visual Recording Code, the decision to continue the interview or terminate it is at the discretion of the interviewing officer. If continued, the officer must inform the complainant that the complaint will be brought to the attention of the custody officer at the conclusion of the interview, which must be done as soon as practicable thereafter.

Other points

The custody record must show the times during which the prisoner was not in the custody of the custody officer and the reason why he was removed from his custody; if a request for the delivery of a prisoner out of that custody was refused, the reason for refusal must be recorded. Decisions to defer breaks must be recorded, with grounds, in the interview record. Assuming he is still at the police station when it is made, the person interviewed must be allowed to read the interview record and to sign it as being correct or to indicate what he considers to be inaccurate, but no person may be kept in custody for this sole purpose.

In conclusion, it should be noted that the Codes of Practice do not prevent a police officer from asking questions at the scene of a crime to elicit an explanation which could provide the arrested person with the opportunity to show that he was innocent. The reason is obvious: since the questions are not asked with a view to establishing admissions on which proceedings can be founded, there is technically no interview for the purposes of the Codes. If, in the course of asking such questions, a suspect makes a confession, it is prima facie admissible (even if the suspect is a juvenile and no appropriate adult is present).

In addition, there is no universal rule that, whenever there is a breach of a Code of Practice in a police interview, all subsequent interviews must be tainted and evidence of them excluded. Such a rule would fetter a judge's discretion under PACE, s 78, which depends upon the facts of the particular case.

DETAINED PERSONS—SPECIAL GROUPS

If a detainee appears deaf or there is doubt about his hearing or speaking ability or ability to understand English and the custody officer cannot establish effective communication, the custody officer must, as soon as practicable, call an interpreter for assistance in the initial action referred to on pp 95–6.

If a detainee is a juvenile, mentally handicapped, or otherwise mentally vulnerable, the custody officer must, as soon as practicable, inform the appropriate adult of the grounds for his detention and his whereabouts, and ask the adult to come to the police station to see the person. It is irrelevant that the person concerned is able to understand procedures and answer questions; this does not obviate the need for the appropriate adult to assist, guide, and protect him. A person appearing to be under 17 must be treated as a juvenile in the absence of clear evidence that he is older.

In the case of a *juvenile*, 'the appropriate adult' means:

(a) his parent or guardian (or, if he is in care, the care authority or organisation). The term 'in care' covers all cases where a juvenile is 'looked after' by a local authority under the Children Act 1989; or

(b) a local authority social worker; or

(c) failing either of the above, another responsible adult aged 18 or over who is not a police officer or employed by the police.

A person, including a parent or guardian, should not be the appropriate adult if he is suspected of involvement in the offence in question, is the victim, is a witness, is involved in the investigation, or has received admissions. If the parent or guardian of a juvenile is estranged from the juvenile, he should not be asked to be the appropriate adult if the juvenile expressly and specifically objects to his presence. The fact that a parent participates in questioning a juvenile during the interview does not disqualify the parent from being the appropriate adult. If a child in care admits an offence to a social worker, another social worker should be the appropriate adult.

Although the Code refers to 'the appropriate adult' in the singular, there may be cases where it is appropriate for more than one adult to be present as 'appropriate adults' during the interview of a juvenile, as where both parents are present or where a parent with language difficulties is present and a second adult is present to assist in questions of language.

In the case of a person *who is mentally disordered or mentally handicapped*, 'the appropriate adult' means:

(a) a relative, guardian, or other person responsible for his care or custody; or

(b) someone who has experience of dealing with persons who are mentally disordered or mentally vulnerable (ie because of their mental state or capacity they may not understand the significance of what is said, of questions or of their replies) but who is not a police officer or employed by the police; or

(c) failing either of the above, some other responsible adult aged 18 or over who is not a police officer or employed by the police.

In the case of people who are mentally disordered or otherwise mentally vulnerable it may in some cases be more satisfactory if the appropriate adult is someone who has experience or training in their case rather than a relative lacking such qualifications. However, if the person himself prefers a relative to a better qualified stranger, his wishes should if practicable be respected.

A solicitor or independent custody visitor who is present at the police station in a professional capacity may not act as the appropriate adult.

A person should always be given an opportunity, when the appropriate adult is called to a police station, to consult privately with a solicitor in the absence of the appropriate adult if he wishes to do so. The appropriate adult is not subject to legal privilege.

If a juvenile is known to be subject to a court order under which a person or organisation is given any degree of statutory responsibility to supervise or otherwise monitor him, reasonable steps must also be taken to notify that person or organisation (the responsible officer). The responsible officer will normally be a member of a youth offending team, except in the case of a curfew order which involves electronic monitoring, when the contractor providing the monitoring will normally be the responsible officer.

A juvenile or a mentally disordered or vulnerable person must not be interviewed regarding his involvement or suspected involvement in a criminal offence or offences, or be asked to provide or sign a written statement under caution or record of an interview, in the absence of the appropriate adult, subject to the special provisions below about urgent interviews authorised by a superintendent. If a juvenile or mentally disordered or vulnerable person is cautioned in the absence of the appropriate adult, the caution must be repeated in the appropriate adult's presence. Such a person may not be asked to give or sign a written statement. An interview is an indivisible process. A failure to involve the appropriate adult in some part of it is a breach of the Detention Code and may render the whole of the interview inadmissible. (Note: There is no requirement for an appropriate adult to be present if someone is detained under the Mental Health Act 1983 for *assessment.*)

If, having been informed of his right to legal advice, the appropriate adult thinks that legal advice should be taken, the provisions of the Code relating to the right to legal advice (see p 99) must be followed.

If the appropriate adult is not at the police station when the provisions of the Code dealing with the juvenile's rights are explained, the provisions must be complied with again in the presence of the appropriate adult once that person arrives.

Juveniles may only be interviewed at their places of education in exceptional circumstances and then only when the principal or his nominee agrees and is present. Every effort should be made to contact both the parents, or other person responsible for the juvenile's welfare, and the appropriate adult (if a different person). A reasonable time should be allowed to enable the appropriate adult to attend. Where this would cause undue delay, and unless the offence is against the educational establishment, the principal or his nominee can act as the appropriate adult for the purposes of the interview.

Juveniles should not be arrested at their place of education unless this is unavoidable. If this occurs, the principal or his nominee must be informed.

A juvenile or someone who is mentally disordered or vulnerable may be particularly open to suggestion. Consequently, special care must always be exercised in questioning such a person, and it is important to obtain corroboration of any facts admitted wherever possible.

If the appropriate adult is present at an interview, he must be told that he is not expected to act simply as an observer. He must also be informed that the purposes of his presence are:

(a) to advise the person being interviewed and to observe whether or not the interview is conducted fairly and properly; and
(b) to facilitate communication with the person being interviewed.

If a person appears to be blind or seriously visually impaired or unable to read, deaf, or unable to speak or has difficulty orally because of a speech impediment, he should be treated as such for the purpose of the Detention Code in the absence of clear evidence to the contrary.

If a person is blind, seriously visually impaired, or unable to read, the custody officer must ensure that his solicitor, relative, the appropriate adult or some other person likely to take an interest in him (and not involved in the investigation) is available to help in checking any documentation. Where the Detention Code requires consent or signing, then the person who is assisting may be asked to sign instead, if the detained person so wishes. However, there is no requirement that the appropriate adult be called solely to assist in checking and signing documentation in such circumstances.

The Detention Code also requires that, where the appropriate adult or the person's solicitor is present at an interview and is still in the police station at the time a written record is made, he must be asked to read it (or any written statement taken down by a police officer) and sign it as correct. If he refuses to sign the record as accurate, the senior officer present must record on the record itself, in the presence of the person concerned, what has happened. If the interview is audibly recorded the arrangements set out in the Code of Practice for the Audio Recording of Police Interviews apply.

Vulnerable suspects: urgent interviews at police stations

Some vulnerable persons may not be interviewed unless an officer of superintendent rank or above considers delay will lead to one of the consequences (potential interference, harm, loss, etc) set out on p 97 and is satisfied that the interview would not significantly harm the person's physical or mental state. They are:

(a) a juvenile or person who is mentally disordered or vulnerable if at the time of the interview the appropriate adult is not present;

(b) any other person who appears to be unable to appreciate the significance of questions and his answers, or to understand what is happening because of the effects of drink, drugs, or any illness, ailment or condition; and

(c) a person who has difficulty understanding English or has a hearing disability, if an interpreter is not present.

Such interviews must not continue once sufficient information has been obtained to avert the consequences referred to above. A record must be made of the grounds for any decision to interview in these circumstances.

Interpreters

Foreign languages

The Detention Code provides:

(1) If a person has difficulty in understanding English, the interviewer cannot himself speak the person's own language and the person wishes an interpreter to be present, he must not be interviewed in the absence of a person capable of acting as an interpreter, unless a superintendent or above considers that delay will lead to one of the consequences set out on p 97, in which case the same rules apply as in the case of urgent interviews with vulnerable suspects.

(2) The interviewer must ensure that the interpreter makes a note of the interview at the time in the language of the person being interviewed for use in the event of his being called to give evidence and that he certifies its accuracy. The interviewer should allow sufficient time for the interpreter to note each question and answer after each is put, given, and interpreted. The person must be given an opportunity to read the record or have it read to him and sign it as correct or to indicate the respects in which he considers it to be inaccurate. If the interview is audibly recorded or visually recorded, the arrangements in the Audio Recording Code or Visual Recording Code respectively apply.

(3) In the case of a person making a statement in a language other than English:

    (a) the interpreter must take down the statement in the language in which it is made;

    (b) the person making the statement must be invited to sign the statement; and

    (c) an official English translation must be made in due course.

The deaf and those with hearing or speech difficulties

The Detention Code provides:

(1) If a person appears to be deaf or there is a doubt about his hearing or speaking ability, he must not be interviewed in the absence of an interpreter unless he agrees in
writing to be so interviewed or special circumstances exist (potential interference,
harm, loss, etc: see p 97). Likewise, an interpreter should also be called if a juvenile
is interviewed and the parent or guardian present as the appropriate adult appears
to be deaf or there is a doubt about his hearing or speaking ability, unless he agrees
in writing that the interview should proceed without one or those special circumstances exist.
(2) The interviewer must ensure that the interpreter is given the chance to read the
record of the interview and to certify its accuracy in the event of being called to
give evidence.

General

Chief officers are responsible for ensuring that arrangements are in place for the provision of interpreters for the deaf and those who cannot speak English. Whenever possible, interpreters should be provided in accordance with national arrangements
approved or prescribed by the Secretary of State.

Interpreters will be provided at public expense and all reasonable attempts should be
made to make this fact clear to a detained person. The interpreter may not be a police
officer or civilian support staff when interpretation is needed for the purpose of obtaining legal advice. In all other cases, a police officer or civilian support staff may only
interpret if the detained person (and the appropriate adult if applicable) agrees in writing or if the interview is audibly recorded or visually recorded.

If a person who has difficulty in understanding English is charged with an offence,
and the interviewer cannot himself speak the person's language, arrangements must be
made for an interpreter to explain as soon as practicable the offence concerned and any
other information given by the custody officer.

Where a person in detention cannot communicate with a solicitor, whether because
of language, hearing, or speech difficulties, an interpreter must be called.

Where a person charged with an offence appears to be deaf, or there is doubt about
his hearing or speaking ability or ability to understand English, and the custody officer
cannot establish effective communication, arrangements must be made for an interpreter to explain as soon as practicable the offence concerned and any other information given by the custody officer.

Documentation and guidance

The action taken to call an interpreter must be recorded, together with any waiver of the
right not to be interviewed in the absence of an interpreter. As the interpreter may be
needed as a witness at the person's trial, a second interpreter will be needed at that trial.

Right to liberty and security and the right to a fair trial under articles 5 and 6 of the European Convention on Human Rights

Article 5(1) provides that everyone has the right to liberty and security of person. No
one shall be deprived of his liberty save in specified cases and in accordance with the
procedure prescribed by law:

(a) the lawful detention of a person after conviction by a competent court;

(b) the lawful arrest or detention of a person for non-compliance with the lawful order of a court or in order to secure the fulfilment of any obligation prescribed by law;

(c) the lawful arrest or detention of a person effected for the purpose of bringing him before the competent legal authority on reasonable suspicion of having committed an offence or when it is reasonably considered necessary to prevent his committing an offence or fleeing after having done so;

(d) the detention of a minor by lawful order for the purpose of educational supervision or his lawful detention for the purpose of bringing him before the competent legal authority;

(e) the lawful detention of persons for the prevention of the spreading of infectious diseases, of persons of unsound mind, alcoholics or drug addicts or vagrants;

(f) the lawful arrest or detention of a person to prevent his effecting an unauthorised entry into the country or of a person against whom action is being taken with a view to deportation or extradition.

By art 5(2), everyone who is arrested must be informed promptly, in a language which he understands, of the reasons for his arrest and of any charge against him; and, by art 5(3), everyone arrested and detained in accordance with (c) above, must be brought promptly before a court and is entitled to trial within a reasonable time or to release pending trial. Release may be conditioned by guarantees to appear for trial.

Article 6 sets out the right to a fair trial. Article 6(1) provides that, in the determination of his civil rights and obligations or of any criminal charge against him, everyone is entitled to a fair and public hearing within a reasonable time by an independent and impartial tribunal established by law. Article 6(3) provides that everyone charged with a criminal offence has the following minimum rights:

(a) to be informed promptly, in a language which he understands and in detail, of the nature and cause of the accusation against him;

(b) to have adequate time and facilities for the preparation of his defence;

(c) to defend himself in person or through legal assistance of his own choosing or, if he has not sufficient means to pay for legal assistance, to be given it free when the interests of justice so require;

(d) to examine or have examined witnesses against him and to obtain the attendance and examination of witnesses on his behalf under the same conditions as witnesses against him;

(e) to have the free assistance of an interpreter if he cannot understand or speak the language used in court.

In effect, the provisions within our laws governing the arrest and detention of persons, and the conduct of police officers, will be measured against the provisions of arts 5 and 6; in addition other articles may also be relevant, for example art 8 (the right to private life). As noted in Chapter 1, a breach of the Convention by a police officer will be an unlawful action for which damages may be awarded. A divisional court, for example, has said that a delay in providing access to legal advice to a vulnerable person who was being interviewed was a breach of art 6.

CHAPTER 5

Treatment, Charging, and Bail of Detainees

GENERAL

A person detained at a police station as a place of safety under the Mental Health Act 1983, s 135 (warrant to search for and remove mental patients) or s 136 (mentally disordered persons found in public places) should not be questioned about any alleged offence or asked to make a statement. However, where, after such detention, such a person is reasonably suspected of having driven a motor vehicle with excess alcohol, it is permissible to commence the breath-testing procedure where the attendance of those required to carry out a medical examination cannot be expeditiously arranged.

Whenever the Detention Code (see p 92) requires a person to be given certain information he does not have to be given it if he is incapable at the time of understanding what is said to him or if he is violent or in urgent need of medical attention, but he must be given it as soon as practicable.

Where video cameras are installed in the custody area, suspects and other people entering should be informed by prominently placed notices that cameras are in use. Any request by a suspect or other person to have video cameras switched off should be refused.

The Detention Code lays down a large number of rules concerning conditions of detention and medical treatment.

RECEPTION OF ARRESTED PERSONS AT POLICE STATIONS

Designated police stations

PACE, s 35(1) requires that the chief officer of police designates the police stations in his area which are to be used for the purpose of detaining arrested persons; his duty is to designate police stations which appear to him to provide sufficient accommodation for detaining arrested persons. By s 35(2A) the Chief Constable of the British Transport Police may designate police stations which (in addition to those designated under s 35(1)) may be used for the purpose of detaining arrested persons.

Custody officers

Where a station is designated under s 35(1) or (2A), s 36(1), (2), and (3) requires that one or more custody officers must be appointed by the relevant chief officer of police or his nominee. They must be of the rank of sergeant (or above), but s 36(4) allows another officer of any rank to perform the duties of a custody officer under PACE at a designated police station if such an officer is not readily available to perform those duties. Such an officer is only not 'readily available' if he is not actually at the police station and cannot, without much difficulty, be fetched there.

None of the functions of a custody officer in relation to a person may be performed by an officer who at the time when the function falls to be performed is involved in the investigation of an offence for which that person is in police detention at that time, except that this does not prevent a custody officer:

(a) performing any function assigned to custody officers by PACE, or by a code of practice issued under PACE;
(b) carrying out the duty imposed on custody officers by PACE s 39 (below);
(c) doing anything in connection with the identification of a suspect; or
(d) doing anything under the Road Traffic Act 1988, ss 7 and 8 (breath, blood, or urine specimens).

Where an arrested person is taken to a non-designated police station any officer not concerned in the investigation of the offence may, by PACE, s 36(7), assume the responsibilities of a custody officer. If no such officer is available, it may be the arresting officer.

Custody officer's duties

A custody officer's duties are laid down by PACE, ss 37 to 39. Basically, and this is provided for by s 39, he is responsible for persons in detention, for ensuring that they and their property are treated in accordance with PACE and the Detention Code, and for maintaining a chronological and contemporaneous record of every aspect of a person's treatment whilst in detention. These responsibilities cannot be overstated. The provisions in relation to detention are quite complex and the requirements for such a log mean that omissions in the keeping of it cannot be corrected. If a duty is carried out but not recorded, the failure to record as required by the Codes is sufficient to raise the issue of disciplinary proceedings. Sections 37 and 38 are dealt with on p 152 and p 159 respectively.

Where PACE and its Codes require that certain things are done by a custody officer, the requirement also applies to a police officer other than a custody officer who is performing the functions of a custody officer.

Where a person has been arrested, a custody officer does not have to satisfy himself that the arrest is lawful before he can hold the arrested person in lawful custody.

A custody officer is required to perform the functions specified in the Detention Code as soon as is practicable. A custody officer is not in breach of the Code in the event of delay provided that the delay is justifiable and that every reasonable step is taken to prevent unnecessary delay. The custody record must indicate where a delay has occurred and the reason why.

Delays might occur in the processing of suspects because, for example, a large number of suspects are brought into the police station simultaneously to be placed in custody, or interview rooms are all being used, or where there are difficulties in contacting the appropriate adult, solicitor, or interpreter.

Police detention

A person is stated by PACE, s 118 to be in police detention for the purposes of the Act if:

(a) he has been taken to a police station after being arrested for an offence, or after being arrested by a police officer under TA 2000, s 41 on reasonable suspicion of being a terrorist; or

(b) he is arrested at a police station after attending voluntarily at the station or accom-
    panying a constable to it,

and he is detained there or is detained elsewhere in the charge of a constable.

In most circumstances, of course, a person's detention begins under (a) on arrival at
a police station under arrest. If a person is subsequently removed from a police station,
eg, to attend an identification parade or to visit the scene of a crime or on transfer to
another station, he is in detention whilst he remains in the charge of a constable. This
is important when periods of detention are to be considered by custody officers. By way
of an exception, s 118 provides that a person who is at a court after being charged is not
in police detention for the purposes of the Act.

As already stated, a separate custody record must be opened as soon as practicable
for each person detained at a police station.

Limitations on police detention

PACE, s 34 provides that a person arrested for an offence (as opposed to a breach of the
peace, which is not an offence) must not be kept in police detention, except in accordance with the provisions outlined below. However, no person in police detention may
be released except on the authority of a custody officer.

Section 34 requires that if at any time a custody officer:

(a) becomes aware, in relation to any person in police detention at that station, that the
    grounds for the detention of that person have ceased to apply; and
(b) is not aware of any other grounds on which the continued detention of that person
    could be justified under the provisions of the Act,

the custody officer must order his immediate release from custody. However, a person
who was unlawfully at large when arrested must not be released under these provisions.

A person released in these circumstances must be released without bail, unless it
appears to the custody officer that there is a need for further investigation of any matter
in connection with which he was detained at any time during the period of his detention, or that in respect of any such matter proceedings may be taken against him or he
may be reprimanded or warned (prospectively, replaced by given a youth caution)
(which is only possible where the offender is under 18), in which case he must be
released on bail.

An investigating officer may bring facts to the notice of a custody officer but issues of
further detention or release are to be decided by the custody officer. It will be appreciated that custody officers may find themselves in dispute with officers of senior rank in
respect of detention issues. If this occurs the superintendent responsible for the police
station must be consulted.

For the above purposes and for the purposes of the detention provisions of PACE
(ss 34–51) in general, a person who:

(a) attends a police station to answer bail under s 30A (p 62),
(b) returns to a police station to answer to bail granted under the detention provi-
    sions, or
(c) is arrested under PACE, s 30D or 46A (pp 63 and 162),

is to be treated as arrested for an offence and that offence is the offence in connection
with which he was granted bail. (This is, however, subject to the rule (p 163) whereby
periods when a person has been on bail are excluded from the calculation of the time
when the person is in police detention.) The above provision does not apply in relation

to a person who is granted bail subject to the duty to attend at a police station appointed by the custody officer for proceedings in relation to a live link direction or any preliminary hearing in relation to which such a direction is given, and who either attends a police station to answer to such bail, or is arrested under s 46A for failing to do so. Provision as to the treatment of such persons is made by s 46ZA.

TREATMENT OF DETAINEES

Conditions of detention

(1)   So far as practicable, not more than one person shall be detained in each cell.

(2)   Cells in use must be adequately heated, cleaned and ventilated. They must be adequately lit, subject to such dimming as is compatible with safety and security to allow people detained overnight to sleep. No additional restraints should be used within a locked cell unless absolutely necessary, and then only approved restraint equipment which is reasonable and necessary in the circumstances having regard to the detainee's demeanour and with a view to ensuring his safety and the safety of others. If the detainee is deaf, mentally disordered, or otherwise mentally vulnerable, particular care must be taken when deciding whether to use any form of approved restraints.

(3)   Blankets, mattresses, pillows, and other bedding supplied should be of a reasonable standard and in a clean and sanitary condition.

(4)   Access to toilet and washing facilities must be provided.

(5)   If it is necessary to remove a person's clothes for the purpose of investigation, for hygiene or health reasons or for cleaning, replacement clothing of a reasonable standard of comfort and cleanliness must be provided. A person must not be interviewed unless adequate clothing has been offered to him.

(6)   At least two light meals and one main meal must be offered in any period of 24 hours. Drinks should be provided at meal times and on reasonable request between meal times. Meals should, so far as practicable, be offered at recognised meal times, or at other times that take account of when the detainee last had a meal. Whenever necessary, advice must be sought from the appropriate healthcare professional (clinically qualified person working within the scope of his practice) on medical or dietary matters. As far as practicable, meals provided must offer a varied diet and meet any special dietary needs or religious beliefs that a person may have. At the custody officer's discretion, the detainee may also have meals supplied by his family or friends at his or their own expense. However, especially in the case of a person detained under the Terrorism Act (TA) 2000, immigration detainees and others likely to be detained for an extended period, a custody officer is entitled to take account of the risk of items being concealed in any food or package and of his (the officer's) duties and responsibilities under food handling arrangements.

(7)   Brief outdoor exercise must be offered daily if practicable.

(8)   A juvenile must not be placed in a police cell, unless no other secure accommodation is available and the custody officer considers that it is not practicable to supervise him if he is not placed in a cell or the custody officer considers that a cell provides more comfortable accommodation than other secure accommodation in the police station.

(9)   A juvenile must not be placed in a cell with a detained adult.

(10) Detainees should be visited at least every hour. If no reasonably foreseeable risk was identified in a risk assessment, a sleeping detainee need not be awakened.

A person suspected of being under the influence of drink or drugs or having swallowed drugs, or whose level of consciousness causes concern, must, subject to any clinical directions given by the appropriate healthcare professional, be visited and roused at least every half hour, have his condition assessed, and clinical treatment arranged if appropriate. His condition must be assessed by entering the cell, calling his name and shaking him gently, before asking his name and where he lives as well as where he thinks he is. He should be asked to open his eyes and to lift one arm and then the other. These provisions apply to a person in police custody by order of a magistrates' court under the CJA 1988, s 152 to facilitate the recovery of evidence where that person has been charged with drug possession or drug trafficking and is suspected of having swallowed the drugs. In the case of the healthcare needs of a person who has swallowed drugs, the custody officer, subject to any clinical direction, should consider the necessity for rousing every half hour. This does not negate the need for regular visiting of the suspect in the cell.

It is important to remember that a person who appears to be drunk or behaving abnormally might be suffering from illness or the effects of drugs or may have sustained injury (particularly a head injury) which is not apparent, and that someone addicted to certain drugs may experience harmful effects within a short time of being deprived of their supply. Consequently, police officers should always err on the side of caution when in doubt about calling an appropriate healthcare professional, and act with all due speed. A detainee may be dependent upon certain drugs, including alcohol, and may experience harmful effects within a short time of being deprived of their supply. In these circumstances an appropriate healthcare professional should be consulted or an ambulance should be called. A record must be made of any intoxicating liquor supplied. Annex G to the Detention Code limits the circumstances in which persons under the influence of drink or drugs, or whose mental state is affected in some other way, may be interviewed. A Home Office Circular states that those detained under the Mental Health Act 1983, s 136 (see p 130) should only exceptionally be detained at a police station; a hospital or care home is a more appropriate place. The same comment can be made about those detained under s 135.

Visits or rousing of detainees carried out in accordance with the Code above, or in accordance with medical advice, do not constitute an interruption to a rest period such that a fresh period must be allowed. Should the custody officer feel in any way concerned about the person's condition, then the officer must arrange for medical treatment.

Documentation

A record must be kept of replacement clothing and meals offered. If a juvenile is placed in a cell, the reason must be recorded. The use of any restraints, the reason for such use and any arrangements for enhanced supervision must be recorded.

Clinical treatment and attention

(1) A custody officer must make sure that a detainee receives appropriate clinical attention as soon as reasonably practicable if that person appears to be suffering from physical illness or mental disorder or to be in need of clinical attention or is injured. This applies even if no request for such attention has been received or if clinical attention has already been received elsewhere. The custody officer must also consider the need for clinical attention in relation to those suffering from the effects of alcohol or drugs.

These rules about seeking medical attention are not intended to delay the transfer of a person to a place of safety under the Mental Health Act 1983, s 136, where that is applicable. Where an assessment under that Act takes place, the custody officer must consider whether an appropriate healthcare professional should be called to conduct an initial check on the detainee. This applies particularly where there is likely to be any significant delay in the arrival of a suitably qualified medical practitioner.

(2) If it appears to the custody officer, or he is told, that a person brought to the police station under arrest may be suffering from an infectious disease or condition, reasonable steps must be taken to safeguard the health of the detainee and others. Advice must be sought from an appropriate healthcare professional. The person and his property may be isolated pending clinical direction.

(3) If a detainee requests a clinical examination, an appropriate healthcare professional must be called as soon as practicable. If a safe and appropriate healthcare plan cannot be provided, the police surgeon's advice must be sought.

(4) If a detainee is required to take or apply any medication in compliance with clinical directions prescribed before his detention, the custody officer must consult the appropriate healthcare professional prior to the use of the medication; such consultation and its outcome must be noted in the custody record. The custody officer is responsible for the safekeeping of any medication and for ensuring that the detainee is given the opportunity to take or apply prescribed or approved medication. However, no police officer may administer medicines which are also controlled drugs subject to the Misuse of Drugs Regulations 2001, Schs 1, 2, or 3. A detainee may administer controlled drugs to himself only under the personal supervision of the registered medical practitioner authorising their use or other appropriate healthcare professional. The custody officer may supervise the self-administration of or authorise other custody staff to supervise the self-administration of drugs listed in Schs 4 or 5 if he has consulted the appropriate healthcare professional authorising their use and both are satisfied self-administration will not endanger the detainee, police officers, or anyone else.

(5) Where appropriate healthcare professionals administer drugs or other medication, or supervise self-administration, it must be within the scope of their practice as defined by their professional body.

(6) If a detainee has in his possession, or claims to need, medication relating to a heart condition, diabetes, epilepsy, or a condition of comparable potential seriousness then, even though (1), above, may not apply, the advice of the appropriate healthcare professional must be obtained.

A record must be made in the custody record of any complaint made, together with a record of any clinical attention received, and of any request for a clinical examination under (3) and arrangements made in response. A note should also be made of any injury, ailment or condition causing such arrangements to be made, together with clinical directions and advice or clarifications given by a healthcare professional. Where applicable, a note should be made of responses made when attempting to rouse a detainee. Should a healthcare professional not record his clinical findings in the custody record, a note must be made in it of where the findings are recorded. Information necessary to ensure ongoing care and well-being of a detainee must be recorded openly in the custody record. A custody record must include all medication in the possession of a detainee on his arrival, together with a note of medication which he claims to need.

Whenever an appropriate healthcare professional is consulted, the custody officer must ask for an opinion concerning risks or problems which need to be taken into account when making a decision about detention, when to carry out an interview if applicable and the need for safeguards. Any doubts concerning directions, particularly in relation to the frequency of visits, must be cleared up.

Nothing in the above provisions prevents the police from calling an appropriate healthcare professional to examine a detainee for the purpose of obtaining evidence relating to an offence in which he is suspected of being involved.

Complaints about treatment

If a complaint is made by or on behalf of a detainee about his treatment since his arrest, or it comes to the notice of any officer that he may have been treated improperly, a report must be made as soon as practicable to an officer of the rank of inspector (or above) who is not connected with the investigation. If the matter concerns a possible assault or the unreasonable use of force, the appropriate healthcare professional must also be called as soon as practicable; a record must be made of any arrangements made.

A record must be made of any complaint reported under the above provisions, together with any relevant remarks by the custody officer.

Independent custody visitors for places of detention

The Police Reform Act 2002, s 51 requires local policing bodies to make arrangements for detainees to be visited by independent custody visitors. The arrangements may provide rights of access to police stations; examination of records; meetings with detainees and the inspection of facilities. Access to a detainee may be denied if:

(a) it appears to an officer of or above the rank of inspector that there are grounds for doing so at the time that it is requested;
(b) those grounds are specified within the arrangements; and
(c) the procedural requirements imposed by the arrangements in relation to a denial of access are complied with.

The Secretary of State has issued a code of practice as to the carrying out of functions under the arrangements. The notice of rights and entitlements given to detainees explains that 'visitors' are members of the community who are allowed access to police stations unannounced to ensure that detainees have access to their rights. It explains that a detainee does not have a right to see an independent custody visitor and that he cannot request to see one; that such a visitor acts independently of the police to check that welfare rights are protected; and that the detainee does not have to speak to such a visitor if he does not wish to do so.

Information to be given to detainees

When the custody officer authorises the detention of a person who has not been charged, he is required by PACE, s 37 to make, as soon as practicable, a written entry on the custody record of the grounds which exist for detention. This must be done in the person's presence and he must be informed at that time of those grounds. If he is asleep he must be woken and told. (However, if at that time a person is incapable of understanding what is said to him or is violent or likely to be so, or is in urgent need of medical treatment, the information may be given as soon as practicable, and in any case before he is questioned for the offence.) At the same time the detainee must be informed clearly of the rights set out on p 95 and the other functions referred to there must be carried out.

Communication with others

See Chapter 4.

Access to legal advice

See Chapter 4.

Searching and retention of property

PACE, s 54 charges the custody officer with a duty to ascertain the property which a person has with him when he is:

(a) brought to a police station after being arrested elsewhere or after being committed to custody by an order or a sentence of a court; or
(b) arrested at a police station or detained there:
    (i)   under s 37 (p 136),
    (ii)   when answering police bail,
    (iii) for failing to answer police bail, or
    (iv) as a person treated by s 46ZA (p 158) as arrested and charged for an offence for which he has been granted live link bail.

A detainee may be searched to the extent considered necessary if the custody officer considers it necessary to ascertain the property which that person has with him, but an intimate search (p 140) may not be carried out for this purpose. A strip search (ie one involving the removal of more than outer clothing) is only permissible if the custody officer reasonably considers that the detainee might have concealed an article which he would not be allowed to keep under the provision below.

The custody officer may record all or any of the items which he finds. In the case of an arrested person, this may be done in the custody record. A strip search may only be carried out if the necessary requirements set out below (p 139) are satisfied.

Articles other than those subject to legal privilege (eg letters from solicitors, etc) may be seized and retained. However, clothes and personal effects (which do not include cash) may only be seized if the custody officer believes that they may be used by the person:

(a) to cause physical injury to himself or another;
(b) to damage property;
(c) to interfere with evidence;
(d) to assist him to escape,

or if the custody officer has *reasonable grounds* for believing that they may be evidence of an offence.

There will be some difficult decisions to be taken by custody officers who are required to allow a person in custody to retain property of a personal, non-dangerous character. Is a woman's handbag mirror likely to cause harm? It will not do so whilst it remains in its original condition but it will certainly do so if it is broken. This, perhaps, leads to a second question for the custody officer: is the woman in a mental state which might lead her to attempt to take her own life? Whatever decision the officer takes, he should apply his mind carefully to the particular situation which confronts him. If personal articles are retained by the custody officer he must explain why.

Section 54 also provides that a constable may at any time search a person who is in custody at a police station, or is in police detention otherwise than at a police station, in order to ascertain whether he has with him any articles which he could use for any of the purposes in (a)–(d) above. A constable may seize and detain anything found in such a search, except that clothes and personal effects may only be seized in the same circumstances as mentioned above.

Any search under s 54 must be by a constable of the same sex as the detainee (s 36).

Where articles are seized under s 54, the person must be told the reason unless he is violent or likely to be violent or is incapable of understanding. Items which are seized on the grounds that they may be used to cause injury or damage, interfere with evidence or assist escape must be returned when the person is released from police detention. The Detention Code states that the custody officer is responsible for the safekeeping of property taken from a person.

Search and examination to ascertain identity

A detainee at a police station may be searched or examined to establish:

(a) whether he has any marks, features, or injuries that would tend to identify him as a person involved in the commission of an offence; or

(b) his identity.

Where the appropriate consent (p 197) has been withheld, or it is not practicable to obtain it, PACE, s 54A permits an officer of at least the rank of inspector to authorise the search and/or examination of a detainee to find marks under (a). If the person concerned has refused to identify himself or the officer has reasonable grounds for suspecting that the person is not who he claims to be, an inspector (or above) may authorise a non-consensual search and/or examination to establish identity under (b). Such an authorisation may be given orally but must be confirmed in writing as soon as is practicable.

Any identifying mark (including features and injuries) which is found may be photographed with consent, or if such consent is withheld or it is not practicable to obtain it, without consent. 'Photographed' covers the use of any means by which a visual image may be produced.

Such searches, examinations, and taking of photographs may only be conducted or taken by constables of the same sex as the person concerned, who may use reasonable force. An intimate search may not be carried out under the authority of s 54A. An examination of the mouth is a non-intimate search and therefore may be undertaken by a constable. A dentist has no power to conduct such examination without consent under these provisions.

Photographs taken under s 54A may be used by or disclosed to, any person for any purpose relating to the prevention or detection of crime, the investigation of an offence, or the conduct of a prosecution. They may be retained after use or disclosure but may not be used or disclosed except for a related purpose.

The references to 'crime' in s 54A include conduct which is an offence (whether under UK law or the law of a country or territory outside the UK) or which is or corresponds to conduct which would be an offence in the UK if it all took place in any part of the UK.

When a person is searched, examined, or photographed under the above provisions, he must be informed of the:

(a) purpose of the search;
(b) grounds on which the relevant authority, if applicable, has been given; and
(c) purposes for which the photograph may be used, disclosed, or retained.

This information must be given before the search or examination commences or the photograph is taken, except if the photograph is to be taken covertly.

A record must be made when a detainee is searched, examined, or a photograph of the person, or any identifying marks found on him, is taken. The record must include the:

(a) identity (subject to the usual exclusion) of the officer carrying out the search, examination, or taking the photograph;
(b) purpose of the search, examination, or photograph and the outcome;
(c) detainee's consent to the search, examination, or photograph, or the reason the person was searched, examined, or photographed without consent; and
(d) giving of any authority, the grounds for giving it and the authorising officer.

If force is used when searching, examining, or taking a photograph in accordance with s 54A, a record must be made of the circumstances and those present.

SEARCHES

Strip searches

A strip search is any search involving the removal of more than outer clothing (which term includes shoes and socks). The Detention Code states that, for such a search to take place, the custody officer must believe it necessary to remove an article which the detainee would not be allowed to keep, which there is reasonable suspicion the person might have concealed. Strip searches should not be routinely carried out where there is no reason for suspicion that articles have been concealed.

Conduct

The following procedures must be observed when strip searches are conducted:

(1) A police officer carrying out a strip search must be the same sex (see p 36) as the person searched.
(2) The search must take place in an area where the suspect cannot be seen by any-one who does not need to be present, or by a member of the opposite sex (except the appropriate adult who has specifically been requested by the person being searched).
(3) Except in cases of urgency, where there is a risk of serious harm to the person detained or to others, whenever a strip search involves exposure of intimate parts of the body, there must be at least two people present other than the person searched, and if the search is of a juvenile or mentally disordered or vulnerable person, one of the people must be the appropriate adult. Except in urgent cases, a search of a juvenile may take place in the absence of the appropriate adult only if the juvenile signifies in that adult's presence that he prefers to be searched in his absence and that adult agrees. A record must be made of the juvenile's decision and signed by the appropriate adult. The presence of more than two people, other than the appropriate adult, may be permitted only in the most exceptional circumstances.

(4) The search must be conducted with proper regard to the sensitivity and vulnerability of the detainee in these circumstances. Every reasonable effort must be made to secure co-operation and minimise embarrassment. Detainees who are searched should not normally be required to have all their clothes removed at the same time; for example, a person should be allowed to remove clothing above the waist and re-dress before removing further clothing.
(5) Where necessary to assist the search, the suspect may be required to hold his or her arms in the air or to stand with his or her legs apart and to bend forward so that a visual examination may be made of the genital and anal areas provided that no physical contact is made with any body orifice.
(6) If, during a search, articles are found, the person must be asked to hand them over. If articles are found within any body orifice other than the mouth, and the person refuses to hand them over, their removal would constitute an intimate search which must be carried out in accordance with the provisions of the Code set out below.
(7) A strip search should be conducted as quickly as possible, and the suspect allowed to dress as soon as the procedure is complete.

Documentation

A note should be made on the custody record of a strip search. It should record the parts of the body searched, who searched, the reason it was considered necessary to undertake it, those present and any result.

Intimate searches

An intimate search is a search which consists of the physical examination of a person's body orifices other than the mouth, ie the nose, ears, anus, and vagina. The intrusive nature of such searches means the actual and potential risks associated with intimate searches must never be underestimated. Intimate searches are governed by PACE, s 55. Before an intimate search is authorised, every effort must be made to persuade a detainee to hand over the article. Whenever possible, a registered medical practitioner or registered nurse should be asked to make a risk assessment. The authorising officer must consider whether the grounds for believing that an article is concealed are reasonable. In cases of doubt, advice should be sought from a superintendent.

Authorisation

An intimate search must be authorised by an inspector (or above). To authorise such a search that officer must have reasonable grounds for believing that:

(a) an article which could cause physical injury to a detainee or others at the police station has been concealed; or
(b) the person has concealed a Class A drug which he intended to supply to another or to export; and
(c) in either case an intimate search is the only practicable means of removing it.

The authorisation of an intimate search may be given orally or in writing, but if orally it must be confirmed in writing as soon as practicable.

An intimate drug offence search may not be carried out without appropriate written consent. Before a detainee is asked to give such consent he must be warned that if he refuses without good cause his refusal may harm his case if it comes to trial. The following form of words may be used to give such a warning:

'You do not have to allow yourself to be searched but I must warn you that if you refuse without good cause, your refusal may harm your case if it comes to trial.'

In appropriate cases the warning may be given in a specified Welsh version. The warning may be given by a police officer or member of police staff. In the case of juveniles, mentally vulnerable, or mentally disordered detainees, the seeking and giving of consent must take place in the presence of the appropriate adult. A juvenile's consent is only valid if his parent's or guardian's consent is also obtained, unless the juvenile is under 14 (in which case his parent's or guardian's consent is sufficient in its own right). If not legally represented, the detainee must be reminded of his entitlement to legal advice, and the reminder must be noted in the custody record. Before the search begins, a constable or a designated detention officer must inform the person of the authorisation and the grounds for giving it and for believing that the item cannot be removed without an intimate search.

Where appropriate consent to a drug offence search is refused without good cause, a court or jury in any proceedings which follow may draw such inferences from that refusal as appear proper.

Execution

Intimate searches may take place only at:

(a) a police station (but not if it is a drug offence search);
(b) a hospital;
(c) a surgery; or
(d) other medical premises.

Before an intimate search takes place, the reasons why it is considered necessary must be explained to the person to be searched and he must be reminded of his entitlement to have legal advice and the reminder must be noted in the custody record.

An intimate search may only be carried out by a registered medical practitioner or registered nurse, unless an inspector (or above) considers that it is not practicable and the search takes place because there are reasonable grounds for believing that an article which could cause physical injury to the detainee or others at the police station has been concealed, in which case it must be carried out by a constable of the same sex (see p 36) and the reason for the impracticability must be recorded. A proposal for a search to be carried out by someone other than a registered medical practitioner or a registered nurse must only be considered as a last resort where the risks involved in retention of the item outweigh those associated with its removal. Except in the case of a juvenile, no one of the opposite sex, other than a doctor or nurse, may be present, nor anyone whose presence is unnecessary, but a minimum of two people, other than the person searched, must be present during the search. A search should be conducted with proper regard to the sensitivity and vulnerability of the suspect in the circumstances.

An intimate search at a police station of a juvenile, or person who is mentally disordered or vulnerable, must take place in the presence of the appropriate adult of the same sex (unless the person specifically requests the presence of a particular adult of the opposite sex who is readily available). The search of a juvenile may take place in the absence of the appropriate adult only if the juvenile signifies in the adult's presence that he prefers it to be done in his absence and that adult agrees. A record should be made of the juvenile's decision and signed by the appropriate adult.

Documentation

After an intimate search has been carried out, an entry must be made as soon as practicable on the custody record, stating the authorisation to carry out the search; the grounds for the authorisation and for believing that the article could not be removed without an intimate search; which parts of the detainee's body were searched; who carried out the search; who was present; and the result. Where the intimate search is a drug offence search, a record must also be made of the necessary warning and the fact that appropriate consent was given or (as the case may be) refused, and if refused, the reason given for the refusal.

The powers of seizure in respect of articles found are the same as those which apply to other searches. If an intimate search is carried out by a police officer, the reason why it was impracticable for a registered medical practitioner or a registered nurse to conduct it must be recorded.

X-rays and ultrasound scans

PACE, s 55A provides that where an inspector (or above) has reasonable grounds for believing that a person arrested for an offence and in police detention may have swallowed a Class A drug (p 900), and was in possession of it with the appropriate criminal intent before his arrest, he may authorise an X-ray or an ultrasound scan (or both) to be taken. An X-ray or ultrasound scan must not take place without the appropriate consent in writing. The detainee must be told beforehand by a police officer or designated detention officer of the authorisation and its grounds. Before being asked for his consent he must be warned that an unjustified refusal may harm his case if it comes to trial. This warning may be given by a police officer or member of police staff. In the case of juveniles, mentally vulnerable, or mentally disordered detainees, the seeking and giving of consent must take place in the presence of the appropriate adult. A juvenile's consent is only valid if his parent's or guardian's consent is also obtained, unless the juvenile is under 14 (in which case his parent's or guardian's consent is sufficient in its own right). A detainee who is not legally represented must be reminded of his entitlement to have free legal advice, and the reminder noted in the custody record. The provisions in relation to the inferences which may be drawn where consent to an intimate drug offence search is refused also apply to refusals to permit X-rays and ultrasound scans to be carried out.

An X-ray or ultrasound scan may only be carried out by a suitably qualified person at a hospital, a doctor's surgery, or at some place used for medical purposes.

If authority is given for an X-ray or an ultrasound scan (or both), consideration should be given to asking a registered medical practitioner or registered nurse to explain to the detainee what is involved and to allay any personal concerns about the effect which such examinations may have upon him. If appropriate consent is not given, evidence of the explanation may, if the case comes to trial, be relevant to determining whether the detainee had good cause for refusing.

A record must be made as soon as practicable in the detainee's custody record of the authorisation, its grounds, the warning, the giving (or otherwise) of the appropriate consent, and of the details of the X-ray or scan (if carried out).

Drug testing

When permitted

PACE, s 63B permits the taking of urine or non-intimate samples from someone *for the purpose of ascertaining whether he has any specified Class A drug (ie cocaine and diamorphine (heroin), their salts, and any preparation containing either drug or its salts)* in his body where:

(a) either the arrest condition or the charge condition is met;

(b) both the age condition and the request condition are met; and

(c) the notification condition is met in relation to the arrest condition, the charge condition, or the age condition (as the case may be).

The arrest condition is that the person concerned has been arrested for an offence but has not been charged with that offence and either:

(a) that offence is a 'trigger offence' (theft, attempted theft, robbery, attempted robbery, burglary, attempted burglary, aggravated burglary, taking a motor vehicle or other conveyance without authority, aggravated vehicle-taking, fraud, possessing articles used in frauds and making or supplying articles used in frauds, attempted fraud, handling stolen goods or attempted handling, going equipped for stealing, etc, and an offence under the Misuse of Drugs Act 1971 if committed in respect of a specified Class A drug associated with producing or supplying a controlled drug, possessing a controlled drug, or possessing a controlled drug with intent to supply, and begging or persistent begging contrary to the Vagrancy Act 1824, ss 3 or 4 respectively); or

(b) an inspector (or above), who has reasonable grounds for suspecting that the misuse by that person of any specified Class A drug caused or contributed to the offence, has authorised such a sample to be taken.

The charge condition is either:

(a) that the person concerned has been charged with a trigger offence; or

(b) that the person concerned has been charged with an offence and an inspector (or above), who has reasonable grounds for suspecting that the misuse by that person of any specified Class A drug caused or contributed to the offence, has authorised the sample to be taken.

The age condition is:

(a) if the arrest condition is met, that the person concerned is 18 or over; or

(b) if the charge condition is met, that he is 14 or over.

The request condition is that a police officer has requested the person concerned to give the sample (which in the case of a person under 17 must be done in the presence of the appropriate adult).

The notification condition is that:

(a) the relevant chief officer has been notified by the Secretary of State that appropriate arrangements have been made for the police area as a whole, or for the particular police station, in which the person is in police detention; and

(b) the notice has not been withdrawn.

Where a sample is taken from a person who satisfies the arrest condition, no other sample may be taken during the same continuous period of detention, but if the charge condition is met during that period, the sample already taken must be treated as one taken after charge. This must be recorded in the custody record.

In circumstances in which a person is arrested for a first offence which satisfies the arrest condition but not the charge condition, and he would normally be liable to be released from custody before a sample is taken but he remains in custody by reason of arrest for another offence not falling within the arrest condition, a sample may be taken before the end of a period of 24 hours following his *initial* arrest.

A sample must not be taken from a person in custody unless he is brought before the custody officer. It may only be taken by a person authorised by the Police and Criminal Evidence Act 1984 (Drug Testing of Persons in Police Detention) Prescribed Persons Regulations 2001 (as amended in 2012), viz a police officer, a person employed by a local policing body, or chief officer of police, or by a contractor engaged by such a body or chief officer, whose duties include taking samples for testing for the presence of specified Class A drugs. A sample may be taken from someone under 17 only in the presence of the appropriate adult.

Disclosure of information obtained

Information obtained from a sample taken under s 63B may be disclosed:

(a) for the purpose of informing any decision about granting bail in criminal proceedings to the person concerned, or about the giving of a conditional caution or a youth conditional caution (YCC);

(b) where the person concerned is in police detention or is remanded in or committed to custody by an order of a court or has been granted such bail, for the purpose of informing any decision about his supervision;

(c) where the person concerned is convicted of an offence, for the purpose of informing any decision about the appropriate sentence to be passed by a court and any decision about his supervision or release;

(d) for the purpose of:

    (i) an initial or follow-up assessment which the person concerned is required to attend;

    (ii) proceedings against the person concerned for an offence of failing to attend such an assessment; or

    (iii) ensuring that appropriate advice and treatment is made available to the person concerned.

Procedure

A request for a sample must be preceded by an explanation (a) of its *purpose*; (b) that failure without good cause to provide a sample may make the person requested liable to prosecution; and, (c) where authorised under (b) of the arrest condition or of the charge condition (see p 143), of the grounds for the authorisation. In addition, the person requested must be reminded of his right to have someone informed of his arrest; of his right to consult privately with a solicitor; of the availability free of charge of independent legal advice; and of the right to consult the relevant code of practice. When warning a person who is asked to provide a urine or non-intimate sample in these circumstances, the following form of words may be used (an alternative warning in Welsh is provided):

'You do not have to provide a sample, but I must warn you that if you fail or refuse without good cause to do so, you will commit an offence for which you may be imprisoned, or fined, or both.'

Custody officers may authorise continued detention for up to six hours from the time of charge to enable a sample to be taken.

Where a sample is taken following authorisation by an inspector (or above), the authorisation and the grounds for suspicion must be recorded in the custody record. An authorisation given by an inspector may be given orally but must subsequently be confirmed in writing as soon as practicable. Details of authorisations and the giving of warnings must be recorded, together with the time of charge and the time at which a sample was given.

A person who fails without good cause to give any sample which may be taken from him is guilty of an offence under s 63B(8).

Assessment of misuse of drugs after positive drug test

Initial assessment   Where an analysis of a sample reveals the presence of a Class A drug a police officer may, at any time before the person's release, require a person of 18 or over to attend an 'initial assessment' and to remain for its duration. A qualified 'initial assessor' will seek to establish dependency or a tendency to misuse any specified Class A drug and whether the person will benefit from further assessment or advice. If an initial assessor finds that a follow-up assessment is appropriate, he must inform the person of the time and place at which it is to take place, confirm this in writing, and warn the person of the consequence of failing to attend.

Follow-up assessment   The police officer may, at the same time as he imposes a requirement on the detainee to attend an initial assessment, require the person to attend a follow-up assessment and to remain for its duration. The officer must inform the detainee that the second requirement will cease to have effect, if at the initial assessment he is informed that a follow-up assessment is not necessary. A follow-up interview will be concerned with a 'care plan'.

Attendance at assessments   A constable must inform the detainee (to be confirmed in writing) that failure to attend either or both forms of assessment and to remain there for its duration without good cause, may result in prosecution. This must be done prior to release from custody and a record must be made in the custody record.

The Drugs Act 2005, s 12(2) provides that a person who is required to attend an initial assessment commits an offence if he fails, without good cause, to attend at the specified time and place, or attends but fails to remain for the duration of the assessment. Where such a failure occurs, any requirement imposed in relation to a follow-up assessment ceases to have effect. It is an offence against s 14(3) to fail, without good cause, to attend a follow-up assessment or to fail to attend for its duration. These offences are not committed if a subsequent analysis of a sample reveals that a specified Class A drug was not present in the person's body. This is because any requirement imposed ceases to have effect.

Any sample taken may not be used for any purpose other than to ascertain whether the person has a Class A drug in his body. It can be disposed of as clinical waste unless it is to be sent for further analysis in cases where the test result is disputed at the point when the result is known, or where medication has been taken, or for quality assurance purposes.

REVIEWS AND MAXIMUM PERIODS OF POLICE DETENTION

The following rules do not apply where a person has been arrested as a suspected terrorist under TA 2000, s 41. In such a case TA 2000, Sch 8 (pp 829) applies.

Reviews

PACE, s 40 requires periodic reviews of the detention of each person in police detention. The review will be carried out:

(a) in the case of a person who has been arrested *and charged*, by the custody officer; and

(b) in the case of a person who has been arrested *but not charged*, by an inspector (or above) who has not been directly involved in the investigation.

The officer by whom the review is carried out is called the 'review officer'.

There will be some designated police stations at which the custody officer will be an officer of the rank of inspector. Where this is so he could carry out both of the above functions.

PACE, s 40 is precise in relation to when these reviews must be carried out:

(a) the first review must be not later than *six hours* after the detention was first authorised;

(b) the second review must be not later than *nine hours* after the first; and

(c) subsequent reviews must be at intervals of *not more than nine hours*.

There is, however, a limited power to postpone a review (see p 148).

Failure to carry out a review in accordance with these rules renders the previously lawful detention unlawful and entitles the detainee to damages for false imprisonment.

The review officer is responsible under PACE, s 40 for determining whether or not a person's detention continues to be necessary.

The case of a person who has been arrested but not charged

Here the review officer must proceed as follows:

(1) Where the person was detained because he was not in a fit state to be charged or released without charge (with or without bail), eg because he was under the influence of drink or drugs, the review officer must consider whether he is now in a fit state to be charged or released. If he is, one or other of these courses must be adopted. If he is not, further detention may be authorised, but consideration should be given to whether there is sufficient evidence to charge him with an offence.

(2) Where, although there is then insufficient evidence to charge him, the detention of the person has been authorised by the custody officer on the basis that there are reasonable grounds to believe that his detention without charge is necessary to secure or preserve evidence relating to an offence for which he is under arrest or to obtain such evidence, the review officer may authorise further detention if this is necessary on the same basis.

PACE, s 40A permits the review of the detention of a person who has been arrested but not charged to be conducted by means of a telephone discussion. (However, if and when regulations are made under PACE, s 45A permitting a review to be carried out by video-conferencing, a review by telephone will not be possible.) A telephone (or (when in use) video-conferencing) review may only be carried out by an inspector (or above). Both telephone (or video-conferencing) reviews may be terminated by the review officer at any stage in favour of a review in person and a record should be made of such a decision.

The decision on whether the review takes place in person or by telephone (or (when permissible) by video conferencing) is a matter for the review officer, who must take full account of the detainee's needs. The benefits of carrying out a review in person should always be considered, based on the particular circumstances with specific additional consideration if the person is:

(a) a juvenile (in which case his actual age should also be considered),

(b) suspected of being mentally vulnerable,

(c) in need of medical attention for other than routine minor ailments, or

(d) subject to presentational or community issues around his detention.

Where a review is conducted over the telephone (or (when permissible) by video-conferencing facilities), the reviewing officer must require another officer at the station to carry out the review officer's functions under PACE, s 40 and the Detention Code by making any record connected with the review in the detainee's custody record in the presence of the detainee (if applicable) and giving the detainee information about the review.

Before deciding whether to authorise continued detention the review officer must give an opportunity to make representations about the detention to the detainee, unless he is asleep; the detainee's solicitor, if available; and the appropriate adult. When a telephone, etc review is carried out, this requirement will be satisfied either orally by telephone, etc or in writing where facilities such as fax or email exist for the immediate transmission of written material. Other people with an interest in the detainee's welfare may also make representations at the authorising officer's discretion.

The case of a person who has been charged

The person must be released, either on bail or without bail, unless:

(a) his name and address cannot be ascertained or there are reasonable grounds to doubt the name and address given; or

(b) there are reasonable grounds to believe that detention is necessary for his own protection or to prevent him causing physical injury to any person or loss of or damage to property; or

(c) there are reasonable grounds to believe that the person will fail to answer bail or that his detention is necessary to prevent him interfering with the administration of justice or with police investigations; or

(d) in the case of an arrested juvenile, detention is necessary in his own interests.

Before deciding whether to authorise continued detention the review officer must give an opportunity to make representations about the detention to:

(a) the detainee (unless the detainee is asleep);

(b) the detainee's solicitor if available at the time; and

(c) the appropriate adult if available at the time.

Other people having an interest in the detainee's welfare may also make representations at the authorising officer's discretion.

General

Representations may be made orally in person, or by telephone or in writing. The authorising officer, however, may refuse to hear oral representations from the detainee if the officer considers him unfit to make representations because of his condition or behaviour.

Any comment the detainee may make if the decision is to keep him in detention must be recorded and, if applicable, the review officer must be informed of the comment as soon as practicable. No officer may put specific questions to the detainee regarding his involvement in any offence, nor in respect of any comments he may make when given the chance to make representations or in response to the decision to keep him in detention. Such an exchange is likely to constitute an 'interview' and would require the safeguard of the Code's provisions concerning interviews generally.

Before conducting a review the review officer must ensure that the detainee is reminded of his entitlement to free legal advice, unless he is asleep. This reminder must be noted in the custody record. The person (unless he is asleep), or the detainee's solicitor if available to attend in person or contactable by telephone or other electronic means at the time of the review, must be given an opportunity by the review officer to make representations to him concerning the detention.

The detainee need not be woken for the review; if he is likely to be asleep at the latest time when a review or extension authorisation may take place, the review officer should bring it forward, if possible, so that the detainee may make representations without being woken up.

If, in the light of the above considerations, the review officer authorises the detention of a person (whether charged or not) to continue, the review officer must make a written record of the grounds for the detention as soon as practicable. A detainee who is asleep at a review and whose continued detention is authorised must be informed about the decision and reason as soon as practicable after waking.

Where a person is in police custody in circumstances which are not subject to statutory review, for example:

(a) someone arrested on warrant for failure to answer to bail or for breach of a condition of bail;

(b) someone in police custody under the Crime (Sentences) Act 1997 for a specific purpose and period;

(c) a convicted or remanded prisoner held on behalf of the Prison Service;

(d) someone detained:
   (i)   to prevent him causing a breach of the peace;
   (ii) on behalf of the UK Border Agency; or
   (iii) under CJA 1988, s 152 by order of a magistrates' court to facilitate the recovery of evidence where that person has been charged with drug possession or trafficking and is suspected of having swallowed drugs,

it is advised that reviews take place periodically to ensure that the power to detain still applies and that detention conditions are being complied with. Such reviews may be conducted by a sergeant.

Postponement of review

PACE, s 40 allows for the postponement of a review:

(a) if, having regard to all the circumstances at the latest time for the review, it is impracticable to carry out the review at that time; or

(b) if at that time the detainee is being questioned by a police officer and the review officer is satisfied that an interruption of the questioning for the purpose of carrying out the review would prejudice the particular investigation; or

(c) if at that time no review officer is readily available.

If a review is postponed it must be carried out as soon as practicable after the normal latest time for it. The reason for any postponement must be recorded in the custody record. The postponement of a review does not affect the time at which any subsequent review must be carried out. Thus, a second review must be carried out nine hours after the latest time at which the first review should have taken place, which time is six hours after the detention was first authorised.

Where the person whose detention is under review has not been charged before the time of the review, the first two paragraphs under the heading 'Duties of custody officer before charge' on p 152 apply with the substitution of 'a person whose detention is under review' for 'person…arrested', and of 'review officer' for 'custody officer', and with the addition of 'asleep' in the list referred to at s 37(4)–(6).

Documentation

A record must be made as soon as practicable of the outcome of each review: if a detainee was asleep when his continued detention was authorised, a record must be made of when he was informed and by whom. The grounds for, and the extent of, any delay in conducting a review must be recorded and reasons for there being a telephone, etc review must also be recorded, together with the place where the review officer was, and the method by which representations were made.

Limits on period of detention without charge

PACE, s 41 provides that a person must not be kept in police detention for more than 24 hours without being charged, except that detention beyond that period may be authorised in certain circumstances by a superintendent (or above) (s 42) or by a magistrates' court (ss 43 and 44). The maximum period of detention without charge is 96 hours, but is only 24 hours where an offence is not indictable.

Calculation of period of detention

PACE, s 41 refers to the 'relevant time', which is the time from which the detention of a particular person is to be calculated. This may be:

(a) in the case where a person, whose arrest is sought in one police area in England and Wales, is arrested in another area, and is not questioned in the area in which he is arrested about the offence for which he has been arrested, *the time at which the person arrives at the first police station in the area in which his arrest is sought, or the time 24 hours after that person's arrest, whichever is the earlier*;

(b) in the case of a person arrested outside England and Wales, *the time at which that person arrives at the first police station to which he is taken in the police area in England and Wales in which the offence for which he is arrested is being investigated, or the time 24 hours after the time of that person's entry into England and Wales, whichever is the earlier*;

(c) in the case of a person who attends voluntarily at a police station, or who accompanies a constable to a police station without having been arrested, and is arrested at the police station, *the time of his arrest*;

(d) in the case of a person who attends a police station to answer bail under s 30A (released on street bail without attending a police station), *the time when he arrives at a police station*; and

(e) in any other case, it is *the time at which the person arrested arrives at the first police station to which he is taken after arrest, unless he is in detention in an area* in England and Wales and his arrest for an offence is being sought *in some other police area* in England and Wales and he is taken to that second area for the purpose of investigating that offence, without being questioned in the first area in order to obtain evidence in relation to it. In such a case the 'relevant time' will be the time 24 hours after he leaves the place where he is detained in the first area or the time at which he arrives at the first police station to which he is taken in the second area, whichever is the earlier.

PACE, s 41 provides a safeguard in relation to a person in police detention who, whilst detained, is arrested for a second offence. The time does not start running again with his arrest for the second offence. It also provides for instances in which a person in police detention is removed to a hospital for medical treatment. Normally the period commencing with his journey to hospital and ending with his arrival back in police custody does not count towards his 24 hours in police custody; in effect, the clock may be stopped. However, any period, either during his journey or whilst in hospital, during which he is questioned by a police officer for the purpose of obtaining evidence in relation to an offence, is included in his period of police detention.

Release from detention after 24 hours

Section 41 provides that, subject to the following paragraph, if a person has not been charged after 24 hours in police detention he *must* be released either on bail or without bail. A person so released must not be re-arrested without a warrant for the same offence unless new evidence justifying a further arrest has come to light since his release, but this does not prevent his arrest for failure to surrender to police bail. It is submitted that evidence justifying further arrest would have to be substantial, probably sufficient in itself to justify arrest.

Release after 24 hours is not required if continued detention is authorised or a warrant of further detention is issued under the powers next discussed.

Authorisation of continued detention

The relevant provisions are set out by PACE, s 42. Where an officer of the rank of superintendent (or above) who is responsible for a police station at which a person is detained has reasonable grounds for believing that:

(a) the detention of that person without charge is necessary to secure or preserve evidence relating to an offence for which he is under arrest or to obtain such evidence by questioning him;

(b) an offence for which he is under arrest is an *indictable* offence; and

(c) the investigation is being conducted diligently and expeditiously,

he may authorise the keeping of that person in police detention for a period expiring at or before 36 hours after the relevant time.

This may not be done if the person has been in detention for more than 24 hours from the relevant time when the authorisation of continued detention is sought, nor may such an authorisation be given before the second review of that person's detention, that is the review at 15 hours after detention was first authorised. If the first period of continued detention given does not take the detention time fully to 36 hours (a superintendent will not necessarily authorise an additional 12 hours), a further period may be authorised if the conditions in the previous paragraph are satisfied, up to the maximum of 36 hours. This further period may be authorised at any time during the first extension, and even though more than 24 hours has elapsed from the relevant time.

The detainee must be informed on all occasions of the grounds for his continued detention and the custody record must be endorsed with them. Before deciding whether to authorise continued detention, the officer responsible must give an opportunity to make representations about the detention to the detainee, or his solicitor if available, and the appropriate adult if available. Any other person having an interest in the detainee's welfare may also make representations at the discretion of the officer authorising continued detention. Representations may be made orally or in writing. During consideration of authorisations of continued detention, specific questions must not be put to a detainee regarding his involvement in an offence or in respect of any comments which he makes. Such an exchange could be considered to be an interview. If, when an extension of detention is authorised, the detainee has not yet exercised his right to have some person informed of his detention, or his right of access to legal advice, the custody officer must inform him of his rights, decide whether he shall be permitted to exercise them, and record his decision in the custody record. Any comment made by a detainee about an authorisation of continued detention must be recorded and, if applicable, the authorising superintendent must be informed of the comment as soon as practicable.

Detaining a juvenile or mentally vulnerable person for longer than 24 hours is dependent upon the circumstances of the case and with regard to the person's special vulnerability, the legal obligation to provide an opportunity for legal representations to be made prior to a decision about extending detention, the need to consult and consider the views of the appropriate adult, and any alternatives to police custody.

A person who has been the subject of continued detention must be released, with or without bail, not later than 36 hours after the relevant time, unless he has been charged, or unless his continued detention is authorised or is otherwise permitted by a warrant of further detention (below). Such a person may not be re-arrested without warrant for the same offence unless new evidence justifying a further arrest has come to light since his release, but this does not apply to a person who fails to surrender to police bail.

Warrant of further detention

Such a warrant is governed by PACE, s 43. A magistrates' court may issue a warrant of further detention following an application on oath by a constable which is supported by a written information. The court must be satisfied that there are reasonable grounds for believing that further detention is justified. A person's further detention is only justified for the purpose of s 43 (or 44 (below)) if the conditions set out on p 150 in relation to s 42 are satisfied.

The detainee must be given a copy of the information and he must be brought before the court. If he is not legally represented, but wishes such representation, the court must adjourn for this to be done and he may be kept in detention during the adjournment.

An application for a warrant of further detention may be made at any time before the expiry of 36 hours after the 'relevant time', or, if it is not practicable for the magistrates' court to sit at that time but it will sit during the six hours following that period, at any time before the expiry of those six hours. In the latter case, the detainee may be kept in police detention until the application is heard, and the custody officer must record in the custody record the fact that (and the reason why) he was detained for more than 36 hours after the relevant time. It is not sufficient for the police to have the application on the court lists for hearing within the sitting of the court. The application must be brought to the notice of the court before the end of the relevant period.

If an application for a warrant of further detention is made after the expiry of 36 hours after the relevant time, and it would have been reasonable for the police to make it before the expiry of that period, the court must dismiss the application. Where on an application for a warrant of further detention a magistrates' court is not satisfied that there are reasonable grounds for believing that the further detention of the person to whom the application relates is justified, it must:

(a) refuse the application; or
(b) adjourn the hearing of it until not later than 36 hours after the relevant time (in which case the detainee may be kept in police detention during the adjournment).

Where an application is refused, the person to whom the application relates shall forthwith be charged or released, either on bail or without bail, but he need not be released:

(a) before the expiry of 24 hours after the relevant time; or
(b) before the expiry of any longer period for which his continued detention is or has been authorised under s 42 above.

Where an application is refused, no further application may be made for a warrant of further detention in respect of the person in question, unless supported by evidence which has come to light since the refusal.

A warrant of further detention must state the time of issue and the period of detention which it authorises, which must not be longer than 36 hours.

A 'magistrates' court' in the present context (and in that of s 44) is a court consisting of two or more justices, sitting otherwise than in open court for the purpose of these provisions.

Where a warrant of further detention is issued, the person must be released from police detention, with or without bail, on or before the expiry of the warrant unless he is charged. He may not be re-arrested for the same offence unless new evidence has come to light since his arrest, but this does not apply to a person who fails to surrender to police bail.

Extension of warrant of further detention

This is dealt with by PACE, s 44. A magistrates' court may extend a warrant of further detention, on an application made in the same way as under s 43, if satisfied that there are reasonable grounds for believing that further detention is justified. The extension may not exceed 36 hours or end later than 96 hours after the relevant time. If an extension ends earlier than 96 hours after that time, it may be further extended, provided that the extension ends no later than 96 hours after that time.

The provisions under s 43 ('Warrant of further detention') apply equally to an application under s 44.

Where an application for an extension is refused, the person to whom the application relates must forthwith be charged or released, either on bail or without bail. However, he need not be released before the expiry of any period for which a warrant of further detention has previously been extended or further extended.

Documentation

A record must be made of the outcome of any determination whether to extend the maximum detention period without charge or an application for a warrant of further detention or its extension. Where an authorisation of continued detention has been given, the record must show the length of time by which the detention was extended or further extended. The same applies where a warrant (or extension) of further detention is granted.

DUTIES OF CUSTODY OFFICER BEFORE CHARGE

PACE, s 37 states that, where a person has been arrested without warrant, or on a warrant which is not endorsed for bail, the custody officer must determine whether he has sufficient evidence to charge him with the offence for which he was arrested. The person may be detained at a police station for such period as is necessary for him to make that decision. The custody officer must record on the custody record the offence(s) for which the detainee has been arrested (and the reasons). He should also note on the custody record any comment the person may make in relation to the arresting officer's account but should not invite comment.

Section 37(2) provides that, if there is insufficient evidence of an offence, the custody officer must release that person either with or without bail, unless he has reasonable grounds for believing that detention is necessary to secure or preserve evidence of the offence or to obtain evidence by questioning him. If the custody officer has reasonable grounds for so believing, he may authorise the arrested person to be kept in police detention. If he authorises a person's detention, he must, as soon as practicable, record the grounds in the custody record. This written record must be made in the presence of the arrested person and at that time that person must be informed by the custody officer of the grounds for detention, unless the arrested person is incapable of understanding what is said to him, violent or likely to become violent or in urgent need of medical attention (s 37(4)–(6)). In any event, he must inform the detainee of the grounds as soon as practicable and in any case before that person is then questioned about any offence. The custody officer must note on the custody record any comment the person may make in respect of the decision to detain him but may not invite comment, nor may he put specific questions to the person concerning his involvement in any offence, nor in respect of any comments he may make in response to the investigating officer's account or the decision to place him in detention. Such an exchange is likely to constitute an interview and would require the necessary safeguards.

Section 37(7) provides that, if the custody officer determines that he has sufficient evidence to charge the person arrested for the offence for which he was arrested, that person must:

(a) be released without charge and on bail, or kept in police detention, for the purpose of enabling the DPP (in practice the CPS) to make a decision about charging or cautioning him;
(b) be released without charge and on bail but not for that purpose;
(c) be released without charge and without bail; or
(d) be charged.

By way of exception, if the person arrested is not in a fit state to be dealt with in this way (eg because he is under the influence of drink or drugs), he may be kept in police detention until he is in a fit state.

By PACE, s 37(7A), the decision as to how a person is to be dealt with under s 37(7) is that of the custody officer, but in making that decision the custody officer must have regard to the DPP's *Guidance on Charging* below.

In relation to (a), it should be noted that Crown Prosecutors are often located at police stations to enable charge decisions to be taken relatively quickly. CPS Direct operates an out-of-hours service linked to the police by a high speed IT and telephony system.

If a person is dealt with under (a), the custody officer must inform him that he is being released, or as the case may be, detained, to enable the DPP to make a decision about charging or cautioning him. In such a case, an officer involved in the investigation must send to the DPP such information as is specified in the DPP's *Guidance on Charging*. The DPP must decide whether there is sufficient evidence to charge the person; must then decide whether he should be charged or given a conditional caution, youth conditional caution, warning or reprimand (prospectively abolished), or (prospectively) a youth caution; and, if so, state the offence. The DPP must notify the officer of his decision, at which stage the person must be charged, cautioned, or told that he has been released from his bail. If a person is arrested for a breach of bail granted under these circumstances he may be charged or released without charge, either on bail or without bail. The custody officer may subsequently appoint a different time, or an additional time, at which the person must attend a police station. A person who surrenders to such bail may be kept in police detention to enable him to be dealt with.

If a person is released without charge under (b) or (c), and a decision has not yet been taken whether he should be prosecuted, the custody officer must inform him of this. A person released without charge and without bail may be dealt with by one of the alternatives to prosecution (see pp 31 and 167).

DPP's Guidance on Charging

Under the DPP's *Guidance on Charging*, the situation is as follows.

The police may charge:

(a) any *summary only* offence (and criminal damage where the value of the loss or damage is less than £5,000) irrespective of plea; and
(b) any *either way offence* anticipated as a guilty plea and suitable for sentence in a magistrates' court, provided it is not:
    (i)   a case requiring the consent of the DPP or Law Officer;
    (ii)   a case involving a death;
    (iii) connected with terrorist activity or official secrets;
    (iv) classified as hate crime or domestic violence under CPS Policies;
    (v)   an offence of violent disorder or affray;
    (vi) causing grievous bodily harm or wounding, or actual bodily harm;
    (vii) a Sexual Offences Act offence committed by or upon a person under 18;
    (viii) an offence under the Licensing Act 2003.

A guilty plea may be anticipated where either:

(a) the suspect has made a clear and unambiguous admission to the offence and has said nothing that could be used as a defence, or
(b) the suspect has made no admission but has not denied the offence or otherwise indicated it will be contested and the commission of the offence and identification of the offender can be established by reliable evidence or the suspect can be seen clearly committing the offence on a good quality visual recording.

A case may be considered suitable for sentence in a magistrates' court unless:

(a) the loss or damage relating to the charge is more than £5,000 or would exceed that sum if more than one offence is charged (or taken into consideration), or
(b) the overall circumstances of the offence are so serious that the court may decide that a sentence of more than six months' imprisonment justifies sending the case to the Crown Court, or
(c) the offence has been committed whilst the suspect was subject to a Crown Court order then in force.

A Crown Prosecutor will make charging decisions in respect of any *offence triable only on indictment, any either way offence not suitable for sentence in a magistrates' court or not anticipated as a guilty plea, and the offences specified in (b)(i)–(viii) above.*

In a case where any offences under consideration for charging by the police include any offence which must be referred to a prosecutor under the *Guidance* then all offences in the case will be referred to a prosecutor to consider which should be charged.

A police inspector may authorise the charging of an offence referable to a prosecutor in accordance with the *Guidance* where the continued detention of the suspect after charge is justified and where it will not be possible to obtain a Crown Prosecutor's authority to charge before the expiry of any relevant PACE time limit applicable to the suspect. Any cases so charged under this provision must be referred to a prosecutor as soon as possible following charge and not later than the time proposed for the first appearance before a magistrates' court.

Police officers should anticipate the PACE custody time limits and seek a charging decision in good time.

Other points

Where the offence for which the person is arrested is one in relation to which a sample could be taken for a drug test under PACE, s 63B (see p 142), and the custody officer is required by s 37(2) to release that person and decides to release him on bail or decides in pursuance of s 37(7) to release that person without charge on bail, the detention of that person may be continued to enable such a sample to be taken, but this does not permit a person to be detained for more than 24 hours after the relevant time (as defined on p 149).

Regulations made under PACE, s 45A may also provide for the functions relating to an arrested person taken to a non-designated police station (which, in the case of an arrested person taken to a designated police station, are a custody officer's functions under PACE, s 37) to be exercised by video link facilities. No regulations are in force at the time of writing.

CHARGING DETAINEES

Procedures

When the officer in charge of the investigation reasonably believes that there is sufficient evidence to provide a realistic prospect of a detainee's conviction, he must without delay inform the custody officer who will be responsible for considering whether or not the detainee should be charged. Where a person has been detained for more than one offence it is permissible to delay informing the custody officer until these conditions are satisfied in respect of all of the offences. If the detainee is a juvenile, or is mentally disordered or vulnerable, any resulting action must be carried out in the presence of the appropriate adult (if present at the time); if not, it must be repeated in that adult's presence on arrival at the police station when the detainee has been released. There is no power under PACE to detain a person and delay action solely to await the arrival of the appropriate adult. Reasonable efforts should therefore be made to give the appropriate adult sufficient notice of the time the decision (charge, etc) is to be implemented so that he can be present. If the appropriate adult is not, or cannot be, present at that time, the detainee should be released on bail to return for the decision to be implemented when the adult is present, unless the custody officer determines that the absence of the appropriate adult makes the detainee unsuitable for bail for this purpose. Where a custody officer determines in accordance with the DPP's *Guidance on Charging* that there is sufficient evidence to charge the detainee, he may detain that person for no longer than is reasonably necessary to decide how that person is to be dealt with under PACE, s 37(7), (see p 153) including, where appropriate, consultation with the duty prosecutor. The period is subject to the maximum period determined by PACE, ss 41 to 44 ('Limits on period of detention without charge'). Where a reference is made to the CPS a custody officer is responsible for ensuring that all specified information is sent with that reference.

Where a person is arrested under the provisions of CJA 2003 allowing a person to be re-tried after being acquitted of a specified serious offence a superintendent (or above) who has not been directly involved in the investigation is responsible for determining whether the evidence is sufficient to charge.

Where a Crown Prosecutor is unable to make a charging decision based upon the information available at the time, a detainee may be released without charge or on bail. A detainee should be informed of the circumstances of such a decision.

Unless the restriction on drawing adverse inferences from silence applies (see p 107), a detainee who is charged or informed that he may be prosecuted for an offence must be cautioned in the relevant terms set out on p 107. If the restriction does apply, the alternative terms of the caution set out on p 108 must be used. The detainee must also be given a written notice showing particulars of the offence charged, which must include the name of the officer (with the usual two exceptions) and the case reference number. The charge must be stated in simple terms but must show the precise offence in law. The notice must begin with the following words:

'You are charged with the offence(s) shown below' [and be followed by the appropriate caution in the particular circumstances].

Where applicable the notice must be given to the appropriate adult.

The giving of a warning or the service of a notice of intended prosecution required by the RTOA 1988, s 1 does not amount to informing a detainee that he may be prosecuted for an offence and so does not preclude further questioning in relation to that offence.

If, after these procedures have been carried out, a police officer wishes to tell a detainee about any written statement or interview with another person relating to the offence, the detainee must either be handed a true copy of the written statement or have the content of the interview record brought to his attention. Nothing must be done to invite a reply or comment except to caution the detainee that he does not have to say anything, but that anything he does say may be given in evidence, and to remind him of his right to legal advice. If the detainee cannot read, the document may be read to him. In relevant cases, the appropriate adult must be given a copy of the document, or the interview record must be brought to his attention.

When a juvenile is charged with an offence and the custody officer authorises his continued detention after charge, the custody officer must arrange for the juvenile to be taken into the care of a local authority to be detained pending appearance in court unless he certifies that:

(a) for any juvenile, it is impracticable to do so; or
(b) in the case of a juvenile at least 12 years old, no secure accommodation is available and other accommodation would not be adequate to protect the public from serious harm from that juvenile.

Questioning after charge

Further questions relating to the offence may not generally be asked of a person after he has been charged with that offence, or informed that he may be prosecuted for it. Exceptions are: where they are necessary to prevent or minimise harm or loss to some other person or to the public, or to clear up ambiguity in a previous answer or statement; or where it is in the interests of justice that the person should have put to him (and have the opportunity to comment upon) new information concerning the offence; or where he volunteers to make a further statement. This could occur where a detainee mentions that property stolen was sold to a second party, or where a reference is made to a day of the week but no date is given; or where the name of a street is given without mention of the town. It could also occur where it would be advantageous to the detainee and in the interests of justice for him to have another offence taken into consideration by the court, should he be prepared to admit responsibility. In such cases the detainee must be cautioned before further questions are put that he does not have to say anything, but that anything he does say may be given in evidence, and the caution must be written at the head of any statement made. He must be reminded of his right to legal advice.

The Counter-Terrorism Act 2008 (C-TA 2008), s 22 permits a judge of the Crown Court to authorise questioning of a person in England and Wales concerning an offence with which he has been charged or informed that he may be prosecuted, where that offence is a 'terrorism offence' or where the judge considers the offence to have a 'terrorist connection'. See further p 836.

Documentation

A record must be made of anything a detainee says when he is charged. Questions put in an interview after a charge and answers given must be recorded in full during the interview on the forms provided and the record must be signed by the detainee or, if he refuses, by the interviewer and any third parties present. If the questions are audibly recorded or visually recorded the arrangements set out in the Audio Recording Code or Visual Recording Code apply.

Detention after charge

PACE, s 46 requires that where a person: (a) is charged with an offence; and (b) after being charged, is kept in police detention or (in the case of a juvenile) is detained by a local authority, he must be brought before a magistrates' court as soon as practicable, and in any event not later than the first sitting after he is charged (or, if he is to be brought before a magistrates' court in another local justice area, not later than the first sitting of that court after his arrival in that area). If the person is to be brought before a magistrates' court in another area, he must be removed to that area as soon as practicable for the above purpose.

If no magistrates' court is due to sit on the day the person is charged (or on the day he arrives in the other area) or on the next day, the custody officer must inform the designated officer for a local justice area that there is a person in the area who has been detained after charge, and that officer must arrange for a sitting of a magistrates' court not later than the day next following the day on which he is charged (or, if he has been transferred to another area, the day next following the day of his arrival in that area). Christmas Day, Good Friday, and any Sunday do not count as 'days next following' for this purpose; thus, for example, the day next following Saturday is Monday.

None of the above provisions requires a person who is in hospital to be brought before a court if he is not well enough.

BAIL

When an investigating officer brings a person arrested for an offence before the custody officer, the custody officer may decide that there is insufficient evidence to justify a charge and that there is unlikely to be other evidence obtained; or that there is enough evidence to charge at that stage; or that there is not sufficient evidence available at that stage to charge the prisoner, but that there probably will be when further inquiries have been made. If the first of the decisions is reached the prisoner must be released at once without charge. If the second decision is reached the detainee may be released on bail if he is charged or pending a decision by the DPP. If the third decision is reached, he may be released on bail if there are no further grounds for keeping him in custody.

PACE, s 47 provides that, for the purposes of police bail, 'bail' refers to bail subject to a duty:

(a) to appear at a magistrates' court at such time and such place as the custody officer may appoint;
(b) to attend at such police station and at such time as the custody officer may appoint for the purposes of (i) proceedings relating to a live link direction (p 27), and (ii) any preliminary hearing in relation to which any such direction is given; or
(c) to attend at such police station at such time, as the custody officer may appoint for purposes other than those mentioned at (b).

PACE, s 46ZA provides that a defendant answering live link bail is not to be treated as being in police detention, except where, at any time before the beginning of proceedings in relation to a live link direction at a preliminary hearing, he is told by a constable that a live link will not be available or where the court determines not to give a live link direction. In such a circumstance, the defendant is to be treated as arrested for and charged with the offence for which he was granted bail, and as if he had been so charged when that circumstance first applied to him. A person arrested under s 46A for failing to attend at a police station to answer to live link bail, and who is brought to such a station, is to be treated as if he had been arrested for and charged with the offence for which he was granted bail and had been so charged when brought to the station.

By PACE, s 54B, a constable may search at any time any person who is at a police station to answer to live link bail; and any article in the possession of such a person. If the constable reasonably believes a thing in the person's possession ought to be seized on any of the grounds that it:

(a) may jeopardise the maintenance of order in the police station;
(b) may put the safety of any person in the police station at risk; or
(c) may be evidence of, or in relation to, an offence,

the constable may seize and retain it or cause it to be seized and retained. Anything so seized and retained must be recorded. Such a search may only be conducted by a constable of the same sex as the person concerned. An intimate search may not be carried out under the authority of s 54B.

PACE, s 54C empowers a constable to retain a thing seized under s 54B until the person from whom it was seized leaves the police station. However, retention beyond that point of time is permissible in two cases:

(a) a constable may retain something seized under s 54B in order to establish the thing's lawful owner, where there are reasonable grounds for believing that it has been obtained in consequence of the commission of an offence; or
(b) where the thing may be evidence of, or in relation to, an offence, a constable may retain it for use as evidence at a trial or for forensic examination or for investigation, if a photograph or copy would be insufficient for that purpose.

Police bail of person charged

Bail here means bail subject to a duty to appear before a magistrates' court. By PACE, s 47(3A), where a custody officer grants bail to a person subject to a duty to appear before a magistrates' court, he must appoint for the appearance:

(a) a date which is not later than the first sitting of the court after the person is charged with the offence; or
(b) where he is informed by the designated officer for the relevant local justice area that the appearance cannot be accommodated until a later date, that later date.

The Magistrates' Courts Act 1980, s 43 enables a magistrates' court to fix a later time for appearance before it.

PACE, s 38 requires that, when a person arrested otherwise than under a warrant endorsed for bail is charged with an offence, the custody officer, subject to CJPOA 1994, s 25 (bail for defendant charged or convicted for homicide or specified sexual offence after previous conviction for such an offence only if exceptional circumstances: p 163), must order his release from police detention, either on bail or without bail, *unless* the charge is murder or unless the following special rules apply.

Arrested person not a juvenile

PACE, s 38 provides that if the person charged (D) is not a juvenile (ie a person appearing to be 17 or over) the custody officer (CO) must order his release from police detention, with or without bail, unless:

(a) D's name and address cannot be ascertained or CO has reasonable grounds for doubting the truth of a name or address provided; or
(b) CO has reasonable grounds for believing that D will fail to appear in court to answer bail;
(c) if D was arrested for an imprisonable offence, CO has reasonable grounds for believing that the detention of D is necessary to prevent him from committing an offence;
(d) in a case where a sample may be taken from D under PACE, s 63B (see p 142), CO has reasonable grounds for believing that the detention of D is necessary to enable a sample to be taken from him;
(e) if D was arrested for a non-imprisonable offence, CO has reasonable grounds for believing that the detention of D is necessary to prevent him from causing physical injury to any other person or from causing loss of or damage to property;
(f) CO has reasonable grounds for believing that the detention of D is necessary (i) to prevent D from interfering with the administration of justice or with the investigation of offences or of a particular offence; or (ii) for D's own protection.

Arrested person a juvenile

PACE, s 38 provides that if the person charged (JD) is a juvenile (ie a person appearing to be under 17) the custody officer (CO) must order D's release from police detention, with or without bail, *unless* one of the above grounds applies or CO has reasonable grounds for believing that JD should be detained in the interests of his welfare. In the case of (d) this only applies if JD has reached the minimum age specified by s 63B (at present 14).

Section 38 also requires that, where CO authorises JD to be kept in police detention, CO must secure that JD is to be taken to local authority accommodation unless CO certifies:

(a) that by reason of such circumstances as are specified in the certificate, it is impracticable to do so; or

(b) where JD is 12 or over, that no secure accommodation is available and that keeping him in other local authority accommodation would not be adequate to protect the public from serious harm from him.

Such a certificate must be produced to the court before which JD is first brought thereafter.

In a case where JD is charged with a violent or sexual offence, the reference in (b) to protecting the public from serious harm is to protection from death or serious personal injury, whether physical or psychological, occasioned by further such offences by him. '*Sexual offence*' in this context means an offence:

(a) under the Protection of Children Act 1978 (indecent photographs of children);

(b) under any provision of the Sexual Offences Act 2003, Part 1, except s 71 (sexual activity in a public lavatory); or

(c) conspiracy or attempt to commit any of these offences.

'*Violent offence*' means an offence contained in a list of 76 offences against the person, firearms offences, explosives offences, public order offences, and road traffic offences which lead, or are intended or likely to lead, to a person's death or to physical injury, and include an offence which is required to be charged as arson (whether or not it would otherwise fall within this definition).

Except as provided above, neither JD's behaviour nor the nature of the offence charged provides grounds for CO to decide that it is impracticable to arrange for the transfer to local authority care on the grounds of impracticability. Similarly, the lack of secure local authority accommodation does not make it impracticable to transfer him. The availability of secure accommodation is only a factor in relation to a juvenile aged 12 or over when the local authority accommodation would not be adequate to protect the public from serious harm from him.

Detention

If the release of a person arrested is not required by PACE, s 38, CO may authorise him to be kept in police detention, but he may not authorise an adult to be so detained for a sample to be taken under PACE, s 63B after a six-hour period running from the charge.

Where CO authorises a person who has been charged to be kept in police detention he must, as soon as practicable, record the grounds in the custody record in that person's presence, unless the usual exceptions (see p 136) apply.

Use of video conferencing

Regulations made under PACE, s 45A may also provide for the functions relating to an arrested person taken to a non-designated police station (which, in the case of an arrested person taken to a designated police station, are a custody officer's functions under PACE, s 38) to be exercised by video link facilities. No regulations are in force.

Release on bail

PACE, s 47 states that a release on bail under the detention provisions of the Act must be a release on bail granted in accordance with the Bail Act (BA) 1976.

By BA 1976, ss 3 and 3A, a custody officer releasing a person on bail and without charge pending a decision of the DPP or after charge has power to require him to comply with such conditions on bail as appear to him to be necessary:

(a) to secure that the person:
    (i)   surrenders to custody;
    (ii) does not commit an offence whilst on bail;
    (iii) does not interfere with witnesses or otherwise obstruct the course of justice whether in relation to himself or any other person; or
(b) for the protection of the person concerned or, if he is under 18, for his own welfare or in his own interests.

However, the custody officer does not have power to impose a requirement to reside in a bail hostel. A custody officer would not have sufficient time to make the necessary inquiries before such a condition might properly be imposed.

The combined effect of provisions in BA 1976, s 3 is to permit the following additional requirements to be made of a person before he is released on bail:

(a) he may be required:
    (i)   to provide a surety or sureties (see below) to ensure his surrender to custody;
    (ii) to give security for his surrender which may be given by him or on his behalf;
(b) if a parent or guardian of a person under 17 consents to be surety for him, the parent or guardian may be required to ensure that the juvenile complies with conditions imposed under (a)(i)–(iii) above, except that no such condition may be imposed where a juvenile will be 17 before the time appointed for surrender, and that a parent or guardian may not be required to secure compliance with any requirement to which his consent does not extend and may not, in respect of those requirements to which his consent does extend, be bound in a sum greater than £50.

Where a custody officer has granted bail in criminal proceedings, he or another custody officer serving at the same police station may vary the condition of bail at the request of the person bailed, and in doing so he may impose conditions or more onerous conditions.

BA 1976, s 5 provides that, where a custody officer grants bail or varies any conditions of bail, or imposes conditions in respect of bail, he must make a record of the decision and, if requested by the person in question, give that person a copy of the record as soon as practicable; in practice this is always done. BA 1976, ss 5 and 5A provide that, where a custody officer imposes conditions in granting bail or varies any condition of bail, he must give reasons for doing so. This is to enable the person concerned to consider requesting the custody officer to vary those conditions. A note of the custody officer's reasons for imposing (or varying) conditions must be made in the custody record and a copy must be given to the person concerned.

A person who is bailed enters into a promise to appear as prescribed. That promise cannot be set against a recognisance from him that, if he fails to appear, a specific sum of money shall be forfeit. Instead BA 1976 provides its own penalties for non- appearance. In serious cases it may be necessary for a defendant to find one or more 'sureties', that is persons who *undertake to secure his attendance*. This is done by each surety entering a recognisance to forfeit a specified sum to the Crown in the event of the non-attendance of the accused. By the Magistrates' Courts Act 1980, s 43, the magistrates' court before whom the person is bailed to appear may enlarge the recognisances of any sureties.

Breach of bail

See p 166.

Police bail of person not charged

The custody officer, when the investigating officer brings the person detained before him, may decide under PACE, s 37 to release the detainee on bail, such bail being conditioned upon his appearance at a police station at a given time, as opposed to appearing at a court. The custody officer may reach this decision because he considers that there is not sufficient evidence at that stage to charge the detainee, but that there probably will be when further inquiries have been made. Alternatively, he may consider that there is sufficient evidence to charge the detainee but decide under s 37 to release him on bail pending a decision by the DPP about charging or for some other purpose. The requirement to attend at a police station may be cancelled at any time by notice in writing from the custody officer.

PACE, s 47(1B) provides that no application by the prosecutor may be made for a reconsideration of a custody officer's decision to grant bail where a person:

(a) is released under s 37 without charge on bail, or
(b) is released without charge on bail following arrest for breach of bail granted under s 37:
   (i) to enable the DPP to make a decision about charging, or
   (ii) for some other purpose.

Where a person is released on conditional bail in such circumstances, that person will not be entitled to apply to a magistrates' court for bail, but may seek variation of such conditions.

Breach of requirements

PACE, s 46A empowers a constable to arrest without warrant any person who, having been released on bail subject to a duty to attend at a police station, fails to attend at that police station at the time appointed for him to do so. In addition, a person who has been released on bail under s 37, or who has been released on bail after being arrested while on bail granted under s 37, may be arrested without warrant by a constable if he has reasonable grounds for suspecting that the person has broken any conditions of his bail.

Such a person must be taken to that police station as soon as practicable after his arrest.

PACE, s 46A(1ZA) and (1ZB) has the effect of extending the power of arrest under s 46A to cover the case where a defendant attends a police station for a live link bail hearing, but (a) leaves the police station before the beginning of the proceedings relating to the live link hearing without informing a constable that he does not intend to give his consent to the direction, or (b) refuses to be searched under PACE, s 54B.

PACE, s 47(2) provides that nothing in BA 1976 prevents a re-arrest without warrant of a person released on bail subject to a duty to appear at a police station if new evidence justifying a further arrest has come to light since his release. If such a person is re-arrested the detention provisions in PACE apply as if he has been arrested for the first time, but this does not apply to a person arrested under s 46A for failure to surrender to police bail at a police station, or who has surrendered to that bail and who accordingly is deemed to have been arrested for that offence, or to a person who is treated under s 46ZA as if he had been arrested.

The Magistrates' Courts Act 1980 (MCA 1980), s 43 permits the enforcement of the recognisance of any surety for a person granted bail which is conditioned upon appearance at a police station in the same way as if conditioned on appearance at a magistrates' court.

PACE, s 47(6), as amended by the Police (Detention and Bail) Act 2011, provides that, where a person who has been granted police bail and either has attended at a police station or has been arrested under s 46A is detained at a police station, any previous time in custody must be included in any calculation of detention time and any time during which he was on bail must not be so included. In practice, his old custody record will be continued.

Offence

See p 166.

Arrest warrant endorsed for bail

The MCA 1980, s 117 allows a person arrested on a warrant endorsed for bail to be released on bail (ie admitted to bail 'on the spot') without being taken to a police station, provided that the endorsement for bail does not demand sureties. If sureties are required, the person must be taken to a police station.

Bail by a court

Section 4 of BA 1976 states that, when a person who is accused of an offence appears before a magistrates' court or the Crown Court in the course of, or in connection with, the proceedings for the offence, or when he applies to a court for bail or for a variation of the conditions of bail in connection with the proceedings, he must be granted bail if none of the exceptions specified in Sch 1 applies. However, this is subject to the provisions of CJPOA 1994, s 25 (bail for defendant charged with or convicted of murder, attempted murder or manslaughter, or any offence under the Sexual Offences Act 2003, ss 1, 2, 4, 5, 6, 8, 30, and 31 (involving rape, non-consensual penetration, or sexual activity, the same activity with children under 13 and mentally disordered persons), or an attempt to commit any such offence, after a previous conviction for such an offence (or an equivalent offence in another EU state) only to be granted if there are exceptional circumstances justifying it). Section 25 also applies to a police officer considering the grant of bail in such circumstances. A court will also have regard, so far as it is relevant, to any misuse of a controlled drug by the defendant.

Bail may only be granted by a Crown Court judge to a person charged with murder.

Exceptions to right to bail: imprisonable offences

An imprisonable offence is one which is punishable in the case of an adult with imprisonment.

The following exceptions (actual or prospective) to the right to bail apply under BA 1976, Sch 1, Part I, where the offence or one of them is imprisonable, except that they do not apply where the offence or each of them is triable only summarily or where the offence is criminal damage or aggravated vehicle-taking only involving damage where the value of the damage is less than £5,000.

(1) Bail need not be granted if the court is satisfied that there are *substantial grounds for believing that the defendant (D), if released on bail (whether subject to conditions or not), would:*
   (a) *fail to surrender to custody; or*
   (b) *commit an offence while on bail; or*
   (c) *interfere with witnesses or otherwise obstruct the course of justice, whether in relation to himself or any other person.*

   This exception does not apply if the defendant falls within (3), (5), or (7) (prospectively (7) only), unless the court is satisfied as mentioned there.

As from a day to be appointed, this exception will not apply where:

(a) D has attained the age of 18,

(b) D has not been convicted of an offence in the proceedings, and

(c) it appears to the court that there is no real prospect that D will be sentenced to a custodial sentence in the proceedings.

(2) As from a day to be appointed, bail need not be granted if the court is satisfied that there *are substantial grounds for believing that D, if released on bail (whether subject to conditions or not), would commit an offence while on bail by engaging in conduct that would, or would be likely to, cause (a) physical or mental injury to an associated person, or (b) an associated person to fear physical or mental injury.*

(3) Where the offence is an indictable offence (including an either way offence) and it appears to the court that D (who is 18 or over) was on bail in criminal proceedings on the date of that offence, it need not grant bail unless it is satisfied that there is *no significant risk of his committing an offence while on bail (whether subject to conditions or not)*; in the case of any other indictable offence (including an either way offence) D need not be granted bail if it appears that D was on bail in criminal proceedings on the date of the offence.

As from a day to be appointed, these provisions will be replaced by a provision that, where the offence is an indictable offence (including an either way offence), D need not be granted bail if it appears that D was on bail in criminal proceedings on the date of the offence. This provision will not apply where:

(a) D has attained the age of 18,

(b) D has not been convicted of an offence in the proceedings, and

(c) it appears to the court that there is no real prospect that D will be sentenced to a custodial sentence in the proceedings.

(4) Bail need not be granted by the court:

(a) if the court is satisfied that D should be kept in custody for his own protection or, if a child or young person (ie under 17, prospectively 18), for his own welfare; or

(b) if he is in custody under a court order or in pursuance of any authority under the Armed Forces Act 2006; or

(c) if the court is satisfied that there has not been sufficient time to obtain information upon which a decision about bail may be made.

(5) Bail need not be granted by a court if D, having previously been released on bail in, or in connection with, the proceedings, has been arrested under BA 1976, s 7. Where the offence is punishable with life imprisonment and D is 18 or over and, having been released on bail, fails to surrender to custody, the bail must not be granted unless the court is satisfied that there is no significant risk that, if released on bail, he would fail to surrender to custody.

As from a day to be appointed, these provisions are replaced by a provision that D need not be granted bail if, having previously been released on bail in, or in connection with, the proceedings, he has been arrested under BA 1976, s 7. This provision will not apply where:

(a) D has attained the age of 18,

(b) D has not been convicted of an offence in the proceedings, and

(c) it appears to the court that there is no real prospect that D will be sentenced to a custodial sentence in the proceedings.

(6) A person charged with murder must not be granted bail unless the court is of the opinion that there is *no significant risk of him committing, while on bail, an offence*

that would, or would be likely to, cause physical or mental injury to any person other than himself.

(7) An alleged drug offender aged 18 or over who is charged may not be granted bail (unless the court is satisfied (prospectively, is of the opinion) that there is no significant risk of his committing an offence while on bail) where:

   (a) a drug test indicates the presence of a Class A drug;

   (b) the offence is one of possession of a Class A drug *or* the court is satisfied that there are substantial grounds for believing that the misuse of a Class A drug caused or contributed to that offence or provided its motivation; and

   (c) the person concerned does not agree to a dependency/propensity to misuse assessment, or has undergone such assessment but does not agree to participate in any relevant follow-up offered.

   However, these provisions only apply in areas where facilities are in place.

In taking decisions about the words italicised in heads (1) to (7), the court must have regard to the nature and seriousness of the offence; the character, antecedents, associations, and community ties of D; D's record in respect of previous grants of bail; the strength of the evidence available (except where the case is merely being adjourned for inquiries or a report); and if there are substantial grounds for believing that D, if released on bail, would commit an offence while on bail, the risk that D may do so by engaging in conduct that would, or would be likely to, cause physical or mental injury to any person other than D.

BA 1976, Sch 1, Part IA applies where *the imprisonable offence (or each of them) is a summary offence or where the offence is criminal damage, or aggravated vehicle-taking only involving damage, and the value of the damage is less than £5,000.*

BA 1976, Sch 1, Part IA provides that D need not be granted bail if:

(a) there has been a previous failure to surrender to bail and the court believes that this will occur again;

(b) D was on bail when the offence was committed and the court believes that, if released on bail, he would commit an offence while on bail;

(c) the court is satisfied that there are substantial grounds for believing that, if released on bail, D would commit an offence by engaging in conduct likely to cause physical or mental injury, or fear of such injury (prospectively) to an associated person;

(d) the court is satisfied that D should be kept in custody for his own protection, or, if under 17 (prospectively 18), for his own welfare;

(e) D is in custody under the sentence of a court or of an officer under the Armed Forces Act 2006;

(f) having been released on bail in proceedings for the same offence, D has been arrested under BA 1976, s 7 for absconding or breaking conditions of his bail, and the court is satisfied that there are substantial grounds for believing that if released on bail (with or without conditions) D would fail to surrender, commit an offence while on bail, interfere with witnesses or otherwise obstruct the course of justice;

(g) it has not been practical to obtain enough information to take the decisions required by Part 1A due to lack of time since the proceedings began; or

(h) the drug users exception (see (7) above) applies.

As from a day to be appointed, (a), (b), and (f) do not apply in relation to bail where:

(i) D has attained the age of 18,

(ii) D has not been convicted of an offence in those proceedings, and

(iii) it appears to the court that there is no real prospect that D will be sentenced to a custodial sentence in the proceedings.

Exceptions to right to bail: non-imprisonable offences

BA 1976, Sch 1, Pt II provides that D charged with a non-imprisonable offence need not be granted bail if (a), (d), (e), or (f) immediately above applies. In respect of (a) and (f), as from a day to be appointed, they will only apply where D is a child or young person, or has been convicted in the proceedings of an offence.

As from a day to be appointed, D need not be granted bail if, having been released on bail in proceedings for the same offence, D has been arrested under BA 1976, s 7 for absconding or breaking conditions of his bail, and the court is satisfied that there are substantial grounds for believing that if released on bail (with or without conditions) D would, or would be likely to, cause physical or mental injury to an associated person, or to cause an associated person to fear physical or mental injury.

Conditions

In granting bail a court may impose conditions for a number of specified purposes, including those specified for the purposes of conditional police bail.

CJA 2003 makes provision for an appeal to the Crown Court by the person concerned against the imposition of conditions relating to residence, provision of surety or giving a security, curfew, electronic monitoring or contact.

Breach of bail by person under duty to surrender into custody of court: arrest

BA 1976, s 7 provides a power to arrest without warrant. A person (D) who has been released on bail in criminal proceedings and is under a duty to surrender into the custody of a court may be arrested without warrant by a constable if:

(a) the constable has reasonable grounds for believing that D is not likely to surrender to custody, or

(b) the constable has reasonable grounds for believing that D is likely to break any of the conditions of his bail or has reasonable grounds for suspecting that D has broken any of those conditions; or

(c) in a case where D was released on bail with one or more sureties, if a surety notifies a constable in writing that D is unlikely to surrender to custody, and that for that reason the surety wishes to be relieved of his obligations as a surety.

Unless D was arrested within 24 hours of the time appointed for surrender to custody, D must be brought before a justice as soon as practicable and in any event within 24 hours. Christmas Day, Good Friday, and any Sunday are excluded from the calculation of 24 hours. If arrested within 24 hours of the surrender time, D must be brought before the court at which he was to have surrendered to custody.

Failure to surrender: offence

By BA 1976, s 6 a person (D) who has been bailed commits an offence if he fails without reasonable cause to surrender to custody as required. 'Surrender to custody' means surrendering into the custody of the court by entering the dock or of a constable (according to the requirements of the grant of bail) 'at the appointed time and place' and not 'at or about' the appointed time. Consequently, it is no defence that D was only slightly late. Moreover, if D had reasonable cause for failing to surrender at the appropriate time, D commits an offence if he fails to surrender to custody at the appointed place as soon after the appointed time as is reasonably practicable.

It is for D to prove 'reasonable cause'.

Where D has been released on bail by a court and subsequently fails to surrender to custody, D must be brought before the court at which proceedings in respect of which bail was granted are to be heard. No information should be laid (or a written charge issued) to commence proceedings for such failure. The court in question should initiate proceedings for an offence of failing to surrender to bail on its own motion, following an express invitation by the prosecutor. On the other hand, where D has been bailed from a police station to appear either at a magistrates' court or at a police station, proceedings for an offence of failure to surrender to bail should be initiated by way of charging him.

Remand to police custody

By the MCA 1980, s 128, a magistrates' court has power to remand a person for a period not exceeding three clear days (24 hours if a person under 18) to 'detention at a police station' where there is a need to question him about other offences. Section 128 also requires that such a person must not be kept in detention at a police station unless there is a need for him to be detained for the purpose of inquiries into other offences. If he is kept in such detention, he must be brought back to the magistrates' court which committed him as soon as the need for detention for the purpose of inquiries ceases. Such a person must be treated as a person in detention for the purposes of PACE (and therefore he must be treated in accordance with the Detention Code and his detention must be subject to reviews as prescribed by PACE).

CAUTIONS AS ALTERNATIVE TO PROSECUTIONS

Cautions, reprimands, and warnings are an alternative to prosecution where someone admits the offence.

Simple cautions by police officers

Only Crown Prosecutors can decide whether to authorise the offer of a simple caution by a police officer for an offence triable only on indictment; a caution in such a case is exceptional. In all other cases, a Crown Prosecutor may direct that such an offer may be made, but otherwise the decision is one for the custody officer, subject only to any specific instructions issued by his chief officer of police. Simple cautions do not have a statutory basis, although their existence is recognised by a number of statutes.

Conditional cautions

Conditional cautions: adults

The Criminal Justice Act (CJA) 2003, Part 3 (ss 22 to 27) makes provision for 'conditional cautions'. An authorised person (ie a constable, investigating officer, or person authorised by a relevant prosecutor (as defined below)) may give a conditional caution to a person aged 18 or over if:

(a) he has evidence that the person has committed the offence;
(b) a relevant prosecutor (the DPP (CPS) or other public prosecutor) or, prospectively, the authorised person has decided that there is sufficient evidence to charge him and that a conditional caution should be given;
(c) the person admits the offence;
(d) the authorised person has explained the effect of the conditional caution to the offender and has warned him that failure to comply with any of the conditions may result in a prosecution for the offence; and
(e) the offender has signed a document which contains details of the offence; an admission of guilt; his consent to being given a conditional caution; and the conditions attached to the caution.

The conditions which may be attached to such a caution are those which have one or more of the following objects:

(a) facilitating the rehabilitation of the offender;
(b) ensuring that the offender makes reparation for his offence; and
(c) punishing the offender.

Typical conditions are payment of compensation, letters of apology, or drink or drugs referral interventions. CJA 2003, Part 3 provides that the conditions may include a condition that the offender pays a financial penalty (but only in respect of offences or descriptions of offences prescribed by the Secretary of State) which must not exceed one-quarter of the maximum fine to which the offender would have been liable on summary conviction or £250, whichever is the smaller. At the time of writing, these provisions for financial penalties apply only in the police areas of Cambridgeshire, Merseyside, Norfolk, Hampshire, and Humberside.

The Criminal Justice Act 2003 (Conditional Cautions: Financial Penalties) Order 2009 provides that the maximum amount in respect of the following offences is £150:

(a) theft;
(b) removal of article from a place open to the public;
(c) abstracting electricity;
(d) false accounting;
(e) handling stolen goods;
(f) going equipped for burglary or theft;
(g) destroying or damaging property;
(h) threatening to destroy or damage property;
(i) possessing articles with intent to destroy or damage property;
(j) making off without payment;
(k) forgery, etc of documents, contrary to the Road Traffic Act 1988, s 173;
(l) forgery or fraudulent use, etc of vehicle licence or trade licence, etc, contrary to the Vehicle Excise and Registration Act 1994, s 44(1);
(m) fraud;
(n) possession, etc of an article for use in fraud;
(o) making, adapting, supplying, or offering to supply an article for use in fraud;
(p) obtaining services dishonestly.

Each of the offences listed above includes an attempt to commit such an offence.

The Order also prescribes particular maximum penalties for certain other prescribed offences:

Causing harassment, alarm, or distress, Public Order Act 1986, s 5.	£100
Any summary offence except an excluded offence (loitering or soliciting for the purpose of prostitution, Street Offences Act 1959, s 1; any offence under Road Traffic Act 1988; or any offence under Road Traffic Offenders Act 1988) for which a person is liable to a maximum fine at level 5 on the standard scale.	£150
Any summary offence except an excluded offence for which a person is liable on conviction to a maximum fine of level 4 on the standard scale.	£100
Any summary offence for which a person is liable on conviction to a maximum fine at level 1, 2, or 3 on the standard scale other than an excluded offence or causing harassment, alarm, or distress, Public Order Act 1986, s 5.	£50

CJA 2003, Part 3 prospectively provides that a condition may be that the offender attend at a specified place at specified times (but not for more than 20 hours in total, excluding attendances required for the purpose of rehabilitation).

In addition, as from a day to be appointed, an amendment (made by the Legal Aid, Sentencing and Punishment of Offenders Act 2012, s 134) will permit a conditional caution given to a 'relevant foreign offender' to have conditions attached to it that have the object of bringing about his departure from the UK and/or ensuring that he does not return to the UK, whether or not these are in addition to conditions with objects specified above. A 'relevant foreign offender' means someone in respect of whom (a) directions for removal from the UK have been, or may be, given under the Immigration Act 1971, Sch 2 or the Immigration and Asylum Act 1999, s 10, or (b) a deportation order is in force under the Immigration Act 1971, s 5.

The Secretary of State has issued a revised Conditional Cautioning Code of Practice and the DPP has issued *Guidance on Adult Conditional Cautioning*. Provision is made for the National Probation Service to provide assistance in deciding whether conditional cautions should be given, the conditions which might be attached and the supervision and rehabilitation of persons so cautioned.

If an offender fails, without reasonable excuse, to comply with any of the conditions attached to the conditional caution, criminal proceedings may be instituted for the original offence and the document signed by him referred to above is admissible in evidence in those proceedings. The caution ceases to have effect with the institution of proceedings.

Youth conditional cautions

The Crime and Disorder Act 1998 (CDA 1998), s 66A provides for a new type of conditional caution, the youth conditional caution (YCC). The Secretary of State has issued a Code of Practice for such cautions. The YCC provisions currently apply only to 16- and 17-year olds within the police areas of Cambridgeshire, Hampshire, Humberside, Merseyside, and Norfolk. A YCC can be given by an 'authorised person' (as defined on p 167) to an offender aged under 18 (italicised words prospectively deleted) *where the offender has not been previously convicted of an offence* and five requirements are satisfied. These requirements are essentially the same as those in respect of 'Conditional cautions: adults' as set out above, substituting 'YCC' for 'conditional caution'. Where an offender is under 16 the requisite explanation and warning must be given in the presence of the appropriate adult.

The conditions which may be attached must have one or more of these objects:

(a) facilitating the offender's rehabilitation;
(b) ensuring that he makes reparation;
(c) punishing him.

A condition may be attached that the offender attend at a specified place at a specified time (but not for more than 24 hours, excluding attendance required for the purpose of rehabilitation). In addition, a condition requiring the payment of a financial penalty may not be attached to a YCC unless the offence committed is a prescribed offence. The Crime and Disorder Act 1998 (Youth Conditional Cautions: Financial Penalties) Order 2009 prescribes the offences in relation to which a financial penalty condition (maximum amount £75) may be attached to a YCC. They are the same as those listed on pp 168–9. The Order also prescribes particular maximum penalties for the offences in the table on p 169. Those penalties are half those which apply in relation to a conditional caution, except that where that penalty is £50 the penalty in relation to a YCC is £30.

Prospectively, if a YCC is given by an authorised officer, he must refer the offender to a Youth Offending Team as soon as possible.

If the offender fails without reasonable excuse to comply with any of the conditions attached to a YCC he may be prosecuted for the offence in question whereupon the YCC ceases to exist. The document signed by the young offender referred to above is admissible in evidence in proceedings for the offence.

Arrest for failure to comply

CJA 2003, s 24A(1), applied to YCCs by CDA 1998, s 66E, provides that, where a constable has reasonable grounds for believing that the offender has failed, without reasonable excuse, to comply with any of the conditions attached to a conditional caution or a YCC, he may arrest him without warrant. A person so arrested must be:

(a) charged with the offence in question;
(b) released without charge and on bail to enable a decision to be made as to whether he should be charged with the offence (in which case the custody officer must inform him that he is being released pending such a decision); or
(c) released without charge and without bail (with or without any variation in the conditions attached to the caution) (s 24A(2)).

The requirements of s 24A(2) also apply:

(i)   where a person who, having been released on bail under (b) above, returns to a police station to answer bail or is otherwise in police detention at a police station;
(ii)   where a person who, having been released on bail elsewhere than at a police station, attends to answer that bail or is otherwise in police detention; and
(iii) where a person has been arrested for failure to answer to police bail.

Section 24A(2) does not require a person who falls within (i) or (ii) above, and is in police detention in relation to another matter, to be so released if he is liable to be kept in detention in relation to that other matter.

A person arrested under s 24A, or any other person to whom s 24A(2) applies, may be kept in police detention:

(a) to enable him to be dealt with in accordance with s 24A(2) (and this includes power to keep him in detention if necessary for the purpose of investigating whether he has failed, without reasonable excuse, to comply with any of the conditions attached to his conditional caution); or
(b) where applicable, to enable a custody officer to appoint a different or additional time for answering to police bail.

Where a person is not in a fit state to be so dealt with, he may be kept in police detention until he is.

CJA 2003, s 24B provides that certain provisions in PACE (those dealing with limitations on police detention, duties of a custody officer, records kept by a custody officer, duties and responsibilities of custody officers, x-rays, and ultrasound scans) apply, with modifications, to persons arrested for suspected breach of a conditional caution or a YCC as they do to offenders arrested in respect of an offence.

PACE, ss 30 to 31, 34, 36, 37(4)–(6), 38, 39, and 55A apply (with any necessary modifications) to a person arrested under CJA 2003, s 24A.

Reprimands and warnings

Circumstances in which they may be given

Where:

(a) a constable has evidence that a person under 18 has committed an offence; or
(b) the constable considers that there is sufficient evidence to charge the offender;
(c) the offence is admitted;
(d) the offender has not previously been convicted of an offence *or given a youth conditional caution* (YCC);
(e) the constable does not consider that the offender should be prosecuted *or given a YCC,*

the provisions of CDA 1998, s 65, relating to reprimand and warning apply. The words italicised apply only in those areas where a YCC can be given.

Reprimand

Where the circumstances are as set out above, the constable may reprimand the offender if he has not been previously reprimanded or warned.

Warning

The constable may warn the offender if he:

(a) has not been previously warned; or
(b) has been previously warned, the offence was committed more than two years after the date of the previous warning, and the constable considers that the offence is not so serious as to merit prosecution or a YCC. However, this special additional warning may only be given once.

Although a warning will not normally be given to an offender who has not previously been reprimanded, it may be given to such an offender if the constable considers the offence to be so serious as to require a warning.

Procedure

A reprimand or warning under CDA 1998, s 65 must be given at a place approved by the Secretary of State. Where the offender is under 17, the appropriate adult must be present.

A constable giving a reprimand or warning must explain that it may be cited in criminal proceedings in the same circumstances as a conviction. In the case of a warning, the constable must refer the offender to a youth offending team as soon as practicable; the constable must explain this to the offender.

As from a day to be appointed, all the above provisions under the heading 'Reprimands and warnings' are repealed and replaced by the Crime and Disorder Act 1998, ss 66ZA and 66ZB, inserted by the Legal Aid, Sentencing and Punishment of Offenders Act 2012. This effect is as follows:

Youth cautions

A constable may give a child or young person (ie someone under 18) (Y) a youth caution under CDA 1998, s 66ZA if:

(a) he decides that there is sufficient evidence to charge Y with an offence,
(b) Y admits to the constable that Y committed the offence, and
(c) the constable does not consider that Y should be prosecuted or given a YCC in respect of the offence.

A youth caution given to someone under 17 must be given in the presence of an appropriate adult. 'Appropriate adult' means:

(a) a parent or guardian of the child or young person;
(b) if the child or young person is in the care of a local authority or voluntary organisation, a person representing that authority or organisation;
(c) a social worker of a local authority; or
(d) if no person falling within paragraph (a), (b), or (c) is available, any responsible person aged 18 or over who is not a police officer or a person employed by the police.

The constable must explain in ordinary language to Y, and where Y is under 17, to the appropriate adult, the effect of a youth caution, and any guidance which has been given.

The Secretary of State is to issue guidance as to the circumstances in which it is appropriate to give youth cautions, the places where youth cautions may be given, the category of constable by whom youth cautions may be given, and the form which youth cautions are to take and the manner in which they are to be given and recorded.

Effect of youth cautions

CDA 1998, s 66ZB provides as follows.

If a constable gives a youth caution to a person (Y), he must as soon as practicable refer Y to a youth offending team (YOT). On a referral, the YOT must assess Y, and unless they consider it inappropriate to do so, must arrange for Y to participate in a rehabilitation programme.

If Y has not previously been referred under the above provision and has not previously been given a YCC, the YOT may assess Y, and may arrange for Y to participate in a rehabilitation programme. Guidance is to be issued as to what should be included in a rehabilitation programme, the manner in which any failure by a person to participate in a programme is to be recorded, and the persons to whom any such failure must be notified.

If:

(a) a person who has received two or more youth cautions is convicted of an offence committed within two years beginning with the date of the last of those cautions, or

(b) a person who has received a YCC followed by a youth caution is convicted of an offence committed within two years beginning with the date of the youth caution,

the court:

(i) must not conditionally discharge him in respect of the offence unless it is of the opinion that there are exceptional circumstances relating to the offence or him that justify it doing so, and

(ii) where it does so, must state in open court that it is of that opinion and its reasons for that opinion.

A youth caution given to a person, and a report on a failure by a person to participate in a rehabilitation programme, may be cited in criminal proceedings in the same circumstances as a conviction of the person may be cited.

CHAPTER 6

Identification Methods

Identification by witnesses who saw the crime committed may be made in a video identification, identification parade, or similar procedure. There may also be an identification by fingerprints or footwear impressions, or by body samples and impressions. The relevant PACE Code of Practice (Code D: the Code of Practice for the Identification of Persons by Police Officers, hereafter referred to as the Identification Code) is concerned with these methods. The Code is also concerned with the keeping of records and with the taking of photographs of arrested people.

GENERAL PRINCIPLES

The Identification Code provides certain general principles, in addition to the general principles in PACE Codes set out on pp 36–7, which apply to all methods by which identification can be made. It provides that:

(1) References to a police officer include a person designated under the Police Reform Act 2002 (p 282) acting in the exercise or performance of powers or duties under his designation.

(2) Where a record is made of any action requiring the authority of an officer of a specified rank, the name (except in the case of terrorism inquiries, where the warrant or other identification number should be given) and rank of the officer must be included in the record.

(3) All records must be timed and signed by the maker (or his warrant or other identification number given in the case of terrorism inquiries).

(4) In the case of a detained person records must be made in the custody record unless otherwise specified.

(5) Where the consent of the suspect to a procedure is required, the consent of a mentally disordered or mentally vulnerable suspect is only valid if given in the presence of the appropriate adult; and in the case of a juvenile his parent or guardian must consent in addition to the juvenile himself (unless he is under 14, in which case his parent or guardian's consent suffices in its own right). These provisions follow the general rules of good practice.

(6) Where a person is blind or seriously visually impaired or unable to read, the custody officer or identification officer must ensure that his solicitor, relative, the appropriate adult or some other person likely to take an interest in him (and not involved in the investigation) is available to help in checking any documentation. Where the Code requires written consent or signification, the person assisting may be asked to sign if the detained person so wishes.

(7) If any information concerning the processes of an identification must be given to or sought from a suspect, it must be given or sought in the presence of the appropriate adult if the suspect is mentally disordered or mentally vulnerable or a juvenile. If the appropriate adult is not present when the information is first given or sought, the procedure must be repeated in his presence when he arrives. If the

suspect is deaf or there is doubt about his hearing ability or his ability to understand, the information must be given through an interpreter.

(8) Any procedure in the Identification Code involving the participation of a witness who is or appears to be mentally disordered, otherwise mentally vulnerable or a juvenile should take place in the presence of a pre-trial support person unless the witness states that he does not want a support person to be present. A support person must not be allowed to prompt any identification of a suspect by a witness. The support person should not be (or not be likely to be) a witness in the investigation.

The terms 'appropriate adult' and 'solicitor' where they appear above have the same meaning as in the Detention Code (see pp 124–5 and p 102).

Persons other than police officers, who are police staff but not 'designated persons', may be allowed to carry out procedures or tasks at the police station if the law allows. Such persons must be employees under the control of the chief officer of police or employed by a person contracted to provide services relating to persons arrested or otherwise in custody. The custody officer or the officer given custody must ensure that the Identification Code is complied with.

IDENTIFICATION AND RECOGNITION OF SUSPECTS

In Code D, the material under this heading is divided into two parts:

(a) Part A: Identification of a suspect by an eye-witness;
(b) Part B: Evidence of recognition by showing films, photographs and other images.

Part A: identification of a suspect by an eye-witness

Part A applies when an eye-witness has seen someone committing the crime or has seen someone in any other circumstances which tend to prove or disprove his involvement in the crime, for example, close to the scene of the crime, immediately before or immediately after it was committed. Part A sets out the procedures to be used to test the ability of that eye-witness to identify a person suspected of involvement in the offence as the person whom he saw on the previous occasion.

(The Identification Code states that, while it concentrates on visual identification procedures, it does not preclude the police making use of aural identification procedures such as a 'voice identification parade', where they judge that appropriate.)

A guidance note to the Identification Code points out that the eye-witness identification procedures in Part A should not be used to test whether a witness can recognise a person as someone he knows and would be able to give evidence of recognition along the lines that 'On (describe date, time location) I saw an image of an individual who I recognised as AB.' In these cases, the procedures in Part B apply. Except where stated, the provisions of Part A do not apply to the procedures described in Part B and the guidance note.

A record must be made of the description of the suspect as first given by a potential witness. This must be made and kept in a form which enables details of that description to be accurately produced from it, in a visible and legible form, which can be given to the suspect or to his solicitor in accordance with the Identification Code. Unless otherwise specified, the record must be made before the witness takes part in any identification procedures. A copy must be provided to the suspect or his solicitor before any procedures under the Code are carried out.

Methods: where the suspect is known and available

Where the identity of the suspect is known to the police and he is available, the methods of visual identification which may be used are:

(1) *Video identification* (where the witness is shown video images of a known suspect, together with similar images of other people who resemble him). Moving images must be used unless the suspect has unusual features and the identification officer does not consider that replication of a physical feature can be achieved or that it is possible to conceal the location of the feature on the image of the suspect. The identification officer may then decide to make use of video identification but using still images. Annex A to the Identification Code (see p 180) governs video identification.

(2) *Identification parade* (where the witness sees the suspect in a line of other people who resemble the suspect: Annex B to the Identification Code (see p 182) governs this).

(3) *Group identification* (where the witness sees the suspect in an informal group of people: Annex C to the Identification Code (see p 184) governs this).

(4) *Confrontation by a witness* (where the suspect is directly confronted by the witness: Annex D to the Identification Code (see p 187) governs this).

A suspect is 'known' for present purposes if there is sufficient information known to the police to justify the arrest of a particular person (the 'suspect') for suspected involvement in the offence. A suspect is 'available' if he is immediately available to take part in the procedure or will become available in a reasonably short time and is willing to take an effective part in at least one of the identification procedures.

The arrangements for, and conduct of, the four methods of identification are the responsibility of an officer *not below the rank of inspector* who must *not be involved in the investigation;* he is called the 'identification officer'. Unless otherwise specified, the identification officer may allow another officer or a member of police staff to make arrangements for, and to conduct any of, these identification procedures. The identification officer must supervise such persons effectively.

No officer or any other person involved with the investigation may take any part in these procedures beyond the extent required by the procedures, or act as the identification officer. There will be a breach of this prohibition, not only if an officer investigating an offence participates in the actual identification process, but also if he takes the witness to the police station at which an identification is to be attempted. This does not prevent an identification officer from consulting the officer in charge of an investigation to determine which procedure to use.

Circumstances in which an identification procedure must be held

Whenever:

(a) a witness has identified a suspect or purported to have identified him prior to any identification procedure having been held; or

(b) there is a witness available, who expresses an ability to identify the suspect, or where there is a reasonable chance of the witness being able to do so, and he has not been given an opportunity to identify the suspect in any procedure,

and the suspect disputes being the person the witness claims to have seen, an identification procedure must be held unless it is impracticable or would serve no useful purpose in proving or disproving whether the suspect was involved in committing the offence, as where the suspect admits being at the scene of the crime and gives an account of what took place and the eye-witness does not see anything which contradicts that, or where it is not disputed that the suspect is already known to the witness who claims to have recognised the suspect when seeing him commit the crime.

An identification procedure may also be held if the officer in charge of an investigation considers it would be useful.

Identification procedures must be held as soon as practicable.

Selecting an identification procedure

If an identification procedure is to be held, the suspect must initially be offered by the officer in charge a video identification, unless:

(a) this is impracticable, or
(b) an identification parade is practicable and more suitable, or
(c) a group identification is practicable and more suitable than the other two methods.

The identification officer and the officer in charge of the investigation must discuss which option is to be offered. An identification parade may not be practicable because of factors such as the number of witnesses, their state of health, availability and travelling requirements. A video identification would normally be more suitable if, in a particular case, it could be arranged and completed sooner than an identification parade. Before an option is offered the suspect must also be reminded of his entitlement to have free legal advice.

Where a suspect refuses the offer of one of these procedures he must state his reason for doing so and may obtain advice from his solicitor and appropriate adult if present. All such persons must be allowed to make representations as to why another identification procedure should be used. A record must be made of these matters. After consideration of such reason and representations the identification officer must, if appropriate, arrange for an alternative which he considers to be suitable and practicable to be offered to the suspect. If he decides that it is not suitable and practicable to offer an alternative, his reasons must be recorded.

Notice to suspect

Before a video identification, an identification parade or a group identification is arranged, the following must be explained to the suspect (S):

(a) the purpose of the video identification, identification parade, or group identification;
(b) S's entitlement to free legal advice;
(c) the procedures for holding it (including S's right to have a solicitor or friend present);
(d) that S does not have to take part in a video identification, identification parade, or group identification;
(e) that, if S does not consent to and take part in a video identification, identification parade, or group identification, his refusal may be given in evidence in any subsequent trial and police may proceed covertly without his consent or make other arrangements to test whether a witness can identify him;
(f) whether, for the purpose of the video identification procedure, images of S have previously been obtained and, if so, that S may co-operate in providing further suitable images to be used instead;

(g) where appropriate, the special arrangements for juveniles or for mentally disordered or mentally vulnerable persons;

(h) that should S significantly alter his appearance between being offered an identification procedure and any attempt to hold it, this may be given in evidence and the identification officer may then consider other forms of identification;

(i) that a moving image or photograph may be taken of S when he attends for any identification procedure;

(j) whether the witness has been shown photographs, a computerised or artist's composite likeness or similar likeness or picture by the police;

(k) that if S changes his appearance before an identification parade it may not be practicable to arrange one on the day in question or subsequently and, because of his changed appearance, the identification officer may consider alternative methods of identification; and

(l) that S or his solicitor will be provided with details of the description of the suspect as first given by any witnesses who are to attend the video identification, identification parade, group identification, or confrontation.

S must also be given a written 'Notice to Suspect' containing this information and a reasonable opportunity to read it. S must then be asked to sign a second copy of the notice to indicate if he is willing to participate in the making of a video or an identification parade or group identification. The identification officer must retain the signed copy.

The above duties of an identification officer may be performed by the custody officer or any other officer not involved in the investigation if:

(a) it is proposed to release S in order that an identification procedure can be arranged and carried out (as where S is bailed to attend an identification parade) and an inspector is not available to act as identification officer before S leaves the station, or

(b) it is proposed to keep S in police detention while the procedure is arranged or carried out, and waiting for an inspector to act as the identification officer would cause unreasonable delay.

Where the identification officer and the officer in charge of the investigation have reasonable grounds to suspect that, if given the above information and Notice, S would take steps to avoid being seen by a witness in any identification procedure, the identification officer may arrange for images of S for use in a video identification procedure to be obtained before giving the information and Notice. If this is done, S may co-operate in providing new images to be used instead, if suitable.

A witness must not be shown photographs, or photofit, identikit, or similar pictures if the identity of the suspect is known to the police and the suspect is available to take part in a video identification, an identification parade, or a group identification.

Where the suspect is known but not available

Where a known suspect is not available or has ceased to be available, the identification officer may make arrangements for a video identification in accordance with the Identification Code. If necessary, the identification officer may follow the video identification procedures but using *still* images. Any suitable moving or still images may be used and these may be obtained covertly if necessary; covert activity must be limited to that which is necessary. Alternatively, the identification officer may make arrangements for a group identification. He may arrange a confrontation where no other option is available. The requirements for the giving of information to, and seeking it from, the suspect, or for the suspect to have the opportunity to view the images before they are shown to a witness, do not apply if the suspect's lack of co-operation prevents the necessary action.

These provisions would apply where a known suspect deliberately makes himself unavailable in order to delay or frustrate arrangements being made for obtaining evidence. They enable any suitable images of the suspect (moving or still) which are available (eg from custody and other CCTV systems) or can be obtained to be used in a video identification.

Where the identity of the suspect is not known

In such cases, a witness may be taken to a neighbourhood or place to see whether he can identify the person whom he saw on the relevant occasion. Although there can be no control over the general mix of people, their age, sex, race and general description or manner of dress, the principles governing the formal identification procedures must be followed so far as practicable. For example:

(1) Where practicable, a record should be made of any description of the suspect given by the witness, before he is asked to make an identification.
(2) The witness's attention should not be directed towards any individual unless this is unavoidable. This does not prevent a witness being told to look carefully at people who are around, or to look towards a group or in a particular direction if this appears necessary to ensure that the witness does not overlook a possible suspect simply because the witness is looking in the opposite direction and also to enable him to make comparisons between any suspect and others in the area.
(3) Where there is more than one witness, every effort should be made to keep them separate and witnesses should be taken to see whether they can identify a person independently.
(4) Once there is sufficient information to justify the arrest of a particular individual, eg, after a witness makes a positive identification, the formal identification procedures must be adopted for any other witnesses in relation to that individual.
(5) The officer or police staff accompanying the witness must record in his pocket book the action taken as soon as practicable and in as much detail as possible. That record should include the date, time, and place of the previous occasion when the witness claims to have seen the suspect; where any identification was made; how it was made and the conditions at the time (eg, the distance which the witness was from the suspect, the weather and light); if the witness's attention was drawn to the suspect; the reason for this; and anything said by the witness or the suspect about the identification or the conduct of the procedure.

If the identity of a suspect is not known, the showing of photographs, or photofit, identikit or similar pictures must be in accordance with Annex E to the Identification Code (see p 188).

Documentation

A record must be made of any video identification, identification parade, group identification, or confrontation. Where an identification officer considers that it is impracticable to hold a video identification or identification parade requested by the suspect, the reasons must be recorded and explained to the suspect. So must a victim's failure or refusal to co-operate in a video identification, identification parade or group identification. If applicable, the grounds for obtaining images must be recorded. Any records relating to these procedures must be made on the forms provided.

Execution: video identification

The following rules are laid down by Annex A to the Identification Code as to how video identification should be carried out.

General

The arrangements for obtaining and ensuring the availability of a suitable set of images to be used in a video identification must be the responsibility of an identification officer who has no direct involvement with the case.

The set of images must include the suspect and at least eight other people who, so far as possible, resemble the suspect in age, general appearance, and position in life. Only one suspect may appear on any set unless there are two suspects of roughly similar appearance, in which case they may be shown together with at least 12 other people.

If the suspect has an unusual physical feature, eg a facial scar, tattoo or distinctive hairstyle or hair colour which does not appear on the images of the other people available to be used, steps may be taken, electronically or otherwise, to:

(a) conceal the location of the feature on the images of the suspect and the other people; or
(b) replicate that feature on the images of the other people.

The identification officer has discretion to choose whether to conceal or replicate the feature and the method to be used. If an unusual physical feature has been described by the witness, the identification officer should, if practicable, have that feature replicated. If it has not been described, concealment may be more appropriate.

If a feature is concealed or replicated, the reason and whether the feature was concealed or replicated must be recorded.

If the witness requests to view an image where an unusual physical feature has been concealed or replicated without that feature being concealed or replicated, the witness may be allowed to do so.

The images used to conduct a video identification must, so far as possible, show the suspect and other people in the same positions or carrying out the same sequence of movements. They must also show the suspect and other people under identical conditions unless the identification officer reasonably believes:

(a) that because of the suspect's failure or refusal to co-operate or other reasons, this is not practicable; or
(b) that any difference in the conditions would not direct a witness's attention to any individual image.

The reason why identical conditions were not practicable must be recorded.

Provision must be made for each person filmed to be identified by number. If police officers are filmed, any numerals or other identifying badges must be concealed. If a prison inmate is filmed, either as a suspect or not, either all or none of the persons filmed should be in prison clothing.

The suspect or his solicitor, friend, or appropriate adult must be given a reasonable opportunity to see the complete set of images before it is shown to any witness. If the suspect has a reasonable objection to the set of images or any of its participants, he must be asked to state his reason. If practicable, steps must be taken to remove the grounds for objection. If this is not practicable, the suspect and/or his representative must be told why his objections cannot be met. The objection, the reason given for it and why it cannot be met must be recorded.

Before the images are shown the suspect or his solicitor must be provided with the details of the first description of the suspect by any witnesses who are to attend the video identification. The suspect or his solicitor must also be allowed to view any material released to the media by the police for the purpose of recognising or tracing the suspect, provided this is practicable and would not unreasonably delay the investigation.

Where practicable, the suspect's solicitor, or where one is not instructed the suspect himself, must be given reasonable notification of the time and place that it is intended to conduct the video identification in order that a legal representative may attend. The suspect may not be present when the film is shown to a witness. In the absence of a person representing the suspect the viewing itself must be recorded on video. No unauthorised person may be present.

Conduct of video identification

The identification officer must ensure that, before they see the set of images, witnesses cannot communicate with each other about the case, see any of the images, see, or be reminded of, any photograph or description of the suspect or be given any other indication as to the suspect's identity, or overhear a witness who has seen the material. There must be no discussion with the witness about the composition of the set of images and the witness must not be told whether a previous witness has made any identification.

Only one witness may see the set of images at a time. Immediately before the images are seen, the witness must be told that the person he saw might or might not appear in the images he is shown and that if he cannot make a positive identification he should say so. The witness must be advised that at any point he may ask to see a particular part of the set of images or to have a particular image frozen for him to study. Furthermore, it should be pointed out to the witness that there is no limit on how many times he can view the whole set of images or any part of them. However, he should be asked to refrain from making any decision until he has seen the entire set at least twice.

Once the witness has seen the whole set of images at least twice and has indicated that he does not want to view the images or any part of them again, the witness must be asked to say whether the individual he saw in person on an earlier occasion has been shown and, if so, to identify him by number. The witness will then be shown that image to confirm the identification.

Care must be taken not to direct the witness's attention to any one individual image, or to give any other indication of the suspect's identity. Where a witness has previously made an identification by photographs, or a photofit, identikit, or similar picture, the witness must not be reminded of such a photograph or picture once a suspect is available for identification by other means in accordance with the Identification Code. Neither must the witness be reminded of any description of the suspect.

Each witness must be asked after the procedure whether he has seen any broadcast or published films or photographs or any description of suspects relating to the offence; his reply must be recorded.

Image security and destruction

The identification officer must ensure that all relevant material containing sets of images used for a specific identification procedure is kept securely and its movement accounted for. In particular, no one involved in the investigation against the suspect may be permitted to view the material prior to its being shown to any witness.

Like any other photograph, where a video film has been made all copies of it must be destroyed with the exceptions set out on p 215. An opportunity of witnessing the destruction must be given to the suspect, if he so requests within five days of being cleared or informed that he will not be prosecuted:

Documentation

A record must be made of all those participating in or seeing the set of images whose names are known to the police.

A record of the conduct of the video identification must be made on the forms provided. This must include anything said by the witness about the identification or the conduct of the procedure and any reasons why it was not practicable to comply with any provisions of the Identification Code governing the conduct of a video identification.

Identification parades

Identification parades must be carried out in accordance with Annex B to the Identification Code, which provides as follows.

A suspect must be given a reasonable opportunity to have a solicitor or friend present, and he must be asked to indicate his wishes in this respect on a second copy of the 'Notice to Suspect'. A parade may take place in a normal room or in one equipped with a screen permitting witnesses to see members of the parade without being seen.

Before the parade takes place the suspect or his solicitor must be provided with the details of the first description of the suspect by any witnesses who are to attend. The suspect or his solicitor should be allowed to view any material released to the media by the police for the purpose of recognising or tracing the suspect, provided it is practicable to do so and would not unreasonably delay the investigation.

Cases involving prison inmates

If a prison inmate is required for identification, and there are no security problems about his leaving the establishment, he may be asked to participate in an identification parade or video identification.

A parade may be conducted in a Prison Department establishment. If it is, it must be conducted as far as practicable under normal parade rules. Members of the public must make up the parade unless there are serious security or control objections to their admission to the establishment. In such cases, or if a video or group identification is arranged within the establishment, other inmates may participate.

If an inmate is the suspect, he should not be required to wear prison clothing for the parade unless the other persons taking part are other inmates in prison clothing or are members of the public who are prepared to wear prison clothing for the occasion.

Conduct of an identification parade

Immediately before the parade, the suspect must be reminded of the procedure governing its conduct and given the appropriate caution (pp 107 and 108). All unauthorised persons must be excluded from the place where the parade is held.

Once the parade has been formed, everything afterwards in respect of it must take place in the presence and hearing of the suspect and of any interpreter, solicitor, friend or appropriate adult who is present (unless the parade involves a screen, in which case everything said to or by any witness must be said in the hearing and presence of the suspect's solicitor, friend or appropriate adult or be video recorded). No investigating officer should enter the room in which the parade is being held.

The parade must consist of at least eight persons (other than the suspect) who, so far as possible, resemble the suspect in age, height, general appearance and position in life. Where a suspect has an unusual physical feature, for example, a facial scar or tattoo or distinctive hairstyle or hair colour which cannot be replicated on other members of the identification parade steps may be taken to conceal the location of that feature on the suspect and other members of the parade if the suspect and his solicitor or appropriate adult agree. The use of a plaster or a hat may achieve such an objective. It is also permissible to take reasonable steps in good faith to make non-suspects resemble the suspect by the use of make-up, but this should not be done if there is an objection.

One suspect only may be included in a parade unless there are two suspects of roughly similar appearance, in which case they may be paraded together with at least 12 other persons. In no circumstances may more than two suspects be included in one parade, and where there are separate parades they must be made up of different persons.

Where all members of a similar group are possible suspects, separate identification parades must be held for each member of the group unless there are two suspects of similar appearance. Where police officers in uniform form an identification parade, numerals or other identifying badges must be concealed.

When the suspect arrives, he must be asked whether he has any objection to the arrangements for the parade or to any of the other participants in it and to state reasons for any objection made. The suspect may obtain advice from his solicitor or friend, if present, before the parade proceeds. If he has a reasonable objection to the arrangements or to any of the participants, steps must, where practicable, be taken to remove the grounds for objection. Where this is impracticable, the officer must explain to the suspect why his objection cannot be met and the objection, the reason for it and why it cannot be met must be recorded on the forms provided.

The suspect may select his own position in the line. Where there is more than one witness, the identification officer must tell the suspect, after each witness has left the room, that he can if he wishes change position. Each position must be clearly numbered, whether by means of a numeral laid on the floor in front of each parade member or by other means.

Appropriate arrangements must be made to ensure, before they attend the parade, that witnesses are not able to:

(a) communicate with each other or overhear a witness who has already seen the parade;
(b) see any member of the parade;
(c) see, or be reminded of, any photograph or description of the suspect, nor are given any other indication of his identity; or
(d) see the suspect, either before or after the parade.

The person conducting a witness to the parade must not discuss with him its composition; in particular, he must not disclose whether a previous witness has made any identification.

Witnesses must be brought in one at a time. Immediately before a witness inspects the parade, he must be told that the person he saw might or might not be on the parade and that if he cannot make a positive identification he should say so. The witness must also be told that he should not make any decision before looking at each member of the parade at least twice. When the officer or police staff member conducting the procedure is satisfied that the witness has properly looked at each member of the parade, he must ask him whether the person he saw in person on an earlier relevant occasion is on the parade and, if so, to indicate the number of the person concerned. Where this takes place behind a screen it is desirable for the witness to be asked to make a note of the number of the person identified so that he may give direct evidence of that fact. However, if a witness is unable to recall that number at a subsequent trial, evidence from the person who conducted the parade as to the number indicated by the witness is admissible as there is statutory authority for its admission. If the witness makes an identification after the parade has ended, the suspect and, if present, his solicitor, interpreter or friend must be informed. Where this occurs, consideration should be given to allowing the witness a second opportunity to identify the suspect.

If a witness wishes to hear any parade member speak, or to see him adopt any specified posture or move, the witness must first be asked whether he can identify any persons on the parade on the basis of appearance only. When the request is to hear members of the parade speak, the witness must be reminded that the participants in the parade have been chosen on the basis of physical appearance only. Members of the parade may then be asked to comply with the witness's request to hear them speak or to see them move or adopt any specified posture.

If the witness requests that the person indicated by him remove anything used to conceal the location of an unusual physical feature, that person may be asked to remove it.

Each witness must be asked after the parade whether he has seen any broadcast or published films or photographs or any description of suspects relating to the offence; his reply must be recorded.

When the last witness has left, the suspect must be asked whether he wishes to make any comments on the conduct of the parade.

Documentation

A video recording of the parade must normally be taken. Where this is impracticable, a colour photograph must be taken. A copy of the video or photograph must be supplied, on request, to the suspect or his solicitor within a reasonable time. The rules about the destruction and retention of such a video or photograph are the same as those described on p 215.

If any person is asked to leave the parade because he is interfering with its conduct, the circumstances must be recorded. A record must be made of all those present at an identification parade whose names are known to the police. A record of the conduct of the parade must be made on the forms provided, including anything said by the witness or suspect about any identifications or the conduct of the procedure, and any reasons why it was not practicable to comply with any provision of the Identification Code.

Group identification

Group identification must be carried out in accordance with Annex C to the Identification Code, which provides as follows.

General

A group identification may take place either with the suspect's consent and co-operation or covertly without his consent.

The location is a matter for the identification officer, although he may take into account representations made by a suspect, appropriate adult, his solicitor or friend. It should be somewhere where other people are passing by, or waiting around informally, in groups so that the suspect is able to join them and is capable of being seen at the same time as others in the group, for example where people are leaving an escalator, walking through a shopping centre, or in queues. Where group identification is carried out covertly, its location depends on where the suspect can be found (along with a number of other people). A suitable location might be a route regularly travelled by the suspect, including buses, trains, and public places frequented by him.

While it is appreciated that the nature and general description of people at the location cannot be controlled, the identification officer must, in selecting it, consider the general appearance and number of persons likely to be present. In particular, he must reasonably expect that persons broadly similar to the suspect will appear from time to time during the period of the witness's observation. A group identification need not be held where the identification officer believes that, because of the unusual appearance of the suspect, none of the practicable locations is likely to make the identification fair.

Immediately after a group identification (whether with or without the suspect's consent) a colour photograph or a video should be taken of the scene, where practicable, so as to give a general impression of the scene and the number of people present. Alternatively, if practicable, the group identification may be video recorded. If such a photograph or video is impracticable, then a photograph or film of the scene may be made later when practicable.

If, at the time of the identification, the suspect is on his own rather than in a group, it remains a group identification.

Before the group identification takes place the suspect or his solicitor must be provided with details of the first description of the suspect by any witness attending it, and should be allowed to view any material released to the media for the purpose of recognising or tracing the suspect, provided that it is practicable to do so and it will not unreasonably delay the investigation. After the procedure each witness must be asked whether he has seen any broadcast or published films or photographs or any descriptions of suspects relating to the offence; his reply must be recorded.

Identification with the consent of the suspect

A suspect must be given a reasonable opportunity to have a solicitor or friend present. He must be asked to indicate his wishes on a second copy of the Notice to Suspect. The witness, person carrying out the procedure, suspect's solicitor, appropriate adult, friend, and any interpreter for the witness may be concealed from the sight of the persons in the group if this facilitates the identification. The person conducting a witness to the location must not discuss the forthcoming group identification nor disclose whether a previous witness has made an identification.

Anything said to or by a witness during the procedure regarding the identification must be said in the presence and hearing of those at the procedure. Witnesses who have not yet attended the identification must not be able; (a) to communicate with each other about the case or overhear a witness who has already been given an opportunity to see the suspect in the group; (b) to see the suspect; or (c) to see or be reminded of any photograph or description of the suspect or to be given any other indication of his identity. Witnesses must be brought to the place singly and must be told that the person they saw might or might not be in the group and that if they cannot make a positive identification they should say so. The witness must then be asked to observe the group; the manner of doing so will depend upon whether the group is stationary or moving.

Moving group   When the group in which the suspect is to appear is moving, eg leaving an escalator, the following provisions apply.

If two or more suspects consent to a group identification, they should each be subject to different identification procedures, which may be conducted consecutively. The person conducting the procedure must ask the witness to observe the group and ask him to point out anyone he thinks he saw on the earlier occasion. The suspect should then be allowed to take up whatever position in the group he prefers. When an identification is made, the witness must, where practicable, be asked to take a closer look to confirm identification. If this is impracticable, or the witness is unable to confirm the identification, the witness must be asked how sure he is that the person is the relevant person. The duration of the identification process must be such as the person conducting the procedure reasonably believes necessary for the witness to be able to make comparisons between the suspect and other individuals of broadly similar appearance.

Stationary group   When the group in which the suspect is to appear is stationary, eg people in a queue, the following provisions apply.

If two or more suspects consent to a group identification, there should generally be two separate procedures. However, if they are of broadly similar appearance, they may appear in the same group. Separate stationary group identifications must consist of different people.

The suspect may select his position. Where there is more than one witness, the suspect must be told, out of sight and hearing of any witness, that he may change his position. The witness must be asked to pass along or amongst the group and to look at each person at least twice before making an identification. Once the witness has done so, he must be asked if the person he saw previously is in the group and to indicate that person by any means considered appropriate by the person conducting the identification. If this is not practicable, the witness will be asked to point out that person. He must, where practicable, be asked to take a closer look and confirm his identification. If this is impracticable, he must be asked how sure he is that the person is the one seen on the earlier occasion.

Rules common to moving and stationary groups   An unreasonable delay by the suspect in joining the group, or (having joined the group) his deliberate self-concealment from the sight of the witness, may be considered as a refusal to co-operate in the identification.

Where a witness identifies someone other than the suspect, that person should be asked if he is prepared to give his name and address. He is not obliged to do so. There is no duty to record persons present in the group or at the place where the procedure is conducted.

At the end of the procedure the suspect must be asked to comment on the conduct of the procedure. Unless previously informed, the suspect must be told of any identifications made by witnesses.

Group identifications without suspect's consent

These should, so far as possible, follow the rules set out above. As such an identification will take place without the suspect's knowledge, no solicitor, etc will be present. Any number of suspects may be identified at the same time.

Group identifications in police stations

These must only take place for reasons of security or safety, or because it is impracticable to hold them elsewhere. The group identification may be in a room equipped with a one-way screen, or elsewhere in a police station. Safeguards applicable to identification parades must be followed where practicable.

Group identifications involving prison inmates

These may only take place in a prison or police station. They must follow the procedure which is applicable to group identifications in a police station. Where a group identification takes place in a prison, other inmates may participate. If the suspect is in prison clothing, all persons taking part must be so dressed.

Documentation

Where a photograph or video is taken a copy must be supplied on request to the suspect or his solicitor within a reasonable time. Such material must be destroyed in accordance with the rules described on p 215. A record of the conduct of the identification must be made on the forms provided, and must include anything said by the witness or suspect about any identification or the conduct of the procedure and any reason why it was impracticable to comply with any of the relevant provisions of the Code.

Confrontation by a witness

A confrontation does not require the suspect's consent.

The rules concerning confrontation, which are set out in Annex D to the Identification Code, are simple.

Before the confrontation takes place:

(a) the witness must be told that the person he saw might or might not be the person he is to confront and that if he cannot make a positive identification he should say so;
(b) the suspect or his solicitor must be provided with the details of the first description of the suspect given by any witness who is to attend the confrontation.

The note should be made available for examination at trial to act as a safeguard against the risk of auto-suggestion. Where a broadcast or publication has been made for the purpose of recognition and tracing of suspects, the suspect or his solicitor should also be allowed to view any material released by the police to the media, provided that it is practicable to do so and would not unreasonably delay the investigation.

Force cannot be used to make the suspect's face visible to a witness.

The suspect must be confronted independently by each witness, who must be asked 'is this the person?' If the witness identifies the person but is unable to confirm the identification he must be asked how sure he is that the person is the person he saw on the earlier relevant occasion. Confrontation must take place in the presence of the suspect's solicitor, interpreter or friend, unless this would cause unreasonable delay.

The confrontation should normally take place in the police station, either in a normal room or one equipped with a screen permitting a witness to see the suspect without being seen. In both cases, the procedures are the same, except that a room equipped with a screen may be used only when the suspect's solicitor, friend or appropriate adult is present or the confrontation is recorded on video.

After the confrontation each witness must be asked whether he has seen any broadcast or published films or photographs or any descriptions of suspects relating to the offence; his reply must be recorded.

Informal identification

Informal evidence of identification may be admitted provided that the evidence was obtained in good faith and has no adverse effect on the fairness of the proceedings.

Where a suspect and a witness are well known to each other, there is less need for any formal out-of-court identification procedure to be used. However, where the suspect asks for a parade, the procedure is governed by the Identification Code and the failure to provide one may result in the exclusion of evidence, whether the suspect and the witness were previously known to one another or not.

Part B: evidence of recognition by showing films, photographs, and other images

Part B of the Identification Code's section on the identification and recognition of suspects applies when any person, including a police officer, is asked if he recognises anyone whose image he sees in a film, photograph or other visual medium as being someone he knows.

A guidance note states that the admissibility and value of evidence of recognition obtained when carrying out the procedures in Part B may be compromised if before the person is recognised, the witness who has claimed to know that person is given or is made, or becomes aware of, information about that person which was not previously known to him personally but which he has purported to rely on to support his claim that the person is in fact known to him.

Part B provides that the films, photographs and other images must be shown on an individual basis to avoid any possibility of collusion and, to provide safeguards against mistaken recognition, the showing must as far as possible follow the procedures for video identification *if the suspect is known* (see p 180) or the procedure in Annex E for identification by photographs if the suspect is not known.

Annex E provides as follows.

An officer of the rank of sergeant or above must be responsible for supervising and directing the showing of photographs, but the actual showing may be done by a constable or police staff. The supervising officer must confirm that the first description of the suspect given by the witness has been recorded before the witness is shown the photographs. If he is unable to confirm that the description has been recorded, he must postpone the showing.

Only one witness may be shown photographs at any one time. He must be given as much privacy as practicable and must not be allowed to communicate with any other witness in the case. The witness must be shown not less than 12 photographs at a time, which, as far as possible, must all be of a similar type.

When the witness is shown photographs, he must be told that the photograph of the person whom he has said that he has previously seen might or might not be among them and that if he cannot make a positive identification he should say so. The witness must be told not to make a decision until he has viewed at least 12 photographs. He must not be prompted or guided in any way but must be left to make any selection without help. If a witness makes a positive identification from photographs then, unless the person identified is otherwise eliminated from the inquiries or is not available, other witnesses must not be shown photographs. However, both they and the witness who has made the identification must be asked to attend a video identification, identification parade or group identification unless there is no dispute about the identification of the suspect. If the witness makes a selection but is unable to confirm the identification the person showing the photographs must ask the witness how sure he is that the photograph indicated is the person that he saw on a previous occasion.

Where the use of computerised or artist's composite likeness or similar likeness has led to there being a known suspect who can be asked to participate in a video identification, an identification parade or a group identification, that likeness may not be shown to other potential witnesses.

Where a witness attending a video identification, an identification parade or a group identification has previously been shown photographs or computerised or artist's composite likeness or similar likeness, the suspect and his solicitor must be informed of this fact before the video identification, identification parade, or group identification takes place. The officer in charge of the investigation is responsible for informing the identification officer of this fact.

None of the photographs used may be destroyed, whether or not an identification is made, since they may be required for production in court. The photographs should be numbered and a separate photograph taken of the frame or part of the album from which the witness made an identification as an aid to reconstituting it.

Documentation

Part B requires that a record of the circumstances and conditions under which the person is given an opportunity to recognise the individual must be made and that the record must include a record of:

(a) whether the person knew or was given information concerning the name or identity of any suspect;
(b) what the person has been told before the viewing about the offence, the person(s) depicted in the images or the offender and by whom;
(c) how and by whom the witness was asked to view the image or look at the individual;
(d) whether the viewing was alone or with others, and if with others the reason for it;
(e) the arrangements under which the person viewed the film or saw the individual and by whom those arrangements were made;
(f) whether the viewing of any images was arranged as part of a mass circulation to police and the public or for selected persons;
(g) the date, time and place images were viewed or further viewed or the individual was seen;
(h) the times between which the images were viewed or the individual was seen;
(i) how the viewing of images or sighting of the individual was controlled and by whom;
(j) whether the person was familiar with the location shown in any images or the place where he saw the individual and if so, why; and
(k) whether or not on this occasion, the person claims to recognise any image shown, or any individual seen, as being someone known to him, and if he does:
   (i)   the reason,
   (ii)   the words of recognition,
   (iii) any expressions of doubt,
   (iv)   what features of the image or the individual triggered the recognition.

The above record may be made by:

(a) the person who views the image or sees the individual and makes the recognition; or
(b) the officer or police staff in charge of showing the images to the person or in charge of the conditions under which the person sees the individual.

Showing films and photographs of incidents and information released to the media

Films, photographs (including video recordings by security cameras) or other images may be shown to the public through the national or local media, or to police officers, for the purposes of recognition and tracing suspects. However, when such material is shown to obtain evidence of recognition, the procedures in Part B apply.

IDENTIFICATION BY FINGERPRINTS AND FOOTWEAR IMPRESSIONS

PACE, ss 61 and 61A and the Identification Code deal with the taking of fingerprints (which term includes palmprints) and footwear impressions. These provisions do not apply in respect of someone arrested as a suspected terrorist under TA 2000, s 41 or someone subject to Terrorist Prevention and Investigation Measures; separate rules apply to such a person (see Chapter 28).

Fingerprints: consent

A person's fingerprints may be taken only with the appropriate consent (which must be in writing if given at a police station) or (in the circumstances set out below) without the appropriate consent. As to 'appropriate consent', see p 197.

Where fingerprints are taken with the appropriate consent, the person must be informed that they may be subject to a speculative search against other fingerprints and that they may be retained in accordance with PACE, s 64 (see p 203 (prospectively replaced). A record must be made of these matters and that the person has been so informed.

Taking fingerprints without consent

Powers to take fingerprints from a person over the age of 10 without the appropriate consent are provided by PACE, s 61. This provides that fingerprints may be taken without the appropriate consent from a person:

(1) If he is detained in consequence of his arrest for a recordable offence (see p 198) (s 61(3)), or he has been charged with such an offence or informed that he will be prosecuted for it, and he has not had his fingerprints taken in the course of the investigation of the offence by the police (s 61(4)). *(By s 61(3A), where such a person has had his fingerprints taken in the course of the investigation by the police, this does not prevent a second set of prints from being taken if the first did not constitute a full set or are of unsatisfactory quality for their purpose.)*

(2) Where he has answered to bail to appear at a court or police station, if the court, or an officer of at least the rank of inspector, authorises them to be taken (s 61(4A)). This may be done where the court or officer reasonably believes that a person who has surrendered to bail is not the person admitted to bail and the person bailed has been previously fingerprinted, or the person who has answered to bail claims to be a different person from the person who had his fingerprints taken on a previous occasion.

(3) If he has been arrested for a recordable offence and released, and:
   (a) in the case of a person who is on bail, he has not had his fingerprints taken in the course of the investigation; or
   (b) in any case, he has had his fingerprints taken in the course of that investigation but s 61(3A) applies (s 61(5A)).

(4) If he has been charged with a recordable offence or informed that he will be reported for such an offence and:
   (a) he has not had his fingerprints taken in the course of the investigation; or
   (b) he has had his fingerprints taken in the course of that investigation but s 61(3A) applies (s 61(5B)).

(5) If he has been convicted of a recordable offence (or, prospectively, in PACE, been found not guilty by reason of insanity or found under a disability but to have done the act charged) or he has been cautioned for an admitted recordable offence, or

(prospectively repealed) he is a child or young person and has been warned or reprimanded under the Crime and Disorder Act 1998, s 65 for such an offence (s 61(6)). Fingerprints may only be taken under this provision (a) if the person has not had his fingerprints taken since he was convicted or cautioned or (prospectively repealed) warned or reprimanded, or (b) if he has had his fingerprints taken since then but s 61(3A) applies (s 61(6ZA)). Fingerprints may only be taken under s 61(6) with the authorisation of an officer of at least the rank of inspector, who may only give such an authorisation if satisfied that taking the fingerprints is necessary to assist in the prevention or detection of crime. Where fingerprints are taken under s 61(6), they may be subjected to a speculative search (s 63A(1E)).

(6) If a constable reasonably suspects that the person is committing or attempting to commit an offence, or has committed or attempted to commit an offence, and the name of the person is unknown to, and cannot be readily ascertained by the constable, or the constable has reasonable grounds for doubting whether a name furnished by the person as his name is his real name (s 61(6A)). This provision will apply to taking fingerprints at a police station or any other place. Before the power under s 61(6A) is exercised, the constable should:

(a) inform the person of the nature of the suspected offence and why he is suspected of committing it;

(b) give him a reasonable opportunity to establish his real name before deciding that his name is unknown etc or that there are reasonable grounds to doubt that a name which he has given is his real name;

(c) as applicable, inform the person of the reason why his name is not known etc or of the grounds for doubting that a name which he has given is his real name, including, for example, the reason why a particular document the person has produced to verify his real name, is not sufficient.

The taking of fingerprints by virtue of s 61(6A) does not count for the purposes of PACE as taking them in the course of an investigation of an offence by the police. Fingerprints taken under this power will have to be destroyed as soon as the purpose for which they were taken has been achieved. They will not be retained or added to the National Automated Fingerprint Identification System (NAFIS). The reason for s 61(6A) is that the police may now use mobile digital fingerprint readers which are connected to NAFIS. This enables the taking of fingerprints (of two fingers) at a place other than a police station. These can immediately be checked to assist an officer in deciding upon a course of action. Such fingerprints will also be subject to a speculative search against the database of fingerprints recovered from crime scenes.

(7) If:

(a) the person has been 'convicted' of an offence under the law in force in a country territory outside England and Wales;

(b) the act constituting the offence would constitute a qualifying offence if done in England and Wales (whether or not it constituted such an offence when the person was convicted); and

(c) either (i) the person has not had his fingerprints taken on a previous occasion under the present provision, or (ii) he has had his fingerprints so taken on a previous occasion but s 61(3A) applies (s 61(6D) and (6E)).

A 'conviction' for these purposes includes a finding equivalent to one of not guilty by reason of insanity or of disability but that the act charged was committed.

Fingerprints may only be so taken with the authorisation of an officer of at least the rank of inspector, who must be satisfied that taking the fingerprints is necessary to assist in the prevention or detection of crime (s 61(6F) and (6G)).

Where fingerprints have been taken under s 61(6D), (6E), they may be subjected to a speculative search (s 63A(1F)).

A 'qualifying offence' means murder, manslaughter, false imprisonment, kidnapping, or an offence under the Offences Against the Person Act 1861, ss 4, 16, 18, 20–24 or 47, the Explosive Substances Act 1883, ss 2 or 3, the Children and Young Persons Act 1933, s 1, the Criminal Law Act 1967, s 4 (in relation to murder), the Firearms Act 1968, ss 16–18, the Theft Act 1968, ss 8 (prospectively), 9 or 10 or (where fatal accident involved) s 12A, the Criminal Damage Act 1971, s 1 (where required to be charged as arson), the Protection of Children Act 1978, s 1, the Aviation Security Act 1982, s 1, the Child Abduction Act 1984, s 2, the Aviation and Maritime Security Act 1990, s 9, the Sexual Offences Act 2003, ss 1–19, 25, 26, 30–41, 47–50, 52, 53, 57–59, 59A (prospectively replacing s 57–59), 61–67, 69, and 70, or the Domestic Violence, Crime and Victims Act 2004, s 5, an offence listed under the Counter-Terrorism Act 2008 (C-TA 2008), s 41, aiding, abetting, counselling, or procuring one of the above offences, attempting or conspiring to commit any of them, or an offence of encouraging or assisting crime in relation to any of them.

Any power under PACE, s 61 to take fingerprints without the appropriate consent must be exercised by a constable. Reasonable force may be used.

Before any fingerprints are taken without the appropriate consent under any power under PACE, s 61, the person must be informed of:

(a) the reason why his fingerprints are to be taken;
(b) the power under which they are to be taken;
(c) the fact that the relevant authority has been given where it is required;
(d) that his fingerprints may be the subject of a speculative search against other fingerprints; and
(e) that his fingerprints may be retained in accordance with PACE, s 64 (see p 203) unless they were taken under the power in s 61(1A) when they must be destroyed after they have been checked. (As to the prospective replacement of s 64, see p 204.)

A record must be made as soon as possible of these matters and of the fact that the person has been so informed. If a person is detained at a police station when the fingerprints are taken, the reason must be noted on his custody record. If force is used a record must be made of the circumstances and those present.

Taking footwear impressions

PACE, s 61A provides that, with the exceptions below, no impression of a person's footwear may be taken without the appropriate consent. Consent to the taking of an impression of a person's footwear must be in writing if it is given at a time when he is at a police station.

Where a person is detained at a police station, a footwear impression may be taken without appropriate consent from a person over the age of 10 if:

(a) he is detained in consequence of his arrest for a recordable offence (p 198), or has been charged with a recordable offence, or informed that he will be reported for a recordable offence, and

(b) he has not had an impression taken of his footwear in the course of the investigation of the offence by the police.

Reasonable force may be used. A record must be made as soon as possible of the reason
for the non-consensual taking and, if force is used, of the circumstances and those
present. If a person mentioned in (a) has already had an impression of his footwear
taken in the course of the investigation of the offence, that fact must be disregarded if the
impression taken previously is incomplete, or is not of sufficient quality to allow satisfactory analysis, comparison or matching (whether in the case in question or generally).
An impression taken without the appropriate consent must be taken by a constable.

In all cases where a footwear impression is taken, the person must be informed
beforehand of the reason the impression is being taken, that the impression may be
retained and may be the subject of a speculative search, and this must be recorded as
soon as practicable. If the person is at a police station, the fact must be recorded in the
custody record. The person must also be informed that, if destruction of the impression
is required, he will be allowed to witness that destruction.

IDENTIFICATION BY BODY SAMPLES, SWABS AND IMPRESSIONS

PACE, ss 62 to 64 (s 64 prospectively replaced) contain the basic provisions in this area,
but (within the terms of these sections) it is the Identification Code which sets out the
detailed procedures. The powers set out below do not apply in respect of a suspected
terrorist arrested under TA 2000, s 41 or of someone subject to Terrorism Prevention
and Investigation Measures; separate rules apply to such a person (see Chapter 28).

Intimate samples

An intimate sample means a sample of blood, semen, or any other tissue fluid, urine, or
pubic hair, a dental impression, or a swab taken from any part of a person's genitals or
from a person's body orifices other than the mouth. Intimate samples are governed by
PACE, s 62.

An intimate sample may be taken from a person in police detention only with the appropriate consent (p 197) in writing and with the requisite authorisation (below) (s 62(1)).

An intimate sample may be taken from a person not in police detention if: (a) in the
course of an investigation into an offence, two or more non-intimate samples have been
taken which have proved unsuitable or insufficient for a particular form of analysis, (b) the
requisite authorisation is given, and (c) the appropriate written consent is given (s 62(1A)).

In these two cases an intimate sample may only be taken if an officer of at least the
rank of inspector authorises it to be taken because he has reasonable grounds for suspecting the involvement of the person in a recordable offence (p 198) and for believing
that the sample will tend to confirm or disprove this involvement.

An intimate sample may also be taken from a person with the appropriate written
consent where:

(a) two or more non-intimate samples suitable for the same means of analysis have
been taken from the person under s 63(3E) and (3F) (persons convicted of offence
outside England and Wales, etc) but have proved insufficient; and
(b) a police officer of at least the rank of inspector (who must be satisfied that taking
the sample is necessary to assist in the prevention or detection of crime) authorises
it to be taken (s 62(2A)).

Before an intimate sample is taken from a person:

(1) He must be informed:
  (a) of the reason;
  (b) that authorisation has been given and the provisions under which it has been given; and
  (c) that a sample taken at a police station may be the subject of a speculative search.

  The reason referred to in (a) must include, except in a case where the sample is taken under s 62(2A), a statement of the nature of the offence in which it is suspected that the person has been involved. After an intimate sample has been taken from a person, the following must be recorded as soon as practicable: the matters referred to in (a) and (b); if the sample was taken at a police station, the fact that the person has been informed as specified in (c); and the fact that the appropriate consent was given.

(2) He must be warned that a refusal without good cause may harm his case in any proceedings against him. The Code suggests the use of the following words:

> 'You do not have to provide this sample/allow this swab or impression to be taken, but I must warn you that if you refuse without good cause, your refusal may harm your case if it comes to trial.'

  The warning must be recorded.

(3) He must be reminded of his entitlement to free legal advice. A record must be made in the custody record of the giving of this reminder if the person is in police custody.

Where a person refuses, without good cause, to consent to the taking of an intimate sample, in any proceedings for an offence, a court may draw such inferences from the refusal as appear proper.

An intimate sample, other than a sample of urine, may only be taken from a person by a registered medical practitioner or a registered nurse or registered paramedic. A dental impression may only be taken by a registered dentist.

Non-intimate samples

There are separate provisions, contained in PACE, s 63, for the taking of a *non-intimate sample*.

A non-intimate sample means hair, other than pubic hair, which includes hair plucked by the root; a sample taken from a nail or under a nail; a swab taken from any part of the body other than a part from which a swab taken would be an intimate sample; saliva; or a 'skin impression' which means any record, other than a fingerprint, which is a record, in any form and produced by any method, of the skin pattern and any other physical characteristics or features of the whole, or any part of, a person's foot or any other part of the body.

Where hair samples are taken for the purpose of DNA analysis (rather than for other purposes such as making a visual match) the suspect should be permitted a reasonable choice as to the part of the body the hairs are to be taken from. When hairs are plucked they should be plucked individually unless the suspect prefers otherwise; no more should be plucked than the plucker reasonably considers necessary for a sufficient sample.

Except in the following cases, a non-intimate sample may be taken from a suspect only with the appropriate consent (p 197) in writing. The exceptional cases are:

(1) A non-intimate sample may be taken from a person without the appropriate consent if:
   (a) he is in detention as a result of an arrest for a recordable offence (p 198), and he has not had a non-intimate sample of the same type and from the same part of the body taken in the course of the investigation of the offence by the police, or he has had such a sample taken but it proved insufficient (s 63(2A)–(2C)); or
   (b) he is being held in custody by the police on the authority of a court, and an officer of at least the rank of inspector has authorised it to be taken without consent (s 63(3)). Such authorisation may only be given where that officer has reasonable grounds to suspect that the offence in question is a recordable offence and that the sample will tend to confirm or disprove the suspect's involvement in it. An authorisation must not be given if the non-intimate sample concerned consists of a skin impression and such an impression has already been taken in the course of the investigation of the offence and that impression did not prove to be insufficient. Where such authorisation is given, the suspect must be informed, before it is taken, of the grounds on which it has been given, including the nature of the suspected offence. He must also be told that any sample taken may be the subject of a speculative search.

(2) A non-intimate sample may be taken from a person without the appropriate consent if he has been arrested for a recordable offence and released and:
   (a) in the case of a person who is on bail, he has not had a non-intimate sample of the same type and from the same part of the body taken from him in the course of the investigation of the offence by the police; or
   (b) in any case, he has had a non-intimate sample taken from him in the course of that investigation but (i) it was not suitable for the same means of analysis, or (ii) it proved insufficient (s 63(3ZA)).

(3) A non-intimate sample may be taken without the appropriate consent from any person (whether or not he is in police detention or held in custody by the police on the authority of a court) if:
   (a) he has been charged with a recordable offence or informed that he will be reported for such an offence; and
   (b) (i) he has not had a non-intimate sample taken from him in the course of the investigation; or
       (ii) he has had a sample taken from him, but it proved unsuitable or insufficient in quantity or quality for a particular form of analysis; or
       (iii) he has had a non-intimate sample taken from him in the course of the investigation and the sample has been destroyed pursuant to s 63R (p 209: not in force at the time of writing) or any other enactment, and it is disputed, in relation to any proceedings relating to the offence, whether a DNA profile (ie information derived from a DNA sample) relevant to the proceedings is derived from the sample (s 63(3A)). A 'DNA sample' means any material that has come from a human body and consists of or includes human cells.

(4) A non-intimate sample may be taken from a person without the appropriate consent if:
   (a) he has been convicted (see p 190) of a recordable offence, or
   (b) he has been given a caution in respect of an admitted recordable offence, or

(c) (prospectively repealed) he has been warned or reprimanded under the Crime and Disorder Act 1998, s 65 for a recordable offence,

and either of the conditions mentioned in s 63(3BA) is met (s 63(3B)), viz:

(i) a non-intimate sample has not been taken from him since the conviction, caution or (prospectively repealed) warning or reprimand; or

(ii) such a sample has been taken from him since then but it was not suitable for the same means of analysis, or it proved insufficient.

A non-intimate sample may only be so taken with the authorisation of an officer of at least the rank of inspector, who must be satisfied that taking the sample is necessary to assist in the prevention or detection of crime.

(5) A non-intimate sample may be taken without appropriate consent from a person detained following acquittal on the grounds of insanity or a finding of unfitness to plead (s 63(3C)).

(6) A non-intimate sample may be taken without the appropriate consent from a person if:

(a) under the law in force in a country or territory outside England and Wales the person has been 'convicted' of an offence under that law;

(b) the act constituting the offence would constitute a qualifying offence (see p 192) if done in England and Wales (whether or not it constituted such an offence when the person was convicted); and

(c) either:

(i) the person has not had a non-intimate sample taken from him on a previous occasion under the present provision, or

(ii) he has had such a sample taken from him on a previous occasion under it but the sample was not suitable for the same means of analysis, or it proved insufficient (s 63(3E), (3F)).

A non-intimate sample may only be so taken with the authorisation of an officer of at least the rank of inspector, who must be satisfied that taking the sample is necessary to assist in the prevention or detection of crime.

A 'conviction' for these purposes includes a finding equivalent to one of not guilty by reason of insanity or of disability but that the act charged was committed.

Reasonable force may be used to take a non-intimate sample without the suspect's consent under the above provisions.

Before any non-intimate sample is taken without the appropriate consent, the person must be informed of:

(a) the reason for taking it;

(b) the power under which it is taken;

(c) the fact that the relevant authorisation (where required) has been given.

The 'reason' for taking the sample must include a statement of the nature of the suspected offence, except in cases under s 63(3B) or (3E), (3F)).

Before a non-intimate sample is taken with or without consent at a police station or elsewhere, the person must be warned:

(i) that his sample or information derived from it may be the subject of a speculative search against other samples and information derived from them; and

(ii) that his sample and the information derived from it may be retained in accordance with PACE, s 64 (PACE, s 64 is prospectively replaced (see p 204)).

A record must be made as soon as practicable of the matters in (a) to (c) and that the person was informed of them and given the two warnings. If force is used a record must be made of the circumstances and those present.

General

Where clothing needs to be removed in circumstances likely to cause embarrassment, no person of the opposite sex (see p 36) who is not a medical practitioner or registered healthcare professional may be present (unless, in the case of a juvenile or a mentally disordered or mentally handicapped person, that person specifically requests the presence of a particular adult of the opposite sex who is readily available), nor shall anyone whose presence is unnecessary. However, in the case of a juvenile this is subject to the overriding proviso that such a removal of clothing may take place in the absence of the appropriate adult only if the juvenile signifies in that adult's presence that he prefers the search to be done in his absence and the appropriate adult agrees.

PACE, s 64 (prospectively replaced) deals with the destruction of samples: see p 204.

IDENTIFICATION BY FINGERPRINTS, FOOTWEAR IMPRESSIONS, AND SAMPLES: GENERAL POINTS

The following general points apply to all these types of identification.

Appropriate consent

'Appropriate consent' means in relation to a person who:

(a) has attained the age of 17 years, the consent of that person;
(b) has not attained that age but has attained 14, the consent of that person and his parent or guardian; and
(c) has not attained 14 years, the consent of his parent or guardian.

A note to the Identification Code contains specimen endorsements in relation to the appropriate consent:

(a) in respect of the case where fingerprints, footwear impressions or samples are requested for the purpose of elimination or as a part of an intelligence-led screening and to be used only for that purpose:

> 'I consent to my [fingerprints/footwear impressions being taken for elimination purposes/ DNA/mouth swab being taken for forensic analysis—as the case may be].
> I understand that the [fingerprints/footwear impressions/swab] will be destroyed at the end of the case and that my [fingerprints/footwear impressions/profile] will only be compared to the [fingerprints/footwear impressions/crime stain profile] from this enquiry.
> I have been advised that the person taking the [fingerprints/footwear impressions/ sample] may be required to give evidence and/or provide a written statement to the police in relation to the taking of it.'

(b) in respect of the case where fingerprints, footwear impressions, or samples are required to be retained for future use (ie speculative search):

> 'I consent to my [fingerprints/footwear impressions/DNA sample and information derived from it—as the case may be] being retained and used only for the purposes related

to the prevention and detection of crime, the investigation of an offence, or the conduct of a prosecution either nationally or internationally.

I understand that my [fingerprints/footwear impressions/this sample] may be checked against other [records/DNA records] held by, or on behalf of, relevant law enforcement authorities, either nationally or internationally.

I understand that once I have given my consent for my [fingerprints/footwear impressions/sample] to be retained and used I cannot withdraw this consent.'

Recordable offence: definition

Some provisions refer to a 'recordable offence'. The following offences are recordable:

(a) any offence punishable with imprisonment (regardless of any prohibition or restriction imposed by or under any enactment on the punishment of young offenders);

(b) persistently loitering or soliciting for the purposes of prostitution (Street Offences Act 1959, s 1);

(c) tampering with a motor vehicle (RTA 1988, s 25);

(d) unauthorised sale or disposal of tickets for a designated football match, and touting for car hire services (CJPOA 1994, ss 166(1) and 167);

(e) giving intoxicating liquor to a child under five, exposing children under 12 to risk of burning, and failing to provide for safety of children at entertainments (Children and Young Persons Act 1933, ss 5, 11, and 12);

(f) being drunk in public place (Criminal Justice Act 1967, s 91);

(g) failing to deliver up authority to possess prohibited weapon or ammunition, possession of assembled shotgun by unsupervised person under 15, and possession of air weapon or ammunition for air weapon by unsupervised person under 14 (Firearms Act 1968, ss 5(6), 22(3) and (4));

(h) trespassing in daytime in search of game, refusal by such trespasser to give name and address, and five or more found armed in daytime in search of game and using violence or refusing to give name and address (Game Act 1831, ss 30, 31, and 32);

(i) being drunk in highway or public place (Licensing Act 1872, s 12);

(j) obstructing authorised person exercising various powers under the Licensing Act 2003 (LA 2003, ss 59(5), 96(5), 108(3), and 179(4));

(k) failing to notify licensing authority of change of name or rules of club, or of convictions, and failing to notify court of the holding of a personal licence (LA 2003, ss 82(6), 123(2), and 128(6));

(l) keeping alcohol on premises for unauthorised sale, etc, allowing disorderly conduct on premises, selling alcohol to drunken person, obtaining it for such a person, failing to leave licensed premises, keeping smuggled goods, and allowing unaccompanied children on certain premises (LA 2003, ss 138(1), 140(1), 141(1), 142(1), 143(1), 144(1), and 145(1));

(m) selling alcohol to children, allowing sale to, purchase by or on behalf of children, allowing consumption by or delivery to children, sending a child to obtain alcohol, delivering alcohol to children, and allowing unsupervised sale by children (LA 2003, ss 146(1) and (3), 147(1), 149(1), (3), and (4), 150(1) and (2), 151(1), (2), and (4), 152(1), and 153(1));

(n) making false statements in applications for licences, etc (LA 2003, s 158(1));

(o) allowing premises to remain open following a closure order (LA 2003, s 160(4));

(p) making false statement in relation to an application for sex establishment licence (Local Government (Miscellaneous Provisions) Act 1982, Sch 3);
(q) falsely claiming professional qualification (Nursing and Midwifery Order 2001, art 44);
(r) taking or destroying game or rabbits by night (Night Poaching Act 1828, s 1);
(s) wearing police uniform with intent to deceive, and unlawful possession of police uniform (Police Act 1996, s 90(2) and (3));
(t) conduct likely to cause harassment, alarm, or distress, failing to give notice of public procession, failing to comply with condition imposed on public procession, taking part in prohibited public procession, failing to comply with a condition imposed on a public assembly, taking part in a trespassory assembly, and failing to comply with directions relating to such an assembly (Public Order Act 1986, ss 5, 11, 12(5), 13(8), 14(5), 14B(2), and 14C(3));
(u) failing to co-operate with preliminary test (RTA 1988, s 6);
(v) in connection with designated sporting events, (i) allowing alcohol to be carried on public vehicle, (ii) being drunk on such a vehicle, (iii) allowing alcohol to be carried in some other vehicles, (iv) being drunk at designated sports ground (Sporting Events (Control of Alcohol, etc) Act 1985, ss 1(2), 1(4), 1A(2), 2(2));
(w) at designated football match, (i) throwing missiles, (ii) indecent or racialist chanting, and (iii) going on to the playing area (Football (Offences) Act 1991, ss 2, 3 and 4);
(x) taking or riding a pedal cycle without the owner's consent (Theft Act 1968, s 12(5));
(y) purchasing or hiring a crossbow (or part) by person under 17, and unsupervised possession by person under 17 (Crossbows Act 1987, ss 2 and 3);
(z) begging, and persistent begging (Vagrancy Act 1824, ss 3 and 4);
(aa) individual subject to a banning order (i) failing to comply with requirement to report etc, (ii) knowingly or recklessly providing false or misleading information in support of application for exemption from a reporting requirement (Football Spectators Act 1989, ss 19(6) and 20(10));
(bb) soliciting, and paying for sexual services of prostitute subjected to force (SOA 2003, ss 51A and 53A).

Fingerprints and samples: requirement to attend

PACE, Sch 2A provides as follows.

Fingerprints

A constable may require a person to attend a police station for the purpose of taking his fingerprints under s 61(5A) (see p 190). This power may not be exercised in a case within s 61(5A)(b) (fingerprints taken on previous occasion insufficient, etc) after six months from the day on which the appropriate officer was informed that s 61(3A) (p 190) applied. The 'appropriate officer' means the officer investigating the offence for which the person was arrested.

A constable may require a person to attend a police station for the purpose of taking his fingerprints under s 61(5B) (see p 190). This power may not be exercised after six months from:

(a) in a case within s 61(5B)(a) (fingerprints not taken previously in the course of investigation), the day on which the person was charged or informed that he would be reported, or

(b) in a case within s 61(5B)(b) (fingerprints taken on previous occasion insufficient, etc), the day on which the appropriate officer was informed that s 61(3A) applied. The 'appropriate officer' means the officer investigating the offence for which the person was charged or informed that he would be reported.

A constable may require a person to attend a police station for the purpose of taking his fingerprints under s 61(6) (see p 190). Where the condition in s 61(6ZA)(a) is satisfied (fingerprints not taken previously), this power may not be exercised after two years from the day on which the person was convicted, cautioned or (prospectively repealed) warned or reprimanded, or, if later, 7 March 2011. Where the condition in s 61(6ZA)(b) is satisfied (fingerprints taken on previous occasion insufficient, etc), this power may not be exercised after two years from the day on which an officer of the investigating police force was informed that s 61(3A) applied, or, if later, 7 March 2011. These provisions do not apply where the offence is a qualifying offence (see p 192) (whether or not it was such an offence at the time of the conviction or caution or (prospectively repealed) warning or reprimand).

A constable may require a person to attend a police station for the purpose of taking his fingerprints under s 61(6D), (6E) (p 191).

Intimate samples

A constable may require a person to attend a police station for the purpose of taking an intimate sample from him under s 62(1A) (see p 193) if, in the course of the investigation of an offence, two or more non-intimate samples suitable for the same means of analysis have been taken from him but have proved insufficient.

A constable may require a person to attend a police station for the purpose of taking a sample from him under s 62(2A) (see p 193) if two or more non-intimate samples suitable for the same means of analysis have been taken from him under s 63(3E), (3F) (see p 196) but have proved insufficient.

Non-intimate samples

A constable may require a person to attend a police station for the purpose of taking a non-intimate sample from him under s 63(3ZA) (see p 195). This power may not be exercised in a case falling within s 63(3ZA)(b) (sample taken on a previous occasion not suitable, etc) after six months from the day on which the appropriate officer was informed of the matters specified in s 63(3ZA)(b)(i) or (ii). The 'appropriate officer' means the officer investigating the offence for which the person was arrested.

A constable may require a person to attend a police station for the purpose of taking a non-intimate sample from him under s 63(3A) (see p 195). This power may not be exercised in a case falling within s 63(3A)(a) (sample not taken previously) after six months from the day on which the person was charged or informed that he would be reported. The above power may not be exercised in a case falling within s 63(3A)(b) (sample taken on a previous occasion not suitable, etc) after six months from the day on which the appropriate officer was informed of the matters specified in s 63(3A)(b) (i) or (ii). The 'appropriate officer' means the officer investigating the offence for which the person was charged or informed that he would be reported.

A constable may require a person to attend a police station for the purpose of taking a non-intimate sample from him under s 63(3B) (see pp 195–6). Where the condition in s 63(3BA)(i) is satisfied (sample not taken previously), this power may not be exercised after two years from the day on which the person was convicted or cautioned (or, prospectively repealed, warned, or reprimanded), or, if later, 7 March 2011. Where the condition in s 63(3BA)(ii) is satisfied (sample taken on a previous occasion not suitable, etc), the above power may not be exercised after two years from the day on which an appropriate officer was informed that the sample was unsuitable or insufficient, or, if later, 7 March 2011. The 'appropriate officer' means an officer of the police force which investigated the offence in question. These time limits do not apply where the offence is a qualifying offence (see p 192).

A constable may require a person to attend a police station for the purpose of taking a non-intimate sample from him under s 63(3E), (3F) (see p 196).

Multiple exercise of power in respect of fingerprints or non-intimate samples

Where fingerprints or a non-intimate sample have been taken from a person under s 61 or s 63 (as the case may be) on two occasions in relation to any offence, he may not be required to attend a police station to have another such sample taken from him under the relevant section in relation to that offence on a subsequent occasion without the authorisation of an officer of at least the rank of inspector. The fact of the authorisation, and the reasons for giving it, must be recorded as soon as practicable after it has been given.

General

A power conferred by Sch 2A to require a person to attend a police station for taking fingerprints or a sample under any provision of PACE may be exercised only where the fingerprints or sample may be taken from the person under that provision (and, in particular, if any necessary authorisation for taking the fingerprints or sample under that provision has been obtained). A requirement under Sch 2A must (except in urgent cases) give at least seven days within which to attend the police station; and may require attendance at a specified time of day or between specified times of day. In urgent cases, a shorter period may be specified if authorised by an inspector (or above). The fact of such authorisation and the reasons for giving it must be recorded as soon as practicable. In specifying a period of time or times of day for attendance, the constable must consider whether the fingerprints or sample could reasonably be taken at a time when the person is for any other reason required to attend the police station. The time, etc at which the person must attend, may be varied by written agreement between him and the constable.

The information and recording requirements referred to in the ante-penultimate paragraphs on p 192 (fingerprints), the first paragraph on p 194 (intimate samples), and the first paragraph on p 197 (non-intimate samples) are applied by the Identification Code to fingerprints taken under Sch 2A.

A constable may arrest without warrant a person who has failed to comply with a requirement under Sch 2A. A guidance note to the Identification Code states that, to justify the arrest without warrant of a person for non-compliance with a requirement under Sch 2A, the officer making the requirement, or confirming in writing an agreed variation of it, should be prepared to explain how, when, and where the requirement was made or the variation was confirmed and what steps were taken to ensure that the person understood what to do and the consequences of not complying with the requirement.

Speculative searches

PACE, s 63A(1) provides that, where someone has been arrested on suspicion of being involved in a recordable offence (p 198), or has been charged with a recordable offence, or has been informed that he will be reported for a recordable offence, fingerprints, footwear impressions, or samples or the information derived from samples taken under any power conferred by PACE from the person may be subjected to speculative searches, ie checked against:

(a) other fingerprints, footwear impressions, or samples to which the person seeking to check has access and which are held by or on behalf of any one or more relevant law enforcement agencies (eg a police force or SOCA), or are held in connection with or as a result of an investigation of an offence;
(b) information derived from other samples if the information is contained in records to which the person seeking to check has access and which are held as described in (a).

When an amendment made by C-TA 2008, s 14 is in force, (a) and (b) will be replaced by the following:

(a) other fingerprints, footwear impressions, or samples—
    (i) to which the person seeking to check has access and which are held by, or on behalf of, any one or more relevant law enforcement authorities or are held in connection with or as a result of an investigation of an offence, or
    (ii) which are held by or on behalf of the Security Service or the Secret Intelligence Service;
(b) information from other samples—
    (i) which is contained in records to which the person seeking to check has access and which are held as mentioned in paragraph (a)(i) above, or
    (ii) which is held by or on behalf of the Security Service or the Secret Intelligence Service.
    Where:

(a) fingerprints, impressions of footwear, or samples have been taken from any person in connection with the investigation of an offence but otherwise than in circumstances to which s 63A(1) applies, and
(b) that person has given his consent in writing to the use in a speculative search of the fingerprints, of the impressions of footwear, or of the samples and of information derived from them,

the fingerprints, etc and that information may be checked against any of the fingerprints, etc or information mentioned in (a) or (b) of s 63A(1) (either version) (s 63A(1C)). A consent given for the above purposes cannot be withdrawn (s 63A(1D)).

Section 63A(1E) and (1F) provide respectively that where fingerprints or samples have been taken:

(a) under ss 61(6) or 63(3B) (persons convicted, etc), or
(b) under ss 61(6D), 62(2A) or 63(3E), (3F) (offences outside England and Wales, etc),

the fingerprints or samples, or information derived from the samples, may be subjected to a speculative search.

Fingerprints taken by virtue of (6) on p 191 (reasonable suspicion that person whose name is not known is committing or has committed an offence, etc) may be checked against other fingerprints to which the person seeking to check has access and which are held by, or on behalf of, any one or more relevant enforcement authorities or which are held in connection with or as a result of an investigation of an offence.

DESTRUCTION, RETENTION, AND USE OF FINGERPRINTS, FOOTWEAR IMPRESSIONS AND SAMPLES SUBJECT TO PACE

Until a day to be appointed, PACE, s 64(1A) provides that where fingerprints, footwear impressions or samples are taken from a person in connection with the investigation of an offence, and s 64(3) does not require them to be destroyed, they may be retained after they have fulfilled the purpose for which they were taken but may not be used *except for purposes related to the prevention or detection of crime, the investigation of an offence, the conduct of a prosecution, or the identification of a deceased person or of the person from whom a body part came.*

Section 64(1A) has been held by the European Court of Human Rights to be incompatible with the European Convention on Human Rights, art 8 (right to respect for private and family life) on the grounds that the blanket and indiscriminate nature of the power under it does not strike a fair balance between competing public and private interests. The Court was particularly concerned by the fact that persons arrested or charged but not subsequently convicted are treated in the same way by s 64(1A) as those convicted. Subsequently, the Supreme Court held that although (in the light of the European Court's decision) the indefinite retention of biometric data of all suspects was an interference which could not be justified under the European Convention on Human Rights, art 8, PACE, s 64(1A) could be read so as *not to require* indefinite retention in all cases. In consequence, it held, no declaration of incompatibility would be granted in respect of s 64(1A) but a declaration would be granted that ACPO's guidelines that there should be indefinite retention, save in exceptional circumstances, was unlawful.

By s 64(1BA), fingerprints taken under s 61(6A) (suspect's name unknown/doubted: p 191) must be destroyed as soon as they have fulfilled the purpose for which they were taken.

Section 64(3) provides that, where fingerprints, footwear impressions or samples are taken from someone who is not suspected of having committed the offence in question (elimination prints), they must be destroyed as soon as they have served the purpose for which they were taken. Fingerprints, footwear impressions and samples are not required to be destroyed under s 64(3):

(1) *Where the non-suspected person consents in writing to the retention of the fingerprints, footwear impressions or sample.* If such consent is given, the use of the fingerprints etc and the information gained from them is not restricted. Such consent cannot later be withdrawn (s 64(3AC)).

(2) *Where the fingerprints, footwear impressions or sample of the non-suspected person (X) were taken for the purpose of an investigation of an offence of which another person from whom such a fingerprint, etc was also taken has been convicted.* This provision was introduced to deal with the case where there were scientific reasons for processing some fingerprints, etc together and it was not technologically possible to separate them afterwards. This could occur where the fingerprints of a number of suspects were all found on a gun and were photographed together (s 64(3AA)).

Where a person is entitled under s 64 (1BA) or s 64(3) to the destruction of any fingerprint, footwear impression or sample, or would be but for s 64(3AA), neither it nor information derived from the sample may be used in evidence against him or for the purposes of the investigation of any offence (s 64(3AB)). Where fingerprints etc are destroyed, any copies must also be destroyed, and access to relevant computer data must be made impossible, as soon as it is practicable to do so. A person must be allowed to witness the destruction of his fingerprints if he so asks. In addition, if his fingerprints are destroyed or rendered inaccessible he is entitled to a certificate, to be issued within three months of his application, certifying destruction or that access to the data has been made impossible.

Section 64 does not apply to suspected terrorists arrested under TA 2000, s 41.

PACE, s 64 (and prospective amendments made by the Crime and Security Act 2010) are prospectively repealed, and replaced, by amendments made by the Protection of Freedoms Act 2012 (PFA 2012). When the prospective replacements are in force the law will be as set out below. The position in relation to the destruction or retention of material taken, or (in the case of a DNA profile), derived from a sample taken, before the commencement day will be dealt with by transitional provisions to be prescribed by the Secretary of State.

PROSPECTIVE RULES ABOUT DESTRUCTION, RETENTION AND USE OF FINGERPRINTS, FOOTWEAR IMPRESSIONS AND DNA PROFILES SUBJECT TO PACE

PACE, ss 63D to 63U, prospectively inserted by PFA 2012, provide as follows.

Destruction rule for fingerprints and DNA profiles

PACE, s 63D prospectively deals with the destruction of:

(a) fingerprints:
    (i)   taken from a person under any power conferred by PACE (as described earlier in this chapter), or
    (ii) taken by the police, with the consent of the person from whom they were taken, in connection with the investigation of an offence by the police, and
(b) a DNA profile derived from a DNA sample taken as mentioned in (a)(i) or (ii).

Fingerprints and DNA profiles to which s 63D applies ('s 63D material') must be destroyed if it appears to the responsible chief officer of police that:

(a) the taking of the fingerprint or, in the case of a DNA profile, the taking of the sample from which the DNA profile was derived, was unlawful, or
(b) the fingerprint was taken, or, in the case of a DNA profile, was derived from a sample taken, from a person in connection with that person's arrest and the arrest was unlawful or based on mistaken identity.

The 'responsible chief officer of police' is the chief officer of police for the police area:

(i) in which the material concerned was taken or derived, or
(ii) in the case of a DNA profile, in which the sample from which the DNA profile was derived was taken (s 63D(2)).

In any other case, s 63D material must be destroyed unless it is retained under any power conferred by ss 63E to 63O (including those sections as applied by s 63P). Section 63D material which ceases to be retained under such a power may continue to be retained under any other such power which applies to it.

Nothing in s 63D prevents a speculative search, in relation to s 63D material, from being carried out within such time as may reasonably be required for the search if the responsible chief officer of police considers the search to be desirable.

Modification of destruction rule for particular circumstances

Retention of s 63 material pending investigation or proceedings

PACE, s 63E prospectively provides that s 63D material taken (or, in the case of a DNA profile, derived from a sample taken) in connection with the investigation of an offence in which it is suspected that the person to whom the material relates has been involved may be retained until the conclusion of the investigation of the offence or, where the investigation gives rise to proceedings against the person for the offence, until the conclusion of those proceedings (for example, the time when charges are dropped or when a verdict is returned).

Further retention of s 63D material: persons arrested for or charged with a qualifying offence

PACE, s 63F prospectively deals with the case where s 63D material:

(a) relates to a person who is arrested for, or charged with, a qualifying offence (see p 192) but is not convicted (p 211 below) of that offence, and
(b) was taken (or, in the case of a DNA profile, derived from a sample taken) in connection with the investigation of the offence.

If the person has previously been convicted (s 65B) of a recordable offence (see p 198) which is not an excluded offence, or is so convicted before the material is required to be destroyed by virtue of s 63F, the material may be retained indefinitely (s 63F(2)). An 'excluded offence', in relation to a person, means a recordable offence:

(a) which:
   (i) is not a qualifying offence,
   (ii) is the only recordable offence of which the person has been convicted, and
   (iii) was committed when the person was aged under 18, and
(b) for which the person was not given a sentence of imprisonment or detention for five years or more.

If a person is convicted of more than one offence arising out of a single course of action, those convictions are treated as a single conviction for the above purposes.

Otherwise, by s 63F(3), material falling within s 63F(4) or (5) may be retained until the end of the retention period below. Material falls within s 63F(4) if it:

(a) relates to a person who is charged with a qualifying offence but is not convicted of that offence, and
(b) was taken (or, in the case of a DNA profile, derived from a sample taken) in connection with the investigation of the offence.

Material falls within s 63F(5) if:

(a) it relates to a person who is arrested for a qualifying offence but is not charged with that offence,
(b) it was taken (or, in the case of a DNA profile, derived from a sample taken) in connection with the investigation of the offence, and
(c) the Commissioner for the Retention and Use of Biometric Material has consented to the retention of the material concerned.

The retention period is three years beginning with the date on which (as the case may be):

(a) the fingerprints were taken, and

(b) the DNA sample from which the profile was derived was taken (or, if the profile was derived from more than one DNA sample, the date on which the first of those samples was taken).

The responsible chief officer of police or a specified chief officer of police may apply within a three-month period ending on the last day of the retention period to a District Judge (Magistrates' Courts) for an order extending the retention period for an additional two years. Appeal lies to the Crown Court against an extension order, or a refusal to make such an order. A 'specified chief officer of police' means:

(a) the chief officer of the police force of the area in which the person from whom the material was taken resides, or

(b) a chief officer of police who believes that the person is in, or is intending to come to, the chief officer's police area.

Consent of Commissioner   Section 63G provides as follows in relation to the consent of the Commissioner for the Retention and Use of Biometric Material referred to above. The responsible chief officer of police may apply in writing to the Commissioner for consent to the retention of s 63D material which falls within s 63F(5)(a) and (b). An application may be made on one of two bases:

(a) that the material was taken (or, in the case of a DNA profile, derived from a sample taken) in connection with the investigation of an offence where any alleged victim (or intended victim) of the offence was, at the time of the offence under the age of 18, a vulnerable adult, or associated with the person to whom the material relates; or

(b) that the material is not material to which (a) relates, but the retention of the material is necessary to assist in the prevention or detection of crime.

The responsible chief officer of police must give the person to whom the material relates (P) written notice of an application under s 63G, and the right to make representations. The notice may, in particular, be given to P by leaving it at his usual or last known address (whether residential or otherwise), by sending it to P by post at that address, or by sending it to P by email or other electronic means. There is no need to give notice if the whereabouts of P is not known and cannot, after reasonable inquiry, be ascertained.

On such application the Commissioner may consent to the retention of material to which the application relates if he considers that it is appropriate to retain the material. Before deciding whether or not to give consent, the Commissioner must consider any representations by P which are made within 28 days beginning with the day on which the notice is given.

Retention of s 63D material: persons arrested for or charged with a minor offence

PACE, s 63H prospectively deals with the retention of s 63D material which:

(a) relates to a person who:
  (i) is arrested for or charged with a recordable offence other than a qualifying offence (see p 192),
  (ii) if arrested for or charged with more than one offence arising out of a single course of action, is not also arrested for or charged with a qualifying offence, and
  (iii) is not convicted of the offence or offences in respect of which he is arrested or charged, and

(b) was taken (or, in the case of a DNA profile, derived from a sample taken) in connection with the investigation of the offence or offences in respect of which the person is arrested or charged.

If, in such a case, the person has previously been convicted of a recordable offence which is not an excluded offence (see p 205), the material may be retained indefinitely.

If a person is convicted of more than one offence arising out of a single course of action, the convictions are treated as a single conviction for the above purpose.

Retention of material: persons convicted of a recordable offence

PACE, s 63I prospectively provides that:

(a) s 63D material (other than material to which s 63K (below) applies) which:
   (i) relates to a person who is convicted (p 211) of a recordable offence, and.
   (ii) was taken (or, in the case of a DNA profile, derived from a sample taken) in connection with the investigation of the offence, or
(b) material taken under s 61(6) (see pp 190–1) or 63(3B) (see pp 195–6) which relates to a person who is convicted of a recordable offence,

may be retained indefinitely.

Retention of material: persons convicted of an offence outside England and Wales

PACE, s 63J prospectively provides that:

(a) fingerprints taken from the person under s 61(6D), (6E) (power to take fingerprints without consent in relation to offences outside England and Wales: see p 191), or
(b) a DNA profile derived from a DNA sample taken from the person under s 62(2A) or 63(3E), (6F) (powers to take intimate and non-intimate samples in relation to offences outside England and Wales: see pp 193 and 196),

which relates to a person who is convicted (p 211) of an offence under the law of any country outside England and Wales may be retained indefinitely.

Retention of s 63D material: exception for persons under 18 convicted of first minor offence

PACE, s 63K prospectively deals with the case where s 63D material, which relates to a person (P) who:

(a) is convicted (p 211) of a recordable offence other than a qualifying offence,
(b) has not previously been convicted of a recordable offence, and
(c) is under 18 at the time of the offence,

was taken (or, in the case of a DNA profile, derived from a sample taken) in connection with the investigation of the offence.

Section 63K(2)–(4) provides as follows:

(a) where P is given a custodial sentence in respect of the offence, the material may be retained until the end of the period consisting of the term of the sentence plus five years (if sentence less than five years), or indefinitely (if the sentence is five years or more);
(b) where P is given a sentence other than a relevant custodial sentence in respect of the offence, the material may be retained until the end of the period of five years beginning with the date on which (as the case may be):

(i)   the fingerprints were taken, and

(ii)   the DNA sample from which the profile was derived was taken, or, if the pro-file was derived from more than one DNA sample, the date on which the first of those samples was taken.

However, if, before the end of the relevant period, P is again convicted of a recordable offence, the material may be retained indefinitely.

Retention of s 63D material: persons given a penalty notice

PACE, s 63L prospectively provides that, where s 63D material relates to a person who is given a penalty notice under the Criminal Justice and Police Act 2001 and in respect of whom no proceedings are brought for the offence to which the notice relates, and was taken (or, in the case of a DNA profile, derived from a sample taken) from the person in connection with the investigation of that offence, the material may be retained for two years beginning with the date on which (as the case may be):

(a)   the fingerprints were taken,

(b)   the date on which the DNA sample from which the profile was derived was taken, or, if the profile was derived from more than one DNA sample, the date on which the first of those samples was taken.

Retention of s 63D material for purposes of national security

PACE, s 63M prospectively provides that s 63D material may be retained for as long as a national security determination made by the responsible chief officer of police (ie a determination that the retention of any such material is necessary for the purposes of national security) has effect in relation to it. Such a determination must be made in writing, has effect for a maximum of two years, and may be renewed.

Retention of s 63D material given voluntarily

PACE, s 63N prospectively provides that fingerprints, or a DNA profile derived from a DNA sample, taken from a person with his consent, may be retained until they or it has fulfilled the purpose for which taken or derived.

Such material which relates to a person who is convicted of a recordable offence, or who has previously been convicted of a recordable offence (other than a person who has only one 'exempt conviction'), may be retained indefinitely. A conviction is exempt if it is in respect of a recordable offence, other than a qualifying offence, committed when the person is under 18.

If a person is convicted of more than one offence arising out of a single course of action, the convictions are treated as a single conviction for the above purpose.

Retention of s 63D material with consent

By PACE, s 63O, fingerprints (other than fingerprints taken under s 61(6A) (see p 191)) to which s 63D applies, and a DNA profile to which s 63D applies, may prospectively be retained for so long as the person to whom the material relates consents to its retention in writing. Such consent can be withdrawn at any time.

Section 63D material obtained for one purpose and used for another

If s 63D material which is taken (or, in the case of a DNA profile, derived from a sample taken) from a person in connection with the investigation of an offence leads to the person to whom the material relates being arrested for or charged with, or convicted of, an offence other than the offence under investigation, ss 63E to 63O (above) and ss 63Q and 63T (below) prospectively have effect in relation to the material as if it was taken (or, in the case of a DNA profile, derived from a sample taken) in connection with the investigation of the offence in respect of which the person is arrested or charged (PACE, s 63P).

Destruction of copies of s 63D material

This is prospectively dealt with by PACE, s 63Q. If fingerprints are required by s 63D to be destroyed, any copies of the fingerprints held by the police must also be destroyed. If a DNA profile is required by s 63D to be destroyed, no copy may be retained by the police except in a form which does not include information which identifies the person to whom the DNA profile relates.

Destruction rules for samples and footwear impressions

Destruction of samples

PACE, s 63R prospectively provides as follows. Samples taken under any power conferred by PACE, or taken by the police, with the person's consent, in connection with the investigation of an offence, must be destroyed if it appears to the responsible chief officer of police (p 204) that:

(a) the taking of the samples was unlawful, or
(b) the samples were taken from a person in connection with that person's arrest and the arrest was unlawful or based on mistaken identity.

Where neither (a) nor (b) applies, (i) a DNA sample so taken must be destroyed as soon as a DNA profile has been derived from the sample, or if sooner, before the end of six months beginning with the date on which the sample was taken; and (ii) any other sample so taken must be destroyed before the end of six months beginning with the date on which it was taken.

The responsible chief officer of police may apply to a District Judge (Magistrates' Courts) for an order to retain a sample beyond the date on which it would otherwise be required to be destroyed by virtue of (i) or (ii) if the sample was taken from a person in connection with the investigation of a qualifying offence, and the responsible chief officer of police considers that the following condition is met. The condition is that, having regard to the nature and complexity of other material that is evidence in relation to the offence, the sample is likely to be needed in any proceedings for the offence for the purposes of disclosure to, or use by, a defendant, or responding to any challenge by a defendant in respect of the admissibility of material that is evidence on which the prosecution proposes to rely. Such application must be made before the date on which the sample would otherwise be required to be destroyed.

If, on such an application, the District Judge is satisfied that the above condition is met, he may make an order which allows the sample to be retained for 12 months beginning with the date on which the sample would otherwise be required to be destroyed, and may be renewed (on one or more occasions) for a further period of not more than 12 months from the end of the period when the order would otherwise cease to have effect. An application for such an order (other than an application for renewal) may be made without notice of the application having been given to the person from whom the sample was taken, and may be heard and determined in private in the absence of that person. A sample retained by virtue of such an order must not be used other than for the purposes of any proceedings for the offence in connection with which the sample was taken. A sample that ceases to be retained by virtue of such an order must be destroyed.

Section 63R does not prevent a speculative search, in relation to samples to which this section applies, from being carried out within such time as may reasonably be required for the search if the responsible chief officer of police considers the search to be desirable.

Destruction of footwear impressions

PACE, s 63S prospectively provides that impressions of footwear taken from a person under any power conferred by PACE, or taken by the police, with the person's consent, in connection with the investigation of an offence, must be destroyed, with the proviso that they may be retained for as long as is necessary for purposes related to the prevention or detection of crime, the investigation of an offence or the conduct of a prosecution.

Supplementary provision for material subject to PACE

Use of Retained Material

PACE, s 63T prospectively deals with the use of material to which PACE, s 63D, 63R, or 63S applies. 'Use of material' includes allowing any check to be made against it and to disclosing it to any person.

Any material to which PACE, s 63D, 63R, or 63S applies must not be used other than:

(a) in the interests of national security,
(b) for the purposes of a terrorist investigation (see p 805),
(c) for purposes related to the prevention or detection of crime, the investigation of an offence or the conduct of a prosecution, or
(d) for purposes related to the identification of a deceased person or of the person to whom the material relates.

For the purposes of s 63T, the reference to crime includes a reference to any conduct which constitutes one or more criminal offences (whether under the law of England and Wales or of any other country or territory), or is, or corresponds to, any conduct which, if it all took place in England and Wales, would constitute one or more criminal offences, and the references to an investigation and to a prosecution include references, respectively, to any investigation outside England and Wales of any crime or suspected crime and to a prosecution brought in respect of any crime in a country or territory outside England and Wales.

Material which is required by PACE, s 63D, 63R, or 63S to be destroyed must not at any time after it is required to be destroyed be used in evidence against the person to whom the material relates, or for the purposes of the investigation of any offence.

Exclusions for certain regimes

PACE, s 63D to 63T do not apply to biometric data held under the Terrorism Act 2000, Sch 8 or the Terrorism Prevention and Investigation Measures Act 2011, Sch 6 (Chapter 28) (PACE, s 63U). A broadly equivalent regime for the destruction, retention, and use of such material operates under these statutes (see p 825) thereto). Nor do PACE, s 63D to 63T apply to material which is or may become disclosable under the Criminal Procedure and Investigations Act 1996 or the Code of Practice under Part II (p 266), or to material taken from someone which relates to another person.

Other supplementary provisions

Cautions treated as convictions

The effect of PACE, s 65B(1) is that, prospectively for the purposes of PACE, s 63D to 63T above, a person who has been given a caution (or, if under 18 at the time, a warning or reprimand) is to be treated in the same way as someone convicted of an offence. So is a person who has been found not guilty by reason of insanity or found to be under a disability and to have done the act charged.

Spent conviction rules do not apply

PACE, s 65B(2) prospectively provides that the provisions of PACE about fingerprints, samples etc apply irrespective of the Rehabilitation of Offenders Act 1974 (under which certain convictions are treated as being spent, and therefore disregarded for most purposes, after the end of a specified expiry period). However, a person is not to be treated as having been convicted of an offence if that conviction is a conviction or caution for the repealed offences of buggery or gross indecency between men and the Secretary of State has ordered it to be disregarded (s 65B(3)).

Inclusion of DNA profiles on National DNA Database

A DNA profile derived from a DNA sample which is retained under PACE, ss 63E to 63L (including those sections as applied by s 63P) will have to be recorded on the National DNA Database (PACE, s 63AA, prospectively inserted by PFA 2012, s 23). This provision puts on a statutory footing the existing National DNA Database, as does PACE, s 63AB, prospectively added by PFA 2012, s 24, which requires the Secretary of State to make arrangements in respect of the National DNA Database Strategy Board whose role is to oversee the National DNA Database. The Board is required to issue guidance about the destruction of DNA profiles taken or retained under the above provisions of PACE in accordance with which chief officers of police must act, and may issue guidance about applications under PACE, s 63G (p 206).

Commissioner for the Retention and Use of Biometric Material

PFA 2012, s 20 provides for the appointment of a Commissioner for the Retention and Use of Biometric Material, whose functions will be to keep under review determinations under PACE, s 63M and corresponding terrorism provisions (see Chapter 28) made by chief officers of police and others that the fingerprints and DNA profiles of a person are required to be retained for national security purposes and the use to which fingerprints and DNA profiles so retained are being put. The Secretary of State is required to issue guidance about the making of such determinations, to which regard must be had (PFA 2012, s 22).

To enable the Commissioner to discharge his functions, s 20 will require persons making national security determinations to notify the Commissioner in writing of the making of a determination, including the reasons for it, and to provide such other information as the Commissioner may require.

The Commissioner will have power under s 20 to order the destruction of the fingerprints and DNA profile held pursuant to it where satisfied that it is not necessary for any material retained under the determination to be so retained. There will be no appeal against such a ruling by the Commissioner save by way of judicial review. The Commissioner may not order the destruction of material that could otherwise be retained pursuant to any other statutory provision.

The Commissioner must also keep under review the retention and use in accordance with PACE, ss 63A and 63D to 63T (or the corresponding terrorism provisions) of any material to which s 63D or 63R (or corresponding terrorism provisions) and any copies of any material to which s 63D (or corresponding terrorism provision) applies.

Destruction, retention and use of national security material not subject to existing statutory restrictions

This is prospectively dealt with by C-TA 2008, ss 18-18E, substituted by PFA 2012 for the original, unimplemented s 18. The prospective provisions are as follows.

The basic provision is s 18 which applies to fingerprints (as defined on p 190), DNA samples (p 195), and DNA profiles that:

(a) are held for the purposes of national security by a law enforcement authority under the law of England and Wales or Northern Ireland, and
(b) are not held subject to existing statutory restrictions.

Such material is described as 's 18 material'.

'Law enforcement authority' means:

(a) a police force,
(b) SOCA,
(c) HM Revenue and Customs Commissioners, or
(d) a foreign authority so far as exercising functions which correspond to those of a police force, or otherwise involve criminal investigation or prosecution.

The prime example of material not held subject to 'existing statutory restrictions' is material on the counter-terrorism DNA database maintained by the Metropolitan Police which comprises DNA material and fingerprints obtained from crime scenes, covert surveillance or from foreign police or intelligence services.

Destruction of material   By C-TA 2008, s 18, material must be destroyed if it appears to the responsible officer that the material has not been:

(a) obtained by the law enforcement authority pursuant to an authorisation under the Police Act 1997, Pt 3 (p 89);
(b) obtained by the law enforcement authority in the course of surveillance, or use of a covert human intelligence source, authorised under the Regulation of Investigatory Powers Act 2000, Part 2 (p 85);
(c) supplied to the law enforcement authority by another law enforcement authority; or
(d) otherwise lawfully obtained or acquired by the law enforcement authority for any of the purposes mentioned in s 18D(1) below.

In any other case, ie where the s 18 material has been so obtained, s 18 material must be destroyed unless it is retained by the law enforcement authority under any power conferred by s 18A or 18B (non-DNA samples: below), but this is subject to a rule that a DNA sample to which s 18 applies must be destroyed as soon as a DNA profile has been derived from the sample, or, if sooner, before the end of the period of six months beginning with the date on which it was taken.

Section 18 material which ceases to be retained under a power conferred by s 18A or s 18B may continue to be retained under any other such power which applies to it.

Section 18 does not prevent s 18 material from being the subject of a speculative search within such time as may reasonably be required for the check, if the responsible officer considers the check to be desirable.

Retention of material: general   By C-TA 2008, s 18A, s 18 material which is *not a DNA sample* and relates to a person who has no previous convictions or only one exempt conviction may be retained by the law enforcement authority until the end of the specified retention period. The retention period is three years beginning with the date on which (as the case may be):

(a) the fingerprints were taken, and
(b) the DNA sample from which the profile was derived was taken (or, if the profile was derived from more than one DNA sample, the date on which the first of those samples was taken).

A person 'has no previous convictions' if he has not previously been convicted in England and Wales or Northern Ireland of a recordable offence (see p 198 and the corresponding Northern Irish legislation), and 'conviction' is defined in the same way as under PACE, s 65B(1) (p 211). 'Spent convictions' are treated in the same way as under PACE, s 65B(2) and (3). A conviction is exempt if it is in respect of a recordable offence, other than a qualifying offence, committed when the person was under 18. A qualifying offence has the meaning as in p 192 and a corresponding meaning in Northern Ireland. Convictions of more than one offence arising out of a single course of action are treated as a single conviction for the purposes of calculating under s 18A whether the person has been convicted of only one offence.

Section 18 material which is *not a DNA sample* and relates to a person who has previously been convicted of a recordable offence (other than a single exempt conviction), or is so convicted before the material is required to be destroyed by virtue of s 18A, may be retained indefinitely.

Section 18 material which is *not a DNA sample* may be retained indefinitely if it is held by the law enforcement authority in a form which does not include information identifying the person (P) to whom the material relates, and the authority does not know, and has never known, the identity of P. Where s 18 material is being so retained by a law enforcement authority, and the authority comes to know the identity of P, and P has no previous convictions or only one exempt conviction, the material may be retained by the authority until the end of the period of three years beginning with the date on which the P's identity comes to be known by the authority.

Retention for purposes of national security   C-TA 2008, s 18B provides that s 18 material which is *not a DNA sample* may be retained for as long as a national security determination made by the responsible officer has effect in relation to it.

A national security determination is made if the responsible officer (ie the chief officer of police in relation to the material obtained or acquired by a police force in England and Wales) determines that it is necessary for any such s 18 material to be retained for the purposes of national security. A national security determination must be written, has effect for a maximum of two years, and may be renewed.

Destruction of copies   C-TA 2008, s 18C provides that, if fingerprints are required by C-TA 2008, s 18 to be destroyed, any copies of the fingerprints held by the law enforcement authority concerned must also be destroyed. If a DNA profile is required by s 18 to be destroyed, no copy may be retained by the law enforcement authority concerned except in a form which does not include information which identifies the person to whom the DNA profile relates.

Use of retained material   By C-TA 2008, s 18D, s 18 material must not be used other than for the same purposes as under PACE, s 63T (p 210).

Subject to this, s 18 material may be subjected to a speculative search if the responsible officer considers the check to be desirable.

Material which is required by s 18 to be destroyed must not at any time after it is required to be destroyed be used in evidence against the person to whom the material relates, or for the purposes of the investigation of any offence.

The references above to using material have the same meaning as under PACE, s 63T (p 210), and so does the reference to crime (with the substitution of 'UK' for 'England and Wales').

PHOTOGRAPHS

(a) Persons detained at a police station

PACE, s 64A provides powers to take a photograph of a detainee with the appropriate consent (p 197), or without such consent where it is withheld or it is impracticable to obtain consent.

(b) Otherwise than at a police station

Section 64A also authorises the taking of a photograph elsewhere than at a police station with the appropriate consent, or without such consent where it is withheld or it is impracticable to obtain it, if the person has been:

(a) arrested by a constable for an offence;
(b) taken into custody by a constable after a citizen's arrest;
(c) required to wait by a community support officer;
(d) given a fixed penalty notice by a constable or designated community support officer or accredited person by virtue of his accreditation; or
(e) given a direction to leave and not return to a specified location for up to 48 hours by a constable (under the Violent Crime Reduction Act 2006, s 27).

General to (a) and (b)

For these purposes, the term 'photograph' includes a moving image. A photograph obtained without the appropriate consent may be obtained by making a copy of an image taken on a camera system installed anywhere in a police station. In the event of non-co-operation, where it is not possible to take the photograph covertly, reasonable force may be used to take the photograph. The use of reasonable force to take the photograph of a suspect elsewhere than at a police station must be carefully considered.

Only a police officer may take a photograph under s 64A. The officer may require the person to remove anything worn on, or over, all or any part of the head or face. In the event of non-compliance, the officer may remove the item or substance. In order to obtain a suspect's consent and co-operation to remove an item of religious headwear to take a photograph, a constable should consider whether in the situation the removal of the headwear and the taking of the photograph should be by an officer of the same sex as the person. It would be appropriate for these actions to be conducted out of public view.

The suspect must be informed of the reason for taking the photograph and the purposes for which it may be used. This must be done beforehand, unless the photograph is taken covertly or by making a copy of an image (in which cases he must be informed as soon as practicable thereafter).

A photograph so taken may be used or disclosed only for purposes related to the prevention or detection of crime (including a foreign crime corresponding to one under UK law), the investigation of an offence, the conduct of a prosecution, or the enforcement of a sentence.

After being so used or disclosed, a photograph may be retained but may only be used or disclosed for the same purposes. Although it appears from this that the photograph may be retained indefinitely, the guidance on the Management of Police Information (MoPI), issued by NPIA, with which chief officers are required to comply by the Code of Practice on MoPI, issued by the Secretary of State, states that all records (including photographs) that are accurate, adequate, up-to-date and necessary will be held for a minimum of six years. Thereafter scheduled reviews must be held to review whether it is still necessary to keep the record for policing purposes. In 2012, a divisional court held that the retention of photographs under the retention rules in the Guidance constituted a breach of the European Convention on Human Rights, art 8 (right to private life) because the retention rules were a disproportionate interference with that right. The court emphasised that the rules failed to distinguish between the photographs of those who were convicted and those who were not charged or who were acquitted. It also expressed concern about the length of the minimum retention period and that the maximum period in some circumstances was the age of 100. Appropriate revision of the Guidance is anticipated.

(c) Persons voluntarily at a police station

When there are reasonable grounds for suspecting the involvement of a person in a criminal offence, but that person is at a police station voluntarily and not detained, the above provisions apply, except that force may not be used to take the person's photograph.

Destruction of photographs

The photograph of a person which is not taken in accordance with the provisions under headings (a) or (b) above or under PACE, s 54A (see p 138), must be destroyed (together with any negatives and copies) unless he:

(a) is charged with, or informed that he may be prosecuted for, or is prosecuted for a recordable offence (p 198);

(b) is cautioned for a recordable offence or (prospectively repealed) given a warning or reprimand in accordance with the Crime and Disorder Act 1998 for such offence; or

(c) gives informed, written consent to the photograph being retained.

Such a person must be given an opportunity to witness the destruction or to have a certificate confirming destruction, if he so requests within five days of notification that the destruction is required.

Documentation

A record must be made of the identity of the photographer (with the usual exceptions), the purpose of the photograph and its outcome, and the detainee's consent (or the reason for taking the photograph without consent).

CHAPTER 7

The Law of Criminal Evidence

The law of criminal evidence determines two things:

(a) the means by which the facts in issue are proved in a court; and

(b) those facts which may (or may not) be proved in a court.

CLASSIFICATION OF EVIDENCE

Certain rules of evidence apply specifically to a particular class of evidence only. Evidence may be classified as follows.

Direct evidence and circumstantial evidence

Direct evidence is evidence which (if believed) directly establishes a particular fact in issue itself. For example, the existence of a firearm alleged to have been possessed by the defendant (D) may be proved by its production in court and the fact that he was in possession of it may be proved by a statement from a person who claims to have discovered D in possession.

Circumstantial evidence is evidence of a fact or facts from which a fact in issue may be inferred. Suppose that D is charged with murder. If an eye-witness gives evidence that he saw D fire a gun at the victim, this is direct evidence of a fact in issue. On the other hand, evidence that D was seen in possession of a gun near the scene of the crime shortly before it was committed is circumstantial evidence since it is evidence of a fact from which the fact in issue (that D fired the gun) may be inferred.

Oral evidence, documentary evidence and real evidence

Oral evidence

Most evidence given in a court is oral evidence. This consists of statements made in court by witnesses concerning matters of which they have knowledge, such as something which they have seen, or heard, or smelt, or touched.

Normally, oral evidence must be given on oath (ie sworn). However, where it is not possible to administer the oath in the manner appropriate to the religious beliefs of the witness (W), or where he objects to being sworn, W may make a solemn affirmation.

Determination of whether a witness should be sworn   The question whether W may be sworn is determined by the court as follows in accordance with the Youth Justice and Criminal Evidence Act 1999 (YJCEA 1999), s 55.

W may not be sworn unless he has reached 14 and he has sufficient appreciation of the solemnity of the occasion and of the particular responsibility to tell the truth which is involved in taking an oath. If W is able to give intelligible testimony, he is presumed to have sufficient appreciation if no evidence is adduced to the contrary. If such evidence is adduced, it is for the party seeking to have W sworn to prove on the balance of probabilities that W has reached 14 and has sufficient appreciation of the specified matters.

Such issues must be dealt with in the absence of the jury.

Reception of unsworn evidence   YJCEA 1999, s 56 deals with a person of any age who is competent to give evidence in criminal proceedings (see p 223) but is not permitted to be sworn by s 55. It provides that the evidence of such a person may be given unsworn. A deposition of unsworn evidence may be accepted as if it had been given on oath.

Unsworn evidence may also be given by a person called simply to produce a document.

Evidence by live link   CJA 2003, Part 8 (ss 51–56) provides as follows.

A 'live link' is a live television link or other arrangement by which a witness, while at a place in the UK which is outside the building where the proceedings are being held, is able to see or hear a person at the place where the proceedings are being held, and to be seen and heard by the defendants, judge and/or justices, jury (if any), legal representatives, and any interpreter.

CJA 2003, s 51 provides that a witness (other than D) may, if the court so directs, give evidence through a live link in criminal proceedings whether at a trial or during an appeal. The court may give such a direction on its own motion or on the application of a party. It cannot make a direction unless it has been notified by the Secretary of State that suitable facilities are available in the area where the proceedings will take place. The court must be satisfied that it is in the interests of the efficient or effective administration of justice for this to take place. In deciding whether to give a direction, the court must consider all the circumstances, including the availability of the witness, the need to attend in person, the importance of the evidence and the views of the witness, the suitability of facilities, and whether giving a direction might inhibit a party to the proceedings from effectively testing the witness's evidence. If the court refuses an application it must state in open court its reasons for doing so.

When such a direction has been given the witness may not give evidence by any other means but a court may rescind a direction if it appears to be in the interests of justice to do so.

Where a magistrates' court wishes to give such a direction and facilities are not available at any place where it can lawfully sit, the court may sit at any place appointed for the purpose of receiving such evidence and this may be outside its local justice area.

Evidence by means of a video recording   The relevant provisions are not in force at the time of writing.

The Criminal Justice Act 2003 (CJA 2003), s 137 permits a court to direct that a video recording of an interview with W (other than D), or a part of such a recording, be admitted as part of the evidence-in-chief in criminal proceedings for an offence triable only on indictment or for prescribed offences triable either way, where W claims to have witnessed an offence (or a part of it) or to have witnessed events closely connected with such events. W must have previously given an account of the events in question (whether in response to questions asked or otherwise) while the events were fresh in his memory.

In such circumstances the court may direct that the recording be admitted, provided that W's recollection of events is likely to be significantly better at the time he gave the recorded account than at the time of giving evidence, and it is in the interests of justice to admit the recording, having regard to the time which has passed since it was made; its quality; and any views of W as to whether the evidence-in-chief should be given orally or by means of the recording.

Any statement given by video recording must be treated as if it had been given in W's oral evidence provided that W in his oral evidence asserts that it is true. Part of a video recording may be admitted, but a court must consider whether admitting only part of it would carry a risk of prejudice to D and, if this is likely, whether the interests of justice nevertheless require it to be admitted in view of the desirability of showing the whole, or substantially the whole, of the recorded interview.

Refreshing memory   Witness statements are usually recorded well in advance of trial. Recognising the difficulties associated with refreshing memory from an audio or video recording, CJA 2003, s 139 states that a witness giving evidence in criminal proceedings may refresh his memory from a document made or verified by him at an earlier time provided that:

(a)   he states in his oral evidence that the document records his recollections of the matter at that earlier time; and
(b)   his recollection of the matter is likely to have been significantly better at that time than it is at the time of his oral evidence.

Where two witnesses have acted together (and this is common in the case of police officers) they may refresh their memories from notes which they made together.

Hostile witness   If, during a trial in a Crown Court, a witness gives evidence which is hostile to the side calling him (it must be 'hostile' as opposed to unfavourable), that evidence may be contradicted by other evidence or, with the leave of the judge, it may be proved that the witness, on another occasion, made a statement which is inconsistent with his present testimony.

Documentary evidence

It is a general rule that the contents of a document (a term which includes not only a written document but also a map or drawing, photograph, disc, tape or the like, and any film or the like) may be proved only by production of the original or an admission as to its contents (primary evidence). However, there are now so many exceptions to this general rule that it has lost much of its importance. When one of these exceptions applies, secondary evidence (eg a copy authenticated in a way approved by the court or oral evidence) of the contents of the document may be given.

The principal exceptions whereby secondary evidence of the contents of a document may be given are as follows:

(1)   Where the original is proved to have been lost or destroyed, secondary evidence of the contents may be given.
(2)   The contents of public documents can always be proved by means of secondary evidence, although some statutes providing this exception for a particular type of public document limit the nature of this secondary evidence. A 'public document' is a document prepared for the purpose of the public making use of it and being able to refer to it. Examples are Registers of Births, Deaths, and Marriages, the contents of which can be proved by a copy of an entry certified by a person who has lawful custody of the register. Judicial notice is taken of Acts of Parliament and their contents, ie they do not have to be proved by evidence. A statutory instrument is proved by production of the Queen's Printer's copy.

(3) By the Bankers' Books Evidence Act 1879, ss 3–5, an examined copy of any entry in a banker's book kept in the ordinary course of business is admissible as prima facie evidence of such entry.

Certain statutory provisions specially provide for evidence to be given by the production of a document. Examples appear in the discussion of the exceptions to the rule against hearsay.

Real evidence

Real evidence is the production of an object for the inspection of the court or jury. Where a document (or other object bearing writing) is produced as evidence of the matter contained in it, as opposed to proof of its physical existence, it is, as we have just seen, documentary evidence. The firearm which was produced by a witness in the example quoted earlier is real evidence. So, it has been held, is a computer printout recording attempts to enter a website. Police officers frequently give evidence of having recovered stolen property; this is oral evidence. When the property is produced for inspection in court, this is real evidence.

Original evidence and hearsay evidence

Original evidence is evidence of a fact by 'first-hand' evidence of it. Hearsay evidence is 'second-hand' evidence, since it consists of any representation of fact or opinion made by whatever means (eg orally, in writing, or by conduct (such as a nod of the head)) by a person, otherwise than in oral evidence in the particular proceedings, which is tendered as evidence to establish the matter stated in it. As an example, a policeman's notebook containing a statement about a stabbing is hearsay evidence of the stabbing. It must be emphasised that not all evidence of what someone else stated is hearsay. If it is produced merely to prove the fact that it was stated, as opposed to being produced with the object of establishing the truth of what was stated, it is original evidence and not hearsay evidence. If D says that he acted under a threat to kill him made by Y, evidence of what he said is original evidence because it is produced as evidence that Y uttered a threat, but, if a witness says that X had told him that Y had broken the windows of a greenhouse, this is hearsay evidence since it is produced as evidence of the truth of what X stated, ie that Y had broken the windows.

The distinction between original evidence and hearsay evidence is important, because hearsay evidence is inadmissible in criminal cases unless its admission is permitted under a variety of rules.

PROOF

The general rule is that the prosecution must prove the existence of any fact on which it relies. There are, however, certain facts which do not need to be proved.

Facts which may be established by means other than proof

Judicial notice

The court may take 'judicial notice' of certain matters which are so notorious or well known that evidence of their existence need not be adduced. One does not have to prove that beer is intoxicating, for example, as this is a matter of general knowledge, whereas it may be necessary to prove that a less well-known drink is intoxicating.

Presumptions

Sometimes there is a presumption of *law* that if a particular fact is proved some other fact *must* be presumed to exist. There are two kinds of presumption of law: irrebuttable and rebuttable.

When the presumption is irrebuttable, no evidence can be received to contradict the presumed fact. An example of an irrebuttable presumption of law is provided by the rule that a child under 10 is incapable of committing an offence.

Where there is a rebuttable presumption of law against D, the jury (or magistrates) must find that the presumed fact existed unless (depending on the presumption) D proves the contrary on the balance of probabilities, or there is evidence raising a doubt that the presumption is rebutted (in which case the prosecution will have to disprove that evidence beyond reasonable doubt). An example of a rebuttable presumption of law is that mechanical instruments are in proper working order, in the absence of evidence to the contrary.

Presumptions of law must be distinguished from presumptions of *fact*. When a jury (or magistrates' court) *may* find that a particular fact (the presumed fact) exists on proof of some other fact, the presumption is one of fact. Presumptions of fact arise in a wide range of cases, because they are suggested by common sense. For example, if D is seen driving a car immediately after an accident, it may be inferred that he was driving at the time of the accident. As a moment's thought shows, presumptions of fact are merely particular and frequently occurring instances of the operation of circumstantial evidence since the nature of circumstantial evidence is that it consists of facts from which other facts may be presumed to exist.

Formal admissions

A formal admission of a fact *dispenses with the need* for proving that fact since it is conclusive evidence of that fact as against the party admitting it. Provision is made for formal admissions, by or on behalf of either prosecution or defence, by the Criminal Justice Act 1967, s 10. Such a formal admission may be made before or at the proceedings. Unless made in court, it must be made in writing and signed by the person making it (or by an officer of the company if made by a company).

CJA 2003, s 118 preserves the common law rules under which in criminal proceedings:

(a) an admission made by D's agent (eg solicitor or counsel), or
(b) a statement made by a person to whom D refers a person for information,

is admissible as evidence against D of any matter stated.

The burden of proof

The burden of proof is often described as the 'persuasive' or 'legal' burden. The general rule is that the prosecution has the burden of proving D's guilt beyond reasonable doubt. In more detail, the position is as follows. The prosecution must prove beyond reasonable doubt that D committed the actus reus of the offence charged with the requisite mens rea. In relation to defences, D normally has the burden of adducing sufficient evidence to raise a defence (an evidential burden); if he does so it is then for the prosecution to disprove the alleged defence beyond reasonable doubt.

Exceptionally, D has the burden of proving a defence on the balance of probabilities. The burden of proof is imposed on D in the following cases:

Defence of insanity This was outlined in Chapter 1.

Express statutory provision A statute sometimes provides that it is a defence if D proves certain facts. For example, under the Homicide Act 1957, s 2, D has the burden of proving the defence of diminished responsibility on a charge of murder.

Provisos and exemptions in statutory offences Where a statute governing any offence provides any exception, exemption, proviso, excuse or qualification, as where it prohibits the doing of an act save in specified circumstances (or by persons of specified classes, or with specified qualifications, or with the licence or permission of specified authorities), the onus of proving such an exception, exemption, etc is impliedly cast on D. This rule is provided in the case of summary proceedings by the Magistrates' Courts Act 1980, s 101, and applies in the case of trial on indictment by virtue of the common law. In exceptional cases, however, the rule will not apply if the court construes the legislation as only imposing an evidential burden.

Rebuttable presumption of law against the defendant where the defendant bears the burden of proving that the presumption is rebutted We dealt with this on p 220.

Placing a persuasive burden on D may be incompatible with the presumption of innocence guaranteed by the European Convention on Human Rights, art 6(2) (see p 270), depending on the nature of the provision which imposes that burden. In each case it depends on whether imposing a persuasive burden serves a legitimate aim and is a justifiable and proportionate response to it; if not it will be incompatible. The Human Rights Act 1998, s 3 gives the courts a liberal power of statutory interpretation which enables them to read an express or implied statutory requirement for D to prove something as simply imposing an evidential burden on D if this makes the provision compatible with the Convention when it would not otherwise be so.

Corroboration

'Corroboration' is evidence from a source (or sources) independent of the witness whose evidence is to be corroborated, which confirms or supports that evidence in some material particular. Corroboration is not generally required as a matter of law. This means that, generally, although corroboration may aid proof, it is possible for the prosecution to discharge its burden of proof by adducing only one item of evidence.

There are, however, exceptional circumstances in which corroboration is required by statute or may be necessary as a matter of practice.

Corroboration required by statute

In cases under this heading the relevant fact is not proved on uncorroborated evidence given on behalf of the prosecution. These cases are:

(a) perjury and other offences under the Perjury Act 1911; and
(b) speeding contrary to the Road Traffic Regulation Act 1984, s 89.

Discretion to give corroboration warning

A judge has a *discretion* to give a warning to the jury about the danger of convicting on the uncorroborated evidence of a witness. For it to be appropriate for a warning to be given, there must be an evidential basis for suggesting that a witness is unreliable; mere suggestions by counsel do not provide such a basis.

Proof of convictions and acquittals

The Police and Criminal Evidence Act 1984 (PACE), s 73 provides that, where the fact that a person has in the UK or in any other EU member state been convicted or acquitted of an offence, otherwise than by a Service court, is admissible in evidence, it may be proved by producing a certificate of conviction or acquittal relating to that offence, and proving that the person named in the certificate is the person whose conviction or acquittal for the offence is to be proved. The certificate must be signed by the 'proper officer' of the court of conviction or acquittal, ie the designated officer in the case of a magistrates' court in England and Wales; the clerk of the court, his deputy, or any other person with custody of the court record in the case of any other court in the UK; or, in relation to a court in another EU state, the officer of the foreign court who equates to a certificate-signatory in the UK. A document purporting to be such a certificate is presumed to be such until the contrary is proved. Where such a certificate is relied on to prove a conviction against D, it must be proved by the prosecution beyond reasonable doubt that D is the person named in that certificate. In respect of any foreign conviction not covered by s 73, there is a corresponding provision in the Evidence Act 1851, s 7. This refers to 'examined copies' or 'authenticated copies' of the foreign court's conviction records.

PACE, s 73 supplements other previous provisions. The Criminal Procedure Act 1865, s 6 provides that if, on a witness being lawfully questioned about a conviction, there is a denial or refusal to answer, the cross-examining party may prove the conviction. To do so, the procedure under s 73 will have to be followed. The Road Traffic Offenders Act 1988, s 31 provides that, where a person is convicted of an offence involving obligatory or discretionary disqualification, any previous conviction for a driving offence endorsed on the counterpart of his driving licence or his driving record is prima facie evidence of that conviction.

In any proceedings where evidence is admissible of the fact that D has committed an offence, he is rebuttably presumed by PACE, s 74 to have committed it if he is proved to have been convicted (ie found guilty) of it by a UK court, by an EU court or by a Service court outside the UK.

PACE, s 74 also provides that the fact that a person *other than* D has been convicted in the UK or any other EU member state or by a Service court outside the UK been convicted of an offence by such a court is admissible in evidence for the purpose of proving that that person committed that offence, where evidence of his having done so is admissible. If that conviction is proved that person is rebuttably presumed to have committed it. However, where D is jointly charged with others who have pleaded guilty, proof of the convictions of those others, in circumstances where the jury is encouraged to rely on that evidence in determining D's guilt, is liable to be held inadmissible by reason of its adverse effect upon the fairness of the proceedings in accordance with PACE, s 78. As to s 78, see p 260.

Although it is possible to prove previous convictions by adducing Police National Computer (PNC) records admitted under CJA 2003, s 117 (see p 238), s 117 cannot be relied on so as to make admissible details on the PNC about the offences (as opposed to the dates of convictions, the offences charged, and the sentences).

COMPETENCE, COMPELLABILITY, AND PRIVILEGE

Who can give evidence? Who is obliged to? When is a witness entitled to refuse to answer questions? The answers to these questions are to be found respectively in the law relating to competence to give evidence, to compellability to give evidence and to various types of privilege.

Competence

YJCEA 1999, s 53 provides that anyone, of whatever age, is competent to give evidence in criminal proceedings unless he is unable to understand questions put to him as a witness, or unable to answer them in a way which can be understood. The Court of Appeal has emphasised that this alone is the test of competence, and that a witness need not understand the special importance that the truth should be told in court, and the witness need not understand every single question or give a readily understandable answer to every question. A witness may need the assistance of 'special measures' (see p 225).

A person charged in criminal proceedings is not competent to give evidence *for the prosecution* (whether or not he is the only person, or is one of two or more persons, charged in the proceedings). This reference to a person charged in criminal proceedings does not include a person who is not, or is no longer, liable to be convicted of any offence in the proceedings (whether because of a guilty plea, or otherwise).

Under s 54, questions of competence are decided by the court and in the absence of the jury if there is one. The party calling the witness must satisfy the court that the witness, on the balance of probabilities, is competent to give evidence.

As a general rule a witness who is competent is also compellable.

Compellability of D's spouse or civil partner

PACE, s 80 deals with the 'compellability' of the *spouse or civil partner of a defendant* to give evidence.

In any proceedings, the spouse or civil partner (W) of a person charged in the proceedings is compellable to give evidence *on behalf of that person*, unless he or she (ie W) is also charged in those proceedings.

In addition, provided that he or she (ie W) is not also charged in those proceedings, W is compellable to give evidence *on behalf of any other person charged in those proceedings*, but only in respect of any specified offence with which that other person is charged, *or to give evidence for the prosecution*, but only in respect of any specified offence with which any person is charged in the proceedings. In relation to W, an offence is a specified offence for these purposes if:

(a) it involves an assault on, or injury or a threat of injury to, W or a person who was at the material time under 16;

(b) it is a sexual offence alleged to have been committed in respect of a person who was at the material time under 16; or

(c) it consists of encouraging or assisting, attempting or conspiring to commit, or of aiding, abetting, counselling, or procuring the commission of, an offence under (a) or (b).

The Court of Appeal has held that (a) is judged by reference to the legal nature of the offence (ie the offence charged must in itself encompass the real possibility of an assault, or injury, or threat of injury), and not its factual circumstances; thus, an offence of threatening to damage another's property fell outside (a), even though in the circumstances there was a threat of injury, because the legal nature of that offence did not involve the real possibility of an assault, or injury, or a threat of injury.

For the purposes of (b), a 'sexual offence' is an offence under:

(a) the Protection of Children Act 1978 (taking, etc indecent photographs, etc of a child);
(b) the Sexual Offences Act 2003, Part 1 (ss 1–79); or
(c) the Sexual Offences Act 1956 or the Indecency with Children Act 1960, both of which have been repealed.

The references above to a person charged in any proceedings do not include a person who is not, or is no longer, liable to be convicted of any offence in the proceedings (whether as a result of pleading guilty or for any other reason).

The failure of a spouse or civil partner of a person charged in any proceedings to give evidence in the proceedings may not be commented on by the prosecution.

An ex-spouse or ex-civil partner is compellable to give evidence as if he or she had never been married to the defendant.

Privilege

Self-incrimination

A person required to answer questions or produce documents may refuse to do so on the grounds that the evidence might incriminate him. Exceptions to this rule are created by a number of statutes concerned with drink-driving, the care and protection of children, and investigations carried out by the Serious Fraud Office. However, the Companies Act 1985, the Financial Services and Markets Act 2000, and similar legislation provide restrictions in relation to the use of evidence obtained within SFO investigations.

Lawyer/client

Communications between a qualified lawyer and his client which are concerned with the giving of legal advice or as to the presentation of material, and those between a qualified lawyer, his client and a third party which are concerned with litigation and legal advice, are privileged. Privilege is not afforded in respect of communications in the furtherance of crime or fraud. In addition, where such communications are disclosed from other sources (document coming into possession of police) or where privilege is waived by the lawyer's client, such evidence may be given.

Public policy and public interest immunity

Privilege on the ground of public interest immunity (PII) relates to the non-disclosure of material held by the prosecution on grounds of the public interest. The approach to be taken where such immunity is claimed is as follows:

(1) Does the material weaken the prosecution case or strengthen the defence case? If it does not, it should not be disclosed. If it does, the 'golden rule' is that disclosure should be made unless PII prevents it.
(2) In determining whether the golden rule can be derogated from, the court must consider whether there is a real risk of serious prejudice to an important public interest. If there is not, PII does not apply and the material must be disclosed.
(3) If the material does give rise to such a risk, the court must consider whether D's interests can be protected without disclosure or whether disclosure can be ordered in a way which would adequately protect the public interest and the interests of the defence. This requires the court to consider whether the prosecution should formally admit what the defence sought to establish or whether limited disclosure could be ordered.

(4) If the court is minded to order limited disclosure it must consider whether what it proposes in order to protect D's interest and the public interest represents the minimum derogation to protect the public interest. If it does not, fuller disclosure should be ordered.

(5) If limited disclosure might render the trial process unfair to D, fuller disclosure should be ordered even if this leads to the discontinuance of the prosecution case. The court must keep the issue of unfairness under review as the trial proceeds.

Where a claim of PII is successful no adverse inference may be drawn from the witness's failure to give evidence. Notice should be given of an intention to claim such privilege.

PII may apply to many police matters: information relied upon for the issue of search warrants; reports to the DPP; the disclosure of the identity of informants or the siting of police observation posts. PII may also apply to files relating to the investigation of complaints (although disclosure of working papers and reports prepared by investigating officers may be ordered where the public interest in disclosure outweighs that in preserving confidentiality) and to disciplinary matters connected with the police. On the other hand, any written complaint made about the conduct of a police officer is not privileged. Nor can privilege be claimed in respect of statements made within a police 'grievance' procedure alleging unlawful discrimination.

PROTECTION OF WITNESSES

Special measures directions in case of vulnerable and intimidated witnesses (other than defendants)

The relevant provisions about such directions are in YJCEA 1999, ss 16–32.

Eligibility for special measures

Witnesses who are eligible for assistance on grounds of age or incapacity   A witness in criminal proceedings may be eligible under YJCEA 1999, ss 16 or 17 for assistance by special measures to help him in giving his evidence.

Section 16 provides that a witness (W) (*other than the defendant*) is eligible for such assistance if:

(a) W is *under 18 at the time of the hearing* (the time when a court must decide whether he is eligible for such assistance); or

(b) if the court considers that the quality of the evidence given by W is likely to be diminished by reason of W:
   (i)   suffering from mental disorder within the meaning of the Mental Health Act 1983; or
   (ii) otherwise having a significant impairment of intelligence and social functioning; or
   (iii) having a physical disability or suffering from physical disorder.

References to the quality of W's evidence are to its quality in terms of completeness, coherence, and accuracy. 'Coherence' refers to W's ability in testifying to give answers which address the questions put to him and can be understood both individually and collectively (ie in relation to a particular question and to his evidence generally).

Witnesses eligible for assistance on ground of fear or distress about testifying   YJCEA 1999, s 17 provides that a witness in criminal proceedings (*other than the defendant (D)*) is eligible for assistance by special measures where the court is satisfied that the quality of evidence given by him is likely to be diminished by reason of fear or distress on his part in connection with testifying in the proceedings. In determining whether it is so satisfied, the court must consider in particular:

(a) the nature and the alleged circumstances of the offence to which the proceedings relate;
(b) W's age;
(c) such of the following matters which appear relevant:
  (i) W's social and cultural background and ethnic origins;
  (ii) W's domestic and employment circumstances; or
  (iii) W's religious beliefs or political opinions, if any;
(d) any behaviour towards W on the part of:
  (i) D;
  (ii) members of the family or associates of D; or
  (iii) any other person who is likely to be a defendant or a witness in the proceedings.

Where the complainant in respect of a sexual offence under the Sexual Offences Act 2003, Part 1 (ss 1 to 79) (Chapters 29 and 30) is a witness in proceedings relating to that offence (or another offence), there is a presumption that the witness is eligible for assistance by special measures unless the witness waives that entitlement.

There is a presumption that a witness in proceedings relating to a relevant offence involving weapons (or to a relevant offence and any other offences) is eligible for assistance by special measures, unless the witness waives that entitlement. For these purposes, an offence is a relevant offence if it is an offence described in Sch 1A, viz:

(a) murder, or manslaughter, where it is alleged that *a firearm or knife* was used to cause the death in question, or where it is alleged that:
  (i) D was carrying such a weapon during the commission of the offence, and
  (ii) a person other than D knew or believed during the commission of the offence that D was carrying such a weapon;
(b) an offence under the Offences Against the Person Act 1861, ss 18, 20, 38, or 47 where it is alleged that *a firearm or knife* was used to commit the offence in question, or in a case where it is alleged that (i) or (ii) above applies;
(c) an offence under the Prevention of Crime Act 1953, s 1 or s 1A or the Criminal Justice Act 1988, s 139 or s 139A or s 139AA (which deal with having an offensive weapon or bladed or pointed article in public places or schools or threatening with such an article);
(d) an offence under the Firearms Act 1968, ss 1, 2(1), 3, 4, 5(1), 5(1A), 16, 16A, 17, 18, 19, 20, 21, 21A, or 24A;
(e) an offence under the Violent Crime Reduction Act 2006, ss 28, 32, or 36.

For the above offences see Chapters 19, 23, and 25.

The reference in (a) and (b) to an offence ('offence A') includes a reference to:

(i) an attempt or conspiracy to commit offence A in a case where it is alleged that the attempt or conspiracy was to commit offence A in a manner or circumstances described in (a) or (b);
(ii) an offence under the Serious Crime Act 2007, Part 2 (encouraging or assisting crime) in relation to which offence A is the offence (or one of them) which the person intended or believed would be committed in a case where it is alleged that the person intended or believed offence A would be committed in the manner or circumstances described in (a) or (b); and

(iii) aiding, abetting, counselling, or procuring the commission of offence A in a case where it is alleged that offence A was committed, or the act or omission charged in respect of offence A was done or made, in the manner or circumstances described in (a) or (b).

A reference in (c)–(e) to an offence ('offence A') includes a reference to:

(i) an attempt or conspiracy to commit offence A;
(ii) an offence under the Serious Crime Act 2007, Part 2 in relation to which offence A is the offence (or one of the offences) which the person intended or believed would be committed; and
(iii) aiding, abetting, counselling, or procuring the commission of offence A.

Special measures direction

By YJCEA 1999, s 18, a range of special measures is made potentially available to witnesses in criminal proceedings who are eligible for special measures under s 16 or s 17. The 'special measures' are set out in detail by ss 23 to 30 (below).

Special measures direction relating to eligible witness YJCEA 1999, s 19(2) provides that, once a court has determined that a witness is eligible for special measures, it must then determine whether any of those measures (or a combination of them) would be likely to improve the quality of the witness's evidence and, if so, determine which of those measures would be likely to maximise so far as practicable the quality of his evidence. Having made this second determination, it must give a 'special measures' direction in relation to the measure or measures so determined. An exception to this approach is provided by s 21.

Special provisions relating to child witnesses YJCEA 1999, s 21 provides special protection for one type of person eligible for 'special measures' under s 16: 'a child witness' (ie someone under 18 at the time of the hearing). It provides that, where in making a determination under s 19, a court determines that a witness (W) is a 'child witness', it must first have regard to the following provisions. Under them the 'primary rule' is that in respect of W it must give a special measures direction providing for a video recording of his evidence-in-chief to be admitted (unless this is contrary to the interests of justice) and providing for any evidence given by him which is not by means of video recording (whether in chief or otherwise) to be given by means of a live link. The primary rule does not apply to the extent that the court is satisfied that compliance with it would not be likely to maximise the quality of W's evidence so far as practicable (whether because the application to that evidence of one or more other special measures available in relation to the witness would have that result or for any other reason).

If W informs the court of his wish that the primary rule should not apply or should apply only in part, the primary rule does not apply to the extent that the court is *satisfied that not complying with the rule would not diminish the quality of W's evidence*. Where, as a consequence of all or part of the primary rule being disapplied under this provision, W's evidence or any part of it would fall to be given as testimony in court, the court must give a special measures direction for W to be screened from D when giving the evidence or that part of it. However, this screening requirement is subject to two limitations:

(a) if W informs the court of his wish that the requirement should not apply, the requirement should not apply to the extent that the court *is satisfied that not complying with it would not diminish the quality of W's evidence*; and
(b) the requirement does not apply to the extent that the court is satisfied that screening would not be likely to maximise the quality of W's evidence so far as practicable.

In making a decision under the italicised provisions, the court must take into account the following factors (and any others it considers relevant):

(a) W's age and maturity;
(b) W's ability to understand the consequences of giving evidence otherwise than in accordance with the requirements of the primary rule or a screening requirement (as the case may be);
(c) the relationship (if any) between W and D;
(d) W's social and cultural background and ethnic origins;
(e) the nature and alleged circumstances of the offence to which the proceedings relate.

Only after it has had regard to the above provisions must the court have regard to s 19(2) (above).

The House of Lords has held that YJCEA 1999, s 21 is not incompatible with D's right to a fair trial guaranteed by the European Convention on Human Rights, art 6.

If a witness is not under 18 at the hearing but was under 18 when a video recording of his evidence-in-chief was made, YJCEA 1999, s 22 provides that the primary rule applies, *so far as relating to the giving of a direction for the recording to be admitted.*

Special provisions relating to sexual offences

Section 22A makes special provisions relating to the trial of a sexual offence (or a sexual offence and other offences) *in the Crown Court where the complainant is a witness in the proceedings and is not under* 18 *at the time of the hearing.* (If the complainant is under 18, YJCEA 1999, s 21 applies.) *Where it applies,* s 22A establishes a rule in favour of admitting the complainant's video-recorded evidence-in-chief. Section 22A does not mean that such evidence is inadmissible in a magistrates' court, but merely that there is no rule in favour of admitting it.

The operation of s 22A is as follows:

(1) If a party to the proceedings applies for a special measures direction in relation to the complainant, that party may request that the direction provide for a video recording of an interview of the complainant to be admitted as evidence-in-chief of the complainant.
(2) If the court determines that the complainant is eligible for assistance by virtue of s 16 (see (b) on p 225) or s 17 (see p 225), it must give such a special measures direction in relation to the complainant, unless:
   (i) it considers that in the interests of justice the recording should not be admitted; or
   (ii) it is satisfied that compliance with such a direction would not be likely to maximise the quality of the complainant's evidence so far as practicable (whether because the application to that evidence of one or more other special measures available in relation to the complainant would have that result or for any other reason).

Special measures available

The special measures are:

(1) *Screening (s 23)*   Screens may be authorised to shield W from D (but the judge, jury, justices, a legal representative from each side, any interpreter, and any person appointed to assist W must be able to see him).
(2) *Evidence by live link (s 24)*   Usually this will be done by closed-circuit television but any technology is permitted. Where a live link direction is given, evidence may

not be given in any other way without the consent of the court. A divisional court has held that evidence being given in this way does not breach D's human right to a fair trial.

(3) *Evidence given in private (s 25)* The court may be cleared of non-essential personnel but this measure is only available in relation to a sexual offence or when the court reasonably believes that someone has tried to intimidate, or will try to intimidate W. At least one member of the press must be allowed to remain in court.

(4) *Removal of wigs and gowns (s 26)* This applies to the judiciary as well as legal representatives.

(5) *Video-recorded evidence-in-chief (s 27)* Where this special measure is directed, it will provide for a video recording of an interview of W to be admitted in evidence-in-chief. However, the direction may not provide for a video recording, or part of it, to be admitted if its admission would not be in the interests of justice. If it is decided to permit only an edited version to be shown, the court must consider whether the exclusion of part of the recording is prejudicial. A court may later exclude a recording if its making is not properly proved, but may nevertheless admit it in such circumstances. The party tendering the evidence must call W, unless a special measures direction provides for cross-examination under s 28 (see (6) below) or the parties have agreed to non-attendance. W may not without the permission of the court give evidence-in-chief otherwise than by means of the recording as to any matter which, in the opinion of the court, is dealt with in his recorded testimony. In giving such permission, the court may direct that the evidence is given by W by means of a live link.

(6) *Video-recorded cross-examination or re-examination (s 28)* The relevant provisions are not yet in force. When they are the law will be as follows. Where a special measures direction provides for video recording of W's evidence-in-chief to be admitted, the special measures direction may also provide that W may be cross-examined before trial and that that cross-examination (and any re-examination) may be recorded for use at trial. This will not occur in the physical presence of D, although D will be able to see and hear it and to communicate with his legal adviser (live link). Nor need it take place in the physical presence of the judge or magistrates and the defence and prosecution legal representatives, although they must be able to see and hear the examination and to communicate with those present. However, a judge or magistrate must control the proceedings and this person will normally be the trial judge or magistrate. Where a recording has been made of the examination of W under the above power, W may not be subsequently cross-examined or re-examined in respect of his evidence unless the court makes a further direction to this effect. Such a further direction may only be given: (a) where the proposed cross-examination is sought by a party to the proceedings as a result of having become aware since the original recording of a matter which he could not with reasonable diligence have ascertained by then, or (b) where it is in the interests of justice to do so.

The following two additional measures under ss 29 and 30 are available only in the case of someone eligible for special measures under s 16:

Examination of witness through intermediary (s 29) An intermediary is an interpreter or someone else whom the court approves to communicate to W the questions asked in court, and then to communicate W's answers. The intermediary may also explain such questions or answers, if necessary to facilitate understanding. An intermediary will normally be a specialist. An intermediary can act however and wherever the examination is conducted. The judge or magistrates, and at least one legal representative for each side, should be able to see and hear W and to communicate with the intermediary. The jury must be able to see and hear W unless the evidence is video recorded.

Aids to communication (s 30)   A special measures direction may require a witness to be provided with an appropriate device to assist communication.

General   Evidence given using any of the special measures set out above must be treated in the same way as oral evidence. However, the judge may give such warning to the jury as he considers necessary to ensure fairness to D.

If a witness who would normally be sworn gives unsworn evidence by means of a video recording, that evidence is admissible. However, where a person authorised to administer an oath is present, the evidence could be taken under oath in appropriate cases.

The *Consolidated Criminal Practice Direction* requires that the party who made the application to admit video-recorded evidence-in-chief must edit the recording in accordance with the judge's directions and send a copy of the edited recording to the appropriate officer of the Crown Court and to every other party to the proceedings.

Where a video recording is to be adduced during proceedings before a Crown Court, it must be produced and proved by the interviewer, or any other person who was present at the interview with the witness, at which the recording was made. The parties may agree to accept a written statement in lieu of the attendance of such a person. The party adducing the video recording must arrange for the operation of the video-playing equipment.

Failure so to prepare, which leads to an adjournment for this to be done, may lead to an appropriate award for costs.

Best practice in questioning child and vulnerable witnesses

The Ministry of Justice has published assistance for those dealing with witnesses subject to special measures and for those preparing video-recorded interviews, *Achieving Best Evidence: Guidance on Interviewing Victims and Witnesses, and Guidance on Using Special Measures.*

The guidance is primarily aimed at police officers conducting visually-recorded interviews with vulnerable, intimidated and significant witnesses, those tasked with preparing and supporting such witnesses during the criminal justice process and those involved at the trial, both in supporting and questioning the witness in court. While the guidance is advisory, compliance with *Achieving Best Evidence* and effective training is likely to maximise the quality of interviews with such witnesses and is likely to benefit the interviewer, the witness, practitioners and the courts alike. Significant departures from the guidance may have to be justified in the courts.

The guidance is complemented by another Ministry of Justice publication, *Vulnerable and Intimidated Witnesses: a Police Service Guide* which provides guidance to assist in the identification of vulnerable and intimidated witnesses.

Evidence of vulnerable defendant

YJCEA 1999, ss 33A to 33BA make provision for the giving of evidence by means of a live link in the case of certain vulnerable defendants.

Live link directions

Section 33A allows a court, on the application of the defendant, D, to direct that D's evidence should be given over a live link. The court must be satisfied that it would be in the interests of justice for D to give evidence through a live link, and:

(a) if D is under 18, that his ability to participate effectively as a witness giving oral evidence is compromised by his level of intellectual ability or social functioning, and that use of a live link would enable him to participate more effectively as a witness;

(b) if D is 18 or over, that he is unable to participate in the proceedings effectively as a witness in court giving oral evidence because he has a mental disorder or a significant impairment of intelligence and social function, and that use of a live link would enable him to participate more effectively, as a witness.

Section 33A is intended to provide a structured approach to decision-making and to ensure that the giving of evidence in this way is reserved for exceptional cases. Where a juvenile is concerned the test is less strict as there is no reference to mental disorder or impairment.

Where a direction has been given under s 33A, D must give all his oral evidence through a live link and cross-examination should be carried out by the same means.

Examination of defendant through intermediary

When s 33BA is in force it will enable a court to direct D's evidence to be given through an 'intermediary' where D is:

(a) under 18 and his ability to participate effectively in the proceedings as a witness giving oral evidence in court is compromised by his level of intellectual ability or social functioning; or

(b) 18 or over and suffers from a mental disorder or otherwise has a significant impairment of intelligence and social function, and is for that reason unable to participate effectively in the proceedings as a witness giving oral evidence in court,

and, in either case, such a direction is necessary to ensure that D receives a fair trial.

The judge or magistrates, and at least one legal representative for each side, should be able to see and hear D communicate with the intermediary. The jury must be able to see and hear D.

Pending the coming into force of s 33BA, it should be noted that a divisional court has held that the courts have a common law duty to appoint an intermediary to help a child defendant (or, indeed, an adult defendant) follow the proceedings and give evidence where he would otherwise not have a fair trial.

Protection of witnesses from cross-examination by defendant in person

Complainants in proceedings for sexual offences

YJCEA 1999, s 34 provides that no person charged with a sexual offence may in any criminal proceedings cross-examine in person a witness who is a complainant, either in connection with the offence, or in connection with any other offence (of whatever nature) with which that person is charged in the proceedings. For these purposes, 'sexual offence' means any offence under the Sexual Offences Act 2003 (SOA 2003), Part 1 (ss 1–79) or any 'relevant superseded sexual offence', ie a corresponding offence superseded by SOA 2003, Part 1.

Child complainants and other witnesses who are children

In relation to an offence to which it applies, YJCEA 1999, s 35 makes similar provisions concerning a 'protected witness'. A 'protected witness' is a witness who:

(a) either is a complainant or a witness to the offence; and

(b) either is a child or falls to be cross-examined after giving evidence-in-chief as a child.

YJCEA 1999, s 35 applies to any offence under SOA 1956, ss 33–36 (brothels), the Protection of Children Act 1978 (taking, etc indecent photographs, etc of a child), and any offence under SOA 2003, Part 1 (ss 1–79) or any 'relevant superseded enactment', ie a statutory enactment containing a corresponding offence or offences superseded by SOA 2003, Part 1. For the purposes of YJCEA 1999, s 35, where an offence is under one of these pieces of legislation, a 'child' is someone under 18.

Section 35 also applies to kidnapping, false imprisonment, child abduction (Child Abduction Act 1984, ss 1 or 2), cruelty to children (Children and Young Persons Act 1933, s 1), or any offence involving an assault on, or injury (or a threat of injury) to, any person. For the purposes of these other specified offences, a 'child' is someone under 14.

Direction prohibiting cross-examination

YJCEA 1999, s 36, which is not limited to sexual offences or the other offences to which s 35 applies, permits a court to prohibit an unrepresented defendant from cross-examining witnesses in other cases, where the provisions of ss 34 and 35 do not apply. This may be done where the court is satisfied that the quality of the evidence given by the witness on cross-examination is likely to be diminished if cross-examination is undertaken or continued by the defendant in person, and would be likely to be improved if a direction was given, and that such a prohibition will not be contrary to the interests of justice.

The term 'witness' does not include any other person who is charged with an offence within the proceedings.

Representation of such persons for the purpose of cross-examination

Where D is prohibited from cross-examining a witness under the provisions of YJCEA 1999, ss 34, 35, or 36, the court must invite D to appoint a legal representative to cross-examine on his behalf. If no such appointment is made within the prescribed time limits, the court must consider whether it is necessary, in the interests of justice, for the witness to be cross-examined by a legal representative. If the court considers that it is necessary, it must appoint a legal representative. Such a court-appointed representative will not have been instructed by D and will not, therefore, be responsible to him. Material relating to the proceedings must be made available to an appointee.

Warning to the jury

Where D is prevented from cross-examining a person by virtue of ss 34, 35, or 36, the judge must give the jury such warning as he considers necessary to ensure that D is not prejudiced:

(a) by any inferences which might be drawn from the fact that he has been prevented from cross-examining in person;

(b) where the witness has been cross-examined by a legal representative appointed by the court, by the fact that such cross-examination was carried out by a representative other than a person acting as D's own legal representative.

Witness anonymity

The Coroners and Justice Act 2009 (C&JA 2009), ss 86–95 provide for the making of witness anonymity orders (WAOs) in criminal proceedings, giving a court power to order that the identity of a witness is withheld from the defendant (D) in such

proceedings. Under s 86, a WAO is an order made by a court that requires such specified measures to be taken in relation to a witness (W) in criminal proceedings as the
court considers appropriate to ensure that the identity of W is not disclosed in or in
connection with the proceedings.

The kinds of measure that may be required to be taken in relation to W include
measures for securing one or more of the following:

(a) that W's name and other identifying features are withheld or removed from mate-
    rials disclosed to any party to the proceedings;
(b) that W may use a pseudonym;
(c) that W is not asked questions of any description specified in the order that might
    lead to his identification;
(d) that W is screened to any extent specified in the order; and
(e) that W's voice is subjected to modulation to any extent specified in the order.

The court cannot require:

(a) W to be screened to such an extent that W cannot be seen by:
    (i)   the judge or other members of the court (if any);
    (ii) the jury (if there is one); or
    (iii) any interpreter or other person appointed by the court to assist W;
(b) W's voice to be modulated to such an extent that W's natural voice cannot be heard
    by any person within (a).

Applications for WAO

By C&JA 2009, s 87, an application for a WAO to be issued in relation to W in criminal
proceedings may be made to the court by the prosecutor or D.

Where an application is made by the prosecutor, the prosecutor:

(a) must (unless the court directs otherwise) inform the court of the identity of W; but
(b) is not required to disclose in connection with the application:
    (i)   W's identity, or
    (ii) any information that might enable W to be identified,

to any other party to the proceedings or his or her legal representatives.

Where an application is made by D, D:

(a) must inform the court and the prosecutor of W's identity; but
(b) (if there is more than one defendant) is not required to disclose in connection with
    the application:
    (i)   W's identity, or
    (ii) any information that might enable W to be identified,

to any other defendant or his legal representatives.

Accordingly, where the prosecutor or D proposes to make an application under s 87,
any relevant material disclosed by or on behalf of that party before the determination
of the application may be disclosed in such a way as to prevent:

(a) W's identity; or
(b) any information that might enable W to be identified,

from being disclosed except as required by the duty to inform the court (and, where
relevant, the prosecutor) of W's identity.

The *Consolidated Criminal Practice Direction* deals further with the procedure on an application.

Conditions for making WAO

The court may make a WAO only if it is satisfied that conditions A to C below are all met (C&JA 2009, s 88).

Condition A is that the measures to be specified in the order are necessary:

(a) in order to protect the safety of W or another person or to prevent any serious damage to property; or
(b) in order to prevent real harm to the public interest (whether affecting the carrying on of any activities in the public interest or the safety of a person involved in carrying on such activities, or otherwise).

In determining whether the measures to be specified in the order are necessary for the purpose mentioned in (a) the court must have regard (in particular) to any reasonable fear on W's part that he or another person would suffer death or injury, or that there would be serious damage to property, if W were to be identified.

Condition B is that, having regard to all the circumstances, the taking of those measures would be consistent with D receiving a fair trial.

Condition C is that the importance of W's testimony is such that in the interests of justice the witness ought to testify and—

(a) the witness would not testify if the proposed order were not made, or
(b) there would be real harm to the public interest if the witness were to testify without the proposed order being made.

When deciding whether Conditions A to C are met in the case of an application for a WAO, the court must have regard to the following considerations:

(a) the general right of a defendant in criminal proceedings to know the identity of a witness in the proceedings;
(b) the extent to which the credibility of W would be a relevant factor when the weight of his identity comes to be assessed;
(c) whether evidence given by W might be the sole or decisive evidence implicating the defendant;
(d) whether W's evidence could be properly tested (whether on grounds of credibility or otherwise) without his identity being disclosed;
(e) whether there is any reason to believe that W has a tendency to be dishonest, or has any motive to be dishonest in the circumstances of the case, having regard (in particular) to any previous convictions of the witness and to any relationship between W and D or any of D's associates; and
(f) whether it would be reasonably practicable to protect W's identity by any means other than by making a WAO specifying the measures that are under consideration by the court (s 89).

The court must also have regard to other matters it considers relevant.

The Court of Appeal has held that, while the calling of anonymous witnesses must not become a routine event, WAOs should not be confined to cases of terrorism or gangland killings.

Warning to jury

By C&JA 2009, s 90, the judge must give the jury such warning as the judge considers appropriate to ensure that the fact that the order was made in relation to the witness does not lead them to prejudice D.

MEANS OF PROOF WHICH MAY BE INADMISSIBLE

Opinion

Opinion evidence is generally inadmissible because it is the function of the court or jury, and not of a witness, to draw conclusions from the facts proved. If a witness alleges that a particular driver was at fault and caused an accident, that evidence is inadmissible because that is the issue which the court or jury must decide. A fine line can sometimes exist between 'opinion' and 'fact', and for this reason evidence as to the identification of a person or thing (which must always be an opinion to some extent) is admissible. In addition, by way of exception to the general rule, the following opinion evidence of experts is admissible:

(a) opinion evidence of experts on matters (outside the knowledge or experience of a jury) of a scientific, technical, or artistic nature, such as doctors of medicine, forensic scientists, metallurgists or literary experts: a police officer can be an expert under this heading in appropriate circumstances; for example, the opinion evidence of a police officer that a quantity of drugs was too great for personal use was held admissible as expert evidence because the officer based his opinion on his 17 years' experience and on published and unpublished material;

(b) opinion evidence from persons who are experts in handwriting comparison; and

(c) opinion evidence by a lawyer shown to have knowledge of a particular system of foreign law.

An expert witness should provide independent, objective assistance to the court in relation to matters within his expertise, and should never assume the role of advocate. An expert is obliged to act in the cause of justice. His duties are owed to the court and override any obligation to those instructing him or by whom he is paid. Consequently, for example, if an expert instructed by the prosecution carries out a test, or knows that a test has been carried out in his laboratory, which casts doubt on his opinion, he must disclose this to his instructing solicitor, who must disclose it to the defence.

Hearsay

As already said, hearsay evidence is 'second-hand' evidence since it consists of any representation of fact or opinion made by whatever means (eg orally, in writing or by conduct) by a person otherwise than in oral evidence in the particular proceedings which is tendered as evidence of any matter stated *in it*. Hearsay evidence is inadmissible, unless its admission is permitted under a variety of rules, because the law of evidence generally requires a fact to be proved by direct evidence of it.

Of course, as already indicated, not all evidence of what someone other than a witness said or wrote is hearsay. If it is produced merely to prove the fact that it was said or written, as opposed to establishing a matter contained in the oral or written statement, it is original evidence and not hearsay evidence, and therefore admissible if relevant to the facts in issue. This distinction can be illustrated as follows.

If a witness says that the deceased, while in hospital with injuries from which he unexpectedly died, told him, 'Fred did this to me', this is hearsay evidence since it is produced as evidence of the truth of what the deceased stated, that is, that Fred caused the injuries.

By way of contrast, it is not necessarily hearsay evidence for evidence to be called to show that D said that he had acted under a threat of death made by Jones, or for a witness to say 'Mrs Bird complained to me that Tate had fondled her breasts'. This is original evidence of the fact that a threat or complaint had been made. The latter statement is, however, hearsay if it is intended to show the fact that the sexual offence has been committed.

The rule against hearsay evidence has gradually been whittled away, culminating in CJA 2003, Part 11, Chapter 2 (ss 114–136) which abolished the common law rules about hearsay evidence and created a set of rules about it.

The cases where a statement is admissible in criminal proceedings as evidence of the truth of its contents under an exception to the rule against hearsay are as follows.

Admissibility of hearsay evidence: the basic provisions

CJA 2003, Part 11, Chapter 2 commences in s 114 by stating in s 114(1) that hearsay evidence is admissible in criminal proceedings as evidence of any matter stated if, but only if:

(a) a statutory provision makes it admissible (considered below);
(b) any rule of law preserved by s 118 (pp 242–4) makes it admissible;
(c) all parties to the proceedings agree to it being admissible; or
(d) the court is satisfied that it is in the interests of justice for it to be admissible.

The Court of Appeal has held that an agreement can be inferred in appropriate circumstances for the purposes of (c) from a failure by a party to object to the admissibility of the hearsay evidence.

In deciding under (d) whether it is in the interests of justice, the court must have regard to the following factors (and any others it considers relevant):

(i)   how much probative value the statement has in relation to a matter in issue (ie how much value is it in determining the matter) or how valuable it is for understanding other evidence;
(ii)   what other evidence has been, or can be, given on the matter or evidence mentioned in (i);
(iii) how important the matter or evidence mentioned in (i) is in the context of the case as a whole;
(iv)   the circumstances in which the statement was made;
(v)   how reliable the maker of the statement appears to be;
(vi)   how reliable the evidence of the making of the statement appears to be;
(vii) whether oral evidence of the matter stated can be given and, if not, why it cannot;
(viii) the amount of difficulty involved in challenging the statement; and
(ix)   the extent to which the difficulty would be likely to prejudice the party facing it.

A court does not have to reach a conclusion about all nine of these factors in order to admit hearsay evidence under (d). The Court of Appeal has held that (d) must be cautiously applied in the case of an absent witness who does not fall within s 116 ('Witness unavailable'); otherwise the conditions in s 116 would be circumvented.

Referring to (iii), the Court of Appeal has stated that only in rare circumstances, if any, could it be right to allow the victim's evidence which was virtually the entirety of the prosecution's case to be adduced under (d) where there had been a failure to take reasonable steps to secure the attendance of the witness.

The Court of Appeal has also held that an anonymous witness statement made by a person whose identity is not known at all, cannot be admitted under the hearsay rules in CJA 2003, Part 11, Chapter 2.

CJA 2003, Part 11, Chapter 2 does not affect the exclusion of evidence of a statement on grounds other than the fact that it is hearsay. For example, a confession (a type of admissible hearsay) might be excluded under the provisions of PACE.

CJA 2003, s 115 provides that, for the purposes of CJA 2003, Part 11, Chapter 2, references to a 'statement' are to any representation of fact or opinion made by a person by whatever means, including a representation made in a sketch, photofit or other pictorial form. By s 115, a 'matter stated' is one to which CJA 2003, Part 11, Chapter 2 applies only if the purpose (or one of the purposes) of the maker of the statement appears to have been to cause another person to believe the matter, or to cause another person to act or a machine to operate on the basis that the matter is as stated. As a result a statement which was not made with such a purpose, but from which a fact may be inferred, is not hearsay evidence and is admissible. Examples would be a statement made in a secret diary or in a text to another person mentioning a fact that the texter believes the other knows. This reverses the old law of hearsay, under which such a statement was hearsay.

We now turn to the exceptions to the hearsay rule to which (a) and (b) above relate.

Witness unavailable

CJA 2003, s 116 provides that in criminal proceedings a statement which is not made in oral evidence in the proceedings is admissible in evidence as evidence of any matter stated if:

(a) oral evidence given by the person making the statement would be admissible as evidence of that matter;
(b) the person who made the statement is identified to the satisfaction of the court; and
(c) that person:
    (i) is dead;
    (ii) is unfit to be a witness because of his bodily or mental condition;
    (iii) is outside the UK and it is not reasonably practicable to secure his attendance;
    (iv) cannot be found although such steps as it is reasonably practicable to take to find him have been taken; or
    (v) through fear does not give (or continue to give) oral evidence in the proceedings, either at all, or in connection with the subject matter of the statement, and the court gives leave for the statement to be given in evidence.

'Unfit to be a witness' in (c)(ii) applies not only to a person's physical inability to attend a court but also to his mental capacity when there to give evidence. The Court of Appeal has said that there is nothing to prevent the written evidence of a witness being admitted where he is too ill to give evidence at the time of the trial, even though his evidence is the only evidence against D.

'Cannot be found' in (c)(iv) includes 'cannot be contacted'.

'Fear' in (c)(v) is to be widely construed and (for example) includes fear of the death or serious injury of another person or of financial loss. There must, if possible, be direct evidence (of fear) from the witness. However, the evidence of fear may, for example, be given by a police officer. Nonetheless, it is important to establish that the fear existed at the time of the trial. The Court of Appeal has said that it is not sufficient that the witness made a statement some months previously in which he said that he was afraid to give evidence because he feared repercussions against himself and his family. Before a court can properly be satisfied as to the requirements, it should be informed of what steps have been taken to persuade the witness to attend or to alleviate his fears. Leave to admit may only be given under (c)(v) where the court considers that the statement ought to be admitted in the interests of justice, having regard to its contents, to the risk of unfairness and, in appropriate cases, to the fact that a special measures direction could be made in relation to the person making the statement, and to any other relevant circumstances.

Any condition in (c)(i)–(v) which is in fact satisfied will be treated as not having been satisfied if any of the circumstances described in (c) effectively are caused by the person in support of whose case it is sought to admit the statement, or by any person acting on his behalf, in order to prevent the person referred to in (c) from giving oral evidence in the proceedings (whether at all or in connection with the subject matter of the statement). It is irrelevant whether the steps which had the relevant effect were taken before or after the commencement of the proceedings.

Business and other documents

CJA 2003, s 117 provides that in criminal proceedings a statement contained in a document is admissible as evidence of any matter stated if:

(a) oral evidence given in the proceedings would be admissible as evidence of that matter;

(b) the following requirements are satisfied:
   (i) the document or the part containing the statement was created or received by a person in the course of a trade, business, profession, or other occupation, or as the holder of a paid or unpaid office;
   (ii) the person who supplied the information contained in the statement (the relevant person) had, or may reasonably be supposed to have had, personal knowledge of the matters dealt with; and
   (iii) each person (if any) through whom the information was supplied from that relevant person to the person mentioned in (i) received the information in the course of a trade, business, profession, or other occupation, or as the holder of a paid or unpaid office; and

(c) additional requirements are satisfied where the statement was prepared for the purpose of pending or contemplated criminal proceedings, or for a criminal investigation, but was not obtained pursuant to a request under the Crime (International Co-operation) Act 2003, s 7, or an order under the Criminal Justice Act 1988, Sch 13 (overseas evidence). The additional requirements referred to are any of the five conditions set out at (c) under the heading 'Witness unavailable' on p 237 above, or that the relevant person cannot reasonably be expected to have any recollection of the matters dealt with in the statement (having regard to the length of time since he supplied the information and all other circumstances).

The persons mentioned in (b)(i) and (ii) may be the same person. Thus, for example, a note made by an operator working for a paging company that messages had been left for a customer would be admissible under s 117.

The provisions of s 117 are obviously sensible. It would be unnecessarily burdensome, and sometimes stultifying, if oral evidence was to be required in every case from a person who was either the creator or keeper of the document, or the supplier of the information contained in the document.

As a result of s 117, entries in a police officer's notebook (or a computerised crime record produced by a police officer) are admissible if the terms of s 117 are satisfied. An example of a case where s 117 was satisfied is where a man presented a stolen debit card at a supermarket checkout and a supervisor saw him making off in a car, the registered number of which she noted; a record made by a second supervisor, at the dictation of the first, was held to be a document created or received in the course of a business, profession, etc for these purposes; the fact that she could recall other matters which occurred at the time (such as the colour of the offender) did not mean that she could be expected to remember the registered number of the car.

It is important to note the limitations of s 117. For example, where a shopper had left the offending vehicle's registration number on the damaged car's windscreen after it had been hit in a supermarket car park and that number had been reported in the police incident log after it had been given by the girlfriend of the owner of the damaged car, the Court of Appeal held that the information in the log should not have been admitted under s 117 because the girlfriend had not received it in the course of trade or business and therefore condition (b)(iii) was not satisfied. The Court of Appeal added that the police record would have been admissible under the rule relating to the admissibility of multiple hearsay (see condition (c) under s 121 on 240).

A statement is not admissible under s 117 if the court makes a direction to that effect, which it can do if satisfied that the statement's reliability as evidence is doubtful, either in its contents, the source of its information, the way or circumstances in which the information was supplied or received, or the way in which the document was created or received.

Inconsistent statements

CJA 2003, s 119 provides that, where a witness (W) in criminal proceedings gives oral evidence and admits making a previous inconsistent statement, or a previous inconsistent statement made by W is proved to have been made, the previous statement is admissible as evidence of any matter in respect of which oral evidence would be admissible. Thus, the fact that W made a previous inconsistent statement does not merely affect W's credibility but it is also some evidence of the truth of the facts which W had previously stated. Evidence may be admitted to show that W has made a statement which is inconsistent with the evidence he has given.

Other previous statements of a witness

Where it is suggested that a witness (W) in criminal proceedings has fabricated oral evidence, a previous statement by W is admissible not only on the issue of credibility but also to prove the truth of the matters previously stated. This is the effect of CJA 2003, s 120(2) which states that any previous statement which W has made is admissible in evidence as evidence of any matter which it contains.

In addition, s 120(3) provides that where W refreshes his memory from a written document and is cross-examined on a statement in that document, and the document is in consequence received in evidence, that statement in the document will become evidence of any matter stated in it. Section 120(3) does not make admissible as truth of the matters stated a statement made in a written document in circumstances where a re-reading of a previous out-of-court document has failed to refresh W's memory when giving oral evidence at the trial. The situation where W has made a previous statement when the matters were fresh in his memory, but does not remember them at the time of the trial, even when he has attempted to refresh his memory, is dealt with specifically by (b) in the following provisions.

By s 120(4)–(7) a previous statement is also admissible as evidence of the facts contained in it if W states that he made the statement and believes it to be true and any one of the following conditions applies:

(a) that the statement describes or identifies a person, object, or place;
(b) that it was made by W when the matters stated were fresh in his memory, and he cannot reasonably be expected to remember the matters stated well enough to give oral evidence of them; or
(c) that:
   (i)   W claims to be a victim of an offence to which the proceedings relate,
   (ii) the statement consists of a complaint by W about conduct which (if proved) would constitute the offence (or part of it),
   (iii) the complaint was not made as a result of a threat or promise, and
   (iv) W gives oral evidence in respect of the matter before the statement is adduced.

Additional requirements for admissibility of multiple hearsay

'Multiple hearsay' refers to the case where the witness has no personal knowledge of the matter stated to him, but repeats a hearsay statement made to him by another, as where X makes a statement to Y who repeats it to Z. Repetition of the statement by Z is multiple (or second-hand) hearsay, whereas if Y gave the statement in evidence it would be first-hand hearsay. CJA 2003, s 121 provides that a hearsay statement is not admissible to prove the fact that an earlier hearsay statement was made unless:

(a) either of the statements is admissible under CJA 2003, ss 117 (business and other documents), 119 (inconsistent statements), or 120 (other previous statements by a witness), or
(b) all parties agree to its admissibility, or
(c) the court is satisfied that the value of the evidence in question, taking into account how reliable the statement appears to be, is so high that the interests of justice require the later statement to be admissible for that purpose.

CJA 2003, ss 116, 117, 119, and 120: general provisions concerning capability to make statements

CJA 2003, s 123 provides as follows.

A statement made under CJA 2003, s 116 (cases where a witness is unavailable), s 119, or s 120 is not admissible in evidence if it was made by a person who did not have the 'required capability' at the time that he made the statement.

In the case of a statement made under s 117 such a statement is not admissible so far as the requirements of para (b) (see p 238) are concerned (created or received by the particular persons in the course of their business, etc) if any person who, in order to be satisfied, must have supplied or received the information concerned (or created or received the document or part concerned) did not at the time have the required capability, or if that person cannot be identified but cannot reasonably be assumed to have had the required capability at that time.

A person has the 'required capability' if he is capable of understanding questions put to him about the matter and of giving answers which can be understood. Where such capability is disputed, the fact must be determined in the absence of the jury (if there is one) and expert evidence may be received as well as that of any person to whom the statement was made. The burden of proof lies upon the party seeking to adduce the statement and the standard of proof is the balance of probabilities.

Evidence from computer records

The ordinary law on evidence applies to computer evidence. In the absence of evidence to the contrary, courts will presume that the computer system was working correctly. If there is evidence that it might not have been, the party seeking to introduce the evidence will need to prove that it was working. Such proof can be satisfied by the evidence of a person familiar with the operation of the computer, who need not be a computer expert. The House of Lords has held that evidence by a store detective that computerised cash tills were working satisfactorily was admissible where it was apparent from the nature of her evidence that she was thoroughly familiar with the operation of the tills and the central computer, even though she did not understand the technical operation of the computer.

CJA 2003, s 129 provides that, where a representation of fact is generated by a machine and depends for its accuracy on information supplied by a person, the representation will only be admissible as evidence of the fact where it is proved that the information was accurate. This is not directly related to proof of the reliability of the machine, but is associated, in that there is a requirement to show that accurate information was fed into the machine.

Procedural rules

The Criminal Procedure Rules 2012, Part 34 requires a party who wants to introduce hearsay evidence under ss 114(1)(d) (evidence admissible in the interests of justice), 116 (witness unavailable), 117(1)(c) (head (c) in relation to business and other documents) or 121 (multiple hearsay) (see respectively p 236, p 237, p 238, and p 240), to give notice to the court officer and all other parties. The prosecutor must give such notice not more than 14 days in the Crown Court (or 28 days in a magistrates' court) after D pleads not guilty. D must give notice of hearsay evidence as soon as reasonably practicable. A party who objects to the introduction of hearsay evidence must apply to the court, within 14 days of the service of the notice or of the service of evidence or of the not guilty plea whichever happens last, for a determination of the objection and serve the application on the court officer and all other parties. Where a party has served notice to introduce hearsay evidence, and no other party objects, the evidence is treated as admissible by agreement. The court may vary these requirements.

Evidence by certificate

The Criminal Justice Act 1948, s 41 provides that a certificate signed by a constable or qualified person certifying that a plan or drawing exhibited in criminal proceedings is a plan or drawing made by him of an identified place or object specified in the certificate, and that the plan or drawing is correctly drawn to a scale so specified, is evidence of the relative position of things shown on the plan or drawing. The plan, etc is admissible to the same extent that oral evidence would be admissible. A 'qualified person' means a registered architect or a chartered engineer of one of certain types.

In order for the certificate to be admissible, a copy of such a plan, etc must be served on D at least seven days before the hearing. Moreover, if D serves the appropriate notice that he requires the attendance of the person who signed the certificate, the certificate will not be admissible.

Proof by written statements

The Criminal Justice Act 1967, s 9 provides for the admissibility of written statements in criminal proceedings. It states that a written statement signed by the person who made it is admissible as evidence to the like extent as oral evidence given by that person. There are certain conditions which must be satisfied:

(a) the statement must contain a declaration by that person to the effect that it is true to the best of his knowledge or belief and that he has made the statement knowing that, if it were tendered in evidence, he would be liable to prosecution if he wilfully stated in it anything which he knew to be false or did not believe to be true;

(b) before the hearing at which the statement is tendered in evidence, a copy of the statement must be served, by or on behalf of the party proposing to tender it, on each of the other parties to the proceedings; and

(c) none of the other parties or their solicitors must, within seven days of such service, have served a notice on the party so proposing objecting to the statement being tendered in evidence under the section.

(b) and (c) do not apply if the parties agree before or during the hearing that the document shall be so tendered.

In practice, statement forms carried by police officers incorporate the declaration at (a) so that the evidence of any witness can be offered in written form if it is accepted by the other side.

It has been held by a judge in the Administrative Court that 'statement' in s 9 means the written assertion of facts made by the person who signed the document, and that what is required by (b) is that the written assertion of facts is contained in a document in identical terms to those in the signed document. Thus, it was irrelevant that the copy of the statement which had been served on the defendant had not been signed by the maker of the written statement; the important thing was that the assertions of facts in the copy were identical to those in the signed statement.

Section 9(3) provides the following additional requirements. A statement made by a person under 18 tendered in evidence under s 9 must state his age; if a statement is made by a person who cannot read, it must be read to him before he signs it and be accompanied by a declaration by the person who so read the statement to the effect that it was so read; and if the statement refers to any other document as an exhibit, the copy served on any other party to the proceedings must be accompanied by a copy of that document or by such information as may be necessary to enable that party to inspect that document or a copy of it.

Copies of such written statements may be served in the same way as a summons or requisition.

Regardless of this procedure having been carried out, the party whose witness it is may nevertheless call that person to give evidence and the court may require that that person attends to give evidence.

Proof of convictions and acquittals

The provisions relating to how such proof may be established, discussed above (p 222), afford another exception to the rule against hearsay.

Statements received as part of the res gestae

An oral statement is part of the res gestae if it relates to a fact so connected with a fact in issue as to explain its nature or form in connection with one continuous transaction. At common law, under the 'res gestae rule', a statement which is part of the res gestae is admissible if the conditions set out below are satisfied.

The res gestae rule is specifically preserved by CJA 2003, s 118 which preserves any rule of law under which, in criminal proceedings, a statement is admissible as evidence of any matter stated if:

(a) the statement was made by a person so emotionally overpowered by an event that the possibility of concoction or distortion can be disregarded;

(b) the statement accompanied an act which can be properly evaluated as evidence only if considered in conjunction with the statement; or

(c) the statement relates to a physical sensation or mental state (such as intention or emotion).

Thus, an oral statement made by a person involved in an unusual, startling or exciting event is admissible as part of the res gestae as evidence of the facts stated, provided it was so clearly made spontaneously that, in the light of the circumstances, the possibility of concoction or distortion can be disregarded. If the issue is one of murder it is probable that a victim's statement 'don't shoot, Sidney', which was made as (or immediately before) the gun was fired, would be admissible as part of the res gestae, although it is hearsay, and that likewise the victim's agitated shout immediately afterwards, 'Look what you've done. Get a doctor, quick', would be admissible. Where a man was stabbed and, whilst being given first aid treatment by a constable, named his attackers, this evidence was admitted as a part of the res gestae at D's trial after the declarant had died.

Another example of the operation of the res gestae rule is provided by a case where two police officers saw V being jostled by two men. The assailants went into a doorway where V's wallet was found. V lunged at the men and said 'They're the ones: these two mugged me of my wallet'. V, although summoned, did not attend the hearing and the issue surrounded whether these statements, which were clearly hearsay when repeated by the police officers, could be admitted as part of the res gestae. It was held that, looking at the nature of the incident as a whole, the statements were relevant and were properly admitted.

Confessions

Although hearsay, a confession is generally admissible. The law relating to confessions is dealt with below. At this point, it needs to be noted that the exception of confessions from the hearsay rule has been held to apply to the case where, in the course of a routine inquiry, a police officer asks someone to identify himself and that person does so by saying 'I am Robin Hood of 15 High Street'. If, in later proceedings against that person the officer cannot independently identify Robin Hood of 15 High Street as the person who spoke to him on the previous occasion, the officer may testify that this person had said 'I am Robin Hood of 15 High Street', despite the fact that this is hearsay, because it amounts to a confession. However, the jury must be directed to be sure that it was D who gave the identification on the previous occasion.

These rules are specifically preserved by CJA 2003, s 118.

Public information

CJA 2003, s 118 preserves the rule of law which permits, in criminal proceedings, the admissibility of:

(a) facts of a public nature stated in published works dealing with matters of a public nature (eg histories, scientific works, dictionaries, maps), or

(b) facts stated in public documents (eg public registers, and returns under public authority with respect to matters of public interest), or in court records, treaties, etc, or

(c) evidence as to a person's age or date or place of birth in a birth certificate.

Expert reports

An expert report is admissible in evidence in criminal proceedings, whether or not the person making it attends to give oral evidence. However, if it is proposed that the maker of the report will not give oral evidence, the report is only admissible with the leave of the court. In determining whether to give leave, the court must have regard to the contents of the report; the reasons why it is proposed that oral evidence will not be given; the likely risk to fairness in relation to the defendant; and any other relevant circumstance. An 'expert report' is one written by a person dealing wholly or mainly with matters on which he is (or if living would be) qualified to give expert evidence.

This common law rule is preserved by CJA 2003, s 118.

Reputation

CJA 2003, s 118 preserves the common law rules whereby, in criminal proceedings, hearsay evidence of a person's reputation is admissible for the purpose of proving his good or bad character, but only in so far as it allows the court to treat such evidence as proving his good or bad character.

Section 118 also preserves the common law rules about the admissibility of evidence of reputation or family tradition for the purpose of proving pedigree or the existence of a marriage, the existence of any public or general right, or the identity of any person or thing. The use of these rules will be rare.

Supplementary points about hearsay

Credibility of hearsay evidence By CJA 2003, s 124, a challenge may be made to the credibility of the maker of a statement admitted in criminal proceedings as hearsay evidence if he does not give oral evidence in the proceedings. In certain circumstances, the person against whom the hearsay evidence has been admitted may produce evidence to discredit the maker of the statement or to show that he has contradicted himself.

Stopping case where hearsay evidence unconvincing A judge has the duty under CJA 2003, s 125 to stop a case and either direct acquittal, or (if the judge considers that there ought to be a re-trial) discharge the jury, if the prosecution case is based wholly or partly on an out-of-court statement which is *so unconvincing that, considering its importance to the case against D, a conviction would be unsafe*. If any untested out-of-court statement is not shown to be reliable and it is a statement which is part of the central body of evidence without which the case cannot proceed, the italicised words will be satisfied.

A magistrates' court would have a similar duty to that under s 125 in the above circumstances.

General discretion to exclude hearsay evidence CJA 2003, s 126 gives a court a discretion to exclude a statement as evidence of a matter stated if the statement was made otherwise than in oral evidence in the proceedings, and the court is satisfied that the case for excluding the statement, taking account of the danger that to admit it would result in undue waste of time, substantially outweighs the case for admitting it, taking account of the value of the evidence. This is in addition to any discretion under PACE, s 78 (p 260) or any other power of a court to exclude evidence.

CONFESSIONS

Confession by one defendant: evidence against co-defendant?

An out-of-court confession by *one defendant is not evidence against another co-defendant* unless the co-defendant expressly or impliedly adopts the statements contained in it.

There are qualifications to this statement. First, the House of Lords has held that, when in a joint trial of two or more for an offence alleged to have been committed jointly, proof of the guilt of one of the defendants, A, is essential in proving the case against another of them, B, and the evidence against A consists solely of his own out-of-court confession, then A's confession will be admissible as evidence, not only against A but also against B in so far as the fact of A's guilt of itself establishes B's guilt. Second, an out-of-court accusation against a co-defendant contained in a confession is *capable* of being admitted as hearsay evidence if it falls within s 114(1)(d) (interests of justice for evidence to be admissible: p 236).

Confession by defendant as evidence against him

For the purposes of the rules which follow, a 'confession' is defined by PACE, s 82 as including 'any statement wholly or partly adverse to the person who made it, whether made to a person in authority or not and whether made in words or otherwise'. A wholly exculpatory statement is not a confession for these purposes. Because of the phrase 'in words or otherwise', a defendant's confession may simply consist of a gesture of acceptance of a statement adverse to him made by another. Statements made which are intended to vindicate a suspect, for example, where he gives explanations intended to justify his possession of goods, and if taken to be true, would do so, do not amount to a confession, even if they are later shown to be false or inconsistent with the maker's evidence. In such a case, however, a record should be made as soon as possible; the reason for there being no contemporaneous notes should be recorded and the suspect should be given an opportunity to check the record.

PACE, s 76(1) allows a confession by the defendant, D, to be given in evidence against him in so far as that confession is relevant to a matter in issue in the proceedings and has not been excluded by the court under s 76(2) on the basis explained below. Thus, if D makes a confession to an offence of burglary and mentions involvement in an offence of wounding on another occasion, his confession to burglary will be admissible at his trial for that offence since it is relevant to a matter in issue but, if he has not also been charged with wounding, his confession to wounding is not admissible since it is not relevant to a matter in issue in the proceedings.

Exclusion

If it is represented by D (or by D's counsel on the basis of material in his possession) that a confession by D was, or may have been, obtained by oppression or in consequence of anything said or done which was likely to render the confession unreliable, the court must not allow the confession to be given in evidence against that person except in so far as the prosecution proves beyond reasonable doubt that the confession (notwithstanding that it might be true) was not obtained by these means.

PACE, s 76(2) provides that a *confession by oppression must always be excluded*. 'Oppression' includes torture, inhuman or degrading treatment, and the use of threats or violence. Apart from this, 'oppression' bears its ordinary dictionary meaning, namely, 'the exercise of power or authority in a burdensome, harsh, or wrongful manner; unjust or cruel treatment'. It will almost inevitably involve some impropriety on the part of the questioner. The fact that a confession has been obtained in circumstances involving a breach of a code of practice does not in itself constitute oppression. However, bullying questioning may exceptionally amount to oppression.

Section 76(2) also provides that a *confession must be excluded if it was obtained in consequence of anything said or done which was likely, in the circumstances existing at the* time, to render unreliable any confession which might be made by D in consequence thereof. An example of something which will be held to be likely to render a confession unreliable is making an untrue inducement to bring about a confession (eg 'if you confess, the matter will go no further'). Another example is the use of hostile and intimidating interview techniques. For such a likelihood of unreliability to be found there is no need for any hint of impropriety. Where a suspect was mentally handicapped and was interviewed without an adult person being present, it was held that once it had been established that there had been a breach of Code C: the Detention Code, the onus was on the prosecution to satisfy the judge beyond reasonable doubt that the confession was not obtained in breach of PACE, s 76(2). The circumstances existing at the time were all important in relation to reliability.

Where it is shown that there has been aggressive and hostile questioning it becomes a matter of degree as to whether the threshold is passed beyond which the behaviour of police officers has made the confession unreliable in all circumstances. However, all the circumstances must be examined. In the course of an interview concerning drug offences an officer interjected, implying that if the suspect (D) did not tell the truth he would be held in custody. Some 16 minutes later D confessed to an offence. The trial judge refused to exclude his confession being satisfied that D was astute, had experience of being interviewed at a police station, and that his will had not been broken. He had continued to deny other offences. The Court of Appeal endorsed the trial judge's decision.

The expert evidence of a psychiatrist or psychologist may be admitted to show that a confession is unreliable because of psychological abnormalities if, but only if, it is to the effect that D was suffering from mental handicap, mental illness, or a personality disorder so severe as to be categorised as mental disorder. It is not enough to allege that D is 'not exceptionally bright and is possibly of dull intelligence and very suggestible'.

It has not yet been decided whether interviewing a drug addict when he is withdrawing falls within the present provision. However, the Court of Appeal has held that, if it is, the question of 'likely to be rendered unreliable' depends on whether or not the addict was fit to be interviewed in the sense that his answers could be relied upon in the circumstances. This, the court held, is a matter for those present at the time. The court held that, where experienced police officers considered a person fit to be interviewed and a doctor who saw him after the interview was of the same opinion, there was no reason to believe that a confession was likely to be unreliable.

Facts discovered as a result of inadmissible confession　PACE, s 76(4) provides that, even if a confession, or a part of it, is excluded under the above provisions, this does not affect the admissibility in evidence:

(a) of any facts discovered as a result of the confession; or
(b) where the confession is relevant as showing that D speaks, writes, or expresses himself in a particular way, of so much of the confession as is necessary to show that he does so.

The effect of (a) is as follows. If evidence of a fact is discovered as a result of a confession, or part of a confession, and that confession, or a relevant part of it, is excluded under s 76(2), that evidence may nevertheless be adduced by the prosecution. However, no reference should be made to the fact that the discovery was the result of a confession; only D, or someone acting on his behalf, may disclose this. Thus, if D is arrested for thefts of motor cars and makes a confession which includes details of the persons to whom he sold the vehicles, and that confession is excluded, the prosecution may give evidence of the recovery of the vehicles from those persons but it may not mention that they were discovered as a result of the excluded confession.

The effect of (b) is that, if there is something in a confession, or part, excluded under s 76, which shows that D writes, speaks or expresses himself in a particular manner, and this serves, for example, to identify him with whoever committed the offence, so much of the confession as is necessary to show the characteristic referred to is admissible.

The Supreme Court has held that s 76(4) is consistent with the right to a fair trial under the European Convention on Human Rights, Art 6.

Confessions given in evidence for co-defendant

PACE, s 76A provides that a confession, as defined by s 82, made by a defendant may be given in evidence for a co-defendant in so far as it is relevant to a matter in issue unless excluded by the court on one of the two grounds under s 76. If it is alleged that one of them applies, the co-defendant seeking to rely on the confession must prove on the balance of probabilities that the confession was not obtained by oppression, etc. The Court of Appeal has held that s 76A does not apply so as to permit evidence of a confession to be given when the defendant who gave the confession has pleaded guilty and is therefore not on trial with the co-defendant; s 76A it said, is designed to cater for the joint trial of the defendant and co-defendant.

The fact that a confession is wholly or partly excluded under s 76A does not affect the admissibility in evidence of the matters referred to in s 76(4).

Confessions by the mentally handicapped

PACE, s 77 is concerned with confessions, as defined by s 82, made by mentally handicapped defendants. Where the case against a defendant (D) depends wholly or substantially upon his confession and the court is satisfied that he is mentally handicapped and that the confession was not made in the presence of an independent person, the jury must be warned of, or the magistrates' court must heed, the special need for caution before convicting D in reliance on the confession. A police officer or member of police staff is not an independent person in this context. Generally speaking, to question a suspect in the absence of an independent person amounts to a breach of the Detention Code.

In establishing whether a defendant is mentally handicapped it is not appropriate to attempt to take figures provided by intelligence tests in one case and then to apply them slavishly to another in order to define some rigid line, the crossing of which would lead automatically to the exclusion of confession evidence. Each case must be looked at on its own facts.

Of course, if a mentally handicapped person's confession is obtained by oppression or by words or conduct likely to make it unreliable (as in a case where D confessed at a fifth interview after 36 hours' detention and without having received any legal advice), the confession will be inadmissible under s 76.

Procedure—tape-recorded confessions: Crown Court

The procedure to be followed in preparation for proceedings in the Crown Court in relation to tape recordings of police interviews with suspects is laid down in the *Consolidated Criminal Practice Direction*. Tapes must be produced and proved by the interviewing officer, or any other officer who was present at the interview; the prosecution must provide a tape machine operator if the officer cannot so act; counsel must indicate the parts of a recording which it may be necessary to play.

DEFENDANT'S RIGHT OF SILENCE

The Criminal Justice and Public Order Act 1994 (CJPOA 1994), ss 34–37 permit a court or jury to draw such inferences from a defendant's (D's) failure to mention facts as appear proper. The circumstances, generally, in which such inferences may be drawn are:

(a) where D has failed, when questioned under caution or on being charged or officially informed that he may be prosecuted (or after being charged when questioned under the Counter-Terrorism Act 2008, s 22), to mention facts later relied upon as part of his defence, and which it is reasonable to expect him to have mentioned (s 34);

(b) where D fails, without good cause, to give evidence or answer questions at trial (s 35);

(c) where an arrested person fails or refuses to account for possession of objects, substances or marks when requested to do so (s 36);

(d) where an arrested person fails or refuses to account for his presence at a particular place, when requested to do so (s 37).

By s 38, an adverse inference drawn under ss 34 to 37 cannot be the sole basis for a finding of a case to answer, for the issue of a notice to transfer, or for a finding of guilt. As a result, the importance of ss 34 to 37 is that an adverse inference under them may enable the judge, jury or magistrates to find that other evidence, when considered with the adverse inference, enables them to be sure beyond reasonable doubt of the truth and accuracy of that other evidence and in consequence of D's guilt.

When evidence is to be offered and admissibility

Subject to any directions given by the court, evidence which tends to establish the particular failure may be given before or after the evidence which tends to establish the fact which the defendant is alleged to have failed to mention. Thus, where the interview is concerned with D's possession of a stolen watch, evidence of his failure to offer an explanation for his possession of it may be given before, or after, evidence of it being found in his possession. In most circumstances, the most appropriate time will be after evidence of his possession of the property has been given. These provisions do not prejudice the admissibility of evidence of his silence or other reaction which would otherwise be admissible (eg reaction to things said in his presence and hearing which relate to his involvement in an offence).

Effect of defendant's silence when questioned under caution or on being charged, etc

The relevant provision is contained in CJPOA 1994, s 34, which applies in relation to:

(a) until a day to be appointed, committal proceedings;

(b) the determination of applications for dismissal of charges made by a person sent to the Crown Court for trial;

(c) the determination of the issue of whether a person accused of an offence (of whatever type) has a case to answer; and

(d) the determination of whether a person is guilty of the offence charged.

By s 34, where it was reasonable to expect D, when questioned under caution or on being charged or officially informed that he may be prosecuted (or after being charged when questioned under the Counter-Terrorism Act 2008, s 22p), to have mentioned facts (as opposed to theory, possibility, or speculation) on which he later relies in his defence, a judge, jury, or magistrate may draw such inferences as appear proper from D's failure to mention any fact which a person could reasonably have been expected to mention in such a situation. The Court of Appeal has held that s 34 does not permit an adverse inference to be drawn from D's failure to leave his police cell to be interviewed because this does not fall within the ambit of 'being questioned'. It has also been held that a person who gives the interviewing officer a prepared statement from which he does not depart when giving evidence at his subsequent trial has 'mentioned facts' and therefore falls outside s 34, notwithstanding that the prepared statement was not given in response to questioning and that he said 'no comment' to all subsequent police questions. The court said that s 34 did not distinctly include police cross-examination of a suspect upon his account of events. Had that been intended, Parliament would have used different language.

Section 34 does not apply in a case where D was at a police station at the time of the failure if he had not been allowed an opportunity to consult a solicitor prior to being questioned, charged, or informed that he might be prosecuted.

It should be noted that there are significant areas of overlap between the rule under s 34 and the rules under ss 36 and 37 (dealt with below). In addition, they share the similarity that drawing an adverse inference under them may infringe the European Convention on Human Rights, art 6 (right to a fair trial). Whether or not it does must be determined in the light of all the circumstances of the case, including any explanation offered for the silence and the compulsion inherent in the situation. It would be contrary to art 6 to base a conviction solely on D's silence. Unlike ss 36 and 37, s 34 is not confined to the questioning of persons who are under arrest. In addition, ss 36 and 37 operate irrespective of whether a fact is relied upon as part of the defence, or irrespective of whether any defence is in fact made. By contrast, it is this reliance which is at the heart of s 34. Lastly, under s 36 or s 37, a constable is under a duty to explain the effect of the requirement in ordinary language, while the key prerequisite in s 34 is the formal caution.

The Court of Appeal has held that there are six formal conditions to be met before an inference may be drawn under s 34 from a failure to mention a fact later relied upon:

(a) there must be proceedings against a person for an offence;
(b) the alleged failure must occur before the person is charged (or—it is submitted—when charged or officially informed of the risk of prosecution);
(c) the alleged failure must occur during questioning under caution by a constable;
(d) the constable's questioning must be directed towards trying to discover whether or by whom the alleged offence had been committed;
(e) the alleged failure must be to mention any fact relied upon in his defence; and
(f) D's failure to mention a fact must relate to a fact which in the circumstances existing at the time D could reasonably have been expected to mention when so questioned. What is reasonable depends on all the circumstances of the case. 'Time' refers to the time of questioning and account must be taken of all the relevant circumstances existing at the time. 'In the circumstances' includes such matters as the time of day, D's age, experience, mental capacity, state of health, sobriety, tiredness, knowledge, personality, and legal advice, which might all be relevant.

For the purposes of (e), a fact can be relied on even though D does not give evidence at his trial, since D can rely on a fact by evidence through a witness on his behalf or through cross-examination of a prosecution witness.

The Court of Appeal has held that legal advice to remain silent cannot in itself prevent an adverse inference from being drawn under s 34, otherwise s 34 would be rendered ineffective. In another case the Court of Appeal held that such advice is a very relevant circumstance to be taken into account in deciding whether it could reasonably have been expected to mention at that time the matter relied on. However, it said that the jury should not be concerned with the correctness of a solicitor's advice, nor with whether it complies with the Law Society guidelines. Another Court of Appeal case has added that a jury may still draw an adverse inference if it is sure that the true reason for D's silence is that he had no, or no satisfactory, explanation consistent with evidence to give.

Subsequently, the European Court of Human Rights has held that the fact that D has been given legal advice to remain silent must be given appropriate weight by a domestic court because there may be good reason for such advice, and that a good reason for not drawing an inference was bona fide legal advice.

In a later statement about silence in reliance on the advice of a solicitor, the Court of Appeal has summarised the law as follows. Where a solicitor's advice is relied upon by D, the ultimate question for the jury remains under s 34 whether the facts relied on at the trial were facts which D could reasonably have been expected to mention at interview. If they were not, that is the end of the matter. If the jury consider that D genuinely relied on the advice, that is not necessarily the end of the matter. It might still not have been reasonable for him to rely on the advice, or the advice might not have been the true explanation for his silence, the true reason being that he had no or no satisfactory explanation consistent with innocence to give.

Although under the Detention Code a juvenile, or mentally vulnerable suspect (hereafter 'vulnerable suspect'), must not be interviewed in the absence of an appropriate adult, except in the case of an urgent interview, s 34 is not confined to questioning that amounts to an 'interview'. However, a note to that Code states that vulnerable suspects may be particularly prone to provide information which is unreliable, misleading or self-incriminating. It goes on to state that special care should always be taken when questioning such a person. This must be true with equal force in respect of any failure to state facts. There is also the distinct possibility that such a person will not understand the significance of the caution, or believe that an obligation to answer exists. For these reasons, considerable caution should be exercised in drawing an inference from a failure of a vulnerable suspect to disclose facts subsequently relied upon, certainly in questioning which occurs in the absence of an appropriate adult.

An inference may be drawn from any failure to mention a fact later relied on as part of D's defence, and which occurs at or prior to charge for the offence, or being officially informed, etc (or after charge in the case of questioning under C-TA 2008, s 22). The fact that D was charged with one offence will therefore not prevent an inference being drawn in respect of another offence for which he is subsequently questioned.

The rule that an inference may only be drawn from a failure to mention facts which D could have been reasonably expected to mention when questioned requires an assessment of the situation at the time of that questioning, not with the benefit of hindsight as at the date of trial. An inference cannot be drawn from a failure to mention a fact of which D was unaware when questioned.

The Court of Appeal has discouraged prosecutors from too readily seeking to activate s 34. Its mischief, it said, was primarily directed at the positive defence following a 'no comment' and/or 'ambush' defence. Where that was not the case, the Court warned against the further complicating of trials and summings-up by invoking s 34.

Effect of defendant's silence at trial

CJPOA 1994, s 35 deals with the case where D fails to give evidence or refuses without good reason to answer a question. It does not apply where:

(a) D's guilt is not in issue, or
(b) it appears to the court (from evidence, and not just from a submission by an advocate) that D's physical or mental condition makes it undesirable (and not just difficult) for D to be called upon to give evidence.

For the purposes of (a), D's guilt will not be in issue if he has pleaded guilty and the hearing is merely concerned to resolve matters relevant to sentencing. Nor will it be in issue in preliminary hearings or in issues concerning the admissibility of evidence. Where the defence wish to rely on (b) they must adduce evidence on the issue referred to in (b).

Where s 35 applies, the court must, at the conclusion of the evidence for the prosecution, satisfy itself (in the presence of the jury where applicable) that D is aware that:

(a) the stage has been reached at which evidence can be given for the defence;
(b) he can, if he wishes, give evidence; and
(c) if he chooses not to give evidence, or, having been sworn, without good cause refuses to answer any question, it will be permissible for the court or jury to draw such inferences as appear proper from such failure or refusal.

This rule will not apply if, at the conclusion of the evidence for the prosecution, it is established that D will give evidence.

For the purposes of (c), a refusal will be taken to be without good cause where a person, having been sworn, refuses to answer any question unless:

(a) he is entitled to refuse to answer the question by virtue of any enactment, whenever passed or made, or on the ground of privilege; or
(b) the court in the exercise of its general discretion excuses him from answering it.

The privilege against self-incrimination and the common law doctrine of legal professional privilege therefore apply. Outside such matters 'good cause' may be limited to relevance and propriety and perhaps where a question may be considered oppressive.

Where s 35 applies, the jury or magistrates in determining whether D is guilty of the offence charged may draw such inferences as appear proper from D's failure to give evidence or his refusal, without good cause, to answer any question.

The Court of Appeal has ruled that, apart from the two exceptions included in s 35 (ie D's guilt not in issue and D's physical or mental condition), it is open to a jury or magistrates to decline to draw an inference from silence where the circumstances of the case justified such a course. However, there must be some evidential basis, or exceptional factors, making that a fair course to take. The inferences permitted by s 35 were only such as 'appear proper'.

The Court of Appeal has highlighted the need for a jury to be told that:

(a) the burden of proof remains on the prosecution;
(b) D is entitled to remain silent;
(c) an inference cannot by itself prove guilt;

(d) the jury must be satisfied that the prosecution has established a case to answer before drawing such an inference; and

(e) if, despite any evidence relied upon to explain silence or in the absence of any such evidence, the jury concludes that silence can only sensibly be attributed to D's having no answer, or none that would stand up to cross-examination, they may draw an adverse inference.

Effect of defendant's failure or refusal to account for objects, marks, etc

CJPOA 1994, s 36 is the relevant provision. Where:

(a) a person is arrested by a constable and there is:
    (i)   on his person; or
    (ii) in or on his clothing or footwear; or
    (iii) otherwise in his possession; or
    (iv) in any place in which he is at the time of his arrest
    any object, substance, or mark, or there is any mark on any such object; and

(b) that or another constable investigating the case reasonably believes that the presence of the object, substance, or mark may be attributable to the participation of the person arrested in the commission of an offence specified by the constable; and

(c) the constable informs the person so arrested that he so believes, and requests him to account for the presence of the object, substance, or mark; and

(d) the person fails or refuses to do so,

then if, in any proceedings (of the type to which s 34 applies) for the offence so specified, evidence of those matters is given, the judge, jury, or magistrates, as appropriate, may draw such inferences from the failure or refusal as appear proper. These provisions of s 36 apply to the condition of clothing or footwear as they apply to a substance or mark thereon. They do not apply unless D was told in ordinary language by the constable when making the request in (c) what the effects of s 36 would be if he failed or refused to comply with the request.

An inference may not be drawn under s 36 where D was at an authorised place of detention (a police station or other authorised place) at the time of the failure or refusal, if he had not been allowed an opportunity to consult a solicitor prior to the request being made.

The provisions of s 36 do not preclude the drawing of inferences from a failure or refusal to account for objects, marks, etc which could properly be drawn apart from s 36.

Effect of defendant's failure or refusal to account for presence at a particular place

CJPOA 1994, s 37 provides that, in the circumstances below, in proceedings of the type to which s 34 applies, a judge, jury, or magistrates may draw such inferences as appear proper from D's failure or refusal to account for certain matters. Such inferences are permitted where:

(a) a person arrested by a constable was found by him at a place at or about the time the offence for which he was arrested is alleged to have been committed; and

(b) that or another constable investigating the offence reasonably believes that the presence of the person at that place and at that time may be attributable to his participation in the commission of the offence; and

(c) the constable informs the person that he so believes, and requests him to account for his presence; and

(d) the person fails or refuses to do so.

Section 37 does not apply unless D was told in ordinary language by the constable when making the request in (c) what the effects of s 37 would be if he failed or refused to comply with the request.

An inference may not be drawn under s 37 where D was at an authorised place of detention (see above) if he had not been allowed an opportunity to consult a solicitor prior to the request being made.

Once again, the provisions of s 37 do not prevent the drawing of any other inference from a refusal or failure to account which could properly be drawn apart from s 37.

EVIDENCE AS TO CHARACTER

By the defendant of his good character

D may always give evidence of his own good character.

If D does so, the judge must direct the jury that evidence of good character must be taken into account in assessing D's credibility. The judge must also direct the jury that D's previous good character must be taken into account as a relevant factor when they are considering whether he was the kind of person who was likely to have behaved in the way alleged by the prosecution. Since good character may be a relative concept, a judge may, if the circumstances justify it, only give one of the above two directions.

The Court of Appeal has held that the fact that, since payment of a fixed penalty by a person issued with a fixed penalty notice under the Criminal Justice and Police Act 2001 (see p 31) does not constitute an admission of the offence or proof that it was committed by him, it does not impugn his good character and has no effect on his entitlement to a good character direction.

Bad character

Evidence of bad character is only admissible if the relevant provisions of CJA 2003, Part 11, Ch 1 (below) are satisfied.

CJA 2003, s 98 provides that references in the relevant provisions to a person's 'bad character' are to evidence of, or of a disposition towards, misconduct on his part, *other than evidence which*:

(a) *has to do with the alleged facts of the offence with which D is charged, or*

(b) *is evidence of misconduct in connection with the investigation or prosecution of that offence.*

'Misconduct' refers to the commission of an offence or other reprehensible behaviour. 'Reprehensible behaviour' is clearly intended to include conduct which is scandalous, disgraceful, dishonest, or improper, without being criminal. Behaviour for which a person has been charged with an offence can clearly amount to misconduct even if the prosecution is later dropped or the person is acquitted.

In relation to (a), the Court of Appeal has held that for evidence 'to do' with the alleged facts of the offence there must be a nexus in time between that offence and the evidence of misconduct; the evidence must be reasonably contemporaneous and closely associated with the alleged facts. However, the Court has subsequently held that there is no 'nexus in time requirement' where the evidence relates to misconduct by D which was alleged to have created the motive for the offence.

The Court of Appeal has held that (b) is not limited to misconduct by the prosecuting authorities and that it could be said to encompass evidence of intimidation or blackmail by a co-defendant which could be said to be connected with the prosecution or investigation of the offence. Thus, it held that evidence that a co-defendant had unsuccessfully tried to blackmail D into paying him £125,000 by threatening to change his statements in order to implicate D was capable of falling within (b) and therefore admissible.

Where the evidence falls within either of the italicised exceptions it is admissible without more ado.

Evidence of non-defendant's bad character

CJA 2003, s 100 provides that, in criminal proceedings, evidence of the bad character of any person other than D is admissible *only* if:

(a) it is important explanatory evidence;
(b) it has substantial probative value in relation to a matter which is in issue in the proceedings and is of substantial importance in the context of the case as a whole; or
(c) all parties in the proceedings agree to its admissibility.

Section 100 applies to a witness, victim, or any other person.

As to (a), 'important explanatory evidence' has the same meaning as it does in respect of s 101 (p 255).

In relation to (b), evidence of a non-defendant's bad character would be of probative value if it assisted in establishing an issue one way or another. In assessing the probative value of evidence for the purposes of (b) the court must have regard to the following factors (and any other relevant factors):

(i)   the nature and number of the events, or other things, to which the evidence relates;
(ii)   when those events or things are alleged to have happened or existed;
(iii) where (*a*) the evidence is evidence of a person's misconduct, and (*b*) it is suggested that the evidence has probative value by reason of similarity between that misconduct and other alleged misconduct, the nature and extent of the similarities and the dissimilarities between each of the alleged instances of misconduct;
(iv)   where (*a*) the evidence is evidence of a person's misconduct, (*b*) it is suggested that that person is also responsible for the misconduct charged, and (*c*) the identity of the person responsible for the misconduct charged is disputed, the extent to which the evidence shows or tends to show that the same person was responsible each time.

As a result of (b) and the above provisions, evidence of a non-defendant's bad character may be admitted, for example, as evidence of *his* propensity to commit the offence in question or of his credibility as a witness.

The Court of Appeal has held that a police report recording unproven allegations against a non-defendant of criminal behaviour is most unlikely to have substantial probative value; first, it is, at best hearsay, and it would fall to be judged by reference to the rules for the admission of hearsay and (given the difficulties of assessing such evidence) it would be rare for it to be judged of substantial probative value; second, if there is no complainant prepared to support the allegation, that robs it of a great deal of probative value. On the other hand, the Court of Appeal has held that 'substantial probative value' does not require, for the admission of a witness's bad character evidence, that it amounted to proof, for example, of a lack of credibility of the witness when credibility was an issue of substantial importance. The question is whether the evidence of bad character is sufficiently persuasive to be worthy of consideration by a fair-minded tribunal upon the issue of, for example, the witness's creditworthiness.

Except in the case of (c), evidence of the bad character of a non-defendant may only be given with the leave of the court.

Under the Criminal Procedure Rules 2012, Part 35, a party who wants to introduce evidence of a non-defendant's bad character must make an application which must be served on the court officer and all other parties to the proceedings as soon as reasonably practicable, and in any event not more than 14 days after the prosecutor has disclosed material on which the application is based (if the prosecutor is not the applicant). A party who objects to the introduction of the evidence must serve notice on the court officer and all other parties to the proceedings not more than 14 days after service of the application. The court may vary these requirements.

Evidence of defendant's bad character

CJA 2003, s 101 deals with such matters. The previous rules which, in most instances, effectively prevented consideration of D's character, were abolished by CJA 2003, s 99.

By s 101, evidence of D's bad character is admissible in criminal proceedings only if one of the following seven gateways is satisfied:

(a) all parties agree to its being admissible;
(b) it is evidence adduced by D himself or is given in answer to a question asked by him during cross-examination and intended to elicit it;
(c) it is important explanatory evidence;
(d) it is relevant to an 'important matter' (ie a matter of substantial importance in the context of the case as a whole) in issue between D and the prosecution;
(e) it has 'substantial probative value' (ie an enhanced capability of proving or disproving) in relation to an 'important matter' in issue between D and a co-defendant;
(f) it is evidence to correct a false impression given by D; or
(g) D has made an attack on another person's character.

Evidence must not be admitted under gateways (d) or (g) if D has made an application to exclude it and the judge or magistrates' court considers that the admission of the evidence would have such an adverse effect on the fairness of the proceedings that it ought not to admit it. The test to be applied is the same as that set out in PACE, s 78 (p 260). On such an application, regard must be had, in particular, to the time which has passed between the matters to which the evidence relates and the matters forming the subject of the offence charged.

By CJA 2003, s 108, which applies in addition to s 101, in proceedings for an offence by D when aged 21 or over, evidence of D's conviction for an offence when under 14 is not admissible unless both offences are triable only on indictment and the interests of justice require the evidence to be admissible.

Where D's conviction under 14 was for an offence under the law of a country outside England and Wales ('the previous offence') and that offence would be an offence under the law of England and Wales ('the corresponding offence') if done in England and Wales at the time of the proceedings with which D is now charged, the previous offence is regarded as triable only on indictment if the corresponding offence is so triable.

Gateway (c): important explanatory evidence

For the purpose of gateway (c) under CJA 2003, s 101, evidence is important explanatory evidence if, in its absence, the jury or court would find it impossible or difficult properly to understand other evidence in the case, and its value for understanding the case as a whole is substantial. In an assault case, for example, evidence may be given that D (who claims that he acted in self-defence) has previously made unprovoked attacks on the victim.

Gateway (d): important matter in issue between defendant and prosecution

CJA 2003, s 103(1) provides that, for the purposes of gateway (d), matters in issue between D and the prosecution include:

(a) the question whether D has a 'propensity' to commit offences of the kind with which he is charged, except where his having that propensity makes it no more likely that he is guilty of the offence; and

(b) the question whether D has a propensity to be untruthful, except where it is not suggested that D's case is untruthful in any respect.

In respect of (b), the Court of Appeal has held that the question whether D has a propensity to be untruthful will not normally be describable as an 'important matter in issue between D and the prosecutor'; the only circumstance where there is likely to be an important issue as to whether D has a propensity to be untruthful is where telling lies is an important element of the offence, and even then the propensity is only likely to be significant if the lying was in the context of committing criminal offences (in which case evidence is likely to be admissible under (a)).

Section 103(2) provides that, where (a) applies, D's propensity to commit offences of the kind with which he is charged may (without prejudice to any other way of doing so) be established by evidence of a previous conviction for an offence of the same description as that with which D is charged, or an offence of the same category as that offence. For these purposes, two offences are of the same description as each other if the statement of the offence in a written charge or indictment would, in each case, be in the same terms, and two offences are of the same category if they are of the same *category of offences as prescribed by order*. The CJA 2003 (Categories of Offences) Order 2004 prescribes two categories of offences: one category is specified offences against the Theft Acts 1968 and 1978, and the other is specified offences against the Sexual Offences Act (SOA) 2003 where the victim was under 16. They are:

The sexual offences category also includes corresponding offences superseded by SOA 2003.

In referring to offences of the same description or category, CJA 2003, s 103(2) is not exhaustive of the types of conviction which may be relied on to show evidence of propensity to commit offences of the kind charged. Indeed, the provision is not limited to previous convictions; the fact that D has previously asked for offences to be taken into consideration can be admitted.

There is no minimum number of convictions necessary to establish such a propensity; but the fewer the number, the weaker the evidence of propensity.

Where the prosecution seeks to adduce evidence of D's bad character, in the form of previous convictions, in order to establish his propensity to commit offences of the kind with which he was charged, there are essentially three questions to be considered:

(1) Did the history of his convictions establish a propensity to commit offences of the kind charged?

(2) Did that propensity make it more likely that the defendant had committed the offence charged?

(3) Was it unjust to rely on the convictions of the same description or category; and, in any event, would the proceedings be unfair if they were admitted?

By CJA 2003, s 103(3), s 103(2) does not apply if the court is satisfied, by reason of the length of time since the conviction or for any other reason, that it would be unjust for it to apply.

CJA 2003, s 103(7) provides that where:

Theft Acts 1968 and 1978

(1)	Theft	TA 1968, s 1
(2)	Robbery	s 8
(3)	Burglary if it was committed with intent to commit an offence of stealing anything in the building or part of a building in question	s 9(1)(a)
(4)	Burglary if the offender stole or attempted to steal anything in the building or that part of it	s 9(1)(b)
(5)	Aggravated burglary where that burglary was of the type described at (3) and (4) above	s 10
(6)	Taking a motor vehicle or other conveyance without authority	s 12
(7)	Aggravated vehicle-taking	s 12A
(8)	Handling stolen goods	s 22
(9)	Going equipped for stealing	s 25
(10)	Making off without payment	TA 1978, s 3
(11)	Aiding, abetting, counselling, procuring, or encouraging or assisting, or attempting the commission of an offence of these descriptions	

Sexual offences (persons under the age of 16)

The offences in the table below are those against the Sexual Offences Act 2003

(1)	Rape if it was committed in relation to a person under 16	s 1
(2)	Assault by penetration if it was committed in relation to a person under 16	s 2
(3)	Sexual assault if it was committed in relation to a person under 16	s 3
(4)	Causing a person to engage in sexual activity if committed in relation to a person under 16	s 4
(5)	Rape of a child under 13	s 5
(6)	Assault of a child under 13 by penetration	s 6
(7)	Sexual assault of a child under 13	s 7
(8)	Causing or inciting a child under 13 to engage in sexual activity	s 8

(9)	Sexual activity with a child	s 9
(10)	Causing or inciting a child to engage in sexual activity	s 10
(11)	Arranging or facilitating the commission of a child sex offence	s 14
(12)	Abuse of position of trust: sexual activity with a child if committed in relation to a child under 16	s 16
(13)	Abuse of position of trust: causing or inciting a child to engage in sexual activity if committed in relation to a person under 16	s 17
(14)	Sexual activity with a child family member if committed in relation to a person under 16	s 25
(15)	Inciting a child family member to engage in sexual activity if committed in relation to a person under 16	s 26
(16)	Sexual activity with a person with a mental disorder impeding choice if it was committed in relation to a person under 16	s 30
(17)	Causing or inciting a person with a mental disorder impeding choice to engage in sexual activity if it was committed in relation to a person under 16	s 31
(18)	Inducement, threat, or deception to procure activity with a person with a mental disorder if committed with a person under the age of 16	s 34
(19)	Causing a person with a mental disorder to engage in or agree to engage in sexual activity by inducement, threat, or deception if committed in relation to a person under 16	s 35
(20)	Care workers: sexual activity with a person with a mental disorder if committed with a person under 16	s 38
(21)	Care workers: causing or inciting sexual activity if committed in relation to a person under 16	s 39
(22)	Aiding, abetting, counselling, procuring, encouraging or assisting or attempting the commission of any of these offences or those in the next paragraph	

(a) D has been convicted of an offence under the law of any country outside England and Wales ('the previous offence'), and

(b) the previous offence would constitute an offence under the law of England and Wales ('the corresponding offence') if it were done in England and Wales at the time of the trial for the offence with which D is now charged ('the current offence'), then for the purpose of determining if the previous offence and the current offence are of the same description or category:

   (i) the previous offence is of the same description as the current offence if the corresponding offence is of that same description, as set out in in the table;

   (ii) the previous offence is of the same category as the current offence if the current offence and the corresponding offence belong to the same category of offences as prescribed by the order referred to above.

Similar provision is also made in respect of a conviction of an offence under a foreign service law which would constitute an offence under the law of England and Wales or a service offence if done in England and Wales by a member of HM forces.

Gateway (e): substantial probative value in relation to an important matter in issue between D and co-defendant

This is intended to deal with 'cut-throat' defences. CJA 2003, s 104 provides that evidence relevant to whether D has a propensity to be untruthful is admissible on that basis under (e) only if the nature or conduct of his defence is such as to undermine the co-defendant's defence. Only evidence adduced by the co-defendant or by a witness in cross-examination by the co-defendant is admissible under (e).

Gateway (f): correcting a false impression

CJA 2003, s 105 provides that, for the purposes of gateway (f), D gives a false impression if he is responsible for the making of an express or implied assertion which is apt to give a false or misleading assertion about D, and that evidence to correct such an impression is evidence which has probative value in correcting it.

D is treated as responsible for the making of an assertion if it is made by D in the proceedings, or by a defence witness, or by any witness in response to a question by D which was intended or likely to elicit it, or if it was made by D when questioned under caution or on being charged with the offence, or if it was made out-of-court by any person and D adduces evidence of it.

The Court of Appeal has held that gateway (f) is too often invoked, particularly in cases where D has done no more than to deny committing the offence in question. Gateway (f), it held, is concerned with attempting to mislead the court in a way that goes beyond denying the offence. The false impression has to be one which is given to the court.

Gateway (g): attack on another person's character

By CJA 2003, s 106, D attacks the character of another person if he adduces evidence to the effect that this person has committed any offence or has behaved in a reprehensible way, or if he asks questions in cross-examination which are intended or likely to elicit such evidence, or if evidence is given of an imputation about the other person by D on being questioned under caution before charge or on being charged or informed that he might be prosecuted. Where evidence of D's bad character has been admitted as a result of his attack upon the character of another person, it can be used, if relevant, to establish a propensity on the part of D to commit offences of the type with which he is charged.

Assumption of truth in assessment of relevance or probative value

CJA 2003, s 109 provides that any reference in the Act's provisions about bad character to the relevance or probative value of evidence is a reference to its relevance or probative value on the assumption that it is true. However, in assessing the relevance or probative value of an item of evidence, a court need not assume that evidence is true if it appears, on the basis of material before it, that no court or jury could reasonably find it to be true.

Notice of introduction of evidence of defendant's bad character

The Criminal Procedure Rules 2012, Part 35 provide as follows.

A prosecutor who wants to introduce evidence of a defendant's bad character must serve notice to the court officer and all other parties to the proceedings. Such notice must be served within 14 days of D's plea of not guilty in the Crown Court, or 28 days in a magistrates' court.

A co-defendant who wants to introduce evidence of a defendant's bad character must serve notice as soon as reasonably practicable, and in any event not more than 14 days after the prosecutor discloses material on which the notice is based, to the court officer and all other parties to the proceedings.

A party who objects to the introduction of the evidence must apply to the court for a determination and serve the application on the court officer and all other parties not more than 14 days after the notice.

A court may vary the above requirements.

Spent convictions etc

The provisions of the Rehabilitation of Offenders Act 1974 whereby an offender's convictions become 'spent' and the offender is thereafter treated as if he had not been convicted do not prevent the admissibility in criminal proceedings of evidence relating to a spent conviction which is otherwise admissible (s 7). A similar rule applies in respect of spent cautions, reprimands, and warnings (Sch 2). A person who has a conviction or caution for the abolished offence of buggery or the abolished offence of gross indecency between men which has been ordered to be disregarded by the Secretary of State under the Protection of Freedoms Act 2012, s 92 is to be treated as if he had not committed, or been charged with, or prosecuted for, or convicted of, or sentenced for, or cautioned for, that offence. In particular, no evidence is admissible to prove any of these matters and he is not, in any court proceedings, to be asked (and, if asked, is not to be required to answer) any question relating to his past which cannot be answered without acknowledging or referring to the conviction or caution or any circumstances ancillary to it (s 96).

Proof of a conviction

See p 222.

EXCLUSION OF UNFAIR EVIDENCE

The purpose of all the rules concerning the gathering of evidence and the manner of its presentation in court is to ensure absolute fairness to an accused person. PACE, s 78 provides that, in any proceedings, a judge or magistrates' court may refuse to allow evidence (including confessions) on which the prosecution proposes to rely to be given if it appears that, having regard to all the circumstances, including the circumstances in which the evidence was obtained, the admission of the evidence would have *such an adverse effect on the fairness of the proceedings that the court ought not to admit it.* 'Fairness of the proceedings' is directed primarily to fairness of the actual conduct of the proceedings but it is not strictly limited to this.

Evidence obtained by a breach by the police of PACE or one of the Codes of Practice does not necessarily render evidence inadmissible under s 78, but it will if it has such an adverse effect on the fairness of the proceedings that it ought not to be admitted. The issue is whether there has been a significant and substantial breach. There is no general requirement for the breach to have been committed deliberately or in bad faith before evidence is excluded under PACE, s 78. Bad faith on the part of police officers will usually lead to the exclusion of evidence (bad faith may make significant and substantial a breach which might not otherwise be so), but evidence may be excluded even though the police acted in good faith if there is a significant and substantial breach of police powers.

An example of the operation of PACE, s 78 is provided by a case where a person had been convicted on evidence based solely on a confession obtained after police had falsely pretended that his fingerprints had been found at the scene of the crime; the Court of Appeal ruled that such evidence should have been excluded under s 78 on the ground that it posed a threat to the fairness of proceedings. Another example is provided by various cases where evidence obtained after a significant and substantial breach of the provisions described in Chapter 4 relating to the right to legal advice or to the conduct of an interview has been excluded on the ground that in the circumstances of the case it would be unfair to admit it.

Section 78 does not affect the common law powers of a court to exclude evidence on the basis that its prejudicial effect is likely to be greater than its probative value, and to exclude self-incriminatory evidence unfairly obtained from the defendant after the commission of the alleged offence. Although s 78 goes much further than the common law power, particularly because it significantly widens the discretion to exclude evidence which has been unfairly or unlawfully obtained, there is one context in which the common law power is more extensive than s 78. This is where the evidence in question has already been adduced. Section 78 does not apply in this context, but if the evidence ought not to have been admitted the court may, under the common law power, take any necessary steps to prevent an injustice, whether by directing the jury to ignore the offending evidence or, if necessary, by discharging the jury.

Sometimes, in cases of unfairness to D, it is more appropriate for the court to stay proceedings on the grounds of an abuse of process on the basis that a fair trial would not be possible or, if it would, that a trial would be contrary to the public interest in the integrity of the criminal justice system, for example because the actions of the police threaten a basic human right. One such case recognised by the House of Lords is police entrapment, ie luring D into committing an offence and then seeking to prosecute him. Alleged entrapment does not prevent D seeking to have the evidence obtained by entrapment excluded as inadmissible, but it must be borne in mind that the tests are different. In staying proceedings the test is that just stated; under s 78 it is whether admitting the evidence would have such an adverse effect on the fairness of proceedings that the evidence ought not to be admitted. The House of Lords has held that in entrapment cases a stay of proceedings should normally be regarded as the appropriate response.

ADVANCE DISCLOSURE OF EVIDENCE

The disclosure provisions

The Criminal Procedure and Investigations Act 1996 (CPIA 1996), Part 1 (ss 1–21) contains provisions relating to the advance disclosure of material which apply where:

(a) a person charged with a summary offence pleads not guilty;
(b) a person of 18 or over charged with an either-way offence, in respect of which a court proceeds to summary trial, pleads not guilty; or
(c) a person under 18 charged with an indictable offence, in respect of which a court proceeds to summary trial, pleads not guilty.

The provisions also apply where a person is charged with an indictable offence and is committed or sent for trial, or proceedings are transferred for trial, to the Crown Court.

For the purpose of the disclosure provisions, 'material' refers to material of all kinds, and in particular refers to information, and to objects of all descriptions.

Initial duty of prosecutor to disclose

By s 3, the prosecutor must:

(a) disclose to the defendant (D) previously undisclosed prosecution material which might reasonably be considered capable of undermining the prosecution case, or of assisting the case for D; or

(b) give to D a written statement that there is no material of a description mentioned in (a).

Material must not be so disclosed to the extent that the court, on an application by the prosecutor, concludes that it is not in the public interest to disclose it and orders accordingly. At the same time as he acts under s 3, the prosecutor must give D any schedule of non-sensitive material previously given to him by the disclosure officer (below) (s 4).

Information need not be disclosed by the prosecutor to the extent that the court, on the prosecutor's application, concludes it is not in the public interest to disclose it and orders accordingly. Nor should it be disclosed if its disclosure is prohibited under the Regulation of Investigatory Powers Act 2000.The Court of Appeal has held that the disclosure responsibilities imposed on the prosecution by the disclosure provisions cannot be sidestepped by not making an enquiry. It stated that a police officer who believed that a person may have information which might undermine the case for the prosecution or assist the case for the suspect or defendant cannot decline to make enquiries of that person in order to avoid the need to disclose what the person might say. The Court therefore allowed appeals against conviction where there had been a failure to disclose a complaint by a prosecution witness against a police officer in case the result of the investigation should require disclosure.

Compulsory disclosure by defendant

The relevant provisions are in CPIA 1996, s 5. Where cases are to be tried on indictment, and the prosecutor complies (or purports to comply) with his initial duty of disclosure, and provided that D has received documents containing the prosecution's case, D is required to provide the court and the prosecutor during the relevant period (p 265) with a defence statement. From a day to be appointed, where there are other defendants, and the court so orders, D will also have to give a defence statement to each other defendant specified by the court. A defence statement may be supplied by D's solicitor.

By s 6A(1), a defence statement must be in writing and must set out the nature of D's defence, including any particular defences which are to be relied upon; indicate the matters of fact on which D takes issue with the prosecution, and why he takes issue; set out the matters of fact on which D intends to rely for the purposes of his defence; and indicate any point of law (including any point as to the admissibility of evidence or an abuse of process) which D wishes to take and any authority upon which he intends to rely. The Court of Appeal has held that if D raises no positive case at all in a defence statement but *simply* requires the prosecution to prove its case, there is no failure to comply with s 6A. It also held that both legal professional privilege and D's privilege against self-incrimination have survived s 6A. Section 6A requires D to disclose what is going to happen at the trial. It does not compel disclosure of his confidential discussions with his advocate. Nor is D obliged to incriminate himself.

Any defence statement which includes an alibi is required by s 6A(2) to give *the name, address, and date of birth of any witness D believes is able to give evidence in support of the alibi, or as many of those details as are known to D, and any other information in his possession which might assist in identifying or finding any such witness where such details are not known to D at that time.* Evidence in support of an alibi is evidence tending to show that, by reason of D's presence at a particular place or area at a particular time, D was not, or was unlikely to have been, at the place where the offence is alleged to have been committed at the time of its alleged commission.

Where a defence statement identifies an alibi witness under s 6A(2) or where D gives a notice under s 6C (p 264) indicating that he intends to call an identified witness at his trial, guidance is provided by a code of practice to police officers and others charged with the duty of investigating offences in relation to arranging and conducting interviews of persons notified. The Code of Practice for Arranging and Conducting Interviews of Witnesses Notified by the Accused provides as follows.

If an investigator wishes to interview a witness identified as above, the witness must be asked whether he consents to being interviewed and informed that:

(a) an interview is being requested following his identification by D as a proposed witness under ss 6A(2) or 6C;
(b) he is not obliged to attend the interview;
(c) he is entitled to be accompanied by a solicitor; and
(d) a record will be made of the interview and he will be sent a copy of it.

If the witness (W) consents to being interviewed, W must be asked whether he:

(a) wishes to have a solicitor present;
(b) consents to a solicitor attending on behalf of D, as an observer; and
(c) consents to a copy of the record being sent to D. If he does not consent, W must be informed that the effect of disclosure requirements in criminal proceedings may nevertheless require the prosecution to disclose the record to D (and any co-defendant) in the course of the proceedings.

The investigator must notify D or D's legal representatives:

(a) that the investigator requested an interview with W;
(b) whether W consented to the interview; and
(c) if W consented to the interview, whether he also consented to a solicitor attending on behalf of D, as an observer.

If D is not legally represented in the proceedings, and if W consents to a solicitor attending the interview on behalf of D, D must be offered a reasonable opportunity to appoint a solicitor to attend it.

The investigator must nominate a reasonable date, time, and venue for the interview and notify W of them and any changes to them.

If W has consented to the presence of D's solicitor, D's solicitor must be notified that the interview is taking place, invited to observe, and provided with reasonable notice of the date, time, and venue of the interview and any changes.

The identity of the investigator conducting the interview must be recorded. He must have sufficient skills and authority, commensurate with the complexity of the investigation, to discharge his functions effectively. He must not conduct the interview if that is likely to result in a conflict of interest, for instance, if he is the victim of the alleged crime which is the subject of the proceedings. The advice of a more senior officer must always be sought if there is doubt as to whether a conflict of interest precludes an individual conducting the interview. If thereafter the doubt remains, the advice of a prosecutor must be sought.

D's solicitor may only attend the interview as an observer if W has consented to his presence as an observer. Provided that D's solicitor was given reasonable notice of the date, time, and place of the interview, the fact that D's solicitor is not present will not prevent the interview from being conducted. If W at any time withdraws consent to D's solicitor being present at the interview, the interview may continue without the presence of D's solicitor.

Where W has indicated that he wishes to appoint a solicitor to be present, that solicitor must be permitted to attend the interview.

If W is under 18 or is mentally disordered or otherwise mentally vulnerable, he must be interviewed in the presence of an appropriate person.

A record must be made of the interview, wherever it takes place. It must be made, where practicable, by audio recording or by visual recording with sound, or otherwise in writing. Any written record must be made and completed during the interview, unless this would not be practicable or would interfere with the conduct of the interview, and must constitute either a verbatim record of what has been said or, failing this, an account of the interview which adequately and accurately summarises it. If a written record is not made during the interview it must be made as soon as practicable after its completion. Written interview records must be timed and signed by the maker.

The Code concludes by providing that a copy of the record must be given, within a reasonable time of the interview, to:

(a) W, and
(b) if W consents, to D or D's solicitor.

Any police officer or other person charged with the duty of investigating offences who arranges or conducts such an interview must have regard to the Code. Any provision of the Code or any failure to have due regard to the Code, either of which is relevant to any question arising in civil or criminal proceedings, can be taken into account by a court or tribunal conducting those proceedings in deciding that question.

Voluntary disclosure by defendant

By s 6, where the case is to be tried summarily, and the prosecutor complies (or purports to comply) with his initial duty of disclosure, D or his solicitor *may* give a defence statement to the prosecutor during the relevant period. If he does so, he must also give the statement to the court.

Updated disclosure by defendant

Section 6B, not in force at the time of writing, provides that where D or his solicitor has given a defence statement, he must during the relevant period give to the prosecutor and the court (and any co-defendant(s) if the court so orders) an updated defence statement or a written statement that he has no changes to make to his defence statement.

Notification of intent to call witnesses

By s 6C, referred to on p 263, D must also give the court and the prosecutor notification of his intention to call witnesses together with their identity or details which might lead to their identification. Changes must be notified.

Continuing duty of disclosure by prosecutor

After the prosecutor has complied (or purported to comply) with his initial duty of disclosure, the prosecutor remains under a continuing duty under s 7A, up to the time of acquittal, conviction or a decision not to proceed with the case, to keep under review whether there is any undisclosed prosecution material which might reasonably be considered capable of undermining the case for the prosecution against D or of assisting D's case. If there is, the prosecution must disclose it as soon as reasonably practicable.

Where D gives a defence statement or an updated defence statement, as a result of which the prosecutor is required by the above provision to make any disclosure, or further disclosure, the prosecutor must do so within the relevant period. If he considers that he is not so required he must give D a written statement to that effect within that period.

Application by defendant for further disclosure

Following compliance (or purported compliance) by the prosecutor with the provision just mentioned, or a failure by the prosecutor to comply with a duty under that provision to disclose, and provided that D has given a defence statement or an updated defence statement, D may apply to the court under s 8 for the disclosure of material which he reasonably believes is required to be disclosed to him but has not been. An order for further disclosure can only be made in respect of material in the possession of the prosecution in connection with the case against D or which the prosecutor has inspected or is entitled to inspect in pursuance of the Criminal Procedure and Investigations Act 1996: Code of Practice under Part II ('Police procedure') or of which in pursuance of that Code the prosecutor is entitled to have a copy; it cannot be made against a third party.

Failure in disclosure by defendant

Section 11 deals with this. It applies in the three cases set out below.

The first case is where s 5 (compulsory disclosure by D) applies and D:

(a) fails to give an initial defence statement; or
(b) gives one out of time; or
(c) is required by s 6B (not yet in force) to give an updated defence statement or a written statement indicating that there is no change but fails to do so; or
(d) gives such a statement out of time; or
(e) sets out inconsistent defences in his defence statement; or
(f) puts forward at his trial a defence which differs from that set out in a defence statement, relies on a matter which, in breach of s 6A, was not mentioned in his defence statement, adduces evidence in support of an undisclosed alibi, or calls a witness to support an alibi about whom he made no disclosure in his defence statement.

The second case is where s 6 applies, D gives an initial defence statement, and D gives that statement after the end of the relevant period for doing so, or does any of the things mentioned in (c) to (f) above.

The third case is where D gives a witness notice but does so after the relevant period for doing so, or at his trial calls a witness (other than himself) not included or adequately identified in a witness notice.

In these three cases, the judge, or any other party (in some cases only with the judge's leave), may make such comment as appears appropriate. In addition, the judge or jury may draw such inferences as appear proper in deciding whether D is guilty of the offence concerned, but a person may not be convicted solely on the basis of such an inference.

Time limits

The Criminal Procedure and Investigations Act 1996 (Defence Disclosure Time Limits) Regulations 2011 provide that the relevant period for compulsory disclosure by D (CPIA 1996, s 5), voluntary disclosure by D, (s 6), or notification of intent to call defence witnesses (s 6C) begins with the day on which the prosecutor complies or purports to comply with the prosecutor's initial duty of disclosure (s 3), and that:

(a) in respect of summary proceedings, the relevant period for s 6 and s 6C expires at the end of 14 days beginning with the first day of the relevant period;

(b) in respect of proceedings in the Crown Court, the relevant period for s 5 and s 6C expires at the end of 28 days beginning with the first day of the relevant period.

Where such a period expires on a weekend, Christmas Day, Good Friday, or a bank holiday, the relevant period is extended so as to expire on the next day which is not such a day.

The Regulations also provide that on an application by the defendant (D) the court may extend, or further extend, the relevant period by so many days as it specifies, if it is satisfied that it would be unreasonable to require D to give a defence statement under s 5 or s 6, or give notice under s 6C, as the case may be, within the relevant period. D's application must be made within the relevant period, specify the ground on which it is made, and state the number of days which D wishes the relevant period to be extended, There is no limit to the number of applications for an extension.

The Regulations do not prescribe a particular period of time in relation to disclosure by the prosecution. However, CPIA 1996, s 13 requires such disclosure as soon as is reasonably practicable in the particular circumstances described in the section.

Police procedure

Police procedure is controlled by the Criminal Procedure and Investigations Act 1996: Code of Practice under Part II. In summary:

The officer in charge of an investigation

The officer in charge of an investigation is any police officer involved in the conduct of a criminal investigation. All investigators are responsible for the recording and retention of materials and this includes negative material resulting from the interview of persons who could give no positive evidence. The officer in charge of an investigation must make such material available to the disclosure officer. While the officer in charge of an investigation may delegate tasks to other investigators, he remains responsible for ensuring that the duties relating to disclosure are properly carried out. All reasonable enquiries, whether pointing towards or away from a suspect must be investigated. Where material is held on a computer, the investigating officer must decide which factors may reasonably be enquired into.

Where an investigating officer believes that other parties may be in possession of relevant material which has not been obtained he may invite those persons to retain the material in case a request for disclosure is received. The disclosure officer should inform the prosecutor that those persons have the material. There is no requirement to make speculative enquiries; there must be some reason to believe that the persons concerned have relevant material.

Material which might be relevant to a criminal investigation but is not recorded must be held in a durable or retrievable form. Information must be recorded at the time at which it is obtained or as soon as is practicable thereafter. There is no requirement to take a statement where it would not otherwise be taken. The investigator has a duty to retain material obtained in a criminal investigation which might be relevant to the investigation. Where material which previously has been examined but not retained becomes relevant, the officer in charge of an investigation must take steps to obtain it or ensure that it is retained. The duty to retain material includes:

(a) crime reports of all descriptions;
(b) custody records;
(c) records derived from tapes of telephone messages containing descriptions of an alleged offence or offenders;
(d) final versions of witness statements (and draft versions if they differ) together with exhibits retained;
(e) interview records in any form with witnesses, potential witnesses or suspects;
(f) communications between police and experts (eg forensic scientists);
(g) records of first descriptions of suspects; and
(h) material casting doubt upon the reliability of a witness.

In addition, the duty to retain material which might be relevant to the investigation includes in particular the duty to retain material which may satisfy the test for prosecution disclosure, such as information provided by D which indicates an explanation for the offence with which he is charged, and material casting doubt on the reliability of a confession or a prosecution witness.

All such material which may be relevant to the investigation must be retained until a decision has been taken whether to institute proceedings against a person for an offence. If proceedings are instituted the material must be retained until the proceedings result in conviction or acquittal or a decision not to proceed has been taken. Where there is a conviction, material must be retained until the person is released from custody, or, in other circumstances, six months from the date of conviction. If a convicted person is released from custody within six months of conviction the material must be retained until the six months has elapsed. Where an appeal is lodged, material must be retained until the appeal is determined.

The disclosure officer

The disclosure officer is the person responsible for examining material retained by the police during an investigation; revealing material to the prosecutor during the investigation and any criminal proceedings resulting from it, and certifying that he has done this; and disclosing material to the defendant at the request of the prosecutor. In any criminal investigation, one or more deputy disclosure officers may be appointed to assist the disclosure officer, and such a deputy may perform any of the above functions of the disclosure officer.

The functions of the disclosure officer may be carried out by the investigator or officer in charge of the investigation. Indeed, the functions of all three roles may be carried out by one person. Where this is not done there must be full consultation between both officers. The disclosure officer is the link between the investigators and the Crown Prosecution Service and is responsible for providing the material for 'primary disclosure' and performing any other tasks required by the prosecutor. He must ensure, by liaison with the officer in charge of the case where that is a different person, that all material is made available for examination.

The disclosure officer or officer in charge of an investigation, or an investigator may seek advice from the prosecutor concerning which items are relevant to the investigation. Material which may be so relevant, which has been retained in accordance with the Code, and which the disclosure officer believes will not form a part of the prosecution case must be listed on a schedule. There must also be a list on a schedule of material which the disclosure officer does not believe to be sensitive. Any material which is believed to be sensitive must be listed on a schedule of sensitive material or, in exceptional circumstances, it may be revealed to the prosecutor separately. If there is no sensitive material this must be recorded by the disclosure officer on a schedule of sensitive material. Sensitive material is material, the disclosure of which, the disclosure officer believes, would give rise to a real risk of serious prejudice to an important public interest. Examples of sensitive material include:

(a)   material relating to national security;
(b)   material received from the intelligence and security agencies;
(c)   material relating to intelligence from foreign sources which reveals sensitive intelligence-gathering methods;
(d)   material given in confidence;
(e)   material relating to the identity or activities of informants, or undercover police officers, or witnesses, or other persons supplying information to the police who may be in danger if their identities are revealed;
(f)   material revealing the location of any premises or other place used for police surveillance, or the identity of any person allowing a police officer to use them for surveillance;
(g)   material revealing, either directly or indirectly, techniques and methods relied upon by a police officer in the course of a criminal investigation, for example covert surveillance techniques, or other methods of detecting crime;
(h)   material the disclosure of which might facilitate the commission of other offences or hinder the prevention and detection of crime;
(i)   material upon the strength of which search warrants were obtained;
(j)   material containing details of persons taking part in identification parades;
(k)   material supplied to an investigator during a criminal investigation which has been generated by an official of a body concerned with the regulation or supervision of bodies corporate or of persons engaged in financial activities, or which has been generated by a person retained by such a body;
(l)   material supplied to an investigator during a criminal investigation which relates to a child or young person and which has been generated by a local authority social services department, an Area Child Protection Committee, or other party contacted by an investigator during an investigation; or
(m)   material relating to the private life of a witness.

In exceptional circumstances, where an investigator considers that material is such that revelation by means of a schedule entry is inappropriate (and this will apply only where compromising the material would be likely to lead directly to the loss of life, or directly threaten national security) the existence of the material may be revealed to the prosecutor separately.

This lengthy list of exceptions illustrates the difficulties which arise following the provisions of a general duty to disclose material gained within an investigation.

In relation to all material, the appropriate schedule must be prepared where:

(a)   the defendant (D) is charged with an offence which is triable only on indictment;
(b)   D is charged with an offence triable either way, and it is considered either that the case is likely to be tried on indictment or that D is likely to plead not guilty at summary trial; or
(c)   D is charged with a summary offence, and it is considered that he is likely to plead not guilty.

In the case of either-way or summary offences a schedule may not be necessary if the offence is admitted, or if it was witnessed by a police officer and the person concerned has not denied it. Where it is believed that D will plead guilty at a summary trial, a schedule need not be prepared in advance. However, if, contrary to this belief, there is a not guilty plea at a summary trial, or if the offence is to be tried on indictment, the disclosure officer must ensure that a schedule is prepared as soon as reasonably practicable thereafter.

All items must be listed separately (provided that it is practicable to do so) and numbered consecutively.

The disclosure officer must give the schedules to the prosecutor at the same time as he gives the file containing the material for the prosecution case (or as soon as possible after a decision concerning mode of trial or plea), drawing attention to retained material which may meet the criteria for prosecution disclosure. Where material is in a form other than in writing, it should be given to the prosecutor in a form agreed between the disclosure officer and the prosecutor.

Where at the time of the preparation of the schedule of non-sensitive material for the prosecutor, the disclosure officer does not know with certainty the material which will form a part of the prosecution case, but these matters are subsequently determined, the disclosure officer must, where necessary, provide an amended schedule listing additional material which may be relevant to the investigation but does not form part of the case against the defendant, which is not already listed in the schedule and which is not believed to be sensitive.

As already mentioned, a continuing duty is imposed on the prosecutor, for the duration of criminal proceedings against D, to disclose material which might reasonably be considered to undermine the case for the prosecution, or which might assist D. After a defence statement has been given, the disclosure officer must look again at the material retained and must bring any material which might have this effect to the attention of the prosecutor.

The disclosure officer must certify that to the best of his knowledge and belief all relevant material which has been retained and made available to him has been revealed to the prosecutor. Further certification must follow subsequent developments.

If material has not already been copied to the prosecutor, and he requests its disclosure to D on the grounds that it satisfies the criteria for disclosure or a court has ordered its disclosure, the disclosure officer must disclose it to D. If material has been copied to the prosecutor, and it is so disclosed, it is a matter for agreement as to who should make the disclosure. Disclosure by the disclosure officer must be made by the provision of a copy or an opportunity to inspect it. Where a request is made for the provision of a copy of inspected material it must be given by the disclosure officer unless he considers that it is not practicable to do so (eg because the material consists of an object which cannot be copied, or because the volume of material is too great), or that it is not desirable (eg where the material is a statement by a child witness in relation to a sexual offence). Where information is recorded other than in writing, it is for the disclosure officer to decide whether it should be given in its original form or by means of a transcript certified as a true record.

If a court concludes that an item of sensitive material satisfies the prosecution disclosure test and that the interests of the defence outweigh the public interest in withholding disclosure, the material must be disclosed if the case is to proceed. The court, however, may in such circumstances direct that parts of the material be blanked out, or that the documents be summarised, or that the prosecutor make an admission concerning the substance of the material under CJA 1967, s 10.

THE RIGHT TO A FAIR TRIAL

Among the 'Convention rights' to which the Human Rights Act 1998 applies is the European Convention on Human Rights, art 6. Article 6 provides:

(1) In the determination of his civil rights and obligations or of any criminal charge against him, everyone is entitled to a fair and public hearing within a reasonable time by an independent and impartial tribunal established by law. Judgment shall be pronounced publicly but the press and public may be excluded from all or part of the trial in the interests of morals, public order, or national security in a democratic society, where the interests of juveniles or the protection of the private life of the parties so require, or to the extent strictly necessary in the opinion of the court in special circumstances where publicity would prejudice the interests of justice.

(2) Everyone charged with a criminal offence shall be presumed innocent until proved guilty according to the law.

(3) Everyone charged with a criminal offence has the following minimum rights:

    (a) to be informed promptly, in a language which he understands and in detail, of the nature and cause of the accusation against him;

    (b) to have adequate time and facilities for the preparation of his defence;

    (c) to defend himself in person or through legal assistance of his own choosing or, if he has not sufficient means to pay for legal assistance, to be given it free where the interests of justice so require;

    (d) to examine or have examined witnesses against him and to obtain the attendance and examination of witnesses on his behalf under the same conditions as witnesses against him;

    (e) to have the free assistance of an interpreter if he cannot understand or speak the language used in court.

The Supreme Court has held that the admission of the statement of an absent, but identified, witness under the rules relating to hearsay evidence does not involve a breach of art 6(1) or (3)(d), even if the evidence of the absent witness is the sole or decisive evidence against D; there are sufficient counter-balancing measures in the legislation to make the trial fair. Subsequently, the European Court of Human Rights has taken a view which is close to this, holding that a conviction may be based on hearsay evidence which is the sole or decisive evidence in the case. The question, it held, in each case is whether there are sufficient counterbalancing factors in place, including measures that permit a fair and proper assessment of the reliability of that evidence to take place. This would permit a conviction to be based on such evidence only if it is sufficiently reliable given its importance in the case. It has been held by the European Court that the Road Traffic Act 1988, s 172, which imposes a duty on the registered keeper of a motor vehicle to give such identity of the driver as may be required to the police, does not violate a person's right of silence and privilege against self-incrimination which are inherent in art 6. See p 424.

CHAPTER 8

The Police

ORGANISATION OF POLICE FORCES

The provisions set out below represent the position as it now is following fundamental changes made by the Police Reform and Social Responsibility Act 2011 (PRSRA 2011), Part 1. Unless otherwise indicated, the provisions referred to below are contained in PRSRA 2011, Part 1.

England and Wales are divided into police areas. Those areas are:

(a) the police areas listed in PA 1996, Sch 1 (which may be increased or reduced in number or extent by the Secretary of State);
(b) the Metropolitan Police district; and
(c) the City of London police area.

Police areas listed in PA 1996, Sch 1

Police and crime commissioners

There must be a police and crime commissioner (PCC) for each police area listed in PA 1996, Sch 1. Such commissioners have replaced police authorities for police areas outside the London area, which have been abolished. They are elected and hold office for four years.

Functions of police and crime commissioners

A PCC must secure the maintenance of the police force for his police area, and secure that the police force is efficient and effective. The PCC must hold the chief constable to account for the exercise of:

(a) the chief constable's functions and duties, including
  (i) the exercise of the duties to have regard to the police and crime plan (see p 274) issued by the commissioner and to the strategic policing requirement and codes of practice issued by the Secretary of State;
  (ii) the effectiveness and efficiency of the chief constable's arrangements for co-operating with other persons in the exercise of the chief constable's functions; and
  (iii) the exercise of duties relating to equality and diversity that are imposed on the chief constable by any enactment; and
(b) the functions of persons under the direction and control of the chief constable.

A PCC has a number of other functions referred to below (p 274).

Neither a PCC, nor a member of his staff, is personally liable for his conduct in the exercise of his functions unless it is shown to have been otherwise than in good faith.

Deputy commissioners, etc

A PCC may appoint a deputy commissioner and may arrange for the deputy commissioner to exercise most of the commissioner's functions.

A PCC may arrange for any person eligible for appointment as a deputy commissioner to exercise some of the PCC's functions.

Scrutiny of police and crime commissioners

Each police area outside the London area must have a police and crime panel with the duties set out below. Such a panel is composed of councillors appointed by local authorities in England and by the Secretary of State in Wales. Provision is made for a panel to co-opt additional members.

A police and crime panel has various powers of scrutiny including:

(a) reviewing or scrutinising decisions or other action by the PCC in connection with the discharge of his functions, and making reports or recommendations to the PCC with respect to such discharge;
(b) reviewing the draft police and crime plan, or draft variation, devised by the PCC, and making a report or recommendations on it to him;
(c) reviewing the PCC's annual report, and making a report or recommendations on it to the PCC;
(d) reviewing the precept proposed by the PCC and (if necessary) vetoing it;
(e) scrutinising, via a confirmation hearing, the proposed appointment by the PCC of a deputy commissioner or the PCC's chief executive or the PCC's chief finance officer. The PCC is not bound by the panel's recommendation about the proposed appointment; and
(f) scrutinising the PCC's proposed appointment of a chief constable or the PCC's requirement of a chief constable to retire or resign.

Suspension of police and crime commissioner   A police and crime panel may suspend the PCC if it appears to the panel that the PCC has been charged in the British Isles with an offence carrying a maximum term of imprisonment exceeding two years. If the PCC is subsequently convicted of any imprisonable offence his office becomes vacant.

Acting police and crime commissioner   The police and crime panel for a police area must appoint a member of the PCC's staff to act as PCC (ie to be 'acting PCC') if no person holds the office of PCC, or the PCC is incapacitated or suspended.

Chief constable

Appointment, suspension and removal   Each police force must have a chief constable appointed by the PCC. A police and crime panel must hold a public confirmation in respect of a proposed appointment and may veto that appointment.

The PCC may suspend from duty the chief constable or require him to resign or retire. A PCC's proposal to require a chief constable to retire or resign is subject to scrutiny by the police and crime panel but the panel can only make recommendations and cannot veto the proposal.

Functions   Subject to any provision in a collaboration agreement, a police force, and the civilian staff of a police force, are under the direction and control of the chief constable of the force.

Deputy and assistant chief constables

Each police force must have one or more deputy chief constables and one or more assistant chief constables. The chief constable must consult the PCC before appointing a person to be a deputy chief constable or an assistant chief constable. Those officers are 'senior police officers'. The chief constable of a police force may suspend from duty a deputy chief constable or an assistant chief constable or require him to resign or retire.

A deputy chief constable (or, where there is more than one, the most senior (as designated by the chief constable after consulting the PCC), or if he is absent, incapacitated, or suspended, the next most senior) may exercise any or all of the powers and duties of the chief constable during any absence, incapacity, or suspension from duty of the chief constable, or during any vacancy in the office of chief constable, or at any other time with the chief constable's consent.

The chief constable must, after consulting the PCC, designate a particular assistant chief constable to exercise any or all of the chief constable's powers if both the chief constable and his deputy (or deputies) are absent, incapacitated or suspended or those posts are all vacant.

Metropolitan Police District

The Mayor's Office for Policing and Crime

A body with the name 'The Mayor's Office for Policing and Crime' (MOPC) whose occupant is the Mayor of London, elected every four years, is established for the Metropolitan Police District. This body has replaced the Metropolitan Police Authority.

The MOPC has the same functions as a PCC (above and below), with the substitution of 'Mayor's Office for Policing and Crime' for 'police and crime commissioner/PCC' and 'Commissioner of Police of the Metropolis' for 'chief constable'.

Neither the occupant of the MOPC, nor a member of his staff, is personally liable for his conduct in the exercise of his functions unless it is shown to have been otherwise than in good faith.

The MOPC may appoint a Deputy Mayor for Policing and Crime and arrange for that Deputy Mayor to exercise most of the function of the MOPC. The MOPC may not appoint the Deputy Mayor until after the end of a confirmation hearing process, or if (after that process) the London Assembly vetoes the appointment of the candidate on the ground that the candidate is not an Assembly member.

The MOPC may also appoint someone who is not the Deputy Mayor for Policing and Crime to exercise some functions of the MOPC.

Scrutiny of Mayor's Office for Policing and Crime

The London Assembly must arrange for the following functions to be discharged on its behalf by a particular committee of the Assembly (the 'police and crime panel'):

(a) reviewing the draft police and crime plan given to the Assembly by the MOPC and making a report or recommendations on the draft plan to the MOPC;
(b) keeping under review the exercise of the functions of the MOPC, insofar as the Assembly is not otherwise required to do so; and
(c) holding a confirmation hearing in respect of appointment of the Deputy Mayor for Policing and Crime by the MOPC.

Commissioner of Police of the Metropolis

The Commissioner of Police of the Metropolis (CPM) is appointed by the Queen on the recommendation of the Secretary of State. Before recommending a person for appointment as the Commissioner the Secretary of State must have regard to any recommendations made by the MOPC. The CPM holds office at Her Majesty's pleasure.

The MOPC may, with the approval of the Secretary of State, suspend the CPM or require him to resign or retire.

The Secretary of State may require the MOPC to exercise the power to require the CPM to retire or resign, or (if the Secretary of State considers that suspension is necessary for the maintenance of public confidence in the metropolitan police force) to suspend the CPM. Where it is proposed to require the exercise of the power to require retirement or resignation, one or more persons must be appointed by, and report to, the Secretary of State after holding an inquiry.

Subject to any provision in a collaboration agreement, the metropolitan police force, and the civilian staff of the metropolitan police force, are under the direction and control of the CPM.

Deputy and Assistant Commissioners

The metropolitan police force has one Deputy Commissioner of Police of the Metropolis, who is appointed and holds office in the same way as the Commissioner, except that before recommending a person for appointment the Secretary of State must also consult the CPM as well as any representations made by the MOPC. The rules about suspending the Deputy CPM, or requiring him to retire or resign are the same as those which apply to the CPM.

The Deputy CPM may exercise any or all of the powers and duties of the CPM:

(a) during any absence, incapacity or suspension from duty of the CPM,

(b) during any vacancy in the office of CPM, or

(c) at any other time, with the consent of the CPM.

The Deputy CPM may not act by virtue of (a) or (b) for a continuous period exceeding three months, except with the consent of the Secretary of State.

The metropolitan police force must have one or more Assistant Commissioners of Police of the Metropolis, one or more Deputy Assistant Commissioners of Police of the Metropolis, and one or more Commanders. These officers are appointed by the CPM. The Commissioner must consult the MOPC before appointing a person to one of these offices. These officers ('senior Metropolitan Police officers') may be suspended by the CPM. After consulting the MOPC, the Commissioner may require a senior Metropolitan Police officer to resign or retire. An Assistant Commissioner of Police of the Metropolis may exercise any of the powers and duties of the CPM with his consent.

Other functions and duties of elected local policing bodies

A police and crime commissioner or the Mayor's Office for Policing and Crime is an 'elected local policing body'.

Police and crime plans

The elected local policing body (ELPB) must issue a police and crime plan within the financial year in which each four yearly election is held and must do so as soon as practicable after taking office. In addition, it may, at any time, issue or vary a police and crime plan. In issuing or varying a police and crime plan, an ELPB must have regard to the strategic policing requirement issued by the Secretary of State (below).

A police and crime plan is a plan which sets out, in relation to the planning period, the following matters:

(a) the ELPB's police and crime objectives;
(b) the policing of the police area which the chief officer of police is to provide;
(c) the financial and other resources which the ELPB is to provide to the chief officer of police for the chief officer to exercise the functions of chief officer;
(d) the means by which the chief officer of police will report to the ELPB on his provision of policing;
(e) the means by which the chief officer of police's performance in providing policing will be measured;
(f) the crime and disorder reduction grants which the ELPB is to make, and the conditions (if any) to which such grants are to be made.

Before issuing or varying a police and crime plan, an ELPB must:

(a) prepare a draft plan or variation,
(b) consult the relevant chief officer of police in preparing that,
(c) send the draft to the relevant police and crime panel,
(d) have regard to any report or recommendations made by the panel (see below), and
(e) give the panel a response to any such report or recommendations, and publish any such response.

If, and to any extent that, the plan or variation differs from the draft plan prepared in accordance with (a), the ELPB must consult the relevant chief officer before issuing or varying the plan.

A plan or variation of it must be published.

After consulting the persons representing the views of police and crime commissioners, the Mayor's Office, the Association of Chief Police Officers (ACPO) and other persons as thought fit, the Secretary of State may give guidance to ELPBs about matters to be dealt with in these plans, and such bodies must have regard to it.

An ELPB and a chief officer of police must have regard to the police and crime plan, and to any guidance issued by the Secretary of State about how this duty to do so is to be complied with. Before giving guidance, the Secretary of State must consult the bodies and persons referred to in the last paragraph.

Information

An ELPB is required to publish information specified by the Secretary of State in the Elected Local Policing Bodies (Specified Information) Order 2011, as amended in 2012, at the times so specified. It must also publish information which it considers necessary to enable local residents to assess its performance and that of the chief officer of police.

Each ELPB must produce and publish an annual report on:

(a) the exercise of its functions in each financial year, and
(b) the progress which has been made in the financial year in meeting the police and crime objectives in its police and crime plan.

The ELPB must attend before the relevant police and crime panel at a public meeting arranged by the panel to present the report to the panel and answer the panel's questions on the report. It must give the panel a response to any report or recommendations on the annual report and publish any such response.

An ELPB must provide the relevant police and crime panel with any information which the panel may reasonably require in order to carry out its functions. This obligation does not apply if disclosure of the information is prohibited by or under an enactment or if the chief officer of police considers that disclosure of the information would prejudice national security or might prejudice the safety of someone, the prevention of crime, the detection or prosecution of offenders, or the administration of justice.

Duties when carrying out functions

In carrying out functions, an ELPB must have regard not only to the local policing plan (see above) but also:

(a) to the views of people in the ELPB's area about policing in that area;

(b) in a particular financial year, to any report or recommendations made by the relevant police and crime panel on the annual report for the previous financial year; and

(c) any financial code of practice issued by the Secretary of State.

Police fund

Each ELPB must keep a 'police fund' into which all receipts must be paid and from which all expenditure must be paid. The Secretary of State, for each financial year, makes a grant from central funds to ELPBs. The remainder of the finance will be met from other grants from the Secretary of State (for capital expenditure or expenditure on safeguarding national security) or local authorities, precepts on local authorities and gifts and loans.

City of London police area

The changes made by PRSRA 2011 do not apply to this area.

The Common Council of the City of London continues to be the police authority for the City of London police area.

The Secretary of State may confer particular functions on the Common Council. Such an order may in particular contain provision requiring the Common Council:

(a) to monitor the performance of the City of London police force in:
    (i) complying with any statutory duty imposed on the force;
    (ii) carrying out its annual policing plan (below);

(b) to secure that arrangements are made for that force to co-operate with other police forces whenever necessary or expedient;

(c) to promote diversity within that force and within the Common Council.

The Common Council must issue an annual policing plan setting out its objectives ('policing objectives') for the policing of the City of London police area, and for the discharge by the City of London Police of its national and international functions during that year, and the proposed arrangements for the policing of that area for the period of three years beginning with that year. In issuing a policing plan, the Common Council must have regard to the strategic policing requirement issued by the Secretary of State.

The Secretary of State may require the Common Council to issue reports concerning the discharge of its functions.

The head of the City of London police force is the Commissioner of Police for the City of London. Its other senior officers are an Assistant Commissioner and a Commander.

Ranks below senior officers

Appointments and promotions to any rank below that of assistant chief constable (or commander) are made by the chief constable (or Commissioner of Police for the

Metropolis or Commissioner of City of London Police). Those ranks are chief superintendent, superintendent, chief inspector, inspector, sergeant, and constable.

The role of the Secretary of State

Strategic policing requirement

Although the courts have ruled that chief officers of police must carry out their duties independently, so that there may be no suggestion of direct government control in relation to law enforcement, by PA 1996, s 37A the Secretary of State is required, from time to time, to issue the 'strategic policing requirement' which sets out what, in the Secretary of State's view, are:

(a) national threats (ie threats to national security, public safety, public order, or public confidence so grave as to be of national importance, or threats which can be countered effectively or efficiently only by 'national policing capabilities' (ie the ability of all English and Welsh police forces)); and

(b) appropriate national policing capabilities to counter those national threats.

A chief officer of police must, in exercising the functions of chief officer, have regard to the strategic policing requirement.

Before issuing the strategic policing requirement, the Secretary of State must obtain the advice of ACPO and of persons representing the views of local policing bodies, and must consult such other persons as the Secretary of State thinks fit.

It will be noted that s 37A does not empower the Secretary of State to interfere in particular law enforcement matters; the Secretary of State is still not permitted to require or prohibit particular investigations or prosecutions.

Policing protocol

The Secretary of State has issued a Policing Protocol. It is contained in the Schedule to the Policing Protocol Order 2011 which contains provisions about ways in which relevant persons should (in the Secretary of State's view) exercise, or refrain from exercising, functions so as to:

(a) encourage, maintain, or improve working relationships (including co-operative working) between relevant persons, or

(b) limit or prevent the overlapping or conflicting exercise of functions.

'Relevant persons' means:

(i) the Secretary of State in the exercise of the Secretary of State's policing functions;
(ii) each ELPB;
(iii) the chief officer of each police force maintained by an ELPB;
(iv) police and crime panels.

Each relevant person must have regard to the policing protocol in exercising that person's function.

Power to give directions

BY PA 1996, ss 40 and 40A, the Secretary of State may direct a local policing body (an ELPB or the Common Council of the City of London) to take specified measures to remedy any defect or potential defect in the discharge of its functions or those of its police force. When directing specified measures, the Secretary of State may require an action plan.

The Secretary of State is also empowered to issue codes of practice relating to the discharge of their functions by chief officers of police (PA 1996, s 39A).

Regulation-making powers

In addition to the regulation-making powers noted above, PA 1996, s 53A empowers the Secretary of State to make regulations requiring police forces in England and Wales to adopt particular procedures or practices. Before making such regulations, the Secretary of State must, after consultation, seek advice from the chief inspector of constabulary.

By PA 1996, s 50, the Secretary of State may, after consultation, make regulations as to the government, administration and conditions of service of police forces. PA 1996, s 53 enables the Secretary of State to make regulations as to the standard and provision of police equipment.

Crime and disorder strategies

The Crime and Disorder Act 1998, ss 5 to 7 makes provision for crime and disorder reduction partnerships in each district council area in England, and each county or county borough area in Wales, in a police area to formulate and implement crime and disorder strategies.

Crime and disorder reduction partnerships

The members of the partnership are the 'responsible authorities', ie:

(a) the district council for the area and, if that council is not a unitary authority, the relevant county council;
(b) every chief officer of police whose police area is in the council's area;
(c) every provider of probation services, every fire and rescue authority and every Primary Care Trust (England) or Local Health Board (Wales) in that area.

The relevant local policing body (or bodies) in relation to two or more local government areas in England may make an agreement with all the responsible authorities in relation to those areas and the Secretary of State for the creation of a 'combined area', in which the functions below will be carried out as if it constituted only one local government area. The 'relevant local policing body' in the present context refers to an ELPB or, in the City of London, the Secretary of State.

Formulation and implementation of crime and disorder strategies

A crime and disorder reduction partnership must formulate and implement:

(a) a strategy for the reduction of crime and disorder in the area (including anti-social and other behaviour adversely affecting the local environment); and
(b) a strategy for combating the misuse of drugs, alcohol and other substances in the area; and
(c) a strategy for the reduction of re-offending in the area.

In exercising functions under (a) to (c), apart from certain functions in Wales where the Welsh Assembly has devolved functions, each of the responsible authorities for a district council area must have regard to the police and crime objectives set out in the police and crime plan for the police area which comprises or includes that local government area.

The responsible authorities for a local government area must, whenever so required by the relevant local policing body (see above), submit to that body a report on such matters connected with the exercise of the above functions, apart from devolved Welsh functions, as requested. The relevant local policing body may require such a report only if it is not satisfied that the responsible authorities for the area are carrying out their above functions in an effective and efficient manner, and it considers requiring a report is reasonable and proportionate.

Collaboration agreements

These are dealt with by PA 1996, ss 22A–23H.

A collaboration agreement is a written agreement containing provision about one or more of the following:

(a) the discharge of functions of members of a police force ('force collaboration provision');
(b) support by a policing body for another policing body ('policing body collaboration provision');
(c) support by a policing body for the police force which another policing body is responsible for maintaining ('policing body and force collaboration provision').

A 'policing body' means an ELPB, the Common Council of the City of London, the British Transport Police Authority, and the Civil Nuclear Police Authority.

Such an agreement may be made by two or more policing bodies, or by the chief officers of police of one or more police forces and two or more policing bodies.

The chief officer of police of a police force must keep under consideration the ways in which the collaboration functions of chief officers or policing bodies could be exercised by the chief officer and by one or more other persons to improve the efficiency or effectiveness of that police force, and one or more other police forces. If the chief officer considers that there is a particular way in which the collaboration functions could be so exercised by the chief officer and by one or more other particular persons ('the proposed collaboration'), he must take the matter up with those other persons.

Similar provisions apply to a policing body in respect of how the collaboration functions could be exercised by it and by one or more other persons to improve:

(a) its efficiency or effectiveness and/or that of its police force; and:
(b) the efficiency and effectiveness of one or more other policing bodies and police forces.

Force collaboration provision in a collaboration agreement involving police forces may, in particular, consist of provision for the joint discharge of functions by members of police forces; for members of a police force to discharge functions in another force's area; for members of a police force to be provided to another force. A collaboration agreement involving police forces may provide for a member of a police force, or a civilian employee, to be under the direction and control of a chief officer specified in or determined in accordance with the agreement.

Policing body collaboration provision, or policing body and force collaboration provision, in a collaboration agreement involving policing bodies may, in particular, consist of provision:

(a) for support to be provided jointly by two or more policing bodies;
(b) for support to be provided for two or more policing bodies or forces jointly;
(c) for a policing body to provide support to another policing body or to a force maintained by another policing body.

In relation to policing body collaboration provision, or policing body and force collaboration provision, references to the provision of support include, in particular, the provision of premises, equipment, staff, services, and facilities. A policing body must consult the chief officer of police of the police force which the body is responsible for maintaining before making a collaboration agreement (unless that chief officer is a party to the agreement).

Where a force collaboration provision, contained in a collaboration agreement, is about the discharge of functions by designated civilian employees of one police force for the purposes of another police force, the force collaboration agreement must specify:

(a) the functions which the designated civilian employees (ie designated under PRA 2002, s 38 (p 282)) are permitted by the collaboration agreement to discharge for the purposes of the assisted force, and
(b) any restrictions or conditions on that permission for the designated civilian employees to discharge those functions.

The force collaboration agreement must not permit the designated civilian employees to discharge functions for the purposes of the assisted police force unless those employees are, by virtue of the relevant s 38 designation, authorised to discharge those functions for the purposes of the assisting force. The force collaboration provision does not authorise the designated civilian employees to discharge functions for the purposes of the assisted police force (but see PRA 2002, s 38B (p 283)).

Powers of Secretary of State

The Secretary of State may give chief officers or policing bodies guidance about collaboration agreements or related matters, to which chief officers and policing bodies must have regard.

The Secretary of State may, by order, require a specified police function to be exercised in relation to all police areas, or all police areas apart from any specified in the order, in accordance with police collaboration provision. The Secretary of State has specified the provision of police air support as such a function in relation to all police areas.

The Secretary of State may give one or more chief officers or policing bodies directions about collaboration agreements. Before giving such a direction the Secretary of State must consult the person or persons to whom it is to be given. A person to whom a direction is given must comply with it. A direction may, in particular, require or prohibit the making or varying of a collaboration agreement, or require the making of a collaboration agreement of a specified description to be considered, or specify terms to be included, or not included, in collaboration agreements. A direction may relate to a particular agreement, agreements of a particular description, or agreements in general.

After consulting the parties to an agreement, the Secretary of State may terminate a collaboration agreement by notice to these parties.

Her Majesty's Inspectors of Constabulary

PA 1996, ss 54 and 55 and Sch 4A govern Her Majesty's Inspectors of Constabulary, who are appointed by Her Majesty.

HM inspectors of constabulary must inspect, and report on the efficiency and effectiveness of, every police force maintained for a police area.

The local policing body for a police area (ie an ELPB or the Common Council of the City of London) may at any time request the inspectors of constabulary to carry out, at its expense, an inspection of a police force maintained for that police area. The request may include a request for the inspection to be confined to a particular part of the force in question, to particular matters, or to particular activities of that force. The Secretary of State has a corresponding power to request an inspection of a police force maintained for any police area; the only difference is that the inspection is not at the expense of the relevant local policing body.

Reports by HM Inspectors of Constabulary must be published. The published report must be sent to the Secretary of State, the relevant local policing body, the chief officer of police, and any relevant police and crime panel.

Where such an inspection leads to a conclusion that the force, or a part of it, or the local policing body, is not efficient or effective, or will cease to be so unless remedial action is taken, the Secretary of State may give a direction under PA 1996, s 40 or 40A to the relevant local policing body to take such remedial measures as are specified in the direction. These measures may include the submission of an action plan.

The chief inspector of constabulary must in each year submit to the Secretary of State a report on the carrying out of inspections and the Secretary of State must lay a copy of that report before Parliament. Such a report must include the chief inspector's assessment of the efficiency and effectiveness of policing for the year reported on.

PA 1996, Sch 4A permits an inspector of constabulary to delegate any of his functions (to such extent as he may determine) to another public authority. A 'public authority' includes any person certain of whose functions are functions of a public nature. The inspectors of constabulary may act jointly with another public authority where it is appropriate to do so for the efficient and effective discharge of their duties.

National police organisations

Serious Organised Crime Agency

The Serious Organised Crime and Police Act 2005 (SOCPA 2005) established SOCA which acts under a Director General appointed by the Secretary of State for a period of five years. Its functions are to prevent and detect serious organised crime and to contribute to the reduction of such crime and to the mitigation of its consequences. It may also investigate revenue frauds and serious frauds, but only with the consent of the Commissioners for Revenue and Customs or the Serious Fraud Office as the case may be. It is also charged with gathering, storing, analysing and disseminating information relevant to the prevention, detection, investigation, or prosecution of offences, or to the reduction of crime by other means or the mitigation of its consequences.

SOCA provides information to police forces, special police forces, and other law enforcement agencies as well as co-operating in other ways. While SOCA was set up to investigate serious crime, it may involve itself in lesser crime if that is the best means of securing a conviction and custodial sentence in respect of an organised criminal. SOCA also has the function of recovery of assets under the Proceeds of Crime Act 2002.

The activities of SOCA are supervised by its Board which consists of a chairman and members appointed by the Secretary of State, the Director General, and other ex officio members. SOCA is obliged to produce an annual plan and an annual report. The Secretary of State is empowered to establish strategic priorities and to issue codes of practice relating to the discharge of the Agency's functions. In addition, SOCA is subject to inspection by HM Inspectors of Constabulary. However, operational control remains with the Director General.

Voluntary arrangements may be made in relation to mutual assistance between SOCA and police forces. Where there is a failure to agree a voluntary scheme, the Secretary of State is empowered to direct that mutual assistance be arranged. SOCA is liable for the actions of any police officer seconded to the Agency.

Where a person becomes a member of staff of SOCA he loses any powers which he held in his previous office as a constable, Revenue and Customs, or immigration officer. Powers may be designated by the Director General, or a designated officer (currently the Deputy Director), according to the needs of the organisation. SOCPA 2005, s 51 creates offences of assaulting, obstructing, or impersonating designated members of SOCA staff.

National Policing Improvement Agency

The Police and Justice Act 2006, s 1 established a National Policing Improvement Agency (NPIA).

NPIA's tasks are to identify, develop, and promulgate good policing practice; to provide police forces with expert operational advice and assistance; to identify and assess opportunities for, and threats to, police forces in England and Wales; to share policing issues with international partners; to provide support to police forces in connection with the provision of information technology, procurement, and training services (such services may be provided by NPIA or by contracted providers); and to carry out the accreditation and training of financial investigators to be used for the recovery of assets under the Proceeds of Crime Act 2002.

NPIA may do anything which it considers to be appropriate to achieve its objectives and has taken over the functions of the Police National Computer.

The Chairman, chief executive, and members are appointed by the Secretary of State. Serving police officers may be seconded to NPIA's staff; they retain their status as constables. Where a serving police officer is appointed to the post of chief executive, he will hold the rank of chief constable.

The Police Reform Act 2002 (PRA 2002), s 16A obliges the Agency to comply with the requirements of an investigation by the Independent Police Complaints Commission (IPCC) and to provide staff for the purposes of an investigation. Section 26B requires the IPCC to enter into agreements with NPIA as to how the IPCC will operate in relation to NPIA's staff, but the IPCC does not have jurisdiction in respect of the direction and control of such staff.

JURISDICTION OF CONSTABLES

In law every member of a police force holds the office of constable, whatever his rank. Although he is not 'a member of a police force', so does a special constable.

PA 1996, s 30 provides that every member of a police force or a special constable has all the powers and privileges of a constable throughout England and Wales and the adjacent UK waters. 'UK waters' means the sea and other waters within the seaboard limits of the territorial seas.

EXERCISE OF POLICE POWERS BY CIVILIANS

PRA 2002, s 38 authorises a chief officer of police to designate a relevant employee as an officer who is under his direction and control as:

(a) a community support officer (CSO);
(b) an investigating officer;

(c) a detention officer;
(d) an escort officer.

By PRA 2002, s 38(11), 'relevant employee' means:
(a) in the case of:
    (i) a police force maintained for an area listed in PA 1996, Sch 1, or
    (ii) the police force maintained for the Metropolitan Police District,
    a member of the civilian staff of that force;
(b) in the case of any other police force, a person who:
    (i) is employed by the police authority maintaining that force, and
    (ii) is under the direction and control of the chief officer making the designation.

A person designated under PRA 2002, s 38 has the powers and duties conferred or imposed on him by the designation as well as (in the case of a CSO) any standard duties and powers conferred on such an officer by an order made by the Secretary of State. The complete range of powers and duties which may be conferred or imposed by a designation are set out in PRA 2002, Sch 4.

By PRA 2002, s 38B, the chief officer of a police force (the 'assisted force') may designate a person (C) who:

(a) is a civilian employee of another police force (the 'assisting force'),
(b) is designated under PRA 2002, s 38 by the chief officer of police of the assisting police force, and
(c) is permitted, under relevant police collaboration provision, to discharge powers and duties specified in that provision for the purposes of the assisted force.

Such a designation (the 'collaboration designation') may designate C as an officer of a particular type, eg CSO, only if the s 38 designation designates C as an officer of that type. C will have the powers and duties conferred or imposed on C by the collaboration designation. However, a power or duty may be conferred or imposed on C by the collaboration designation only if C is permitted, under the relevant police collaboration provision, to discharge that power or duty for the purposes of the assisted force. The collaboration designation must specify the restrictions and conditions to which C is subject in the discharge of the powers and duties conferred or imposed by the collaboration designation. Those restrictions and conditions must include the restrictions and conditions specified in the relevant police collaboration provision.

A community support officer

Examples of powers which may be conferred on a CSO are as follows.

A designation may confer on a CSO the power to issue prescribed fixed penalty notices:

(a) under the Criminal Justice and Police Act 2001 (CJPA 2001) (fixed penalty notices for offences of disorder: p 31), except in relation to offences of theft against the Theft Act 1968, s 1 and of leaving litter against the Environmental Protection Act 1990 (EPA 1990), s 87;
(b) under education legislation, in respect of failure to secure attendance of a pupil at school or of the presence of an excluded pupil in a public place;
(c) under the Anti-social Behaviour Act 2003, s 43, in respect of graffiti or fly-posting.

The above offences are all described as 'relevant fixed penalty offences'.

In addition, a designation may confer on a CSO the power to remove truants and excluded pupils to designated premises, to disperse groups in areas of persistent anti-social behaviour and remove those under 16 to their place of residence, to serve closure notices for licensed premises persistently serving children, to enter to investigate licensing offences, to stop vehicles for testing, and to control traffic for purposes of escorting a load of exceptional dimensions.

A person designated as a CSO has the standard powers and duties of a CSO conferred by the Police Reform Act (Standard Powers and Duties of Community Support Officers) Order 2007 made by the Secretary of State under PRA 2002, s 38A in addition to any powers conferred on him by designation as set out in Sch 4, Part 1.

The standard powers and duties of a CSO are set out in the Schedule to the 2007 Order which makes the following powers in PRA 2002, Sch 4, Part 1 standard powers:

(a) issue of fixed penalty notices applying to offences of cycling on a footway or litter (against EPA 1990, s 88) and in respect of offences under dog control orders. Such offences are also 'relevant fixed penalty offences';

(b) requirement of name and address if the CSO has reason to believe that the person has committed a 'relevant offence' (ie a relevant fixed penalty offence, or an offence which appears to have caused injury, alarm or distress, to another or any damage to another's property, or certain other offences) or a relevant licensing offence. It is an offence for a person to fail to comply with such a requirement. (In addition, *a designation may* provide a power permitting a CSO who is so designated and who has made a requirement for a name and address to require the other person to remain with him for a period, not exceeding 30 minutes, for the arrival of a constable, where the CSO has reasonable grounds for suspecting that the person has given a false or inaccurate name or address. When making that requirement, the officer may enforce it by a gesture. The alleged offender may elect to accompany the CSO to a police station as an alternative to waiting. Such a person, on arrival at a police station, is under a duty to remain there until his custody is transferred to a constable. Failure to wait, or making off, is an offence. A *designation may* also empower search of a person asked to wait or the use of reasonable force to prevent an individual making off when subject to a requirement to give his name and address or while accompanying the officer to a police station);

(c) requirement of name and address of person reasonably believed to have been active or to be acting in an anti-social manner;

(d) requirement of name and address under RTA 1988, ss 165 or 169 (power to require name and address following failure to comply with a traffic direction or failure by a pedestrian to comply with a direction given by a police officer in uniform or a traffic officer respectively);

(e) exercise of a constable's powers in respect of alcohol consumption in designated public places;

(f) exercise of a constable's powers to confiscate alcohol or tobacco from a young person. (A designation may give an associated power of search and seizure);

(g) confiscation of controlled drugs found in a young person's possession. (A designation may give an associated power of search and seizure);

(h) entry to save life or limb or prevent serious damage to property;

(i) seizure of vehicles used to cause alarm, etc (entry to premises to do so only in company, and under supervision, of a constable);

(j) exercise of powers in respect of abandoned vehicles;

(k) stopping cycles;

(l)   control of traffic for purposes other than escorting a load of exceptional dimensions;

(m)   carrying out road checks;

(n)   placing traffic signs;

(o)   exercise of constable's powers under the Terrorism Act 2000, s 36 in cordoned areas;

(p)   exercise of specified stop, search, and seizure powers under the Terrorism Act 2000, s 47A (p 817); and

(q)   photographing persons arrested, detained or given fixed penalty notices.

An investigating officer

A designation may empower an investigating officer to exercise the powers under the Police and Criminal Evidence Act 1984 (PACE), s 8 to apply for a warrant to enter and search premises to be issued to him and to seize and retain articles found during a search. The safeguards, etc provided by PACE in relation to searches apply equally to an officer so designated. A designation may permit a search warrant to be issued, and executed, under the Theft Act 1968, s 26 or the Misuse of Drugs Act 1971, s 23, by an officer in respect of whom the designation applies these provisions. A designation may give the powers of a constable under PACE, s 9(1) (access to excluded and special procedure material) to an investigating officer. The various procedural matters prescribed by PACE in relation to such matters apply to such an officer. Powers under PACE, ss 18, 19, and 21 to enter, search, seize, and copy things seized may also be given by a designation, as may powers to arrest for a further offence at a police station for another offence. In addition, a designation may give powers under CJPOA 1994 to require arrested persons to account for certain matters, or powers under the UK Borders Act 2007, ss 44, 45, and 46 to enter and search premises and to seize nationality documents where a person, who is suspected of not being a British citizen, has been arrested on suspicion of having committed an offence under that Act. Authorised persons have the same search and seize powers as are possessed by an investigating officer whom they accompany.

The exercise of these powers must be on the written authority of an officer of at least the rank of inspector.

A detention officer

A designation may authorise a detention officer to require a person to attend a police station for the taking of a sample or fingerprints (and to take those fingerprints without consent); to photograph a detained person; to carry out intimate or non-intimate searches; to search a person answering live link bail; to carry out a search and examination to establish identity (including the taking of a photograph of an identifying mark); to take impressions of footwear; and to carry out a search of someone attending a police station to answer live link bail, and to seize articles found.

A designation may authorise a detention officer to keep under control detainees at a police station (or to assist others in doing so) and to secure that persons in detention do not escape; reasonable force may be used for these purposes. A designation may authorise a detention officer to carry out specified duties to give information in relation to intimate searches, X-rays and ultrasound scans carried out in respect of Class A drug searches.

An escort officer

An escort officer may be designated to take an arrested person to a police station or to escort a person in police detention. An escort officer designated to escort a person in police detention may also use reasonable force to keep the detainee under control. A designated escort officer remains in control until the detainee is handed over to the custody officer or other responsible person, and may use reasonable force to prevent that person escaping and to keep him under his control. A designated escort officer may carry out an intimate search of the detainee.

Community safety accreditation schemes

PRA 2002, s 40 authorises a chief officer to establish and maintain a 'community safety accreditation scheme' for the exercise in his area, by persons accredited by him under s 41, of powers related to community safety and security and (in co-operation with the local police) combating crime and disorder, public nuisance, and other forms of anti-social behaviour. Any such scheme must contain provisions for arrangements to be made with employers who are carrying on a business in the police area for those employers to supervise the carrying out of such functions for the purposes of which accreditation powers are provided. Chief officers must ensure that the employer has made satisfactory arrangements for the handling of complaints relating to the exercise of those powers.

The powers which may be conferred on accredited persons are set out in PRA 2002, Sch 5, namely powers to give fixed penalty notices:

(a) under CJPA 2001, except in respect of offences of drunkenness, theft, criminal damage, or leaving litter (contrary to EPA 1990, s 87);
(b) in respect of offences relating to dog control orders, cycling on a footpath, failing to secure attendance of a pupil at school, being an excluded pupil in a public place, graffiti or fly-posting, and litter under EPA 1990, s 88.

Accredited persons may also be given powers to deal with alcohol consumption in a designated public place, confiscation of liquor, tobacco and abandoned vehicles, stopping vehicles for testing, and controlling traffic for the purpose of escorting a load of exceptional dimensions.

Accredited persons may be authorised to require names and addresses in relation to certain traffic offences, to control traffic, and to photograph persons given fixed penalty notices.

Accreditation of weights and measures inspectors

PRA 2002, s 41A provides that weights and measures inspectors (trading standards officers) may be accredited ('an accredited officer') by a chief officer of police. An accredited officer may be accredited to issue fixed penalty notices under CJPA 2001, to require the name and address of someone reasonably believed to have committed a fixed penalty offence for the purposes of CJPA 2001 and/or to photograph someone to whom he has given such a notice. The powers may only be exercised by such an accredited officer in the exercise of his duties as a trading standards officer. PRA 2002, s 41B authorises the Secretary of State to apply these provisions related to an accredited officer to persons of a description specified by order.

General

A designated person or person accredited under PRA 2002, s 41 or s 41A must produce evidence of his designation or accreditation if requested to do so when exercising one of his powers. In addition, such a person is restricted in the exercise of powers to times when he is wearing approved uniform or badge. However, a police officer of or above the rank of inspector may direct a particular investigating officer not to wear uniform for the purposes of a particular operation. PRA 2002, s 46 creates offences of assault on designated persons, accredited persons or other persons assisting such persons, in the execution of their duties; resisting or wilfully obstructing such persons; and, with intent to deceive, impersonating a designated or accredited person or making a statement or doing an act calculated falsely to suggest that a person is designated or accredited. A designated or accredited person commits an offence if he makes any statement or does any act calculated falsely to suggest that he has powers as a designated or accredited person which exceed his actual powers.

These auxiliary personnel must have regard, in the discharge of their duties, to the provisions of the Codes of Practice under PACE. A person lawfully in the custody of such a person must be treated as in police detention.

Where any power exercised by one of the above types of person includes power to use reasonable force to enter premises, that power may only be exercised in the company, and under the supervision of, a constable or to save life or limb or to prevent serious damage.

REPRESENTATION

The Association of Chief Police Officers, the Superintendents' Association and the Police Federation represent the interests of the various members of police forces. A member of a police force is not permitted to be a member of a trade union, or of any association having as one of its objects control or influence over pay, pensions, or conditions of service of any police force. However, persons who were members of trade unions before joining the police force may retain that membership with the approval of their chief constable.

LIABILITY

A constable will be liable to pay damages if his conduct is unlawful in civil law, as where he commits a tort or acts in breach of a Convention right under the Human Rights Act 1998.

PA 1996, s 88 states that a chief officer of police is vicariously liable in civil law for any unlawful conduct of his constables (or an international joint investigation team which has been formed under the leadership of a constable who is a member of his force) in the performance or purported performance of their duties. This means that civil claims may be pursued against a chief officer, as well as against (or instead of against) the officer alleged to have committed a wrongful act or to have failed to comply with a duty of care owed to another. The chief officer can even be liable for the off-duty unlawful conduct of a constable if it was committed at a time when the constable was apparently acting in his capacity as a constable. However, it has been held in the High Court that a chief officer is not necessarily liable for conduct in the purported performance of a constable's duty if the conduct was clearly for a purpose unrelated to the constable's duty—as where he offers not to report an illegal immigrant in return for sexual favours. Special provision is made by PA 1996, s 97 in relation to officers seconded to central service; it is the Secretary of State (and not their chief constable) who is vicariously liable for their unlawful conduct.

Although the House of Lords has held that no action lies against a constable or his chief constable for injury caused to a person (X) by a negligent failure to identify and arrest a criminal where that failure results in the criminal committing further offences or for a negligent failure to give X reasonable protection, this does not necessarily mean that an action would never lie in respect of the negligent exercise of some other police function. The European Court of Human Rights has held that an absolute immunity would be a breach of the European Convention on Human Rights, art 6 (right to a fair trial). The Court held that while the immunity may be permissible, it is open to an English court not to apply it if the public interest does not require the immunity.

An officer conducting disciplinary proceedings (or his chief constable) cannot be liable under civil law to the officer under investigation if he negligently conducts the proceedings or acts in breach of his duty under the relevant regulations (see p 308). Nor can a constable (or his chief constable) be liable to someone who suffers injuries in a foreseeable attempt to escape, nor to a road user for injuries caused by a constable's failure to give warnings of hazards of which the constable was aware but for which he was not responsible.

As a matter of public policy, chief constables are not generally liable to their subordinates who are injured by rioters in the course of controlling serious public disorder. Nor are they liable to a person in respect of whom they provide inaccurate information for criminal records purposes. Statutes providing powers to make a closure order or notice in respect of premises generally provide that neither a constable nor his chief officer will be liable for any thing done or omitted in the course of a constable's performance of his functions under the relevant provisions unless the act or omission is shown to have been in bad faith or to be unlawful because of the Human Rights Act 1998.

A police officer (or, vicariously, his chief officer) may be liable under the Equality Act 2010 for discrimination on grounds of race, sex, sexual orientation, gender reassignment, age, disability, religious belief, marriage or civil partnership, pregnancy, or maternity.

Any costs or damages awarded against a chief officer on the grounds of his vicarious liability must be paid out of police funds. Those awarded against the constable concerned may be paid or part-paid from police funds at the discretion of the local policing body, and it has been held that they should be so paid if the constable acted in good faith.

IMPERSONATING A POLICE OFFICER AND CAUSING DISAFFECTION AMONGST MEMBERS OF A POLICE FORCE

Impersonation

A person who, with intent to deceive, impersonates a member of a police force or a special constable, or makes any statement or does any act calculated falsely to suggest that he is such a member or constable, commits an offence against PA 1996, s 90(1). It is also an offence against s 90(2) for a person who, not being a member of a police force or a special constable, wears any article of police uniform in circumstances where it gives him an appearance so nearly resembling that of a member of a police force as to be calculated to deceive. Section 90(3) makes it an offence to possess an article of police uniform, unless it was obtained lawfully and is possessed for a lawful purpose.

Causing disaffection

A person who causes, or attempts to cause, or does any act calculated to cause, disaffection amongst members of any police force, or induces, or attempts to induce, or does any act calculated to induce, any member of a police force to withhold his services commits an offence against PA 1996, s 91(1). The section applies to special constables appointed for a police force as it does to members of a police force.

HANDLING OF COMPLAINTS AND CONDUCT MATTERS, ETC RELATING TO PERSONS SERVING WITH THE POLICE

The foundations of the system

PRA 2002 established the Independent Police Complaints Commission (IPCC). The investigation of many complaints is carried out by police forces. Investigations may be carried out by a person serving with the police (of the force concerned or any other force), or a member of staff of SOCA or a member of staff of NPIA. Except in the case of NPIA, there is no requirement that the investigator must be a police officer. In addition, the IPCC is empowered to carry out its own investigation of complaints and to supervise or manage other investigations.

Under PRA 2002, s 9 and Sch 2, IPCC consists of a chairman (appointed by the Queen) and not less than five other members (appointed by the Secretary of State). The Secretary of State may appoint not more than two deputy chairmen from the membership. These appointments are for a maximum period of five years at a time. The Secretary of State may remove members from office for various reasons.

The functions of the IPCC include securing the maintenance by the IPCC itself, and by police and crime commissioners, etc and chief officers, of suitable arrangements for:

(a) the handling of complaints about the conduct of persons serving with the police;
(b) the recording of matters from which it appears that there may have been conduct by such persons which constitutes or involves a criminal offence or behaviour justifying disciplinary proceedings;
(c) the recording of matters from which it appears that a person has died or suffered serious injury during, or following, contact with a person serving with the police; and
(d) the manner in which such complaints or any such matters are investigated or otherwise handled and dealt with.

The IPCC is required to enter into arrangements with the chief inspector of constabulary for the purpose of securing co-operation between the IPCC and the Inspectorate. PRA 2002 does not confer any function on the IPCC in relation to any part of a complaint or conduct matter which relates to the direction and control of a police force by a chief officer of police. In respect of the Metropolitan Police District, and elsewhere from a day to be appointed, the previous sentence should be deleted (PRSRA 2011, Sch 14). Thenceforth, the provisions of PRA 2002, Sch 3 about complaints or conduct matters apply to a complaint or conduct matter relating to the direction and control of a police force by a chief officer of police (or a person for the time being carrying out his functions). Such a matter is referred to in the amended Sch 3 as a 'direction and control matter'.

The IPCC, its officers and employees have equivalent powers to use directed or intrusive surveillance, to use covert human intelligence sources, and to enter property to interfere with property or wireless telegraphy, to those exercisable by the police.

Complaints

The rules under PRA 2002 about complaints set out below apply whatever the rank of the officer against whom the complaint is made. As will be seen, various functions relating to complaints are carried out by the 'appropriate authority'. The 'appropriate authority' is the chief officer of police of the officer who is subject to the complaint. (The chief officer may delegate his powers and duties in respect of complaints to an officer above the rank of chief superintendent (or, in the case of local resolution below, to anyone serving with the force).) Where a complaint relates to the chief officer, his local policing body is the 'appropriate authority'.

By PRA 2002, s 12, a 'complaint' is any complaint, written or otherwise, about the conduct of a person serving with the police which is made by:

(a) a member of the public claiming to be the person in relation to whom the conduct took place;
(b) any other member of the public claiming to have been adversely affected by the conduct;
(c) a member of the public claiming to have witnessed the conduct; or
(d) a person acting on behalf of a person in (a) to (c) above.

A judge in the Administrative Court has held that the word 'conduct' in PRA 2002, s 12 (and elsewhere in PRA 2002) does not carry with it the notion that the behaviour had to be of a particular quality, good or bad; 'conduct' in PRA 2002 is not limited to bad behaviour, misconduct or personal misconduct.

For the purposes of the provisions about complaints, (b) does not include a complaint made by or on behalf of a person who claims to have been adversely affected as a result only of having seen or heard the conduct, or any of its alleged effects, unless:

(i) it was only because that person was physically present, or sufficiently nearby, when the conduct took place or the effects occurred that he was able to see or hear the conduct or its effects; or
(ii) unless the adverse effect is attributable to, or was aggravated by, the fact that the person in relation to whom the conduct took place was already known to the person claiming to have suffered the adverse effect.

A person is taken to have witnessed conduct only if he acquired his knowledge in a manner which would make him a competent witness capable of giving admissible evidence, or if he has in his possession or under his control anything which would constitute admissible evidence.

A person within (a) to (c) is not taken to have authorised another to act on his behalf unless that other person is designated by the IPCC as a person through whom a complaint may be made, or is a person who has been authorised in writing by the person on behalf of whom he is acting.

Handling of complaints

PRA 2002, Sch 3, Part 1, as amended by PRSRA 2011, Sch 4, deals with this.

Duties to preserve evidence relating to complaints

Where a complaint about the conduct of a person serving under his direction or control is submitted to a chief officer of police, or that chief officer becomes aware that such a complaint has been made to the IPCC or to a local policing body, he must, as soon as reasonably practicable, take any steps appearing to him to be desirable to obtain or preserve evidence relating to the conduct complained of. The term 'a person serving under his control and direction' includes members of a police force, local policing body employees under the direction and control of a chief officer, and special constables.

Initial handling and recording of complaints

Where a complaint is made to the IPCC, it must determine whether the complainant consents to the local policing body or chief officer who is the appropriate authority being notified; if he does it must give that notification. Where no consent is given, but the IPCC believes that it is in the public interest for the subject matter of the complaint to be brought to the attention of the appropriate authority and recorded, the IPCC may bring the matter to the attention of the appropriate authority as if it were a 'recordable conduct matter'; where this is done the provisions of PRA 2002, Sch 3 have effect as if it were such a matter. In respect of the Metropolitan Police District, and elsewhere as from a day to be appointed, these provisions are substituted by a provision that, where a complaint is made to the IPCC, it must notify the appropriate authority, unless it considers that there are exceptional circumstances that justify its not being given.

Where a complaint is made to a local policing body and it determines that it is not the appropriate authority it must notify the chief officer who is the appropriate authority in relation to the officer etc against whom the complaint was made. Where a complaint is made to a chief officer and he determines that he is not the appropriate authority, because the complaint relates to an officer in another force or to a senior officer, he must notify the appropriate authority. Where notification of a complaint is given to an appropriate authority, the person who gave the notification must notify the complainant.

If a chief officer determines that he is the appropriate authority in relation to a complaint, or if he is notified that he is, he must record the complaint. However, a complaint need not be recorded where the subject matter of the complaint has been, or is already being, dealt with by means of criminal or disciplinary proceedings, where the complaint has been withdrawn or (the courts have held) where the complaint lacks the degree of specificity without which a sensible proportionate investigation would be impossible.

There is no need to record any complaint about any conduct if it is considered that the complaint falls within a description of complaints specified in the Police (Complaints and Misconduct) Regulations 2012 (P(CM)R 2012), namely:

(a) the matter is already the subject of a complaint made by or on behalf of the same complainant;
(b) the complaint discloses neither the name and address of the complainant or other interested parties and such a name or address cannot reasonably be ascertained;
(c) the complaint is vexatious, oppressive, or otherwise an abuse of the complaints procedures; or
(d) the complaint is repetitious or fanciful.

Non-notification or recording of a complaint

Where a complaint has been received by, or notified to, an appropriate authority and the authority decides to take no action in relation to recording it, or notifying the appropriate authority, it must notify the complainant of the decision, the grounds for it, and the complainant's right of appeal. The complainant has a right of appeal to the IPCC against that decision. If the IPCC thinks that action should have been taken, it must give directions to the appropriate authority which are binding. All parties must be notified. P(CM)R 2012 govern the procedures to be followed.

As from a day to be appointed, the right of appeal referred to under this heading is not available where:

(a) there is no need to record the complaint because it relates to criminal or discipli-nary proceedings or has been withdrawn; or
(b) the complaint relates to a direction and control matter, and the appeal relates to a failure by a local policing body.

Reference of complaints to the IPCC

A complaint must be referred to the IPCC if:

(a) it alleges that the conduct complained of has resulted in death or serious injury;
(b) it is of a description specified in P(CM)R 2012; or
(c) the IPCC notifies the appropriate authority that it requires the matter to be referred for consideration.

P(CM)R 2012 provide that a complaint of serious assault, a serious sexual offence, seri-ous corruption, a criminal offence or behaviour which is liable to lead to a disciplinary sanction and which in either case was aggravated by discriminatory behaviour on the grounds of race, sex, religion, or other status identified in guidance issued by the IPCC, murder or an offence carrying seven or more years' imprisonment, are complaints for the purposes of (b) above.

In cases other than those in which reference is mandatory, an appropriate authority may refer a complaint to the IPCC if it considers that it would be appropriate to do so in view of the gravity of the subject matter or other exceptional circumstances. Such references may be made regardless of the fact that the complaint is already being con-sidered by the IPCC. Such action must be notified to the complainant and, except where any future investigation may be prejudiced, to the person complained against. In addi-tion, where a death or serious injury matter comes to the attention of a local policing body, or a chief officer who is the appropriate authority, the matter must be recorded and if this has not been done the IPCC may direct that it be done. Following the inves-tigation of such matters a report will be submitted and IPCC may make recommenda-tions or give advice. Where such an investigation reveals a conduct matter (a criminal or disciplinary offence) the matter will be treated as a conduct matter.

As from an appointed day, where a complaint relates to a direction and control matter, and it is not a case where the appropriate authority must refer the complaint to the IPCC, the appropriate authority may refer the complaint to the IPCC under those provisions only if the IPCC consents.

Where a complaint is referred to the IPCC, the IPCC must determine whether or not investigation of the complaint is necessary. Where it considers that investigation is unneces-sary, it may refer the complaint back to the appropriate authority to be dealt with under the rules under the following heading, and inform the complainant and (unless this might prej-udice an investigation of the complaint) the person complained against that it has done so.

Handling of complaints by the appropriate authority

Where a complaint has been recorded by the appropriate authority, it must deter-mine whether or not the complaint is suitable for being subjected to local resolution. If the appropriate authority determines that the complaint is suitable for being subjected to local resolution, it must make arrangements for it to be so subjected. If the appropriate authority determines that the complaint is not so suitable, it must make arrangements for the complaint to be investigated by the authority on its own behalf.

A determination that a complaint is suitable for being subjected to local resolution may not be made unless the appropriate authority is satisfied that:

(a) the conduct complained of (even if proved) would not justify the bringing of any criminal or disciplinary proceedings against the person whose conduct is complained of; and

(b) the conduct complained of (even if proved) would not involve the infringement of a person's rights under the European Convention on Human Rights, art 2 (right to life) or 3 (prohibition of inhuman or degrading treatment).

The above provisions do not apply to a complaint if it is one that has been, or must be, referred to the IPCC (see p 292), unless the complaint is for the time being:

(a) referred back to the authority under the provisions referred to in the last paragraph under the heading just mentioned; or

(b) the subject of a determination by the IPCC as to the form of an investigation referred to under the heading 'Power of IPCC to determine the form of an investigation' (p 299).

Where (b) applies, a determination that the complaint is suitable for being subjected to local resolution may not be made without the IPCC's approval.

Disapplication of requirements

Where a complaint has been recorded, and not referred to the IPCC, and the appropriate authority considers that it should be handled otherwise than in accordance with the procedures set out in PRA 2002, Sch 3, or that no action should be taken in relation to that complaint, and that the complaint falls within a description of complaints specified in P(CM)R 2012, the appropriate authority may handle the complaint in whatever manner (if any) it thinks fit. The specified description of complaints is where the appropriate authority considers that:

(a) the incident is more than 12 months old and there is no good reason for the delay;

(b) the matter is already the subject of a complaint by or on behalf of the complainant;

(c) the complaint does not disclose the name and address of the complainant or other interested party and such an address cannot reasonably be ascertained;

(d) the complaint is vexatious, oppressive, or otherwise an abuse of the complaint procedures;

(e) the complaint is repetitious; or

(f) it is not reasonably practicable to investigate the complaint.

The appropriate authority is not required to apply for (and obtain) permission from the IPCC to handle the complaint in an alternative manner, except in a case where the complaint:

(a) has been, or must be, referred to the IPCC, and has been referred back to the authority, or

(b) is the subject of a determination as to the form of an investigation (see 'Handling of complaints by the appropriate authority').

Where the appropriate authority has decided to handle the case in an alternative manner, it must notify the complainant of this.

Where an application to the IPCC for permission to handle the case in an alternative manner has been made, the appropriate authority must notify the complainant of this.

Where the complaint is to be handled in whatever manner (if any) the authority thinks fit (whether or not the IPCC's permission is needed), the authority need do no more under Sch 3 than preserve the evidence, and may take any action which it considers appropriate, or no action at all.

Where the appropriate authority is required to apply to the IPCC for permission to handle the complaint in an alternative manner, and does so, and the IPCC does not grant permission, the appropriate authority must consider whether the complaint is suitable for local resolution.

The complainant has a right of appeal to the relevant appeal body against any decision by the appropriate authority to handle the complaint otherwise than in accordance with Sch 3 or to take no action in relation to it. By way of exception, the complainant has no right of appeal if the appeal relates to a decision for which the IPCC has given permission, or the complaint relates to a direction and control matter. The relevant appeal body is:

(a) the IPCC, where the relevant complaint falls within a description of complaints specified in regulations made by the Secretary of State; or

(b) the chief officer of police who is the appropriate authority in relation to the relevant complaint, in any other case.

The procedural rules for an appeal are set out in P(CM)R 2012.

On such an appeal, the relevant appeal body must:

(a) determine whether any decision by the appropriate authority should have been taken in the case in question; and

(b) if the relevant appeal body finds in the complainant's favour, give such binding directions as it thinks appropriate to the local policing body or chief officer as to the action to be taken for handling the complaint in accordance with Sch 3 or otherwise.

However, this provision does not apply where a particular chief officer of police is both the person in respect of whose decision the appeal is made and the relevant appeal body in relation to the appeal. In such a case:

(i) the appeal must determine whether any decision taken by the appropriate authority should have been taken in the case in question; and

(ii) if the appeal finds in the complainant's favour, the chief officer of police must take such action as the chief officer thinks appropriate for handling the complaint in accordance with Sch 3 or otherwise.

Local resolution of complaints

Where there is to be a local resolution of a complaint, the arrangements made by the appropriate authority for subjecting a complaint to local resolution may include the appointment of a person, who is serving with the police and is under the direction and control of the chief officer of police of the relevant force, to secure the local resolution of the complaint. P(CM)R 2012 deal with the procedural requirements. Any statement made for the purpose of such resolution is not admissible in any subsequent criminal, civil or disciplinary proceedings except to the extent that it consists of an admission relating to a matter which has not been subjected to local resolution.

If, after attempts to achieve local resolution, it appears to the appropriate authority that local resolution is impossible, or that the matter is unsuitable for local resolution, it must arrange for an investigation, and any attempt at local resolution must be discontinued. Such an attempt must also be discontinued if there is a requirement for the matter to be referred to the IPCC or it is otherwise referred. Any person who has been involved in an attempt at local resolution is barred from participation in subsequently investigating the complaint.

Appeals relating to complaints dealt with other than by investigation

Unless the complaint relates to a direction and control matter, the complainant has a right of appeal to the 'relevant appeal body' (as defined on p 294 against the outcome of any complaint that is subjected to local resolution, or handled otherwise than in accordance with Sch 3. P(CM)R 2012 deal with the procedural requirements.

On such an appeal, the relevant appeal body must:

(a) determine whether the outcome of the complaint is a proper outcome; and
(b) if the relevant appeal body finds in the complainant's favour, give such binding directions as it thinks appropriate to the appropriate authority as to the action to be taken in relation to the complaint.

However, this provision does not apply if a chief officer of police is the relevant appeal body in relation to the appeal. In such a case:

(i)   the appeal must determine whether the outcome of the complaint is a proper outcome; and
(ii) if the appeal finds in the complainant's favour, the chief officer of police must take such action as the chief officer thinks appropriate in relation to the complaint.

Withdrawn and discontinued complaints

P(CM)R 2012 provide that, where an appropriate authority receives written notification, signed by the complainant or by his solicitor or other authorised agent, that he withdraws his complaint or does not wish any further action to be taken, that withdrawal must be recorded. The procedures will be discontinued unless the appropriate authority decides, notwithstanding the withdrawal, to treat the matter as a recordable conduct matter, in which case the provisions of Sch 3, Part 2 below apply.

Circumstances in which an investigation or other procedure may be suspended

The IPCC or the appropriate authority may suspend any investigation or other procedure which, if it were to continue, would prejudice any criminal proceedings. The IPCC, however, may direct an appropriate authority to continue an investigation if of the view that it is in the public interest to do so.

Where the investigation of a complaint has been suspended pending the outcome of criminal proceedings, the IPCC or the appropriate authority must contact the complainant after that outcome to establish whether or not he wishes the investigation to continue. If he does not wish to do so, or fails to reply within 21 days, the IPCC or the appropriate authority must decide whether or not it is in the public interest to treat the complaint as a recordable conduct matter.

Handling of conduct matters

PRA 2002, Sch 3, Part 2, as amended by PRSRA 2011, Sch 14, deals with this.

A 'conduct matter' is a matter which is not and has not been the subject of a complaint but in respect of which there is an indication that the person serving with the police might have committed a criminal offence or might have behaved in a manner which would justify disciplinary proceedings.

Conduct matters arising in civil proceedings

Where a local policing body or a chief constable has received notification that civil proceedings have been brought by a member of the public against it or him, or are likely to be brought, and it appears that these proceedings would involve a conduct matter, it or he should follow a similar procedure as in respect of a complaint about determining the appropriate authority (and, if necessary, notifying that authority). The appropriate authority must determine whether the matter is one which it or he is required to refer to the IPCC (see p 297) or is one which it would be appropriate to so refer. If it or he determines that the matter is, it or he must record the matter. In any other case, the appropriate authority must determine whether the matter falls within a description of matters specified in regulations made by the Secretary of State. If it determines that it does not, it or he must record the matter. Otherwise, the appropriate authority may (but need not) record the matter. In a case where the appropriate authority:

(a) records a matter under the above provisions, and
(b) is not required to refer the matter to the IPCC (see p 297) and does not do so,

the appropriate authority may deal with the matter in such other manner (if any) as it or he may determine.

Recording etc of conduct matters in other cases

Where a conduct matter comes (otherwise than as arising in civil proceedings) to the attention of a local policing body or chief officer of police in some other way from that just mentioned and it is conduct:

(a) which appears to have resulted in the death of any person;
(b) as a result of which a member of the public has been adversely affected; or
(c) which is a serious assault, a serious sexual assault, serious corruption, a criminal offence or behaviour liable to lead to a disciplinary sanction and which in either case was aggravated by discriminatory behaviour on the grounds of race, sex, religion, or other status identified in guidance by the IPCC, murder or an offence carrying a maximum of seven or more years' imprisonment, *conduct whose gravity or other exceptional circumstances make it appropriate to record the matter*, and conduct in the same incident as one in which the above conduct (besides that italicised) is alleged,

the appropriate authority must determine whether the matter is one which it or he is required to refer to the IPCC (see p 297), or is one which it would be appropriate to so refer. If the appropriate authority determines that it is, it or he must record the matter.

In any other case, the appropriate authority must determine whether the matter is a 'repetitious conduct matter' (ie a conduct matter concerning substantially the same matter as a previous complaint or conduct matter with no significant fresh information and no fresh evidence not reasonably available at the previous time). If it determines that it is not, the matter must be recorded. If the appropriate authority determines that the matter is a repetitious conduct matter, it may (but need not) record the matter. Where the appropriate authority:

(a) records a matter under the above provisions, and

(b) is not required to refer the matter to the IPCC and does not do so,

the appropriate authority may deal with the matter in such other manner (if any) as it or he may determine.

No conduct matter which has already been dealt with by means of criminal or disciplinary proceedings need be recorded.

The IPCC may direct the appropriate authority to record a matter that has come to its attention and that it considers to be a 'recordable conduct matter' if it has not otherwise been recorded. A 'recordable conduct matter' is a conduct matter which must be recorded under this or the previous heading by the appropriate authority or has been so recorded.

Duties to preserve evidence relating to the conduct matters

The appropriate authority must, as soon as practicable, obtain and preserve evidence related to a recordable conduct matter.

Reference of conduct matters to the IPCC

The same matters as in (c) on p 296 besides that italicised must be referred as in the case of complaints and there are similar arrangements in respect of voluntary references. Similar conditions apply in relation to notifications to interested parties.

Where reference has been made, it is the duty of the IPCC to decide whether or not an investigation is necessary. Where an investigation is considered unnecessary, it may refer the matter back to the appropriate authority to be dealt with in such manner (if any) as the authority determines.

P(CM)R 2012 deal with the recording and reference of conduct matters. Those matters are similar to those applying in the case of a complaint, together with conduct the gravity of which, or other exceptional circumstances, make it appropriate to record such conduct.

Delegation of powers and duties by chief officer

A chief officer may delegate all or any of his powers or duties above in relation to handling conduct matters to:

(a) a senior officer, in the case of a complaint or conduct matter concerning the conduct of a senior officer, and

(b) a member of a police force of at least the rank of chief inspector, in any other case,

or to a police staff member who, in the opinion of the chief officer, is of at least a similar level of seniority.

A chief officer may not delegate any such power or duty to a person whose involvement in the role could reasonably give rise to a concern as to whether he could act impartially.

A chief officer may delegate all or any of his powers or duties in relation to the local resolution of complaints to any person serving with the police.

Handling of death and serious injury matters

PRA 2002, Sch 3, Part 2A deals with this.

A 'death or serious injury matter' ('DSI matter') means circumstances (other than those which are or have been the subject of a complaint or which amount to a conduct matter) in or in consequence of which a person has died or has sustained serious injury and in relation to which one or other of the following requirements is satisfied:

(a) at the time of the death or serious injury the person had been arrested by a person serving with the police and had not been released from that arrest, or was otherwise detained in the custody of a person serving with the police, or

(b) at or before that time the person—directly or indirectly—had contact with a person serving with the police who was acting in the execution of his duties and there is an indication that the contact may directly or indirectly have caused or contributed to the death or serious injury.

Duty to record DSI matters

Where a DSI matter comes to the attention of the local policing body or chief officer who is the appropriate authority in relation to that matter, the appropriate authority must record that matter.

If it appears to the IPCC:

(a) that any matter that has come to its attention is a DSI matter, but

(b) that that matter has not been recorded by the appropriate authority,

the IPCC may direct the appropriate authority to record that matter, and that authority must comply with the direction.

Duty to preserve evidence relating to DSI matters

Where:

(a) a DSI matter comes to the attention of a local policing body, and

(b) the relevant officer in relation to that matter is the chief officer of the force maintained by that local policing body,

that body must secure that all appropriate steps are taken, both initially and thereafter, to obtain and preserve evidence relating to that matter.

Where:

(a) a chief officer becomes aware of a DSI matter, and

(b) the relevant officer in relation to that matter is a person under his direction and control,

he must take all such steps as appear appropriate as soon as practicable to obtain and preserve evidence relating to that matter. After that, he must, until he is satisfied that it is no longer necessary to do so, continue to take the steps from time to time appearing appropriate for obtaining and preserving evidence relating to the matter.

A local policing body must comply with all such directions as may be given to it by the IPCC in relation to the performance of its duty to obtain and preserve evidence relating to the matter.

The chief officer must take all such specific steps for obtaining or preserving evidence relating to any DSI matter as he may be directed to take by the local policing body maintaining his force or by the Commission.

Reference of DSI matters to the IPCC

The appropriate authority must refer a DSI matter to the IPCC by the end of the day, whether or not a working day, following the day on which the IPCC directs a referral or the matter comes to the attention of the relevant authority.

Duties of the IPCC on reference

The IPCC must, in the case of every DSI matter referred to it by a local policing body or a chief officer, determine whether or not it is necessary for the matter to be investigated. Where the IPCC determines that it is unnecessary for a DSI matter to be investigated, it may if it thinks fit refer the matter back to the appropriate authority to be dealt with by that authority in such manner (if any) as that authority may determine.

Investigations and subsequent proceedings

PRA 2002, Sch 3, Part 3, as amended by PRSRA 2011, Sch 14, deals with these.

Power of the IPCC to determine the form of an investigation

Where a complaint, recordable conduct matter or DSI matter has been referred to the IPCC and it decides that an investigation is necessary, the form of the investigation will depend upon the seriousness of the case and the public interest but must consist of:

(a) an investigation by the appropriate authority on its own behalf;
(b) an investigation by that authority under the supervision of the IPCC;
(c) an investigation by that authority under the management of the IPCC; or
(d) an investigation by the IPCC.

The form of the investigation may be changed by the IPCC at any time and the IPCC may give directions to that effect.

Investigations by the appropriate authority on its own behalf

The appropriate authority must appoint a person serving with the police (whether under the direction and control of the chief officer of police of the relevant force or of another force) or a member of staff of SOCA or a member of staff of NPIA who is a constable to investigate the complaint or matter.

Under P(CM)R 2012 no one may be appointed to carry out an investigation by the authority on its own behalf *or when the investigation is supervised or managed by the IPCC* (below):

(a) unless he has an appropriate level of knowledge, skills, and experience to plan and manage the investigation,
(b) if there could be any reasonable appearance of bias,
(c) if he works, directly or indirectly, under the management of the person being investigated, and
(d) where the officer concerned is a senior officer, if he is the chief officer of the police force concerned, or a member of the same force as the officer concerned.

Heads (c) and (d) do not apply in a case where the investigation is of a complaint in relation to a direction and control matter. Where the investigation is of a complaint in relation to a direction or control matter, the fact that a person:

(i) works, directly or indirectly, under the management of the person whose conduct is being investigated; or
(ii) is the chief officer of the police force concerned or a member of the same force as the officer concerned,

does not, without more, constitute reasonable grounds for concern as to whether that person could act impartially for the purposes of (b).

Where the person being investigated is a chief officer, no one under the chief officer's direction and control may be appointed to carry out the investigation.

Investigations supervised by the IPCC

The IPCC may require that no appointment as an investigating officer may be made without its approval. If an appointment has already been made a further approved appointment must be made as soon as practicable.

The person appointed to investigate the complaint or matter must comply with directions from the IPCC which are authorised by regulations.

Investigations managed by the IPCC

The same conditions apply as apply in the case of supervised investigations with the addition that the investigator must be under the direction and control of the IPCC.

Investigations by the IPCC itself

The IPCC must designate a member of its own staff to take charge of the investigation on its behalf; it must also designate other members of its staff to assist that person. Any member of the IPCC's staff so designated who does not already have all the powers and privileges of a constable throughout England and Wales and the adjacent UK waters has, for the purposes of carrying out the investigation and all purposes connected with it, all those powers and privileges of a constable.

Special procedure where investigation relates to a police officer or special constable

Where it appears to an investigating officer that there is an indication that a member of a police force or a special constable under investigation may have committed a criminal offence, or behaved in a manner which would justify the bringing of disciplinary proceedings, the investigator must certify the investigation as one subject to special requirements and make a severity assessment as soon as reasonably practicable in relation to the conduct. A similar requirement is included in relation to the investigation of a recordable conduct matter, in which case such an assessment must be made as soon as reasonably practicable after it is recorded. A 'severity assessment' is an assessment as to whether the conduct, if proved, would amount to misconduct or gross misconduct, and if the conduct were to become the subject of disciplinary proceedings, the form which those proceedings would be likely to take. The appropriate authority must be consulted in respect of the assessment. Such assessments may be revised and if so, the person concerned must be notified.

Following such an assessment, the person under investigation must be given a written notice (unless the investigator considers that doing so might prejudice the investigation or any other investigation, including in particular, any criminal investigation), containing information prescribed by P(CM)R 2012.

Under P(CM)R 2012, the person appointed to investigate must notify the person under investigation in writing of his appointment and the notification must state:

(a) the conduct that is the subject matter of the allegation and how that conduct is alleged to fall below the Standards of Professional Behaviour set out on p 319;
(b) that there is to be an investigation into the matter, and the identity of the investigator;
(c) the investigator's assessment of whether that conduct, if proved, would amount to misconduct or gross misconduct;

(d) whether, if the matter was referred to misconduct proceedings, those would be likely to be a misconduct meeting or a misconduct hearing;

(e) that if the likely form of any misconduct proceedings to be held changes, further notice (with reasons) will be given;

(f) that he has the right to seek advice from his staff association or any other body and of the effect of provisions permitting him to choose to have a police officer, police staff member, or, where he is member of a police force, someone nominated by his staff association to act as his police friend;

(g) the effect of reg 14C (person concerned or police friend must provide any relevant statement or notice within 10 working days of written notification referred to above unless period extended) and of PRA 2002, Sch 3, para 19C (duty to consider submissions from person whose conduct is being investigated) and of the Police (Conduct) Regulations 2008, reg 7(1) to (3) (legal or other representation); and

(h) that, while he does not have to say anything, it may harm his case if he does not mention when interviewed or when providing any information under reg 14C or the Police (Conduct) Regulations 2008, reg 22 (procedure on receipt of notice of referral to misconduct proceedings: p 313) something which he later relies on in any misconduct proceedings, special case hearing, an appeal meeting or appeal hearing.

P(CM)R 2012 go on to provide that, if the investigator revises his assessment of the conduct or his determination of the likely form of any misconduct proceedings to be taken, the investigator must, as soon as practicable, give the person concerned written notice of that revised assessment.

As indicated above, the officer or police friend must provide documents for the investigator within 10 clear working days. The investigator must, if reasonably practicable, agree a date for any interview with the officer but may specify a date in the absence of agreement, but that date may be postponed by agreement.

Procedure where conduct matter revealed during DSI investigation

If, during an investigation into a DSI matter, it appears to the investigating officer that there is an indication that the person (P) whose conduct is in question may have committed a criminal offence or behaved in a way justifying disciplinary proceedings, he must make a submission to that effect to the IPCC (if the IPCC appointed him) or to the appropriate authority (if it appointed him). If the appropriate authority or the IPCC (as the case may be) determines that there is such an indication, it must act as follows:

(a) in the case of the IPCC, notify the appropriate authority and send it a copy of the submission;

(b) in the case of the appropriate authority, if it is not the appropriate authority in relation to P, it must notify the other authority of its determination and send it a copy of the submission, and, in any event, it must notify the IPCC of its determination and send it a copy of the submission.

Once notified, the appropriate authority must record the DSI matter as a conduct matter, and the investigating officer must continue the investigation thereafter as a conduct matter investigation.

Restrictions on proceedings pending the conclusion of an investigation

No criminal or disciplinary proceedings may be brought in relation to any matter subject to an investigation (unless it has been discontinued) until the appropriate authority has certified the case as a 'special case' or a report has been submitted to the IPCC or the appropriate authority. However, these provisions do not apply to proceedings by the Director of Public Prosecutions (DPP) in exceptional cases where delay is undesirable.

Accelerated procedure in special cases

There is an accelerated procedure in respect of a complaint or a recordable conduct matter in 'special cases'. These are where the investigating officer believes that the appropriate authority would be likely to consider that there is sufficient written evidence to establish on the balance of probabilities that the police officer or special constable in question is guilty of gross misconduct and that his dismissal without delay is in the public interest. In such cases the investigator must submit a report to the appropriate authority before the completion of the investigation to enable disciplinary proceedings to be brought earlier than would otherwise have been possible. The DPP should be consulted in such cases and he may order the continuation of the investigation regardless of the disciplinary proceedings. It is difficult to see how any following trial for an alleged criminal offence will not be affected by the outcome of disciplinary proceedings in respect of which there are reduced standards of proof and majority verdicts.

Power to discontinue an investigation

The IPCC may by order require the discontinuance of the investigation of a complaint or matter if (whether on the application of the appropriate authority or otherwise) it appears to the IPCC that:

(a) the complaint or matter is of a description specified in P(CM)R 2012, and
(b) discontinuance of the investigation is within the IPCC's power.

The appropriate authority that is investigating a complaint or matter may discontinue the investigation if it appears to that authority that:

(a) the complaint or matter is of a description specified in P(CM)R 2012, and
(b) discontinuance of the investigation is not within the IPCC's power.

For the above purposes:

(a) the descriptions of conduct or matter specified by P(CM)R 2012 are any complaint or matter:
   (i)   in which the complainant refuses to co-operate to the extent that it is not reasonably practicable to continue the investigation;
   (ii) which the appropriate authority has determined is suitable for local resolution;
   (iii) which is vexatious, oppressive, or otherwise in abuse of the procedures for dealing with complaints, conduct matters, or DSI matters;
   (iv) which is repetitious; or
   (v)   which is such as to make it not reasonably practicable to proceed with the investigation;
(b) discontinuance of the investigation of a complaint is within the IPCC's power if (i) the investigation is being undertaken by the appropriate authority on its own behalf and the complaint is one required to be referred to IPCC under the provisions (p 292); or (ii) the investigation is under the supervision or management of the IPCC;
(c) discontinuance of the investigation of a matter other than a complaint is within the IPCC's power if the investigation is under the supervision or management of the IPCC.

Where the investigation is being conducted by the IPCC itself, the IPCC may only discontinue it if the complaint or matter falls within (a) immediately above.

Where an investigation is discontinued *by order* of the IPCC, the IPCC may give the appropriate authority directions as to steps (specified in P(CM)R 2012) to be taken and may itself take such steps of a description specified in P(CM)R 2012 as it considers appropriate for the purposes connected with the discontinuance, and neither the appropriate authority nor the IPCC may take any further action in accordance with Sch 3 in relation to that complaint or matter. Where the appropriate authority decides (ie otherwise than by order of the IPCC) to discontinue an investigation, the appropriate authority may take such steps (specified in P(CM)R 2012) as it considers appropriate in connection with the discontinuance, and neither the appropriate authority nor the IPCC may take any further action in accordance with Sch 3 in relation to that complaint or matter.

The IPCC or the appropriate authority (as the case may be) must notify the complainant (if the investigation is of a complaint) and every person entitled to be kept informed about the investigation of the discontinuance.

Except if the complaint relates to a direction and control matter, the complainant has a right of appeal to the relevant appeal body against any discontinuance decision by the appropriate authority.

The relevant appeal body is:

(a) the IPCC, where the relevant complaint falls within a description of complaints specified in P(CM)R 2012 or
(b) the chief officer of police who is the appropriate authority in relation to the relevant complaint, in any other case.

On such an appeal, the relevant appeal body must:

(a) determine whether any decision taken by the appropriate authority should have been taken; and
(b) if the relevant appeal body finds in the complainant's favour, give such binding directions as the relevant appeal body thinks appropriate to the local policing body or chief officer as to the action to be taken for investigating the complaint.

If, however, a particular chief officer of police is both the person in respect of whose decision an appeal is made and the relevant appeal body in relation to the appeal:

(i) the appeal must determine whether any decision taken by the appropriate authority should have been taken in the case in question; and
(ii) if the appeal finds in the complainant's favour, the chief officer of police must take such action as the chief officer thinks appropriate for investigating the complaint.

P(CM)R 2012 deal with the procedural requirements which apply before and after a discontinuance decision is taken and as to appeals against such a decision.

Final reports on investigations

On completion of an investigation of a complaint or conduct matter, the investigating officer must submit his report to the appropriate authority. Where the investigation was supervised, or managed by the IPCC, the investigating officer must send a report to the IPCC and a copy to the appropriate authority. Where the IPCC carries out the investigation itself, the investigating officer must report to the IPCC. In all of these cases, the investigator is not prevented by any obligation of secrecy from including all such matters in his report as he thinks fit.

The report must provide an accurate summary of the evidence; attach or refer to any relevant document; and indicate the investigator's opinion as to whether there is a case to answer in respect of misconduct or gross misconduct, or whether there is no case to answer.

Action by the IPCC in response to an investigation report

Where the IPCC receives a report on an investigation which it has supervised, managed, or carried out itself, it must send a copy to the appropriate authority and determine whether or not a criminal offence is disclosed. If it considers that such an offence is disclosed it must notify the DPP and send him a copy of the report, and it must notify the appropriate authority of this notification. The DPP must notify the IPCC of his decision to take, or not to take, action in respect of the matter or matters investigated. If criminal proceedings are brought by the DPP, the IPCC must inform, in the case of a complaint, the complainant and every person entitled to be kept informed in relation to the complaint; in the case of a recordable conduct matter, every person entitled to be kept informed of that matter must be informed. On receipt of the report of an investigation supervised, managed, or carried out by itself, the IPCC must also notify the appropriate authority that it must:

(a) determine in accordance with regulations:
   (i)   whether any person to whose conduct the investigation related has a case to answer in respect of misconduct or gross misconduct or has no case to answer
   (ii) whether or not any such person's performance is unsatisfactory; or
   (iii) what action (if any) the authority is required to, or will in its discretion, take in respect of the matters dealt with in the report, and
(b) determine what other action (if any) the authority will in its discretion take in respect of those matters.

On receipt of such a notification the appropriate authority must make those determinations and submit a memorandum to the IPCC which sets out the determinations the authority has made, and, if it has decided that disciplinary proceedings should not be brought, sets out its reasons for so deciding. On receipt of the memorandum, the IPCC must determine whether or not to make recommendations under the provisions on p 307 about duties with respect to disciplinary proceedings, and make such recommendations (if any) as it thinks fit. The complainant and other entitled persons must be informed of the report's findings, IPCC's determination and the recommended action.

Action by appropriate authority in response to an investigation report

The appropriate authority must determine whether an investigation report submitted or sent to it indicates that a criminal offence may have been committed by the person whose conduct has been investigated, and that it is appropriate for the report to be considered by the DPP. If it determines that it has, it must notify the DPP and send a copy of the report. It must notify the complainant and every other person entitled to be kept informed of its determination and of a reference to the DPP. If the DPP brings criminal proceedings, the appropriate authority must notify the above persons.

On receipt of an investigation report, the appropriate authority must also:

(a) determine:
   (i)   whether any person to whose conduct the investigation related has a case to answer in respect of misconduct or gross misconduct or has no case to answer;

    (ii) whether or not such person's performance is unsatisfactory; and

    (iii) what action (if any) the authority is required to, or will in its discretion, take in respect of the matters dealt with in the report, and

(b) determine what other action (if any) the authority will in its discretion take in respect of those matters.

The complainant and other entitled persons must be informed of the report's findings, the authority's determinations, and the complainant's right of appeal. Except so far as it may be otherwise directed by regulations, an appropriate authority may (notwithstanding any obligation to secrecy imposed by any rule of law) give such a person notification of the findings by sending the person a copy of the report.

Final reports on DSI investigations and actions in response

On completion of an investigation into a DSI matter in respect of which neither the IPCC nor the appropriate authority has made a determination (see p 301) that a person serving with the police (P) *may* have committed a criminal offence or behaved in a way justifying disciplinary proceedings, the investigating officer must send a report to the IPCC and a copy to the appropriate authority. The IPCC must then determine whether the report indicates P may have committed a criminal offence or so behaved. If it determines that the report does so indicate, it must notify the appropriate authority which must record the matter as a conduct matter and the investigating officer must investigate the matter as a conduct matter investigation.

Complaints or conduct matters concerning officers who are no longer serving or whose identity cannot be ascertained

By P(CM)R 2012, where a complaint or conduct matter is recorded against an ex-officer, the preceding conditions apply as if they did not include a requirement on the part of the appropriate authority to determine whether disciplinary proceedings should be brought.

P(CM)R 2012 also make it clear that, where a complaint or conduct matter relates to the conduct of an unidentified person, all provisions concerning notices to be given to such a person and the determination of whether or not there may be criminal liability or liability to disciplinary proceedings do not apply.

Appeals with respect to an investigation

Unless the complaint relates to a direction and control matter, a complainant whose complaint has been investigated by the appropriate authority on its own behalf or under the supervision of the IPCC has a right of appeal to the *relevant appeal body*:

(a) on the grounds that he has not been provided with adequate information about the findings of the investigation or any proposals in relation to the taking or not taking of action;

(b) against the findings of the investigation;

(c) against a determination by the appropriate authority that a person investigated has a case to answer in respect of misconduct or gross misconduct or has no case to answer, or that his performance is, or is not, unsatisfactory;

(d) against any determination of the appropriate authority to take, or not to take, action in respect of any of the matters dealt with in the report; and

(e) against a determination by the appropriate authority about whether a criminal offence may have been committed and whether the case should be considered by the DPP, as a result of which it is not required to send the DPP a copy of the report.

The relevant appeal body is the IPCC, where the relevant complaint falls within a description of complaints specified in P(CM)R 2012. Otherwise it is the chief officer of police who is the appropriate authority in relation to the relevant complaint.

The complaints specified by P(CM)R 2012 are any complaint:

(a) about the conduct of a senior officer;
(b) in the case of which the appropriate authority is unable to satisfy itself, from the complaint alone, that the conduct complained of (if it were proved):
  (i) would not justify the bringing of criminal or misconduct proceedings against a person serving with the police; or
  (ii) would not involve the infringement of a person's rights under the European Convention on Human Rights, art 2 (right to life) or 3 (inhuman or degrading treatment);
(c) that has been, or must be, referred to the IPCC;
(d) arising from the same incident as a complaint to which (a), (b), or (c) applies;
(e) to any part of which (a), (b), (c), or (d) applies.

The relevant appeal body must notify all persons concerned that an appeal with respect to an investigation has been lodged. If such an appeal is brought, the IPCC may require the appropriate authority to submit a memorandum specifying whether it has made a determination of the type referred to in (c) on p 305; whether any action is proposed to be taken (and, if it is, specifying the nature of that action); where no disciplinary proceedings are proposed, specifying the reasons for so deciding; and, where a determination of the type referred to in (e) on p 305 has been made, the reasons for it. In addition, where the investigation was carried out by the appropriate authority on its own behalf, and the IPCC so requires, the IPCC must be supplied with a copy of the report of the investigation.

If the relevant appeal body considers that the complainant has not been provided with adequate information:

(a) where the IPCC is the relevant appeal body, the IPCC must direct the appropriate authority to provide such information; and
(b) where the appropriate authority is the relevant appeal body, that authority must take such steps as it considers appropriate for securing that the complainant is properly informed.

If, in a case where the IPCC is the relevant appeal body, the IPCC determines that the findings of the investigation need to be reconsidered, it must either:

(a) review those findings without an immediate further investigation; or
(b) direct that the complaint be re-investigated; and

in a case where the appropriate authority is the relevant appeal body, that authority must re-investigate the complaint.

Where the relevant appeal body determines that the appropriate authority has not made a determination as to whether there is a case to answer that the relevant appeal body considers appropriate, or determines that the appropriate authority has not made a determination as to whether or not there is unsatisfactory performance, or determines that the appropriate authority is not proposing to take appropriate action, the situation is as follows:

(a) if the IPCC is the relevant appeal body, it may make such recommendations as it thinks fit;

(b) if the chief officer of police is the relevant appeal body, he must take such steps as he thinks fit in relation to bringing disciplinary proceedings.

Any determination or recommendation made by the relevant appeal body as a result of determining an appeal must be notified to all persons concerned.

P(CM)R 2012 deal with the appeal procedures relating to an appeal.

Review and re-investigations following an appeal

On a review of the findings of an investigation based upon the existing report, the IPCC may:

(a) uphold the findings in whole or in part;
(b) give the appropriate authority such directions as to the review by the authority of the findings, as to the information to be provided to the complainant, and generally in respect of the handling of the matter in future, as it thinks fit; or
(c) direct that the complaint be re-investigated in a specified form.

All persons concerned must be informed by the IPCC of any such determination or direction.

Duties with respect to disciplinary proceedings

Certain duties are imposed on the appropriate authority in the case of any investigation, where it has given, or is required to give, notification to entitled persons of its proposed action, or it has submitted, or is required to submit, a memorandum setting out its proposed action.

Subject to any recommendations or directions given by the IPCC, the authority must take any action notified and, where that action consists of or includes disciplinary proceedings, it must secure that those proceedings are taken to a proper conclusion.

Where a memorandum has been submitted to the IPCC, the IPCC may recommend to the appropriate authority in respect of a person serving with the police that:

(a) the person has a case to answer in respect of misconduct or gross misconduct or has no case to answer;
(b) (from a day to be appointed) the person's performance is or is not unsatisfactory;
(c) disciplinary proceedings in the form specified are brought in respect of the person's conduct, or (from a day to be appointed) efficiency or effectiveness; and
(d) any disciplinary proceedings brought are modified so as to deal with such aspects of that person's conduct, or (from a day to be appointed) efficiency or effectiveness, as may be specified.

The appropriate authority is then obliged to notify the IPCC as to whether it accepts the recommendation and (if it does) to set out its proposed steps. Where the appropriate authority does not take steps to carry out the IPCC's recommendations, the IPCC may direct it to do so, setting out the steps to be taken, and the authority must comply. The IPCC must supply a statement of its reasons for giving such a direction. The authority must keep the IPCC informed of the action which it takes.

Information for complainant etc about disciplinary recommendations

The complainant, and all other persons entitled to be informed of such matters, must be notified by the IPCC of any steps which it recommends to be taken by the appropriate authority unless the authority has not notified its acceptance of the recommendation. If the appropriate authority notifies the IPCC that it does not accept the recommendations, or fails to effect them, the IPCC must determine what further steps, if any, should be taken. The IPCC must also notify such persons of any determination not to take further steps or of the outcome of a determination to take further steps.

HANDLING OF COMPLAINTS AND CONDUCT MATTERS, ETC IN RELATION TO POLICE AND CRIME COMMISSIONERS AND THE LIKE

The Elected Local Policing Bodies (Complaints and Misconduct) Regulations 2012 set out the functions of police and crime panels and the IPCC in relation to the handling of complaints and other matters concerning the conduct of police and crime commissioners, deputy commissioners, the holder of the Mayor's Office for Policing and Crime, and the Deputy Mayor for Policing and Crime. The Regulations set out the process to be followed in dealing with these complaints and matters. They also provide for complaints alleging criminal conduct, and all conduct matters (those matters which indicate that criminal conduct may have occurred), to be referred to the IPCC and investigated either by the IPCC itself or a police force under the management of the IPCC. The Regulations provide for any other complaint to be resolved informally by the police and crime panel, except in the case of the holder of the Mayor's Office for Policing and Crime, or the Deputy Mayor for Policing and Crime if that person is a member of the London Assembly (in which cases the complaint will be passed to the monitoring officer of the Greater London Authority, who is responsible for dealing with complaints about the conduct of the Mayor and other Assembly members). The Regulations are modelled on the provisions of PRA 2002 and associated regulations about the handling of complaints and conduct matters in relation to persons serving with the police. In some instances, the Regulations apply those provisions, with or without modifications.

POLICE DISCIPLINARY PROCEEDINGS

Introduction

The Police (Conduct) Regulations 2008 (P(C)R 2008) govern disciplinary procedures in respect of misconduct by police officers and special constables. Matters connected with unsatisfactory performance or attendance are dealt with by the Police (Performance) Regulations 2008. In addition, the Police Appeals Tribunal Rules 2008 provide for appeals to the Police Appeals Tribunal against findings and specific outcomes resulting from the procedures set out in the two sets of regulations.

The Police (Conduct) Regulations 2008

P(C)R 2008 apply where an allegation comes to the attention of an appropriate authority which indicates that the conduct of a police officer may amount to misconduct or gross misconduct. This includes an allegation contained within a complaint, recordable conduct matter or DSI matter referred to the IPCC in accordance with PRA 2002, except that Part 3 (Investigations) of P(C)R 2008 (see p 310) does not apply in such cases because PRA 2002, Sch 3 (see p 299) deals with the investigation of them. Except for the Metropolitan Police, the 'appropriate authority' is, in the case of an allegation involving a senior officer (ie an officer above the rank of chief superintendent), the local policing body, and in any other case the chief officer of police of the force concerned (who may delegate his functions to a chief inspector (or above) or a police staff member of at least a similar level of seniority, although a delegate's decision to suspend or to refer a case to a special case hearing must be authorised by a senior officer). In the case of the Metropolitan Police, the appropriate authority in respect of the Commissioner or Deputy or Assistant Commissioner exercising functions of the Commissioner is the Mayor's Office for Policing and Crime, and in any other case the Commissioner. What follows describes the procedure which applies to those other than senior officers. In respect of the latter there are some variations from what is said below.

The harm test

In what follows reference is occasionally made to the 'harm test'. Information in documents which are stated to be subject to the harm test must not be supplied to the officer concerned in so far as the appropriate authority considers that preventing disclosure to him is:

(a) necessary for the purpose of preventing the premature or inappropriate disclosure of information that is relevant to, or may be used in, any criminal proceedings;
(b) necessary in the interests of national security;
(c) necessary for the purpose of the prevention or detection of crime, or the apprehension or prosecution of offenders;
(d) necessary for the purpose of the prevention or detection of misconduct by other police officers or police staff members or their apprehension for such matters;
(e) justified on the grounds that providing the information would involve disproportionate effort in comparison to the seriousness of the allegations against the officer concerned;
(f) necessary and proportionate for the protection of the welfare and safety of any informant or witness; or
(g) otherwise in the public interest.

Representation by a 'police friend'

The officer concerned (member of a police force or special constable) may choose a person who is not otherwise involved in the matter and is a police officer, a police staff member, or where the officer concerned is a member of a police force, a person nominated by his staff association, to act as his police friend. Such a 'friend' may:

(a) advise the officer throughout proceedings under the P(C)R 2008;
(b) unless the officer has the right to legal representation and chooses to be so represented, represent the officer at the misconduct proceedings, special case hearing, or appeal meeting;
(c) make representations to the appropriate authority concerning any aspect of the proceedings; and
(d) accompany the officer to any interview, meeting, or hearing forming part of the proceedings.

Where a 'friend' is a police officer or police staff member, a chief officer must permit such a person to use a reasonable amount of duty time for such purposes. Except where the officer has the right to be legally represented and chooses to be so represented, he may only be represented by a police friend.

Legal representation

An officer has a right to legal representation by a lawyer of his choice at a misconduct *hearing* or a special case hearing. Should an officer choose not to be legally represented he may be dismissed or receive any other outcome under regs 35 or 55 without his being so represented. (Regulation 35 deals with the possible outcomes of misconduct proceedings and reg 55 with the possible outcomes following a special case hearing; both are dealt with below). The appropriate authority may also be similarly represented.

Possibility of criminal proceedings

Before referring a case to misconduct proceedings (ie a misconduct meeting or misconduct hearing (p 312) or a special case hearing (p 318), the appropriate authority must decide whether such proceedings would prejudice any criminal proceedings. If the authority decides that it would, no misconduct or special case proceedings may take place.

Where a witness who is or may be a witness in criminal proceedings is to be or may be asked to attend misconduct proceedings, the appropriate authority must consult the relevant prosecutor before making a decision about whether misconduct proceedings or a special case hearing would be prejudicial.

Suspension

The appropriate authority may suspend with pay an officer from his office of constable and (in the case of a member of a police force) his membership of a police force but there must be no suspension unless:

(a) the authority has determined that temporary redeployment to alternative duties or an alternative location is not appropriate; and

(b) it appears to the authority that *either* the effective investigation of the case may be prejudiced unless the officer concerned is suspended, *or*, having regard to the nature of the allegation and any other relevant considerations, the public interest requires that he should be suspended.

These are called 'the suspension conditions'.

Where an officer is suspended, that suspension continues until either it has been decided that there will be no referral to misconduct proceedings or a special case hearing, or until such proceedings have ended. He must be informed (if orally, to be confirmed in writing within three clear working days) of an intention to suspend and given a summary of the reasons. The officer (or his police friend) may make representations before the end of seven clear working days after the suspension, or at any time during the suspension if he reasonably believes that there has been a change in relevant circumstances. On receipt, the appropriate authority must review the suspension conditions. In any case, where there has been no previous review, it must review the suspension conditions before the end of four weeks of the first working day after the suspension. In addition, the authority must review the suspension conditions within four weeks of the day after the last review. If it is decided to continue suspension, the officer must be informed in writing within three clear working days of the review and given a summary of the reasons.

In appropriate cases, the authority must consult the IPCC.

Investigations

These are governed by P(C)R 2008, Part 3, as explained below. As already indicated, these provisions do not apply to a case in which investigations are being conducted under PRA 2002, Sch 3, referred to on p 299.

Assessment of conduct

By reg 12(1), the appropriate authority must assess whether the alleged conduct, if proved, would amount to misconduct (breach of the Standards of Professional Behaviour: see p 319) or gross misconduct (breach of the Standards of Professional Behaviour which is so serious that dismissal would be justified).

If it decides that the conduct amounts to neither, the appropriate authority may take no action; take management action (advice intended to improve the conduct of the officer); or refer the matter to be dealt with under the Police (Performance) Regulations 2008.

Where the authority considers that, if proved, the conduct would amount to misconduct, it must decide whether it merits investigation and:

(a) if so, the matter must be investigated and the authority must further decide whether, if the matter were referred to misconduct proceedings, those proceedings would be likely to be a misconduct *meeting* (officer may be dealt with by disciplinary proceedings up to and including a final written warning) or misconduct *hearing* (officer may be dealt with by disciplinary action up to and including dismissal); or

(b) if not, the appropriate authority may take no action or take management action.

Where it is decided that the conduct, if proved, would amount to gross misconduct the matter must be investigated.

Appointment of investigator

Where a matter is to be investigated in accordance with P(C)R 2008, Part 3, the appropriate authority must appoint an investigator. An investigator must have the appropriate level of knowledge, skills, and experience to plan and manage the investigation; must not be an interested party; and must not work, directly or indirectly, under the management of the officer concerned.

Written notices

As soon as reasonably practicable after appointment an investigator is required by P(C)R 2008, reg 15(1) to cause the officer concerned to be given a written notice:

(a) describing the conduct and how it is alleged that it falls below the Standards of Professional Behaviour;

(b) of the appropriate authority's assessment of whether that conduct, if proved, would amount to misconduct or gross misconduct;

(c) that there is to be an investigation into the matter, and the identity of the investigator;

(d) of whether, if the matter were to be referred to misconduct proceedings, those would be likely to be a misconduct meeting or a misconduct hearing and the reason for this;

(e) that if the likely form of any misconduct proceedings to be held changes, further notice (with reasons) will be given;

(f) informing him that he has the right to seek advice from his staff association or any other body and of the effect of the provisions above about the appointment of a 'police friend';

(g) of the effect of the provisions above about legal and other representation and of the provisions below about representations to the investigator; and

(h) informing him that, whilst he does not have to say anything, it may harm his case if he does not mention, when interviewed or providing any information under reg

16(1) (oral statement or document: see below) or 22(2) (written statements of acceptance, mitigation or challenge in reply: see p 313), something which he later relies upon in misconduct proceedings or a special case hearing.

The notice requirement does not extend to circumstances where a notice might prejudice the investigation or any other investigation (including a criminal investigation). Any revision of an assessment of conduct must be notified as soon as practicable, indicating any change in likely outcomes. Where there has been no previous notification following the issue of a notice, an officer must be notified of the progress of the investigation within four weeks of the first working day after the start of the investigation. In any other case, notification of progress must be given before the end of four weeks beginning with the first working day after the previous notification.

Representations to an investigator and interviews during an investigation

By reg 16(1), within 10 clear working days of the service of the notice, an officer may provide a written or oral statement and any relevant document to the investigator.

If a date and time for an interview cannot be agreed, the investigator must specify a date and time. In the case of non-availability of the officer or his police friend, the interview must be postponed if the officer proposes an alternative time which is reasonable and falls within five working days after the day specified by the investigator. The investigator should supply in advance such information as he considers appropriate in the circumstances of the case to enable the officer to prepare for the interview.

Report of investigation

On completion of his investigation, the investigator must as soon as practicable submit a written report to the appropriate authority, providing an accurate summary of the evidence, attaching or referring to relevant documents and giving his opinion as to whether there is a case to answer in respect of misconduct or gross misconduct or whether there is no case to answer. If at any time during his investigation an investigator believes that the appropriate authority would be likely to determine that the *special conditions* (ie there is sufficient evidence in the form of written statements or other documents to establish on the balance of probabilities that the conduct of the officer constituted gross misconduct, and it is in the public interest for the officer concerned to cease to be a police officer without delay) are satisfied, he must inform that authority of the grounds for his belief and supply a written report of the investigation up to that point.

Misconduct proceedings

P(C)R 2008, Part 4 deals with misconduct proceedings.

Subject to the fast track procedure for special cases (p 317), the appropriate authority must on receipt of a written report from an investigator, including a final report under PRA 2002, Part 3, determine as soon as practicable whether or not an officer has a case to answer in respect of misconduct or gross misconduct or whether there is no case to answer.

If the answer is 'no case' it may decide to take no further action; take management action; or refer the matter to be dealt with under the Police (Performance) Regulations 2008.

If the appropriate authority determines that there is a case to answer in respect of:

(a) *gross misconduct* it must refer the case to a misconduct hearing;
(b) *misconduct* it may refer the case to misconduct proceedings (ie a misconduct meeting or misconduct hearing) or take management action against the officer.

Where there is a referral, no such proceedings may take place during any period when they would prejudice any criminal proceedings. Where the authority accepts a recommendation that proceedings are brought at a misconduct meeting or misconduct hearing it must notify the officer of this within 15 clear working days. Where it decides to take management action, the officer must be informed as soon as practicable.

Withdrawal of a case

At any time before the beginning of misconduct proceedings, the appropriate authority may withdraw a case and take no further action; take management action; or refer the matter to be dealt with under Performance Regulations. The authority must give the officer written notice of its decision and, where the investigation has been completed, provide the officer on request and subject to the 'harm test' with a copy of the investigator's report, or such parts of it which refer to the officer. As said more fully on p 309, information in documents which are stated to be subject to the harm test must not be supplied to the officer concerned in so far as the authority considers that preventing disclosure is necessary or justified: to prevent premature or inappropriate disclosure of information relevant to criminal proceedings; for reasons of national security; to prevent or detect crime or the apprehension or prosecution of offenders; to prevent or detect misconduct by other officers or police staff members or their apprehension for such matters; on the grounds that providing the information would involve disproportionate effort in comparison to the seriousness of the allegations; for the protection of the welfare and safety of any informant or witness and are proportionate; or otherwise in the public interest.

These provisions about withdrawal of a case do not apply to a case in which investigations are being conducted under PRA 2002, Sch 3, referred to on pp 299–300 (investigations by an appropriate authority or the IPCC, or supervised or managed by the IPCC).

Notice of referral to misconduct proceedings

Written notice of a referral must be given to the officer as soon as practicable informing him of the conduct in question and how it is alleged to amount to misconduct or gross misconduct, the name of the person appointed to conduct or chair the misconduct proceedings, and the officer's entitlement to legal representation. In addition, he must be given a copy of any statement made to the investigator and, subject to the 'harm test', the investigator's report (or the part of it relating to him), any document attached to it, and any other relevant document. As soon as practicable, the officer must be informed of the names of advisers and panel members (where the proceedings are to be so conducted). He may object to the appointment of any of these persons, including the chair, within three clear working days after being given notice.

Within 14 clear working days of receipt of such a notice an officer must give to the appropriate authority written notice of whether or not he accepts that his conduct amounted to misconduct or gross misconduct. If the officer does so accept, he may by P(C)R 2008, reg 22(2) make any written submission he wishes to make in mitigation. If he does not so accept, he must indicate the allegations which he disputes and any points of law he wishes to be considered by the person or persons conducting the misconduct proceedings. The officer must provide the authority with a copy of any document which he intends to rely on in the misconduct proceedings. Within three clear working days each side must provide the other with a list of proposed witnesses which includes a brief indication of the details of their individual evidence. The person conducting or chairing the misconduct proceedings will then determine which witnesses should attend.

Timing of misconduct proceedings

After the documents have been supplied to an officer, any misconduct meeting must take place within 20 clear working days and any misconduct hearing within 30 clear working days. If reasonably practicable, the date and time of the misconduct proceedings should be agreed between the person conducting or chairing the misconduct proceedings and the officer.

Persons conducting misconduct proceedings

Misconduct meeting　Such a meeting must be conducted by a person who is not an interested party and who:

(1) (a)　in the case of a police officer who is a member of a police force, is another police officer at least one rank higher than the officer concerned;
    (b)　in the case of a special constable, is a sergeant or above or a senior human resources professional; or
(2)　unless the case substantially involves operational police matters, is a police staff member who, in the opinion of the appropriate authority, is more senior than the officer.

A person so appointed must be supplied with all of the relevant documents (referred to above) relating to the case.

Misconduct hearing　Such a hearing must be conducted by a panel of not more than three persons appointed by the appropriate authority, the chair being a senior officer (ie above the rank of chief superintendent) or senior human resources professional (ie someone who, in the opinion of the appropriate authority, has sufficient seniority, skills, and experience, to be a panel chair). Where the chair is a senior officer the second member is a superintendent or above or a human resources professional; where the chair is a senior human resources professional that member is a superintendent or above. The third member is selected from a list maintained by a local policing body.

A person so appointed must be supplied with all the relevant documents referred to above.

Attendance of persons at misconduct proceedings

The officer concerned must attend the misconduct proceedings, but where he informs the person who is to conduct or chair the proceedings that he is unable to attend and his reasons appear to be reasonable, that person may allow attendance by way of video link or other means. Whether or not the officer attends and participates in the proceedings, he may be represented by his police friend, or in the case of a misconduct hearing, by a lawyer and his police friend. The investigator or a nominated person must attend if required to do so by the person conducting or chairing the proceedings.

The IPCC may attend misconduct proceedings to make representations in any case in which it has been involved, or has made a recommendation, or has given a direction. When the IPCC attends, it may instruct a lawyer to represent it and it must notify the complainant or any interested person. The person conducting or chairing the proceedings must notify the officer in these circumstances.

In the case of misconduct proceedings arising from investigations conducted under PRA 2002, Sch 3, referred to on pp 299–300 (investigations by an appropriate authority or the IPCC, or supervised or managed by the IPCC), the complainant must be notified of the time and place of the proceedings. The following may attend as an observer up to the point at which the person conducting or chairing the proceedings considers the question of disciplinary action: the complainant, or any interested person, and in respect of each such person one other person (and, where the complainant or interested party has a 'special need' (ie a person with a disability, learning difficulty, or insufficient knowledge of English), one further person to accommodate that need). The person conducting or chairing proceedings may impose conditions in respect of such attendance (including circumstances in which attendees may be excluded) in order to facilitate the proper conduct of proceedings. In addition, where it appears that a person, in giving evidence may disclose something which, under the 'harm test' ought not to be disclosed to any persons attending the proceedings, such attendees may be required to withdraw while the evidence is being given. A complainant, interested party, or any person accompanying him who is to give evidence within the proceedings, must not be allowed to attend the proceedings before giving evidence.

In a case involving investigation by the IPCC, the IPCC may direct that the hearing be in public if it considers that it is in the public interest to do so. Before doing so, it must consult the appropriate authority, the officer concerned, the complainant or interested person, and any other witness. Any decision so to direct must be notified to such persons within five clear working days.

Procedure at misconduct proceedings

The person conducting or chairing the proceedings must determine the procedure and inform the officer of the nature of those proceedings and his rights in relation to representation.

The person representing the officer may present the case for him; sum up that case; respond on his behalf to any view expressed in the proceedings; make representations concerning any aspect of the proceedings; ask questions of any witness; and confer with the officer. Where, at a *misconduct hearing*, the officer is represented by a lawyer, the police friend may also confer with the officer. However, a lawyer or police friend may not answer questions which are put to the officer.

The person conducting or chairing misconduct proceedings has discretion as to whether or not questions should be put to a witness. He may also allow any document to be considered even though a copy of it has not been supplied by or to the officer. Where evidence is given or considered to the effect that the officer on being questioned by an investigator after being given written notice under P(C)R 2008, reg 15(1) or the equivalent notice under the Police (Complaints and Misconduct) Regulations, or in submitting written information, failed to mention any fact relied upon in his case at the misconduct proceedings, which the officer could reasonably have been expected to mention or provide, the person or persons conducting the misconduct proceedings may draw such inferences from that failure as appear to be proper.

The person conducting the proceedings or the panel, as the case may be, must then decide: in the case of a misconduct *meeting*, whether the conduct of the officer amounted to misconduct or not; and, in the case of a misconduct *hearing*, to misconduct, gross misconduct, or neither. The officer's conduct may not be found to amount to misconduct or gross misconduct unless the person or persons conducting the proceedings is or are satisfied on the balance of probabilities that this is the case, or the officer admits that it is. Where the issue is to be decided by a panel, the decision will be based on a majority. The Chairman has a casting vote.

The outcome of misconduct proceedings

Under P(C)R 2008, reg 35, as amended in 2011, the person or panel conducting the misconduct proceedings may impose any of the disciplinary action below, or, where he or they find the conduct amounts to misconduct but not gross misconduct, record a finding of misconduct but take no further action.

The disciplinary action available at or after a misconduct *meeting* is:

(a) management advice;
(b) written warning; or
(c) final written warning.

The disciplinary action available at or after a misconduct *hearing* is:

(a) to (c) above; or
(d) dismissal with notice; or
(e) dismissal without notice.

The Court of Appeal has held that, because of the importance of maintaining public confidence in the police service, personal mitigation is likely to have a limited effect on the outcome, and that where there has been a finding of operational dishonesty the sanction of dismissal would usually be the outcome.

In the case of dismissal with notice the persons imposing the disciplinary action must decide the period of notice, subject to a minimum of 28 days. Where there is a finding of misconduct (as opposed to gross misconduct) an officer may not be dismissed, with or without notice, unless he has previously received a final written warning which is in force on that date.

Where a written warning is in force at the time, an officer may not be given a written warning. Where a final written warning is in force, that final written warning may, in exceptional circumstances, be extended for a further 18 months, but this may only occur on one occasion.

Where there is a finding of gross misconduct and it is decided that the officer shall be dismissed, the dismissal must be without notice.

Before the nature of disciplinary action is decided, the officer, his police friend, or, at a misconduct hearing, his lawyer, must be given an opportunity to make oral or written representations. So must the appropriate authority or person appointed to represent that authority. The person or persons considering the question of disciplinary action must have regard to the officer's record of service as shown on his personal record and may receive evidence from a witness where that evidence might assist him or them in determining that question.

The officer must be notified as soon as practicable of the outcome and any disciplinary action imposed. He must also be given a written notice of these matters, and a summary of the reasons, before the end of five clear working days from the end of the misconduct proceedings.

Where there is a finding of misconduct or gross misconduct that notice must include details of the officer's right to appeal.

A record must be made of misconduct proceedings; in the case of a misconduct hearing, that record must be verbatim. On request, an officer must be supplied with a copy of such records.

Appeal from finding etc of misconduct meeting

Where an officer whose case was determined by a misconduct meeting has admitted misconduct, he may appeal against the disciplinary action imposed. Where he denied misconduct he may appeal against a finding of misconduct or any disciplinary action imposed at a misconduct meeting. The only grounds for such an appeal are:

(a) that the finding or disciplinary action was unreasonable; or
(b) that there is evidence that could not reasonably have been considered at the misconduct meeting; or
(c) that there was a serious breach of the procedures or other unfairness, which could have materially affected the finding or decision on disciplinary matters.

Such an appeal must be commenced by giving written notice to the appropriate authority (1) within seven clear working days from the giving of the notice of outcome and summary reasons, and (2) stating the grounds of the appeal and whether a meeting is requested. Where the person who conducted the misconduct meeting was a member of a police force, such an appeal will be determined by an officer appointed by the appropriate authority of at least one rank higher than that person, or (unless the case substantially involves operational policing matters) by a police staff member more senior than that person. Where the person who conducted the misconduct meeting was a police staff member, the appeal will be determined by a member of the police force more senior than that person or by a more senior police staff member.

An officer has a right to make a written objection to the appointment of any person to determine the appeal (or to advise that person) within three clear working days of being notified of the name(s) of such person(s), setting out his grounds for objection.

Appeal meeting, procedure, and finding

Where the person determining the appeal considers that there are arguable grounds of appeal, an appeal meeting with the officer must be arranged within five clear working days. If he determines that it does not, he must dismiss the appeal. The Regulations make provision for the establishment of a suitable time and date for all parties involved in the appeal to attend.

The person determining the appeal must determine the procedure at the meeting. Any interested person or complainant may attend an appeal meeting as an observer but only up to the point where a decision is to be made about disciplinary action. Conditions on attendance may be imposed on the same basis as at misconduct proceedings.

The person determining the appeal may:

(a) confirm or reverse the decision appealed against;
(b) deal with the officer concerned in any manner in which the person conducting the misconduct meeting could have dealt with him in the first instance.

The officer must be given written notice of the outcome of the appeal together with a summary of the reasons within three clear working days of its determination. Should the IPCC have been involved in the investigation of the conduct, the IPCC be given the same information.

Appeal from finding etc of misconduct hearing

As to appeals by an officer against whom a finding of misconduct or gross misconduct has been made at *a misconduct hearing*, see p 330.

Fast track procedure for special cases

This is dealt with by P(C)R 2008, Part 5.

Referral of case to special hearing

As stated earlier, if at any time during his investigation an investigator believes that the appropriate authority would be likely to determine that the *special conditions* are satisfied (ie there is sufficient written evidence to establish on the balance of probabilities that the conduct of the officer constituted gross misconduct, and it is in the public interest for the officer concerned to cease to be a police officer without delay) he must submit to that authority a statement of his belief and the grounds for it and provide a written report of his investigation so far. The authority must then determine whether such grounds exist either at that time or, should special case proceedings have been delayed on the grounds that their continuance would prejudice criminal proceedings, when that matter has been resolved. If it determines that the special conditions are satisfied, the authority must certify the case as a special case and refer it to a special case hearing, unless it considers that circumstances make this inappropriate. If it does not certify the case, it must refer the matter back to the investigator for completion of the investigation, where the investigation is incomplete, or, in any other case, proceed with misconduct proceedings.

Where a case is referred to a special case hearing, the officer must as soon as practicable be informed by written notice of a decision to 'fast track' the proceedings and be supplied with a copy of the certificate that the case is a special case, any statement which the officer may have made to the investigator, and, subject to the 'harm test' referred to on p 309, the investigator's report or such parts as relate to him (together with any document attached to or referred to in that report which relates to him) and any other relevant document.

The notice must describe the conduct in question and indicate how it is alleged to amount to gross misconduct.

A date for a special case hearing not less than 10 and not more than 15 clear working days of the written notice being given must be specified by the appropriate authority, and must immediately be communicated (with a time and place) to the officer. Within seven clear working days of being given the written notice, the officer must provide written notice of whether or not he accepts that his conduct amounted to gross misconduct. If he does so accept, he must within that time also provide any written submission which he wishes to make in mitigation. Where he does not so accept, he must within that time provide written notice of the allegations which he disputes and his account of events, and of any arguments on points of law he wishes to be considered. He must also provide the appropriate authority within that time period with a copy of any document he intends to rely on at the hearing.

Hearing of special cases

A special case hearing where the metropolitan police force is the force concerned will be conducted by an assistant commissioner. Otherwise, it will be conducted by the chief officer of the force concerned, except that, where that chief officer is an interested party or is unavailable, the hearing must be conducted by the chief officer of another force or an assistant commissioner of the Metropolitan Police.

Prior to the hearing, the officer must be supplied with a list of the documents supplied to the person conducting the proceedings together with a copy of any such documents with which he has not already been supplied.

The rules about attendance and representation are the same as in the case of misconduct proceedings (see p 314).

The Regulations also provide for the attendance of the IPCC where it has been involved in the investigation.

Where the special case hearing arose from a conduct matter or complaint, the complainant or interested party may attend the hearing as an observer and be accompanied by one other person and a 'special needs' assistant up to the point where disciplinary action is being considered.

Procedure at special case hearing

The person conducting the hearing must determine the procedure. The hearing must not proceed unless the officer has been informed of his right to legal representation. No witnesses other than the officer concerned may give evidence. The role of the person representing the officer is the same as at misconduct proceedings (see p 315). The person conducting the hearing may allow a document to be considered notwithstanding that it has not been supplied by the officer to the appropriate authority as required (p 318) or has not been supplied to the officer as required (p 318).

The same rule applies as in misconduct proceedings (see p 315) where the officer relies at the hearing on evidence which he had previously failed to mention. The person conducting the hearing must not decide whether the conduct of the officer amounted to gross misconduct unless satisfied, on the balance of probabilities, that this is the case.

Outcome of special case hearing

This is dealt with by P(C)R 2008, reg 55. On a finding of gross misconduct, disciplinary action may be taken by way of a final written warning; the extension of a final written warning; or dismissal without notice. Where a final written warning was already in force a final written warning may not be given but, in exceptional circumstances, may be extended (only once) for a period of 18 months. Where it is found that the conduct did not amount to gross misconduct, the person conducting the proceedings may dismiss the case or return the case to the appropriate authority to be dealt with at a misconduct meeting or (if the officer had a final written warning in force at the time of the assessment of his conduct under reg 12(1) (see p 311) or the corresponding assessment under the Police (Complaints and Misconduct) Regulations (2004) at a misconduct hearing.

Where the question of disciplinary action is being considered at a special case hearing, the person conducting the proceedings must have regard to an officer's record of service, may consider relevant documentary evidence, and must give the officer, his police friend, and his legal representative, an opportunity to make oral or written representations on the officer's behalf.

The officer must be informed as soon as practicable of the finding and any disciplinary action imposed or the return of the case to the appropriate authority. In any event, he must within five clear working days of the conclusion of the special case hearing be provided with written notice of these matters and a summary of the reasons.

A verbatim record must be made of a special case hearing and the officer concerned must be supplied with a copy if he so requests.

Records of disciplinary proceedings generally

A chief officer of police must cause a record to be kept of disciplinary proceedings and special case proceedings brought against officers, together with the finding and decision on disciplinary action and the decision in any appeal by the officer concerned.

Standards of Professional Behaviour

The Standards of Professional Behaviour expected of police officers, which are referred to in the Police (Conduct) Regulations 2008, are set out in the Schedule to the Regulations.

Honesty and integrity

1.   Police officers are honest, act with integrity and do not compromise or abuse their position.

Authority, respect and courtesy

2.   Police officers act with self-control and tolerance, treating members of the public and colleagues with respect and courtesy.
3.   Police officers do not abuse their powers or authority and respect the rights of all individuals.

Equality and diversity

4.   Police officers act with fairness and impartiality. They do not discriminate unlawfully or unfairly.

Use of force

5.   Police officers only use force to the extent that it is necessary, proportionate and reasonable in all the circumstances.

Orders and instructions

6.   Police officers only give and carry out lawful orders and instructions.
7.   Police officers abide by Police Regulations, force policies and lawful orders.

Duties and responsibilities

8.   Police officers are diligent in the exercise of their duties and responsibilities.

Confidentiality

9.   Police officers treat information with respect and access or disclose it only in the proper course of police duties.

Fitness for duty

10.   Police officers when on duty or presenting themselves for duty are fit to carry out their responsibilities.

Discreditable conduct

11.   Police officers behave in a manner which does not discredit the police service or undermine public confidence in it, whether on or off duty.
12.   Police officers report any action taken against them for a criminal offence, any conditions imposed on them by a court or the receipt of any penalty notice.

Challenging and reporting improper conduct

13.   Police officers report, challenge or take action against the conduct of colleagues which has fallen below the Standards of Professional Behaviour.

POLICE PERFORMANCE PROCEEDINGS

General

The Police (Performance) Regulations 2008 (P(P)R 2008) are concerned with the unsatisfactory performance or attendance of members of a police force below the rank of chief superintendent and special constables. 'Unsatisfactory performance or attendance' means an inability or failure to perform the duties of the role or rank that the officer is currently undertaking to a satisfactory standard or level. 'Gross incompetence' means a serious inability or serious failure of a police officer to perform the duties of his rank or the role he is currently undertaking to a satisfactory standard or level, to the extent that dismissal would be justified, except that no account should be taken of his attendance when considering whether or not he has been grossly incompetent. Under the Regulations, the appropriate authority (chief officer of police) may delegate functions to an officer not below the rank of chief inspector, or a police staff member of a similar level of seniority. Where this is done, any decision to require a third stage meeting without a first or second stage meeting (see p 326) must be authorised by an officer of above the rank of chief superintendent.

Police friend

The officer concerned may choose a police officer; police staff member; or (where the officer is a member of a police force) a person nominated by his staff association, to act as his 'police friend' A police friend may advise the officer throughout the proceedings; unless the officer has a right to legal representation and so chooses, represent the officer at a meeting; make representations to the appropriate authority concerning any aspects of the proceedings; and accompany the officer to any meeting which the officer is required to attend. Where a police friend is a police officer or police staff member he must be permitted by his chief constable to use a reasonable amount of time for these purposes.

Legal representation

Where a police officer is required to attend a third stage meeting without a first or second stage meeting (see below) he has the right to be legally represented at that meeting by a lawyer of his choice. If legal representation is declined, the officer may be dealt with and may be dismissed or receive any other outcome without such representation, and the panel conducting the meeting may nevertheless receive legal advice on the proceedings and on any question of law at that meeting. Except in a case where the officer has the right to be legally represented and chooses to be so represented, he may be represented only by a police friend. The officer concerned must be informed of these provisions.

Provision of notices or documents

Notices or documents must be given to the officer personally or left with some person at, or sent by recorded delivery to, his last known address.

Procedure at meetings under the regulations

Where an officer does not attend a meeting under P(P)R 2008, or where he participates in a third stage meeting by video link or any other means, he may be represented at that meeting by a police friend, or in the case of a third stage meeting, by his lawyer. Where the officer does not attend such a meeting or participates in a third stage meeting by video link or other means, the meeting may proceed and be concluded in his absence whether or not he is so represented.

Representatives may put the case; sum it up; respond on the officer's behalf to any views expressed at the meeting; make representations in relation to any aspect of the proceedings; in the case of a third stage meeting, ask questions of any witness; and confer with the officer. Where a third stage meeting is being conducted by a video link or other means, representatives may similarly participate. However, representatives may not answer questions on behalf of an officer. Whether any question should be put to a witness at a third stage meeting must be decided by the panel chair. There must be no finding of unsatisfactory performance or attendance or gross incompetence unless such is satisfied on the balance of probabilities, or unless the officer consents to such a finding. The person conducting or chairing a meeting may permit a document to be considered notwithstanding that a copy of it has not been supplied to the officer in accordance with the Regulations, or has not been made available to each panel member or given to the officer concerned in accordance with the Regulations.

First stage

Circumstances and arrangements

When the line manager (ie the person with immediate supervisory responsibility for the officer) considers that the performance or attendance of that officer is unsatisfactory, he may require him to attend a first stage meeting to discuss his performance or attendance. The officer must be given a written notice requiring his attendance at a first stage meeting; informing him of the procedures for determining the time and place of the meeting; summarising the reasons for considering performance or attendance to be unsatisfactory; informing him of the possible outcomes of first, second, and third stage meetings; informing him that a human resources professional or police officer may attend to advise the line manager; informing him that, if he consents, any other person specified in the notice may attend; where the person concerned is a member of a police force, informing him that he may seek advice from a representative of his staff association; informing him that he may be accompanied and represented by a police friend; and informing him that he must supply the line manager in advance of the meeting with a copy of any document he intends to rely upon at the meeting. The line manager's notice must be accompanied by any document relied upon by the line manager in coming to a decision that performance or attendance is unsatisfactory.

If reasonably practicable, the date and time for the meeting must be agreed. If they are not, the line manager must specify and notify in writing a date and time. If the officer or his police friend is unavailable on that date but the officer proposes a reasonably acceptable alternative time falling before the end of five clear working days after the date specified by the line manager, the meeting must be postponed until that time. The officer must provide the line manager with a copy of any document he intends to rely upon, in advance of the meeting.

Procedure at first stage meeting

The line manager will conduct the meeting. The line manager must explain the reasons why he considers the performance or attendance of the officer to be unsatisfactory; give the officer an opportunity to make representations; and give the police friend (if there is one) an opportunity to address the meeting.

If, after considering such representations, the line manager finds that the officer's performance or attendance has been unsatisfactory, he must inform him:

(a) in which respects this is so;
(b) of the respects in which improvement is required;
(c) that, if sufficient improvement is not evident within a *specified reasonable period* (not greater than 12 months), the line manager may require attendance at a second stage meeting;
(d) that he will receive a written improvement notice; and

(e) that, if the 'sufficient improvement' referred to in (c) is not maintained during any part of the *validity period* of such notice remaining after the expiry of the period specified in accordance with (c), he may be required to attend a second stage meeting.

Procedure following first stage meeting

As soon as practicable, a written record of the meeting must be prepared and, where performance or attendance was found unsatisfactory, a written improvement notice. Where the officer concerned has failed to attend a first stage meeting, and the line manager finds his performance or attendance unsatisfactory, a written improvement notice must be prepared as soon as reasonably practicable; and if a police friend of the officer concerned attended the meeting a written record of the meeting must be prepared.

An improvement notice must record the matters of which the officer concerned was informed (or would have been informed had he attended the meeting); state the validity period (ie the period of validity of the notice), which is 12 months, and be signed and dated by the line manager. A copy must be given to the officer concerned of any written record and any written improvement notice as soon as practicable. Where an improvement notice has been prepared, the line manager must, when supplying these documents, inform the officer in writing that he may appeal:

(a) against the finding of unsatisfactory performance or attendance; or
(b) against (i) the respect in which his performance or attendance was considered to be unsatisfactory, (ii) the improvement required, or (iii) the length of the period for improvement specified,

on the grounds that the finding was unreasonable, or that any of the relevant terms of the improvement notice are unreasonable, or that there is material evidence that could not reasonably have been considered at the first stage meeting, or that there was a breach of the procedures set out in the Regulations or other unfairness which could have materially affected the finding or any of the relevant terms of the improvement notice. At the same time the line manager must inform the officer concerned of the name of the person to whom written notice of appeal must be given, and of his entitlement to submit written comments on any written record if he does not appeal.

The entitlement just referred to is that the officer concerned may submit written comments on any matter contained in any written record within seven clear working days following the day on which a copy is received.

In the case of an appeal, the officer must give written notice to the second line manager before the end of seven clear days from the receipt of any written record or any written improvement notice. The second line manager is the person appointed by the appropriate authority to act as the second line manager for the purposes of P(P)R 2008 in relation to the officer concerned and who is either (a) a member of the police force concerned having supervisory responsibility for the line manager, and who (in a case where the line manager is a member of the force) is senior in rank to the line manager, or (b) a police staff member who has supervisory responsibility for the line manager.

As soon as reasonably practicable after receipt of such a notice, the second line manager must inform the officer in writing of the procedures for determining the date and time of the appeal meeting and of who may attend it (same rules as apply to a first stage meeting). The equivalent rules apply for fixing a date for the appeal meeting as apply to a first stage meeting p 322), substituting 'second line manager' for 'line manager'.

Procedure at first stage appeal meeting

The meeting will be conducted by the second line manager. Other persons may attend as specified for a first stage meeting (p 322). The officer must be allowed to make representations and his police friend (if there is one) must be allowed to address the meeting. After considering such representations, the second line manager, may:

(a) confirm or reverse the finding of unsatisfactory performance or attendance; or
(b) confirm or vary the relevant terms of the written improvement notice.

Where the second line manager has reversed the finding of unsatisfactory performance or attendance, he must also revoke the written improvement notice. As soon as reasonably practicable after the end of the meeting, the officer concerned must be given written notice of the second line manager's decision and a written summary of the reasons for it. In any event the officer must be given written notice of the decision within three clear working days from the end of the meeting. Where the decision of the second line manager differs from that at the first stage hearing it takes effect by way of substitution for it to the extent that it differs.

Second stage

Circumstances in which second stage meeting may be required

As soon as reasonably practicable after the relevant *specified period* for improvement, the line manager must assess the performance or attendance of the officer concerned in consultation with the second line manager or a human resources professional (or both) and notify the officer in writing whether he considers that there has been sufficient improvement within that period. If he does not consider that there has been sufficient improvement, he must at the same time notify the officer in writing that he is required to attend a second stage meeting to consider his performance or attendance.

Where an officer has not been so required to attend a second stage meeting, or has been so required to attend but a finding of unsatisfactory performance or attendance was not made at that meeting, the officer may be required to attend a second stage meeting if, in the opinion of the line manager, the officer concerned has failed to maintain sufficient improvement during any part of the *validity period* of the written improvement notice remaining after the expiry of the specified period for improvement.

The performance or attendance considered at any second stage meeting must be unsatisfactory performance or attendance similar to or concerned with that referred to in the improvement notice.

Arrangements for second stage meeting

Where the line manager requires the officer to attend a second stage meeting, he must as soon as reasonably practicable provide the officer with a written notice setting out similar information to that required to be given for a first stage meeting, except that it must inform the officer that the meeting will be with the second line manager (to whom documents sent in advance by the officer must be sent). The notice must be accompanied by any document relied upon by the line manager when he reached his decision. The same rules apply to the arrangements for the meeting as apply to a first stage meeting.

Procedure at and following second stage meeting

The second line manager must conduct the meeting. The line manager may attend. Otherwise, the meeting follows the format of a first stage meeting. Following the meeting, the second line manager must get prepared (a) a written record of the meeting, and (b) where he found unsatisfactory performance or attendance, a final written improvement notice setting out the respects in which the officer's performance or attendance is unsatisfactory and the other matters set out in relation to a first stage meeting, but with reference to the fact that if such improvement is not maintained throughout the specified period, he may be required to attend a third stage meeting. On this occasion, the notice will be a final written improvement notice. It must state the period for which it is valid (the 'validity period'), a period of 12 months, and must be signed and dated by the second line manager.

The second line manager must give the officer a copy of the written record and any final written improvement notice as soon as reasonably practicable after preparation. Where a final written improvement notice has been prepared, the second line manager must at the same time also notify the officer of the appeal process and of the person to whom a written notice of appeal must be given and of his entitlement to submit written comments to the second line manager within seven clear working days. No written comments on the written record may be made by the officer if he has exercised his right to appeal.

Appeal against the finding and outcome of second stage meeting

The officer may appeal against (a) the finding, (b) any of the matters specified in the Regulations (the same as those specified in respect of a first stage appeal) and recorded in the final written improvement notice, or (c) the line manager's decision to require the officer to attend the second stage meeting.

The only grounds of appeal are:

(i)   in relation to (c), that the officer should not have been required to attend the second stage meeting as that meeting did not concern unsatisfactory performance or attendance similar to or connected with performance or attendance referred to in the written improvement notice;

(ii) that the finding of unsatisfactory performance or attendance was unreasonable;

(iii) that any of the terms of the final written improvement notice are unreasonable;

(iv) that there is evidence which might have been considered at the second stage meeting which could have materially affected the finding or any of the relevant terms of the final written improvement notice, or

(v)   that there was a breach of the procedure prescribed by the Regulations or other unfairness which could have materially affected the finding or any relevant terms of the notice.

The officer must give written notice of appeal, setting out the grounds and accompanied by any evidence upon which he relies, to the senior manager within seven clear days of receipt of the copies of any written record and written formal improvement notice. The arrangements to be made in respect of the second stage appeal meeting are similar to those applying to a first stage appeal. The 'senior manager' means (a) the police officer or police staff member who is the supervisor of the second line manager, or (b) in the absence of such a supervisor, the police officer or police staff member nominated by the appropriate authority to carry out the functions of such a supervisor under the Regulations (who must be of at least the same rank (or equivalent) as the second line manager just mentioned).

Procedure at second stage appeal meeting

The meeting will be conducted by the senior manager and will follow a similar procedure to that at a first stage appeal. When the officer concerned has been provided with an opportunity to make representations and his police friend has had an opportunity to address the meeting, the senior manager may (a) make a finding that the officer concerned should not have been required to attend a second stage meeting and reverse the finding made at it; (b) confirm or reverse the finding of unsatisfactory performance or attendance made at it; (c) confirm or vary the relevant terms of the final written improvement notice appealed against. Where the senior manager reverses the finding of unsatisfactory performance or attendance, he must also revoke the final written improvement notice.

As soon as reasonably practicable after the end of the meeting, the officer must be given written notice of the senior manager's decision and a written summary of his reasons. In any event, he must be given written notice within three clear working days. Where the senior manager has reversed a finding of unsatisfactory performance or attendance or varied any of the relevant terms of the final written improvement notice, his decision takes effect by way of substitution for the finding, final notice, or the relevant terms of the final notice appealed against from the date of the second stage meeting.

Third stage

Assessment following second stage meeting

As soon as reasonably practicable after the period for improvement *specified* in the final written improvement notice ends, the line manager must assess the officer's performance or attendance during that period in consultation with the second line manager or a human resources professional (or both). The line manager must notify the officer in writing as to whether he considers that sufficient improvement has taken place. If he considers that it has not, he must at the same time notify the officer in writing that he is required to attend a third stage meeting at which his performance or attendance will be considered.

Where the officer concerned has not been required to attend a third stage meeting under the above provisions, or he has been required to attend such a third stage meeting but the panel did not make a finding of unsatisfactory performance or attendance at that meeting, he may be required to attend a third stage meeting if, in the line manager's opinion, he has failed to maintain sufficient improvement during any part of the validity period of the final written improvement notice after the expiry of the specified period.

The performance or attendance to be considered at a third stage meeting must concern unsatisfactory performance or attendance similar to or connected with that referred to in the final written improvement notice.

Arrangement of third stage meeting

Where the line manager requires an officer's attendance at a third stage meeting, the senior manager must give him written notice setting out similar information to that required in the case of first and second stage meetings. That notice must be accompanied by a copy of any document relied upon by the line manager in forming his view that performance or attendance is unsatisfactory. A third stage meeting may not take place unless the officer has been informed of his right to representation by a police friend.

Third stage meeting without prior first or second stage meeting

Where an appropriate authority considers that an officer's performance constitutes gross incompetence it may inform him in writing that he is required to attend a third stage meeting, notwithstanding that he has not attended a first or second stage meeting. In such a case, the authority must give the officer similar information to that referred to in the last paragraph.

Appointment of panel members

The third stage hearing must be conducted by a panel of three, appointed by the appropriate authority, consisting of:

(a) a chair, who must be a senior officer (ie chief superintendent or above) or a senior human resources professional (ie such professional who, in the appropriate authority's opinion, has sufficient seniority, skills and experience to be a panel chair);

(b) a superintendent (or above) or a human resources professional who, in the authority's opinion, is of equivalent rank; and

(c) a police officer or a police staff member of the rank of superintendent (or so equivalent).

At least one panel member must be a police officer and one a human resources professional. No panel member may be of lower rank (or equivalent) than the officer concerned or be an interested party. Once panel members have been appointed, the officer must be notified as soon as reasonably practicable of their names. He must be provided with any document which was available to the line manager in relation to the first stage meeting; or to the second line manager in relation to the second stage meeting; or which was prepared or submitted under the Regulations to be made available to him and to each panel member.

The officer may make written objection to the appointment of any panel member within three clear working days of notification, setting out the grounds of his objection. If the authority accepts the objection, it must appoint a new member and as soon as reasonably practicable so inform the officer in writing. The officer has the same right to object to the new appointment but no further objections are allowed.

Procedure on receipt of notice of third stage meeting

Within 14 clear working days of receipt of the notification of panel members the officer must inform the appropriate authority as to whether or not he accepts that his performance or attendance has been unsatisfactory, or that he has been grossly incompetent, as the case may be. If he so accepts, he may make a written submission in mitigation. Where he does not so accept, or where he disputes all or part of the matters referred to in the notice to attend a third stage meeting, he must give written notice of the matters which he disputes, together with his account of the relevant events, and any arguments on points of law he wishes to be considered by the panel. He must also provide the authority with a copy of any documents which he intends to rely upon at the third stage meeting.

Within three clear working days of the above submission of notice, each side must provide the other with a list of proposed witnesses, together with brief details of the evidence which it will give, or give notice that it does not have such witnesses. Where there are proposed witnesses, the officer must, if reasonably practicable, agree a list of proposed witnesses with the senior manager. If no such list is agreed, the officer must supply the appropriate authority with his list of proposed witnesses. As soon as reasonably practicable after any such list has been agreed or supplied by the officer to the appropriate authority, the authority must supply the panel chair with a list of its proposed witnesses. The panel chair should then determine which of the list(s) of proposed witnesses should be allowed to attend, and may determine that witnesses not named in the list(s) may attend the third stage meeting. No witness may give evidence at a third stage meeting unless the panel chair reasonably believes that it is necessary in the interests of fairness for that witness to do so. Where he requires a police officer to attend as a witness, he must have that person ordered to attend; in any other case, he must cause the witness to be given notice that his attendance is necessary.

Timing and notice of third stage meeting

The third stage meeting must take place within 30 clear working days after notice has been given to the officer. The meeting should take place, where possible, on an agreed date, but where such agreement is not reached the chair must specify a date and time. In the event of non-availability of the officer or his police friend, the meeting must be postponed to a time submitted by the officer, provided that that time is a reasonable one and within five clear working days after the day specified by the chair. The chair must give the officer written notice of the time and date of the meeting determined under these provisions and of its place. Where the officer informs the chair in advance that he is unable to attend the meeting on grounds which the chair considers reasonable, the chair may permit participation by video link or other means.

Procedure at third stage meeting

The panel chair will determine procedure. The meeting will be held in private. A human resources professional and a police officer may attend as advisers to the panel on the proceedings, and a lawyer may attend to advise the panel on the proceedings and on any question involving a point of law. Other persons specified in the notice requiring the officer concerned to attend a third stage hearing may attend with that officer's consent. The officer must be given an opportunity to make representations in relation to matters specified in that notice and his police friend (if he has one) must be allowed to address the meeting in relation to them; where the meeting is being held without first or second stage meetings a lawyer representing the officer fulfils the role otherwise fulfilled by the police friend. As to legal representation of the officer see p 321. A verbatim record of the meeting must be made, and the officer, on request, must be supplied with a copy.

Finding

The panel must make a finding as to:

(a) whether or not the officer's performance or attendance during the specified period has been satisfactory, or
(b) whether or not it has been satisfactory during any part of the validity of the written notice after the specified period, or
(c) where the officer is attending a third stage meeting without having attended a first or second stage meeting in respect of his performance, whether his performance constitutes gross incompetence, unsatisfactory performance or neither.

The panel must prepare its decision in writing, and must state the reasons for a finding of unsatisfactory performance or attendance or gross incompetence, together with any outcome which they order. Any finding or decision may be based on a simple majority but must not indicate whether it was taken unanimously or by a majority. The officer and the line manager must be given copies of the decision as soon as reasonably practicable. In any event, the officer must be given written notice of the finding within three clear working days of the end of the meeting. Where the finding has been one of unsatisfactory performance or attendance or gross incompetence, the copy of the decision given to the officer must be accompanied by a notice setting out the circumstances in which, and the timetable within which, a police officer may appeal to the Police Appeals Tribunal.

Outcomes

In the case of a finding *at a third stage meeting after first and second stage meeting* that there has not been sufficient improvement within the period specified in the written improvement notice, or any period of validity remaining in such notice, the panel may order one of outcomes (a), (b), or (c):

(a) dismissal with notice, the period of which is to be decided by the panel, subject to a minimum period of 28 days;
(b) except where the officer is a special constable or the meeting relates to his attendance, reduction in rank of the officer concerned with immediate effect;
(c) redeployment to alternative duties (which may involve a reduction in rank) within the police force concerned.

Where the panel is satisfied that there are exceptional circumstances which justify it, it may order an extension of the final written improvement notice. In such a case, a reasonable period for improvement (not more than 12 months) must be specified and the notice will be valid for 12 months (the 'validity period') from the date of extension. The notice must state that the officer may be required to attend another third stage meeting if he fails to make sufficient improvement within the specified period.

In the case of a finding *at a third stage meeting not preceded by a first or second stage meeting* that the performance of the officer constitutes gross incompetence, the panel may order:

(a) dismissal with immediate effect;
(b) reduction in rank of the officer concerned with immediate effect;
(c) the issue of a final written improvement notice; or
(d) redeployment to alternative duties (which may involve a reduction in rank) within the police force concerned.

Where the finding *in such a case* is one of *unsatisfactory* performance, the panel must issue a written improvement notice.

Where an improvement notice or a final written improvement notice is issued after a finding at a third stage meeting, it must:

(a) state in what respect the officer's performance or attendance (as the case may be) is considered unsatisfactory or grossly incompetent;
(b) state the improvement in his performance or attendance required;
(c) state that, if a sufficient improvement is not made within such reasonable period (not greater than 12 months) as the panel specifies, the officer may be required to attend a second stage meeting (in the case of a written improvement notice) or another third stage meeting (in the case of a final written improvement notice) and state the date on which this period ends;
(d) state that it is valid for a period of 12 months from the date of the notice (the 'validity period');
(e) state that, if the sufficient improvement referred to in (c) is not maintained during any part of the validity period after the expiry of the period specified in accordance with (c), he may be required to attend a second stage meeting (in the case of a writ-

ten improvement notice) or another third stage meeting (in the case of a final written improvement notice); and

(f) be signed and dated by the panel chair.

Assessment of performance or attendance following third stage meeting

Where a written improvement notice has been issued following a third stage meeting, the officer's performance or attendance will be assessed by his line manager in consultation with the second line manager or a human resources professional (or both). Where, as a result, the officer is required to attend a second stage meeting, that meeting must be concerned with unsatisfactory performance which is similar to or connected with the unsatisfactory performance referred to in the written notice.

Where a final written improvement notice has been issued or extended following a third stage meeting, then, as soon as possible after the expiry of the reasonable period for improvement specified in the notice, (a) the panel must assess the officer's performance or attendance (as the case may be), and (b) the panel chair must notify him whether the panel considers that there has been sufficient improvement. If it considers that there has not been sufficient improvement, the chair must, at the time he gives notification under (b), also notify the officer that he is required to attend another third stage meeting to consider his performance or attendance.

Where the officer concerned has not been so required to attend a third stage meeting, or has been so required to attend a third stage meeting but the panel did not make a finding of unsatisfactory performance or attendance at that meeting, the officer may be required to attend a third stage meeting if the panel considers that he has failed to make sufficient improvement during any part of the validity of the final written improvement notice (or extended final notice) remaining after the expiry of the specified period.

A third stage meeting under the above provisions must concern unsatisfactory performance or attendance which is similar to or connected with that referred to in the final written improvement notice (or extended final notice).

For the purposes of the above provisions, the panel must be that which conducted the initial third stage meeting, subject to the appointment of a substitute in accordance with the rules about panel composition where a panel member is unable to continue. In such a case the officer must be notified in writing of the appointment of a new member and he may object to that appointment in the same way as in the case of the appointment of the original panel.

Following such a third stage meeting, a panel may not order the extension of the final written improvement notice.

APPEAL TO POLICE APPEALS TRIBUNAL

Composition of tribunal

PA 1996, Sch 6 provides as follows.

In the case of an appeal by a member of a police force (other than a senior officer) or a special constable, the Police Appeals Tribunal consists of three members appointed by the relevant local policing body, of whom:

(a) the chair is qualified for judicial appointment,

(b) one is a senior officer, and

(c) one is a retired member of a police force who, at the time of his retirement, was a member of an appropriate staff association.

In the case of an appeal by a senior officer, the Police Appeals Tribunal consists of three members appointed by the Secretary of State, of whom:

(a) the chair is qualified for judicial appointment,
(b) one is an inspector of constabulary, and
(c) one is the permanent secretary to the Home Office or his nominee.

The relevant rules are contained in the Police Appeals Tribunals Rules 2008 (PATR 2008).

Right of appeal

A police officer against whom a finding has been made of misconduct or gross misconduct at a misconduct hearing, or of gross misconduct at a special case hearing, may appeal to the Police Appeals Tribunal against that finding or the disciplinary action which was taken, on one or more of the grounds that:

(a) the finding or disciplinary action imposed was unreasonable; or
(b) there is evidence that could not reasonably have been considered at the original hearing which could have materially affected the finding or decision on disciplinary action; or
(c) that there was a breach of the procedures set out in P(C)R 2008, P(CM)R 2012, PRA 2002, Sch 3, or other unfairness which could have materially affected the finding or decision on disciplinary action.

However, a police officer may not appeal to a tribunal against a *finding* where he accepted that his conduct amounted to misconduct or gross misconduct.

A police officer against whom a finding of unsatisfactory performance or attendance or gross incompetence has been made at a third stage meeting under P(P)R 2008 may appeal to the Police Appeals Tribunal. Where there has been a finding of unsatisfactory performance or attendance following a third stage meeting which was preceded by first and second stage meetings, the officer may appeal against the finding or against dismissal with notice or reduction in rank in consequence of the finding. Where there has been a finding of gross incompetence or unsatisfactory performance following a third stage meeting without a prior first or second stage meeting, the officer may appeal against the finding or consequent dismissal without notice; reduction in rank; redeployment to alternative duties; the issue of a final written improvement notice; or the issue of a written improvement notice.

The grounds of appeal are:

(a)   that the finding or outcome imposed was unreasonable; or
(b)   that there is evidence that could not reasonably have been considered at the original hearing which could have materially affected the finding or decision on the outcome; or
(c)   that there was a breach of the procedures set out in P(P)R 2008 or other unfairness which could have materially affected the finding or decision on the outcome; or
(d)   that, where the police officer was required to attend the third stage meeting following a second stage meeting, he should not have been required to attend that meeting as it did not concern unsatisfactory performance or attendance similar to or connected with the unsatisfactory performance or attendance referred to in the final written improvement notice.

Notice of appeal

A police officer who wishes to appeal to the tribunal must give to the relevant local policing body written notice of the appeal within 10 clear working days after the day on which he is supplied with a written copy of the relevant decision. The officer may request a transcript of the proceedings at the original hearing in his notice of appeal.

The 10-day rule does not apply where an officer gives reasons with his notice which persuade the chair that it was not reasonably practicable for the officer to give notice within the period and that the notice was given within a reasonable time after the end of that period.

Procedure on notice of appeal

As soon as reasonably practicable, the local policing body must supply a copy of the notice of appeal to the respondent (the relevant chief officer of police (or person designated by the relevant local policing body if the appellant is a senior officer)), and to IPCC where it is involved. Within 15 clear working days the respondent must supply the body with a copy of the relevant decision, any documents made available to the panel, and a copy of the transcript made at the hearing which has been requested by the appellant officer concerned. A copy of the transcript must at the same time be given to the appellant. In turn, the appellant must supply the local policing body with:

(a) a statement of the decision reached at the hearing and his grounds for appeal;
(b) any supporting documents;
(c) where the appellant is permitted to adduce witness evidence, a list of proposed witnesses together with a copy of their statements; and
(d) indicate whether he consents to the appeal being determined without a hearing.

Such documents must be supplied by the appellant within 20 clear working days of his receipt of a copy of the transcript or within 35 clear working days if no transcript was requested in the notice of appeal. For the purposes of (c), an appellant is only permitted to adduce witness evidence where his ground of appeal is that there is material evidence that could not reasonably have been considered at the original hearing, and a 'proposed witness' is a person whose evidence was not and could not reasonably have been considered at the original hearing and could have materially affected the relevant decision.

The local policing body must supply the respondent with a copy of the documents referred to in (a) to (d) as soon as practicable after their receipt, and the respondent must supply the local policing body, within 20 clear working days, with a statement of his response together with supporting documents and, where the respondent is permitted to adduce witness evidence, a list of proposed witnesses together with their statements. The respondent must also indicate in writing whether he consents to the appeal being dealt with without a hearing. The respondent is only permitted to adduce witness evidence where the appellant is relying on the ground of appeal that there is material evidence that could not reasonably have been considered at the original hearing, and a 'proposed witness' can give evidence relevant to all or part of the evidence on which the appellant is relying in relation to that ground.

The appellant or the respondent may apply to a local policing body for an extension to any of the time limits of 15, 20, or 35 working days. An extension may be arranged by agreement of the parties; otherwise the chair must determine whether the relevant period should be extended and, if so, for how long.

Review of appeal

On receipt of the above documents the chair must determine whether the appeal should be dismissed on the basis that there is no real prospect of success and no other compelling reason for proceeding. If the chair considers that it should be dismissed on this ground, he must, before making his determination, inform both sides in writing of his view and his reasons. Both parties may make written representations in response within 10 clear working days. Having considered them, the chair must give the appellant, respondent and local policing body written notice of his determination. In the case of dismissal of the appeal, the reasons must be given.

Where an appeal is not so dismissed, the chair must decide whether the appeal should be determined at a hearing. The chair may only determine that the appeal be determined without a hearing if the appellant consents. If there is to be a hearing, both sides must be given the name of the chair and his contact address, and the following rules apply.

Power to request disclosure of documents

At any time after the provision of documents by the appellant and the respondent as described above, either may apply to the chair for disclosure of any document by the other party which is relevant to the appeal. The chair may request such disclosure. A copy of a document so disclosed must be given to the chair and the requesting party. Where a party fails to comply with a request for disclosure, that party must provide the chair with reasons.

Notice of the hearing

The chair must get both parties provided with 20 clear days' notice of a hearing (or a shorter period if agreed). He must also determine which, if any, witnesses shall give evidence at the hearing. Witnesses who may be allowed to give evidence are those who the chair reasonably believes it is necessary to hear.
Where:

(a) the appellant is relying on the ground of appeal that there is material evidence that could not reasonably have been considered at the original hearing, and
(b) either the appellant or the respondent (or both) have proposed witnesses,

the chair must determine which, if any, witnesses must give evidence at the hearing. No witness may give evidence, unless the chair reasonably believes that it is necessary for him to do so, in which case the chair must, where the witness is a police officer, get that person ordered to attend the hearing, and, in any other case, cause the witness to be given notice that his attendance is necessary and of the date, time and place of the hearing.

Legal and other representation

An appellant has the right to choose representation by a lawyer or a police friend. Where he is represented by a lawyer, he may also be accompanied by a police friend. The respondent may also be represented by a lawyer or an officer of the police force or by the chief executive or other officer or employee of the local policing body.

Procedure at hearing

The procedure at a hearing is determined by the tribunal. The tribunal may proceed in the absence of either party, whether represented or not, if it appears to be just and proper to do so. Usually, the appellant's evidence must be adduced first and witnesses giving evidence may be subject to questioning and cross-questioning. Issues relating to admissibility, or whether any question should or should not be put to a witness must be determined by the tribunal. A verbatim record of the evidence must be taken and retained by the local policing body for at least two years.

The tribunal may admit as evidence a witness statement of a proposed witness supplied under the above rules, notwithstanding that the proposed witness is not to be called as a witness at the hearing, provided that such evidence would have been admissible if given orally. A written statement purporting to be made and signed by a person and witnessed by another person is presumed to have been made by that person unless the contrary is shown.

A hearing must be in private, although the tribunal may allow attendance of an observer for the purposes of training.

In the case of a 'complaint' which was certified as subject to special requirements under the special procedure referred to on p 300, the chair must get the complainant or any interested party notified of the hearing at the same time as notice is given to the appellant and respondent, and either, or both, may attend as an observer and be accompanied by one other person. If either has a 'special need' a further person may also attend to accommodate that need. Where a complainant, interested person or accompanying person is a proposed witness and is to give evidence, none of these persons may attend before that evidence is given. The chair may put questions to the appellant that the complainant or interested person has requested to be put.

In the case of a 'specified appeal' (one arising from a complaint or conduct matter in which the IPCC was involved in the investigation) the IPCC must be notified of the hearing, and may attend as an observer.

On the application of either the appellant or the respondent, the chair may require any observer to withdraw from the hearing. The chair may impose conditions in respect of the attendance at the hearing of an observer (or person accompanying a complainant or interested person) in order to facilitate its proper conduct.

Statement of tribunal's determination

The tribunal must determine whether the ground(s) of appeal have been made out. The determination may be by a simple majority and must not indicate whether it was unanimous or not. The chair must prepare a written statement of the determination and of the reasons for the decision.

Copies of the statement must be given to the appellant, respondent and local policing body as soon as reasonably practicable. In any event, the appellant must be given written notice of the decision within three clear working days. Where the decision followed a complaint which was certified as subject to special requirements under the special procedure, the local policing body must notify the complainant and any interested party of the tribunal's decision. In the case of a 'specified appeal', the local policing body must notify the IPCC of the decision.

RECORDING IN PERSONAL RECORDS OF OUTCOMES OF DISCIPLINARY OR PERFORMANCE PROCEEDINGS

The Police Regulations 2003 provide that records of service of officers must include particulars of:

(a) disciplinary action other than 'management advice' taken under P(C)R 2008 or ordered following an appeal to the Police Appeals Tribunal under PATR 2008;
(b) written improvement notices and final written improvement notices issued under the Police (Performance) Regulations 2008 following a first or second stage meeting respectively; and
(c) outcomes, other than redeployment to alternative duties, ordered under P(P)R 2008 following a third stage meeting or ordered following an appeal to the Police Appeals Tribunal under PATR 2008.

A written warning given under P(C)R 2008 must be expunged from the record of service after the period of 12 months, and a final written warning under those provisions must be expunged after a period of 18 months, subject in each case to the exclusion of any time taken as a career break. Where a final written warning was extended it must be expunged from the record on the expiry of that extended warning. A record of a reduction in rank must be expunged after a period of five years. Lastly, a record of a written improvement notice or final written improvement notice issued or extended must be expunged at the end of the period of validity as defined in P(P)R 2008, or at the end of any extended period.

However, a written warning or final written warning must not be expunged where, before the expiry of the relevant notice, a written notice is served on the officer notifying him of the appointment of an investigating officer to investigate an allegation that the officer's conduct has fallen below the Standards of Professional Behaviour set out on p 319, in which cases the written warning or final written warning will remain on the record until the conclusion of those disciplinary proceedings.

Where, following an appeal under either of P(C)R 2008, or a first or second stage appeal under P(P)R 2008, or an appeal to the Police Appeals Tribunal under PATR 2008, the person or persons hearing the appeal reverse, revoke, vary the terms of, or impose a different disciplinary action, outcome, or notice, the previous disciplinary action, outcome, or notice must be expunged forthwith.

RESTRICTIONS UPON PRIVATE LIVES OF MEMBERS OF POLICE FORCES

General

The Police Regulations 2003 impose a number of general restrictions upon the private lives of members of a police force. Schedule 1 to the Regulations lists the restrictions:

(1) A member of a police force must at all times abstain from any activity which is likely to interfere with the impartial discharge of his duties, or which is likely to give rise to the impression amongst members of the public that it might so interfere. A member of a police force must not take any active part in politics, nor belong to any organisation specified or described in a determination of the Secretary of State.
(2) A member of a police force must not reside at premises which are not for the time being approved by his chief officer of police.
(3) A member of a police force must not, without the previous consent of his chief officer, receive a lodger in a house or quarters with which he is provided by the local policing body or sublet any part of the house or quarters.
(4) A member of a police force must not, unless he has previously given notice to his chief officer, receive a lodger in a house in which he resides and in respect of which he receives a rent allowance or sublet any part of the house.

(5) A member of a police force must not wilfully refuse or neglect to discharge any lawful debt.

While not representing a 'restriction', the Police Regulations provide that every member of a police force must, on appointment, have a sample of hair or saliva taken. Such a specimen must be kept separate from specimens obtained under the provisions of PACE, s 63 and must be destroyed when the officer leaves the service. In addition, regulations provide the power to test for controlled drugs in respect of applicants to police forces, officers who give cause to suspect that they have used such drugs, probationers, officers whose work involves dealing with drugs, and officers in specialist roles. In the case of officers in specialist roles, a power to test for alcohol is also provided. The Secretary of State is given power to set out in a determination the consequences of testing positive in any of these situations.

Business interests

For the following purposes, a person has a 'business interest' if:

(a) being a member of a police force, he holds any office or employment for hire or gain (otherwise than as such a member) or carries on any business; or
(b) being a member of a police force or a relative of a member, he holds or possesses a pecuniary interest in a liquor or betting and gaming licence or permit (or certain similar types of licence) in his force area.

The Police Regulations 2003, as amended in 2012, require a member of a police force to give notice to his chief officer in writing of any actual or proposed business interest of himself or of a relative, ie his spouse or civil partner (not separated), cohabitee, parent, child, or sibling, unless that interest has previously been disclosed. However, in the case of a business interest held by a relative, the duty to notify arises only where the member is of the opinion that the interest could interfere with the discharge of his duties. On receipt of notification, the 'appropriate officer' (a person responsible for maintaining professional behaviour standards who has been authorised by the chief constable) must decide whether or not that business interest is compatible with the member's duties as a police officer. In making his decision, an appropriate officer must have regard to whether, as a result of the interest, the officer's conduct fails, or would fail, to meet the appropriate standard in the statutory Standards of Professional Behaviour (p 319).

Where the appropriate officer is minded to decide that the business interest is not compatible, or is not compatible unless conditions are imposed, he must:

(a) notify the member in writing of this preliminary view and the reasons for it;
(b) give the member the opportunity to make representations in writing, at a meeting, or both, at the discretion of the member; and
(c) take any such representations into account.

Whether or not such notification is given, the appropriate officer must, within 28 days of receipt of the member's notice, notify the member of his decision. Where the decision is that the business interest is not compatible, or is not compatible unless conditions are imposed, the notification must:

(a) include a statement of the reasons for the decision;
(b) be accompanied by copies of any document on which the officer relies in support of the decision; and
(c) inform the member of the existence of the right of appeal to the chief officer.

Where, on such an appeal, it appears to the chief officer that the member has adduced substantive reasons why he should be permitted to have the business interest, or why conditions should not be imposed, or that in reaching his determination the appropriate officer failed to apply fair procedures, he may remit the matter back to the appropriate officer for redetermination. Otherwise he must determine the appeal.

Where a business interest has been held by the appropriate officer to be incompatible with continued membership of the force, and either no appeal has been made or such an appeal has been made and the chief officer has upheld the decision of the appropriate officer, the decision of the appropriate officer is regarded as a lawful order for the purposes of the Standards of Professional Behaviour and, in the event of any failure to abide by the decision, as though the appropriate authority had determined under the Police (Conduct) Regulations 2008 that the member had a case to answer in respect of gross misconduct.

The above functions of the chief officer may be exercised only by the chief officer personally or by an acting chief officer.

PROBATIONARY SERVICE

The Police Regulations 2003 provide that a member of a police force appointed in the rank of constable is always on probation for such period as the Secretary of State determines. This applies to all members of a police force appointed in the rank of constable other than a member who transfers to the force from another force, having completed the required period of probation therein. Where, in the opinion of the chief officer of police (which term hereafter includes an assistant commissioner in the Metropolitan Police), the period of probation was seriously interrupted by a period of absence from duty, by reason of injury or illness, probation may be extended for a longer period, not exceeding 12 months, as determined in the particular circumstances. Such an extension may be made after the expiry of the initial probationary period if the probationer constable was on sick leave at the time of expiry. It may also be extended for other reasons. The power to extend a constable's period of probation may be delegated to an assistant chief constable, but a decision to dispense with the services of a probationer constable may only be taken by the chief officer himself.

An officer who transfers from one force to another and has already successfully completed not less than one year of probationary service in that or any other police force will thereafter be on probation for one year (unless extended as above). However, the chief officer may reduce this period, provided that the total probationary service is not less than two years.

This period of probationary service is used to establish whether or not a person is fitted mentally and physically to perform the duties of a constable. A probationer constable may be discharged at any time if his chief officer considers that he is not so fitted. The word 'mentally' is not used to indicate a level of academic acceptability. The demands of the job can be considerable and the pressures can be too much for those who are not equipped to handle certain situations.

The chief officer may also dispense with the services of a probationer if he considers that he is not likely to become an efficient or well-conducted police officer. A judge in the Administrative Court has held that this power to discharge does not apply where the reason is the misconduct of the probationer constable; the only way in which a probationer constable can be dismissed on grounds of misconduct is as a result of formal misconduct proceedings.

Where a chief officer is considering dispensing with the services of a probationary constable under these regulations, the probationer constable must be shown any report containing judgements and opinions on him. However, it has been held that where the grounds for dispensing with his services are that, in the opinion of medical officers, he is too overweight to carry out his duties satisfactorily, there would be no purpose in such action as any further observation could not alter the decision.

DATA PROTECTION

The Data Protection Act 1998 (DPA 1998) is concerned with the regulation of processing of information relating to individuals, including the obtaining, holding, use or disclosure of such information.

Principles

Unless exempted by the Act, a 'data controller' is obliged to comply with certain 'data protection principles' in relation to all 'personal data' in relation to which he is data controller. A 'data controller' is a person who (alone or jointly or in common with others) determines the purposes for which and the way in which any personal data are, or are to be, processed. It follows that each chief constable is a data controller.

The 'data protection principles' are:

(1) Personal data must be processed fairly and lawfully and, in particular, must not be processed unless:
   (a) the data subject (DS) has given his consent, or the processing is necessary for the performance of a contract to which DS is a party (or for the taking of steps at the request of DS with a view to entering into a contract), or is required by law, or is necessary to protect the vital interests of DS, or is necessary in the interests of the administration of justice, or in certain other cases, and
   (b) in the case of 'sensitive personal data' (eg an individual's racial origin, political or religious belief, health or commission (or alleged commission) of an offence), DS has given his explicit consent, or the processing is necessary for exercising or performing any right or duty imposed by law on the data controller in connection with employment, or is necessary to protect the vital interests of DS (if the consent of DS cannot be given or cannot reasonably be expected to be obtained), or is necessary in the interests of justice, or in certain other cases.
   The application of this principle does not usually apply to the processing of personal data for the purpose of preventing or detecting crime.
(2) Personal data must be obtained only for one or more specified and lawful purposes, and may not be further processed in any manner incompatible with it or them.
(3) Personal data must be adequate, relevant and not excessive in relation to the purpose or purposes for which processed.
(4) Personal data must be accurate and, where necessary, kept up to date.
(5) Personal data processed for any purpose or purposes may not be kept longer than necessary for it or them.
(6) Personal data must be processed in accordance with the rights of data subjects under the DPA 1998.

(7) Appropriate technical and organisational measures must be taken against unauthorised or unlawful processing of personal data and against accidental loss or destruction of, or damage to, personal data.

(8) Personal data must not be transferred to a country or territory outside the EEA unless that country or territory ensures an adequate level of protection for the rights and freedoms of data subjects in relation to the processing of personal data.

'Data' means information which:

(a) is being processed by means of equipment operating automatically in response to instructions given for that purpose;

(b) is recorded with the intention that it should be processed by means of such equipment;

(c) is recorded as part of a relevant filing system or with the intention that it should form part of a relevant filing system;

(d) does not fall within paragraphs (a), (b) or (c) but forms part of an educational, health or accessible public record of a prescribed type; or

(e) is recorded information held by a public authority and does not fall within (a) to (d).

'Personal data' means data which relate to a living individual who can be identified:

(a) from those data, or

(b) from those data and other information which is in the possession of, or is likely to come into the possession of, the data controller,

and includes any expression of opinion about the individual and any indication of the intentions of the data controller or any other person in respect of the individual.

There is no statutory constraint on the purposes for which personal data may be retained, other than that a purpose must be lawful. In particular, the police are entitled to retain personal data relating to convictions, including spent convictions, however old or minor, not only for core purposes (the prevention and detection of crime, the investigation and apprehension of offenders, or the maintenance of law and order) but also for non-core purposes (eg to supply accurate records of convictions to the CPS or the courts).

Registration

'Data controllers' must register with the Information Commissioner in order for 'personal data' to be processed if that personal data falls within types (a) or (b) *of the definition of 'data' above*, but not (normally) in the case of the other types of data. Thus, the manual files retained within command and control systems do not require registration, but data stored on the Police National Computer does.

By DPA 1998, s 21(1), it is an indictable (either way) offence to process personal data unless an entry in respect of the data controller has been registered.

Unlawful obtaining, etc of personal data

DPA 1998, s 55(1) provides it is an offence knowingly or recklessly, without the consent of the data controller, to:

(a) obtain or disclose personal data or the information contained in personal data; or

(b) procure the disclosure to another person of the information contained in personal data.

It is a defence to show:

(a) that the obtaining, disclosing or procuring:
  (i) was necessary to prevent or detect crime (as where the data is passed from one police force to another for this purpose); or
  (ii) was required or authorised by or under any law or court order;

(b) that the defendant reasonably believed that he had in law the right to obtain or disclose the data or information or, as the case may be, to procure the disclosure of the information to the other person;

(c) that he reasonably believed that he would have had the consent of the data controller if the data controller had known of the obtaining, disclosing, or procuring and the circumstances of it;

(d) from a day to be appointed, that he acted:
  (i)   for the special purposes (ie the purposes of journalism, artistic purposes, and literary purposes),
  (ii) with a view to the publication by any person of any journalistic, literary, or artistic material, and
  (iii) in the reasonable belief that in the particular circumstances the obtaining, disclosing, or procuring was justified as being in the public interest; or

(e) that in the particular circumstances the obtaining, disclosing or procuring was justified as being in the public interest.

By DPA 1998, s 55(4), a person who sells personal data is guilty of an offence if he has obtained the data in contravention of s 55(1). Section 55(5) provides that a person who offers to sell personal data commits an offence if he has obtained it in contravention of s 55(1) or if he subsequently does so.

Offences under s 55 are indictable (either way) offences.

Prohibition of requirement as to production of certain records

DPA 1998, s 56(1) prospectively provides that a person must not, in connection with:

(a) the recruitment of another person as an employee;

(b) the continued employment of another person; or

(c) any contract for the provision of services to him by another person,

require that other person or a third party to supply him with a relevant record or to produce a relevant record to him.

Likewise, DPA 1998, s 56(2) prospectively provides that a person concerned with the provision (for payment or not) of goods, facilities or services to the public or a section of the public must not, as a condition of providing or offering to provide any goods, facilities or services to another person, require that other person or a third party to supply him with a relevant record or to produce a relevant record to him.

Breach of either of these provisions is an indictable (either way) offence. A 'relevant record' in these provisions includes any record of a conviction or caution obtained by a data subject from a data controller who is a chief officer of police or the Director General of SOCA.

DPA 1998, s 56(1) and (2) do not apply to a person who shows that:

(a) the imposition of the requirement was required or authorised by or under any enactment, by any rule of law or by the order of a court; or

(b) in the particular circumstances the imposition of the requirement was justified as being in the public interest (which it will not be if the alleged justification is that it would assist in the prevention or detection of crime; in such a case one of the various types of certificate of criminal record under the Police Act 1997, Pt V will be available from the Disclosure and Barring Service (DBS), which has been formed out of a merger of the Criminal Records Bureau and the Independent Safeguarding Authority).

CHAPTER 9

Traffic: General Provisions

TERMINOLOGY

Mechanically propelled vehicle

The means of propulsion may be petrol, diesel, gas, steam, or electricity. Whether or not a vehicle is mechanically propelled is a question of fact. Motor cars which are broken down on a road remain mechanically propelled vehicles; it is irrelevant that they might not be driven at that particular time. Before a vehicle can cease to be a mechanically propelled vehicle it must be in such a condition or in such circumstances that there is no reasonable prospect of it ever being driven again. Where a vehicle has been immobilised the extent of the immobilisation is the critical factor when considering whether it remains a mechanically propelled vehicle. A motor car in a scrap yard, stripped of all of its mechanical means of propulsion and without any reasonable prospect of the restoration of motive power, is obviously not a mechanically propelled vehicle. However, a motor car similarly stripped down in a garage to effect repairs remains a mechanically propelled vehicle as there is a reasonable prospect of it being restored to its former mobility.

Motor vehicle

This is defined by the Road Traffic Act 1988 (RTA 1988), s 185 as a mechanically propelled vehicle intended or adapted for use on a road. The words *'intended or adapted for use on a road'* are important. 'Adapted' does not mean 'altered'; it simply means 'fit and apt'. Some vehicles are quite obviously 'mechanically propelled' but they are not 'intended or adapted for use on a road'.

Whether or not a mechanically propelled vehicle is intended or adapted for use on a road depends on whether a reasonable person looking at the vehicle would say that one of its uses is general use on a road. On this basis, for example, it has been held that three types of motorised scooter known as a 'Segway', 'Go-ped', and 'City Mantis' were motor vehicles within s 185. A 'Segway' consisted of a small gyroscopically stabilised platform mounted on two wheels, on which the traveller stood, powered by a battery driven electric motor. A vertical joy-stick was used to steer. Speed was controlled by leaning forward (to go faster) or standing up straight (to slow down). A divisional court held that, although the expectations, advice and intentions of the manufacturer were that it should not be used on a road, they did not provide the answer to the question whether a Segway was a motor vehicle; the judge had not been wrong in concluding that a Segway was a motor vehicle within s 185. A 'Go-ped' consisted of a small foot platform attached to a sub-frame on which the person using the Go-ped would stand. It was powered by a 22.5 cc engine attached to the rear. It was capable of a maximum speed of 20 mph. The braking system was such that it could not stop the vehicle if it was travelling at any great speed, or when the brakes were applied in an emergency situation. Severe braking caused the rear wheel to lift from the road surface. A divisional court said that the roadworthiness of a conveyance or its capability to be used safely on a road were not conclusive in relation to whether or not its use on a road was contemplated. There was no obvious place in which a Go-ped could be used, other than on a road. It could not travel on rough ground, soft or uneven surfaces. It was not designed for use in a place other than a road. Regardless of the fact that the manufacturers said that it was not to be used on a road it would be and the reasonable person would recognise that to be so. Likewise, a divisional court has held that a 'City Mantis' electric scooter was a motor vehicle. It was battery operated and capable of a speed of 10 mph. The court considered that the vehicle could only be used on smooth and even surfaces and a reasonable person might well conclude that the best place to find such surfaces was on a road.

The above test does not depend on the owner's or manufacturer's intention. Unless there is evidence of regular use on a road, the particular use to which the vehicle is put at the time is irrelevant to the above test. In one case, a dumper truck, which was used on a site for the transport of material around that site and was occasionally driven on adjoining roads for short distances, was held not to be a motor vehicle because there was no proof of general (as opposed to occasional) use on roads. On the other hand, in another case, a Euclid earth scraper, which was primarily used to dig up earth on a building site and carry that earth under its own power to other places, was held to be intended for use on a road when evidence of its general use on roads and of its capability of reaching a speed of 45 mph was given. Evidence was also offered to prove that the earth scraper was too large to be transportable and generally travelled from site to site by road.

RTA 1988, s 189 expressly provides that pedestrian-controlled lawnmowers and 'electrically assisted pedal cycles' (p 451) are not motor vehicles. Mechanically propelled invalid carriages of a prescribed type are expressly excluded from the definition of motor vehicle in s 185; mobility scooters are therefore not motor vehicles.

A mechanically propelled vehicle originally manufactured for use on a road may cease to be a 'motor vehicle' for the purposes of RTA 1988, s 185 if it is subsequently altered, but only if such alterations are very substantial.

Road

This is defined by RTA 1988, s 192 as meaning any highway and any other road to which the public has access and including bridges over which a road passes.

Highway

A 'highway' is defined by the common law. It is a way over which there exists a public right of passage on foot, riding, accompanied by a beast of burden or with vehicles and cattle. The term is therefore wide enough to embrace public footpaths, bridleways and carriageways, defined below. It is presumed that the boundary of the highway is defined by the buildings, hedges, fences, walls or the like along its route. Consequently, grass verges are generally a part of the highway. If, for example, a fence behind a grass verge was erected by the highway authority it would clearly mark the limits of the highway. If it was erected by an adjoining landowner this would not necessarily be so.

A footpath is a highway over which the public has a right of way on foot alone.

A bridleway is a highway over which the public has a right of way while on foot, on horseback or leading a horse. By the Countryside Act 1968, s 30, the public also has a right to ride a pedal bicycle on a bridleway (provided that the cyclist gives way to pedestrians and persons on horseback). The right to ride a pedal cycle on a bridleway may be controlled by a local authority order. There may be a right on some bridleways to drive animals and such bridleways may be referred to locally as 'droves' or 'driftways'.

A carriageway is a way constructed or comprised in a highway, being a way (other than a cycle track) over which the public has a right of way on foot, on horseback, or with vehicles or cattle.

Road

Apart from a highway, 'road' in the road traffic legislation means any road (ie a definable way for passage between two points) to which the public has access. The essential factor is whether or not, as a question of fact, the public in general has access to the road. A private road leading to a farmhouse, which was maintained by the farmer, has been held to be a 'road' on evidence being offered that there was no gate and that it was regularly used by persons who had no business at the farm. Likewise, a divisional court has held that justices were entitled to find that tarmacked roadways across a caravan park to a beach, which had road markings and were easily definable as routes leading from one point to another on a map and to which the public had unrestricted access, were 'roads'. It has been decided that any road may be regarded as a road to which the public has access, if members of the public are to be found on it who have not obtained access either by overcoming a physical obstruction or in defiance of a prohibition, express or implied. A pavement which is partly publicly owned and partly privately owned is a road if the public has access to the whole of it. It is essential to show that the public in general has access. Access which is restricted to certain classes of person is not usually sufficient to make a road 'public'.

Where a road within a housing estate has not been adopted by the local authority, the determining factor is not whether the road is repairable at public expense but whether the public has access to it. If members of the public are seen there, and their presence is tolerated, it is a road.

The House of Lords has ruled that a road is provided for the purpose of moving from one place to another as opposed to parking a car. It said that even though a part of a car park might be made up of routes giving access to parking bays this, by itself, was not enough if those routes merely gave access to parking bays and were not for the purpose of travelling from one place to another. In another case where a driver was charged with driving on a 'road' within a station car park on the grounds that station staff drove through it in order to reach their own private car park, a divisional court held that such use was insufficient to permit the car park to be described as a road. In a third case the 'road' concerned was within a caravan and camping site which contained privately owned residential caravans, but guests and campers were also permitted entry. A tarmac road encircled the site but driving could only be proved to have taken place on the grass area of the site. A divisional court rejected the magistrates' finding that this area was a 'road' and observed that the justices appeared to have decided that a road was a place to which the public had access. The place was not a road for the purposes of RTA 1988.

REGISTRATION

For a variety of reasons, all vehicles used or kept on roads in the UK must be registered with the Secretary of State. A 'vehicle' for this purpose is a mechanically propelled vehicle, or anything (whether or not a vehicle) that has been, but has ceased to be, a mechanically propelled vehicle. All records relating to vehicles are retained by the Driver and Vehicle Licensing Agency (DVLA) at Swansea (or Coleraine, in the case of Northern Ireland). One of the purposes of central registration is to ensure the payment of vehicle excise duty; another is separately to identify all vehicles used or kept on roads by allocating to each a registration mark which is different from any mark assigned to any other vehicle.

The Road Safety Act (RSA) 2006, s 49 provides statutory authority for the Secretary of State to disclose information held by him under the Vehicle Excise and Registration Act (VERA) 1994, (registration of vehicles) to the authorities of a country or territory outside the UK in respect of registration particulars. RSA 2006, s 49A contains a corresponding provision for the disclosure by the Secretary of State to specified bodies (generally government departments) of information in foreign registers which has been obtained.

The Road Vehicles (Registration and Licensing) Regulations (RV(R&L)R) 2002 provide a single set of Regulations for the whole of the UK.

VERA 1994, s 21 provides that it is the duty of the Secretary of State to register a vehicle on the first issue by him of a vehicle licence or a nil licence (ie a licence for a vehicle exempt from excise duty), or where particulars in respect of the vehicle are received by the Secretary of State from a motor dealer before the first licence is issued. The registration mark assigned to a vehicle must be fitted in the prescribed manner. Since it is the Secretary of State's responsibility to register vehicles, the use of an unregistered vehicle on a road simply constitutes the offence of use without a vehicle excise licence. If it has been registered, but registration plates have not been fixed on it, an offence under s 42(1) is committed by the driver or, if the vehicle is not being driven, by the person keeping the vehicle.

In addition to the assignment of a registration number on initial registration, the Secretary of State has power to assign new registration numbers to a vehicle in place of its existing ones. The Secretary of State also has power to assign to a vehicle (whether on first registration or not) registration numbers previously assigned to another vehicle. It is these powers which give effect to the practice of trading in personalised number plates. The Secretary of State may also grant to a person the right to retain a registration number by transferring it from one vehicle registered in that person's name to another such vehicle.

VERA 1994, s 22 authorises the Secretary of State to make regulations concerning vehicle registration. RV(R&L)R 2002, reg 10 authorises the Secretary of State to register a vehicle in either the Great Britain or Northern Ireland records as he considers appropriate and to issue a registration document. He may require the keeper of a vehicle to produce it for inspection or to produce other evidence that the vehicle accords with the particulars furnished with the application. If he is not satisfied that the vehicle accords with the particulars, he may refuse to issue a registration document or replacement registration document. Regulation 11 provides that, where a keeper of a vehicle requests that a particular registration mark is assigned to it, that mark having been previously assigned to another vehicle, that other vehicle shall be made available for inspection by the Secretary of State.

VEHICLES: REGISTRATION MARKS AND DOCUMENTS

Registration document

When the Secretary of State registers a vehicle a registration document is issued and, unless a registration mark has already been assigned by a motor dealer who has received a 'block' of numbers, a registration mark is assigned to that vehicle. Even if a vehicle is exempt from the requirement to be licensed, it must still be registered. A registration document contains the registered particulars of the vehicle and the name and address of the person shown in the register as the owner or keeper of the vehicle. The Secretary of State has power to issue, without charge and on surrender of the existing registration document, a registration document which complies with Community Directive 1999/37/EC in relation to dimensions, composition and the information to be contained in it.

On first registration of a vehicle registered in another member state of the EU or Gibraltar, the Secretary of State must retain for not less than six months the former registration document surrendered and notify the appropriate member state or Gibraltar in which the vehicle was previously registered.

The Secretary of State may issue a registration document in a microprocessor smart card format and may issue that type of registration document without charging a fee where the old type of document is surrendered.

The registered owner of a vehicle is not necessarily its legal owner, and possession of a registration document is not in itself proof of ownership.

RV(R&L)R 2002, reg 13 provides that where a registration document has been, or may have been, lost, stolen, destroyed, or damaged, or it contains any particulars that have become illegible, the registered keeper must apply for a replacement. In the case of damage or illegibility, the document must accompany the application. In any other case an oral application by telephone may be accepted. Provided that the Secretary of State is satisfied as to the circumstances, the Secretary of State must issue a replacement document. Before this is done, the keeper of the vehicle may be required to produce the vehicle, or evidence that it accords with its currently registered particulars.

RV(R&L)R 2002, reg 15(3) and Sch 3 provide for the issue of a new registration document in certain circumstances where an insurer has informed the Secretary of State that it has 'written off' the vehicle concerned and destroyed the registration document, or the registration document has been surrendered on a change of keeper; the Schedule requires the production and examination of the vehicle in order to ascertain that it is the vehicle concerned.

By reg 12, the keeper of a vehicle must produce a registration document for inspection if required to do so at any reasonable time by a constable or person acting on the Secretary of State's behalf. There are no provisions for later production.

VERA 1994, s 28A requires a person *using* a vehicle in respect of which a registration document has been issued to produce it for inspection by a constable or a person authorised by the Secretary of State (who must produce his authority). Failure to do so is an offence. However, no offence is committed if the person produces the document personally at a police station specified by him within seven days or as soon as is reasonably practicable. Nor is an offence committed if a vehicle is on lease or hire, and the vehicle is not registered (nor required to be registered) in the name of the lessee or hirer, and he personally produces appropriate evidence of the lease or hire agreement in the same way as just described. However, he must reasonably believe (or it must be reasonable for him to expect) that the lessor, etc is able to produce, or require production, of the registration document.

The Road Traffic (Vehicle Testing) Act 1999 provides a statutory basis for the establishment of a central computer database of motor vehicles. This provides the option of vehicle relicensing online.

Notification of change of ownership

RV(R&L)R 2002, reg 22 is concerned with changes of ownership affecting vehicles. *Where there is a 'private' sale or transfer of a vehicle*, ie to a person other than a motor vehicle trader, the registered keeper must give to the new keeper the part of the registration document which provides for particulars of a new keeper, and must forthwith send to the Secretary of State the remainder of the registration document giving:

(a) the name and address of the new keeper;
(b) the date of transfer;
(c) a signed declaration that this information is correct to the best of his knowledge; and
(d) a signed declaration made by the new keeper to the effect that this information is correct.

By reg 23, *where the new keeper is a vehicle trader*, the registered keeper must notify the Secretary of State, on the part of the registration document which relates to the transfer to a vehicle trader of the name and address of the vehicle trader and the date on which the transfer took place, and he must send declarations from both himself and the vehicle trader to the effect that the transfer occurred on the specified date. On or before the 'appropriate date', the trader must notify the Secretary of State of the date of his acquisition of the vehicle (reg 24). The 'appropriate date' is the earliest of the day of first use or keeping of the vehicle on a public road otherwise than under a trade licence, or the day following the expiry of a three-month period. If there is a transfer to another vehicle trader within the three-month period, the registration document must be transferred with the vehicle.

Where a vehicle trader transfers the vehicle to a person other than another vehicle trader or transfers the vehicle to another trader outside the three-month period, he must, on the appropriate part of the registration document, inform the Secretary of State of:

(a) the name and address of the new keeper;
(b) the date of transfer;
(c) sign a declaration to the effect that he transferred the vehicle to the new keeper on the date specified; and
(d) sign a declaration from the new keeper that the vehicle was transferred to him on the date specified.

Where all parts of the registration document have been, or may have been, lost, stolen or destroyed, the new keeper *whether or not a trader* must submit an application for a new registration document and send the prescribed fee. If the new keeper can produce that part of the registration document which is to be given to the new keeper, no fee need be sent.

Failure to notify the Secretary of State is not a continuing offence and therefore the time limitation upon proceedings runs from the day of the transfer of the vehicle. If, therefore, a period of six months has passed since the transfer of a vehicle no proceedings may be taken against either of the parties to the transaction if they have failed to comply with the requirement to notify the Secretary of State forthwith.

Notification of other changes

An owner of a registered vehicle who changes his name or address is required by RV(R&L)R 2002, reg 18 forthwith to notify the Secretary of State and deliver the registration document to him. Where the registration document has been, or may have been, lost, stolen or destroyed, notification must be accompanied by a fee.

In the event of a vehicle being sent permanently out of Great Britain or Northern Ireland, reg 17 requires notification of that fact and the surrender of the registration document. Regulation 17A requires that where an 'end-of-life' vehicle is transferred to an authorised treatment facility (facility operating under a waste disposal site licence) the facility must, in addition to issuing a 'certificate of destruction' to the last holder/owner of the vehicle, inform the Secretary of State of the issue of that certificate. No further records may then be made which are related to that vehicle.

RV(R&L)R 2002, reg 16 is concerned with procedures which must be followed when any alteration to a vehicle renders the particulars in the registration document incorrect, as where it is resprayed a different colour or has a different engine fitted. Such alterations must be notified to the Secretary of State in writing by the owner and the registration document surrendered for amendment. Once again, if the registration document is not available, an application must be made for a new registration document and be accompanied by a fee. Should the alteration necessitate changes to the vehicle excise licence, it must also be surrendered by the owner for amendment.

Offence of using incorrectly registered vehicle

VERA 1994, s 43C(1) and (2) provides that it is an offence to use a vehicle on a public road or in a public place if excise duty is chargeable in respect of it, or it is an exempt vehicle which requires a 'Nil' licence, where the name and address of its keeper are not recorded in the register, or any particulars recorded in the register are incorrect.

It is a defence for the defendant (D) to show that there was no reasonable opportunity, before the material time, to furnish:

(a) the name and address of the keeper of the vehicle; or
(b) particulars correcting the incorrect particulars (s 43C(3)).

It is also a defence for D to show:

(a) that he had reasonable grounds for believing, or it was reasonable for him to expect, that the name and address of the keeper or the other particulars of registration (as the case may be) were correctly recorded in the register; or
(b) that any prescribed exception is met. No such exception has been prescribed at the time of writing (s 43C(4)).

The offence under s 43C has the effect of extending responsibility for ensuring that correct details are recorded in the register to those who use vehicles, subject to the defences provided.

Regulation of motor salvage operators

The Vehicles (Crime) Act 2001 (V(C)A 2001) was passed to tackle the problem caused where vehicles are stolen, and then either broken up for their parts or 'ringed' (ie the true identity of the car is swapped for a written-off car).

Part I deals with motor salvage operators. It requires that all persons who carry on a business as 'motor salvage operators' must be registered with the local authority. The term 'motor salvage operator' covers those who carry on a business consisting:

(a) wholly *or partly* in the recovery for re-use or sale of salvageable parts from vehicles and the subsequent sale or other disposal for scrap of the remainder of the vehicle concerned (which definition covers scrap metal dealers);
(b) wholly *or mainly* in the purchase of written-off vehicles and their subsequent repair and resale;

(c) wholly *or mainly* in the sale or purchase of motor vehicles which are to be subject (whether immediately or on a subsequent resale) to any of the activities at (a) and (b); or

(d) wholly *or mainly* in activities falling within (b) and (c).

It will be noted that V(C)A 2001 refers to *motor vehicles* to which the Act gives a special definition. In the present context a 'motor vehicle' is one whose function is or was to be used on a road as a vehicle.

A local authority may refuse to register a person whom it considers to be unfit to carry on such a business. An appeal lies to a magistrates' court against such a decision. V(C)A 2001, ss 1(1), 7(4), and 8(3) create offences of failure to register, failure to keep appropriate records, and failure to notify the Secretary of State of the destruction of a motor vehicle. By ss 10(1) and 11(4), respectively, a person commits an offence if he makes a false statement in an application for registration, or if he fails to give notice of any change in the registered information. V(C)A 2001, s 12 makes it an offence for any person to give a false name or address to a motor salvage operator when selling a vehicle to him.

V(C)A 2001, s 9 provides a constable with a power of entry at any reasonable time into registered premises which are occupied as a 'motor salvage yard' by a person carrying on a business as a motor salvage operator or are occupied by him in relation to that business. At any reasonable time a constable may require the production of, and inspect, motor vehicles, salvageable parts or records, and may take copies or extracts of entries. Provision is also made for the issue of a warrant authorising entry and inspection. Force may not be used in respect of general entry, but it may be used in association with the execution of a warrant. When effecting entry without a warrant, a constable must, if required by or on behalf of the owner or occupier or person in charge of the premises, produce evidence of identity, and of his authority for entering, before doing so.

V(C)A 2001, s 8 provides for regulations to be made requiring registered motor salvage operators to notify the Secretary of State of the destruction of motor vehicles. No such regulations have been made at the time of writing. The Motor Salvage Operators Regulations 2002 require motor salvage operators to keep records of such vehicles passing through their hands. The records must contain a range of specified information about a vehicle: registration number; vehicle identification number; make; model; colour; identity of supplier or receiver of the vehicle; details of proof of his identity and the condition of the vehicle; and the date on which the information was entered. It is an offence under V(C)A 2001, s 7(4) to fail to record any of this information, except information relating to proof of identity or the vehicle's condition.

Registration marks

Generally

VERA 1994, s 42(1) and (3) makes it an offence to drive a motor vehicle or (when it is not being driven) to be its keeper when a registration mark is not fixed to it as required by VERA 1994, s 23. D has a defence if he proves that he had no reasonable opportunity to register the vehicle and that it was being driven for the purpose of being registered (s 42(4)).

The Road Vehicles (Display of Registration Marks) Regulations 2001 (RV(DRM)R 2001) deal with the forms of registration marks and the manner in which they are fixed to vehicles.

RV(DRM)R 2001, reg 10 and Sch 2 introduce a mandatory requirement for the use of registration plates made of retro-reflecting material conforming to British Standard specification BS AU 145a or an equivalent standard laid down by a European Economic Area (EEA) state on all vehicles first registered on or after 1 September 2001, and on all vehicles registered before that date but on or after 1 January 1973 if an existing plate is replaced. Regulation 10 and Sch 2 also set out the requirements for vehicles registered on or after 1 January 1973 and before 1 September 2001 in other circumstances (reflex-reflecting plates conforming to British Standard specification BS AU 145a or an equivalent standard laid down by an EEA state) but such vehicles *may* carry the forms of plates prescribed for vehicles first registered on or after 1 September 2001. In either case they must have black characters on a white background on a front plate; and black characters on a yellow background on a rear plate.

Schedule 2 also deals with vehicles registered before 1 January 1973. It provides optional specifications by requiring that where the plate is such that it may be illuminated from behind by virtue of the translucency of its characters they must be white translucent characters on a black background, and when illuminated the characters must appear white against a black background. Otherwise, plates must comply with BS AU 145 carrying black characters on a white background at the front and black characters on a yellow background at the rear; alternatively, they must be white, silver, or light grey letters and numbers on a black surface which are indelibly inscribed on the plate and cannot readily be detached.

Permitted layouts

RV(DRM)R 2001, reg 13 and Sch 3 govern this. Registration marks in any non-permitted format are unlawful. The marks may be, for example, a group consisting of two letters and two numbers followed by a group of three letters (eg DE51 ABC); a group consisting of a single letter and not more than three numbers followed by a group of three letters (eg A123 ABC); a group of three letters followed by a group consisting of not more than three numbers and a single letter (eg ABC 123A); a group of four numbers followed by a single letter or a group of two letters (eg 1234 A, 1234 AB); a group of not more than three numbers followed by a group of not more than three letters (eg 123 ABC, 123 AB, 12 A); a group of not more than three letters followed by a group of not more than three numbers (eg ABC 123, AB 123, A 12); a single letter or group of two letters followed by a group of four numbers (eg A 1234, AB 1234); and in Northern Ireland, a group of three letters followed by a group of four numbers (ABZ 1234) or a group of four numbers followed by a group of three letters (eg 1234 ABZ).

It is not necessary that these letters and numbers all follow one another. The plates may be square permitting the letters and characters to be placed in two or three rows, except that plates containing three rows of characters are not permitted on vehicles first registered on or after 1 September 2001 or a replacement plate fixed to a vehicle first registered before then but on or after 1 January 1973. Plates containing all of the letters and numbers in a straight line are not permitted on motor cycles.

Character sizes and fonts

RV(DRM)R 2001, reg 14 and Sch 3 deal with the size and spacing of characters. Regulation 14 provides that the registration marks of vehicles must be 79 mm high. In respect of vehicles first registered before 1 September 2001 the registration marks may be 78 mm high instead of 79 mm, except where the vehicle was first registered on or after 1 January 1973 and the mark is displayed on a new registration plate. By way of further exception, the required height is 64 mm in relation to a motor cycle, motor tricycle, quadricycle, agricultural machine, works truck or road roller. The width of characters, spacing, and margins are all precisely prescribed by Table B in Sch 3.

Regulation 14A applies special rules to a vehicle imported into the UK which does not have EC Whole Vehicle Type Approval and is so constructed that the area available for the fixing of the registration plate precludes the display on the plate of a registration mark in conformity with the requirements of reg 14. In such a case the prescribed height of characters is 64 mm; the width (except for the letter 'I' or figure '1') must be 44 mm; the width of every part of a stroke and the spacing of characters within a group must be 10 mm, the vertical spacing between groups of characters and the width of a margin between the mark and the top and lateral sides of the registration plate must not be less than 5 mm; and the space between the bottom of the mark and the bottom of the registration plate must not be less than 13 mm.

RV(DRM)R 2001, reg 12(2) permits deviation from the prescribed height of characters provided that the deviation is not more than 1 mm either way. In the case of other dimensions, including spaces, the permitted deviation is 0.5 mm either way.

RV(DRM)R 2001, reg 15 and Sch 4 deal with the font of characters displayed on a registration plate fixed to a vehicle first registered on or after 1 September 2001, or on a new registration plate fixed to any other vehicle (except where the vehicle was first registered before 1 January 1973). They require that each of the characters must be in the prescribed font. In relation to other cases, characters must be in the prescribed font or in a style which is substantially similar to the prescribed font so that the character is easily distinguishable but, in the latter case, characters must not be formed in italic script (or other script which is not vertical), or in script in which the curvature or alignment of the lines of the strokes is substantially different from the prescribed font, or in script using multiple or a broken stroke or in such a way that a character, or characters, appear like a different character or characters. A character will not be treated as substantially different solely on the grounds that it has, or does not have, serifs (small lines at the extremity of a main stroke).

Fixing of rear registration plates: post-1938 vehicles

RV(DRM)R 2001, reg 5 (which applies to all vehicles first registered on or after 1 October 1938 other than works trucks, road rollers and agricultural machines) requires a rear registration plate to be fixed on the rear of the vehicle or (where it is towing a trailer) to the rear of the trailer or the rearmost trailer. However, where a vehicle or trailer has been constructed for rear plates to be fixed in accordance with relevant EC type approval directives the plate may be fixed in the space provided in accordance with the directives. Regulation 9 requires a plate of the present type to be lit in accordance with the regulation when used on a road between sunset and sunrise.

Unless fitted in a space provided in accordance with a European type approval directive, a rear registration plate must be fitted vertically (or, if that is not reasonably practicable, as close to vertical as is reasonably practicable) in such a position that the characters are easily distinguishable from a distance of 22 m (where the characters are of a width of 57 mm); 21.5 m (where the characters are of a width of 50 mm); and 18 m (where the characters are of a width of 44 mm). Regulation 9 provides that, except where a plate is fitted and lit in accordance with EC type approval requirements, the plate should be lit so that it is easily distinguishable from a distance of 18 m, but 15 m is substituted where the characters are of a width of only 44 mm.

Fixing of front registration plates: post-1938 vehicles

RV(DRM)R 2001, reg 6 deals with registration plates on a vehicle first registered on or after 1 October 1938, with the same exceptions as above in relation to rear plates.

It requires that a front registration plate must be fixed vertically (or if that is not reasonably practicable, as close to vertical as is reasonably practicable) so that its characters are easily distinguishable from the rest of the plate in normal daylight. Regulation 6 requires that, in the case of motor cycles or motor tricycles which do not have a body of a type which is characteristic of the body of a four-wheeled vehicle, there must not be a front registration plate if the vehicle was first registered on or after 1 September 2001. A front registration plate need not be fitted if such a vehicle was registered before that date.

Pre-1938 vehicles, works trucks, road rollers and agricultural machines

RV(DRM)R 2001, reg 7 deals with registration plates fitted to the front of vehicles registered before 1 October 1938 and to their rear (and the rear of any trailer or rearmost trailer). It requires vertically fitted plates which are easily distinguishable.

There are similar provisions in respect of reasonable practicability and distinguishability of the characters on a plate as under regs 5 and 6. Likewise, there is no need for a front plate to be fitted to a motor bicycle or motor tricycle. The lighting requirements of reg 9 apply to the rear plates of these vehicles.

Regulation 8 is concerned with works trucks, road rollers and agricultural machines. Registration plates must be fitted vertically on both sides of the vehicle and on its rear, so that the characters on the mark are easily distinguishable from the sides and rear respectively. When the vehicle is towing a trailer and the plate is not fixed to the sides of the vehicle, a plate must be fixed on the trailer (or rearmost trailer) so that the characters of the mark are easily distinguishable from behind the trailer. In the case of a towing machine which is an agricultural machine (tractor, off-road tractor, light agricultural vehicle, agricultural engine or mowing machine) the plate displayed on the trailer may be that of any agricultural machine kept by the keeper of the towing vehicle. The lighting requirements of reg 9 do not apply to these vehicles.

Use of reflex-reflecting material and other impediments to true photographs

RV(DRM)R 2001, reg 11 prohibits the application of reflex-reflecting material to any part of the registration plate or the treatment of the plate in such a way as to cause the registration mark to become retroreflective. In addition, it requires that the surface of a registration plate must not comprise nor incorporate any design, pattern or texture, or be treated in any way which gives to any part of the plate the appearance of a design, pattern or texture. It also prohibits any treatment of a registration plate which has the effect of making it less distinguishable or would prevent or impair the making of a true photograph. The use of a screw or bolt or other fixing device in a manner which has the effect of changing the appearance or legibility of any characters of a registration mark, or would impair the making of a true photograph, is also prohibited.

GB plates

RV(DRM)R 2001, reg 16 provides that no material other than a registration mark and the following material may be displayed on a registration plate. 'The following material' refers to the international distinguishing sign of the UK ('GB') *or* (unless the vehicle is recorded in the part of the register relating to Northern Ireland) the displayed letters denoting in full or by a specified abbreviation one of the constituent countries of Great Britain, Great Britain (as a whole), or the United Kingdom (as a whole) accompanied by an image of the Union Flag or the national flag of one of those countries. Thus, registration marks may identify vehicles as belonging to the UNITED KINGDOM (UK), GREAT BRITAIN (GB), ENGLAND (ENG), SCOTLAND (SCO), or WALES/CYMRU

(CYM) by capital letters or (except GB) a mixture of initial capital letters followed by lower case and by the respective flags of those nations.

Exemptions

RV(DRM)R 2001, regs 3 and 18 preserve the exemption of small purpose-built invalid carriages and pedestrian-controlled vehicles from the requirement to carry registration marks. The use of old-style number plates on 'classic' vehicles is also preserved.

Breach of the Regulations: offences

VERA 1994, s 59 provides that a contravention of, or a failure to comply with, RV(DRM)R 2001 is an offence. An offence under s 59 is a fixed penalty offence if it relates to a failure to fix prescribed registration marks to a vehicle in accordance with the regulations relating to the size, shape and character of registration marks.

Offences relating to registration marks

VERA 1994, ss 42(1) and 43(1) provide, respectively, that, if a registration mark is not fixed on a vehicle as required, or if a registration mark is obscured, the driver (or, if it is not being driven, its keeper) is guilty of an offence.

Forgery, fraud, or falsity

VERA 1994, s 44(1) and (2) makes it an offence to forge, alter, fraudulently use on a public road, fraudulently lend, or fraudulently allow another to use on a public road, a registration mark to be fixed to a vehicle. These offences which are indictable (either way) offences also apply to trade plates, registration documents, and vehicle licences.

Registration plates

Regulation of suppliers of registration plates

V(C)A 2001, Part 2 is concerned with the regulation of suppliers of registration plates.

By V(C)A 2001, s 17(1), a person commits an offence if he carries on business as a registration plate supplier without being registered with the Secretary of State. A person carries on a business as a registration plate supplier if his business consists wholly or partly in selling registration plates and he is not exempt from the provisions of the Act. The Vehicles Crime (Registration of Registration Plate Suppliers) Regulations 2008, reg 3 exempts a dealer in vehicles who has arranged a first registration in the UK on behalf of the intended purchaser or keeper, or where the registration plate was not fixed to the vehicle by the dealer or on his behalf.

Under V(C)A 2001, s 18, on payment of any prescribed fee, the Secretary of State must supply information from the register of registration plate suppliers on request by any person (subject to exceptions provided by regulations). Where a request is so made, and subject to any prescribed exception and fee, the Secretary of State must supply the information in the form of a certified copy of the register or of an extract from it. Any such certified copy is evidence of the matters mentioned in it. The Secretary of State may make all the information contained in the register, or prescribed parts of it, available to the National Policing Improvement Agency for use by constables, civilian employees (ie members of the civilian staff of a police force or persons employed by the Common Council of the City of London who are under the direction and control of the Commissioner of the City of London Police) in the investigation of offences against Part 2. Regulations limit the further disclosure by constables of information to which they have been given access.

By V(C)A 2001, s 19(3), a person who, in applying for registration, makes a statement which he knows to be false in a material particular, or recklessly makes a statement which is so false, commits an offence. On conviction, a court may make an order under s 20 providing for the removal of the entry relating to him in the register, and/or prohibiting him from making an application for registration within a period not exceeding five years specified by the court.

Under V(C)A 2001, s 21, the Secretary of State may cancel a person's registration if satisfied that the person is not carrying on the business of a registration plate dealer and has not, while registered, been doing so for the past 28 days, but may not do so without serving notice under s 22 and allowing time for representations. An appeal lies to a magistrates' court within 21 days.

Information to be obtained from prospective purchasers of plates

The Vehicles Crime (Registration of Registration Plate Suppliers) Regulations 2008 require registered persons who are in the course of selling registration plates to obtain prescribed information from the prospective purchasers before the completion of the sale. They also require registered persons to keep records of prescribed matters.

The information to be obtained by a registered supplier from a prospective purchaser is prescribed by reg 6. He is required to obtain:

(a) where the prospective purchaser is a partnership or is one or more partners of a partnership (or a limited liability partnership (LLP) or registered company) purchasing on behalf of such an organisation, the firm's name and the address of the principal place of business (the registered name and office, and principal place of business if different, in the case of a LLP or company);

(b) where the prospective purchaser is not as set out above at (a), the purchaser's name and residential or other address;

(c) where a person is acting as an agent for a prospective purchaser, the name and address of that agent;

(d) the registration mark to be displayed on the plate;

(e) the connection of the prospective purchaser with the registration mark or the vehicle on which the registration plate is intended to be fixed.

The information in (a)–(c) must be verified by the registered person.

Part 1 of the Schedule to the 2008 Regulations lists the ways in which the name or address must be verified by the registered person:

(a) a valid driving licence containing a photograph;

(b) a valid driving licence (whether or not issued in the UK);

(c) a registration document or registration certificate provided it is also used to verify the prospective purchaser's connection with the registration mark or vehicle (see below);

(d) a valid passport whether or not it is issued in the UK;

(e) a valid national identity card (whether or not issued in the UK);

(f) a valid debit card or credit card issued by a bank or building society;

(g) a police warrant card;

(h) a valid armed forces identity card;

(i) a dated bill or statement of account issued in respect of the supply of gas, electricity, water or telecommunications services to premises at a specified address;

(j) a dated council tax bill or statement of account;

(k) a dated bill or statement of account issued in respect of rates payable in Northern Ireland; or

(l) a dated statement relating to an account held at a bank or building society.

If not dated, documents referred to in (i) to (l) must relate to a period ending no earlier than six months before that time.

In addition, the registered person must verify the purchaser's connection with the registration mark or the vehicle by one of the following documents listed in Part 2 of the Schedule to the 2008 Regulations: the registration document or registration certificate, or that part of such document or certificate relevant to the transfer of a vehicle; a certificate of entitlement to a registration mark; a retention document relating to the right of retention of a registration mark; a vehicle licensing reminder issued to the registered keeper; a temporary registration certificate; an authorisation issued by the Secretary of State for the purchase of a number plate; or an authorisation for the purchase of the number plate issued by a company owning more than one vehicle stating that it holds the registration document or the registration certificate and giving the reference number of that document or certificate.

By V(C)A 2001, s 25(3), a person who contravenes any provision in reg 6 commits an offence, unless he shows that he took all reasonable steps and exercised all due diligence to avoid committing the offence.

Regulation 7 of the 2008 Regulations requires a registered person to keep records at his principal place of business or at any other premises at which he carries on the business of a registration plate supplier. Records must be retained for a period of three years from the date of registration. Such records must contain:

(a) the information required by reg 6;

(b) the registration mark displayed on the registration plate (where not recorded under (a)); and

(c) details of all documents used for verification in accordance with reg 6 and those details must include:

　(i) in the case of a document listed in Part 1 of the Schedule which is used for verification, such particulars or numbers (if any) appearing on the document as purport to make it, or those particulars or numbers (or both), unique to the purchaser and which, in the case of a driving licence, must be the driver number, or

　(ii) in the case of a registration document or certificate the reference number of that document, and in the case of an authorisation to purchase the number plate, issued by a company owning more than one vehicle, the reference number referred to in that document.

Failure to comply with these provisions as to records is an offence against V(C)A 2001, s 24(4), unless the defendant shows that he took all reasonable steps and exercised all due diligence to avoid committing the offence.

Supplementary provisions and offences

V(C)A 2001, s 26 empowers a constable, or person authorised by the Secretary of State or the local authority for the area, to enter and inspect the registered premises of registered persons at any reasonable time. The constable or authorised person has power to require production of, and to inspect, any plates kept at the premises and any records which are required to be kept under Part 2, and to take copies or extracts. Provision is also made for the issue to a constable or authorised person of a warrant. While force may not be used to obtain entry in normal circumstances, it may be used in the exercise of the constable or authorised person's powers under the authority of a warrant. When effecting entry without a warrant, a constable or authorised person must, if required by or on behalf of the owner or occupier or person in charge of the premises, produce evidence of identity, and of his authority for entering, before doing so. This also applies to an authorised person when executing a warrant. Section 26(7) also creates an offence of obstruction of an authorised person in the exercise of his powers under the section. The Secretary of State is authorised to prosecute offenders.

A person registered under V(C)A 2001, Part 2 is required by s 27 to give notice of changes of circumstances. Section 27(4) creates the offence of failure to do so. The same due diligence defence as is set out above in relation to ss 24 and 25 is available to a person accused of this offence.

V(C)A 2001, s 28 is concerned with counterfeit registration plates and those which do not conform with regulations. It creates three offences:

(a) selling a plate or other device which is not a registration plate as a registration plate, knowing that it is not such a plate or being reckless as to whether it is a registration plate (hereafter 'unlawful activity') (s 28(1));

(b) selling a plate or other device which is not a registration plate because the mark does not comply with regulations or is displayed otherwise than as permitted by regulations (s 28(1A)); and

(c) supplying a plate, device or other object to a person who is carrying on a business which consists wholly or partly in such unlawful activity and he knows or reasonably suspects that the plate, device or other object will be used for the purposes of that other person's unlawful activities (s 28(2)).

V(C)A 2001, s 29(1) creates the offence of supplying a plate, device or other object to an unregistered person (other than an exempt person to be defined by regulations) who is carrying on a business which consists wholly or partly in selling registration plates, knowing or reasonably suspecting that the plate, device or other object will be used for the purpose of that other person's business as a registration plate or as part of a registration plate.

LICENSING

VERA 1994, s 1 provides that vehicle excise duty must be charged in respect of:

(a) every mechanically propelled vehicle that is:
   (i) registered under the Act, or
   (ii) (if not so registered) is used, or kept, on a public road.
   As we have seen, it is not necessary to prove that such a vehicle was intended or adapted for use on roads. Any mechanically propelled vehicle, including a go-kart, which is actually used or kept on a public road requires a vehicle excise licence regardless of whether or not it was intended or adapted for use on a road; and

(b) every thing (whether or not it is a vehicle) that has been, but has ceased to be, a mechanically propelled vehicle and:
   (i) is registered under the Act, or
   (ii) (if not so registered) is used, or kept, on a public road.

Vehicle excise duty charged in respect of a vehicle is paid on a vehicle licence.

In the rest of VERA 1994 'vehicle' means a mechanically propelled vehicle or any thing (whether or not it is a vehicle) that has been, but has ceased to be, a mechanically propelled vehicle.

VERA 1994, s 29(1) provides that if any person *uses* or *keeps* a vehicle for which no vehicle licence or trade licence (see p 365) is in force, not being a vehicle exempted from duty under the Act, he is guilty of an offence. Prior to the removal of the reference to a 'public road' by the Finance Act 2008, the offence could only be committed if the vehicle was used or kept on a public road. The offence may now be committed in any place other than:

(a) any place which is in the curtilage of, or in the vicinity of, a dwelling house, mobile home or houseboat, and which is normally enjoyed with it; or
(b) any place which is in the curtilage of, or in the vicinity of, a building consisting entirely (apart from common parts) of two or more dwellings and which is normally enjoyed only by the occupiers of one or more of those dwellings.

Section 29(2A) provides that the offence under s 29(1) does not apply if the vehicle is an exempt vehicle requiring a 'nil' licence and such a licence is in force, or if it is an exempt vehicle not required by regulations to have a 'nil' licence. Neither does it apply if the vehicle is (a) neither being used or kept on a public road, (b) a statutory declaration has been made, and (c) the terms of that declaration have not been breached (s 29(2B)). Nor does s 29(1) apply if the vehicle is kept by a motor trader or vehicle tester at his business premises (s 29(2C)). Section 29(2E) provides that a defendant is not entitled to the benefit of any of these exception from s 29(1) unless evidence is adduced which is sufficient to raise an issue with respect to that exception, but where evidence is so adduced it is for the prosecution to prove beyond reasonable doubt that the exception does not apply.

In addition, if a registered vehicle is unlicensed the registered keeper is guilty of an offence contrary to VERA 1994, s 31A(1), unless it is an exempt vehicle of one of the types referred to in s 29(2A) above. However, s 31B provides a number of exceptions. The registered keeper does not commit an offence under s 31A if *at the relevant time*:

(a) he is not the person keeping the vehicle and, if previously he was the person keeping it, he has by the relevant time complied with *any requirements to furnish particulars or make declarations which apply on surrendering or not renewing a licence, or when keeping an unlicensed vehicle*;
(b) he is keeping the vehicle, it is neither kept nor used on a public road and he has complied with any requirement italicised in (a);
(c) the vehicle has been stolen and has not been recovered, and within 14 days he has notified a member of a police force with prescribed details about the theft; or
(d) the period of 'grace days' has not expired since the expiry of the last licence and a licence is taken out within the 14 'grace days'.

RV(R&L)R 2002, reg 26A deals with the 'requirements to furnish particulars', etc referred to in (a). They are the requirements in relation to the surrender or destruction of a registration document; delivery of a registration document to the Secretary of State; notification of transfer to a vehicle trader; and notification by a vehicle trader of a sale or transfer.

These sections of VERA 1994 contain a number of terms which require definition.

Definitions

Uses

This term is described in Chapter 10. An employer is liable for use by his employee even though blamelessly unaware of what the employee is doing. It is not good practice to proceed against the employee in normal circumstances.

Keeps

VERA 1994, s 62 states that a person keeps a vehicle on a public road if he causes it to be on such a road for any period, no matter how short, when it is not in use there. If the description 'use' cannot be applied to the vehicle's presence on the road at any particular time, it is 'kept' on that road by any person who causes it to be there. It is a question of fact in each case who that person is. It may be a driver who has parked it there whilst the vehicle still remains under his control. It may be the owner who allows it to remain in a back street unlicensed, or it may be some person in temporary possession. If an unlicensed vehicle is repaired at a garage and placed outside on the road by the proprietor when the repairs have been effected, the garage proprietor is keeping the vehicle on a road without there being an excise licence in force.

Public road

A public road is one which is repairable at public expense. Whether or not a road is repairable at public expense can be established by the local authority who will be able to say whether it has been 'adopted' in the sense that a highway authority is responsible for its maintenance under the Highways Act 1980 or another enactment. In most instances, particular reference to authorities is unnecessary as the road concerned is commonly known to be a public road and justices are entitled to apply their knowledge to such matters. Inquiries are advisable when use on roads within new housing estates is alleged, as the roads may still be the responsibility of the builder if development work is still continuing or has recently finished.

Licence is in force

The prosecutor invariably offers evidence of the lack of a vehicle excise licence but this does not strictly need to be proven. Once (a)(i) or (ii) or (b)(i) or (ii) on p 356 is established, the defendant must prove that it was licensed. A 'licence' in this context includes a trade licence (p 365). Where a licence is obtained by means of a cheque which is dishonoured the licence is void from the time of issue.

Not being exempted

Exemptions are listed in VERA 1994, Sch 2.

The most significant exemptions from the necessity to be licensed are police vehicles, fire engines, ambulances and health service vehicles, veterinary ambulances, invalid carriages not exceeding 10 cwt, vehicles for export, vehicles imported by members of foreign armed forces, vehicles which are used only for purposes related to agriculture, horticulture or forestry and are on public roads only in passing between different areas of land occupied by the same person and the distance so travelled on public roads in doing so does not exceed 1.5 km, off-road tractors, agricultural engines, hedge and verge-cutting tractors, mowing machines, electrically propelled vehicles, snow ploughs and gritters. An electrically assisted pedal cycle is also an exempt vehicle.

When used for particular purposes, a vehicle may also be exempt for that purpose only. One case is where the vehicle is used only for the purpose of submitting it by prior arrangement for examination or re-examination for a test certificate (or a vehicle weight test or identity check) or of taking it from such an examination or re-examination. This exemption also applies to a charge of 'keeping'. Thus, if a driver parks whilst on his way to the testing station simply for the purpose of buying something in a shop, such 'keeping' of the vehicle on a public road is exempt because it is still possible to say that the vehicle was on the road *solely* for the purpose of going to the testing station. Another exemption is where the vehicle is used in the course of an examination; another is where, having been refused a test certificate, a vehicle is taken by prior arrangement for repair, etc.

A vehicle used by or for persons with particular disabilities may, in certain circumstances, be exempt.

A vehicle constructed before 1 January 1973 is exempt, *except*:

(a) a vehicle for which an annual rate is specified in Sch 1, Parts III, V, VI, VII, and VIII (buses, recovery vehicles, vehicles used for exceptional loads, haulage vehicles and goods vehicles); or
(b) a special vehicle (other than digging machine, works truck, mobile crane, mobile pumping vehicle or road roller) where:
   (i) it is designed or adapted for use for the conveyance of goods or burden of any description (or for use with a semi-trailer attached);
   (ii) it is put to a commercial use on a public road; and
   (iii) that use is not a use for the conveyance of goods or burden of any description (or in a case where that use is a use with a semi-trailer attached, the semi-trailer is not used for the conveyance of goods or burden of any description).

A foreign vehicle is exempt if brought temporarily into the country for a period of one year. The term 'foreign' includes vehicles from the Isle of Man and the Channel Islands. A visitor from abroad may purchase a vehicle in this country with the intention of exporting it and then use it here without licensing it before taking it out of Great Britain. Northern Ireland licences are treated as licences issued here. RV(R&L)R 2002, Sch 5 exempts vehicles imported by members of visiting forces, members of a headquarters or other organisation, or a dependant of such a person. This exemption lasts for a period of 12 months only.

Documentary evidence of commission of offence of using or keeping

RTOA 1988, s 20 provides that evidence of a fact relevant to proceedings for an offence to which it applies may be given by the production of a record produced by a prescribed device, accompanied by a certificate as to the circumstances in which it was produced, signed by a constable or a person authorised by or on behalf of a chief officer of police. An offence under VERA 1994, s 29 is prescribed as an offence to which RTOA 1988, s 20 applies and in respect of it a prescribed device is one designed or adapted to register:

(a) an image of a vehicle and its registration mark; and
(b) the time at which the image is registered,

and to record that information if, according to data stored by or otherwise accessible by the device, that vehicle is unlicensed. See p 460 for more about s 20.

Duration and issue of licence

Excise licences may be issued for a period of 12 months or for six months for vehicles in respect of which the annual rate of duty exceeds £50. In addition, where an application is made for an excise licence, the Secretary of State may issue a temporary licence for 14 days or such other period as is prescribed by regulations. Other than temporary licences, licences are valid from the first day of the month on which they are taken out. An application may be made out by any person who must make a declaration and furnish particulars which are prescribed. V(C)A 2001 extended the provisions of VERA 1994 to permit the Secretary of State to require, in addition to the declaration and particulars originally required by VERA 1994, s 7, any other document or evidence prescribed. This is intended to counter the practice of 'ringing' stolen vehicles to assume the identity of legitimate vehicles.

The licence is issued to the vehicle, not the applicant, and it does not authorise that person to use or keep any other vehicle. On the sale of a vehicle the licence must either be returned to DVLA with an application for a rebate of duty, or be transferred with the vehicle. It cannot be transferred to a new vehicle.

It has been the practice for many years to allow 14 days' grace for the renewal of vehicle excise licences. The period of grace only applies where an application for a licence was made before the previous one expired and it is limited to a period of 14 days immediately following the expiry of the previous licence. It would not therefore apply to a new vehicle or to one which had been laid up for the winter and then brought back into use. If a licence is not obtained within the 14-day period, proceedings will probably be taken for unlicensed use whenever it occurred during that period, even though a licence was obtained in the currency of the rest of the month in question. Although the idea of this period of grace is to allow for postal delays in respect of licences which were applied for within the currency of the previous licence, proceedings are not usually taken in respect of use within the following 14-day period if a licence is applied for (and obtained) within that period. The period of grace cannot apply to the circumstances set out in the next paragraph.

Statutory off-road notification

RV(R&L)R 2002, reg 26 and Sch 4 require that, where a person surrenders a licence, does not renew it on expiry or keeps an unlicensed vehicle, he must make a 'required declaration' to the Secretary of State (in writing, orally or by electronic means) not later than the day upon which the licence ceases to be in force (or three months after such expiry in the case of motor traders). The declaration is to the effect that (except for use under a trade licence) (a) the vehicle is not intended for the time being to be used or kept on a public road and (b) a licence will be taken out before any such use. It is an offence to fail to make such a declaration. If there is a transfer of such a vehicle during an unlicensed period and a licence is not taken out, a 'required declaration' must be made by the new owner.

Supplement payable on late renewal

A supplement of £80 is payable where a licence for a vehicle has expired and no vehicle licence is issued for the vehicle before the expiry of a period of one month from the date of expiry of the licence and no 'statutory off-road notification' has been made. That sum may be reduced to £40 if it is paid within 28 days of the registered keeper being notified by the Secretary of State that a supplement may or has become payable. This supplement is payable by the person in whose name the vehicle is registered at the date of expiry of the licence by reason of whose late renewal the supplement became payable.

Rates of duty

Licences cost differing amounts depending upon the nature of the vehicle and its particular use. VERA 1994, Sch 1 sets out the various rates of duty. It sets the basic rate (which applies where no other rate is set by the schedule) and this is the rate which applies to many private cars. Buses are charged according to their seating capacity and goods vehicles are charged according to their 'revenue weight'. This is, in most circumstances, the plated gross or plated train weight of the vehicle but where a vehicle does not have such a plated weight there will be a 'design weight certificate' in force in respect of the vehicle and the weight shown on that certificate is the revenue weight for the purposes of VERA 1994.

Provision is made by RV(R&L)R 2002, reg 5 for reduced rates of duty for certain buses, haulage vehicles, and heavy goods vehicles which have been adapted to reduce pollution. Where this is so, a 'reduced pollution certificate' will be in force.

Some vehicles, which would otherwise have fallen within the goods vehicle rates of duty, are declared by Sch 1 to be 'special vehicles' or recovery vehicles.

Special vehicles

The basic rate of goods vehicle duty is payable in respect of *special vehicles* regardless of their revenue weight. Such vehicles have a revenue weight exceeding 3,500 kg and are digging machines, mobile cranes, mobile pumping vehicles, works trucks or road rollers.

'Digging machines' are machines designed for use for trench digging, excavating or shovelling which are used on public roads for such a purpose or for getting to or from the place where they will so operate. 'Mobile cranes' are cranes designed for use on site which are used on public roads only in connection with work in the immediate vicinity of that road or in travelling to or from that place.

A 'works truck' is a goods vehicle (other than a straddle carrier) designed for use on private premises and used on public roads only for carrying goods between such premises and a vehicle on a road in the immediate vicinity, or in passing from one part of any such premises to another or to other private premises in the immediate vicinity, or in connection with roadworks while at or in the immediate vicinity of the site of such works. A drive of one-and-a-half miles through congested roads is not from one set of premises to another which is in the immediate vicinity, nor is a journey of six-tenths of a mile. 'Immediate vicinity' connotes a very considerable degree of closeness.

A vehicle which is designed or adapted for use for the conveyance of goods or burden of any description, but not so used, or not so used for hire or reward or in connection with a trade or business, is a special vehicle. So is a vehicle which is designed or adapted for use with a semi-trailer attached but which is not so used or, if it is used, the semi-trailer is not used for the conveyance of goods or burden of any description.

Recovery vehicles

The rate of duty applicable to a recovery vehicle is the basic goods vehicle rate where the revenue weight exceeds 3,500 kg but does not exceed 25,000 kg, and 2.5 times that rate if the revenue weight exceeds 25,000 kg.

A 'recovery vehicle' is a vehicle which is constructed or permanently adapted primarily for the purpose of lifting, towing and transporting a disabled vehicle or for any one or more of those purposes. For a vehicle to be classified as a recovery vehicle for the purpose of attracting a lower rate of duty, it must be being used for:

(a) the recovery of a disabled vehicle;
(b) the removal of a disabled vehicle from where it became disabled to premises where it is to be repaired or scrapped;
(c) the removal of a disabled vehicle from premises where it was taken for repair, to other premises where it is to be repaired or scrapped;
(d) carrying fuel and other liquids required for its propulsion and tools and other articles required for the operation of or in connection with integral or permanently mounted apparatus designed to lift, tow or transport a disabled vehicle;

(e) repairing a disabled vehicle at the place where it became disabled or to which it had been moved in the interests of safety after becoming disabled; or

(f) drawing or carrying one trailer if the trailer was, immediately before a vehicle became disabled, being drawn or carried by the disabled vehicle (VERA 1994, Sch 1 and RV(R&L)R 2002, Sch 7).

When recovering or removing a disabled vehicle from the place where it became disabled, a recovery vehicle may carry the driver, passenger and any load which was in or on the vehicle immediately before it became disabled and persons and their personal effects from the place where the vehicle is to be repaired to their destinations. Such a vehicle may also be used to remove vehicles at the request of a constable or local authority, and whilst proceeding to and from permitted assignments. If a recovery vehicle is used outside these purposes, it is no longer a recovery vehicle for the purposes of the Act. Nor is it a recovery vehicle if it is used to recover more than two vehicles at any time.

Exhibition of licences

An excise licence must be fixed to a vehicle in a holder sufficient to protect the licence from the effects of the weather to which it would otherwise be exposed. Consequently, an externally displayed licence must be completely enclosed in a waterproof container. RV(R&L)R 2002, reg 6 sets out the requirements. An excise licence must be exhibited on the vehicle so that the particulars are clearly visible in daylight from the nearside of the road, as follows:

(a) on an invalid carriage, tricycle, or bicycle, on the nearside of the vehicle;

(b) on a bicycle with sidecar, on the nearside of the handlebars or the nearside of the sidecar;

(c) on a vehicle with a windscreen extending across the vehicle, on or adjacent to the nearside of the windscreen; or

(d) on any other vehicle, on the nearside window of the driver's cab (if it has one), or on the nearside of the vehicle in front of the driver's seat and not less than 760 mm and not more than 1.8 m above the surface of the road.

Immobilisation of unlicensed vehicles

The Vehicle Excise Duty (Immobilisation, Removal and Disposal of Vehicles) Regulations 1997 authorise the immobilisation and removal of stationary unlicensed vehicles in places other than the curtilage of a dwelling in circumstances in which an 'authorised person' (a person, such as a police officer or local authority employee, authorised by the Secretary of State) has reason to believe that an offence is being committed under VERA 1994, s 29(1) (unlicensed vehicle used or kept at a place other than the curtilage of a dwelling). Such persons are given power to enter any such place for the purpose of enforcement.

The vehicle may be wheelclamped where it stands, or moved to another place and wheelclamped there. This may be done by the authorised person or a person acting under his direction. An immobilisation notice must be fixed to the vehicle indicating that the device has been fitted, warning that no attempt should be made to move the vehicle until it has been released from the device, and providing other information, including the charge for release, removal and disposal. Before an authorised person can release such a vehicle:

(a) the prescribed 'release charge' must be paid;

(b) (i) evidence must be produced that no offence contrary to s 29(1) was being committed at the time of clamping or removal;

(ii) a valid excise licence must be produced;

(iii) the prescribed 'surety payment' (a sum payable where no such licence is produced) must be made; or

(iv) a declaration must be made to the effect that a licence was in force at the specified time, that a statutory off-road notice was in force, or that the vehicle was an exempt vehicle which did not require a 'nil' licence.

A voucher will be issued to a person who makes a 'surety payment'. Where a licence cannot be obtained immediately the 'surety payment' permits the vehicle to be used unlicensed for a period of 24 hours. The payment will be returned upon production of a valid vehicle excise licence.

The Regulations authorise the removal of a vehicle which has been clamped for a period of 24 hours without release; it may be removed to the custody of an authorised 'custodian'. Where this has been done, a removal fee will be charged additionally, together with charges for storage.

The 1997 Regulations create the following offences:

(a) unauthorised removal of or interference with an immobilisation notice: reg 7(1) and (2);

(b) unauthorised removal, or attempted removal, of an immobilisation device: reg 7(3);

(c) false declaration with a view to securing release of vehicle from an immobilisation device: reg 8(2);

(d) false declaration with a view to securing possession of impounded vehicle: reg 13(1);

(e) making declaration in connection with obtaining voucher or refund relating to a surety payment, knowing that it is false or in a material respect misleading: reg 16(1) and (3); and

(f) forgery, fraudulent alteration, fraudulent use, or the fraudulent lending, of a voucher relating to surety payment: reg 16(2) and (3).

The offences under (c), (d), (e), and (f) are indictable (either way) offences.

Offences related to licences

The most common offences committed contrary to VERA 1994 are:

(a) using or keeping a vehicle without having in force a vehicle licence or trade licence in respect of it: s 29(1) (described above);

(b) using or keeping a vehicle on a public road without the requisite licence being fixed to and exhibited on the vehicle in the prescribed way: s 33(1). Section 33(1B) provides that a person is not guilty of the offence by using or keeping a vehicle on a public road during any of the five working days following the time when a licence or a relevant statutory off-road declaration ceases to be in force if an application for a licence has been received within that time—a 'working day' is any day other than Saturday, Sunday, Christmas Eve, Christmas Day, Good Friday, or a bank holiday;

(c) forging, fraudulently altering, fraudulently using, fraudulently lending, or allowing to be used by any other person, a vehicle licence or nil licence (s 44(1) and (2)). Where a person is charged with forging a licence it is not essential to prove an intention to avoid paying duty, it is sufficient to prove an intention to induce a person exercising a public duty to accept it as genuine and, by reason of so accepting it, to act or refrain from acting in a way which he would otherwise not have done, to his own or another's prejudice. Thus, the alteration of a licence, to avoid attracting attention while an application for an excise licence was pending, is a forgery for the purpose of s 44;

(d) making, in connection with an application for the issue of a licence, a declaration which to the defendant's knowledge is false or in a material respect misleading: s 45(1);

(e) supplying or producing false information or documents which the defendant knows (or is reckless as to) are false or in a material respect misleading in relation to the design weight of a vehicle (for the purposes of establishing the revenue weight): s 45(3A);

(f) forgery, alteration or use of a certificate (design weight certificate) with intent to deceive, or lending or allowing such a certificate knowing or believing that it will be used for deception, or without reasonable excuse making or possessing a document so resembling such a certificate as to be calculated to deceive: s 45(3B);

(g) exhibiting anything which is intended to be, or could reasonably be, mistaken for a licence: s 59 and RV(R&L)R 2002, reg 7.

An offence under (c), (d), (e), or (f) is an indictable (either way) offence.

Proceedings for offences and admissibility of evidence

VERA 1994, s 47 provides that proceedings for offences of using, etc without a licence, of using a trade licence outside permitted uses (see p 366), and of using a licensed vehicle for a purpose which attracts a higher rate of duty than that paid, can only be instituted by the Secretary of State or a constable; such a person is known as the authorised prosecutor. Moreover, no prosecution may be instituted by a constable for these offences without the approval of the Secretary of State; proof of such approval is required at the outset of proceedings in court.

Proceedings instituted by an authorised prosecutor for one of the above offences or for an offence under VERA 1994, s 44 or 45 (forgery or false statements, etc) may be instituted within six months from the date on which sufficient evidence came to the prosecutor's knowledge to warrant proceedings, subject to a maximum limit of three years from the commission of the offence. This means that, if the Secretary of State institutes proceedings as the authorised prosecutor, the six-month time limit runs from the time when the required evidence came to his knowledge. The six-month limit replaces the normal rule requiring that proceedings for summary offences be taken within six months from the commission of the offence. VERA 1994, s 47 allows proof of the date upon which evidence came to the knowledge of the authorised prosecutor, or proof that the Secretary of State has approved the institution of a prosecution by a constable, to be given by means of a certificate signed by or on behalf of the authorised prosecutor or, as the case may be, the Secretary of State. Such a certificate is conclusive evidence of the facts stated, and is deemed to be properly signed unless the contrary is proved.

VERA 1994, s 52 allows certified extracts from DVLA records to be admissible to the same extent as oral evidence. Evidence may therefore be offered of the last date upon which a vehicle was licensed by means of such a certified extract.

VERA 1994, s 46 requires that, where an offence under ss 29 above or 34 (p 366) is alleged to have been committed in relation to a particular vehicle, the person keeping the vehicle must give such information as he may be required by or on behalf of a chief officer of police or the Secretary of State to give as to the identity of any person concerned in the offence. Failure to do so is an offence under s 46(4), unless the defendant keeper proves that he did not know, and could not with reasonable diligence have ascertained, the identity of the person(s) concerned (s 46(6)). A divisional court has held that where there is evidence of using or keeping a vehicle on a road and a notice has been sent in accordance with s 46 to which the keeper does not respond, the justices should draw an adverse inference from the failure to respond and that this, coupled with the other evidence of using or keeping, is sufficient to support a conviction under s 46. The requirement to respond also extends to any person other than a 'keeper', and (in the case of a s 29 offence) to the person alleged to have been using the vehicle. Both types of person commit an offence under s 46(4) if they fail to give such information as to identity as it is in their power to give. A request under s 46 is, in practice, made by serving on a person a form requiring the specified information. A reply to such a request must be made in writing.

TRADE LICENCES

Without modification, the requirement that all vehicles (as defined on p 356) which are registered, or which are used or kept on a road, should be individually licensed under VERA 1994 would cause considerable problems for motor traders, through whose hands many vehicles pass, most of which are retained for a short period of time. The purpose of trade licences is to permit traders temporarily to use vehicles for restricted purposes without the necessity for licensing in the manner described above. Trade licences are inexpensive and in consequence their permitted uses are carefully defined.

Who may apply for a trade licence?

By VERA 1994, s 11, a motor trader may apply to the Secretary of State for a licence to cover all vehicles which are from time to time temporarily in his possession in the course of his business as a motor trader. Any motor trader who is a manufacturer may also be granted a licence for the purpose of allowing him to carry out research and development work in the course of his business as a manufacturer, and for all other vehicles which are from time to time submitted to him by other manufacturers for testing on roads in the course of that business.

The term 'motor trader' means a manufacturer or repairer of, or dealer in, vehicles. A person is treated as a dealer in vehicles if he carries on a business consisting wholly or mainly of collecting and delivering vehicles.

A person whose business is that of modifying vehicles (by fitting accessories or otherwise) or of 'valeting' vehicles (which means the thorough cleaning of a vehicle prior to first registration or in order to prepare it for sale, and includes removing wax and grease from the exterior, engine, and interior) is also a 'motor trader'.

A vehicle tester may also apply for a trade licence to cover his use of vehicles submitted to him for testing in the course of his business. A vehicle tester is a person, other than a motor trader, who regularly in the course of his business engages in the testing on roads of vehicles belonging to other persons.

Persons who satisfy the Secretary of State that they intend to commence business as motor traders or vehicle testers may also take out trade licences. Trade licences may be taken out for a period of 12 months. Shorter-term licences are also available but are seldom used.

Trade plates

The holder of a trade licence is issued with a set of two plates (which are generally referred to as 'trade plates') in respect of each licence held. These plates consist of red letters on a white background and show the registration mark assigned to the holder of the licence. One of the plates contains a means by which the licence may be fixed to the plate; it must be displayed at the front of the vehicle so as to be clearly visible at all times during daylight. The licence is therefore available for inspection by police officers and the registration mark itself is traceable to the motor trader who holds that licence. If the trader satisfies the Secretary of State that the vehicles which he will use in the course of his business will include motor cycles as well as other vehicles, he may be issued with a single additional plate for the motor cycles only. Trade licences for motor cycles only are much cheaper. The plates remain the property of the Secretary of State and must be returned when the trader ceases to be the holder of the licence.

Non-permitted uses of trade licences

VERA 1994, s 12 provides that the holder of a trade licence is not entitled by virtue of *that* licence:

(a) to use more than one vehicle at any one time; or
(b) to use any vehicle for any purpose other than a permitted one (see below); or
(c) to keep any vehicle on a road if it is not being used thereon.

However, there is nothing to prevent a motor trader from holding more than one licence to permit use of more than one vehicle at any one time.

It is an offence, contrary to VERA 1994, s 34(1), for the holder of a trade licence to use on a public road a greater number of vehicles than permitted by his licence (or licences), or to use a vehicle for a non-permitted purpose. Section 34(1) also punishes the keeping on a public road of a vehicle using a trade licence, if it is not being used at that time.

Restrictions on use of trade licences

RV(R&L)R 2002, reg 37 and Sch 6 provide that the holder of a trade licence must not permit any person to display a trade licence or trade plates on a vehicle other than one which that person is using for the purpose of the licence-holder's business, or other than when the vehicle is being used for one or more of the prescribed permitted purposes. However, this does not prevent a person driving a vehicle on a road with the consent of the licence-holder, when the vehicle is being used for the licence-holder's business. Thus, an employee may drive vehicles in the course of his employer's (the licence-holder's) business. Breach of the above provision is an offence.

Permitted purposes

The use of vehicles by a motor trader under a trade licence is controlled by RV(R&L)R 2002, regs 38 to 42 and Sch 6, breach of which is an offence.

Regulation 38 and Sch 6 prescribe the purposes for which the holder of a trade licence may use a vehicle by virtue of a trade licence. Those purposes do not include the carrying of any person on the vehicle or any trailer drawn by it except a person carried in connection with such a purpose. The prescribed purposes are without prejudice to the provisions of VERA 1994, s 11(2) to (4) which specify classes of vehicle which a trade licence is for, in relation respectively to a motor trader who is a manufacturer of vehicles, any other motor trader and a vehicle tester.

Schedule 6, para 10 authorises a motor trader who is the holder of a trade licence to use a vehicle on a public road for purposes which meet each of the following requirements:

(a) business purposes, as specified by para 11;
(b) purposes specified by para 12; and
(c) purposes that do not include the conveyance of goods or burden of any description except specified loads (as defined by para 13).

Business purposes, para 11

A vehicle is used for 'business purposes' if used for purposes connected with the motor trader's business:

(a) as a manufacturer or repairer of or dealer in:
    (i) vehicles; or
    (ii) trailers carried on in conjunction with his business as a motor trader;
(b) of modifying vehicles (whether by the fitting of accessories or otherwise); or
(c) of valeting vehicles.

Paragraph 12 purposes

A vehicle is used for a para 12 purpose if it is used:

(a) for the test or trial of the vehicle, or its accessories or equipment, in the ordinary course of construction, modification or repair, or after completion;
(b) for proceeding to or from a public weighbridge to ascertain its unladen weight, or to or from any place for its registration or inspection by someone acting on the Secretary of State's behalf;
(c) for its test or trial for the benefit of a prospective purchaser, including going either to or from a place of such test or trial at the instance of the prospective purchaser;
(d) for its test or trial for the benefit of a person interested in promoting publicity in regard to the vehicle, including going either to or from a place of such test or trial at the instance of such a person;
(e) for delivering it to a purchaser;
(f) for demonstrating the operation of the vehicle or its accessories or equipment when handed over to a purchaser;
(g) for delivering it between parts of the motor trader's own premises or to the premises of another manufacturer, dealer, or repairer or bringing it back from there directly to his own premises;
(h) for proceeding to or from a workshop where a body, or a special type of equipment or accessories, is to be or has been fitted to it or where it is to be or has been painted, valeted or repaired;
(i) for proceeding from the premises of a manufacturer, repairer or dealer to a railway station, airfield or shipping dock for the purpose of transportation, or for proceeding to such premises from a railway station, etc to which it has been transported;
(j) for proceeding to or from any garage, auction room or storage place where vehicles are usually stored or offered for sale and at which the vehicle is to be or has been stored or offered for sale as the case may be;

(k) for proceeding to or from a place of testing; or

(l) for proceeding to a place to be broken up or otherwise dismantled.

The use of a vehicle with a trailer is regarded as the use of a single vehicle under the licence.

Specified loads

Schedule 6, para 13 defines the 'specified loads' referred to in para 10 above as follows:

(a) a load which is carried by a vehicle being used for the purpose of testing or demonstrating the vehicle, or its accessories or equipment, within the terms of (b), (d), (e), or (g), above, and is carried solely for that purpose, and which is returned to the place of loading without having been removed from the vehicle (except in the case of an accident or for demonstrating its operation to a purchaser when handed over to him, or when the load consists of water, fertiliser, or refuse);

(b) in the case of a vehicle which is being delivered or collected and is being used for a relevant purpose (as described in (f) to (k) above), a load consisting of another vehicle used or to be used for travel to or from the place of delivery or collection;

(c) any load built in as a permanent part of the vehicle or permanently attached to it;

(d) in the case of a vehicle which is being used for a purpose falling within (h), (i), or (j) above, a load which consists of a trailer or of parts, accessories or equipment designed to be fitted to the vehicle and of tools for fitting them.

The effect of these provisions is simply to prohibit the carriage of goods on vehicles being used under a trade licence in all but the narrowest of circumstances. It may be that a 'test and trial' will necessarily involve the use of a vehicle with a load. If so, the provisions limit the carriage of the load to the duration of that trial. In most circumstances in which a goods vehicle is observed being used under a trade licence while carrying a load, an offence will be committed. Some vehicles have what might be described as built-in loads, such as essential engineering equipment, and vehicles which are on their way to have accessories, etc fitted may carry these accessories, etc with them for that purpose. None of these loads is being carried for a commercial purpose connected with the use of the vehicle in the accepted sense of the word 'commercial'.

Research and vehicle testing purposes

The regulation makes similar restrictions in respect of use by vehicle researchers and vehicle testers.

RV(R&L)R 2002, Sch 6, paras 14 and 15 deal respectively with manufacturers' research vehicles and use by vehicle testers. The first restricts use to manufacturers for research and development purposes and the second restricts testing to vehicles and trailers drawn thereby, or any accessory or equipment on the vehicle or trailer, in the course of a business as a vehicle tester.

No other permitted purposes

The purposes listed under the heading 'Permitted purposes' (see p 367) are the only ones for which vehicles may be used under a trade licence, and even then only in the course of the business of the holder. If an employee used the trade plates and licence to remove his own private car to a paint shop for spraying, not in the course of his employer's business, the use would be unlawful. If the holder of the licence used under trade plates a vehicle which was in his possession in the course of his business to visit a cinema in the evening, that use of the motor vehicle would be unlawful as it would not be in the course of his business as a motor trader.

Trade plate and trade licence offences

Breach of the regulations relating to loads or passengers is also an offence under VERA 1994, s 34(1) (above).

RV(R&L)R 2002, Sch 6, para 3 provides that the holder of a licence must not, or must not permit any person to, exhibit on any vehicle any trade licence or trade plate which has been altered, defaced, mutilated or added to; upon which the figures or particulars have become illegible; or upon which the colour has been altered by fading or otherwise. Breach of such prohibition is an offence.

By VERA 1994, s 44(1) and (2), forgery, fraudulent alteration or use, or fraudulent lending or allowing to be used by any other person, of trade licences and trade plates is an indictable (either way) offence. So is the false declaration under VERA 1994, s 45(1) (p 364) which also applies in respect of an application for such a licence.

DRIVING LICENCES, PENALTY POINTS AND DISQUALIFICATION

Driving licences

The licensing of drivers of motor vehicles is dealt with by RTA 1988, Part III (ss 87 to 109C) and the Motor Vehicles (Driving Licences) Regulations 1999 (MV(DL)R 1999).

For driving licence purposes, motor vehicles are divided by MV(DL)R 1999 into various categories and sub-categories and it is essential that licences are checked, not only to establish the identity of the driver, but also to ascertain that he is authorised to drive the particular vehicle in which he is found. Amendments made to MV(DL)R 1999 with effect from 19 January 2013 provide for the introduction of new categories and sub-categories of vehicles (principally mopeds and motor cycles). The categories and sub-categories of vehicles for licensing purposes is set out in MV(DL)R 1999, Sch 2, as amended, as follows:

Category or sub-category	*Class of vehicle included*	*Additional categories and sub-categories covered*
	Part 1	
	A licence authorising the driving of motor vehicles of a class included in a category or sub-category shown in Part 1 may be granted to a person who is entitled thereto by virtue of:	
	(a) holding or having held a full licence, full Northern Ireland licence, full British external licence, full British Forces licence, exchangeable licence or Community licence authorising the driving of vehicles of that class, or	
	(b) having passed a test for a licence authorising the driving of motor vehicles of that class of a Northern Ireland or Gibraltar test corresponding to such a test.	

(continued)

Category or sub-category	*Class of vehicle included*	*Additional categories and sub-categories covered*
AM	Mopeds: two- or three-wheel vehicles with a maximum design speed (MDS) not exceeding 45km/h (excluding those with MDS less than 25km/h) and light quadricycles: quadricycles with unladen mass not exceeding 350kg (excluding batteries in case of electric vehicles), MDS not exceeding 45km/h, and engine capacity not exceeding 50cc (spark ignition) or maximum net power output not exceeding 4kw (other internal combustion engine) or maximum continuous rated power not exceeding 4kw (electric motor)	Q
A	Motor bicycles and motor tricycles: motor vehicles with three symmetrically arranged wheels with MDS exceeding 45km/h and engine capacity exceeding 50cc (if internal combustion engine)	Q, AM, A1, A2, and K
A1	A sub-category of A comprising A1 motor cycles: motor bicycles with engine capacity not exceeding 125cc, power not exceeding 11kw and power to weight ratio (PWR) not exceeding 0.1kw/kg and A1 motor tricycles: motor tricycles with power not exceeding 15kw	Q and AM
A2	A sub-category of A comprising A2 motor cycles: motor bicycles of power not exceeding 35kw, PWR not exceeding 0.2kw/kg and not being derived from a vehicle of more than double its power	Q, AM, and A1
A3	A sub-category of A comprising A3 motor bicycles: motor bicycles (a) of power exceeding 35kw or PWR exceeding 0.2kw/kg, or (b) of power not exceeding 35kw with PWR not exceeding 0.2kw/kg and derived from a vehicle of more than double its power and A3 motor tricycles: motor tricycles with power exceeding 15kw	Q, AM, A1, A2, and K
B	Motor vehicles, other than vehicles included in category Q, AM, A, F, or K, having maximum authorised mass (MAM) not exceeding 3.5 tonnes and not more than 8 seats in addition to driver's seat, including: (a) combination of any such vehicle and trailer where trailer has MAM not exceeding 750kg, and (b) combination of any such vehicle and trailer where MAM of combination does not exceed 3.5 tonnes	Q, AM F, and K

Category or sub-category	Class of vehicle included	Additional categories and sub-categories covered
B + E	Combinations of motor vehicle (being tractor vehicle in category B) and trailer or semi-trailer where (a) combination does not fall within category B or B96; and (b) MAM of trailer or semi-trailer does not exceed 3.5 tonnes	None
C	Motor vehicles having MAM exceeding 3.5 tonnes, other than vehicle falling within category D, F, G, or H, designed and constructed for the carriage of no more than 8 passengers in addition to the driver, and including such vehicle drawing trailer having MAM not exceeding 750kg	None
C1	A sub-category of C comprising motor vehicles having MAM exceeding 3.5 tonnes but not exceeding 7.5 tonnes, designed and constructed for the carriage of no more than 8 passengers in addition to the driver, and including such vehicle drawing trailer having MAM not exceeding 750kg	None
D	Motor vehicles constructed or adapted for the carriage of passengers having more than 8 seats in addition to driver's seat, including such vehicle drawing trailer having MAM not exceeding 750kg	None
D1	A sub-category of D comprising motor vehicles having more than 8 seats but not more than 16 seats in addition to driver's seat with maximum length not exceeding 8m, and including such vehicle drawing a trailer with MAM not exceeding 750kg	None
C + E	Combination of motor vehicle and trailer where the tractor vehicle is in category C but the combination does not fall within that category	B + E
C1 + E	A sub-category of C + E comprising combinations of motor vehicle in category B, or in sub-category C1, and trailer or semi-trailer where combination's MAM is no more than 12 tonnes and: (a) if tractor vehicle is in category B, MAM of trailer or semi-trailer exceeds 3.5 tonnes, or (b) if tractor vehicle is in sub-category C1, MAM of trailer or semi-trailer exceeds 750kg	B + E
D + E	Combination of motor vehicle and trailer where tractor vehicle is in category D but the combination does not fall into that category	B + E

(continued)

Category or sub-category	*Class of vehicle included*	*Additional categories and sub-categories covered*
D1 + E	A sub-category of D + E comprising any combination of motor vehicle and trailer where:	B + E
	(a) tractor vehicle is in sub-category D1, and	
	(b) MAM of trailer exceeds 750kg but not the unladen weight of the tractor vehicle	
F	Agricultural or forestry tractors, including any such vehicle drawing trailer but excluding any motor vehicle included in category H	K
G	Road rollers	None
H	Track-laying vehicles steered by their tracks	None
K	Mowing machines, not falling within category A, or vehicle controlled by pedestrian	None

Part 2

A licence authorising the driving of motor vehicles of a class included in any category or sub-category shown in Part 2 may not be granted to a person unless, at a time before 1 January 1997:

(a) in the case of a person applying for a full licence, (i) he held a full licence authorising the driving of motor vehicles of that class or a class which by virtue of MV(DL)R 1999 corresponds to a class included in that category or sub-category, or (ii) he passed a test which at the time it was passed authorised the driving of motor vehicles of such a class or a Northern Ireland test corresponding to such a test;

(b) in the case of a person applying for a provisional licence, he held a provisional licence authorising the driving of vehicles of that class or a class which by virtue of MV(DL)R 1999 corresponds to a class included in that category or sub-category

C1 + E (8.25 tonnes)	A sub-category of category C + E comprising combinations of motor vehicle and trailer in sub-category C1 + E where MAM of trailer exceeds 750kg and may exceed unladen weight of tractor vehicle, and MAM of combination does not exceed 8.25 tonnes	None

Category or sub-category	Class of vehicle included	Additional categories and sub-categories covered
D1 (not hire or reward)	A sub-category of category D comprising motor vehicles in sub-category D1 driven otherwise than for hire or reward	None
D1 + E (not hire or reward)	A sub-category of D + E comprising motor vehicles in sub-category D1 + E where: (a) motor vehicle driven otherwise than for hire or reward, and (b) MAM of trailer exceeds 750kg and may exceed unladen weight of tractor vehicle	None
L	Vehicle propelled by electrical power	None

Part 3

B1 (invalid carriage)	A sub-category of category B comprising motor vehicles which are invalid carriages	None

Part 4

A licence authorising the driving of motor vehicles of a class shown in column 2 of Part 4 opposite a former category or former sub-category (as the case may be) shown in column 1 may not be granted to a person unless, before 19 January 2013, that person held a licence authorising the driving of motor vehicles of that class or passed a test for a licence authorising the driving of motor vehicles of that class

Former sub-category B1 (vehicle with three or four wheels and unladen weight not exceeding 550kg)	Motor vehicles having four wheels and unladen weight not exceeding 550kg, except light quadricycles	None
Former category B + E (as column 2)	Combination of motor vehicle and trailer where tractor vehicle is in category B and MAM of trailer exceeds 3.5 tonnes	None
Former sub-category D1 (as column 2)	Motor vehicles having more than 8 but not more than 16 seats in addition to driver's seat with maximum length exceeding 8m and including any such vehicle drawing trailer with MAM not exceeding 750kg	None

(continued)

Category or sub-category	Class of vehicle included	Additional categories and sub-categories covered
Former sub-category D1 + E (as column 2)	Combination of motor vehicle and trailer where: (a) tractor vehicle is in former sub-category D1, (b) MAM of trailer exceeds 750kg but not unladen weight of tractor vehicle, (c) MAM of combination does not exceed 12 tonnes, and (d) trailer is not used for carriage of passengers	None
Former category P (vehicles having fewer than four wheels, MDS not exceeding 50km/hr and, if internal combustion engine, not exceeding 50cc)	Motor vehicle with fewer than four wheels, MDS exceeding 45km/hr but not exceeding 50km/hr and, if internal combustion engine, maximum 50cc	None

Part 5

| Q These would be mopeds but for maximum speed limit of 25km/hr | Category Q vehicles: motor vehicle with less than four wheels which: (a) if propelled by internal combustion engine, has a cylinder capacity not exceeding 50cc and, if not equipped with pedals capable of propelling vehicle, MDS not exceeding 25km/hr; and (b) if not propelled by internal combustion engine, has MDS not exceeding 25km/hr A licence authorising the driving of category Q vehicles may not be granted to a person unless he is entitled to be granted a full licence authorising the driving of motor vehicles of a class included in category AM, A, or B, or category P vehicles | None |

Category or sub-category	Class of vehicle included	Additional categories and sub-categories covered
B96	Combinations of motor vehicle and trailer where: (a) tractor vehicle is in category B, (b) MAM of trailer exceeds 750kg, (c) MAM of combination exceeds 3.5 tonnes but not 4.25 tonnes A B96 licence is only granted if person holds or has held a Community licence to drive B96 vehicle	None

So far as vehicles of category B1 (invalid carriages) are concerned, MV(DL)R 1999, reg 5 provides that no licence may be issued for that sub-category to a person who did not hold one for a B1 vehicle or a corresponding class before 12 November 1999.

The term 'maximum authorised mass' has the same meaning:

(a) in relation to goods vehicles as 'permissible maximum weight' in RTA 1988, s 108(1); and
(b) in relation to any other vehicle or trailer as 'maximum gross weight' in the Road Vehicles (Construction and Use) Regulations 1986, reg 3(2), namely the weight which the vehicle is designed or adapted not to exceed when on a road.

As amended with effect from 19 January 2013, MV(DL)R 1999 parallel categories of vehicle with the previous categories introduced by regulations in 1987 (the older categories which were themselves replaced by regulations in 1996 (the 'old categories')). As amended, the 1999 Regulations provide that licences (whether full or provisional) granted before 1 January 1997 or 19 January 2013, as the case may be, are valid in respect of the new categories of vehicle, as set out in the table to the regulations.

Where a licence (whether full or provisional) granted before 19 January 2013 authorises the driving of:

(a) standard motor bicycles only, or
(b) standard motor bicycles and side-car combinations only,

any reference in that licence to motor vehicles in category A (save for those in sub-category A1) is a reference:

(i) where the standard access period (two years commencing on the day when the test to drive a standard motor bicycle was passed excluding any period of disqualification or any period when the licence was not in force) has not expired, to motor vehicles in sub-category A2; and
(ii) where that period has expired, to motor vehicles in category A.

Entitlement on passing a test

MV(DL)R 1999, reg 43 provides that, where a person passes a test prescribed in respect of any category for a licence which authorises the driving of motor vehicles included in that category or in a sub-category of that category, the Secretary of State must grant him a licence authorising him to drive vehicles of all classes included in that category or sub-category unless his licence is restricted to such vehicles fitted with automatic transmission, or vehicles specially adapted for the disabled, in which cases his entitlement will be so restricted. Such holders are also authorised to drive those vehicles shown in column 3 above as additional categories or sub-categories with the same limitations as set out above, should the test have been taken on those types of vehicle. However, where the additional category is Q, AM, F or K the limitation in respect of 'automatics' will not apply.

In relation to a person passing the test of competence to drive a vehicle in category B on or after 1 February 2001, a licence to drive a vehicle in category B does not confer entitlement to drive vehicles in category Q or category AM unless that licence-holder has successfully completed an approved training course for motor cyclists.

Where a person has passed the test of competence to drive a vehicle in category AM in a three-wheeled moped or light quadricycle, reg 44A provides for the grant of a licence restricted to three-or four-wheeled vehicles in category AM.

AM. When licence-holder reaches the prescribed age

Full driving licences issued to those who have passed the appropriate test are granted until the holder reaches 70. After that, the licence can be renewed for three-year periods. When the time for renewal arrives, it is the licence-holder's duty to apply for renewal: there is no requirement for reminders, nor are there any days of grace. Those licences which authorise the holder to drive prescribed goods or passenger-carrying vehicles will be renewable on the holder's 45th birthday, or after five years, whichever is the longer, or where the licence is issued to a person between 45 and 65 for the period ending on his 66th birthday or after five years, whichever is the shorter. A licence granted after the age of 65 will remain in force for one year only.

Other licences

RTA 1988, s 88 provides that it is lawful for a person to drive provided that the driver has held a driving licence, a Community licence, a Northern Irish licence, a British external licence or British forces licence, or an exchangeable licence, for the class of vehicle in question or a corresponding licence, and a 'qualifying application' for a licence under Part III of the Act which includes that time has been received.

Grant of licences

RTA 1988, s 97(1), requires the Secretary of State to issue a licence to a person who applies in the prescribed manner, pays the appropriate fee, and supplies necessary evidence to support his application. A prospective amendment of s 97 permits the grant of a licence subject to prescribed conditions:

(a) for a prescribed period; or
(b) until the happening of a prescribed event.

This will permit for example, the imposition of conditions where a person disqualified for drink/driving had accepted a court order requiring participation in an alcohol ignition interlock programme, limiting driving to driving in accordance with that programme.

RTA 1988, s 98 requires the licence to be in the form of a photocard of a description specified by the Secretary of State, or in such other form as he may specify. Photocard licences were introduced in 1998, but existing licences remain in force until they expire or the holder's details expire. Where a photocard licence is issued an applicant must supply the Secretary of State with a photograph which is a current likeness of him and with a specimen signature which can be electronically recorded and reproduced on the licence. If any other form of licence is granted, the holder must forthwith sign the licence in ink. Defaced or lost licences may be replaced by the Secretary of State. If a lost licence is subsequently found it must be returned to the authority. By RTA 1988, s 99, as amended in 2012, where a photocard licence remains in force after the end of the administrative validity period, its holder must nevertheless surrender the licence and its counterpart to the Secretary of State not later than the end of that period. The administrative validity period will generally be five years for a licence to drive any prescribed class of goods vehicles or passenger-carrying vehicle, or ten years in other cases, with provision for replacement licences issued during those periods. If a licence expires before the end of the standard five- or ten-year period (for instance in the case of licences issued for shorter periods on medical grounds), its administrative validity period will end on the expiry date of the licence. Subject to exceptions, the surrender of a photocard will be followed by the grant of a new one.

RTA 1988, s 98A prospectively authorises the making of an order for the surrender of old-form licences and creating an offence of failure without reasonable excuse to do so (s 98A(7)).

By RTA 1988, s 89(1), a person applying for a full licence for the first time must have passed a test within the previous two years. Prospectively, a different period may be prescribed by regulations.

Compulsory driver training courses

RTA 1988, ss 99ZA–99ZC provide for the making of regulations about compulsory driver training courses which may provide that persons who have not successfully completed a driver training course:

(a) may not take a test of competence to drive motor vehicles of a prescribed class (or a prescribed part of such a test);

(b) are not authorised to drive motor vehicles of a prescribed class (before having passed a test of competence to drive them) by a provisional licence (or by RTA 1988, ss 98(2) or 99A(5)) (use of full licence as provisional);

(c) are not granted a licence authorising the driving of motor vehicles of a prescribed class by virtue of regulations under RTA 1988, s 89(6)(b) or (c) (authority to drive vehicles of other classes); or

(d) are not authorised to drive motor vehicles of a prescribed class in prescribed circumstances (despite having passed a test of competence to drive them).

Exemptions are made by s 99ZB in respect of (b), (c), and (d) where the person is undergoing training on a driver training course and is driving a motor vehicle as a part of that training. In addition, the regulations may provide exemptions in other circumstances.

No regulations have been made at the time of writing.

Disqualification of persons under age

A person may be disqualified from driving a particular class of vehicle by reason of age. A person is disqualified from holding or obtaining a licence to drive a motor vehicle of a particular class if he is under the age applicable to that class of vehicle. The minimum ages at which persons may drive particular classes of vehicles are listed by RTA 1988, s 101, which provides that a person below the minimum age to drive a particular class of vehicle is disqualified from holding a licence to drive that class of vehicle. The requirements of s 101 are amplified by MV(DL)R 1999, reg 9, as amended in 2012. The minimum ages are as follows:

(a) *16 years*:
   (i)   invalid carriage,
   (ii) vehicle in category AM (moped and light quadricycle) or category Q,
   (iii) agricultural or forestry tractor, provided it is a wheeled vehicle not exceeding 2.45 m in width and driven without a trailer (other than a two-wheeled or close-coupled four-wheeled trailer not exceeding 2.45 m in width); the driver must have passed a test for category F or be proceeding to or from such a test, or
   (iv) disability living allowance: 16-year-olds in receipt of a higher rate disability living allowance under the Social Security Contributions and Benefits Act 1992 may drive a small vehicle (except a motor tricycle or light quadricycle) if it is driven without a trailer;

(b) *17 years*:
   (i)   A1 motor cycle or A1 motor tricycle,
   (ii) small vehicle, which means a motor vehicle (other than an invalid carriage, or a vehicle in category AM or category Q, or a motor tricycle) which:
      (*a*) is not constructed or adapted to carry more than nine persons inclusive of the driver, and
      (*b*) has a maximum gross weight not exceeding 3.5 tonnes, and includes a combination of such a vehicle and a trailer, but does not include a motor tricycle or light quadricycle,
   (iii) incomplete large vehicle not exceeding 3.5 tonnes, or
   (iv) road roller which is not steam propelled, whose unladen weight does not exceed 11.69 tonnes, which has no pneumatic, soft, or elastic tyres, and which is not constructed or adapted to carry a load other than equipment of the vehicle;

(c) *18 years*:
   (i)   medium-sized goods vehicle, which means a motor vehicle constructed or adapted to carry or haul goods and not adapted to carry more than nine persons inclusive of the driver, with a permissible maximum weight exceeding 3.5 tonnes but not 7.5 tonnes, and includes a combination of such a vehicle and a trailer where the relevant maximum weight of the trailer does not exceed 750 kg. However, the age of 21 applies if such a vehicle is drawing a trailer and the maximum authorised mass of the combination exceeds 7.25 tonnes,

    (ii) motor-vehicle-and-trailer combination of sub-category C1 + E the maximum authorised mass of which does not exceed 7.5 tonnes,

    (iii) motor vehicle of a class included in category C or C + E where that person:

        (*a*) has an initial qualification (Certificate of Professional Competence (CPC) (see Appendix 1 contained in the companion website to this book <http://www.oup.com/>)) to drive a vehicle of that class;

        (*b*) has been issued by the Secretary of State with a document authorising him to drive the relevant vehicle for a specified period of up to 12 months while undertaking a vocational training course; or

        (*c*) is using the vehicle in the course of a lesson leading to the grant of a licence or a CPC test;

    (iv) motor vehicle of a class included in category C or C + E where being used by the fire service or for maintaining public order or is undergoing road tests for repair or maintenance purposes,

    (v) motor-vehicle-and-trailer combination which is in sub-category C1 + E and the maximum authorised mass of the combination does not exceed 12 tonnes,

    (vi) motor vehicle of a class included in category D or D + E, other than sub-category D1 of D1 + E, where the person driving the vehicle:

        (*a*) has an initial qualification authorising him to drive motor vehicles of that class and is either (*i*) engaged in the carriage of passengers on a regular service over a route which does not exceed 50 km, or (*ii*) is not engaged in the carriage of passengers;

        (*b*) is using the vehicle in the course of a driving lesson or driving test for the purpose of obtaining a driving licence or CPC; or

        (*c*) has been issued by the Secretary of State with a document authorising him to drive the relevant vehicle for a specified period of up to 12 months while undertaking a vocational training course;

    (vii) motor vehicle of a class included in sub-category D1 (more than eight but not more than 16 seats in addition to driver's seat) or D1 + E, where:

        (*a*) the person driving the vehicle has an initial qualification authorising him to drive vehicles of that type, in which case (*i*) or (*ii*) of (*a*) in (vi) do not apply, or

        (*b*) one of (*b*) or (*c*) in (vi) applies; or

    (viii) incomplete large vehicle exceeding 3.5 tonnes but not exceeding 7.5 tonnes;

(d) *19 years:*

A2 motorcycle;

(e) *20 years:*

motor vehicle of a class included in category D or D + E, other than sub-category D1 or D1 + E, where the driver has an initial qualification authorising him to drive motor vehicles of that class and is engaged in the carriage of passengers otherwise than on a regular service restricted to 50 km; and

(f) *21 years:*

    (i) motor vehicle of a class included in category D or D + E, other than sub-category D1 or D1 + E, where the vehicle is being used by the fire service or for maintaining public order or is undergoing road tests for repair and maintenance purposes, and

(ii)   all other motor vehicles not referred to in (a) to (g);
(g) *24 years:*
   (i)   A3 motorcycle or A3 motor tricycle,
   (ii) subject to (c)(vi), and (e), a motor vehicle of a class included in category D or D + E, other than sub-category D1 or D1 + E, save where the vehicle is being used by the fire service or for maintaining public order or is undergoing road tests for repair and maintenance purposes, or in respect of a person under the age of 24 who was entitled to a licence to drive a vehicle of that class before 19 January 2013, in which case the minimum age is 21.

The regulations permit members of the armed services, aged 17 or over, to drive A2 or A3 motorcycles, A3 motor tricycles and medium and large goods vehicles which are owned by the Secretary of State for Defence and are being used subject to his orders. Clearly this exemption is not a general one and the nature of the use of the vehicle at the time must be taken into account.

A1 motorcycles or A1 motor tricycles, A2 motorcycles, and A3 motorcycles can be ridden at 16, 18, and 20 respectively in the case of a person holding a Community licence authorising the driving of vehicles of that particular sub-category. An A3 motorcycle or A3 motor tricycle can be driven by a person at 21 where, for two or more years, he has held a full licence for A2 motorcycles. An A2 motorcycle or A3 motorcycle can be driven at 17 by someone who passed a test before 19 January 2013 in respect of a motorcycle (other than one with an engine with maximum net power output of 11kw or less) and the standard access period has elapsed. An A3 motorcycle can be driven by a person who passed an appropriate driving test after 18 January 2013 on a vehicle of a class in category B or sub-category A2 or A3, and was entitled, before 19 January 2013, to a licence to drive a motor bicycle with an engine having a maximum net power output exceeding 25kw or a power to weight ratio exceeding 9.16kw per kg. An A3 motor tricycle can be driven at 17 by someone who was, before 19 January 2013, entitled to drive vehicles having three or four wheels and an unladen weight not exceeding 550kg.

Although these provisions appear to be complex at first sight, the vehicles with which police officers are generally concerned are motor cycles, private saloon cars, goods vehicles and public service vehicles and the age limits which generally apply are as follows: mopeds may be ridden at 16, motor cycles (unless they are A2 or A3 motorcycles) and private cars at 17, vehicles between 3.5 tonnes and 7.5 tonnes at 18, and those in excess of 7.5 tonnes at 21 (18 in the circumstances described above in relation to initial qualifications) in most circumstances. Small passenger vehicles, which are generally private cars (as the seating of such a vehicle must not exceed nine) may be driven at 17. Passenger vehicles with more than nine seats, with the exceptions outlined, may only be driven by a person of 21; most vehicles of the 'Transit' type fall within this category.

Grant of licences

A person may apply for a driving licence at any time within two months of the date from which the licence will take effect. Where the application is for a large goods or passenger-carrying vehicle driver's licence, it must be made within three months of such date.

Full licences

Where the application is for a full licence, an applicant must satisfy the Secretary of State that he has passed a test at the time of his application. In support of his application he must produce a valid test certificate.

MV(DL)R 1999, Part III deals with the constituent parts of driving tests, and the certificates to be issued to those who take tests. It requires that a test for a licence to drive a category B vehicle (eg the typical private motor car) must be in accordance with reg 40(2A) or (2B).

Regulation 40(2A) provides that a test thereunder must consist of two parts: (a) the standard test of driving theory and the standard test of hazard perception; and (b) the practical test of driving skills and behaviour.

Regulation 40(2B) provides that a test thereunder must consist of three parts: (1) the safe road use test; (2) the abridged standard test of driving theory and the standard test of hazard perception; and (3) the practical test.

In either type of test the theory part must be passed before the practical part is taken.

Where a person has been awarded the Safe Road User Award before 1 May 2010, the test for a category B licence is conducted in two parts, parts (2) and (3) as mentioned above.

As to driving tests for licences for other types of vehicle, see p 386 (motor bicycles) and Appendix 1 (buses and lorries) contained in the companion website to this book <http://www.oup.com/>.

MV(DL)R 1999 include a requirement that, where a person produces to an examiner an appropriate licence which does not include a photograph, he must satisfy the person conducting the test as to his identity by producing a document to establish his identity as prescribed by Sch 6 (all of which have a photograph) or a document of a like nature. However, if the person's identity is clearly apparent from the facts known to, or other evidence in the possession of, the person conducting the test, this will be satisfactory.

Provisional driving licences

Full licences to drive a class of vehicle may only be granted to those who have passed the relevant driving test to drive that class of vehicle. Provisional licences are issued to those who wish to learn to drive motor vehicles and are issued subject to conditions set out in MV(DL)R 1999, reg 16. These conditions are concerned with the need for supervision, distinguishing marks, the drawing of trailers, and the carriage of passengers. However, these conditions do not apply where a provisional licence-holder has passed a test by virtue of which he is entitled to be granted a licence authorising him to drive a vehicle of the class then being driven.

Supervision With the exceptions listed below, a provisional licence-holder must not drive or ride a motor vehicle otherwise than under the supervision of a qualified driver who is present with him in or on the vehicle (MV(DL)R 1999, reg 16).

A person is a qualified driver if he:

(a) is 21 years of age or over;
(b) holds a relevant licence (see below);
(c) has the relevant driving experience (see below); and
(d) in the case of a disabled driver, is supervising a provisional licence-holder who is driving a vehicle of a class included in categories B, C, D, C + E or D + E and would in an emergency be able to take control of the steering and braking functions of the vehicle in which he is a passenger.

However, for the purposes of supervising the holder of a provisional licence driving a vehicle of a class included in sub-category C1, C1 + E, D1, or D1 + E ('the learner vehicle') which the holder is authorised to drive by that licence, a person is not a qualified driver unless that person has, in addition to meeting the above requirements, passed a test in which the vehicle used in the practical test fell within the same sub-category as that of the learner vehicle.

Subject to provisions below relating to a disabled driver, a '*relevant licence*' means a *full licence authorising the driving of vehicles of the same class as the vehicles being driven by the provisional licence-holder*. However, subject to the provisions relating to a disabled driver, where a person holds a full licence authorising the driving of vehicles of the same class as that being driven by the provisional licence-holder, which class is included in a category or sub-category specified in column 1 of the table below, and that person has held the licence for less than three years, 'relevant licence' has a special meaning. It means a full licence authorising:

(a) where that class of vehicle is included within any sub-category specified in column 1 of the table below, the driving of vehicles in the sub-category specified in column 2 which is opposite that sub-category; or

(b) where (a) above does not apply, the driving of vehicles in the category specified in column 2 of that table which is opposite the category specified in column 1 that includes the class of vehicle being driven by the provisional licence-holder.

For the above purposes, the term 'full licence' includes a Northern Ireland licence and a Community licence.

In the case of a (supervising) disabled driver who holds a licence authorising the driving of vehicles in category B, a relevant licence must authorise the driving of vehicles other than a quadricycle or vehicles in sub-category B1 (invalid carriages). A 'disabled driver' is a person who holds a relevant licence which is limited by virtue of a declaration made with his application for the licence or a notice under RTA 1988, s 92(5)(b) to vehicles of a particular class.

Where the above italicised definition of 'relevant licence' only applies, a person has '*relevant driving experience*' if he has held the relevant licence for a minimum period of three years. Where the definitions in (a) and (b) above apply, a person has *relevant driving experience* if he has held the relevant licence authorising the driving of vehicles:

(a) of the same class as the vehicle being driven by the provisional licence-holder for a minimum period of one year; and

(b) in the category or sub-category specified in column 2 of the table below for a minimum period of three years.

For the purpose of meeting the requirements in this paragraph the minimum period of time for holding a full licence may be met either by holding that licence continuously for that period or for periods amounting in aggregate to not less than that period.

A period before 1 May 2010 during which a person ('the supervising driver') has held a licence authorising the driving of vehicles included in sub-category C1, C1+E, D1, or D1+E may only be taken into account in assessing whether the supervising driver has the relevant driving experience to supervise the holder of a provisional licence driving such a vehicle, if the supervising driver has passed a test before 1 May 2010 in which the vehicle used for the practical test fell within one of those sub-categories.

The table referred to above is as follows:

Column (1)	Column (2)
Categories and sub-categories which include the vehicle being driven by the provisional licence-holder	Categories and sub-categories authorised by the relevant licence
C	D
C1	D1
C + E	D + E
C1 + E	D1 + E
D	C
D1	C1
D + E	C + E
D1 + E	C1 + E

The conditions requiring that a qualified driver is over 21 and that he has relevant driving experience do not apply to a member of the armed forces of the Crown acting in the course of his duties. In addition, reg 8 provides that such a person may drive a dual-purpose vehicle (p 430) when it is being used to carry passengers for naval, military, or air force purposes:

(a) where it does not exceed 3.5 tonnes, with a category B (not former sub-category B1 or sub-category B1) licence;
(b) where it exceeds 3.5 tonnes but does not exceed 7.5 tonnes, a C1 licence; and
(c) in any other case, a C licence (other than C1).

The supervisor's duty is to make up for any deficiencies in the skill of the learner; as part of his duty he must participate in the driving to such extent as could reasonably be expected to prevent danger to other persons or property. Because he has a right of control over the learner driver, a supervisor can be convicted as an accomplice to a driving offence committed by the learner driver if he deliberately fails to prevent it when he could reasonably have done so.

A provisional licence-holder is not required to be supervised while undergoing a test. Although an examiner will be with him, the examiner is there for the purpose of assessing his competence, not for the purpose of supervision (and therefore not for the purpose of interference when a lack of skill is evident). The examiner is not, therefore, similarly exposed to charges of aiding and abetting offences by the learner.

A provisional licence-holder is not required to be supervised if he:

(a) is driving a motor vehicle constructed to carry only one person which is not adapted to carry more than one person and which is a vehicle in sub-category B1 (invalid carriages), a motor tricycle, a motor vehicle having four wheels and an unladen weight not exceeding 550 kg, or a motor vehicle of a class included in category F, G, H, or K;
(b) is driving a motor vehicle of a class included in former sub-category B1 which is adapted to carry only one person, and the licence-holder has at any time between 1 August 2002 and 1 March 2003 had the use of an NHS invalid carriage that was issued to him by reason of his having a relevant disability. Category B1 vehicles may have three or four wheels and an unladen weight not exceeding 550 kg;

(c) is riding a moped, or motor bicycle with or without a sidecar, a former category P vehicle, or a category Q vehicle; or

(d) is driving a motor vehicle, other than a vehicle of a class in category C, C + E, D or D + E, on a road in an exempted island (a term which covers small islands like Lundy and the Isles of Scilly other than St Mary's).

It follows, for example, that a small three- or four-wheeler with two seats requires a supervisor in order to be driven by a provisional licence-holder, whereas if it is constructed with only one seat it does not (unless it has since been adapted to carry more than one person). The removal of a seat from a two-seater does not alter the position since it will have been constructed with two. It must be emphasised that there is a total exemption for two-wheeled motor bicycles, whether fitted with a sidecar or not.

Other licence conditions   Motor vehicles which are driven or ridden by persons holding a provisional driving licence must display on the front and on the back of the vehicle the letter 'L' (or 'D' in Wales) in such a manner that it is clearly visible from a reasonable distance to other persons using the road. It is an offence under RTA 1988, s 87(1) for the holder of a provisional licence to drive a vehicle which is not so marked.

The drawing of trailers by a motor vehicle driven by the holder of a provisional licence is prohibited, except that the holder of a provisional licence may do so in relation to the category of vehicles specified if his provisional licence authorises the driving of a vehicle of a class included in category B + E, C + E, D + E or F (combination vehicles where the tractor falls in category B, C or D respectively but the combination does not, or agricultural or forestry tractors).

Holders of provisional licences authorising the driving of a moped, a motor bicycle with or without a sidecar, or a former category P vehicle, or a category Q vehicle, must not drive such a vehicle while carrying on it another person.

The holder of a provisional licence authorising the driving of a motor bicycle other than an A1 motor cycle must drive under the supervision of a 'direct access instructor' who is accompanying him on another motor bicycle or, if the instructor is suffering from a relevant disability of such a nature that he is unable to ride a two-wheeled vehicle, a three-wheeled vehicle in category AM or A; is able to communicate with him by radio other than a hand-held radio; is supervising only that person or, at the most, one additional provisional licence-holder; and is carrying a valid certificate issued by the Secretary of State. The 'learner' and the supervisor must both wear fluorescent or (during hours of darkness) luminous apparel. The holder of a provisional licence authorising the driving of an A1 motorcycle must drive under the supervision of an instructor who is accompanying him on another two-wheeled vehicle in category AM or A or a former category P vehicle and who is supervising him and no more than three other persons, all provisional licence-holders. The requirements concerning communication by radio do not apply to a person who has impaired hearing provided that a suitable means of communication with the instructor is arranged in advance. Direct access instructors hold additional qualifications in respect of larger motor cycles.

It is a condition of a provisional licence to drive a moped or A1 motor cycle that, when undergoing 'relevant training' (receiving professional tuition from a paid instructor in driving on a road after compulsory basic training), the holder of the licence cannot be in a group of more than three other such learners. Such an instructor must be present with him and riding a moped, or A1 motor bicycle, or a category P vehicle.

Offences

By RTA 1988, s 87(1), it is an offence for any person to drive on a road a motor vehicle of any class otherwise than in accordance with a licence authorising him to drive a motor vehicle of that class. Once the prosecution has proved that D has driven a motor vehicle on a road, the onus is upon D to prove that he is licensed to drive as this is a fact peculiarly within his own knowledge. It is desirable that there should be, where possible, a statutory demand for production of the relevant licence, but there is no obligation to do so.

It is an offence, under RTA 1988, s 87(2), for a person to cause or permit another person to drive on a road a motor vehicle of any class otherwise than in accordance with a licence authorising that other person to drive a motor vehicle of that class. For the meaning of 'permit' and 'cause' see p 434.

RTA 1988, s 3ZB created the indictable (either way) offence of causing death by driving when unlicensed. The offence is committed when it is shown that the defendant was driving otherwise than in accordance with a licence issued under RTA 1988, s 87(1) and the death of another person was caused by the driving of that vehicle. There is no requirement to prove any form of negligence.

The activities which may be described as 'driving' in relation to a motor vehicle are discussed in Chapter 14 and it is sufficient to bear in mind that the essence of 'driving' is the use of the driver's controls (or, at least, one of them) in order to control the movements of the vehicle, however that movement is produced, provided that what occurs can in any sense be described as driving.

It should be noted that, when a police officer discovers an offence of driving without a driving licence in circumstances in which the offender's driving would not have been in accordance with any licence that could have been granted to him, the police officer should include in the report reference to whether or not the conditions applicable to that licence were being complied with. The reason is that this is important to the court in relation to the penalty points awarded for the offence.

Motor bicycles: some special rules

Restrictions on provisional licences: two-wheeled vehicles   These are set out in MV(DL) R 1999, reg 15A. A provisional licence granted in respect of a vehicle in category AM or A is restricted to such vehicles as have no more than two wheels save where the applicant declares that he is suffering from a relevant disability of such a nature that he is unable to ride a vehicle which has two wheels. A provisional licence granted in respect of a vehicle with two wheels is restricted to vehicles of a class within category AM or A.

Approved training course   Motor cyclists and moped riders must undertake the two-part practical training which is applicable to them, within an approved training course for motor cyclists and moped riders. The first part is concerned with the basic handling and control of machines. The training for the first part can be undertaken without the necessity to ride on a road. The second part is the normal 'on the road' training to drive which takes place under the supervision of instructors.

A provisional licence does not authorise a person, before he has passed a test of competence to drive, to drive on a road a motor bicycle or moped, except where he has successfully completed an approved training course for motorcyclists or is undergoing training on such a course and is driving a motor bicycle or moped on a road as part of the training. Certificates will be issued to those who have successfully completed such courses.

A certificate is not valid:

(a) if the person to whom it is issued is at the time of issue ineligible to undertake the training course; and

(b) after whichever is the earliest of the following dates, namely:

   (i) in a case where the person to whom the certificate was furnished is subsequently disqualified by order of a court under the RTOA 1988, s 36, the date on which the order is made,

   (ii) in a case where the licence of the person to whom the certificate was furnished is subsequently revoked by the Secretary of State under the Road Traffic (New Drivers) Act 1995 (see p 403), the date on which the revocation has effect,

   (iii) in a case where the certificate was issued before 1 February 2001, the last day of the period of three years beginning with the date of the certificate, or

   (iv) in a case where the certificate was issued on or after 1 February 2001, the last day of the period of two years beginning with the date of the certificate.

MV(DL)R 1999, reg 69 provides that the requirement that a person is not authorised, unless he has passed a driving test of competence, to drive a motor bicycle on a road without having successfully completed an approved training course, does not apply to a person who is a provisional entitlement holder by virtue of having passed a test in respect of former category P (mopeds) on or after 1 December 1990 and before 19 January 2013, or passes the test in respect of category AM (mopeds and light quadricycles), and such a person is also exempt from the need to produce a certificate of such a pass on applying for a driving test to drive a motor bicycle. Similar exemptions exist in favour of persons resident on exempted islands.

The general proposition, that no person may be permitted to take a test of competence to drive a vehicle in category A (motor bicycles and motor tricycles) unless he produces the prescribed certificate of completion of an approved training course, is subject to the following qualifications contained in reg 69. It does not apply to a person who is for the time being the holder of a full licence for a class of vehicle included in category A in respect of a test of competence to drive a vehicle of any other class included in that category. Such a holder is also exempt from the restrictions imposed by RTA 1988, s 97(3) (which prevent the driving of a vehicle in category AM or category A on a road, by the holder of a provisional licence, before he has successfully completed an approved training course for motorcyclists) in respect of his driving of a vehicle of any class included in category AM or A. However, these qualifications do not apply in relation to the holder of a full licence authorising him only to drive a vehicle in category A having automatic transmission in respect of a test to drive vehicles with manual transmission or the driving of such a vehicle.

Driving test   By MV(DL)R 1999, reg 40(1A), the driving test for a licence for a category AM (mopeds and light quadricycles) or a category A vehicle (motor bicycles and motor tricycles) must be conducted in three parts: (a) the standard test of driving theory and the standard test of hazard perception; (b) the manoeuvres test; and (c) the practical test. All three parts must be passed and must be passed in the same category or subcategory of vehicle. Test (a) must be passed before test (b) is taken and test (b) must be passed before test (c) is taken.

Entitlement upon passing a test to drive a category AM vehicle   MV(DL)R 1999, reg 44A provides that, where a person has passed a test for a licence authorising the driving of vehicles included in category AM, the Secretary of State must grant:

(a) in a case where the test was passed on a three-wheeled moped or a light quadricycle, a licence authorising the driving of all vehicles having three or four wheels
included in category AM;

(b) in any other case, a licence authorising the driving of all vehicles included in category AM.

Full licence as provisional licence

RTA 1988, ss 98(2) (and 99A(5)) provide that a full licence (or Community licence) may act
as a provisional licence for any other classes of vehicle, unless the holder is below the minimum age at which the other class of vehicle may be driven. However, by MV(DL)R 1999,
reg 19, this does not apply to a full licence which is restricted to a specially adapted vehicle
for a person with a physical disability, nor does it authorise a person who has not passed a
moped or motor bicycle test to drive a former category P or a category Q vehicle.

MV(DL)R 1999, reg 19 provides that RTA 1988, s 98(2) applies as follows. It provides
that the holder of a full licence which authorises the driving of motor vehicles of a class
included in a category or sub-category specified in column (1) of the table below may
drive motor vehicles:

(a) of other classes included in that category or sub-category, and

(b) of a class included in each category or sub-category specified, in relation to that
category or sub-category, in column (2) of the table,

as if he were authorised by a provisional licence to do so.

Column (1)	*Column (2)*
Full licence held	Provisional entitlement included
AM	A, B, F and K
A1	A, B, F and K
A2	A, B, F and K
A3	B, F and K
B	A, B + E, G and H
C1	C1 + E
C	C1 + E, C + E
D1	D1 + E
D	D1 + E, D + E
F	Q, AM and B
G	H
H	G

In the case of a full licence granted before 19 January 2013 which authorises the driving of a class of standard motor bicycles, other than motor bicycles with an engine the
maximum net power output of which is 11 kilowatts or less, such licences do not
authorise the driving of an A3 motorcycle before the expiration of the standard access
period. Nor do they authorise the driving, as if authorised by a provisional licence, of
vehicles of any class included in category B96.

Except to the extent indicated in the table, ss 98(2) and 99A(5) do not apply in so far as they authorise the full or Community licence-holder to drive vehicles of any class included in category B + E, C + E, D + E, or K or in sub-category B1 (invalid carriages), C1 or D1 (not for hire or reward).

Holders of full licences restricted to vehicles with automatic transmissions may use those licences as provisional licences to drive manually controlled vehicles of a category or sub-category as specified in the table above. A corresponding provision applies to holders of Community licences.

Physical fitness of drivers

RTA 1988, s 92 provides that an applicant for a driving licence must declare his physical fitness to drive, stating whether or not he is suffering, or has in the past suffered, from any relevant or prospective disability. The term 'disability' for the purposes of the section includes disease and the persistent use of drugs or alcohol, whether or not such misuse amounts to dependency, and:

(a) a *relevant disability* means any *prescribed disability* and *any other disability likely to cause* the driving of a vehicle by him to be a source of danger to the public; and

(b) prospective disability means any other disability which, by virtue of its intermittent or progressive nature, may become a disability of the type specified in (a) in course of time.

For the purposes of the prescribed disabilities, licences are divided into Group 1 and 2 licences. Group 1 licences are those for vehicles in categories AM, A, B, B + E, F, G, H, K and L and the former category N (vehicles travelling six or less miles on public roads per week between two pieces of land in same occupation). Group 2 licences cover the other categories of licence; the rules relating to them are more stringent.

In respect of Groups 1 and 2 licences, the disabilities prescribed for the purposes of (a) above are:

(i)   epilepsy;

(ii)   severe mental disorder;

(iii) liability to sudden attacks of disabling giddiness or fainting;

(iv)   liability to sudden attacks of giddiness or fainting due to a heart condition for which a 'pacemaker' has been fitted; or

(v)   persistent misuse of drugs or alcohol, whether or not such misuse amounts to dependency.

The Secretary of State must refuse an applicant a licence if satisfied that the applicant is suffering from a relevant disability (unless in the case of (iii) he is satisfied that the person's driving is unlikely to endanger the public and that that person has adequately arranged regular medical supervision and is conforming to those arrangements).

The Secretary of State may not refuse a licence on account of a relevant disability if the applicant has had a previous licence and his disability is one of absence of a limb, deformity, or loss of use of a limb provided that the condition has not become more acute, or if the application is for a provisional licence.

An epileptic must not be refused a Group 1 licence if free from attacks for one year or (if not so free) for the past three years attacks have been restricted to times while asleep, provided that in either case the following conditions are satisfied: so far as practicable, the applicant must comply with medical directions including directions concerning regular check-ups given to him by a registered medical practitioner supervising his treatment; if required by the Secretary of State, the applicant must provide a signed declaration that he will observe such conditions; and the Secretary of State must be satisfied that the driving of a vehicle in accordance with the licence is not likely to be a danger to the public.

An epileptic may be granted a Group 2 licence if, during the previous 10 years, he has been free from any epileptic attack, he has not required any medication to treat epilepsy, and the driving of a vehicle by him in accordance with the licence is not likely to be a source of danger to the public.

In respect of Group 1 licences, the following are also prescribed as relevant disabilities:

(a) inability in good daylight (with the aid of corrective lenses if worn) to read at a distance of 20.5 m a vehicle registration mark containing characters which are 79 mm high and 57 mm wide, at a distance of 20 m characters which are 79 mm high and 50 mm wide. In the case of mowing machines and pedestrian-controlled vehicles the distance is 12.3 m in the former case and 12 m in the latter;

(b) diabetes mellitus. Where the person is being treated with medication which carries a risk of inducing hypoglycaemia and has experienced two or more episodes of severe hypoglycaemia during the previous one year period, or has impaired awareness of hypoglycaemia, there are no qualifications; the grant of a licence must be refused. On the other hand, where the person is being treated with insulin, he is not prevented from obtaining a licence if he:

   (i) has had no more than one episode of severe hypoglycaemia during the past year;

   (ii) does not have impaired awareness of hypoglycaemia;

   (iii) can demonstrate an understanding of the risks of hypoglycaemia and adequate control of the condition;

   (iv) undertakes regular glucose monitoring;

   (v) is under regular medical review; and

   (vi) is a person in respect of whom the Secretary of State is satisfied that the driving of a vehicle in accordance with the licence is not likely to be a source of danger to the public.

In respect of Group 2 licences, the following are also prescribed as relevant disabilities:

(a) defective eyesight as in (a) above;

(b) except in the case of an excepted licence-holder (holder of categories C1 and C1 + E (8.25 tonnes) licence which was in force before 1 January 1997), such abnormality of sight in one or both eyes as not to meet the relevant standard of visual acuity. Certain other eyesight conditions are also prescribed;

(c) liability to seizure other than epilepsy;

(d) diabetes mellitus. Where the person is being treated with medication which carries a risk of inducing hypoglycaemia and has experienced one or more episodes of severe hypoglycaemia during the previous one-year period, or does not have full awareness of hypoglycaemia, there are no qualifications; the grant of a licence must be refused. On the other hand, the person is not prevented from obtaining a licence in the following cases:

   (i) where he is being treated with insulin and:

      (*a*) has undergone treatment with insulin for at least four weeks, has full awareness of hypoglycaemia, and has not, during the past year, had an episode of severe hypoglycaemia, and (*b*) regularly monitors his condition and, in particular, undertakes blood glucose monitoring at least twice daily and at times relevant to driving (and provides a signed declaration as to his understanding and preparedness to report significant changes in his condition, to follow medical advice, and to provide evidence as to monitoring); or

(ii) where he is being treated with a medication which carries a risk of inducing hypoglycaemia, other than insulin, and has full awareness of hypoglycaemia; and

    (*a*) has not, during the previous year, had an episode of severe hypoglycaemia;

    (*b*) regularly monitors his condition and, in particular, undertakes blood glucose monitoring at least twice daily and at times relevant to driving (and provides a signed declaration as to his understanding and preparedness to report significant changes in his condition, to follow medical advice, and to provide evidence as to monitoring); and

    (*c*) a specialist confirms responsible diabetic control and minimal risk of impairment due to hypoglycaemia; and electronic monitoring is used.

The Secretary of State may, by notice, require a person to be examined by one of his officers rather than a registered medical practitioner, if he suffers from visual defects, limb disabilities or impairment of cognitive function.

Existing licences (including Community licences of persons normally resident in Great Britain) may be revoked totally if such a disability as described above actually arises, or may be revoked and replaced with shorter-term licences if a prospective disability (as described above) arises.

Licences may be issued which allow the driving of vehicles of a special construction—for example, a vehicle fitted with hand controls for a person who has lost both legs—or they may allow driving subject to certain specified conditions.

Persons holding driving licences who suffer an actual or prescribed disability must notify the Secretary of State forthwith. Failure without reasonable excuse to do so is an offence under RTA 1988, s 94(3). Driving after such a failure is an offence under s 94(3A).

A person who holds a licence and drives a motor vehicle of the class authorised on a road commits an offence under s 92(10) if he knowingly made a false declaration in relation to a relevant disability to obtain the licence. A person who drives a motor vehicle on a road, otherwise than in accordance with a licence, commits an additional offence under s 94A(1) if a licence has earlier been refused or revoked on account of such a disability. These offences may also be committed by holders of Community licences normally resident in Great Britain.

RTA 1988, s 96(1) creates the offence of driving a motor vehicle on a road with uncorrected defective eyesight. The offence lies in driving while the eyesight is such that the requirement to read registration marks at the specified distances given above cannot be complied with. The defect in eyesight may be one which cannot be corrected or one which is not for the time being sufficiently corrected to enable the driver to satisfy the above requirement. Thus, a registered blind person necessarily commits the above offence if he drives on a road, whilst a person with impaired vision does not if his vision is sufficiently corrected by wearing spectacles (provided, of course, that he wears them).

A constable may require a person driving a motor vehicle to submit to an eyesight test; it is an offence under s 96(3) to refuse to submit to such a test.

Licences to drive passenger-carrying vehicles or large goods vehicles

Definitions

There are two types of passenger-carrying vehicle (PCV).

A vehicle is a '*large PCV*' if it is used to carry passengers and is constructed or adapted to carry more than 16 passengers, whether or not for hire or reward. The various forms of large PCVs are included in variations of category D types of vehicles under MV(DL) R 1999.

A vehicle is a '*small PCV*' if it is used to carry passengers *for hire or reward* and constructed or adapted to carry more than eight but not more than 16 passengers. Small PCVs are category D1 type vehicles.

A large goods vehicle (LGV) is a motor vehicle (not being a medium-sized goods vehicle as defined on p 378) which is constructed or adapted to carry or to haul goods and the permissible maximum weight of which exceeds 7.5 tonnes. The permissible maximum weights of goods vehicles are as follows:

(a) in the case of a motor vehicle which neither is an articulated goods vehicle nor is drawing a trailer, the relevant maximum weight of the vehicle;

(b) in the case of an articulated goods vehicle:

  (i) when drawing only a semi-trailer, the relevant maximum train weight of the articulated goods vehicle combination;

  (ii) when drawing a trailer as well as a semi-trailer, the aggregate of the relevant maximum train weight of the articulated goods vehicle combination and the relevant maximum weight of the trailer;

  (iii) when drawing a trailer but not a semi-trailer, the aggregate of the relevant maximum weight of the articulated goods vehicle and the relevant maximum weight of the trailer;

  (iv) when drawing neither a semi-trailer nor a trailer, the relevant maximum weight of the vehicle;

(c) in the case of a motor vehicle (not being an articulated goods vehicle) which is drawing a trailer, the aggregate of the relevant maximum weight of the motor vehicle and the relevant maximum weight of the trailer.

The 'relevant maximum weight' of a goods vehicle is the maximum gross weight which is shown on the relevant plate of the vehicle. The relevant plate is always the Ministry plate if the vehicle has then been fitted with one. If it has not, then the relevant maximum weight will be shown on the vehicle.

The 'relevant maximum train weight' of an articulated goods vehicle combination is the gross weight of the unladen motor vehicle and its unladen trailer plus the maximum weight which the combination is permitted to carry. This is shown under the column marked 'gross train weight' on the plate attached to the vehicle.

Matters relating to the weights of goods vehicles are discussed further in Appendix 2 contained in the companion website (<http://www.oup.com/>).

A driving licence issued under RTA 1988, Part III (ss 87 to 109C) is required to cover the driving of PCVs or LGVs or any class thereof on a road. However, by RTA 1988, s 110, licences under RTA 1988, Part III to drive such vehicles must be granted by the Secretary of State in accordance with RTA 1988, Part IV (ss 110 to 122) and, in so far as they authorise the driving of PCVs or LGVs, are subject to Part IV as well as Part III.

Licensing requirements

By s 112, the Secretary of State may not grant a PCV driver's licence or LGV driver's licence unless satisfied, having regard to his conduct, that he is a fit and proper person to hold the licence applied for. Any issue relating to an applicant's conduct may be referred to the traffic commissioner for the area for a determination as to whether the applicant is, having regard to his conduct, a fit person to hold a PCV licence or LGV licence (s 113).

Someone who drives a PCV or LGV without holding a driving licence authorising the driving of a PCV or LGV of the class in question commits an offence under s 87(1), and so does a person who permits him to do so.

By s 114, it is an offence to fail without reasonable excuse to comply with conditions of a PCV or LGV licence

Other provisions of RTA 1988, Part IV are referred to on pp 405–6.

Exemptions

MV(DL)R 1999, reg 50(1) provides that the provisions of RTA 1988, Part IV and the provisions of MV(DL)R 1999, regs 54 (below) and 55, 56 and 57 (special provisions relating only to LGV and PCV drivers' licences) do not apply to LGVs of a classs included in categories F, G or H (some tractors, road rollers and track-laying vehicles) or to sub-category C1 + E (8.25 tonnes), or exempted vehicles. The list of other exempted vehicles is extensive, covering military vehicles, a variety of vehicles used in public works, industry, agriculture, articulated vehicles the unladen weight of which does not exceed 3.5 tonnes, unladen goods vehicles manufactured before 1 January 1960, and emergency vehicles. In addition, by reg 50(2) and (3), RTA 1988, Part IV and the provisions of regs 54 to 57 of the Regulations do not apply to:

(a) a PCV manufactured more than 30 years before the date upon which it is driven and not used for hire or reward or for the carriage of more than eight passengers;
(b) a PCV driven by a constable for the purpose of removing or avoiding obstruction to other road users or to other members of the public, for the purpose of protecting life or property (including the PCV and its passengers) or for other similar purposes.

LGV licences granted to persons under 21

These may be of two types. To permit those aged 18 or over but under 21 to be taught to drive a LGV within a training agreement, provisional trainee drivers' licences may be issued. Other learner drivers will be issued with a standard provisional driving licence.

MV(DL)R 1999, reg 54(1) provides that a LGV driver's licence granted to a person under 21 is subject to the following additional conditions.

A LGV trainee driver's licence is subject to the condition that its holder must not drive a LGV unless he is a registered employee of a registered employer, and the vehicle is a LGV to which his training agreement applies and which is owned or operated by that employer or by a registered LGV driver training establishment (reg 54(2)).

A full LGV driver's licence authorising the driving of a vehicle of category C is subject to the condition that its holder may not drive LGVs in category C + E (other than vehicles included in sub-category C1 + E whose maximum authorised mass does not exceed 7.5 tonnes) as if he were authorised to do so by a provisional licence before the expiry of six months commencing on the date on which he passed a test for category C (reg 54(4)). Thus, a trainee driver could pass a test for category C vehicles (exceeding 3.5 tonnes + trailer not exceeding 750kg) but would be unable to use his full licence for category C vehicles as a provisional licence in respect of category C + E vehicles (combinations of motor vehicles and trailers which fall outside category C) until he has held that full licence for a period of six months.

It is an offence to fail without reasonable excuse to comply with any of these conditions (RTA 1988, s 114(1)), or knowingly to cause or permit someone under 21 to do so (s 114(2)).

Other matters

Other matters relating to the driving of PCVs and LGVs are dealt with in Appendices 1 and 2 on the companion website (<http://www.oup.com>).

Foreigners and driving licences

Community licence-holders

By RTA 1988, s 99A, a Community licence-holder (a holder of a licence issued within the EEA) may drive in Great Britain a motor vehicle of any class which he is authorised by his Community licence to drive, provided that he is not disqualified for holding or obtaining a licence under RTA 1988.

By RTA 1988, s 99A, the holder of a Community licence who becomes resident in Great Britain is authorised to drive here without the need to exchange his licence for a British licence within a year of becoming resident. He does, however, have a right to exchange his licence. Where matters of validity, standards of health and fitness, and disqualification are concerned, the exchange of licences is mandatory. A resident Community licence-holder is subject to the same medical requirements as holders of a British licence. A Community licence-holder resident in Great Britain who wishes to drive medium-sized or large goods vehicles and passenger-carrying vehicles of any class must, after a period of 12 months' residence, deliver his licence to the Secretary of State and provide details prescribed by RTA 1988, s 99B. He will be issued with a counterpart. The right to a British driving licence is restricted to persons normally resident in the UK. A Community licence-holder is also entitled to be licensed to drive a taxi or private hire vehicle or to drive small buses for charitable or similar purposes provided that his Community licence authorises him to drive cars.

Drivers other than Community licence-holders

The Motor Vehicles (International Circulation) Order 1975, art 2 states that it is lawful for *a person resident outside the UK who is temporarily in Great Britain* to drive for a period of 12 months from the date of his last entry into the UK if he holds a Convention driving permit (see below) or a domestic driving permit of a country outside the UK authorising him to drive the vehicle in question, provided he is not disqualified (eg by age) for holding or obtaining a British licence.

What has just been said is subject to qualification in respect of large passenger-carrying vehicles, privately operated passenger-carrying vehicles (vehicles not used for carrying passengers for hire or reward which are constructed or adapted to carry more than eight but not more than 16 passengers), large goods vehicles and medium-sized goods vehicles (vehicles constructed or adapted to carry or haul a load which is not adapted to carry more than nine persons including the driver and exceeds 3.5 tonnes but does not exceed 7.5 tonnes). A holder of either type of permit may drive such a vehicle if he is resident in an EEA (European Economic Area) state, the Isle of Man, Jersey, or Guernsey. Other holders of such a permit may only drive such a vehicle if it has been temporarily brought into Great Britain. In the cases set out in this paragraph no other licence is required.

Generally, any person may cause or permit holders of such Convention or domestic driving permits to drive vehicles which they are authorised by their permit to drive. In the phrase 'temporarily in Great Britain', 'temporarily' is an element other than simply a time element. It involves a presence for casual purposes, for example a holiday, as contrasted with regular habits. For example, an overseas student studying here is not 'temporarily' resident here.

A Convention driving permit is usually referred to as an 'international driving licence'. In Britain it is issued by the AA or RAC. The term 'domestic driving permit' refers to the licence issued by the driver's own country and it is therefore lawful for a visitor to Great Britain to drive for a one-year period on the authority of his own, local driving licence. Article 2, above, merely recognises that persons visiting from abroad would experience difficulty in undertaking a test in Great Britain while they are temporarily in this country. These permits are treated as driving licences in every respect and a constable's powers to demand production of a licence and to demand the holder's date of birth apply equally to them.

MV(DL)R 1999, reg 80 makes the same provision for a person from abroad who becomes resident in Great Britain, the one-year period in this case running from when he became a resident. Someone from abroad who is in this country but who falls outside the term 'temporarily in Great Britain', for example an overseas student, will be resident in Great Britain.

The holder of a relevant permit who becomes resident in Great Britain and is not disqualified for holding or obtaining a licence in Great Britain is, during the one-year period after he becomes so resident, treated as the holder of a licence authorising him to drive all classes of small vehicles (generally vehicles not constructed or adapted to carry more than nine persons inclusive of the driver and vehicles not exceeding 3.5 tonnes, including a combination of such a vehicle and a trailer), motor cycles, or mopeds which he is authorised to drive by that permit. A 'relevant permit' is a 'domestic driving permit', or a 'Convention driving permit'. Where a question arises as to whether a person is normally resident in Great Britain or the UK, a person is deemed to be normally resident if he shows that he will have lived there for not less than 185 days preceding a test appointment.

Persons who become resident in Great Britain and who hold British external licences granted in the Isle of Man, Guernsey, or Jersey authorising the driving of large goods vehicles or passenger-carrying vehicles, and who are not disqualified for holding or obtaining a licence in Great Britain, may drive such vehicles under the authority of those licences for a one-year period from the date upon which they became resident.

People permitted to drive in this country under a domestic driving permit, etc who take out a provisional licence during the one-year period in order to take a driving test need not comply with the normal conditions applicable to a learner driver if they are still driving under the authority of their domestic permit, etc at the time (ie within the one-year period).

RTA 1988, s 108(2) empowers the Secretary of State to designate a non-EEA country for the purpose of 'exchangeable licences' where he is satisfied that the driving test in that country is satisfactory. He may, however, restrict approval to the grant of exchange licences to particular circumstances, impose conditions to which they are subject, and limit the exchanged licence to particular classes of vehicles. An up-to-date list of the countries specified by order is contained in the Driving Licences (Exchangeable Licences) Order 2007.

Production of driving licences

By virtue of RTA 1988, s 164(1), a constable or vehicle examiner (ie an examiner appointed under RTA 1988, s 66A by the Secretary of State) may demand the production of a driving licence and its counterpart by the following people:

(a) a person driving a motor vehicle on a road; or
(b) a person whom a constable or vehicle examiner has reasonable cause to believe has been the driver of a vehicle at the time when an accident occurred owing to its presence on a road; or
(c) a person whom a constable or vehicle examiner has reasonable cause to believe has committed an offence in relation to the use of a motor vehicle on a road; or
(d) a person who is supervising the holder of a provisional licence while the holder is driving a motor vehicle on a road; or
(e) a person whom the constable or vehicle examiner has reasonable cause to believe was supervising the holder of such a licence when an accident occurred owing to the presence of the vehicle on a road or when an offence is suspected of having been committed by the holder in relation to the use of a vehicle on a road.

When a licence is produced to a constable or vehicle examiner pursuant to a request under RTA 1988, s 164(1), he is entitled to ascertain the name and address of the holder of the licence, its date of issue, and the authority by which it was issued. RTA 1988, s 164(2) also provides a power whereby a constable may require a person (A) in circumstances prescribed by MV(DL)R 1999 to state his date of birth. These circumstances are:

(a) where A fails to produce forthwith for examination his driving licence on being required to do so by a constable; or
(b) where, on being so required, A produces a licence which the constable has reason to suspect:
  (i)   was not granted to A, or
  (ii) was granted to him in error, or
  (iii) contains an alteration in its particulars made with intent to deceive; or
(c) where, on being so required, A produces a licence in which the driver number has been altered, erased or defaced; or
(d) where A is a person supervising the holder of a provisional licence while he is driving a motor vehicle on a road, or is someone whom the constable reasonably suspects to have been supervising such a person when an accident occurred or an offence was committed, and the constable has reasonable cause to suspect that A is under 21.

RTA 1988, s 164(4A) provides that, where a constable to whom a provisional licence has been produced by a person driving a motor bicycle has reasonable cause to believe that the holder was not driving it as a part of the training being provided on a training course for motorcyclists, the constable may require him to produce the prescribed certificate of completion of such a course.

A traffic warden is empowered to demand the production of a driving licence where he has reasonable cause to believe that an offence has been committed in contravention of the pedestrian crossing regulations or by leaving a vehicle in a dangerous position.

The term 'licence' means a licence under RTA 1988, Part III or a Community licence.

Police officers have direct access to details of driving licences and their holders through the Police National Computer.

RTA 1988, s 164(3) provides that:

(a) where a licence has been revoked by the Secretary of State but the holder has not surrendered it and its counterpart; or

(b) where the holder has failed to produce his licence and its counterpart to a court when lawfully required to do so; or

(c) where the Secretary of State has served notice on a Community licence-holder in pursuance of s 99C (relevant disability) or s 115A (conduct of holder of LGV or PCV Community licence) requiring delivery of the licence to him,

a constable or vehicle examiner may require the holder to produce them and on production may seize them. RTA 1988, s 164(4) empowers a constable to require the holder of a licence to produce it and its counterpart where he has reasonable cause to believe that a false statement was knowingly made to obtain it.

A person who fails to produce his licence and its counterpart, or a certificate of completion of a training course for motorcyclists, or fails to state a date of birth, when required to do so under any of the provisions of RTA 1988, s 164 commits an offence under RTA 1988, s 164(6).

An offence of failing to produce a licence is not committed if the person produces a current receipt for the surrender of the licence issued under the fixed penalty procedure (see p 473) and, if required, produces the licence in person immediately on its return at a police station specified at the time of the request, or if within seven days of the request he produces the receipt in person at that police station and, if requested, produces the licence there in person immediately on its return. In addition, in proceedings for an offence of failing to produce a licence it is a defence for the defendant to show that:

(a) within seven days after the production of his licence and its counterpart was required he produced them in person at such police station as may have been specified by him at the time its production was required; or

(b) he produced them in person there as soon as was reasonably practicable; or

(c) it was not reasonably practicable for him to produce them there before the day on which proceedings commenced.

If a licence is not produced at the time its production was required, it is the usual practice of the police to make out a form HO/RT1 which will be produced at the police station nominated, together with the driving licence. This is merely a practice followed by the police and there is no statutory requirement that this be done.

Disqualification by a court and penalty points

Revision of system of recording penalty points

The relevant provisions of RTA 1988 (ie Part III) and the fixed penalty provisions of RTOA 1988 have been amended. The previous provisions were such that a fixed penalty notice in respect of an endorsable offence could only be issued to a person holding a driving licence and a counterpart. Fixed penalty notices could not therefore be issued to unlicensed drivers. Nor could they be issued to non-GB residents unless they held a counterpart (to a Northern Ireland or EEA Community driving licence) recording any penalty points previously awarded. Persons holding such licences may apply for counterparts but few do. The new system therefore makes provision for the issue of fixed penalty notices to drivers who do not have counterparts.

Provision is made by the RTOA 1988, s 97A for the Secretary of State to maintain an instantly accessible 'driving record' which will contain details of endorsements for driving offences. The introduction of the revised system involves two stages.

(1) In the first stage, which is in force, records are made of *offences by unlicensed and foreign drivers other than those holding counterparts to their driving licences.* RTOA 1988, s 97A defines the term 'driving record' as a record in relation to the person maintained by the Secretary of State and designed to be endorsed with particulars relating to offences committed by the person under the Traffic Acts (RTA 1988, RTOA 1988, and RTRA 1984).

   RTOA 1988, s 44A, added in 2006 and brought into force in 2009, provides for the endorsement of the driving record of unlicensed drivers or foreign drivers not having a counterpart who have been given a fixed penalty notice in respect of an offence involving obligatory endorsement. Section 44A provides for a constable or vehicle examiner to issue a fixed penalty notice to such a driver where the driver's record maintained by the Secretary of State indicates that the driver would not be liable to a 'totting-up' disqualification. Section 44A also deals with the case where the constable or vehicle examiner cannot satisfy himself at the time about whether the driver would be liable to such a disqualification. In such a case, the officer or vehicle examiner may give the driver a notice stating that if he delivers the notice back to a constable or authorised person at the police station specified in the notice within seven days, or, if the notice is given by a vehicle examiner, the offender returns it to the Secretary of State within 14 days, and the recipient of the notice is satisfied that the offender would not be liable to a 'totting-up' disqualification, he will then be given a fixed penalty notice.

   Under RTOA 1988, s 57A, the driving record of an unlicensed driver or of a foreign driver not having a driving licence with a counterpart who has been given a fixed penalty notice for an offence carrying obligatory endorsement is endorsed, without the need for a court hearing, at the end of a suspended enforcement period unless he gives notice requesting a hearing and has not paid the fixed penalty.

(2) The second stage is not yet in force. It will involve all drivers within the new system and counterparts will become redundant. However, there will be two categories of drivers identifying those who hold GB licences and those who do not. Holders of GB licences will be required to produce their licences in order to be given a fixed penalty notice. Those Community and Northern Ireland licence-holders who previously held counterparts will no longer be treated in the same way as GB licence-holders and will be dealt with in the same way as unlicensed and foreign drivers.

All references to 'counterparts' will be removed from existing legislation as these measures come into effect. However, it is likely to be some time before counterparts become obsolete so far as GB licence-holders are concerned.

Obligatory disqualification

RTOA 1988, s 34(1) deals with disqualification for driving following a conviction for an offence involving obligatory disqualification. On such a conviction, a court must order disqualification for at least a specified minimum period, unless the court for special reasons thinks fit to order a shorter period of disqualification or not to order disqualification at all. These offences, which are all offences under RTA 1988 unless otherwise indicated, are:

(a) manslaughter (common law offence);
(b) causing death by dangerous driving (s 1);
(c) causing serious injury by dangerous driving (s 1A);
(d) dangerous driving (s 2);
(e) causing death by careless or inconsiderate driving (s 2B);
(f) causing death by driving unlicensed, disqualified, or uninsured (s 3ZB);
(g) causing death by careless driving when under the influence of drink or drugs (s 3A);
(h) driving or attempting to drive whilst unfit through drink or drugs (s 4(1));
(i) driving or attempting to drive with excess alcohol in breath, blood, or urine (s 5(1) (a));
(j) failure to provide specimen for analysis (where specimen required to assess ability or alcohol level at time offender was driving or attempting to drive) to see whether person guilty of an offence under s 3A, 4(1), or 5(1)(a) (ss 7(6) and 7A(6));
(k) motor racing and speed trials on a public highway (s 12);
(l) aggravated vehicle-taking (Theft Act 1968, s 12A).

In the case of most of these offences, the specified minimum period of disqualification is 12 months. However, in the case of the offences of manslaughter, causing death by dangerous driving, causing serious injury by dangerous driving, or causing death by careless driving while under the influence of drink or drugs, it is two years.

The same minimum period applies in relation to a person on whom more than one disqualification for a fixed period of 56 days or more has been imposed within the three years immediately preceding the commission of the offence. (When RTOA 1988, s 35A is in force any extension period (see p 402) should be disregarded in computing the period). However, a disqualification imposed as a result of an offence committed by using vehicles in the course of crime or in respect of a conviction for stealing or attempting to steal a motor vehicle, joyriding, or going equipped to steal, etc a motor vehicle, or attempting to commit any such offence, is disregarded for this purpose, as is an interim disqualification on committal for sentence.

If the conviction is for any of the above offences which are connected with the drink-driving laws, that is an offence under RTA 1988, ss 3A, 4(1), 5(1)(a), 7(6), or 7A(6) referred to above, and there has been a previous conviction for such an offence within the preceding 10 years, a court *must* order disqualification for a period of not less than three years, unless there are special reasons for not doing so.

'*Special reasons*' are reasons special to the circumstances of the offence, as opposed to special to the offender. It is of no consequence that the loss of a driving licence will lose the offender his job, that he is a man of previous good character and/or that he has driven for many years without having been convicted of any motoring offence. The courts' approach is strict in this respect. They have refused to accept as special reasons the hardship to a country doctor and his patients or the problems caused for a disabled man. An example of a case where there would be reasons special to the offence is where someone has his supposed non-alcoholic drink 'laced' without his knowledge. In such a case, it is open to the court in its discretion to mitigate the period of disqualification, or not to disqualify at all, because of special reasons. Special reasons might have been found in the case of the country doctor if the country doctor had been called out to a man suffering a heart attack in circumstances in which no other doctor could reasonably have been summoned to attend.

Discretionary disqualification

RTOA 1988, s 34(2) deals with discretionary disqualification. Where a person is convicted of an offence which is shown in Sch 2 to the Act to be one which carries discretionary disqualification and either:

(a) the penalty points to be taken into account on that occasion number fewer than 12; or
(b) the offence is not one involving obligatory endorsement,

the court may disqualify for any period which it thinks fit. Disqualification may not be for an indefinite period, since the court must state the period of disqualification (although it may be for life). Particulars of any disqualification must be endorsed on the licence or its counterpart (or the driving record). Offences which carry discretionary disqualification usually carry obligatory endorsement.

Endorsement and penalty points

RTOA 1988, s 44 provides that, unless there are special reasons not to do so, where a person is convicted of an offence involving obligatory endorsement the court must order particulars of the conviction to be endorsed on his licence or the driving record of an unlicensed or foreign driver (or on the driving record of any driver when the driving record scheme applies to all drivers) and the endorsement must also include:

(a) if the court orders disqualification, particulars of the disqualification; or
(b) if the court does not order disqualification, particulars of the offence (including its date) and the number of penalty points to be attributed as shown in respect of the offence in RTOA 1988, Sch 2 (or, where a range of numbers is so shown, a number falling within the range).

It follows that, where an offender is convicted and the court imposes disqualification under RTOA 1988, s 34, no penalty points are to be attributed for that offence or any other offence in respect of which he is convicted on that occasion. This prevents the possibility of 'double disqualification'.

Where a person is convicted of two or more offences included in Sch 2, all of which are committed on the same occasion, the number of points awarded is generally the highest single figure applicable to one of those offences.

RTOA 1988, Sch 2 lists the offences which carry penalty points. Where a person is convicted for aiding and abetting offences involving obligatory disqualification the number of penalty points to be attributed to the offence is 10. The offences of dangerous driving, causing death by careless driving when under the influence of drink or drugs, driving or attempting to drive vehicles when under the influence of drink or drugs or with excess alcohol in breath, blood, or urine, failing to provide a specimen for analysis, all carry obligatory endorsement of 3–11 penalty points, in addition to obligatory disqualification, unless there are special reasons. However, as indicated above, if disqualification is ordered the licence will not be endorsed with penalty points.

The offence of failing to stop after an accident carries 5–10 points, as does that of failing to report an accident. Insurance offences carry 6–8, careless driving 3–9, and failing to provide a specimen for a screening breath test 4. Any contravention of the construction and use regulations which constitutes an endorsable offence carries 3 points, as does a failure to comply with traffic directions, with the directions of school crossing patrols, or with pedestrian crossing regulations. All offences of exceeding a speed limit carry 3–6 penalty points or 3 (fixed penalty). However, this is prospectively amended by RSA 2006, s 17 which extends the range of penalty points which may be given in respect of speeding to 2–6 or appropriate penalty points (fixed penalty). Offences concerned with driving licences carry 3–6 penalty points, except driving whilst disqualified by a court order which carries 6 points.

Unless there are special reasons for not doing so a court *must* endorse a person's licence if he is convicted of an offence shown in RTOA 1988, Sch 2 to be one in respect of which endorsement is obligatory.

Attendance on courses—effect upon penalty points

RTOA 1988, ss 30A, 30B, 30C and 30D (added in 2006 but none of which is in force at the time of writing) authorise courts to order a reduction in penalty points, to take effect on completion of a training course, where a person has been convicted of careless driving, inconsiderate driving, failing to comply with traffic signs, use of motorway contrary to scheme or regulations, or speeding, and is not disqualified but has his licence endorsed. There must be at least 7 but no more than 11 penalty points to be taken into account at the time of conviction. If such a person successfully completes a course within 12 months after the order, 3 points (or less if the court endorsed less) will cease to be taken into consideration under 'totting-up' considerations.

This option will not be available where a person has committed one of these offences within the preceding three years and has successfully completed such a course, nor to a person who committed the offence during his probationary period under the Road Traffic (New Drivers) Act 1995.

Endorsement—holders of Community licences

RTOA 1988, s 91A provides that within those sections of the Act concerned with the production of a licence to a court in the event of conviction for an offence involving obligatory or discretionary disqualification, the term 'licence' includes references to a Community licence. RTOA 1988, s 91A(4) (prospectively repealed) requires a court to notify the Secretary of State of any endorsement made to a Community licence and s 91A(5) requires a court to send to the Secretary of State a Community licence and its counterpart (if any) in the event of a convicted person being disqualified from driving. The Secretary of State will notify the EEA state concerned of the disqualification.

Duty to notify EU member state of driving disqualification of non-UK resident

The Crime (International Co-operation) Act 2003 (C(IC)A 2003), Part 3, Chapter 1 (ss 54 to 75) deals with this as well as the matters described under the next heading. C(IC)A 2003, s 55 provides that where an individual normally resident in another EU member state is disqualified by a UK court for holding or obtaining a driving licence, the appropriate Minister must generally notify the state in which the individual is normally resident of the details of the disqualification.

EU member states are similarly obliged to notify the UK about the disqualification by their courts of a UK resident.

Recognition of disqualification imposed in another EU state, Northern Ireland, etc

By virtue of C(IC)A 2003, Part 3, Chapter 1, where an individual normally resident in the UK is convicted in another EU member state of an offence of reckless or dangerous driving, drink-driving, speeding, driving while disqualified, or certain other offences, and is disqualified in that state for holding or obtaining a driving licence, and provided certain conditions are satisfied, the appropriate Minister in the UK must give a notice disqualifying that individual for holding or obtaining a licence for the unexpired period of the foreign disqualification beginning 21 days from the giving of the notice; where the unexpired period is less than one month the Minister is not required to give such a notice but may do so. The unexpired period of the foreign disqualification is the period of that disqualification less any period of that disqualification which is treated by regulations as having been served in the foreign state. By the Mutual Recognition of Driving Disqualifications (Great Britain and Ireland) Regulations 2008 the period to be treated for this purpose as having been served in Ireland starts on the day the disqualification became operative in Ireland and ends on the day immediately before the beginning of the 21-day notice period; any time during which the disqualification was suspended is disregarded in determining the period.

RTA 1988, s 102A also provides that a person disqualified for holding or obtaining a driving licence by a court in Northern Ireland, the Isle of Man, any of the Channel Islands or Gibraltar, is disqualified for holding or obtaining a licence in Great Britain for the period of the disqualification.

Obligatory disqualification for repeated offences

RTOA 1988, s 35 applies to an offence involving discretionary disqualification and obligatory endorsement and to an offence involving obligatory disqualification in respect of which no order is made under s 34. Section 35 requires that where, on conviction for such an offence, the award of the penalty points for the offence, together with those already endorsed on the licence, brings the total to 12, the offender must be disqualified for a minimum period of six months if the points have been accumulated within three years of the commission (and not the conviction) of the offence for which penalty points are then awarded, unless the court is satisfied that there are grounds for mitigating the normal consequences of the conviction and thinks fit to order a shorter period of disqualification or not to order disqualification. If the total is in excess of 12 this may be recognised by disqualification for a longer period. The minimum period is one year's disqualification if there is a previous disqualification in the above period, or two if there is more than one. No account is to be taken, as a ground for mitigating the normal consequences, of any circumstances which are alleged to make the offence or any of the offences not a serious one; nor of any hardship other than exceptional hardship; nor of any circumstances which, within the preceding three years, have already been taken into account in ordering the offender to be disqualified for a shorter period or not to be ordered to be disqualified at all. Exceptional hardship which would be caused to a person other than the offender (for example a dependent, invalid wife) may be taken into account.

It follows from the above rules that, even if a court decides not to order disqualification when it is discretionary in relation to the offence in question, because of mitigating circumstances, it may be required to disqualify under RTOA 1988, s 35 as a result of the 'totting-up' of the penalty points attributed for the offence with previous penalty points.

A person who is already the holder of a driving licence authorising him to drive a vehicle of a particular class is disqualified by RTA 1988, s 102 for holding another licence for that class of vehicle. This is to prevent a person from holding more than one licence. If he was able to do so he could share out his penalty points by holding two licences indicating different addresses.

Once the disqualification has been imposed the driving licence is in effect wiped clean. However, 'wiping clean' is restricted to disqualification under s 35 for repeated offences. Where a disqualification is imposed under s 34 for a specific offence, the penalty points previously accumulated remain effective at the end of the period of disqualification until the expiry of three years from the date of the offence for which they were imposed.

Extension of disqualification period where immediate custodial sentence also imposed

When RTOA 1988, s 35A comes into force, where the offender has been sentenced to an immediate term of imprisonment for the offence for which he is to be disqualified, the court must add to the period of disqualification determined under s 34 or s 35 an extension period (broadly, the custodial period which must be served). This is designed to require that the former period of disqualification takes effect after the offender's release from imprisonment.

Use of vehicle in commission of crime: discretion to disqualify

On conviction of an offender in the Crown Court of an offence punishable with imprisonment for a term of two years or more, or when sentencing such a person after his conviction before a magistrates' court for such an offence, the Crown Court, if satisfied that a motor vehicle was used (by the person convicted or anyone else) for the purpose of committing or facilitating the commission of the offence, may disqualify the person convicted for such a period as it thinks fit for holding or obtaining a licence to drive (Powers of Criminal Courts (Sentencing) Act 2000, s 147). 'Facilitation' will include use after the offence for disposal of property or avoiding apprehension or detection.

Disqualification: offenders in general

The Powers of Criminal Courts Crime (Sentencing) Act 2000, s 146 empowers a court on conviction of any offence to order the offender to be disqualified. The Court of Appeal has held that this power is not limited to offences connected with the driving of a motor vehicle. However, there may be human rights implications where such disqualification is ordered for an offence, the commission of which was not aided, in any respect, by the use of a motor vehicle and which could not be prevented by the removal of the right to drive.

Legislation also empowers a magistrates' court to order disqualification in a case of default in paying a fine.

Effect of an order of disqualification

RTOA 1988, s 37(1) provides that, where a licence-holder is disqualified by order of a court, the licence is to be treated as revoked with effect from the beginning of the period of disqualification. However, where the disqualification is for a fixed period shorter than 56 days in respect of an offence involving obligatory endorsement or the order is made under s 26 (interim disqualification), this does not prevent the licence from again having effect at the end of the period of disqualification. When an amendment by the Coroners and Justice Act 2009 is in force, any extension period must be disregarded in calculating the length of the disqualification for the purposes of s 37 (and s 42, below).

Removal of disqualification

RTOA 1988, s 42 provides that a person who has been disqualified by a court may apply to have the disqualification removed as follows:

(a) if the disqualification is for less than four years, after two years;

(b) if it is for less than ten but more than four years, when half the disqualification has expired; or

(c) in any other case (life or ten or more years), when five years have passed.

Disqualification until passing of driving test

RTOA 1988, s 36 provides that, where a person is disqualified under s 34 (obligatory disqualification) on conviction for manslaughter by the driver of a motor vehicle, or for causing death by dangerous driving, or for causing serious injury by dangerous driving, or for dangerous driving, for causing death by careless driving while under the influence of drink or drugs, or is disqualified under ss 34 or 35 (repeated offences) in such circumstances or for such period as the Secretary of State may prescribe, or is convicted of an offence involving obligatory endorsement which may be prescribed by the Secretary of State, the court must order him to be disqualified until he has passed the appropriate driving test.

Where a person is disqualified under s 34 on conviction for any other offence carrying obligatory endorsement, the court may order him to be disqualified until he has passed the appropriate driving test.

An order of disqualification until the passing of a driving test ends when a certificate of competence is produced to the Secretary of State.

The term 'appropriate driving test' is prospectively amended by RSA 2006, s 37 so as to mean an extended driving test in such circumstances as the Secretary of State prescribes and, otherwise, a test of competence to drive which is not an extended driving test. Currently, an extended driving test is required where a person is convicted of an offence involving obligatory disqualification or is disqualified under the totting-up provisions (RTOA 1988, s 35), and the ordinary driving test is required in any other circumstances.

A person disqualified until he has passed a driving test is permitted by RTOA 1988, s 37(3) to take out a provisional licence, once any fixed period of disqualification has expired, in which case he may drive under the conditions applicable to such a licence. A person who drives under a provisional licence granted by virtue of s 37(3), but who does not comply with the conditions attached to such a licence, commits an offence contrary to RTA 1988, s 103(1), of driving whilst disqualified. A person charged with driving while disqualified who relies on RTOA 1988, s 37(3) has the burden of proving that he is the holder of a provisional licence and that he was driving in accordance with the provisions of such a licence.

Revocation of licence of 'new driver'

Under the Road Traffic (New Drivers) Act 1995, where a qualified driver commits an offence involving obligatory endorsement during his 'probationary period' (two years from becoming a qualified driver) and the penalty points to be taken into account on that occasion number six or more, the court must send the Secretary of State a notice containing the particulars to be endorsed on the counterpart of the person's licence together with the licence (and counterpart). A similar requirement is made of a fixed penalty clerk, where a fixed penalty offence is involved. The Secretary of State must, by notice, revoke that licence. Such a licence may not be granted (restored) until the person concerned has passed a relevant driving test (ie re-test); the re-test must be within two years of that revocation. There are similar provisions about the revocation of a provisional licence and test certificate where the driver has not applied for a full licence.

The prescribed probationary period ends early:

(a) where an order is made under RTOA 1988, s 36 (disqualified until a test is passed); or
(b) where, after revocation of the licence (or provisional licence plus test certificate) by the Secretary of State (see above), the full licence is granted after the person has passed a re-test.

Obtaining licence, or driving, while disqualified

RTA 1988, s 103 creates two offences which can be committed by a person disqualified *by a court*: obtaining a licence while so disqualified (s 103(1)(a)), and driving a motor vehicle on a road whilst so disqualified (s 103(1)(b)). RTA 1988, s 3ZB created a more serious, indictable (either way) offence of causing death by driving when disqualified, which does not require proof of negligence.

An order of disqualification remains valid unless it is suspended pending an appeal or is subsequently revoked. A subsequent revocation does not excuse driving whilst the order was in force. The prosecution must prove not only the order of disqualification (by means of certificate of conviction or entry in a court register), but that the person before the court is the person so disqualified. There is no prescribed way that the identification of the defendant (D) as the person disqualified must be proved; it can be proved by any admissible means. Proof of identity may be given, for example, by an admission under the Criminal Justice Act (CJA) 1967, s 10, or by evidence of a person who was present in court when the disqualification was imposed. In addition, a written statement made under CJA 1967, s 9, which refers to a person whom the deponent knew and stating that the deponent knew him under a particular name, may provide sufficient evidence of identification. It will normally be possible to establish a prima facie case on the basis of a match between the personal details of D and those recorded on the certificate of conviction. Indeed, where D has a highly unusual name it may not be necessary for the date of birth on the certificate to correspond with his. If D calls no evidence to contradict a prima facie case, it is open to the court to be satisfied that it has been proved that D was the person disqualified. In addition, if it is proper and fair to do so and warning has been given, a failure to give contradictory evidence can additionally give rise to an adverse inference under the Criminal Justice and Public Order Act 1994, s 35, dealt with on p 251.

In terms of proof of the order of disqualification, a divisional court has ruled that justices are not entitled to consult their own computerised records of convictions in order to establish whether D is a person who has, on a previous occasion, been disqualified from driving; the prosecutor is obliged to prove that D was a disqualified driver.

Offender escaping consequences of endorsable offence by deception

RTOA 1988, s 49 covers the case where, in dealing with a person convicted of an endorsable offence (ie one involving obligatory or discretionary endorsement), a court was deceived regarding any circumstances that were or might have been taken into account in deciding whether, or for how long, to disqualify him. It provides that, if the deception constituted or was due to an offence committed by that person and he is convicted of *that* offence, the court has the same powers of disqualification as the court which was deceived. However, the court must take account of the order made by the first court on his conviction for the endorsable offence.

Revocation of passenger-carrying vehicle or large goods vehicle drivers' licences

RTA 1988, s 115 requires that a passenger-carrying vehicle or large goods vehicle driver's licence:

(a) must be revoked by the Secretary of State if, in relation to its holder, prescribed circumstances occur; or
(b) must be revoked or suspended by the Secretary of State if the holder's conduct is such as to make him unfit to hold such a licence. A divisional court has held that 'conduct' such as to make a driver 'unfit to hold such a licence' refers to conduct 'as a driver of a motor vehicle'.

RTA 1988, s 115A makes similar provision in respect of the holder of a LGV Community licence or a PCV Community licence where that person ceases to be authorised to drive a LGV or PCV (as the case may be).

The 'prescribed circumstances' referred to in (a) are set out in respect of a large goods vehicle driver's licence or a LGV Community licence by MV(DL)R 1999, reg 55. They are that, in the case of the holder of such a licence who is *under 21*, the holder has been convicted, or is by virtue of RTOA 1988, s 58 (*effect of endorsement without hearing under fixed penalty points provisions*) to be treated as if he had been convicted, of an offence as a result of which more than three penalty points are to be taken into account. Where such large goods vehicle licences are revoked, the cases in which such persons must be disqualified indefinitely or for a fixed period must be determined by the Secretary of State. Where it is determined that the disqualification shall be for a fixed period, such a person must be disqualified until he reaches 21 or for such longer period as the Secretary of State may determine. No corresponding provisions have been made in respect of large passenger-carrying vehicle licences.

Regulation 56 applies where large goods vehicle or passenger-carrying vehicle drivers' licences are treated as revoked by RTOA 1988, s 37 (effect of disqualification by order of court). RTA 1988, s 117 is modified by reg 56 to provide that, where the licence to be treated as revoked is a large goods vehicle driver's licence held by a person under 21, the Secretary of State must order that person to be disqualified either indefinitely or for a fixed period, and where the Secretary of State determines that it shall be for a fixed period, he must be disqualified until he reaches 21 or for such longer period as the Secretary of State determines. Where the licence revoked is held by *any other person*, or is a large passenger-carrying vehicle driver's licence:

(a) the Secretary of State may order that person to be disqualified either indefinitely or for a fixed period; or
(b) the Secretary of State may order him to be disqualified for holding or obtaining a full licence until he passes the test if it appears that, owing to that person's conduct, it is expedient to require him to comply with the prescribed conditions applicable to provisional licences until he passes a test. This does not apply where the licence is a provisional licence.

Where the Secretary of State orders disqualification until a test is passed, the test must be a test for a licence authorising the driving of any class of vehicle in Category C (other than C1), C + E, D, or D + E which, prior to his disqualification by order of the court, the offender was authorised to drive by his revoked licence.

By RTA 1988, s 117 or 117A respectively, where a person's licence is revoked under s 115 or s 115A the Secretary of State must order that that person be disqualified. Such a disqualification for more than two years may be removed after two years if the disqualification is for less than four years, or after half the disqualification period if that period is between four and 10 years, or five years if it is 10 years or more, provided the applicant for removal has not incurred any penalty points (while disqualified) (MV(DL)R 1999, reg 57).

Access to driver licensing records

The Motor Vehicles (Access to Driver Licensing Records) Regulations 2001, reg 2 provides that the purposes for which constables may be given access to information made available to the National Policing Improvement Agency (NPIA) are:

(a) the prevention, investigation, or prosecution of a contravention of any provision of the following enactments:
   (i)   the RTA 1988,
   (ii) the Road Traffic Offenders Act (RTOA) 1988,
   (iii) the Road Traffic (Northern Ireland) Orders 1981 and 1995,
   (iv) the Road Traffic Offenders (Northern Ireland) Order 1996,
   (v)   the Vehicle Drivers (Certificates of Professional Competence) Regulations 2007; and
(b) ascertaining whether a person has had an order made in relation to him under:
   (i)   the Child Support Act 1991, s 40B(1) or (5) (disqualifications from driving: further provisions) (prospectively repealed by the Welfare Reform Act 2009),
   (ii) the Criminal Procedure (Scotland) Act 1995, ss 248A(1) (general power to disqualify offenders) or 248B(2) (power to disqualify fine defaulters), or
   (iii) the Crime (Sentences) Act 1997, ss 39(1) (offenders) or 40(2) (fine defaulters).

Regulation 3 provides that information to which constables have been given access may be further disclosed to an employee of a police authority, local policing body, or chief officer of police for any purpose ancillary to, or connected with, the use of the information by constables.

In addition, RV(R&L)R 2002, reg 27 authorises the Secretary of State to make available particulars contained in the register to:

(a) a local authority for the purpose of an investigation of an offence or for any purpose connected with its activities as an enforcement authority under the Traffic Management Act 2004, Part 6 (see p 468);
(b) a chief officer of police;
(c) the Motor Insurers' Bureau in connection with its functions relating to the enforcement of the offence of keeping a vehicle which does not meet insurance requirements; or
(d) any person who can show satisfactory cause for requiring the information.

Regulation 28 authorises the Secretary of State to sell such particulars to such persons as he considers fit, provided that the information does not identify any person or contain anything enabling such identification.

MOTOR VEHICLE INSURANCE

Using, causing or permitting use of, a motor vehicle on a road without insurance

RTA 1988, s 143(1) states that a person must not use, or cause or permit any other person to use, a motor vehicle on a road or other public place unless there is in force in relation to the use of that vehicle by that person or that other person, as the case may be, such a policy of insurance or such security in respect of third-party risks as complies with the requirements of RTA 1988, Part VI. By s 143(2), breach of s 143(1) is an offence. Section 143(4) states that Part VI does not apply to invalid carriages not exceeding 254 kg unladen weight; a mobility scooter is a type of invalid carriage. Since electrically assisted pedal cycles are not motor vehicles (unless they fall outside the relevant regulations), the provisions dealing with insurance do not apply to them.

As in the case of driving without a driving licence, the onus is upon a defendant (D), who is proved to have used a motor vehicle on a road or other public place, to prove the existence of insurance as this is a fact peculiarly within his knowledge. However, a divisional court has said that it is *desirable* that there should be, where possible, a statutory demand for its production.

For the meaning of 'road' and 'public place' see pp 343 and 531 respectively. The terms 'use', 'cause' and 'permit' are discussed in Chapter 10. Basically, a person who drives a vehicle 'uses' it, but 'using' is not limited to driving. 'Use' means 'have the use of', with the result that, for example, if someone parks a motor vehicle on a road he can be said to be using it while it is parked, and it has been held that this is so even though the vehicle has been totally immobilised. Where an employee drives a motor vehicle owned by his employer in the course of his employment, his employer is regarded in law as also using it. A person 'causes' a vehicle to be used when, being in a position to do so, he expressly orders or authorises the vehicle to be used; and he 'permits' a vehicle to be used when he allows another person to use it. In each case, of course, the use must be on a road or other public place without there being in force in relation to the use of the person using the vehicle a requisite third-party policy of insurance or security.

The prohibition in s 143(1) against using, or causing or permitting the use of, an uninsured vehicle is strict in the sense that it is no defence that D reasonably believed that he, or the person allowed, etc to drive, was covered by an insurance policy, etc. There is one exception: under RTA 1988, s 143(3) it is a defence for a person charged with *using* an uninsured vehicle to prove that it did not belong to him and was not in his possession under a contract of hiring or loan, and that he was using it in the course of his employment and neither knew nor had reason to believe that it was not properly insured, etc.

Can a person be said to permit his vehicle to be used on a road or other public place without insurance when he has lent it out on the express condition that it should only be used if its use is covered by insurance and its subsequent use is not so covered? The law provides a rather odd answer. If the condition is directly communicated to the person who uses the vehicle without insurance, the person imposing the condition does not permit his vehicle to be used without insurance. This seems sensible. How can you permit something which you have expressly forbidden? Thus, it is somewhat surprising that a divisional court has held that, if the condition as to use being covered by insurance has not been directly communicated to the user but has been communicated to someone else, for example to someone who borrows the vehicle, with a view to it being driven by the user, and it is used in breach of that condition, the person imposing the condition does in law permit uninsured use.

A person cannot permit another's use if he was not in a position to forbid it. Thus A, who supervises B, a learner driver, in B's own car cannot be convicted of permitting its uninsured use.

Causing death by driving uninsured

RTA 1988, s 3ZB creates an indictable (either way) offence of causing death by driving when uninsured. The offence is committed when it is shown that the defendant was using a motor vehicle on a road or public place while uninsured or unsecured against third-party risks, contrary to RTA 1988, s 143, and that the death of another person was caused by the driving of that vehicle. There is no requirement to prove any form of negligence.

Keeping vehicle not meeting insurance requirements

Section 144A creates an offence of keeping a motor vehicle which does not meet the insurance requirements. No use on a road or other public place is required. A vehicle will meet the insurance requirements if it is covered by a policy of insurance or a security complying with RTA 1988 and either the policy or security, or a related certificate, identifies the vehicle covered by its registration mark or the policy or security covers any vehicle, or any particular type of vehicle, owned by the person named in it or a related certificate. There are no penalty points to be imposed for this offence.

Section 144B specifies exceptions which are generally the same as those set out in s 144 (vehicles of local authorities, the police, and National Health Service, etc: see p 417).

Other exceptions may apply where the vehicle is no longer kept by the registered keeper, it is not kept for use on a road or other public place or it has been stolen. However, these exceptions only apply if a 'prior statement' has been made in respect of the vehicle. The Motor Vehicles (Insurance Requirements) Regulations (MV(IR)R) 2011, regs 2–4 set out the following requirements for the 'prior statement':

(1) In the case of the exception relating to a vehicle no longer kept by the registered keeper:
   (a) where the vehicle has been sold or transferred by the registered keeper (other than to be destroyed or sent permanently out of Great Britain) the registered keeper must, by the relevant time and in relation to that vehicle, have furnished the information and documents and made the declarations in accordance with the appropriate requirements;
   (b) where the vehicle has been sold or transferred by the registered keeper for the purpose of its destruction, that keeper must, by the relevant time and in relation to that vehicle, have furnished the information and documents and made the prescribed declarations, or been given a certificate of destruction; and
   (c) where the vehicle has been sent permanently out of Great Britain, the registered keeper must, by the relevant time and in relation to that vehicle, have notified the Secretary of State of that fact (reg 2).

(2) In the case of the exception relating to a vehicle not kept for use on a road or other public place, the registered keeper must, by the relevant time and in relation to that vehicle, have made a statutory off-road notification (reg 3).

(3) In the case of the exception relating to a vehicle which has been stolen, the registered keeper must, by the relevant time and in relation to that vehicle, have given notification of the theft to a member (or employee) of a police force (reg 4).

MV(IR)R 2011, reg 5 adds to 144B a further exception to an offence under RTA 1988, s 144B, namely that:

(a) the registered keeper is at the relevant time keeping the vehicle;
(b) neither a licence nor a nil licence under VERA 1994 was in force on 31 January 1998;
(c) neither a licence nor a nil licence has been taken out for the vehicle for a period starting after that date; and
(d) the vehicle has not been used or kept on a public road after that date.

Section 144C authorises the Secretary of State to serve a fixed penalty notice on a person whom he believes to have committed an offence against s 144A. That penalty is £100 but it is reduced to £50 if that amount is paid within 21 days of notice being given that a RTA 1988, s 144A offence has been committed.

Immobilisation, removal, and disposal

The Motor Vehicles (Insurance Requirements) (Immobilisation, Removal and Disposal) Regulations (MV(IR)(I, R and D)R) 2011 provide for the clamping of vehicles by an authorised person (AP) who has reason to believe that a s 144A offence has been committed, and their removal and disposal. An AP is a person authorised by the Secretary of State for the purposes of MV(IR)(I, R and D)R 2011. An AP may be a local authority, an employee of a local authority, a member of a police force or any other person. Different persons may be authorised for different purposes, but a person who is an AP for the purposes of reg 14 (appeals: below) must not act as an AP for any other purpose (reg 3).

By reg 4, MV(IR)(I, R and D)R 2011 do not apply where:

(a) a current disabled person's badge is displayed on the vehicle;
(b) the vehicle appears to an AP to have been abandoned;
(c) the vehicle is a public service vehicle being used for the carriage of passengers;
(d) the vehicle is being used for the purpose of the removal of any obstruction to traffic, the maintenance, improvement or reconstruction of a public road, or the laying, erection, alteration, repair or cleaning in or near a road of any traffic sign or sewer or of any main, pipe or apparatus for the supply of gas, water or electricity, or of any telegraph or telephone wires, cables, posts or supports; or
(e) the vehicle is being used by a universal service provider in relation to the provision of a universal postal service and each side of the vehicle is clearly marked with the name of the universal service provider concerned.

Power to immobilise vehicles   Where an AP has reason to believe that an offence under RTA 1988, s 144A is being committed as regards a vehicle which is stationary on a road or other public place, he (or a person acting under his direction) may:

(a) fix an immobilisation device to the vehicle while it remains in the place where it is stationary, or
(b) move it from that place to another place on the same or another road or public place and fix an immobilisation device to it in that other place.

The exercise of this power does not prevent a prosecution for an offence under RTA 1988, Part VI (ss 143 to 162) (reg 5).

Where an immobilisation device is so fixed to a vehicle, the person fixing it must also fix to the vehicle an immobilisation notice which:

(a) indicates that the device has been fixed to the vehicle and warns that no attempt should be made to drive it or otherwise put it in motion until it has been released from the device;
(b) states the reason why the device has been fixed;
(c) specifies the steps to be taken to secure its release, including the charges payable under MV(IR)(I, R and D)R 2011 and the person to whom and the means by which those charges may be paid; and
(d) states the right of the owner, or person in charge of the vehicle at the time it was immobilised, to appeal, and specifies the steps to be taken and the address to which representations to an AP should be sent.

Except in relation to a vehicle which is the subject of a hiring agreement or a hire-purchase agreement, references to the 'owner' of a vehicle at a particular time are to the person by whom it was then kept and the registered keeper at a particular time is to be taken, unless the contrary is shown, to be the person by whom the vehicle was kept at that time (MV(IR)(I, R and D)R 2011, reg 2).

For the purposes of regs 5 (above), 11 (below), and 12 (below), 'owner', in relation to a vehicle which is the subject of a hiring agreement or hire-purchase agreement, means a person who is a party to such an agreement (reg 2).

Release of immobilised vehicles (reg 6)   A vehicle to which an immobilisation device has been fixed in accordance with reg 5:

(a) may only be released by, or under the direction of, an AP; and
(b) subject to (a), is to be released:
  (i) where an AP is satisfied that the vehicle was immobilised in any of the circumstances specified in reg 4; or
  (ii) if the following two requirements are met, viz.
    (*a*) that the prescribed charge (£100) for the release of the vehicle from the immobilisation device is paid in any manner specified in the immobilisation notice, and
    (*b*) that, in accordance with any instructions specified in the immobilisation notice, prescribed evidence is produced which establishes that any person who proposes to drive the vehicle away will not in doing so be guilty of an offence under RTA 1988, s 143, and that the registered keeper is not, at the point of release, guilty of an offence under RTA 1988, s 144A as regards the vehicle.

For the purposes of MV(IR)(I, R and D)R 2011, 'prescribed evidence' means any of the following: a policy or certificate of insurance, or a policy or certificate of security in respect of third party risks.

Removal of or interference with immobilisation notice or device   An immobilisation notice must not be removed or interfered with except by or under the authority of an AP; it is an offence to do so (reg 7(1) and (2)).

Any person who, without being authorised to do so in accordance with reg 6, removes or attempts to remove an immobilisation device fixed to a vehicle is guilty of an offence (reg 7(3)).

Other offences connected with immobilisation (reg 8)   Where MV(IR)(I, R and D)R 2011 would apply to a vehicle but for the fact that a current disabled person's badge is displayed on it and the vehicle was not, at the time it was stationary, being used:

(a) in accordance with the 'Badges Regulations' made under regulations under the Chronically Sick and Disabled Persons Act 1970 (p 485), and

(b) in circumstances falling within the Road Traffic Regulation Act 1984, s 117(1)(b) ((b) on p 486), the person in charge of the vehicle at that time is guilty of an offence.

Removal of vehicles (reg 9)   Where an AP has reason to believe that an offence under RTA 1988, s 144A:

(a) is being committed as regards a vehicle which is stationary on a road or other public place, or

(b) was being committed as regards a vehicle at the time when an immobilisation device which is fixed to the vehicle was fixed to it and:

   (i)   24 hours have elapsed since the device was fixed to the vehicle, and
   (ii) the vehicle has not been released in accordance with MV(IR)(I, R and D)R 2011,

the AP, or a person acting under his direction, may remove the vehicle and deliver it to a person authorised by the Secretary of State to keep vehicles so removed ('the custodian').

Disposal of removed vehicles (reg 10)   The custodian of a vehicle delivered in accordance with reg 9 may dispose of it by selling it or dealing with it as scrap, as he thinks fit.

   Where the owner of a vehicle has disclaimed all rights of ownership of that vehicle, it may be disposed of at any time.

   In any other case, a vehicle must not be disposed of before:

(a) the end of a period, beginning with the date on which the vehicle was removed in accordance with reg 9, of either:
   (i)   in the case of a vehicle of no economic value, seven days, or
   (ii) in any other case, 14 days;

(b) the custodian has, for the purpose of ascertaining the owner of the vehicle, taken steps to ascertain from GB records or, as the case may be, Northern Irish records, the name and address of the registered keeper, or, if the vehicle does not carry a GB or Northern Irish registration mark, the custodian has made such inquiries as appear to be practicable to ascertain the identity of the owner of the vehicle, and

(c) either:
   (i)   the custodian has failed to ascertain the name and address of the owner; or
   (ii) the owner has failed to comply with a notice in accordance with the following requirements served on the owner by first class post. The requirements are that the notice must be a notice addressed to the owner which states—
      (*a*)   the registration mark and make of the vehicle;
      (*b*)   the place where the vehicle was found before it was immobilised;
      (*c*)   the place to which it has been removed;
      (*d*)   the steps to be taken to obtain possession of it in accordance with reg 12 (below); and
      (*e*)   that unless it is removed by the owner on or before the date as specified below, the custodian intends to dispose of it;
      and requires the owner to remove the vehicle from the custody of the custodian—
      (*f*)   in the case of a vehicle which is of no economic value, within three days of the date on which the notice is served; or
      (*g*)   in any other case, within seven days of that date.

For these purposes, a vehicle is of no economic value if the custodian is satisfied that the total prescribed charges for the removal of the vehicle and its storage for seven days exceed the resale or scrap value of the vehicle.

Where it appears to a custodian of a vehicle that more than one person is the owner, such one of them as the custodian thinks fit is treated as the owner for the above purposes.

Except in relation to a vehicle which is the subject of a hiring agreement or a hire-purchase agreement, references to the 'owner' of a vehicle at a particular time are to the person by whom it was then kept and the registered keeper at a particular time is to be taken, unless the contrary is shown, to be the person by whom the vehicle was kept at that time (reg 2).

For the purposes of regs 10 and 13, 'owner', in relation to a vehicle which is the subject of a hiring agreement or hire-purchase agreement, means the person who, being a party to such agreement, has given up possession of the vehicle in return for payment under the agreement (reg 2).

Recovery of prescribed charges (reg 11)   Where a vehicle has been removed and delivered into the custody of a custodian in accordance with reg 9, the Secretary of State or the custodian may (whether or not any claim is made under reg 12 or 14 (below)) recover from the person who was the owner of the vehicle when the vehicle was removed the prescribed charges for:

(a) its removal and storage; and
(b) its disposal, if the vehicle has been disposed of.

The relevant prescribed charges are:

Removal of a vehicle where possession is taken within the first 24 hours of such removal	£100
Removal of vehicle where the above does not apply	£200
Storage of vehicle for each period of 24 hours or part thereof	£21
Disposal of vehicle	£50

For the above purposes, 'owner' has the same meaning as for the purposes of reg 5 (p 410).

Where, by virtue of (a) above, any sum is recoverable in respect of a vehicle by a custodian, the custodian is entitled to retain custody of it until that sum is paid.

Where it appears to a custodian of a vehicle that more than one person is the owner, such one of them as the custodian thinks fit is to be treated as the owner for the purposes of this regulation.

Taking possession of a vehicle (reg 12)   A person ('the claimant') may take possession of a vehicle which has been removed and delivered to a custodian and has not been disposed of under reg 10, if:

(a) the claimant satisfies the custodian that the claimant is the owner of the vehicle, or a person authorised by the owner to take possession of the vehicle;
(b) except where the claimant produces evidence that no offence under RTA 1988, s 144A was committed or the custodian is satisfied that MV(IR)(I, R and D)R 2011 did not apply to the vehicle at the time it was immobilised or removed, the claimant pays to the custodian:

   (i)   the prescribed charge in respect of the removal of the vehicle; and

   (ii) the prescribed charge for the storage of the vehicle during the period it was in the custody of the custodian; and

(c) prescribed evidence (p 410) is produced which establishes that—

   (i)   any person who proposes to drive the vehicle away will not in doing so be guilty of an offence under RTA 1988, s 143; and

   (ii) the registered keeper is not, at the point of release, guilty of an offence under RTA 1988, s 144A as regards the vehicle.

On giving the claimant possession of a vehicle pursuant to the above, the custodian must give the claimant a statement of the right of the owner, or person in charge of the vehicle at the time it was immobilised or, where it was not immobilised, it was removed, to appeal, of the steps to be taken in order to appeal and of the address to which representations to an AP made as mentioned in reg 14 should be sent.

Where it appears to a custodian of a vehicle that more than one person is the owner or person authorised by the owner, such one of them as the custodian thinks fit is to be treated as the owner, or authorised person, for the purposes of reg 12.

For the above purposes, 'owner' has the same meaning as in reg 5 above.

Claim by owner of a vehicle after its disposal (reg 13)   If, after a vehicle has been disposed of by a custodian pursuant to reg 10, a person claims to have been the 'owner' (as defined for the purposes of reg 10: p 412) of the vehicle at the time when it was disposed of and:

(a) the person making the claim satisfies the custodian that that person was the owner of the vehicle at the time it was disposed of; and

(b) the claim is made before the end of the period of one year beginning with the date on which the vehicle was disposed of,

the custodian must pay that person an amount calculated by deducting from the proceeds of sale the prescribed charges for the removal, storage and disposal of the vehicle.

Where it appears to a custodian of a vehicle that more than one person is the owner, such one of them as the custodian thinks fit is treated as the owner for the purposes of this regulation.

Appeal (reg 14)   Where a dispute has arisen because:

(a) a person ('the claimant') has paid a charge in accordance with reg 6 or 12 in order to secure the release or to obtain possession of a vehicle and alleges that the charge ('the disputed charge') should be refunded to him on the ground that, at the time the vehicle was immobilised or, where it was not immobilised, at the time it was removed:

   (i)   an offence under RTA 1988, s 144A was not being committed; or

   (ii) any of the circumstances specified in reg 4 applied to the vehicle (*ground 1*); and

(b) the person to whom the disputed charge was paid refuses to refund the charge (*ground 2*),

the claimant may appeal against the refusal of a refund by sending, to the AP whose name is given for this purpose in the immobilisation notice under reg 5 or the statement under reg 12 of the right of the owner etc at the address so given, written representations stating the grounds on which a refund is claimed.

The AP to whom the appeal is made may disregard representations and evidence received later than 28 days from the date on which the vehicle was released, or as the case may be, on which possession was taken.

The AP to whom the appeal is made must uphold the appeal if he accepts that:

(a) *ground 1* above has been established and the AP who immobilised or removed the vehicle did not have reason to believe that an offence under s 144A was being committed as regards the vehicle at the time it was immobilised or removed, as the case may be; or

(b) *ground 2* above has been established.

Where the AP upholds an appeal, he must inform the claimant of the decision and the Secretary of State must refund the disputed charge.

Where the AP rejects the appeal, he must inform the claimant of the decision and of the right to make a further appeal.

A claimant who has made an appeal to an AP may make a further appeal to a magistrates' court:

(a) if the claimant's appeal has been rejected and the further appeal is made within 28 days of the claimant being served with notification to that effect; or

(b) if the AP has not notified the claimant of the outcome of the appeal and 56 days have elapsed since the claimant appealed.

If the court finds that:

(a) *ground 1* above has been established and the AP did not have reason to believe that an offence under s 144A was being committed as regards the vehicle at the time it was immobilised or removed, as the case may be; or

(b) *ground 2* above has been established,

it must order the Secretary of State to refund the disputed charge.

Provision of information

RTA 1988, s 159A authorises the making of regulations requiring the Motor Insurers' Information Centre to provide information to prescribed persons for the purpose of their functions under the insurance provisions of RTA 1988. MV(IR)R 2011, reg 7 provides that the Motor Insurers' Information Centre must make available to the Secretary of State, for the purpose of enforcing the s 144A offence, information relating to vehicle insurance policies in the UK and to vehicles which are permitted to be used on the road without insurance.

Third-party insurance policies

Certificate of insurance

The requirement made by RTA 1988, s 143 is that there must be a policy of insurance (or a security: see later) in respect of third-party risks in accordance with Part VI (ie ss 143 to 162) of that Act in relation to the use of the vehicle by the person using it. By s 147, no policy of insurance has effect unless the insurer has delivered to the person insured a certificate of insurance in the prescribed form. Delivery of the certificate may be by electronic transmission, or via a website, with the insured's consent. 'Telephone insurance' is not valid; no certificate has been delivered at that time giving evidence of a contract between insurer and insured. Police officers frequently exercise discretion in circumstances in which a company has clearly accepted liability for third-party risks but some technicality has delayed delivery of a certificate. A cover note is a certificate.

What must be covered

RTA 1988, s 145 provides that, in order to comply with the requirements of Part VI, a policy must be issued by an 'authorised insurer' and must insure such person, persons or classes of persons as may be specified in it in respect of any liability which may be incurred by him or them in respect of the death of or bodily injury to any person (other than the driver) or damage to property up to a maximum value of £1,000,000 caused by, or arising out of, the use of the vehicle on a road or other public place in Great Britain.

The policy must also cover him or them:

(a) in respect of any liability for the emergency treatment of persons injured;
(b) in the case of a vehicle normally based in Great Britain, in respect of any liability which may be incurred as a result of its use within the territory of any member state of the EU, according to the law on compulsory insurance against civil liability in that state or, if it would give higher cover, according to the law which would be applicable if the vehicle was used in Great Britain; and
(c) in the case of a vehicle normally based in another EU state, in respect of any liability which may be incurred as a result of the use of the vehicle in Great Britain if, under the law of that other state, he or they would be required to be insured in respect of a liability which would arise under it had the event occurred in that state, and the cover required by that law is higher than that required as indicated in the previous paragraph.

Extent of cover

The nature of the policy held will be specified in the certificate. A policy covering use for social, domestic and pleasure purposes does not cover business use. However, to give a lift to a friend who is on business at the time is not a business use of the vehicle. To help move household goods for a friend without payment is not a business use, but it might be if payment was made. It is usual for non-business policies to exclude use for hire or reward, but RTA 1988, s 150 makes specific provisions for 'car-sharing' schemes. Provided that arrangements are made before the journey, that payment is in respect of running costs and depreciation only, and that the vehicle used is not adapted to carry more than eight passengers, the use is not for hire or reward.

The extent of cover is the cover specified in the policy of insurance. In disputed cases this depends on the construction of the insurance policy rather than the views of the insurance company or its willingness to meet liabilities.

Some policies allow persons to drive with the permission of the insured person if such a person 'holds or has held a driving licence' and is not disqualified. If a person has at any time held a licence, whether full or provisional, it is sufficient in law to satisfy such a requirement. The terms of the policy will have to be examined in circumstances in which the class of vehicle which the person is licensed to drive is different to the class of vehicle which is being driven. If the policy demands that such a person holds or has held a licence to cover the same class of vehicle as is covered by the policy, then use by a person who does not hold (and has not held) such a licence will amount to uninsured use, unless the licence which he holds may act as a provisional one to cover use of the vehicle in question. Similarly, where a person has borrowed a vehicle subject to an implied limitation, of which he was aware, concerning the purpose for which the vehicle was to be driven, he does not have the consent of the owner for a purpose outside that limitation. Where, therefore, insurance cover was dependent upon the driver having 'the consent of the owner thereof', use outside that limitation was uninsured use.

The use of trailers in Great Britain does not expressly need to be covered in respect of third-party risks, whereas this is essential in other EU countries. However, the use of trailers in Great Britain is generally covered in all policies of insurance and would seem to be within the use of the motor vehicle in any case. Injury caused to a person by a trailer is certainly caused due to the use of the motor vehicle on a road or other public place.

Validity

When a policy has been taken out it remains in force until it expires or is validly set aside. If a disqualified driver obtains insurance by failing to disclose his disqualification, then, although such insurance is obtained by means of a false declaration, it remains valid until the company takes steps to set aside the policy. If the company does set it aside, this only invalidates the policy for the future.

It is the practice of some insurance companies to insert restrictive clauses in their policies which can affect their validity in particular circumstances. However, RTA 1988, s 148 states that the third-party requirement of s 143 must be covered by companies regardless of restrictions which might be inserted covering the age, mental or physical condition of a driver; the condition of the vehicle; the number of persons carried; the load; the times or areas of use; the horsepower cylinder capacity or value of the vehicle; the carrying of any special apparatus, or the carrying on the vehicle of special identification marks.

When a person is apprehended for taking motor vehicles without consent, it is good practice to check any certificate of insurance held by him in respect of motor vehicles. It is the terms of the policy which are important, not the moral implications. If his policy covers the use by him of another vehicle not owned by him or hired to him by a hire-purchase agreement, that policy will cover such use even though the vehicle has been taken illegally. It would be different if the use covered was similar but 'with the consent of the owner of such vehicle'.

Securities and other exemptions from insurance requirements

Securities

A security, rather than a policy of insurance, can satisfy the provisions of RTA 1988, Part VI if it satisfies certain conditions set out in s 146. The security must consist of an undertaking by the giver of the security (who must be an authorised insurer or some body of persons in the business of giving securities which has deposited with the Accountant General of the Senior Courts the sum of £500,000 in respect of that business). The undertaking must be to make good, subject to any conditions specified therein, any failure by the person covered by the security duly to discharge any third-party liability for which insurance would otherwise be required under Part VI of the Act. Use of securities is frequently made by large undertakings, such as bus companies, which would experience unnecessary difficulties in negotiating separate insurance in respect of a large fleet of vehicles. A security is of no effect for the purposes of Part VI unless there is a 'certificate of security' in force in relation to the vehicles.

Exemptions

The offences relating to use without third-party insurance or security, which are provided by RTA 1988, s 143, are subject to exemptions provided by RTA 1988, s 144. RTA 1988, s 144 exempts from the requirement for third-party insurance or security:

(a) a vehicle owned by a local authority, a National Parks Authority or the Broads Authority at a time when it is being driven under the owner's control;

(b) a vehicle owned by a local policing body or police authority being driven under its control, or a vehicle driven by a person for police purposes by or under the direction of a police constable, or by a person employed by a local policing body, etc or by a member of the civilian staff of the police force; a police officer on duty using his own car for police purposes falls within this exemption;

(c) a vehicle being driven for salvage purposes pursuant to the Merchant Shipping Act 1995, Part IX;

(d) a vehicle owned by a health service body, or an ambulance owned by an NHS Trust, or NHS foundation trust, at a time when it is being driven under the owner's control;

(e) a vehicle made available by the Secretary of State to any person, body or local authority under the National Health Service Act 1977 at a time when it is being used within the terms on which it is being made available; or

(f) a vehicle used by the Care Quality Commission, at a time when the vehicle is being used under the owner's control.

The reasoning behind these exemptions is clear: the vehicles are either owned by or being used by undertakings which are in a position to meet liabilities which might be incurred. Crown vehicles appear to be similarly exempt, as RTA 1988, s 183, which deals with the application of the provisions of the Act to the Crown, does not mention RTA 1988, s 143.

Other requirements in respect of motor vehicle insurance

RTA 1988, s 147(4) and (4A) requires that where an insurance policy or security to which a certificate of insurance or security relates becomes cancelled, either by mutual consent or by virtue of the provisions of the policy or security, the insured must within seven days surrender the certificate, or electronically transmit to the insurer a statement that the policy in question has ceased to have effect. If a certificate has been lost or destroyed, a statutory declaration or electronically transmitted statement to that effect must be made within that period. An offence is committed by a person who fails to comply with these provisions (s 147(5)).

RTA 1988, s 154 requires any person against whom a claim is made in respect of any such liability as is required to be insured against by s 145 (see p 415) to provide particulars of his insurance cover in respect of that liability. It is an offence under s 154(2) to fail to do so without reasonable excuse, or wilfully to make a false statement in reply to such a demand. Section 154 allows the administrative officers of hospitals, etc to recover the cost of emergency treatment from vehicle insurers.

Disclosure of vehicle insurance information to NPIA

SOCPA 2005, s 153 empowers the Secretary of State to make regulations requiring the Motor Insurers' Information Centre to make available 'relevant motor vehicle insurance information' to the National Policing Improvement Agency (NPIA) for it to process with a view to making the processed information available for use by police officers. 'Relevant motor vehicle insurance information' means information relating to vehicles whose use was, but is no longer, insured. The Disclosure of Vehicle Insurance Information Regulations 2005 authorise the provision of such information at intervals specified by NPIA. That organisation may process the information in a form which will be of assistance to a police officer in establishing whether or not an offence of uninsured use of a vehicle has been committed. Chief officers of police may further process that information to assist a police officer in deciding whether or not to demand production of evidence of insurance. All such information must not be disclosed other than for the purposes of proceedings.

Fraud, forgery, etc

By RTA 1988, s 174(5), it is an offence to make a false statement, or to withhold any material information, for the purpose of obtaining the issue of a certificate of insurance or security, or any other document which may be produced in lieu of a certificate of insurance or security. Any person who issues such a document which to his knowledge is false in any material particular commits an offence against RTA 1988, s 175(1).

The alternative documents to which RTA 1988, s 174(5) refers are specified by the Motor Vehicles (Third-Party Risks) Regulations 1972, reg 7 as follows:

(a) duplicates of certificates of security;
(b) certificates of deposit;
(c) a certificate signed by a specified body, local policing body, police authority, etc; or
(d) in the case of a vehicle normally based in another EU country, or Finland, Norway, or Switzerland, a document issued by the insurer in the prescribed form.

The making of false statements to obtain insurance is not uncommon. The disclosure of previous convictions for motoring offences, particularly those involving endorsement, can lead to high premiums which can be avoided by non-disclosure. In this context, the Rehabilitation of Offenders Act 1974 is important. The Act provides for convictions to become 'spent'. It also provides that where a question seeking information with respect to a person's previous convictions is put to him, otherwise than in proceedings before a judicial authority, the question must be treated as not relating to spent convictions and answers may be made accordingly. Most road traffic offences will have resulted in a fine and as a result will become spent after a period of five years.

The offence of making a false statement contrary to s 174(5) is a strict liability offence and it is not necessary to prove that the person who made the statement was aware of its falsity (or even of the risk that it might be false). It is submitted, however, that it would be essential to prove a deliberate act of 'withholding'.

RTA 1988, s 173(1) makes it an indictable (either way) offence for a person, with intent to deceive, to forge, alter, use, lend for use, or allow to be used, a certificate of insurance or a document which may be used in lieu thereof. Section 173(1) also provides an indictable (either way) offence of making, or having in possession, with intent to deceive, any document or other thing so closely resembling a document or other thing of the above types as to be calculated (ie likely) to deceive. Uncompleted insurance forms can be documents for this purpose; so can an expired certificate, if used with intent to deceive.

Persons temporarily in Great Britain

The Motor Vehicles (International Motor Insurance Card) Regulations 1971, reg 5 authorises a visitor to Great Britain to use his motor vehicle under the internationally recognised 'green card' insurance provision. 'Green cards' are referred to in the regulations as 'valid insurance cards'. A peculiarity of this provision is that a green card remains valid after the expiry date shown. This is to prevent the complications which would otherwise arise if holiday visitors decided to extend their stay. A constable's powers in respect of insurance certificates, etc apply to 'green cards'.

Certificates of insurance or security issued in Northern Ireland are, of course, valid in Great Britain.

Police powers in relation to motor vehicle insurance

RTA 1988, s 165 states that:

(a) a person driving a motor vehicle, other than an invalid carriage, on a road; or
(b) a person whom a constable or vehicle examiner reasonably believes to have:
    (i) been the driver of such a motor vehicle on a road or other public place when an accident occurred, etc; or
    (ii) committed an offence in relation to the use of such a motor vehicle on a road,

must, on being required by a constable or vehicle examiner, give his name and address and the name and address of the owner of the vehicle, and produce for examination the relevant certificate of insurance (or electronic access to a copy of it where it was transmitted electronically or made available via a website by the insurer), etc. The Court of Appeal has held that the 'relevant certificate of insurance' is a certificate covering the driving of a vehicle, whether or not the vehicle is identified in the certificate (as where a borrower of the vehicle is driving it on his insurance). Failure to do any of these things is an offence. The usual provisions concerning production of documents apply, allowing seven days for production; or production as soon as reasonably practicable; or proof that production was not reasonably practicable before the day on which proceedings were instituted. The documents (unlike a driving licence) need not be produced in person.

The provisions of RTA 1988, s 165 requiring a person to give his name and address and the name and address of the owner of the vehicle also apply to a supervisor of a provisional licence-holder in each of the circumstances set out above.

Police powers of seizure of vehicles being driven without a driving licence or insurance

RTA 1988, s 165A provides that:

(a) where a constable in uniform requires, under RTA 1988, s 164, the production of a licence and counterpart (p 395), or under s 165, the production of evidence of insurance; and
(b) the documents are not produced; and
(c) the constable has reasonable grounds for believing that the vehicle was being driven in contravention of s 87(1) (requirement to have a driving licence) or s 143 (requirement to have insurance),

the constable may seize the vehicle and remove it.

RTA 1988, s 165A also provides that:

(a) where a constable in uniform has required, under s 163, a person driving a motor vehicle to stop it; and

(b) there is a failure to do so, or a failure to do so for a sufficient time to allow the constable to make appropriate enquiries, and the constable has reasonable grounds for believing that the vehicle is being driven in contravention of s 87(1) (driving without licence) or 143 (uninsured driving),

he may seize and remove it.

Section 165A empowers the constable to enter any premises (other than a private dwelling house) on which he has reasonable grounds for believing the vehicle to be in order to seize it. The constable may use reasonable force to seize and remove the vehicle or to enter premises to seize and remove it.

Before seizing a vehicle under s 165A, and provided it is practicable to do so, a constable must warn the person by whom it appears that the vehicle is, or was being, driven in contravention of either s 87(1) or s 143 that he will seize the vehicle if the relevant documents are not produced. On seizing a vehicle under s 165A, a constable must give a seizure notice (below) to the driver unless the circumstances make it impracticable to do so.

Where there has been a failure to stop, the power of seizure is valid for a period of 24 hours.

Retention and disposal of vehicles seized under powers provided by RTA 1988, s 165A

The Road Traffic Act 1988 (Retention and Disposal of Seized Motor Vehicles) Regulations 2005 provide for the retention, safe-keeping and disposal by an AP (ie a constable or other person authorised by the chief officer of police) of vehicles seized under RTA 1988, s 165A.

Such a vehicle must be passed into and remain in the custody of an authorised person (AP) until the AP permits it to be removed from his custody by a person appearing to him to be the registered keeper or owner of the vehicle, or until it has been disposed of in accordance with the Regulations.

An AP must, as soon as is reasonably practicable after he has taken a vehicle into his custody, take such steps as are reasonably practicable to give a seizure notice to the person who is the registered keeper of the vehicle and to the owner, where that person appears to be someone different, unless (a) the AP is satisfied that a seizure notice has already been given, by a constable on seizing the vehicle, to the registered keeper and to the owner, where it appears that the owner is a different person; or (b) the vehicle has been released from his custody in accordance with the Regulations.

A seizure notice must contain information which can be or could have been ascertained from an inspection of the vehicle, or has been ascertained from another source, as to the registration mark and make of the vehicle. It also must include a statement as to the place of seizure and the place where the vehicle is now being kept; a requirement that the keeper or owner claim the vehicle from an AP on or before a date specified in the notice (not less than seven working days from the date upon which the notice is given); a statement that unless the vehicle is claimed on or before that date, an AP intends to dispose of it; a notice that charges are payable and that the vehicle may be retained until they are paid and a notice that the registered keeper or owner must either:

(a) produce at a specified police station a valid insurance certificate covering his use of that vehicle and a valid licence authorising him to drive that vehicle; or

(b) nominate for this purpose a third person who produces at a specified police station such a valid certificate and such a valid licence.

The notice must also make clear that the vehicle may be retained until (a) or (b) is satisfied.

A seizure notice may be given:

(a) by delivering it to the person to whom it is directed;
(b) in the case of the registered keeper, by leaving it at the registered address or by sending it by registered post to that address;
(c) in the case of the owner, by leaving it at his usual or last known address, or by sending it by registered post to that address;
(d) in the case of a body corporate, by delivering it to the secretary or clerk of the body at its registered or principal office, or by sending it by registered post addressed to that secretary or clerk at that office.

Where, before a relevant motor vehicle is disposed of, a person satisfies an AP that he is the registered keeper or owner of that vehicle, pays the appropriate charge and produces at a police station specified in the notice a valid insurance certificate covering his use of the vehicle and a valid driving licence authorising him to drive the vehicle (or such documents are produced by a nominated person), the AP must permit him to remove the vehicle from custody. An AP may consider any documentary evidence produced to him in determining whether a person who claims to be the owner of a motor vehicle is in fact the owner.

A person, who would otherwise be liable to pay the appropriate charge, is not liable to pay it if he was not driving the vehicle at the time when it was seized under s 165A; did not know that the vehicle was being driven at that time; had not consented to it being driven; and could not, by taking reasonable steps, have prevented it from being driven.

An AP is empowered to dispose of a vehicle if:

(a) where the registered keeper and the owner appear to be the same person, that person fails to comply with any requirement in the seizure notice, or an AP was not able, after taking reasonably practicable steps, to give a seizure notice to that person;
(b) where the owner and registered keeper appear to be different:
  (i) where the seizure notice was given to both of those persons, neither the registered keeper nor the owner complies with all the requirements of the seizure notice;
  (ii) where, having taken such steps as were reasonably practicable, the AP was only able to give a seizure notice to one of them, that person fails to comply with any requirement in that seizure notice; or
  (iii) where, after taking reasonably practicable steps, the AP was not able to give a seizure notice to either the registered keeper or the owner.

An AP may not dispose of a vehicle:

(a) during the period of 14 days starting with the date of seizure; or
(b) if that date has expired, until after a date specified in the seizure notice; or
(c) if not otherwise covered by (a) or (b), during the period of seven working days starting with the date on which the vehicle is claimed under the above provisions.

Where there is a disposal by way of sale, the net proceeds of that sale must be paid to any person who, within a one-year period beginning with the date of sale, satisfies an AP that at the time of the sale he was the owner of the vehicle. Where it appears that there may be more than one owner, the proceeds must be paid to such one of them as the AP thinks fit. The term 'net proceeds' refers to that part of the money remaining after the deduction of charges under the legislation.

INFORMATION AS TO IDENTITY OF DRIVER IN SPECIFIED CASES

The requirement to give information

RTA 1988, s 172(2) provides that where the driver of a vehicle is alleged to be guilty of an offence to which the section applies:

(a) the person keeping the vehicle must give such information as to the identity of the driver as he may be required to give by or on behalf of a chief officer of police. A requirement made with the express or implied authority of the chief officer is given on his behalf; and

(b) any other person must if required as stated above give any information which is in his power to give and may lead to the identification of the driver.

The expression 'any other person' includes the driver himself.

Section 172 applies to:

(a) all offences against RTA 1988, except an offence under Part V (driving instruction), or s 13 (promoting motoring events on highway), s 16 (wearing of protective headgear), s 51(2) (certain test conditions—goods vehicles), s 61(4) (certain type approval requirements), s 67(9) (obstructing a vehicle examiner), s 68(4) (failing to proceed to place of vehicle inspection), s 96 (driving with uncorrected defective eyesight), or s 120 (offence against regulations dealing with licensing of drivers of large goods vehicles and passenger-carrying vehicles);

(b) an offence under RTOA 1988, s 25 (information as to date of birth and sex after conviction), s 26 (interim disqualification), or s 27 (production of a licence on conviction);

(c) any offence against any other enactment relating to the use of vehicles on roads; and

(d) manslaughter by the driver of a motor vehicle.

A requirement may be made by way of written notice and served by post. Where it is so made it has effect as a requirement to give the information within the 28-day period beginning on the day on which the notice is served. Where there are joint keepers and they live at the same address, it suffices that one notice is addressed to them jointly at that address.

The offence

By RTA 1988, s 172(3), a person who fails to comply with such a requirement commits an offence. However, by s 172(4), a person who *keeps* the vehicle is not guilty of the offence if he shows that he did not know, and could not with reasonable diligence have ascertained, who the driver of the vehicle was. A divisional court has held that the answer to the question of whether the driver's identity was known or could have been ascertained with reasonable diligence is to be assessed from the date the requirement is made and not earlier; the keeper is not required to keep a written record of those to whom he lends the vehicle. Section 172(4) is subject to s 172(6) in the case of a corporate body; s 172(6) provides that s 172(4) does not apply unless the alleged offender also shows that no record of those who drove the vehicle was kept and that the failure to do so was reasonable. Any other person must be proved to have had the information within his power to give.

The fact that the defendant (D) does not know the driver's identity does not excuse him if he simply fails to respond to a requirement for information (as opposed to responding and saying that he does not know). There must be evidence of the notice and that a requirement under s 172 has been made. This can be done by annexing a copy of the notice and requirement to a written statement under CJA 1967, s 9. By s 172(7)(b), D is not guilty of the offence if he shows that he gave the information as soon as reasonably practicable after the end of that period or that it had not been reasonably practicable for him to give it. A divisional court has held that it is not necessary to prove that D knew that he was required to provide the specified information, but that in an appropriate case D might be able to show that it was not reasonably practicable for him to be aware of the notice, in which case s 172(7)(b) would apply.

Where more than one individual is registered as the keeper of a vehicle (eg where husband and wife are joint keepers), a notice under s 172 may be sent to them jointly; if there is a failure to comply and no defence is shown under s 172(4) or (7)(b) each is guilty of the offence under s 172(3).

Procedure in respect of the notice

The police are not required to specify the nature of the offence alleged to have been committed. Where a notice has been produced from an official source and has every appearance of authenticity, justices may draw an inference as to the validity of the notice.

A divisional court has held that the obligation to respond is an obligation to respond in the manner specified in the notice. In that case the notice required (as usual) that information be given in writing and signed. The driver had not done so but had provided the required information by telephone to an employee in the relevant fixed penalty office of the constabulary. The court held that the driver was guilty of failing to comply with the requirement for information.

RTOA 1988, s 12 permits a court to accept a signed form as evidence that the signatory was the driver of the vehicle at the time in question. A divisional court has held that where the name of the driver had been inserted in block capitals, but there was no signature, this could not be a statement in writing purporting to be signed by D for the purposes of s 12 in the circumstances. Anyone could have written out the form. All such completed forms should be carefully examined when they are returned to ticket offices to avoid such difficulties arising.

Where a registered keeper endorsed the form sent by the police, 'please see covering letter enclosed', a divisional court allowed an appeal by the keeper against his conviction for failing to provide the required information. Within the letter the keeper had admitted that he was the keeper but explained that the vehicle concerned was one of a number of vehicles held by his medical practice and he could not ascertain who had been driving at the relevant time. The court said that while it had been decided that an oral reply to such a notice did not meet the statutory requirement, the letter had been written and signed. In a case where the keeper of a vehicle responded by claiming that it was also used by a friend and that neither he nor his friend could recall driving at the time, date and place alleged, a divisional court upheld the keeper's conviction for failing to disclose the identity of the driver, holding that he had had relevant information in his possession, had been required to give any information in his power which would lead to the identification of the driver and had failed to provide the identity of his friend.

Human rights implications

The Privy Council has concluded, and its finding has since been endorsed by the European Court of Human Rights, that the use of an admission by a keeper obtained in pursuance of a requirement under RTA 1988, s 172(2)(a) is not incompatible with the defendant's human rights under the European Convention on Human Rights, art 6(1). Section 172(2)(a) merely provides for the putting of one simple question. The answer to that question cannot, by itself, incriminate the suspect. It does not permit prolonged questioning of a nature similar to that which is objectionable under the Convention. A divisional court, having been asked to consider the position of 'any other person' required to provide information under s 172(2)(b), concluded that the position was no different. Conclusive evidence should be admitted unless there is good reason for not doing so. The fact that, in this case, evidence could have been given by the driver's employer was not such a reason. It could not be unfair to admit the defendant's own answer to a requirement made under the section. Parliament had sought to facilitate the giving of evidence as to the identity of drivers by means of written statements.

DANGEROUS ACTIVITIES

Dangerous parking

RTA 1988, s 22 makes it an offence for a person to cause or permit a vehicle or trailer drawn by it to remain at rest on a road in such a position, or in such condition or in such circumstances, as to involve danger of injury to other persons. The danger may be caused by the manner of the parking, the condition of the bodywork, etc which may come into contact with persons, or other circumstances. It has been held that, where a vehicle has been parked without the brake being properly set and the vehicle moves and injures a pedestrian, the offence is committed. See below for other offences of causing danger on or near roads.

Causing danger to road users

By RTA 1988, s 22A, a person commits an indictable (either way) offence if he intentionally and without lawful authority or reasonable cause:

(a) causes anything to be on or over a road; or
(b) interferes with a motor vehicle, trailer or cycle; or
(c) interferes (directly or indirectly) with traffic equipment,

in such circumstances that it would be obvious to a reasonable person that to do so would be dangerous. If the danger would have been obvious to a *reasonable* person, it is irrelevant that the defendant was unaware of it. In relation to (b), it has been held that 'interferes' suggests 'tampering' with the vehicle and that a person who stands in front of a vehicle does not interfere with it.

'*Dangerous*' refers to danger either of injury to any person while on or near a road, or of serious damage to property on or near a road. In determining what would be 'obvious' to a reasonable person in a particular case, regard must be had not only to the circumstances of which he could be expected to be aware but also to any circumstances shown to have been within the knowledge of the defendant.

With regard to (a) above, where persons are seen on a bridge over a motorway in possession of large pieces of concrete, and then are seen to *balance* these objects on the parapet, they certainly cause those objects to be over a road and it is submitted that it would be obvious to a reasonable person that what they are doing is dangerous. Protesters who erect a barrier across a road will not normally be guilty of an offence under s 22A if the barrier is solid and easily seen. Although their actions are otherwise unlawful, the essential element of 'danger' is normally missing in such circumstances. However, the stretching of a thin rope or wire across a road would cause the type of danger which the section seeks to outlaw.

A person who deflates a car tyre to a low pressure or interferes with its brakes or steering clearly interferes with it for the purposes of (b), above, in such circumstances that it would be obvious to a reasonable person that to do so would be dangerous.

For the purposes of (c) above, 'traffic equipment' means:

(a) anything lawfully placed on or near a road by a highway authority;
(b) a traffic sign lawfully placed on or near a road by a person other than a highway authority;
(c) any fence, barrier, or light lawfully placed on or near a road, to protect street works or undertakings, or items placed by a constable or person acting on the instructions (whether general or specific) of a chief officer of police.

Any such thing placed on or near a road is, unless the contrary is proved, deemed to have been lawfully placed.

Thus, all official road signs, those indicating temporary works or obstructions, road accidents, or diversions are covered by s 22A. The intentional interference with any such sign must be shown to have created the danger envisaged by s 22A. A person who removes a hazard warning sign will commit an offence provided that the hazard still exists. If the sign indicates the existence of a hazard associated with roadworks and those works have been completed (so that no danger then exists), there will be no offence under s 22A. Where a sign is removed which merely indicates the direction of a town, nuisance has certainly been caused but there is no danger associated with such removal in normal circumstances. If road surfacing operations are marked at night by a series of lamps, the removal of one lamp might or might not cause the type of danger which s 22A seeks to prevent. If lamps are set at intervals of inches, it might be that the removal of one lamp is insignificant. If there are few lamps and a gap is left completely unmarked, the situation changes.

For another offence of dangerousness, see p 426.

LAW RELATING TO HIGHWAYS

Highways

The meaning of the term 'highway' for the purposes of the Highways Act 1980 (HA 1980) is given in HA 1980, s 328. Section 328 states that the term includes the whole or part of a highway other than a ferry or waterway. Where a highway passes over a bridge or through a tunnel, the bridge or tunnel is, for the purposes of the Act, a part of the highway. HA 1980, s 328 does not define 'highway'; instead, that term is defined by common law (see p 343).

Obstruction of highway

By HA 1980, s 137(1), it is an offence for a person, without lawful authority or excuse, in any way wilfully to obstruct the free passage along the highway.

Whether or not there was an *obstruction* is a question of degree for a court to decide; a complete blockage of the highway is not required. Whether or not a use of the highway amounts to an obstruction depends upon whether or not it was unreasonable having regard to all the circumstances of the case, including where it occurs, its duration, its nature, its extent and its purpose, and whether there is an actual, as opposed to a potential, obstruction. Where a supermarket left trolleys in a pedestrian precinct for the convenience of shoppers there was an obstruction even though no complaint had been made by a member of the public. In another case there was held to be an obstruction where for 15 years a bridleway had been completely blocked by farm gates, tied by twine to hedges and held closed by a loop of twine, which could be opened easily. Simply to cause fear to users of a highway cannot amount to an obstruction. A divisional court so held in a case where the defendant allowed his Rottweiler dogs to act in a menacing way behind a fence separating his land from a path constituting a highway. Pedestrians on the path were put in fear but, said the court, the highway was not obstructed.

The term *'wilfully'* in this context means that the particular obstruction was occasioned by some deliberate act which was freely carried out by the defendant; consequently, a motorist who stops at a traffic light showing red does not wilfully obstruct the highway. In one case, a man who addressed a crowd, whose assembly interfered with traffic although traffic movement was not completely stopped, was held to have caused a wilful obstruction because, by the exercise of free will, he caused that obstruction to take place. On the other hand, if a queue forms outside a shop because many customers are attracted to it, it cannot be said that the shopkeeper has committed a deliberate and wilful act which caused the obstruction, as he is trading in a normal way. It would be different if the obstruction was caused because he was trading in an unusual way, for example through the window, as that unusual act would be wilful and would lead to an obstruction.

The question of whether or not a person has *'lawful authority or excuse'* will always be a question for the court to decide. PACE authorises police officers to set up road blocks in certain circumstances (see p 50). Clearly, a road block established in accordance with PACE would have lawful authority. 'Lawful excuse' embraces activities lawful in themselves which are a reasonable use of the highway or incidental to the right of passage. On the other hand, the right to protest does not give a right to obstruct the highway; consequently there is no lawful authority or excuse for such obstruction.

Danger or annoyance on highway

HA 1980, s 161 makes it an offence for any person, without lawful authority or excuse:

(a) to deposit anything on a highway in consequence of which a user is injured or endangered (s 161(1)); or

(b) to light any fire on or over a highway which consists of or comprises a carriageway, or to discharge any firearm or firework within 50 feet of the centre of such a highway, if in consequence a user of the highway is injured, interrupted or endangered (s 161(2)).

HA 1980, s 161A(1) prohibits a person from lighting a fire on any land not forming part of a highway which consists of or comprises a carriageway, or from directing or permitting such a fire to be lit, when in consequence a user of any highway which consists of or comprises a carriageway is injured, interrupted or endangered by, or by smoke from, that fire or any other fire caused by that fire. However, s 161A(2) provides a defence if it can be proved that at the time the fire was lit the person was satisfied on reasonable grounds that it was unlikely that users of any such highway would be injured, interrupted or endangered by the fire or by smoke from it, or from any other fire caused by it, and *either* that before or after the fire was lit he did all that he reasonably could to prevent the consequences *or* that he had reasonable excuse for not doing so. Section 161A is aimed at preventing smoke clouds, caused by straw burning in surrounding fields, blowing over motorways and main roads.

HA 1980, s 161(4) also punishes those who, without lawful authority or excuse, allow filth, lime or dirt, or other offensive matter or thing, to run on to a highway from any adjoining premises. Section 161(3) prohibits the playing of football or any other game on a highway to the annoyance of a user of the highway. This offence creates many problems for police officers. Usually a complaint is received by telephone from a householder who wishes to complain that he is being annoyed by children playing football in the street. The offence is only committed when the game is 'to the annoyance of a user of the highway'; a person sitting in his house is not a 'user' in the sense intended by the section. A person who was not using the highway when annoyed cannot be subsequently annoyed by walking into the street unless the game continues to his annoyance when on the highway.

It is an offence contrary to HA 1980, s 162 to place, for any purpose, a rope, wire or other apparatus across a highway in such a manner as to be likely to cause danger to persons using the highway, unless the defendant proves that he had taken necessary means to give adequate warning. A washing line in a back street with white sheets suspended from it certainly involves the stretching of a rope across the highway, but in the circumstances it can easily be proved that adequate warning was given. However, if the washing is taken in and only the rope is left, it will be harder to prove that the necessary steps were taken to give adequate warning.

Builders' skips

HA 1980, s 139 provides that a builder's skip must not be deposited on the highway without the permission of the highway authority; otherwise an offence is committed under s 139(3).

Such permission must be in writing; it is granted to a named person and the highway where the skip is to be located is specified. Each skip must be authorised on each occasion; a general permission to place skips is not possible. The authority may impose conditions on its permission. These may refer to the siting of the skip, its dimensions, the painting of the skip to make it visible, the care and disposal of its contents, the manner in which it is to be lighted or guarded and its removal at the end of the authorised period. Skips must be fitted with two oblong plates of diagonal red and yellow fluorescent or reflective material, similar to those fitted to heavy goods vehicles.

HA 1980, s 139 also provides that, whatever the conditions imposed, an owner must secure that the skip is properly lit during the hours of darkness, that it is clearly and indelibly marked with the owner's name and with his telephone number or address, that it is removed as soon as possible after it has been filled, and that all conditions of the permission are complied with. Failure to do so is an offence under s 139(4) on the part of the owner. The term 'owner' in relation to a skip which is hired for a month or more, or one which is the subject of a hire-purchase agreement, means the person in possession of the skip under the hiring agreement. 'Otherwise deposits in' is extremely wide and means no more than 'places or puts'.

Where the commission by any person of an offence under s 139 is due to the act or default of some other person, that other person is also guilty and may be convicted whether or not proceedings are taken against the first-mentioned person.

It is a defence to a charge under HA 1980, s 139 for the defendant to prove that the commission of the offence was due to the act or default of another and that the defendant took all reasonable precautions and exercised all due diligence to avoid the commission of the offence by himself or any other person under his control.

HA 1980, s 140 provides that, regardless of whether or not permission has been obtained, the highway authority or a constable in uniform may require the owner of a skip to remove it, or reposition it, or cause it to be removed or repositioned. To fail to do so as soon as possible is an offence. A request by a constable must be made in person; a request by telephone, for example, is not sufficient.

Use of loudspeakers

The Control of Pollution Act 1974, s 62 bans the operation of loudspeakers in a street between 9 pm and 8 am the following morning for any purpose. It also bans their use at any other time for the purpose of advertising any entertainment, trade or business. Breach of these bans is an offence under s 62(1). The term 'street' means any highway and any other road, footway, square or court which is for the time being open to the public. The ban is therefore effective both in built-up areas and in the country, provided, in either case, the loudspeaker is operated in a 'street'.

The exemptions to these provisions are predictable. They are: use for police, fire and rescue or ambulance purposes; by the Environment Agency or a water undertaking in the exercise of its functions, or by a local authority; 'in-vehicle' entertainments or announcements; telephones; use by showmen at a pleasure fair; and use in an emergency provided that the loudspeaker is operated so as not to give reasonable cause for annoyance to persons in the vicinity.

The most common exception to the general rule against the use of loudspeakers for advertising is in favour of those who have a loudspeaker fixed to a vehicle used for the conveyance of a perishable commodity for human consumption, which is used solely for the purpose of informing the public (by means other than words) that the commodity is on sale from the vehicle. Such a loudspeaker must be operated so as not to give reasonable cause for annoyance to persons in the vicinity and it may only be used between noon and 7 pm of the same day. Thus 'ice-cream chimes' can be used between these times, but at no other.

SPECIAL EVENTS ON ROADS

The Road Traffic Regulation Act 1984, ss 16A and 16B permit traffic authorities to make temporary orders restricting/prohibiting traffic in connection with special events or entertainments on a road. By s 16C(1), contravention of such an order is an offence.

An order may not be made in relation to motor racing, and may only be made in respect of a motor 'competition or trial' or a bicycle race or speed trial if authorised by or under RTA 1988, s 13 or s 31 (see pp 528 and 451). For a time trial or bicycle race to be authorised, a promoter must in either case give 28 days' written notice to the police, giving times, dates, routes, start, finish, maximum number taking part, arrangements for marshalling and supervision, and such particulars as show that it is a time trial or is a bicycle race complying with the conditions above.

OFF-ROAD DRIVING

RTA 1988, s 34(1) prohibits a person from driving a mechanically propelled motor vehicle, without lawful authority, on to or on any common land, moorland or land of any other description which is not a part of the road, or on any road which is a footpath, bridleway or restricted byway. However, s 34 provides that driving within fifteen yards of a road upon which a motor vehicle may be driven is not an offence if the driving is only for the purpose of parking. Nor is it an offence under s 34 for a person with an interest in the land, or a visitor to it, to drive to it along a road which before 2 May 2006 (England) or 16 November 2006 (Wales) was shown in a definitive map and statement as a road used as a public path. It is a defence to prove that the vehicle was driven for saving life, or extinguishing fire, or for dealing with any other similar emergency.

The Police Reform Act 2002, s 59 provides powers for the seizure of vehicles in pre-scribed circumstances: see p 517.

CHAPTER 10

Use of Vehicles

TERMINOLOGY

Unless otherwise indicated, the following terms used in this chapter are defined as set out below by the Road Traffic Act (RTA) 1988 or Road Vehicles (Construction and Use) Regulations 1986 (RV(C&U)R 1986). All of them are concerned with mechanically propelled vehicles, and hereafter 'vehicle' must be understood in this sense.

A '*motor car*' is a vehicle for the carriage of a load or passengers whose unladen weight does not exceed: (a) 3,050 kg (3 tonnes), if it is constructed solely for the carriage of passengers and adapted to carry no more than seven of them exclusive of the driver, or if it is constructed for the conveyance of goods; or (b) 2,540 kg (2.5 tonnes) in any other case.

A '*heavy motor car*' is a vehicle (not being a motor car) constructed to carry a load, whether goods or passengers, and whose unladen weight exceeds 2,540 kg (2.5 tonnes). Although this definition covers buses and coaches, there are some requirements of the regulations which are specific to them. For this reason 'bus', 'large bus', and 'coach' are separately defined.

A '*bus*' is a vehicle constructed or adapted to carry more than eight seated passengers in addition to the driver, and '*large bus*' is a vehicle constructed or adapted to carry more than 16 such passengers. A '*coach*' is a large bus with a maximum gross weight of more than 7.5 tonnes and a maximum speed exceeding 60 mph.

A '*dual-purpose vehicle*' is a vehicle constructed or adapted for the carriage both of passengers and of goods or burden, being a vehicle whose unladen weight does not exceed 2,040 kg, and which either:

(a) is so constructed or adapted that the driving power of the engine is, or can be, transmitted to all the wheels of the vehicle; or

(b) (i) is permanently fitted with a rigid roof;

(ii) has at least one row of transverse, upholstered seats for two or more passengers permanently fitted;

(iii) has on each side and at the rear a window or windows having an overall area of not less than 1,850 square cms on each side and not less than 770 square cms at the rear; and

(iv) is such that the distance between the rearmost part of the steering wheel and the back-rests of the row of transverse seats in (ii) (or, if there is more than one such row of seats, the distance between the rearmost part of the steering wheel and the back-rests of the rearmost such row) is not less than one-third of the distance between the rearmost part of the steering wheel and the rearmost part of the floor of the vehicle.

A '*motor tractor*' is defined as a vehicle which is not constructed itself to carry a load (other than one concerned with its own propulsion or maintenance) and the unladen weight of which does not exceed 7,370 kg (7.25 tonnes). A '*locomotive*' is a similar vehicle, the unladen weight of which exceeds 7,370 kg (7.25 tonnes); there are two types: 'light locomotive'—unladen weight not exceeding 11,690kg (11.5 tonnes), 'heavy locomotive'—unladen weight in excess of this.

ROAD VEHICLES (CONSTRUCTION AND USE) REGULATIONS 1986

RV(C&U)R 1986 are made under RTA 1988, s 41. They are divided into two main parts: Part II dealing with the construction, equipment and maintenance of motor vehicles and trailers, and Part IV dealing with the various uses of motor vehicles and trailers on roads. The 'construction' elements of the regulations are aimed at manufacturers in the main, as they amount to specifications for vehicle production. Many of these provisions are being replaced in relation to most modern vehicles by requirements of an international nature relating to 'type approved' vehicles. The date of manufacture or first registration of vehicles will normally be the conclusive factor in deciding whether the 'construction' elements of RV(C&U)R 1986 apply, or those directed towards type approval. A vehicle which complies with the relevant type approval and has the relevant certificate of type approval or manufacturer's certificate of conformity to the type approval is exempt from certain parts of RV(C&U)R 1986, Part II concerned with the construction of motor vehicles. Police officers are much more frequently concerned with offences relating to the use of vehicles in contravention of the Regulations.

Certain special types of vehicle are authorised under the Road Vehicles (Authorisation of Special Types) General Order 2003 and do not have to comply with all of the requirements of the RV(C&U)R 1986. The clue to the nature of such vehicles lies within the term 'special'. The vehicles concerned are likely to be track-laying vehicles; those used for special engineering and maintenance purposes; military vehicles; and vehicles used for life-saving operations.

The type approval system is backed up by two offences under RTA 1988, ss 63 and 65:

(a) using, or causing or permitting to be used, on a road, a vehicle subject in whole or part to compulsory type approval, without a certificate; and

(b) selling, supplying, offering to sell, supplying, or exposing for sale a vehicle which does not have a certificate.

By RTA 1988, ss 64A and 65A–H respectively, there are specific offences relating to the use on a road of a motor cycle or tractor which is not covered by a type approval certificate, or to the sale of an unregistered motor cycle without such a certificate being in effect.

CONSTRUCTION AND USE OFFENCES: GENERAL

RTA 1988, ss 40A, 41A, 41B, 41D, and 42 provide various offences which may be committed in relation to the use of a vehicle in a dangerous condition and/or in contravention of the RV(C&U)R 1986.

Using vehicle in dangerous condition

RTA 1988, s 40A makes it an offence for a person to use, cause or permit another to use a motor vehicle or a trailer on a road when:

(a) the condition of the motor vehicle or trailer, or of its accessories or equipment; or

(b) the purpose for which it is used; or

(c)   the number of passengers carried by it, or the manner in which they are carried; or

(d)   the weight, position, or distribution of its load, or the manner in which it is secured,

is such that the use of the motor vehicle or trailer involves danger of injury to any person. The question of whether there was a danger for the purposes of RTA 1988, s 40A is a matter which the justices must consider by reference to the matters set out above; the fact that an accident has occurred is irrelevant. On the other hand, they can take into account the nature of the locality and the classification of the road.

Breach of requirements as to brakes, steering-gear, or tyres

RTA 1988, s 41A makes it an offence for a person to:

(a)   contravene or fail to comply with a construction and use requirement as to brakes, steering gear, or tyres; or

(b)   use on a road a motor vehicle or trailer which does not comply with such a requirement, or cause or permit a motor vehicle or trailer to be so used.

Offences against RTA 1988, ss 40A and 41A carry discretionary disqualification; the endorsement of three penalty points is obligatory. However, if a s 40A offence is committed within three years of a previous conviction for such offence, disqualification is obligatory. Such obligatory disqualification will be for not less than six months.

Breach of requirement as to weight: goods and passenger vehicles

RTA 1988, s 41B punishes offences in relation to 'weight'. By s 41B(1), a person who:

(a)   contravenes or fails to comply with a construction and use requirement as to any description of weight applicable to:
   (i)   a goods vehicle; or
   (ii)   a motor vehicle or trailer adapted to carry more than eight passengers; or

(b)   uses on a road a vehicle which does not comply with such a requirement, or causes or permits a vehicle to be so used,

commits an offence. Where the alleged contravention relates to any description of weight applicable to a goods vehicle, it is a defence to prove either that the vehicle was going to or coming from a weighbridge, or, where the relevant weight limit is not exceeded by more than 5 per cent, that this weight was not exceeded at the time of loading and this load had not been added to (s 41B(2)). Those who contravene RTA 1988, s 41B are not thereby liable to disqualification or endorsement.

Breach of requirements as to control of vehicle, mobile telephones, etc

RTA 1988, s 41D makes it an offence for a person to contravene or fail to comply with construction and use requirements as to a driver being in such a position that he can retain proper control of the vehicle, or a full view, or as to not using a mobile telephone. Such an offence carries discretionary disqualification; the endorsement of three penalty points is obligatory.

Breach of other construction and use requirements

RTA 1988, s 42 is concerned with contraventions of a construction and use requirement other than one dealt with by ss 41A, 41B, and 41D. It provides that a person
who:

(a) contravenes or fails to comply with such a requirement; or
(b) uses on a road a motor vehicle or trailer which does not comply with such a require-
    ment, or causes or permits a motor vehicle or trailer to be so used,

commits an offence.

An offence of using on a road a trailer which does not comply with regulations is an
offence distinct from that of using a defective motor vehicle.

Those who contravene RTA 1988, s 42 are not liable to disqualification or to
endorsement.

Use

This term should be given its ordinary meaning. A person uses a vehicle if he controls,
manages, operates, or otherwise has the use of it as a vehicle.

In law, a person can 'use' a vehicle, even though he does not do so personally. This is
because, if a driver of a vehicle is about his employer's business, the employer is also
using the vehicle (and can therefore be held vicariously liable), and the words 'causing'
or 'permitting' should not be considered. The offence of 'using' covers most eventualities where there is an employer/employee relationship.

RTA 1988, ss 40A to 42 impose strict liability upon those who use motor vehicles in
contravention of RV(C&U)R 1986; consequently, it is irrelevant that the defendant did
not know of the defect, etc, nor ought to have known of it.

It is quite possible that the owner of a motor vehicle may be totally unaware that an
offence of using in breach of RV(C&U)R 1986 is being committed in relation to his
vehicle which is being driven by an employee of his many miles away from his operating centre. Nevertheless, if the vehicle is on the road, driven by an employee in the
course of his employment, the employer is using it in addition to his employee-driver,
and both he and his employee can be convicted of the offence.

In one case, a self-employed driver was paid on a daily basis. He paid his own tax
and National Insurance contributions, and did not work exclusively for the company.
When he did work for the company, he wore its uniform, drove its vehicle and collected and delivered loads from and to specified locations. A divisional court held that
the company was not 'using' the vehicle. It said that *a person is a user only if he is the
driver or the owner of the vehicle, but an owner only uses his vehicle if the driver is
employed by him under a contract of service and at the material time he is driving on his
employer's business,* which the driver in the case was not. A divisional court has
remarked upon the illogicality and artificiality caused by its insistence upon the need
for a strict employer/employee relationship. The court on one occasion said that it
found it difficult to accept that, if a man can 'use' his vehicle through the hands of his
employee, he cannot be said to use it at the hands of someone else who, at his specific
request, drives it on a journey at the express orders and with the full knowledge of the
owner. Illogical or not, the court has persistently refused to extend the meaning of
'use' on the grounds that a line must be drawn somewhere. Where such a strict
employer/employee relationship cannot be established, a charge of 'causing' or 'permitting' must be considered.

Where a vehicle is hired out with a driver for use by another firm, the driver will usually remain the employee of the owner of the vehicle, so that a 'using' by the driver will be a 'using' by the owner. Thus, where a haulier (BRS) hired a vehicle together with its driver to another haulier for a period of five years, and that other haulier operated the vehicle under its own livery, BRS was held to be using that vehicle when it was found to be overloaded. BRS had been in the business of hiring out vehicles with drivers who remained their employees and the vehicles were being used in the course of that business. Similarly, where the driver of a vehicle who was employed by company A was ordered by telephone to pick up a return load on behalf of company B, company B being responsible for loading the vehicle, its documentation, and the selection of route, a divisional court held that company A was guilty of using the vehicle when it was found to be overloaded. The court said that, while it might be correct to argue that company B was using the vehicle, this did not mean that company A was not. It was their vehicle and their driver and that driver was employed under a contract of service.

Where a company hires another company to transport its goods, the first company is not 'using' the vehicle at the time the second company is doing so. The first company is not 'operating' the vehicle at the time in question; it would be different if it had hired the vehicle and operated it itself.

As is apparent from the above, someone who lends his private motor car to his friend is not liable for 'using' that vehicle if RV(C&U)R 1986 are contravened by the friend. However, in certain circumstances, he could be guilty of permitting its use in contravention of the Regulations.

Where a trailer is towed by another vehicle and the offence concerned relates to the trailer, as, for example, where there is a defective part on the trailer, or it carries an insecure load, the information or written charge should specify that it was the trailer which was defective or improperly used. This is essential where the tractor unit and the trailer are owned by different persons or companies.

Cause the use

This term, together with 'permitting the use', covers circumstances in which charges of aiding and abetting would otherwise normally be appropriate. To be guilty of causing the use of a vehicle in contravention of RV(C&U)R 1986, a defendant must actually have known of, or been wilfully blind as to, the contravention in question, and have been in a position to exercise some control over the driver. To 'cause' involves some express or positive command or direction from the person 'causing' to the person 'using'. If the foreman of a haulage depot, knowing that a vehicle has a defective tyre, orders an employee to drive the vehicle, the foreman 'causes' the driver to commit the offence. He is in a position to give orders to the employee in relation to the use of the vehicle and does so, and he knows of the defect. In such a case the haulage company would also be guilty of using the vehicle as it was used on their business and knowledge is not an essential ingredient of that offence.

A person who tows another vehicle is causing it to be used on a road.

Permit the use

Like 'causing the use' of a vehicle, 'permitting' a vehicle to be used in contravention of RV(C&U)R 1986 requires proof that the defendant actually knew of, or was wilfully blind as to, the contravention in question. However, the meaning of 'permitting' is much wider than the meaning of 'causing' because there does not need to be any express or positive mandate to use a motor vehicle by a person in a position to exercise control over the driver, and a general or particular permission to use a vehicle will be sufficient. However, for a person to be guilty of 'permitting' he must be in a position to forbid another person to use the vehicle.

Many employees are given general permission to use their employers' vehicles in any way they choose. Having given such a general permission, it is unlikely that such an employer will be liable for contraventions of the RV(C&U)R 1986 in respect of that vehicle, but in some circumstances he may. There is a distinction between knowledge that the vehicle is being used and knowledge that it is being used unlawfully. A sales representative may be given total use of a motor car. As a driver he will be responsible for its use in such contravention but his employers will not normally be liable for *permitting* such use, as they are unlikely to have knowledge of the particular unlawful use. However, if the vehicle is being used on company business, a charge of using may be appropriate.

Someone who lends his car to his friend permits him to use it. That permission does not extend to unlawful use of a warning instrument as no permission has been given in that respect. On the other hand, if the tyres were defective, it would be a question of fact as to whether the owner of the vehicle knew of the defect when permission was given to use it.

PARTICULAR REGULATIONS UNDER RV(C&U)R 1986, PART II

Brakes

The differing braking systems with which different types of vehicles must be fitted are dealt with in regs 15 and 16 and Sch 3. These provisions include exemptions from RV(C&U)R 1986 if type approval has been given. However, the fitting of various systems is not a matter of prime concern to police officers. On the other hand, the maintenance of brakes is. Regulation 18 deals with the maintenance of brakes and applies quite generally to braking systems (where fitted under these, or other, regulations).

Regulation 18(1) requires every braking system and the means of operation thereof fitted to a vehicle to be maintained in good and efficient working order, and properly adjusted. This applies to any vehicle to which a braking system is fitted, including a trailer which is not required to have a braking system fitted.

By reg 18(3), braking systems must be so maintained that service braking systems and secondary braking systems have prescribed braking efficiencies set out in detail in the following table.

	Service	Secondary
(a) if the vehicle's construction, etc complies with Community Directive 79/489, 85/647, 88/194 or 91/422:		
(i) not drawing trailer	50%	25%
(ii) drawing trailer	45%	25%
(b) vehicles first used on or after 1 January 1968 and complying with reg 16:		
(i) when not drawing trailer or drawing trailer manufactured after 1 January 1968	50%	25%
(ii) drawing trailer manufactured before 1 January 1968	40%	15%

(c) goods vehicles and buses first used before 1 January 1968
     having an unladen weight exceeding 1,525 kg being rigid
     vehicles with two axles (not artics):

(i) when not drawing trailer	45%	20%
(ii) when drawing trailer	40%	15%

(d) vehicles not shown at (a)–(c) having at least one means of   **50%   25%**
     operation applying to at least four wheels (not a bus or artic)

(e) vehicles not shown at (a)–(c) having three wheels and at   **40%   25%**
     least one means of operation applying to all three wheels
     (not a motorcycle and sidecar) when not drawing a trailer,
     or when drawing a trailer if three-wheeler is classed as a
     motorcycle

(f) other vehicles not shown at (a)–(c) when not drawing a   **30%   25%**
     trailer or, in the case of a motorcycle, when drawing a trailer

In certain circumstances where a defect arises in an ABS braking system during the course of a journey, it is permissible for the vehicle to complete its journey, or to be driven to a place where the ABS is to be repaired, without there being a breach of the requirement under reg 18(1) that every part of a braking system must be maintained in good and efficient working order. However, the affected braking system must still meet the braking efficiencies specified in reg 18(3).

Seat belts

RV(C&U)R 1986, regs 46 and 47 deal the fitting of anchorage points and seat belts. These provisions are of particular relevance to manufacturers and others engaged in the motor trade.

Wearing of seat belts

The circumstances in which seat belts must be worn by passengers in motor vehicles are now prescribed in the Motor Vehicles (Wearing of Seat Belts) Regulations (MV(WSB)R) 1993 and the Motor Vehicles (Wearing of Seat Belts by Children in Front Seats) Regulations (MV(WSBCFS)R) 1993 and not by RV(C&U)R 1986. The 1993 Regulations implement the requirements of Council Directives 91/671/EEC and 2003/20/EC which apply to vehicles of less than 3.5 tonnes with four or more wheels and a design speed of more than 25 kph, and to large and small buses and light goods vehicles. Directive 2003/20/EC requires additional measures in respect of the wearing of child-restraining devices and places obligations upon bus operators to require the wearing of seat belts fitted to large and small buses.

The offences committed by breaches of the Seat Belt Regulations are punishable under RTA 1988, ss 14 and 15 and not by RTA 1988, s 42. The requirements created by the 1993 Regulations are not always confined to the description of vehicles set out in the Directive.

Adult passengers   MV(WSB)R 1993, reg 5 requires that every person:

(a) driving a motor vehicle (other than a two-wheeled motor cycle with or without a sidecar); or

(b) riding in a front or rear seat of a motor vehicle (other than a two-wheeled motor cycle with or without a sidecar)

must wear an adult seat belt. The regulation does not apply to a person under the age of 14.

Condition (b) does not apply to a person riding in a small or large bus (p 440) being used to promote a 'local service', or which is constructed or adapted for standing passengers and on which standing is permitted. Failure to comply with reg 5 is an offence under RTA 1988, s 14(3).

Regulation 6 provides the following exemptions from the requirement to wear a seat belt made by reg 5:

(a) a person holding a medical certificate to the effect that it is inadvisable for him to wear a seat belt;

(b) the driver of or a passenger in a motor vehicle constructed or adapted for carrying goods, while on a journey which does not exceed 50 metres and which is undertaken for the purpose of delivering or collecting anything;

(c) a person performing a manoeuvre which includes reversing;

(d) a qualified driver supervising a learner carrying out such a manoeuvre;

(e) a person by whom a test of competence to drive is being conducted where wearing a seat belt would endanger himself or another person;

(f) a person driving or riding in a vehicle being used for fire and rescue, or police or Serious Organised Crime Agency (SOCA) purposes, or for carrying a person in lawful custody who is included in the exemption;

(g) the driver of a licensed taxi whilst being used to seek hire or answer a call, or when carrying a passenger for hire, or a private hire car whilst it is being used to carry a passenger for hire;

(h) a person in a vehicle being used under a trade licence for investigating or remedying a fault;

(i) a disabled person who is wearing a disabled person's belt; or

(j) a person riding in a vehicle whilst in a procession organised by or on behalf of the Crown.

There are two other exemptions. A person who is riding in a vehicle which is participating in a procession which is held to mark or commemorate an event is exempt from the requirement to wear a seat belt if the procession is one commonly or customarily held in a police area or areas, or if notice in respect of the procession has been given in accordance with the Public Order Act 1986, s 11 (see p 761). The second requirement in reg 5 relating to a person riding in a front or rear seat of a motor vehicle other than a two-wheeled motor cycle with or without a sidecar does not apply to a person riding in a small or large bus which is being used to provide a local service (within the meaning of the Transport Act (TA) 1985) in a built-up area (ie entirely on restricted roads) or which is constructed or adapted for the carriage of standing passengers and on which the operator permits standing. TA 1985, ss 6 – 9 deal with this.

A 'local service' is a service, using one or more public service vehicles, for the carriage of passengers by road at separate fares other than:

(a) a journey organised privately by persons acting independently of the vehicle operators, etc; or

(b) a service within which every vehicle used is operated under a permit granted under TA 1985, s 19 (minibuses and buses operated by educational, religious, social, recreational, and other beneficial bodies); or

(c) a service in relation to which (except in an emergency) *either* the place where each passenger is set down is 15 miles or more, measured in a straight line, from the place where he was taken up *or* some point on the route between those places is 15 miles or more from that place or both (limited stop vehicles).

Front-seat child passengers   It is an offence, contrary to RTA 1988, s 15(1) and (2), for a person, without reasonable excuse, to drive a motor vehicle on a road if a child under 14 is in the front of that vehicle, unless the child is wearing a seat belt in conformity with MV(WSBCFS)R 1993, reg 5. Generally, it is irrelevant that a seat belt is not provided or available for the seat. The Regulations set out the rules with which a driver must conform. A 'front seat' is one which is wholly or partially in the front of the vehicle. The Regulations do not apply to two-wheeled motor cycles, with or without sidecars.

The description of the seat belts which satisfy the requirements of the above Regulations relating to children is prescribed in reg 5 thereof:

(a) in the case of a 'small child', the seat belt must be a child restraint with a marking required under RV(C&U)R 1986, reg 47(7) or a child restraint approved by another EU member state;

(b) in the case of a 'large child', the seat belt must be a child restraint approved under reg 47(7) or an adult belt.

For the purposes of the Regulations, a 'small child' is a child who is under 12 and under 135 cm in height, and a 'large child' is a child under 14 who is not a 'small child'.

MV(WSBCFS)R, reg 7 exempts from these provisions:

(a) a 'small child' aged three or more who is riding in a bus and is wearing an adult belt if an appropriate seat belt is not available for him in the front or rear of the vehicle;

(b) a child for whom there is a medical certificate; or;

(c) a disabled child who is wearing a disabled person's belt.

In addition, the prohibition created by RTA 1988, s 15(1) does not apply in relation to a child riding in a bus which is being used to provide a local service within the meaning of the Transport Act 1985, or which is constructed or adapted for the carriage of standing passengers and on which the operator permits standing. The prohibition does not apply in relation to a 'large child' if no appropriate seat belt is available for him in the front of the vehicle.

RTA 1988, s 15(1A) requires that where:

(a) a child is in the front seat of a motor vehicle other than a bus;

(b) that child is in a rear-facing child restraining device; and

(c) the passenger seat where the child is placed is protected by a front air bag,

a person must not, without reasonable excuse, drive the vehicle on a road unless the air bag is deactivated. 'Deactivation' includes the case where a bag is designed or adapted in such a way that it cannot inflate enough to pose a risk of injury to a child travelling in a rear-facing child restraining device in the seat in question. It is an offence contrary to s 15(2) for the person to drive a motor vehicle in contravention of s 15(1A).

For the purposes of s 15, 'bus' means a motor vehicle with at least four wheels, constructed or adapted for the carriage of passengers, with more than eight seats in addition to the driver's seat, and with a maximum design speed exceeding 25 kph.

Rear-seat child passengers   RTA 1988, s 15(3) provides that a person must not, without reasonable excuse, drive a motor vehicle on a road if:

(a) a child under the age of three is in the rear of that motor vehicle; or
(b) a child of or over that age but under the age of 14 is in the rear of the motor vehicle and any seat belt is fitted in the rear of that vehicle,

unless the child is wearing a seat belt in conformity with MV(WSB)R 1993, reg 8. Regulation 8 is identical to the requirements which apply to children in front seats, ie MV(WSBCFS)R 1993, reg 5 (see p 438).

RTA 1988, s 15(3A) provides that a person must not, without reasonable excuse, drive a passenger car on a road where a child under the age of 12 and less than 150 cm in height is in the rear of the car and no seat belt is fitted in the rear of that car, but a seat in the front of the passenger car is provided with a seat belt and is not occupied by any person.

Exemption from these prohibitions is provided by MV(WSB)R 1993, regs 9 and 10. Regulation 9 provides that they do not apply where the motor vehicle is a large bus, or where the vehicle is a licensed taxi or licensed hire car in which (in each case) the rear seats are separated from the driver by a fixed partition. Regulation 10 provides that the prohibitions in s 15(3) and (3A) do not apply in relation to:

(a) a child for whom there is a medical certificate;
(b) a small child aged under three who is riding in a licensed taxi or a licensed hire car if no appropriate seat belt is available for him in the front or rear of the vehicle;
(c) a small child aged three or more who is riding in a licensed taxi, a licensed hire car, or a small bus and wearing an adult belt if an appropriate seat belt is not available for him in the front or rear of the vehicle;
(d) a small child aged three or more who is wearing an adult belt and riding in a passenger car or light goods vehicle where the use of child restraints by the child occupants of two seats in the rear of the vehicle prevents the use of an appropriate seat belt for that child and no appropriate seat belt is available for him in the front of the vehicle;
(e) a small child who is riding in a vehicle being used for the purposes of the police, security or emergency services to enable the proper performance of their duty;
(f) a small child aged three or more who is wearing an adult belt and who, because of an unexpected necessity, is travelling a short distance in a passenger car or light goods vehicle in which no appropriate seat belt is available for him; or
(g) a disabled child who is wearing a disabled person's belt or whose disability makes it impracticable to wear a seat belt where a disabled person's belt is unavailable to him.

In addition, by reg 10, the prohibition in s 15(3) does not apply in relation to a child under three riding in a rear seat of a small bus. Nor does it apply to a small child aged three or more riding in the rear of a small bus if neither an appropriate seat belt nor an adult seat belt is available for him in the front or rear of the vehicle. In addition, it does not apply in relation to a 'large child' in any vehicle, if no appropriate seat belt is available for him in the rear of the vehicle. Lastly, the prohibition in s 15(3) does not apply to a child riding in a small bus which is being used to provide a local service (within the meaning of the Transport Act 1985) in a built-up-area (ie entirely on restricted roads) or which is constructed or adapted for the carriage of standing passengers and on which the operator permits standing.

Regulation 10 also provides that the prohibition in s 15(3A) does not apply to a child if no appropriate seat belt is available for him in the front of the vehicle.

For the purposes of the seat belt regulations 'large buses' and 'small buses' are 'buses' as defined on p 438. The difference between them is that a large bus has a maximum laden weight exceeding 3.5 tonnes and a small bus see has a maximum laden weight not exceeding 3.5 tonnes. A 'light goods vehicle' is a motor vehicle with at least four wheels, a maximum design speed of more than 25 kph, and a maximum laden weight not exceeding 3.5 tonnes. 'Small child' and 'large child' have the same meaning as in respect of 'child front seat passengers' (p 438). 'Operator' has the same meaning as in RTA 1988, s 15B.

Breach of RTA 1988, s 15(3) or (3A) is an offence under s 15(4).

Wearing of seat belts in buses   RTA 1988, s 15B(1) requires bus operators to notify passengers of the need to wear seat belts. It provides that, subject to s 15B(6), the operator of a bus in which any of the passenger seats are equipped with seat belts must take all reasonable steps to ensure that every passenger is notified that he is required to wear a seat belt at all times when:

(a) he is in a seat equipped with a seat belt, and
(b) the bus is in motion.

'Operator' means the owner of the bus or, if the bus is in the possession of any other person under an agreement for hire, or hire-purchase, conditional sale, loan or otherwise, that person. 'Bus' has the same meaning as in RTA 1988, s 15.

Notification may be made by an official announcement, or an audio-visual presentation, made when the passenger joins the bus or within a reasonable time of his doing so, or a sign (a symbol of a seated figure wearing a belt) prominently displayed at each passenger seat equipped with a seat belt.

Section 15B(6) provides that the offence against s 15B(1) does not apply in relation to a bus which is being used to provide a local service (within the meaning of the Transport Act 1985) in a built-up area (ie entirely on restricted roads) *or* which is constructed or adapted for the carriage of standing passengers and on which the operator permits standing.

The operator commits an offence against s 15B(4) if he fails to comply with the requirements of s 15(1). Where an offence committed by a body corporate is proved to have been committed with the consent or connivance of, or attributable to, any neglect on the part of a director, manager, secretary, or other similar officer, or any person purporting to act in such a capacity, that person is equally liable.

'Availability' of seat belts   MV(WSB)R 1993, Sch 2, and MV(WSBCFS)R 1993, Sch 2, describe in the same terms the circumstances in which a seat belt will be regarded as not being available. They are where:

(a) another person is wearing the relevant belt;
(b) a child is occupying the relevant seat and wearing a child restraint which is an appropriate child restraint for that child and this renders use of the seat belt impracticable;
(c) a person holding a medical certificate is occupying the relevant seat;
(d) a disabled person (not being the person in question) is occupying the relevant seat and wearing a disabled person's belt and this renders use of the seat belt impracticable;
(e) by reason of his disability, it would not be practicable for the person in question to wear the relevant belt;
(f) the person in question is prevented from occupying the relevant seat by the presence of a child restraint which could not readily be removed without the aid of tools; or

(g) the relevant seat is so designed that it can be adjusted to increase the space available for goods and effects and when it is so adjusted the seat cannot be used.

Speedometer

By RV(C&U)R 1986, reg 35 every motor vehicle (with very limited exceptions) must be fitted with a speedometer. Regulation 35 also provides that speedometers fitted to vehicles first used after 1 April 1984 must indicate speed in both miles per hour and kilometres per hour; otherwise the indication given by a speedometer may be either in miles per hour or kilometres per hour. Instead of complying with reg 35, a vehicle may comply with the relevant Community directive or EC regulations.

The following vehicles do not need to have speedometers fitted:

(a) invalid carriages, motor cycles not exceeding 100 cc, and works trucks (provided in each case they were first used before 1 April 1984);
(b) agricultural vehicles which are not driven at more than 20 mph;
(c) vehicles which legally or physically cannot exceed 25 mph; and
(d) vehicles first used before 1 October 1937.

Regulation 36 requires that a speedometer must be kept free from any obstruction which might prevent its being easily read and must at all times be maintained in good working order. On a charge involving a breach of this requirement, it is a defence to prove that the defect occurred in the course of the journey being then undertaken or that steps had already been taken to have repairs or replacements effected as soon as possible. These defences cover so many possibilities, and if alleged are so hard to disprove, that enforcement is almost limited to admitted long-standing defects in respect of which no repairs have been arranged or when the instrument registers incorrectly.

Mirrors

RV(C&U)R 1986, reg 33 sets out detailed requirements about the fitting of mirrors. Instead of complying with the above requirements about mirrors, a vehicle may comply with the relevant Community directive. The various requirements are of particular relevance to the manufacturers and others in the motor trade.

Windscreen wipers and washers

By RV(C&U)R 1986, reg 34(1), all vehicles fitted with windscreens must be fitted with one or more efficient automatic windscreen wipers, unless the driver can obtain an adequate view to the front without looking through the windscreen, for example by opening the windscreen or looking over it (as is the case with many cars produced before the 1950s). Regulation 34(1) also requires that the wipers fitted must be capable of clearing the windscreen so that the driver has an adequate view of the road in front of both sides of the vehicle and to the front of the vehicle.

Regulation 34(6), which deals with maintenance, requires that every windscreen wiper required by the Regulations to be fitted is, at all times while the vehicle is used on a road, maintained in good and efficient working order and is properly adjusted. As stated, reg 34(1) demands one or more wipers. If the driver's wiper provides the view ahead and to both sides, as required, any other wiper is not subject to the maintenance requirement.

By reg 34(2), a windscreen washer must be fitted to any vehicle which requires one or more automatic wipers, except an agricultural motor vehicle (other than one first used on or after 1 June 1986 and driven at more than 20 mph), a track-laying vehicle, a vehicle incapable of exceeding 20 mph, or a vehicle being used to provide a local bus service. The washer must be such that, in conjunction with the wipers, it is capable of cleaning the area of the windscreen swept by the blades of mud or similar deposits.

In the alternative to the above requirement, a vehicle may comply with the relevant Community directive.

Audible warning instrument

The following provisions are made by RV(C&U)R 1986, reg 37. All motor vehicles with a maximum speed of more than 20 mph must be fitted with a horn (but, in the case of an agricultural motor vehicle, only if it is being driven at more than 20 mph). In the case of motor vehicles first used on or after 1 August 1973 the sound emitted by any horn must be continuous and uniform and not strident. This is to ensure that the horns of such vehicles give a sound which is not offensive to the ear.

With the exception of police vehicles, SOCA vehicles, emergency vehicles, vehicles of HM Revenue & Customs used in the investigation of serious crime, and vehicles owned and operated by the Secretary of State for Defence and used by the special forces in response (or training or practising in responding) to a national security emergency, no motor vehicle may be fitted with a bell, gong, siren, or two-tone horn; consequently, horns which play snatches of tunes, such as 'Colonel Bogey', are prohibited. However, vehicles may be fitted with an instrument or apparatus (not being a two-toned horn) to give a sound informing the public that goods are for sale from the vehicle; thus, ice-cream chimes, etc are not prohibited. The rule against fitting gongs, etc does not apply to an anti-theft device nor to an alarm to summon help to a public service vehicle. Any anti-theft device fitted must have a cut-out limiting its use to five minutes. Where a horn can operate as an anti-theft device, such a cut-out must be fitted if the motor vehicle was first used on or after 1 October 1982.

A 'reversing alarm' fitted to a vehicle to warn persons that the vehicle is reversing or about to reverse, or a 'boarding aid alarm' fitted to a bus to warn that a power-operated ramp or lift is in operation is exempted from the requirement that the sound of a warning instrument shall be continuous and uniform but it must not be strident. The sound emitted must be such that it is not likely to be confused with the sound emitted from a pedestrian crossing (reg 99). A reversing alarm may only be used on a stationary vehicle if the vehicle's engine is running and it is about to move backwards or the vehicle is in danger from another moving vehicle.

Horns and other audible warning instruments must be maintained in good and efficient working order at all times.

Instead of complying with the provisions mentioned above concerning the nature and maintenance of audible warning instruments, a vehicle may comply with the relevant Community directive or regulation.

Regulation 99 provides that no person shall sound, or cause or permit to be sounded, the horn or other audible warning device of a motor vehicle when it is stationary on a road at any time. The only exception is when there is danger due to another moving vehicle on or near the road. In addition, it provides that no person shall sound, or cause or permit to be sounded, in a vehicle in motion on a restricted road, a horn, etc, between 11.30 pm and 7 am on the following day. This does not, of course, apply to anti-theft alarms, reversing devices, or boarding aid alarms. Instruments to advise the public of goods for sale from a vehicle must only be used for that purpose and must not be used between 7 pm and 12 am on the following day.

Silencer

RV(C&U)R 1986, reg 54 requires every vehicle propelled by an internal combustion engine to be fitted with an exhaust system including a silencer, and exhaust gases from the engine not to escape into the atmosphere without first passing through its silencer. Specified noise levels are prescribed but they are directed at the manufacturers. Police officers detect faulty silencers by the nature of the sound emitted which indicates that the exhaust gases are escaping into the atmosphere without first passing through a silencer. This will occur where there is a break or large hole in the pipe. Instead of complying with the above provisions, a vehicle may comply with the relevant Community directive.

Alterations or replacements to exhaust systems are not permitted if they have the effect of increasing the noise.

Although not directly concerned with silencers, regs 97 and 98 also deal with noise. Regulation 97 prohibits the use, etc of a motor vehicle in a manner so as to cause excessive noise which could reasonably have been avoided by the driver. Regulation 98 requires the driver of a stationary vehicle to stop the action of machinery attached to it, or forming part of the vehicle, so far as may be necessary for the prevention of noise or of exhaust emissions.

Wings

RV(C&U)R 1986, reg 63 requires the following to be fitted with wings or similar fittings to catch, as far as practicable, mud or water thrown up by the wheels:

(a) invalid carriages;
(b) heavy motor cars, motor cars and motor cycles, not being agricultural motor vehicles or pedestrian-controlled vehicles;
(c) agricultural motor vehicles driven at more than 20 mph; and
(d) trailers.

The requirements in relation to trailers are restricted to the rear wheels, if the trailer has more than two wheels.

Works trucks, unfinished vehicles, living vans and some agricultural trailed appliances are exempt from the above requirements. Trailers used for or in connection with the carriage of round timber and the rear wheels of the motor vehicle parts of articulated vehicles whose semi-trailer is so used are also exempt.

Instead of complying with these requirements, a vehicle may comply with the relevant Community directive.

Dangerous vehicles, etc

RV(C&U)R 1986, reg 100(1) requires that a motor vehicle, every trailer and all parts and accessories of such vehicle or trailer are at all times in such a condition that no danger is caused or is likely to be caused to any person in or on the vehicle or trailer or on a road. The provision is concerned with danger, and a distant possibility of such danger is not enough. For example, in a case where the radiator grille was missing, the court would not accept that sufficient danger existed of persons coming into contact with the revolving fan blades, because the engine was transverse.

Regulation 100(1) applies to a vehicle which in its manufactured condition is inherently likely to cause danger to other road-users, as well as to a vehicle which has become dangerous through lack of maintenance. In relation to the requirement that all parts and accessories must be in such condition that no danger is caused, it is immaterial that parts may be in reasonable condition if they are dangerous because they are not in working order. In a case where a tow bar was in good condition, but the trailer was incorrectly coupled, its user was guilty of using it in a dangerous condition. Separate and distinct offences are involved in using a defective motor vehicle and using a defective trailer. This equally applies to articulated vehicles.

Regulation 100(1) also requires that the number of passengers carried, or the manner of their carriage, is such that no danger is caused or is likely to be caused to any person in or on the vehicle or trailer or on a road.

Regulation 100(1) also requires that the weight, packing, distribution and adjustment of a load is such that no such danger is caused, or likely to be caused. This prohibition is really aimed at a badly loaded vehicle; insecure loads are dealt with by reg 100(2).

Regulation 100(2) requires that the load carried by a motor vehicle or trailer must at all times be so secured, if necessary by physical restraint other than its own weight, and be in such a position, that neither danger nor nuisance is likely to be caused to any person or property by reason of the load or any part of it falling or being blown from the vehicle or by reason of any other movement of the load or a part of it. In effect, this deals with insecure loads which for any reason cause danger or nuisance. It is necessary to specify which of these alternatives resulted from the insecurity of the load. Where a substantial part of a solid load falls onto a busy road there is little doubt that danger is caused. In circumstances where a goods vehicle, loaded with gravel, sheds part of its load steadily into the path of following traffic, there is no doubt that there is a breach of the requirement so to secure the load that no nuisance to persons or property is likely.

In considering whether a load has been adequately secured so that neither danger nor nuisance is likely to be caused one has to consider four things:

(a) the nature of the journey;
(b) the way in which the load was secured;
(c) the way in which the load was positioned; and
(d) the journey to be taken.

What might be secure for one journey in fine weather and on good roads might not be secure for another journey in poor weather and on less good roads. If the load is a high one, and too high to go under a bridge on the route, so that it is inevitable that the load will be knocked off, the load will not have been so secured that neither danger nor nuisance was likely.

Regulation 100(3) prohibits the use of a motor vehicle or trailer for any purpose for which it is so unsuitable as to cause danger or nuisance to any person on the vehicle or trailer, or on a road. The crucial question is whether the vehicle or trailer was unsuitable. If it is not properly loaded and it is the load which causes the danger or nuisance, this does not affect the suitability of the vehicle itself. In a case where an excavator which was loaded onto a trailer struck a bridge, it was held that the trailer did not become unsuitable when it was so loaded. It was the manner of the loading which was at fault; reg 100(1) was the relevant provision.

Reference has already been made on p 431 to the offences under RTA 1988, s 40A of using, causing or permitting the use of a motor vehicle or trailer which is in a dangerous condition because of the condition of the vehicle's accessories or equipment, the purpose of its use, the number of passengers carried or the manner of their carriage and the weight, or the distribution and security of the load, etc. It is submitted that most offences involving dangerous vehicles will now be charged under RTA 1988, s 40A and not under s 42 for a breach of reg 100(1), since a conviction of an offence under s 40A involves the risk of discretionary disqualification and requires the obligatory endorsement of three penalty points. Where there is a conviction under s 42 for a breach of reg 100 there can be no disqualification or endorsement of the offender's driving licence.

Some aspects of reg 100(2) and (3) have also been overtaken by the arrival of RTA 1988, s 40A as they also deal with elements related to danger being caused to persons in consequence of the use of the motor vehicle or trailer in the manner prohibited by s 40A.

Maintenance of glass

All glass or other transparent material fitted to motor vehicles is required, by RV(C&U)R 1986, reg 30(3), to be maintained in such condition that it does not obscure the vision of the driver while the vehicle is being driven on a road. This regulation is not limited to the windscreen but applies to all glass affecting the driver's vision, such as the rear window and side windows through which he needs to look.

Maintenance of fuel tank

By RV(C&U)R 1986, reg 39 a fuel tank on a motor vehicle must be maintained so that any leakage of liquid or vapour from it is adequately prevented (except that this does not prevent a tank being fitted with a pressure release valve). Instead of complying with these requirements, a vehicle may comply with the corresponding requirements contained in EC directives and regulations.

Maintenance of tyres

RV(C&U)R 1986, reg 27(1) prohibits the use, on a road, of any motor vehicle or trailer, a wheel of which is fitted with a pneumatic tyre, if:

(a) the tyre is unsuitable for the use to which the vehicle or trailer is being put or to the type of tyres fitted to its other wheels;
(b) it is wrongly inflated for such use;
(c) it has a cut in excess of 25 mm or 10 per cent of the section width of the tyre, whichever is the greater, measured in any direction on the outside of the tyre and deep enough to reach the ply or cords;
(d) it has a lump, bulge, or tear caused by separation or partial failure of its structure;
(e) it has a portion of the ply or cord exposed; or
(f) the tyre is not maintained in such condition as to be fit for the use to which the vehicle or trailer is being put or has a defect which might in any way cause damage to the surface of the road or damage to persons on or in the vehicle or to other persons using the road.

Also prohibited is the use on a road of:

(a) a passenger vehicle, other than a motor cycle, constructed or adapted to carry no more than eight seated passengers in addition to the driver;
(b) a goods vehicle with a maximum gross weight which does not exceed 3,500 kg; and
(c) a light trailer not falling within (b),

where a pneumatic tyre on a wheel does not have in grooves of the tread pattern a depth of at least 1.6 mm throughout a continuous band comprising the central three-quarters of the breadth of the tyre and round the entire circumference of the tyre. There are special provisions for tyres on a vehicle first used before 3 January 1933.

In relation to large goods vehicles, motor cycles and other vehicles not included above, their use on a road is prohibited if a wheel is fitted with a pneumatic tyre and:

(a) the base of any groove which showed in the original tread pattern of the tyre is not clearly visible; or

(b) either it does not have a depth of 1 mm in the grooves of the tread pattern throughout a continuous band measuring at least three-quarters of the breadth of the tyre and round its entire circumference; or, if the grooves of the original tread pattern of the tyre did not extend beyond three-quarters of the breadth of the tread, any groove which showed in the original tread pattern does not have a depth of at least 1 mm.

As can be seen, all forms of damage to tyres which may result in danger are covered by this regulation. Potential danger is, of course, the reason for the requirement that the contact area of a tyre must have visible tread which must be at least 1.6 mm or (as the case may be) 1 mm deep for three-quarters of that contact area (subject to special provisions which apply to special tyres with narrow contact areas).

Regulation 27(2) makes special provision to allow for the use of tyres designed to be used safely when deflated. There are general exemptions in favour of agricultural trailed appliances, agricultural motor vehicles not driven at more than 20 mph and broken-down vehicles being towed at a speed not exceeding 20 mph. The tread pattern and minimum depth of tread provisions do not apply to three-wheelers not exceeding 102 kg with a maximum possible speed of 12 mph or less, nor to pedestrian-controlled works trucks. In addition, the minimum depth of tread provisions do not apply to motor cycles not exceeding 50 cc.

Regulation 27(5) prohibits the fitting on a motor vehicle or trailer of a recut pneumatic tyre if its ply or cord has been cut or exposed in the process of recutting. Heavy-duty tyres fitted to goods vehicles can usually be recut without causing danger, but tyres fitted to saloon cars do not usually have sufficient thickness of rubber to accept the process.

Special provision is made by reg 27(3) to allow passenger vehicles (not buses) to fit a temporary-use spare tyre, provided the vehicle does not exceed 50 mph.

Mixture of tyres

RV(C&U)R 1986, reg 26(1) provides that pneumatic tyres of different types of construction must not be fitted to the same axle of a vehicle. The regulation mentions three types of tyre:

(a) diagonal-ply tyres, which are commonly known as cross-ply tyres;

(b) bias-belted tyres, which are as above but have a reinforcing band around the outer circumference of the tyre under the tread, but on top of the cords; and

(c) radial-ply tyres.

Regulation 26(2) provides that a motor vehicle having only two axles must not be fitted with the following combinations of tyres:

(a) cross-plys or bias-belted tyres on the rear axle and radials on the front; or

(b) cross-ply on the rear axle and bias-belted on the front.

This regulation is designed to prevent a gripping tyre from being fitted to the 'steering' wheels, whilst a tyre which is not so stable is fitted to the rear.

Not to emit smoke, etc

RV(C&U)R 1986, reg 61(5) provides that no person shall use, or cause or permit to be used, on a road a motor vehicle from which is emitted any smoke, visible vapour, grit, sparks or oily substance which causes, or is likely to cause, damage to property or injury or danger to any person who is, or who may reasonably be expected to be, on the road. This could occur where oil spillage made the road unsafe or fumes badly affected visibility.

Regulation 61(1) provides that a vehicle must be maintained so as not to emit any avoidable smoke or avoidable visible vapour.

CONDITIONS UNDER R(C&U)R 1996, PART IV RELATING TO USE

Position to retain proper view and control

RV(C&U)R 1986, reg 104 provides that a driver must at all times be in such a position that he retains full control and has a full view of the road and traffic ahead. Someone who drove with a sheepdog on his lap has been held to be in breach of this provision.

Reversing

By RV(C&U)R 1986, reg 106, no person shall drive, or cause or permit to be driven, a motor vehicle backwards on a road further than may be requisite for the safety or reasonable convenience of the occupants of the vehicle or other traffic.

Unnecessary obstruction

RV(C&U)R 1986, reg 103 provides that a person in charge of a motor vehicle or trailer must not cause or permit it to stand on a road so as to cause any unnecessary obstruction. The various exemptions within local no-waiting orders in favour of goods vehicles which are loading or unloading has led to a belief by some van drivers that they may double park and even completely block roads for these purposes. This is not so. Any unreasonable use of the road which leads to the obstruction of other road users is an offence against reg 103. An obstruction can be caused by taking up so much of the road that normal two-way traffic is reduced to a one-way flow. In considering whether a particular use was reasonable or unreasonable, a court will apply its mind to the facts, including the duration of the obstruction, the nature of the place where it occurred, the purpose for which the vehicle was there and the *actual* (as opposed to potential) obstruction caused.

Parking facing the wrong way at night

RV(C&U)R 1986, reg 101 provides that, except with the permission of a uniformed police officer, a person must not cause or permit a motor vehicle to stand on a road between sunset and sunrise otherwise than with the left or nearside of the vehicle as close as may be to the edge of the carriageway. If lights are not displayed in a place where parking lights are required to be shown, two offences are committed.

The exemptions from the prohibition under reg 101 are predictable: vehicles being used for fire and rescue, police or ambulance purposes; taxi stands and bus stops; one-way streets; emergency operations, etc.

Stopping engine and setting parking brake

RV(C&U)R 1986, reg 107 provides that no person shall leave, or cause or permit to be left, on a road any motor vehicle which is not attended by a person duly licensed to drive it, unless the engine has been stopped and the parking brake effectively set. The exceptions include a vehicle being used for fire and rescue authority, police or ambulance purposes and special vehicles which use their engines for particular operations other than the driving of the vehicle. Although there is a requirement to do two things, that is stop the engine and set the handbrake, the failure to carry out either of these operations completes the offence under RTA 1988, s 42.

Opening of doors

RV(C&U)R 1986, reg 105 provides that *no person* may open, or cause or permit to be opened, the door of a motor vehicle on a road so as to cause injury or danger to any person. It is not necessary to prove negligence: if the action causes injury or danger that is sufficient.

Mobile telephones

RV(C&U)R 1986, reg 110(1) prohibits the driving of a motor vehicle on a road if the driver is using a hand-held mobile telephone, or a hand-held device of any kind, other than a two-way radio, which performs an interactive communication function by transmitting and receiving data.

For the purposes of reg 110 a mobile telephone or device is classified as 'handheld' if it is, or must be, held at some point during the course of making or receiving a call or performing any other interactive communication function. The term 'interactive communication function' includes:

(a) sending or receiving oral or written messages, or
(b) facsimile documents, or
(c) still or moving images; and
(d) providing access to the internet.

The term 'two-way radio' refers to wireless telegraphy apparatus which is designed or adapted for the purpose of transmitting or receiving spoken messages and to operate on any frequency except a number of ranges. Such equipment is fitted to vehicles used by the emergency services and is therefore exempted from these provisions.

Regulation 110(2) prohibits causing or permitting any other person to drive a motor vehicle on a road while using a hand-held mobile telephone or hand-held device of the specified type. Regulation 110(3) forbids a person supervising a provisional licence holder to use a hand-held mobile telephone or such a hand-held device at a time when the provisional licence holder is driving a motor vehicle on a road.

Regulation 110(5) provides that there is no contravention of reg 110 where:

(a) the use is to call the emergency service on 112 or 999;
(b) it is in response to a genuine emergency; and

(c) it is unsafe or impracticable to cease driving in order to make the call, or for the provisional licence holder to cease driving while the call is made.

Trailers

RV(C&U)R 1986, reg 86 provides that, where a motor vehicle is drawing a trailer by means of a rope or chain, the length of the rope or chain must not exceed 4.5 m, and must not exceed 1.5 m unless the rope or chain is made clearly visible to other road users within a reasonable distance from either side.

Regulation 86A provides that trailers to which reg 15 (see p 435) applies, which are not fitted with an automatic stopping device operative in the event of separation, must not be used on a road unless a secondary coupling is attached to the drawing vehicle and its trailer in such a way that, in the event of separation, the drawbar of the trailer would be prevented from touching the ground and there would be some residual steering of the trailer.

Trailers to which reg 15 applies which are fitted with a device which is designed to stop the trailer automatically in the event of separation must not be used on a road unless the secondary coupling is properly attached to the drawing vehicle and trailer.

Trailers which are living vans and have less than four wheels (or have two close-coupled wheels on each side) are prohibited by reg 90 from being used for the carriage of passengers. The only exception is in favour of testing, when a repairer, etc may be carried in the van for that purpose.

Regulation 83 limits the number of trailers which may be drawn by a motor vehicle on a road. It limits locomotives to a maximum of three trailers, motor tractors to one laden trailer or two unladen trailers, and heavy motor cars and motor cars to one trailer. For the purposes of reg 83, a vehicle drawn by a steam-powered vehicle and which is used solely to carry water for the purpose of the drawing vehicle is not a trailer.

Miscellaneous

RV(C&U)R 1986, reg 53 provides that mascots, emblems or other ornamental objects fitted to vehicles first used on or after 1 October 1937 must not be in such a position that they are likely to strike persons with whom the vehicle may collide unless the nature of the mascot is such that injury is not liable to be caused.

Regulation 109 provides that no person shall drive, or cause or permit to be driven, a motor vehicle on a road if the driver is in such a position as to be able to see, whether directly or by reflection, a television receiving apparatus or other cinematographic apparatus used to display anything other than information concerning the vehicle or its journey.

INTERFERING WITH MOTOR VEHICLES

Tampering with motor vehicles

RTA 1988, s 25 provides that if, while a motor vehicle is on a road or on a parking place provided by a local authority, a person:

(a) gets on to the vehicle, or
(b) tampers with the brake or other part of its mechanism,

without lawful authority or reasonable cause he is guilty of an offence.

Holding or getting on to motor vehicle in order to be towed or carried

If, for the purpose of being carried, a person without lawful authority or reasonable cause takes or retains hold of, or gets on to, a motor vehicle or trailer while in motion on a road he is guilty of an offence under RTA 1988, s 26(1).

If, for the purpose of being drawn, a person takes or retains hold of a motor vehicle or trailer while in motion on a road he is guilty of an offence under s 26(2).

CYCLES

Use of motor cycles

RTA 1988, s 23 restricts the carriage of passengers on a motor bicycle to one person who must be carried sitting astride the cycle on a proper seat securely fixed to the vehicle behind the driver's seat. Interestingly, a pillion passenger need not be carried facing the front. The driver commits an offence if a passenger is carried in contravention of s 23. RV(C&U)R 1986, reg 102 prohibits the carriage of a passenger on a motor bicycle (whether it has a sidecar attached to it or not) on which there are not available suitable supports or rests for the feet for him.

RTA 1988, s 16 empowers the Secretary of State to make regulations requiring persons driving or riding on a specified type of motor cycle (other than in a sidecar) which is on a road to wear protective headgear. The type of headgear is prescribed by the Motor Cycles (Protective Helmets) Regulations 1998. For the purpose of these Regulations, 'motor cycle' means a motor bicycle, including one with a sidecar, and motor tricycles where the paired wheels are less than 460 mm apart. A divisional court has held that the BMW C1 motor cycle (which has a rigid rider cell in the form of a cab) is a motor cycle for these purposes. The Regulations do not apply to mowing machines, motor cycles being propelled by a person on foot, or followers of the Sikh religion while wearing a turban. Helmets must comply with various British Standard or EEA specifications. Breach of the Regulations is an offence contrary to RTA 1988, s 16(4). However, it is not an offence to aid and abet the failure to wear a crash helmet, unless the other party is under 16.

By virtue of RTA 1988, s 18(3), it is an offence to drive or ride on a motor cycle on a road without wearing eye protectors of the type prescribed by the Motor Cycles (Eye Protectors) Regulations 1999. For the purposes of s 18, the Regulations define 'motor cycle' in the same way as in relation to protective helmets. The present requirement does not apply to a person driving or riding on a mowing machine nor does it apply to a person driving or riding on a motor cycle temporarily brought into Great Britain by a foreign resident, if it has been here for less than one year. In addition, the requirement does not apply to a member of the armed forces of the Crown who is driving or riding on a motor cycle on duty, if he is wearing an eye protector which is part of his service equipment. A person propelling a motor cycle on foot is not required to wear an eye protector.

Use of pedal cycles

By RTA 1988, s 24 the carriage of more than one person on a road on a bicycle not propelled by mechanical power is an offence by each of the persons carried, unless it is *constructed* or *adapted* for the carriage of more than one person. A tandem is a cycle *constructed* for the carriage of more than one person, and a cycle which has a seat fitted to permit the carriage of a child has been *adapted* for the carriage of more than one person.

The wilful riding of a pedal cycle on a footpath or causeway by the side of any road made or set apart for the use or accommodation of foot passengers remains an offence contrary to the Highways Act 1835, s 72. A person rides a cycle, even if he merely sits astride it and propels himself with his feet.

Races or speed trials

RTA 1988, s 31 provides that a person who promotes or takes part in a race or speed trial for pedal cycles on a highway commits an offence, unless that race or speed trial is authorised under, and conducted in accordance with, the Cycle Racing on Highways Regulations 1960. Time trials and bicycle races are dealt with separately by the Regulations.

Regulation 2 defines 'time trials' as a cycle race or trial of speed involving either single competitors, or groups of not more than four competitors, starting at intervals of not less than one minute. In the case of groups they must not compete against one another. The result must depend upon the time taken by a competitor, or if a group any member of it, to reach a finishing point; or on the distance covered in a fixed time.

A 'bicycle race' is defined by reg 2 as a race or trial of speed which is not a time trial. In order for it to be authorised, the following additional requirements must be satisfied. The numbers taking part are restricted to, in not more than two races a year selected by the British Cycling Federation, 100 competitors, and in any other approved race, 80. Races must not take place during the hours of darkness. If they follow a circuitous route, they must travel at least 10 miles before passing the same point on a highway twice (in whichever direction). No continuous part of the race may be on more than one-and-a-half miles of any road subject to a speed limit of 40 mph or less, and no further continuous part in a 40 mph-restricted section may be within three miles of the previous one. A chief officer of police is empowered to make directions as to traffic movement and routes, including the closure of sections of roadway on such occasions.

Electrically assisted pedal cycles

An 'electrically assisted pedal cycle' is not a motor vehicle for the purpose of the Road Traffic Acts; such a cycle is a pedal cycle which has a kerbside weight not exceeding 40 kg, or if a tandem 60 kg, is fitted with pedals, and has an electric motor of rated output not exceeding 0.2 kw (0.25 kw in the case of a tandem) and incapable of propelling the vehicle when it is travelling at more than 15 mph. In other words, it is basically a pedal cycle with an auxiliary electric motor which cuts out when the vehicle is travelling in excess of 15 mph. A divisional court has held that, to satisfy the definition of an electrically assisted pedal cycle, the nature of the pedals fitted to such a cycle must be such that they are reasonably capable of propelling the vehicle in a safe manner in normal day-to-day use.

The Pedal Cycles (Construction and Use) Regulations 1983, reg 4, requires such pedal cycles to have a plate showing, inter alia, the continuous rated output of the motor. The battery must not leak so as to be a source of danger and the cycle must be fitted with a device, biased to the off position, which switches on the motor. Breach of reg 4 is an offence contrary to RTOA 1988, s 91.

Electrically assisted pedal cycles may be driven by anyone aged 14 or over. Unlike motor vehicles, their use does not require an excise licence or insurance. Nor do the requirements of testing, driving licences and protective headgear apply.

Brakes on pedal cycles

The Pedal Cycles (Construction and Use) Regulations 1983 deal with the fitting and maintenance of brakes on pedal cycles and with matters affecting electrically assisted pedal cycles generally. The Regulations also refer to fixed-wheel and free-wheel cycles, and these are defined as follows. Fixed-wheel cycles are those so constructed that one or more of the wheels is incapable of rotating independently of the pedals. Free-wheel cycles are those which are not so constructed.

Regulation 4 provides that no person may ride, or cause or permit to be ridden, on a road an electrically assisted pedal cycle unless it is fitted with braking systems which comply with cl 6 of the 1981 British Standard. Regulation 5 prohibits a person from riding, or causing or permitting to be ridden, on a road such a cycle when the brakes have not been maintained in efficient working order.

The braking systems of pedal cycles which are not electrically assisted are also governed by these Regulations. Regulation 6 provides that no person shall ride, or cause or permit to be ridden, a pedal cycle which does not comply with the braking-system requirements in regs 7 or 8. Regulation 7 requires that at least one braking system be fitted to pedal cycles.

Pedal cycles manufactured on or after 1 August 1984 are subjected by reg 7 to additional braking requirements if the saddle height (fully raised and tyre fully inflated) is 635 mm (about 25 inches). The additional requirements are that fixed-wheel cycles must have a braking system acting on the front wheel or on at least two front wheels if there are more than one. Free-wheel cycles must have two independent systems, one acting upon the front wheel, or at least two front wheels if more than one is fitted, and the other acting upon the rear wheel, or at least two rear wheels if more than one is fitted. In the case of pedal cycles manufactured before 1 August 1984, these additional requirements apply under reg 8 to pedal cycles, any wheel of which exceeds 460 mm (approx 18 inches) in diameter including the fully inflated tyre, except that the braking system acting upon the rear need only act upon one rear wheel even if there is more than one rear wheel fitted. A non-goods tricycle, whenever manufactured, may instead have two independent systems both acting upon the front wheel if it has two rear wheels (and vice versa).

Regulation 9 provides that nothing in reg 7 or 8 applies to pedal cycles on which the pedals act directly on the wheel rather than through a gearing system (eg a penny-farthing) and those temporarily in Great Britain when ridden by a visitor, such a cycle having a braking system or system complying with provisions of the International Convention on Road Traffic.

Regulation 10 prohibits riding, or causing or permitting to be ridden, on a road a pedal cycle the braking system of which, fitted in accordance with these Regulations, is not in efficient working order. This is the offence most frequently dealt with by police officers but it is not uncommon to find that one of two systems has been removed from a cycle.

Breach of regs 4, 5, 6, or 10 is an offence contrary to RTOA 1988, s 91. A constable in uniform is empowered by reg 11 to test and inspect a pedal cycle for the purpose of ascertaining that the braking requirements are satisfied. This may be done on a road, or on any premises where the cycle is if the cycle has been involved in an accident (provided that the test and inspection are carried out within 48 hours of the accident with the consent of the owner of the premises).

TESTING AND INSPECTION

Testing vehicles on roads: RTA 1988, s 67

Authorised examiners may test a motor vehicle on a *road* to ascertain whether the requirements relating to its construction and use are being complied with, and also whether there is compliance with the requirement that the condition of the vehicle is not such that its use on a road would involve danger of injury to any person. There are two principal types of authorised examiners for the purposes of s 67: (a) police officers specially authorised by their chief constables for this purpose, and (b) vehicle examiners (ie examiners appointed under RTA 1988, s 66A by the Secretary of State). For the purpose of testing a vehicle an examiner may require the driver to comply with his reasonable instructions and may drive the vehicle. All authorised examiners must produce their authority if required to do so.

The provisions of s 67 do not mean that the requirement of RTA 1988 and RV(C&U)R 1986 may only be enforced on a road by an authorised examiner. Particular offences may still be reported by a constable who is not an authorised examiner. In addition, any constable may test a vehicle with the owner's consent. This is borne out by a case where a constable who was not an authorised examiner tested the efficiency of a handbrake with the driver's consent; evidence of his findings was admitted even though he was not an authorised examiner. It is submitted that there is a difference between a power to make a general examination of a vehicle and the examination of a particular part of it because of the suspicion of an offence. If the wall of a tyre is badly split and the fabric exposed, this is observable by any police officer and the examination of the whole vehicle is unnecessary in order to deal with the particular infringement. It does not take a vehicle examiner to notice that the entire exhaust system of a motor vehicle is hanging off.

Where an examination of the vehicle under RTA 1988, s 67 is required by an authorised examiner, the driver may elect that the test shall be deferred to a time and place to be arranged within the next 30 days.

The right to defer does not apply:

(a) when it appears to a constable that, following an accident on a road, the test must be taken forthwith. If this is so and the constable is not an authorised examiner, he may require that the vehicle is not taken away until the test has been carried out (s 67(7)); or

(b) when the vehicle appears to a constable to be so defective that it ought not to be allowed to proceed (s 67(8)).

Testing vehicles off roads: RV(C&U)R 1986

Regulation 74 empowers any police constable in uniform or vehicle examiner to test and inspect the brakes, silencers, steering gear, and tyres, of any motor vehicle or trailer on any *premises* where that motor vehicle or trailer is, *subject to the consent of the owner of the premises*. This represents the basic difference between these powers and those set out above.

Because the consent of the *owner of the premises* is necessary, there is no power of entry onto premises for the purpose of inspection under reg 74. In addition, the test and inspection cannot be carried out without the consent of the *owner of the vehicle*, unless notice of it has been served personally upon him at least 48 hours before the test, or 72 hours before it if service is effected by recorded delivery. The consent of the *owner of the vehicle* is not required if it has been involved in an accident within the preceding 48 hours.

Prohibition of unfit vehicles

RTA 1988, s 69 empowers an authorised constable to issue an immediate prohibition notice if, on an inspection under ss 41, 45, 49, 61, 67, 68, or 77, it appears to him that, owing to any defects in the vehicle, driving it (or driving it for any particular purpose or purposes or for any except one or more particular purposes) would involve a danger of injury to any person. The sections referred to deal with powers in relation to construction and use requirements; test certificates generally; inspections related to plated weights of goods vehicles, public service vehicles, and vehicles adapted to carry more than eight passengers which are not public service vehicles; and the testing of the condition of used vehicles at sale rooms, etc. A notice under s 69 may prohibit use absolutely, or for one or more specified purposes, or except for one or more specified purposes.

Vehicle examiners have a similar power.

The Road Vehicles (Prohibition) Regulations 1992 make provision for a vehicle which is subject to a prohibition issued by an authorised constable, or vehicle examiner, to be driven on a road solely for the purpose of submitting it, by prior arrangement, for test with a view to removal of that prohibition, or for it to be driven in the course of any test for the purpose of the removal of the prohibition, or (within three miles from where it is being, or has been, repaired) to be driven solely for the purpose of its test or trial with a view to the removal of the prohibition.

TEST CERTIFICATES

RTA 1988, ss 45 to 47 are concerned with tests of the satisfactory condition of motor vehicles, other than goods vehicles to which s 49 applies. The relevant provisions with regard to such goods vehicles are discussed in Appendix 2 contained in the companion website to this book (<http://www.oup.com/>). The Secretary of State is authorised by RTA 1988, s 45 to make regulations for the examination of all vehicles to which ss 45 to 47 apply and the Secretary of State has made the Motor Vehicles (Tests) Regulations 1981.

By RTA 1988, s 47(1), a person commits an offence if he uses, or causes or permits to be used, at any time on a road a motor vehicle to which s 47 applies, and as respects which no test certificate has been issued within the appropriate period before the said time. In relation to 'use', 'cause', or 'permit', see pp 433–4. Once it is proved that the defendant has used, etc a vehicle on a road, the burden shifts to him to prove that there was in force a test certificate for the vehicle.

The vehicles to which s 47 applies

The answer to the question which vehicles must be tested depends on the *type of vehicle* and its *age*.

The following must be examined and receive a test certificate annually, *after the period of three years* defined in the next paragraph:

(a) passenger vehicles with not more than eight seats, excluding the driver's seat;
(b) rigid goods motor cars, the unladen weight of which does not exceed 1,525 kg;

(c) dual-purpose vehicles;

(d) motor cycles (including three-wheelers and mopeds); and

(e) motor caravans.

RTA 1988, s 47 applies to motor vehicles of the above types which were first registered not less than three years before the time in question (ie the time of the alleged use without a test certificate). If, for any reason, a vehicle is used on a road in Great Britain or elsewhere before being registered, a test certificate must be obtained three years from the date of manufacture. Thus, a serviceman returning from duty abroad who brings into this country a vehicle which is more than three years old must have it tested immediately.

RTA 1988 requires annual tests for the following motor vehicles *after one year from first registration* or three years from manufacture if used pre-registration:

(a) motor vehicles used for the carriage of passengers and with more than eight seats, exclusive of the driver's (mainly public service vehicles);

(b) taxis licensed to ply for hire; and

(c) ambulances.

Exemptions

The Motor Vehicles (Tests) Regulations 1981 exempt a range of vehicles including:

(a) goods vehicles with a design gross weight exceeding 3,500 kg;

(b) articulated vehicles other than articulated buses;

(c) invalid carriages not exceeding 306 kg unladen weight (or 510 kg if supplied by the Department of Health);

(d) vehicles temporarily in Great Britain for a 12-month period;

(e) police vehicles maintained in police workshops, or a vehicle provided for the purposes of SOCA;

(f) electrically propelled goods vehicles with a design gross weight not exceeding 3,500 kg;

(g) some licensed hackney carriages and private hire cars;

(h) any vehicle at a time when it is being used on a public road during any calendar week if it is being used only in passing from land in the occupation of its keeper to other land in his occupation, and it has not been used on public roads for more than an aggregate of six miles in that calendar week;

(i) heavy locomotives, light locomotives, motor tractors, track laying vehicles, agricultural motor vehicles and works vehicles; and

(j) vehicles which have a Northern Ireland test certificate.

The Regulations also permit use without a test certificate when a vehicle is being taken to a testing station by previous arrangement for a test, or when it is being brought away from such a test, or while it is being so tested by an authorised person or under his direction. In circumstances in which a test certificate is refused, the vehicle may be moved without a test certificate for the purpose of work being done (once again, by previous arrangement), or for the purpose of delivering it, by towing, to a place where it is to be broken up. Imported vehicles which need to be tested may be driven on arrival in this country to the place of residence of the owner of the motor vehicle.

Test certificate

The contents of a test certificate are not prescribed. A certificate must be in a form supplied by the Secretary of State. A certificate has a serial number; indicates that the vehicle complied with the requirements on the date of the examination; shows the registration mark of the vehicle, the vehicle testing station number, the date of issue of the certificate, the date of expiry, and bears the signature of the person issuing the certificate. A signature may be a facsimile of the signature of the examiner or of a person so authorised by the Secretary of State. If the previous certificate had expired at the time of the examination, the serial number of the previous certificate may also be shown. Tests can only be conducted at testing stations authorised by the Secretary of State.

Requirement to produce test certificate

RTA 1988, s 165 empowers a constable or vehicle examiner to require a person driving, or reasonably believed by him to have been driving, when an accident occurred or when an offence was committed, to give his name and address and the name and address of the owner of the vehicle and to produce certain documents, including a test certificate (if one is required for the vehicle). As with other types of document, there is a proviso which permits production within seven days at a specified police station; or production as soon as reasonably practicable; or proof that production was not reasonably practicable before the day on which proceedings were commenced. Production in person is not required.

CHAPTER 11

Control of Vehicles

TRAFFIC SIGNS AND DIRECTIONS

These are governed by the Road Traffic Regulation Act 1984 (RTRA 1984) and regulations thereunder.

For the purposes of RTRA 1984, the term 'traffic sign' is defined by s 64 as any object or device (fixed or portable) for conveying, to traffic on roads or any specified class of traffic, warnings, information, requirements, restrictions or prohibitions of any description:

(a) specified by regulations made by the relevant Ministers acting jointly; or
(b) authorised by the Secretary of State,

and any line or mark on a road for so conveying such warnings, information, requirements, restrictions or prohibitions.

Section 64 authorises the making of regulations in respect of the size, colour, and type of traffic signs. The current regulations are the Traffic Signs Regulations and General Directions 2002. Equipment used in connection with traffic signs must be of a type approved in accordance with the Directions.

Powers to place traffic signs

RTRA 1984, s 65 empowers *highway authorities* to cause or permit traffic signs to be placed on or near any road in their area.

RTRA 1984, ss 66 and 67 empower *a constable, or a traffic officer in uniform (in the case of s 67), or a person acting under the instructions (whether general or specific) of the chief officer of police*, to place on a road such authorised traffic signs indicating prohibitions, restrictions, or requirements relating to vehicular traffic as may be required:

(a) to prevent an obstruction on public occasions or near public buildings or at an authorised cycle race (s 66). Section 66 permits police officers to place emergency signs on the road at special events such as air displays;
(b) to prevent or mitigate congestion or obstruction of traffic, or danger to or from traffic, in consequence of extraordinary circumstances (s 67). Among other things, s 67 empowers the police to place emergency signs on the road at the scene of an accident. Such signs may be maintained for a maximum period of seven days. The time starts when the signs are placed, so that a sign placed at 2 pm must be removed by 2 pm seven days after placement. The important feature of s 67 is that it deals with temporary signs in respect of extraordinary circumstances. If the need is a permanent one the matter must be dealt with by the highway authority.

Failure to comply with a sign placed under the provisions of RTRA 1984, ss 65, 66, and 67 is an offence contrary to the Road Traffic Act 1988 (RTA 1988), s 36 (p 458).

Quite apart from the above, the Traffic Signs (Temporary Obstructions) Regulations 1997 authorise *persons not otherwise authorised to do so* to place specified traffic signs on roads in connection with temporary obstructions, other than roadworks. The indications given by the signs are specified in regs 4 to 7 and the form which the signs take is prescribed by regs 8 to 14.

Regulation 15 of the 1997 Regulations permits a 'keep right sign' to be placed by the *crew of an emergency or breakdown vehicle* which is causing a temporary obstruction. Non-compliance is an offence against RTA 1988, s 36.

In addition, reg 15 authorises *any person* to place a 'road vehicle sign' on a vehicle, and to place on any road:

(a) a minimum of four 'flat traffic delineators', 'traffic cones', or 'traffic pyramids';
(b) a 'traffic triangle' (at least 45 metres from the obstruction); or
(c) a 'warning lamp' (but only in conjunction with one of any of the reg 15 signs, including the 'keep right sign' and 'road vehicle sign'),

for the purpose of *warning* traffic of a temporary obstruction, other than roadworks. Non-compliance with such a sign is not in itself an offence. A 'road vehicle sign' consists of a flexible sheet on which there is a triangle the outer edges of which are red, the inner part being either reflectorised white or fluorescent yellow. It is designed to be fixed to a stationary vehicle, facing approaching traffic. A 'traffic delineator', 'traffic cone', or 'traffic pyramid' is of the 'lane marker' type of device frequently used by emergency services and a 'traffic triangle' or 'warning lamp' (flashing amber signal) is the type of device frequently used by individual motorists.

The placing of signs otherwise than as prescribed is of no legal effect. Persons do not have a right to paint 'No Parking' on the roadway, or on a sign, outside their premises.

Drivers to comply with traffic signs

RTA 1988, s 36(1) states that an offence is committed by a person driving or propelling a vehicle who fails to comply with the indication given by an authorised traffic sign, a term which includes a road marking. It is no defence for a driver to allege that he did not see a traffic sign.

RTA 1988, s 36 applies to any traffic sign which indicates a statutory prohibition, restriction, or requirement or to any other traffic sign where it is expressly provided by or under RTA 1988 or RTRA 1984 that RTA 1988, s 36 shall apply to the sign; such express provision has been made by the Traffic Signs Regulations and General Directions 2002 (TSR&GD 2002), reg 10. Examples of signs to which s 36 applies are described in the next three paragraphs, which deal in turn with signs indicating a prohibition, a restriction, and a requirement.

Examples of signs which indicate a *prohibition* are 'No entry', 'No right turn', 'No U turn', 'Lorries prohibited', and 'No overtaking' signs. These signs frequently involve the use of symbols only. Except in the case of a 'No Entry' sign, these consist of a red circle with the enclosed symbol in black on a white background. Thus a sign prohibiting entry to lorries would carry the symbol of a lorry with a red circle around it.

Signs dealing with *restrictions* include those dealing with waiting restrictions. These signs have a red outer circle with a blue background and a red band cutting across the face from the top left to bottom right of the sign as seen by approaching drivers. Information concerning the nature of the restrictions in force is provided on a plate, usually attached to the post supporting the sign. A yellow plate with the words 'at any time' in black indicates a total ban on parking, while the words '8.00 am–6.00 pm' would indicate a restriction upon waiting between those hours. Where waiting is limited rather than prohibited, the sign will be of white lettering on a blue background. Restrictions on waiting may be additionally indicated by signs placed on the roadway but such a sign is only effective to create the prohibition or restriction if used in conjunction with a restriction sign or plate of the type referred to above. A single continuous yellow line running parallel with the kerb restricts waiting (other than for loading or unloading) for a period of at least eight hours between 7 am and 7 pm on a minimum of four days a week. A double continuous yellow line indicates that, additionally, the restrictions may extend on occasions beyond those hours. Broken yellow lines indicate other waiting restrictions, usually unilateral parking schemes, restricting waiting on particular sides of the road on particular days of the week.

Those signs which deal with *requirements* under the section are those which require a driver, etc to do something. 'Stop', 'Give Way', 'Keep Right', 'Keep Left', 'Traffic Lights' are all signs which indicate a requirement. The driver must stop his vehicle, turn it in a particular direction or give way to other traffic. These signs vary in appearance. The modern 'Stop' sign is octagonal and coloured red with 'Stop' in white capitals on it, although variations still exist. Other statutory requirements relating to stopping are red traffic lights and manually operated 'stop' signs at road works. 'Give way' signs consist of a red inverted triangle on a white, circular background with the words 'give way' inside the triangle. White arrows on a blue background indicate the route which a driver must follow. Another example of a sign making a requirement is one requiring certain drivers to telephone for permission to cross automatic level crossings.

For the purposes of RTA 1988, s 36, traffic signs placed on or near a road are deemed to be of the prescribed size, colour and type, and to have been lawfully placed, unless the contrary is proved. Consequently, the prosecution does not normally have to offer evidence of the nature of the sign beyond that which satisfies the court of the nature of the restriction, prohibition or requirement in question. However, if the sign is proved not to be of the prescribed size, etc, or not to have been lawfully placed, it will not be a valid sign and no offence can be committed in relation to it, unless the breach of the requirement is trivial. There is a presumption that automatic traffic lights are in working order, unless the contrary is proved.

Where the provisions of s 36 do not apply to a sign but it is governed by regulations concerning traffic control made by the Secretary of State, the Road Traffic Offenders Act 1998 (RTOA 1988), s 91 states that contravention or failure to comply is an offence under that section.

Particular signs

Certain signs indicate particular requirements. A 'Stop' sign requires that:

(a) every vehicle must, before entering the major road, stop at the transverse lines at the junction, or, if the lines are not visible, at the major road; and

(b) no vehicle may proceed past the transverse line painted nearest to the major road, or, if the lines are not visible, may not enter the major road, in such a manner or at such a time as is likely to cause danger to the driver of any other vehicle on the major road, or such as to necessitate the driver of any such other vehicle to change its speed or course in order to avoid an accident.

The latter provision (ie (b)) also applies to 'Give Way' signs. Thus, it is not sufficient to stop, or give way, and then to proceed, if the results of so proceeding are as described. There should be no interference with traffic on the major road. To emerge in such circumstances also indicates an element of carelessness which might amount to careless driving.

TSR&GD 2002, reg 26 deals with double white lines, which consist of either two continuous white lines or one continuous white line together with a broken white line painted along the middle of the carriageway itself. Any white unbroken line must be immediately preceded by a white warning arrow painted on the road; otherwise the line is not valid as a sign. If there are two continuous white lines vehicles travelling in both directions are required to keep to the nearside of the nearest continuous white line. A broken line with a continuous line requires vehicles to keep to the nearside of the continuous white line when that line is the nearer of the two to the vehicle. Neither of these rules applies if it is both safe to do so and necessary to do so:

(a) to enable the vehicle to enter, from the side of the road on which it is proceeding, roadside property or a side road joining that road;
(b) to pass a stationary vehicle;
(c) owing to circumstances outside the control of the driver;
(d) to avoid an accident;
(e) to pass a road maintenance vehicle which is in use, is moving at a speed not exceeding 10 mph, and is displaying to the rear a specified sign (angled white arrow on blue background within white edged circle, which may be mounted on a square or rectangular background);
(f) to pass a pedal cycle moving at a speed not exceeding 10 mph;
(g) to pass a horse that is being ridden or led at a speed not exceeding 10 mph; or
(h) to comply with any direction of a constable in uniform, or a traffic officer in uniform or a traffic warden.

No vehicle may stop on either side of the road with only one traffic lane in each direction where there is a double white line marking of either description unless it is done:

(a) to pick up or set down passengers, to load or unload, or for building operations;
(b) in connection with road or public utility works;
(c) by a vehicle used for police, traffic officer, fire, special forces, SOCA or ambulance purposes;
(d) by a pedal cycle without a sidecar (auto-assisted or not);
(e) to avoid an accident or because it is impossible to proceed; or
(f) with the permission or at the direction of a constable in uniform or a traffic officer in uniform, or in accordance with the direction of a traffic warden.

Records produced as evidence

RTOA 1988, s 20 provides that evidence of a fact related to an offence involving a driver's failure to comply with a traffic sign, contrary to RTA 1988, s 36(1), may be given by the production of a record produced by a device of a description specified by the Secretary of State. However, evidence may only be so given if (in the same or another document) there is a certificate as to the circumstances in which it was produced, signed by a constable, or by a person authorised by (or on behalf of) the chief police officer for the area. The effect of s 20 is that the record and certificate can be tendered in evidence without the need for a witness to be called to prove them. The device must be of a type approved by the Secretary of State; it has been held that this requirement has been satisfied by the Secretary of State's approval of 'a device designed or adapted for recording by photographic or other image recording means the position of vehicles in relation to light signals' as a prescribed device. The device must be used in accordance with conditions subject to which the approval was given.

For a document of the type referred to above to be admissible under s 20, a copy of it must be served on the defendant (D) not less than seven days before the hearing or trial.

If D, not less than three days before the hearing or trial, requires the attendance of the person who signed the document, the evidence of the circumstances in which the record was produced will not be admissible, although the record produced by the device will.

Where the prosecution does not serve the record and certificate on D within the seven days before the trial, a police officer may nevertheless attend as a witness to produce and prove those items as real evidence.

Drivers to comply with traffic directions

RTA 1988, s 35(1) provides that, where a constable or a traffic officer in uniform is for the time being engaged in the regulation of traffic in a road, a person driving or propelling a vehicle who neglects (ie fails) or refuses:

(a) to stop the vehicle; or
(b) to make it proceed in, or keep to, a particular line of traffic,

when directed to do so by a constable in the execution of his duty, is guilty of an offence. The Functions of Traffic Wardens Order 1970 extends the above offence to failure to comply with the directions of a uniformed traffic warden employed in the control and regulation of traffic. Disqualification or endorsement cannot be ordered if the failure is to comply with the directions of a traffic warden.

Traffic surveys

RTA 1988, s 35(2) provides that, where a traffic survey is being conducted, a constable or a traffic officer in uniform may direct a person driving or propelling a vehicle to stop or to proceed in a line of traffic or to a particular point, but no requirement to give information may be made; non-compliance is an offence. By s 35(3), no unreasonable delay must be caused to a person who does not wish to provide information. RTA 1988, s 36(4) also provides that signs such as 'Stop at Census Point' and 'Census Point—Stop if required' are traffic signs to which s 36 applies.

Other powers to stop drivers and pedestrians

Apart from the powers given to the police by RTA 1988, s 35, RTA 1988, s 163 requires that a person driving a mechanically propelled vehicle or riding a cycle on a road must stop his vehicle on being required to do so by a constable in uniform or a traffic officer in uniform. Failure to do so is an offence against s 163(2). The Functions of Traffic Wardens Order 1970 extends the offence to failure to comply with the directions of a uniformed traffic warden employed in the control and regulation of traffic.

In addition, by RTA 1988, s 37, a person on foot who fails to comply with the signals of a uniformed constable or traffic officer on traffic control commits an offence. Failure to give a name and address in such circumstances is a further offence. The Functions of Traffic Wardens Order 1970 extends these offences to failure to comply with the directions of a uniformed traffic warden employed in the control and regulation of traffic. At common law, a constable (whether or not in uniform) can engage a person's attention to question him, provided that his actions go no further than generally acceptable standards of conduct. If the person does not stop there is no common law power to detain him short of an arrest.

Under the Fire and Rescue Services Act 2004, s 44 an authorised employee of a fire or rescue authority may close off streets, or stop or regulate traffic in any street, whenever he reasonably believes this is necessary for rescue or fire fighting purposes. It is an offence, contrary to the Emergency Workers (Obstruction) Act 2006, s 1, without reasonable excuse to obstruct or hinder a fire and rescue authority employee taking action under s 44.

PEDESTRIAN CROSSINGS

The Regulations described below govern 'Zebra', 'Pelican', and 'Puffin' crossings. Zebra crossings are uncontrolled; Pelican and Puffin crossings are light-controlled. By RTRA 1984, s 25(5), a person who contravenes the regulations is guilty of an offence.

'Zebra' crossings

The 'Zebra', 'Pelican' and 'Puffin' Pedestrian Crossing Regulations and General Directions 1997 prescribe the nature of uncontrolled crossings and the rules governing them. The *limits* of the crossing itself (the walking area for the pedestrians) are indicated by lines of studs between which is an area marked by alternate black and white stripes. Flashing yellow globes indicate the presence of such a crossing to approaching drivers. The globes are mounted on poles which are also marked by black and white stripes. There must be a globe at either side of the crossing; if there is a central reservation or street refuge on the crossing, one or more globes may be placed there. The failure of the lamps does not invalidate a 'Zebra' crossing; the regulations must still be complied with.

The approach to the crossing from each direction is marked out as a 'controlled area'. It is in effect a defensive area and drivers are made aware that they are entering it by white lines situated at each kerb and in the crown of the road on the approaching driver's side. This is known as the 'terminal line' and from it three zig-zag lines stretch to a distance of one metre from the crossing itself where they join a broken white line which is the 'give way' line.

These regulations only apply to 'Zebra' crossings when traffic is not being controlled by a uniformed police constable, traffic officer or traffic warden. Immediately such a person takes control of traffic movements at such a crossing, the crossing ceases to be an uncontrolled one and the regulations cease to apply until that control ceases.

Precedence at a zebra crossing

Regulation 25 states that every pedestrian on the carriageway within the limits of an uncontrolled crossing has precedence within these limits over any vehicle. That precedence must be afforded by a driver before any part of his vehicle enters the pedestrian limits of the crossing itself. Where there is a central refuge each side of it is treated as a separate crossing. A pedestrian only has precedence when he or she is within the limits of the crossing before the vehicle enters the limits of the crossing. A pedestrian waiting at the kerbside is awaiting the courtesy of drivers who care to stop; such a person is not entitled to any precedence until he steps on to the crossing.

The driver of a vehicle must always approach an uncontrolled crossing in such a manner that he will be able to stop before reaching it unless he can see that there is no one in the vicinity. Evidence of a failure to take reasonable care is unnecessary; the duty to accord precedence is strict and its discharge requires an approach to such crossings that will allow precedence to be given in any circumstances. The only exceptions are where there is a sudden defect in the vehicle or it is pushed on to the crossing by the vehicle behind; in such circumstances a driver is clearly unable through no fault of his to discharge his duty to accord precedence. It is important to recognise that the issue of precedence does not arise until there is the question of who goes first. Clear evidence should be offered that the passage of a pedestrian was interfered with by the passage of a motor vehicle over the limits of the crossing. Taken to extremes, where a crossing spans a very wide street, a vehicle might pass over the limits while a pedestrian was on the crossing without the progress of that pedestrian being in any way interfered with. Alternatively, where a vehicle is stopped at a crossing and the pedestrians have passed the point at which it is waiting, the driver is free to proceed. If another pedestrian then steps on the crossing as the vehicle moves off, the driver commits no offence (provided no issue of 'who goes first' is raised).

'Pelican' and 'Puffin' crossings

By reg 23, when a red light is being displayed at a pelican or puffin crossing a driver of a vehicle must not cause it to 'proceed beyond the stop line' or, if that line is not visible, the post on which the light signal is mounted. At a puffin crossing, a red with amber signal denotes an impending change to green, but it conveys the same prohibition as a red signal. At either type of crossing a steady amber signal when shown alone conveys the same prohibition as a red signal (with the usual proviso applicable to traffic lights), and there may be a green arrow showing, which signals that traffic may cross the stop line to proceed in a particular direction. As to flashing amber lights at a pelican crossing, see below.

Both pelican and puffin crossings will have 'controlled areas' on each side of the crossing (or on one side in the case of one-way traffic), indicated by two or more zig-zag lines stretching from the terminal line to the stop line (a line which is met before the limits of the crossing itself are reached). The primary signals shown to both drivers and pedestrians are by synchronised light signals. Whilst a steady green light is shown to drivers, a steady red light is shown to pedestrians, and vice versa. The light signals to pedestrians are, in the case of pelican crossings, steady red, steady green and flashing green figures reinforced by the illumination of a sign which reads 'WAIT'. Those at puffin crossings are by means of red and green figures.

Audible signals may be used at pelican crossings to indicate to pedestrians when it is safe to cross.

Precedence at a pelican or puffin crossing

This is determined to a major extent by the light signals which are showing at the time. There are specific offences within the Regulations, dealing with failure to comply with such signals.

However, at pelican crossings (but not puffin crossings) a driver may encounter a flashing amber signal which indicates that pedestrians, who are on the carriageway or a central reservation within the limits of the crossing before any part of the vehicle has entered those limits, must be accorded precedence by the driver of a vehicle.

Prohibition on waiting

Regulation 18 prohibits a driver from stopping his vehicle in the limits of any of the three types of crossing unless he is prevented from proceeding by circumstances beyond his control or it is necessary to avoid an accident. Moreover, reg 20 prohibits the driver of a vehicle from causing the vehicle or any part of it to stop in a 'controlled area' (the zig-zag area). However, this does not apply to pedal cycles without sidecars, whether mechanically assisted or not. Regulations 21 and 22 exempt from reg 20 vehicles:

(a) whose drivers have stopped to comply with requirements of the Regulations or to avoid an accident; or

(b) whose drivers have been prevented from proceeding by circumstances beyond their control; or

(c) which have stopped for fire, ambulance, police, SOCA, defence or special forces purposes, or in connection with building works, road works, or repairs to public utilities.

Vehicles may also halt to make right or left turns. Public service vehicles may stop to pick up or set down passengers but only on the far side of the crossing itself, not on its approach.

Regulation 19 prohibits a pedestrian remaining within the limits of a crossing longer than necessary for the purposes of crossing with reasonable despatch.

Prohibition on overtaking

By reg 24, a driver within a 'controlled area' of any of the three types of crossing must not overtake *on the approach side* to a crossing a moving motor vehicle or a stationary motor vehicle according precedence to a pedestrian on the crossing. For these purposes, a vehicle overtakes another if any part of the vehicle passes ahead of the foremost part of another vehicle. The aim of reg 24 is to prevent pedestrians from being struck by overtaking vehicles. It is not surprising, therefore, that reg 24 limits the prohibition on overtaking to cases where the vehicle overtaken is the only other vehicle in the controlled area, or is the foremost vehicle. If this was not so, where there were two lines of traffic approaching a crossing, it would not be possible for the traffic on the offside to close up. In relation to the prohibition on overtaking a vehicle which has stopped to accord precedence, such a vehicle includes one which has stopped for this purpose even though a pedestrian intending to cross has not yet stepped on to the crossing.

Because of the drafting of reg 24, the ban on overtaking does not apply where the overtaking vehicle was actually on the crossing when it passed ahead of the foremost part of the overtaken vehicle.

School crossing patrols

RTRA 1984, s 26 authorises an appropriate local authority to make arrangements for patrolling places where children cross roads on their way to or from school (or from one part of the school to another).

The stopping of vehicles at school crossings is dealt with by RTRA 1984, s 28.

When a vehicle is approaching a place in a road where a person is crossing or seeking to cross the road, a school crossing patrol wearing an approved uniform is empowered, by exhibiting a prescribed sign, to require the person driving or propelling the vehicle to stop it. When such a person has been required to stop:

(a) he must cause the vehicle to stop before reaching the place where the person is crossing or seeking to cross and so as not to stop or impede his crossing; and

(b) the vehicle must not be put in motion again so as to reach the place in question so long as the sign continues to be exhibited.

As long as a prescribed sign has been properly exhibited, a driver must stop even if the persons have cleared the road and there are no others seeking to cross. A divisional court has held that the words 'so as not to stop or impede his crossing' in (a), above, merely describe the manner in which a driver should stop (ie he must not halt across the path which those children would take) and are not meant to indicate that drivers can ignore a properly displayed sign if, in doing so, they would not directly impede pedestrians. Drivers must, therefore, stop and remain stopped while the sign is exhibited. The duty to stop is absolute.

It is an offence under s 28(2) for a person to fail to comply with (a) or for him to cause a vehicle to be put in motion contrary to (b). These are separate offences.

The duty to stop only exists if the patrol was wearing a uniform approved by the Secretary of State. The approved uniform is a cap, beret or yellow turban and a coat with or without a fluorescent overgarment. Alternatively, a high visibility coat may be worn. The stopping of traffic may only be effected by exhibiting a sign prescribed by the School Crossing Patrol Sign (England and Wales) Regulations 2006. That sign will display the word 'Stop' in black letters with a black bar on a yellow fluorescent background surrounded by a red fluorescent border. Where the sign is displayed by a school crossing patrol it will be presumed that it is a prescribed sign and, if displayed in circumstances in which it was required to be illuminated, that it was so illuminated. A sign is exhibited if an approaching driver can see the words on it; but it need not be proved that it was full face to oncoming traffic.

REMOVAL OF VEHICLES

The police have powers to require the removal of vehicles and to remove them themselves. Local authorities are legally obliged to remove abandoned vehicles.

Powers of police

The Removal and Disposal of Vehicles Regulations 1986 (RDVR 1986), reg 3, as amended in 2012, allows a constable to require the owner, driver or other person in charge or control of a vehicle which:

(a) has broken down, or been permitted to remain at rest, on a road or other land in such a position, condition or circumstances as to cause obstruction to other persons using the road or land concerned, or as to be likely to cause danger to such other persons; or

(b) has been permitted to remain at rest or has broken down and remained at rest on a road or other land in contravention of a prohibition or restriction in or under any enactment mentioned in Sch 1 to the Regulations,

to move or cause it to be moved. The reference to 'other land' is not limited to land in the open air; the land could, for example, include an underground car park.

In determining, for the purposes of (a), the question of 'obstruction', a different interpretation is given to that term from that accorded to it in the Highways Act 1980, s 137 and the Road Vehicles (Construction and Use) Regulations 1986, reg 103 (see p 425 and p 447). This was stated by the Court of Appeal which held that 'obstruction' in (a) means more than simply impeding the free access of members of the public to every part of the highway; what is required is obstructing their passage by hindering or preventing them getting past. That 'obstruction', said the Court, need not be an actual one; it includes obstructing people who might be expected to be using the highway. On the other hand, the Court held, mere unreasonable use of a highway does not make it an obstruction. No doubt a corresponding meaning applies in respect of 'other land'.

The statutory prohibitions or restrictions included in Sch 1, referred to in (b) above, are concerned with parking in 'No waiting' areas, in the controlled areas of pedestrian crossings or in contravention of traffic signs—including police 'No waiting' signs. The constable's requirement may include a requirement to move the vehicle to some other place which may be a road or other land, or a requirement that it shall not be moved to such road or other land as may be specified.

It is an offence against RTOA 1988, s 91 to fail to move or cause a vehicle to be moved as soon as practicable when required under the provisions of reg 3.

RDVR 1986, reg 4, as amended in 2012, allows a constable to remove or arrange for the removal of a vehicle which is on a road or other land in the circumstances outlined in (a) or (b), above. He may also do so if the vehicle, having broken down on a road or other land, appears to have been abandoned without lawful authority, or if the vehicle has been permitted to remain at rest on a road or other land in such a position or circumstances as to appear to have been abandoned without lawful authority.

The power to remove vehicles from land occupied by any person is subject to giving notice as prescribed by RTRA 1984, s 99 and RDVR 1986, reg 8. The power under reg 4 is very useful when the driver, person in charge or owner of a vehicle cannot be found or that person refuses to move the vehicle.

Other powers

Regulation 4A empowers a traffic warden, a community support officer, or a person accredited for this purpose under a community safety accreditation scheme to remove a vehicle parked or broken down on a road and causing an obstruction, where it is likely to cause danger to road-users, or where an offence is being committed in relation to a statutory prohibition or restriction included in Sch 1 to the Regulations, referred to above.

Regulation 5A empowers civil enforcement officers acting on behalf of a local authority within the terms of the Regulations to remove vehicles which are parked in contravention of a prohibition or restriction order. Regulation 5C extends such powers to enforcement officers acting within a civil enforcement area (p 468). In both cases the power may not be exercised until fifteen minutes have passed since the expiry of authorised parking.

The Removal and Disposal of Vehicles (Traffic Officers) (England) Regulations 2008 permit uniformed traffic officers to remove, or require the removal of, vehicles from 'relevant roads', ie trunk roads (other than certain lengths of the M4 and M48) in England, and from other roads if necessary to prevent danger or obstruction on a relevant road. Regulation 3 enables a uniformed traffic officer to require the owner, driver, or other person in control or in charge of a vehicle which has broken down or been permitted to remain at rest and is causing an obstruction, is likely to cause danger to others or is in contravention of certain statutory restrictions or prohibitions to move the vehicle or have it moved.

Regulation 4 enables a uniformed traffic officer to remove or arrange for the removal of such a vehicle as well as a vehicle which appears to have been abandoned.

The powers under regs 3 and 4 also apply to roads which are not relevant roads but may only be exercised to avoid danger to persons or other traffic using a relevant road or preventing risks of any such danger arising, or to prevent an obstruction to anything on or near to a relevant road, or for a purpose incidental to either of these purposes (reg 7).

Regulation 8 enables a uniformed traffic officer to remove, or arrange for the removal of, any vehicle that appears to have been abandoned without lawful authority on other land which is adjacent to a relevant road.

Associated with the two powers relating to abandoned vehicles are the provisions of RTRA 1984, ss 100–102 (interim and absolute disposal of vehicles and charges for removal, storage and disposal).

Duties of local authorities

The Refuse Disposal (Amenity) Act 1978, s 3(1) obliges local authorities to remove motor vehicles abandoned without lawful authority on any land in the open air or on any other land forming part of the highway within their area. Before removing vehicles from land other than a road the local authority must serve notice on the occupier of the land which is involved; if the occupier objects the authority is not entitled to remove the vehicle. It is an offence contrary to s 2 so to abandon a vehicle or part of a vehicle dismantled there without lawful authority: see p 664.

TRAFFIC OFFICERS APPOINTED UNDER THE TRAFFIC MANAGEMENT ACT 2004

The Secretary of State (in England) or the Welsh Assembly (in Wales), the 'national authority', may designate individuals as traffic officers and may authorise other persons to make such appointments. Appointments may be subject to limitations and conditions. The designation of individual officers will be in writing and will specify such limitations or conditions and its period of validity. Traffic officers must be employed by, or by persons providing services to, the authorised person. Because they are not designated by a chief officer of police, traffic officers are not police support officers. However, they are officers who will perform enforcement functions and are therefore dealt with within this chapter.

The Traffic Management Act 2004, Part 1 deals with the appointment of 'traffic officers' in England and Wales, and their jurisdiction and powers. Traffic officers may be appointed by order made by, or authorisation given by, the Secretary of State or the Assembly to perform duties connected with the management of traffic on the network of 'relevant roads' in England or Wales, depending on which national authority appointed them. A uniformed traffic officer can exercise his powers over any 'relevant road', ie road for which the national authority has responsibility, unless his designation is limited or subject to conditions which will be specified. He may also be authorised to perform any other function of the national authority (in its capacity as a traffic authority or highway authority). The powers of a uniformed traffic officer are referred to on pp 458, 461, and 466. In cases referred to on p 466, a traffic officer has powers exercisable elsewhere than on a relevant road.

Traffic officers are required to comply with any directions given by a constable. Subject to that limitation, they must comply with any direction given by the appropriate national authority. A traffic officer's powers must only be exercised for the purpose of maintaining or improving the movement of traffic on a relevant road; preventing or reducing the effect of anything causing (or which has the potential to cause) congestion or other disruption to the movement of traffic; avoiding danger to persons or other traffic (or preventing it arising); preventing damage to the road, or to anything on or near a road; or for a purpose incidental to any of those purposes.

It is an offence to assault, or to resist or wilfully obstruct, a traffic officer in the execution of his duty (TMA 2004, s 10(1) and (2) respectively), or with intent to deceive to impersonate such an officer or to make a statement or perform an act calculated to suggest that that person is a traffic officer (s 10(3)). A traffic officer commits an offence if he suggests that he has powers which he does not have (s 10(3)).

PARKING GENERALLY

RTRA 1984 permits local authorities to make traffic regulation orders (outside Greater London) and similar orders (Greater London). Most of these will be 'No waiting' orders.

Generally, such orders contain exemptions in favour of particular persons or particular types of vehicles. The offences which are committed when the provisions of such orders are contravened are contained in RTRA 1984, ss 5 (outside Greater London) and 8 (Greater London).

In addition, RTRA 1984, s 32 empowers a local authority to provide off-street parking places and to authorise the use as a parking place of any part of a road outside Greater London within their area. RTRA 1984, s 35 permits local authorities to make parking place orders in respect of places so provided. RTRA 1984, ss 45 and 46 permit local authorities to designate parking places on highways within their areas and permit the imposition of charges in respect of such parking. It is an offence against s 47(1) to fail to comply with the requirements of any order so made.

RTRA 1984, ss 104 to 106 deal with the immobilisation of vehicles illegally parked in contravention of any statutory prohibition or restriction. Such vehicles may be immobilised within areas specified by the Secretary of State, following an application by a local authority or the Traffic Director for London. Where a vehicle has been immobilised, a notice must be affixed warning against attempting to release the vehicle and specifying the steps to be taken to secure its release. The vehicle will be released on payment of the appropriate sum. An offence is committed by any person who removes or interferes with any notice attached to such a vehicle (s 104(5)), or who removes or attempts to remove an immobilisation device (s 104(6)). A person who damages an immobilisation device in order to release his vehicle commits an offence of criminal damage.

Civil enforcement of parking and some other contraventions

TMA 2004, Part 6 (ss 72 to 93) provides for civil enforcement in relation to penalty charges for 'road traffic contraventions' (ie parking contraventions, bus lane contraventions, London lorry ban contraventions, and moving traffic contraventions) committed in a 'civil enforcement area', under regulations made by the 'appropriate national authorities'. The appropriate national authority in England is the Secretary of State, and in Wales the Welsh Assembly. These regulations must include provisions specifying the person or persons by whom a penalty charge must be paid (who may be the owner of the vehicle, its driver or any other appropriate person).

Civil enforcement areas

In Greater London, 'civil enforcement area' means the whole of Greater London for contraventions relating to parking places, bus lanes and lorry bans, or such parts of Greater London as may be designated in respect of parking contraventions not related to parking spaces and of moving traffic contraventions. Outside Greater London, the term means any area in respect of which an order has been made, by the appropriate national authority, designating the whole or part of a local authority area as such a civil enforcement area for the purpose of parking contraventions, bus lane contraventions and/or moving traffic contraventions. An area which, immediately before the coming into force of the above provisions under TMA 2004, Part 6, was designated as a special parking area or permitted parking area under the Road Traffic Act 1991 is a civil enforcement area for parking contraventions.

Civil enforcement officers

'Civil enforcement officers' (CEOs) may be appointed to deal with civil enforcement matters. TMA 2004, s 76 authorises a local authority to employ CEOs for the enforcement of road traffic contraventions for which it is the enforcement authority. Such an officer must be employed by the local authority or, where the authority has made arrangements with any person for these purposes, an individual employed by that person to act as a CEO. When exercising specified functions a CEO must wear uniform.

TMA 2004, s 76 also provides that a local authority parking attendant, ie a parking attendant appointed by a local authority which is an enforcement authority under RTRA 1984, s 63A, is a CEO in relation to parking contraventions for which the authority is the enforcement authority; such a person may also be appointed a CEO in relation to other road traffic contraventions for which that authority is the enforcement authority.

The specified functions of CEOs are those of fixing notices to vehicles and handing notices to offenders; immobilisation of vehicles; and removal of vehicles.

The system of civil enforcement is subject to the Civil Enforcement of Parking Contraventions (England) General Regulations 2007 (and corresponding regulations in Wales). Hereafter all these regulations will be referred to as 'the Regulations'.

Penalty charges

The Regulations provide for penalty charges to be imposed for parking contraventions and for the charge to be payable by the owner of the vehicle concerned (except where, in response to a notice to the owner, representations made were accepted by the enforcement authority), or by the hirer of a vehicle. The Regulations state that a penalty charge should not be imposed except on the basis of a record produced by device approved by the Secretary of State or information given by a civil enforcement officer as to conduct observed by him.

The Regulations prohibit criminal proceedings and fixed penalty notices under RTOA 1988 in respect of parking contraventions in civil enforcement areas, but an exception is made for a pedestrian crossing contravention. A penalty charge may not be imposed in such a case where the conduct is subject to criminal proceedings or a fixed penalty notice under RTOA 1988, s 52 has been given in respect of that conduct.

Where a CEO has reason to believe that a penalty charge is payable for a stationary vehicle, he is empowered by the Regulations to fix a penalty charge notice to a vehicle or hand it to a person appearing to be in charge of the vehicle. Such a notice may also be served by an enforcement authority by first class post if:

(a) the authority has reason to believe, in consequence of a record produced by an approved device, that a penalty charge is payable; or

(b) a CEO attempted to serve a penalty charge notice but was prevented from doing so by some person; or

(c) a CEO had begun to prepare a penalty charge notice for service but the vehicle concerned was driven away before he had finished preparing the notice, or had served it.

It is an offence against reg 11(1) to interfere with a penalty charge notice served by being fixed to a vehicle, except by or under the authority of the owner or person in charge of the vehicle or the enforcement authority.

Setting level of charges

In London the level of charges under TMA 2004, Part 6 is set through a joint committee of local authorities.

Elsewhere it is set by enforcement authorities (ie the relevant local authority). The level of charges must accord with guidelines given by the appropriate national authority, except where that authority permits an authority to depart from them. The guidelines distinguish between higher level penalty charges (street parking, etc contraventions) and lower ones (other contraventions including those on car parks, loading areas, etc). An enforcement authority may set penalty charges in accordance with different bands (Bands 1 and 2) in different parts of its area, provided that all charges in each part of its area are set in accordance with the same band. The normal higher level penalty will be £60 (Band 1 or £30 if paid early) or £70 (Band 2 or £35 if paid early). Lower level penalty charges will be £40 (Band 1 or £20 if paid early) and £50 (Band 2 or £25 if paid early). However, in respect of higher level penalty charges which are paid after a charge certificate (payment overdue) has been served, the charges will be £90 (Band 1) and £105 (Band 2); for lower level contraventions paid after such service the charges will be £60 (Band 1) and £75 (Band 2).

Immobilisation

Regulation 12 deals with the immobilisation of vehicles. It defines the circumstances where an immobilisation device may be fixed and requires that a notice be affixed to the vehicle at the time of immobilisation. Regulation 12(4) creates offences of removing or interfering with the notice, or removing or attempting to remove the device. Exceptions to the general power to immobilise vehicles are provided by reg 13 in favour of vehicles displaying a current disabled person's badge etc (as specified in the Chronically Sick and Disabled Persons Act 1970). Release from an immobilisation device may only be effected by an authorised person upon payment of the penalty charge in respect of the parking contravention and a release charge.

Removal

See RDVR 1986, reg 5A (p 466).

Adjudicators

Adjudicators are appointed to deal with appeals against decisions of enforcement authorities.

Enforcement of penalty charges

After a period of 28 days specified in the notice as the time allowed for payment has passed and no payment has been made, the enforcement authority may serve a 'notice to owner' containing specified information. Such a notice may not be served after a six-month period. Where the penalty is not paid following service of a notice to owner, an authority may serve a charge certificate setting out details of an applicable surcharge added to the original penalty charge. Where this is not paid before the end of a 14-day period beginning with the date of service, an enforcement authority may, if a county court so orders, recover the increased charge as payable under a county court order.

Special enforcement areas

In TMA 2004, ss 85 and 86 and Sch 10, special provision is made in respect of 'special enforcement areas' designated for their purposes. An area which immediately before the commencement of TMA 2004, Part 6 was designated as a special parking area became a special enforcement area. TMA 2004, s 85 prohibits double parking in special enforcement areas by providing that parking more than 50 cm from the edge of the carriageway is prohibited in places other than a designated parking place or where loading cannot be reasonably carried out (but not for more than twenty minutes). The usual exemptions apply in respect of essential works, etc. Parking is prohibited by s 86 in most instances in a special enforcement area where there is a 'dropped footway, cycle track, or verge' (ie where the footway, etc has been lowered at its join with the carriage-way to assist pedestrians or cyclists or vehicles when entering or crossing the carriageway), or where the carriageway has been raised to meet the level of the footway, etc for the same purpose. However, special exemption is made by s 86(3) in respect of parking outside residential property by or with the consent of the occupier, but this does not apply if permission is given for reward. Local authorities are not obliged to provide traffic signs indicating that such prohibitions exist.

Congestion charging

Although not exclusively directed at parking offences, mention must be made of orders which restrict the use generally of motor vehicles within 'charging areas'.

The Road User Charging (Charges and Penalty Charges) (London) Regulations 2001 deal with the procedures relating to the imposition of charges and penalty charges (road user charging, commonly known as 'congestion charging') in Greater London. The Regulations include requirements concerning the imposition, setting, and liability for charges and penalty charges; the examination of, and entry to, vehicles; powers of seizure and immobilisation; removal and disposal of vehicles; recovery of penalty charges in respect of removed vehicles; and taking possession of vehicles, and claims by owners of vehicles after their disposal.

Charges may also be imposed in respect of release from immobilisation; removal; storage and release; and the sale or destruction of vehicles.

An 'authorised person' (a local authority or its employee or an employee of Transport for London, a constable, or any other person authorised in writing by the charging authority) may examine a vehicle to ascertain whether any document required by a charging scheme is displayed; whether required equipment has been fitted, is in work-ing order, or has been interfered with due to intent to avoid payment, and whether conditions of use are being complied with. He may enter a vehicle on a road where he reasonably suspects that such equipment has been interfered with or that a false docu-ment is being used. He may seize anything (if necessary by detaching it from the vehi-cle) and retain it as evidence. An authorised person who is not a constable may exercise these powers only when in the presence of a constable.

The Transport for London Act 2008, s 5 provides that a Transport for London (TfL) scheme may provide that any person who, without reasonable excuse, contravenes or fails to comply with any specified requirement of the congestion charging scheme com-mits an offence. Offences so created must not consist only of a failure to pay a penalty charge, or any other contravention or failure to comply with a requirement of the scheme by which a penalty charge imposed by regulations made under the Greater London Authority Act 1999 is payable. Section 6 provides powers of examination, immobilisation, and removal where stationary vehicles are found in a charging area. However, TfL may not enter public off-street parking places for the purpose of enforce-ment without the prior consent of the operator.

While the effect of these Regulations is limited to Greater London, the Transport Act 2000 makes provision for such schemes to be introduced elsewhere.

There are procedures for the enforcement and adjudication of road-user charging schemes in Greater London. They deal particularly with notification, adjudication, and enforcement, the determination of disputes, appeals against such determinations, the appointment of persons to hear appeals, and the admissibility of evidence in such proceedings.

Wheelclamping on private property

Private wheelclampers and other people who without statutory authority seek to prevent vehicles being driven away commit an indictable offence of immobilising etc a vehicle, contrary to the Protection of Freedoms Act 2012 (PFA 2012), s 54. Section 54(1) provides that a person commits an indictable (either way) offence who, without lawful authority:

(a) immobilises a motor vehicle by the attachment to the vehicle, or a part of it, of an immobilising device (eg a wheel clamp), or
(b) moves, or restricts the movement of, such a vehicle by any means (eg by a barrier, by towing it away, or by blocking it in with another vehicle),

intending to prevent or inhibit the removal of the vehicle by a person otherwise entitled to remove it. For these purposes, a motor vehicle is a mechanically propelled vehicle or a trailer for it.

A person who immobilises a motor vehicle under a statutory power, eg the powers referred to on pp 362–4, 468, 469, 470, 471, and 483 has lawful authority. On the other hand, the express or implied consent (whether or not legally binding) of a person otherwise entitled to remove the vehicle to the immobilisation, movement or restriction concerned is not lawful authority for the purposes of s 54(1) (s 54(2)), except that where the restriction of the movement of the vehicle is by means of a fixed barrier and the barrier was present (whether or not lowered into place or otherwise restricting movement) when the vehicle was parked, any express or implied consent (whether or not legally binding) of the driver of the vehicle to the restriction is lawful authority for the restriction (s 54(3)).

Thus, although a driver who parks in a commercially-run car park may have impliedly consented to the terms and conditions (including enforcement mechanisms in respect of payment of the charges), s 54(2) means that this implied consent does not provide lawful authority for the vehicle's immobilisation in accordance with the terms and conditions. The only exception would be where the consent relates to the restriction of the vehicle's movement by a barrier which was present when the vehicle was parked. Here the special rule in s 54(3) would apply.

A person who is entitled to remove a vehicle cannot commit an offence under s 54 in relation to that vehicle (s 54(4)).

The requirement of an intention to prevent or inhibit removal of the vehicle by someone entitled to do so means that a person who moves an obstructively parked vehicle a short distance in order to access his property (and without intending to prevent its driver removing it) does not commit the offence; neither does a person who wheelclamps his own vehicle to prevent it being stolen.

It has always been possible for a landowner to bring civil proceedings against the *driver of* a vehicle in respect of unpaid parking charges for which the driver is liable under the terms of a parking contract with the landowner, or for damages for trespass by unauthorised parking. In such cases, the particulars of the keeper of the vehicle can be obtained from DVLA which is empowered to release such information to persons having cause to seek it. However, before PFA 2012, Sch 4 came into force, the landowner could not recover money from the keeper or anyone else if the driver's identity was disputed and was not known.

PFA 2012, Sch 4 makes provision for the recovery from the keeper or hirer of a vehicle (in a civil action) of unpaid parking charges for which the *driver* is liable under the terms of a parking contract with the landowner, or for the pre-estimated damages resulting from unauthorised parking, in cases where the name and address of the driver of the vehicle when the charges were incurred are unknown.

Exposing vehicles for sale, or repairing vehicles, on a road

The Clean Neighbourhoods and Environment Act 2005 (CNEA 2005), s 3(1) provides that a person is guilty of an offence if he leaves two or more motor vehicles parked within 500 m of each other on a road or roads where they are exposed or advertised for sale, or causes two or more motor vehicles to be so left. However, a person is not guilty if he proves that he was not acting for the purpose of a business of selling motor vehicles.

By CNEA 2005, s 4(1), the carrying out of restricted works on a motor vehicle on a road is an offence. 'Restricted works' means works for the repair, maintenance, servicing, improvement or dismantling of a motor vehicle or of any part or accessory, or works for the installation, replacement or renewal of any part or accessory. However, because the offence is aimed at 'commercial works', a person is not guilty if he proves that the works were not carried out in the course of, or for the purposes of, a business of carrying out restricted works, or for gain or reward. This defence does not apply where carrying out the works gave reasonable cause for annoyance to persons in the vicinity. A further defence exists where the works carried out were works of repair which arose from an accident or breakdown in circumstances where repairs on the spot or elsewhere on the road were necessary, and were carried out within 72 hours of the accident or breakdown or were, within that period, authorised to be carried out at a later time by the local authority for the area.

By s 6, an authorised officer of the local authority may issue a fixed penalty notice for £100 in respect of an offence against s 3 or s 4. A prosecution may not be instituted if payment is made within 14 days. Under s 7, an officer proposing to give a notice may require an offender to provide his name and address. It is an offence under s 7(2) to fail to do so or to provide a false or inaccurate name and address.

FIXED PENALTY OFFENCES

The application of the law on fixed penalties for road traffic offences requires police officers to be aware not only of the list of offences which can be dealt with by the fixed penalty procedure but also to be aware of those offences which carry obligatory endorsement of penalty points. RTOA 1988, Sch 3, as amended by the Fixed Penalty Offences Order 2009, lists the offences which are 'fixed penalty offences'. Schedule 2 indicates the offences which carry obligatory endorsement. To assist the memory of police officers in this respect, aides memoire have been prepared listing the various offences which are non-endorsable fixed penalty offences and those which are endorsable. The aide memoire in relation to endorsable fixed penalty offences also indicates the number of penalty points which apply, and gives a code number for each offence. The aide memoire for non-endorsable fixed penalty offences includes advice concerning enforcement policies existing within a police force, particularly where a vehicle rectification scheme is in operation.

The non-endorsable fixed penalty offences are generally concerned with those involving minor defects in the vehicle or its parts; vehicle registration and vehicle excise offences; failure to display goods vehicle plates; stopping on the verge or hard shoulder of a motorway; contravention of certain traffic directions (eg 'Give way', 'No entry', 'No U turn', 'One-way' signs, and temporary traffic signs); obstruction; waiting and parking offences;

lighting and noise offences; offences relating to loads (other than dangerous loads); use of a vehicle without a test certificate; trailer offences; offences peculiar to motorcycles; offences of carrying more than one person on a pedal cycle and of cycling on a footway; and other miscellaneous motoring offences (eg failing to wear a seat belt).

The endorsable fixed penalty offences include those in the Road Vehicles (Construction and Use) Regulations 1986 which are concerned with danger (parts, loads, tyres, etc); failure to comply with 'Stop' signs, double white lines, traffic lights, directions of a constable; illegal waiting at pedestrian crossings, overtaking a moving or stationary vehicle at such a crossing and failure to accord precedence, contrary to the 'Zebra', 'Pelican' and 'Puffin' regulations; speeding; stopping or reversing on the carriageway of a motorway; driving on a hard shoulder or central reservation; driving on a motorway by a provisional licence-holder; use of offside lane of three-lane motorway by a large goods vehicle or passenger-carrying vehicle; breaches of conditions of provisional licences; use, etc of a vehicle without insurance; failure to identify the driver; not exhibiting a licence; offences relating to motorcycle passengers; leaving a vehicle in a dangerous position; use of a vehicle in a designated play street; and driving or riding a motorcycle without wearing eye protectors of a prescribed type or using them in contravention of the relevant regulations.

Fixed penalty notices should not be given to juveniles as there are other recommended procedures for dealing with juveniles which recognise all the circumstances of each case.

The provisions discussed under this heading are contained in RTOA 1988, unless otherwise indicated.

The issue of a fixed penalty notice for a non-endorsable offence

RTOA 1988, s 54 states that a fixed penalty notice for a non-endorsable offence may be issued on the spot by a constable in uniform who has reason to believe that a person he finds *is committing or has committed* a fixed penalty offence. It cannot be issued where inquiries are necessary to trace the driver of a vehicle. In such a case the conditional offer of a fixed penalty procedure (see p 482) will have to be used or a prosecution will have to be instituted.

Only one fixed penalty notice may be issued on any one occasion. If more than one offence is committed on a particular occasion a constable should either issue a fixed penalty notice for one offence and administer a verbal warning in respect of all other offences, or report the offender in the normal way for all offences committed. However, this will not apply when offences are subsequently detected, as would occur when documents which were subsequently produced were found to be defective in some respect. These offences, subsequently detected, will be dealt with by the officer reporting the offender with a view to prosecution, even though a fixed penalty notice has been issued for the original offence.

Traffic wardens may also issue fixed penalty notices for non-endorsable offences but their power is restricted to those offences described in the Functions of Traffic Wardens Order 1970.

Where the driver is absent a notice may be fixed to the vehicle: see p 477 below.

The issue of a fixed penalty notice for an endorsable offence

RTOA 1988, s 54 states that, *subject to the provisions described below,* a fixed penalty notice for an endorsable offence may be issued by a constable in uniform who finds a person on any occasion and has reason to believe that on that occasion *he is committing or has committed* a fixed penalty offence. If it is not so issued the conditional offer of a fixed penalty procedure (see p 482) will have to be instituted.

The Secretary of State has power, by order, to permit the use of traffic wardens to deal with fixed penalty offences which involve obligatory endorsement where the vehicle concerned is stationary. At the time of writing, an order has been made specifying the offence of leaving a vehicle in a dangerous position. Hereafter, references to a constable include a traffic warden for this purpose.

When licence produced at time

Where it appears to a constable that the fixed penalty offence involves obligatory endorsement, and the offender is a holder of a licence, he may give the offender (O) a fixed penalty notice on-the-spot in respect of the offence if:

(a) O produces his driving licence for inspection by the constable;
(b) the constable is satisfied on inspecting the licence that O would not be liable to be disqualified because the total number of penalty points would number 12 or more if he was convicted of the fixed penalty offence; and
(c) O surrenders his driving licence to the constable to be retained and dealt with in accordance with RTOA 1988.

In determining whether O would be liable on conviction to disqualification it must be assumed, where the offence carries a range of penalty points, that the points to be attributed to the offence would be the lowest in the range.

If O is able to produce his licence, and does so, and provided that the number of penalty points is not such that O will be liable to disqualification if points for the fixed penalty offence are added, the constable may issue a full fixed penalty notice. When the constable has examined the driving licence and is satisfied that he is able to issue a fixed penalty notice, because the addition of penalty points for the offence will not combine to a total of 12 or more, he should invite O to surrender his driving licence. Care must be taken in the choice of words. A constable might say:

> 'Your licence indicates that you may have this offence dealt with by fixed penalty notice. Are you willing to surrender your licence to me? You will be given a receipt.'

Part 3 of the fixed penalty notice gives advice on the procedure to be followed if O wishes to request a court hearing. If O contests the issue of a fixed penalty notice, his attention should be drawn to this part of the notice. Constables completing fixed penalty notices should, wherever possible, obtain the full postcode as well as O's address, as this assists the registration of subsequent penalties with O's home court.

RTOA 1988, s 56 requires a receipt to be given for a driving licence so surrendered. The receipt given is incorporated in the fixed penalty notice. It is valid for one month from the date of issue (or such longer period as may be prescribed). However, a person to whom the penalty is paid may issue a new receipt on the application of the licence-holder, which will expire on such date as may be specified in it. In any event, a receipt ceases to have effect on the return of the licence to the holder. Section 56 enables the receipt to be produced in place of a licence, subject to the same conditions concerning later production, on a request being made by a constable under RTA 1988, s 164, provided that, if required to do so, the licence-holder subsequently produces his driving licence at the specified police station immediately it is returned.

When licence not produced at time

The procedure to be followed when an offender (O) does not produce his driving licence at the time of the offence is dealt with as follows by RTOA 1988, s 54. In any case where:

(a) the offence appears to the constable to be one involving obligatory endorsement;
(b) O is the holder of a licence; and
(c) O does not produce his licence for inspection by the constable,

the constable may give O a provisional fixed penalty notice. A notice issued by a constable must state that if, within *seven days* after the notice is given, O *personally* delivers the notice together with his driving licence *to a constable or an authorised person* at *the police station* specified in the notice (being a police station chosen by O) and the requirements in the next paragraph are met O will then be given a fixed penalty notice in respect of the offence. (An 'authorised person' is a person at a police station authorised for this purpose by the chief officer of police.)

Where the constable or the authorised person etc to whom the licence is delivered is satisfied that O would not be liable to a 'totting-up disqualification' because of accumulated penalty points and O surrenders his driving licence to be retained and dealt with in accordance with RTOA 1988, he must give O a fixed penalty notice in respect of the offence.

It must be stressed that these provisions are concerned with extending the fixed penalty provisions to those drivers who are not in possession of their licence at the time of their offence. No offence is committed if O fails to produce his driving licence as a result of an offer made under these provisions.

If O fails to produce his licence under the provisions of RTOA 1988, or on production it is found that O's penalty points are such that the issue of disqualification arises, O will be prosecuted for the offence in the normal way and the provisional fixed penalty notice is of no further effect.

The form HO/RT 2 deals with the production of driving licences consequent upon the issue of provisional fixed penalty notices and the production of driving licence receipts. When HO/RT 2 forms are made out specifically in connection with a provisional fixed penalty notice, the number of the notice should be included on the HO/RT 2.

Endorsements of licences without hearing

RTOA 1988, s 57 authorises the endorsement by the designated officer of the court (without any order of a court) of a driving licence surrendered by a person given a fixed penalty notice under s 54. A licence may not be endorsed if a request for a hearing has been received before the end of the suspended enforcement period.

Licences so surrendered will be endorsed either at the time at which the fixed penalty is paid, if this occurs before the end of the suspended enforcement period, or, if it does not, when the fixed penalty plus one-half of that penalty has been registered for enforcement as a fine. Details of the endorsement must be sent to the Secretary of State.

By RTOA 1988, s 28(3), the number of penalty points to be attributed to an offence where a fixed penalty notice has been issued is:

(a) where both a range of numbers and a number followed by the words '(fixed penalty)' is indicated in Sch 2, that number;
(b) where a range of numbers followed by the words 'or appropriate penalty points (fixed penalty)', the appropriate number of penalty points for the offence (such number imposed by order under s 28(3A) and (3B);
(c) where only a range of numbers is shown, the lower number in that range.

Section 28(3A) and (3B) permit the making of orders prescribing the appropriate number of penalty points for offences; such an order may make provision for the fixed penalty for an offence to be different depending upon the circumstances, including, in particular, the nature of the offence, its seriousness, the area or place at which it was committed, or that the offender has committed an offence specified in the order during a specified period. No such order has yet been made.

RTOA, s 57A provides that where a fixed penalty notice is given to a person who is not the holder of a driving licence in respect of an offence involving obligatory endorsement, the Secretary of State may endorse the person's driving record accordingly without any order of a court on receipt of the details from the person paid the fixed penalty.

RTOA 1988, s 83 deals with the case where the appropriate person is deceived into endorsing a licence in circumstances in which the licence-holder should have been disqualified under the totting-up procedure and the deception constituted, or was due to, an offence committed by the licence-holder. It provides that if the licence-holder is convicted of that offence, the court before which he is convicted will have the same powers to disqualify as it would have had if it was convicting him of the endorsable offence.

Fixing notices to vehicles

RTOA 1988, s 62(1) provides that where a constable or vehicle examiner (ie an examiner appointed under RTA 1988, s 66A by the Secretary of State) has reason to believe that a fixed penalty offence is being or has been committed in respect of a stationary vehicle, he may affix to that vehicle a fixed penalty notice in respect of the offence unless the offence appears to him to involve obligatory endorsement.

Notice to owner

In cases in which a fixed penalty notice is affixed to a vehicle under s 62 and the fixed penalty has not been paid within the suspended enforcement period, *a notice to owner* may be served under s 63 by or on behalf of the chief officer of police (Secretary of State, if notice fixed by vehicle examiner) on *any person who appears to him* to be the owner of the vehicle (or a person authorised to act on such person's behalf). Such a notice must give particulars of the offence in question, of the fixed penalty concerned, and of the period allowed for response to the notice. It must also indicate that, if the fixed penalty is not paid before the end of that period, the person on whom the notice is served must furnish, before the end of that period, a statutory statement of ownership. The period allowed for response to such a notice is 21 days from the service of the notice. However, a notice need not be served when a request for a hearing has been made with an admission by the person making the request that he was the driver of the vehicle on that occasion. If a person on whom a notice has been served was not the owner of the vehicle at the relevant time, and he furnishes in time a statutory statement to that effect, he is not liable for the offence in question. Otherwise, where a notice is served within six months of the commission of that offence and the fixed penalty has not been paid within the period allowed, a sum equal to the fixed penalty, plus one-half of that penalty, may be registered against the person on whom the notice to owner was served as a fine.

Where person receiving was not the driver

There will be occasions when the person who receives a notice to owner will not have been the driver at the relevant time. RTOA 1988, s 63 therefore requires that the notice must indicate that, before the end of the period permitted for response, the person on whom it is served may either:

(a) request a hearing; or
(b) if he was not the driver and someone purporting to have been the driver wishes to give notice requesting a hearing, furnish, together with a statutory statement of ownership, a statutory statement of facts which has the effect of the actual driver requesting a hearing. (If such a driver is prepared to accept responsibility for the fixed penalty it is implied that he will do so by paying the penalty on behalf of the person to whom the notice is addressed.)

Once a statutory statement of facts has been supplied, the person named in the notice to owner is relieved of further responsibility and any sums due by way of fixed penalty may not be registered for enforcement. Once a fixed penalty has been registered for enforcement as a fine against a person on whom a notice to owner has been served, however, no proceedings can be brought against any other person in respect of that offence.

Special provisions are applied to hire vehicles, ie a vehicle hired for temporary use, by RTOA 1988, s 66. Provided a form of agreement has been drawn up between the hire firm and the hirer under the Road Traffic (Owner Liability) Regulations 2000, and provided the hire firm produces a copy of this to the police (together with a statement of hirer liability signed by the hirer under that hiring agreement), liability is removed from the hire firm; and the hirer of the vehicle becomes its owner for the purpose of the fixed penalty provisions.

Fixed penalty offences generally

Discretion

The issue of a fixed penalty notice for an endorsable offence (or a non-endorsable offence) is a matter for the constable's discretion so far as this is permitted by force policy. Within the limits of such policy, a constable may decide to give a verbal warning for the offence; issue a fixed penalty notice provided that existing penalty points permit such a course of action; or report O with a view to proceedings by way of summons or requisition.

When considering whether to deal with the offence by way of fixed penalty, and before he asks to see O's driving licence, the constable must ensure that O is aware of the implications of such a procedure. It is suggested that, in the case of an endorsable offence, he uses a form of words which convey the following message:

'I am considering the issue to you of a fixed penalty notice for the offence of…It will be necessary for me to examine your driving licence and any penalty points which may be endorsed on it. If after examination I find that it is appropriate to issue you with a fixed penalty notice it will be necessary to surrender your licence to me.'

Whatever form of words is used, O must not be given the impression that he must permit the examination of penalty points endorsed on his licence or that he must surrender it. There is no power to require those things.

Proceedings

No proceedings may be brought for an offence to which a fixed penalty notice relates until 21 days have passed since the day of the notice (or such longer period as may be specified in the notice). This period of time is referred to as the suspended enforcement period.

Where a fixed penalty notice has been given to an offender (O), no proceedings may be brought unless O has given notice requesting a hearing before the end of the suspended enforcement period. If no such notice has been received and the fixed penalty has not been paid before the end of the suspended enforcement period, a sum equal to the fixed penalty plus one-half of that amount may be registered against O as a fine.

Payment of penalties

Fixed penalties must be paid to the designated officer for a magistrates' court in a manner specified within the notice and the money must be dealt with as if it was a fine imposed on summary conviction. Payment may be made by way of a properly addressed, pre-paid letter. The payment is regarded as having been made at the time that the letter would be delivered in the course of normal post. In any proceedings a certificate from a fixed penalty clerk is admissible to prove that a fixed penalty was or was not received by a date specified in the certificate, or that a letter was marked as posted on a date so specified. If a fixed penalty is paid before the end of the suspended enforcement period, no further proceedings may be brought.

By RTOA 1988, s 53, the amount of the fixed penalty to be paid in respect of an offence is such amount as the Secretary of State may by order prescribe, or one-half of the maximum fine for it on summary conviction, whichever is less. The Secretary of State may provide for the fixed penalty for an offence to differ depending on the circumstances.

The amounts prescribed by the Secretary of State are currently contained in the Fixed Penalty Order 2000. The penalty for use, etc of a motor vehicle without insurance is fixed at £200; for failure to identify a driver £120; and for offences involving obligatory endorsement £60. Where the offence is non-endorsable the penalty is normally £30. However, where the non-endorsable offence consists of a fixed penalty parking offence committed in Greater London the penalty is £60 if it is committed on a red route, or £40 if it is committed otherwise than on a red route. 'Fixed penalty parking offence' means:

(a) an offence under RTRA 1984 which does not involve obligatory endorsement and is committed in respect of a stationary vehicle; and
(b) road obstruction offences under a variety of statutory provisions.

A 'red route' means a length of road on which there are traffic signs bearing the words 'red route' or red lines or marks.

The fixed penalty for offences against RTA 1988, ss 14 and 15(2) and 15(4) (seat belt offences: p 436) and those against VERA 1994, ss 42(1), 43(1) and 59 (registration plate offences: pp 345, 353, and 364) is £60. The fixed penalty for use without a MOT certificate or for not exhibiting a licence is £60. The fixed penalty for an offence under the Transport Act 1985, ss 98(4), 99(4), 99ZD(1), or 99C, the Road Traffic (Foreign Vehicles) Act 1972, s 3(1), the Public Passenger Vehicles Act 1981, s 12(5), RTA 1988, s 71(1), RTOA 1988, s 90D(6), or GV(LO)A 1995, s 2(5) is £200.

Graduated fixed penalties

RTOA 1988, s 53 permits fixed penalties to be different depending upon the circumstances including (in particular):

(a) the nature of the contravention or failure constituting the offence;
(b) how serious it is;
(c) the area, or sort of place, where it takes place; and

(d) whether the offender appears to have committed any offence or offences of a specified description, during the period so specified.

The Fixed Penalty Order 2000, Sch 2, as amended in 2010, specifies the fixed penalty
to be paid for offences by reference to the matters set out above. Graduated fixed penalties apply to offences under the:

(a) Transport Act 1968 (TA 1968), s 96 (drivers' hours) and vary from £60 to £200
depending upon the number of hours in excess of those permitted or the extent of
the failure to take rest;
(b) TA 1968, s 97 (recording equipment) and vary from £60 to £200 depending upon
the nature of the contravention or failure;
(c) RTA 1988, s 41A (tyres) and the penalty is £120 (£60 in the case of a motor cycle)
for failure to have a tread pattern of at least 1 mm;
(d) RTA 1988, s 41B (weight limit offences) and vary from £60 to £200 depending
upon the percentage of the excess weight; and
(e) RTA 1988, s 42 (speed limiters and danger in respect of passengers or load) and
vary from £60 to £120.

Fixed penalty notices given by vehicle examiners

RTOA 1988, Part 3 allows vehicle examiners to issue fixed penalty notices in respect of
offences which they are empowered to enforce. The system is operated independently
of the police by the Secretary of State who is responsible for administering the system,
collecting the penalties, and the endorsement of the licences or driving records. The
Fixed Penalty (Vehicle Examiner) Regulations 2009 prescribe certain information or
further information to be included in a fixed penalty notice issued by a vehicle examiner, the receipt for a driving licence (if held), and the registration certificate in the case
of non-payment of the fixed penalty. They also provide for the return of a driving
licence (if so held) to the licence-holder if the period in which no enforcement proceedings can be brought ('the suspended enforcement period') has expired, the fixed
penalty has not been paid, and the recipient of the notice has either requested a hearing
or the fixed penalty has not been registered for enforcement.

Penalty registered against person who has no knowledge of the offence

It is obvious that there will be occasions when a penalty is registered against a person
who, for some reason, has no knowledge of the offence. This may occur when fixed
penalty notices are affixed to vehicles which have changed ownership without DVLA
records being amended, or where a driver of someone else's vehicle does not inform the
owner of the notice.

RTOA 1988, ss 72 and 73 deal with this issue. By s 72, if registration has followed
non-receipt of a request for a hearing and the fixed penalty has not been paid, a statutory declaration may be made to the effect (a) that the declarant was not the person to
whom the fixed penalty notice was given or (b) that he had requested a hearing before
the end of the suspended enforcement period. Section 73 provides that, where the registration has followed service of 'notice to owner', and the penalty has not been paid, the
statutory declaration must state either that:

(i)   the declarant did not know of the penalty, or fixed penalty notice, or notice to
owner, until he received notice of the registration; or
(ii)   he was not the owner at the time of the offence alleged and that he has reasonable
excuse for failing to comply with the notice to owner; or
(iii) he requested a hearing as permitted by the notice to owner.

A declaration must be served on the proper officer of the relevant court, within 21 days of receipt of the notification of registration. With the exception of (b) and (iii) respectively, the effect of the declaration is that the relevant notice, registration, or endorsement (as the case may be) is void; in case (b), the declarant will be treated as if he had given notice requesting a hearing. In the case of (iii), the effect is to re-activate the 21-day response period referred to in the notice.

Miscellaneous points

RTOA 1988, s 30 requires that, if a person is convicted of an offence involving obligatory endorsement and the court is satisfied that he is liable to have penalty points endorsed upon his licence or his driving record within the fixed penalty procedure for an offence committed on the same occasion as those for which he is convicted, the court must reduce the number of penalty points endorsed on the licence by the number which will be attached in consequence of the fixed penalty offence.

It is an offence contrary to RTOA 1988:

(a) s 62(2), to remove or interfere with a notice affixed to a vehicle under s 62(1) (p 477) unless it is done by or under the authority of the driver or person in charge of the vehicle or the person liable for the offence in question;

(b) s 67, recklessly to furnish a statement which is false in a material particular, in response to a notice to owner, or to furnish such a statement knowing it is false in that particular.

Financial penalty deposits

RTOA 1988, Part 3A (ss 90A–90F) empowers a constable or vehicle examiner, who has reason to believe that a person is committing, or has on that occasion committed, a prescribed motor vehicle offence, to require from him the payment of a financial penalty deposit if he does not provide a satisfactory address in the UK. This power only exists where the person and the circumstances, as well as the offence, are within descriptions specified by regulation. Under the Road Safety (Financial Penalty Deposits) Order 2009, the offences in respect of which financial penalty deposits may be required are specified. The specified person is the person in charge of the vehicle at the time and the specified circumstances are that the offence is being, or has been, committed on a road or other public place. The Road Safety (Financial Penalty Deposits) (Appropriate Amount) Order 2009, as amended in 2010, provides that the term 'appropriate amount' is that required to be made to the Secretary of State as specified in the Schedules to the Order. The Regulations set out the offences and the circumstances in which a financial penalty deposit requirement can be imposed.

Police and vehicle examiners are empowered to prohibit the moving of the vehicle if the deposit is not paid immediately, although written permission may be given to remove it to a specified place. The Road Safety (Immobilisation, Removal and Disposal of Vehicles) Regulations 2009 provide for the detention, etc of vehicles prohibited from being driven following the imposition of a prohibition: see p 483. The prohibition continues until the deposit is paid, or (where the offender has received a fixed penalty notice or conditional offer) the offender has paid the fixed penalty, or the offender is convicted or acquitted of the offence or informed that he will not be prosecuted for it, or a 12-month period has elapsed since the deposit requirement. It is an offence to fail to comply with a prohibition, to cause or permit a vehicle to be driven in contravention of it, or to fail to comply within a reasonable time with a direction requiring the person in charge of the vehicle to remove it to a specified place (RTOA 1988, s 90D(6)).

Thus, a means is provided to secure a deposit where an enforcement officer is not satisfied that a penalty or fine could be enforced in the UK. If a person who has paid a financial penalty deposit is subsequently acquitted of the offence, the deposit, with interest, will be returned to him; otherwise it will be set against any penalty imposed.

Evidence in court proceedings in fixed penalty notice cases

RTOA 1988, s 79 permits the service of the statement of evidence of a constable or a vehicle examiner together with a fixed penalty notice or notice to owner. Such a statement will be deemed to have been served for the purposes of the Criminal Justice Act 1967, s 9 (referred to on p 241).

RTOA 1988, s 68 and Sch 4 permit 'statutory statements of ownership or of facts' to be used in evidence. A statutory statement of ownership is one where the declarant states whether or not he was the owner of the vehicle at the relevant time. If he was not it will state whether he was ever the owner and, if so, when. A statutory statement of facts is one where the declarant states that he was not the driver of the vehicle at the relevant time and states the name and address of the person who was.

Conditional offer of fixed penalty

RTOA 1988, s 75 provides as follows. Where a constable or vehicle examiner has reason to believe that a fixed penalty offence has been committed and *no fixed penalty notice has been given at the time or fixed to the vehicle concerned*, a notice of 'conditional offer' may be sent to the alleged offender (O) by, or on behalf of, the chief officer of police (by the Secretary of State in the case of a vehicle examiner). A conditional offer must:

(a) give particulars of the circumstances and reasonable information about the alleged offence;
(b) state the amount of the fixed penalty; and
(c) state that proceedings cannot be commenced for the offence until the end of 28 days following the date of issue of the conditional offer (or such longer period as may be specified in it).

Where O is the holder of a licence, a conditional offer must indicate that if:

(a) within the above 28-day period (or whichever longer period is specified), O pays to the appropriate person the fixed penalty and, where the offence concerned involves obligatory endorsement, at the same time delivers his licence to the clerk; and
(b) where his licence is delivered, the appropriate person is satisfied that, if the O was convicted, O would not be liable to disqualification under RTOA 1988, s 35 (disqualification for repeated offences),

liability to conviction will be discharged. Similar provisions apply where O is not the holder of a licence, except that there is no reference to a licence being delivered, reference being made instead to the appropriate person accessing O's driving record. In assessing liability to such disqualification, it is assumed (where penalty points awardable for the offence are within a range) that the number to be attributed for the offence would be the lowest in the range.

A person issuing a conditional offer must notify the fixed penalty clerk. If payment is made in accordance with the offer and the licence is delivered, no proceedings will be taken for the offence to which the conditional offer relates. The fixed penalty clerk must endorse the licence or driving record in appropriate cases and return it to the holder.

The fixed penalty clerk must notify the Secretary of State of any endorsement made on the licence in accordance with these procedures.

Special provisions for dealing with offences by way of fixed penalty

The Road Traffic (Vehicle Emissions) (Fixed Penalty) (England) Regulations 2002 (2003 in Wales) make provision for specified local authorities to authorise persons to issue fixed penalty notices to users of vehicles within their areas who contravene, or fail to comply with, RV(C&U)R 1986, reg 61 (emission of oil, smoke, vapour, gases, oily substances, etc) or reg 98 (stopping of engine when vehicle stationary).

PROHIBITION ON DRIVING: IMMOBILISATION, REMOVAL, AND DISPOSAL OF VEHICLES

In consequence of the introduction of RTOA 1988, Part 3A (financial penalty deposits: p 481), the Road Safety (Immobilisation, Removal and Disposal of Vehicles) Regulations 2009 provide for the immobilisation of prohibited vehicles and their removal and disposal. The Regulations apply to a vehicle which has been prohibited from being driven: in connection with a contravention of drivers' hours rules (TA 1968, s 99A); under powers to prohibit the driving of foreign goods vehicles and foreign public service vehicles (Road Traffic (Foreign Vehicles) Act 1972, s 1) or under powers to prohibit the driving of unfit or overloaded vehicles (RTA 1988, ss 69 or 70); or under powers to prohibit the driving of vehicles on failure to make payment in compliance with a financial penalty deposit requirement (RTOA 1988, s 90D). The Regulations do not apply to a vehicle displaying a current disabled person's badge.

Under the Regulations an authorised person or person acting under his direction may fix an immobilisation device, or may remove the vehicle or require the driver or person in charge of it to move it for the purpose of fixing the device. A notice must be fixed to the vehicle and must include steps to be taken to secure the release of the vehicle. A release fee of £80 will be required.

The Regulations also empower an authorised person, or someone acting under his direction, to remove a vehicle or require the driver or person in charge of it to remove it on grounds of safety, because of lack of space at the site, or because it appears abandoned.

The Regulations create offences of:

(a) failing to comply within a reasonable time with a requirement to move, or direct the removal of a vehicle, to enable the fitting of an immobilisation device (reg 5);
(b) unauthorisedly removing or interfering with an immobilisation notice (reg 6);
(c) unauthorisedly removing or attempting to remove an immobilisation device (reg 7);
(d) making a false or misleading statement in order to secure the release of a vehicle (reg 8);
(e) failing to comply within a reasonable time with a direction to remove a vehicle for safety reasons or to deliver the vehicle into custody (reg 16); and
(f) making false or misleading statements to secure possession of a vehicle in custody (reg 17).

The offences in (d) and (f) are indictable (either way) offences.

PARKING BY DISABLED DRIVERS

The Chronically Sick and Disabled Persons Act 1970 (CS&DPA 1970), s 21 requires that a 'blue badge' of the prescribed form be issued by local authorities in England, Wales and Scotland for motor vehicles driven by, or used for the carriage of, disabled persons resident within their areas.

Badges may also be issued to organisations concerned with the care of the disabled.

Badges are normally valid for three years.

The Disabled Persons (Badges for Motor Vehicles) (England) Regulations 2000 and the Disabled Persons (Badges for Motor Vehicles) (Wales) Regulations 2000 (the Badges Regulations) prescribe the forms of the badges to be issued and the Schedule to the regulations shows the contents and various forms of badges. Badges issued before the dates below are made from card and details completed by hand. The background on the front and reverse sides of the badge is coloured light blue and includes a pattern of wheelchair symbols. The square box which contains the wheelchair symbol and the rectangular box containing the country identifier are coloured dark blue. All other boxes contained within the badge are coloured white. With effect from 1 January 2012 (England) and 1 April 2012 (Wales) badges issued are new style badges. These are electronically printed and completed and have a unique hologram, a unique serial number, and (in the case of an individual's badge) a digital photograph. There are no white boxes on the new style badge.

CS&DPA 1970, ss 21A and 21C set out a system for the recognition in England and Wales of badges issued under equivalent provisions in Northern Ireland or under corresponding provisions in those foreign jurisdictions set out in regulations. At the time of writing no such regulations have been made. The Badges Regulations provide that badges issued in Scotland are valid in England and Wales.

Exemptions conferred by badge

The Local Authorities' Traffic Orders (Exemptions for Disabled Persons) (England) Regulations 2000 and the Local Authorities' Traffic Orders (Exemptions for Disabled Persons) (Wales) Regulations 2000 (the Exemptions Regulations) require that, except in respect of certain areas in central London, all 'No waiting' orders, etc made by local authorities must contain exemptions in favour of a vehicle displaying a disabled person's badge. The exemptions in favour of a disabled person's vehicle are in respect of orders prohibiting vehicles waiting beyond a specified period of time, of orders prohibiting waiting for vehicles at all times of day or during specified periods of the day (whether in relation to some types or all vehicles), of orders prescribing charges and time limit restrictions at parking meters. The only restriction which may apply to disabled persons' vehicles is that, where there is a prohibition on waiting for a period of more than three hours, a vehicle displaying a disabled person's badge is exempt for a maximum of three hours (and must not return to the same road for an hour), and is only so exempt if a parking disc is displayed showing the time of arrival (disc parking scheme). Any exemption required to be made in no waiting orders may be limited to vehicles of the same class as those to which the no waiting order applies.

The badge scheme does not permit parking:

(a) during the time a ban on loading or unloading is in force (indicated by one, two or three yellow marks on a kerb, at a time shown on a post-mounted plate);

(b) where there is a double white line in the centre of the road even if one of the lines is broken;

(c) in a bus or cycle lane when it is in use;

(d) on Zebra, Puffin, or Pelican crossings or on the zig-zag markings before or after these crossings;

(e) in parking places reserved for specific users, eg loading bays, residents, taxis or cycles; and

(f) in suspended meter bays or when the use of the meter is prohibited.

Display of badge

A badge issued under the CS&DPA 1970, s 21 may be displayed on a vehicle either inside or outside the area of the issuing authority.

The Badges Regulations require that a disabled person's badge be exhibited on the dashboard or fascia of the vehicle, or where the vehicle is not fitted with a dashboard or fascia, the badge is exhibited in a conspicuous position, in either case, so that the front of the badge is clearly legible from outside the vehicle. Similar provisions are made by the Exemptions Regulations for the display of parking discs, so that the quarter-hour period during which the period of waiting begins is legible from outside the vehicle.

The Badges Regulations set out the circumstances in which a disabled person's badge may be displayed while the vehicle is being *driven*. These are:

(a) the holder is either driving or being carried in the vehicle; or

(b) the vehicle is being used solely to collect the holder; or

(c) the vehicle is leaving the place where the holder has got out.

For (b) and (c) to apply, it is necessary that a disabled person's concession (other than one relating to parking) would be available to a vehicle displaying such a badge; and it would not have been practicable for the vehicle to be lawfully driven to, or to stop at, or to have left the place where the holder is collected.

By the Badges Regulations, the circumstances in which an individual's disabled person's badge may be displayed while the vehicle is *parked* are:

(a) it has been driven by the holder, or has been used to carry him, to the place where it is parked; or

(b) it is to be driven by the holder, or is to be used to carry him, from that place.

CS&DPA 1970, s 21(4B) makes it an offence for a person to drive a motor vehicle which is displaying a badge purporting to be in a form prescribed under s 21 otherwise than in a manner or in circumstances prescribed by the Regulations.

Production of badge

CS&DPA 1970, s 21(4BA)–(4BD) makes provision for the inspection of badges. Section 21(4BA) provides that, where it appears to a constable or enforcement officer that there is displayed on any motor vehicle a badge purporting to be of prescribed form, he may require anyone who:

(a) is in the vehicle, or

(b) appears to have been in, or to be about to get into, the vehicle, to produce the badge for inspection.

'Enforcement officer' means:

(a) a traffic warden;
(b) a civil enforcement officer (see p 469);
(c) a local authority parking attendant.

The power conferred on an enforcement officer is exercisable only for purposes connected with the discharge of his functions in relation to a stationary vehicle.

A person who, without reasonable excuse, fails to produce a badge when required to do so under s 21(4BA) commits an offence against s 21(4BD).

Wrongful use of badge

RTRA 1984, s 117 provides that a person is guilty of an offence if, when he commits some other offence under the Act (eg contravention of an order relating to parking made under it), the following conditions are satisfied:

(a) there was displayed on the motor vehicle a badge purporting to be of a prescribed form;
(b) he was using the vehicle in circumstances where a disabled person's concession would be available to a disabled person's vehicle,

but he is not guilty of an offence under s 117 if the badge was properly issued and displayed.

DRIVING INSTRUCTION

RTA 1988, s 123 prohibits the giving of paid driving instruction (ie for money or money's worth) unless the instructor is a registered approved instructor or the holder of a licence authorising him to give such instruction. There must be fixed to, and exhibited on, the motor car the current licence or certificate of registration, in a similar position to that occupied by the vehicle excise licence. Free instruction given as a perk when buying a car from a motor trader is deemed to be given for payment. RTA 1988, s 123 only applies to motor cars, but RSA 2006, Sch 6 prospectively substitutes s 123. When in force, the substituted s 123 will apply to any paid driving instruction of a type prescribed in regulations unless the instructor is registered and the registration is not suspended. RTA 1988, s 123 does not apply to police instructors.

Licensed instructor

To enable persons to gain experience with a view to undergoing the practical test of ability and fitness to instruct, which is part of the official driving instructor's examination for registration purposes, RTA 1988, s 129 allows the Registrar to grant a licence to give instruction in the driving of a motor car. Section 129 is prospectively repealed by RSA 2006, Sch 6. An applicant must have passed the written part, and the practical test of driving ability and fitness to drive, of the official driving instructors' examination. Licence-holders may only give instruction from premises named in the licence. If the premises are a driving school the licence-holder may only give instruction if properly employed in accordance with rules that there can be no more than one licence-holder to each registered instructor.

For the first three months of any licence (other than the second of two consecutive ones) the holder either must be under the direct personal supervision of a registered instructor for at least one-fifth of that time and keep a log to that effect, or must undertake a minimum of 20 hours' supplementary training. In the case of the latter alternative he must undertake five further hours of training in a second consecutive period.

Disabled persons

Disabled persons may be registered or licensed as driving instructors, but only if they hold a current disabled person's limited driving licence and a current emergency control certificate. Such a certificate is only granted after assessment of the person's ability to take control of a motor car of a class covered by his disabled person's driving licence (with or without modifications).

Offences

By RTA 1988, s 123(4), a person giving instruction in breach of s 123 commits an offence, as does his employer if he is employed for that purpose. It is a defence to prove that he did not know and had no reasonable cause to believe that his name, or that of his employee, was not in the register.

A person to whom a certificate of registration or a licence has been granted must produce it to a constable or authorised person on being required to do so. Failure to do so is an offence, contrary to s 137(3). However, it is a defence to prove in any proceedings for non-production:

(a) that the licence was produced within seven days at a police station specified by the constable or at a place specified by the authorised person; or

(b) that the document was produced at that police station or place as soon as reasonably practicable; or

(c) that it was not reasonably practicable for it to be so produced before the day on which proceedings commenced.

By RTA 1988, s 135(2), it is an offence for any unregistered person to wear or display a badge or certificate or to use any name, title or description which is prescribed or which implies that he is registered. Section 135(3) makes it an offence for someone carrying on a driving instruction business to use any such title or description in respect of an unregistered employee, or to issue any advertisement, etc which is misleading in that respect. It is a defence to an offence under s 135(2) or (3) for the defendant to prove that he did not know, and had no reasonable cause to believe, that his name, or that of his employee, was not in the register at the material time. Section 135 is prospectively substituted in similar terms by RSA 2006, Sch 6.

If an applicant for registration fails, without reasonable excuse, to disclose a relevant or prospective disability, he commits an offence (s 125A(4)). So does a registered or licensed disabled instructor who fails, without reasonable excuse, to disclose such a disability or who gives paid instruction without an emergency control certificate or in an unauthorised motor car (s 133C(4) and s 133D(2) and (3) respectively). A person who employed him to give that instruction is also liable if an offence under s 133D is committed.

RESTRICTIONS ON THE USE OF MOTORWAYS

The Motorways Traffic (England and Wales) Regulations 1982 impose various restrictions on drivers on motorways of the classes of vehicles permitted to use motorways. Contravention of the Regulations is an offence.

Vehicles which may use motorways

Under the 1982 Regulations, Class I and Class II vehicles are, in normal circumstances, permitted to use motorways. Class I includes heavy and light locomotives, motor tractors, heavy motor cars, motor cars and motorcycles of not less than 50 cc and trailers drawn by such vehicles. (These terms are defined in Chapter 10.) Track-laying vehicles are not within Class I. To be in Class I vehicles must be fitted with pneumatic tyres, must not be agricultural motor vehicles or machines and must not be pedestrian-controlled. All such vehicles must be capable of attaining a speed of 25 mph when unladen.

Class II vehicles are those specially made to transport abnormal, indivisible loads, and large vehicles (eg tank transporters) used by the armed services. In addition, earth movers and similar engineering plant are Class II vehicles if they are capable of attaining 25 mph when unladen.

Direction of driving

The 1982 Regulations, reg 6 requires the observance of 'No entry' and 'No left or right turn' signs. It also requires that vehicles always have the central reservation on their right or offside, and that, if there is no central reservation, they continue to travel in the direction which was permitted on entry to the motorway and that they are not driven or moved so as to cause them to turn and proceed in, or face, the opposite direction.

Stopping

Regulation 7 of the 1982 Regulations requires that no vehicle may stop or remain at rest on a carriageway of a motorway. When a stop becomes necessary due to breakdown, mechanical defect, lack of fuel, accident, illness or other emergency, or to permit someone carried in the vehicle to recover or move an object which has fallen on to the motorway, or to permit someone to give help to another in any of those circumstances, the vehicle must, as soon and in so far as is reasonably practicable, be driven or moved off the carriageway on to a contiguous hard shoulder where it may stop and remain at rest. Such a vehicle must remain at rest in such a position that, as far as reasonably practicable, no part of it or its load obstructs or causes danger to vehicles using the carriageway. It must not remain for longer than necessary for such purpose.

The regulation makes the obvious exception in favour of drivers prevented from proceeding by 'traffic jams'. It also provides for stopping to pay motorway tolls.

Reversing

The driving or moving of a vehicle backwards is prohibited by reg 8 of the 1982 Regulations, unless it is necessary to do so to allow it to move forward or be connected to another vehicle.

General use

Regulations 9 and 10 of the 1982 Regulations prohibit driving, stopping or remaining at rest on a hard shoulder (in circumstances other than those permitted) or on a central reservation. Regulation 11 prohibits the driving of motor vehicles on motorways by persons who are authorised to drive the vehicle which they are driving only by virtue of being the holder of a provisional licence. The regulation applies to:

(a) a motor vehicle in category A or B or sub-category C1 + E (8.25 tonnes), D1 (not for hire or reward), D1 + E (not for hire or reward), or P; and

(b) a motor vehicle in category B + E or sub-category C1 if the provisional licence authorising the driving of such a motor vehicle was in force at a time before 1 January 1997.

The Motor Vehicles (Driving Licences) Regulations 1999 provide for separate driving tests for motor cars with trailers (category B + E), trucks and vans of between 3.5 tonnes and 7.5 tonnes maximum authorised mass (sub-categories C1 and C1 + E), and for buses having more than eight but not more than 16 passenger seats in addition to the driver's seat whether or not they carry passengers for hire or reward (sub-categories D1 and D1 + E). Provisional licences to drive such vehicles may only be issued to persons holding at least a full licence to drive motor cars (category B). Such holders of provisional licences are authorised to drive on motorways while holding provisional licences (as they are full licence-holders in respect of category B).

Regulation 14 of the 1982 Regulations provides that the person in charge of an animal shall, so far as is practicable, ensure that it is not removed from or permitted to leave the vehicle while on a motorway. If it escapes or it is necessary for it to be removed from or permitted to leave the vehicle, it must not go on or remain on any part of a motorway other than a hard shoulder, where it must be held on a lead or otherwise kept under proper control.

Use of right or offside lane

Regulation 12 of the 1982 Regulations prohibits the following motor vehicles from using the offside lane of a three-lane motorway at any place where all three lanes are open to traffic:

(a) a goods vehicle which has a maximum laden weight exceeding:
  (i) 7.5 tonnes; or
  (ii) 3.5 tonnes but not exceeding 7.5 tonnes, to which RV(C&U)R 1986, reg 36B applies (speed limiters) or would apply but for the fact that it is en route for repair or installation of a limiter or its limiter has broken down en route;
(b) a passenger vehicle which is constructed or adapted to carry more than eight seated passengers in addition to the driver, the maximum laden weight of which:
  (i) exceeds 7.5 tonnes; or
  (ii) does not exceed 7.5 tonnes, to which RV(C&U)R 1986, reg 36A applies (speed limiters) or would apply but for one of the exceptions in (a)(ii);
(c) a vehicle drawing a trailer; and
(d) a motor tractor or a locomotive.

The only occasion upon which such vehicles may enter the offside lane of a three-lane motorway, when all lanes are open, is when this is necessary to overtake a wide load.

Regulation 12 does not require a vehicle to change lane during a period when it would not be reasonably practicable for it to do so without involving danger of injury to any person or inconvenience to property.

Exceptions and relaxations of effect of regulations

Regulation 15 of the 1982 Regulations provides as follows. Vehicles other than those within Classes I and II are permitted to use motorways in emergencies and certain other cases. There are occasions upon which vehicles which would normally be banned must be present to carry out maintenance work or repairs, etc. In addition, the Secretary of State may authorise limited use to allow excluded traffic access on occasions or in an emergency or to enable it to cross a motorway to gain access to premises abutting on or adjacent to a motorway. Lastly, a chief officer of police (or a superintendent acting on his behalf) may authorise use by excluded traffic for a period of time during which the use of an alternative road is rendered impossible or unsuitable. The regulation also permits pedestrian use where this is authorised by a constable or appointed person to enable tolls to be paid.

Regulation 16 permits the use of a motorway otherwise than in accordance with the Regulations, on the direction of a constable in uniform or traffic officer in uniform or in compliance with a traffic sign; with the permission of a constable in uniform or traffic officer in uniform for the purpose of the investigation of an accident; where necessary to prevent an accident or give help as a result of an accident or emergency; where the act is done in exercise of the duty of a constable, traffic officer (when in uniform), member of SOCA for the purposes of that Agency, or member of a fire and rescue authority or of an ambulance service; or where necessary in connection with motorway maintenance or the removal of vehicles.

Offence

A person who uses a motorway in contravention of the above regulations commits an offence under RTRA 1984, s 17(4).

CHAPTER 12

Lights and Vehicles

The lighting requirements for vehicles are set out in the Road Vehicles Lighting Regulations 1989. Unless otherwise indicated, all references in this chapter to 'the Regulations' or to a regulation are to these Regulations, or a regulation in them.

The Regulations define certain terms which are used throughout as follows:

Daytime hours   The time between half an hour before sunrise and half an hour after sunset.

Hours of darkness   The time between half an hour after sunset and half an hour before sunrise.

Obligatory lamp, reflector, rear marking or device
A lamp, reflector, rear marking or device with which a vehicle, its load, or equipment, is required by the Regulations to be fitted.

Optional lamp, reflector, rear marking or device
A lamp, reflector, rear marking or device with which a vehicle, its load, or equipment, is not required by the Regulations to be fitted.

OBLIGATORY LAMPS, REFLECTORS, REAR MARKINGS, AND DEVICES

Required equipment

By reg 18, a person must not use a vehicle on a road, or cause or permit it to be so used, unless it is equipped with obligatory lamps, reflectors, devices or markings as specified by Sch 1 to the Regulations. Column 1 of Sch 1 lists the type of lamp, reflector, rear marking, or device required; column 2 the installation (including height and lateral positioning) and performance requirement (by reference to other Schedules); and column 3 any exceptions to the general rule. The various types of obligatory lamp, etc are as follows:

Front position lamp   A lamp used to indicate the presence and width of a vehicle when viewed from the front, ie a side lamp.

Dim-dip lighting device   A device capable of causing a dipped beam headlamp to operate at reduced intensity.

Running lamp   A lamp (not being a front position lamp, an end-outline marker lamp, headlamp, or front fog lamp) used to make the presence of a moving motor vehicle readily visible from the front. (An alternative to a dim-dip device; in effect, a higher intensity front position lamp.)

Dipped beam headlamp   'Dipped beam' means a beam of light emitted by a lamp which illuminates the road ahead of a vehicle without causing undue dazzle or discomfort to oncoming drivers or other road users.

Main beam headlamp   'Main beam' means a beam of light emitted by a lamp which illuminates the road over a long distance ahead of the vehicle.

Direction indicator   A lamp on a vehicle used to indicate to other road users that the driver intends to change direction to the right or to the left.

Hazard warning signal device   A device capable of causing all the direction indicators with which a vehicle, or a combination of vehicles, is fitted to operate simultaneously.

Side marker lamp   A lamp fitted to the side of a vehicle or its load and used to render the vehicle more visible to other road users.

Rear position lamp   A lamp used to indicate the presence and width of a vehicle when viewed from the rear.

Rear fog lamp   A lamp used to render a vehicle more readily visible from the rear in conditions of seriously reduced visibility.

Stop lamp   A lamp used to indicate to road users that the brakes of a vehicle or combination of vehicles are being applied.

End-outline marker lamp   A lamp fitted near the edge of a vehicle in addition to the front and rear position lamps to indicate the presence of a wide vehicle.

Rear registration plate lamp   A lamp used to illuminate the rear registration plate.

Side retro reflector   A reflector fitted to the side of a vehicle or its load and used to render the vehicle more visible from the side.

Rear retro reflector   A reflector used to indicate the presence and width of a vehicle when viewed from the rear.

Rear marking   A marking as indicated in Sch 19, Part I, to the Regulations, ie a 'long vehicle' marking.

Conspicuity marking   A device intended to increase the conspicuity of a vehicle, when viewed from the side or rear, by the reflection of light emanating from a light source not connected to the vehicle, the observer being situated near the source, ie high visibility 'conspicuity marking tape'.

Each of these lamps, reflectors, devices, and markings is obligatory for motor vehicles (with exceptions mentioned later) and some of them are obligatory for trailers drawn by motor vehicles and for other vehicles. Such lamps, etc must be fitted in the manner described by the Regulations.

As the requirements have increased, the position of vehicles manufactured before new requirements were made has had to be safeguarded. The various regulations therefore specify the date of application by applying the requirements to vehicles first used on or after a given date. However, reg 4 provides that, even if a motor vehicle is first used on or after that date, it will be exempt from the requirements of the particular regulation if manufactured more than six months in advance of that date. In some instances this provision is expressly repeated in a particular regulation but generally it must be implied into a particular regulation from reg 4. For example, a motor vehicle first used on or after 1 April 1980 is required to have a rear fog lamp fitted, but (by virtue of reg 4) such a vehicle is exempt from the requirement if it was manufactured before 1 October 1979.

The Regulations require that obligatory lamps, reflectors, rear markings, and devices are fitted and performing satisfactorily at all times. However, there are certain understandable exceptions to this rule. The Regulations do not require any lamp or reflector to be fitted between sunrise and sunset to:

(a) an incomplete vehicle proceeding to a works for completion,
(b) a pedal cycle,
(c) a pedestrian-controlled vehicle,
(d) a horse-drawn vehicle,
(e) a combat vehicle (ie a tank, armoured car, field gun, and the like, and vehicles constructed for the carriage of such a thing or of other weapons or ammunition), or
(f) a vehicle being taken to, or removed from, a testing station by an authorised vehicle examiner in order to submit the vehicle for an examination there in order to ensure that the examination carried out at the station is correctly carried out.

To that list is added a vehicle which is not fitted with any front or rear position lamps, so that if a person is building a motor car from parts and has not yet installed such lights he will not commit an offence by using the vehicle on a road during daylight hours. In addition, the regulations relating to fitting do not apply to a vehicle based outside Great Britain which is on a journey in this country, provided that it has not been here for more than 12 months and that it complies with international requirements. Vehicles going to a port for export are similarly exempt. Hand-propelled vehicles whose overall width does not exceed 800 mm do not require lamps or reflectors if pushed close to the nearside of the carriageway.

For the purpose of the Regulations, a lamp is not treated as being a lamp if it is so painted over or masked that it is not capable of being immediately used or readily put to use, or if it is an electric lamp which is not provided with any system of wiring by means of which that lamp is (or can readily be) connected with a source of electricity.

Front lights

Front position lamps

Vehicles with three or more wheels (other than invalid carriages and pedal tricycles) require two front position lamps.

Pedal cycles, solo motor bicycles, hand-propelled vehicles whose width (with load) does not exceed 1,250 mm, and invalid carriages require only one front position lamp, which must be fitted on the centre line or offside of the vehicle. Motorcycle combinations with a headlamp on the motor bicycle require a front position lamp on the centre line of the sidecar, or on the side of the sidecar furthest from the motor bicycle. A solo motor bicycle fitted with a headlamp need not be fitted with a front position lamp.

All front position lamps must be white in colour, unless they are incorporated in a yellow headlamp, in which case they may be yellow. They must be visible from a reasonable distance.

Dipped beam headlamps

Two dipped beam headlamps are required by motor vehicles with three or more wheels in most circumstances. Solo motor bicycles or combinations, and three-wheelers first used before 1 January 1972, or with an unladen weight of not more than 400 kg and an overall width of not more than 1,300 mm, require only one headlamp on the centre line of the motor vehicle itself. A bus first used before 1 October 1969 need only have one dipped beam headlamp.

The light emitted by a dipped beam headlamp must be white or yellow. The lamp itself must be so constructed that the direction of the beam of light can be adjusted whilst the vehicle is stationary. Where two dipped beam headlamps are required to be fitted, they must form a matched pair and be capable of being switched on and off simultaneously and not otherwise.

Main beam headlamps

The provisions concerning the number of obligatory headlamps to be fitted are the same as those relating to dipped beam headlamps, except that a bus must have two main beam headlamps, even if first used before 1 October 1969. (This means that a bus must have two headlamps, although only one of them needs to be capable of being dipped.) The outer edges of the illuminated areas must not be outside those of the dipped beam headlamps; there is no maximum distance which should separate a pair of such lamps.

Main beam headlamps must emit a white or yellow light and must be constructed so that they can be deflected at the will of the driver to become a dipped beam, or so that they can be extinguished by the operation of a device which at the same time switches on a dipped beam or causes another lamp to emit a dipped beam. Thus headlamps of the 'long-range' type are invariably wired so that as they are extinguished a dipped beam is emitted from the normal headlamps. Main beam headlamps must be constructed so that the direction of the beam can be adjusted whilst the vehicle is stationary.

Dim-dip devices

Dim-dip devices must be provided on motor vehicles with three or more wheels first used on or after 1 April 1987. Vehicles having a maximum speed of 40 mph or less and home forces vehicles are exempt, as are vehicles which comply with Community Directive 76/756/EEC. A running lamp may be fitted as an alternative.

Rear lights

Rear position lamps

Most vehicles with three or more wheels require two rear position lamps. The following vehicles, some of which have three or more wheels, require only one rear position lamp: buses first used before 1 April 1955; solo motor bicycles; pedal cycles with less than four wheels; trailers drawn by pedal cycles; trailers (the overall width of which does not exceed 800 mm) drawn by solo or motorcycle combinations; invalid carriages having a maximum speed not exceeding 4 mph; and vehicles propelled by hand. (See p 493 for the exemption for hand-propelled vehicles not exceeding 800 mm in width.) Some motor vehicles of maximum speed not exceeding 25 mph, and their trailers, require four rear position lamps; the details are in Sch 10 to the Regulations.

In cases in which only one rear position lamp is required it must be fitted on the centre line of the vehicle or on its offside.

All rear position lamps must be red.

Rear fog lamps

If it was first used on or after 1 April 1980, any motor vehicle having three or more wheels, and any trailer drawn by a motor vehicle, must, unless specifically dealt with elsewhere in the Regulations, have at least one rear fog lamp fitted, at or near the rear, on the centre line or offside of the vehicle. If two lamps are fitted there is no requirement concerning the distance these lights are placed from the sides of the vehicle. No more than two lamps may be fitted.

Vehicles first used before 1 April 1980 do not need to be fitted with rear fog lamps. Nor do motor vehicles whose maximum speed is 25 mph or less, nor motor vehicles or trailers which are no more than 1,300 mm in width, nor agricultural vehicles or works trucks first used before 1 April 1986. If one of these exempt vehicles is fitted with such lamps there are no restrictions in relation to the number of lamps which may be fitted, but any which are fitted must not be capable of illumination by a braking system.

A rear fog lamp must show a red light. It must not be fitted so that it can be illuminated by the application of any braking system of the vehicle. A tell-tale must be fitted to show that the lights are in operation. If two lamps are fitted to a motor vehicle first used on or after 1 April 1986, or on a trailer manufactured on or after 1 October 1985, they must form a matched pair. If two rear fog lamps are fitted, the rules for obligatory fog lamps apply to both of them.

Stop lamps

Stop lamps must show a red light. Motor vehicles having three or more wheels, and trailers drawn by a motor vehicle, must, unless otherwise stated, be fitted with two stop lamps. Solo motor bicycles, combinations, invalid carriages, and trailers drawn by motor cycles, together with motor vehicles or trailers first used before 1 January 1971, need only be fitted with one stop lamp. Motor bicycles of less than 50 cc first used before 1 April 1986 do not require any stop lamp, nor does any type of motor vehicle first used before 1 January 1936 or a motor vehicle whose maximum speed is 25 mph or less or an agricultural vehicle or works truck first used before 1 April 1986.

If two stop lamps are fitted they should be on each side of the longitudinal axis of the vehicle. If only one is fitted it should be on the centre line or offside.

The lamps must be operated by the application of the service braking system of the motor vehicle, and this also applies to the stop lamps of any trailer attached to that vehicle. Where two stop lamps are required to be fitted, they must form a pair.

Rear registration plate lamp

All vehicles which are required to be fitted with a rear registration plate must have lighting which is capable of adequately illuminating the rear registration plate.

Other obligatory lamps

Direction indicators

The requirements for direction indicators are as follows:

(1) Motor vehicles first used before 1 April 1936 and trailers manufactured before that date *may* have any arrangement of indicators but they are not required to have any at all.
(2) Motor vehicles first used on or after that date and before 1 April 1986, and trailers manufactured between 1 January 1936 and 1 October 1985, *must* be provided with any arrangement of indicators so as to satisfy the requirement of visibility to front and rear (or rear only in the case of a trailer).
(3) Motor vehicles first used on or after 1 April 1986, and trailers manufactured on or after 1 October 1985, are subject to detailed restrictions. Motor vehicles with three or more wheels, other than motorcycle combinations, must have a single front indicator, one side repeater indicator, and one rear indicator on each side. One additional optional rear indicator may be fitted and any number of side repeater indicators may be added. Trailers manufactured after the specified date must have

a rear indicator on each side. Additional optional indicators may be fitted as above. Motor bicycles and combinations must have a single front and a single rear indicator on each side of the vehicle.

The colour of the light shown by direction indicators is amber in most instances. Motor vehicles first used before 1 September 1965, and the trailer of such a vehicle, may show white or amber to the front or red or amber to the rear. However, if such an indicator is visible from both the front and the back it must show an amber light regardless of the date of first use. All indicators on any side of a vehicle or its trailer must be operated by one switch. There must be a tell-tale to show that the indicators are in operation. Flashing indicators must flash constantly at a rate of not less than 60 and not more than 120 times per minute.

Vehicles whose maximum speed does not exceed 15 mph or invalid carriages having a maximum speed not exceeding 4 mph are not required to have direction indicators fitted, nor are vehicles first used before 1 August 1986 which are agricultural vehicles, industrial tractors, or works vehicles.

Agricultural vehicles having an unladen weight not exceeding 255 kg do not require direction indicators.

End-outline marker lamps

These are required on motor vehicles first used on or after 1 April 1991, except those with a maximum speed not exceeding 25 mph; those having an overall width not exceeding 2,100 mm; and incomplete vehicles proceeding to works, etc. Their purpose is to indicate the presence of a wide vehicle.

There must be two white lights fitted to the front and two red lights to the rear, not more than 400 mm from the side of the vehicle. Each set must be a matched pair. Any number may be fitted.

Hazard warning signals

These signals are obligatory on motor vehicles having three or more wheels and first used on or after 1 April 1986, except vehicles which are not required to be fitted with direction indicators. Hazard warning signals which are optionally fitted to other vehicles must comply with the same provisions. Each device must be operated by one switch which causes all direction indicators with which the vehicle or combination of vehicles is equipped to flash in phase. There must be a tell-tale, and the device must be capable of operation without the ignition being switched on.

Side marker lamps

Some motor vehicles with three or more wheels, and trailers drawn by motor vehicles are required to have side marker lamps on each side. Most are not, since motor vehicles first used before 1 April 1991 and trailers, the overall length of which does not exceed 6m (or 9.15m if manufactured before 1 October 1990), are not required to have side marker lamps, and nor are the following first used on or after that date:

(a) motor vehicles whose maximum speed does not exceed 25 mph;
(b) passenger vehicles;
(c) incomplete motor vehicles;
(d) those not exceeding 6m in length;
(e) those first used before 1 April 1996 complying with Community Directive 76/756/ EEC (and trailers manufactured before 1 October 1985 which comply with this Directive);

(f) trailers, whose overall length, excluding any drawbar and any fittings for its attachment, exceeds 6m (9.15m if manufactured before 1 October 1990);
(g) agricultural and works trailers;
(h) caravans and boat trailers; and
(i) trailers complying with the Community Directive.

A side marker lamp is a lamp which will show an amber light, if fitted to a vehicle first used on or after 1 October 1990, unless it is placed within 1m of the rear of the vehicle, when it may be red. Trailers manufactured before that date may have lamps which show a white light to the front and a red light to the rear.

The requirements are to have two, on each side, and as many more as are sufficient to ensure that the maximum distance from the front of the vehicle (including any drawbar) to the first lamp is 4m and the maximum distance from the rear in respect of the rearmost side marker lamp is 1m. The maximum separation distance of adjacent obligatory lamps on the same side of the vehicle is 3m or, if this is not practicable, 4m.

A vehicle, or a combination of vehicles whose overall length (including any load) exceeds 18.3m, must have additional side marker lamps, one lamp being no more than 9.5m from the foremost part of the vehicle or vehicles and one lamp no more than 3.05m from the rear (including loads in both circumstances). Other lamps must be placed to ensure that no more than 3.05m separates the lamps.

Where the length exceeds 12.2m but not 18.3m and the load is supported by any two vehicles, lamps must be placed behind the rearmost part of the drawing vehicle, but not more than 1,530 mm to the rear of that point. If the supported load extends more than 9.15m to the rear of the drawing vehicle, the lamp must not be forward of, or more than 1,530 mm to the rear of, the centre of the length of the load. These provisions do not apply to articulated vehicles.

Obligatory reflectors, etc

Rear retro reflectors

Generally, all vehicles must be equipped with two rear retro reflectors. By way of exception, the following only require one retro reflector: solo motor bicycles; pedal cycles with less than four wheels (with or without a sidecar); trailers drawn by pedal cycles; trailers not exceeding 800 mm drawn by solo motorcycles or combinations; invalid carriages having a maximum speed not exceeding 4 mph; and hand-propelled vehicles. Some restricted vehicles (maximum speed 25 mph) require four reflectors.

Reflectors must be fitted at or near the rear of the vehicle. Where there is only one reflector it must be on the centre line or offside of the vehicle.

The colour of all rear reflectors must be red. A triangular-shaped rear reflector may only be fitted to a trailer or broken-down vehicle under tow.

Side retro reflectors

Side reflectors are obligatory on certain motor vehicles with three or more wheels and their trailers. The relevant requirements do not apply to a passenger vehicle (including private cars), nor to an incomplete vehicle travelling to a works for completion, etc, mobile cranes, plant, and certain earth-removal vehicles, nor to a vehicle having a maximum speed not exceeding 25 mph. Nor do they apply to a goods vehicle whose overall length does not exceed 6m (if first used on or after 1 April 1986) or 8m (if first used before that date).

The requirements therefore are restricted to long goods vehicles. In the case of such vehicles, first used before 1 April 1986, and trailers manufactured before 1 October

1985, there must be two side retro reflectors on each side of the vehicle. In the case of those first used or manufactured on or after the relevant date, there must be two on each side of the vehicle and as many more as are required by Sch 17 to the Regulations. Side retro reflectors must be amber or, within 1m of the rear of the vehicle, they may be red. They must not be triangular in shape.

Rear markings

The rear markings provisions relate to 'long vehicle' markings, and therefore most vehicles are exempted from them. In the case of those motor vehicles first used before 1 April 1996 which are not exempted, those which do not exceed 13m in length need only carry the marker boards with diagonal lines, whereas those which exceed 13m must carry marker boards with the words 'long vehicle' in black on a yellow background surrounded by a red border or, as an alternative, boards of yellow retro reflective material surrounded by a red fluorescent border. Those used on or after 1 April 1996, which are not exempted, must carry boards of red and yellow diagonal stripes if they do not exceed 13m in length; if they exceed 13m, they must carry boards of yellow retro reflective material surrounded by a red fluorescent border. The same markings are required on certain trailers forming part of a combination of vehicles. In the case of a trailer manufactured on or after 1 October 1995 which does not, in combination, exceed 11m, it must carry a board of red and yellow diagonal stripes; if it exceeds 11m but not 13m it must carry boards of such red and yellow stripes or of yellow surrounded by red; and if it exceeds 13m, the boards must be of yellow surrounded by red. In the case of a trailer manufactured before 1 October 1995, the overall length does not exceed 11m, the marking must be of the diagonal line variety; if between 11m and 13m the marking may be of any approved variety; and if it exceeds 13m it must be the 'long vehicle' type, or a board of yellow reflective material surrounded by a red fluorescent border.

A vehicle fitted with conspicuity markings to the rear where the fitting complies with the relevant ECE conspicuity requirements is exempt from the rear marking requirements.

Conspicuity markings

A goods vehicle which is—

(a) a motor vehicle first used on or after 10 July 2011, or
(b) a trailer manufactured on or after 10 July 2011,

must be fitted with conspicuity markings complying with the relevant ECE conspicuity requirements (hereafter 'conspicuity markings').

This requirement does not apply to a goods vehicle which is—

(a) a motor vehicle with a maximum gross weight not exceeding 7,500kg;
(b) a trailer with a maximum gross weight not exceeding 3,500kg;
(c) an incomplete vehicle proceeding to a works for completion or to a place where it is to be stored or displayed for sale; or
(d) a motor car or heavy motor car intended to form part of an articulated vehicle.

A goods vehicle to which the above requirement applies is known as a 'relevant goods vehicle'.

If the overall length of a relevant goods vehicle does not exceed 6m, conspicuity markings need not be fitted to the side of that vehicle.

If the overall width of a relevant goods vehicle does not exceed 2.1m, conspicuity markings need not be fitted to the rear of that vehicle.

Pedal retro reflectors

Pedal cycles manufactured on or after 1 October 1985 must be provided with two amber reflectors on each pedal.

OPTIONAL LAMPS, REFLECTORS, REAR MARKINGS, AND DEVICES

The requirements above relate to obligatory lights and equipment to be fitted to the vehicles described. However, in most instances the Regulations do not prevent the fitting of optional lamps, etc, ie lamps, etc which are not obligatory under the Regulations. Regulation 20 provides that every optional lamp, etc fitted to a vehicle must comply with provisions set out in the respective Schedules to the Regulations. A table included in the Regulations describes the types of optional lamps, etc and requires compliance with certain parts of the directions given in the relevant Schedule.

Optional lamps, etc can be divided into two categories:

(a) those which are additional to obligatory lamps, etc; and
(b) those which are not additional in that sense; there is no absolute requirement to have any lamp, etc of the particular type.

Additional lamps, etc

The position is:

(1) Any number of optional front position lamps may be fitted (except that a solo motor bicycle first used on or after 1 April 1991 may not be fitted with a total of more than two front position lamps). They must be white or, if incorporated in a yellow headlamp, yellow.
(2) Dim-dip devices in addition to running lamps and vice versa may be fitted optionally.
(3) Any number of optional dipped beam headlamps may be fitted. Additional ones must be white or yellow, comply with maximum and minimum height requirements, and be capable of adjustment while the vehicle is stationary.
(4) Any number of optional main beam headlamps may be fitted. They must be white or yellow, electrically connected so that they deflect or extinguish by the dip switch, and be capable of adjustment while the vehicle is stationary.
(5) Any number of rear position lamps may be fitted. They must be red.
(6) The number of rear fog lamps is controlled in the case of vehicles first used on or after 1 April 1980 (or, in the case of trailers, manufactured on or after 1 October 1979). No more than two such lamps are permitted in such a case. Rear fog lamps must be red.
(7) Any number of stop lamps can be fitted. If additional lamps are fitted they must comply with the provisions for obligatory stop lamps, except those relating to position and angles of visibility. Motor vehicles first used on or after 1 April 1991 are subject to control in relation to the intensity of the light projected through the rear windows. Rear stop lamps must be red.
(8) Any number of side retro reflectors may be fitted. They must be amber except that, in respect of a vehicle used for the following purposes, the following colours are permitted:

Police—amber, yellow, blue, white*
Fire and Rescue Authority—amber, yellow, red

Ambulance—amber, yellow, green, white*
VOSA (Vehicle and Operators Service Agency)—amber, yellow, silver, white*
Traffic officer— amber, yellow, white.

(*Or, if within 1m of the rear of the vehicle, red.)
They may not be triangular.
(9) Any number of rear retro reflectors may be fitted. Optional rear retro reflectors must be red, except that, in respect of a vehicle used for police, fire and rescue authority, VOSA or traffic officer purposes, the following colours are permitted: red, yellow, or orange (or any combination). Optional rear retro reflectors may not be triangular, except in the cases referred to on p 497.

Non-additional optional lamps, etc

If such lamps are fitted they must comply with the following requirements.

Front fog lamps

These must be white or yellow lamps. Where a pair of front fog lamps is used in conditions of seriously reduced visibility in place of the obligatory dipped beam headlamps, they must not be more than 400 mm from the side of the vehicle.

Motor vehicles (other than motor bicycles) first used on or after 1 April 1991 may not have more than two front fog lamps.

Reversing lamps

Such a lamp must show a white light. Not more than two, facing the rear, may be fitted. In the case of a motor vehicle first used on or after 1 July 1954, they must be such that they cannot be illuminated other than automatically by the selection of the reverse gear or otherwise there must be a tell-tale.

If a vehicle has an overall length in excess of 6m and is a bus or a vehicle which is not a passenger vehicle four reversing lamps may be fitted. If four are fitted to such a vehicle the configuration must be four to the rear or two to the rear and one on each side. If such side lamps are fitted:

(a) it must not be possible for them to be illuminated unless the front and rear position lamps of the vehicle are illuminated; and
(b) they must be switched on and off by the manual operation of one switch which has no other function; but
(c) they must switch off automatically if the vehicle is moving forward at a speed of 10km/h or more.

Warning beacons

The lights of such warning beacons must flash between 60 and 240 times per minute at constant intervals. Their colour is prescribed by reg 11:

(1) Blue—a blue-and-white chequered light is permitted from a chequered domed lamp fitted to a police control vehicle and intended for use at the scene of an emergency; a blue light is permitted from a warning beacon or rear special warning lamp on an emergency vehicle, or on a special forces vehicle used in response to, or for training or practising to respond to, a national security emergency.
(2) Amber—permitted on road-clearance, refuse, or breakdown vehicles; those with an overall width exceeding 2.9m; road-service vehicles; special vehicles carrying

abnormal loads; on vehicles escorting an abnormal load; vehicles used for escort purposes other than escorting an abnormal load, while they are travelling at a speed not exceeding 25 mph; and vehicles of HM Customs and Excise (fuel-testing vehicles). Regulation 17 requires motor vehicles with four or more wheels, other than those first used before 1 January 1947, which have a maximum speed which does not exceed 25 mph, or any trailer which they are drawing, to be fitted with, and display, at least one amber warning beacon when being driven on an unrestricted dual carriageway road. The Regulations do not apply to such vehicles when merely crossing such a road in the quickest possible manner.

(3) Green—permitted to be used by registered medical practitioners.

(4) Yellow—permitted to be used by airport vehicles.

Only permitted vehicles may be fitted with a warning beacon of the appropriate type. However, where a permitted vehicle which is fitted with a warning lamp is used for a purpose other than that to which the permission relates, as where an ambulance is used to take children to school, there is no requirement that the lamp should be covered or removed.

Conspicuity markings

To the extent that a relevant goods vehicle (see p 598) is exempt from the requirement to be fitted with conspicuity markings, conspicuity markings may be fitted to the side or rear (as the case may be).

A vehicle, other than:

(a) a passenger vehicle (except a bus);

(b) a trailer with a maximum gross weight not exceeding 750 kg,

which is not a relevant goods vehicle may be fitted with conspicuity markings.

USE OF LAMPS, REFLECTORS, ETC

No red lights to the front

By reg 11(1), no vehicle may be fitted with a lamp or retro reflective material which is capable of showing a red light to the front. The important word is 'capable': the provision is not confined to the hours of darkness, nor is it necessary that the light is actually shown. The exceptions to the provision are obvious; they are (1) red-and-white chequered lamps or beacons fitted to a fire service vehicle for emergency purposes, (2) a red side marker lamp or a red side retro reflector, (3) red retro reflective material or a red side retro reflector fitted to any wheel or tyre of a pedal cycle (or its trailer or sidecar), a motor bicycle or motor-bicycle combination or an invalid carriage, and (4) a traffic sign attached to a vehicle.

Red lights to the rear

Regulation 11(2) provides that no vehicle may be fitted with a lamp or retro reflective material which is capable of showing a light to the rear other than a red light. The same comments apply to 'capable' as made above. The exceptions are plentiful and include direction indicators, reversing lamps, conspicuity markings, interior illumination, rear number plates, public service vehicle route indicators, retro reflective material or side retro reflectors fitted to bicycles (or their sidecar or trailer), motor bicycles (or motor-bicycle combinations), and invalid carriages, and the various emergency lights described above. Pedal cycles may show an amber light to the rear from lamps fitted to their pedals. Pedal cycles, their trailers or sidecars may show a white or amber light to the rear from lamps fitted to their wheels or tyres if the lamp is designed to emit primarily to the side.

Maintenance of lamps, reflectors, rear markings, and devices

Regulation 23(1) prohibits a person using, or causing or permitting to be used, on a road any vehicle unless every front position lamp, rear position lamp, headlamp, rear registration plate lamp, side marker lamp, end-outline marker lamp, rear fog lamp, retro reflector, and rear marking with which it is required to be fitted is in good working order and, in the case of a lamp, clean.

Regulation 23, therefore, requires correct maintenance of all of the lamps, reflectors, markings and devices with which a vehicle is *required* to be fitted. Moreover, reg 23 goes on to require that all stop lamps, running lamps, dim-dip devices, headlamp levelling device, hazard warning signalling devices, and direction indicators, even if they are in excess of those required by law, must be maintained at all times. However, reg 23 does not apply to rear fog lamps on a vehicle which is a part of a combination of vehicles, if any part of the combination is not required to have a rear fog lamp. Nor does reg 23 apply to a rear fog lamp on a vehicle drawing a trailer; nor to any defective lamp reflector, dim-dip device, or headlamp levelling device where the defect arose in the course of the journey on a vehicle in use in the daytime (ie between sunrise and sunset), or if arrangements have been made to remedy the defect with all reasonable expedition; nor, during the daytime, to a lamp, reflector or rear marking fitted to a combat vehicle.

Driving or parking without lights

Regulation 24 prohibits a person using, or causing or permitting to be used, a vehicle on a road between sunset and sunrise or (while the vehicle is in motion) during daytime hours in seriously reduced visibility unless every obligatory front position lamp, rear position lamp, rear registration plate lamp, side marker lamp and end-outline marker lamp is kept lit and unobscured. Except as indicated below, it also prohibits allowing (or causing or permitting to be allowed) a vehicle to remain at rest (ie parked) in similar circumstances between sunset and sunrise. There are variations to these provisions in respect of motorcycles and trailers not required to be fitted with front position lamps, since the prohibitions are not breached if there are fitted to these vehicles 'ad hoc' front position lamps.

Regulation 24 also provides that vehicles of certain classes may lawfully park between sunset and sunrise on roads subject to speed limits of 30 mph or less, without showing such lights. These are goods vehicles with gross vehicle weight not exceeding 2,500 kg, passenger vehicles other than buses, invalid carriages, and motorcycles, or pedal cycles (in either case with or without a sidecar). The exemption does not apply if the vehicle has a trailer attached or is carrying a load which requires lamps.

The exemption only applies to vehicles parked in:

(a) designated parking places on roads; or
(b) a lay-by which is clearly shown to be such; or
(c) elsewhere, provided, if the vehicle is parked on a one-way road, it is facing in the correct direction on either side of the road as close as possible to the kerb, or, if it

is parked on an ordinary road, it is properly parked and facing the correct way, and in either case no part of the vehicle is less than 10m from a junction with the road upon which it is parked, whether the junction is on the same side of the road or not. Where a curving kerb exists, the 'junction' begins where the kerb begins to curve.

The lighting requirements under reg 24 do not apply to a solo motorcycle or pedal cycle, which is being pushed close to the nearside kerb, a pedal cycle which is halted and waiting to proceed (eg at traffic lights) if it is kept to the nearside, or a vehicle which is parked at roadworks and properly outlined by lamps or traffic signs.

Use of headlamps

Regulation 25 provides that a person must not use, or cause or permit to be used, on a road a vehicle which is fitted with obligatory dipped beam headlamps unless every such lamp is kept lit:

(a) during the hours of darkness, except on a road which is a restricted one by virtue of a system of street lighting, when those lights are lit; and

(b) during daylight hours in seriously reduced visibility.

There are certain permitted variations; for example, motor vehicles with one obligatory dipped beam headlamp are exempt from the above requirement if a main beam or fog lamp is kept lit. Vehicles which are being towed, those which are parked, and those propelling snow ploughs are exempt from the above requirement. In addition, in the case of a motor vehicle other than a motor tricycle or motor-bicycle combination, a pair of main beam lamps may be used as an alternative or, in seriously reduced visibility, a pair of front fog lamps may be used, provided that they are not more than 400 mm from the outer edges of the vehicle.

Prohibition of particular use of lamps or devices

Regulation 27 provides that a person must not use, or cause or permit to be used, on a road any vehicle on which any lamp, hazard signal warning device or warning beacon of a specified type is used in the manner listed below.

Headlamps may not be used so as to cause undue dazzle or discomfort to other persons using the road and shall not be lit when a vehicle is parked. These prohibitions also apply to front fog lamps, with the addition of a prohibition upon use at any time other than in conditions of seriously reduced visibility.

The use of rear fog lamps is similarly restricted but the reference to undue dazzle or discomfort is predictably restricted to following drivers. They must also not be used when a vehicle, other than an emergency vehicle, is parked.

Reversing lamps must not be used for any purpose other than that of reversing. Similarly the use of hazard warning signal devices is restricted to warning road users of a temporary obstruction (or the presence of a school bus which is stationary and loading or unloading school children under 16) when the vehicle is at rest, or, on a motorway or unrestricted dual carriageway, to warn of a temporary obstruction ahead, or, in the case of a bus, to summon assistance for the driver or conductor or an inspector who is on the vehicle.

Blue lamps and special warning lamps may only be used at the scene of an emergency, or to indicate the urgency of the journey or the presence of a hazard on the road.

The use of amber lights is similarly restricted but they may also be used in connection with breakdowns or slow-moving vehicles on dual carriageways. Green lights may only be used whilst the vehicle is occupied by a registered medical practitioner and used in an emergency. Yellow light beacons may not be lit on a road. Work lamps must not dazzle, etc and must not be used other than for illuminating a working area, accident, breakdown, or works in the vicinity of the vehicle. No other lamp which is fitted to a vehicle may ever be used so as to cause undue dazzle or discomfort to other persons using the road.

Movement of lamps or reflectors and nature of light

Regulation 12 provides that no person shall use, or cause or permit to be used, on a road a vehicle fitted with a lamp or reflector capable of being moved (by swivelling, deflecting, or otherwise) while the vehicle is in motion. There are some obvious exceptions, eg dipping headlights, lamps which may be adjusted to compensate for loads, retracting headlamps, etc, amber pedal reflectors, and retro reflective material fitted to any wheel or tyre of pedal cycles or their trailer or sidecar.

Steady light

By regulation 13, the light shown by lamps covered by the Regulations must be a steady light, in that flashing lights are not permitted. There are exceptions for warning beacons prescribed for emergency vehicles, etc, and flashing front or rear position lamps fitted to pedal cycles (or their trailer or sidecar).

Overhanging or projecting loads

Regulation 21 prohibits a person using, or causing or permitting to be used, on a road:

(a) any trailer projecting laterally beyond the preceding vehicle in the combination; or
(b) any vehicle or combination of vehicles carrying a load or equipment,

which (in either case) does not comply with the following specifications:

(a) a trailer, which (or whose load) projects laterally more than 400 mm from the outermost part of the obligatory front position light on that side of the vehicle in front of it, must have white lights to the front which are not more than 400 mm from the outermost projection of the trailer (or, as the case may be, of the load);
(b) a vehicle whose load projects laterally more than 400 mm must have lights at the front and rear not more than 400 mm from the outermost projection of the load;
(c) a vehicle whose load projects more than 1m to the front or to the rear must have a front or rear lamp not more than 1m from the foremost or rearmost projection of the load (except that that distance is 2m in the case of an agricultural vehicle or a vehicle carrying a fire escape); or
(d) a vehicle carrying a load which obscures any obligatory lamps, reflector or rear markings must show a lamp, etc in the prescribed position.

These requirements only apply when the vehicle/trailer is being used between sunset and sunrise or in circumstances of reduced visibility, except that in relation to stop lights and direction indicators in (d) the requirement applies in all circumstances.

TESTING AND INSPECTION OF LIGHTING EQUIPMENT, ETC

Regulation 28 applies the provisions of reg 74 of the Road Vehicles (Construction and Use) Regulations 1986 to lighting equipment and reflectors with which a vehicle is *required* by the Regulations to be fitted. Regulation 74 empowers a constable in uniform to test and inspect lighting equipment on motor vehicles and trailers on any premises, subject to the consent of the owner of the premises.

OFFENCES

Contravention of, or failure to comply with, any regulation contained in the Road Vehicles Lighting Regulations 1989 is an offence contrary to RTA 1988, s 42 except that a breach which relates to a pedal cycle is an offence contrary to the Road Traffic Offenders Act 1988, s 91.

It is also an offence under RTA 1988, s 42 for a person to use on a road a motor vehicle or trailer which does not comply with these Regulations or to cause or permit a vehicle to be so used.

CHAPTER 13

Traffic Accidents

DUTY TO STOP, ETC

Where, owing to the presence of a mechanically propelled vehicle (MPV) on a road or other public place, an accident occurs by which:

(a) personal injury is caused to someone other than the driver of that MPV; or
(b) damage is caused to a vehicle other than that MPV or a trailer drawn by it, or to an animal other than an animal in or on that vehicle or a trailer drawn by it, or to any other property constructed on, fixed to, growing in or otherwise forming part of the land on which the road or other public place in question is situated or land adjacent to such land (Road Traffic Act 1988 (RTA 1988), s 170(1)),

the driver of the MPV is required by RTA 1988, s 170(2) to stop and, if required to do so by any person having reasonable grounds for so requiring, give his name and address, and also the name and address of the owner and the identification marks of the vehicle. If an accident might occur owing to the presence of two or more vehicles on a road, the driver of each vehicle must stop, etc if the consequences set out above occur.

The driver of a MPV, owing to whose presence on a road or other public place an accident occurs, is not obliged by RTA 1988, s 170 (or any other provision) to stop, etc if:

(a) no one (besides that driver) is injured; and
(b) no vehicle (besides that vehicle or its trailer) is damaged; and
(c) no animal (other than one in that vehicle or its trailer) is injured; and
(d) no property forming part, etc of the road or land adjacent to it is damaged.

Section 170 places duties only upon the *drivers of MPVs*; the rider of a pedal cycle has no obligations to stop, etc under it (or any other provision).

An accident must have occurred owing to the presence of a motor vehicle on a road or other public place

The terms 'MPV' and 'road' have already been discussed in Chapter 9 (pp 342 and 343). As to 'public place', see p 531.

The requirement that the *accident* must have occurred *owing to the presence* of a MPV on a road or other public place involves the following additional points. First, if the words 'owing to the presence' were to be given their widest possible meaning they would embrace circumstances in which a person, who had been allowed to cross a road by the courtesy of a driver who had stopped to allow him to do so, tripped over the kerb on turning to acknowledge this courtesy. This would clearly be ridiculous. The rule is, therefore, that there must be a direct causal connection between the presence of the MPV and the occurrence of the accident. If the driver of a vehicle brakes sharply on approaching a pedestrian who is crossing the road and the noise of that braking so startles the pedestrian that he falls and is injured, there is a direct causal connection between the vehicle and the accident. Likewise, if a cyclist collides with a motor car waiting at traffic lights, it is reasonable to accept that the accident occurred because the vehicle was on the road. There is a direct causal connection between the presence of the vehicle and the accident in that the cyclist was in contact with it.

The second point is the meaning of the word 'accident'. A divisional court has held that that word bears its ordinary popular meaning (as opposed to any technical meaning) and that the question is whether an ordinary person would say that an accident has occurred. It also held that there can be an accident even though part of the chain of events leading to the injury or damage was a deliberate act on someone's part. For the obligations in s 170 to apply to the driver of a MPV, it is not necessary that his vehicle is involved in an accident in the sense that it is in collision. For example, if D, the driver of a motor car, carelessly drives it across a junction with a major road, causing vehicles on the major road to take avoiding action which causes them to collide with each other, D certainly causes that accident although he is not involved in the collision. In such a case, the obligations in s 170 will have to be discharged by D, as well as by the drivers of the other motor vehicles.

The accident must have caused one of the specified consequences

As we have seen, these specified consequences are:
(1) Personal injury to a person *other than the driver* of the MPV owing to whose presence on a road or other public place the accident occurred.

   'Injury' presumably bears its ordinary meaning and, as such, includes cases of shock. It is irrelevant whether the person injured is a passenger in the driver's vehicle, the driver or a passenger in another vehicle, or someone else.
(2) Damage to a vehicle *other than the MPV, or its trailer*, owing to whose presence on a road or other public place the accident occurred.

   The term 'vehicle' should be given its dictionary meaning (ie carriage, cart, or other conveyance by land) so as to include all types of wheeled vehicles, such as fairy cycles, prams or barrows, but not, it is submitted, skateboards or roller skates, since they are not produced for some form of conveyance in a general sense.
(3) Damage to any animal *other than an animal in or on the MPV, or its trailer*, owing to whose presence on a road or other public place the accident occurred.

   'Animal' means any horse, cattle, ass, mule, sheep, pig, goat, or dog. Poultry are not included, nor are cats (no matter how valuable they may be).
(4) Damage to any other property constructed on, fixed to, growing in or otherwise forming part of the land on which the road or other public place in question is situated or land adjacent thereto.

   Examples of such property are buildings, traffic signs, street lamps, fences, hedges and trees, provided they 'form part' of the land on which the road is situated or of land adjacent thereto. By way of example, if a motor car collides with a traffic bollard causing damage to it, it causes damage to property which is either constructed on or fixed to land on which the road or other public place is situated or land adjacent thereto. It will be a question of fact to be determined by the justices whether or not property which is damaged forms part of, or is adjacent to, such land. If a car collides with the petrol pumps in a filling station adjacent to the road there is little doubt that a court would consider the petrol pumps to be on land adjacent to land on which a road is situated. Should damage be occasioned to a dwelling house which is immediately at the roadside, that house is undoubtedly constructed on land which is at least adjacent to land on which the road is situated.

It is probable that, even if a garden exists at the front of the house, justices would consider that the house was constructed on land adjacent to the road. If, because of the presence on the road or other public place of a motor car, an accident occurs and the motor car leaves the road or other public place and is driven through a fence into a field of corn, the accident certainly causes damage to both the fence and the crops which are on land adjacent to the road.

The driver of the motor vehicle must stop and, if required by a person having reasonable grounds for so requiring, must give certain information

The term '*driver*' means the person who takes the vehicle out on a road; he remains its 'driver' until that particular journey is over or someone replaces him as 'driver'. Someone who parks his car, in order to post a letter or for some other purpose of his own, can be found to have remained its driver, because he is still en route on a journey, notwithstanding that an accident is caused by a passenger releasing the car's handbrake; the passenger lacks sufficient control to have replaced him as the driver. On the other hand, RTA 1988, s 170 would not apply if the accident was caused by the car's presence on the road or other public place after he had parked it outside his place of work at the end of his journey.

The obligation to stop arises immediately the accident occurs. Thus, in one case, where a bus driver had injured a passenger by braking sharply and had driven on to a rendezvous with an ambulance which he had arranged by radio, a divisional court held that he had failed to stop as required by s 170. Because the duty to stop is an immediate one, a driver who leaves the scene and later returns to it does not 'stop' for the purpose of s 170.

The term 'stop' means that the driver should stop and remain where he has stopped for such a period of time as in the circumstances will provide a sufficient period of time to enable persons who have reasonable grounds for so doing to require of him directly and personally the information which the driver may be required to supply. In determining what that period should be, particular regard should be paid to the character of the road or the place where the accident occurred. The duty is that of the driver and his responsibilities cannot be discharged by some other person whom he leaves at the scene. The driver must remain sufficiently near to the vehicle throughout this period of time to allow any person to make the requests permitted by the section. Common sense must be applied when considering the duty to stop. If a driver collides with a vehicle parked in a deserted country lane, it would be unreasonable to expect him to remain there indefinitely. The reasonable approach would be to consider whether his 'stop' was sufficient to allow any person who was nearby and aware of the accident to make such a request. In the case of a stationary vehicle, its driver cannot stop in the physical sense, but must 'stop at the scene' for sufficient time to permit persons to request information.

As already implied, the duty to stop does not cast on the driver the duty to go and seek persons to whom to give the above information.

Section 170 also requires *the driver to provide certain information if required so to do by 'any person having reasonable grounds for so requiring'*. Such a person will usually be the driver of any other vehicle involved in the accident, a person injured, or the owner of property or of an animal. However, there are other persons who might quite reasonably demand information from the driver of a MPV; for example, a relative or friend of a person who has been injured, or a person who witnessed the accident and who is a friend of the owner of damaged property. It will be a matter for the courts to determine in cases of doubt. They may well look differently upon a demand made by a 'nosey parker' as opposed to one made by some person who quite genuinely had the other party's interests at heart.

If the requirement is made by a person having reasonable grounds, s 170 obliges the driver to give:

(a) his name and address;
(b) the name and address of the owner of the vehicle; and
(c) the identification mark of the vehicle.

Section 170 can be satisfied by giving an address other than a home address, for example the address of the driver's solicitor or the driver's business address, provided the driver can be contacted via that address reasonably swiftly and easily.

This obligation is absolute in the sense that, if the requirement is made by a person having reasonable grounds to make it, the driver must supply this information. However, if this information is supplied at the scene the obligations of the driver cease and there is no need to report the accident to the police. (If injury to some person is occasioned there is also a need to produce evidence of insurance; see p 510)

DUTY TO REPORT TO THE POLICE

RTA 1988, s 170(3) deals with a driver's obligation to report an accident to the police. Its wording is important: if for any reason the driver of the MPV does not give his *name and address* as required above, he must report the accident. If a driver gives his name and address to a person reasonably requiring information, but refuses to give the name and address of the owner or the identification mark of the vehicle, he will not be obliged to report the accident to the police, although he will commit an offence under s 170 in consequence of his refusal to give the other information.

The obligation to report an accident to the police arises whenever the driver has not given his name and address at the scene of the accident, whether or not he was requested to do so by anyone there (and indeed, even though he was known personally to any person with reasonable grounds to request his name and address). Thus, a divisional court has held, the obligation to report arises even though the driver could not have given his name and address at the scene of the accident because he was unconscious throughout the time he was there. The obligation is not negated by the fact that police are in attendance at the scene of an accident from which an unconscious driver is taken to hospital. Second, the obligation to report is to do so at a police station or to a constable as soon as reasonably practicable and, in any case, within 24 hours of the occurrence of the accident and it can only be performed officially and personally; telling a friend who is a police officer will not do, nor will a telephone message to a police station.

The obligation to report, of a driver who does not give his name and address at the scene of the accident, is subject to the following rules as to time. The driver must report the accident at a police station or to a constable 'as soon as practicable and, in any case, within 24 hours'. 24 hours is, therefore, the maximum period in which the report may be made, so that if the driver does not report until 24 hours or more have elapsed since the accident he is necessarily in breach of his obligation under s 170. Even if the report is made within 24 hours, the driver will nevertheless be in breach of his obligation if he has not made it 'as soon as reasonably practicable'. What is 'reasonably practicable' is a matter for the court to decide on in the particular circumstances. If a driver who is not seeking urgent medical attention drives from the scene of an accident and past a police station, in order to go to his home, and only reports the accident 20 hours later, a court is unlikely to find that he reported the accident as soon as reasonably practicable. On the other hand, in a case where a motorist's car left the road and collided, causing damage, at 11 pm and the motorist left his address in his car at the scene and was interviewed by the police at 8.30 am the next day (at which point of time he reported the accident), the divisional court held that the justices were entitled to conclude that in the circumstances there had been no failure to report as soon as reasonably practicable.

OFFENCES

A person who fails to comply with any requirement of RTA 1988, s 170(2) or (3) commits an offence against s 170(4). In fact, if he fails to stop (or to give his name and address, etc), contrary to s 170(2), and also fails to report the accident to the police, contrary to s 170(3), he commits two offences. The first offence can be committed in two ways, either by failing to stop *or* having stopped, failing to provide the information which is required to be given by a person with reasonable grounds; neither failure is excused by a subsequent report to the police.

A person charged with the first offence under s 170(4) has a defence if he proves that he did not know that an accident had occurred. However, in the case of the second offence, if, although unaware of the accident at the time of it, he subsequently becomes aware of it within the 24-hour period and fails to report it to the police, he can be convicted of that offence since he will be obliged to report the accident and his failure at that time will be with knowledge of the accident.

INJURY ACCIDENTS: REQUIREMENT TO PRODUCE INSURANCE

RTA 1988, s 170(5) provides that if, in the case of a *personal injury* accident to which s 170 applies, the driver of the motor vehicle does not at the time of the accident produce a certificate of insurance or security, or other evidence prescribed by regulations:

(a) to a constable; or
(b) to some person who, having reasonable grounds for so doing, has requested him to produce it,

the driver must report the accident and produce such a certificate or other evidence. It is, of course, not sufficient to wave a certificate of insurance in front of the eyes of a person requesting such information; it must be produced in the sense that the person is able to satisfy himself that an effective insurance is in force.

As in the case of the duty to report an accident under s 170(3), the driver must report the accident (and produce his insurance certificate, etc) at a police station or to a constable and must do so as soon as reasonably practicable, within 24 hours. It is an offence, contrary to s 170(7), to fail to do so. However, the offence is subject to the proviso that a person is not to be convicted of it by reason *only* of a failure to produce a certificate, etc if, within seven days after the accident, the certificate, etc is produced at the police station specified by him when the accident was reported.

CHAPTER 14

Driving Offences

INTRODUCTION

Statutory offences were created in the nineteenth century to deal with carriages and the like. Although these provisions were enacted before the days of mechanically propelled vehicles, they can be applied to such vehicles. This is important in relation to the third provision next mentioned. The Highways Act 1835 prohibits certain acts in relation to 'carriages', and the Town Police Clauses Act 1847, s 28 deals with the furious driving in a street of any horse or carriage. The Offences Against the Person Act 1861, s 35 still punishes as an offence triable only on indictment the causing of bodily harm by wanton or furious driving on a road or otherwise by a person having charge of a carriage or vehicle; this charge can be useful in circumstances in which the negligent driving of a mechanically propelled vehicle did not take place on a road or other public place. However, for all practical purposes, driving offences that are committed in relation to mechanically propelled vehicles are governed by the Road Traffic Act 1988 (RTA 1988). Those offences contain a number of general terms, which are defined below or elsewhere in this book.

'Driving'

The essence of 'driving' is the use of the driver's controls (or at least one of them) in order to control the movement of the vehicle, however that movement is produced, provided that what occurs can in any sense be regarded as 'driving'. Thus, a person who releases the handbrake and 'coasts' downhill in a car is 'driving' it (and this is so even though the steering is locked). A person who propels a moped by 'paddling' with his feet, sitting astride it and steering it, is driving it. A person in the driving seat of a car which is being towed is driving if he has the ability to control its movements by means of the brakes or steering. This is so even if the vehicle is attached by means of a rigid tow bar which is attached to the towing vehicle by means of a ball hitch, and to the vehicle being drawn by means of a shackle. Such a combination leaves the person holding the steering wheel of the towed vehicle with a substantial potential for directional control because he is able (indeed he is required) to keep the towed vehicle in line with the towing vehicle by means of the steering wheel. In such a case it would be irrelevant that the towed vehicle does not have any brakes; directional control through steering is enough. On the other hand, a person in the driving seat of a vehicle on a fixed tow is not driving it, since he cannot control its movements by the use of any of the driver's controls. Nor is a person who is pushing a car and steering it with his hand through the window driving it because this cannot in any sense be described as driving.

Two people may be driving a vehicle at the same time. For example, if A who is in the driving seat operates the clutch and brakes and gear shift but allows his passenger, B, to steer the vehicle, both A and B are driving.

The Road Traffic Act 1988 (RTA 1988), s 192 provides that, except for the purposes of the offence of causing death by dangerous driving, where a separate person acts as steersman of a motor vehicle he is driving the vehicle (as well as any other person engaged in driving it). This covers the case where one person is primarily concerned with the propulsion of the vehicle and another acts as its steersman. It is relevant only in the case of traction engines and the like.

A limited company cannot be convicted of an offence of driving physically committed by one of its employees; nor can any other employer.

It must be proved that the person alleged to have been driving was driving at the time of the alleged offence. Difficulties in this respect have arisen in cases in which a witness has reported an incident to a police officer and at the same time has provided, from memory, the registration mark of the vehicle. Even with the modern rules about hearsay evidence, there may be problems if the officer seeks to say in evidence that he was told that the number of the car involved in the incident was that given by the witness. In such cases, it would be good practice for the officer to record the number given to him in his notebook and to have the witness endorse the entry as being correct and sign it. Such a record then becomes 'joint' and may be referred to by either. The witness's statement should also include the fact that he gave that particular number to the officer and that it was the number of the vehicle seen on that occasion.

Other terms

Mechanically propelled vehicle   See p 342.

Motor vehicle   See p 342.

Road   See p 343.

Public place   For discussion as to what may or may not be a public place, in particular circumstances, see p 531.

DANGEROUS DRIVING, CAUSING DEATH OR SERIOUS INJURY BY DANGEROUS DRIVING

Dangerous driving

RTA 1988, s 2 provides that it is an offence for a person to drive a mechanically propelled vehicle dangerously on a road or other public place. The offence is an indictable (either way) offence.

The ways in which driving may be dangerous are set out in RTA 1988, s 2A.

Dangerous manner

RTA 1988, s 2A(1) provides that a person is to be regarded as driving dangerously if:

(a) the way that he drives falls far below what would be expected of a competent and careful driver; and

(b) it would be obvious to a competent and careful driver that driving in that way would be dangerous.

This test in RTA 1988, s 2A(1) is concerned with whether the manner of D's driving falls *far* below what would be expected of a careful and competent driver in circumstances where it would be obvious to a competent and careful driver that driving in that way would be dangerous. The presence of the word '*far*' separates offences of dangerous driving from those which should more appropriately be charged as careless driving.

It would be no defence that D was doing his incompetent best, nor that he did not intend to drive dangerously. This was held by the Court of Appeal in a case where a bus driver unintentionally pressed the accelerator when he meant to press the brake; as a result the bus travelled across a pedestrian island and pedestrians were killed. The court held that the driver's lack of an intention to drive dangerously was no defence.

The objective standards to be applied will vary according to the prevailing conditions and to exceptional circumstances which might have existed. In fog, the competent and careful driver would drive in a manner quite different from that which he would adopt in dry, clear conditions. Whilst driving at a speed of 70 mph in an area restricted to 30 mph might be described as dangerous, it would not often be so on a dual carriageway. If it occurred in the middle of the night when the road was not being used by any other person or vehicle, such driving in a restricted area might not be 'dangerous', whilst driving at that speed on a dual carriageway which is restricted by road works might be.

The opinion of witnesses as to whether or not D drove dangerously is, of course, inadmissible.

Once it has been established that the actual driving fell far below standards of a competent and careful driver, it becomes necessary to consider whether or not it would be 'obvious' to a competent and careful driver that such driving would be dangerous. Section 2A(3) states that 'dangerous' refers to danger either of injury to any person or of serious damage to property. It also states that, for the purpose of s 2A(1) and (2) (see under 'Dangerous state of the vehicle'), in determining what would be expected of, or obvious to, a competent and careful driver in a particular case, regard must be had not only to the circumstances of which he could be expected to be aware but also to any circumstances shown to have been within the defendant's knowledge. Regard must not be had to any circumstance which D wrongly believed to exist. Consequently, it has been held that, where a police officer pursued a stolen car at speed through traffic lights at red, his mistaken belief that the junction was being controlled by other officers (so that he could cross safely) was irrelevant to the issue of dangerous driving. The Court of Appeal has held that D's special skill as a driver (eg D had taken a police advanced driving course) is an irrelevant consideration when considering whether driving was dangerous: to take it into account would be inconsistent with the objective test of the competent and careful driver.

A breach of the Highway Code does not necessarily mean that an offence has been committed, but the Code's provisions can be considered by a jury or magistrates, provided that it is clearly explained that they do not provide a 'standard'.

Dangerous state of the vehicle

The second way in which driving may be dangerous is provided by RTA 1988, s 2A(2) which provides that a person is also to be regarded as driving dangerously if it would be obvious to a competent and careful driver that driving the vehicle in its current state would be 'dangerous' (in the sense defined by s 2A(3)). In determining the state of the vehicle, regard may be had to anything carried on or in it, and the manner in which it is attached or carried.

Because the danger involved in driving the vehicle in its current state must be obvious, the offence will not be committed if the defect involved is a latent one. A danger is 'obvious' in this context only if it could be seen or realised at first glance by a competent and careful driver. It is not enough that such a driver would have taken steps to check out whether the vehicle was in a condition which was not dangerous, and by doing so would have discovered the defect, perhaps by examining the underside of the vehicle.

'Current state' in s 2A(2) implies a state different from the original or manufactured state. Thus, where the alleged danger relates solely to something inherent in the original design of the vehicle (eg spikes forming part of a grab unit at the front of an agricultural vehicle) dangerous driving is not committed. It would be different if the original, unaltered state made the *manner* of the driving dangerous.

As with s 2A(1), in determining what would be obvious to a competent and careful driver, regard must be had not only to the circumstances of which he could be expected to be aware but also to any circumstances shown to have been within D's knowledge. Apart from such knowledge, the state of D's mind is irrelevant.

Driving in a dangerously defective state through intoxication or consumption of drugs

Evidence of consumption of alcohol or drugs cannot by itself establish the fact that a driver has committed an offence of dangerous driving. The offence is concerned with the dangerous nature of the driving, not with the dangerous nature of the driver due to drink. The Court of Appeal has held that, while evidence of alcohol consumption is admissible in respect of an offence of dangerous driving if the amount of alcohol is proved or admitted, even though the driver's blood alcohol level is below the legal limit, it cannot be conclusive. The consumption of a drug, even if the amount is unquantified, has been held by the Court of Appeal to be admissible in respect of such an offence, although it cannot be conclusive. In either case, there must be evidence that the vehicle was driven dangerously within the definition in RTA 1988, s 2A.

Dangerous cycling

A person who rides a bicycle or tricycle dangerously on a road commits a separate and less serious offence contrary to RTA 1988, s 28. A person is to be regarded as riding dangerously if he rides in a *manner* which equates to the manner of driving described above.

Causing death by dangerous driving

RTA 1988, s 1 provides that a person who causes the death of another person by driving a mechanically propelled vehicle dangerously on a road or other public place is guilty of an offence. The offence is triable only on indictment.

Proof of the offence requires proof that D drove a mechanically propelled vehicle on a road or other public place dangerously (in the sense just explained) and that the dangerous driving caused the death of another person (including someone else in D's vehicle).

It is not necessary to show that the dangerous driving was the sole cause of death, since it is sufficient that it is a more than minimal cause. An example is a case where two drivers were engaged in a high-speed chase and one of them was killed when she collided with an oncoming car; the other driver was convicted of this offence. His dangerous driving had been a cause of the death of the first driver and that 'cause' had been more than 'slight or trifling', ie more than minimal. By way of a further example, if a driver deliberately accelerates towards people who are crossing at a pedestrian crossing and knocks down one of them, who later dies, he can be convicted of causing that death by dangerous driving. It will not assist him to allege that the victim was not seriously injured and would not have died if a heart condition from which he suffered had not been aggravated by the shock. His driving is a cause of that death and it is certainly not a minimal cause in such circumstances.

No mens rea need be proved as to the risk of death resulting from the dangerous driving; it follows that it is irrelevant that the risk in question was unforeseen or unforeseeable, as would be the case where the only obvious risk was of damage to property.

It is not necessary that the driver should have been driving the vehicle (ie it need not have been in motion) at the time that the fatal injury was caused. It is enough that there has been dangerous driving by the driver and that this driving is more than a minimal cause of death. This is shown by a case where a driver took his lorry on to a motorway after having been warned that his brake air-pressure gauges were not working (which constituted dangerous driving), and the handbrake system was activated due to loss of air pressure. The trailer unit blocked the nearside lane of the motorway. Some 12 minutes later a lorry collided with it and the driver of that vehicle was killed. The Court of Appeal held that the consequences of dangerous driving are capable of outlasting the time the driver spends at the wheel. It held that the dangerous driving must have played a part, not simply in creating the occasion of the fatal accident, but in bringing it about. On the facts the consequences of the dangerous driving were not 'spent' and too remote from the accident, and were more than a minimal cause of the death. As a result the driver's conviction for causing death by dangerous driving was upheld.

Causing death by dangerous driving is a serious offence and it is important that the evidence offered to a court is well presented. Identification of the person fatally injured is of extreme importance. Medical evidence will be given at the Crown Court concerning the cause of death of the person injured in the accident. It is essential that a police officer, who was at the scene of the accident and saw the injured person, identifies that person to the pathologist who carries out the post mortem examination. In the absence of such evidence, there is nothing to connect the person upon whom the post mortem examination was carried out with the person injured in the accident. In addition, a careful note must be made of everything observed at the scene of the accident at the particular time at which it occurred. Whether driving can be described as dangerous will often depend upon the particular circumstances existing at the time, such as the state of street lighting and the nature and volume of traffic at that time of day. All fatal traffic accidents must be handled carefully and the possibility of the need for forensic evidence should be considered. There is little purpose in tracing a damaged vehicle suspected of having been involved in a fatal accident if samples of glass, paint, and other vehicle debris were not collected at the scene at the time of the accident.

The ingredients of the offences of manslaughter by gross negligence and of causing death by dangerous driving (a less serious offence in terms of punishment) are similar. CPS policy is to charge manslaughter only if the evidence shows a very high degree of risk, making the case one of the utmost gravity.

Causing serious injury by dangerous driving

A person commits an offence under RTA 1988, s 1A if he causes serious injury to another person by driving a mechanically propelled vehicle dangerously on a road or other public place. 'Serious' injury means physical harm which amounts to grievous bodily harm for the purposes of the Offences against the Person Act 1861 (p 681). The offence under s 1A is an indictable (either way) offence.

CARELESS OR INCONSIDERATE DRIVING, CAUSING DEATH BY CARELESS OR INCONSIDERATE DRIVING

Offences of careless driving

RTA 1988, s 3 creates two separate offences by providing that if a person drives a mechanically propelled vehicle on a road or other public place without due care and attention, or without reasonable consideration for other persons using the road or place, he is guilty of an offence. The level of 'bad' driving which must be proved in a charge of careless or inconsiderate driving is considerably less than that required in cases of dangerous driving.

Driving without due care and attention

RTA 1988, s 3ZA provides that a person is to be regarded as driving 'without due care and attention' if (and only if) the way he drives falls below what would be expected of a competent and careful driver. In determining what would be expected of a competent and careful driver in a particular case, regard must be had not only to the circumstances of which he could be expected to be aware but also to any circumstances shown to have been within the knowledge of the defendant (D). The definition of driving without due care and attention differs from that relating to dangerous driving in relation to the extent to which D's driving falls below the standard of a competent and careful driver. While dangerous driving requires a fall 'far' below what would be expected of a competent and careful driver, simply 'falling below' that standard, however marginally, suffices for careless driving.

The standard is an objective standard, impersonal and universal, fixed in relation to the safety of the other users of the highway. It is in no way related to the degree of proficiency or degree of experience attained by the individual driver, and it is unaffected by the fact that the driver was driving to an emergency.

Bearing in mind the objective approach to be applied, it is no defence that, as a learner, the driver was doing his best, if that best falls short of the standard which might be expected from a competent and careful driver. If a learner driver applies the accelerator instead of the footbrake and causes an accident he is guilty of driving without due care and attention. There is only one standard of competence and his actions fall short of it. In circumstances where a competent driver wears shoes with smooth leather soles and this causes his foot to slip from the brake pedal, the court will have to consider whether in the circumstances a competent and careful driver would have been aware of the possibility of this happening and would not have driven the car with such shoes. In the same way, it is essential to keep in mind that experienced drivers or specially trained drivers do not in consequence of that experience or training owe some higher standard of care. For example, the driver of a police vehicle owes the ordinary standard of care to other persons on the road.

There is no limit to the forms which this offence may take. If a driver gives false direction signals this amounts to driving without due care and attention since it falls below the standard of a competent and careful driver in the circumstances because such a driver, realising the possible risks of deluding other road users as to the intended movements of his vehicle, would ensure that he did not give false signals. There are numerous circumstances in which this offence is quite clearly committed. Road markings at the junctions of roads frequently indicate that no vehicle shall pass the line markings in a side street in circumstances which will impede other traffic on the main road. If a collision occurs because a vehicle emerges from such a side street, having passed over the road markings, this provides clear proof that the driver was not paying sufficient attention.

In applying the appropriate test as to whether D has driven without due care and attention, all the circumstances of the case can be considered, including evidence that D had been affected by drink or that D had taken such an amount of drink as would be likely to affect a driver, since such evidence may indicate a lack of due care on D's part in driving as he did.

Failure to observe a provision of the Highway Code does not of itself establish driving without due care and attention, but any such failure may be relied on as evidence of it.

In some cases the facts are such that, unless D offers some explanation consistent with him having taken due care, which is not disproved, the only proper inference is careless driving, in which case the justices must convict him (and if they do not a divisional court will order them to do so).

Driving without reasonable consideration

RTA 1988, s 3ZA provides that a person is to be regarded as driving without reasonable consideration for other persons only if those persons are inconvenienced by his driving. Those persons must be shown to have been inconvenienced. Thus, a driver may deliberately drive at speed through a pool of water, but will only commit this offence if other persons were either dampened or forced to flee.

Once again, an objective test should be applied as to whether particular forms of driving are carried out without reasonable consideration for other persons using the road or place. Thus, the question is whether D drove without showing the consideration to other road users which would be shown by a considerate driver. The driver who occupies the fast lane of a motorway, or even the outside lane of a dual carriageway, in circumstances in which there is nothing to prevent him from regaining the nearside lane, is unreasonably interfering with the progress of other drivers. The irresponsible use of full-beam headlamps may also amount to driving without reasonable consideration. A considerate driver certainly does not drive towards opposing traffic in this manner. A person may drive without reasonable consideration for other persons using the road even where his lack of consideration is to his own passenger.

A point about both offences

Because RTA 1988, s 3 creates two offences, an information or written charge alleging both alternatives is likely to fail for duplicity. It is sufficient to allege that a person drove without due care and attention at a particular time or place, or, as the case may be, to allege that he drove without reasonable consideration at a time and place, since it is not necessary to specify the nature of his negligence in the information or written charge.

Vehicle used in manner causing alarm, distress or annoyance

The Police Reform Act 2002 (PRA 2002), s 59(1) provides that, where a constable in uniform has reasonable grounds for believing that a mechanically propelled vehicle (MPV) *is being used* in a manner which contravenes RTA 1988, s 3 (careless or inconsiderate driving) and which is causing, or is likely to cause, alarm, distress, or annoyance to members of the public, he has the powers under PRA 2002, s 59(3) set out below.

A constable in uniform additionally has the powers under s 59(3) where he has reasonable grounds for believing that a MPV *has been used* on any occasion in a manner falling within PRA 2002, s 59(1).

The powers set out in s 59(3) are:

(a) if the vehicle is moving, to order the person driving it to stop it;
(b) to seize and remove the vehicle;
(c) for the purposes of exercising a power falling within (a) or (b), to enter any premises other than a 'dwelling house', which term does not include any garage or other structure occupied with the dwelling house, or any land appurtenant to the dwelling house, on which he has reasonable grounds for believing the vehicle to be;
(d) to use reasonable force, if necessary, in the exercise of any power conferred by (a)–(c).

Section 59(4) provides that the power of seizure may not be exercised unless:

(a) the constable has warned the person appearing to him to be the person whose use falls within s 59(1) that he will seize the vehicle if that use continues or is repeated; and
(b) it appears to him that the use has continued or been repeated after the warning.

However, a warning need not be given if:

(a) the circumstances make it impracticable;
(b) the constable has already on that occasion given a warning under s 59(4) in respect of any use of that vehicle or of another MPV by that person or any other person;
(c) the constable has reasonable grounds for believing that such a warning has been given on that occasion otherwise than by him; or
(d) the constable has reasonable grounds for believing that the person whose use of that MPV on that occasion would justify the seizure is a person to whom a warning has been given (whether or not by that constable or in respect of the same vehicle or the same or a similar use) on a previous occasion in the previous 12 months.

It is an offence under s 59(6) to fail to comply with an order under s 59(3) to stop a MPV.

The Police (Retention and Disposal of Motor Vehicles) Regulations 2002 provide for the safe keeping, retention, release and disposal of a vehicle seized under s 59(3). They provide that a person who would otherwise be liable to charges is not liable to pay if the use which caused the seizure was not a use by him and he did not know of the use of the vehicle in the manner which led to its seizure, had not consented to its use in that manner and could not, by the taking of reasonable steps, have prevented its use in that manner.

These powers also apply where a uniformed constable reasonably believes that an offence against RTA 1988, s 34 (prohibition of off-road driving, see p 429) has been committed, and that the manner in which the vehicle is being used is causing, or is likely to cause, alarm, distress, or annoyance to members of the public.

Causing death by careless or inconsiderate driving

RTA 1988, s 2B provides that a person who causes the death of another person by driving a mechanically propelled vehicle on a road or other public place without due care and attention, or without reasonable consideration for other persons using the road or place, is guilty of an offence. The offence is an indictable (either way) offence. It is not necessary to show that the careless driving was the sole cause, since it is sufficient that it is a more than minimal cause. No mens rea need be proved as to the risk of death resulting from the careless driving; it follows that it is irrelevant that the risk in question was unforeseen or unforeseeable. These points also apply to the next offences and to the offence under RTA 1988, s 3ZB on p 520.

Causing death by careless driving when under the influence of drink or drugs

RTA 1988, s 3A(1) provides that it is an offence for a person to cause the death of another person by driving a mechanically propelled vehicle on a road or other public place without due care and attention, or without reasonable consideration for other persons using the road or place, where he:

(a) is, at the time when he is driving, unfit to drive through drink or drugs; or
(b) has consumed so much alcohol that the proportion of it in his breath, blood, or urine at that time exceeds the prescribed limit;
(c) is, within 18 hours after that time, required under s 7 to provide a specimen, but without reasonable cause fails to provide it; or
(d) is required by a constable to give his permission for a laboratory test of a specimen of blood taken from him under s 7A, but without reasonable excuse, fails to do so.

The offence is triable only on indictment.

In essence, to be guilty of an offence under RTA 1988, s 3A(1), D must be proved to have committed one or other of the offences of careless driving and thereby killed another, and to fall within one of the drink/drive elements in (a)–(d) above.

The term 'unfit to drive through drink or drugs' is explained in Chapter 15, as are other references to drink or drugs, prescribed limits, etc. Other matters concerned with the evidential linking of the driver to the person who received fatal injuries are discussed above.

Despite the wording of RTA 1988, s 3A(1), the offences at (b), (c), and (d), which are based upon the consumption of alcohol in excess of the prescribed limit and upon failure within the specified circumstances to provide a specimen or permit its analysis, apply only to persons driving motor vehicles as opposed to mechanically propelled vehicles.

Careless cycling

There are separate, and less serious, offences, contrary to RTA 1988, s 29, of riding a bicycle or tricycle on a road without due care and attention, or without reasonable consideration for other persons using the road.

DEFENCES TO OFFENCES INVOLVING DANGEROUS OR CARELESS DRIVING

Duress of circumstances and duress by threats

Where a person is compelled to drive dangerously or carelessly in order to avoid the threat of death or serious injury to himself or some other person, as where his car is being hotly pursued by an armed gang or where his car has been hijacked by an armed gang who order him to outdistance a pursuing police car, he may have the defence of duress of circumstances or of duress by threats. The requirements of these defences are set out on p 9.

Unless the defence of duress of circumstances applies, police officers, firefighters, and ambulance drivers may not use the emergency nature of their mission as a defence to a charge of dangerous or careless driving, as they owe the same duty of care to the public at all times.

Automatism

Generally, as in the case of other offences, it is a defence that D was in a state of automatism (see p 8). Consequently, a driver who suffers a completely unexpected epileptic fit and suffers a total loss of control over his limbs, or who is overcome by a swarm of bees and prevented from exercising any directional control over the vehicle cannot be convicted of dangerous or careless driving.

However, by way of *exception*, it must be remembered that automatism does not excuse a person from liability for the crimes discussed in this chapter if his automatism resulted from his voluntary intoxication. Nor will automatism excuse such a person if, before he became an automaton, he appreciated the risk that something which he did or failed to do was likely to make him unpredictable or uncontrollable with the result that he might endanger others (as opposed to simply becoming an automaton) and he deliberately ran the risk or otherwise disregarded it.

Moreover, by way of further *exception*, a defendant who, for example, falls asleep at the wheel or goes into a hypoglycaemic coma at the wheel can be convicted of dangerous or careless driving under the ordinary principles of liability, not in relation to the time when he was an automaton but in relation to the time when he realised or should have realised that he was about to become unconscious and should have stopped driving. The reason is clear: to drive in such a case falls below the standard of a reasonable and prudent driver (who would have stopped).

Mechanical defect

The fact that the driving complained of was due to the sudden mechanical failure of an essential part of a vehicle can provide a defence to charges of dangerous or careless driving, provided that the defect was not known by D to exist prior to the occurrence which forms the basis of the charge, and was not such that it should have been discovered by a reasonably prudent driver. Thus, where a driver knew that the brakes of his vehicle pulled to the off-side but nevertheless drove it, the defence of mechanical defect was held not to be open to him.

Like the defence of automatism, the essence of this defence is that the dangerous situation was caused by a sudden loss of control which was in no way due to the fault of the driver.

CAUSING DEATH BY DRIVING UNLICENSED, UNINSURED OR DISQUALIFIED

RTA 1988, s 3ZB provides that a person is guilty of an offence if he causes the death of another person by driving a motor vehicle on a road and, at the time when he is driving, the circumstances are such that he is committing an offence under:

(a) RTA 1988, s 87(1) (driving otherwise than in accordance with a licence);
(b) RTA 1988, s 103(1)(b) (driving while disqualified); or
(c) RTA 1988, s 143 (using a motor vehicle while uninsured or unsecured against third-party risks).

These offences (which are indictable (either way) offences) are mentioned here because of the 'causing death' provisions, but are also noted within Chapter 9 under the appropriate headings.

SPEEDING

In considering offences of exceeding speed limits it is essential to separate them into those which are related to restricted roads, to roads subjected to a speed limit order, to speed limits on motorways, to speed limits introduced by temporary orders, and to speed limits which affect particular vehicles in particular places.

Restricted roads

By RTRA 1984, s 81 it is not lawful for a person to drive a motor vehicle on a restricted road at a speed exceeding 30 mph. It is an offence contrary to RTRA 1984, s 89(1) to do so.

In the present context, a 'restricted road' is basically defined by RTRA 1984, s 82 as one upon which there is provided a system of street lighting furnished by means of lamps placed not more than 200 yards apart. A divisional court has held that an error of 12 yards between two lamps in a system of 24 does not prevent the road from being restricted. In addition to this basic definition, s 82 provides that a direction may be given by the traffic authority that a specified road with street lighting as described above shall cease to be a restricted road for the purpose of s 81 or that a road which is not provided with such lighting shall be a restricted road for the purpose of s 81. Such directions are made by the traffic authority, ie the Secretary of State (in England) or the Welsh Ministers (in Wales) in the case of trunk roads, and by the local authority in the case of other roads (except that Transport for London is the traffic authority for a GLA road).

Signage

A road with street lighting which has been de-restricted by a direction must show the prescribed de-restriction signs (including repeater signs). Likewise, a road without such lighting which has been made a restricted road (or subjected to some other speed limit) must be provided with the prescribed restriction signs (including repeater signs). If these are not in place on the relevant part of the road, a driver cannot be convicted of exceeding the indicated speed limit. Moreover, even if they are, it is a requirement that the relevant signs can reasonably be expected to indicate the limit to an approaching driver in sufficient time to reduce from the previous lawful limit to a speed within the new limit. Thus, where a driver proved that the restriction sign, because of an overgrowing hedgerow, was not visible until the sign itself was reached, a divisional court allowed his appeal against conviction for speeding. Subject to this qualification, where signs are correctly placed, it is no defence to such a charge that the driver simply did not see the signs. The de-restriction or restriction signs which must be used are prescribed by the Traffic Signs Regulations and General Directions 2002.

The requirement for restriction signs does not apply to a road which is restricted by virtue of having a system of street lighting with lamps not more than 200 yards apart. Consequently, it is no defence for a driver accused of exceeding 30 mph on such a road that no signs were provided.

Roads subject to speed limit orders

Quite apart from the 'restricted' roads just discussed, there are many other roads which are subject to speed limits. RTRA 1984, s 84 empowers a traffic authority to make an order prohibiting the driving of motor vehicles on a specified road at a speed exceeding that specified in the order (either at any time or during specified periods) or at a speed exceeding that indicated by traffic signs in accordance with the order. By s 89(1), a person who drives a motor vehicle at a speed in excess of that specified for the particular road is guilty of an offence. If a speed limit order is made under s 84, the specified road must bear the prescribed restriction signs (including repeater signs). If it does not at the point of enforcement, a person cannot be convicted of driving in excess of the specified limit.

Speed limits on motorways

The Motorways Traffic (Speed Limit) Regulations 1974 impose an overall speed limit of 70 mph on any motor vehicle using a motorway. If a section of motorway is subject to a lesser limit, this is expressly listed and that section must bear the prescribed signs indicating the lower limit (otherwise a driver cannot be convicted of exceeding that limit). Contravention of the Regulations is an offence contrary to RTRA 1984, s 17(4).

Temporary speed limits

RTRA 1984, s 88 permits temporary speed limit orders to be made by the Secretary of State or the Welsh Ministers when it is desirable to do so in the interests of safety or for the purpose of facilitating the movement of traffic. Such orders may impose temporary maximum speed limits.

The 70 mph, 60 mph, and 50 mph (Temporary Speed Limit) Order 1977, which was made under the predecessor to s 88 and was continued in force indefinitely in 1978, imposes a maximum limit of 60 mph on single carriageways and of 70 mph on dual carriageways. These are general limits which apply to all roads (other than motorways) unless some other speed limit operates by virtue of the provisions described in this chapter.

The 1977 Order also imposes a limit of 60 mph on certain specified lengths of dual carriageway and of 50 mph on certain specified lengths of single carriageway. Such lengths must be provided with the prescribed restriction signs (including repeaters).

By RTRA 1984, s 89(1), it is an offence for a person to drive a motor vehicle on a road in excess of an applicable temporary speed imposed under the Order.

Minimum speed limits

RTRA 1984, s 88 also permits orders to be made imposing minimum speed limits, subject to such exceptions as may be specified. Signs must be displayed if a minimum speed limit is in force in respect of any road. By s 88(7), breach of such an order is an offence. Neither disqualification nor endorsement can be ordered on a conviction for this offence. Such a minimum speed limit only applies, of course, to motor vehicles.

Temporary maximum limits by traffic authorities

RTRA 1984, s 14 permits traffic authorities to impose temporary speed limits because of roadworks or work which is being undertaken near a road, or because of the likelihood of danger to the public or of serious damage to the road, or for the purpose of cleaning or clearing litter. Such an order cannot continue in force for more than 18 months unless the Secretary of State or Welsh Ministers consents to its further continuance.

A person who contravenes a speed limit imposed under RTRA 1984, s 14 commits an offence contrary to RTRA 1984, s 16 but a divisional court has held that persons committing this offence should be charged under RTRA 1984, s 89(1).

Speed limits on particular vehicles

Quite apart from the various speed limits which apply to roads, speed limits are also imposed on various types of vehicle. The result is that the driver of such a vehicle must not only observe the *speed limit applying to the road* in question but also the *speed limit applying to his vehicle on that road*. RTRA 1984, s 86 provides that it is unlawful for a person to drive a motor vehicle on a road at a speed in excess of a speed limit applicable to that vehicle. By RTRA 1984, s 89(1), a person who does so is guilty of an offence.

RTRA 1984, Sch 6 sets out the speed limits applying to particular classes of vehicles as follows:

	Class of vehicle	*M/ways*	*Dual carr*	*Other roads*
1	Invalid carriage	n/a	20	20
2	Passenger vehicle, motor caravan, car-derived van, or dual purpose vehicle drawing one trailer	60	60	50
3	Vehicle of the type mentioned in 2, drawing more than one trailer	40	20	20
4	Goods vehicle (except car-derived van) up to 7.5 tonnes mlw (maximum laden weight) not drawing a trailer	70	60	50
5	Articulated goods vehicle up to 7.5 tonnes mlw, and goods vehicles drawing one trailer where the combined mlw does not exceed 7.5 tonnes	60	60	50
6	Articulated goods vehicle over 7.5 tonnes mlw, goods vehicle over 7.5 tonnes mlw, and goods vehicles drawing one trailer where the combined mlw exceeds 7.5 tonnes	60	50	40
7	Goods vehicle, other than a car-derived van, drawing more than one trailer	40	20	20
8	Motor tractor, light loco, heavy loco	20	20	20
9	Motor tractor, light loco, heavy loco with certain requirements as to springs and wings being met	40	30	30

(continued)

Continued

Class of vehicle		M/ways	Dual carr	Other roads
10	Works truck	18	18	18
11	Passenger vehicle exceeding 3.05 tonnes unladen weight or adapted to carry more than eight passengers:			
	Not exceeding 12 m length	70	60	50
	Exceeding 12 m length	60	60	50
12	Agricultural motor vehicle	40	40	40

The term 'car-derived van' means a goods vehicle which is constructed or adapted as a derivative of a passenger vehicle and which has a maximum laden weight not exceeding 2 tonnes. It is treated as if it was a passenger vehicle of the type from which it was derived.

A recovery vehicle equipped with a special boom for lifting vehicles is not a motor tractor. It is constructed to carry a load and is not, therefore, restricted to 40 mph on a motorway.

Exemptions for emergency services

RTRA 1984, s 87 exempts motor vehicles which are being used for fire and rescue, ambulance or police purposes from the statutory provisions imposing speed limits on motor vehicles, if the observance of any such provision would be likely to hinder the use of the vehicle for the purpose for which it is being used on that occasion. Section 87 also applies in relation to vehicles being used for SOCA purposes, or for training drivers for use for SOCA purposes, as it applies to a vehicle being driven for police purposes. However, other than in the case of training, s 87 does not apply in relation to a vehicle being driven for SOCA purposes unless it is being driven by a person trained to drive vehicles at high speeds.

When the relevant provisions of RSA 2006, s 19 are brought into force the exemptions will expressly apply where the vehicle is being used for training purposes for any of the above emergency services, but only if the driver has successfully completed a high-speed driving course, or is driving as a part of such a course. The Secretary of State will be authorised to make regulations concerning training in the driving of high-speed vehicles.

Exemptions for special forces

The Road Traffic Exemptions (Special Forces) (Variation and Amendment) Regulations 2011 vary statutory provisions which impose speed limits to provide exemptions for drivers who are members of the special forces using vehicles in response to a national security emergency or whilst being trained or practising to do so.

It is a condition of the exemptions that drivers have been trained in the driving of vehicles at high speeds.

Regulation 2 provides that speed limits imposed by or under:

(a) RTRA 1984, s 81 (p 521);

(b) existing orders or notices under RTRA 1984, s 14 (p 522);

(c) existing orders under RTRA 1984, ss 16A (prohibitions or restrictions on road in connection with sporting event, social event, or entertainment held on road), 84 (p 521) or 88 (p 522);

(d) motorway speed limits regulations (p 522);

(e) any local Act,

are varied so as to exempt special forces drivers using vehicles in response to a national security emergency or whilst being trained or practising to do so.

Procuring, etc speeding: a special provision

RTRA 1984, s 89(4) provides that, if a person who employs others to drive motor vehicles on roads publishes or issues any timetable or schedule, or gives any directions, under which any journey or part of a journey is required to be completed within a specified time, and it is not practicable for that journey (or part) to be completed in the specified time without the commission of an offence under s 89(1), that publication or issue, or giving of directions, may be produced as evidence that the employer procured or (as the case may be) encouraged or assisted his employees to commit such an offence.

Proof

RTRA 1984, s 89(2) states that a person must not be convicted of an offence of speeding contrary to s 89(1) solely on the evidence of one witness to the effect that, in the opinion of the witness, the person prosecuted was driving the vehicle at a speed exceeding the specified limit. Section 89(2) requires corroborative evidence; it does not require that there must necessarily be more than one witness. Although, technically, there is no reason why an offender should not be convicted on the evidence of two witnesses, where one corroborates the other by stating that in his opinion the vehicle was, for example, exceeding a limit of 30 mph, the courts would generally not be satisfied with two such opinions unless the speed was estimated to be far in excess of the limit imposed. Corroboration is therefore usually provided by some mechanical device, which is read by an operator (normally a police officer) who may then give evidence of its reading. These readings will provide corroboration of the operator's opinion of the speed of the vehicle in question. However, a divisional court in judicial review proceedings refused to interfere with a conviction where two experienced traffic officers saw a vehicle enter a built-up area at a speed which they both said was at least 45 mph. The court said that it was a matter for the court of trial to decide on the facts whether it accepted the evidence of the police officers or the explanation given by the defendant. It was not its function, on an application for judicial review, to consider whether that court had reached the right conclusion; it could only interfere if the conclusion reached was such that no reasonable court, properly considering the evidence before it, could have reached. The court added that it would have reached the same conclusion.

Corroboration of speed may be obtained by the use of stopwatches to assess speeds over a measured distance, but it is usually provided by a speedometer, fixed camera, radar speed meter, VASCAR, or similar approved device. Where a speedometer is used, it is important to establish that the police vehicle containing the speedometer maintained an even distance from the vehicle being checked as this is relevant to the issue of speed.

A police officer's opinion of a vehicle's speed may also be corroborated from scientific calculations made by him (or another) based, for example, on damage to the vehicle and skid marks where it has crashed. It has been held by a judge in the Administrative Court that a police officer is entitled to corroborate his own opinion of whether a vehicle was exceeding a speed limit by reference to a prescribed device even if that device is not of a *type* approved by the Secretary of State (so that RTOA 1988, s 20 (below) cannot be relied on).

In instances where two police officers are involved in detecting speeding offences, they may keep one record of the transaction provided that both check and acknowledge the accuracy of that record at the time. This frequently occurs where one officer is engaged in checking the speed of the vehicle, whilst another stops and deals with the offending driver.

Radar meters are extremely accurate devices, and the courts will accept evidence of speed which is based upon meter readings provided that the operator can satisfy the court that he is a trained operator and that there is clear evidence of the identity of the particular motor vehicle alleged to have exceeded the speed limit. The vehicle will have been stopped by another officer and clear proof will be required that the vehicle stopped by the second officer was the one which had exceeded a statutory speed limit. Hand-held radar guns have been criticised in the courts but, in the instances in which the readings obtained by such guns have been rejected, it is operator-error which has been the cause of the difficulties. Hand-held guns are accurate, provided the batteries are fully charged or, if they are operating from another source, provided they are properly connected. However, their accuracy is affected if they are operated within a quarter of a mile of powerful VHF or UHF transmissions or within 100 yards of high-voltage cables. Care must also be taken to ensure that the beam is not bounced off metal objects and that it could not have picked up a reading from another moving object. In the case of devices such as the LT1 20.20 which can measure the speed of vehicles at a distance of 1,000 metres, it is essential that the device is aimed at one spot and does not waver. A small movement of the 'spot' directed at the vehicle can lead to a false reading.

VASCAR and similar devices are also in common use within police forces. They record speeds averaged by a vehicle over a specified distance. Operators must be carefully trained as the device is operated by a series of switches. It is essential that the operator is able to satisfy a court that the switches were operated at the right time to ensure that correct distances are recorded, and that the vehicle was properly identified, together with the precise moment when it passes the object which marks the limit of the distance over which it is checked.

The above devices are prescribed devices (see below).

Evidence produced by prescribed devices

RTOA 1988, s 20 provides that a record produced by a prescribed device (ie a device of a description prescribed by the Secretary of State) in an order made by statutory instrument is evidence of a fact related to any offence of speeding. The Road Traffic Offenders (Prescribed Devices) Order 1992 prescribed devices designed or adapted for measuring by radar the speed of motor vehicles. An identically named Order in 1993 prescribed devices designed or adapted for measuring speed by means of sensors or cables on or near the surface of a highway and those activated by means of a light beam or beams. Another identically named Order in 1999 prescribed cameras designed or adapted to record speed by correlating the image of the motor vehicle as it passes two positions, digitally recording each image and the time it is photographed, and calculating the average speed between the two positions. The cameras do not require film but transmit computer images to a computer centre. They are capable of measuring the speed of vehicles in different lanes. Another order with the same title in 2008 approved the use of manually operated devices that record the speed of a vehicle (vehicle A) from another vehicle (vehicle B) by (a) measuring the time it takes for vehicle A to travel between two points, (b) recording the distance between those points by means of the odometer pulses of vehicle B as it travels between the two points, and (c) calculating vehicle A's average speed between the two points by reference to the time in (a) and the distance calculated under (b) or measured manually.

The record must provide (in the same or another document) a certificate as to the circumstances in which the record was produced, signed by a constable or a person authorised by, or on behalf of, a chief police officer for the area in which the offence is alleged to have been committed.

A record produced by a prescribed device is inadmissible unless the device is of a type proved to have been approved by the Secretary of State and was used in accordance with conditions subject to which the approval was given.

The Orders referred to above show that a statutory instrument specifying a 'prescribed device' is drafted in general terms (as permitted by the legislation). On the other hand, approval of a type of device is given specifically in relation to a particular make and model. Evidence of the approval of the particular type of device used may be required and should be offered in the absence of judicial notice having been taken of its existence. This may be done by production of a valid copy of the instrument of approval or oral evidence may be given from a police officer who has knowledge of the approval, but approval may not be inferred merely from the fact that the device is in general use within police forces. A divisional court has held that the fact that a device is not properly used, in particular that a pre-operative test has not been performed, does not mean that the device is not of an approved type. The court went on to uphold a conviction for speeding where the expert evidence indicated that the failure properly to calibrate a laser speed device did not give rise to any material error.

The purpose and effect of RTOA 1988, s 20, is to enable a record relying on an accompanying certificate to be tendered in evidence without the necessity of a witness being called to prove them. A copy of evidence obtained by means of an approved device must be served on the person charged with the offence not less than seven days before the hearing or trial. If, not less than three days before the hearing or trial, the defendant requires the attendance of the person who signed the document, the evidence of the circumstances in which the record was produced will not be admissible, although the record produced by the device will. Where the record and certificate are not served on the defendant seven days before the trial, the magistrates should allow them to be produced by a police officer as real evidence.

Notices under RTA 1988, s 172

Notices may be sent under s 172, requiring the owner of the vehicle to identify the driver within 28 days. See further p 422.

Speed-assessment equipment detection devices

RTA 1988, s 41 is prospectively amended to permit the making of regulations to prohibit the fitting of a 'speed assessment equipment detection device' and to create an offence of using a vehicle fitted with such a device. The device is defined as 'a device, the purpose, or one of the purposes, of which is to detect, or interfere with the operation of, equipment used to assess the speed of motor vehicles'.

Motor racing and rallies

It is an offence contrary to RTA 1988, s 12 to promote or take part in a race or trial of speed between motor vehicles on a highway. Thus, there is a complete ban on racing motor vehicles on a highway.

RTA 1988, s 13(1) creates the offence of promoting or taking part in a 'competition or trial' (other than a race or trial of speed) which involves the use of motor vehicles *on a highway* unless the event is authorised and conducted in accordance with any conditions imposed. The Motor Vehicles (Competitions and Trials) Regulations 1969 deal with such events. Competitions or trials are authorised without the need for an application if:

(a) there are no more than 12 vehicles involved and the event does not take place within eight days of another similar event promoted by the same person or club;

(b) no merit is attached to completing the event with the lowest mileage and, in respect of any part of the event on a public highway, there are no performance tests and no route, competitors are not timed or required to visit the same places, although they may be required to finish at the same place by a specified time;

(c) in respect of any part of the event on the public highway, merit is attached to a competitor's performance only in relation to good road behaviour and compliance with the Highway Code; or

(d) all competitors are members of the armed forces of the Crown and the event is designed solely for the purpose of service training.

Regulation 6 permits the authorisation of other events by the Royal Automobile Club Motor Sports Association Ltd (events, or part of events, in England) or RAC (events, or part of events, in Wales). Applications for such events must be made not less than two months before the event is due to be held (or, if it is to be held on more than one date, the date the event is due to begin). Except in the case of a specified event, which is an event which is run not more than once a year, for example the 'Veteran Car Run', and is specified in the schedule to the Regulations, the application must not be made more than six months before the event.

RTA 1988, s 13A states that a person is not guilty of an offence under RTA 1988, ss 1, 1A, 2, or 3 by virtue of driving a vehicle *in a public place other than a road* if he shows that he was driving in accordance with an authorisation for a motoring event given under regulations. The Motor Vehicles (Off Road Events) Regulations 1995 authorise a number of bodies to issue such authorisations.

RTA 1988, s 33(1) prohibits the promoting or taking part in a trial of any description between motor vehicles on a footpath, bridleway or restricted byway unless the holding of it has been authorised by the local authority. Contravention of s 33(1), or breach of a condition of an authorisation, is an offence under s 33(3).

NOTICE OF INTENDED PROSECUTION

If not interviewed by the police at the time of a driving offence, a driver may experience considerable difficulty in recalling the circumstances some weeks after the event. For this reason, RTOA 1988, s 1 states that, in relation to certain named offences, a person may not be convicted unless:

(a) he was warned at the time of the possibility of prosecution for the offence; or

(b) he was served with a summons or requisition for the offence within 14 days of its commission; or

(c) a notice of intended prosecution specifying the nature of the alleged offence and the time and place where it is alleged to have been committed was served within 14 days on him or the person, if any, registered as the keeper of the vehicle at the time of the commission of the offence. (In the case of dangerous or careless cycling the notice must be served on the rider.)

These requirements are deemed to have been complied with unless and until the contrary is proved.

The following offences require notice in one of these forms:

(a) Road Traffic Act 1988, s:
  2 Dangerous driving
  3 Careless, or inconsiderate, driving
  22 Leaving vehicle in a dangerous position
  28 Dangerous cycling
  29 Careless, or inconsiderate, cycling
  35 Failing to conform with the indication given by constable engaged in the regulation of traffic
  36 Failing to comply with the indication given by traffic sign

(b) Road Traffic Regulation Act 1984, s:
  16 Exceeding temporary speed restrictions imposed under s 14
  17(4) Exceeding speed restriction on special road (ie a motorway)
  88(7) Exceeding temporary speed limit imposed by order
  89(1) Speeding offences generally

(c) Aiding and abetting any of the above offences.

However, such notice need not be given in relation to an offence in respect of which a full or provisional fixed penalty notice has been given or fixed under RTOA 1988.

Warning at the time of the offence

The words 'at the time of the offence' mean at the *time of the incident and not the moment of the offence*. In one case, a warning, given by a police officer at the scene of an incident 35 minutes after its occurrence and while it was still being dealt with, was held to have been given 'at the time'. In other circumstances, where the police immediately traced the driver but the process took two-and-a-half hours, the notice was held to have been given 'at the time'. However, there is obviously a limit, and the matter should be judged in the context of the warning being given as a part of the continuous process of initial investigation, a question of fact and degree. If there has been any delay at the scene, it is best to send a written notice.

The warning must be heard and understood by the person concerned, and it must be to the effect that the question of prosecuting him for one or other of the above offences will be taken into consideration. There is no prescribed form of words and any clear statement to the above effect will do. It is appreciated that it is not always possible to decide whether the prosecution might be for dangerous or merely careless driving but a warning that it might be for either will suffice as the evidence upon which the charge will be based will be similar.

Service of summons, requisition or notice of intended prosecution

Where an oral notice is not given at the time, then either a summons or requisition or a written notice of intended prosecution must be served within 14 days. The day on which the offence was committed is ignored.

A notice of intended prosecution may be served by delivering it to the person or addressing it to him and leaving it at his last known address. In addition, a notice may be served by sending it to the person by registered post, recorded delivery service or first class post addressed to the person concerned at his last known address. There is a difference between the first two postal methods and the third. A notice sent by registered post or recorded delivery service is irrebuttably deemed to have been served on a person if addressed to him at his last known address, and this includes being irrebuttably deemed to have been served within the period of 14 days. On the other hand, there is no such irrebuttable presumption in respect of a notice sent by first class post; consequently, if it is proved that a letter so sent was delivered after the end of the 14-day period it will not have been effectively served.

In the absence of personal service of notice on the offender, it is obviously advisable to serve a notice by sending it by registered post or recorded delivery since in such a case he is deemed to have been served if the notice was addressed to him at his last known address, notwithstanding that the notice is returned as undelivered or is for some other reason not received by him.

As to service of a summons or requisition see p 18.

It has been held that service of a notice on the defendant's wife by handing her the notice was valid, since she was authorised to accept and deal with her husband's mail. It would be different if the notice was left with a hall porter, as he would not be so authorised.

Circumstances where non-compliance is no bar to conviction

By RTOA 1988, s 2(3), a failure to comply with the above requirements is no bar to conviction if the court is satisfied that the defendant's or the vehicle's registered keeper's name and address could not with reasonable diligence have been ascertained in time for service of a summons, requisition or notice or that the defendant by his own conduct contributed to the failure.

RTOA 1988, s 2(1) waives the requirements of s 1 in relation to any offence if, at the time of the offence or immediately thereafter, an *accident occurs owing to the presence on a road of the vehicle* in respect of which the offence was committed. This exemption exists because, in such circumstances, the offender will normally be aware of the circumstances surrounding the offence and the risk of prosecution. It does not apply, therefore, if the accident was so trivial that the driver was unaware that the accident had occurred. Here, the requirements of s 1 apply. On the other hand, the waiver of the requirements of s 1 does apply if the driver was unaware of the circumstances of an accident owing to the severity of his injuries, because subsequently the driver will be only too aware that the accident has occurred.

'Accident' in s 2(1) is given a commonsense meaning and is not restricted to unintended consequences having an adverse physical effect. It is for the prosecution to prove beyond reasonable doubt that an 'accident' has occurred. The words 'owing to the presence on a road of the vehicle' require there to be a direct causal link between the vehicle on the road and the accident.

CHAPTER 15

Drinking or Drug-Taking and Driving

The Road Traffic Act 1988 (RTA 1988), ss 4 to 11 contain various offences relating to drinking and driving. The principal types of offence are driving or attempting to drive a motor vehicle with an alcohol concentration in excess of the prescribed limit (s 5), and driving or attempting to drive a mechanically propelled vehicle when unfit to drive through drink or drugs (s 4) (p 534).

Apart from cases where the defendant is unfit through drugs or he is below the prescribed limit or the mechanically propelled vehicle is not a motor vehicle, it is the almost invariable practice to prosecute for an offence under RTA 1988, s 5 rather than one under s 4. This is because s 5 lays down an objective test; whereas under s 4 it is necessary for the prosecution to prove that the defendant's ability to drive properly was for the time being impaired by drink or drugs, which is a question of fact for the justices.

DRIVING, ETC WITH EXCESS ALCOHOL

Under RTA 1988, s 5(1) it is an offence for a person:

(a) to drive or attempt to drive a motor vehicle on a road or other public place; or
(b) to be in charge of a motor vehicle on a road or other public place,

after consuming so much alcohol that the proportion of it in his breath, blood or urine exceeds the prescribed limit.

The charge must state whether the person was driving, attempting to drive or in charge of the vehicle and the nature of the specimen in which the prescribed limit was exceeded. If it does not it is likely to fail for duplicity.

Road or other public place

Road

See p 343.

Public place

The term 'other public place' means a place (other than a 'road') to which the public, whether on payment or otherwise, have access with at least the tolerance of the landowner or proprietor. It is irrelevant whether the public could have access; the question is whether they actually have access to the place in question. The term therefore includes car parks which are open to the public at the time, and fields in which public events are taking place (such as galas, shows or race meetings); they will be public places at the time when the public have access to them. A distinction must be drawn between the car park of a public house and that of a members' club. The first is open to the public at large during licensing hours and is therefore a public place during those hours, but that of the members' club is restricted to members of that club and their guests and therefore it is never a 'public place'. A car park situated within the business premises of a motor dealer for use by customers has been held to be a public place as members of the public using the car park did not cease to be members of the public and become a special class of persons merely because they used the car park as customers.

A place can be a 'public place' even though access to it is only permitted after a person has been screened. If those who are admitted pass through a screening process because of a special characteristic or reason personal to themselves (eg because they are members of the caravan club to whose site they seek access, or because they are workers at a factory to whose car park they seek access), the place in question is not a public place. On the other hand, if anyone can pass through the screening process and gain access simply by paying an entry fee (eg a site fee at a caravan park), or by satisfying conditions imposed by the landowner (eg access only for private vehicles or the possession of a boarding pass), the place is a public place.

The absence of a physical obstruction or of a notice forbidding entry does not of itself mean that the public have access.

Driving, attempting to drive or in charge of motor vehicle

Driving

'Driving' in the present context bears its normal meaning in road traffic offences. The essence of 'driving' is the use of the driver's controls (or, at least, one of them) in order to control the movement of the vehicle, however that movement is produced, provided that what occurs can in any sense be regarded as 'driving'. See, further, p 511. A divisional court has held that D was 'driving' in circumstances where the vehicle was stationary. D was sitting in the driver's seat of a vehicle on a grass verge engaging in an activity which he described as 'wheel spinning'. This involved the use of the engine, accelerator, clutch and steering wheel with the vehicle in gear but the handbrake applied preventing any form of movement. The court held that the ordinary meaning of the word 'driving' included a situation where someone was ensuring that there was no movement but the wheels were spinning.

Attempting to drive

As explained in Chapter 39, what is required is the doing of an act which is more than merely preparatory to the commission of the full offence, coupled with the intention to commit the full offence. For example, if someone gets no further than sitting in the driving seat of a motor car on a road and searching his pockets for the ignition keys, it is almost certain that the justices would find that his acts were merely preparatory and that he was not attempting to drive (although he could be convicted of the offence of being in charge with excess alcohol). On the other hand, if he finds the keys and gets as far as placing them in the ignition switch and turning it it is almost certain that the justices would find that the act was more than merely preparatory, and that therefore he was attempting to drive.

A person may be guilty of an attempt even though the facts are such that the commission of the full offence is not possible. Consequently, someone who attempts to drive in circumstances where it is impossible for him to do so is guilty of attempting to drive.

The offence of 'attempting to drive' is convenient where a driver with excess alcohol is stopped in a private place, eg a private car park, as he drives towards a road. In such circumstances he can be convicted of an attempt to drive on a road with excess alcohol.

Being in charge

Generally, once a person takes a vehicle out on a road or other public place he remains in charge of it until he has taken it off the road or public place, unless he puts someone else in charge of it (as where he hands the ignition keys to another to prevent himself from being able to drive it) or loses effective control over the vehicle in some other way (as where it is stolen or where he has gone to bed). Persons other than the owner or someone in lawful possession or control of the vehicle may assume charge of it. In such cases consideration must be given to whether and where such a person was in the vehicle or how far from it, what he was doing, whether he was in possession of a suitable ignition key, evidence of intention to take control by driving or otherwise, and the position and circumstances of other persons who were also in the vehicle. Because more than one person can be in charge of a vehicle, someone sitting in a passenger seat supervising a learner driver is in charge of the vehicle.

The defence under s 5(2)   RTA 1988, s 5(2) provides that it is a defence for a person charged with 'being in charge of a motor vehicle', etc to prove that, at the time he is alleged to have committed the offence, the circumstances were such that there was no likelihood of his driving the vehicle whilst the proportion of alcohol in his breath, blood or urine remained likely to exceed the prescribed limit. In determining whether there was such a likelihood the court may disregard any injury to him and any damage to the vehicle (s 5(3)). Normally, the defendant (D) will only succeed in proving this defence if there is expert evidence as to the rate of alcohol destruction by the body which indicates that his alcohol level would not have been above the limit at the time he was likely to drive.

A divisional court has held that the defence is not primarily concerned with D's intentions, although they might be a factor to be considered. D's subjective intentions cannot be decisive in circumstances where he was affected by alcohol at a level well over the prescribed limit and has no means of knowing or proving when his alcohol levels had fallen below that limit.

The House of Lords has ruled that D bears a persuasive burden of proof of the s 5(2) defence (ie on the balance of probabilities), and that this is not incompatible with the presumption of innocence under the European Convention on Human Rights, art 6(2).

Motor vehicle

See p 342.

Driving motor vehicle on a road or other public place

A divisional court has held that for a vehicle to be driven 'on' a road or other public place it is not necessary that its wheels should be on the road etc or for the entirety of the vehicle to be on the road etc. It is enough that the vehicle materially encroaches on the road. The court, therefore, upheld a conviction where the boot of a car being manoeuvred in a private driveway had projected into a road and collided with a car parked there.

After consuming so much alcohol that the proportion of it in breath, blood or urine exceeds the prescribed limit

'Consuming' is a wide enough term to include other methods of ingestion than through the mouth. Thus, for example, an alcohol level which may have, in part, resulted from the injection of a substance, comes about through 'consumption'.

The prescribed limits

These are defined by RTA 1988, s 11 which states that the 'prescribed limit' means, as the case may require:

(a) 35 microgrammes of alcohol in 100 millilitres of breath;
(b) 80 milligrammes of alcohol in 100 millilitres of blood; or
(c) 107 milligrammes of alcohol in 100 millilitres of urine,

or such other proportion as may be prescribed by regulations made by the Secretary of State. So far, the Secretary of State has not prescribed any other proportion.

The 35 microgrammes is roughly equivalent to the 80 and 107 milligrammes of the two other levels.

DRIVING, ETC UNDER INFLUENCE OF DRINK OR DRUGS

RTA 1988, s 4(1) and (2) provides that:

(1) A person who, when driving or attempting to drive a mechanically propelled vehicle on a road or other public place, is unfit to drive through drink or drugs is guilty of an offence.
(2) Without prejudice to subsection (1), a person who, when in charge of a mechanically propelled vehicle which is on a road or other public place, is unfit to drive through drink or drugs is guilty of an offence.

The charge must state whether the person was driving, attempting to drive or in charge.

Many of the elements of these offences have been dealt with already in relation to s 5. It is worth noting that s 4 applies to a mechanically propelled vehicle (see p 342), whereas s 5 is limited to a motor vehicle, and that s 4(3) provides a similar defence for persons charged with 'being in charge' to that provided by s 5(2) for those charged with the corresponding offence under s 5, namely, that it is a defence for the defendant to prove that there was no likelihood of his driving the vehicle while he remained unfit through drink or drugs.

It remains to be added that 'drink' means alcoholic drink and 'drug' means any intoxicant other than alcohol, including medicines and glue.

Unfitness to drive

Section 4(5) provides that a person is to be taken to be unfit to drive if his ability to drive properly is for the time being impaired. The evidence before the court on this point will normally include evidence of the defendant's driving before his vehicle was stopped; any evidence of driving apparently outside the pattern of normal driving is relevant in that it may show some impairment of the ability to drive properly. In addition, the evidence of the defendant's speech after he was stopped, together with his general manner and demeanour and any apparent lack of co-ordination or control over bodily movements, may be important. The evidence before the court will also normally include the report of a medical examination by a medical practitioner, which is extremely important since the practitioner will have required the defendant to carry out a series of tests indicative of his ability (or lack of ability) to drive properly. Lastly, the evidence may include the result of the analysis of a specimen of breath, blood or urine required under s 7. The procedure relating to such specimens, and the rules relating to the use of their analysis as evidence, are essentially the same as for the offences of driving, etc with excess alcohol. It must be remembered that the presence of a drug can be detected by a blood or urine test, but not by a breath test.

PROCEDURE

The procedures which will normally precede a person being charged with an offence under RTA 1988, s 5 are regulated by RTA 1988. These procedures will usually begin with a police officer on the beat requiring a preliminary test; followed by an arrest (whether as a result of a positive test or of a failure to provide a breath specimen for it) which then must be followed by a requirement for a specimen of breath (for an evidential breath test) or, in limited cases, a specimen of blood or urine (for analysis).

A charge under RTA 1988, s 3A (causing death by careless driving when unfit through drink or drugs or with excess alcohol (p 519)) or s 4 (driving etc when unfit through drink or drugs) will also normally be preceded by a preliminary test.

PRELIMINARY TESTS

Under RTA 1988, s 6, there are three types of preliminary test whose purpose is to give an indication as to a defendant's 'impairment' in consequence of consumption of alcohol and/or of taking drugs, by means of a breath test, an impairment test or a drugs test.

Power to require preliminary tests

RTA 1988, s 6(1) provides that where any of s 6(2) to (5) applies, a constable may require a person to co-operate with one or more preliminary tests administered to that person by that constable or another.

Section 6(2) provides that such a test may be required *if a constable reasonably suspects that the person*:

(a) *is driving, is attempting to drive or is in charge* of a motor vehicle on a road or other public place; and
(b) *has alcohol or a drug in his body or is under the influence of a drug.*

Section 6(3) authorises a test where a constable *reasonably suspects* that the person:

(a) *has been driving, attempting to drive or in charge of* a motor vehicle on a road or other public place *while having alcohol or a drug in his body or while unfit to drive because of a drug*; and
(b) *still has alcohol or a drug in his body or is still under the influence of a drug.*

Section 6(4) authorises a test where a constable *reasonably suspects* that the person:

(a) *is or has been driving or attempting to drive or in charge* of a motor vehicle on a road or other public place; and
(b) *has committed a traffic offence while the vehicle was in motion.*

The type of traffic offence which the constable must reasonably suspect to have been committed is defined by RTA 1988, s 6(8), which provides that 'traffic offence' in this context means an offence under any provision of the Public Passenger Vehicles Act 1981, Part II (fitness of vehicles and PSV operator's licence), the Road Traffic Regulation Act (RTRA) 1984, the Road Traffic Offenders Act (RTOA) 1988 except Part III (offences relating to fixed penalty procedures), or any provision of RTA 1988 except Part V (driving instruction for payment without being licensed or registered and other driving instructor offences). This effectively covers the range of road traffic offences which could be described as 'moving traffic offences'. All offences which are set out in regulations made under those Acts are also included within this description; for example, offences contrary to the Road Vehicles (Construction and Use) Regulations 1986 or the Road Vehicles Lighting Regulations 1989.

Section 6(5) authorises a test if:

(a) an *accident occurs* owing to the presence of a motor vehicle on a road or other public place; and
(b) a constable *reasonably believes* that the person *was driving, attempting to drive or in charge of the vehicle at the time* of the accident.

The tests required (other than in the case of a test under s 6(5) (road traffic accidents)) may only be administered by a constable in uniform. Whether or not a constable was in uniform is a question of fact in each case. A constable wearing his uniform except for his helmet has been held to be in uniform so long as he is easily identifiable as a constable. A court is entitled to assume that a constable was in uniform unless this point is disproved.

The necessary suspicion or belief need not arise while the vehicle is in motion. Indeed, a uniformed constable may stop motorists, under his common law or statutory powers to do so, in order to see whether there is a reasonable suspicion that they have consumed alcohol, and if a reasonable suspicion then emerges of such consumption, go on to require a preliminary test. Thus, random stopping of motorists is not prohibited, although random preliminary tests are.

A constable does not have to administer a caution before requiring a preliminary test. It is only where the motorist has failed such a test (or failed to take it) that a caution needs to be administered.

Special circumstances which apply where an accident has occurred

As already stated, there is a power, under RTA 1988, s 6(5), to require a 'preliminary' test if an accident occurs owing to the presence of a motor vehicle on a road or other public place. A constable may require any person whom he has *reasonable cause to believe* was driving or attempting to drive or in charge of the vehicle at the time of the accident to provide a preliminary test, subject to s 9 (hospital procedure: p 555).

'Accident' in this context bears its ordinary meaning, and it has been held that a crash which is deliberately caused falls within that meaning. The person's vehicle need not have been physically involved but there must have been a direct causal connection between his vehicle being on the road and the accident occurring. Where a sequence of events begins on a road and leads to a vehicle leaving the road and colliding with an object some distance from the road, there is an accident for the purposes of s 6(5).

Of course, the fact that an accident has occurred owing to the presence of a motor vehicle on a road or other public place does not entitle a constable to require a specimen of breath under s 6(5) from anyone; that provision only empowers him to make such a requirement of any person whom he has *reasonable cause to believe was driving or attempting to drive or in charge of* the vehicle at the time of the accident.

The reader will remember that the power to require a breath specimen under the other provisions of RTA 1988, s 6 is framed in terms of a constable having *reasonable cause to suspect* the specified things. In contrast, s 6(5) uses the term '*has reasonable cause to believe*', which requires more than 'reasonable suspicion' since 'believe' requires more than mere suspicion and refers to being virtually certain (ie having no substantial doubt) about the facts.

The nature of preliminary tests

Preliminary breath test

RTA 1988, s 6A provides that a preliminary breath test is a procedure whereby the person to whom the test is administered provides a specimen of breath to be used for the purpose of obtaining, by means of a device approved by the Secretary of State, an indication whether the proportion of alcohol in the person's breath or blood is likely to exceed the prescribed limit.

A preliminary breath test may be administered under s 6(2) to (4) only at or near the place where the requirement to co-operate with the test is imposed; where it is administered under s 6(5) (ie following an accident), it may be administered at or near that place or, if the constable who imposes the requirement thinks it expedient, at a police station specified by him.

Preliminary breath test devices used by police officers must be approved by the Secretary of State. Currently, the Secretary of State has approved two types of device, one which might be described as the 'blow in the bag' type of device and the other 'electronic'.

Approved devices of the 'blow in the bag' type are the Draeger Alcotest 80, the Alcotest R80A, and the Lion Alcolyser. The containers of such devices show the dates beyond which the devices should not be used and it is important that these dates are checked.

A number of electronic devices have been approved by the Secretary of State. There are various types of some of these devices (because new models have been approved as a particular device has been developed). In the following list the latest model of devices currently available is given: the Lion Alcolmeter 500 B, the AlcoQuant 6020, the Alcosensor FST and the Alcotest 6810 GB. The Alcolmeter 500 B is a battery-operated device of compact size into which a plastic tube is inserted. The suspect breathes into the tube and the result is displayed on a back-lit screen. The instrument incorporates a sensor which will respond to alcohol only and it is not affected by other breath contaminants. The Alcotest 6810 GB is a device of high accuracy which gives both audible and (via LCD and illuminated display) visible indications of a positive test. The Alcosensor FST has a back-lit LCD display and a 'lever and snap' mouthpiece insertion. The AlcoQuant is a three-button device with a back-lit display.

The instructions which accompany all preliminary breath test devices warn that a breath test should not be given until at least 20 minutes have elapsed since the last intoxicating drink was taken. The reason for this is that it is the alcoholic content of deep-lung air which is to be measured, not mouth alcohol. If a drink has been taken within that period the constable should wait until 20 minutes have elapsed before carrying out the test. If a suspect is smoking he should be asked to stop and to take two or three deep breaths to clear the lungs of smoke. A divisional court has held that the failure by a police officer to follow these instructions did not render inadmissible the result of the analysis of a specimen subsequently provided for analysis.

Code C: The Code of Practice for the Detention, Treatment and Questioning of Persons by Police Officers (the Detention Code) referred to in Chapter 4, excludes the 'specimens for analysis' procedures under RTA 1988, s 7 (p 543) from the provisions of the Code which relate to 'interviews'; no similar exclusion is made in relation to s 6 procedures. It is therefore advisable that, where there is conversation between an officer and a suspect which relates to his condition, that conversation is recorded and read and signed by the suspect. A divisional court, however, refused to interfere with a decision of the justices not to exclude evidence subsequently obtained following an officer's inquiry as to whether a suspect had been drinking, to which the suspect replied, 'Yes, I've had a couple of pints'. It said that the justices, although recognising that there had been a breach of the Detention Code, were entitled to find that this breach had not been sufficiently 'significant and substantial' to merit exclusion of the evidence.

Nevertheless, care must be taken when engaging in conversation with drivers suspected of drink/drive offences. In one case police officers spoke to a man on three occasions, at his home prior to arrest and before caution; after his arrest and caution at his home; and in a police car, in the course of which he admitted that he had been to a funeral and had taken alcohol afterwards, that his last drink ('a couple of cans') had been taken at about 4 pm and that he had last driven his car at 5 pm and had not since taken a drink. It was held that these three conversations were 'interviews' for the purpose of the Detention Code. Additionally, it was stated that at the first interview at his home he had been entitled to legal advice which had not been offered. In this case the matter became unimportant as there was a subsequent 'untainted' interview at the police station but perhaps there is scope for some further guidance concerning the need for legal advice at such an exploratory stage as, if this line of argument is extended, police officers will have to be accompanied by solicitors when on patrol.

The preliminary impairment test

Such a test is designed to indicate whether a person is unfit to drive, and, if he is, whether or not this is due to drink or drugs.

RTA 1988, s 6B provides that a preliminary impairment test is a procedure whereby the constable administering the test observes the person to whom the test is administered in his performance of tests specified by the constable, and makes such other observations of the person's physical state as the constable thinks expedient. Section 6B requires that such tests may only be administered by a constable approved for the purpose by his chief officer of police. It may be administered at or near the place where the requirement to co-operate with the test is imposed or, if the constable who imposes the requirement thinks it expedient, at a police station specified by him.

Under s 6B the Secretary of State has issued the Code of Practice for Preliminary Impairment Tests for the use of constables trained and authorised to carry out such tests, to which a constable administering a preliminary impairment test must have regard.

The Code of Practice provides that in each of the preliminary impairment tests described below the officer must give a full explanation of what is required, demonstrating actions which a subject is required to perform where this is essential to understanding and establishing whether or not a disability, injury or illness exists, whether physical or mental, which might affect performance during the test. Obesity and age may be factors. The tests are:

A pupillary examination   which involves the subject looking straight ahead with eyes wide open. The constable should establish whether or not he is wearing contact lenses. A gauge is held adjacent to the appropriate side of the subject's face to enable, by a process of comparison, the size of the pupils of the eyes to be estimated. Conditions in which a subject's eyes are 'watering' or 'reddening' should also be noted.

The Modified Romberg Balance Test is concerned with a person's internal clock and ability to balance. He should be required to stand with heels and toes together and arms by his side and retain that position while tilting the head back slightly and closing the eyes and then to bring the head forward, open the eyes and say 'stop' when he thinks that 30 seconds have passed. A record will be made of ability to balance while being so instructed, whether he steps, sways or raises his arms and whether the eyes were opened, or the head straightened, during the test, together with the actual number of seconds which elapsed.

The walk and turn test enables an assessment to be made of a person's ability to divide attention between walking, balancing, and processing instructions. The constable should identify a line (other than a kerb or other place where a person might fall) and instruct the person to place his left foot on the line, his right foot on the line in front of the left foot touching heel to toe, put arms down by the side and keep them there throughout the test and to maintain that position while further instructions are given. On the instruction 'start', the subject should take nine heel-to-toe steps along the line; after these nine steps, leave the front foot on the line and turn around using a series of small steps with the other foot (these manoeuvres can be demonstrated by the constable). After turning, the subject should take another nine heel-to-toe steps back along the line. The officer should count each step out loud.

A record must be made of whether a subject was able to stand still while being instructed, whether he started too soon, turned correctly, occasions when he stopped walking, missed heel-to-toe connection, stepped off the line, or raised his arms. A record must also be made of whether the steps were correctly counted; the point of any deviation from the straight line should be marked on a diagram on the appropriate form.

The one-leg stand tests balance and ability to count out loud. The subject should be instructed to stand with his heels and toes together and arms by his sides; to maintain that position while receiving instructions and not to begin until told to do so. On the instruction 'start' he should raise his right foot 6 to 8 inches or 15 to 20 cms off the ground; keep the elevated leg straight with the toes pointing forward and the foot parallel with the ground; keep his arms by his side; keep looking at the elevated foot throughout the test; and while doing so to count out loud 'one thousand and one, one thousand and two, one thousand and three' and so on progressively until told to stop. The test should be carried out using each foot in turn.

A record will be made over a timed period of 30 seconds, for each foot, of any instances in which a subject sways, hops, puts a foot down, or raises the arms, together with the point in the test where that occurred.

The finger-to-nose test is designed to test depth of perception and balance. A subject must stand with both feet together and extend both arms in front, palms uppermost with the fists closed and the index finger of each hand extended (this must be carefully demonstrated) and he must maintain this position while waiting to be told to perform the remainder of the test. On being told to start he should tilt his head back slightly and then close his eyes and, when told which hand to use, should attempt to touch the tip of his nose with the tip of the index finger then, having done so, to lower the hand, as the constable calls out the order in which each hand should be used—Left, Right, Left, Right, Right, Left.

A record should be made where the subject steps, sways or raises an arm, and whether the correct hand was used, or touched a part of the face other than the tip of his nose and whereabouts.

Safety and site conditions   The safety of the subject must be considered. A hard, level, non-slippery surface should be chosen wherever possible in a well-lit unobstructed area out of the public view and in appropriate weather conditions. Where this is not possible, consideration must be given to the possibility of the test being conducted at another nearby location or at a police station. If not, appropriate allowance must be made in interpreting the tests. If the nature of footwear may be an impediment, the subject should be given the opportunity to remove it.

A constable should not close his eyes when demonstrating a test. He should always stand away from the subject and remain still.

Disabilities, injuries or illness   Any such factors must be recorded, whether physical or mental, if they might affect the performance of the subject during a test. Obesity or age must be recorded if likely to affect the test.

Where such factors are evident or claimed, an officer may continue to require co-operation with the test. However, he must be particularly mindful of the possibility of the effect which this might have on performance when interpreting test results.

General   A constable may decide, in consequence of these tests, that there is sufficient evidence to justify an arrest on reasonable suspicion of an offence under RTA 1988, s 3A or 4 (pp 519 and 534). There is no pass/fail standard, nor a scoring system. A decision must be based upon overall observation during the tests and the records made of those performances.

The preliminary drugs test

This is dealt with by RTA 1988, s 6C. A preliminary drugs test is a procedure by which a specimen of sweat or saliva is obtained and used for the purpose of obtaining, by means of a device of a type approved by the Secretary of State, an indication whether the person to whom the test is administered has a drug in his body. It may be administered at or near the place where the requirement to co-operate with the test is imposed or, if the constable who imposes the requirement thinks it expedient, at a police station specified by him.

At the time of writing, no details of these tests have been published, nor has a device of this nature been approved by the Secretary of State.

Arrest

Positive preliminary breath test

RTA 1988, s 6D(1) provides that a constable may arrest a person without warrant if as a result of a preliminary *breath* test the constable reasonably suspects that the proportion of alcohol in the person's breath or blood exceeds the prescribed limit. The suspect must be requested to provide a breath specimen before he can be arrested under s 6D, even if his conduct makes this difficult. Where an officer is assaulted by the suspect and thus prevented from making a proper request, the suspect should be arrested under another appropriate provision. The fact that evidential specimens of breath have been provided under s 7 (see p 543) by the person concerned does not prevent s 6D(1) having effect if the constable who imposed on him the requirement to provide the specimens has reasonable cause to believe that the device used to analyse the specimens has not produced a reliable indication of the proportion of alcohol in the breath of that person (s 6D(1A)).

Failure to co-operate

By RTA 1988, s 6D(2), a constable may arrest a person without warrant if:

(a) the person fails to co-operate with a *preliminary test* in pursuance of a requirement imposed under s 6, and

(b) *the constable reasonably suspects that the person has alcohol or a drug in his body or is under the influence of a drug.*

Section 11(2) provides that 'fails' includes 'refusal'. If a person is given an opportunity to do something and does not do it, there is a failure to comply with that request. Where a person refuses to reply to such a clear request, there has been a failure and it is no defence to allege that the refusal to reply was consequent upon a previous caution. It is essential that the constable makes it clear to the person concerned that he is required to co-operate in the test.

In a case where a driver refused to wait until a preliminary breath test device arrived at the scene, having been properly required to provide a specimen, it was held that he had failed to provide a specimen of breath. A demand that a test be deferred until the arrival of a solicitor amounts to a refusal. There can be no acceptance subject to conditions.

Section 11(3) provides that a person does not co-operate with a preliminary test unless his co-operation is sufficient to enable the test to be carried out, and is provided in such a way as to enable the objective of the test to be satisfactorily achieved. The importance of this can be shown by reference to the preliminary breath test. The various preliminary breath test devices require breath to be supplied in various ways to allow a sufficient sample to be obtained. If sufficient breath has not been supplied there has been a failure. Where a preliminary breath test device requires the illumination of two lights before a satisfactory specimen has been obtained, there is a 'failure' where only one of those lights is illuminated and a police officer is not required to 'read' such a specimen.

An important point to note about the power to arrest after a failure to co-operate is that, before effecting an arrest, the constable must have reasonable cause to suspect that the person has alcohol or a drug in his body or is under the influence of a drug.

General

Section 6D(2A) provides that a person arrested under s 6D, instead of being taken to a police station, be detained at or near the place where the preliminary test was, or would have been administered, with a view to imposing on him there a requirement for an evidential test under RTA 1988, s 7. Thus, a means is provided to carry out an evidential test at the roadside as an alternative to taking the person concerned to a police station.

Clear words must be used in all cases to indicate the reason for arrest and that the person concerned is being compulsorily taken to a police station in consequence of such a failure.

Normally, a constable will exercise his power of arrest in the above two cases but this is not a pre-condition of further steps in the procedure being adopted and is unnecessary if the person concerned is quite happy to proceed to the next stage in the procedure.

No arrest of hospital patient

A person may *not* be arrested under s 6D *while at hospital as a patient* (RTA 1988, s 6D(3)).

Power of entry

By RTA 1988, s 6E a constable may enter any place (using reasonable force if necessary) for the purpose of:

(a) imposing a requirement by virtue of s 6(5) following an accident in a case where the constable reasonably suspects that the accident involved injury of any person; or

(b) arresting a person under s 6D following an accident in a case where the constable reasonably suspects that the accident involved injury of any person.

Clearly, the power to enter to require a preliminary test is limited to cases where the entry is for the purpose of requiring a person to provide a preliminary test under s 6(5) *in a case where a constable has reasonable cause to suspect that the accident involved injury of any person*. A constable is therefore empowered by s 6E to enter premises to test a driver involved in an 'injury' accident or to arrest under s 6D where there has been an 'injury' accident, but he will not be empowered by s 6E to enter to arrest a person under s 6D who, having provided a positive test, or having failed to provide one, seeks sanctuary on private premises before arrest, in any case in which there has not been an 'injury' accident.

It must be emphasised that, with the one exception in (a), police officers do not have power to enter a place without the express or implied consent of the occupier for the purpose of requiring a preliminary breath, impairment or drug test. Likewise, police officers, with the one exception in (b), do not have power to enter a place without the express or implied consent of the occupier for the purpose of making an arrest under s 6D.

Offence of failure to co-operate with a preliminary test under s 6

RTA 1988, s 6(6) provides that a person commits an offence if without reasonable excuse he fails to co-operate with a preliminary test in pursuance of a requirement imposed under s 6. This offence can be committed notwithstanding that the defendant has not been warned that refusal to co-operate will be an offence. Such warning is not required.

As to what constitutes a 'failure to co-operate', see p 541. There cannot be a conviction for this offence unless the co-operation has been required under s 6, and it will not have been so required if the requirement made is invalid for some reason. For example, if the constable is a trespasser at the time of requiring a preliminary breath test he will be behaving unlawfully and his requirement will not be valid.

In addition, where there is a preliminary breath test, there cannot be a conviction for failing to provide a specimen if the requisite procedure is not validly administered, as will be the case if the device used is not an approved one, or if it is defective, or if the constable fails to comply with the manufacturer's instructions as to *assembly*. However, if the constable realises the defect or mistake he may validly require another breath test to be taken on another device. Provided the constable acts in good faith and not negligently, non-compliance by him with the manufacturer's instructions as to the use of the device does not invalidate the test unless the non-compliance is prejudicial to the defendant.

A person cannot be convicted of failing to co-operate with a preliminary test unless his failure was without reasonable excuse. It is not a reasonable excuse that the defendant did not think that he had consumed any alcohol, nor that he mistakenly believed that the requirement made was invalid, nor that he had consumed alcohol after driving.

It has been stated in a number of cases that no excuse can be adjudged reasonable unless the defendant was physically or mentally unable to provide the specimen or its provision would entail a substantial risk to his health. This covers cases such as where the defendant was unable to supply a sufficient specimen of breath because of a medical condition, eg bronchitis or shock, or where he was concussed and unable to appreciate the requirement made of him. However, it has also been held that a foreigner who is unable to understand the purpose of the requirement and the penal consequence of a failure to comply has a reasonable excuse. Not surprisingly, someone who has made himself so drunk as to be unable to understand these matters does not have a reasonable excuse, nor does someone who fails to provide a specimen because he is in a state of self-induced agitation. See also p 560.

PROVISION OF SPECIMEN FOR ANALYSIS

RTA 1988, s 7(1) provides that, in the course of an investigation into whether a person has committed an offence under ss 3A, 4 or 5, a constable may, subject to s 9 (p 555), require him to provide:

(a) two specimens of breath for analysis by means of a device of an approved type (s 7(1)(a)); or
(b) a specimen of blood or urine for a laboratory test (s 7(1)(b)).

No need for prior preliminary test or arrest

The fact that a requirement under s 7(1) can be made 'in the course of an investigation' into whether a person has committed an offence under ss 3A, 4 or 5 indicates that it is not necessary that a preliminary test should have been required (although it normally will have been) and that, if there has been such a test, it is irrelevant that there has been some breach in the procedure relating to it.

In most circumstances, a person required to provide a specimen for analysis will have been arrested under RTA 1988, s 6D after a preliminary breath test. However, s 7 also permits the procedure to be followed if a person has not been arrested, or if he has been arrested on reasonable suspicion of driving etc while unfit through drink or drugs or on reasonable suspicion of a non-drink/drive offence, or if he has been unlawfully arrested. Thus, if a driver reports an accident at a police station, and it is suspected that he has alcohol in his body, he may be required to provide specimens for analysis. No matter how a person came to be at a police station, if he is there in the course of an investigation into whether an offence under ss 3A, 4 or 5 has been committed by him, a specimen may be required under s 7. In addition, a person who alleges that he was a passenger, not the driver of a car, at the time in question, may lawfully be required to provide a specimen as 'a person under an investigation for an offence under either ss 3A, 4 or 5'. It is not necessary to show that he was driving or in charge. Although, of course, liability for an offence under ss 3A, 4 or 5 will depend on proof that he was driving, attempting to drive or in charge at the material time, he can be convicted under s 7 of failing to provide a specimen even if he was not driving, etc.

As already stated, the procedure under s 7 does not constitute an 'interview' for the purposes of the Detention Code referred to in Chapter 4. However, under PACE, s 78, the evidence obtained from the analysis of a specimen can be excluded if it appears to the court that, having regard to all the circumstances, including non-compliance with the preliminary test procedure under s 6, the admission of that evidence would have such an adverse effect on the fairness of the proceedings that the court ought not to admit it. PACE, s 78 was so applied in a case where a preliminary test was improperly required (because the officer did not have one of the requisite reasonable suspicions specified by s 6). A divisional court held that, since the defendant had been denied the protection afforded by s 6, the prosecutor had obtained evidence which he would not otherwise have obtained and, as a result, the defendant was significantly prejudiced in resisting the charge. The magistrates, it held, were therefore entitled to exclude the evidence.

We now turn to the procedure to be adopted under s 7; it should be noted that where the person in question is a patient at a hospital a special procedure, governed by s 9 (p 555), must be followed. It should also be noted that, because time is of the essence, it is only where the delay would be very short that the procedure can be delayed to enable the person to obtain legal advice. The courts have held that, except in such a case: (a) evidence obtained under the procedure will not have been obtained in breach of PACE, s 58, and (b) there will be no reasonable excuse should the person fail to provide a specimen.

Breath specimens

The important part of the procedure under RTA 1988, s 7 is s 7(1)(a) whereby a constable may require two specimens of *breath*. It is only in exceptional circumstances that alternative samples may be required under s 7(1)(b).

Where breath specimens can be required

Section 7(2) provides that a requirement under s 7 to provide specimens of breath can only be made at:

(a) a police station;
(b) a hospital; or
(c) near a place where a relevant breath test has been administered to the person concerned or would have been so administered but for his failure to co-operate with it.

For the purposes of s 7, s 7(2A) provides that 'a relevant breath test' is a procedure involving the provision by the person concerned of a specimen of breath to be used for the purpose of obtaining an indication whether the proportion of alcohol in his breath or blood is likely to exceed the prescribed limit.

Section 7(2B) states that a requirement under s 7 to provide specimens of breath may not be made at or near a place mentioned in (c) above unless the constable making it:

(a) is in uniform; or
(b) has imposed a requirement on the person concerned to co-operate with a relevant breath test in circumstances in which s 6(5) applies (ie after an accident: see p 536).

By s 7(2C), where a constable has imposed a requirement on the person concerned to co-operate with a relevant breath test at any place, he is entitled to remain at or near that place in order to impose on him there a requirement under s 7.

Section 7(2D) provides that if a requirement under s 7(1)(a) has been made at a place other than a police station, such a requirement may subsequently be made at a police station if (but only if):

(a) a device or a reliable device of the type mentioned in s 7(1)(a) was not available at that place or it was for any other reason not practicable to use such a device there, or

(b) the constable who made the previous requirement has reasonable cause to believe that the device used there has not produced a reliable indication of the proportion of alcohol in the breath of the person concerned.

The result of the analysis of a roadside evidential breath specimen is admissible in evidence to the same extent as the analysis of a specimen at a police station.

A constable requiring a person to provide a breath specimen under s 7 is required by s 7(7) to warn him that a failure to supply it may result in his prosecution. The results of a breath test under s 7 taken in the absence of a warning are inadmissible, even if no prejudice to the person results from the lack of a warning.

Specimen of breath

RTA 1988, s 7 requires that the two specimens of breath which have been required under it be analysed by means of a device approved by the Secretary of State. Someone who has provided one specimen of breath which exceeded the prescribed limit but has failed to provide a second specimen cannot, on the basis of that specimen, be convicted of driving with excess alcohol. He can, however, be convicted of failing to provide a specimen of breath (p 559).

Section 11(3) provides that a person does not provide a specimen of breath for analysis unless his co-operation is sufficient to enable the analysis to be carried out, and is provided in such a way as to enable the objective of the analysis to be satisfactorily achieved. This is an important provision, as it is necessary for the person providing the specimen to continue blowing until the indicator lights signify that sufficient breath has been obtained for analysis. If sufficient is not provided, there has been a 'failure'.

For the purposes of the legislation relating to the provision of 'specimens of breath', 'breath' does not mean deep-lung air but should be given its ordinary dictionary definition, ie 'air exhaled from anywhere'; therefore there is no need for the prosecution to prove that the reading from an approved device related solely to deep-lung alcohol and was not related to mouth alcohol.

Approved devices

Currently, the devices approved by the Secretary of State are as follows.

Camic datamaster The machine measures the amount of ethyl alcohol present in a person's breath. It looks only for ethyl alcohol and rejects any other substance which is present in a specimen of breath. The breath analyser is concerned with infrared absorption as a means of determining the presence of alcohol. The machine is combined with a microprocessor (computer) which calculates the validity of any sample provided. A 'run' button initiates the process of analysis and a 'print' button initiates a print-out of the last test. Accuracy checks are fully automatic. Print-outs from the Datamaster show the standard details from satisfactory specimens and record any circumstances in which a non-valid specimen has been detected. The machine detects and records the presence of 'interfering substances'. The clock can be reset by the operator to run in local time in the same way as setting a clock on the standard type of video recorder.

Lion intoxilyzer 6000 UK   This is a microprocessor-controlled, multi-filtering infrared spectrometer. It works on the principle that the greater the concentration of alcohol in the breath, the greater the amount of infrared light which is absorbed. It will detect any interfering substance. The machine indicates its status. When ready for use it indicates 'standby'. It indicates that it is fully powered-up and ready for analysis, or has started to analyse a specimen, when it indicates 'analyse'. The print-outs include the standard details where there is a satisfactory specimen and otherwise indicate the defect which has been detected. So far as the clock is concerned, the computer software changes the reading between summer and winter time without intervention from the operator.

Intoximeter EC/IR   The machine incorporates two separately controlled systems dealing with the analytical functions of the machine and the input/output control system which controls all aspects of the user interface and controls test sequences and protocols. The flow of electrons through the fuel cell is measured and this indicates the amount of alcohol consumed by the fuel cell. The infrared analysis system follows the general pattern of analysis and detects the presence of ethanol. Mouth alcohol and other 'interfering substances' are detected. The use of the 'enter' key initiates a test and the 'P' key produces a print-out of the latest test. The machine incorporates an internal clock and calendar.

Analysis of breath by approved devices

Procedure   The devices have been designed to overcome the problems likely to arise from an evidential viewpoint. At the outset the devices are correctly calibrated but in actual use the devices check themselves for accuracy. They check their correct calibration both before and after each of the two breath samples and a record is made of those calibration checks on the eventual print-out slip. The slip therefore shows two separate readings of alcohol levels sandwiched between records of calibration checks to ensure that the devices are operating correctly. The defendant is present throughout the procedure and has the opportunity to see the device at work. The officer carrying out the test is not obliged to explain to the defendant that the second specimen must be provided within three minutes of the first, or the test will abort.

The devices provide a timed and dated print-out which gives evidence of two separate readings of alcohol content in the breath of the defendant. The normal procedure thereafter is that the constable who has operated the device certifies all copies of the print-out, which shows, in addition to the readings, the particulars of the person from whom the sample is obtained, the signature of the officer, and the signature of the person (or a record that such a signature was refused). The constable's statement declares the lower of the two readings given by the device to be at the specified level and certifies that copies of the statement were signed by him and by the defendant, or that the defendant refused. Where a print-out is not produced in evidence and no oral evidence is given in relation to correct calibration, it is open to a court to find that calibration was correct where there is evidence that the machine was used by a trained operator.

The three devices are computers. In the absence of evidence to the contrary, courts will presume that the computer system was working correctly. If there is evidence that it might not have been, the party seeking to introduce the evidence will need to prove that it was working. It is therefore desirable that police officers record on the appropriate procedural forms the fact that the computer was operating correctly, together with any appropriate observations.

The officer also certifies that he handed a copy of the statement to the defendant who accepted, or declined to accept it. The mere fact that the copy handed to the defendant is not signed by the officer does not affect the validity of the original. RTOA 1988, s 16(3) requires that a copy is either 'handed to' a defendant at the time, or is served upon him not later than seven days before the hearing. Where a defendant signed all the copies of the statement but refused to accept one, a divisional court held that s 16(3) had been complied with when the defendant was offered a copy although there had been no physical transfer of possession of the document. Nevertheless, it will be good practice in such circumstances subsequently to serve a copy of the statement upon the defendant in accordance with s 16(3).

Evidence, however, of the test is not restricted to documentary evidence. Oral evidence may be given of the results of a test should the prosecutor, for some reason, choose not to use the simplified procedure. If this is done, oral evidence of calibration should also be given. It will be advisable, in such cases, to serve a copy of the evidence of the police operator on the defendant in accordance with the Criminal Justice Act 1967, s 9. A divisional court has said that, where an officer is giving oral evidence of the result of an analysis, there is no difference between those results having been seen on the screen, and seen on a print-out.

Defence lawyers have no right to obtain documents kept in relation to breath-testing devices, such as the log, repair reports and memory roll, with a view to searching for material which might support a submission that the device was defective. They must rely upon the prosecution to carry out its duty to disclose material evidence which might be of assistance to the defence. The reliability of the approved device which has been used can be challenged either by direct evidence of some malfunctioning or by evidence from which the inference of unreliability can reasonably be drawn. On the other hand, the reliability of the device used cannot be challenged on grounds relating to all devices of the prescribed type because the type of device has been approved by the Secretary of State.

Only the lower reading is evidence   RTA 1988, s 8 provides that it is only the lower of the two readings given by the machine which may be used as evidence; the other must be disregarded. Where one of the two required readings is not obtained within the same operating cycle of the machine, a second cycle must be commenced. In such a case it is the lower specimen in the first cycle taken and the first of the second cycle which should be recognised. However, where neither of the specimens in the first cycle is valid, a second cycle is undertaken and third and fourth specimens are, effectively, the first and second specimens recognised by the machine.

Where only one satisfactory specimen of breath has been obtained due to a failure of the breath-testing machine and, in consequence, an alternative blood or urine specimen has been obtained and a charge has been preferred alleging an excess of alcohol in that alternative specimen, evidence of the proportion of alcohol found in the one specimen of breath is inadmissible, as it is not relevant to a charge of excess alcohol in another specimen. However, where the accuracy of the analysis of the alternative specimen is challenged, the prosecution is required to prove beyond reasonable doubt that the blood/urine analysis was reliable and if the breath test result is broadly equivalent to the analysis of the alternative specimen then, notwithstanding the reason for requiring the alternative specimen, such evidence is at least capable of tending to support the reliability of the analysis of the alternative specimen. Provided that the significance of the relationship between the two analyses is explained by an expert, the evidence may be relevant.

Blood or urine specimens

Section 7(3) provides that a requirement to provide a specimen of *blood* or *urine* can only be made at a *police station* or at a *hospital*; and that it cannot be made at a police station unless:

(a) the constable making the requirement has reasonable cause to believe that for medical reasons a specimen of breath cannot be provided (because of inability) or should not be required (for some other reason, such as the taking of a drug which affects blood/alcohol levels). Provided that a reasonable cause to believe that there are medical reasons exists, it is irrelevant that the constable himself does not believe that for medical reasons a breath specimen cannot be provided or should not be required. The constable is not required to seek medical advice; the question is whether on the facts before the constable he had reasonable cause to believe that medical reasons exist;

(b) specimens of breath have not been provided elsewhere and, at the time the requirement is made, an approved device or a reliable approved device is not available at the police station or it is then for any other reason not practicable to use such a device there;

(c) an approved device has been used (at the police station or elsewhere) but the constable who required the specimen of breath has reasonable cause to believe that the device has not produced a reliable indication of the proportion of alcohol in the breath of the person concerned;

(d) as a result of the administration of a preliminary drug test, the constable making the requirement has reasonable cause to believe that the person required to provide a specimen of blood or urine has a drug in his body; or

(e) the suspected offence is one under ss 3A or 4 and the constable making the requirement has been advised by a medical practitioner that the condition of the person required to provide the specimen might be due to some drug;

but may then be made notwithstanding that the person required to provide the specimen has already provided or been required to provide two specimens of breath.

The fact that, where the alleged offence is one under ss 3A or 4, the constable has been advised by a medical practitioner that the person's condition may be due to some drug may be proved by oral evidence from the practitioner or by the police officer testifying to what the practitioner said to him. In addition, where unchallenged evidence has been given by the custody officer as to what the practitioner said and did and as to his completion of a procedural form recording the signed observations of the practitioner, justices are entitled to find that this advice had been given. While the endorsement signed by the practitioner is, in its contents, hearsay, the fact that the medical practitioner had signed the endorsement and said things which led the officer to complete the remainder of the form in a particular way, indicating that it was concerned with impairment through drugs after medical advice, has been held to be a matter to which the justices were entitled to have regard.

Reliable approved device not available or not practicable to use it

A '*reliable device*' referred to in (b) is one which the police officer concerned reasonably believes to be reliable. The police officer must reasonably believe that the device *is* unreliable, *not* that it *might be*. Where a police officer thought that the device might be unreliable, because the defendant did not appear to be as badly affected as the device indicated, and required an alternative specimen, the conviction was quashed on the grounds that a belief that the device might be unreliable is insufficient. It is 'not practicable to use a device' if there is no officer available at the station who has been trained to use the device.

Where a defendant has provided two specimens of breath on a machine which is then found to be defective, he may lawfully be required to provide two further specimens of breath for analysis by another device instead of being required to provide blood or urine. Where this involves a suspect being taken to another police station, a divisional court has said that it might be wise, *as a matter of an abundance of caution*, to repeat, at the second police station, the statutory warning that failure may render him liable to prosecution.

Unreliable indication reasonably believed

Under (c) an alternative specimen may be required where a breath-testing device has been used and the constable who required the specimens has reasonable cause to believe that the device has not produced a *reliable indication* of the proportion of alcohol in the breath of the person concerned. Thus, if a device produces two readings which indicate significant differences in the levels of alcohol, it is open to the constable to require an alternative specimen if he reasonably believes that the device has not produced a reliable indication of alcohol in the breath. The latest breath-testing devices incorporate new software which enable them to identify and flag up automatically where it is suspected an interfering substance may be present, or the alleged offender produces mouth alcohol, or the difference between the readings of two specimens is greater than 15 per cent. In such situations a constable will be able to require blood or urine as an alternative.

Reliance on the guidance contained in procedural instructions about the use of breath-testing devices, which leads to the conclusion that an indication is unreliable, will mean that the constable has reasonable grounds to believe that the device has not produced a reliable reading.

It has been held that, where the constable has reasonable cause to suspect that the unreliable indication is due not to the unreliability of the device but to the way in which the individual provided the breath specimens, the officer may offer the individual the opportunity to provide further breath specimens (instead of requiring him to provide a blood or urine specimen).

Decision as to blood or urine

RTA 1988, s 7(4) provides that, if the provision of a specimen other than a specimen of breath may be required in pursuance of s 7, the question whether it is to be a specimen of blood or a specimen of urine and, in the case of a specimen of blood, the question who is to be asked to take it shall be decided (subject to s 7(4A)) by the constable making the requirement. The limitation in s 7(4A) is that there must be no requirement to provide a blood specimen if:

(a) the medical practitioner who is asked to take the specimen is of the opinion that, for medical reasons, it cannot or should not be taken; or
(b) the registered healthcare professional who is asked to take it is of that opinion and there is no contrary opinion from a medical practitioner.

A 'registered healthcare professional' is a registered nurse, or a registered member of a healthcare profession designated by an order made by the Secretary of State. A registered paramedic is so designated. If the constable knows of a medical reason affecting this issue he must pass on that knowledge.

RTA 1988, s 7(4A) also provides that where, by virtue of s 7(4A), there can be no requirement to provide a specimen of blood, the constable may require a specimen of urine instead.

Where a constable requires blood as an alternative and the person required to give blood refuses but offers urine as an alternative, there is a 'failure' to provide a specimen as required under s 7 unless a medical reason exists.

Information to be given to suspect

On requiring a person to provide a specimen of blood or urine, a constable:

(a) must warn him that a failure to provide it may render him liable to prosecution; and

(b) state the reason why a breath specimen cannot be taken or used.

Both requirements (the first made by RTA 1988, s 7(7) and the second by the House of Lords) are mandatory; non-compliance with either of them renders the analysis of a blood or urine specimen inadmissible, even if no prejudice to the person results from the absence of a warning.

In addition, in order to ensure that the person is aware of the role of the medical practitioner or healthcare professional, the constable should tell him that it is for the constable to decide whether the specimen is to be of blood or urine and, if (as is usually the case) the constable decides to require blood, ask the person if there are any medical reasons why a blood specimen cannot or should not be taken from him by a medical practitioner or healthcare professional. Failure to do so will not lead to a dismissal of the charge unless the court has a reasonable doubt as to whether or not the person was prejudiced by not being told about the role of the practitioner or professional. Thus, for example, if he was aware that a practitioner would take the blood specimen, the charge will not be dismissed.

The House of Lords has held that there is no statutory requirement, nor any consideration of fairness, which requires a police officer to ask a suspect if any non-medical reason exists in consequence of which a specimen of blood should not be taken. Any such matter might support 'a reasonable excuse for failure to provide a specimen' but that is a matter for a court.

There is no need to give the person a chance to indicate his preference as to the alternatives of blood or urine.

Where a medical reason is given (for example that the suspect is taking tablets) there must be evidence that the police officer took this into account or had considered whether it could be a medical reason. Although medical possibilities might appear to be far-fetched, it is impossible to *know* that this is so. There must be evidence that the officer has asked questions. Where a 'medical reason' offered is capable of being valid the officer must refer the matter to a medical practitioner. If he does not, a requirement will not have been made pursuant to the Act and evidence of the resulting analysis will be inadmissible.

Taking of blood specimen

RTA 1988, s 11(4) provides that a person supplies a specimen of blood if and only if:

(a) he consents to the taking of such a specimen from him; and

(b) the specimen is taken from him by a medical practitioner or, if it is taken in a police station, either by a medical practitioner or by a registered healthcare professional.

Specimens of blood taken from a person incapable of consenting

RTA 1988, s 7A deals with the taking of blood specimens from a person who has been involved in an accident and is, for some reason, incapable of giving a valid consent to the taking of a specimen of blood.

Section 7A(1) provides that a constable may request a medical practitioner to take a specimen of blood from a person ('the person concerned') irrespective of whether that person consents if:

(a) that person is a person from whom the constable would (in the absence of any incapacity of that person and of any objection under s 9 referred to on p 556) be ntitled under s 7 to require the provision of a specimen of blood for a laboratory test;

(b) it appears to that constable that this person has been involved in an accident which constitutes or is comprised in the matter that is under investigation or the circumstances of that matter;

(c) it appears to that constable that this person is or may be incapable (whether or not he has purported to do so) of giving a valid consent to the taking of a specimen of blood; and

(d) it appears to that constable that this person's incapacity is attributable to medical reasons.

Section 7A(2) provides that a request under s 7A:

(a) must not be made to a medical practitioner who for the time being has any responsibility (apart from the request) for the clinical care of the person concerned; and

(b) must not be made to a medical practitioner other than a police medical practitioner unless:

   (i) it is not reasonably practicable for the request to be made to a police medical practitioner; or

   (ii) it is not reasonably practicable for such a medical practitioner (assuming him to be willing to do so) to take the specimen.

A 'police medical practitioner' is a medical practitioner who is engaged under any agreement to provide medical services for purposes connected with the activities of a police force.

By s 7A(3), it is lawful for a medical practitioner to whom a request is made:

(a) to take a specimen of blood from the person concerned irrespective of whether that person consents; and

(b) to provide the sample to a constable.

Section 7A(4) states that, if a specimen is taken pursuant to a request under s 7A, the specimen must not be subjected to a laboratory test unless the person from whom it was taken:

(a) has been informed that it was taken; and

(b) has been required by a constable to give his permission for a laboratory test of the specimen; and

(c) has given his permission.

On requiring a person to give permission for the purposes of s 7A for a laboratory test of a specimen, a constable is required by s 7A(5) to warn him that a failure to give the permission may render him liable to prosecution.

It is an offence under s 7A(6) for a person, without reasonable excuse, to fail to give permission for a laboratory test of a specimen of blood taken from him under s 7A. It is a defence that a warning was not given under s 7A(5) or has not been understood by the person in question.

Other provisions about blood or urine specimens

Blood   If a specimen of blood is taken, RTOA 1988, s 15(4) provides that a specimen of blood must be disregarded unless:

(a) it was taken from the defendant (D) with his consent and, if taken in a police station, was taken by a medical practitioner or a registered healthcare professional, or, if taken elsewhere, was taken by a medical practitioner; or
(b) it was taken from D by a medical practitioner under RTA 1988, s 7A and D subsequently gave his permission for a laboratory test of the specimen.

Evidence that a specimen of blood was taken from D with his consent by a medical practitioner (or a registered healthcare professional) may be given by the production of a document purporting to certify that fact and to be signed by a medical practitioner (or registered healthcare professional). Blood specimen kits are provided by the forensic science laboratories and are kept at police stations.

Urine   A urine specimen must, by RTA 1988, s 7(5), be provided within one hour of the requirement and after the provision of a previous specimen. This means that a specimen must be taken and discarded, and another provided (for analysis) within one hour of the requirement. A police officer is not obliged to extend the time but, if he does accept a second specimen of urine outside the time limit, the result of the analysis of that specimen is nevertheless admissible. It has been held that a constable is entitled to require a specimen of urine where, the breath-analysis device being inoperable, he had required blood but a doctor was unable to obtain such a specimen when the defendant's vein collapsed. The rule is that an unproductive request for one specimen (ie the specimen is not provided) does not prevent a subsequent request for another specimen from being valid.

A divisional court has held that, where a urine sample is taken from someone who is catheterised, a specimen is provided for the purposes of s 7(5) each time the catheter bag is emptied, rather than at the point the urine leaves the body.

Providing D with part of specimen   RTOA 1988, s 15(5) provides that where, at the time a blood or urine specimen was provided by D, he asked to be provided with such a specimen, evidence of the proportion of alcohol or any drug found in the specimen is inadmissible on behalf of the prosecution unless:

(a) the specimen is one of two parts into which the specimen was divided at the time it was provided; and
(b) the other part was given to D.

'At the time' does not mean 'then and there' nor 'in the presence of D'. It suffices that the division is closely linked in time and part of the same event as the taking of the sample. It is, however, desirable that the division takes place in D's presence. There is no obligation to inform D that he may request part of the specimen. Provided that at his request the specimen has been divided and one part has been given to him, but it is handed back to the police for some reason, it is irrelevant that he never collects it; the statutory requirement is satisfied, and evidence of the alcohol level in the part retained by the police is admissible. Where someone is not in a position to take receipt of the second part of a sample, it may be provided to him for present purposes by handing it to someone else for safe-keeping. This was held by a divisional court in a case where D was detained at a hospital and both of his arms had been incapacitated. The second part of a blood sample which he had provided was given to a friend for safe-keeping. There were no locker facilities available in the ward. The divisional court upheld a finding that D had been given a specimen.

RTOA 1988, s 15(5A) provides that, where a specimen was taken under RTA 1988, s 7A, evidence of the proportion of alcohol or any drug found in the specimen is not admissible on behalf of the prosecution unless:

(a) the specimen in which the alcohol or drug was found is one of two parts into which it was divided at the time it was taken; and

(b) any request to be supplied with the other part of the specimen taken from D, which was made by him when he gave his permission for a laboratory test of the specimen, was complied with.

Labelling   When a specimen of blood or urine has been obtained, the labels identifying it with that person must be carefully made out and attached securely to the specimen which must then be sent to the forensic science laboratory.

Statutory option to replace specimen of breath with an alternative specimen

The prescribed limit in relation to alcohol in the breath is 35 microgrammes of alcohol in 100 millilitres of breath. RTA 1988, s 8(2) provides that, *if the specimen with the lower proportion of alcohol contains no more than* 50 *microgrammes of alcohol in* 100 *millilitres of breath*, the person may claim that it should be replaced by a specimen of blood or urine. This is called the 'statutory option'. The burden is upon the person from whom the specimen is required to exercise that option. However, he must be informed of the fact italicised and of his right to exercise the option, unless he makes this impossible (as where he refuses to listen and walks away). Police officers must take care, when explaining this right, not to say anything which might have the effect of dissuading a person from exercising this right, or of depriving him of the opportunity to exercise the option, or of causing him to exercise it in a different way from that which he would have adopted if everything had been explained. If they do say something which might have one of these effects, any conviction resulting from the original analysis will be quashed. If the person who makes such a claim under s 8(2) was required to provide specimens of breath for analysis under s 7 at or near a place where a preliminary breath test was administered, a constable will have to take him to a police station for an alternative specimen to be provided. A power of arrest without warrant is provided by s 8(2A).

Decision as to whether blood or urine

Subject to RTA 1988, s 7(4A) (see p 550), the decision whether a 'replacement specimen' shall be of blood or urine is for the constable.

It is not necessary to invite the person concerned to express a preference as to whether the specimen should be of blood or urine (since it suffices that he is told that, if he exercises the right to have a replacement specimen taken, it will be for the police officer to decide whether that specimen is to be of blood or urine).

In addition to telling the suspect that a specimen of blood will be taken by a medical practitioner (or, at a police station, a registered health care professional) unless a medical practitioner considers that there are medical reasons for not taking blood, a constable who has decided to require blood should ask the suspect if there are any medical reasons why a specimen of blood could or should not be taken by such a person. Failure to do so will not lead to a dismissal of the charge unless the person was prejudiced by being deprived of the opportunity to exercise the option, or being caused to exercise it in a way which he would not have done if everything had been said. The suspect should be told of the role of the medical practitioner at the outset of the procedure.

Where a police officer has, at the outset, explained the whole procedure to a suspect who then exercises the option, it is not essential that the whole procedure be repeated when the suspect exercises the option. The reason is that the information will still be present and effective in the suspect's mind.

A divisional court has held that it is not *strictly* necessary for a police officer to inform the suspect that the breath specimen which that person has provided exceeds the statutory limit, since the fact that an alternative is being offered makes it obvious that the specimen provided shows an alcohol content in excess of the limit. A divisional court has also held that a person exercising his statutory option is not required to give his consent *to the police officer* to the taking of blood.

Where a suspect gives a reason for not giving blood, which may amount to a medical reason (eg a medically recognised phobia against needles), the police officer should ask him for an explanation of that reason (because this may establish that the alleged reason is unfounded) or, if necessary, call a medical practitioner to establish whether there is a medical reason. If this is not done, the prosecution cannot rely on the specimen of breath supplied. On the other hand, where a suspect says that he would prefer to provide urine as he does not like needles but accepts that there was no reason why a specimen of blood could not, or should not, be taken by a medical practitioner and then refuses to supply blood, the police officer is under no obligation to make further inquiries about the suspect's fear of needles. The suspect's two replies, taken together, do not create sufficient doubt as to a medical reason. Consequently, the prosecution will be entitled to rely upon evidence of the breath specimen.

It is a question of fact whether a suspect's statement to the effect that he cannot provide blood raises a potential medical reason for not providing a blood specimen. A divisional court has held that, where a driver replied 'I do take tablets' when asked if there was a medical reason why he could not or should not give blood, this was capable in principle of being a valid reason and the police officer should not have gone on to arrange for a specimen of blood to be taken without making inquiries as to the nature of the medication and seeking medical advice if necessary.

Exercise of statutory option

A suspect has no right to legal advice before deciding whether or not to exercise the option; the requirements of fairness inherent in the statutory option entitle him to know of his option but do not entitle him to legal advice as to the result of exercising it. If a person, having been refused access to legal advice, declines to exercise his option, the original specimen is admissible. It would seem that if a suspect does not understand that the option exists, because, for example, of a breakdown in communication, the original specimen could be excluded by the court, although it will not be if the suspect's inability to understand is due wholly or partly to his consumption of alcohol. Where the option has been offered and refused, but the suspect then changes his mind, it is for the justices to decide, in accordance with the evidence, whether the procedure had come to an end at a time when the suspect changed his mind. It is likely that a more or less immediate change of mind will be acceptable as in other similar circumstances such words have been held to be 'relevant words and conduct to be taken into account'. However, once the procedure has moved on to the next stage, justices will have grounds to support a conclusion that the issue of acceptance or refusal had been finalised, in which case a claim to exercise the option would be ineffective. It has also been held that, if a suspect initially indicates that he wishes to exercise the statutory option but later unequivocally indicates that he will not provide the sample requested, this constitutes an abandonment of the option, with the result that his lower breath specimen can be used to prove the offence.

New specimen replaces breath specimen

If the option to provide a blood or urine specimen is taken and a blood or urine specimen is provided, the results of the analysis of that specimen at the laboratory replace the lower of the readings of the breath specimen obtained by the machine for evidential purposes, regardless of whether the reading is higher or lower.

Miscellaneous

Where a suspect has opted to replace the analysis of a specimen of breath with that of a specimen of blood which he opts to provide, it is not necessary for the prosecution to prove the calibration of the breath-testing device. The positive specimen of breath, in such circumstances, is no more than a prerequisite for the supply of a specimen of blood; the analysis of the breath specimen ceases to have any probative value in proving the offence.

If a suspect given the statutory option is asked to provide a blood specimen, but the police officer is unable to contact a medical practitioner or healthcare professional, the police officer has power to ask the suspect to provide a urine specimen instead. If the suspect is unable to do so (eg because he has visited the lavatory in the meanwhile), the lower of the two breath specimens can be used in evidence since the statutory option procedure only prohibits either specimen of breath being used if a blood or urine specimen is provided under it.

HOSPITAL PATIENTS

RTA 1988, s 9 lays down a special procedure which applies while a person is at a hospital as a patient.

Section 9(1) states that, while a person is at a hospital as a patient, he must not be required to co-operate with a preliminary test or to provide a specimen under RTA 1988, s 7 unless the medical practitioner in immediate charge of his case has been notified of the proposal to make the requirement, and:

(a) if the requirement is made, it must be for co-operation with a test administered, or for the provision of a specimen, at the hospital; but
(b) if the medical practitioner objects on the ground specified in s 9(2) (below), the requirement must not be made.

This procedure is concerned with whether the practitioner objects to a preliminary test of, or a specimen being provided by, a patient, and not whether the practitioner objects to a particular type of test or specimen.

Section 9(1A) provides that, while a person is at a hospital as a patient, no specimen of blood may be taken from him under s 7A (person incapable of consenting) and he must not be required to give his permission for a laboratory test of a specimen taken under s 7A unless the medical practitioner in immediate charge of his case:

(a) has been notified of the proposal to take the specimen or to make the requirement; and
(b) has not objected on the ground specified in s 9(2).

By s 9(2), the ground on which the medical practitioner may object is:

(a) in a case within s 9(1), that the requirement or the provision of the specimen or (if one is required) the warning required by s 7(7) (p 545) would be prejudicial to the proper care and treatment of the patient; and
(b) in a case within s 9(1A), that the taking of the specimen, the requirement or the warning required by s 7A(5) (p 551) would be so prejudicial.

A divisional court has held that where a police officer has knowledge of a medical reason affecting the decision as to whether a blood sample should be taken he must pass on such knowledge to the medical practitioner dealing with the defendant.

If the medical practitioner objects on the ground that the requirement, or the provision of a specimen, or the warning about the consequences of failing to provide it would be prejudicial to the proper care and treatment of the patient, the requirement in question must not be made.

It should be noted that if a preliminary test undergone by a patient proves positive, or he fails to undergo it, he may not be arrested, but this does not prejudice the rest of the procedure being followed (s 6D(3)).

Procedure

The procedure in relation to hospital patients is strictly controlled. The steps which a constable should take in a 'hospital case' in normal circumstances (ie where the patient does not appear incapable of consenting to the taking of a blood specimen) are as follows:

(a) seek out the medical practitioner in charge of the case;
(b) request his consent to the provision of a preliminary breath test explaining the method of operating the particular device to be used;
(c) obtain that consent before proceeding further: the doctor may not object if the process is not prejudicial to care or treatment;
(d) if the medical practitioner does not object, require a preliminary test;
(e) if the test is negative, explain that there will be no further action;
(f) if the test is positive or the patient fails to provide it, obtain the medical practitioner's consent to the provision of two specimens of breath or the taking of a specimen for laboratory analysis, after having explained the procedure; and
(g) if the medical practitioner does not object, obtain two specimens of breath, or obtain a specimen of blood with the consent of the person, the sample being taken by a medical practitioner, or obtain a urine specimen followed within one hour by a second urine specimen (the evidential specimen).

It has been held in Scotland that, where a police officer has received the consent of a medical practitioner in immediate charge of a patient at a hospital, he is not required to obtain the further consent of another one to whose charge the patient has been transferred.

It is not strictly necessary to obtain a preliminary test before requiring a specimen for analysis but an explanatory circular states that it is assumed that this will be done. It is good practice to give a person the opportunity quickly to clear himself of suspicion.

Where a requirement to provide a specimen of blood has been made at a hospital but the patient is discharged before the specimen can be taken, that requirement is not varied or discharged by the mere fact that the person to whom the requirement was made is then taken to a police station. The specimen of blood may be taken there. The only exception is if a police officer abrogates the procedure started at the hospital by asking for breath specimens and thereby setting in train the procedure under s 7.

EVIDENCE IN PROSECUTIONS UNDER ROAD TRAFFIC ACT 1988, s 3A, 4 OR 5

By RTOA 1988, s 15(2), evidence of the proportion of alcohol or any drug in a specimen of breath, blood or urine provided by or taken from a defendant (D) must, in all cases, be taken into account and it *must be assumed* that the proportion of alcohol in D's breath, blood or urine at the time of the alleged offence was not less than that found in the specimen. Evidence of a breath, blood or urine specimen is not the only admissible evidence. The result is that, if the analysis or test reveals a proportion below the prescribed limit, but the magistrates are sure from expert evidence that, given the lapse of time between the alleged offence and the provision of the specimen, the proportion of alcohol at the time of the alleged offence was over the prescribed limit, they may convict D of an offence under ss 3A, 4 or 5. On the other hand, since D's alcohol level *must be assumed to be not less* than that found in the sample, he is not permitted to adduce evidence at trial that, although above the limit when the specimen was taken, he was below it when actually driving.

The assumption made by s 15(2) does not apply if there is evidence that the evidential device was unreliable or that a blood or urine specimen is unreliable (eg because analysis of the part given to D is below the limit). A divisional court held that justices can assume that a device was reliable unless there is evidence that it was not, and that if there is evidence that a device was unreliable the prosecution are obliged to prove its reliability. Presumably, the same approach as taken in that case applies where the challenge is to the reliability of a blood or urine specimen. Evidence relating to unreliability may be direct evidence, but—depending on the disparity between the claimed consumption and the analysis—evidence of the unreliability may be provided by reference to the amount of alcohol allegedly consumed before the specimen was provided. Expert evidence of the reading which could be produced in the circumstances by D is not essential.

Although s 15 says that the proportion of alcohol or any drug in a specimen provided by D must in all cases be taken into account, there are exceptions. This is because s 15(4) expressly states that evidence derived from a specimen of blood must be disregarded unless:

(a) it was taken with D's consent (i) in a police station by a medical practitioner or a registered healthcare professional, or (ii) elsewhere by a medical practitioner; or
(b) it was taken from D by a medical practitioner under RTA 1988, s 7A (without consent) and D subsequently gave his permission for a laboratory test of the specimen.

In addition, as seen on p 552, in the case of a blood or urine specimen, the evidence derived from it is inadmissible if D's request for one of the parts into which it was divided was not properly complied with.

Breaches of the procedure laid down by RTA 1988, ss 7 to 9 will render the evidence obtained from the specimen inadmissible, because a specimen obtained in breach of that procedure cannot be said to have been obtained under the Act, as RTOA 1988, s 15(2) requires.

Hip-flask defence

RTOA 1988, s 15(3) allows D what is often described as the 'hip-flask' defence. It provides that, in cases under RTA 1988, s 3A, 4 or 5, the assumption as to alcohol level must not be made if the defendant proves that:

(a) he consumed alcohol before he provided the specimen or had it taken from him; and
   (i) in relation to an offence under s 3A, after the time of the alleged offence, and
   (ii) otherwise, after he had ceased to drive, attempt to drive or be in charge of a vehicle on a road or other public place; and
(b) had he not done so the proportion of alcohol in his breath, blood or urine would not have exceeded the prescribed limit and, if the proceedings are for an offence under RTA 1988, s 4, would not have been such as to impair his ability to drive.

It has been held that the burden of proof placed on D is a persuasive one, ie proof on the balance of probabilities, and that this is not incompatible with the presumption of innocence under the European Convention on Human Rights, art 6(2).

The hip-flask defence can arise where D, having been required to provide a preliminary test, locks the door of his car and drinks from a flask in the hope that he will then be in a position to allege that his alcohol level was so increased. It may also arise where D has driven home, following an accident, and has then taken a number of drinks in order to make it almost impossible to establish what the level might have been prior to his 'post-incident' drinking. While s 15(3) does not eliminate such possibilities, it places the burden on D of satisfying a court that, had he not done so, he would not have exceeded the prescribed limit in a specimen provided for analysis.

In such cases it will almost invariably be necessary for D to call expert medical or scientific evidence in order to discharge this burden of proof, unless in rare cases the non-expert evidence which is called is such that a layman would reliably and confidently say that the subsequent drinking was the explanation for the excess alcohol.

Defendants who are able to prove the hip-flask defence may nevertheless be liable for the offence of wilfully obstructing a constable in the execution of his duty. In any event, such deliberate consumption is liable to be self-defeating since D will often still be in charge of the vehicle at the time of the additional imbibing. It is therefore good practice, in instances in which D drinks from a bottle before submitting to testing procedures, to charge D with an offence of 'being in charge, etc' should tests prove to be positive.

Use of certificates

RTOA 1988, s 16(1) provides that evidence of the proportion of alcohol in a specimen of breath may be given by the production of the print-out produced by the breath-analysis device together with the certificate signed by a constable (normally the operator) (which certification may be made on the print-out). As already explained, that certification is to the effect that the print-out relates to a specimen provided by D at the date and time shown in it. The print-out and certificate are only admissible in evidence on behalf of the prosecution if a copy of it (or both) has been handed to D when the print-out was produced, or has been served on him not later than seven days before the hearing. Moreover, the certificate is not so admissible if D, not later than three days before the hearing or within such further time as the court may allow, has served notice on the prosecution requiring the attendance at the hearing of the constable who signed the certificate. While the Act makes specific provision for print-outs to be offered in evidence, it does not require that this be done. Consequently, a constable may give oral evidence of the readings obtained on the screen of the device, provided that he is able to testify that the device was working properly and was accurately self-calibrating.

RTOA 1988, s 16(1) also provides that evidence of the proportion of alcohol or a drug in a specimen of blood or urine may be given by the production of a certificate signed by an authorised analyst as to the proportion of alcohol or any drug found in the specimen identified in the certificate. However, such a certificate is only admissible in evidence on behalf of the prosecution if a copy of it has been served on D not later than seven days before the hearing. In default of this, evidence of the analysis can be given by the authorised analyst attending as a witness. In addition, the certificate is not admissible under s 16(1) if, not later than three days before the hearing or within such further time as the court may allow, D has served notice on the prosecutor requiring the attendance at the hearing of the analyst who signed the certificate. However, a divisional court has held that, if the analyst is unable to attend, a court is entitled to admit the evidence of a certificate of analysis as hearsay under CJA 2003, s 116.

A divisional court has held that the s 16(1) requirement for an analyst to be authorised only applies to the giving of a certificate under s 16 and does not apply to, or prevent, the giving of oral evidence or a statement under CJA 1967, s 9 (p 241).

OFFENCE OF FAILING TO PROVIDE A SPECIMEN REQUIRED UNDER s 7

RTA 1988, s 7(6) makes it an offence for a person, without reasonable excuse, to fail to provide a specimen when required to do so in pursuance of s 7. Where a person is charged with failure to provide a specimen of blood for laboratory analysis in circumstances in which an approved breath-testing device was not available, and the validity of the request for a sample of blood is challenged, the non-availability of the device must be proved in accordance with the laws of evidence. However, where a defendant (D) contended that there was no direct evidence to prove that there was no approved device available at the police station, as there could have been a second machine there, a divisional court ruled that evidence that the device failed to operate together with evidence that D was told that it was not therefore possible to take specimens of breath was sufficient. As in the case of the offence under s 6(6), there cannot be a conviction under s 7(6) if the requirement made for a specimen is invalid for some reason; the fact that the person was brought to the police station after a wrongful arrest or after a trespass by the police does not render the requirement invalid.

Fail

As already said 'fail' includes 'refuse'. However, where D refused to supply a specimen of breath, but within five seconds said that he wanted to change his mind, there was no refusal. A divisional court said that the justices had ignored the motorist's words five seconds after his refusal. Regard must be had to all words and conduct in reaching a conclusion. It is submitted that, in the light of this and other rulings, the right to change one's mind will exist until the constable has moved on to the next stage of the procedure. Where a person declines to provide a specimen of breath, alleging a medical reason which is discounted by a medical practitioner, there is a failure to provide a specimen without reasonable excuse. The police officer is not obliged to start the procedure all over again. If it were otherwise, recalcitrant persons could play the system to gain some delay. Once D is required to provide a specimen an offence is committed if, without reasonable excuse, D does not provide it.

In addition, where D refuses to supply specimens of breath and it is subsequently found that, because of his limited lung capacity, he would have been unable to supply specimens, this cannot amount to a reasonable excuse. There must be a causative link between the refusal and the excuse and this cannot be so where the condition was not known to exist at the time of the refusal.

A person fails to provide a specimen of breath if the specimen is insufficient for analysis, or is so provided that it cannot be analysed.

Reasonable excuse

A foreigner who is unable to understand the purpose of the requirement and the penal consequences of a failure to comply has a reasonable excuse. In addition, there would be a reasonable excuse for failing to provide a specimen of blood where D has refused to sign a form of consent (to providing a specimen of blood) until he has read it. Apart from these instances an excuse cannot be adjudged reasonable unless D was physically or mentally unable to provide the specimen requested, or its provision would entail a substantial risk to his health. While an invincible repugnance, amounting to a medically recognised phobia, to blood being taken is a reasonable excuse, the fear of the sight of blood is not; D can always close his eyes or look away.

A divisional court has held that there is no obligation on D, asked to provide a specimen of breath for analysis, to declare a medical condition which might make it difficult or impossible for him to provide the specimen. However, D's failure to communicate a medical condition of which he was aware at the time of the request will normally result in the court concluding that a belatedly proffered medical excuse is not acceptable and indicates a wilful failure to provide a specimen. Where D claimed before a court that he had a 'phobia' in relation to needles but had made no mention of this to the police officer requiring the specimen, and had made no attempt to provide a specimen, a divisional court held that there could be no question of him having a reasonable excuse.

Stress caused by self-precipitated agitation cannot amount to a reasonable excuse for failure to provide breath, nor can mental anguish caused by a constable's conduct which D considered to be oppressive. There would have to be a causal connection between such anguish and the failure. Such a connection was found in one borderline case where the justices found that there had been a reasonable excuse where D was said by her doctor to be suffering from a condition in which any stress would cause her to suffer from extremes of agitation which would require chemical intervention. D had not taken medication which controlled her condition within the preceding week or so. The justices found that D had been suffering from a panic attack at the police station and this had prevented her from supplying specimens of breath. They noted the doctor's opinion that she would have understood the procedure and that there would be nothing of a physical or mental nature to prevent her from supplying breath, but considered that there was a causative link between her physical condition and her inability to supply breath. A divisional court refused to interfere with this finding.

The fact that D was so drunk that he could not understand the procedure which was being followed does not amount to a reasonable excuse because it does not relate to his *capacity* to supply a specimen. However, where D failed to provide two specimens of breath and two police officers gave evidence that he appeared to be too drunk to do so, a divisional court refused to overturn a decision of the justices that he had had a reasonable excuse for not providing a specimen due to stress resulting from adverse personal and family circumstances which had led to recent breathlessness, although no medical evidence was offered. The justices had reached their decision on unimpeachable findings of fact and the divisional court would not interfere.

While a fear of AIDS is not a reasonable excuse for not providing a specimen of blood, a medically recognised *phobia* in relation to contracting AIDS is, as stated above. The wording of the relevant provisions is such that a person who fails to provide a specimen under s 7 on the grounds that he has been unlawfully arrested also does not have a reasonable excuse.

Someone who has not been given time to read the Detention Code, or to refer to a law book, does not have a reasonable excuse for not providing a specimen in consequence of that lack of opportunity, nor does someone who has been advised by his solicitor not to provide a specimen. Nor does someone who refuses to supply a specimen unless he can first consult a solicitor, unless the consultation will only cause a very short delay to the taking of the specimen.

D does not have the burden of proving reasonable excuse. There must, however, be evidence in support of facts which could constitute a reasonable excuse, otherwise the prosecution does not have to prove that there was no reasonable excuse. In almost every imaginable case of alleged physical or mental incapacity, that evidence must be medical evidence; in exceptional cases, however, other evidence—even that of D—can suffice. An example of such an exceptional case was where D had provided one specimen of breath but began to lose composure, sobbing continuously and experiencing difficulty in breathing. She was unable to provide a second specimen. A divisional court ruled that the justices were entitled to conclude that D was physically incapable of providing a specimen, whilst accepting that the case was close to the borderline. The need for medical evidence on such a point could not be accepted in absolute terms.

Other points

As already indicated, on requiring a person to provide a specimen in pursuance of RTA 1988, s 7, a constable must warn him that a failure to provide it may render him liable to prosecution (s 7(7)). Although an omission to warn is no defence to a charge of failing to co-operate with a preliminary test, contrary to s 6(4), it is a defence to a charge under s 7(6) that such a warning has not been given or has not been understood by the person from whom the specimen is required.

In terms of available punishment, an offence under s 7(6) is as serious as the one under ss 4 or 5 in respect of which the specimen was sought (but less serious than one under s 3A).

Because there is only one offence under s 7(6), an information or written charge framed in terms of s 7(6) alone, without reference to the circumstances in which the requirement was made, is unlikely to fail for duplicity. It would be *good practice* to inform D of the circumstances surrounding the charge as soon as they have been established. In most cases, the issue of whether he was driving, attempting to drive or in charge of the vehicle will be known at the time of his arrest. It is therefore preferable that the charge should specify whether the investigation was being carried out under RTA 1988, ss 3A, 4(1), 4(2), 5(1)(a), or 5(1)(b).

DETENTION OF PERSONS AFFECTED BY ALCOHOL

RTA 1988, s 10(1) provides that a person who has been required under ss 7 or 7A to provide a specimen of breath, blood or urine may be detained at a police station (or, if the specimen was provided otherwise than at a police station, arrested and taken to and detained at a police station) if a constable has reasonable grounds for believing that, if he was released and drove or attempted to drive, he would commit an offence against either s 4 or 5. In practice this may often involve detention until a negative preliminary test. On any question under s 10 whether a person's ability to drive properly is or might be impaired through drugs, a constable must consult a medical practitioner and must act on his advice (s 10(4)).

Section 10(1) does not apply to a person if it ought reasonably to appear to the constable that there is no likelihood of his driving or attempting to drive while his ability to drive properly is impaired or while the proportion of alcohol in his breath, blood or urine exceeds the prescribed limit (s 10(2)).

A hospital patient may not be arrested and taken to a police station if it would prejudice his proper care and treatment (s 10(3)).

SPECIAL PROVISIONS—DRINK-DRIVE OFFENCES

Alcohol ignition interlocks

New sections 34D, 34E, 34F, 34G, and 41B are prospectively inserted into RTOA 1988 by the Road Safety Act 2006 (RSA 2006). Their effect is to empower courts to allow offenders to participate, at their own expense, in an 'alcohol ignition interlock programme'. Agreement permits the court to reduce a period of disqualification. The option applies to those convicted of a second 'relevant drink-driving offence' within a period of 10 years who would otherwise have to be disqualified for no less than two years. The programme must last for not less than 12 months but must not exceed one-half of the original unreduced period of disqualification. It cannot be offered to a person in respect of whom a drink-drive offenders' rehabilitation order is made.

The main feature of the programme is that the offender is restricted to driving a vehicle which is fitted with an approved alcohol interlock device which is designed to prevent the vehicle from being driven until an acceptable specimen of breath has been provided (nine microgrammes of alcohol in 100 millilitres of breath). Such devices will be approved by the Secretary of State. Failure to comply with a condition will result in the restoration of the full period of disqualification.

Reduced disqualification period for attendance on course for drink-drive and other specified offences

Such disqualification is available where a person is disqualified under RTOA 1988, s 34 for a period of not less than 12 months (disregarding any extension period, when such periods are brought into force) after conviction for a listed 'drink-drive' offence. The provisions are contained in RTOA 1988, ss 34A to 34C.

Offences under RTA 1988, ss 3A, 4, 5, and 7 are listed for the purposes of RTOA 1988, ss 34A to 34C. RTOA 1988, ss 34A to 34C are prospectively substituted, and s 34BA is prospectively added, by RSA 2006.

Under the prospective provisions, the scheme relates to 'relevant offences' under RTA 1988 and 'specified offences' against RTA 1988 and RTRA 1984. Relevant offences are those against RTA 1988, s 3A (where the offence relates to alcohol); s 4 (where the offence relates to alcohol); and ss 5, 7, and 7A. Specified offences are not relevant for the purposes of this chapter but are those against RTA 1988, s 3 (careless or inconsiderate driving) and s 36 (failing to comply with a traffic sign), RTRA 1984, s 17(4) speeding on motorway) and s 89(1) (speeding elsewhere).

Under RTOA 1988, ss 34A to 34C (in their original and substituted forms) courts are empowered to reduce a period of disqualification where an offender agrees to undergo a training course at his own expense, upon the successful completion of the course, by an amount specified in the order. The reduced period must not be less than three months, nor more than one-quarter of the disqualification period.

The option is only available where the offender has been disqualified for not less than 12 months (disregarding any extension period, when such periods are brought into force). It is not available to those who have committed one of the above offences within the preceding three years and successfully completed an approved course in consequence of such offences, nor to a person who is within his probationary period under the Road Traffic (New Drivers) Act 1995.

OTHER OFFENCES

Cycling while unfit

By RTA 1988, s 30, it is an offence to ride a cycle with two or more wheels on a road or other public place while unfit to ride through drink or drugs. Being in charge of such a cycle in such circumstances is not an offence under RTA 1988, but it is an offence under the Licensing Act 1872, s 12, which is described in the next paragraph.

Drunk in charge of a carriage, horse, etc

By the Licensing Act 1872, s 12 (p 612) it is an offence for a person to be drunk while in charge on any highway or other public place of any carriage, horse, cattle or steam engine. A motor vehicle, trailer, bicycle or tricycle is a 'carriage' for this purpose, but a person liable to be charged with an offence of driving or being in charge of a motor vehicle when unfit to drive through drink or drugs should not be charged with the present offence since its maximum punishment is far less severe than that for the appropriate offence under RTA 1988.

Drinking—guided public transport systems and airports

The Transport and Works Act 1992 (TWA 1992), s 27 applies to transport systems which are used, or are intended to be used, wholly or partly for the carriage of members of the public. Its provisions are restricted to railways, tramways, and other *guided transport systems* specified by the Secretary of State. The guided transport systems at Birmingham International Airport; Merry Hill Centre, West Midlands; and Gatwick and Stansted Airports have been so specified. The first two systems are, however, no longer in operation.

TWA 1992, s 27 creates two offences involving drink or drugs on such transport systems which can be committed by the following workers:

(a) drivers, guards, conductors, signalmen and others who control or affect the movement of vehicles operating under one of these systems;

(b) persons who couple or uncouple such vehicles or check that they are working properly;
(c) persons maintaining the permanent way (or other support or guidance structures), signalling systems and power supply used by such vehicles; and
(d) supervisors of, and look-outs for, persons engaged in the functions set out in categories (b) or (c) above.

An offence is committed where:

(a) a person in one of the above categories carries out his duties when unfit to carry out that work through drink or drugs; or
(b) a person in one of those categories carries out his duties after consuming so much alcohol that the proportion of it in the breath, blood or urine exceeds the prescribed limit (which is the same limit as prescribed by RTA 1988).

A constable in uniform is empowered by TWA 1992, s 29 to require a preliminary breath test where he has reasonable cause to suspect that:

(a) a person working on a transport system has alcohol in his body; or
(b) a person has been working on a transport system with alcohol in his body and still has alcohol in his body.

This power is extended to circumstances in which there has been *an accident or dangerous incident* and a uniformed constable has reasonable cause to suspect that, at the time of that event, the person was working in one of the above capacities and that his act, or omission, while so working, might have been the cause of the accident or incident. A 'dangerous incident' means an incident which, in the constable's opinion, involved a danger of death or personal injury.

Failure without reasonable excuse to comply with a request under s 29 is an offence.

The appropriate powers under RTA 1988 in relation to arrest and entry, obtaining specimens for analysis, the option to have a breath specimen replaced if the alcohol content in it does not exceed 50 microgrammes in 100 millilitres of breath, failure to comply with a request, and hospital patients, are applied with modifications, together with the provisions of RTOA 1988 in respect of the use of specimens and documentary evidence. There is, of course, no power of disqualification from driving. The consent of the Secretary of State or the DPP is required before proceedings for such offences may be instituted.

These provisions are important to all police officers. Following a train crash, it is the first police officer on the scene who will be expected to require a screening breath test if it applies.

The Road Traffic (Drink and Drugs) (Cambridgeshire Guided Busway) Regulations 2011 apply RTA 1988, ss 4–11 (pp 531–62) to vehicles on the Cambridgeshire Guided Busway with modifications whereby 'road' in those sections includes the Busway and 'motor vehicle' includes a mechanically propelled vehicle intended or adapted for use on the Busway.

Persons involved in shipping or aviation: alcohol and drugs

Although, like the provisions just discussed, these matters are not concerned with the subject 'drinking and driving' they are outlined here as a matter of convenience. Police officers on duty at ports and airports may be required to act under powers provided by Railways and Transport Safety Act 2003 (RTSA 2003) which are related to the consumption of alcohol or drugs by those involved in marine or aviation activities.

Persons involved in marine activities

RTSA 2003, s 78 provides that a professional master of a ship, a professional pilot of a ship, or a professional seaman while on duty on a ship, commits an indictable (either way) offence if his ability to carry out his duties is impaired because of drink or drugs. He also commits an indictable (either way) offence if the proportion of alcohol in his breath, blood or urine exceeds the prescribed limit. A master, pilot, or seaman is 'professional' if (and only if) he is so acting as a master, pilot, or seaman in the course of a business or employment.

By s 79, a professional seaman in a ship who is off duty but who in the event of an emergency would or might be required by the nature or terms of his engagement or employment to take action to protect the safety of passengers commits an indictable (either way) offence if his ability to take such action is impaired because of drink or drugs, or the proportion of alcohol in his breath, blood or urine exceeds the prescribed limit.

By s 80, which has not been brought into force at the time of writing, non-professionals (eg yachtsmen) on board a ship under way, who are exercising or purporting to exercise a navigational function, may commit the same offences.

The 'prescribed limit' in all of these cases is the same as that provided by RTA 1988 (p 534). The appropriate powers under RFA 1988 to administer preliminary tests, to obtain specimens for analysis, the option to have a breath specimen replaced if the alcohol content in it does not exceed 50 microgrammes in 100 millilitres of breath, protection for a hospital patient and detention of persons affected by alcohol or drugs are applied with modifications to these circumstances, together with the provisions of RTOA 1988 in relation to the use of specimens and documentary evidence.

A marine official is empowered to detain a ship if he reasonably suspects that a person on board is committing, or has committed, an offence under RTSA 2003, ss 78 to 80, provided that before doing so, or as soon as possible after doing so, he requests the presence of a constable.

Police powers   RTSA 2003, s 85 provides that, unless the person concerned is a patient at a hospital, a constable may arrest a person without warrant if he reasonably suspects that the person is committing an 'under the influence' offence under ss 78 to 80 or has committed such an offence and is still under the influence of drink or drugs.

By s 86, a constable in uniform may board a ship, or enter any place, if he reasonably suspects that he may wish to exercise a power under s 83 (to obtain specimen) or s 85 in respect of a person who may be on that ship, or in that place. He may use reasonable force to board a ship or enter a place and may be accompanied by one or more persons.

Persons involved in aviation activities

RTSA 2003, s 92 provides that a person commits an indictable (either way) offence if he performs an aviation function at a time when his ability to perform the function is impaired because of drink or drugs, or if he carries out an activity which is ancillary to an aviation function at a time when his ability to perform the function is impaired because of drink or drugs.

An 'aviation function' for the purposes of RTSA 2003 is any of the following (and only any of the following):

(a) acting as a pilot, flight navigator, flight engineer or radio-telephony engineer of an aircraft during flight;

(b) acting as a member of the cabin crew of an aircraft during flight;

(c) attending the flight deck during flight to give or supervise training, to administer a test, to observe practice or to monitor or record the gaining of experience;

(d) acting as a licensed air traffic controller (other than a licensed student); or

(e) acting as a licensed aircraft maintenance engineer.

An 'ancillary function' means an activity which is undertaken by a person who has reported for a period of duty in respect of the function, and is carried out as a requirement of, for the purpose of or in connection with the performance of, the function during that period. A person who, in accordance with the terms of an employment or undertaking, holds himself ready to perform an aviation function if called upon to do so is to be treated as carrying out an activity ancillary to the function. Where someone sets out to perform an aviation function anything which he does as preparation to perform it is to be treated as an activity ancillary to it.

By RTSA 2003, s 93, it is an indictable (either way) offence for a person to perform an aviation function or a function which is ancillary to an aviation function at a time when the proportion of alcohol in his breath, blood or urine exceeds the prescribed limit. The prescribed limit in relation to 'aviation functions' is:

(a) in the case of breath, 9 microgrammes of alcohol in 100 millilitres;

(b) in the case of blood, 20 milligrammes of alcohol in 100 millilitres; and

(c) in the case of urine, 27 milligrammes of alcohol in 100 millilitres.

This limit does not, however, apply in respect of a licensed aircraft maintenance engineer. In that case the higher limits which apply to motor vehicle drivers, those involved in guided transport systems and those on ships apply.

The appropriate powers under RTA 1988 to administer preliminary tests, to obtain specimens for analysis under s 7 and s 7A, the option to have a breath specimen replaced if the alcohol content in it does not exceed 50 microgrammes in 100 millilitres of breath, protection for a hospital patient and detention of persons affected by alcohol or drugs are applied with modifications to these circumstances, together with the provisions of RTOA 1988 in relation to the use of specimens and documentary evidence.

Police powers   RTSA 2003, s 97 provides that, unless the person concerned is a patient at a hospital, a constable may arrest a person without warrant if he reasonably suspects that this person is committing such an offence or has committed an offence under s 92 and is still under the influence of drink or drugs.

A constable in uniform may board an aircraft, or enter any place, if he reasonably suspects that he might wish to exercise a power under s 96 (to obtain a specimen) or 97 on the aircraft, or in that place. For the purpose of boarding an aircraft or entering a place a constable may use reasonable force and may be accompanied by one or more persons.

CHAPTER 16

Children and Young Persons

The various statutes dealing with children and young persons are partly concerned with punishing adults, particularly those under a duty to care for a child or young person, whose conduct is physically or mentally harmful to him or otherwise harmful to his proper development. They are also concerned with the responsibilities of local authorities to receive a child or young person into their care, with the power of family proceedings courts to put a child or young person into care, when this is necessary on specified grounds for his welfare, with the power of a court to make a child safety order or parenting order, and with barring unsuitable people from working in a range of activities with children.

MEANING OF TERMS

Various terms are used in the relevant legislation with particular meanings. The most common of these terms are:

Child

For most legal purposes of relevance to a police officer, a child is a person under 14. However, there are occasions when the term is used in relation to persons who are 14 or over. For example, the Education Act 1996 defines 'child' for the purposes of the legislation relating to child employment as meaning any person not over compulsory school age. In the legislation relating to street trading and performances abroad a 'child' means someone under 18, and the same is the case in enactments dealing with the responsibilities of a local authority in relation to the welfare of children under the Children Act 1989 (ChA 1989) and in the Safeguarding of Vulnerable Groups Act 2006 relating to barring.

For the purposes of law, a person attains an age on the relevant anniversary of his birth. The Children and Young Persons Act 1933 (CYPA 1933), s 99 states that when a person is brought before a court, other than as a witness, the issue of whether or not he is a child or young person must be decided upon inquiry by the court as to the age of the person. If it is later found that the age was different from that established by the court, any judgment or order will not be invalidated.

Young person

For the purpose of the CYPAs 1933 and 1969, in which the term is frequently used, a 'young person' is a person who has reached 14 and is under 18.

Guardian

Generally, the CYPAs are concerned with 'guardians' in the wide sense of including any person who, in the opinion of the court, has for the time being the care of the child or young person. This covers a much wider range of people than 'legal guardian'. A 'legal guardian' is a person appointed to have parental responsibility by a signed and witnessed document (including a will) or by order of a court.

RESPONSIBILITIES OF PARENT OR GUARDIAN

By CYPA 1933, s 34A where a child or young person is charged with an offence or is, for any other reason, brought before a court, the court may in any case, and must in the case of a child or young person who is under 16, require a person who is a parent or guardian of his to attend court during all stages of the proceedings, unless and to the extent that the court is satisfied that it would be unreasonable to require such attendance. 'Parent or guardian' in this context includes a local authority which has parental responsibility for a child or young person, and which has him in its care, or in accommodation which it provides under ChA 1989.

Where a child or young person under 16 is convicted of an offence, the court is obliged by the Powers of Criminal Courts (Sentencing) Act 2000 (PCC(S)A 2000), s 137 to order that a fine, surcharge, costs or compensation be paid by the parent or guardian (or by a local authority with parental responsibility for the child or young person if it is in the authority's care or accommodation), unless the court is satisfied that such parent or guardian cannot be found, or it would be unreasonable to make an order for payment, having regard to the circumstances of the case. In the case of a young person of 16 or more, the court may make such an order. These provisions also apply to circumstances in which such fines result from failure to comply with a community order.

PCC(S)A 2000, s 150 empowers a court, where a child or young person is convicted of an offence, to order a parent or guardian to enter into a recognisance not exceeding £1,000 to take proper care of him and to exercise proper control over him. In the case of a child or young person under 16, the court is obliged to exercise these powers where it is satisfied, having regard to the circumstances of the case, that it is desirable in the interests of preventing him from committing further offences to do so. Where it does not exercise these powers, it must state in open court that it is not so satisfied and give its reasons for so finding. Such a recognisance may be for a period not exceeding three years. The order must not extend beyond the date upon which the person becomes 18. A parent or guardian must consent to the making of such an order. If he refuses and the court considers his refusal unreasonable, it may order him to pay a fine not exceeding £1,000.

Such orders may not be made in respect of the binding over of a parent or guardian where a referral order is made under the Youth Justice and Criminal Evidence Act 1999.

Where a court has made a youth rehabilitation order it may include in such a recognisance a condition that the minor's parent or guardian ensures that the minor complies with the requirements of that sentence.

OFFENCES OF CRUELTY TO PERSON UNDER 16

Responsibilities are placed upon social agencies by various Acts of Parliament and this has had the effect of relieving the police of some of their burdens. 'Child abuse' is dealt with by the criminal law by the offences of cruelty towards children and young persons which are governed by CYPA 1933, s 1. This provides that someone who has attained the age of 16 and has the responsibility for any child or young person under that age commits an indictable (either way) offence, if he wilfully assaults, ill-treats, neglects, abandons, or exposes him, or causes or procures him to be assaulted, ill-treated, neglected, abandoned, or exposed, in a manner likely to cause him unnecessary suffering or injury to health.

CYPA 1933, s 1 can be broken down into the following elements.

Responsibility for a child

For a person to be guilty of an offence contrary to CYPA 1933, s 1(1), he or she must have attained the age of 16 and have the responsibility for the child or young person under that age.

In this context a person is presumed to have responsibility for a child or young person if:

(a) he has parental responsibility for him under ChA 1989 (which the mother and father will both have if they were married to each other when the child or young person was born, or which only the mother will have if the mother and father were not so married, or which another person (including the father in the instance just given) or a local authority may acquire by operation of law); or

(b) he is otherwise liable to maintain him; or

(c) he has care of him.

The basic elements of the offence

CYPA 1933, s 1(1) specifies several ways in which an offence of cruelty can be committed by a person (of 16 or over) with responsibility for a child or young person. It specifies the following, each of which must occur wilfully:

(a) assaulting;

(b) ill-treating;

(c) neglecting;

(d) abandoning; or

(e) exposing,

a child or young person under 16 *in a manner likely to cause him unnecessary suffering or injury to health* (including injury to or loss of sight, or hearing, or limb, or organ of the body, and any mental derangement).

In what follows it must not be forgotten that those who have the responsibility for a child or young person are also guilty if they cause or procure the commission of one of these offences by someone else.

CYPA 1933, s 1 does not prevent a parent, or other person with the right to do so, administering punishment to a child or young person. As explained in Chapter 23, the right to administer corporal punishment is now very limited.

Wilfully

'Wilfully' makes it clear that any offence under CYPA 1933, s 1 requires mens rea on the part of the defendant (D) as to the risk of unnecessary suffering or injury to health. For example, on a charge of wilfully neglecting, D must be aware of the risk of unnecessary suffering or injury to health resulting from the neglect, and if (to continue the example) that charge involves failure to provide adequate medical aid, the requirement of wilfulness can only be satisfied where D was aware that the child or young person's health might be at risk if he was not provided with medical aid or where D's non-awareness of this risk was due to his not caring whether the child's health was at risk or not.

Assault

'Assault' for the purpose of CYPA 1933, s 1 requires more than a mere common assault or battery. An assault or battery may amount to no more than frightening a person or giving him a light slap, but this could hardly be done 'in a manner likely to cause unnecessary suffering or injury to health'. Although consent could be an issue in some minor assaults, it must be remembered that, particularly in the case of children, mere submission to a person in authority does not signify consent.

Ill-treat

This signifies a continuous course of conduct leading to unnecessary suffering. A series of assaults, each of which, if considered on its own, would not amount to an offence against s 1, might together form ill-treatment over a period of time. Likewise, persistent frightening or bullying will suffice if it is likely to cause unnecessary suffering.

Neglect

This signifies a want of adequate care. The likelihood of causing unnecessary suffering or injury to health can be caused by a deliberate omission to supply medical or surgical aid. Direct proof of such likelihood is not always strictly necessary as this may be inferred from the evidence of neglect and its actual effect. Section 1(2) provides that a parent or other person legally liable to maintain a child or young person or his legal guardian is deemed to have neglected him in a manner likely to cause injury to health if he has failed to provide adequate food, clothing, medical aid or lodging for him or if, having been unable to provide such food, clothing, medical aid or lodging, he has failed to take steps to procure it to be provided under the enactments applicable in that behalf.

Section 1(2) also declares that if the death of an infant under three years of age is caused by suffocation (other than by disease or a foreign body in the throat) while the infant was in bed with a person of 16 or over who went to bed under the influence of drink, that person will be deemed to have neglected the infant in a manner likely to cause injury to health.

Abandon or expose

It is helpful to consider these terms together since an abandonment frequently leads to exposure. To abandon a child means leaving it to its fate. If a woman separated from her husband takes her child to her husband's home and leaves the child at his door, she abandons that child. From the moment of abandonment the child is exposed and, if that exposure leads to suffering, the child has been abandoned and exposed in a manner likely to cause unnecessary suffering. If the husband becomes aware that the child has been left on his doorstep and allows it to remain there, he cannot then disclaim his custodial responsibilities. This exposure does not cover exposure to risk. A father, who took his son and other boys on to a baulk of timber and floated the timber into deep water in London Docks, was not guilty of an offence under s 1, because this was not the type of exposure to which the section refers.

Police action in cruelty cases

It is now standard procedure to refer reports of cruelty to children to officers of the National Society for the Prevention of Cruelty to Children. The NSPCC attempts, through a process of encouragement, persuasion, and warnings, to remedy the situation without recourse to the law whenever possible.

In all cases of non-accidental injury to children the police are likely to become involved at the outset when carrying out their role as one of the emergency services. Local authorities, social services, the NSPCC and the police have the power to initiate any civil proceedings before a family proceedings court when a child appears to be in need of care. The police have power to detain children who appear to be in need of care and to take them to safe places. We deal with these matters later in this chapter. Police officers must never feel that the other social agencies have assumed responsibility for these matters. It is still the duty of the police to take some initial action to ensure the safety of any child in circumstances where a report of child abuse is received. Such cases may, in appropriate circumstances, be referred to other agencies later.

OTHER OFFENCES

There are a number of offences under CYPA 1933 which require little explanation. These offences are committed in relation to children of a specified age, which varies from offence to offence.

Brothels

By CYPA 1933, s 3(1), it is an offence for any person who has responsibility for a child or young person who has attained the age of four, but is under 16, to allow that child or young person to reside in or frequent a brothel. What is and what is not a brothel is discussed in Chapter 30. It is important to remember that a woman who is a prostitute and receives men in her own room, but does not allow other women to use her room, is not keeping a brothel. This is the most likely situation to come to the notice of the police. Although an offence is not committed in these circumstances, care proceedings (see later) could perhaps be considered (as they should in the case of a brothel).

Begging

Causing or procuring a child or young person under 16 to be in any street, premises, or place for the purpose of begging or receiving alms, or of inducing the giving of alms (whether or not there is any pretence of singing, playing, performing, offering anything for sale or otherwise) is an offence contrary to CYPA 1933, s 4(1). There is a similar offence under the Vagrancy Act 1824, s 3.

It is an offence under CYPA 1933, s 4(1) for the person having the responsibility for such a child or young person to allow him so to act. Such a person allows a child or young person to beg in the street if he fails to prevent this when he could and should have prevented it. If it is proved that a child or young person was in a street, etc for the purpose of begging, etc and that a person with responsibility for him allowed him to be in the street, etc, that person is presumed to have allowed him to be there for that purpose, until the contrary is proved.

Intoxicating liquor

It is an offence, contrary to CYPA 1933, s 5, to give, or cause to be given, intoxicating liquor to a child under the age of five, otherwise than on the orders of a duly qualified medical practitioner or in an emergency.

Tobacco

By CYPA 1933, s 7(1), it is an offence to sell tobacco or cigarette papers to any person under 18 whether for his own use or not. The sale is not required to be face-to-face. It is irrelevant that the under-18-year-old is acting as an agent for someone else. 'Tobacco' includes cigarettes and any product containing tobacco intended for oral or nasal use, and smoking mixtures intended as a substitute for tobacco. Selling tobacco or cigarette paper to a person under the age of 18 is an offence of strict liability. The proprietor of a shop is guilty even when he has played no part in the transaction and knows nothing about it. However, s 7(1A) provides that it is a defence for a defendant to prove that he took all reasonable precautions and exercised all due diligence to avoid the commission of an offence. The fact that all possible precautions have not been taken does not rule out this defence. Thus, where shop staff had been provided with written instructions setting out a procedure to be followed when in doubt about a customer's age, such procedures being regularly reviewed and supervised, a divisional court ruled that the justices were entitled to find the defence made out, even though the defendant shop proprietor could have done other things to try to prevent the offence.

CYPA 1933, s 7(3) places responsibilities upon constables and uniformed park keepers to seize tobacco or cigarette papers from a person apparently under 18 whom they find smoking in any street or public place. These articles will then be disposed of by the appropriate authorities.

None of the above provisions about sale to a child applies to a child who is an employee of a tobacconist or a uniformed messenger employed by a messenger company.

The Children and Young Persons (Protection from Tobacco) Act 1991, s 3(1) provides that it is an offence for a person carrying on a retail business to sell to anyone unpacked (ie unpackaged) cigarettes. Section 4(1) makes it an offence not to display on retail premises where tobacco is sold notices concerning the illegality of tobacco sales to persons under 18.

Restricted premises orders and restricted sales orders

CYPA 1933 s 12A governs 'restricted premises orders' which may be made where a person (X) is convicted of an offence against s 7. The person who brought the proceedings may, by way of complaint, apply for such an order in respect of the premises where the offence was committed. An order prohibits the sale on the premises of any tobacco or cigarette papers to any person and remains in force for a specified period (no more than one year). Notice must have been given of the intention to apply for such an order to persons affected by the order who may make representations.

By s 12B, a 'restricted sale order' may also be made. Such an order has the effect of prohibiting X (above) from selling tobacco or cigarette papers and from having any management function in respect of such sales on the premises.

These orders may only be made where a court is satisfied that on at least two occasions within the past two years the offender had committed other 'tobacco offences'.

An offence is committed under s 12C(1) if a person sells tobacco or cigarette papers in contravention of a restricted premises order and knew, or ought reasonably to have known, that the sale was in contravention of the order. It is an offence under s 12C(2) to fail to comply with a restricted sales order but it is a defence to prove that the defendant took all reasonable precautions and exercised all due diligence to avoid the commission of the offence.

Risk of burning

If a person of 16 or over, having responsibility for a child under 12, allows the child to be in a room containing an open fire grate or any heating appliance liable to cause injury to a person by contact with it, and it is not sufficiently guarded against the risk of the child being burnt or scalded without taking reasonable precautions against that risk and in consequence the child is killed or seriously injured, that person commits an offence contrary to CYPA 1933, s 11.

It will be noted that death or serious injury must result from the unguarded fire or appliance and it is almost certain that civil proceedings for a 'care order' (see below) would result from any incident likely to be charged as an offence under s 11, which is punishable only by a fine.

Section 11 goes on to say that a prosecution under s 11 will not affect a person's liability to prosecution for any indictable offence. For example, if a child died as a result of his injuries it is probable that proceedings on indictment for manslaughter would follow.

Safety at entertainments

CYPA 1933, s 12(1) provides that, wherever an entertainment is provided in a building for an audience mainly of children, then, if there are more than 100 children attending the entertainment, there must be a sufficient number of adult attendants, properly stationed and instructed in their duties, to prevent more people being admitted than can properly be accommodated and to control the movement of those entering and leaving and general safety. If these provisions are not complied with, the person providing the entertainment is guilty of an offence under s 12(2). A constable may enter any building in which he has reason to believe that such an entertainment is taking place, or is about to take place, to ensure that this is being done. Section 12 does not apply to any entertainment in a dwelling house.

Street trading

By CYPA 1933, s 20(1), no child may engage in, or be employed in, street trading. By way of exception, by-laws made by a local authority may authorise children who have attained the age of 14 to be employed by their parents in street trading and may regulate such trading by a child so authorised (s 20(2)). By-laws must specify the days and hours during which, and the places at which, such children may engage or be employed in street trading.

In the event of a breach of s 20(1) or a by-law made under s 20(2), the employer etc commits an offence under s 2(1). A child who breaches s 20(1) or such a by-law commits an offence under s 21(3).

Dangerous performances

By CYPA 1933, s 23, no person aged 16 or under may take part in any performance in which his life or limbs are endangered without a local authority licence. Anyone who causes or procures this to be done, or a parent or guardian who allows it, commits an offence. No proceedings may be brought under s 23 except by or with the authority of a chief officer of police. The types of performance referred to are those in respect of which a charge is made, or which take place in licensed premises or registered clubs, or which are live or recorded broadcast performances, or performances filmed for public exhibition.

LOCAL AUTHORITY CARE

The Children Act 1989 (ChA 1989) makes various provisions for children to be brought into the care of a local authority (ie the council of a county (including a unitary authority) or a metropolitan district or London borough council or the Common Council of the City of London (in England) or a county or county borough council (in Wales)). For the purposes of these provisions, a 'child' is a person under 18, unless otherwise stated. ChA 1989 emphasises that the child's welfare is paramount in all matters, particularly those concerned with his upbringing, and that delay in deciding such matters is likely to prejudice the child's welfare. The guiding principle of ChA 1989 is that the court should not make an order unless to do so is considered better for the child than making no order. Most of the Act's provisions relate to the functions of local authorities and the social service agencies. Those matters which most directly affect the police are considered later. ChA 1989, s 21 requires local authorities to make provisions for the reception and accommodation of children, including a child who is in police protection (see p 576). A child whom a custody officer has authorised to be kept in police detention after arrest must be received by a local authority where that officer so requests.

Care and supervision orders

ChA 1989, s 31 provides that, on the application of a local authority or authorised person (NSPCC or other body authorised by the Secretary of State), a family proceedings court (ie that part of a magistrates' court hearing proceedings under the 1989 Act) may make an order:

(a) placing the child with respect to whom the application is made in local authority care; or
(b) putting him under local authority supervision or the supervision of a probation officer.

A court may only make a care or supervision order if it is satisfied:

(a) that the child concerned is suffering, or is likely to suffer, significant harm; and
(b) that the harm, or likelihood of harm, is attributable to:
  (i) the care given to the child, or likely to be given to him if the order were not made, not being what it would be reasonable to expect a parent to give him; or
  (ii) the child being beyond parental control.

'Harm' means ill-treatment or the impairment of health or development, including, for example, impairment suffered from seeing or hearing the ill-treatment of another.

Such an order may not be made with respect to a child who has reached the age of 17 (or 16 in the case of a child who is married). A care order may not be made until the court has considered a care plan. On an application for a care order the court may make a supervision order, and vice versa.

As can be seen, where a child has been the victim of offences of cruelty or sexual abuse or neglect, an application may be made by a local authority or an authorised person for either of the above orders to be made. In addition, the provisions at (b)(ii), above, supply a means of obtaining a care order in circumstances in which a child who is below the age of criminal responsibility (10) habitually commits a crime, or where a child receives adequate care from his parents but is so out of control that he is likely to harm himself.

Care and supervision orders are civil orders, as are the other orders under ChA 1989 mentioned below. In consequence, the standard of proof required of an applicant for one of these orders is only proof on the balance of probabilities.

Child assessment orders

ChA 1989, s 43 permits a local authority or authorised person to apply to a family proceedings court for such an order where difficulties are being experienced in making an assessment of the needs of such a child. This may be due to lack of co-operation by those who have parental responsibility for the child. Such an order permits assessment to be made over a period not exceeding seven days and may require any person to produce the child to a person named in the order and to comply with specified instructions. However, a court should not make such an order if it is satisfied that there are grounds for making an emergency protection order and that it ought to do so rather than make a child assessment order.

Emergency protection order

There will be occasions upon which action must be taken immediately to protect a child. ChA 1989, s 44 empowers a court, on the application of any person, to make an emergency order for the protection of a child. It may do so if it is satisfied that:

(a) there is reasonable cause to believe that the child is likely to suffer significant harm if:
  (i) he is not removed to accommodation provided by or on behalf of the applicant, or
  (ii) he does not remain in the place in which he is then being accommodated;
(b) in the case of an application made by a local authority:
  (i) inquiries are being made with respect to the child under the authority's duty to investigate where it reasonably suspects that a child is suffering, or is likely to suffer, significant harm, and
  (ii) these inquiries are being frustrated by access to the child being unreasonably refused to a person authorised to seek access and that the applicant has reasonable cause to believe that access to the child is required as a matter of urgency; or
(c) in the case of an application made by an authorised person:
  (i) the applicant has reasonable cause to suspect that the child is suffering, or is likely to suffer, significant harm,
  (ii) the applicant is making inquiries with respect to the child's welfare, and
  (iii) those inquiries are being frustrated by access to the child being unreasonably refused to a person authorised to seek access and the applicant has reasonable cause to believe that access to the child is required as a matter of urgency.

An emergency protection order directs any person in a position to do so to produce the child, and authorises the child's removal to accommodation provided by or on behalf of the applicant or the prevention of the removal of the child from a hospital or other place. It also gives the applicant parental responsibility for the child. An emergency protection order has effect for such period, not exceeding eight days, as is specified by the court, but the court has power (on one occasion only) to extend it for up to a further seven days. An emergency protection order can include an exclusion requirement in specified circumstances. Such a requirement enables the child to stay in its home by excluding someone else, such as a suspected child abuser, from it.

By s 44(15), it is an offence intentionally to obstruct a person exercising the power (under an order) to remove or prevent the removal of a child.

Removal and accommodation of children by police in emergencies

ChA 1989, s 46 empowers police officers to take a child into 'police protection' in pre-scribed circumstances. It also places responsibilities upon 'designated police officers', that is officers designated by chief officers of police to conduct inquiries into such cases.

Where a constable has reasonable cause to believe that a child would otherwise be likely to suffer significant harm, he may:

(a) remove the child to suitable accommodation and keep him there; or
(b) take such steps as are reasonable to ensure that the child's removal from any hospi-tal, or other place, in which he is then being accommodated is prevented.

Where a police officer knows that an emergency protection order p 575 is in force in respect of a child, he should not exercise the power of removal under ChA 1989, s 46, unless there are compelling reasons to do so.

As soon as is reasonably practicable after taking a child into police protection, as above, the constable must:

(a) inform the local authority within whose area the child was found of the steps that have been, or are proposed to be, taken with respect to the child and the reasons for taking them;
(b) give details to the local authority within whose area the child is ordinarily resident ('the appropriate authority') of the place at which the child is being accom-modated;
(c) inform the child (if he appears capable of understanding);
    (i) of the steps that have been taken and of the reasons for taking them, and
    (ii) of the further steps which may be taken with respect to him under s 46;
(d) take such steps as are reasonably practicable to discover the wishes and feelings of the child;
(e) secure that the case is inquired into by a designated officer; and
(f) where the child was taken into police protection by being removed to accommoda-tion which is not provided:
    (i) by or on behalf of a local authority, or
    (ii) as a refuge (ie a voluntary home or registered children's home certified as a refuge),
    secure that he is moved to accommodation which is so provided.

The constable must also, as soon as reasonably practicable, inform:

(a) the child's parents;
(b) any other person who has parental responsibility for him; and
(c) any other person with whom the child was living immediately before being taken into police protection,

of the steps that he has taken under s 46 with respect to the child, the reasons for taking them and the further steps that may be taken with respect to him under the section.

When the case has been inquired into by the designated officer, he must release the child from police protection unless he considers that there is still reasonable cause for believing that the child would be likely to suffer significant harm if released.

No child may be kept in police protection for more than 72 hours. However, at any time while the child is in police protection, the designated officer may apply *on behalf of the appropriate local authority* for an emergency protection order to be made with respect to the child. Such an application may be made whether or not the local authority knows of it or agrees to its being made.

Whilst a child is in police protection, the designated officer must do what is reasonable in all the circumstances of the case for the purpose of safeguarding or promoting the child's welfare (having regard in particular to the length of the period during which the child will be so protected).

The designated officer must allow:

(a) parents;
(b) any other person with parental responsibility;
(c) any person with whom the child was living immediately before he was taken into police protection;
(d) where there is a 'contact order' (an order permitting contact by named persons), any such named person; and
(e) any person acting on behalf of any of these persons,

to have such contact (if any) with the child as, in the opinion of the designated officer, is both reasonable and in the child's best interest. However, if a child taken into police protection is in accommodation provided by, or on behalf of, the appropriate authority, these contact responsibilities are those of the authority rather than the designated officer.

Abduction of children in care, etc

It is an offence against ChA 1989, s 49(1) for any person, knowingly and without lawful authority or reasonable excuse, to take a child to whom s 49 applies from the responsible person, or to keep such a child away from the responsible person, or to induce or assist or incite such a child to run away or stay away from the responsible person. These offences apply to a child who is in care, the subject of an emergency protection order, or in police protection. A 'responsible person' means any person who for the time being has care of him by virtue of the care order, the emergency protection order, or ChA 1989, s 46 (p 576).

Where such abduction has occurred, ChA 1989, s 50 permits a court to issue a 'recovery order'.

Police powers

By ChA 1989, s 48, an emergency protection order may include a requirement directed to a person to disclose the whereabouts of the child and may authorise an applicant to enter premises specified by the order and search for the child. Such a warrant may authorise a constable to assist an applicant where entry is being, or is likely to be, denied. It may also direct that a constable be accompanied by a registered medical practitioner, registered nurse or registered midwife.

If a child or young person is absent without the consent of the responsible person:

(a) from a place of safety to which he has been taken under PCC(S)A 2000, Schs 1 or 8 (pending court appearance after referral by youth offender panel, or after breach of reparation order or for revocation or amendment of order), CJIA 2008, Sch 2 (pending court appearance for breach of youth rehabilitation order) or under the Street Offences Act 1959, Sch (p 880);

(b) from local authority accommodation in which he is required to live as a requirement of a youth rehabilitation order; or

(c) from local authority accommodation:
   (i)   in which he is required to live by a youth rehabilitation order,
   (ii) to which he has been remanded under the Street Offences Act 1959, Sch,
   (iii) to which he has been remanded after an arrest for referral back to the appropriate court, or for breach of a reparation order, or
   (iv) to which he has been remanded or committed for trial or sentence,

CYPA 1969, s 32 authorises a constable to arrest such a child or young person without a warrant. When so arrested he must be conducted to a place of safety, local authority accommodation, or such other place as the responsible person may direct.

Arrest of young offenders in breach of remand conditions

CYPA 1969, s 23A provides that a constable may arrest without warrant someone under 18 who has been remanded (or committed) to local authority accommodation in respect of any breach of a condition of that remand (or committal) if the constable has reasonable grounds for suspecting that the offender has broken any of those conditions.

The arrested person must be brought before a justice as soon as is practicable and in any event within 24 hours of his arrest. In reckoning any period of 24 hours, no account shall be taken of Christmas Day, Good Friday, or any Sunday.

Section 23A is prospectively replaced by the Legal Aid, Sentencing and Punishment of Offenders Act 2012, s 97 which makes the same provision as above except that it omits the words in brackets.

CHILD SAFETY ORDERS

These are governed by the Crime and Disorder Act 1998 (CDA 1998), ss 11 to 13.

A child safety order is an order which:

(a) places a child under 10, for a period specified in the order, under the supervision of the responsible officer; and

(b) requires the child to comply with such requirements as are so specified.

The permitted maximum period of supervision for the above purposes is 12 months.

The requirements that may be specified under (b) are those which the court considers desirable in the interests of:

(a) securing that the child receives appropriate care, protection and support and is subject to proper control; or

(b) preventing any repetition of the kind of behaviour which led to the child safety order being made.

The main responsibility of the responsible officer will be to the child and paramount to that will be the need to supervise the child and to ensure full compliance with the requirements of the order. However, the officer also has an important role to play in relation to the child's family circumstances.

The 'responsible officer' will be one of the following who is specified in the order:

(a) a social worker of a local authority; and

(b) a member of a youth offending team.

The child safety order is directed to the child and requires or prohibits conduct specified in it. Where it is linked with a parenting order (below) that order could make associated requirements of the parent. For example, if the child safety order requires a child to be home by 7 pm, the associated parenting order could require the parent to ensure that the child is home by then.

Child safety orders are made by magistrates' courts sitting as family proceedings courts. A court can make an order only if it is convinced that, with respect to a child under 10, one or more of the following conditions is satisfied:

(a) the child has committed an act which, if he had been 10 or over, would have constituted an offence;

(b) a child safety order is necessary to prevent the child committing such an act; or

(c) the child has acted in a manner that caused or was likely to cause harassment, alarm or distress to one or more persons not of the same household as himself.

A child safety order cannot be made without an application by a local authority (defined in the same way as on p 574).

Breach of a child safety order

Proceedings for breach of a child safety order must be brought by the responsible officer.

If on such an application it is proved that the child has failed to comply with any requirement in the order, a magistrates' court sitting as a family proceedings court may make an order varying the order in the same way as on a variation after an application for discharge.

Breach of a child safety order may also result in the making of a parenting order; it is one of the triggers of such an order.

PARENTING ORDERS

Parenting orders

A parenting order can be made under CDA 1998, ss 8 or (prospectively) 8A, or under the Anti-social Behaviour Act 2003 (A-sBA 2003), ss 20, 26, 26A, or 26B.

A parenting order is a court order requiring a parent or guardian (ie the person for the time being with care):

(a) to comply, for a period not exceeding 12 months, with such requirements ('the compliance requirements') as are specified in the order; and

(b) to attend, for a concurrent period not exceeding three months, such counselling and guidance programme as may be specified in directions given by the responsible officer.

A parenting order need not include a counselling and guidance-session requirement under (b) if the parent has previously been made subject to a parenting order, although it may do so.

The 'responsible officer', eg a probation officer, social worker or youth offending team member, who is to specify the counselling or guidance sessions to be attended will be specified in the order.

The responsible officer's role is also to ensure that parents attend whatever sessions are specified in his directions and to ensure compliance with the order and any requirements under it.

The compliance requirements which may be specified are those which the court considers desirable in the interest of preventing any repetition of the kind of conduct which 'triggers' the making of a parenting order or (as the case may be) the commission of any further offence of the type which is a 'trigger'. Examples of compliance requirements are a requirement to exercise control over the child and a requirement to ensure that he is home by a certain time of night.

Parenting orders under CDA 1998, s 8

When can an order be made under s 8?

By CDA 1998, s 8, a parenting order may be made in any court proceedings where:

(a) a child safety order is made in respect of a child or the court determines that a child has failed to comply with such an order;

(b) an anti-social behaviour order (ASBO) or sexual offences prevention order (SOPO) is made in respect of a child or young person (ie someone aged under 18);

(c) a child or young person is convicted of an offence (except, prospectively, breach of an ASBO);

(d) a person is convicted of an offence under the Education Act 1996, s 443 (failure to comply with a school attendance order) or s 444 (failure to secure regular attendance at school of registered pupil); or

(e) a parental compensation order is made in relation to a child's behaviour.

If the court is satisfied that 'the relevant condition' is met, it may (or must, see below) make a parenting order in respect of a person who is the parent or guardian of the child or young person or (as the case may be) the person convicted of an offence referred to in (d).

The 'relevant condition' is that the parenting order would be desirable in the interests of preventing:

(a) in a case falling within (a), (b) or (e) above, any repetition of the kind of behaviour which led to the child safety order, ASBO, SOPO or a parental compensation order being made;

(b) in a case falling within (c) above, the commission of any further offence by the child or young person; and

(c) in a case falling within (d) above, the commission of any further offence referred to there.

CDA 1998 provides that a court is not normally obliged to make a parenting order if one of the relevant conditions under s 8 is satisfied; it simply has the power to do so. There are two exceptions, both provided by CDA 1998, s 9, in relation to a child or young person under 16. If it is satisfied that the relevant condition is satisfied, a court must make a parenting order (a) where such a person has been convicted of an offence (prospectively, other than breach of an ASBO); and (b) where a court makes an ASBO against such a person. If such a person is convicted or subjected to an ASBO but the court is not so satisfied, it must say so in open court and give its reasons why it is not so satisfied. (a) does not apply where the court makes a referral order in respect of the offence.

Parenting orders on breach of anti-social behaviour order

CDA 1998, s 8A, prospectively added by the Crime and Security Act 2010, s 41, provides that, where someone under 16 is convicted of breach of an ASBO, the court by or before which he is convicted must make a parenting order in respect of his parent or guardian, unless of the opinion that there are exceptional circumstances that would make a parenting order inappropriate. The parenting order must specify such requirements as the court considers would be desirable in the interests of preventing:

(a) any repetition of the kind of behaviour which led to the ASBO being made, or
(b) the commission of any further offence by the person convicted.

If the court does not make a parenting order because it is of the opinion that there are exceptional circumstances that would make it inappropriate, it must state in open court that it is of that opinion and what those circumstances are.

Parenting orders in cases of exclusion or potential exclusion from school

The provisions already existing in respect of parenting orders for parents convicted of a school attendance offence are complemented by the provisions of A-sBA 2003, s 20. These enable applications for a parenting order to be made to a magistrates' court in relation to the parent of a pupil who has been excluded (or whose behaviour warrants his exclusion) from school on disciplinary grounds, provided any prescribed conditions (below) are satisfied. A local authority (or, in England, the school governors) may apply for a parenting order as a first measure, or where a parent refuses to sign a 'parenting contract'.

Conditions have been prescribed for England by the Education (Parenting Contracts and Parenting Orders) (England) Regulations 2007, and for Wales by the Education (Parenting Contracts and Parenting Orders) (Wales) Regulations 2010.

In the case of a child *who has been excluded for a fixed period*, the prescribed condition is that the application must be made within whichever of the following is applicable (if both are applicable whichever expires the later):

(a) the period of 40 school days beginning with:
　　(i) the next school day after the day on which consideration of the exclusion was completed by the school governors, (or, in the case of an exclusion from a pupil referral unit, the local authority), or
　　(ii) if it was not so considered, the day on which it began;
(b) the period of six months beginning with the day on which a parent of the pupil entered into a parenting contract.

In the case of a pupil *excluded permanently*, the application must be made within whichever of the following is applicable (if both are applicable whichever expires the later):

(a) the period of 40 school days beginning with:
　　(i) the next school day after the day on which a review panel decided to uphold the exclusion, or
　　(ii) the day when the parent indicated in writing that he will not apply for a review, or
　　(iii) the day when a review was abandoned, or

(iv) if there was no review, the last day on which a review could have been applied for; or

(b) the period of six months beginning with the day on which a parent of the pupil entered into a parenting contract.

In Wales, the references to a 'review panel' and 'review' are replaced by references to 'appeal panel' and 'appeal'.

In the case of a child whose behaviour warrants his exclusion, the prescribed condition is that an application must be made within whichever of the following is applicable (if both are applicable whichever expires the later): (a) the period of 40 school days beginning with the next school day after the day on which the relevant behaviour occurred; (b) the period of six months beginning with the day on which a parent of the pupil entered into a parenting contract.

The court may make such an order in respect of a pupil's parent if the prescribed condition is met and the court is satisfied that an order is desirable in the interests of improving the pupil's behaviour.

In deciding whether to make a parenting order under A-sBA 2003, ss 20 or 26 (below), a court must consider any refusal by a parent to enter into a parenting contract, or a failure by the parent to comply with any requirement of a contract. In the case of a person under 16, it must consider the pupil's family circumstances and the order's likely effect upon them.

Parenting orders in respect of criminal conduct and anti-social behaviour: youth offending teams

Similar provision is made by A-sBA 2003, s 26 for a parenting order where a youth offending team applies to a magistrates' court for such an order in respect of a child or young person who has been referred to the team. If the court is satisfied that such a child or young person has engaged in criminal conduct or anti-social behaviour and that the making of the order is desirable in preventing further criminal conduct or anti-social behaviour, it may make such an order. Only a member of a youth offending team can be the responsible officer in respect of an order under s 26.

Parenting orders in respect of anti-social behaviour: local authorities and registered social landlords

A-sBA 2003, ss 26A and 26B respectively enable a local authority or registered social landlord to apply to a magistrates' court for a parenting order against a parent in respect of anti-social behaviour by his or her child or young person. Such an application may also be made to a county court as an adjunct to other proceedings in that court.

General points about parenting orders

As long as a parenting order of any type is in force, it is an offence for a parent to fail without reasonable excuse to comply with any requirement included in a parenting order, or specified in directions given by the responsible officer (CDA 1998, s 9(7)).

The process of enforcement envisaged is that the responsible officer will report to the police an alleged breach of a parenting order. The police will investigate the allegation, taking statements, etc and proceed from there. This can be contrasted with breach of a community order where it is the Probation Service which brings proceedings and conducts them.

A-sBA 2003, s 28A makes provision for the Secretary of State (in Wales, the Welsh Assembly) to enable, by order, a local authority to 'contract out', to a person specified in the order, its functions in respect of parenting orders.

REMOVAL OF TRUANTS AND EXCLUDED PUPILS TO SCHOOLS OR DESIGNATED PREMISES

CDA 1998, s 16 empowers a constable to remove a juvenile of compulsory school age whom he has found in a public place if he has reasonable grounds to believe that the juvenile is truanting or excluded from school on disciplinary grounds. This power can only be exercised if a direction has been made under s 16.

In order for a direction to be given under s 16, a local authority must have designated premises to which children and young persons of compulsory school age may be removed under s 16, and must have notified the chief constable for the police area concerned of the designation. The designated place could be a social services department; it could be a school where there are suitable facilities and staff able to deal with children who might have come from other schools.

Where premises have been designated in a police area under s 16, a police officer of, or above, the rank of superintendent may direct that the powers set out below conferred on a police officer under s 16 are to be exercisable as respects any area falling within the police area that is specified in the direction. The powers will only be exercisable during the period specified in the direction. A British Transport Police superintendent (or above) has power to make such a direction but in such a case the powers set out below are only exercisable in any area or in the vicinity of any premises policed by the British Transport Police or in the premises themselves.

A direction will probably be made only after discussions between a school and the police about a perceived truanting problem.

Section 16 provides that, where a police officer has reasonable cause to believe that a child or young person found by him in a public place in a specified area during a specified period:

(a) is of compulsory school age; and
(b) is absent from a school without lawful authority, or has been excluded from school on disciplinary grounds and has no justification for being in a public place,

he may remove the child or young person to designated premises, or to the school from which he is so absent. Condition (b) only applies to an excluded juvenile where he is so found during school hours.

Surprisingly, the constable does not have to be in uniform. The child must be 'found in a public place' by a police officer. There is no power to enter private premises (eg the child's home) nor to remove a truant found on private premises on which the police officer is already lawfully present. 'Public place' means any highway and any place to which at the material time the public or any section of the public has access, on payment or otherwise, as of right or by virtue of express or implied permission. Streets, shopping centres, local authority parks, recreation grounds and swimming pools, and amusement arcades, in many of which truanting children tend to congregate and make a nuisance of themselves, are all 'public places' within this definition.

For the purpose of the requirement of a reasonable belief in the juvenile's absence from a school without lawful authority, a child's absence is deemed to be without lawful authority unless (a) it is absent with leave, or (b) because attendance at school is prevented by sickness or any unavoidable cause, or (c) because the absence is on a day exclusively set aside for religious observance by the religious body to which his parent belongs.

If it transpired that the police officer did not have the necessary reasonable belief, or the child was not found in a public place, any force used by the officer would be unlawful and he would not be acting in the execution of his duty.

PENALTY NOTICE FOR AN OFFENCE OF FAILURE TO SECURE REGULAR ATTENDANCE AT SCHOOL

The offence of failure to secure regular attendance at a relevant school of a registered pupil under the Education Act 1996, s 443 is one in respect of which a penalty notice may be given in England by an authorised officer. An 'authorised officer' for these purposes is a constable, a community support officer, an accredited person, an authorised local authority officer, or an authorised staff member (head teacher or staff member authorised by the head teacher). A relevant school is a maintained school, a pupil referral unit, an Academy, a city technology college, or a city college for the technology of the arts.

The Education (Penalty Notices) (England) Regulations 2007 prescribe the form of the notice and allow a period of 42 days during which no proceedings will be taken. The Regulations require that a code of conduct be drawn up by each local authority in consultation with other parties, to ensure consistency in the issuing of penalty notices. Records of the issue of notices must be kept by the education authority. The penalty to be paid is £60 where payment is made within 28 days of receipt of the notice and £120 where paid within 42 days of receipt of the notice.

DISQUALIFICATION FROM WORKING WITH CHILDREN

The Safeguarding of Vulnerable Groups Act 2006 (SVGA 2006), amended by the Protection of Freedoms Act 2012 (PFA 2012), and regulations under it provide the framework for a central Vetting and Barring Scheme for a range of people whose activities give them significant access to children (ie persons under 18). Hitherto, the Scheme has been operated by the Independent Safeguarding Authority, but as from December 2012 it is operated by the Disclosure and Barring Service (DBS) formed by a merger of the Independent Safeguarding Authority and the Criminal Records Bureau.

Those subject to the previous system of barring have been included or considered for inclusion in the barred lists under SVGA 2006. There is a similar system in respect of those whose work gives them access to vulnerable adults.

Where a person who is not already barred is convicted of an offence the court may, or must, in specified circumstances, order him to be disqualified from working with children. The relevant provisions are prospectively repealed by SVGA 2006. A person disqualified on conviction under those provisions will be automatically included in the children's barred list (see p 585) in due course by virtue of his conviction.

How the SVGA 2006 scheme works

Regulated activity

SVGA 2006 refers to a 'regulated activity', a term which covers a range of activities, such as being a teacher or registered child-minder, or a range of paid or voluntary activities involving close contact with children. The DBS must establish and maintain two barred lists, the 'children's barred list' (CBL) listing those barred from engaging in regulated activity with children, and the 'adults' barred list' listing those barred from engaging in such activity with vulnerable adults.

The children's barred list

SVGA 2006, Sch 3, as amended by PFA 2012, contains provisions for determining whether an individual is included in the CBL.

Automatic inclusion   If the Secretary of State has reason to believe that any of the criteria prescribed for automatic inclusion might apply to a person, the Secretary of State must refer the matter to the DBS. If (whether or not the Secretary of State has made a reference to it) the DBS is satisfied that a person has met the prescribed criteria for automatic barring it is required to include him in the CBL.

Inclusion subject to consideration of representations   If the Secretary of State has reason to believe that the criteria prescribed for this type of inclusion might apply to a person, and the person is or has been, or might in future be, engaged in regulated activity relating to children, the Secretary of State must refer the matter to the DBS. If (whether or not the Secretary of State has referred the matter to it) the DBS is satisfied that the prescribed criteria apply and that the person is or has been, or might in future be, engaged in regulated activity relating to children, it must seek representations from the person before reaching a decision as to whether to include him in the CBL. If the person does not make representations in the prescribed time, and the DBS is satisfied that the prescribed criteria apply and has reason to believe that the person is or has been, or might in future be, engaged in regulated activity relating to children, it must include him in the CBL. If the person does make representations in the prescribed time, the DBS must include him in the CBL if it is satisfied that the prescribed criteria apply, has reason to believe that the person is or has been, or might in future be, engaged in regulated activity relating to children, and is satisfied that it is appropriate to include him in the CBL.

Inclusion on grounds of relevant conduct   Where it appears to the DBS that the person has (at any time) engaged in relevant conduct, and is or has been, or might in future be, engaged in regulated activity relating to children, and the DBS proposes to include him in the CBL, it must give him the opportunity to make representations as to why he should not be included in the list. Representations must be made within eight weeks. The DBS must include the person in the CBL if it is satisfied that the person has engaged in relevant conduct, it has reason to believe that the person is or has been, or might in future be, engaged in regulated activity relating to children, and it is satisfied that it is appropriate to include the person in the list.

'Relevant conduct' is defined as follows:

(a) conduct which endangers a child, or is likely to endanger a child;
(b) conduct which, if repeated against or in relation to a child, would endanger that child or would be likely to endanger him;
(c) conduct involving sexual material relating to children (including possession of such material);
(d) inappropriate conduct of a sexual nature or involving sexually explicit images or depicting violence against human beings (including possession of such images).

Inclusion on grounds of risk of harm   Where it appears to the DBS that a person may:

(a) harm a child;
(b) cause a child to be harmed;
(c) put a child at risk of harm;
(d) attempt to harm a child; or
(e) incite another to harm a child;

and is or has been, or might in future be, engaged in a regulated activity relating to children, and the DBS proposes to include him in the CBL, the DBS must give the person opportunity to make representations within eight weeks as to why he should not be included in the list. The DBS must include the person in the CBL if it is satisfied that the person falls within (a)–(e), it has reason to believe that the person is or has been, or might in future be, engaged in regulated activity relating to children, and it is satisfied that it is appropriate to include the person in the list.

Supplementary

Having included a person's name in the CBL, the DBS must take all reasonable steps to notify an individual of his inclusion.

SVGA 2006, s 50A empowers the DBS to provide information it holds to the chief officer of police for use in the prevention, detection and investigation of crime, the apprehension and prosecution of offenders, the appointment of persons under his direction and control, or any prescribed purpose. It must provide to a chief officer on request, for use for any of these purposes, a barred list or information as to whether a person is barred.

Effect of inclusion in barred list

A person included in the CBL, or the corresponding lists in Scotland and Northern Ireland, is barred from regulated activity relating to children.

After the specified minimum barred period, which varies depending on the circumstances, has elapsed, and provided he has made no other such application in the prescribed period ending with the time when he does so, a barred individual may apply to the DBS for permission to apply for a review of his inclusion. The DBS must not grant permission unless it thinks that the applicant's circumstances have changed since he was included in the list or last applied for permission and that the change is such that permission should be granted.

SVGA 2006, s 4 provides for an appeal by the barred individual to the Upper Tribunal against a decision of the DBS to include him (except in the case of automatic inclusion), or to keep him (on a review), in the CBL. Such an appeal may be made only on a point of law or on a finding of fact made by the DBS.

Offences

By SVGA 2006, s 7(1), an individual commits an indictable (either way) offence if he:

(a) seeks to engage in regulated activity from which he is barred;
(b) offers to engage in regulated activity from which he is barred;
(c) engages in regulated activity from which he is barred.

It is a defence for a person charged with in offence under s 7(1) to prove that he did not know, and could not reasonably be expected to know, that he was barred from that activity. It is also a defence for a person charged with an offence under s 7(1) to prove that:

(a) he reasonably thought that it was necessary for him to engage in the activity for the purpose of preventing harm to a child;

(b) he reasonably thought that there was no other person who could engage in the activity for that purpose; and

(c) he engaged in the activity for no longer than was necessary for that purpose.

Indictable (either way) offences are also committed by employers who use, or employment agencies who supply, a barred person for a regulated activity.

CHAPTER 17

Licensed Premises, Licensed Persons, Clubs, Places of Entertainment, and Offences of Drunkenness

INTRODUCTION

The Licensing Act (LA) 2003 introduced a system of licensing operated by licensing authorities, essentially local authorities, who are empowered to issue various types of authorisation. The activities to which the provisions of the Act apply are not restricted to matters involving the sale or supply of alcohol; they extend to the control of various forms of entertainment and to the provision of late-night refreshment.

The key to understanding the regime under LA 2003 is that premises where the above activities occur must always be authorised by a premises licence (or sometimes a club premises certificate or temporary event notice), and, in addition, a personal licence is required by a person selling alcohol by retail or supplying it by, or on behalf of, a club to, or to the order of, a member of the club on premises which have a premises licence.

On certain occasions it is an offence under LA 2003 intentionally to obstruct an authorised person (ie an officer of a licensing authority or a person with a health, safety or environmental role appointed or authorised by certain bodies). These officers share powers with a constable in relation to the enforcement of many provisions of the Act. On each of these occasions it will also, of course, be an offence against the Police Act 1996, s 89(2) wilfully to obstruct a constable in the execution of his duties.

By s 4, a licensing authority must carry out its functions under LA 2003 with a view to promoting the licensing objectives under that section:

(a) the prevention of crime and disorder ('and' has been held to mean 'and/or');
(b) public safety;
(c) the prevention of public nuisance; and
(d) the protection of children from harm.

TERMINOLOGY
Licensable activities and qualifying club activities

These are the activities which are regulated by LA 2003 and require authorisation by the relevant licensing authority.

Licensable activities

By LA 2003, s 1(1), the following are licensable activities:

(a) the sale by retail of alcohol;
(b) the supply of alcohol by or on behalf of a club to, or to the order of, a member of the club, otherwise than a sale by retail;
(c) the provision of regulated entertainment; and
(d) the provision of late-night refreshment.

The reference to 'sale by retail' in (a) means that 'business-to-business' wholesale sales are outside the provisions of the Act. The reference to 'otherwise than a sale by retail' in para (b) of this definition can be explained as follows. In the case of a members' club (as opposed to a proprietary one) the property of the club belongs to its members for the time being jointly in equal shares. Consequently if alcohol is supplied to a member at a price, this is not a sale by retail but a release by the other members of their interest in the drink supplied. This would not be covered by para (a), although a supply at a price to a guest of a member of the club would be.

LA 2003, s 173 excludes activities which would otherwise be licensable activities from being so if they are carried on in particular places, for example aboard an aircraft, hovercraft or train on a journey, at an approved wharf at a designated port or hoverport, on board a vessel on an international journey, or at an examination station at a designated international airport (area beyond security check-in). Premises permanently or temporarily used for the purpose of the armed forces are also exempted.

LA 2003, s 175 provides that the promotion of an incidental non-commercial lottery will not constitute a licensable activity by reason only of one or more of the prizes in the lottery consisting of or including alcohol, provided that the alcohol is in a sealed container.

Qualifying club activities

By LA 2003, s 1(2), the following licensable activities are also qualifying club activities:

(a) the supply, otherwise than a sale by way of retail, of alcohol by or on behalf of a club to, or to the order of, a member of the club;
(b) the sale by retail of alcohol by or on behalf of a club to a guest of a member of the club for consumption on the premises where the sale takes place; and
(c) the provision of regulated entertainment where that provision is by or on behalf of a club for members of the club or members of the club and their guests.

A number of terms in the above definitions are defined as follows.

Alcohol

'Alcohol' in LA 2003 means spirits, beer, wine, cider or any other fermented, distilled or spirituous liquor, except alcohol with a strength not exceeding 0.5 per cent and obvious exceptions like perfume, medicinal or veterinary products, and liqueur confectionery.

Regulated entertainment

LA 2003, Sch 1 provides that 'the provision of regulated entertainment' means the provision of one of the following types of entertainment:

(a) a performance of a play;
(b) an exhibition of a film;

(c) an indoor sporting event;
(d) a boxing or wrestling entertainment;
(e) a performance of live music;
(f) any playing of recorded music;
(g) a performance of dance; or
(h) entertainment of a similar description to that falling within (e), (f), or (g),

where the entertainment takes place in the presence of an audience and is provided for the purpose, or for purposes which include the purpose, of entertaining that audience, provided that the following two conditions are satisfied.

The first condition is that the entertainment is provided:

(a) to any extent for members of the public or a section of the public;
(b) exclusively for members of a club (or members and their guests) which is a qualifying club in relation to the provision of regulated entertainment; or
(c) in any case not falling within (a) or (b), for consideration and with a view to profit.

The second condition is that the premises on which the entertainment is provided are made available for the purpose, or for purposes which include the purpose, of enabling the entertainment concerned.

Exemptions   The following are not regulated entertainments:

(a) playing of live TV and radio programmes;
(b) background music in a shop, or a piano in a restaurant or the like;
(c) films used for product demonstration, advertisement, information, education or instruction, or in an exhibition in a museum or art gallery;
(d) entertainment incidental to a religious service or at a place of religious worship;
(e) entertainment at a garden fete;
(f) Morris dancing or dancing of similar type;
(g) entertainment provided on vehicles in motion;
(h) lap dancing and other sexual entertainment (which are subject to a separate licensing regime operated by local authorities);
(i) live music on premises in respect of which there is a premises licence or club premises certificate, provided:
    (i) the premises are then open for the supply of alcohol for consumption on the premises,
    (ii) the live music is unamplified or (if amplified) the audience does not exceed 200,
    (iii) the live music takes place between 0800 and 2300 on the same day (or, where a special occasion order (see p 595) has effect, between the hours specified in that order), and
    (iv) conditions have not been included in the licence or certificate by virtue of LA 2003, s 177A(3) or (4) (referred to on p 611));
(j) live music at a workplace provided:
    (i) the place is not licensed under LA 2003 (or is so licensed only for the provision of late night refreshment),
    (ii) the audience does not exceed 200, and
    (iii) the live music takes place between 0800 and 2300 on the same day; and
(k) subject to s 177A(3) and (4), live unamplified music which takes place between 0800 and 2300 on the same day.

Late-night refreshment

LA 2003, Sch 2 provides that 'late-night refreshment' means the supply at any time between 2300 and 0500 of hot food or hot drink for consumption on or off the premises: (a) to members of the public (or a section of it), or (b) when members of the public (or a section of it) are admitted to any premises, to any persons, (or to a person of a particular type) on or off those premises. 'Hot' for the purposes of the Act means food or drink which is heated on the premises or elsewhere or that which, after it is supplied, may be heated on the premises.

There are exemptions:

(a) supply to persons staying at hotels, camping sites or other premises supplying accommodation as their main purpose;
(b) supply to members of recognised clubs;
(c) supply to employees of particular employers (works canteens, etc);
(d) premises already licensed under other Acts, eg 'near beer' premises in London;
(e) supply free of charge provided no charge has been made for admission to the premises or some other item;
(f) supply by a charity;
(g) supply by means of a vending machine; and
(h) supply on a vehicle not permanently or temporarily parked.

PREMISES LICENCES, CLUB PREMISES CERTIFICATES AND TEMPORARY EVENT NOTICES

Premises licence

Premises licences are governed by LA 2003, Part 3 (ss 11 to 59). They authorise premises to be used for one or more licensable activities.

A premises licence is granted by the licensing authority for the area in which the premises are situated and authorises its holder to use the premises to which the licence relates for licensable activities (see p 589).

In addition to the general right to apply for a review of a premises licence, an involved process, a chief officer of police may apply for an expedited review of a premises licence. A chief officer may do so where a superintendent or above has certified that he considers that premises which are licensed are associated with serious crime or disorder. A serious crime is one defined by the Regulation of Investigatory Powers Act 2000, s 81 (generally, those crimes for which a sentence of imprisonment for at least three years may be imposed and offences involving violence, resulting in substantial gain or involving a large number of persons in pursuit of a common purpose). Interim steps may be taken in accordance with regulations without the licence-holder being given an opportunity to make representations.

Where it is intended to build or extend premises a person may apply to the relevant licensing authority for a provisional statement about whether, if the work is done as proposed, it would be appropriate to attach conditions to the premises licence, exclude a licensable activity, refuse to accept a specified person as premises supervisor, or refuse a premises licence.

By LA 2003, s 59, a constable or authorised person (see p 588) may enter the premises to which an application for a premises licence or provisional statement relates, before that application has been determined, in order to assess the likely effect on the promotion of the licensing objectives of the grant of the application. An authorised person must produce evidence of his authority, if requested. It is an offence against s 59(5) intentionally to obstruct an authorised person exercising such a power.

A licence granted by a licensing authority will be granted subject to conditions consistent with the operating schedule and any mandatory conditions which are appropriate.

The premises licence-holder must ensure that the licence (or a certified copy) and a list of relevant mandatory conditions is kept on the premises in his custody or control or that of an employee there nominated in writing, and that the summary of the licence (or a certified copy) and the position of any nominee referred to above are prominently displayed on the premises. Non-compliance by the premises licence-holder, without reasonable excuse, is an offence under LA 2003, s 57(4). A constable or authorised person may require production of the premises licence (or a certified copy) or a list of relevant mandatory conditions. An authorised person must, on request, produce evidence of his authority. Non-compliance without reasonable excuse with such a request is an offence under LA 2003, s 57(8).

Club premises certificates

These are dealt with by LA 2003, Part 4 (ss 60 to 97).

Club premises certificates will be granted to a qualifying club by the licensing authority for the area in which the club is situated and will authorise the use of club premises for qualifying club activities specified in the certificate (see p 589).

A club may wish to provide entertainment to members of the public on certain occasions and, in consequence, it may hold a club premises certificate in respect of its day-to-day activities and a premises licence authorising the provision of entertainment.

A club premises certificate will be subject to conditions in the same way as a premises licence.

A club premises certificate may authorise the supply of alcohol to its *members* for consumption off the premises. In general:

(a) a club premises certificate may not authorise the supply of alcohol for consumption off the premises unless it also authorises its supply to members for consumption on the premises;

(b) a club premises certificate authorising the supply of alcohol for consumption off the premises must include three conditions:

    (i) the supply must be made at a time when the premises are open for the purposes of supplying alcohol, in accordance with the club premises certificate, to members of the club for consumption on the premises,

    (ii) any alcohol supplied for consumption off the premises must be in a sealed container, and

    (iii) any supply of alcohol for consumption off the premises must be made to a member of the club in person.

Sale of alcohol by retail to a guest is not authorised by the certificate.

No conditions attached to a club premises certificate may prevent the sale by retail of alcohol or the provision of regulated entertainment to associate members of a club or their guests if those are permitted activities.

A club premises certificate has effect until withdrawn or surrendered. A constable or authorised person may require production of a certificate (or certified copy) or a list of relevant mandatory conditions. Failure to comply, without reasonable excuse, is an offence against s 94(9). The club secretary must ensure that the certificate (or certified copy) is held on the club's premises by a person nominated by him, and the nominated person must ensure that a summary of the certificate and notice of the nominated individual responsible for it on the premises are prominently displayed. Failure to comply with one of these requirements, without reasonable excuse, is an offence against s 94(5) (failure by secretary to ensure holding) or (6) (failure to ensure display).

By LA 2003, s 96, on production of his authority a constable authorised by the chief officer of police or an authorised person may enter and inspect premises in respect of which an application has been made for the grant of a certificate. 48 hours' notice must have been given to the club. It is an offence against s 96(5) intentionally to obstruct an authorised person exercising these powers.

By s 97 a constable may enter and search club premises (by force, if necessary) where he has reasonable cause to believe that an offence in respect of controlled drugs has been, is being, or is about to be, committed or that there is likely to be a breach of the peace.

Temporary event notices

Sometimes, a person wishes to carry out licensable activities at premises which are not licensed, eg to provide bar facilities at a wedding reception on premises not licensed for the sale of alcohol, or to set up a disco in premises which, although licensed for the sale of alcohol, are not licensed for the provision of entertainment. This can be achieved under the provisions of LA 2003, Part 5 (ss 98 to 110) which deals with permitted temporary activities. Under Part 5, licensable activities can occur on premises which do not have a premises licence or club premises certificate on a temporary basis (for a period not exceeding 168 hours) subject to conditions and limitations.

A licensable activity is a 'permitted temporary activity' if:

(a) it is carried out in accordance with:
    (i) a temporary events notice given to the relevant licensing authority; and
    (ii) where relevant, any conditions imposed; and
(b) it satisfies the following conditions:
    (i) the temporary event notice has been duly acknowledged (if required (no requirement if licensing authority has issued counter-notice following police objection or if permitted limits already exceeded)) by the licensing authority;
    (ii) the temporary event notice has not been subsequently withdrawn by the individual giving the notice; and
    (iii) no counter-notice has been issued by the relevant licensing authority.

The individual who gives the temporary event notice is called the 'premises-user'.

The temporary event notice

A notice must contain details including:

(a) the licensable activities to be carried out;
(b) the date(s) when the licensable activities are to be carried out (and the total length of the event);
(c) the times during the event at which the licensable activities are to be carried out;
(d) the maximum number of people to be allowed on the premises at any one time, which must be less than 500;

(e) whether any alcohol sales are to be made for consumption on or off the premises (or both).

If the proposed licensable activities include the supply of alcohol, the notice must include the condition that all supplies will be made by, or under the authority of, the premises-user.

Where the police consider that if the temporary event should proceed it would undermine the crime prevention objective, the premises-user and the relevant licensing authority must be informed by an objection notice, setting out the reasons, before the end of the second working day following the day on which the temporary event notice was received. If there is a police objection there must be a hearing unless all parties agree that it is unnecessary. Where the licensing authority accepts the objection it must give the premises-user a counter-notice preventing the event from taking place; this must be done at least 24 hours before the proposed event. If the counter-notice is not given as required, the premises-user may proceed with the event.

Where there has been a police objection, at any time before a hearing the chief officer of police may, with the consent of the premises-user, modify the terms of the temporary event notice. If this is done the notice takes effect with those modifications.

In addition to the case where a police objection is accepted, a licensing authority must give a counter-notice in certain cases; the effect is to prevent the event taking place.

LA 2003, s 108 provides that a constable or an authorised officer of the licensing authority may, at any reasonable time, enter premises to assess the probable impact of the proposed event upon the crime prevention objective. An authorised officer must produce evidence of his authority, if requested. It is an offence intentionally to obstruct such an officer (s 108(3)).

The premises-user must ensure that a copy of the notice together with any statement of conditions is displayed on the premises or is kept there under his control or that of a nominated person; where the notice and any statement of conditions is in the custody of a nominated person, the premises-user must ensure that a notice to that effect is prominently displayed on the premises. A constable or authorised officer may require production of a notice. It is an offence against LA 2003, s 109 for a premises-user, without reasonable excuse, to fail to comply with one of these requirements.

Where a temporary event notice or any statement of conditions is not displayed and there is no notice displayed as to its whereabouts, a constable or authorised officer may require the premises-user to produce the temporary event notice or statement of conditions. Where a notice relating to a 'nominated person' is displayed on the premises such a person may require the nominated person to produce the actual notice or statement of conditions. It is an offence under s 109(8) for a person to fail, without reasonable excuse, to produce a temporary event notice or statement of conditions when requested to do so.

Opening hours of premises in respect of which there is a premises licence or club premises certificate

LA 2003 does not prescribe 'permitted hours' within which alcohol may be sold or supplied for consumption on or off the premises. In addition, there are no general restrictions placed upon any other licensable activity. An applicant for a premises licence or a club premises certificate may choose the hours within which it would like to be authorised to carry out the licensed activities. The licence will be granted on those terms unless, following representations, the authority considers it necessary to reject the application or alter its terms bearing in mind the 'licensing objectives' set out on p 558.

The Secretary of State is empowered by LA 2003, s 172 to make an order to permit premises with a premises licence or a club premises certificate to open for specified, generally extended hours, on special occasions of international, national or local significance.

Early morning alcohol restriction orders

LA 2003, s 172A empowers a licensing authority to make an early morning alcohol restriction order if it considers it appropriate for the promotion of the licensing objectives.

An order will provide that premises licences and club premises certificates granted by the authority, and temporary event notices given to the authority, do not have effect to the extent that they authorise the sale or supply of alcohol during the period specified in the order. The period that may be specified in the order must begin no earlier than 2400 and end no later than 0600. The order would, therefore, apply not only to pubs, bars and nightclubs but also to non-profit clubs such as sports, political, and working men's clubs, supermarkets and convenience stores, and temporary events. An order may have effect (a) in relation to the same period of every day on which the order is to apply, or in relation to different periods of different days, (b) every day or only on particular days (eg particular days of the week or year), (c) in relation to the whole or part of the licensing authority's area, or (d) for a limited or unlimited period.

The Licensing Act 2003 (Early Morning Restriction Orders) Regulations 2012 prescribe exceptions from the effect of an early morning alcohol restriction order. The prescribed exceptions are:

(a) premises which are a hotel, guest house, lodging house or hostel at which the supply of alcohol between 2400 and 0600 on any day may only be made to persons staying at the premises for consumption in their rooms (eg alcohol supplied by room service or by virtue of a mini-bar);

(b) premises which are authorised to supply alcohol for consumption on the premises between 2400 and 0600 only on 1 January in every year.

Thus, premises of these descriptions may continue to supply alcohol notwithstanding that they are situated in an area to which an early morning alcohol restriction order applies. An order made under s 172A is subject to an order made under s 172 (unless the s 172 order provides otherwise).

PERSONAL LICENCES

A personal licence is a licence granted by a licensing authority to an individual which authorises him to supply alcohol, or to authorise the supply of alcohol, in accordance with a premises licence. Supplying alcohol in this context means selling it by retail, or supplying it by or on behalf of a club to, or to the order of, a member of the club. On any premises with a premises licence authorising their use for the sale or supply of alcohol, the person nominated for the day-to-day running of the premises must hold a personal licence and is known as the 'designated premises supervisor'. There may be more than one personal licence-holder on the licensed premises, but it is not necessary for all members of staff to have personal licences. However, all supplies of alcohol under a premises licence must be made by or under the authority of a personal licence-holder.

A personal licence is one which relates solely to the supply of alcohol. A personal licence is not required in respect of the other activities regulated by LA 2003 (ie regulated entertainment or late-night refreshment).

Personal licences are dealt with by LA 2003, Part 6 (ss 111 to 135). The licensing authority must grant a personal licence if it appears to it that:

(a) the applicant is aged 18 or over;
(b) he possesses a recognised qualification or is a person of a prescribed description;
(c) no personal licence held by him has been forfeited in the five-year period ending with the date of application; and
(d) he has not been convicted of any 'relevant offence' (a long list of offences ranging from theft to possession of drugs) or any 'foreign offence' (an offence (other than a relevant offence) under the law of any country outside England and Wales).

A licensing authority must reject an application if the applicant is under 18, or if he does not possess the required qualification, or if he has had a licence forfeited in the previous five years.

If an applicant is 18 or over, has the required qualification and has not had his licence forfeited in the previous five years, but has a conviction for a relevant offence or a foreign offence, the authority must notify the chief officer of police for its area. If the chief officer is satisfied, by reference to any conviction for a relevant offence or any conviction for a foreign offence which he considers comparable to a relevant offence, that granting a personal licence to the applicant would undermine the crime prevention objective of LA 2003, he must within 14 days give the authority an objection notice. If he does not, the authority must grant the personal licence; if he does the authority must hold a hearing to consider the objection notice and decide whether or not to grant the personal licence.

A licence specifies the holder's name and address, the authority which granted it, and convictions for relevant or foreign offences. The holder is under a duty to notify the authority of any change in name or address. It is an offence to fail, without reasonable excuse, to do so (LA 2003, s 127(4)).

The system of personal licences permits licensed persons to move from one set of premises to another, regardless of area.

Where the holder of a personal licence is on premises to sell or authorise the sale of alcohol by virtue of a premises licence or temporary event notice, he may be required by a constable or an authorised officer of the licensing authority to produce his licence; if requested an authorised officer must produce his authority. Failure to comply with such a request, without reasonable excuse, is an offence against LA 2003, s 135(5).

LICENSING OFFENCES

Unauthorised licensable activities

It is an offence against LA 2003, s 136(1)(a) for a person to carry on, or attempt to carry on, or against s 136(1)(b) for a person knowingly to allow to be carried on, a licensable activity on or from any premises otherwise than under or in accordance with an authorisation provided by a:

(a) premises licence;
(b) club premises certificate; or
(c) temporary event notice.

A divisional court has held that the offence under s 136(1)(a) is directed at persons who, as a matter of fact, actually carry on, or attempt to, a licensable activity otherwise than in accordance with such authorisation. Thus, for example, where premises subject to a premises licence are used in breach of a condition under the premises licence the premises licence-holder is not automatically guilty of the offence. This is of obvious importance where (as in the case referred to) the premises licence-holder owns the licensed premises but lets them to someone else who actually carries out the licensable activity there and who breaches a condition of the licence unknown to the licence-holder.

Exposing alcohol for unauthorised sale

It is an offence against LA 2003, s 137(1) to expose, on any premises, alcohol for sale by retail in circumstances where the actual sale by retail of that alcohol would be an unauthorised licensable activity because there is no applicable premises licence, club premises certificate, or temporary event notice. As can be seen, a sale, or an attempted sale, is not necessary.

Keeping alcohol on premises for unauthorised sale

LA 2003, s 138(1) creates the offence of possessing, or having under control, alcohol, with the intention of selling it by retail, or supplying it, where that sale or supply would be an unauthorised licensable activity.

Defence of due diligence

By LA 2003, s 139, it is a defence to an offence under ss 136(1)(a), 137, or 138 that the defendant's act was due to a mistake, or to reliance on information given to him, or to an act or omission of another person, or to some cause beyond his control, and he took all reasonable steps and exercised all due diligence to avoid committing the offence.

DRUNKENNESS AND DISORDERLY CONDUCT

Allowing disorderly conduct on licensed premises, etc

LA 2003, s 140(1) and (2) makes it an offence knowingly to allow disorderly conduct on licensed premises, premises in respect of which a club premises certificate is in force, or premises which may be used for a permitted temporary activity. The offence can be committed by any person who works on the premises in a capacity, paid or unpaid, which gives him the authority to prevent such conduct. On premises with a premises licence, the offence can also be committed by the premises licence-holder or designated premises supervisor. In the case of a club, the offence can also be committed by an officer or member of the club who is present when the disorderly conduct takes place and who has the authority to prevent it. Members of a club committee would obviously be in such a position. In the case of a temporary event the offence can also be committed by the premises-user.

Sale of alcohol to a person who is drunk or obtaining alcohol for such a person

It is an offence, contrary to LA 2003, s 141, knowingly to sell, or attempt to sell, alcohol to a person who is drunk, or to allow alcohol to be sold to such a person, on premises in respect of which there is a premises licence, or a club premises certificate, or premises which may be used for a permitted temporary activity. The offence also applies to the supply of alcohol by or on behalf of a club.

The offence may be committed by the same category of persons to which s 140 applies.

The s 141 offence is a 'penalty offence' for the purposes of the Criminal Justice and Police Act 2001, and may be dealt with under a fixed penalty procedure: see p 31.

By s 142(1), it is an offence for a person knowingly to obtain, or attempt to obtain, alcohol for consumption on the above types of premises by a person who is drunk.

Failure to leave licensed premises, etc

A person commits an offence against LA 2003, s 143(1) and (2) if he is drunk and disorderly and fails, without reasonable excuse, to leave relevant premises as defined by s 159 (ie premises in respect of which there is a premises licence, or a club premises certificate, or premises which may be used for a permitted temporary activity), at the request of a police constable or:

(a) any person who works at the premises in a capacity, paid or unpaid, which gives him the authority to make that request;
(b) a premises licence-holder or designated premises supervisor;
(c) an officer or member of a club who is present at the time and has authority to make that request; and
(d) a premises-user who has given a temporary event notice in respect of the event.

A person who is drunk and disorderly also commits an offence under s 143(1) and (2) if, without reasonable excuse, he enters, or attempts to enter, such premises when requested not to do so by any such persons.

Section 143(4) requires a constable to assist in the expulsion of persons who are drunk and disorderly from such premises, or to help prevent such a person from entering, if requested to do so by any of the persons described above.

OFFENCES IN RELATION TO CHILDREN

Unaccompanied children prohibited from certain premises

It is an offence against LA 2003, s 145(1) for a person, knowing that 'relevant premises' (as defined below) are within s 145(4), to allow a child under 16 to be on certain categories of relevant premises if he is not accompanied by an adult (18 or over) and the premises are open for the supply of alcohol for consumption on the premises. 'Relevant premises' are within s 145(4) if:

(a) they are exclusively or primarily used for the supply of alcohol for consumption on the premises; or
(b) they are open for the purpose of being used for the supply of alcohol for consumption on the premises by virtue of LA 2003, Part 5 (permitted temporary activities)

and, at the time the temporary event notice in question has effect, they are exclusively or primarily used for such supplies.

It is also an offence against s 145(1) to allow an unaccompanied child under 16 to be on 'relevant premises' at a time between the hours of 2400 and 0500 when the premises are open for the supply of alcohol for consumption there.

'*Relevant premises' in the various offences under LA 2003 in relation to children means licensed premises, premises with a club premises certificate, and premises which may be used for a permitted temporary activity.*

By s 145(3), these offences may be committed by a person working on the premises in any capacity, paid or unpaid, with the authority to ask the child to leave; the premises licence-holder or designated premises supervisor; an officer or member of a club with that authority; or the premises-user who has given temporary notice in respect of the premises.

No offence is committed where the unaccompanied child is merely passing through the premises, where this is the convenient route.

A person charged with an offence under LA 2003, s 145 by reason of his own conduct has a defence if he believed the child to be 16 or over, or that an individual accompanying him was 18 or over, and had either taken all reasonable steps to establish the individual's age, or no one could reasonably have suspected from the individual's appearance that he was aged under 16 or 18, as the case may be. A person will be treated as having taken all reasonable steps to establish an individual's age if he asked for evidence of it and the evidence would have convinced a reasonable person. Where a person is charged because of the default of some other person, it is a defence to show that he had exercised all due diligence to avoid committing the offence.

Sale of alcohol to children

LA 2003, s 146(1) prohibits the sale of alcohol to an individual aged under 18 *anywhere*. Section 146(2) provides that a club commits an offence if alcohol is supplied by or on its behalf to, or to the order of, a member under 18, or to a person under 18 to the order of a member of a club. A person who supplies alcohol on behalf of a club in such circumstances commits an offence contrary to s 146(3).

LA 2003, s 146(4) provides a defence where the person charged with an offence under s 146 believed that the purchaser was 18 or over and either:

(a) the person charged took all reasonable steps to establish the purchaser's age; or
(b) no one could reasonably have suspected from the purchaser's appearance that he was under 18.

A defendant will be deemed to have taken all reasonable steps if he asked the individual for evidence of his age and the evidence would have convinced a reasonable person. In the latter respect, the prosecution may show that the evidence of age produced was such that no reasonable person would have been convinced by it (it might be an obvious forgery or obviously belong to some other person).

Where a sale or supply was made by some other person than the person charged (as where a barman supplies a drink on behalf of a manager) it is a defence to show that the person charged exercised all due diligence to avoid committing the offence.

An offence under s 146(1) or (3) is a 'penalty offence' for the purposes of the Criminal Justice and Police Act 2001, and may be dealt with under a fixed penalty procedure: see p 31.

It is an offence against LA 2003, s 147(1) for a person knowingly to allow the sale of alcohol to a person under 18 on 'relevant premises' as defined on p 599. The persons who can commit this offence are those workers, paid or unpaid, with authority to prevent sale or supply. An officer or member of a club, or a worker in it, with that authority commits an offence under s 147(3) if he allows alcohol to be supplied to or to the order of a member under 18, or to someone under 18 to the order of such a member.

Although liqueur confectionery is not alcohol for the purposes of LA 2003, it is an offence to sell liqueur confectionery to a person under the age of 16 (s 148(1)), or for a club or person on behalf of a club to supply it to, or to the order of, a member under 16 or to a person under 16 to the order of a member (s 148(2)). The same defences apply as in the case of unlawful sales under s 146.

Persistently selling alcohol to children

LA 2003, s 147A(1) provides that an offence is committed if, on two or more different occasions in a period of three consecutive months, alcohol is unlawfully sold on the same premises, which *at the time of each sale* are licensed by a premises licence or upon which a permitted temporary activity is taking place, to an individual who is under 18. The offence is committed by a person who was a 'responsible person' in relation to the premises *at each such time*. A person is a 'responsible person' for the purposes of s 147A(1) if, *at that time*, he is the person (or one of the persons) who holds the premises licence or who is the premises-user in respect of a temporary event notice. For the purposes of s 147A, alcohol is unlawfully sold to an individual under 18 if the person making the sale believed the individual to be under 18 or did not have reasonable grounds for believing him to be 18 or over. A person has reasonable grounds for so believing only if he asked for evidence of age and the evidence produced was such that it would have convinced a reasonable person, or if no person could reasonably have suspected from the individual's appearance that he was less than 18. The sales mentioned in s 147A(1) might, but need not, be to the same individual. The same sale may not be counted in respect of different offences for the purpose of enabling the same person to be convicted of more than one offence under s 147A, or for the purpose of enabling the same person to be convicted under s 147A and an offence under s 146 (sale of alcohol to children) or s 147 (allowing such a sale) referred to above. The purpose of s 147A is to provide a much larger penalty for persistent sales by responsible persons.

For the purposes of establishing the offence under s 147A, evidence in respect of a conviction, caution, or fixed penalty notice for an offence under s 146 in respect of a sale to *that individual on those premises on that occasion* is admissible as evidence that there has been an unlawful sale of alcohol to an individual under 18 on any premises on any occasion.

LA 2003, s 147B provides that, on conviction of a premises licence-holder for an offence against s 147A, the court may make an order suspending the premises licence for a period of not more than three months in respect of retail sales of alcohol. Such an order may be suspended pending an appeal.

As an alternative to a prosecution under LA 2003, s 147A, LA 2003, s 169A permits a 'relevant officer' (superintendent or above or an inspector of weights and measures) to issue a closure notice in the prescribed form in relation to any premises if:

(a) there is evidence of the commission of an offence against s 147A;
(b) the relevant officer considers that the evidence provides a realistic prospect of a conviction; and

(c) the offender is still the premises licence-holder (or one of them) in respect of the premises in question.

Such a notice proposes a prohibition of the sale of alcohol at the premises in question for a period specified in the notice and offers the offender the chance to discharge all criminal liability for the alleged offence against s 147A by the acceptance of the prohibition proposed by the notice. The length of the prohibition specified in the order must not exceed 336 hours. The period specified in the notice as the *start time* for closure must not be less than 14 days following service of the notice. Service of a notice must take place when licensable activities are taking place. The notice has the effect of temporarily suspending the premises licence. If sales take place during the period of prohibition, those sales will be unlawful in terms of LA 2003, s 136 referred to on p 596.

Purchase of alcohol by children or on their behalf

LA 2003, s 149(1) makes it an offence for a person under 18 (a) to buy or attempt to buy alcohol, or (b) if he is a member of a club, for him to have alcohol supplied to him by the club in circumstances in which he initiates the supply, or for him to attempt to do so. Test purchasing on behalf of a constable or trading standards officer is excepted from these provisions.

LA 2003, s 149(3) makes it an offence for a person to act as an agent for a child in purchasing, or attempting to purchase, alcohol.

LA 2003, s 149(4) provides an offence which is committed on 'relevant premises' (see p 599) by prohibiting a person from buying or attempting to buy alcohol for consumption by a person under 18 on those premises. This would cover any relative or friend of a child who buys a drink for a child, or tries to do so, on 'relevant premises'. However, the offence is not committed by an adult who buys beer, wine, or cider for a person aged 16 or 17 to consume with a table meal (ie a meal eaten by a person seated at a table, counter or other structure used as a table by seated persons) taken on those premises in the company of an adult.

The offences under s 149(3) and (4) also apply in respect of the *supply* of alcohol in premises in respect of which there is in force a club premises certificate.

A s 149 offence is a 'penalty offence' for the purposes of the Criminal Justice and Police Act 2001, and may be dealt with under a fixed penalty procedure: see p 31.

Consumption of alcohol by children

It is an offence against LA 2003, s 150(1) for an individual under 18 knowingly to consume alcohol on 'relevant premises'. Because of the presence of 'knowingly' the offence will not be committed where a child accidentally consumes alcohol, being unaware of the nature of his drink, or where something has been furtively added to it.

LA 2003, s 150(2) makes it an offence for a person knowingly to allow such consumption to take place on 'relevant premises'. This offence can be committed by a worker at the premises who has authority to prevent the consumption or by a member or officer of a club in a capacity to do so.

These offences do not apply to a person of 16 or 17 who consumes beer, wine, or cider with a table meal on licensed, etc premises and is accompanied by a person of 18 or over.

Delivering alcohol to children

LA 2003, s 151(1) is concerned with the delivery of alcohol to a person under 18. Delivery is a term which avoids 'sale or supply'. The offence lies in a person who works on 'relevant premises', knowingly delivering to a person under 18, alcohol which is sold on the premises or supplied by a club. It may be that his mother has bought and paid for a quantity of drink and has left it at the off-licence to be picked up. If a child goes to pick up the alcohol and it is handed over to that child, there has been a delivery. It is an offence (by s 151(2)) for a person working on the premises with the necessary authority to prevent the delivery to allow it to take place. A similar offence under s 151(4) applies to clubs.

None of the offences under s 151 is committed if alcohol is delivered to a home or workplace, nor does it apply where the job of a minor involves the delivery of alcohol, nor where alcohol is sold or supplied for consumption on the 'relevant premises' (as other offences are committed in this circumstance).

An offence under LA 2003, ss 150 or 151 is a 'penalty offence' for the purposes of the Criminal Justice and Police Act 2001, and may be dealt with under a fixed penalty procedure: see p 31.

Sending child to obtain alcohol

In view of the offences involving delivery to a person under 18, it is not surprising to find that 'sending' such a person to obtain alcohol sold, or to be sold, on 'relevant premises', or supplied or to be supplied by a club, is an offence against LA 2003, s 152(1). Thus where a parent orders by telephone from an off-licence and sends a child to seek the order, an offence against the section is committed. Section 152 provides that the offence is committed whether the child is sent to the licensed premises, etc or to some other delivery point. Thus, if the 'order' has been sent to a distribution centre and it is collected from those premises, the offence is still committed. No offence is committed where the minor works at the premises in a capacity involving the delivery of alcohol, nor if the child is assisting a constable or trading standards officer.

Unsupervised sales by children

It is an offence against LA 2003, s 153(1) for a responsible person knowingly to allow on 'relevant premises' a person under the age of 18 to sell or, in the case of a club, supply alcohol, unless each sale or supply has been specifically approved by a responsible person. A 'responsible person' means:

(a) in the case of licensed premises, the holder of the premises licence or the designated premises supervisor or an adult authorised by such a person to prevent the sale; or
(b) in the case of club certificate premises, any member or officer present in a capacity to prevent the supply; or
(c) at a temporary permitted activity, the premises-user or an adult authorised by him to prevent the sale,

as appropriate. Many of the checkout personnel in supermarkets which are authorised to sell for off-consumption are under 18, but provided that each sale is specifically approved no offence is committed. Such youngsters are seen to gain the approval of more senior personnel. Section 153 exempts sales in a restaurant of alcohol to be taken with a table meal. Thus waiters and waitresses under 18 may serve drinks in such a part of the premises.

CONFISCATION OF ALCOHOL–YOUNG PERSONS

The Confiscation of Alcohol (Young Persons) Act 1997 (CA(YP)A 1997), s 1 provides that, where a constable reasonably suspects that a person in any public place other than licensed premises, or any place (other than a public place) to which a person has unlawfully gained access, is in possession of alcohol and that either:

(a) he is under 18; or
(b) he intends that any of the alcohol should be consumed by a person under the age of 18 in that or another similar place; or
(c) a person under the age of 18 who is, or has recently been, with him, has recently consumed alcohol in that or another similar place,

the constable may require that person to surrender anything which he possesses which is, or the constable reasonably believes to be, alcohol, or a container for it. A constable who imposes such a requirement on a person must also require him to state his name and address and may, if the constable reasonably suspects that he is under 16, remove him to his place of residence or to a place of safety. A person who, without reasonable excuse, fails to comply with a surrender of alcohol requirement or a name and address requirement commits an offence under s 1(3). A constable who makes a surrender requirement must inform the person concerned of his suspicion and that failing without reasonable excuse to comply with either type of requirement is an offence.

The Act provides a means by which the nuisance caused by youngsters assembling in public places and drinking may be removed. The provisions of the CA(YP)A 1997, s 1 effectively embrace all persons likely to be in such a group, including those who are 18 or over if, as they are almost certain to be, they are associated with drinking by those who are under age. Where a person of 18 or over is with a young person who is or has been drinking in such a place, (b) and (c) above require the surrender of alcohol in the adult person's possession. The terms of CA(YP)A 1997 are such that everyone in a group containing some under-18-year-olds with alcohol in their possession may be required to surrender it.

A constable may dispose of anything surrendered to him under CA(YP)A 1997 in such a manner as he considers appropriate.

OTHER PROHIBITIONS UPON THE SALE OR CONSUMPTION OF ALCOHOL AND FALSE STATEMENTS

Offence of persistently possessing alcohol in a public place

P&CA 2009, s 30(1) provides that a person under 18 is guilty of an offence if, without reasonable excuse, he is in possession of alcohol in any relevant place on three or more occasions within a period of 12 consecutive months.

'Relevant place', in relation to a person, means any public place, other than excluded premises, or any place, other than a public place, to which the person has unlawfully gained access. 'Excluded premises' means:

(a) premises which may by virtue of LA 2003, Parts 3 or 5 (see pp 591 and 593) be used for the supply of alcohol,

(b) premises which may by virtue of Part 4 (see p 592) be used for the supply of alcohol to members or guests.

Prohibition of sale of alcohol on moving vehicles

LA 2003, s 156(1) creates the offence of selling alcohol by retail on or from a vehicle which is not permanently or temporarily parked. It is a defence where the sale was mistaken; was due to the seller relying on information given to him; was the fault of another person; or was due to some cause beyond the seller's control, provided (in each case) that he took all reasonable precautions and exercised due diligence to avoid committing the offence. This could occur where it was believed that the refreshment served was non-alcoholic and there was some good reason to have held that belief.

Power to prohibit sale of alcohol on trains

Section 157 provides for a magistrates' court to make an order prohibiting the sale of alcohol at specified stations or on trains travelling between specified stations for a particular period. A prohibition order may be made on the application of a police officer of at least the rank of inspector, if the magistrates are satisfied than an order is necessary for the prevention of disorder. A copy of the order must be served by the police upon the operator or operators concerned. Thus, provision is made for 'dry' soccer specials, at least so far as the operating companies are concerned.

Making false statements in applications for licences and certificates and in notices

It is an offence against LA 2003, s 158(1) for a person knowingly or recklessly to make a false statement in or in connection with (a) an application for the grant, variation, transfer or review of a premises licence or club premises certificate, (b) an application for a local authority provisional statement in respect of a premises licence, (c) a temporary event notice or any other notice under the Act, or (d) an application for the grant or renewal of a personal licence. For the purposes of s 158 a person is treated as making a false statement if he produces, furnishes, signs or otherwise makes use of a document that contains a false statement.

Alcohol consumption in designated public places

The Criminal Justice and Police Act 2001 (CJPA 2001), ss 12 to 16 address the issue of disorder and nuisance associated with such consumption.

CJPA 2001, s 12 gives a constable certain powers where he reasonably believes that a person is, or has been, consuming alcohol in a designated public place, or intends to consume alcohol in such a place. These are powers to require the person concerned not to consume, in the designated place, anything which is, or which the constable reasonably believes to be, alcohol, and to surrender anything in his possession which is, or which the constable reasonably believes to be, alcohol or a container for alcohol. Anything so surrendered may be disposed of by the constable in a manner which he considers to be appropriate. Failure without reasonable excuse to comply with such a requirement is an offence under s12(4). However, the constable making the requirement must inform the person concerned that failing without reasonable excuse to comply with the requirement is an offence.

As can be seen, it is not essential in order for a requirement to be made that an officer sees a person consuming alcohol. If a person has alcohol in a glass or an open container it raises the inference that he intends to drink it. Where alcohol is in a sealed container, notice will have to be taken of the surrounding circumstances. Possession of a 'four-pack' by a person who is walking home differs from possession by groups of persons assembled at that place for the purpose of drinking.

By s 13, a 'designated public place' is, subject to s 14, a public place within the area of a local authority which is identified in an order made by that authority. A local authority may make such an order where it is satisfied that:

(a) nuisance or annoyance to members of the public, or a section of the public; or
(b) disorder,

has been associated with the consumption of alcohol in that place.

By s 14, a place is not a designated public place if it is:

(a) premises in respect of which a premises licence has effect which authorises the premises to be used for the sale or supply of alcohol;
(b) premises in respect of which a club premises certificate has effect which certifies that the premises may be used for the sale or supply of alcohol;
(c) a place within the curtilage of premises described at (a) or (b);
(d) premises which by virtue of LA 2003, Part 5 (permitted temporary activities) may for the time being be used for the supply of alcohol or could have been so used within the last 30 minutes; or
(e) a place where facilities or activities relating to the sale or consumption of alcohol are for the time being permitted by virtue of a permission granted under the Highways Act 1980, s 115E (council permission to set up objects and structures on a highway for the purpose of producing income).

Where premises within (a) are licensed premises in respect of which a local authority holds the premises licence, or which are occupied by such an authority or managed by it or on its behalf, they are not a designated public place only during the hours when alcohol is being sold or supplied there and for thirty minutes thereafter.

The Local Authorities (Alcohol Consumption in Designated Public Places) Regulations 2007 apply to procedural matters relating to orders.

CLOSURE OF LICENSED PREMISES DUE TO DISORDER OR DISTURBANCE

Closure orders for identified premises

LA 2003, s 161 provides that a senior police officer (ie inspector or above) may make a closure order in relation to any 'relevant premises' (in this context, premises in respect of which there is a premises licence or a temporary events notice) if he reasonably believes that:

(a) there is, or is likely imminently to be, disorder on, or in the vicinity of and related to, the premises and their closure is necessary in the interests of public safety; or
(b) a public nuisance is being caused by noise coming from the premises and the closure of the premises is necessary to prevent that nuisance.

A closure order requires the premises to be closed for a period not exceeding 24 hours. An officer making a closure order must consider, in particular, any conduct of each appropriate person in relation to the disorder or nuisance. 'Appropriate person' means a premises licence-holder, any designated premises supervisor, premises-user in relation to a temporary event notice, or a manager of the premises. A closure order is effective as soon as notice of it has been given to the licensee or a manager of the premises.

A person who permits relevant premises to be open in contravention of a closure order, without reasonable excuse, commits an offence under s 161(6).

Extension of closure order

Where, before the end of the closure period, the responsible senior police officer reasonably believes that:

(a) a magistrates' court will not have determined whether to exercise its powers under s 165(2) (below) before the end of the closure period; and
(b) the conditions for an extension are satisfied,

he may extend the closure period for a further 24 hours. The conditions for an extension are:

(a) in the case of an order made on the grounds of public safety because of disorder, that those conditions still exist;
(b) in the case of an order made on the grounds of nuisance, that those conditions still exist.

To have effect, such a notice of extension must be given before the original period has expired.

Cancellation of a closure order

The responsible senior officer may cancel a closure order or any extension of it at any time between the making of the appropriate order and determination by the magistrates. Such an officer must cancel an order if he does not believe that the original conditions which merited its making continue to exist. Notice of cancellation must be given.

The 'responsible senior police officer' is the senior officer who made the order or another senior officer designated by the chief officer of police.

Procedure following the making of an order

As soon as reasonably practicable after the making of the order, the responsible senior police officer must apply to a relevant magistrates' court for it to consider the order. The magistrates' court must as soon as reasonably practicable hold a hearing and may:

(a) revoke the order and any extension of it;
(b) order that closure continues until the matter is considered by the relevant licensing authority;
(c) order the premises to remain closed until that time subject to any stated exceptions; or
(d) order closure until that time unless prescribed conditions are satisfied (s 165(2)).

The magistrates must notify the licensing authority of their decision in relation to any premises in respect of which a premises licence is in force. The licensing authority is required to review the premises licence within 28 days of receiving notification from the justices. Regulations deal with notification to the holder of a premises licence.

Where it has been ordered that premises remain closed an offence is committed under LA 2003, s 165(7) by a person who, without reasonable excuse, allows them to remain open. Such premises are open if a person (other than a licence-holder or person living there) enters the premises and is supplied with food or drink, or, while he is there, the premises are used for entertainment. Entries to premises which are not associated with licensable activities are outside these provisions.

Police powers

By LA 2003, s 169, a constable may use such force as may be necessary for the purpose of closing premises in compliance with a closure order. Neither a constable nor his chief officer will be liable for any damage which occurs in the course of such duties unless the act or omission is shown to have been in bad faith or to be unlawful because of the Human Rights Act 1998.

Closure of all premises in an identified area

LA 2003, s 160 deals with situations in which there is, or there is expected to be, disorder in a local justice area. In such cases, a magistrates' court acting for that area may make a closure order for a period not exceeding 24 hours, in relation to all premises situated at or near the place of the disorder or expected disorder and in respect of which a premises licence or a temporary event notice has effect. Application for such an order must be made by a superintendent (or above) and the order must not be made unless the court is satisfied that it is necessary to prevent disorder.

It is an offence under s 160(4) for a manager of premises, the holder of a premises licence, the designated premises supervisor, or the premises-user in the case of a temporary event, to knowingly keep open premises to which the order relates, or to allow any such premises to be kept open, during the currency of that order.

By s 160(7), a constable may use such force as may be necessary to close such premises.

Closure of unlicensed premises under provisions of the Criminal Justice and Police Act 2001

Where a constable or a local authority is satisfied that premises are being, or within the last 24 hours have been, used for unauthorised sale of alcohol for consumption on, or in the vicinity of, the premises, CJPA 2001, s 19 provides that he or it must serve a closure notice on a person having control of, or responsibility for, the activities carried on at the premises. A closure notice must also be served on any person occupying any other part of the building whose access would be impeded by the order. It may also be served on any other person with control of, or responsibility for, the activities on the premises, or any person with an interest in the premises. A closure notice must specify the nature of the alleged use of the premises, state the effect of s 20 (below), and set out the steps which may be taken to ensure that the alleged use of the premises ceases or (as the case may be) does not recur. Closure notices issued by a constable or a local authority may be cancelled at any time.

CJPA 2001, s 20 provides that when a closure notice has been served the constable or local authority may seek an order from the justices, not less than seven days, and not more than six months, after the service of the notice. An order should not be sought where the constable or local authority is satisfied that the offending use of the premises has ceased and that there is no reasonable likelihood of resumption. Where the justices on hearing the case are satisfied that a notice was properly served under s 19, and that the premises and/or the vicinity of those premises continue to be used for the offending purpose or that there is a reasonable likelihood that there will be such use, they may make a closure order under CJPA 2001, s 21, requiring in particular:

(a) immediate closure of the premises to the public until the constable or local authority (as the case may be) has certified that the need for the order has ceased (such an order may include conditions relating to admission and access to other parts of the building);

(b) any offending use to be discontinued immediately; and

(c) any defendant to pay into court a sum of money which will not be released until the other requirements of the order have been complied with.

The constable or local authority (as the case may be) must fix a copy of the order to the premises.

Affected persons may seek discharge of the order. If the justices are satisfied that the need for the order has ceased, they may discharge it.

A person who, without reasonable excuse, permits premises to be open in contravention of a closure order, or who otherwise fails to comply with it, commits an offence.

Police powers

BY CJPA 2001, s 25(1) and (2), where a closure order has been made a constable or an authorised person, who identifies himself if so required, may enter the premises at any reasonable time, if need be by reasonable force, and do anything reasonably necessary to secure compliance with the order.

It is an offence contrary to s 25(3) for a person intentionally to obstruct a constable or an authorised person in the exercise of these powers.

Closure of noisy premises with premises licence or temporary event notice

The Anti-social Behaviour Act 2003, s 40 empowers the chief executive officer of a local authority or environmental health officer authorised by him to make a closure order in relation to premises in respect of which a premises licence or temporary event notice is in effect if he reasonably believes that a public nuisance is being caused by noise coming from the premises and the closure is necessary to prevent that nuisance. Such an order requires the specified premises to remain closed during a specified period (maximum 24 hours) and begins when the manager of the premises receives written notice of it. It is an offence, without reasonable excuse, to permit premises to be open in contravention of a closure order.

Notice of the order must be given as soon as reasonably practicable to the licensing authority. A closure order may be cancelled by the chief executive officer or authorised officer by written notice, and must be cancelled as soon as reasonably practicable if he believes that it is no longer necessary.

DIRECTIONS TO INDIVIDUALS WHO REPRESENT A RISK OF DISORDER

The Violent Crime Reduction Act 2006 (VCRA 2006), s 27 empowers a constable in uniform to give to an individual aged 10 or over who is in a public place a direction:

(a) requiring him to leave the locality of that place; and

(b) prohibiting the individual from returning to that locality for such period (not exceeding 48 hours) from the giving of the direction as the constable may specify.

Such a direction may only be given if:

(a) the presence of the individual in that locality is likely, in all the circumstances, to cause or to contribute to the occurrence of alcohol-related crime or disorder in that locality, or to cause or to contribute to a repetition or continuance there of such crime or disorder; or

(b) the giving of such a direction to that individual is necessary for the purpose of removing or reducing the likelihood of there being such crime or disorder in that locality during the period for which the direction has effect or of there being a repetition or continuance in that locality during the period of such crime or disorder.

A direction under s 27:

(a) must be in writing;

(b) may require the individual to whom it is given to leave the locality in question either immediately or by such time as the constable giving the direction may specify;

(c) must clearly identify the locality to which it relates;

(d) must specify the period for which the individual is prohibited from returning to that locality;

(e) may impose requirements as to the manner in which that individual leaves the locality, including his route; and

(f) may be withdrawn or varied (but not extended so as to apply for a period of more than 48 hours) by a constable.

A constable may not give a direction under s 27 that prevents the individual to whom it is given:

(a) from having access to a place where he resides;

(b) from attending at any place which he is:
    (i) required to attend for the purposes of his work, or
    (ii) expected to attend for the purposes of education or training or of receiving medical treatment; or
    (iii) required to attend by any obligation imposed on him by or under an enactment or court order.

A constable who gives a direction under s 27 must make a record of the terms of the direction and the locality to which it relates; the individual to whom it is given; the time at which it is given; and the period during which that individual is required not to return to the locality.

Failure to comply with a direction under s 27 is an offence contrary to s 27(6).

A constable who gives a direction under s 27 may, if he reasonably suspects that the individual to whom it is given is under 16, remove the person to a place where the person resides or a place of safety.

MISCELLANEOUS MATTERS

Exclusion of persons convicted of offences of violence from licensed premises

The Licensed Premises (Exclusion of Certain Persons) Act 1980 permits courts to make exclusion orders in respect of someone convicted by or before them of offences of violence or threats of violence on premises in respect of which a premises licence authorising the supply of alcohol for consumption on the premises is in force, prohibiting such a person from entering specified licensed premises without the express consent of the licensee, his employee or agent. A person who enters in breach of an exclusion order commits an offence under s2(1). By s 3, the licensee, his employee or agent may expel a person who has entered, or whom he reasonably suspects of entering, in breach of an order. A constable must, on the demand of a licensee, his employee or agent, help to expel any person whom the constable reasonably suspects of being in breach of an exclusion order. The 1980 Act will be unnecessary where drinking banning orders can be made by a court on conviction. It is prospectively repealed by VCRA 2006, Sch 5.

Drinking banning orders

VCRA 2006, Part 1, Ch 1 (ss 1 to 14) makes provision for drinking banning orders to be made, the effect of which is to exclude persons aged 16 or over who are responsible for alcohol-related disorder from licensed premises and clubs in a specified area for a period of time specified in the order. Such an order may be made by a magistrates' or county court on application by a relevant chief constable or local authority (in force) or on conviction (in force in certain areas). The order must have effect for not less than two months and not more than two years. Other relevant matters may be dealt with by the order. Provision is also made for a reduction in the duration of the order if an individual agrees to complete an approved course.

Breach of an order (or interim order) without reasonable excuse is an offence under VCRA 2006, s 11(1).

Alcohol disorder zones

VCRA 2006, Part 1, Ch 2 (ss 15 to 20) provides that, with the consent of the police, local authorities may designate a locality as an alcohol disorder zone where problems are experienced with nuisance or annoyance to members of the public, or disorder, associated with the consumption of alcohol supplied at premises in that locality, which are likely to be repeated. This can lead to the drafting of action plans to try to deal with the problem. Such a plan might require the funding of services such as late transport. Local authorities may impose charges on the holders of premises licences and club premises certificates related to provision of alcohol where they do not implement such an action plan. The Local Authorities (Alcohol Disorder Zones) Regulations 2008 set out the procedures involved in obtaining a designation under VCRA 2006, Part 1, Ch 2. The provisions relating to alcohol disorder zones are prospectively repealed by the Police Reform and Social Responsibility Act 2011.

Prohibition of sales of alcohol at service areas, garages, etc

LA 2003, s 176 provides that no premises licence, club premises certificate or temporary event notice has effect to authorise the sale by retail or supply of alcohol on or from excluded premises. These are premises on the land of a motorway authority being used for the provision of facilities at motorway service stations or premises used primarily as a garage or which form part of such premises. The nature of prohibited premises may be altered by order. The Secretary of State may, for example, wish to exempt certain premises in rural areas where the business concerned with the provision of petrol, etc is only a part of the business concerned.

Dancing in certain small premises

LA 2003, s 177 is concerned with the situation where (a) a premises licence or a club premises certificate authorises dancing and the sale of alcohol for consumption on the premises, and (b) the premises are used primarily for the sale of alcohol for consumption on the premises and have a capacity limit of up to 200. Section 177 provides that, at any time when the premises are open for the supply of alcohol for consumption on the premises and are being used for dancing, any conditions imposed in respect of music entertainment (ie live music or dancing) by the licensing authority, other than those set out in the licence-holder's operating schedule, will be suspended unless they were imposed for public safety or the prevention of crime and disorder.

Section 177 may be disapplied in relation to conditions in respect of particular premises following a review of the licence or certificate.

The LA 2003, s 177A, added by the Live Music Act 2012, provides that, where live music takes place on premises authorised to be used for the supply of alcohol for consumption on the premises by a premises licence or club premises certificate, and:

(a) at the time of the live music, the premises are open for the purposes of being used for the supply of alcohol for consumption on the premises,

(b) the live music is unamplified, or (if amplified) the audience does not exceed 200,

(c) the live music takes place between 0800 and 2300 on the same day (or, where a special occasion order (p 595) has effect, between the hours specified in that order),

any condition of the premises licence or club premises certificate which relates to live music does not have effect in relation to the live music, unless, on a review of the licence or certificate, s 177A is disapplied in relation to that condition (s 177A(3)) or a condition is added relating to live music as if it were regulated entertainment and the licence or certificate licensed it (s 177A(4)). For the purposes of s 177A, 'condition' means a condition included in a premises licence or club premises certificate, other than one which is a mandatory one, including one added by way of variation at the request of the licence-holder or the club, as the case may be.

Police powers

LA 2003, s 179(1) provides for a police officer or authorised person (see p 588) to enter premises where he has reason to believe that the premises are being, or are about to be, used for a licensable activity to ensure that the activities are being carried on under and in accordance with the appropriate authorisations. An authorised person must produce his authority if requested. Reasonable force may be used if necessary. By s 179(4), it is an offence to obstruct an authorised person.

LA 2003, s 180 provides that a police officer may enter and search premises where there is reason to believe an offence under the Act has been, is being or is about to be, committed, and may use reasonable force to gain entry.

OFFENCES OF DRUNKENNESS AND POLICE POWERS

Drunkenness is not in itself an offence but becomes so in certain circumstances, which are described below. Drunkenness in this context is limited to intoxication through drink and does not include intoxication through drugs or through glue-sniffing.

A divisional court has held that 'drunkenness' requires that the defendant has voluntarily consumed alcohol and that this has resulted in his becoming drunk. 'Drunk' bears its ordinary natural meaning; whether a defendant was drunk is a question of fact in each case.

The offence of being drunk at a designated sports ground is dealt with in Chapter 27.

Simple drunkenness

The term 'simple drunkenness' is one of practice and not of law. Police officers have for many years used the term to separate the offence of being found drunk from various offences dealing with aggravated forms of drunkenness. This offence of simple drunkenness is often referred to, although not strictly accurately, as one of being drunk and incapable. The offence is governed by the Licensing Act (LA) 1872, s 12 which provides that a person is guilty of an offence if he is found drunk on any highway or other public place, whether a building or not, or on any licensed premises. The general arrest provisions of PACE, s 24 will apply to such circumstances. It is particularly worth remembering that this section permits an arrest if it is necessary to prevent the person from suffering serious physical harm. Such harm would be likely if he was left unconscious in the open.

This offence under LA 1872, s 12 is a 'penalty offence' for the purposes of CJPA 2001 and may be dealt with under a fixed penalty procedure: see p 31.

Drunk and disorderly

The Criminal Justice Act 1967, s 91 states that any person who in any public place is guilty, while drunk, of disorderly behaviour commits an offence. A divisional court has held that whether the defendant's behaviour was disorderly is a simple question of fact. What is required is that his behaviour, viewed objectively, was disorderly. 'Disorderly behaviour' does not involve any element of mens rea. Where there is an intercom system and locks on the entrance to a block of flats, so that only those admitted by the occupiers are given access to the area, the landing area outside the flats is not a public place for the purposes of this offence. Nor would it be for the purposes of the offence of simple drunkenness.

An offence under CJA 1967, s 91 is a 'penalty offence' for the purposes of CJPA 2001 and may be dealt with under a fixed penalty procedure: see p 31.

Drunk in charge of particular things

LA 1872, s 12 also makes it an offence for a person to be drunk while in charge on any highway or other public place, of a carriage, horse, cattle, or steam engine, or to be drunk when in possession of a loaded firearm. 'Carriage' includes a motor vehicle, but if a person is drunk in charge of such a vehicle the appropriate offence is that under RTA 1988, s 4 (discussed in Chapter 15) and not the present one, since it is a more serious offence which reflects the gravity of the situation. Although a bicycle is a 'carriage', *riding* a cycle while unfit through drink is also an offence under RTA 1988, s 30, and if a person rides while unfit he should be dealt with under that section. However, a person *in charge*, eg pushing a pedal cycle, in such a condition commits an offence only against LA 1872, s 12. The Act does not define the term 'firearm' for the purposes of the section, but that term bears its everyday meaning and includes an airgun.

Drunk in charge of a child

The Licensing Act 1902, s 2 creates the offence of being found drunk on any highway or other public place, whether a building or not, or on any licensed premises, while having the charge of a child apparently under the age of seven.

CHAPTER 18

Dogs

CONTROL OF DOGS

Collars

The Control of Dogs Order 1992 requires that while on a highway or in a place of public resort every dog must wear a collar with the owner's name and address inscribed upon it, or on a plate or badge attached to it. This does not apply to:

(a) any pack of hounds;
(b) any dog while being used:
    (i) for sporting purposes;
    (ii) for the capture or destruction of vermin;
    (iii) for the driving or tending of cattle or sheep;
    (iv) used on official duties by a member of the armed forces or Revenue and Customs or by the police force for any area; or
    (v) in emergency rescue work; or
(c) any dog registered with the Guide Dogs for the Blind Association.

The owner or the person in charge of a dog who, without lawful authority or excuse, the proof whereof is on him, causes or permits the dog to be in a highway or place of public resort without the requisite collar is guilty of an offence under reg 3.

Leads and muzzles

The Road Traffic Act 1988, s 27 empowers local authorities to make orders designating lengths of roads within their areas as roads upon which dogs must at all times be kept on a lead. The chief officer of police must be consulted before such an order is made and the local authority is required to publish it and to place signs on the designated length of road subject to the order. When such an order is in force, it is an offence under s 27(1) to cause or permit a dog to be on such a length of road if it is not held on a lead. Section 27 permits exceptions to be made by the order, and it expressly provides that the offence does not apply to dogs tending cattle or sheep in the course of a business nor to those being used for sporting purposes.

See also the offences under the CNEA 2005 and the Dangerous Dogs Act 1991, s 1(2) and (7) considered in this chapter.

Dogs fouling land

The Clean Neighbourhoods and Environment Act 2005 (CNEA 2005) makes provision for dog control orders to be made by local authorities which may include requirements in relation to this matter.

Dog control orders

CNEA 2005, s 55 provides local authorities with powers to make dog control orders providing for offences in relation to the control of dogs in respect of any land in its area. For these purposes an offence relates to the control of dogs if it relates to one of the following matters:

(a) fouling of land by dogs and the removal of dog faeces;
(b) the keeping of dogs on leads;
(c) the exclusion of dogs from land; and
(d) the number of dogs which a person may take onto any land.

Dog control orders may apply to any land open to the air to which the public are entitled or permitted to have access, with or without payment. Covered land which is open to the air on at least one side is land open to the air.

Land may be designated by statutory instrument as land to which these provisions do not apply. The Controls on Dogs (Non-application to Designated Land) Order 2009 and the Controls on Dogs (Non-application to Designated Land) (Wales) Order 2007 designate the following as such: land which is placed at the disposal of the Forestry Commission (for the purpose of making any dog control order), and land which is or forms part of a road (for the purpose of making a dog control order which provides for an offence relating to the exclusion of dogs from land).

The offences which are provided for in a dog control order are prescribed by regulations. The Dog Control Orders (Prescribed Offences and Penalties, etc) Regulations 2006, Schs 1 to 5 (England) and the Dog Control Orders (Miscellaneous Provisions) (Wales) Order 2007, Schs 1 to 5 prescribe the offences of:

(a) failing to remove faeces deposited by a dog on land in respect of which a Fouling of Land by Dogs Order applies;
(b) failing to keep a dog on a lead on land;
(c) failing to put, and to keep, a dog on a lead when directed to do so by an authorised officer, on land in respect of which a Dogs on Leads by Direction Order applies;
(d) permitting a dog to enter land in respect of which a Dogs Exclusion Order applies; and
(e) taking more than the maximum number of dogs onto land in respect of which a Dogs (Specified Maximum) Order applies.

These offences must be committed without reasonable excuse or without the consent of the owner, occupier or other person or authority who has control of the land. Persons who are registered blind or who have some other disability which makes them dog-dependent cannot commit the offences at (a) and (d).

CNEA 2005, s 59 makes provision for offences to be dealt with by an authorised officer of the local authority by way of a fixed penalty. The amount of the fixed penalty may be specified in the order. If not specified it is currently £75. An authorised officer is empowered to require a person to whom he intends to give a notice to give his name and address. Failure to do so, or the giving of a false or inaccurate name and address, is an offence.

Community support officers and accredited persons may be authorised to deal with these matters by way of a fixed penalty.

STRAY DOGS

The Environmental Protection Act 1990 (EPA 1990), s 149 requires every local authority to appoint an officer to deal with stray dogs found in its area. Where the appointed officer has reason to believe that any dog found in a public place or on any other land or premises is a stray dog, he must, where possible, seize it and detain it. Where the place concerned is not a public place, he may only seize and detain the dog with the consent of the owner or occupier of the place. Where the dog wears a collar on which appears a person's name and address, or its owner is known, a notice must be served on that person, stating that the dog will be liable to be disposed of if it is not claimed within seven clear days and the expenses of its detention met. After the dog has been detained for seven clear days (or, where a notice has been served, if it has not been claimed and the expenses paid within seven clear days after service of the notice) the dog may be disposed of by way of sale, gift, or destruction. The ownership of a dog so sold or given is vested in the buyer if he acts in good faith.

The officer must keep a register giving particulars of all dogs so seized and disposed of. The register must be available for inspection by the public without charge.

EPA 1990, s 150 requires the finder of a stray dog to:

(a) return it to its owner; or
(b) take the dog to the appointed local authority officer for the area or to the nearest police station;

and to inform that officer or the police officer in charge of where the dog was found. Failure to do so is an offence (s 150(5)). Where a dog has been taken to an appointed officer, the finder may keep the dog, if he wishes, on informing the officer of this and his name and address. In such a case the finder must keep the dog for at least a month; he commits an offence if he fails to do so (s 150(5)).

DANGEROUS DOGS

Order to keep under control

If it appears to a magistrates' court that a dog is dangerous and not kept under proper control, it may, under the Dogs Act 1871, order the owner to keep it under control or order the dog's destruction. The proceedings must be by way of complaint. Complaints may be preferred by a police officer.

Such an order may be made whether or not the dog is shown to have injured any person. It may specify the measures to be taken for keeping the dog under control, whether by muzzling, keeping on a lead or by excluding it from specified places or otherwise. Such an order may also require the neutering of a male dog.

A divisional court held that it is not necessary that the dog is dangerous to mankind; it is enough that it is dangerous to other animals of whatever kind. However, in one case, a dog which killed two pet rabbits was held by a divisional court not to be dangerous as it was within the natural instincts of a dog to chase, wound, or kill other small animals. This is a surprising view. If followed generally it would undermine the Dogs Act 1871. In contrast, in a more recent case, where a Japanese Akita dog slipped its lead and attacked a Jack Russell terrier which died as a result of its injuries, a divisional court held that a dog could be dangerous and not under proper control even if the only danger it presented was to another dog. It held that 'dangerous' was to be given its ordinary everyday meaning and was not limited to danger to mankind or particular species of animals or birds.

The Dangerous Dogs Act 1989, s 1 empowers a magistrates' court, when it makes a destruction order under the 1871 Act, to appoint a person to undertake the destruction and to require the custodian to deliver it up. It may also disqualify the owner from having custody for a specified period; an owner who has custody of a dog while disqualified commits an offence under s 1(6).

The 1989 Act. s 1(6) also creates offences of failing to keep a dog under proper control as ordered under the 1871 Act, and failing to deliver up a dog for destruction. The punishment can include disqualification from having custody of a dog for a specified period.

Specific offences in relation to dangerous dogs

The Dangerous Dogs Act 1991 (DDA 1991), ss 1 and 3 make further provisions in relation to dangerous dogs.

Possession or control of dogs bred for fighting

DDA 1991, s 1(3) provides that no person may have in his possession or control a dog to which s 1 applies, ie any dog of the type known as pit bull terrier, Japanese tosa and any other type of dog designated by order of the Secretary of State, currently the dogo argentino and the fila braziliero. Breach of s 1(3) is an offence under s 1(7). 'Type' has a wider meaning than 'breed'. Determining the limits of a type is a question of fact for determination by the magistrates or Crown Court. They are entitled to look at the American Dog Breeders' Association (ADBA) breed standard as a guide. The fact that a dog does not meet that standard in every respect is not conclusive that it is not one of the specified types. Thus, for example, it has been held that the fact that a dog is near to, or has a substantial number of, characteristics of a pit bull terrier as set out in the ADBA standard is sufficient for the dog to be found to be of the pit bull terrier type. It is relevant to consider whether the dog exhibited the behavioural characteristics of a pit bull terrier but that evidence would not be conclusive.

Breeding, selling, etc of dogs bred for fighting

DDA 1991, s 1(2) and (7) makes it an offence to breed, sell, exchange, give or offer to give, advertise or expose for sale, exchange or gift, a dog specified above in relation to s 1(3).

Section 1(2) and (7) also make it an offence for the owner to abandon such a dog, or for the owner or person in charge of it to allow it to stray.

Finally, s 1(2) and (7) make it an offence for the owner, or person for the time being in charge, of such a dog to allow it to be in a public place without being muzzled and kept on a lead. 'Public place' is defined on p 618. This prohibition in s 1 is a strict one. If a dog of the requisite type is in a public place, it must not be allowed to be unmuzzled and must be kept on a lead. Thus, where an owner removed the muzzle from a pit bull terrier because it developed kennel cough and it was therefore cruel to muzzle it, it was held that neither the Act nor the common law allowed a person in control of such a dog to make a value judgement between the safety of the public or the well-being of the dog, and that there were no circumstances in which the necessity of the situation could overtake the prohibition.

Keeping dogs under proper control

Where any dog is dangerously out of control in a public place, the owner or the person for the time being in charge of it is guilty of an offence under DDA 1991, s 3(1). There is an aggravated, indictable (either way) offence if the dog, whilst so out of control, injures any person. Strict liability is imposed by s 3(1) on the owners or handlers of such dogs. The test is objective and the state of mind of the owner is irrelevant. However, an owner has a defence if he can prove that at the time of the offence the dog was in the charge of a person whom he reasonably believed to be a fit and proper person to be in charge of it. A divisional court has held that the defence only applies if there is plain evidence that 'charge' has been transferred to an identified person.

Allowing entry to unpermitted place

The owner or person in charge of a dog commits an offence against DDA 1991, s 3(3) if he allows it to enter a place which is not a public place but where it is not permitted to be and, while it is there, it injures any person, or there are grounds for reasonable apprehension that it will do so. There would be such grounds, for example, if a dog attacks someone without prior warning. The offence can be committed by omission if it results in the dog entering the place in question. Consequently, for example, a person who fails to take adequate precautions to prevent a dog escaping into another place 'allows' it to enter that place. Where a dog was secured by a chain which proved to be inadequate and it escaped from a garden, entered a place where it was not permitted to be, and bit the face of a young child, the owner was held to have 'allowed' the dog to enter that place, even though he thought that the chain was adequate. A divisional court has held that more than one person may be in charge of a dog at the same time, as where D1, who is taking a dog for a walk, hands its lead temporarily to D2.

Like the offence under s 3(1), the present offence is one of strict liability. If the dog does injure any person in these circumstances, an aggravated, indictable (either way) offence is committed.

Public place

In DDA 1991, a 'public place' means any street, road, or other place (whether or not enclosed) to which the public have or are permitted to have access whether for payment or otherwise, including the common parts of a building containing two or more separate dwellings (eg a block of flats) (s 10). A front garden or driveway is not a public place in this context and neither is any other type of place which people enter by express or implied invitation. On the other hand, a dog in a private car on a public highway is in a public place.

Destruction and disqualification orders

These are dealt with by DDA 1991, s 4 or s 4A

Immediate destruction order

Section 4(1) provides that, where a person is convicted of an offence against ss 1 or 3, the court may order destruction of the dog concerned. Indeed, it must do so in the case of an offence under s 1 or an aggravated offence contrary to s 3, unless it is satisfied that the dog would not constitute a danger to public safety.

A court may also order a person convicted of any of these offences to be disqualified from keeping a dog for such a period as it thinks fit. Dogs may not be destroyed during the period allowed for notice of, and determination of, any appeal.

Similar provisions are made in DDA 1991 to those set out in the Dangerous Dogs Act 1989, in relation to the appointment of a person to undertake the destruction of a dog and requiring it to be delivered up for that purpose.

Offences are committed against s 4(8) where a person has custody of a dog while disqualified, or where he fails to deliver up a dog for destruction as ordered.

Contingent destruction order

Section 4A provides that where:

(a) a person is convicted of an offence under s 1 or an aggravated offence under s 3(1) or (3);
(b) the court does not order destruction of the dog under s 4; and
(c) in the case of an offence under s 1, the dog is subject to the prohibition under s 1(3),

the court must order that, unless the dog is exempted on specified grounds by DEFRA from that prohibition within the requisite period, the dog shall be destroyed. The requisite period, currently two months, may be extended by the court.

Section 4A also provides that, where a person is convicted of a simple offence under DDA 1991, s 3(1) or (3), the court may order that, unless its owner keeps it under proper control, the dog must be destroyed. Such an order may specify the measures to be taken to keep the dog under control whether by muzzling, keeping on a lead, excluding it from specified places or otherwise, and, if it appears to the court that the dog is a male and would be less dangerous if neutered, may require that the dog be neutered.

Dogs owned by young persons

DDA 1991, s 6 provides that, where a dog is owned by a person who is under 16, the term 'owner' in the above provisions includes a reference to the head of the household, if any, of which that person is a member.

Police powers

By DDA 1991, s 5(1), a constable (or authorised local authority officer) may seize any dog:

(a) which appears to be a dog to which s 1 applies and which is in a public place; or
(b) which is in a public place and which appears to be dangerously out of control.

The additional powers of seizure provided by the Criminal Justice and Police Act 2001, s 50 apply to this power of seizure.

If a justice of the peace is satisfied by information on oath that there are reasonable grounds to believe that one of the above offences has been committed, or that evidence of such an offence is to be found on any premises, he may issue a warrant authorising a constable to enter and search them and to seize any dog or other thing which is evidence of such an offence. This power is given by DDA 1991, s 5(2).

DDA 1991, s 4B makes provision for an order of destruction which may be made by a justice of the peace in respect of a dog which has been seized under s 5(1) or (2) where there is no prosecution, or where the dog cannot be released without contravention of s 1(3). A justice is not required to make such an order if he is satisfied that the dog would not be a danger to public safety.

DOGS WORRYING LIVESTOCK

The Dogs (Protection of Livestock) Act 1953 (D(PL)A 1953), s 1(1) declares that the owner of a dog, and, if it is in the charge of a person other than the owner, that person also, is guilty of an offence if the dog worries livestock on any agricultural land.

By s 1(2), the term 'worry livestock' covers attacking livestock, or chasing livestock in such a way as might reasonably be expected to cause injury or suffering to it, or, in the case of females, abortion, or loss of or diminution in their produce. It also covers a dog being at large (ie not on a lead or under close control) in a field or enclosure in which there are sheep, but not where the dog is owned by, or in the charge of, the occupier of the field or is a police dog, guide dog, trained sheepdog, working gun dog or, perhaps unexpectedly, a pack of hounds.

'Livestock' means cattle, sheep, goats, swine, horses (including asses and mules), or poultry. Thus 'livestock' can generally be described as farm animals. 'Agricultural land' means land used as arable, meadow or grazing land or for the purposes of poultry farming, pig farming, market gardens, allotments, nursery grounds or orchards.

Defences

The owner of the dog has a defence if he proves that at the time in question the dog was in the charge of some other person, whom he reasonably believed to be a fit and proper person to be in charge, as where he has allowed a reliable person to take the dog for a walk.

If the dog which attacks the livestock is owned by, or in the charge of, the occupier of that land or a person authorised by him, a defence is open to that person provided that he did not cause the dog to attack the livestock.

Police powers

By D(PL)A 1953, s 2(2), a constable is empowered to seize a dog, found anywhere, which he reasonably believes to have been worrying livestock on agricultural land and to retain it until the owner is found and has paid the expenses of its detention. This power cannot be exercised if there is a person present who admits to being the owner of the dog or in charge of it.

If, on an application by a constable, a justice is satisfied that there are grounds for believing that:

(a) an offence under the Act has been committed; and
(b) the dog in question is on premises specified in the application,

he may issue a warrant under s 2A authorising a constable to enter and search the premises in order to identify the dog.

GUARD DOGS

The Guard Dogs Act 1975 sets out to control the use of guard dogs on premises. It is an offence under s 5(1) to use or permit the use of a guard dog on any premises unless a person ('the handler') who is capable of controlling the dog is present on the premises and the dog is under the direct control of the handler at all times while it is being so used except while it is secured so that it is not at liberty to go freely about the premises.

The handler of a guard dog must keep the dog under his control at all times while it is being used as a guard dog at any premises except:

(a) while another handler has control over the dog; or
(b) while the dog is secured so that it is not at liberty to go freely about the premises.

Failure to do so is an offence under s 5(1).

However, the Act is concerned with what might be described as the commercial use of guard dogs, rather than the family watchdog. It therefore excludes from the term 'premises' agricultural land and land in the curtilage of a dwelling house, thus exempting farm dogs and those confined within a dwelling house or its yard or garden.

When guard dogs are kept upon 'premises' warning notices must be clearly displayed at all entrances to the premises; failure to display such notices is an offence under s 5(1).

A 'guard dog' is one which is used either to protect the premises or property on them, or to protect a person guarding the premises or property. If the dog is properly secured it is not necessary for the handler to be on the premises all the time. If secured on a long chain, it is a question of fact, for the justices to determine, whether the dog was at liberty to go freely about the premises.

WELFARE OF DOGS

The welfare of dogs is dealt with in Appendix 4 (Animals, Birds and Plants) on the companion website: see under the heading ANIMAL WELFARE.

CHAPTER 19

Firearms and Weapons

The Firearms Act 1968 (FiA 1968) controls the possession, use, manufacture, transfer and acquisition of firearms or ammunition. Other Acts punish the possession of firearms on particular occasions and deal with other forms of weapon.

FIREARMS: DEFINITIONS

FiA 1968, s 57 defines 'firearm' for the purposes of that Act as a *lethal barrelled weapon* of any description *from which any shot, bullet or other missile can be discharged*. This is the basic definition. Section 57 also provides that 'firearm' includes any *prohibited weapon*, whether or not it is such a lethal weapon, and any *component part* of such a lethal or prohibited weapon, and any *accessory* to any such weapon designed or adapted *to diminish the noise or flash caused by firing the weapon*.

Nothing in the FiA 1968 relating to firearms applies to an antique firearm which is sold, transferred, purchased, acquired or possessed as a curiosity or ornament.

Firearms: the basic definition

Lethal weapon

It is clear from judicial decisions that a 'lethal weapon' means a weapon which in itself is capable of causing injury from which death might result. It need not be designed or manufactured for the purpose of causing such injury; if it is not, it is enough that it is capable of causing such injury if misused. Consequently, even though the purpose of its designer and manufacturer was to produce a toy, a spring pistol which can fire pellets through a barrel will be a firearm if, albeit only through misuse, it is capable of causing an injury from which death might result. By way of further example, a signalling pistol which fired an explosive magnesium and phosphorus flare, and which was capable of killing at short range, has been held to be lethal; the fact that the manufacturer did not produce it for the purpose of killing or injuring was immaterial. Many air guns would normally only cause a trivial injury but they may be classed as lethal since they could cause death by a pellet striking an extremely vulnerable part of the body, for example, an eye.

Whether or not a weapon is lethal must be assessed in relation to the particular weapon in question, and not to weapons of its type. If the particular weapon is not in working order and is therefore incapable of causing injury from which death might result *it* is not a lethal weapon, even though a weapon of its type is so capable when in working order.

Under the *basic* definition of a 'firearm', the 'lethal weapon' must be *barrelled* and capable of *discharging* any shot, bullet or other *missile*.

Barrelled

A barrel, in relation to a gun, is a tube through which a bullet or shot is discharged.

Shot, bullet, or other missile

The terms 'shot' and 'bullet' are self-explanatory, and the term 'other missile' should be taken to relate to some similar solid object which can be discharged from some form of 'barrelled weapon'. It is unlikely that much difficulty will be experienced in relation to this term as the only 'guns' which are excluded thereby are those weapons designed or adapted to discharge some form of gas, and these are almost certain to be 'prohibited weapons', and therefore a firearm, in any case. However, a weapon which simply discharged compressed air would not be a prohibited weapon for the purposes of FiA 1968.

Prohibited weapon

As already indicated, such weapons are firearms, whether or not they are lethal barrelled weapons from which any shot, bullet or other missile can be discharged. See p 631 for the definition of prohibited weapons.

Changes in type

A weapon which at any time has been classified as a prohibited weapon (or as a FiA 1968, s 1 firearm or as a shotgun) remains so classified notwithstanding anything done to convert it into a weapon of another type (eg prohibited weapon into a s 1 firearm).

Component parts and accessories

The fact that any *component part* of a lethal barrelled weapon or prohibited weapon is stated by FiA 1968, s 57 to be a firearm in itself is of importance.

The only *accessories* which are included within the term 'firearm' by FiA 1968, s 57, and are therefore controlled by the Act, are those designed or adapted to diminish noise or flash, ie silencers and flash eliminators. Any other accessory to a firearm is not included. A telescopic sight is an accessory but it is not an 'accessory' for the purposes of FiA 1968.

Imitation firearms

Under the Firearms Act 1982, s 1 the provisions of FiA 1968 concerned with a firearm to which FiA 1968, s 1 (firearms requiring a firearm certificate: p 624) applies are made to apply (with limited exceptions) to an imitation firearm which has the appearance of being a firearm to which FiA 1968, s 1 applies and which is so constructed or adapted as to be readily convertible into such a firearm. The limited exceptions are indicated in the text. An imitation firearm is '*readily* convertible' if it can be converted into a firearm without special skill and without equipment or tools not in common use. '*Convertible*' refers to converting an item from which a missile could not be discharged into one from which a missile could be discharged. It does not matter whether that process would involve the permanent alteration of the item (eg by drilling) or some more temporary result; an item can be converted by altering its construction or by adapting the way it could be used (eg by making it capable of discharging a missile by the use of an external implement).

Antique firearms

As already said, antique firearms are exempt from the provisions of FiA 1968 relating to firearms, provided they are sold, transferred, purchased, acquired or possessed as a curiosity or ornament. The term 'antique' is not defined. Basically, it is a question of fact and degree for the court to decide; it is unlikely that a court will consider that anything made in this or the last century is an antique.

Ammunition

For the purposes of FiA 1968, 'ammunition' is defined by s 57 as meaning ammunition for any firearm; a blank cartridge is ammunition. Section 57 provides that the term also includes grenades, bombs and other missiles, whether capable of use with a firearm or not, and also includes prohibited ammunition. A 'bomb' is any explosive substance in a case, or a case containing poison gas, smoke, or inflammable material which might be dropped from an aircraft, fired from a gun, or thrown or placed by hand.

POSSESSION, PURCHASE OR ACQUISITION OF FIREARMS OR AMMUNITION

Section 1 firearms and ammunition

FiA 1968, s 1(1) states that, subject to any exemption under FiA 1968, it is an offence for a person:

(a) to have in his possession, or to purchase or acquire, a firearm to which s 1 applies without holding a firearm certificate in force at the time, or otherwise than as authorised by the certificate; or

(b) to have in his possession, or to purchase or acquire, any ammunition to which s 1 applies without holding a firearm certificate, or otherwise than as authorised by such a certificate, or in quantities in excess of those so authorised.

The offence is an indictable (either way) offence.

Section 1 applies to every firearm except:

(a) a shotgun, as defined on p 625; and

(b) an air weapon (ie an air rifle, air gun or air pistol which does not fall within FiA 1968, s 5(1) (p 631) and is not of a type declared by rules made by the Secretary of State under FiA 1968 to be specially dangerous (p 625)).

FiA 1968, s 1(1) applies to ammunition for a firearm except:

(a) cartridges containing five or more shot, none of which exceeds .36 inch in diameter;

(b) ammunition for any air gun, air rifle or air pistol; and

(c) blank cartridges not more than 1 inch in diameter.

A person can be in possession of a firearm or ammunition even though he does not have physical custody of it nor keeps it in his home; it is enough that he knowingly has more than momentary control of it (as where he stores a firearm at the home of a relative for safe-keeping). Indeed, someone can be in possession of a firearm or ammunition even though he does not know or suspect that he has a firearm, etc under his control. For example, if someone has custody of a firearm in a holdall which he knows contains something without giving thought to the nature of its contents, he is in possession of the firearm (as well as the other contents). The fact that possession was brief, or that he did not know or could not reasonably have been expected to know that it contained a firearm, affords no defence. Because the defendant need not know or suspect that the article possessed was a firearm or ammunition within the relevant meaning of those terms, an honest and reasonable mistaken belief that the article is not a firearm or is an antique firearm is no defence. There is one exception; where the alleged offence involves an imitation firearm which is readily convertible into a firearm to which s 1 applies, it is a defence for the defendant to prove that he did not know and had no reason to suspect that it was readily convertible.

It is an indictable (either way) offence under s 3(2) for a person to sell or transfer a firearm or ammunition to which s 1 applies to a person other than a registered firearms dealer or person who has a firearm certificate authorising its purchase or acquisition.

Shotguns and ammunition

For the purposes of FiA 1968, a 'shotgun' is a smooth-bore gun (not being an airgun) which:

(a) has a barrel not less than 24 inches in length and does not have any barrel with a bore exceeding 2 inches in diameter;

(b) either has no magazine or has a non-detachable magazine incapable of holding more than two cartridges; and

(c) is not a revolver gun.

If the barrel of a shotgun is shortened to less than 24 inches it is no longer a shotgun, but becomes a firearm to which FiA 1968, s 1 applies.

Shotguns are excepted from the provisions of FiA 1968, s 1 but FiA 1968, s 2 states that, subject to any exemption under FiA 1968, it is an offence for a person to have in his possession, or to purchase or acquire, a shotgun without holding a certificate under FiA 1968 authorising him to possess shotguns. The reason for these special provisions in relation to shotguns is that the conditions for obtaining a shotgun certificate are different from those which apply in the case of FiA 1968, s 1 firearms. Shotgun ammunition, other than that to which FiA 1968, s 1 applies, does not require a firearm certificate, shotgun certificate or any other form of certificate for its possession, acquisition, or purchase.

What was said about possession and a defendant's state of mind in relation to FiA 1968, s 1 is equally applicable here.

It is an indictable (either way) offence under s 3(2) for a person to sell or transfer a shotgun to a person other than a registered firearms dealer or person who has a shotgun certificate authorising its purchase or acquisition.

Air weapons and ammunition

Air weapons essentially operate by the release of compressed air. However, the Firearms (Amendment) Act 1997, s 48 provides that any reference in the firearms legislation to an air rifle, air pistol or air gun also includes a reference to a rifle, pistol or gun powered by compressed carbon dioxide. An 'air weapon' (ie an air rifle, air gun or air pistol) which is not a prohibited weapon and which has not been declared by the Secretary of State to be specially dangerous does not require a firearm certificate or any other form of certificate for its possession, acquisition or purchase. Nor does ammunition for any air weapon, even if declared especially dangerous. The Secretary of State has declared that an air weapon will be specially dangerous (and therefore a firearm to which FiA 1968, s 1 applies) if:

(a) on discharge from the muzzle there is a kinetic energy in excess of 6 ft/lb in the case of an air pistol, or 12 ft/lb in the case of a weapon other than a pistol; or

(b) it is disguised as another object.

Firearm certificates and shotgun certificates

Firearm certificates

To obtain a firearm certificate an applicant must apply to the chief officer of police of the area in which he resides and must state such particulars as may be required by the form. Information concerning previous names, residence, and convictions, other than those for minor traffic offences, must be given. The applicant must sign a statement to the effect that the statements are true, rather than believed to be true. It is an indictable (either way) offence under FiA 1968, s 3(5) knowingly or recklessly to make a statement false in a material particular. An applicant must provide up to four photographs and the names and addresses of two persons who have agreed to act as referees. Before considering the application, the chief officer will verify the particulars included in the application and the likeness to the applicant of the photographs provided. The information which the applicant is required to give on the application form must be verified by each of two referees by a signed statement that the information is, to the best of his knowledge and belief, correct. In addition, each referee must provide a reference to the effect that he knows of no reason why the applicant should not possess a firearm.

FiA 1968, s 27 states that a firearm certificate must be granted by the chief officer of police if he is satisfied that:

(a) the applicant is fit to be entrusted with a firearm to which FiA 1968, s 1 applies and that he is not prohibited by FiA 1968 (see p 628) from possessing such a firearm;

(b) he has good reason for having in his possession, or for purchasing or acquiring, the firearm or ammunition in respect of which the application is made;

(c) in all the circumstances the applicant can be permitted to have the firearm or ammunition in his possession without danger to the public safety or peace.

The certificate must specify the nature and number of firearms to which it relates and certain other matters. A chief officer may impose conditions subject to which the firearm certificate is held. These conditions may refer to the nature of the storage of the weapons or their use. Conditions can be varied at any time by notice in writing to the holder, who may be required to return his certificate for variation.

A person under 18 who applies for such a certificate is capable of having a good reason for possessing or acquiring it *only* if he has no intention of using it, before that age, for a purpose other than an authorised purpose under the European Weapons Directive. An authorised purpose is a sporting purpose, the shooting of vermin, a purpose related to estate management activities, competition shooting, or target shooting, and use as or with a slaughtering instrument. Such purposes are likely to be specified in the certificate.

Police officers are required to carry out inquiries on behalf of the chief officer and, with these provisions in mind, they are required to check upon the intended usage of the weapon. The officer conducting the inquiry should always check the secure place in which the weapon will be stored.

If a firearm certificate is granted, the holder must on receipt sign it in ink. He must at all times keep the firearm and ammunition in a safe place and must inform the chief officer of the theft or loss of the firearm or a change of address.

Shotgun certificates

The rules relating to applications for shotgun certificates are not quite so strict. An application must be made in the prescribed form to the chief officer of police and there are similar requirements in respect of the submission of photographs, verification and a reference by one referee, signature of the certificate, and notification of the loss or theft of the certificate or of a change of address. The 'false statement offence' under FiA 1968, s 3(5) also applies to an applicant for a shotgun certificate.

By FiA 1968, s 28, such a certificate must be granted by the chief officer of police if he is satisfied that the applicant can be permitted to possess a shotgun without danger to the public safety or to the peace, unless he has reason to believe that the applicant is prohibited by FiA 1968 from possessing a shotgun (see p 628), or is satisfied that the applicant does not have a good reason for possessing, purchasing or acquiring one. It has been held that a refusal to grant a certificate to the wife of a man with two previous convictions for drug offences was justified, where they both continued to associate with drug users.

A sporting or competitive purpose is declared by FiA 1968 to be a good reason. A person under 18 is deemed not to have a good reason for possessing or acquiring a shotgun if it is his intention to use the shotgun, before he attains that age, for a purpose not authorised by the European Weapons Directive.

If a shotgun certificate is granted, the holder must on receipt sign it in ink. He must at all times keep the shotgun and ammunition in a safe place and must inform the chief officer of the theft or loss of the shotgun or a change of address.

A shotgun certificate must specify the description of the shotguns to which it relates including, if known, the identification numbers of the guns.

Transfer of firearms, etc between authorised persons

The Firearms (Amendment) Act 1997 (Fi(A)A 1997), s 32 requires that where:

(a) a s 1 firearm or ammunition is sold, let on hire, lent or given; or
(b) a shotgun is sold, let on hire, given, or lent for a period of more than 72 hours,

by any person, to a person who is not a firearms dealer nor exempt from holding a certificate, the following requirements must be complied with:

(a) the transferee must produce to the transferor the appropriate certificate or permit (eg a firearm certificate);
(b) the transferor must comply with any instructions contained in the certificate, etc; and
(c) the transferor must hand the firearm to the transferee personally.

Failure to comply with these requirements is an offence under s 32(3); in the case of a s 1 firearm or ammunition, the offence is an indictable (either way) offence.

Each party to the transfer (as described above) of a s 1 firearm or ammunition or of a shotgun who is the holder of a firearm or shotgun certificate must give notice of the transfer within seven days to the chief officer of police by registered post, the recorded delivery service or permitted electronic means. It is an offence under s 33(4) to fail to do so; in the case of a s 1 firearm or ammunition, the offence is an indictable (either way) offence.

De-activation, destruction or loss of firearms or shotguns

Fi(A)A 1997, s 34 requires that where a firearm to which a firearm certificate or shotgun certificate relates is de-activated, destroyed or lost, the certificate holder must give notice to the chief officer of police within seven days by registered post, the recorded delivery service or permitted electronic means. It is an offence under s 34(4) to fail to do so without reasonable excuse; in the case of a s 1 firearm or ammunition, the offence is an indictable (either way) offence.

Grant, refusal, revocation, etc

There is a right of appeal to the Crown Court against a refusal to grant a person a firearm or shotgun certificate or to vary a certificate or condition therein.

A firearm certificate may be revoked if the chief officer of police has reason to believe that the holder:

(a) is of intemperate habits or unsound mind or is otherwise unfitted to be entrusted with a firearm; or

(b) can no longer be permitted to have the firearm or ammunition to which the certificate relates without danger to the public safety or peace;

(c) is prohibited from possessing a s 1 firearm (below); or

(d) no longer has a good reason for possessing, purchasing or acquiring the firearm or ammunition which the certificate authorises him to have, etc.

A firearm certificate may also be revoked if the holder has failed to comply with a notice requiring him to deliver up his certificate.

In addition, a chief officer may partially revoke a firearm certificate in relation to any particular firearm or ammunition held under its authority if satisfied that the holder no longer has a good reason for possessing, purchasing or acquiring it.

A shotgun certificate may be revoked only if the holder becomes a 'prohibited person', or cannot be permitted to possess a shotgun without danger to the public safety or to the peace. It has been held that a chief officer, in deciding whether to revoke a shotgun licence, is entitled to take into account irresponsible conduct by the licence holder which does not involve the use of a shotgun. It is a matter for the chief officer's discretion to what extent he should investigate a particular offence.

Where a certificate is revoked the holder must be notified in writing and required to surrender his certificate. It is an offence to fail to comply with such a notice within 21 days of the date of the notice.

Persons prohibited from possessing a firearm

FiA 1968, s 21 prohibits the possession of any firearm or ammunition by a person who has been convicted of a crime and been sentenced to:

(a) custody for life or preventive detention, or to imprisonment, corrective training, youth custody or detention in a young offender institution for three years or more; such a person is banned for life; or

(b) imprisonment or youth custody or detention in a young offender institution from three months to three years, or has been subject to a secure training order or a detention and training order; such a person is banned for five years from the date of his release.

Suspended sentences do not count unless they are actually served at a later date. Air weapons are included in the prohibition.

Lawful possession without a certificate

Permits

Persons who hold a permit under FiA 1968, s 7 from the chief officer of police of the area in which they reside may, without holding a firearm certificate, possess a firearm (including a shotgun and ammunition) in accordance with the terms of the permit. Such permits are frequently issued where the holder of a firearm certificate dies and a relative requires some form of authority to possess the firearm pending its sale or disposal. It is unusual for such permits to be valid for more than one month.

Exemptions

Firearms dealers (if registered: see p 641) and their employees may possess firearms and ammunition without a certificate.

Other people may lawfully possess firearms and ammunition without holding a certificate. The principal exemptions provided by FiA 1968, ss 9 to 15 and 54 and the Firearms (Amendment) Act 1988 (Fi(A)A 1988), ss 15 and 16 are as follows:

(a) an auctioneer, carrier, warehouseman, or the employee of such a person is frequently required to handle other people's firearms and ammunition in the course of his duties. Sensibly this is permitted, but it is necessary for such persons to take reasonable precautions for safe custody and to report loss or theft forthwith to the police;

(b) a slaughtering instrument and its ammunition may be possessed by a licensed slaughterman;

(c) a person carrying a firearm or ammunition belonging to another person who is the holder of a certificate may possess that firearm or ammunition under instructions from, and for the use of, that other person for sporting purposes only. The person carrying the firearm, etc can best be described as a 'gun bearer'. However, where the person carrying the firearm or ammunition is under 18, this exemption only applies if the other person is 18 or over;

(d) if aged 18 or over, a starter at an athletic meeting may possess a firearm for the purpose of starting races only. The exemption does not allow a starter to possess ammunition, so that he is restricted to blanks not exceeding one inch in diameter (which do not, of course, require a certificate);

(e) subject to any exclusion of the club or restriction to specified types of rifle by the Secretary of State, a member of an approved rifle club (including a miniature rifle club) or of an approved muzzle-loading pistol club may possess a firearm and ammunition when engaged as such a member in connection with target shooting. An approval of a club may be limited to specified weapons;

(f) possession at a miniature rifle range (usually a side show at a fair) provided that no weapons are used exceeding .23 inch calibre. It should be noted that the owner of the range, unless only air weapons are used, will have to have a firearm certificate listing the weapons in use;

(g) a person who does not hold a shotgun certificate may borrow a shotgun from the occupier of private premises and use it on those premises, provided the occupier is present, but if the borrower is under 18 the occupier must be 18 or over;

(h) a person of 17 or over, without holding a firearm certificate, may borrow a rifle from the occupier of private premises and use it on the premises in the presence of the occupier or an employee of the occupier, if that person holds a firearm certificate in respect of that rifle, the borrower's possession and use complies with any conditions in the certificate, and, where the borrower is 17, the person present is 18 or over;

(i)   a person may use a shotgun at a time and place approved by the chief officer of police for shooting at artificial targets. This exemption is designed to cover a person who is interested in shooting or wishes to receive instruction, but has not got a shotgun certificate. Commonly approved places at which the exemption permits him to shoot include agricultural shows and permanent shooting grounds run by firearms dealers;

(j)   a person taking part in a theatrical performance, rehearsal or film may possess a firearm during the performance etc. This exception does not extend to ammunition, so that any ammunition used would have to be blanks not more than one inch in diameter;

(k)   signalling apparatus or ammunition for it may be possessed on board an aircraft or at an aerodrome as a part of its equipment. It may also be transferred at an aerodrome from one aeroplane to another, or from or to an aeroplane at an aerodrome to or from an appointed place of storage there;

(l)   a firearm and ammunition may be possessed on board a ship as a part of its equipment. However, if it is to be removed from or to a ship a permit to do so must be obtained from a constable (a similar permit is required if the signalling apparatus described at (k) is to be removed from or to an aeroplane or aerodrome);

(m)   a Northern Ireland shotgun certificate authorises possession of a shotgun in Great Britain; and

(n)   any Crown servant or member of a police force or of the staff of the Serious Organised Crime Agency or the Scottish Crime and Drug Enforcement Agency who is in possession of a firearm or ammunition in his capacity as such does not require a certificate.

Fi(A)A 1988, s 17 makes provision for 'visitors permits' issued by a chief officer of police in relation to both s 1 firearms and shotguns. A firearm permit permits a person to possess a firearm and ammunition and to acquire ammunition for it, and a shotgun permit permits a person to possess or acquire a shotgun (although there are exceptions in the case of a shotgun with a magazine). 'Group' applications may be made for not more than 20 permits. These will cover persons visiting Great Britain to take part in competitions.

Fi(A)A 1988, ss 16A and 16B authorise, respectively, persons under the supervision of a member of the armed forces to possess a firearm and ammunition on service premises without holding a firearm certificate, and persons being trained or assessed under the supervision of a member of the Ministry of Defence Police to do so on premises used for any purpose of the Ministry of Defence Police. The sections also authorise such persons in such circumstances to possess a prohibited weapon or prohibited ammunition without obtaining the Secretary of State's authority.

Prohibited weapons and ammunition

Because weapons and ammunition of this type can only properly be regarded as suitable for official use, FiA 1968, s 5(1) and (1A) provide that a person commits an offence if he has in his possession, or purchases or acquires, any prohibited weapon or ammunition to which s 5(1) or (1A) respectively apply without the written authority of the Secretary of

State. An offence under FiA 1968, s 5(1) or s 5(1A) is one of strict liability as to the fact that the weapon or ammunition is prohibited, so that it is no defence that the possessor is reasonably unaware of the characteristic which makes the weapon or ammunition prohibited. The offence under s 5(1) (except in relation to a prohibited weapon within (h) below) and the offence under s 5(1A) in relation to a firearm disguised as another object are triable only on indictment; otherwise the above offences are triable either way.

The controls under s 5(1) and (1A) apply over and above the need for a firearm certificate.

Prohibited weapons

For the purposes of the offence under FiA 1968, s 5(1), a prohibited weapon is:

(a) any firearm which is so designed or adapted that two or more missiles can be successively discharged without repeated pressure on the trigger;

(b) any self-loading or pump-action rifled gun other than one chambered for .22 inch rim-fire cartridges;

(c) any firearm which either has a barrel less than 30 cm in length or is less than 60 cm in length overall, other than an air weapon, a muzzle-loading gun or a firearm designed as a signalling apparatus;

(d) any self-loading or pump-action smooth-bore gun which is not an air weapon (as defined on p 625) or chambered for .22 inch rim-fire cartridges and either has a barrel of less than 24 inches in length or is less than 40 inches in length overall;

(e) any smooth-bore revolver gun other than one which is chambered for 9 mm rim-fire cartridges or a muzzle-loading gun;

(f) any rocket launcher, or any mortar designed for line-throwing or pyrotechnic purposes or as a signalling apparatus;

(g) any air rifle, air gun or air pistol which uses, or is designed or adapted for use with, a self-contained gas cartridge system; and

(h) any weapon of whatever description designed or adapted for the discharge of any noxious liquid, gas or other thing.

In relation to (a) above, the Court of Appeal has held that the words 'so designed or adapted that two or more missiles can be successively discharged without repeated pressure on the trigger' relates to what is objectively possible and not to the intention of the designer of the weapon. Thus, if that effect could be brought about, even if only in expert hands, the weapon is designed as a prohibited weapon.

For the purposes of (c) and (d), any detachable, folding, retractable or other movable butt-stock is disregarded in measuring the length of any firearm.

References to muzzle-loading guns in (c) and (e) are references to guns which are designed to be loaded at the muzzle end of the barrel or chamber with a loose charge and a separate ball (or other missile).

An air weapon referred to at (g) possessed on 30 April 2004 may be retained subject to the need to obtain a firearm certificate. A chief officer may not refuse an application for a firearm certificate in such circumstances, nor an application for renewal, on the ground that the person does not have a good reason for having the weapon.

Head (h) covers a wide variety of weaponry including a flamethrower and a high-voltage electric stunning device. The fact that a stun-gun designed for an electrical charge is not working due to some unknown fault does not change its character as a prohibited weapon. The words 'designed or adapted' mean that any other type of weapon which is converted in any way for these purposes is a prohibited weapon as it has been 'adapted'. These weapons do not need to be either lethal or barrelled *provided* they are capable of discharging noxious liquid, gas or other thing. If the weapon is capable of discharging such a substance, and was either designed or adapted for that purpose, it is prohibited. A water pistol used to discharge gas would not be a prohibited weapon if it was used in an unaltered state, since it would not have been designed to discharge one of the prohibited substances, nor adapted in any way to allow it to do so. The same applies to a washing-up liquid bottle filled with hydrochloric acid. The container was neither designed nor adapted for the discharge of a noxious liquid. 'Noxious' before 'liquid, gas or other thing' must apply to all three things. A substance is noxious if it is harmful, hurtful, or injurious. All forms of gas projector are therefore prohibited, from the tear-gas gun to the small gas pistol.

Slaughtering instruments, humane killers, shot pistols used for killing vermin, starting pistols, trophies of war, firearms of historic interest, and weapons used for treating animals are exempted from the prohibitions imposed upon weapons falling within (c) above (or, in the case of weapons used for treating animals, within (c) or (g)) subject to conditions set out in the Firearms (Amendment) Act 1997.

For the purposes of FiA 1968, s 5(1A), the following are prohibited weapons:

(a) any firearm which is disguised as another object; and
(b) any launcher or other projecting apparatus, not a prohibited weapon under s 5(1), which is designed to be used with any rocket or ammunition designed to explode on or immediately before impact and is prohibited ammunition under s 5(1) or s 5(1A).

In relation to FiA 1968, s 5(1A) only, there are a number of exemptions in terms of weapons and of ammunition. They relate principally to collectors and to possession, purchase, or acquisition for use for certain authorised purposes, namely slaughtering animals, sporting purposes, shooting vermin, estate management purposes, and competition and target shooting purposes.

Prohibited ammunition

Prohibited ammunition for the purposes of FiA 1968, s 5(1) is:

(a) any cartridge with a bullet designed to explode on or immediately before impact (eg a 'dum-dum bullet');
(b) any ammunition which contains, or is designed or adapted to contain, any noxious liquid, gas or other thing; and
(c) if capable of being used with a firearm of any description, any grenade, bomb (or other like missile), or a rocket or shell designed to explode on or immediately before impact,

other than ammunition used for treating animals.

Therefore containers designed or adapted to contain any noxious gas, etc for use as a missile or bomb are prohibited ammunition, whether filled or not. The other types of prohibited ammunition are explosive bullets and (if capable of being used with a firearm) grenades, bombs, rockets and shells.

Prohibited ammunition for the purposes of FiA 1968, s 5(1A) is:

(a) any rocket or ammunition which is not prohibited ammunition (under (c) above) for the purposes of FiA 1968, s 5(1) which consists in or incorporates a missile designed to explode on or immediately before impact and is for military use;
(b) any ammunition for military use which consists in or incorporates a missile designed so that a substance contained in the missile will ignite on or immediately before impact;

(c) any ammunition for military use which consists in or incorporates a missile designed, on account of its having a jacket and hard-core, to penetrate armour plating, armour screening or body armour;

(d) any ammunition which incorporates a missile designed or adapted to expand on impact;

(e) anything which is designed to be projected as a missile from any weapon and is designed to be, or has been incorporated in:

    (i) any ammunition falling within any of the above definitions; or

    (ii) any ammunition which would fall within any of those definitions but for its being specified in FiA 1968, s 5(1).

Museum licences

By virtue of Fi(A)A 1988, s 19 and Sch 1 specified museums do not need to have a firearm certificate, shotgun certificate, or s 5 authority, as the case may be, in relation to exhibits displayed or stored at the museum if they have a museum firearm licence granted under those provisions. Specified museums are those registered with the Museums and Galleries Commission for the purpose of making them eligible for a museum firearm certificate.

European Firearms Pass

The Firearms Act 1968, s 32A governs the issue of a European Firearms Pass. Persons holding such passes are entitled to acquire in another EU member state firearms to which the pass relates. Such 'passes' are issued in Great Britain by the chief officer of police to holders of an appropriate firearm certificate. A European Firearms Pass must be produced on demand by a constable.

POSSESSION OR ACQUISITION BY YOUNG PERSONS

FiA 1968, ss 22 to 24 deal with the possession or acquisition of all types of firearms by juveniles.

Section 1 firearms

If a person under 18 wishes to have a s 1 firearm, or ammunition for it, he cannot buy or hire it himself; if he does so he commits an offence under FiA 1968, s 22(1). Under s 24(1), the seller or person letting it on hire also commits an offence, unless he can prove that he reasonably believed that the other person was 18 or over. However, provided that someone is 14 or over he may receive a firearm, together with ammunition, by way of a gift or loan. Where an adult wishes to buy a firearm as a gift for such a youth, he must obtain a firearm certificate and so must the youth. The seller may then sell to the adult, who may then transfer the weapon to the youth, both notifying the chief officer of police of the transaction by registered post, recorded delivery or permitted electronic means within 48 hours. Certificates granted to persons under 18 are endorsed to the effect that firearms or ammunition cannot be sold or hired to them until the specified date, which is the date of their 18th birthday.

It is an offence under s 24(2)(a) to give or lend a s 1 firearm or ammunition to a person under 14 years of age. It is an offence under ss 22(2) and 24(2)(b) respectively for such a person to possess such a thing, or for someone to part with possession of such a thing to such a person, with certain exceptions. In recalling these exceptions it is helpful to consider those persons who are permitted to possess s 1 firearms without a certificate and to identify the exceptions which might apply to persons under 14. The exceptions are when:

(a) he is carrying the firearm or ammunition for another for sporting purposes, and that other person is 18 or over and the holder of a firearm certificate; or

(b) he is using the firearm or ammunition at a shooting gallery or miniature rifle range where the only weapons used do not exceed .23 inch calibre; or

(c) as a member of an approved rifle club, he is engaged in connection with target shooting.

If proved, a reasonable belief that the other person was 18 or over is a defence to a charge under s 24(2)(a) or (b).

It is an offence under s 22(1A) for a firearm certificate holder under 18 to use a firearm covered by it for a purpose not authorised by the European Weapons Directive referred to on p 626.

Shotguns

It is an offence under s 22(1) for a person under 18 to purchase or hire any shotgun or ammunition. Likewise, someone who sells or lets it on hire to such a person commits an offence under s 24(1). It is an offence under s 24(3) to make a gift of a shotgun to a person under 15. (These rules also apply to ammunition for a shotgun.) It is, of course, possible for a person of 15, 16, or 17 lawfully to acquire a shotgun by the same process as that outlined in relation to s 1 firearms. If proved, a reasonable belief that the other person was 18 or over is a defence to a charge under s 24(1) or (3).

All young persons in possession of shotguns must have a shotgun certificate. Although FiA 1968 does not prescribe a minimum age at which a shotgun certificate may be granted, control is exercised by the chief officer of police who must consider the grant of such a certificate in the context of public safety.

Even if he has a shotgun certificate, it is an offence under s 22(3) for a person under 15 to 'have with him' an assembled shotgun, except:

(a) while under the supervision of a person of 21 or more; or

(b) while it is so securely fastened with a gun cover that it cannot be fired.

In addition, a holder of a shotgun certificate who is under 18 may not use the weapon for a purpose which is not authorised by the European Weapons Directive; to do so is an offence under s 22(1A).

Air weapons

The same general rule applies. By FiA 1968, s 22(1), it is an offence for a person under 18 to purchase or hire an air weapon or ammunition. The seller or person who lets on hire in such a case also commits an offence under s 24(1); if proved, a reasonable belief that the other person was 18 or over is a defence. There are, however, restrictions in relation to possession and they are predictable.

By s 22(4) a person under 18 commits an offence if he has with him an air weapon or ammunition for it except when:

(a) he is under the supervision of someone aged 21 or over (s 23(1)), but the supervisor commits an offence under s 23(1) if he allows the juvenile to fire a missile beyond the premises (unless he can prove that the occupier of the other premises into or across which the missile was fired had consented to this). The supervisor will have a defence if he shows that the only premises into or across which the missile was fired were premises occupied by a person who had consented to this;

(b) as a member of an approved club, he is engaged in connection with target shooting (s 23(2)(a));

(c) he is using the weapon or ammunition at a shooting gallery or miniature range where the only firearms used are either air weapons or miniature rifles not exceeding .23 inch calibre (s 23(2)(b)); or

(d) he is aged 14 or over and is on private premises with the consent of the occupier (s 23(2)(c)).

In relation to the exception under (a), it may be noted that a person of any age commits an offence under s 21A if he fires a missile from an air weapon beyond the premises where he is, unless he shows that the occupier of the premises into or across which the missile is fired had consented to this.

It is an offence under s 24(4)(a) for any person to make a gift of an air weapon or ammunition to a person under 18. By s 24(4)(b), it is an offence to part with the possession of an air weapon or ammunition to a person under 18 except where that person is not prohibited from having it with him by virtue of one of the exceptions in s 23. If proved, a reasonable belief that the person was 18 or over is a defence.

Section 24ZA(1) and (2) provides that it is an offence for a person in possession of an air weapon to fail to take reasonable precautions to prevent any person under the age of 18 from having the weapon with him, unless, by virtue of s 23, that person is not prohibited from having the weapon with him. It is a defence to show that the defendant reasonably believed that the other person was 18 or over. A person is taken to have shown these matters if sufficient evidence of them is adduced to raise an issue with respect to them, and the contrary is not proved beyond a reasonable doubt.

Purchase of imitation firearm by or sale to minors

FiA 1968, s 24A(1) and (2) respectively make it an offence for a person under 18 to purchase an imitation firearm, or for anyone to sell an imitation firearm to such a person. In relation to 'selling', it is a defence to show a reasonable belief that the person was 18 or over. The defence will be taken to have been made out where sufficient evidence is given to raise the issue and the contrary is not proved by the prosecution. In this offence, 'imitation firearm' is defined by FiA 1968, s 57 (and not by the Firearms Act 1982, s 1), as meaning anything which at the material time has the appearance of being a firearm (other than a weapon for the discharge of a noxious liquid, gas or other thing) whether or not it is capable of discharging any shot, bullet or other missile.

FIREARMS OFFENCES RELATING TO PREVENTION OF CRIME AND PUBLIC SAFETY

Conversion of firearms

It is an indictable (either way) offence under FiA 1968, s 4(1) to shorten the barrel of a shotgun within the meaning of FiA 1968 (see p 625) to a length of less than 24 inches. It is not an offence for a registered firearms dealer to shorten a barrel for the sole purpose of replacing a defective part so as to produce a barrel not less than 24 inches in length.

It is an indictable (either way) offence under s 4(3) for anyone other than a registered firearms dealer to convert into a firearm anything which, though having the appearance of a firearm, cannot discharge a missile through its barrel.

Possession with intent to endanger life

Under FiA 1968, s 16 it is an offence triable only on indictment to possess a firearm or ammunition with intent by means thereof to endanger life, or to enable another person by means thereof to endanger life, whether an injury has been caused or not.

There are two factors to prove:

(a) that the defendant was in possession of a firearm or ammunition; and
(b) that at the time of that possession he had an intention by means thereof to endanger life or to enable another by means thereof to endanger life.

A person who carries a loaded gun merely to give it to a colleague to use, should he be challenged, is guilty. So is an accomplice who carries ammunition for a gunman for use, if necessary, in a bank raid. However, possession of a firearm, etc with intent that another person should, by means thereof, endanger life, means more than merely making it available to known criminals who might endanger life. An intention to endanger the life of a person abroad is sufficient for s 16; consequently, it covers possession by terrorist groups who might intend their mischief elsewhere. Possession with intent to commit suicide is not covered by s 16; an intent to endanger life must relate to the life of another.

The present offence is not committed by a person who intended to endanger life for a lawful purpose, as where a person whose house is besieged by an armed gang threatened them with his firearm in self-defence. This defence, however, is only available in circumstances where there is a specific risk of imminent attack: it does not apply where there is only a potential risk.

Possession with intent to cause fear of violence

By FiA 1968, s 16A, a person commits an offence triable only on indictment if he has in his possession any firearm or imitation firearm with intent:

(a) by means thereof to cause; or
(b) to enable any other person by means thereof to cause,

any person to believe that unlawful violence will be used against him or another.

In this offence, 'imitation firearm' is defined by FiA 1968, s 57 (and not by the Firearms Act 1982, s 1), as meaning anything which at the material time has the appearance of being a firearm (other than a weapon for the discharge of a noxious liquid, gas or other thing) whether or not it is capable of discharging any shot, bullet, or other missile. An automatic pistol with the firing pin removed has been held to be such an imitation firearm; clearly, it fell within the definition. So may things which have the appearance of being firearms in particular circumstances on specific occasions, but not in others. A piece of roughly fashioned wood held in the hand in a darkened room might certainly have the appearance of being a firearm. It would be a matter for the jury to decide whether something actually did have the appearance of being a firearm in the circumstances in question. The House of Lords has held that fingers positioned in a jacket so as to appear to be a gun are not in law capable of constituting a firearm.

The Court of Appeal has held that FiA 1968, s 16A is not limited to cases where the intent specified in s 16A was formed before the material time. It held that, provided there is a coincidence of possession and intent, s 16A also embraces the situation where the defendant forms an intention to cause fear of violence at or immediately before the time of his actions which were designed to cause such fear.

Use of firearms to resist arrest

It is an offence by FiA 1968, s 17(1) for a person to make, or attempt to make, any use whatsoever of a firearm or imitation firearm with intent to resist or prevent the lawful arrest or detention of himself or another person. The offence is triable only on indictment. If a firearm or imitation firearm is used in resisting lawful arrest or detention, whether of the person using the firearm, or some other person, the offence is complete. The important words are 'to make, or attempt to make use of' the firearm and the issue of in whose possession the firearm was before that moment does not arise. Someone who grabbed a gun from the person arresting him and made use of it in this way would be guilty. It must be proved that the firearm was used intentionally for such a purpose. The offence would not be made out, for example, if the firearm was used with the intention of preventing a search of premises and an arrest was not intended at that time.

FiA 1968, s 17(2) creates a second indictable-only offence of possessing a firearm or imitation firearm *at the time of committing or being arrested* for an offence specified in FiA 1968, Sch 1, unless the defendant can show that he possessed it for a lawful object. The offences in Sch 1 include theft, robbery, burglary, blackmail, taking a conveyance, assaulting a constable in the execution of his duty, assaulting a prison custody officer acting in pursuance of prison escort arrangements or performing custodial duties at a contracted-out prison, assaulting a secure training centre custody officer in the execution of his duty, rape, assault by penetration, causing a person to engage in sexual activity without consent where the activity caused involved penetration, rape of child under 13, assault of a child under thirteen by penetration, causing or inciting a child under 13 to engage in a sexual activity where any activity involving penetration was caused, sexual activity with a person with a mental disorder impeding choice where the touching involved penetration, causing or inciting a person with a mental disorder impeding choice to engage in sexual activity where penetration was caused, criminal damage, malicious wounding, assault occasioning actual bodily harm, and assault with intent to resist arrest. For example, a person who takes a motor car whilst in possession of an air pistol, or even an imitation firearm, commits this offence. Even if he had not possessed the firearm at the time of taking the conveyance, he would be equally liable if he was in possession of it at the time of his arrest. Where the case is one of possession *at the time of arrest*, there is no requirement that the prosecution prove that the defendant actually committed the specified offence. It is only necessary to prove that the defendant was in possession of the firearm when lawfully arrested for a specified offence. The physical possession of the firearm is not essential. The Court of Appeal has said that 'possession' in s 17(2) simply refers to 'custody and control'. Consequently, for example, a person remains in possession of a firearm for the purposes of s 17(2) if he has left it in a nearby van at the time of committing a specified offence elsewhere.

For the purposes of both subsections of FiA 1968, s 17, a 'firearm' does not include a component part or accessory. Subject to this, 'imitation firearm' in s 17(1) and (2) has the same meaning as in FiA 1968, s 16A (see p 636).

Having firearm with criminal intent

FiA 1968, s 18(1) deals with the offence committed by a person who has with him a firearm or imitation firearm with intent to commit an indictable offence, or to resist arrest or prevent the arrest of another, in either case while he has the firearm or imitation firearm with him. The offence is triable only on indictment.

'Imitation firearm' has the same meaning as in FiA 1968 s 16A (see p 636).

The intent required by s 18 is a particular one. It is not sufficient that the defendant (D) intended to commit an indictable offence or to resist, etc the arrest. D must also intend to have a firearm or imitation firearm with him at the time of that commission or resistance. On the other hand, D does not have to intend to use or carry the gun in furtherance of the indictable offence. Section 18(2) provides that proof that D had a firearm or imitation firearm with him and intended to commit an offence, or to resist or prevent arrest, is evidence that he intended to have it with him while doing so.

Having firearm in a public place

A person commits an offence contrary to FiA 1968, s 19 if, without lawful authority or reasonable excuse (the proof whereof lies on him), he has with him in a public place:

(a) a loaded shotgun;
(b) an air weapon (whether loaded or not);
(c) any other firearm (whether loaded or not) together with ammunition suitable for use in that firearm; or
(d) an imitation firearm (same meaning as in ss 16A to 18: see p 636).

Such an offence is an indictable (either way) offence with the following exceptions. If it is committed in relation to a prohibited weapon under s 5(1) (on p 631) (other than that at (h)), a prohibited weapon of type (a) under s 5(1A) (p 632) or prohibited ammunition of type (a) under s 5(1A) (p 632), the offence is triable only on indictment. If the offence relates to an air weapon it is a summary offence.

A shotgun which has a loaded magazine is loaded, even though there is no round in the breach.

This is another offence which refers to 'having with him' rather than 'possessing'. The former term is a narrower one. As we have seen, a person can be in possession of a firearm if he has control of it, even though it is not in his physical custody and is not immediately available to him, as where it is in his home in Norwich while he is in London. In contrast, although a person can have a firearm with him, even though he is not carrying it, he must have a close physical link with it and it must have been readily accessible to him. A man who has a gun in his pocket clearly has it with him, and the same is true if it is in a bag which he is carrying or in the glove compartment of the car which he is driving. Provided that the firearm is readily accessible to him, a person may even have with him at the time a firearm which he has left in his car which he has parked down the street. A person does not 'have with him' something of whose presence he is unaware, such as a firearm which has been slipped into his bag; but once he knows of its presence it is no excuse that, at the material time, he has forgotten about it, as where he puts a firearm in the glove compartment of his car but has forgotten about it when he is stopped by a patrol car a month later.

The offence under s 19 is one of strict liability as to the nature of the item in question as defined above. Thus, knowledge or suspicion as to its nature is not required, and even a reasonably mistaken belief that it is not of that nature will not excuse.

It is difficult to imagine circumstances in which someone could, with lawful authority or reasonable excuse, have with him a loaded shotgun in a public place. The possession of a shotgun certificate certainly does not authorise this. Depending on the circumstances, a gamekeeper, crossing a public highway in the course of his duties, might be considered to have a reasonable excuse for having a loaded shotgun with him. Someone going to his rifle club with a .22 rifle in his hand and ammunition in his pocket would doubtless be able to prove a reasonable excuse for having the rifle and ammunition with him, provided that he possessed a firearm certificate.

Trespassing with a firearm

An indictable (either way) offence is committed against FiA 1968, s 20(1) if a person, while he has any firearm or imitation firearm with him, enters or is in any building or part of a building as a trespasser and without reasonable excuse (the proof whereof lies on him). A less serious offence is committed under FiA 1968, s 20(2) where the trespass is on land; the other ingredients of this offence are identical to those in s 20(1). 'Imitation firearm' bears the same meaning as in FiA 1968, s 16A (see p 636).

'Enters' requires the bodily presence of the defendant to some degree. As to 'trespasser', see p 938. 'Building' refers to a structure which has a roof and is of a reasonably permanent nature; the term 'part of a building' covers instances where a person might have a right to be in a building, for example a hotel, but is a trespasser in someone else's room, which would be a part of that building. For the purposes of FiA 1968, s 20(2), the expression 'land' includes land covered with water, so that a person with a firearm trespassing in a boat on a lake is guilty of this offence.

POLICE POWERS

Stop and search in certain cases

FiA 1968, s 47(1) authorises a constable to require any person whom he has reasonable cause to suspect:

(a) of having a firearm, with or without ammunition, with him in a public place; or
(b) to be committing or about to commit, elsewhere than in a public place, an offence of 'having with him' a firearm or imitation firearm with intent to commit an indictable offence or to resist arrest (contrary to s 18, above), or an offence of trespassing with a firearm (contrary to s 20, above),

to hand over the firearm or ammunition for examination. Failure to comply with such a demand is an offence (s 47(2)). Imitation firearm bears the same meaning as on p 636.

FiA 1968, s 47(3) also provides that a constable who has reasonable cause to suspect the existence of one of the above circumstances (ie (a) or (b)) may search that person and may detain him for the purpose of doing so. This power extends to the search of vehicles and the constable may require a driver to stop for that purpose (s 47(4)).

A constable may enter any place to exercise his powers under s 47.

Production of certificates

FiA 1968, s 48(1) states that a constable may demand, from any person whom he believes to be in possession of a firearm or ammunition to which s 1 applies, or of any shotgun, the production of his firearm certificate or (as the case may be) his shotgun certificate.

FiA 1968, s 48(1A) provides that, where a constable has made a demand under s 48(1) and the person to whom it is made fails:

(a) to produce a firearm certificate or (as the case may be) a shotgun certificate; or
(b) to show that he is a person who is not entitled to be issued with a document identifying that firearm under any provisions which in the other EU states correspond to the provisions under FiA 1968 for the issue of European Firearms Passes; or
(c) to show that he is in possession of the firearm only in his capacity as a recognised firearms collector of another EU state,

the constable can demand from that person the production of a valid European Firearms Pass issued to that person in another EU state relating to the firearm in question. Failure to comply with such a demand is an offence (s 48(4)).

If a person on whom a demand has been made under s 48 fails to produce the certificate or document or to permit the constable to read it, or to show that he is exempt from the requirement to have a certificate, the constable may seize and detain the firearm, ammunition or shotgun and may require the person immediately to declare his name and address (s 48(2)). It is an offence under s 48(3) to refuse or fail to give a true name and address.

Search warrant

By FiA 1968, s 46(1), a justice, who is satisfied by information on oath that there is reasonable ground for suspecting that:

(a) an offence relevant for the purposes of s 46 has been, is being, or is about to be committed; or
(b) in connection with a firearm or ammunition, there is a danger to the public safety or to the peace,

may grant a search warrant. The warrant will authorise a constable or civilian officer:

(a) to enter at any time any premises or place specified, if necessary by force, and to search them and every person found there;
(b) to seize and detain anything found on the premises or place, or on any such person, in respect of which or in connection with which he has reasonable grounds for suspecting that:
  (i)   a relevant offence has been, is being or is about to be committed, or
  (ii) in connection with a firearm, imitation firearm or ammunition there is a danger to the public safety or to the peace (s 46(2)).

A 'relevant offence' is any offence under FiA 1968 except that under s 22(3) (person under 15 having assembled shotgun otherwise than under supervision) or an offence relating specifically to air weapons (ie under ss 22(4), 22(5), 23(1), 24(4), or 24ZA).

The power of seizure and detention includes power to require information which is stored in any electronic form and is accessible from the premises or place to be produced in a form in which it is visible and legible (or from which it can readily be produced in such form) and can be taken away. The additional powers of seizure provided by the Criminal Justice and Police Act 2001, s 50 apply where a search warrant is executed under FiA 1968, s 46.

The Court of Appeal held that the police may use reasonable force to restrain or detain the occupants of premises when executing a warrant under FiA 1968, s 46.

It is an offence intentionally to obstruct a constable or civilian officer in the exercise of these powers (s 46(5)).

Entry into rifle clubs

By Fi(A)A 1988, s 15(7), a constable duly authorised in writing by a chief officer of police, on producing (if required) his authority, may enter any premises occupied or used by an approved rifle club and inspect those premises, and anything on them, for the purpose of ascertaining whether the requirements relating to its use and any limitations in the approval are being complied with.

FIREARMS OFFENCES UNDER OTHER ACTS

Drunk in possession

It is an offence contrary to the Licensing Act 1872, s 12 to be drunk when in possession on any highway or other public place of any loaded firearm (including a loaded air rifle).

Discharge near the highway

By the Highways Act 1980, s 161(2)(b), a person commits an offence if, without lawful authority or excuse, he discharges any firearm within 50 feet of the centre of any highway which consists of or comprises a carriageway, *and in consequence thereof* a user of the highway is injured, interrupted (eg by being forced to make a detour), or endangered. For the meaning of 'highway', see p 343.

Wanton discharge in a street

By the Town Police Clauses Act 1847, s 28 it is an offence wantonly to discharge a firearm in any street to the obstruction, annoyance, or danger of residents or passengers.

BUSINESS TRANSACTIONS RELATING TO FIREARMS

A 'firearms dealer' is defined by FiA 1968, s 57 as a person who, by way of trade or business, *manufactures, sells, transfers, repairs, tests or proves firearms or ammunition to which FiA 1968, s 1 applies or shotguns, or sells or transfers air weapons.*

It is an indictable (either way) offence under FiA 1968, s 3(1), for a person to:

(a) do any of these things,
(b) expose for sale or transfer any firearm and/or ammunition to which s 1 applies, or a shotgun or air weapon,
(c) possess such a firearm or ammunition or a shotgun for sale, transfer, repair, or proof, or
(d) possess an air weapon for sale or transfer,

without being registered under FiA 1968 as a firearms dealer.

By way of exception, it is not an offence for an auctioneer to sell by auction a firearm or ammunition without being registered as a firearms dealer, provided he holds a police permit for that purpose (s 9(2)).

The Violent Crime Reduction Act 2006 (VCRA 2006), s 32(1) and (2) makes it an offence to sell an air weapon by way of trade or business to a person who is not a registered firearms dealer when this is not done face to face.

The sale or transfer of a s 1 firearm or ammunition or of a shotgun to a person other than a registered firearms dealer is an indictable (either way) offence under FiA 1968, s 3(2), unless that person produces the necessary certificate, or shows he is legally entitled to purchase or acquire the firearm or ammunition without a certificate.

The chief officer of police must keep a register of firearms dealers. An applicant must provide details of every place of business (including storage places) in the area, at which he proposes to carry on business as a firearms dealer, and details of the precise nature of the business which he intends to conduct. A registered firearms dealer or his employee is permitted to keep, purchase or acquire firearms and ammunition in the ordinary course of his business without holding firearm certificates in respect of them, and this is so even though the place where the firearm or ammunition is possessed, purchased or acquired by the dealer or employee is not the dealer's place of business or has not been registered as his place of business.

Except on certain specified grounds, the chief officer of police must enter the applicant's name and place(s) of business in the register and grant him a certificate of registration. The chief officer of police may, however, impose conditions upon registration. These conditions are generally concerned with ensuring the safe-keeping of firearms. They usually include the following conditions; that:

(a) the dealer must, on being given reasonable notice, allow a police officer authorised in writing by the chief officer to enter and inspect his premises;
(b) hand-guns must be kept in a locked safe;
(c) other weapons must be chained together by the trigger guards and locked in a rack;
(d) ammunition is to be stored separately and locked up;
(e) rifle bolts must be removed and kept separately;
(f) the windows of cabinets for storage must be illuminated at night; and
(g) glass door panels and windows must be barred.

In addition, conditions are usually imposed concerning notification of dealings in various types of weapon.

FiA 1968 does not permit registration for particular purposes. A person is either a firearms dealer or he is not; there is no right to restrict dealings to shotguns. All certificates of registration are renewable every three years. A new place of business must be notified to the chief officer and must be registered by him, unless the use of those premises for firearms dealing would endanger the public safety or the peace. A registered dealer may be removed from the register if he ceases to deal in firearms, or to have a business place within the area, or if he cannot be permitted to continue in business without danger to the public safety or the peace. Failure to comply with conditions also provides reason for removal from the register. Particular premises may be removed from the register on safety grounds.

Dealer to keep records

A dealer must keep a register of transactions. He must within 24 hours enter in his register the particulars of persons to whom firearms and ammunition (excluding those to which FiA 1968, s 1 does not apply: see p 624) are sold or transferred.

Registered dealers must allow police officers or civilian officers, authorised in writing by the chief officer of police, to enter and inspect all stock in hand and must produce their registers for inspection. It is an offence to fail to do so, or knowingly or recklessly to make any false entry in a register (FiA 1968, s 40(5)). A police officer who is author-ised in writing by his chief officer of police to carry out these duties must produce that written authority if required to do so.

Manufacture, import, and sale of realistic imitation firearms

VCRA 2006, s 36(1) makes it an offence to manufacture, import, or sell a realistic imita-tion firearm (ie an imitation firearm which has an appearance that is *so realistic as to make it indistinguishable*, for all practical purposes, from a real firearm, and is neither a de-activated firearm nor itself an antique). Such an imitation firearm is not to be regarded as '*so distinguishable*' if it is distinguishable only by an expert, on close exami-nation or by attempting to load or to fire it. Defences are provided by s 37 in relation to things done for specified legitimate purposes.

The Violent Crime Reduction Act 2006 (Realistic Imitation Firearms) Regulations 2007 specify the sizes and colours of imitation firearms which are to be regarded as unrealistic for the purposes of the definition of 'realistic imitation firearm'. The Regulations provide that an imitation firearm is not a 'realistic' one if:

(a) it is less than 38 mm high and 70 mm in length; or
(b) it is of one of the following colours: bright
    (i) red,
    (ii) orange,
    (iii) yellow,
    (iv) green,
    (v) pink,
    (vi) purple, or
    (vii) blue;
    or is made of transparent material.

The Regulations provide a defence to a charge under s 36 for the defendant to show that his conduct was for the purpose only of making the imitation firearm available for the organisation and holding of permitted activities in respect of which there were insurance arrangements in respect of third-party liabilities, or for the purpose of dis-play at a permitted event. 'Permitted activities' means the acting-out of military or law enforcement scenarios for the purpose of recreation (eg historical re-enactments of battles); and 'permitted events' means a commercial event at which firearms or realistic imitation firearms (or both) are offered for sale or displayed. The defendant will have shown such a matter if there is sufficient evidence to raise an issue and the contrary is not proved beyond reasonable doubt.

OFFENSIVE WEAPONS IN PUBLIC PLACES

The Prevention of Crime Act 1953 (PCA 1953), s 1(1) provides that any person who with-out lawful authority or reasonable excuse, the proof whereof lies on him, has with him in any public place any offensive weapon is guilty of an indictable (either way) offence. The court may make an order as to the disposal of a weapon following conviction.

'Has with him' was defined on p 638. The defendant need not know of the facts which render the article an offensive weapon within the meaning of the statute.

An offensive weapon is defined by s 1(4) as any article made or adapted for use for causing injury to the person, or intended by the person having it with him for such use by him or by some other person. This definition includes two classes of offensive weapon.

Articles made or adapted for causing injury to the person

These weapons are described as offensive per se (ie in themselves).

Examples of articles *made* for causing injury to the person are bayonets, coshes, knuckledusters, swords, flick knives and butterfly knives. The Court of Appeal has held that an article which has all the characteristics of one made for causing injury to the person (in the instant case a flick knife) is a weapon offensive per se despite the fact that it has a harmless secondary characteristic, eg of being a lighter.

Examples of articles *adapted* for causing injury to the person are a piece of chain whose links have been sharpened and someone's cap in the peak of which a razor blade has been inserted with the cutting edge exposed. In such cases, articles which are harmless in themselves are made offensive weapons by their deliberate adaptation for use for causing personal injury.

Articles intended to be used for causing injury to the person

This class covers articles which are inoffensive per se (ie in themselves), because they have not been made or adapted for causing personal injury, but which are rendered offensive by the defendant's intention to use them for causing injury to the person. Such articles include belts, shoes, walking sticks (or umbrellas), and dog leads, provided it can be shown that there was an intention to use the article for causing injury to the person. The difficulty of proving such an intention increases in proportion to the generally non-offensive character of the article in question.

It is not enough that someone, who is in innocent possession of an article, suddenly uses it for an offensive purpose. Thus, where a carpenter took a hammer from his tool bag during a fight and used it, a divisional court held that he was not guilty of an offence under PCA 1953, s 1, as he did not have the hammer with him for causing injury to the person. This is a stricter rule than applies to similar wording in the offence of aggravated burglary (see p 942).

Public place

The defendant must have with him the offensive weapon in a public place; this can include having it with him in a vehicle which is in a public place. By PCA 1953, s 1(4), 'public place' includes any highway, and any other premises or place to which at the material time the public have or are permitted (ie invited or tolerated) to have access, whether on payment or otherwise. The issue is generally whether the public have access, or are permitted to have it if they wish. Public access is a matter of fact and if access is restricted to certain classes of person, it must be restricted to some considerable degree before it will be accepted that the public are not admitted. A dance restricted to those under 25 is a public dance as all classes of those under that age have a right of access. A soccer ground is a public place if paying spectators are admitted; it would be unlikely to be considered so if entry was restricted to elected members, but regard would have to be paid to the nature and restriction of membership. If the ground was generally available to the public without interview or election by the committee it would probably be different.

The fact that a person is found with an offensive weapon in a private place may lead to a conviction for the present offence. For example, if a visitor to a dwelling house produces an offensive weapon, this gives rise to a strong inference that he brought it with him through the streets and therefore had it with him in a public place.

Lawful authority or reasonable excuse

A person does not commit the offence if he has lawful authority or reasonable excuse for having with him the offensive weapon; the defendant has the onus of proving such authority or excuse.

Those who may have offensive weapons with lawful authority include members of the armed services, or police forces, who may carry weapons which are offensive in themselves as part of their duty. On the other hand, it has been held that private security guards do not have lawful authority to carry truncheons or the like. Whether there is reasonable excuse depends on whether a reasonable person would think it excusable in the circumstances to carry the weapon in question, but as a matter of law limitations have been imposed by the courts on what a reasonable man might think in this context. Thus, it has been held that he would not think it reasonable for a person to have with him a weapon for self-defence unless that person reasonably believes that there is an imminent and particular threat to him (as opposed to a constant one), nor would he think it reasonable for a person to have with him a weapon in order to commit suicide with it or for a security guard at a dance hall to carry a truncheon 'as a deterrent' and 'as part of his uniform'. The Court of Appeal has held that a claim by a person who has been proved to be in possession of a weapon which is offensive per se, that he did not know that the article in question was an offensive weapon, cannot amount to a reasonable excuse. It has also held that the fact that the defendant had forgotten that the article was in his possession in itself cannot amount to a reasonable excuse.

Threatening with offensive weapon in public

Under the Prevention of Crime Act 1953, s 1A(1), added in 2012, a person is guilty of an indictable (either way) offence if he:

(a) has an offensive weapon (as defined on p 644) with him or her in a public place (as defined on p 644),
(b) unlawfully and intentionally threatens another person with the weapon, and
(c) does so in such a way that there is an immediate risk of serious physical harm to that other person.

For these purposes, physical harm is serious if it amounts to grievous bodily harm for the purposes of the Offences against the Person Act 1861.

Unlike the offence under PCA 1953, s 1 this offence carries a mandatory minimum custodial sentence. The only exception to this minimum is where it would be unjust in the circumstances, having regard to the offence or the offender.

ANCILLARY OFFENCES TO THOSE UNDER PCA 1953

Having article with blade or point in a public place

The Criminal Justice Act 1988 (CJA 1988), s 139 provides an ancillary offence which is useful where a knife or the like cannot be proved to have been made, adapted or intended to cause injury to the person. Section 139(1) makes it an indictable (either way) offence for a person to have with him in a public place an article which is sharply pointed or with a blade, other than a folding pocket knife with a blade not exceeding three inches. 'Has with him' has, and 'public place' essentially has, the same meaning as under PCA 1953.

A butter knife without a handle and with no cutting edge and no point has been held to be a bladed article within CJA 1988, s 139. A folding knife which is secured in an open position by a locking device and can only be released from the open position by the pressing of a release button is not a folding pocket knife within the meaning of CJA 1988, s 139.

A defendant (D) has a defence if he proves lawful authority or good reason for having the article with him in a public place, or that he had it with him there for use at work, for a religious reason or as part of any national costume (s 139(4) and (5)). Whether D was in possession of such a knife 'for use at work' is a matter for the court or jury as the statute uses ordinary, everyday language. Whether D had a good reason is a matter for the court or jury. A judge should not tell a jury what 'good reason' means, but in a clear case the judge can rule that D's explanation cannot amount to a good reason. For example, the Court of Appeal has held that D's forgetfulness that he has the article is not a good reason, but that forgetfulness combined with another reason may be. A fear of attack may be a good reason, depending on how imminent, how likely, how specific the perceived threat, and how serious the anticipated attack. The Court of Appeal has also held that requiring the defendant to prove one of these defences is not in conflict with the presumption of innocence under of the European Convention on Human Rights, art 6(2).

Having article with blade or point (or offensive weapon) on school premises

CJA 1988, s 139A makes it an indictable (either way) offence for a person to have any article to which CJA 1988, s 139 applies with him on school premises. It creates a similar either way offence in relation to an offensive weapon to which PCA 1953 applies. The term 'school premises' means land used for the purpose of a school excluding any land occupied solely as a dwelling by a person employed at the school. Similar defences exist; a person who proves that he had good reason or lawful authority for having the article or weapon with him on the premises has a defence. So has a person who proves that he had the article or weapon with him for the purposes set out above in relation to CJA 1988, s 139. In addition, he may show possession 'for educational purposes'.

Threatening with article with blade or point (or offensive weapon)

Under the Criminal Justice Act 1988, s 139AA(1), added in 2012, a person is guilty of an indictable (either way) offence if he:

(a) has an article to which s 139AA applies with him in a public place (as defined for s 139: p 644) or on school premises (as defined for s 139A: above),
(b) unlawfully and intentionally threatens another person with the article, and
(c) does so in such a way that there is an immediate risk of serious physical harm (as defined on p 645) to that other person.

In relation to a public place, s 139AA(1) applies to an article to which s 139 applies (above). In relation to school premises, s 139AA(1) applies to an article to which 139 applies, and to an offensive weapon within the meaning of PCA 1953, s 1.

Unlike the offences under CJA 1988, ss 139 and 139A, the new offence carries a mandatory minimum custodial sentence. The only exception to this minimum is where it would be unjust in the circumstances, having regard to the offence or the offender.

Power of entry to search for articles with a blade or point and offensive weapons

CJA 1988, s 139B provides a constable with a power of entry, using reasonable force if necessary, into school premises and the power to search those premises and any person on those premises for articles to which CJA 1988, s 139 applies, or to which PCA 1953, s 1 applies, if he has reasonable grounds for suspecting that an offence under CJA 1988, s 139A or s 139AA (above) is being, or has been, committed. He may seize any articles or weapons discovered in the course of such a search which he reasonably suspects to be such articles or weapons.

RESTRICTION OF OFFENSIVE WEAPONS

Manufacture, sale, etc of flick knives and gravity knives

The Restriction of Offensive Weapons Act 1959 is concerned with the manufacture and distribution of flick knives and gravity knives. It is an offence under s 1(1) for any person to manufacture, sell, hire, offer for sale or hire, or to expose or have in his possession for the purpose of sale or hire, or to lend or give to any person, either of these weapons.

A 'flick knife' is any knife which has a blade which opens automatically by hand pressure applied to a button, spring or other device in or attached to the handle of the knife. A 'gravity knife' is one which has a blade which is released from the handle or sheath thereof by the force of gravity or the application of centrifugal force and which, when released, is locked in place by means of a button, spring, lever, or other device. The flick knife is therefore one with an up-and-over blade and a gravity knife is one which allows the blade to be shaken from the handle.

Manufacture, sale, etc of specified weapons

By CJA 1988, s 141(1), a person who manufactures, sells or hires, or offers for sale or hire, exposes or has in his possession for the purpose of sale or hire, or lends or gives to any other person, any weapon specified by order by the Secretary of State, commits an offence.

The specified weapons

The Secretary of State has made the Criminal Justice Act 1988 (Offensive Weapons) Order 1988 listing the knuckleduster, swordstick, handclaw, belt buckle knife, push dagger, hollow kubotan (small truncheon with spikes), footclaw, death star, butterfly knife, telescopic truncheon, blow-pipe, kusari gama (sickle and chain), kyoketsu shoge (hooked knife and chain) and maurik kusari or kusari (weights joined by chain).

An order in 2002 added a disguised knife, ie any knife which has a concealed blade or concealed sharp point and is designed to appear to be an everyday object of a kind commonly carried on the person or in a handbag, briefcase or other hand luggage (such as a comb, brush, writing instrument, cigarette lighter, key, lipstick, or telephone).

An order in 2004 added (a) a stealth knife, that is a knife or spike, which has a blade or a sharp point, made from a material that is not readily detectable by apparatus used for detecting metal, and which is not designed for domestic use or for use in the processing, preparation or consumption of food or as a toy, and (b) a straight, side-handled or friction-lock truncheon (sometimes known as a baton).

An order in 2008 added a sword with a curved blade 50 cm or more in length (for which purpose the length of the blade is the straight line distance from the top of the handle to the tip of the blade). It is a defence to a charge under s 141 in relation to such a sword to show:

(a) that the weapon in question was made before 1954 or was made at any other time according to traditional methods of making swords by hand;
(b) that the conduct was for the purpose of making the weapon available for the purposes of the organisation and holding of a permitted activity (historical re-enactment or a sporting activity) in respect of which public liability insurance is held; or
(c) that the defendant's conduct was for the purpose only of making the weapon available for the purposes of use in religious ceremonies.

A person shows (a), (b), or (c) if sufficient evidence as to it is adduced to raise an issue with respect to it and the contrary is not proved beyond reasonable doubt.

General defences

It is a defence to a charge under CJA 1988, s 141 to show that the conduct in question was only for the purpose of making the weapon available to a public museum or gallery. It is also a defence to show that the conduct in question was for the purpose only of making the weapon available for theatrical performances (or rehearsals) or the production of films or television programmes. A person shows one of these defence elements if sufficient evidence of the matter is adduced to raise an issue with respect to it and the contrary is not proved beyond reasonable doubt.

Police powers

A justice may issue a warrant under CJA 1988, s 142 authorising entry and search on the application of a constable if he is satisfied that there are reasonable grounds for believing that there are on those premises knives such as are mentioned in the Restriction of Offensive Weapons Act 1959, s 1(1) or weapons to which CJA 1988, s 141 applies, that an offence under either of these provisions has been or is being committed in relation to them, and that one of the normal essential conditions for a search warrant exists.

Sale of knives, etc to persons under 18

By CJA 1988, s 141A(1), it is an offence to sell to a person under the age of 18 a knife, knife blade or razor blade, any axe, and any other article which has a blade or which is sharply pointed and which is made or adapted for use for causing injury to the person. Section 141A does not apply to articles already controlled by the Restriction of Offensive Weapons Act 1959 or CJA 1988, s 141, or described in an order made by the Secretary of State under CJA 1988, s 141A. The Secretary of State has made an order in respect of a folding pocket knife with a blade which does not exceed three inches and razor blades permanently enclosed in a cartridge or housing.

Section 141A provides a defence for a person who proves that he took all reasonable precautions and exercised all due diligence to avoid commission of the offence.

Marketing etc of combat knives

Marketing

The Knives Act 1997 (KA 1997), s 1(1) provides that it is an indictable (either way) offence to market a knife in a way which:

(a) indicates, or suggests, that it is suitable for combat; or
(b) is otherwise likely to stimulate or encourage violent behaviour involving the use of the knife as a weapon.

The term 'market' includes selling or hiring, offering or exposing for sale or hire, or possession for the purpose of sale or hire. A 'knife' is an instrument which has a blade or is sharply pointed; 'suitable for combat' means suitable for use as a weapon for inflicting injury on a person or causing a person to fear injury; and 'violent behaviour' means an unlawful act inflicting injury on a person or causing a person to fear injury.

Publication

KA 1997, s 2 creates the indictable (either way) offence of publishing any written, pictorial or other material in connection with the marketing of any knife, which:

(a) indicates, or suggests, that the knife is 'suitable for combat'; or
(b) is otherwise likely to stimulate or encourage 'violent behaviour' involving the use of the knife as a weapon.

Defences

In relation to the offence under KA 1997, s 1, proof that the knife was marketed for use by the armed forces of any country, or as an antique or curio is a defence.

In relation to the offence under s 2, it is a defence to prove that:

(a) the material was published in connection with marketing a knife for use by the armed forces of any country or as an antique or curio; and
(b) it was reasonable for the knife to be marketed in that way; and
(c) there were no reasonable grounds for suspecting that a person into whose possession the knife might come in consequence of the way in which it was marketed would use it for an unlawful purpose.

It is also a defence to a charge under KA 1997, s 1 or s 2 for the defendant to prove that he did not know or suspect, and had no reasonable grounds for suspecting, that the way the knife was marketed (s 1), or the material (s 2), amounted to an indication or suggestion that the knife was 'suitable for combat', or was likely to stimulate or encourage 'violent behaviour' involving the use of the knife as a weapon. Lastly, it is a defence to either offence for the defendant to prove that he took all reasonable precautions and exercised due diligence to avoid committing the offence.

Police powers

KA 1997, s 5 provides for the issue of search warrants authorising entry, search and seizure in respect of knives and publications. Reasonable force may be used in exercising the powers under the warrant. The additional powers of seizure provided by the

Criminal Justice and Police Act 2001, s 50 apply where such a search warrant in respect of publications is executed.

USING SOMEONE TO MIND A WEAPON

VCRA 2006, s 28 provides that a person is guilty of an offence triable only on indictment if:

(a) he uses another to look after, hide or transport a dangerous weapon for him; and
(b) he does so under arrangements or in circumstances that facilitate, or are intended to facilitate, the weapon being available to him for an unlawful purpose.

For this purpose, the cases where a dangerous weapon is to be regarded as available to a person for an unlawful purpose include any case where it is available for him to take possession of it at a time and place at which his possession of the weapon would constitute, or be likely to involve or to lead to, the commission by him of an offence. A 'dangerous weapon' is a firearm other than an air weapon or a component part of, or accessory to, an air weapon, or a weapon to which CJA 1988, s 141 or 141A applies (specified offensive weapons, knives, and bladed weapons: see pp 647–8).

CROSSBOWS

The Crossbows Act 1987 creates specific offences in respect of crossbows with a draw weight of at least 1.4 kg.

By s 1, it is an offence for any person to sell or let on hire such a crossbow or part of a crossbow to a person under the age of 18. No offence is committed if the seller or hirer believes the person so acquiring to be 18 or older, provided he has reasonable ground for that belief. Similarly, by s 2, it is an offence for a person under 18 to purchase or hire a crossbow or part of a crossbow.

Section 3 provides that, unless he is under the supervision of a person who is 21 or older, a person under 18 who has with him a crossbow which is capable of discharging a missile, or parts of a crossbow which together (and without any other parts) can be assembled to form a crossbow capable of discharging a missile, is guilty of an offence.

Where a constable suspects with reasonable cause that a person is committing or has committed an offence under s 3, he may:

(a) search that person for a crossbow or part of a crossbow; or
(b) search any vehicle, or anything in or on a vehicle, in or on which the constable reasonably suspects there is a crossbow or part of a crossbow connected with the offence.

A person or vehicle may be detained by the constable for the purpose of such a search and anything appearing to be a crossbow (or part) may be seized. The constable may enter any land other than a dwelling house to exercise these powers. These powers are provided by s 4.

CHAPTER 20

Explosives

FIREWORKS

Offences under the Fireworks Act 2003

The Fireworks Regulations 2004 made under the Fireworks Act 2003 contain a number of prohibitions. The Fireworks Regulations 2004, reg 12 requires chief officers of police to enforce the provisions of the Regulations in relation to offences of possession or use. The enforcement of the parts of the Fireworks Regulations relating to licensing and storage is a matter for the local weights and measures authority, except that in a metropolitan county licensing enforcement is a matter for that county's fire and rescue authority.

The Fireworks Act 2003, s 11 provides that any person who contravenes a prohibition imposed by fireworks regulations, or who fails to comply with a requirement imposed by or under such regulations, is guilty of an offence. The defence of 'due diligence' provided by the Consumer Protection Act 1987, s 39 applies to these offences. The offence is a 'penalty offence' for the purposes of the Criminal Justice and Police Act 2001 (p 31).

Prohibition on possession

Regulation 4 of the Fireworks Regulations 2004 provides that no person under 18 may possess an adult firework in a public place. The term 'public place' bears its usual meaning.

Regulation 5 prohibits anyone from possessing a 'category 4 firework'. This is a firework classified as category 4 under Part I of BS 7114.

However, reg 6 provides that nothing in regs 4 and 5 prohibits the possession of any firework by:

(a) any person employed by, or in business as, a professional organiser or operator of firework displays who possesses the firework in question for such purposes;
(b) any person employed in, or whose trade or business (wholly or partly) is, the manufacture of fireworks or assemblies containing fireworks who possesses the firework in question for the purposes of his trade, employment or business;
(c) any person employed in, or whose trade or business (wholly or partly) is, the supply of fireworks or such assemblies in accordance with Pyrotechnic Articles (Safety) Regulations 2010;
(d) any person employed by a local authority, or the UK government, who possesses the firework in question for the purpose of a display or in connection with a national public celebration, or in the course of carrying out enforcement powers in relation to fireworks (or, in the case of government employees, use for research or investigation);
(e) any person for use, in the course of a trade, business or employment, for special effects purposes in the theatre, on film or on television;

(f) any person in business as or employed by a supplier of goods designed and intended for use in conjunction with fireworks or assemblies containing fireworks who possesses the firework in question for testing those goods in connection with safety; and

(g) any person employed by a naval, military or air force establishment who possesses the firework in question for the purpose of a display or at a public celebration or a national commemorative event.

Prohibition of use at night

The Fireworks Regulations 2004, reg 7 prohibits the use of an adult firework during 'night hours' (11 pm to 7 am) otherwise than on a permitted fireworks night or by a local authority employee in the course of a local authority display or at a national public celebration or commemorative event. Permitted fireworks nights are Chinese New Year (11 pm to 1 am); 5 November (11 pm to midnight); the day of Diwali (11 pm to 1 am); and 31 December (11 pm to 1 am).

Throwing fireworks

It is an offence to throw, cast, or fire any fireworks in or onto any highway, street, thoroughfare, or public place. This offence, provided by Explosives Act 1875 (EA 1875), s 80, is extremely useful. Although there are other offences in relation to the use of fireworks in streets and public places, eg under the Highways Act 1980, s 161 and the Town Police Clauses Act 1847, 28, this offence is the most easily proved. There are no exceptions to the offence; even the celebration of 'Guy Fawkes Night' must be restricted to the use of fireworks otherwise than in streets or public places.

The offence under EA 1875, s 80 is a 'penalty offence' for the purposes of the Criminal Justice and Police Act 2001.

EXPLOSIVE SUBSTANCES ACT 1883

The Explosive Substances Act 1883 (ESA 1883) deals with many offences which can be committed in relation to 'explosive substances'.

Explosive substance

The term is defined by ESA 1883, s 9, which declares that an explosive substance is deemed to include:

(a) any material for making any explosive substance;
(b) any apparatus, machine, implement, or materials used, or intended to be used, or adapted for causing, or aiding in causing, any explosion in or with any explosive substance; and
(c) any part of any such apparatus, machine, or implement.

This wide definition covers, for example, an ingredient which would go into the making of an explosive substance, an empty bomb case, and a detonator for a bomb.

ESA 1883 does not define the essential term 'explosive' but the Court of Appeal has held that 'explosive' should be interpreted in the light of the definition of 'explosive' in EA 1875, s 3, which states that the term means:

(a) gunpowder, nitro-glycerine, dynamite, gun-cotton, blasting powder, fulminate of mercury or of other metals, coloured fires, and every other substance, whether similar to those already mentioned or not, used or manufactured with a view to producing a practical effect by explosion or a pyrotechnic effect; and

(b) includes fog-signals, fireworks, fuses, rockets, percussion caps, detonators, cartridges, ammunition of all descriptions, and every adaptation or preparation of an explosive as above defined.

'Explosive substance' is, therefore, a wide term. A petrol bomb has been held to be an 'explosive substance'.

Causing an explosion likely to endanger life

ESA 1883, s 2 makes it an offence for any person unlawfully and maliciously to cause by an explosive substance any explosion of a nature likely to endanger life, or to cause serious injury to property, whether such injury or damage occurs or not.

'Unlawfully' means without lawful justification, ie otherwise than in self-defence, prevention of crime, or the like, which will rarely be the case. 'Maliciously' simply requires the defendant to have intended to cause some unlawful harm to another or to property, or to have been reckless as to the risk of this resulting from the explosion. It does not mean or require spite or ill-will.

Nothing is required to result from the explosion. If someone, without lawful justification or excuse, intending to cause unlawful bodily harm or damage to property, causes an explosion of such a nature that its likely result will be to endanger life or cause serious damage to property, the fact that the explosion has occurred is all that is necessary for the offence to have been completed.

Attempt to cause explosion; making or keeping explosives with intent

ESA 1883, s 3(1) creates two offences. The first offence is concerned with acts done with the specified intent to cause an explosion, and the second with making or possessing an explosive substance with the specified intent. The offences relate to consequences in the UK or elsewhere.

In examining circumstances which might lead to the identification of offences contrary to s 3, one should think in terms of those who have not yet caused an explosion (and are therefore not caught by ESA 1883, s 2) but are doing some act with that intention in mind. Section 3 extends, by its terminology, the normal concept of an 'attempt' by making punishable acts which would normally be considered to be preparatory acts.

The offences are unlawfully and maliciously:

(a) to do any act with intent to cause by an explosive substance an explosion of a nature likely to endanger life or cause serious injury to property; or

(b) to make or have in one's possession or under one's control an explosive substance with intent by means thereof to endanger life or cause serious injury to property, or to enable any other person to do so.

'Unlawfully' has the same meaning as in s 2. 'Maliciously' is redundant in this offence because of the specific nature of the required intent.

Making or possessing an explosive under suspicious circumstances

There will often be practical difficulties associated with proving that explosive substances were made or possessed for the purpose of causing explosions likely to endanger life, etc. On occasions, the circumstances of the finding, any admissions, and the nature of the explosive device itself may tend to support a charge under ESA 1883, s 3, but on other occasions there may be difficulties in proving a particular intention. ESA 1883, s 4 is useful in such cases.

Section 4(1), as interpreted by the Court of Appeal, provides that any person who knowingly makes or knowingly has in his possession or under his control any explosive substance, under such circumstances as to give rise to a reasonable suspicion that he is not making it or does not have it in his possession or under his control for a lawful object, commits an offence. If the defendant claims that he made, possessed or controlled it for a lawful object, he must prove that this was so, in which case the offence is not committed.

Section 4 does not define what constitutes a 'lawful object' but it has been held that it requires a positive object which is lawful, and not simply the absence of a criminal purpose. Thus, it has been held, making a bomb by following instructions on the Internet with no intention of exploding it would not be making an explosive substance for a lawful object. On the other hand, it has been held that self-defence or the like against an imminent attack would be a lawful object if the defendant intended to use the explosive in a way which was no more than reasonably necessary to meet the imminent attack.

The two offences under ESA 1883, s 4 (making and possession/control) cover many modes of involvement. If several persons are concerned in the making, they are equally guilty of the offence; so are those who 'control' the explosive substances as well as those who actually possess them. Each person in a group, if such group has a common design, is responsible for the conduct of a member of that group within the common design: if that amounts to 'possession', all will be guilty.

General

An offence under ESA 1883 is triable only on indictment. A prosecution for such an offence may not be instituted without the consent of the Attorney General.

OTHER OFFENCES IN RELATION TO EXPLOSIVES

ESA 1883 deals with the likely activities of a bomber quite extensively but police officers should always remember, when considering charges which can be preferred in relation to the activities of terrorist bombers, that the Offences Against the Person Act 1861 and the Criminal Damage Act 1971 also deal with similar offences to those set out in ESA 1883. (These offences are described in Chapters 23 and 37.)

GENERAL POLICE POWERS AND DUTIES IN RESPECT OF EXPLOSIVES

By EA 1875, s 73, a constable may enter at any time, by force if necessary, any place (including a building, vehicle, or vessel) upon reasonable cause for believing that any offence has been or is being committed in that place with respect to an explosive if he is in possession of:

(a) a justices' warrant granted following information on oath; or

(b) a written order from a superintendent (or above), which may be issued if the case is one of emergency and delay in obtaining a warrant would be likely to endanger life,

and to search for explosives, and take samples of any explosives and ingredients of an explosive. It is suggested that if information is received that explosives are stored upon any premises in a locality in which people normally reside, the case will be one in which delay would be likely to endanger life.

There are certain duties which must be carried out by the police when thefts of explosives are reported. The Hazardous Substances Division of the Health and Safety Executive should be informed of the exact nature and quantity of explosives stolen, the circumstances of the theft, whether the explosives have been stolen from a store or conveyance, and the use to which the explosives are normally put. The Division also requires the identity of the caller and details of place, time, and date of the theft, together with details of any explosives left behind by the thieves. Where explosives are found, similar notification should be given to the Division.

The HSE Explosives Inspectorate requires details of all cases of illegal manufacture of explosives, even in the case of trivial experimentation by children. The usual details of the person, time, date, etc, of offence are required together with details of police action or court action, and of any forensic report on the substance. The Inspectorate also likes to know where the persons concerned obtained their knowledge of the manufacture of explosives.

BOMB HOAXES

The offences which generally attract the description of bomb hoaxes are those dealt with by the Criminal Law Act 1977 (CLA 1977), s 51.

Placing or dispatching an article

CLA 1977, s 51(1) creates two indictable (either way) offences. The first is committed by any person who places an article in any place whatsoever with the intention of inducing some other person to believe that it is likely to explode or ignite and thereby cause personal injury or damage to property. Section 51(1) states that the term 'article' includes any substance. The offence would be committed by someone who produced a parcel in a tube train, or in an arena or elsewhere, to which wires were attached together with something which resembled a timing device. If he then, in view of other passengers, pushed the parcel under the seat or elsewhere and left the train, arena, etc, he would quite clearly intend to induce others to believe that it was an explosive device.

The second offence is dispatching any article by post, rail, or any other means from one place to another with the intention to induce in some other person a belief that it is likely to explode or ignite and thereby cause personal injury or damage to property. If someone sends through a post office sorting office a number of false devices with the intention of causing fear of an explosion to be aroused in the staff of that office, the offence is complete.

Neither offence requires the defendant to have any particular person in mind as the person in whom he intends to induce the relevant belief.

False messages

CLA 1977, s 51(2) is concerned with false messages to the effect that an explosive device has been planted. It states that it is an indictable (either way) offence for a person to communicate any information, which he knows or believes to be false, to another person, with the intention of inducing in him or any other person a false belief that a bomb or other thing liable to explode or ignite is present in any place or location whatever. The use of the words 'there is a bomb' by a hoaxer is sufficient to give rise to the offence. It is not a necessary ingredient that the person communicating the false information should identify a location.

This offence is aimed partly at the hoax telephone caller. It must be proved that the defendant knew or believed that the information which he passed was false. If a man asked a boy to ring the manager of a cinema to warn him of the presence of a bomb on the premises and the boy, believing the story to be true, made the call, the boy would commit no offence as he did not know or believe that the story was false. On the other hand, the man would commit the offence because he knowingly communicated false information to the boy, with the intention of inducing him to believe that a bomb was liable to explode at the cinema.

When police officers receive such a call, it is essential to gain as much information as possible from the caller, or from the person who is passing on a message received from such a caller. The details should include sex, estimated age, urgency in voice, emotion, and accent, together with details of the time, date, duration of call, whether from a private telephone or a call box, and any background voices. All information given by the caller must be established; where, when, and why the bomb is likely to explode, description of the type of bomb and its appearance, and as many of the actual words used as can be recalled.

Although the offence is most commonly committed by means of a telephone call, it can be committed by any form of communication. It is not necessary that the defendant had any particular person in mind in whom he intends to induce the relevant belief.

CHAPTER 21

Railways

The enforcement of much of the legislation relating to railways frequently falls to police officers other than those of the British Transport Police because they happen to be the first to arrive on the scene.

RAILWAY TRESPASS

Trespass offence

A person is a trespasser if he is on the land of another without a right by law to do so or any express or implied permission of the occupier (or his authorised agent). There may also be occasions where the original entry onto the premises was authorised, but became unauthorised. For example, a person who is permitted to enter a railway station to meet a passenger becomes a trespasser if he unauthorisedly goes on the track. A person who is validly requested to leave a railway station becomes a trespasser after the expiry of a reasonable time for him to leave has elapsed from the withdrawal of his permission to remain.

Trespass on the railway is an offence under the British Transport Commission Act 1949 (BTCA 1949), s 55. This offence is committed when any person trespasses upon any of the lines of railway or sidings, or in any tunnel, or upon any railway embankment, cutting or similar work belonging, leased to or worked by a successor to the British Railways Board (essentially Network Rail, but also BRB (Residuary) Ltd) or by Transport for London, or trespasses upon any other lands of such a body in dangerous proximity to any such lines of railway or other works or to any electrical apparatus used for, or in connection with, the working of the railway. However, a person may not be convicted of this offence unless it is proved to the satisfaction of the court that public warning has been given to persons not to trespass upon the railway by a notice clearly exhibited at the station on the railway nearest to the place where the offence is alleged to have been committed. The notice must be renewed as often as it is obliterated or destroyed; if it is not, a person cannot be convicted of the offence. The significance of such a notice at railway stations is difficult to assess as the station is likely to be miles distant from the scene of trespass.

The offence only applies to trespassing on the track, land, etc. Thus, it does not apply where a person who is not trespassing on such land jumps onto (and thereby trespasses on) a passing train, nor does it apply where the trespass is on the track, land, etc of one of the various companies running restored steam trains. It is useful to police officers to be aware of the provisions of BTCA 1949, but it is preferable to leave enforcement to the British Transport Police and to railway officials. However, in the interests of the safety of such trespassers it may be necessary for any police officer to take action in such cases. A refusal by a trespasser to leave railway property on such an occasion will amount to an obstruction of a police officer in the execution of his duty, contrary to the Police Act 1996, s 89(2).

The offence under BTCA 1949, s 55 is a 'penalty offence' for the purposes of the Criminal Justice and Police Act 2001 (see p 31).

Offence of refusal to quit

The Railway Regulation Act 1840, s 16 states that it is an offence for any person wilfully to trespass upon the railway or any station or premises connected therewith and to refuse to quit upon request by any officer or agent of the railway company. This offence of trespass is not restricted to the operational areas of a railway system, as is the case under BTCA 1949. It can occur anywhere on railway property but the offence is not complete until there is a refusal to quit at the request of any officer or agent of the railway company. Police officers, other than officers of the British Transport Police, are not 'officers of the company'. There is no need to prove that notices are displayed in such a case.

ENDANGERING THE SAFETY OF PASSENGERS

Interfering with the railway system with intent

The Offences Against the Person Act 1861 (OAPA 1861), s 32 provides that it is an offence triable only on indictment for any person unlawfully and maliciously to carry out certain acts *with intent to endanger the safety of any person travelling or being on a railway*. Basically, these acts involve interference with the railway system itself by doing or causing something to be done, eg the placing of obstructions on a railway, the displacing of parts of it, the moving of points and similar fittings, the showing of a false signal, or the concealment of a real one.

Throwing things with intent

OAPA 1861, s 33 provides that it is an offence triable only on indictment for any person unlawfully and maliciously to throw, or cause to fall or strike, any wood, stone, or other matter or thing, at, against, into or upon any engine, tender, carriage, or truck used upon any railway *with intent to injure or endanger the safety of any person on the train*.

Endangering passengers

There are, of course, occasions where it may not be possible to prove that the act was carried out with an intention to injure anyone or to endanger anyone's safety. To cover such eventualities, OAPA 1861, s 34 creates a less serious indictable (either way) offence which can be committed by any person who, by any unlawful act, or by any wilful omission or neglect, endangers or causes to be endangered the safety of any person conveyed or being in or upon a railway.

The general nature of OAPA 1861, s 34 requires examination. If young persons throw stones at railway trains but cannot be shown to have done so with the intention to injure or endanger, as specified in OAPA 1861, s 33, they may nevertheless be convicted of an offence under s 34 since, by their unlawful acts, they have endangered the safety of railway passengers. The same would be so where someone who placed an obstruction on a railway line cannot be proved to have had the intent to endanger a person on the train, which is required by OAPA 1861, s 32, provided that the obstruction is of such a nature as to endanger passengers. In respect of such conduct, and any other conduct covered by s 34, it is irrelevant whether or not the defendant ever considered the consequences of his conduct. Section 34 also punishes wilful omissions or neglect.

These offences are likely to be committed by railwaymen. A driver who neglected to keep a lookout for signals would certainly be guilty of this offence.

Stone throwing on railway

BTCA 1949, s 56 creates an offence of throwing stones and other objects at locomotives, carriages and other things on railways belonging or leased to or worked by any of the organisations referred to in relation to s 55. This is a 'penalty offence' for the purposes of the Criminal Justice and Police Act 2001 and may be dealt with under a fixed penalty procedure: see p 31.

OBSTRUCTION, ETC OF ENGINES AND THE LIKE

In considering the offences committed in circumstances involving obstruction, etc by objects being unlawfully placed upon a railway line it is helpful to consider from the outset the parallel offences under OAPA 1861 and the Malicious Damage Act 1861 (MDA 1861). MDA 1861, ss 35 and 36 almost repeat the substance of the offences under OAPA 1861, ss 32 and 34.

Interfering with the railway system with intent

MDA 1861, s 35 is almost identical to OAPA 1861, s 32. The only difference is in relation to intent. The intention required by MDA 1861 must be to obstruct, upset, overthrow, injure, or destroy an engine, tender, carriage, or truck using such railway. An offence under MDA 1861, s 35 is triable only on indictment.

Obstructing engines or carriages

MDA 1861, s 36 parallels the offence previously described in OAPA 1861, s 34. There must have been an unlawful act, or a wilful omission or neglect, which led to the obstruction of an engine or carriage using a railway (as opposed to endangering the safety of passengers as required by OAPA 1861, s 34). If, therefore, persons unlawfully obstruct a line, they commit an offence of the same gravity, whether they do so in such a way that the safety of passengers is threatened, or merely in such a way that an engine, etc was obstructed. A person who causes a train to stop or to slacken speed by altering signals or by making unauthorised signals with the arms is guilty of obstructing a train contrary to MDA 1861, s 36. The offence is also committed by those who cause an obstruction to take place. It is an indictable (either way) offence.

TICKET OFFENCES

Generally, all offences related to tickets will be dealt with by a railway employee or by British Transport Police officers, but there may be occasions upon which a police officer from a local force may be called to a dispute centred upon whether or not a person has committed a ticket offence.

Travelling without a ticket

The Regulation of Railways Act 1889 (RRA 1889), s 5(1) provides that every passenger on a railway, on request by an officer or agent or servant of the railway company, must either produce, and if requested deliver up, a ticket showing that his fare is paid, or pay his fare from the place where his journey started, or give his name and address (ie his true name and address), so that the fare may be recovered from him by civil process, if necessary. In default of doing so, the passenger commits an offence.

Travelling with intent to avoid paying fare

One of two offences may be involved here, both provided by RRA 1889, s 5(3).

Section 5(3) provides, first, that if any person travels, or attempts to travel, on a railway without having previously paid his fare, and with intent to avoid payment thereof, he commits an offence. The intention to avoid payment may be proved by showing that the passenger has ignored opportunities to pay his fare or has taken measures to avoid a ticket inspector. A person who leaves a train without paying his fare when there has been an opportunity to do so indicates such an intention. In addition, a person who travels on a ticket issued to another person, which is not transferable, clearly indicates an intention to avoid payment. A person, therefore, who produces a concessionary ticket issued to a young person or a senior citizen to which he is not entitled, clearly shows an intention to avoid payment of his true fare. In this respect the term 'fare' means the correct fare for the particular journey and the class of carriage by which the person travels. A person who travels in a first-class carriage with a standard-class ticket may be convicted of travelling without having previously paid his fare, if an intention to avoid payment of the correct fare is indicated by his refusal to pay the excess.

Second, it is also an offence under s 5(3) knowingly and wilfully to proceed by train beyond the distance for which a fare has been paid. Opportunities exist on all trains to obtain an additional ticket for the excess journey and if opportunities to do so are ignored on the journey, this may be taken to indicate a knowing and wilful act.

Penalty fares

The Railways (Penalty Fares) Regulations 1994 make provision for the charging of penalty fares for failure to produce, when required to do so, a ticket or other authority authorising a person to travel by train or to be present in a compulsory ticket area at a station. The Regulations apply to all train operators.

By reg 3, subject to the provisions of the regulations, and to any rules made under them:

(a) any person travelling by, present on, or leaving a train must, if required by or on behalf of the train operator, produce a ticket or other authority authorising his travelling by or his being present on that train, as the case may be; and

(b) any person present in or leaving a compulsory ticket area must, if so required, produce a ticket or other authority authorising him to be present in or leave that area.

Failure to produce a ticket or other authority when so required renders the person liable to be charged a penalty fare by the train operator or someone acting on its behalf. A person is not liable to pay a penalty fare in a case covered by (a) if, when he boarded the train (or a preceding train on his journey, which was operated by the same operator):

(i)   there were no ticket etc facilities available for the journey in question;

(ii) there was no notice in a prescribed form indicating the penalty fare scheme;

(iii) at the station where and when he commenced his journey, a notice was displayed indicating that it was permissible to travel without having such ticket or authority; or

(iv) a person in authority (or apparently in authority) at the originating station gave permission to travel without a ticket etc.

These exemptions do not exempt a person who had the opportunity to obtain a fare ticket while on the train (or one of them used on the journey).

There are similar exemptions from liability to pay a penalty fare in respect of a case covered by (b) above.

A person who fails to pay a penalty fare at once must provide his name and address on being required to do so by an authorised person.

In an action to recover a penalty fare, which is a civil action, a defendant may provide the claimant with a 'relevant statement' explaining his failure to produce a ticket etc and including particulars of his journey, which must be submitted within 21 days. Where this has been done it will be for the claimant to show that the facts of the case do not fall within the exemptions provided by the Act. In any other case it is for the defendant to show that the facts of the case fall within those exemptions.

If a person has been charged a penalty fare in respect of his failure to produce a ticket or other authority when required and he is then prosecuted under RRA 1889, s 5(3) (see p 660) or for breach of a railway byelaw in respect of the lack of a ticket etc, he ceases to be liable to pay the penalty fare. If he has already paid it, it must be refunded.

CHAPTER 22

Nuisances, Collections, Vagrancy, Peddling, and Scrap Metal

NUISANCES

Common law offence of public nuisance

It is a common law indictable (either way) offence to cause a public nuisance. To constitute the offence, the act concerned must obstruct or cause inconvenience or damage to the public in the exercise of their rights. The essence of the offence is that the act is a nuisance to the public in general and not to an individual, or a restricted group of people. An act which is specifically authorised by law cannot be a public nuisance if carried out as prescribed. Despite its width, this common law offence is little used as most 'nuisances' are covered by statutes.

Nuisances related to noise

Because of difficulties experienced by local authorities and police officers in dealing with 'noise' nuisances, the Noise Act 1996 (NA 1996) provides powers for local authorities to serve warning notices in respect of a dwelling ('the offending dwelling') or premises in respect of which a premises licence or a temporary event notice (see p 591) has effect ('the offending premises') from which excessive noise is emanating, such noise being heard during the night. For these purposes, 'night' is the period between 11 pm and 7 am. Local authorities are equipped with approved measuring devices which establish noise levels. A local authority which receives a relevant complaint must secure that an officer of the authority takes reasonable steps to investigate the complaint.

Where a warning notice has been served in respect of an offending dwelling, it is an offence under NA 1996, s 4(1) for any person responsible for the noise to emit from it, within a period specified in the notice, noise which exceeds the permitted level, as measured from within the complainant's dwelling or premises. This offence is subject to a defence of 'reasonable excuse', the onus of proving which is on the defendant.

Where a warning notice has been served in respect of other premises and noise is emitted from them, within a period specified in the notice, which exceeds the permitted level, as measured from within the complainant's dwelling, the responsible person in respect of the offending premises commits an offence under s 4A(1). No defence of reasonable excuse is provided.

If an authorised local authority officer has reason to believe that a person has committed or is committing one of the above offences, he may give that person a fixed penalty notice. Where this has been done, no proceedings may be instituted for the offence within 14 days following the date of the notice. Payment of the fixed penalty within that period is a bar to conviction of the offence in question.

Local authority officers have a power of entry to a dwelling or other premises in respect of which a warning notice has been issued. It is an offence to obstruct such an officer. The Act provides powers of seizure and disposal of equipment causing such a noise nuisance.

Depositing litter

There are several provisions dealing with forms of defacement which might generally be described as 'litter'. The Environmental Protection Act 1990 (EPA 1990), s 87, which deals with land 'in the open air' (a term including a covered place open to the air on at least one side), provides that a person commits an offence if he *throws down, drops or otherwise deposits*, any litter in *any* place open to the air in the area of a principal litter authority, *and leaves it*. However, s 87 does not apply to a covered place open to the air on at least one side if the public does not have access to it, with or without payment. The offence of depositing litter is committed whether the litter is deposited on land or on water.

No offence is committed where the depositing of litter is authorised by law or is done with the consent of the owner or occupier or other person having control of the place where it is deposited. Consent may only be given to the depositing of litter in a lake, pond or watercourse by the owner, occupier or other person having control of all of the land adjoining that lake, pond or watercourse and all of the land into which water from those places directly or indirectly discharges, otherwise than by means of a public sewer.

The term 'litter' includes the discarded ends of cigarettes and like products and discarded chewing gum and the like.

A divisional court has held that 'leave' for these purposes does not mean abandon, and that an article deposited with no intention to remove it can be 'left' after only a short period of time. Someone who throws down fish wrappers, and refuses to pick them up immediately, commits the offence of depositing and leaving litter. He has no intention of removing the wrappers and this is evidenced by his refusal.

The offence under EPA 1990, s 87 is a 'penalty offence' for the purposes of the Criminal Justice and Police Act 2001 (see p 31).

Where the offence under EPA 1990, s 87 is dealt with by a local authority '*litter warden*' (who must be authorised in writing so to act on behalf of a litter authority), EPA 1990, s 88 permits the use of a fixed penalty procedure under *that* section.

Abandonment of property

Things other than motor vehicles

The Refuse Disposal (Amenity) Act 1978 (RD(A)A 1978), s 2(1)(b) provides the offence of abandoning, without lawful authority, on any land in the open air, or on any other land forming part of a highway, anything other than a motor vehicle which has been brought to the land for the purpose of being abandoned there. This deals with instances where someone takes refuse quite deliberately into the countryside and abandons it there. Such a person may leave an old mattress at the side of the road or throw it over the fence into a field; in either event he commits an offence.

Motor vehicles

RD(A)A 1978, s 2(1)(a) deals with the abandonment of motor vehicles in similar circumstances. The difference is that it is not necessary to prove that a motor vehicle was brought to the land for the purpose of abandonment. The offence is committed by someone who, without lawful authority, abandons on any land in the open air, or on any other land forming part of a highway, a motor vehicle or anything which formed part of a motor vehicle and was removed from it in the course of dismantling the vehicle on the land. RD(A)A 1978, s 2A provides for the offence under s 2(1)(a) to be dealt with as a fixed penalty offence by an authorised local authority officer.

General

Section 2(2), which applies to s 2(1)(a) and (b), deals with a person who leaves anything on land in such circumstances or for such a period that he may reasonably be assumed to have abandoned it or to have brought it to the land for the purpose of abandoning it there. It provides that such a person is deemed to have abandoned it there or, as the case may be, to have brought it to the land for that purpose, unless the contrary is shown.

Nuisance on educational premises

These offences are provided by the Education Act 1996, s 547 (which deals with schools) and the Further and Higher Education Act 1992, s 85A (which deals with further education colleges and 16 to 19 Academies). Both sections create an offence which may be committed by a person who is present on educational premises to which they apply, without lawful authority, who causes or permits nuisance or disturbance to the annoyance of persons who lawfully use those premises (whether or not any such persons are present at the time). 'Premises' includes playgrounds, playing fields and other premises for outdoor recreation. A constable or an authorised local authority officer may remove a person from the premises if he has reasonable cause to suspect that he is committing or has committed such an offence.

STREET AND HOUSE-TO-HOUSE COLLECTIONS

Street collections

The Police, Factories, etc (Miscellaneous Provisions) Act 1916, s 5 permits local authorities or the Mayor's Office for Policing and Crime to make regulations with respect to the places where and the conditions under which persons may be permitted, in any street or public place within their area, to collect money or sell articles for *the benefit of charitable or other purposes*. It also provides that a contravention of any regulations so made is an offence. When the Charities Act 2006, Part 3, Ch 1 (see p 665) comes into force, the words 'any purpose in circumstances not involving the making of a charitable appeal' will be substituted for the words italicised.

House-to-house collections

The House to House Collections Act 1939 prohibits house-to-house collections for charitable purposes unless the collection is authorised. Such a collection may be authorised by a licence (issued by a district council, the Commissioner of the Metropolitan Police, or the Common Council of the City of London), or an order of exemption (granted by the Minister for the Cabinet Office where the charitable purpose is to be pursued throughout the whole of England or a substantial part of it), or a certificate of exemption (granted by a chief officer of police in respect of a collection which is local in character and likely to be completed within a short period of time).

The House to House Collections Regulations 1947 deal with such matters as badges, certificates of authority, collecting boxes and receipt books, and duties of collectors and promoters. They prescribe a minimum age of 16 in respect of collectors. The 1947 Regulations do not apply to a collection under a certificate of exemption. Breach of the regulations is an offence under s 4(3) of the 1939 Act.

The House to House Collections Act 1939, s 5 punishes the unauthorised use of pre-scribed badges or certificates of authority, or a thing so closely resembling those articles as to be calculated to deceive.

A constable may require any person whom he believes to be acting as a collector for the purposes of a collection for charitable purposes to declare to him his name and address and to sign his name. Failure to comply with such a requirement is an offence under s 6.

Charities Act 2006

The Charities Act 2006, Part 3, Ch 1 (ss 45 to 66), the substantive provisions of which are not in force at the time of writing, establishes a regime for the conduct and regula-tion of public charitable collections. It defines two types: collections in a public place, and door-to-door collections.

Section 48 provides that a collection in a public place cannot be undertaken unless the organisation (a) holds a public collections certificate and (b) has obtained a permit from the relevant local authority. There is exemption from (a) and (b) if the collection is a 'local, short-term collection'.

By s 49, a door-to-door collection cannot be undertaken unless the organisation (a) holds a public collection certificate and (b) has (within a prescribed period) notified the local authority of specified matters, such as the purpose for which the collection is being raised and when and where it is to be conducted. There is an exemption from (a) and (b) if the collection is a 'local, short-term collection'.

To be a 'local, short-term collection' the collection must be for an appeal which is local in character. For it to be exempt the promoters must give advance notice of its purpose and when and where the collection is to be conducted.

Breach of s 48 or s 49 is an offence under s 48(3) or s 49(3) on the part of each pro-moter. Each promoter of an exempt local short-term collection which does not comply with s 48 commits an offence if there is non-compliance with the notification require-ment (s 50(6)).

Public collections certificates will be issued by the Charity Commission.

VAGRANCY OFFENCES

Begging

The Vagrancy Act 1824 (VA 1824), s 3 punishes persons who wander abroad, or place themselves in any public place, street, highway, court or passage, to beg or gather alms, or who cause, procure or encourage any child to do so. A divisional court has held that the offence does not cover those who collect alms in an orderly manner for a specific purpose, eg striking workers who seek assistance by asking for contributions towards their cause.

VA 1824, s 4 deals with the aggravated forms of begging by the exposure of wounds or deformities in public or by going about seeking charitable contributions of any kind by false pretences.

Sleeping out, etc

It is an offence contrary to VA 1824, s 4 for any person, wandering abroad and lodging in any barn or outhouse, or in any deserted or unoccupied building, or in the open air, or under a tent, or in any cart or waggon, not to give a good account of himself.

People holidaying at a static caravan site and genuine hikers who, being tired and hungry, rest in a barn or outhouse are not guilty of this offence because they can easily give a good account of themselves by explaining their presence. In contrast, a tramp found sleeping in a barn would find it much more difficult to give a good account of himself, particularly if he has made a temporary home in that building.

Two important limits were imposed on the offence by the Vagrancy Act 1935. First, the Act amended VA 1824, s 4 by providing that the reference to a person lodging under a tent or in a cart or waggon does not include a person lodging under a tent, cart, or waggon with or in which he travels. It was thereby made quite clear that the present offence was not concerned with gypsies travelling in their own waggons, nor with persons sleeping out in their own tents.

The Vagrancy Act 1935 also requires that before a person can be guilty of the present offence, it must be proved either that:

(a) on the occasion in question, he had been directed to a reasonably accessible place of free shelter and that he failed to apply for, or refused, accommodation there; or

(b) he is a person who persistently wanders abroad and, notwithstanding that a place of free shelter is reasonably accessible, lodges or attempts to lodge in a way described above; or

(c) by, or in the course of, lodging in a way described above he caused damage to property, infection with vermin, or other offensive consequence, or he so lodged in such circumstances as to appear to be likely to do so.

As a result, the present offence is of little practical significance to police officers. The reason is that there are few places of free shelter to which people may be directed, or which are reasonably accessible to the person who persistently sleeps out. The provision of greatest practical significance is that at (c), which can apply to the roadster who destroys hay or feed in a barn by his presence, or who causes the barn or outbuilding to become verminous by his presence.

PEDLARS

The Pedlars Act 1871 (PA 1871) still exists to provide some element of control over those who engage in some forms of door-to-door trading. Not the least of the reasons for this control is that peddling provides for those who commit crime a convenient cover or excuse to visit houses, where they may take advantage of opportunities to steal.

'Pedlar'

'Pedlar' is defined by PA 1871, s 3 as meaning a hawker, pedlar, petty chapman (another name for a pedlar), tinker, caster of metals, or other person who, without any horse or other beast bearing or drawing burden, travels and trades on foot, and goes from town to town or to other men's houses, carrying to sell, or exposing for sale, any goods, wares, or merchandise, or procuring orders for goods etc immediately to be delivered.

An important part of this definition is 'travels and trades on foot', which has been held to require that, to be a pedlar, a person must *go round* selling things; he must *trade as he travels on foot*, although he may stop to conduct a particular sale, rather than simply selling from a stall or pitch. Thus, a door-to-door salesman is a pedlar, but someone who stands in one place with a pitch, soliciting custom, is not. Nor is a person who moves a barrow from place to place, waiting at each place for customers to come to him. Provided the words of the definition are satisfied, it is irrelevant that the trade is carried out on a part-time basis or on the basis that the proceeds of sale will go (wholly or partly) to a charity.

Pedlars' certificates

A person who acts as a pedlar without a pedlar's certificate commits an offence, contrary to PA 1871, s 4, subject to certain exceptions. A pedlar's certificate is obtained from the chief officer of police of the district in which the applicant has resided during the month preceding his application. Before granting a certificate the chief officer must be satisfied that the applicant is above 17, is of good character, and in good faith intends to carry on the trade of a pedlar.

The certificate is renewable annually and authorises the holder to carry on the trade of a pedlar in any part of the UK. It also permits the pedlar to sell vegetables and fruits within the limits of a market, but only in the district in which it was granted. A chief officer of police may not deprive a pedlar of his certificate during its currency. The only way in which a pedlar may be deprived of a certificate is by order of a court in circumstances set out in s 16.

Chief officers of police must maintain a register of certificates.

PA 1871 permits a chief officer to delegate his functions under PA 1871. In practice, certificates are usually issued within police divisions and signed by the divisional commander on behalf of the chief officer.

An applicant may appeal to the justices against a refusal to issue a pedlar's certificate; the applicant must give to the chief officer, within one week of the refusal, written notice of his wish to appeal.

Exemption from need for a certificate

PA 1871, s 23 states that it is not necessary for certain persons to obtain pedlar's certificates, and these are:

(a) commercial travellers or other persons selling or seeking orders for goods, wares or merchandise, to or from dealers therein, and who buy to sell again;
(b) those who sell or seek orders for books as agents authorised in writing by the publishers of such books;
(c) sellers of vegetables, fish, fruit or victuals; and
(d) persons selling or exposing for sale goods etc in any public market or fair which is legally established.

In relation to (c), a High Court judge has held that lavender is a vegetable and that those who sell lavender from door to door are exempt from the necessity to obtain a pedlar's certificate. The exemption in (d) appears to be unnecessary as market traders do not go to other men's houses in any case.

Other offences

It is an offence for a pedlar to refuse on demand to show his pedlar's certificate to a justice or constable or to a person to whom he offers his goods for sale (or upon whose private grounds or premises he is found), or to refuse to allow it to be read (PA 1871, s 17).

It is an offence to make a false representation with a view to obtaining a pedlar's certificate (s 12).

SCRAP METAL DEALERS

Registration of dealers

The Scrap Metal Dealers Act 1964 (SMDA 1964), which is aimed at the prevention of dealings in stolen metal, requires every district council (hereafter 'the local authority') to maintain a register of persons carrying on business in their area as scrap metal dealers.

It is an offence under s 1(7) for a person to carry on a business as a scrap metal dealer in the area of a local authority unless he is registered with that authority.

Carrying on a business in area of a local authority

For the purposes of SMDA 1964, a person carrying on business as a scrap metal dealer is treated as carrying on that business in the area of a local authority if, but only if:

(a) a place in that area is occupied by him as a scrap metal store; or
(b) no place is occupied by him as a scrap metal store, whether in that area or else-where, but:
    (i)   he has his usual place of residence in that area; or
    (ii) a place in that area is occupied by him wholly or partly for the purposes of that business.

'Place' includes land, whether enclosed or not, and a 'scrap metal store' means a place where scrap metal is received or kept in the course of the business of a scrap metal dealer.

Business as a scrap metal dealer

A person carries on business as a scrap metal dealer if he carries on a business which consists wholly or partly of buying and selling scrap metal, whether the scrap metal sold is in the form in which it was bought or otherwise, other than a business in the course of which scrap metal is not bought except as materials for the manufacture of other articles or as part of the carrying on of a business as a 'motor salvage operator' and is not sold except as a by-product of such manufacture or of such a business or as surplus materials bought but not required for such manufacture or of such a business. A 'motor salvage operator' is someone who carries on a business which consists:

(a) wholly or partly in the recovery for re-use or sale of salvageable parts from motor vehicles and the subsequent sale or other disposal for scrap of the remainder of the vehicle concerned;
(b) wholly or mainly in the purchase of written-off vehicles and their subsequent repair and resale;
(c) wholly or mainly in the sale or purchase of motor vehicles which are to be the sub-ject (whether immediately or on a subsequent resale) of any of the activities set out at (a) and (b) above; or
(d) wholly or mainly in activities falling within (b) and (c).

The above definition of carrying on business as a scrap metal dealer is quite complex and difficult to follow unless it is broken up into pieces. In the first instance, the person must carry on a business which consists wholly or partly of buying and selling scrap metal. Therefore, persons who merely buy scrap metal are not scrap metal dealers, nor are those who merely sell it. If this was not so, a farmer who quite regularly sells scrap metal which gathers about the farm might be considered to be carrying on business as a scrap metal dealer if it could be said that his business was partly that of selling scrap metal. If a person both buys and sells it does not matter that the metal is sold in a different form. Consequently, a person who buys scrap washing machines and crushes them into cubes of metal, which he then sells to some other person, is quite clearly a scrap metal dealer.

In terms of the exclusion of motor salvage operators from the definition of 'carrying on business as a scrap metal dealer', such operators are subject to the special regulatory regime under the Vehicles (Crime) Act 2001 The Vehicles (Crime) Act 2001, s 2 requires local authorities to establish and maintain a register of persons carrying on business as motor salvage operators. Registration with the local authority may be cancelled if the authority is satisfied that the person (or a director of or partner in a company) concerned is not a fit and proper person to conduct such a business.

The Motor Salvage Operators Regulations 2002 provide for the keeping of records by registered motor salvage operators.

If a motor salvage operator also deals in scrap in ways falling outside the above list, he must comply with SMDA 1964. SMDA 1964, s 4A prospectively empowers the Secretary of State to make regulations providing for the notification by persons registered as scrap metal dealers of the destruction of motor vehicles and for the keeping of appropriate records. Section 4A(3) creates an offence of failure to comply with such regulations.

Scrap metal

SMDA 1964 describes scrap metal as including any old metal, and any broken, worn out, defaced, or partly manufactured articles made wholly or partly of metal, and any metallic wastes, and also as including old, broken, worn out or defaced tooltips or dies made of any of the materials commonly known as hard metals or of cemented or sintered metallic carbides. References to metals, other than 'hard metals' or 'metallic carbides', are references to aluminium, copper, iron, lead, magnesium, nickel, tin, and zinc, or, subject to the next sentence, to brass, bronze, gun metal, steel, white metal, or any other alloy of these metals. However, if any alloy has 2 per cent or more of gold, silver, platinum etc, it is not treated as such an alloy. It follows that a person who deals only in precious metals is not a scrap metal dealer.

Alteration in registered particulars

Dealers must notify the local authority within 28 days of any change in their registered particulars, or if they cease to carry on business as a scrap metal dealer. This requirement is the same as that imposed on motor salvage operators.

Records of dealings

The relevant provisions are contained in SMDA 1964, s 2. They seek to ensure that, from the moment that scrap metal is received by the dealer, the records will provide a continuing history of its origin, including the person from whom it is obtained, through its processing to its ultimate disposal.

A scrap metal dealer must keep a bound record book at each place occupied by him as a scrap metal store. He must make entries concerning:

(a) all scrap metal received at that place; and
(b) all scrap metal either processed at, or despatched from, that place.

Any bound book and, prospectively, anything required to be kept with it, must be retained for two years after the last entry in it.

He may, if he wishes, keep two separate bound books recording matters at (a) and (b) separately but otherwise may not extend the book-keeping by keeping any other books recording dealing in that store.

Records of metals received

The records must show:

(a) the description and weight of the scrap metal;
(b) the date and time of receipt of the scrap metal;
(c) if the scrap metal is received from another person, his full name and address;
(d) the price, if any, payable, if ascertained at the time of the entry;
(e) as from a day to be appointed, if the price has been so ascertained, any part of the price unpaid at the time of the entry;
(f) if the price has not been so ascertained, the dealer's estimate; and
(g) if the scrap metal has been delivered by mechanically propelled vehicle, the registration mark of the vehicle (even if it is the dealer's).

Records—metals processed or despatched

The records must show:

(a) the description and weight of the scrap metal;
(b) the date of processing and the process applied, or, as the case may be, the date of despatch;
(c) if despatched on sale or exchange, the full name and address of the person to whom the scrap is sold or with whom it is exchanged, and the consideration for which it is sold or exchanged; and
(d) if processed or despatched otherwise than on sale or exchange, the value of the scrap before its processing or despatch as estimated by the dealer.

Records of payments for scrap metal

As from a day to be appointed, if a scrap metal dealer pays at any time for scrap metal received at a place occupied by him as a scrap metal store:

(a) he must keep, with the book containing the entry relating to receipt of the scrap metal, a copy of the cheque (if the payment was by cheque), or any receipt identifying the transfer (if the payment was by electronic transfer and such a receipt was obtained), and
(b) the particulars required by s 2 to be entered include
    (i)   the full name and address of any person who makes the payment acting for the dealer;
    (ii) the full name and address of the person to whom the payment is made;
    (iii) in the case of an electronic transfer where no receipt identifying the transfer was obtained, particulars identifying the transfer.

Anything kept by virtue of (a) must be marked so as to identify the scrap metal by reference to the entry relating to receipt of the metal. An entry under (b) must be made immediately after the payment is made, and, if not made at the same time as the entry relating to receipt of the scrap metal, must identify the metal by reference to that entry.

Non-compliance with any of the requirements under s 2 as to records of dealings is an offence, contrary to s 2(6).

Itinerant collectors

Where a person who is registered by a local authority as a scrap metal dealer satisfies the authority that he carries on, or proposes to carry on, the business of a scrap metal dealer as part of the business of an 'itinerant collector', and not otherwise, the authority may make an order under SMDA 1964, s 3 exempting him from keeping the records set out above, but making him subject to the following requirements:

(a) that, when he sells scrap metal, he obtains a receipt from the purchaser showing its weight and aggregate price; and
(b) that he keeps such receipts for two years in such a way that he can produce them on demand to any authorised person.

Before making an order of the above type, the local authority must consult the chief officer of police for their area. This order, limiting the need to keep records, may be revoked by the local authority at any time. Failure to comply with the requirement to keep records as an itinerant collector is an offence, contrary to SMDA 1964, s 3(4).

An 'itinerant collector' is a person regularly engaged in collecting waste materials, and old, broken, worn out or defaced articles, by means of visits from house to house. Most 'tinker' collectors will fit this description as they are regularly engaged in such activities.

Offence of buying scrap metal for cash etc

SMDA 1964, s 3A provides that a scrap metal dealer must not pay for scrap metal except:

(a) by a cheque which is not transferable, or
(b) by an electronic transfer of funds (authorised by credit or debit card or otherwise).

'Paying' includes paying in kind (with goods or services). Section 3A does not apply if the payment is made in the carrying on of the dealer's business as a scrap metal dealer as part of the business of an itinerant collector, and at the time of the payment an order under s 3 is in force in relation to the dealer.

If a scrap metal dealer pays for scrap metal in breach of s 3A, each of the following is guilty of an offence under s 3A(4):

(a) the scrap metal dealer;
(b) a person who makes the payment acting for the dealer;
(c) a manager who fails to take reasonable steps to prevent the payment being made.

'Manager' means a person who works in the carrying on of the dealer's business as a scrap metal dealer in a capacity, whether paid or unpaid, which authorises the person to prevent the payment being made.

Police powers of entry

SMDA 1964, s 6(1) empowers a constable at all reasonable times:

(a) to enter and inspect any place registered as a scrap metal store, or as a place occupied by a scrap metal dealer wholly or partly for the purposes of his business; and

(b) to require production of, and to inspect, any scrap metal kept at that place and any book which the dealer is required to keep at that place, or, as the case may be, any receipt (itinerant dealers), and to take copies of or extracts from any such book or receipt.

The term 'reasonable times' is not defined, and must therefore be given a normal, commonsense meaning. Any time during working hours would be reasonable unless particular circumstances (such as some internal operation within the yard which demanded the dealer's uninterrupted attention) indicated the contrary.

Entry to inspect can only be effected by force on the authority of a justice's warrant.

A justice's warrant may be issued under s 6(3) if a justice is satisfied by information on oath that admission is reasonably required in order to secure compliance with the provisions of the Act, or to ascertain whether those provisions are being complied with. The warrant authorises those having a right of entry to enter within one month, if necessary by force.

Whether or not a place is one to which a constable has a right of entry under s 6(1), a justice of the peace may, by s 6(3A), also issue a warrant authorising entry at any time within one month if satisfied by information on oath that there are reasonable grounds for believing that the place:

(a) is a scrap metal store where scrap metal paid for contrary to s 3A is or has been received or kept, or

(b) is a place to which admission is reasonably required in order to ascertain whether that section is being complied with.

A constable entering a place under such a warrant has a right (i) to inspect that place, (ii) to require production of, and to inspect, any scrap metal kept there, any book, receipt or copy which the dealer is required to keep there under SMDA 1964, and to take copies of the book, copy or receipt, and (iii) to require production of, and to inspect, any other record kept there relating to payment for scrap metal, and to take copies of the record.

It is an offence under s 6(5) for any person to obstruct the exercise of a right of entry or inspection under s 6, or to fail to produce a book or other document which a person has a right to inspect thereunder.

Power of courts to impose additional requirements

Where a person is convicted of carrying on business as a scrap metal dealer without being registered, or (being registered) he is convicted of failing to keep records or of any offence involving dishonesty, the court may make an order subjecting him to certain additional requirements in respect of his scrap metal store, namely that:

(a) no scrap metal shall be received between 6 pm and 8 am; and

(b) all scrap metal received at such place shall be kept in the form in which it is received for a period of not less than 72 hours.

An order may not exceed two years. Non-compliance with the requirements of an order is an offence under s 4(4). A further order may be made against someone convicted under s 4(4).

Miscellaneous offences

It is an offence, contrary to SMDA 1964, s 5(1), for a scrap metal dealer to acquire scrap metal from a person apparently under 16, whether that metal is offered on his own behalf or on behalf of someone else. The accused dealer has a defence if he proves that the person from whom he acquired the scrap metal was in fact 16 or over.

By s 5(2), a person who gives a false name or false address to a scrap metal dealer, on selling him scrap metal, commits an offence.

CHAPTER 23

Non-Fatal Offences Against the Person

The various non-fatal offences against the person are distinguishable in a number of ways, such as the degree of harm caused, the way in which it is inflicted and the status of the victim.

The first two offences to be discussed are the separate offences of common assault and battery, contrary to the Criminal Justice Act 1988, s 39. Rather confusingly, the word 'assault' is used in some statutes to refer to assault or battery.

COMMON ASSAULT AND BATTERY

Assault

A person is guilty of the separate offence of assault if he intentionally or recklessly causes another person to apprehend the immediate application to himself of unlawful force.

The actus reus which must be proved is some act by the defendant (D) which causes another person (V) to fear the immediate application of unlawful force against him.

Any act, even mere words, can suffice if it has the requisite result. An example would be where, during an argument in a pub, someone holding a beer glass loses his temper and shouts out to his antagonist, 'I'll glass you for that'. Although words alone can constitute an assault, threatening words are more likely to be prosecuted as an offence under the Public Order Act 1986, ss 4, 4A or 5.

The requirement that the immediate application of unlawful force must be apprehended means that it is an assault to aim a blow at V, whether or not that blow hits him, unless V is blind, or the blow is aimed from behind him or there is some other circumstance which means that he does not apprehend force. The requirement of 'immediacy' has been given a liberal interpretation by the courts. In one case, where a woman (V) had been caused psychiatric harm after repeated telephone calls and letters from D, the last two of which contained threats, the Court of Appeal held that the jury were entitled to find that the last letter had caused V fear of immediate force. It emphasised that D, who was known to V, lived near her and she thought that something could happen at any time. In a curious statement, the Court of Appeal, albeit accepting the requirement of the apprehension of immediate force, said that it was enough for the prosecution to prove fear of force 'at some time not excluding the immediate future', which seems to require a fear of the application of force at some time in the future, including the immediate future. Cases involving repeated conduct such as that just described are now better dealt with by bringing a prosecution for an offence under the Protection from Harassment Act 1997, described later in this chapter.

If V is put in fear of immediate force, it is irrelevant that D could not in fact carry out his threat; for example, pointing an unloaded gun or an imitation gun at someone who is unaware of its harmlessness can be an assault.

The force apprehended must be unlawful; see p 683.

The mens rea required for an assault is an intention to cause the other person to apprehend the immediate application of unlawful force or recklessness as to whether he might so apprehend. Recklessness requires that D was aware of the risk that his act might cause the apprehension of immediate unlawful force and that, in the circumstances known to D, it was unreasonable to take the risk.

Rowdies who throw bottles at passers-by on the opposite pavement clearly indicate an intention to cause them to fear being hit (ie immediate unlawful force) if they take deliberate aim; if they lob the bottles in the general direction of the passers-by, this may indicate recklessness as to whether any of the passers-by might be put in fear of immediate unlawful force.

Battery

A person is guilty of battery if he intentionally or recklessly applies unlawful force to another person. Most batteries are preceded by an assault, but this is not always so. If a person is clubbed down from behind there is certainly a battery but, if he was unaware that the blow was coming, there cannot be an assault, because there would have been no apprehension by him of the immediate application of unlawful force.

The actus reus of the offence of battery is some conduct on the part of D which results in unlawful force being applied to another (V). Technically, the slightest degree of force, even a mere touching, suffices, but a prosecution is most unlikely unless some harm has been caused. The force can be applied directly, as where D hits V with his fist or an instrument, or indirectly, as where D puts a tripwire across an alley over which V trips or D puts acid in a hand drier which is blown onto the hands of the next user. The fact that a battery requires an application of force, whether by a fist, an implement, a projectile or a liquid, means that those who cause harm in some other way than by applying force, for example by poisoning, do not commit a battery. Causing someone psychiatric harm by a threat does not involve a battery because it does not involve the application of force.

Normally, the force must be applied as a result of an act by D. However, liability can also be based on an omission (with the appropriate mens rea) to take such steps as are in D's power to counteract a dangerous situation created by him, even if inadvertently. This was held by a divisional court in a case where V, a police officer, approached D and told him that she intended to carry out a full body search. V asked D to turn out his pockets. D did so and produced some syringes without needles. V asked D if he had any needles on him and he replied 'No'. When V searched one of D's pockets her finger was pierced by a hypodermic needle, at which D smirked. Clearly, D had failed to counteract a danger, which his assurance had created, by not warning V not to put her hand in the pocket. As a result force (the needle) had been applied to V's finger and there could be a conviction for battery since D had the mens rea for that offence.

The force applied must be unlawful; see p 683.

The mens rea required for a battery is an intention to apply unlawful force to the other or recklessness as to whether unlawful force might be so applied. It follows that, if D punches V mistakenly believing that V is attacking him, there is no battery because, as we shall see, he will not have intended, nor been reckless as to, the application of *unlawful* force.

Clearly, it is not a battery to hit someone accidentally (since there is no intention to apply force to another), unless D can be proved to have realised the risk that his act, eg of swinging his arm, might possibly result in unlawful force being applied to another and unreasonably run that risk (in which case he would be proved to have been reckless as to the risk).

Procedural matters

Where the person has been merely 'put in fear' (ie common assault) D must be charged that he 'did assault' that person. If force has been applied (ie common battery), the charge should allege 'did assault by beating'.

Certificate of dismissal

If, on a charge of common assault or battery brought by or on behalf of the victim, the justices find that the charge is not proved, or that the assault or battery was justified or so trifling as not to merit punishment, they must make out a certificate of dismissal which (like a conviction for common assault or battery) has the effect of releasing the person concerned from all further proceedings in relation to that offence, whether criminal or civil (ie for damages). Clearly it is important that the victim realises this before a written charge is issued, or an information is laid.

AGGRAVATED ASSAULTS

There are a number of offences of aggravated assault. Among them are assault with intent to rob, and racially or religiously aggravated assault, discussed later. Like the aggravated assaults discussed below, they require an assault or battery which is accompanied either by a particular intention or by a special circumstance or consequence.

Assault occasioning actual bodily harm

It is an indictable (either way) offence, contrary to the Offences Against the Person Act 1861 (OAPA 1861), s 47, to assault any person, thereby occasioning him actual bodily harm. What is required is an assault or battery which has occasioned actual bodily harm. Actual bodily harm means any injury which is not so trivial as to be wholly insignificant. It must be more than transient but it need not be permanent. 'Bodily' refers to injury to any part of the body (including a person's hair) or an identifiable psychiatric injury brought about by psychological factors (eg post-traumatic stress disorder, or battered wife syndrome, or reactive depression) but not mere emotions such as fear, distress, or panic which are not themselves evidence of an identifiable clinical condition. Consequently, to cause someone psychiatric injury by a threat of 'immediate' force can amount to an offence under s 47. Where V claims to have suffered psychiatric illness or injury as a result of a non-physical assault, there must be psychiatric evidence as to whether the symptoms alleged by V amount to a psychiatric illness or injury. A judge in the Administrative Court has held that loss of consciousness falls within the meaning of 'harm', because it involves an injurious impairment to the victim's sensory functions. He added that, even though the loss of consciousness was momentary, the bodily harm was 'actual'.

There must be a direct connection between the 'assault' and the bodily harm occasioned and in most circumstances this will be apparent. If D punches V in the face and causes actual bodily harm, for example cuts or bruises, there has been a battery and the harm has been occasioned thereby. It may be, however, that D chases V who, fearful of the consequences of being caught, attempts to jump over a fence and thereby injures himself. In such circumstances there has been an assault, ie the putting of another in fear of immediate force, and that assault has led to the harm done. It is a question of sufficient connection between the two elements. To attempt to escape in that way is reasonable and there is therefore sufficient connection. Only if the action taken by the person assaulted, which led to the bodily harm, was unreasonable in the circumstances would there be an insufficient connection.

The mens rea required for this offence is the mens rea required for an assault or battery (as the case may be). It is not necessary to establish that D intended to cause some bodily harm or was reckless as to the risk of doing so.

Assault with intent to resist arrest

It is an indictable (either way) offence under OAPA 1861, s 38 for someone to assault (ie by an assault or by a battery) any person with intent to resist or prevent the lawful apprehension or detaining of himself, or any other person, for any offence. Section 38 deals with assaults on any person effecting an arrest, and therefore protects members of the public who are making 'citizens' arrests'. It does not apply, however, if the arrest is for a breach of the peace (which is not itself an offence) or in civil process; it is limited to an arrest for an offence.

An offence under s 38 is proved if it is established that the arrest was lawful; that D intended to resist it; and that he knew that the person whom he assaulted was seeking to arrest him. The issue of whether or not an offence which merited arrest had been committed is irrelevant as is an alleged belief on D's part that he had not committed the offence.

Assault on a constable in the execution of his duty

The Police Act 1996 (PA 1996), s 89(1) makes it an offence for a person to assault (by an assault or by a battery) a constable in the execution of his duty. While, of course, D must have the necessary mens rea for the assault or battery which he commits, it is irrelevant that he does not know that V was a constable acting in the execution of his duty. However, if D, ignorant that V is a constable, applies force to V who is exercising one of his powers, and that force would have been reasonable on the ground of self-defence if V had not been a constable, D does not commit an offence. He will not have intentionally or recklessly applied unlawful force (the mens rea for a battery) because of his ignorance of V's status.

The key point about this offence is that the constable must be acting in the execution of his duty. At first sight the offence seems to be quite straightforward as there is a tendency to assume that police officers are in the execution of their duty at all times while they are carrying out duties in the course of their routine work. This is not so, and it is important to remember that on every occasion upon which it is alleged that this offence has been committed the particular duty which was being executed at the time will be examined by the courts.

To be acting in the execution of his duty, a constable must be acting within the general scope of a duty imposed on him by law (such as his duties to protect life and property, to keep the peace, to prevent and investigate crimes and to prevent obstruction of the highway) and he must not be acting unlawfully at the time. Thus, even if a constable is acting within the general scope of one of his duties, he is not acting in the execution of his duty if he has no power to do the thing in question (and is, therefore, committing a trespass against a person or his property). In one case, a man kicked a constable, used foul language, and started to walk away. The constable laid a hand on the man's shoulder, not with the intention of arresting him but to detain him for further conversation. This was held to be an unlawful detention against the man's will and therefore the constable was held not to be acting in the execution of his duty in so acting. It would have been different if the constable had been exercising a power of arrest. Where police officers arrest a man and it is not practicable to give the reason for that arrest at the time, the arrest will be lawful and an assault upon the police officers will, at that time, be committed while they are in the execution of their duty. This is so even if the arrest is subsequently made unlawful by a failure to give the reason for arrest as soon as it is practicable to do so.

The test whether a police officer is acting in the execution of his duty is judged objectively. Thus, for example, an officer who makes an unlawful arrest is not acting in the execution of his duty even though he believes that he has the necessary reasonable grounds for making an arrest. Officers who arrive on the scene and assist a colleague in what turns out to be an unlawful arrest will also not be acting in the execution of their duty.

A constable who arrested a man who was wanted on a warrant for non-payment of a fine, without having the warrant in his possession, has been held not to be acting in the execution of his duty as what he did was unlawful. Police officers who arrest without warrant are not acting in the execution of their duty if a power does not exist in the circumstances. It is always essential for police officers to show that an arrest without warrant was necessary and this factor will have to be taken into account when considering whether an officer was acting in the execution of his duty.

A constable does not act outside the execution of his duty if what he does involves no more than a trivial touching; indeed there is probably not an assault or battery in any event (see p 684). In one case, for example, a constable, who touched a man on the shoulder to attract his attention because he wished to speak to him in relation to an offence, was held to have been acting in the execution of his duty. It would not have been so if he had tried to detain him where there was no power to arrest.

Assaults upon constables frequently occur in police stations and, once again, the nature of the duties being undertaken at the time must be examined before a charge under s 89(1) is preferred. A person who has not been arrested is entitled to leave a police station at any time unless he is detained under particular provisions which allow detention. An officer who attempts to prevent him from leaving a police station is not acting in the execution of his duty. In one case, two policewomen, in searching a prisoner in accordance with their interpretation of the chief constable's instructions, removed her brassiere and were assaulted by the prisoner. It was held that, regardless of those instructions, they were not acting in the execution of their duty if they had not personally considered whether such a search was necessary for a lawful purpose, or whether the removal of that garment was necessary for that particular person's protection. This is an interesting decision which clearly places responsibility for lawful search upon the officer conducting it.

Police officers are frequently asked to assist with the expulsion of persons from premises, where the owner of the premises considers them to be intruders or for some other reason they are unwelcome. An officer may lawfully assist the owner of property in these circumstances, but he is not bound to do so. Unless there are particular circumstances which demand such expulsion, for example, the removal of violent, quarrelsome, disorderly persons from various premises as required by law (see, eg, p 598), or where a breach of the peace is taking place or apprehended, it is unlikely that he will be considered to have been acting in the execution of his duty.

Most assaults upon police officers still occur when they are dealing with disorderly persons in the street. The onerous nature of these duties is very much appreciated, as is the immediate pressure placed upon the officer and the suddenness with which assaults occur. However, whether or not the actions of the officer were in the execution of his duty will always be considered in the calm of the courtroom!

On occasions constables are given the authority to enter premises, and if they enter under such an authority they are acting in the execution of their duty. For example, the common law authorises a constable to enter premises to deal with a breach or reasonably apprehended breach of the peace (and it also authorises him to remain for this purpose if he is already on the premises); such a constable is acting in the execution of his duty. Response to a burglar alarm gives police an implied authority to enter premises for a reasonable time for the purpose of a search, but there is no legal right to enter premises found insecure at night. Where a constable is invited to enter premises by a member of the family and is later told to leave by the occupier, and he is assaulted by the occupier while he is immediately complying with that request, it is an assault upon him in the execution of his duty. On the other hand, he would no longer be in the execution of his duty if he did not comply with the request within a reasonable time because he would become a trespasser; if he was assaulted after the expiry of such a time an offence under s 89(1) would not be committed.

It has been held in the Administrative Court that, where a constable has acted unlawfully, eg by making an unlawful stop, it does not follow that the constable's subsequent exercise of his powers is also unlawful (and therefore outside the execution of the constable's duty).

Obstructing or resisting a constable in the execution of his duty

It is an offence under PA 1996, s 89(2) for a person to resist or wilfully obstruct a constable in the execution of his duty, or a person assisting him.

To '*obstruct*' is to do any conduct which prevents or makes it more difficult for a constable to carry out his duty, and in this sense those who give warning of police speed checks may obstruct the constables in the execution of their duty. It has been held that someone who warns motorists of a police speed check is only guilty of obstructing a constable in the execution of his duty if the prosecution proves that the motorists warned were in fact speeding or were likely to be speeding at that location. Someone who deliberately drinks alcohol after an accident to negate the breath-testing procedure is also guilty of this offence.

The obstruction must be 'wilful', which in this context means that:

(1) D's conduct which has resulted in the obstruction must have been deliberate and intended by him to bring about a state of affairs which, in fact, prevented or made it more difficult for the constable to carry out his duty, whether or not D realised that that state of affairs would have that effect.

(2) Also, D must have had no lawful excuse. Police officers often experience difficulty in obtaining names and addresses from offenders but a refusal to give such information will not amount to a wilful obstruction unless that person has a duty to give that information, because otherwise he will have a lawful excuse for his refusal. Nor, for the same reason, is it a wilful obstruction to advise someone not to answer police questions which he is not obliged to answer, even if the advice is given in an

abusive way. Much of the traffic legislation imposes a duty to give particular types of information, but there is no such requirement in relation to most offences. Just as in the case of a failure to provide information, so in the case of other failures to assist the police (eg by failing to accord entry to a constable), there is only a wilful obstruction if the constable has the right to require the assistance in question, so that D is under a legal duty to provide it. An example would be where a constable has a statutory right of entry. A refusal to admit the constable in breach of the duty to admit him would be a wilful obstruction.

It has been held that a defendant who believed that the person obstructed was not a constable could not be convicted of the present offence.

Like obstruction, *resistance* does not require an assault or battery. Probably, any resistance is also an obstruction, but resistance is a more appropriate word in certain cases (such as where a person arrested by a constable tears himself away).

What was said above about 'acting in the execution of his duty' is equally applicable to the offences of obstruction and resistance. Thus, for example, where a person seeks to prevent an arrest which, in the circumstances, is not a lawful arrest, he is not guilty of a wilful obstruction of a police officer acting in the execution of his duty since the officer will not be acting *in the execution of his duty*.

Other points

By PA 1996, s 89(3) the offences under s 89 may also be committed against constables of Scottish forces or the Police Service of Northern Ireland who are executing warrants or acting in England and Wales by virtue of any enactment. Similar amendments have been made to the laws of those countries to apply equivalent offences to acts against police officers of England and Wales so acting in those countries. Section 89 also applies to a constable of the British Transport Police Force in the same way as it applies to other constables in England and Wales (Railways and Transport Safety Act 2003, s 68). A foreign police or customs officer carrying out surveillance in England and Wales under the Regulation of Investigatory Powers Act 2000, s 76A is treated as if he were acting as a constable in the execution of his duty (Crime (International Co-operation) Act 2003, s 84).

Under s 89(1) and (2) it is also an offence to assault, obstruct, or resist a person assisting a constable in the execution of his duty. The reference in s 89 to 'a person assisting a constable in the execution of his duty' includes reference to any person who is neither a constable nor in the company of a constable but who is a member of a joint investigation team (ie an investigation team established under an EU framework directive or a specified treaty) led by a member of a police force.

The Police Reform Act 2002, s 46 creates similar offences in relation to assaults on, or the obstruction of, a designated or accredited person acting in the execution of his duty, or someone assisting such a person: see p 287.

OFFENCES INVOLVING WOUNDING OR GRIEVOUS BODILY HARM

Malicious wounding or infliction of grievous bodily harm

OAPA 1861, s 20 provides two indictable (either way) offences: malicious wounding and malicious infliction of grievous bodily harm. Section 20 provides that a person who unlawfully and maliciously wounds or inflicts any grievous bodily harm on any other person, either with or without any weapon or instrument, is guilty of an offence.

Both offences have two elements in common: 'unlawfully' and 'maliciously'. The difference between them relates to their actus reus: 'wounding' and 'infliction of grievous bodily harm', and these terms will be discussed first.

Wounding or infliction of grievous bodily harm

The term 'wound' indicates a breaking of the continuity of both layers of the skin. Consequently, all injuries involving broken bones are excluded unless the bone pierces the skin. However, such injuries will normally amount to grievous bodily harm.

'Grievous bodily harm' means really serious harm, but 'really serious' appears to mean no more than 'actually serious'; 'bodily harm' can include psychiatric injury or loss of consciousness but, of course, such injury must be serious in order to be grievous. It is not necessary that the nature of the harm should be either permanent or dangerous.

A wound can be caused or grievous bodily harm can be 'inflicted' even though it does not result from the application of force; it is enough, instead, that it directly results from something done by D, as where D infects V with the HIV virus or some other serious disease (which D conceals from V) by having intercourse with V. A further example would be where D shouts through the locked door of a third-floor flat, threatening to kick it down and injure its occupant, and the terrified occupant jumps out of a window and breaks a leg when he hits the ground. In these situations convictions for unlawfully and maliciously inflicting grievous bodily harm have been upheld on appeal.

Unlawfully

This means 'without lawful justification' and is merely intended to except from the offence, in certain circumstances, acts done with a justification rendering the harm lawful, for example harm lawfully caused in self-defence.

Maliciously

The mens rea of an offence under OAPA 1861, s 20 is that D should have wounded or inflicted grievous bodily harm 'maliciously'. This does not mean that D must have acted out of spite or ill-will. Instead, what is required is that D must have intended his act to cause some unlawful harm to another, or been reckless as to whether some unlawful harm might result from his act (and this means that D must have realised the risk that some unlawful harm might result but unreasonably (on the facts known to him) persisted in taking that risk). It must be emphasised that it is not necessary that D should have intended or foreseen harm of the gravity described in s 20, ie a wound or really serious harm; foresight that some harm, albeit of a minor character, might result, is enough.

Because D must have been aware that his act might cause some *unlawful* bodily harm, a defendant who mistakenly believes that he is acting in self-defence or has some other legal justification is not guilty under s 20 if he wounds or inflicts grievous bodily harm on someone.

The fact that recklessness as to the risk of causing some unlawful bodily harm to another suffices for s 20 means that if D, knowing that he has the HIV virus or some other serious sexually transmitted disease, and therefore aware of the risk of infecting V, has intercourse with V who consents to the intercourse in ignorance of D's disease, as D knows, D will be guilty of the present offence if V becomes infected with the disease and suffers grievous bodily harm in consequence.

Wounding or causing grievous bodily harm with intent to do grievous bodily harm or to resist or prevent arrest

OAPA 1861, s 18 provides that a person who unlawfully and maliciously by any means whatsoever wounds or causes grievous bodily harm to any person with intent to do grievous bodily harm to any person, or with intent to resist or prevent the lawful apprehension or detainer of any person, is guilty of an offence triable only on indictment.

An offence under s 18 is a very serious one; the nature of the maximum punishment (life imprisonment) is a factor to bear in mind when deciding which of the various non-fatal offences against the person to charge.

OAPA 1861, s 18 provides two offences: wounding with intent to do grievous bodily harm or with intent to resist the lawful apprehension or detaining of any person, and causing grievous bodily harm with one of these intents.

What was said in relation to OAPA 1861, s 20 in relation to the words 'unlawfully', 'wound', and 'grievous bodily harm' is equally applicable to OAPA 1861, s 18. However, s 18 specifies that grievous bodily harm must be 'caused' (as opposed to 'inflicted'). This difference in terminology between s 18 and s 20 raises the question of whether there is a difference of substance. Grievous bodily harm can be 'caused' by a deliberate and culpable omission to act; but opinions differ as to whether such harm can be 'inflicted' by a deliberate and culpable omission to act.

Mens rea

If D is charged with wounding with intent to do grievous bodily harm, or with causing grievous bodily harm with such intent, the word 'maliciously', the meaning of which was explained above, is rendered redundant by the stricter requirement of an intent to do grievous bodily harm. The grievous bodily harm intended need not be grievous bodily harm to the particular victim. D may be convicted of wounding V with intent, even though D thought that V was X, or even though D fired at X and hit V by accident. If a person fires a gun into a group of people without taking particular aim, but intending to harm someone, he may be charged with a s 18 offence against the person whom he hits.

The basic distinction between wounding or causing grievous bodily harm with intent to do grievous bodily harm and attempted murder is that, in the former offences, only an intent unlawfully to do grievous bodily harm is required, while the latter requires an intent unlawfully to kill.

Where D is charged with wounding with intent to resist or prevent the lawful apprehension or detaining of any person (whether himself or another), or with causing grievous bodily harm with such intent, 'maliciously' is relevant. It must be proved that D intended his conduct to cause *some* unlawful harm to another (or was reckless as to this occurring), ie that he was 'malicious', *and* that he intended to resist or prevent the lawful apprehension or detaining of himself or another. The lawful arrest which D intends to resist or prevent need not be for an offence; it could be for a breach of the peace or in civil process.

Differences between Offences Against the Person Act 1861, s 18 and s 20

It is interesting to consider the essential differences between offences described in OAPA 1861, ss 18 and 20. If, during an argument, D strikes a person with a stick, causing a cut to his head which requires stitches, there has certainly been a wound which was unlawful, in that it could not legally be excused. Maliciousness was apparent, as the act indicated a decision on D's part to do some unlawful bodily harm. All the essential points required under s 20 to be proved are therefore capable of proof. If we are to consider whether an offence contrary to s 18 is disclosed, we must ask ourselves if it can be proved that D intended to cause unlawful grievous bodily harm when the blow was struck. The surrounding circumstances will help; any words said by D at the time, the ferocity of the attack, and the nature of the weapon used. If the stick used was light in weight and one blow was struck, this would not support the allegation that D intended to cause grievous bodily harm. If the stick was heavy and metal tipped, the blow struck was severe, and it could be shown that D shouted an intention to do serious harm to the person injured, then an intention to cause such harm could be more easily established.

UNLAWFUL FORCE OR HARM

It is an integral part of the offences referred to above that the requisite force (apprehended or applied) or harm (as the case may be) must be unlawful. In this context, the essential point is that, if the victim has given a valid consent to the force or harm, or if D has acted in self-defence, prevention of crime or the like, it is lawful.

Consent

Consent can validly be given to an act which does not cause actual bodily harm. 'Actual bodily harm' means any injury which is not so trivial as to be wholly insignificant. See, further, p 676.

Consent cannot validly be given if an act causes actual bodily harm which D intended or foresaw *unless the case falls within one of a number of recognised exceptions or a new exception is recognised on public interest grounds.* The result of all this is that if a person intentionally causes another actual bodily harm or the actual bodily harm caused was foreseen, it is generally irrelevant whether or not the latter has consented, since, generally, he cannot give a valid consent in such a case. Thus, assuming the other elements of the offence are proved, there can generally be a conviction for an assault occasioning actual bodily harm or some other offence involving harm to the person in such a case, despite the victim's apparent consent. For example, men who fight each other to 'settle a score' and cause actual bodily harm commit an assault occasioning actual bodily harm when they fight each other, despite their consent to such harm since actual bodily harm is clearly intended or foreseen. For the same reason, willing and enthusiastic participants in harmful sado-masochistic acts of violence for the sexual pleasure engendered in the giving and receiving of pain can be convicted of an assault occasioning actual bodily harm (or a more serious non-fatal offence).

The recognised exceptions

A person can give a valid consent to 'any actual bodily harm' caused by reasonable surgical operations or procedures; if he could not, the surgeon would commit a battery or an assault occasioning actual bodily harm or some more serious offence against the person.

It has been held that a valid consent can be given to ear piercing, to being tattooed or, even, to being branded with one's spouse's initials, since the bodily harm caused by these activities is not contrary to public policy.

Those who agree to take part in a lawful sport consent to the rules of that sport and, if those rules allow forms of physical contact, they validly consent to the risk of actual bodily harm which is likely to result from physical contact which is within the rules or is a minor infringement of them. For example, a blow struck in a boxing match under the Queensberry Rules (in which boxers wear approved gloves) is not a battery or any other offence, regardless of the injury caused, unless the blow is struck in circumstances far outside the rules (eg hitting an opponent when he is lying unconscious on the floor, or hitting an opponent with a glove in which is concealed a heavy object). Likewise, in soccer and rugby, the participants consent to the risk of actual bodily harm resulting from something within the rules of the game or not too far removed from them, but not to the risk of such harm resulting from something which is far outside the rules, such as a head-butt or deliberately kicking a player who is on the ground. The fact that the play is within the rules of the game gives a firm indication that what has happened is not criminal. In judging whether conduct is criminal or not, it must be remembered that, in highly competitive sports, conduct outside the rules can be expected to occur in the heat of the moment, and even if the conduct justifies a sending-off, it still may not reach the threshold level required for it to be criminal. That level is an objective one and does not depend upon the views of individual players. The type of the sport, the level at which it is played, the nature of the act, the degree of force used, the extent of the risk of injury and the state of mind of the defendant are all likely to be relevant in determining whether the defendant's actions go beyond the threshold.

Not all sports are lawful. For example, a prize-fight, where gloves are not worn and the fight continues until one of the participants can no longer continue, is an unlawful sport. Thus, the participants cannot give a valid consent to the actual bodily harm intended or foreseen, with the result that the force which they apply to each other is always unlawful.

Other points on consent

Sometimes when a person has consented to the application of force, his consent is invalid, even though actual bodily harm is not caused by the force. This occurs where he is so young or mentally impaired as not to be able to make a rational decision whether or not to consent, or where his apparent consent has been procured by duress or has been given under a mistake as to the identity of the other party or as to the nature of the act or its purpose.

When considering a claim of consent one must consider what it is that is supposed to have been consented to. A person does not consent to something if he does not give an 'informed consent' to it. Suppose that someone consents to have intercourse with an AIDS sufferer in ignorance of that person's disease. While he will have consented to the intercourse (bodily contact) involved, this does not mean that he will have consented to run the risk of becoming diseased with the HIV virus (grievous bodily harm). In such a case, the consent to contact means that there will not be a battery but there can be liability for a more serious offence (see pp 680–3) based on the infliction or causing of grievous bodily harm.

Assuming it is valid, a consent need not be express; it can be implied from the circumstances. Everyday living demands a certain amount of physical contact. People are often touched in order to attract their attention, and there are constant collisions in shopping precincts, and the consent of people to such things can normally be implied. It is, of course, different if the person touched has indicated that he does not want to be touched. If V tells D, who has been pestering him, to go away, V clearly does not impliedly consent to D touching him soon after in order to attract his attention. Of course, there is a limit to what a person impliedly consents to. There is certainly no consent to a violent blow, allegedly to attract attention, perhaps as a person walked away after an argument. Similarly, one does not impliedly consent to collisions in a shopping precinct caused by hooligans charging about.

Another way of expressing cases based on implied consent is that they fall within a general exception embracing all physical contact which is generally acceptable in the ordinary conduct of daily life.

Normally, the consent of sports players referred to above is implied from their participation in the game, rather than being expressly given.

Other factors which render force lawful

Disciplinary use of force and corporal punishment

Subject to the limitations below, parents and other people in loco parentis are entitled as a disciplinary measure to apply a reasonable degree of force to their children or charges old enough to understand its purpose. In relation to the following offences:

(a) wounding or causing grievous bodily harm with intent, or unlawful wounding or infliction of grievous bodily harm;
(b) assault occasioning actual bodily harm; or
(c) cruelty to a person under 16,

battery of a child cannot be justified on the ground that it constituted reasonable punishment.

Teachers are no longer entitled by virtue of their position as such to apply reasonable corporal punishment as a disciplinary measure. However, the prohibition on corporal punishment by teachers does not affect the power of members of school staff to use reasonable force to restrain a pupil from:

(a) committing an offence or continuing to do so;
(b) causing or continuing to cause personal injury or damage to property; or
(c) behaving or continuing to behave in a way prejudicial to good order and discipline at school or among the pupils.

Prevention of crime or effecting arrest

The Criminal Law Act 1967, s 3 provides that it is lawful to use such force as is reasonable in the circumstances in the prevention of crime (ie a crime under the law of England and Wales) or in effecting (or assisting in) the lawful arrest of offenders, suspected offenders, or persons unlawfully at large. The effecting of an arrest will almost always involve some form of restraint, even if it is only symbolic, and this would be a battery but for the present defence. It must be emphasised that, if the force used to prevent a crime or to make an arrest is unreasonable in the circumstances, it will be unlawful and the person using it will not have a defence to a charge of battery or of another offence against the person. Like anyone else, a police officer has no defence, even though he uses reasonable force, if he is acting in furtherance of an unlawful arrest. Nor does he have a defence if he uses force to restrain someone whom he does not intend or purport to arrest, even though an arrest would have been justified.

Self-defence and defence of property or of another

Self-defence and the defence of property or of another are common law defences. They are limited to defence against an actual or imminent unlawful (ie criminal or tortious) act. However, a person who acts in defence of himself or another or of property is almost invariably acting in the prevention of crime, in which case he also has the defence under the Criminal Law Act 1967, s 3. For practical purposes, the terms of both the common law and the statutory defences are identical in their requirements.

Use of force against an innocent person

The Court of Appeal has held that self-defence and the defence under the Criminal Law Act 1967, s 3 extends to the use of force against an innocent third party where such force is used to prevent a crime being committed by someone else. Two examples of cases where the defence is capable of arising include a police constable bundling a man out of the way to get to another man who is about to detonate an explosive device, and where a person knocks car keys out of the hands of a third party to prevent the keys being given to a drunk person who is attempting to drive.

Applicable principles

The Criminal Justice and Immigration Act 2008, s 76 (as prospectively amended by the Legal Aid, Sentencing and Punishment of Offenders Act 2012, s 148), which applies to the common law defences of self-defence or defence of another (or, from a day to be appointed, defence of property) and the defences under the Criminal Law Act 1967, s 3(1) of the use of force in the prevention of crime or making of a lawful arrest, is intended to clarify the operation of those defences. It seeks to do so by putting into statutory form principles established by the case law.

Section 76 provides that the question whether the degree of force used by D was reasonable in the circumstances is to be decided by reference to the circumstances as D believed them to be, and that in connection with deciding that question:

(a) if D claims to have held a particular belief as regards the existence of any circumstances:
  (i) the reasonableness or otherwise of that belief is relevant to the question whether he genuinely held it, but
  (ii) if it is determined that D did genuinely hold it, he is entitled to rely on it, whether or not it was mistaken or (if it was mistaken) the mistake was a reasonable one to have made;
  but (ii) does not enable D to rely on any mistaken belief attributable to intoxication that was voluntarily induced;

(b) the degree of force used by D is not to be regarded as having been reasonable in the circumstances as D believed them to be if it was disproportionate in those circumstances;

(c) as from a day to be appointed, in deciding whether the degree of force used by D was reasonable in the circumstances, a possibility that D could have retreated is to be considered (so far as relevant) as a factor to be taken into account, rather than as giving rise to a duty to retreat;

(d) in deciding whether the degree of force used by D was reasonable in the circumstances, the following considerations are to be taken into account (so far as relevant in the circumstances of the case):
  (i) that a person acting for the purpose of crime prevention, effecting a lawful arrest, self-defence or defence of another (or, from a day to be appointed, defence of property) ('a legitimate purpose') may not be able to weigh to a nicety the exact measure of any necessary action, and

(ii) that evidence of a person's having only done what the person honestly and instinctively thought was necessary for a legitimate purpose constitutes strong evidence that only reasonable action was taken by that person for that purpose.

The law on defence of property is currently governed by common law rules essentially the same as set out above.

For the avoidance of doubt, it must be stated that the mere fact that a person who has used force against another was provoked to lose self-control (as opposed to acting in self-defence, etc) is no defence.

RACIALLY OR RELIGIOUSLY AGGRAVATED NON-FATAL OFFENCES AGAINST THE PERSON

The Crime and Disorder Act 1998 (CDA 1998), s 29 provides that a person is guilty of an indictable (either way) offence under this section if he commits:

(a) an offence under OAPA 1861, s 20;
(b) an offence under OAPA 1861, s 47;
(c) common assault (or battery),

which is racially or religiously aggravated for the purposes of this section.

On a charge of an offence under CDA 1998, s 29, the prosecution must prove that D has committed one of the relevant specified basic offences and that it (the basic offence) was racially or religiously aggravated.

Racially or religiously aggravated

By CDA 1998, s 28, any of the specified basic offences is racially or religiously aggravated if:

(a) at the time of committing the offence, or immediately before or after doing so, the offender demonstrates towards the victim of the offence hostility based on the victim's membership (or presumed membership) of a racial or religious group (s 28(1)(a)); or
(b) the offence is motivated (wholly or partly) by hostility towards members of a racial or religious group based on their membership of that group (s 28(1)(b)).

In (a), 'membership', in relation to a racial or religious group, includes association with members of that group; 'presumed' means presumed by the offender.

Religious group

'Religious group' means a group of persons defined by reference to religious belief or lack of religious belief. Muslims and Rastafarians are religious groups, for instance.

Racial group

'Racial group' means a group of persons defined by reference to race, colour, nationality (including citizenship) or ethnic or national origins. These words are given a broad, non-technical interpretation. Two points may be made about them:

(1) A group of people will be a racial group defined by reference to race if, in ordinary speech, those people would be regarded as belonging to a named race. In one case, for example, it was held by a divisional court that 'African' described a racial group

defined by reference to race because in ordinary language 'African' denotes a limited group of people regarded as common stock and as one of the major divisions of humankind having distinct physical features in common; it 'denotes a person characteristic of the blacks in Africa'. This was said to be so despite the fact that, strictly, 'African' is capable of covering Egyptians and white South Africans who would not fit the 'common stock' definition of 'Africans'. This broad, non-technical approach has been taken further where the victims of the words 'bloody foreigners' were Spanish. The House of Lords considered that these words were capable of satisfying the requirements of s 28(1)(a). It held that people who are not of British origin constitute a racial group for the purposes of the definition of 'racial group'. Thus, a racial group can be defined exclusively by reference to what its members are not in terms of race, colour, nationality or ethnic or national origins, eg non-British or non-white, as well as inclusively by reference to what they are in such terms, eg Spanish or black.

(2) Although a cultural or religious group is not per se defined by reference to its ethnic origins, 'ethnic' is used in a sense wider than the strictly racial or biological. A Law Lord said in a widely quoted passage that, for a group to constitute an ethnic group, it must regard itself, and be regarded by others, as a distinct community by virtue of certain characteristics, some essential and others not (although one or more of them will commonly be found and will help to distinguish the group from the surrounding community).

The Law Lord said that conditions which were essential are:

(a)   a long shared history, of which the group is conscious as distinguishing it from other groups, and the memory of which keeps it alive, and

(b)   a cultural tradition of its own, including family and social customs and manners, often but not necessarily associated with religious observance.

The relevant non-essential conditions were:

(c)   either a common geographical origin, or descent from a small number of common ancestors,

(d)   a common language,

(e)   a common literature peculiar to the group,

(f)   a common religion different from that of the neighbouring groups or from the general community surrounding it, and

(g)   being a minority or being an oppressed or a dominant group within a larger community.

In the light of this statement, it is clear that Jews are a group defined by reference to their ethnic origins, and so are the Sikhs (as well as being a religious group) and Romany gypsies. On the other hand, tinkers or travellers are not.

Section 28(1)(a)

Because s 28(1)(a) does not require D's conduct to be motivated by racial or religious hatred, but simply requires the demonstration of such hatred (as defined), it is possible for D to fall within s 28(1)(a) even though he is of the same colour, etc as the victim of his conduct. This was held by a divisional court in a case where it upheld the conviction of D whose conduct had demonstrated hostility based on the victim's membership of a racial group which was the same as D's.

For the test under s 28(1)(a) to be satisfied, D must have formed the view that the victim was a member of a racial group (or religious group, as the case may be) and D must have done or said something which demonstrated hostility towards the victim

(V) based on that membership. Words used need not expressly identify the racial or religious group to which the victim belongs. This was held by the Court of Appeal in a case where V was Indian and brown-skinned. He was called an 'immigrant doctor' by D immediately before D assaulted him. The Court of Appeal held that it was open to the jury to conclude that D had identified V as falling within the racial groups 'Indian' and 'brown-skinned' and that the use of 'immigrant' demonstrated hostility based on the victim's membership of such groups.

Section 28(1)(a) does not require the hostility demonstrated to be based only on V's membership of a racial or religious group, or even principally on it. Thus, in one reported divisional court case, the fact that the hostility demonstrated was based more on a dispute over food at a kebab shop rather than racial hostility did not prevent racial aggravation being proved under s 28(1)(a). However, the more incidental the words or other conduct with a racial or religious content, the more difficult it will be to prove that D has demonstrated racial or religious hostility. In this context it must be emphasised that it is not enough simply to refer, for example, to V's race or religion; D must be proved to have demonstrated 'hostility' based on V's membership, or presumed membership of a racial or religious group. Where a man of Asian origin attacked an Asian caretaker at a community centre and called him a 'white man's arse licker' and a 'brown Englishman' it was held that what he said was not in any material sense based upon the caretaker's membership of the Asian race but upon hostility to the caretaker's conduct on that night. The phrases used did not, therefore, make the assault into a racially aggravated one. The Court of Appeal said that an offence of racially aggravated common assault might be made out if a white man was to assault another white man and make such a remark as 'nigger lover' when noting that man's association with a group of black persons.

The word 'immediately' in s 28(1)(a) qualifies 'after' as well as 'before'; s 28(1)(a) strikes at words uttered or acts done in the immediate context of the basic substantive offence. Thus, a divisional court held that a racially aggravated offence was not made out where D demonstrated racial hostility to the victim only 20 minutes after committing the basic offence, while being questioned by the police.

Section 28(1)(b)

Section 28(1)(b) requires that the offence is motivated (wholly or partly) by hostility towards members of a racial or religious group based on their membership of that group. Section 28(1)(b) does not require D to be motivated by racial or religious hostility towards the victim of the offence but 'merely' by hostility 'towards members of a racial or religious group'. Hostility towards one member of a racial or religious group based on his membership of that group is sufficient to qualify so long as it forms part of the motivation for the conduct. Normally the victim will be a member of that group (and thus included within the ambit of that hostility) or at least be associated with it but this is not a requirement of s 28(1)(b). For example, a person who, motivated by hostility towards members of the Jewish religious community, attacked a bricklayer whom he knew was not Jewish who was building a synagogue would fall foul of s 28(1)(b).

Although s 28(1)(a) requires proof of what D did at the time of committing the offence, s 28(1)(b) can be established by evidence relating to what D might have said or done on other occasions (since such evidence may be relevant to D's motivation at the time of the offence).

PROTECTION FROM HARASSMENT ACT 1997

Prohibitions of harassment

The Protection from Harassment Act 1997 (PHA 1997) sets out two prohibitions of harassment. The first, contained in s 1(1), prohibits a person from pursuing a course of conduct:

(a) which amounts to harassment of another person; and
(b) which he knows or ought to know amounts to harassment of the other person.

The second prohibition of harassment, contained in PHA 1997, s 1(1A) prohibits a person from pursuing a course of conduct:

(a) which involves harassment of two or more persons; and
(b) which he knows or ought to know involves harassment of those persons; and
(c) by which he intends to persuade any person (whether or not one of those mentioned above),
    (i)   not to do something that he is entitled or required to do, or
    (ii) to do something that he is not under any obligation to do.

Section 1(1A) was added to protect company employees from harassment by animal rights groups. Section 1(1) does not protect such employees if they are only harassed on one occasion.

Course of conduct

In the case of conduct relating to a single person (see PHA 1997, s 1(1)), a 'course of conduct' must involve conduct on at least two occasions in relation to that person. In the case of conduct in relation to two or more persons (see s 1(1A)), a 'course of conduct' must involve conduct on at least one occasion in relation to each of those persons. Publishing a series of articles in a newspaper can constitute a course of conduct.

The term 'conduct' in PHA 1997 includes speech. By s 7(3A), a person's (X's) conduct on any occasion which is aided, abetted, counselled, or procured by another (Y) is taken:

(a) also to be on that occasion the conduct of Y; and
(b) to be conduct in relation to which Y's knowledge and purpose (and what Y ought to have known) are the same as they were in relation to what was contemplated or reasonably foreseeable at the time of the aiding, abetting, etc.

This means in relation to the wording in s 1(1) that there can be a breach of the prohibition on harassment by Y if, for example, on one occasion the harassing conduct is by X aided and abetted by Y and on the second occasion is by Y himself, provided that the two pieces of conduct can be regarded as a 'course' and that part (b) of s 7(3A) is satisfied. The same principle will apply to conduct aimed at different company employees so far as s 1(1A) is concerned.

By s 1(2), for the purposes of ss 1 and 2A (see p 692) the person whose course of conduct is in question ought to know that his conduct amounts to or involves harassment of another if a reasonable person in possession of the same information would think the course of conduct amounted to or involved harassment of the other. The reasonable person in this context is not imbued with any mental illness or other characteristic which the defendant has.

Although, a company cannot be harassed for the purposes of PHA 1997, it can be liable for harassment.

Harassment

By s 7(2), 'harassment' in PHA 1997 includes alarming another person or causing that person distress. The Court of Appeal has held that s 7(2) does not provide a comprehensive definition of harassment. 'To harass' means 'to torment by subjecting to constant interference or intimidation'. The Court of Appeal has held that, in addition to the statutory requirement, the conduct must be unacceptable to a degree that would sustain criminal liability and also must be oppressive; it must be targeted at an individual, and it must be calculated to produce alarm or distress.

A course of conduct which begins with a legitimate inquiry may become harassment by reason of the persistence and manner in which it is pursued. Thus, where D had telephoned to find out why his partner had not got a job, but did not get an explanation, and then telephoned the original recipient 95 times in an hour and a half, setting his telephone to automatic re-dial and saying at one point that he was 'set for the night', a divisional court held that that conduct was capable of amounting to harassment for the purposes of PHA 1997.

While s 1 was fashioned with 'stalkers' in mind (in this respect note s 2A on p 692), its terms are wide enough to embrace situations in which harassment is caused to neighbours or to persons living in a particular area in which unruly juveniles tend to congregate. Section 1 can also cover the activities of political protesters and members of the 'paparazzi', and more mundane things like sending a series of letters demanding payment of a debt, if the other elements are established.

Exceptions

By PHA 1997, s 1(3), the prohibitions of harassment in s 1(1) and (1A) do not apply to a course of conduct if the person who pursued it shows that it was pursued for the purpose of preventing or detecting crime (it has been held that this must be his sole purpose); or that it was pursued under any enactment or rule of law or to comply with a condition or requirement lawfully imposed; or that, in the particular circumstances, the pursuit of the course of conduct was reasonable. It has been stated in a divisional court that whether conduct was reasonable involves balancing the interests of the victim against the purpose and nature of the course of conduct pursued, including the right to peaceful protest.

Offence of harassment

PHA 1997, s 2(1) makes it an offence to break either of the prohibitions of harassment.

Civil remedy

PHA 1997, s 3 makes provision for an actual or apprehended breach of the prohibition of harassment under s 1(1) to be the subject of a civil claim by the victim. Damages may be awarded for (among other things) any anxiety caused by the harassment and any financial loss resulting from the harassment. An employer can be liable in damages for a breach of the prohibition of harassment by an employee. The High Court or a county court may grant an injunction for the purpose of restraining a defendant from pursuing any course of conduct which amounts to harassment.

Section 3A permits an injunction to be sought where there is an actual or apprehended breach of s 1(1A). It permits a person who is or might be the victim of the course of conduct in question, or anyone who is or might be a person falling within s 1(1A)(c), to apply to the High Court or a county court for an injunction to forbid such conduct.

Victims should be made aware of these possibilities. Breach of an injunction under s 3 or s 3A is an indictable (either way) offence.

Offence of stalking

PHA 1997, s 2A, added by the Protection of Freedoms Act 2012 (PFA 2012), s 111, provides that a person is guilty of an offence if (a) he pursues a course of conduct *in breach of the prohibition of harassment in PHA 1997, s 1(1)*, and (b) the course of conduct amounts to stalking (PHA 1997, s 2A(1)). For the purposes of (b), a person's course of conduct amounts to stalking of another person if:

(a) it amounts to harassment (p 691) of that person,
(b) the acts or omissions involved are ones associated with stalking, and
(c) the person whose course of conduct it is knows or ought to know that the course of conduct amounts to harassment of the other person (PHA 1997, s 2A(2): see p 690).

Section 2A has been enacted as a more appropriate offence than that under s 2 to deal with stalkers. However, the offence of stalking may alternatively be dealt with by a prosecution under PHA 1997, s 2.

PHA 1997, s 2A(3) gives the following examples of acts or omissions which, in particular circumstances, are ones associated with stalking:

(a) following a person,
(b) contacting, or attempting to contact, a person by any means,
(c) publishing any statement or other material
     (i)   relating or purporting to relate to a person, or
     (ii) purporting to originate from a person,
(d) monitoring the use by a person of the internet, email or any other form of electronic communication,
(e) loitering in any place (whether public or private),
(f) interfering with any property in the possession of a person,
(g) watching or spying on a person.

Power of entry in relation to offence of stalking

PHA 1997, s 2B, added by the PFA 2012, s 112, provides that a justice of the peace may, on an application by a constable, issue a warrant authorising a constable to enter and search premises (as defined on p 64) if the justice of the peace is satisfied that there are reasonable grounds for believing that:

(a) an offence under s 2A has been, or is being, committed,
(b) there is material on the premises which is likely to be of substantial value (whether by itself or together with other material) to the investigation of the offence,
(c) the material is likely to be admissible in evidence at a trial for the offence, and does not consist of, or include, items subject to legal privilege, excluded material, or special procedure material (as defined on p 71), and
(d) either entry to the premises will not be granted unless a warrant is produced, or the purpose of a search may be frustrated or seriously prejudiced unless a constable arriving at the premises can secure immediate entry to them.

A constable may seize and retain anything for which a search has been so authorised. The additional powers of seizure provided by the Criminal Justice and Police Act 2001, s 50 apply to this power of seizure. A constable may use reasonable force, if necessary, in the exercise of any power conferred by virtue of PHA 1997, s 2B.

Putting people in fear of violence

PHA 1997, s 4 creates the indictable (either way) offence of putting people in fear of violence. Section 4(1) provides that a person whose course of conduct causes another to fear, on at least two occasions, that violence will be used against him, is guilty of an offence if he knows or ought to know that his course of conduct (p 690) will cause that other person so to fear on each of those occasions. The Court of Appeal has held that the course of conduct must amount to harassment of another. Direct evidence from the victim that he was caused to fear such violence is not essential, because a court may infer such fear if there is other evidence entitling it to do so, but without direct evidence from the victim proof may be difficult.

For the purposes of s 4, the person whose course of conduct is in question ought to know that it will cause another to fear that violence will be used against him on any occasion if a reasonable person in possession of the same information would think the course of conduct would cause the other so to fear on that occasion.

Section 4 provides similar defences to those under s 1(3) with the substitution of 'circumstances in which the pursuit of his course of conduct was reasonable for the protection of himself or another or for the protection of his or another's property', for 'the pursuit of the course of conduct being reasonable in the circumstances'.

The Court of Appeal has stated that s 4 is not normally appropriate for use as a means of criminalising conduct, not charged as violence, during incidents in a long and predominantly affectionate relationship in which both parties persisted and wanted to continue. Description of a number of acts of violence spread over nine months during a close and affectionate relationship does not, it said, satisfy the course of conduct requirement or the requirement that it is conduct amounting to harassment.

Stalking involving fear of violence or serious alarm or distress

PHA 1997, s 4A(1), added by PFA 2012, s 111, provides that a person (D) whose course of conduct:

(a) amounts to stalking, and
(b) either:
    (i) causes another (V) to fear, on at least two occasions, that violence will be used against V, or
    (ii) causes V serious alarm or distress which has a substantial adverse effect on V's usual day-to-day activities,

is guilty of an indictable (either way) offence if D knows or ought to know that D's course of conduct will cause V so to fear on each of those occasions or (as the case may be) will cause such alarm or distress.

For the purposes of s 4A, D ought to know that his course of conduct will cause V to fear that violence will be used against V on any occasion if a reasonable person in possession of the same information would think the course of conduct would cause V so to fear on that occasion; and D ought to know that his course of conduct will cause V serious alarm or distress which has a substantial adverse effect on V's usual day-to-day activities if a reasonable person in possession of the same information would think the course of conduct would cause V such alarm or distress.

The same defences are available as apply to an offence under s 4.

The offence under s 4A may alternatively be dealt with by a prosecution under s 4.

Breach of restraining order

PHA 1997, s 5, which empowers a court to make a restraining order when sentencing a convicted person for *any* offence, is of particular importance in respect of cases under PHA 1997. It provides that, in addition to any other sentence imposed, the court may make an order protecting the victim of the offence (who must be named), or any other person mentioned in the order, from further conduct which amounts to harassment or will cause a fear of violence.

PHA 1997, s 5A permits a court before which a defendant is acquitted of an offence under PHA 1997 or otherwise, if it considers that it is necessary to do so to protect a person from harassment by the defendant, to make an order prohibiting the defendant from doing anything specified in the order.

If, without reasonable excuse, a person does anything which is prohibited by a restraining order, he commits an indictable (either way) offence (ss 5(5) and 5A(2)).

Police directions stopping the harassment, etc of a person at his home

The Criminal Justice and Police Act 2001 (CJPA 2001), s 42 provides that a constable who is at the scene may give a direction to a person if:

(a) this person is present outside, or in the vicinity of, premises used by someone (the resident) as a dwelling;

(b) that constable believes, on reasonable grounds, that this person is there for the purpose (by his presence or otherwise) of representing to the resident or another individual, or of persuading the resident or other individual that:

(i)   he should not do something which he is entitled or required to do, or

(ii) he should do something which he is not under any obligation to do; and

(c) the constable also believes on reasonable grounds that the presence of this person (either alone or together with others who are likely to be present):

(i)   amounts to, or is likely to result in, the harassment of the resident, or

(ii) is likely to cause alarm or distress to the resident.

A direction under CJPA 2001, s 42 is one which requires its addressee to do things which the constable considers to be necessary to prevent the harassment of the resident or the causing of alarm or distress to the resident. It may be given orally, either to an individual or a group. Requirements that may be made under s 42 include:

(a) a requirement to leave the vicinity of the premises in question; and

(b) a requirement to leave that vicinity and not to return to it within such period as the constable may specify, not being longer than three months.

A requirement to leave may be to do so immediately or after a specified period. A direction includes exceptions and may make exceptions subject to conditions, including conditions as to the distance from the premises in question at which, or the location where, those who do not leave must remain, and conditions as to the numbers, or identity, of the persons who are authorised by the exception to remain in the vicinity.

When there is more than one officer at the scene, only the senior officer present may give the direction. The power to give a direction under CJPA 2001, s 42 does not include the power to direct a person to refrain from activity which is lawful under the Trade Union and Labour Relations (Consolidation) Act 1992, s 220 (see p 797). Any direction given may be varied or withdrawn.

A person who knowingly fails to comply with a requirement in a direction (other than a requirement not to return under (b) above) commits an offence (s 42(7)). A person who in breach of a requirement under (b) returns to the vicinity of the premises within the period specified for the purpose of persuading the resident or another individual as described above also commits an offence (s 42(8)).

Offence of harassment etc of a person in his home

CJPA 2001, s 42A provides that a person also commits an offence if:

(a) he is present outside or in the vicinity of any premises that are used by any individual (the resident) as a dwelling; and
(b) he is there to represent to the resident or another individual, or to persuade the resident or other person, that he should not do something which he is entitled or required to do, or should do something he is not obliged to do;
(c) he intends his presence to amount to harassment, alarm or distress to the resident, or knows or ought to know that his presence is likely to do so; and
(d) his presence amounts to, or is likely to result in, harassment, or alarm or distress to, of the resident, a person in the resident's building or a person in another dwelling in the vicinity of the resident's dwelling.

RACIALLY OR RELIGIOUSLY AGGRAVATED HARASSMENT OFFENCES

A person commits an indictable (either way) offence under CDA 1998, s 32 if he commits an offence under PHA 1997, ss 2 to 4A, which is racially or religiously aggravated.

By CDA 1998, s 28, an offence is racially or religiously aggravated for the purposes of s 32 if:

(a) at the time of committing it, or immediately before or after doing so, the offender demonstrates towards the victim hostility based on that person's membership (actual or presumed) of a racial or religious group; or
(b) the offence is motivated (wholly or partly) by hostility towards members of a racial or religious group based on their membership of that group.

In (a) 'membership of a racial or religious group' includes association with members of that group, and 'presumed' means presumed by the offender. A 'racial group' means a group of persons defined by reference to race, colour, nationality (including citizenship) or ethnic or national origins. A 'religious group' is a group of persons defined by reference to religious belief or lack of religious belief. Section 28 was discussed on pp 687–9; what was said there is equally applicable here.

OTHER NON-FATAL OFFENCES

OAPA 1861, ss 21 to 24 include other offences which are associated with the causing, or attempted causing, of forms of bodily harm. These offences, which are all triable only on indictment, should be considered when circumstances are presented involving actual or attempted harm to a person.

Attempting to choke, etc

This offence, provided by OAPA 1861, s 21, consists of:

(a) an attempt by D, by any means whatsoever, to choke, suffocate, or strangle any other person, or

(b) an attempt by D, by any means calculated to choke, suffocate, or strangle, to render any other person insensible, unconscious, or incapable of resistance,

with intent thereby to enable D or another person to commit any indictable offence, or with intent to assist another to do so.

Using chloroform, etc to commit an indictable offence

By OAPA 1861, s 22, D commits an offence if he unlawfully applies or administers to, or causes to be taken by, any person a stupefying or overpowering drug, matter, or thing, with intent thereby to enable himself or another person to commit any indictable offence, or with intent to assist another to do so.

Administering poison, etc so as thereby to endanger life, etc or with intent to injure, etc

OAPA 1861, s 23 provides that a person is guilty of an offence if he unlawfully and maliciously administers to, or causes to be administered to or taken by, any other person any poison, or other destructive or noxious thing, *so as thereby to endanger the life of such person, or so as thereby to inflict upon such person any grievous bodily harm.*

OAPA 1861, s 24 provides that a person is guilty of an offence if he unlawfully and maliciously administers to, or causes to be administered to or taken by, any other person any poison, or other destructive or noxious thing, *with intent to injure, aggrieve, or annoy such person.*

A 'poison' means a recognised poison, in whatever quantity it may be administered, etc; a 'noxious thing' is any other drug or thing which is harmful in the dosage in which it was administered, etc. 'Administer' does not necessarily involve the application of direct physical force and covers, for example, the spraying of tear gas from a distance. Where D acts in concert with V who self-injects a drug (for example by holding a tourniquet around V's arm while V self-injects or by preparing and giving V the drug for immediate self-injection), D does not *thereby* administer the drug. If the act of self-injection by V was not free, or not deliberate or not informed, as where V was forced to self-inject, D would cause the thing to be administered by V.

A poison, or other destructive or noxious thing, is caused to be taken if it is left for a person who then drinks it in ignorance of what it is or under duress. To leave it for the purpose of it being taken would be to attempt to cause it to be taken.

The consent of the person to whom the poison is given is no defence to charges under OAPA 1861, ss 23 or 24. For example, heroin can be a noxious substance for the purposes of these offences. If a shot of heroin is administered to another with his consent, this will amount to an administration for the purposes of this section.

The distinction between the offences under OAPA 1861, ss 23 and 24 lies partly in the fact that the offence under OAPA 1861, s 23 requires the additional element that the administration must be such as thereby to endanger life or to inflict grievous bodily harm, and partly in the fact that the requirement of mens rea is not the same for each offence. The differences between the two offences are shown by the words italicised in the definitions given above.

The mens rea required is as follows. In the case of the offence under OAPA 1861, s 23, the Court of Appeal has held that where endangering of life or grievous bodily harm is caused directly (eg by injection) the requirement of malice is satisfied by its deliberate administration; no mens rea is required to be proved as to the risk of injury. The Court stated that where the endangering of life etc was caused indirectly (eg by causing the victim to inhale gas) foresight of injury must be proved. In the case of an offence under s 24 not only must an intentional or reckless administration, etc of a poison or other destructive or noxious thing be proved but also an intention to injure, aggrieve, or annoy.

Torture

The offence of torture, which is triable only on indictment, is governed by the Criminal Justice Act 1988, s 134.

By s 134(1), a public official or person acting in an official capacity, whatever his nationality, commits the offence of torture if he intentionally inflicts severe physical or mental pain or suffering on another in the performance or purported performance of his official duties.

By s 134(2), a person not acting in such an official capacity commits the offence of torture if he intentionally inflicts severe physical or mental pain or suffering on another at the instigation or with the consent or acquiescence of a public official or person acting in that capacity, and the official or other person is performing or purporting to perform his official duties when he instigates the commission of the offence or consents to or acquiesces in it.

It is immaterial whether the pain or suffering is physical or mental and whether it is caused by an act or omission. It is a defence for a person to prove that he had lawful authority, justification, or excuse for that conduct.

The consent of the Attorney General is required for a prosecution for the offence of torture.

CHILD ABDUCTION

Two indictable (either way) offences of child abduction are provided by the Child Abduction Act 1984 (CAA 1984). These offences contain a number of common features; these will be dealt with after the separate offences have been outlined.

Abduction from the United Kingdom by parent, etc

By CAA 1984, s 1(1), a person connected with a child under 16 commits an offence if he takes or sends the child *out of the UK* without the appropriate consent. A person is regarded as 'sending' a child if he causes the child to be sent. A person connected with a child does not commit an offence if the appropriate consent has been given for a child to be removed from the UK for a defined period but the child is kept out of the UK after the end of that period and the appropriate consent no longer exists.

For the purposes of the offence, a person is 'connected with' a child if:

(a) he is the child's parent; or
(b) in the case of a child, whose parents were not married to each other at the time of his birth, there are reasonable grounds for believing that he is its father; or
(c) he is a guardian or special guardian of the child; or
(d) he is the person in whose favour a residence order is in force in respect of the child.

Only persons falling within these categories can commit the present offence.

The reference to the 'appropriate consent', in relation to the removal or sending of the child out of the UK, means:

(a) the consent of *each* of the following:
    (i)   the child's mother,
    (ii)   the child's father, if he has parental responsibility for him,
    (iii) any guardian or special guardian of the child,
    (iv)   any person in whose favour a residence order is in force with respect to the child, and
    (v)   any person who has custody of the child; or
(b) the leave of the court granted under or by virtue of the Children Act 1989, Part II; or
(c) if any person has custody of the child, the leave of the court which granted custody to him.

It is irrelevant that the child consents to what occurs.

A person does not commit the present offence by taking or sending a child out of the UK without the appropriate consent:

(a) if he is the person in whose favour there is a residence order in respect of the child and he takes or sends the child out of the UK for a period of less than one month; or
(b) if he is a special guardian of the child and takes or sends it out of the UK for a period of less than three months,

unless he is in breach of an order under the Children Act 1989, Part II.

A person does not commit the present offence by doing anything without the consent of another person whose consent is required if:

(a) he does it in the belief that the other person has consented or would consent if he was aware of all the relevant circumstances; or
(b) he has taken all reasonable steps to communicate with the other person but has been unable to communicate with him; or
(c) the other person has unreasonably refused to consent.

However, condition (c) does not apply where the person who refused consent is a person in whose favour there is a residence order, or who is a special guardian of the child, or who has custody of the child; or where the taking or sending out of the UK is in breach of an order made by a court in the UK.

There are special provisions where the child is in the care of a local authority or a voluntary organisation, detained in a place of safety, remanded to local authority accommodation, or the subject of proceedings (or an order) for adoption, or is in a place of safety.

The offence under CAA 1984, s 1 cannot be prosecuted without the DPP's consent.

The Court of Appeal has held that the defence of duress of circumstances is not available on a charge under CAA 1984, s 1; the remedy where serious bodily harm to the child is believed to be imminent is, it said, to seek the protection of the courts.

Abduction of child by other persons

This offence is governed by CAA 1984, s 2. It can be committed by anyone other than:

(a) the father or mother (if they were married when the child was born) or the mother (if they were not); or
(b) the child's guardian or special guardian;
(c) a person with a residence order in respect of the child; or
(d) a person with custody of the child.

Other important differences from the offence under CAA 1984, s 1 are that the child need not be abducted from the UK and that the offence can be committed by taking *or detaining* a child.

Section 2(1) provides that anyone, other than someone mentioned above, commits an offence if, without lawful authority or reasonable excuse, he takes or detains a child under 16 so as either to remove him from the lawful control of anyone having lawful control of him or to keep him out of the lawful control of any person entitled to it. Removal from control does not require any removal in a geographical sense; it suffices to deflect the child from what, with the consent of those having lawful control of him, he would be otherwise doing into some activity induced by D, as where D finds a child in a park pursuing a particular activity (eg playing football) and induces it to go elsewhere in the park for another activity (eg to look for an alleged lost bicycle).

There can be a 'taking' for the purposes of s 2 despite the fact that a child consents provided that D's acts were a cause of the child accompanying him and such acts are more than just peripheral or inconsequential. If D's acts are an effective cause of the child accompanying him, that is sufficient.

A person is regarded as detaining a child if he causes him to be detained or induces the child to remain with him or another.

Although it must be proved that there was an intentional or reckless taking by D, the objective consequence of which was to remove or keep the child from the lawful control of anyone having lawful control of the child, it does not have to be proved that D intended or was reckless as to this consequence occurring.

It is a defence for D to prove that, at the time of the alleged offence, he believed the child was 16 or over. Alternatively, in the case where the father and mother of 'the child in question' (ie the child taken or detained) were not married to each other at the time of birth, it is a defence for D to prove that he is the father of the child taken or detained or that he had reasonable grounds to believe he was that child's father. Lastly, D is not guilty of an offence under s 2 if he mistakenly believed, reasonably or not, in facts which—if they had been as he believed—would have given him a lawful authority or reasonable excuse. On this basis, a man who takes a child, thinking that it is his child whereas in truth it is another child, will not be guilty if, on the facts as he believes them to be, he would have a lawful authority or reasonable excuse for taking the child.

General

For the purposes of both offences, a person is regarded as taking a child if he causes or induces the child to accompany him or any other person, or causes the child to be taken.

KIDNAPPING

The offence involves four requirements:

(a)   The taking or carrying away of one person by another

This can include the case where a person is induced to walk or drive away himself, if the other elements of the offence are fulfilled (as where his car is hijacked and he drives away under the instructions of the hijackers). Although the person taken or carried away is often secreted thereafter, this is not a requirement of the offence.

(b)   The taking or carrying away must be by force or by fraud

'Force' is not limited to physical force or the threat of it. It encompasses any conduct which, coupled with the taking or carrying away (requirement (a)), overrides the true consent of the person taken or carried away (requirement (c)). Thus, the exercise of mental or moral power or influence to compel another to do something against his will can suffice if it overcomes his will. Any fraud which induces the victim to consent to being taken or carried away will suffice, and will invalidate the victim's apparent consent.

(c)   The taking or carrying away must be without the consent of the person taken or carried away

This requirement must be satisfied whatever the age of that person. However, there can be a kidnapping, even though the person carried away consents at first, if he changes his mind and ceases to consent while still being carried away. A very young child does not have the understanding or intelligence to give consent so that the absence of consent will be a necessary inference from its age. In the case of an older child, it is a question of fact for the jury whether the child had sufficient understanding or intelligence to give consent and, if so, whether absence of consent has been proved. Unlike child abduction, the presence or absence of consent on the part of the person having custody or care and control of a child victim is immaterial (except that such consent may support a defence of lawful excuse). Likewise the presence or absence of consent on the part of other people, such as the spouse of a person who is taken, is immaterial.

It must be proved that a person charged with kidnapping knew or was reckless that he did not have the victim's consent.

(d)   The taking or carrying away must be without lawful excuse

Clearly, for example, a parent (or other person) with custody of a child will often have a lawful excuse for taking or carrying away the child. An exception would be where this contravenes a court order in relation to the child.

Procedural points

Kidnapping is triable only on indictment. The House of Lords has held that the conduct of a parent who snatches his own child in defiance of a court order relating to its custody or care and control (such as one making the child a ward of court) should normally be dealt with as a contempt of court rather than as the subject matter of a prosecution for kidnapping, unless the parent's conduct was particularly bad.

The Court of Appeal has held that where both child abduction and kidnapping have been committed by a parent, it does not necessarily follow that for policy reasons a charge of kidnapping is always inappropriate.

CAA 1984, s 5 provides that the consent of the Director of Public Prosecutions to the institution of a prosecution for kidnapping is required wherever the victim is under 16 or where the prosecution is against a person connected with the child (parent or guardian, etc).

HOSTAGE TAKING

The Taking of Hostages Act 1982, s 1 provides that a person of any nationality commits an offence triable only on indictment if he detains any other person ('the hostage') and, in order to compel any state, international governmental organisation, or person to do or abstain from doing any act, he threatens to kill, injures or continues to detain the hostage. The consent of the Attorney General is required before a prosecution may be brought for this offence.

CONTAMINATION OF GOODS, ETC WITH INTENT

The Public Order Act 1986 (POA 1986), s 38(1) provides that it is an indictable (either way) offence for a person to contaminate or interfere with goods, or make it appear that goods have been contaminated or interfered with, or to place goods which have been contaminated or interfered with, or which have that appearance, in a place where goods of that description are consumed, used, sold or otherwise supplied, with the intention:

(a) of causing public alarm or anxiety;
(b) of causing injury to members of the public consuming or using the goods;
(c) of causing economic loss to any person by reason of (i) the goods being shunned by members of the public, or (ii) steps taken to avoid any such alarm or anxiety, injury or loss.

Section 38(2) makes it an indictable (either way) offence for a person to threaten that he or another will do, or claim that he or another has done, any of the acts referred to in s 38(1) with such intention as is mentioned in (a) or (c) above. This does not include someone who, in good faith, reports or warns that such acts have been, or appear to have been, committed. Thus, the broadcast of a warning received, if carried out in good faith, is excused.

By s 38(3), possession of contaminated goods, apparently contaminated goods, or materials with which to contaminate goods or to make it appear that goods have been contaminated, is also an indictable (either way) offence.

Thus, the activities of groups, including animal rights groups, calculated to hit at businesses with which they are not in sympathy are made punishable. However, it must be remembered that such activities may also amount to attempts to commit offences (for example, attempted murder, if poisons are placed in foodstuffs with an intention of killing, since the placing of the contaminated goods is more than merely a preparatory act which can amount to an attempt). In addition, if someone actually consumes a contaminated product and suffers harm, there will be liability for the relevant 'full' offence against the person, depending on the degree of harm.

GUNPOWDER, ETC OFFENCES

OAPA 1861, ss 28 to 30 and 64 create a number of offences triable only on indictment related to the use or possession of explosives.

OAPA 1861, s 28 provides that anyone, who unlawfully and maliciously, by the explosion of gunpowder or other explosive substance, *burns, maims, disfigures, disables, or does any grievous bodily harm to any person*, is guilty of an offence.

OAPA 1861, s 29 provides that anyone, who unlawfully and maliciously causes an explosion, or sends or delivers an explosive substance (or any other dangerous or noxious thing), or places or throws at someone any corrosive fluid or any destructive or explosive substance, *with intent to burn, maim, disfigure, or disable any person, or to do some grievous bodily harm to any person*, is guilty of an offence, whether or not any bodily injury is effected.

OAPA 1861, s 30 provides that it is an offence unlawfully and maliciously to place or throw in, into, upon, against, or near any building or vessel an explosive substance *with intent to do any bodily injury to any person, whether or not any explosion occurs and whether or not anyone is injured.*

It has been held that a petrol bomb is an explosive substance under s 29. This decision is equally applicable to the meaning of 'explosive substance' in ss 28 and 30.

Clearly, there is a good deal of overlap between the three offences, especially those under ss 28 and 29. The major distinguishing feature of each offence is indicated by the words italicised. The basic distinction is that s 28 is concerned with where serious bodily harm is actually caused by an explosion, while it suffices for s 29 that D caused an explosion with intent to cause such harm, whether or not harm occurred; in fact, s 29 does not require an explosion to occur since it is also concerned with sending, etc explosives and certain other substances with such intent. Section 30 does not require an explosion nor that anyone is harmed but it does require D to act with the specified intent to do bodily injury (which need not be serious injury).

OAPA 1861, s 64 makes it an offence to make, manufacture, or knowingly possess any explosive substance or machine, engine, or instrument with intent to commit any offence under OAPA 1861, or for the purpose of enabling others to do so.

When circumstances are being considered involving explosives, it must be remembered that offences under the Criminal Damage Act 1971 and the Explosive Substances Act 1883 must also be considered. However, if the bomber, etc has the requisite specified intent to cause grievous bodily harm (OAPA 1861, s 29) or bodily injury (OAPA 1861, s 30), or actually causes grievous bodily harm (OAPA 1861, s 28), an offence will always be committed under OAPA 1861.

CHAPTER 24

Disputes

Quite a large part of a police officer's time is spent in advising members of the public of action which they may take in relation to disputes involving them and their spouses, cohabitants, other members of their families, landlords, and the like. On occasions it is appropriate to have recourse to the criminal law, but on most occasions the most useful approach may be to put them in touch with one of the various agencies which are equipped to deal with such situations. In many cases civil remedies are available and particularly appropriate. Because the police service offers an immediate, round-the-clock response, police officers will most often be involved in disputes, or incidents, when they occur or very soon afterwards.

DOMESTIC VIOLENCE

For convenience, we shall refer to the victim of domestic violence as a woman but it must not be forgotten that sometimes the victim in such a case is a man. A woman who has been injured by her husband, civil partner or cohabitant is competent and compellable to give evidence against that person in a criminal court in relation to the offence in question, and may wish to do so. Likewise, a family member who has been subject to domestic violence is competent and compellable. However, it will be appreciated that this is frequently an extremely difficult decision for a wife, partner or family member to make. Many women, for example, feel trapped and helpless and, being unable to face up to life on their own, prefer to remain with a husband who treats them badly. In such circumstances they will not wish to give evidence against their husbands because of their fear that this will lead to a final breakdown of the marriage. The social services are experienced in the handling of these situations and will help if the wife will accept such aid.

Non-molestation orders

Where a woman (or member of a family who is a child) has been subjected to domestic violence, the courts can assist without the necessity for the woman to give evidence in a criminal court. She can seek assistance by applying in civil family proceedings for a non-molestation order under the Family Law Act 1996 (FLA 1996), s 42, which is not limited to proceedings between spouses (or ex-spouses), civil partners (or ex-civil partners) or cohabitants (or ex-cohabitants).

A non-molestation order under FLA 1996, s 42 is an order containing either or both of the following provisions:

(a) prohibiting a person (the respondent) from molesting another person who is associated with the respondent; and

(b) prohibiting the respondent from molesting a relevant child.

A non-molestation order may be made:

(a) on the application (whether in other family proceedings or without any other family proceedings being instituted) of a person who is associated with the respondent; or
(b) during family proceedings to which the respondent is a party, if the court considers that such an order will benefit any other party or a relevant child even though no application has been made.

By FLA 1996, s 62, a person is 'associated with' the respondent if they are spouses (or ex-spouses), civil partners (or ex-civil partners), or cohabitants (or ex-cohabitants), or members (or ex-members) of the same household, or relatives, or are or have been engaged, or have or have had an intimate personal relationship which is or was of significant duration, or are parties to family proceedings other than proceedings for a non-molestation order. In addition, in relation to a child (ie someone under 18), a person is associated with the respondent if each of them is a parent of the child or has had parental responsibility for it. Where a child has been adopted or freed for adoption, two persons are associated with each other if one is its natural parent (or a parent of such a natural parent) and the other is the child or someone who is its adoptive parent (or an applicant for adoption) or with whom the child has been placed for adoption.

A 'relevant child' in relation to such proceedings is any child who is living with or might reasonably be expected to live with either party to the proceedings, or any child in relation to whom an order under the Adoption Act 1976, the Adoption and Children Act 2002 or the Children Act 1989 is in question in the proceedings, or any other child whose interests the court considers relevant.

In deciding whether to make a non-molestation order, the court must consider all the circumstances, including the need to secure the health, safety and well-being of the applicant or any relevant child.

A non-molestation order may refer to molestation in general, to particular acts of molestation, or both. It may be made for a specified period, or until a further order is made. An order which is made in other family proceedings ceases to have effect if those proceedings are withdrawn or dismissed.

Application without notice to the other party

Where it appears to be just and convenient to do so a court may, under FLA 1996, s 45(1), make a non-molestation order even though the party against whom the complaint is made (the respondent) has not been given notice of the proceedings. In such cases, the court must consider:

(a) the risk of significant harm if the order is not made immediately;
(b) whether if such an order is not made the applicant is likely to be deterred or prevented from pursuing the application; and
(c) whether there is reason to believe that the respondent is aware of the proceedings but is deliberately evading service of the notice and the applicant, or a relevant child, will be seriously prejudiced by the delay involved in effecting service (or substituted service) of the proceedings.

Where an order is made on an application without notice to the respondent, it must afford the respondent an opportunity to make representations as soon as just and convenient at a full hearing.

Arrest warrant

Where a non-molestation order has been made, and the applicant considers that the respondent has failed to comply with it, the applicant may apply to the court for a warrant to arrest the respondent.

Offence of breaching non-molestation order

Under FLA 1996, s 42A(1), a person who without reasonable excuse does anything that he is prohibited from doing by a non-molestation order is guilty of an indictable (either way) offence. In the case of an order made without notice to the other party, a person can be guilty of the offence only in respect of conduct engaged in when he was aware of the existence of the order. Where a defendant has adduced evidence which raises the issue of reasonable excuse, the prosecution has the burden of disproving reasonable excuse beyond reasonable doubt.

Undertakings

Where a non-molestation order could be made, a court may accept an undertaking from any party to the proceedings. Where such an undertaking is given breach of it is not an offence. However, the undertaking is enforceable in civil law in the same way as a court order, except that no power of arrest attaches to its breach. Where a power to arrest appears to be appropriate, an undertaking should not be accepted by a court.

Domestic violence protection notices and orders

The Crime and Security Act 2010 empowers a superintendent (or above) to issue a domestic violence protection notice (DVPN). A DVPN prohibits a suspected perpetrator (P) from molesting a victim of domestic violence (V) and, where they cohabit, may require P to leave those premises. Sections 24 to 26 deal with DVPNs.

The issue of a DVPN triggers an application for a domestic violence protection order (DVPO), which is an order lasting between 14 and 28 days. A DVPO prohibits P from molesting V and may also make provision about access to shared accommodation by P and V. Sections 27 to 30 deal with DVPOs.

Under the scheme the police and courts can protect V when V is most vulnerable, in the immediate aftermath of an attack, by preventing P from contacting V or returning home for up to 28 days. This helps victims who may otherwise have had to flee their home and gives them the space and time to access the support they need and to consider their options.

The scheme is intended to plug a gap in protection for victims of domestic violence due to either the police being unable to charge the perpetrator due to lack of evidence (so V cannot be protected through strict bail conditions) or the process for granting longer-term injunctions taking several days or weeks to apply for.

At the time of writing, the provisions relating to DVPNs and DVPOs are only in force (as pilots) in three police areas: Greater Manchester, West Mercia, and Wiltshire.

DVPN

The conditions and considerations that must be met in order for a DVPN to be issued are set out in s 24. A DVPN may be issued to P, if P is aged 18 or over, where the authorising officer (superintendent (or above)) has reasonable grounds for believing that:

(a) P has been violent, or has threatened violence, towards an associated person, V, and
(b) the issue of a notice is necessary in order to protect V from violence or the threat of violence by P.

An 'associated person' has the same meaning as in FLA 1996, s 62 (see p 704).

Before issuing a DVPN, the authorising officer must consider the welfare of any child whose interests the officer considers relevant. He must take reasonable steps to find out the opinion of V as to whether the DVPN should be issued. Consideration must also be given to any representation P makes in relation to the issuing of the DVPN. Where the DVPN is to include conditions in relation to the occupation of premises shared by P and V, reasonable steps must also be taken to find out the opinion of any other associated person who lives in the premises. The issue of the DVPN does not require V's consent, as the authorising officer may nevertheless have reason to believe that V requires protection from P.

A DVPN must contain provision to prohibit P from molesting V for the duration of the DVPN, which may be expressed so as to refer to molestation in general, particular acts of molestation, or both.

Where P and V share living premises, the DVPN may explicitly:

(a) prohibit P from evicting or excluding V from the premises;
(b) prohibit P from entering the premises;
(c) require P to leave the premises; or
(d) prohibit P from coming within a certain distance of the premises (as specified in the DVPN) for the duration of the DVPN.

It does not matter for these purposes whether the premises are owned or rented in the name of P or V.

Where a DVPN is issued which prevents P from entering (or requires P to leave) premises, and the authorising officer believes that P is subject to service law and the premises are service living accommodation, he must make reasonable efforts to inform P's commanding officer that the notice has been issued.

The DVPN must state the grounds for issuing a DVPN; that a constable may arrest without warrant if he has reasonable grounds to believe that P is in breach of the DVPN; that the police will make an application for a DVPO which will be heard in court within a 48-hour period and a notice of the hearing will be given to P; that the DVPN will continue to be in effect until the DVPO application is determined; and the provision that may be included in a subsequent DVPO. A DVPN must be in writing and only be served on P personally by a constable. The constable serving the DVPN must ask P to supply an address in order to enable P to be given notice of the hearing for the DVPO.

If he has reasonable grounds to believe that P is in breach of the DVPN, a constable may arrest P without warrant as set out above. P must then be held in custody and brought within a period of 24 hours before the magistrates' court that will hear the application for the DVPO. In calculating the end of that period, a Sunday, Christmas Day, Good Friday, or a Bank Holiday is disregarded. However, if the DVPO hearing has already been arranged to take place within that 24-hour period, then P must be brought before the court for *that* hearing. If P is brought before the court in advance of the DVPO hearing, the court may remand P; it may also remand P if it adjourns the hearing.

DVPO

Once a DVPN has been issued, a constable must apply by complaint to a magistrates' court for a DVPO. The magistrates' court hearing must be no later than 48 hours (calculated as for a DVPN) after the time when the DVPN was served. Notice of the hearing must be given to P. Where no address has been given by P, the court must be satisfied that reasonable efforts have been made to give P the notice of the hearing. The Magistrates' Courts (Domestic Violence Protection Order Proceedings) Rules 2011 provide that a notice of hearing is deemed to be a summons, but that this does not enable a warrant of arrest to be issued for failure to appear in answer to any such notice.

If the hearing of the application is adjourned, the DVPN continues in effect until the application is determined by the court. V is not compelled to attend the hearing of an application for a DVPO, or to answer questions (unless V has given oral or written evidence at the hearing).

Two conditions must be met for a DVPO to be made:

(a) the court must be satisfied on the balance of probabilities that P has been violent, or threatened violence, towards an associated person, V;

(b) the court must think that the DVPO is necessary to secure the protection of V from violence, or the threat of violence, by P.

Before making a DVPO, the court must consider: the welfare of any person under 18 whose interests the court considers relevant to the DVPO: the opinion (if known) of V; and, where the DVPO is to include conditions in relation to the occupation of premises shared by P and V, the opinion (if known) of any other associated person who lives in the premises. The court may issue a DVPO regardless of whether or not V consents.

A DVPO must contain provision explicitly prohibiting P from molesting V for the duration of the DVPO. The prohibition may be expressed so as to refer to molestation in general, particular acts of molestation, or both. Where P and V share living premises, the DVPO may explicitly: prohibit P from evicting or excluding V from the premises; prohibit P from entering the premises; require P to leave the premises; or prohibit P from coming within a certain distance of the premises (as specified in the DVPO). The DVPO must state that a constable may arrest P without warrant if he has reasonable grounds for believing that P is in breach of the DVPO.

A DVPO may be in force for a minimum of 14 days, and a maximum of 28 days, from the day on which it is made. It must state the period for which it is to be in force.

If P is arrested under the above-mentioned power for breach of a DVPO, P must be held in custody and brought before a magistrates' court within a 24-hour period. In calculating the end of that period a Sunday, Christmas Day, etc is disregarded. If the matter is not disposed of when P is brought before the court, the court may remand P.

General

Like an anti-social behaviour order and various other orders, a DVPO is a civil order. As to the implications of this on the rules of evidence, see pp 745 and 912. Note, however, that the 2011 Rules disapply, in respect of a DVPO, the normal requirement in civil proceedings that notice must be given of a proposal to adduce hearsay evidence.

Rights associated with the matrimonial home

Where domestic disputes occur, regardless of whether or not a non-molestation order or, where available, a DVPO has been sought, the issue of rights of occupation in relation to the home still remains. FLA 1996 seeks to ensure that all sides to a dispute are protected from eviction.

Where one spouse has no estate, etc

FLA 1996, s 30 provides that, where one spouse or civil partner (A) is legally entitled to occupy a dwelling house and the other spouse or civil partner (B) has no such legal entitlement, B has 'home rights' which means that:

(a) if B is in occupation, B has a right not to be evicted or excluded from the dwelling house or any part of it by A without the leave of the court under FLA 1996, s 33 (occupation order provisions); and

(b) if B is not in occupation, B has a right with the leave of the court under FLA 1996, s 33 to enter and occupy the dwelling house.

There is, therefore, no lawful way by which one party to a marriage or civil partnership can be removed from the matrimonial home without the circumstances being examined by a civil family proceedings court.

Occupation orders

FLA 1996, s 33 provides for the making of an occupation order where the applicant has an estate or interest, etc entitling him to occupy a dwelling house or has home rights (see p 707) in it and the dwelling house is or has been the home of the applicant and of someone else with whom he is associated (or was intended by both such people to be their home). If an occupation order is made it may:

(a) enforce the applicant's occupation rights as against the other person (the respondent);
(b) require the respondent to permit the applicant to enter and remain in that dwelling house or part of it;
(c) regulate the occupation by either or both parties;
(d) if the respondent is entitled via an estate or interest etc to occupy, prohibit, restrict or suspend the exercise by him of his occupation rights;
(e) if the respondent has home rights and the applicant is the other spouse, restrict or terminate those rights;
(f) require the respondent to leave the dwelling house or part of it; or
(g) exclude the respondent from a defined area in which the dwelling house is included.

In deciding whether to make an occupation order and (if so) in what manner, the court must have regard to all of the circumstances including the housing needs and housing resources of both parties and any relevant child (as defined on p 704), the financial resources of both parties, the likely effect of any order (or of a failure to make an order) on the health, safety or well-being of each party and any relevant child, and the conduct of the parties in relation to each other and otherwise.

Former spouse, etc not entitled to occupy, and situations in which neither spouse, former spouse, etc entitled to occupy

FLA 1996 makes similar provisions for occupation orders in relation to former spouses or civil partners, and cohabitants or former cohabitants, where one of them is legally entitled to occupy a dwelling house, and the other is not. It also makes provision for occupation orders in circumstances in which neither spouse or civil partner or cohabitant (or ex-spouse or ex-civil partner or ex-cohabitant) has a legal entitlement to occupy a dwelling house which is (or was) the matrimonial home. These provisions are set out in FLA 1996, ss 35 to 38.

Breaches of occupation order and other points

Under FLA 1996, s 47, there is a power to arrest without warrant for breach of an occupation order where such a power has been attached to the order; otherwise an application must be made for an arrest warrant. 'Undertakings' and orders without notice to the other party may be made in respect of these orders in the same way as in the case of non-molestation orders.

Police action

Arrest for offences

Serious or minor offences may have been committed, or be reasonably suspected within domestic incidents. If so, a constable will have the normal power of arrest if the requirements of PACE, s 24 are satisfied.

The common law powers of arrest in relation to breaches of the peace may also be relevant.

Police action—when contact is first made

When a first contact is made with the police, it should be determined whether immediate response is required or whether there is no immediate danger. Such complaints must be recorded. Existing records should be checked to establish whether there is any previous record of incidents involving the complainant. Generally, if the victim claims to have been violently assaulted, reconciliation should not be attempted. Where the victim is a woman, a woman police officer should attend such incidents where possible as a woman who has been assaulted may prefer to be dealt with by another woman. A woman police officer should also attend where the victim is a girl or young boy. Any interview at the time should not take place in the presence of the alleged assailant. However, if a complainant wishes to repeat any allegation in the presence of the alleged assailant, she may do so and any reply made by the assailant should be noted.

If hospital treatment is not required, a victim may be taken to a victim examination suite if one is available. A medical examination by a police surgeon or some other doctor with forensic science training is preferable to examination by her own general practitioner. It is important to ensure that children are adequately cared for throughout this procedure. Other members of the family, or neighbours, may prove to be good witnesses in such cases, particularly where the victim is reluctant to become involved.

In domestic violence cases it is essential that the CPS is fully informed of the circumstances surrounding the family relationships involved, the domestic circumstances, and the likely course of future events including whether there is any likelihood of any lasting reconciliation.

It is important to ensure that victims continue to receive help and guidance in such cases from bodies such as Women's Aid Federation, Refuge, and Childline. It may also be necessary to remove the victim to a place of shelter (or, in the case of children, a place of safety) before making long-term arrangements with some other social agency. Some police forces have domestic violence units which specialise in such matters. Where it is necessary for the victim to live elsewhere, the police should assist in taking her to a place of refuge. If she subsequently wishes to visit the home for any reason she should be accompanied by a police officer.

Where complainant subsequently withdraws complaint

Where a victim subsequently decides to withdraw her complaint and states that she will be unwilling to give evidence in court she should be asked to make a statement to that effect. This will be taken into account by the Crown Prosecutor who may, nevertheless, take steps to compel the complainant to give evidence in criminal proceedings against her husband.

The Crown Prosecutor will also wish to take into account the views of the officer who recorded that statement concerning the validity of the complainant's reasons and her likely reaction to being compelled to give evidence. Where a victim refuses to give evidence it might be possible to continue the case by offering her statement in evidence in accordance with the rules set out on p 237.

EVICTION AND HARASSMENT

The Protection from Eviction Act 1977 (PEA 1977), s 1 provides three indictable (either way) offences whose aim is to protect tenants: the offence of eviction and two offences of harassment. The Act specifically authorises district councils to institute proceedings for these offences. Both offences use the term 'residential occupier' and this must first be explained.

A 'residential occupier', in relation to any premises, means a person occupying the premises as a residence, whether under a contract or by virtue of any enactment or rule of law giving him the right to remain in occupation or restricting the right of any other person to recover possession of the premises. Therefore, a tenant, or even a lodger who is living in a furnished room under an agreement with the owner, is a residential occupier. However, someone like a lodger who simply had a contractual licence which has expired is not a residential occupier.

Eviction

PEA 1977, s 1(2) provides that if any person unlawfully deprives the residential occupier of any premises of his occupation of the premises or any part thereof, or attempts to do so, he is guilty of an offence unless he proves that he believed, and had reasonable cause to believe, that the residential occupier had ceased to reside in the premises.

It is not necessary that any form of violence or intimidation is used; it would be sufficient if the residential occupier was tricked into leaving so that the owner could regain occupation, or that the owner entered by stealth during the residential occupier's absence. The offence requires something in the nature of an eviction. The deprivation of occupation need not be permanent. Consequently, a person who unlawfully excludes a residential occupier from his premises, intending the exclusion to be permanent, can he convicted under s 1(2) even though he repents almost immediately and lets the occupier back in.

The commission of the offence is not restricted to the owner or any person having an interest in the property; it can be committed by anyone who unlawfully deprives, or attempts to deprive, a residential occupier of his premises. This is meant to prevent the use of other persons to apply pressure in an attempt to dispossess. The only defence, which must be proved by the defendant, is one of reasonable belief that the residential occupier has ceased to reside in the premises. The House of Lords has held that putting the onus of proving this defence on the defendant is not incompatible with the presumption of innocence under the European Convention on Human Rights, art 6(2).

Harassment

PEA 1977, s 1(3) deals with harassment and provides that if any person with intent to cause the residential occupier of any premises:

(a) to give up the occupation of the premises or any part thereof; or

(b) to refrain from exercising any right or pursuing any remedy in respect of the premises or part thereof;

does any act likely to interfere with the peace or comfort of the residential occupier or members of his household, or persistently withdraws or withholds services reasonably required for the occupation of the premises as a residence, he is guilty of an offence.

Section 1(3) is therefore concerned with persons who, with the requisite intent, either do some act likely to interfere with the peace or comfort of the residential occupier, etc or persistently withdraw services. The actus reus may, therefore, consist of any *act*, such as intimidation, threats, or even interference with the building, perhaps by removing window frames or doors on the pretence that they are to be replaced. Alternatively it can consist of a *lack of action* which results in services reasonably required for the occupation of the premises being persistently withdrawn or withheld, as where the landlord fails to pay for essential services to the premises occupied by the tenant. The use of the word 'persistently' which is used as an adverb to both 'withdraws' and 'withholds' indicates that this must be done for some period of time.

The intention must be to cause a *residential occupier* to give up permanently occupation of the premises or to refrain from exercising any right or pursuing any remedy in respect of the premises or part of them. A s 1(3) offence therefore cannot be committed in relation to squatters who are in occupation of premises without agreement or any form of residential status.

Where an act likely to interfere with the peace or comfort of the residential occupier or members of his household is carried out with intent to cause the residential occupier *to give up occupation*, it is irrelevant that the act in question is not wrongful in civil law. This was stated by the House of Lords in a case where it held that a landlord who had disconnected a tenant's doorbell could be convicted of an offence under PEA 1977, s 1(3), even though the tenant was not entitled under his tenancy agreement to a front door bell (so that the disconnection was not a civil wrong).

Proof of the requisite intention under s 1(3) may not always be easy. Consequently, s 1(3A) provides that the landlord of a residential occupier or an agent of the landlord commits an offence if he does acts likely to interfere with the peace or comfort of the residential occupier or members of his family, or if he persistently withdraws or withholds services reasonably required for the occupation of the premises, and (in either case) *he knows or has reasonable cause to believe that this conduct is likely to cause* the residential occupier to give up occupation of the whole or part of the premises or to refrain from exercising any right or pursuing any remedy in respect of the whole or any part of the premises. A person is not guilty under s 1(3A) if he proves that he had reasonable grounds for doing the acts or withdrawing or withholding the services in question.

Disputes involving anti-social behaviour

Under the Housing Act 1996 local authorities, housing action trusts, and social landlords have powers to deal with anti-social behaviour in social housing. In particular, they may apply in the civil courts for an anti-social behaviour injunction. Where there are persistent reports of anti-social behaviour on housing estates in which the properties are owned or administered by such persons or organisations, the attention of the appropriate person or authority should be drawn to any conduct alleged to be that of tenants or their families.

As to the availability of anti-social behaviour *orders*, see p 744.

Caravans: eviction and harassment

The Caravan Sites Act 1968 (CSA 1968), s 3 provides similar indictable (either way) offences to those under PEA 1977 in relation to residential caravans.

Eviction

It is an offence for any person, during the subsistence of a residential contract, unlawfully to deprive the occupier of his occupation on a *'protected site'* of any caravan which the occupier is entitled by the contract to station and occupy, or to occupy, as his residence on that site (CSA 1968, s 3(1)(a)).

Moreover, even after a residential contract has expired or been ended, it is an offence for a person to enforce, otherwise than by court proceedings, a right to exclude the occupier from *the protected site* or from any such caravan, or to remove or exclude the caravan from the site (s 3(1)(b)).

A defence to either of these offences is available to a person if he proves that he believed and had reasonable cause to believe that the occupier of the caravan had ceased to reside on the site.

Harassment

A person commits an offence if, whether during or after a residential contract, with intent to cause the occupier to abandon occupation of the caravan or remove it from the site or to refrain from exercising rights or remedies, he does acts likely to interfere with the peace or comfort of the occupier or persons residing with him, or persistently withdraws or withholds services or facilities reasonably required for the occupation of the caravan as a residence on the site (s 3(1)(c)).

In addition, the owner of *a protected site* or his agent is guilty of an offence if, whether during the subsistence or after the expiration or determination of a residential contract, he does acts likely to interfere with the peace or comfort of the occupier or persons residing with him, or he persistently withdraws or withholds services or facilities reasonably required for the occupation of the caravan as a residence on the site, and (in either case) he knows, or has reasonable cause to believe, that this conduct is likely to cause the occupier to abandon occupation of the caravan or remove it from the site or to refrain from exercising rights or remedies (s 3(1A)).

It is a defence to either of these offences to prove that the defendant had reasonable grounds for doing the acts or withdrawing or withholding the services or facilities in question.

Definitions

A 'protected site' is:

(a) any land in respect of which a site licence is required under the Caravan Sites and Control of Development Act 1960, Part I; or
(b) a gypsy or other local authority site exempt from the necessity of becoming so licensed.

The term 'protected site' does not extend to those which are for holiday use only or are part-time sites.

'The occupier' for these purposes includes a person who was the occupier within the terms of a residential contract which has expired or been terminated. In the event of the death of the occupier, the widow, widower or surviving civil partner of that person (provided they were then residing together) or, in default, any member of the occupier's family (if then residing with the occupier) is 'the occupier'.

Police action

The primary duty of police officers will always be the prevention of a breach of the peace. When allegations are made concerning a dispute affecting a landlord and tenant a police officer should make all inquiries which are possible at that time at the scene of the dispute. If it appears that there might have been an offence in relation to the provisions outlined above in respect of dwellings or caravans, the officer should explain the provisions to the landlord and should warn him of the possibility of prosecution. However, whether or not such a warning is issued at the time, a comprehensive report of the circumstances should be sent to the local housing authority immediately. In appropriate cases, the police should inform the complainant in writing that the complaint has been referred to the housing authority.

HOMELESSNESS

The Housing Act 1996, Part VII requires every local housing authority to secure that advice and information about homelessness, and the prevention of homelessness, is available free of charge.

In addition, if someone applies to the authority for accommodation, or assistance in obtaining it, and the authority has reason to believe that he is or may be homeless or threatened with homelessness, the authority is required by Part VII to inquire into his eligibility for assistance (persons from abroad who are not eligible for housing assistance are not eligible for assistance under Part VII, nor are asylum seekers or their dependants in any event) and the circumstances.

In cases of apparent priority need, the authority must provide temporary accommodation while it makes its inquiries.

If the authority is satisfied as a result of its inquiries that the applicant is intentionally homeless but has a priority need, it is required to ensure that accommodation is available for such period thereafter as will give him reasonable opportunity to find accommodation, and to give him advice and assistance in finding it; if a person found intentionally homeless does not have a priority need, he is only entitled thereafter to advice and assistance.

If the authority is satisfied that the applicant is homeless, but not intentionally so, and is satisfied that he does not have a priority need, its obligation thereafter is simply to provide advice and assistance in finding accommodation; it has power, however, to secure that accommodation is made available to him. On the other hand, if it is aware that an applicant who is not homeless intentionally has a priority need, the authority must secure that accommodation is made available to him; this duty comes to an end in certain circumstances specified by the Act.

Persons who are apparently homeless and seek advice from police officers should be referred to the local housing authority, whether or not the persons concerned have been previously resident in that area.

CHAPTER 25

Homicide and Related Offences

Offences of homicide are categorised as follows: murder, manslaughter, infanticide, corporate manslaughter, causing death by careless driving while under the influence of drink or drugs, causing death by dangerous driving, causing death by careless driving, and causing death by driving when the driver was unlicensed, disqualified or uninsured. The 'death by driving' offences were dealt with in Chapter 14.

MURDER

Murder continues to be a common law offence triable only on indictment. It is defined as follows. The crime of murder is committed where a person of sound mind and discretion unlawfully kills any reasonable creature in being, and under the Queen's peace, with intent unlawfully to kill or cause grievous bodily harm.

In three types of exceptional case a person is not guilty of murder, but only of voluntary manslaughter, even though the definition of murder is satisfied. Those exceptions are where the defendant (D): was suffering from diminished responsibility, has the defence of loss of control or was acting in pursuance of a suicide pact.

With the exception of the reference to D's intent, the terms of the definition of murder also apply to involuntary manslaughter, which is discussed later in this chapter.

Person of sound mind and discretion

This phrase is really redundant. It simply refers to the general rules (see Chapter 1) that a person is not legally liable if he is legally insane or under 10 (the age of criminal responsibility).

Unlawfully

A killing is unlawful unless it falls within one of the following categories:

Prevention of crime or effecting arrest

It is lawful to use such force as is *reasonable* in the circumstances as D believed them to be in the prevention of a crime under the law of England and Wales or in effecting (or assisting in) the lawful arrest of offenders, suspected offenders, or persons lawfully at large. See, further, p 685. It follows that a police officer who accidentally causes the death of someone whom he is lawfully arresting is not guilty of manslaughter, let alone murder, provided that the force used by him was reasonable in the circumstances as he believed them to be (including the degree of resistance offered by the deceased).

Self-defence and defence of another or of property

Self-defence and defence of another or of property are common law defences, and they render a killing lawful if the force used is *reasonable* in the circumstances as D believed them to be. See, further, p 685. A police officer who shoots an armed terrorist who is shooting at him (or someone else) would clearly be using reasonable force, assuming that there is no other way of preventing the terrorist continuing to fire, and he can successfully plead the statutory defence of prevention of crime or the common law defence of self-defence (or defence of another).

Misadventure

Death is caused by misadventure where the killing is not murder, manslaughter, or any other offence of homicide. As an example, if a patient dies as a result of a lawful operation carried out by a surgeon with proper care, the killing is by misadventure, and so not unlawful, and therefore the surgeon is not guilty of any offence of homicide.

Kills

Generally, some form of action is required which proves to be a substantial cause of death. However, 'substantial' in this context simply means 'more than minimal'. Although generally some 'act' is required, if D is under a legally recognised duty to act (as where a parent or similar person has the care of a child or helpless person), and fails to act, that failure being a substantial cause of death, he may be convicted of an offence of homicide. Normally an act's contribution to the death will be easily proved, for example shooting, stabbing, pushing over a cliff, or violently assaulting, a person with fatal consequences, but the act does not need to be violent. Thieves who lock bank staff in a sealed, airtight vault to secure their escape without an alarm being raised kill their victims as surely as they would by any direct act. A person who steals the food and water left to sustain an injured man who is lost on the fells, while his companion seeks assistance, kills that man if he dies from the lack of sustenance, even though the man is not touched in any direct way.

If D's original act was a substantial cause of death it does not matter that some other intervening event finally caused the death, provided that this intervening event (as opposed to its details) was reasonably foreseeable in the ordinary course of things. If D knocks V unconscious on the beach and V is killed by the incoming tide, D's act is regarded in law as the cause of V's death because the incoming tide was clearly reasonably foreseeable. On the other hand, if two men (D and V) fight in a park and D leaves V unconscious but not seriously hurt and V is later killed by a tree which falls upon him when it is blown down by a gale, the fact that the fall of the tree was not reasonably foreseeable means that D's act is not regarded in law as a cause of V's death. A similar rule applies where D threatens someone who takes evasive action and is killed in doing so, as where a woman jumps out of a first-floor window to avoid rape. Provided that the evasive action is likely, the threat will be a cause of death if it was a substantial cause (as almost inevitably it will be).

If the injuries inflicted by D are an operating cause of death it is irrelevant that an intervening act by a third party also contributed to the death, provided that D's act was a substantial contribution. Suppose that D causes such serious injuries to V that V can only be kept alive by a life-support machine. If, subsequently, because there is no hope of recovery, doctors switch off that machine, D has still killed that person as his act was a substantial and operating cause of death. Suppose, on the other hand, that D's act is not an operating cause of death but merely provides the setting in which an intervening act by a third party is the immediate cause of death. D's act will not be a legal cause of death unless the third party's act is not free or not deliberate or not informed. In one case D in attempting to evade arrest, snatched a girl in front of him as he fired at police officers. The officers fired back instinctively, killing the girl. Although the officers' act resulted in the girl's death, it was held that D's act was in law a cause of the girl's death; the officers' reaction was instinctive (and therefore not deliberate) and was done in self-defence (and therefore not free).

Even where negligence in the treatment of a victim was the immediate cause of death, this does not exclude D's responsibility, unless the original injury had ceased to be an operative cause of death and the negligent treatment was so independent of D's acts and itself so potent in causing death that D's contribution was insignificant.

Sometimes a victim contributes to his death by doing something (other than taking evasive action, dealt with above) after D's act. The normal rule here is that if the victim's intervening act is not free, or is not deliberate, or is not informed, D's act will be a legal cause of death, whereas if the victim's act was free, deliberate, and informed D's act will not be a legal cause of death.

If an act is committed which leads to death, it is legally immaterial that the person injured had a medical condition rendering him more susceptible to death (eg haemophilia or a weak heart) or refused medical treatment. A person who commits violent acts must take his victim as he finds him, including the victim's mental condition or, even, the victim's religion. Where a girl, who was a Jehovah's witness, was stabbed by an assailant and refused a blood transfusion required before surgery and died, the act of her attacker was held to be a cause of her death.

Reasonable creature in being

Any human being, however deformed or subnormal, is a 'reasonable creature in being' and therefore protected by the law of homicide, provided that it is 'in being' at the material time.

This raises the question of the point of time at which a foetus becomes a human being and therefore a 'reasonable creature in being'. To be a reasonable creature in being a child must have completely emerged into the world and have a separate existence from its mother. To have had that separate existence it is not essential that the cord has been severed or even that the afterbirth has been expelled, but it must have breathed.

The wilful destruction of a child capable of being born alive before it is born alive may amount to the offence of child destruction, while the intentional procuring of a miscarriage may constitute the offence of abortion; see p 727. If someone injures a pregnant woman, and as a result of the attack she goes into premature labour and her child, although born alive, subsequently dies owing to its prematurity, the assailant is guilty of manslaughter but cannot be convicted of murder despite the fact that he intended to kill the woman or seriously harm her. It would make no difference that he intended also to destroy the foetus in the womb because such an intent does not suffice for murder.

Under the Queen's peace

For the purposes of murder, all persons are under the Queen's peace whether they are Her Majesty's subjects or not. The only persons who are not under the Queen's peace are alien enemies (and possibly rebel subjects) in the actual heat and exercise of war. However, while it is not murder to kill an alien enemy in battle, it is murder intentionally to kill an alien enemy in other circumstances (as when he is a prisoner of war).

Lapse of time between act and death

An offence of homicide may be committed by a person who carries out an appropriate act with the necessary mens rea regardless of the time which has passed since the injury, etc was inflicted. However, where the injury alleged to have caused the death was sustained more than three years before the death occurred, or where the person whom it is intended to prosecute for an offence of homicide has already been convicted of an offence in circumstances alleged to be connected with the death, no prosecution for an offence of homicide may be brought without the consent of the Attorney General. These provisions also apply to the offences of encouraging or assisting suicide and of causing or allowing the death of a child or vulnerable adult.

Intent unlawfully to kill or cause grievous bodily harm

The mens rea required for murder is an intent unlawfully to kill another human being or unlawfully to cause grievous bodily harm to another human being. This is described as 'malice aforethought'. To apply the term 'malice' strictly to the offence of murder can be misleading. The killing itself need not be such that it would normally attract the description 'malicious'; it might even be compassionate, as when a person kills a close relative, who is suffering considerably in the final stages of an incurable illness, by means of a drug overdose. In addition, the word 'aforethought' is also misleading because it suggests that the killing must have been premeditated, which is certainly not a legal requirement. Provided that D's fatal act was done with intent unlawfully to kill or cause grievous bodily harm, it is irrelevant that he acted on the spur of the moment, the intention only being formed a brief second before the killing. A person who intends to kill or cause grievous bodily harm will not intend to do so unlawfully if on the facts, as he believes them, his use of force is reasonable to prevent crime or in self-defence.

Provided that D intends unlawfully to kill or cause grievous bodily harm to another human being he is guilty of murder, even though the person whom he killed was not the intended victim. Thus if D fires at X, intending to kill him, but misses and kills V, D is guilty of murder: see p 5.

MANSLAUGHTER

Manslaughter is a term which covers a variety of unlawful homicides which do not amount to murder. Manslaughter continues to be a common law offence triable only on indictment. There are two varieties: voluntary and involuntary manslaughter.

Voluntary manslaughter

Voluntary manslaughters embody all the characteristics of murder including the necessary malice aforethought. It is the presence of particular circumstances acting upon the mind of the defendant, which has the effect of reducing the nature of the crime. These circumstances are: where the person was acting under 'loss of control' at the material time; where the person was suffering from 'diminished responsibility' at that time; and where a killing occurred in consequence of a suicide pact. Where their terms are satisfied, the rules relating to loss of control, diminished responsibility and suicide pacts operate as a partial *defence* to a charge of murder, reducing liability to manslaughter. A person cannot, for example, be charged with manslaughter under loss of control.

Loss of control

The Coroners and Justice Act 2009 (C&JA 2009), ss 54 and 55 replace the common law defence of provocation with a defence to murder of loss of control.

C&JA 2009, s 54(1) provides that where a person (D) kills or is a party to the killing of another (V), D is not to be convicted of murder if:

(a) D's acts and omissions in doing or being a party to the killing resulted from D's loss of self-control,

(b) the loss of self-control had a qualifying trigger, and

(c) a person of D's sex and age, with a normal degree of tolerance and self-restraint and in the circumstances of D, might have reacted in the same or in a similar way to D.

The fact that one party to a killing is by virtue of the defence of loss of control not liable to be convicted of murder does not affect the question whether the killing amounted to murder in the case of any other party to it.

Section s 54(2) provides that it does not matter whether or not the loss of self-control was sudden. However, by s 54(4) the defence does not apply if, in doing or being a party to the killing, D acted in a considered desire for revenge.

Qualifying trigger   D's loss of self-control must have had a qualifying trigger. By s 55(2)–(5), a loss of self-control would have a qualifying trigger if D's loss of self-control was attributable to:

(a) D's fear of serious violence from V against D or another identified person; or

(b) a thing or things done or said (or both) which—

(i)   constituted circumstances of an extremely grave character, and

(ii) caused D to have a justifiable sense of being seriously wronged; or

(c) a combination of the above matters.

There are two limits to the first trigger (ie (a)):

- the fear of serious violence must be of violence from V, the person killed; and
- the fear must be of such violence to D or some other identified person.

In determining whether a loss of self-control had a qualifying trigger, D's fear of serious violence must be disregarded to the extent that it was caused by a thing which D incited to be done or said for the purpose of providing an excuse to use violence.

The second trigger (ie (b)) deals with cases of gross provocation. In determining whether a loss of self-control had a qualifying trigger:

- a sense of being seriously wronged by a thing done or said is not justifiable if D incited the thing to be done or said for the purpose of providing an excuse to use violence;
- the fact that a thing done or said constituted sexual infidelity must be disregarded. (However, the Court of Appeal has held that, although sexual infidelity must be disregarded where it is the only element in support of a qualifying trigger, sexual infidelity may be relied on when it is not the only element relied on in support and is integral to and forms an essential part of the context.)

Objective requirement   Assuming the other two requirements in s 54(1) are satisfied, D is not guilty of murder if a person of D's sex and age, with a normal degree of tolerance and self-restraint and in the circumstances of D, might have reacted in the same or in a similar way to D. As can be seen this requirement is not wholly objective. It is not simply concerned with whether someone with a normal degree of tolerance and self-restraint might have reacted as D did (ie might he have reacted, and if so might he have reacted as D did?) but also whether a person of D's sex and age (the latter in particular may be relevant to tolerance and self-restraint) and in D's circumstances might have reacted as D did. However, not all D's circumstances can be taken into account. This is because s 54(3) provides that the reference in s 54(1)(c) to 'the circumstances of D' is a reference to all of D's circumstances other than those whose only relevance to D's conduct is that they bear on D's general capacity for tolerance or self-restraint. The closing words of s 54(3) make it clear that characteristics or other circumstances whose only relevance to D's conduct is that they bear on D's general capacity for tolerance or self-restraint cannot be referred to in applying the present requirement. Thus, the fact that D was intoxicated or intolerant or irritable or excessively jealous or had problems in controlling his impulses or otherwise had impaired powers of self-control must be ignored.

Function of judge and jury   If sufficient evidence is adduced to raise an issue with respect to the defence under s 54(1), the jury must assume that the defence is satisfied unless the prosecution proves beyond reasonable doubt that it is not. For these purposes, sufficient evidence is adduced to raise an issue with respect to the defence if evidence is adduced on which, in the opinion of the trial judge, a jury, properly directed, could reasonably conclude that the defence might apply.

Diminished responsibility

The Homicide Act 1957, s 2 governs this defence. Section 2(1) provides that a person (D) who kills or is a party to the killing of another is not to be convicted of murder if D proves that he was suffering from an abnormality of mental functioning which:

(a) arose from a recognised medical condition;
(b) substantially impaired D's ability to do one or more of the things mentioned below; and
(c) provides an explanation for D's acts and omissions in doing or being a party to the killing.

The things referred to in (b) are set out in s 2(1A). They are:

(a) to understand the nature of D's conduct;
(b) to form a rational judgement;
(c) to exercise self-control.

By s 2(1B), an abnormality of mental functioning provides an explanation for D's conduct if it causes, or is a significant contributory factor in causing, D to carry out that conduct. This means that abnormality of mental functioning need not be the sole cause of D's conduct. Thus, for example, the fact that other explanations or causes were also operative does not in itself negate the defence of diminished responsibility.

Although acute intoxication is a recognised medical condition, the Court of Appeal has held that the defence of diminished responsibility cannot be based on it.

Suicide pacts

The Homicide Act 1957, s 4 declares that it is manslaughter, and not murder, for a person to kill another or be party to someone else killing another, if he was acting in pursuance of a suicide pact between himself and the person killed. This is a matter for the defence to prove.

A 'suicide pact' is a common agreement between two or more persons, having for its object the death of them all, whether or not each is to take his own life. Nothing done by a person entering into a suicide pact may be treated as in pursuance of such a pact unless it is done while he has the settled intention of dying in pursuance of the pact.

Involuntary manslaughter

This category covers cases where D, who has unlawfully killed another (ie has committed the actus reus of murder), is not guilty of murder because he lacked malice aforethought (ie an intent unlawfully to kill or cause grievous bodily harm) but acted with some lesser degree of mens rea.

There are three types of involuntary manslaughter, between which there is a degree of overlap:

(a) killing by an unlawful and dangerous act;
(b) killing by gross negligence; and
(c) killing with recklessness as to death or serious bodily harm.

Killing by an unlawful and dangerous act

This mode of committing manslaughter is commonly known as 'constructive manslaughter'. It cannot be committed by an omission to act; an unlawful act by D is required. Three elements must be proved by the prosecution:

(1) *That D has committed the actus reus of an offence (other than homicide) with the mens rea required for that offence*; proof of this is proof of the 'unlawful act'. In most cases the offence will be a battery, but constructive manslaughter is certainly not limited to that offence; for example it is not unusual for a constructive manslaughter conviction to be based on an offence of administering a noxious thing (see p 696). However, the mere supplying of a noxious thing to another who then freely, deliberately and voluntarily injects himself with it will not amount to an offence of administration of a noxious thing and therefore is not an unlawful act and cannot make the supplier guilty of constructive manslaughter. Dangerous driving or careless driving which results in death can never constitute constructive manslaughter.

(2) *That the unlawful act was dangerous.* For an unlawful act to be dangerous it must be such that all sober and reasonable people would inevitably recognise that it must subject another person to the risk of some physical harm (including physical harm—eg a heart attack—resulting from shock), albeit not serious harm. This element is applied on the basis of the facts known to D at the time of his unlawful act or, if the act continues over a period of time, which became known during that period. Suppose that D, a burglar, being confronted by the householder and becoming aware that the householder is old and physically frail, continues his burglarious trespass. If the householder suffers a heart attack and dies in consequence of that trespass and on the facts which became known to D all sober and reasonable people would inevitably recognise that his burglarious trespass must subject the householder to the risk of some physical harm, the burglar is guilty of manslaughter.

(3) *That the unlawful and dangerous act was a cause of death.* It is not enough that some other act by D caused the death. As to the requirement of causation, see p 715.

Killing by gross negligence

This type of manslaughter may be committed by an act or by a failure to act (if D has failed in breach of a legal obligation to do an act); it is irrelevant whether or not D's act or omission would have constituted an offence if death had not resulted.

The requirements of manslaughter by gross negligence are:

(1) *The existence of a duty of care.* Such a duty arises when it is foreseeable to D that negligence will cause injury to the victim (V); there is a relationship of sufficient proximity between D and V, and it would be 'just and reasonable' to impose liability.

(2) *A gross breach of duty.* Normally, proof of negligence simply involves proof that, whether or not he realised the risk (of which he should have been aware), the person subject to the duty did something, or failed to do something, in a way which fell below the standard of conduct expected of a reasonable person in all the circumstances (including D's expertise and training, if they are relevant in the context). This is not enough in the case of gross negligence. For there to be gross negligence, D's conduct must have involved a risk of death to another and in respect of that risk his conduct must have fallen so far below the standard to be expected of a reasonable person, ie be so bad, that it should be judged criminal.

(3) *The breach must cause death.* This simply repeats the requirement of causation.

Killing with recklessness as to death or serious bodily harm

In this context, a person is reckless as to a risk of death or serious bodily harm if he himself foresees that risk as a highly probable consequence of the fatal act or omission and he takes that risk, and in all circumstances it is unreasonable for him to do so.

The present type of involuntary manslaughter will often overlap with constructive manslaughter and manslaughter by gross negligence, but it will not do so where the fatal act is not otherwise unlawful and there is no risk of death.

CORPORATE MANSLAUGHTER

The offence

The Corporate Manslaughter and Corporate Homicide Act 2007 (CMCHA 2007) creates the offence of 'corporate manslaughter' which is triable only on indictment. CMCHA 2007, s 1(1) provides that an organisation to which s 1 applies is guilty of an offence if the way in which its activities are managed or organised:

(a) causes a person's death; and

(b) amounts to a gross breach of a relevant duty of care owed by the organisation to the deceased.

By s 1(3), an organisation is guilty of an offence under CMCHA 2007, s 1 only if the way in which its activities are managed or organised by its senior management is a substantial element in the breach referred to in s 1(1). Because the offence requires a gross breach of a duty of care this offence is one requiring proof of gross negligence within its terms.

CMCHA 2007 has abolished the common law offence of manslaughter by gross negligence in its application to corporations and in any application it had to the other organisations listed below.

Organisations to which CMCHA 2007, s 1 applies

Section 1 applies to:

- a corporation;
- a government department or other public body listed in CMCHA 2007, Sch 1;
- a police force; and
- a partnership, or a trade union or employers' association, that is an employer (s 1(2)).

Senior management

'Senior management', in relation to an organisation, means the persons who play significant roles in:

(a) the making of decisions about how the whole or a substantial part of its activities are to be managed or organised; or
(b) the actual managing or organising of the whole or a substantial part of those activities.

Relevant duty of care

Section 2 states that a relevant duty of care in relation to an organisation means any of the following duties owed by it under the law of negligence:

(a) a duty owed to employees to provide safety at work;
(b) a duty owed as occupier of buildings or land to provide for the safety of persons on the premises;
(c) a duty owed in connection with the use or keeping of any plant, vehicle or other thing;
(d) a duty owed in connection with supplying goods or services;
(e) a duty owed in connection with carrying on any other activity on a commercial basis;
(f) a duty owed in connection with carrying on construction or maintenance operations; or
(g) a duty owed to a person who is held in detention. 'Detention' means detention in a prison or similar establishment or in a custody area at a court or police station, or detention in service custody premises, or detention in immigration detention facilities, or transportation under escort to such places, or placement in secure accommodation for children and young persons, or detention under mental health provisions.

It will be noted that a 'relevant duty of care' does not exist in respect of policing and law enforcement activities which are not covered by the Act. Thus, response to emergency calls (circumstances that are life-threatening or which are causing, or threatening to cause serious injury or illness, or serious harm to the environment or buildings or other property), the general conduct of police operations, witness protection, and the arrest of suspects fall outside the provisions of the Act.

Whether or not a duty of care was owed to a particular individual is a matter of law to be decided by a judge.

Exclusions

Sections 3 to 7 set out exclusions from the 'relevant duty of care'.

Decisions relating to public policy taken by public authorities such as government departments and local authorities are excluded, as are activities involved in carrying out statutory inspections unless the duty is connected to the organisation's duty as an employer or occupier of premises.

Other exclusions include those relating to policing and law enforcement. CMCHA 2007, s 5 provides an exclusion from the relevant duty of care in favour of the police and other enforcement agencies in respect of:

(a) operations for dealing with terrorism, civil unrest or serious disorder, which involve policing or law enforcement activities in the course of which officers or employees of the authority come under attack or face the threat of attack or violent resistance;
(b) activities carried on in preparation for, or directly in support of, such operations; or
(c) training of a hazardous nature, or training carried out in a hazardous way, which it is considered needs to be carried out, or carried out in that way, in order to improve or maintain the effectiveness of officers or employees of the public authority with respect to such operations.

Exclusions from the relevant duty of care exist for fire and rescue services, NHS bodies, ambulance services and the armed forces in respect of the way in which they respond to emergencies, and for child-protection and probation functions.

Gross breach of duty

By s 1(4)(b), a breach of a duty of care by an organisation is 'gross' if the conduct alleged to amount to a breach of that duty falls far below what can reasonably be expected of the organisation in the circumstances.

Authorisation of prosecutions

The DPP's consent is required before proceedings may be instituted.

INFANTICIDE

The offence of infanticide arose out of a desire to separate certain acts committed by a disturbed mother, who had recently given birth to a child, from the then mandatory death penalty for murder. It is not now, however, limited to mothers who would otherwise be guilty of murder. The Infanticide Act 1938, s 1 states that where a woman by any wilful act or omission causes the death of her child, being a child under the age of 12 months, but at the time of that act or omission the balance of her mind was disturbed by reason of not having fully recovered from the effect of giving birth to the child, or by reason of the effect of lactation consequent on the birth of her child, then if the circumstances were such that, but for the Infanticide Act 1938, the offence would have amounted to murder or manslaughter she is guilty of infanticide.

The basis of the law on infanticide is that depression after childbirth, or the effect of breast-feeding a child, are factors which can cause a mother to act out of character by committing some wilful act, or omitting to do something which a caring mother would do, that act or omission leading to the death of a child. The Infanticide Act 1938 only refers to children under the age of 12 months and this is not surprising, as Parliament had in mind a nursing mother who, in a fit of depression, killed the child which she was nursing. However, it leads to problems when such a mother kills more than one of her children, the other being over the age of 12 months. A charge of infanticide will lie in respect of the child who is under the age of 12 months and one of murder in respect of the child who is over that age. However, the defence of diminished responsibility would normally be available to the mother in respect of the killing of the older child.

Infanticide may be charged in the first instance as an offence triable only on indictment or may be raised as a defence to a charge of murder or manslaughter.

CAUSING OR ALLOWING A CHILD OR VULNERABLE ADULT TO DIE OR SUFFER SERIOUS PHYSICAL HARM

In cases of child abuse, or of abuse of a vulnerable adult, where the victim has died or been injured as a result of the act or default of someone in the same household, it is sometimes difficult to prove who perpetrated the crime, or to prove that either A aided and abetted B to do so or B aided and abetted A to do so (so that both can be convicted of an offence of homicide described above or a non-fatal offence, as the case may be).

This problem has been resolved by the Domestic Violence, Crime and Victims Act 2004 (DVCVA 2004), s 5, as amended by the addition of references to serious physical harm by the Domestic Violence, Crime and Victims (Amendment) Act 2012. DVCVA 2004, s 5(1) provides that a person (D) is guilty of an offence triable only on indictment if:

(a) a child under 16 or vulnerable adult (V) dies or suffers serious physical harm as a result of the unlawful act of a person who:
   (i) was a member of the same household as V, and
   (ii) had frequent contact with him;
(b) D was such a person at the time of that act;
(c) at that time there was a significant risk of serious physical harm being caused to V by the unlawful act of such a person; and
(d) either D was the person whose act caused the death or serious physical harm, or:
   (i) D was, or ought to have been, aware of the risk mentioned in para (c),
   (ii) D failed to take such steps as he could reasonably have been expected to take to protect V from the risk, and
   (iii) the act occurred in circumstances of the kind that D foresaw or ought to have foreseen.

The prosecution does not have to prove whether it is the first alternative in (d) or the second ((i)–(iii)) that applies.

There are two offences under s 5(1), one where death has occurred, and one where only serious physical harm has occurred.

If D was not the mother or father of V:

(a) D may not be charged with an offence under s 5 if he was under 16 at the time of the act that caused the death or serious physical harm;
(b) for the purposes of (d)(ii), D could not have been expected to take any such step as is referred to there before attaining 16.

For the purposes of s 5:

- 'act' includes a course of conduct and also includes omission;
- an 'unlawful' act is one that constitutes an offence, or (except where the act is by D) would constitute an offence but for being the act of a person under 10 or of a person who has the defence of insanity;

- 'vulnerable adult' means a person aged 16 or over whose ability to protect himself from violence, abuse or neglect is significantly impaired through physical or mental disability or illness, through old age or otherwise; and
- a person is to be regarded as a 'member' of a particular household, even if he does not live in that household, if he visits it so often and for such periods of time that it is reasonable to regard him as a member of it.

It is important to note that, although s 5 was introduced to deal with the case where it is unclear which of two defendants killed the vulnerable person, its drafting is not limited to this type of case. Consequently, it can apply to make one person guilty under it where it is clear that another person killed a child or vulnerable person and that the former person failed to protect the person killed.

The Court of Appeal has emphasised that, even if D had the awareness or foresight specified in (d)(i) and (iii), or ought to have had it, he cannot be convicted unless he failed to take the steps which could reasonably be expected to protect the child or vulnerable adult ((d)(ii)), and that this means 'reasonably expected *of the defendant*' (taking into account his characteristics and all the circumstances).

The Court of Appeal went on to hold, in relation to (d)(iii) that the act or conduct in question must occur in circumstances of *the kind* which were, or ought to have been, foreseen by D, as opposed to being identical.

The Court of Appeal added that the state of vulnerability envisaged by s 5 does not need to be longstanding. It may be short, or temporary. A fit adult may become vulnerable as a result of accident, or injury, or illness. The anticipation of a full recovery may not diminish the individual's temporary vulnerability.

THREATS TO KILL

By the Offences Against the Person Act 1861 (OAPA 1861), s 16 it is an indictable (either way) offence for any person, without lawful excuse, to make to another person a threat to kill him or a third person, intending that that other person would fear that it would be carried out. An unborn child is not 'a third person' for the purposes of this section.

It is not necessary that the person making the threat intends to kill. If D writes or telephones to another and says that he is a member of a terrorist group and that the group intends to kill that person or someone else, the offence is complete if D intends that the person receiving the message should fear that the threat will be carried out. Whether or not D is a member of that organisation is immaterial. However, if a similar telephone call was made by D to his friend as an intended joke, and D admitted at the end of the call that it was a joke, this would be clear evidence that D had not intended that it be taken seriously.

Self-defence can amount to lawful excuse for a threat provided that the threatened force is reasonable in the circumstances as the maker of the threat believes them to be. A householder who, hearing a burglar in his house, arms himself with a gun and threatens to kill the burglar with it when the burglar threatens him with a crowbar, might be found by a jury to have threatened reasonable force in self-defence.

SOLICITING ANOTHER TO COMMIT MURDER

It is an offence contrary to OAPA 1861, s 4 for a person to solicit, encourage, persuade or endeavour to persuade, or to propose to any person, to murder any other person. There must be some form of communication and this may be in any form. It is not essential that the person solicited, etc was affected by the communication. The offence is triable only on indictment.

ENCOURAGING OR ASSISTING SUICIDE

The Suicide Act 1961 (SA 1961) provides as follows.

By SA 1961, s 2(1) a person (D) commits an offence if:

(a) D does an act capable of encouraging or assisting the suicide or attempted suicide of another person; and
(b) D's act was intended to encourage or assist suicide or an attempt at suicide.

Section 2A elaborates on what constitutes an 'act capable of encouraging or assisting the suicide or attempted suicide of another person'. It provides that:

(a) if D arranges for D2 to do an act that is capable of encouraging or assisting the suicide or attempted suicide of another person and D2 does that act, D is also to be treated as having done it. Thus, if D tells D2 to assist in the commission of suicide by T, and D2 does so, D is treated as having done the act of assistance done by D2. Both of them can be convicted of an offence of encouraging or assisting suicide;
(b) where the facts are such that an act is not capable of encouraging or assisting suicide or attempted suicide, it is to be treated as so capable:
  (i) if the act would have been so capable had the facts been as D believed them to be at the time of the act (as where D wrongly believes that the harmless drugs which he supplies to assist another's suicide are lethal); or
  (ii) had subsequent events happened in the manner D believed they would happen (as where D posts a lethal drug to another to assist the other's suicide but this is lost in the post); or
  (iii) both;
(c) a reference to a person (P) doing an act that is capable of encouraging the suicide or attempted suicide of another person includes a reference to P doing so by threatening another person or otherwise putting pressure on another person to commit or attempt suicide.

A reference to an act in SA 1961 includes a reference to a course of conduct, and a reference to doing an act is to be read accordingly.

Section 2(1A) provides that the person referred to in SA 1961, s 2(1)(a) need not be a specific person (or class of persons) known to, or identified by, D. Thus, provided the necessary mens rea can be proved, a person who posts information about how to commit suicide to a suicide chat room may be convicted of the present offence. By s 2(1B), D may commit an offence under s 2 whether or not a suicide, or an attempt at suicide, occurs; it may be difficult, for example, in the case of information posted to a suicide chat room to prove that any reader committed suicide or attempted to do so.

A prosecution for the offence requires the DPP's consent. The DPP has published a policy outlining public interest factors for and against such a prosecution. The offence is triable only on indictment.

Information society services providers

In order to ensure that SA 1961, s 2 is compatible with the UK's obligations under the EU's E-Commerce Directive, the Crime and Justice Act 2009, Sch 12 makes special provision in connection with the operation of SA 1961 in relation to information society services providers.

CHILD DESTRUCTION

Murder requires the killing of a 'reasonable creature in being'. It does not protect a child yet unborn. It was therefore necessary to protect unborn children, and this is now done by the statutory offences of child destruction and abortion, both of which are triable only on indictment. The offence of child destruction is associated with those unborn children who are capable of being born alive.

The Infant Life (Preservation) Act 1929 (ILPA 1929) is concerned with persons who, with intent to destroy the life of a child capable of being born alive, by any wilful act cause a child to die before it has an existence independent of its mother.

A child is capable of being born alive when it has reached a state of development in the womb in which it is capable, if born then, of living and breathing through its own lungs without any connection with its mother. ILPA 1929 provides a presumption that a child is capable of being born alive at any time after the 28th week of pregnancy. However, the offence can be committed in relation to a younger child if it is proved that it was capable of being born alive. Provided that the child was capable of being born alive, it is irrelevant that it is not capable of sustained survival.

There is a proviso to the offence, namely that a person is not guilty of it unless it is proved by the prosecution that D did not act in good faith for the purpose only of preserving the life of the mother. This proviso has been construed by the judges as including acting to preserve the mother's physical or mental health. In addition, the Abortion Act 1967 (AA 1967), s 5(1) provides that no offence under ILPA 1929 is committed by a registered medical practitioner who terminates a pregnancy in accordance with the provisions of AA 1967, explained on p 728.

Perhaps this offence is best understood by examining extreme circumstances. If a man deliberately shoots his pregnant girlfriend in the stomach, her child having developed beyond seven lunar months, and the child is born dead, the man will be guilty of child destruction. However, if the child had been born alive and had died after having an existence independent of its mother, the man would be guilty of manslaughter.

ABORTION

The offence under OAPA 1861, s 58 commonly known as abortion is somewhat misleadingly described in this way, because the relevant offence does not require the abortion (miscarriage) of a foetus but merely that one of a number of specified acts should be done with intent to procure a miscarriage, ie the expulsion of an ovum implanted in the uterus (whether or not this occurs). Because there must be such an intent, someone who does something to *prevent* the implantation of a fertilised ovum in the uterus (as where the 'morning-after' pill is used) does not commit an offence under s 58 because a pregnancy only begins, and a miscarriage can only occur, after implantation.

The woman herself

OAPA 1861, s 58 states that it is an offence for a woman, being with child and with intent to procure her own miscarriage, unlawfully to administer to herself any poison or other noxious thing, or unlawfully to use any instrument or other means whatsoever.

As can be seen, s 58 provides that the woman must be pregnant if she is charged with abortion upon herself; it is not sufficient for her to imagine that she is pregnant. There are a number of means by which the offence can be committed. She may unlawfully administer to herself any poison or other noxious thing. 'Poison' has been defined as a recognised poison. If such a thing is taken, etc, it is irrelevant that the quantity is too small to cause harm. The term 'noxious thing' means any substance, other than a recognised poison, which is harmful in the dosage in which it was administered even though it might be harmless in smaller quantities. Clearly 'noxious thing' is a wide term. If a dosage is insufficient to render a substance a noxious thing, although D believes it is, there can be a conviction for an attempt to commit an offence under OAPA 1861, s 58. The term 'instrument' would cover the range of surgical instruments usually associated with medical operations and also the instruments used by the back-street abortionist, such as knitting needles. The term 'other means whatsoever' embraces any other way in which a person may seek to bring about an abortion, such as manual manipulation with the fingers. These comments concerning the nature of substances and instruments are equally valid in relation to the offence when carried out by some other person.

Any other person

OAPA 1861, s 58 goes on to provide that anyone (other than the woman herself) who, with intent to procure the miscarriage of any woman, unlawfully administers to her, or causes to be taken by her, any poison or other noxious thing, or who, with the same intent, unlawfully uses any instrument or other means whatsoever commits an offence, *whether or not the woman is pregnant.* The words italicised indicate an important distinction between the offence committed by the woman herself and the offence committed by other persons.

Unlawfully: the effect of the Abortion Act 1967

By AA 1967, s 5(2) anything done with intent to procure a woman's miscarriage (or, in the case of a woman carrying more than one foetus, her miscarriage of any foetus) is unlawfully done unless authorised by s 1.

AA 1967, s 1 legalises abortions (including abortion operations which are unsuccessful or not completed) carried out by a registered medical practitioner where two registered medical practitioners are of the opinion formed in good faith that:

(a) the pregnancy has not exceeded its 24th week and that the continuance of the pregnancy would involve risk, greater than if the pregnancy was terminated, of injury to the physical or mental health of the pregnant woman or any existing children of her family (a question in the determination of which account may be taken of the mother's actual or reasonably foreseeable environment); or

(b) the termination is necessary to prevent *grave* permanent injury to the physical or mental health of the pregnant woman (a question in the determination of which account may be taken of the woman's actual or reasonably foreseeable environment); or

(c) the continuance of the pregnancy would involve risk to the life of the pregnant woman, greater than if the pregnancy was terminated; or

(d) there is a substantial risk that if the child were born it would suffer from such physical or mental abnormalities as to be seriously handicapped.

In order to be lawful, any treatment for the termination of pregnancy must be carried out in a NHS hospital, Primary Care Trust hospital (prospectively deleted), NHS Trust hospital (prospectively deleted except in Wales), NHS Foundation Trust hospital or other approved place.

In an emergency any treatment for the termination of pregnancy may be carried out by a registered medical practitioner without complying with the above requirements if it is necessary to do so immediately to save the life of a pregnant woman, or to prevent grave permanent injury to her physical or mental health. This might occur during an operation upon the woman or at the scene of, or immediately following, a serious road accident.

The person supplying or procuring the means

OAPA 1861, s 59 punishes those who unlawfully supply or procure any poison or other noxious thing, or any instrument or physical thing whatsoever, knowing that it is intended to be unlawfully used or employed with intent to procure the miscarriage of any woman, whether she be or be not with child. Like abortion, the offence is triable only on indictment. 'Supply' should be given its ordinary meaning of transferring physical control of something from one person to another. 'Procure' in s 59 means to obtain possession of something for some other person. As to 'intent to procure miscarriage', see p 727.

CONCEALMENT OF BIRTH

OAPA 1861, s 60 provides that, if any woman is delivered of a child, every person who, by any secret disposition of the dead body of that child, endeavours to conceal its birth is guilty of an indictable (either way) offence. It is irrelevant whether the child died before, at or after its birth. However, in the case of a stillborn child, it must have reached a sufficient state of maturity that, but for some accidental circumstance, it might have been born alive.

The secret disposition may be done by anyone, but typically it is done by the mother following an unattended birth. In such a case, the offence is of importance where it cannot be proved how and/or when a child died, so that the mother cannot be convicted of an offence of homicide or of child destruction.

The abandonment of the child's body is not enough. There must be a secret disposition of it in an endeavour to conceal its birth from the world at large, but there can be such an endeavour even though some of the defendant's confidantes know of the birth. Clearly, a secret disposition in an endeavour to conceal the birth from a particular person does not constitute the offence.

CHAPTER 26

Public Order other than Offences Related to Sporting Events or Industrial Disputes

BREACH OF THE PEACE

To be a breach of the peace, the conduct in question does not have to be disorderly. However, there cannot be a breach of the peace on the part of a person unless there is an incidence of violence on his part; verbal abuse is insufficient.

There is a breach of the peace whenever and wherever (even on private premises):

(a) harm is *actually done*, or is *likely* to be done, to a person, whether by the conduct of the person against whom a breach of the peace is alleged or by someone whom it provokes; or

(b) harm is *actually* done, or is *likely* to be done, to a person's property in his presence; or

(c) a person is genuinely in fear of harm to himself or to his property in his presence as a result of an assault, affray, riot, or other disturbance.

Mere agitation or excitement does not amount to a breach of the peace where there is no question of harm or threat of harm. It is for the justices to decide whether or not there has been a breach of the peace in particular circumstances.

A breach of the peace is not in itself a criminal offence, but it (or the risk of it) can result in an arrest without warrant being lawfully made or in other steps being lawfully taken or in a binding-over order being made.

A police officer (and, indeed, every citizen) has power to arrest without a warrant or to take other reasonable preventive steps where:

(a) a breach of the peace occurs in his presence; or

(b) he reasonably believes that such a breach is about to occur by the person arrested although that person has not yet committed any breach.

The House of Lords has confirmed that the power to prevent a breach of the peace does not arise when it is believed (however reasonably) that a breach of the peace is *likely to become imminent* and that it is reasonable to take action to prevent it; it must be believed that the breach of the peace is *actually imminent*.

An example of the exercise of the power to take preventive steps in relation to a reasonably apprehended imminent breach of the peace is 'kettling' (containment of people within a police cordon during a violent demonstration). The European Court of Human Rights, affirming a decision of the House of Lords, has held that 'kettling' does not amount to a deprivation of the right to liberty, guaranteed by art 5 of the European Convention on Human Rights, of those kettled so long as it was rendered unavoidable as a result of circumstances beyond the control of the authorities, was necessary to avert a real, imminent risk of serious injury or damage, and was kept to the minimum required for that purpose. The Court of Appeal has held that kettling of a group of relatively peaceful demonstrators to prevent another group of protesters, who were violent, taking over the former demonstration was legally permissible because there had been a reasonably believed risk of imminent and serious breaches of the peace.

Where a person's conduct is lawful but provocative, preventive steps cannot be taken against him if his behaviour is reasonable; if it is, preventive steps can be taken against opponents who are likely to react violently to the provocation if this reaction would be unreasonable. For example, where a person concerned in a lawful activity, eg a demonstration against neo-fascists, acts reasonably in making a reasoned but impassioned speech against neo-fascism, which is likely to produce violence from his opponents, preventive steps can be taken not against him but against them if their violent reaction would be unreasonable. It would be different if it is the speaker's conduct which is unreasonable.

A constable is entitled to enter private premises (or to remain on them if he is already there), to deal with a breach of the peace or reasonably apprehended breach of the peace.

BINDING OVER

'Binding over' is a precautionary measure; it is not a conviction or punishment. It should not be ordered for some act that is past and not likely to be repeated.

The powers of a magistrates' court to bind over a person may be exercised either as a complaint (under the Magistrates' Courts Act 1980, s 115) or on the court's own motion, at any stage of court proceedings, under the Justices of the Peace Act 1361 and common law powers. Other courts can also bind over on their own motion, but we shall limit ourselves to the powers of a magistrates' court.

The importance of the fact that a magistrates' court can bind over of its own motion is that a person can be bound over in criminal proceedings whether or not he has been convicted of an offence; if he has been so convicted, the binding over may be in addition to any punishment imposed.

Where the magistrates act on complaint under the Magistrates' Courts Act 1980 they can only bind a person over if the facts complained of have been proved beyond reasonable doubt. If they act of their own motion, it must be proved beyond reasonable doubt that there is a risk of a breach of the peace or of an offence in the future.

The process of binding over is effected by requiring the individual to enter into a recognisance, with or without sureties, to keep the peace.

A person enters into a recognisance if he undertakes to pay a sum of money fixed by the court if he fails within the time specified by the court to comply with the terms of the recognisance, and a person becomes a surety if he agrees to pay a sum so specified if that other person so fails to comply.

Before a person is bound over, he will be told by the court of its intention to do so, and he, the complainant and their witnesses will be heard by the court. The court cannot impose a binding over if the person does not consent but, in the event of a refusal to be so bound, or to find sureties, the person concerned may be committed to prison for a fixed term not exceeding six months or until he complies with the requirements of the court, if sooner.

RIOT

The Public Order Act 1986 (POA 1986), s 1(1) provides that, where 12 or more persons who are present together use or threaten unlawful violence for a common purpose and the conduct of them (taken together) is such as would cause a person of reasonable firmness present at the scene to fear for his personal safety, each of the persons using unlawful violence for the common purpose is guilty of riot. Riot is triable only on indictment. It is the most serious offence against public order.

Basically, what is required is that a defendant (D) uses unlawful violence in the circumstances that:

(a)   12 or more persons (including D) who are present together use or threaten unlawful violence for a common purpose; and

(b)   the conduct of them (taken together) is such as would cause a person of reasonable firmness present at the scene to fear for his personal safety; and

(c)   D's use of unlawful violence was for the common purpose.

Riot may be committed in private as well as in public places. Thus, a riot can take place at factory premises, in a club, in a college, or—even—in someone's home.

Use of unlawful violence

A person does not perpetrate the offence of riot merely by threatening unlawful violence; he must actually use violence in the prescribed circumstances. If 12 or more people simply threaten violence for a common purpose in a frightening way, but none of them uses violence, riot is *not* committed.

On the other hand, provided one of 12 or more people actually uses violence for the common purpose, the offence of riot is perpetrated by him (or by all those who so use violence if more than one does). Those who merely threaten violence for the common purpose can, however, be convicted as accomplices to riot if they aid, abet, counsel or procure the use of violence by another (like anyone else who does so).

'Violence' is defined by POA 1986, s 8 as 'violent conduct'. It is not limited to violent conduct towards a person or persons since it includes violent conduct towards property (for example, smashing shop windows or overturning cars). Nor is it limited to conduct causing or intended to cause personal injury or damage to property, since it 'includes any other violent conduct (for example, throwing at or towards a person a missile of a kind capable of causing injury which does not hit or falls short)'. Swinging a knife at someone or firing a gun in his direction is violence under the definition in s 8, even though he is not hit.

The requirement that the violence be unlawful excludes from riot the use of violence which is justified by law (for example, under the rules relating to the use of reasonable force in self-defence, the defence of another or of property, or the use of such force in the prevention of crime or the effecting of an arrest).

Use or threat of unlawful violence for a common purpose by 12 or more present together

The Court of Appeal has held that 'present together' was intended to denote nothing more than being present in the same place. Thus, the 12 or more people need not form a cohesive group or be present pursuant to an agreement to come together.

The same comments apply to 'violence' as have been made above. If, during public disorder, the residents of a street use or threaten reasonable violence for the common purpose of defending themselves or their property from attack, their use or threat of violence does not constitute a riot because their violence is not unlawful.

In relation to threats, they may be by gestures alone (eg the brandishing of a weapon or the pointed display of it) or be by words alone, or be by a combination of both.

POA 1986, s 1(2) provides that it is immaterial whether or not the 12 or more use or threaten violence simultaneously. Equally, it is immaterial whether or not *any* of the others used or threatened violence at the time of the use of violence by the defendant. Provided that 12 or more persons who use or threaten violence are present *together* throughout, and that the violence is used or threatened by 12 or more for a common purpose, the offence of riot can be committed. Thus, it covers the situation where violence is used or threatened in one part of a crowd, then dies away, only to break out in another part at a later time.

It must be proved that the use or threat of violence by the 12 or more present together was for a purpose common to them (or at least to 12 of them). The question is not whether the 12 or more were present for a common purpose but whether they threatened or used violence for a common purpose. The common purpose need not be violence and it need not be an unlawful purpose (although, no doubt, it will normally be so). The common purpose may be inferred from the conduct of those involved; if a large group advance towards police officers, shouting 'kill the pigs', it may be inferred that they are threatening violence for a common purpose.

Conduct such as would cause fear

The question is not whether the conduct of an individual defendant would cause fear but whether the conduct of the '12 or more present together...' is such as would, *taken together,* cause fear (ie alarm or apprehension). The conduct of the 12 or more must be such as *would* cause a person (ie a third-party bystander) of reasonable firmness present at the scene to fear for his *personal safety*; it does not matter whether it actually caused fear to a person present at the scene or even *might* have.

No person of reasonable firmness need actually be, or be likely to be, present at the scene; in fact, no one else (beside the 12 or more) need be present or likely to be present at the scene. No doubt the case where there are no bystanders will be exceptional; where it occurs proof of the riot may be particularly difficult.

Mens rea

By POA 1986, s 6(1), a person is guilty of riot only if he intends to use violence or is aware that his conduct may be violent. POA 1986, s 6(5) provides that, for the purposes of the offence of riot, a person whose awareness is impaired by intoxication shall be taken to be aware of that of which he would be aware if not intoxicated, unless he shows either that his intoxication was not self-induced (as where his drink has been 'laced') or that it was caused solely by the taking or administration of a substance in the course of medical treatment. 'Intoxication' here means any intoxication, whether caused by drink, drugs, or other means (eg glue), or by a combination of means.

VIOLENT DISORDER

POA 1986, s 2(1) provides that, where three or more people who are present together use or threaten unlawful violence and their conduct (taken together) is such as would cause a person of reasonable firmness present at the scene to fear for his personal safety, each of the persons using or threatening unlawful violence is guilty of violent disorder, an indictable (either way) offence.

To perpetrate the offence, an individual defendant (D) must use or threaten unlawful violence in the circumstances that:

(a) three or more people (including D) together use or threaten unlawful violence (whether towards persons or towards property);
(b) the conduct of them (taken together) is such as would cause a person (ie a third-party bystander) of reasonable firmness present at the scene to fear for his personal safety. No person of reasonable firmness need actually be, or be likely to be, present at the scene.

As in the case of riot, violent disorder may be committed in private as well as in public places.

The prohibited conduct for this offence is substantially the same as that of riot (and the comments made when discussing the identical elements in riot are equally applicable here) with the exceptions that:

(a) D is guilty if he uses or *threatens* unlawful violence;
(b) only three persons (including D) who are present together are required to use or threaten unlawful violence;
(c) neither D nor the other participants are required to use or threaten unlawful violence for a common purpose.

The operation of the above can be illustrated as follows. If a racist march or static demonstration takes place in the centre of an immigrant community, accompanied by threats of immediate violence which would make a person of reasonable firmness fear for his personal safety, the offence is committed; but not if the taunts are merely of a racist nature highly offensive to local inhabitants, although they might give rise to an offence under POA 1986, ss 4A, 5, or 18 or the Crime and Disorder Act 1998, s 31 (pp 739, 756 and 742).

By POA 1986, s 6(2) a person is guilty of violent disorder only if he intends to use or threaten violence or is aware that his conduct may be violent or threaten violence.

As in the case of riot, a person whose awareness is impaired by intoxication is to be taken to be aware of that of which he would be aware if not intoxicated, unless he shows either that his intoxication was not self-induced or that it was caused solely by the taking or administration of a substance in the course of medical treatment.

Violent disorder is a useful offence to charge since it is not restricted to incidents which might be described as serious public disorder. If three or more gather outside a pub using or threatening violence against others, they can be convicted of violent disorder if they are acting collectively and their conduct (taken together) is sufficiently frightening to be liable to affect a person of reasonable firmness.

AFFRAY

POA 1986, s 3(1) provides that a person is guilty of affray, an indictable (either way) offence, if he uses or threatens unlawful violence towards another and his conduct is such as would cause a person of reasonable firmness present at the scene to fear for his personal safety.

The prohibited conduct is that:

(a) D must use or threaten violence *towards* another; and

(b) his conduct must be such as would cause a person of reasonable firmness present at the scene to fear for his personal safety.

Like riot and violent disorder, affray may be committed in private as well as in public places. One result is that, if a fight breaks out at a party in someone's home, those who participate in it can be guilty of affray if the terms of the offence are satisfied. In fact any assault—even a domestic one—wherever committed, accompanied by the use or threat of violence, is an affray if it would cause a person of reasonable firmness present at the scene to fear for his personal safety. *Most* of the elements of the actus reus are common to riot and violent disorder.

Use or threat of unlawful violence towards another

Unlike the position in riot and violent disorder, 'violence' here does not include violent conduct towards property.

Another important difference between affray and riot and violent disorder is that a threat of violence cannot be made by the use of words alone, whether the words are uttered orally or displayed or distributed in writing, and however aggressively they are expressed. Of course, an affray can be committed where a threat of violence is made by a combination of words and gestures (such as shouting out, 'I'll get you for that', while brandishing a weapon or even shaking a fist) as well as by gestures alone. As in the case of riot and violent disorder, the overt possession of weapons which are not waved or brandished can amount to a threat of violence. A threat or use of violence must be directed towards a person or persons actually present at the scene.

It has even been held that inciting an excited dog off the lead to attack someone can constitute a threat of violence. It would be different, of course, if a person merely said 'seize him' to a quiet dog lying at his feet, since the threat would be by words alone.

An affray, like riot and violent disorder, can only be committed if the violence is 'unlawful' as defined on p 732. Thus, a person who fights another in self-defence cannot be guilty of an affray, although his assailant can be if his use of violence would make a person of reasonable firmness fear for his personal safety.

Where two people use or threaten unlawful violence there is no need for them to do so for a common purpose.

Conduct such as would cause a person of reasonable firmness present at the scene to fear for his personal safety

This requirement provides an important limit on the offence, and excludes many fights from it. For example, it is most unlikely that a fight between two people, arising out of a personal quarrel but without any danger of the involvement of others, would consti-tute an affray.

The reference to the hypothetical person 'present at the scene' is to an 'innocent member of the public within sight or earshot' of the violence.

Where two or more people use or threaten the unlawful violence, it is the conduct of them taken together that must be considered for the purpose of ascertaining whether the conduct would have the required effect.

As in the case of riot and violent disorder no one besides the participants (ie no bystander) need be present, or be likely to be present, at the scene, and it is expressly provided by POA 1986, s 3(4) that no person of reasonable firmness need actually be, or be likely to be, present at the scene. The offence of affray is, in reality, concerned with *three* persons: a person using or threatening unlawful violence (D), a person towards whom the violence or threat is directed (V), and a notional person of reasonable firmness. It is not enough that the victim of the violence or threat is put in fear for his personal safety. The question is whether, *if the notional person of reasonable firmness* had been so present, he would have been caused to fear for *his* personal safety (as opposed to that of D or V or someone else).

Mens rea

By POA 1986, s 6(2), a person is guilty of affray only if he intends to use or threaten violence or is *aware* that his conduct may be violent or threaten violence. As in the case of riot, a person whose awareness is impaired by intoxication—whether by drink, drugs, or other means (or a combination of these)—must be taken to be aware of what he would have been aware of if not intoxicated, unless he shows that his intoxication was not self-induced or that it was caused solely by the taking or administration of a substance in the course of medical treatment.

FEAR OR PROVOCATION OF VIOLENCE

POA 1986, s 4(1) provides that a person is guilty of an offence if he:

(a) uses towards another person threatening, abusive or insulting words or behaviour; or
(b) distributes or displays to another person any writing, sign or other visible representation which is threatening, abusive or insulting,

with intent to cause that person to believe that immediate unlawful violence will be used against him or another by any person, or to provoke the immediate use of unlawful violence by that person or another, or whereby that person is likely to believe that such violence will be used or it is likely that such violence will be provoked.

Threatening, abusive or insulting

The words 'threatening, abusive or insulting' do not bear an unusual legal meaning. Instead, the magistrates will decide as a question of fact whether D's conduct was threatening, abusive or insulting in the ordinary meaning of those terms, and this is to be judged according to the impact which the conduct would have on a reasonable member of the public. Behaviour is not threatening, abusive or insulting merely because it gives rise to a risk that immediate violence will be feared or provoked, nor simply because it gives rise to anger, disgust or distress. This is shown by a case where D's activities in disrupting a tennis match at Wimbledon (by running onto No 2 court and distributing leaflets) caused anger among spectators, some of whom tried to hit him as he was removed. The House of Lords did not disturb the magistrates' finding that, albeit annoying and irritating, D's behaviour was not threatening, abusive or insulting.

If conduct is threatening, abusive or insulting, it does not matter whether or not anyone who witnessed it felt himself to be threatened, abused or insulted.

The distribution or display of any writing, sign or other visible representation which is threatening, abusive or insulting covers handing out leaflets (distribution) or holding up a banner or placard (display).

POA 1986, s 4 requires that threatening, abusive or insulting words or behaviour must be used *towards another person* or that threatening, etc written material be distributed or displayed *to another*. In relation to the use of threatening, abusive or insulting words or behaviour, 'towards another' imports a requirement that the words or behaviour in question must be directed towards (ie deliberately aimed at) another particular person or persons; if they are not, one must rely on the offence under POA 1986, s 4A or the lesser offence under POA 1986, s 5. Conduct is not used towards another if he is not present, in the sense that he can perceive with his own senses the threatening words or behaviour, etc. Thus, a person who makes a threat against a person who is out of earshot and only learns of it through a third party who is not under the control or direction of the maker of the threat cannot be convicted of an offence under s 4. However, whilst the person towards whom the behaviour was aimed must have been present to perceive it, this does not mean that the only means of proving that the victim perceived the behaviour is by hearing evidence from that person. Justices may rely solely on evidence from a bystander and may draw the inference that the victim did perceive what was said and done by an accused.

The insertion of 'to another' after 'distributes or displays' requires that the written material be directed towards another particular person or persons (or brought to his notice), rather than simply being distributed (eg by leaflets being left lying around in a shopping centre) or displayed (eg by pinning a poster to a wall in the middle of the night).

Public or private place

With one exception, an offence under POA 1986, s 4 can be committed in private places, such as factory premises, clubs or college premises, as well as in public places, such as football grounds, restaurants, public car parks and shopping precincts. Thus, an offence can be committed by pickets who threaten working colleagues, whether the pickets are inside or outside factory premises, or by protesters who invade a military base.

The exception is that, in order to exclude domestic disputes, s 4 has the effect of providing that the use of words or behaviour inside a dwelling is only an offence if the addressee (ie another person towards whom the words or behaviour are used or the writing, etc is displayed) is not inside that dwelling or any other dwelling. Thus, to use threatening, abusive or insulting words towards someone else in the same house cannot be an offence under s 4, and the same is true if such words are shouted to someone in the house next door. On the other hand, if such words are shouted in a house at a next-door neighbour who is in his back garden, an offence under s 4 will be committed, provided that the other elements of the offence are satisfied.

For the above purpose, 'dwelling' means any structure or part of a structure occupied as a person's home or as other living accommodation (whether the occupation is separate or shared with others) but does not include any part not so occupied, such as a garage, a shop with accommodation over, or the communal parts of a block of flats. Thus, if threatening words are shouted from a flat to a shop below, an offence under s 4 may be committed, and so may it if the words are shouted from the shop to the flat upstairs. 'Structure' here includes a tent, caravan, vehicle, vessel or other temporary or movable structure. A police cell is not a home or other living accommodation and is therefore not a dwelling for these purposes.

Mens rea

D must either intend the words, behaviour or writing, etc to be threatening, abusive or insulting or be aware that they or it might be. The result of this requirement is that a person, who uses words which are seemingly innocuous but which are addressed to, or heard by, persons to whom (unknown to him) they are highly insulting, is not guilty of the present offence.

A person whose awareness is impaired by intoxication must be taken to be aware of that of which he would be aware if not intoxicated, unless he shows either that his intoxication was not self-induced or that it was caused solely by the taking or administration of a substance in the course of medical treatment.

POA 1986, s 4 also requires that D's use of the words or behaviour towards another (hereafter described as 'an addressee'), or D's distribution or display to an addressee of the writing, etc, must be intended by D or be likely (whether or not D realises this) either:

(a) to provoke the immediate use of unlawful violence by an addressee or another; or
(b) to cause an addressee to believe that immediate unlawful violence will be used against him or another.

It will be noted, under para (a), that it is not necessarily an addressee who must be intended or likely to be provoked to immediate violence. It is sufficient that someone else present, towards whom the threatening, etc behaviour, etc was not directed, was intended or likely to be provoked. Thus, if X shouts at an Asian person whom he knows cannot speak English, 'Paki bastard, go home', intending that this should provoke immediate violence on the part of a group of racists who are in the near vicinity, the present offence is committed. On the other hand, for the purposes of para (b) (fear of immediate violence, intended or likely), the fear must be felt by an addressee (although it need not be fear of violence against himself, nor of violence by D).

It is important to note that the offence under s 4, unlike those under ss 1 to 3, is not concerned with the reactions of a hypothetical person of reasonable firmness. Instead, for example, a speaker must take his audience as he finds it. If he uses insulting words at a meeting, he is guilty of the present offence if they are likely to provoke the immediate use of violence by the particular audience he is addressing, even though he does not intend to provoke this and even though his words would not be likely to cause a reasonable person so to react, provided that he intends his words to be insulting or is aware that they might be.

It has been held that, since constables are under a common law duty to preserve the peace, they are unlikely to respond to threatening, abusive or insulting conduct by using violence. Nevertheless, such conduct directed towards a constable will constitute an offence under s 4 if it is intended or likely to put him in fear of immediate unlawful violence or is intended to provoke him to such violence. If the conduct is so serious as to amount to a breach of the peace and make it likely that a constable to whom it is addressed will have to use violence in the exercise of his common law power to arrest for a breach of the peace, an offence under s 4 will not be committed because the violence likely to be provoked will not be unlawful.

The fact that the unlawful violence which is intended or likely to be feared or provoked must be *immediate* must be emphasised. However, that term has been given a liberal interpretation by a divisional court. 'Immediate' does not mean 'instantaneous'. Instead violence will be 'immediate' if it is likely to result in a relatively short period of time and without any intervening occurrence.

As indicated above, the immediate violence which is intended or likely to be feared or provoked will not be unlawful if it is reasonable force in self-defence, or in prevention of crime, or is otherwise legally justified.

In the reference to an intention to cause, or the likelihood of causing, the apprehension of immediate unlawful violence or the provocation of it, 'violence' has the same meaning as in riot and related offences: see p 732.

HARASSMENT, ALARM OR DISTRESS

POA 1986, s 4 does not deal with many minor acts of hooliganism or other anti-social behaviour which are prevalent, particularly in inner city areas. Such conduct is a particular cause for concern when it is directed at members of especially vulnerable groups, such as the elderly, who may feel unable to act themselves to remove the nuisance or who may be deterred from participating in everyday activities or even from leaving their homes. It is at problems such as these, in particular, that the offences under POA 1986, ss 4A and 5 are aimed.

POA 1986, s 4A provides that a person is guilty of an offence if, with intent to cause a person harassment, alarm or distress, he:

(a) uses threatening, abusive or insulting words or behaviour, or disorderly behaviour; or
(b) displays any writing, sign or other visible representation which is threatening, abusive or insulting,

thereby causing that or another person, harassment, alarm or distress.

POA 1986, s 5 provides that a person is guilty of an offence if he:

(a) uses threatening, abusive or insulting words or behaviour, or disorderly behaviour; or
(b) displays any writing, sign or other visible representation which is threatening, abusive or insulting,

within the hearing or sight of a person likely to be caused harassment, alarm or distress thereby.

As these two definitions indicate, there is much common ground between these two offences. We shall deal with this first and then consider the elements which distinguish the two offences.

Common elements

The common elements are that a person must use threatening, abusive or insulting words or behaviour, or disorderly behaviour, or display any writing, sign or other visible representation which is threatening, abusive or insulting. The words 'threatening, abusive or insulting' have already been discussed and what is said there is equally applicable here. A similar approach applies to 'disorderly', a term with which magistrates are familiar via the offence of being drunk and disorderly. Thus, it is a question of fact for the magistrates whether the defendant's conduct was disorderly in the ordinary meaning of the term. A divisional court, in confirming this, has held that an element of 'violence' is not essential for there to be disorderly behaviour, and that neither is any feeling of insecurity, in an apprehensive sense, on the part of a member of the public.

Another common element is that harassment, alarm or distress must be caused (s 4A) or be likely (s 5). 'Harassment, alarm or distress' are not defined by POA 1986. They are somewhat vague terms. It has been held that 'harassment' does not require any apprehension about one's personal safety, nor (probably) does 'distress'.

A divisional court has ruled in the context of s 4A that 'distress' requires emotional disturbance or upset. That emotional disturbance does not have to be grave but the requirement should not be trivialised. There must be something amounting to real emotional disturbance or upset. These statements are equally applicable to s 5.

It has been held by a divisional court that a person could be harassed for the purposes of 'harassment' in ss 4A and 5 without experiencing emotional disturbance or upset. The court added that the words or behaviour in question must be likely to cause some real, as opposed to trivial, harassment; although that harassment need not be grave it must be more than trivial. On this basis it held to be sustainable a finding by a youth court that in the circumstances the likely effect of D's abusive words directed at a police officer during an incident in which for a period he was making it impossible for the officer to detain a suspect was to cause the officer some real harassment. The divisional court rejected the argument that s 5 is not available when police officers alone are the likely audience or target.

In relation to any threatening, abusive or insulting writing, sign, or other visible representation, the offences are limited to displaying and cannot (unlike an offence under s 4) also be committed by distribution. One result is that handing out threatening, abusive, or insulting leaflets is not caught by s 4A or s 5, unless the leaflets are so printed, and so held, that their contents can be said to be displayed in the sight of another. An important application of s 5 will be the display of graffiti or slogans likely to cause racial harassment.

Another distinction between the offences under s 4A and s 5 and that under s 4 is that the words or behaviour need not be used *towards* another person (nor need writing, etc be displayed to another). It follows that words or behaviour need not be directed towards another, nor need written material be deliberately brought to the attention of another.

An offence under s 4A or s 5 may be committed in a public or a private place, except that no offence is committed where the words or behaviour are used, or the writing, sign or other visible representation is displayed, by a person inside a dwelling and the other person who is harassed, alarmed or distressed thereby (s 4A), or, within whose sight or hearing it occurs and who is likely to be harassed, alarmed or distressed thereby (s 5), is also inside that or another dwelling. Consequently, displaying an abusive poster in the front window of a house adjacent to the street is capable of being an offence under s 4A or s 5, whereas if the poster was displayed in a place where it could only be seen by a person in the house or by a person in the first-floor flat of the house next door a s 4A or s 5 offence would not be committed.

The separate elements: POA 1986, s 4A

While D's conduct need not be directed towards another (and written material need not be displayed by him to another), there must be a victim in the sense that someone else is actually caused harassment, alarm or distress.

A decision of a divisional court provides a good illustration of the operation of s 4A. D, aged 12 and four feet nine inches tall, had been in the company of his sister when she was arrested for criminal damage. D made masturbatory gestures and called the police officers involved 'wankers'. V, one police officer, who was over six feet tall and weighed over 17 stones, arrested him for an offence under s 4A. At the boy's trial, V stated that he was not personally annoyed by his behaviour but that he found it distressing that a boy of D's age would be out in the early hours and acting as he did. A youth court found that V had been distressed by D's behaviour and found D guilty of an offence under s 4A. D appealed successfully to the divisional court. The Divisional Court held:

(a) D's behaviour was truly anti-social but there was nothing to suggest that it caused V emotional disturbance or upset and therefore the youth court could not properly conclude that V was distressed by D's behaviour;

(b) D had doubtless intended to insult or annoy V but there was no material upon which the youth court could have found that D had intended to cause real emotional disturbance or upset (ie distress) to him.

The fact that there has to be an identifiable victim means that some (possibly many) cases falling within s 4A will not be prosecuted under that section because victims of harassment might well be reluctant to give evidence for fear of reprisals, and without such evidence it will normally be impossible to prove that a particular person was caused harassment, alarm or distress. The offence is intended to protect the vulnerable, and the vulnerable are most likely to be influenced by the fear of reprisals.

D must either intend his words or behaviour, or the writing, etc, to be threatening, abusive or insulting or be aware that they or it may be threatening, abusive or insulting, or (as the case may be) intend his conduct to be or be aware that it may be disorderly.

D must also intend his threatening, etc words or behaviour or his display of threatening, etc, writing, etc to cause a person harassment, alarm or distress; it is irrelevant that the person who was actually caused the harassment, etc was not the intended victim.

Section 4A(3) provides two defences. Section 4A(3)(a) provides a defence for a defendant who alleges that he was inside a dwelling at the material time. It states that it is a defence for him to prove that he was inside a dwelling and had no reason to believe that the words or behaviour used, or the writing, sign or other visible representation displayed, would be heard or seen by a person outside that or any other dwelling.

Section 4A(3)(b) provides that it is a defence for a defendant to prove that his conduct was reasonable, reasonableness being judged objectively. It would be reasonable, for example, to shout a threat at a pickpocket across the street to deter him. This is an exceptionally vague defence and proving it may often be difficult.

The separate elements: POA 1986, s 5

While D's conduct need not be directed towards another (and written material need not be displayed by him to another), there must be a victim in the sense that what D does must be within the hearing or sight of a person likely to be caused harassment, alarm or distress thereby, although no likelihood of violence being provoked or feared is required. Whilst there must be evidence that someone was able to see or hear the words or behaviour complained of, the prosecution does not have to call evidence that the words or behaviour were actually heard or seen. However, if it does call a witness who says nothing in giving evidence about experiencing harassment, alarm or distress it cannot be inferred that he was likely to be caused harassment etc.

It is not necessary that a person who is likely to be alarmed should be alarmed for his own safety; it suffices that he is likely to be alarmed about the safety of someone unconnected with him.

D must either intend his words or behaviour, or the writing, etc, to be threatening, abusive or insulting or be aware that it may be threatening, abusive or insulting, or (as the case may be) intend his conduct to be or be aware that it may be disorderly. Consequently, a person who gives no thought to the nature of his conduct, or who honestly believes that there is no risk of it being threatening, etc, does not commit this offence. The provisions of s 6(5) concerning intoxication, discussed on p 733, apply equally to an offence under s 5.

Although D's conduct must be in the hearing or sight of a person likely to be caused harassment, alarm or distress thereby, D is not required to intend this or to be aware that it might occur. On the other hand, s 5(3)(a) provides that it is a defence for D to prove that he had no reason to believe that there was any person within hearing or sight who was likely to be caused harassment, alarm or distress.

Section 5(3)(b) provides a defence identical to that under s 4A(3)(a) above.

Section 5(3)(c) provides a defence (conduct reasonable) identical to that under s 4A(3)(b) above. A divisional court has held that if the prosecution proves, as it must, that D's conduct was threatening, abusive, insulting or disorderly, and that he intended it to be, or was aware that it might be, it would in most cases follow that his conduct was objectively unreasonable. The court also stated that, in considering whether conduct was reasonable, the court must have regard to all the circumstances, and to the European Convention on Human Rights, art 10(2), which sets out the grounds on which the freedom of expression may be interfered with. See, further p 781.

Offences against POA 1986, s 5 are 'penalty offences' for the purpose of the Criminal Justice and Police Act 2001, as explained on p 31.

RACIALLY OR RELIGIOUSLY-AGGRAVATED PUBLIC ORDER OFFENCES

A person commits an offence under the Crime and Disorder Act 1998 (CDA 1998), s 31 if he commits an offence under POA 1986, ss 4, 4A, or 5, which is racially or religiously aggravated. There are three separate offences under s 31, each based on one of the three basic offences under POA 1986. Those based on ss 4 or 4A are indictable (either way) offences.

By CDA 1998, s 28(1), an offence is racially or religiously aggravated for the purposes of CDA 1998, s 31 if:

(a) at the time of committing it, or immediately before or after doing so, D demonstrates towards the victim of the offence (or, in the case of a basic offence under POA 1986, s 5, the person likely to be caused harassment, alarm or distress) hostility based on that person's membership (actual or presumed) of a racial or religious group; or
(b) the offence is motivated (wholly or partly) by hostility towards members of a racial or religious group based on their membership of that group.

A divisional court has held that (a) envisages the presence of the victim of the offence and hostility based on the victim's membership of a racial group, whereas (b) concerns D's motivation in relation to a racial group, no member of which need be present.

What was said on p 687 about (a) and (b) is equally applicable here.

PROTECTION OF ACTIVITIES OF ANIMAL RESEARCH ORGANISATIONS

Interference with contractual relationships so as to harm animal research organisation

The Serious Organised Crime and Police Act 2005 (SOCPA 2005), s 145 provides that a person commits an offence if, with the intention of harming an animal research organisation, he:

(a) does a relevant act; or
(b) threatens that he or someone else will do a relevant act,

in circumstances in which that act or threat is intended or likely to cause a second person (B):

(a) not to perform any contractual obligation owed by B to a third person (C) (whether or not such non-performance amounts to a breach of contract);

(b) to terminate any contract B has with C; or

(c) not to enter into a contract with C.

The offence is an indictable (either way) offence.

A 'relevant act' is an act amounting to a *criminal offence*, or to a *tortious act* (ie an act giving rise to liability for damages) causing B to suffer loss or damage of any description. For these purposes, a tortious act does not include an act which is actionable on the ground *only* that it induces another person to break a contract with B.

'Contract' includes any other arrangement, and to 'harm' an animal research organisation means to cause the organisation to suffer loss or damage *of any description*, or to prevent or hinder the carrying-out by the organisation of any of its activities.

Section 145 does not apply to any act done wholly or mainly in contemplation or furtherance of a trade dispute within the meaning of the Trade Union and Labour Relations (Consolidation) Act 1992 (TULR(C)A 1992) which deals with similar acts committed in contemplation or furtherance of trade disputes.

Section 145 seeks to limit the activities of animal rights groups which have, for many years, targeted animal research organisations in an effort to compel them to cease activities authorised by law. Other legislation dealing with forms of harassment and disorder left many gaps which could be exploited by those who engaged in activities of various kinds aimed at 'persuading' such organisations to abandon all forms of research which involved the use of animals. Targeting was not restricted to the actual animal research establishments, since it was also aimed at other organisations which were alleged to have any form of business dealings with such animal research establishments, or with other organisations which had such dealings.

Intimidation of persons connected with animal research organisation

Animal rights groups are extremely well organised and encounter few difficulties in acquiring the names and addresses of directors and employees of organisations alleged to have connections with animal research establishments. Many research establishments, and the business premises of organisations with a connection with such establishments, are able to take effective measures to protect their property, to a large extent, but the residences of employees present an easier target to protesters, leading to houses being damaged and cars covered with paint stripper.

SOCPA 2005, s 146 therefore provides that a person (D) commits an offence if, with the intention of causing a second person (V) to abstain from doing something which V is entitled to do (or do something which V is entitled to abstain from doing):

(a) D threatens V that D or somebody else will do a relevant act; and

(b) D does so wholly or mainly because V is:
  (i) an employee or officer of an animal research organisation,
  (ii) a student at an educational establishment that is an animal research organisation,
  (iii) a lessor or licensor of premises occupied by an animal research organisation,
  (iv) a person who has a financial interest in, or who provides financial assistance to, such an organisation,
  (v) a customer or supplier of such an organisation,
  (vi) a person contemplating becoming someone within (iii), (iv), or (v),

(vii)   a person who is, or is contemplating becoming, a customer or supplier of someone within (iii), (iv), (v), or (vi),

(viii) an employee or officer of someone within (iii), (iv), (v), (vi), or (vii),

(ix)   a person with a financial interest in, or who provides financial assistance to, someone within (iii), (iv), (v), (vi), or (vii),

(x)   a spouse, civil partner, friend, or relative of, or a person known personally to, someone within (i)–(ix),

(xi)   a person who is, or is contemplating becoming, a customer or supplier of someone within (i), (ii), (viii), (ix), or (x), or

(xii)   an employer of someone within (x).

The offence is an indictable (either way) offence.

The provisions s 146 do not apply to trade disputes within the meaning of TULR(C) A 1992.

'Relevant act' has the same meaning as in s 145 referred to on p 743, except that the limitation whereby a tortious act does not include an act actionable only because it induces a breach of contract does not apply.

General

Proceedings for an offence under SOCPA 2005, ss 145 or 146 may not be taken without the consent of the DPP.

'Animal research organisation' means any person or organisation (a) who or which is the owner, lessee, or licensee of premises licensed or designated by the Animals (Scientific Procedures) Act 1986 or (b) who or which is the employer of, or engages under a contract of service, a person who is the holder of a licence under that Act or who is specified by it.

ANTI-SOCIAL BEHAVIOUR ORDERS

ASBOs made by a magistrates' court

CDA 1998, s 1 empowers a relevant authority, ie:

(a) a council for a local government area;

(b) a county council (in England);

(c) a chief officer of police (including the British Transport Police (BTP));

(d) a non-profit registered provider of social housing which provides or manages any houses or hostel in a local government area;

(e) any person registered under the Housing Act 1996, s 1 as a social landlord who so provides or manages;

(f) a housing action trust;

(g) the Environment Agency (EA); or

(h) Transport for London (TfL),

to apply by way of complaint to a magistrates' court for an anti-social behaviour order to be made in respect of any person aged 10 or over. Before applying for an order, a council must consult the local chief officer of police (and vice versa) before making an application. A registered social landlord or housing trust must consult the council and the chief officer of police before making an application. A chief officer of police can delegate the consultation process and the application for an order to officers in his force.

By CDA 1998, s 1(1), an application may be made by a relevant authority if it appears to it that:

(a) the person has acted in an anti-social manner, that is to say, in a manner that caused or was likely to cause harassment, alarm or distress to one or more persons not of the same household as himself; and
(b) such an order is necessary to protect relevant persons from further anti-social acts by him.

The defendant must have so acted within the previous six months of the making of the complaint. However, provided there is evidence of some conduct within that period, evidence of events which took place more than six months before the complaint is made are admissible to prove either limb of s 1(1).

In the case of a complaint by a council or a chief officer of police (other than BTP), 'relevant persons' are those within the council or county council area, or police area, respectively. In the case of a complaint by the chief officer of BTP 'relevant persons' are those who are within (or are likely to be within) areas which may briefly be described as railway land within the jurisdiction of the BTP. In the case of a complaint by a registered social landlord or a housing action trust or a non-profit registered provider of social housing, 'relevant persons' are people who are residing (or are likely to be) in the premises subject to their control or in the vicinity of those premises. The relevant persons in relation to the EA are persons who are (or are likely to be) on or in the vicinity of land in relation to which the EA has a statutory function. The relevant persons in relation to TfL are persons who are (or are likely to be) on or in the vicinity of land or vehicles used for a TfL transport service.

When an amendment made by the Crime and Security Act 2010 is in force, before making an application in respect of an under-16-year-old the relevant authority will have to prepare a report on that person's family circumstances in accordance with regulations.

If the conditions in (a) and (b) above are satisfied, the magistrates' court may make an ASBO, which prohibits the defendant from doing anything described in the order. In considering whether to make such an order, the court must disregard any acts which are shown to have been reasonable.

Evidential rules

The House of Lords has held that, although the proceedings described above to obtain anti-social behaviour orders are civil (and not criminal) in nature, condition (a) (anti-social behaviour) must be proved beyond reasonable doubt, and that condition (b) (ASBO necessary) involves an exercise of judgement and evaluation and does not involve a standard of proof. The court can also take into account evidence of bad character untrammelled by the conditions for doing so in criminal proceedings under CJA 2003, s 101. In determining whether the conditions are met the court can also take into account hearsay evidence admissible under the Civil Evidence Act 1995 (CEA 1995).

Under CEA 1995, s 1, subject to certain safeguards in later sections, hearsay evidence is admitted in civil cases.

CEA 1995, s 1 does not give a party to a civil action an unfettered right to introduce hearsay evidence in proceedings. In particular, a statement is not admissible at all if the maker of it (not the witness but the person whose words it is sought to admit) would not have been a competent witness. In addition a number of sections provide specific safeguards:

(1) Section 2 provides that a party proposing to adduce hearsay evidence must give notice to that effect and provide further details if requested to do so by the other party to the action. The Magistrates' Courts (Hearsay Evidence in Civil Proceedings) Rules 1999 require a party who desires to give hearsay evidence to serve a hearsay notice not less than 21 days before the date fixed for the hearing. Failure to give notice (or provide further details if requested) does not affect the admissibility of the evidence but may affect the weight that is given to it.

(2) Section 4 provides that in estimating the degree of weight which is given to the statement the court 'shall have regard to any circumstances from which any inference can reasonably be drawn as to the reliability or otherwise of the evidence'. Section 4(2) lists a number of factors to which the court should have regard in assessing weight but does not restrict the court to these factors. Factors listed include whether it would have been reasonable and practicable to call the maker of the statement, whether the statement was contemporaneous with events narrated in it, and whether the statement involved multiple hearsay.

(3) Section 5 allows the credibility of the maker of the statement to be impeached and also allows the admission of inconsistent statements made by the maker of the statement. With the leave of the court the maker of the statement, if available, may be called as a witness.

Section 9, which complements s 1, permits the admission of certain documents in evidence. While documents admissible under this section would also be admissible under s 1, the advantage of using s 9 is that the safeguards just outlined do not apply, although a court may direct that s 9 shall not apply having regard to the circumstances of the case. Thus, if there was doubt as to the authenticity of the document or as to whether it was genuinely contemporaneous with the information it purported to record, a court might reject it wholly or in part.

If what is relied on are oral statements to a police officer, the officer should give direct evidence of what was said and the circumstances in which it was said.

Other points

The prohibitions which may be included in an order are those necessary for the purpose of protecting persons (whether relevant persons or persons elsewhere in England and Wales) from further anti-social acts by the defendant.

Variation of an order may be applied for by way of complaint but no order can be discharged before the end of the period of two years other than with the consent of both parties. Its duration may be extended by way of variation.

The Police Reform Act 2002 (PRA 2002), s 50 provides that if a constable in uniform has reasonable grounds to believe that a person has been acting in an anti-social manner within the meaning of CDA 1998, s 1, he may require that person to give his name and address. Failure to do so, or the provision of a false or inaccurate name and address, is an offence.

ASBOs in county court proceedings

By CDA 1998, s 1B, a relevant authority additionally may apply for an anti-social behaviour order within county court proceedings concerning future behaviour. A relevant authority may apply to have a person who is not a party to the principal proceedings in a county court, but whose behaviour is material, to be joined in those proceedings so that an order can be applied for.

ASBOs on conviction in criminal proceedings

By CDA 1988, s 1C, an anti-social behaviour order can also be made on conviction in criminal proceedings, if a court considers that the conditions set out in CDA 1998, s 1 have been met, and this may be done whether or not an application has been made. The order must be additional to a sentence for the offence or an order of conditional discharge.

Individual support order

CDA 1998, s 1AA requires that where a court makes an ASBO in respect of a defendant who is a child or young person (10–17 inclusive) it must consider whether individual support conditions are met, and if they are must make an individual support order (ISO). This provision also applies where a child or young person is subject to an ASBO made on a previous occasion and a relevant authority applies for an ISO; this is useful where an ISO was not made when the ASBO was made. The individual support conditions are:

(a) that it would be desirable in the interests of preventing any repetition of the behaviour which led to the order;
(b) the defendant is not already subject to an ISO; and
(c) the court has been notified that arrangements are in place for implementing such orders.

If all of those conditions are met, the court must make an ISO for a period not exceeding six months. Such an order requires the defendant to comply with its requirements and to comply with directions given by a 'responsible officer' (social worker, education officer, or member of a youth offending team), eg, to participate in specified activities, or to comply with educational arrangements, but attendance at an appointed place may not be required on more than two days each week. Before the court makes such an order it must obtain information from the local authority or a member of a youth offending team. An ISO will cease if the ASBO to which it is linked ceases.

Breach of order

Breach of an order under CDA 1998, s 1, 1AA, 1B, or 1C or of an interim ASBO under s 1D without reasonable excuse is an offence (s1(10) (in respect of ss 1, 1B, 1C, or 1D) and s 1AB(3) (in respect of s 1AA)). Except in the case of breach of a s 1AA order, such an offence is an indictable (either way) offence. Where a defendant has adduced evidence which raises the issue of reasonable excuse, the prosecution has the burden of disproving it beyond reasonable doubt. What constitutes a reasonable excuse depends on the circumstances of the case in the context of the offence to which it relates; matters going to the defendant's state of mind, such as forgetfulness or a misunderstanding of the meaning of the order or an accidental breach may be relevant.

When an amendment made by the Crime and Security Act 2010 is in force, where a person under 16 is convicted of breach of an anti-social behaviour order, the court must make a parenting order unless it considers that there are exceptional circumstances making this inappropriate.

Miscellaneous

Review

CDA 1998, s 1J provides for an annual review of orders made under CDA 1998, s 1, 1B, or 1C which are made against a child or young person under 17. Such reviews will be carried out by the authority which applied for the order.

Contracting out of functions

CDA 1998, s 1F permits local authorities to 'contract out' their functions under the above provisions. The Secretary of State may by order specify a person to whom local authorities may contract out these functions. Such an order may specify conditions and may empower a local authority to make its own conditions.

Intervention order

CDA 1998, s 1G permits a relevant authority, which is applying for an ASBO under s 1 or under s 1B in respect of a person of 18 or over, to also apply for an 'intervention order' where it has received a report relating to the effect of the use of controlled drugs upon a person's behaviour. In such circumstances a court may, additionally, make such an order in the interests of preventing further such behaviour. Such an order may be valid for no more than six months and will require the person to comply with requirements specified in the order. In the event of failure to comply, the appointed supervisor must inform the relevant authority.

Failure, without reasonable excuse, to comply with a requirement of the order is an offence under s 1H.

Special measures

CDA 1998, s 1I makes provision for special measures under the Youth Justice and Criminal Evidence Act 1999 (see p 225) to apply to vulnerable and intimidated witnesses in the context of ASBO proceedings under s1 or 1C or proceedings for an interim ASBO.

VIOLENT OFFENDER ORDERS

Nature of orders and applications for such orders

CJIA 2008, Part 7 provides that a 'violent offender order' may be made in respect of a qualifying offender imposing such prohibitions, restrictions or conditions as a court considers necessary for the purpose of protecting the public from the risk of serious violent harm caused by the offender. Such an order will have effect for not less than two, nor more than five, years as specified in the order. The reference to protecting the public includes the public in the UK, or any particular members of the public in the UK, from the risk of serious physical or psychological harm caused by that person committing one or more 'specified offences'.

'Specified offences' are:

(a) manslaughter;
(b) an offence under OAPA 1861, s 4 (soliciting murder);
(c) an offence under s 18 or s 20 of that Act (wounding with intent to cause grievous bodily harm or malicious wounding);
(d) attempting to commit murder or conspiracy to commit murder; or
(e) a corresponding service offence.

A 'qualifying offender' is a person aged 18 or over who has been convicted of a specified offence and given a custodial sentence of at least 12 months or a hospital order, or a person found not guilty of such an offence by reason of insanity but made subject to a hospital order or a supervision order, or a person found to be under a disability to be tried and to have done the act charged who has been made subject to such an order. A person is also a qualifying offender if the above terms are satisfied in respect of proceedings outside England and Wales in respect of equivalent offences under the corresponding foreign law.

A chief officer of police may apply by way of complaint to a magistrates' court for a violent offender order in respect of a person who resides in his area, or who he believes is in, or intends to come to, that area, if it appears that: (a) that person is a qualifying offender; and (b) he has acted in such a way as to give reasonable cause to believe that it is necessary for such an order to be made. That application may be made to any magistrates' court whose area includes any part of the chief officer's police area, or any place in which it is alleged that he so acted. An order may be made if conditions (a) and (b) above are satisfied. It may not be made so as to come into force at any time when the offender is subject to a custodial sentence, on licence, or subject to a hospital order or supervision order, in respect of an offence.

A violent offender order may contain prohibitions, restrictions, or conditions preventing the offender from going to specified premises or places (whether at all or at specified times), attending specified events or having any (or specified) contact with a specified individual.

Provision is made for interim orders which apply before determination of an application.

Notification requirements

Offenders who are for the time being subject to violent offender orders (or interim orders) must notify the police, within three days of the making of the order, of particulars specified in CJIA 2008, s 108 (personal particulars including date of birth, name/s on the relevant date, National Insurance number, home address, and other addresses at which the offender may be found) and any other information to be prescribed by regulations. Changes must be notified within three days of the change in circumstances occurring. In addition, the offender must renotify the police annually of the information required to be given on initial notification; in respect of renotification of addresses (other than a home address) at which the offender may be found, provision is made for some other renotification period to be prescribed in regulations. The periodic renotification requirement does not apply in the case of an interim order. In addition, the time periods referred to above are suspended while a person is remanded in custody, in prison, or detained in hospital. The Criminal Justice and Immigration Act 2008 (Violent Offender Orders) (Notification Requirements) Regulations 2009 impose notification requirements in respect of travel outside the UK.

Offences

It is an indictable (either way) offence against CJIA 2008, s 113 for a person to fail, without reasonable excuse, to comply with any prohibition, restriction or condition contained in an order or interim order, or with any notification requirement; or to fail to provide fingerprints and/or a photograph if requested when making a notification. Knowingly providing false information when making a notification is also an indictable (either way) offence under s 113.

INJUNCTIONS TO PREVENT GANG-RELATED VIOLENCE

These injunctions, which are intended to be used against members of violent street gangs, are dealt with by the Policing and Crime Act 2009 (P&CA 2009), Part 4 (ss 34–50).

Those involved in gang-related violence should be prosecuted for a criminal offence if there is sufficient evidence and it is in the public interest, but there may be instances where criminal proceedings have not yet been brought and applying for a gang-related violence injunction may be an appropriate response.

Power to grant injunctions to prevent gang-related violence

P&CA 2009, s 34 empowers the High Court or a county court to grant an injunction against a respondent aged 14 or over to prevent gang-related violence if two conditions are met:

(a) that the court is satisfied on the balance of probabilities that the respondent has engaged in, or has encouraged or assisted, gang-related violence; and
(b) that the court thinks it is necessary to grant the injunction for either or both of the following purposes:
   (i)   to prevent the respondent from engaging in, or encouraging or assisting, gang-related violence;
   (ii) to protect the respondent from gang-related violence.

'Gang-related violence' means violence or a threat of violence occurring in the course of, or otherwise related to, the activities of a group that:

(a) consists of at least three people,
(b) uses a name, emblem or colour or has any other characteristic that enables its members to be identified by others as a group, and

is associated with a particular area. 'Violence' includes violence against property.

An injunction under s 34 may (for either or both of purposes (i) and (ii) above) prohibit the respondent from doing anything described in the injunction, or require the respondent to do anything described in the injunction.

The prohibitions and requirements included in the injunction must, so far as practicable, be such as to avoid any conflict with the respondent's religious beliefs and any interference with the times at which the respondent normally works or attends any educational establishment.

An injunction granted under s 34 may not include a prohibition or requirement that has effect after the end of the period of two years beginning with the day on which the injunction is granted ('the injunction date').

The court may attach a power of arrest in relation to any prohibition in the injunction, or to any requirement in the injunction (other than one which has the effect of requiring the respondent to participate in particular activities). If the court attaches a power of arrest, it may specify that the power is to have effect for a shorter period than the prohibition or requirement to which it relates.

Applications for injunctions

By P&CA 2009, s 37, an application for an injunction under s 34 may be made by:

(a) the chief officer of police for a police area,
(b) the chief constable of the British Transport Police Force, or
(c) a local authority.

A chief officer of police can delegate the application for an injunction to an officer in his force.

An application can be made 'with notice' or 'without notice'.

Applications with notice

These require the applicant to notify the respondent of the application for the injunction. In addition, before applying for an injunction under P&CA 2009, s 37, the applicant must comply with the consultation requirement, ie must consult:

(a) any local authority, and any chief police officer, that the applicant thinks it appropriate to consult,

(b) the youth offending team(s) in the area(s) where it appears to the applicant that the respondent resides if the respondent is under 18 (and will be under 18 when the application is made), and

(c) any other body or individual that the applicant thinks it appropriate to consult.

If the court adjourns the hearing of a 'with notice' application for an injunction under s 34, the court may grant an interim injunction if it thinks that it is just and convenient to do so. Such an interim injunction may include any provision which the court has power to include in an injunction granted under s 34 (including a power of arrest).

Applications without notice

By P&CA 2009, s 39, an application under s 37 may be made without the respondent being given notice, in which case the above consultation requirement does not initially apply. If an application without notice is made the court must either:

(a) dismiss the application, or

(b) adjourn the proceedings until a full hearing, in which case the applicant must comply with the consultation requirement before the date of the first full hearing (ie a hearing of which notice has been given to the applicant and respondent in accordance with rules of court).

Section 41 provides that, if an application without notice is made by virtue of s 39, and the proceedings are adjourned (otherwise than at a full hearing), the court may grant an interim injunction if it thinks that it is necessary to do so. Such an interim injunction may not have the effect of requiring the respondent to participate in particular activities. Otherwise, such an interim injunction may include any provision which the court has power to include in an injunction granted under s 34 (including a power of arrest).

Applications without notice should not be routine but may be appropriate if an injunction is urgently required, if there is a risk that the respondent may flee if given prior notice of an injunction application, or if giving notice would endanger witnesses.

Variation and discharge of injunctions

The court has power under P&CA 2009, s 42 to vary or discharge an injunction after a review hearing, or on an application to vary or discharge the injunction made by the applicant for the injunction or the respondent. If such an application is dismissed no further application may be made by anyone without the consent of the court.

Breach of injunction and enforcement

Punishment

An injunction is a civil order. Breach of an injunction is not a criminal offence; it is punishable as a contempt of court. Special provision is made by Sch 5A in respect of the punishment of a respondent under 18. Breach of an injunction must be proved beyond reasonable doubt. If the respondent's behaviour constitutes a criminal offence, it should be dealt with as such.

Arrest without warrant

This is governed by P&CA 2009, s 43, which applies if a power of arrest is attached to a provision of an injunction under Pt 4.

A constable may arrest without warrant a person whom the constable has reasonable cause to suspect to be in breach of the provision. If a constable arrests a person under this power, he must inform the person who applied for the injunction. The person arrested must be brought before a relevant judge within the period of 24 hours beginning with the time of the arrest. In calculating when the period of 24 hours ends, Christmas Day, Good Friday, and any Sunday are to be disregarded. 'Relevant judge' means a High Court judge where the injunction was granted by the High Court, and a judge, or district judge, of any county court where the injunction was granted by a county court.

By Sch 5, if the matter is not disposed of when the person is brought before the judge, the judge may remand the person in custody (if aged 18 or over) or on bail.

Issue of warrant of arrest

If the person who applied for the injunction considers that the respondent is in breach of any of its provisions, the person may apply under P&CA 2009, s 44 to a relevant judge for the issue of a warrant for the arrest of the respondent. A relevant judge may not issue a warrant on such an application unless he has reasonable grounds for believing that the respondent is in breach of any provision of the injunction.

By Sch 5, if a person is brought before a court by virtue of such a warrant, but the matter is not disposed of, the court may remand the person in custody (if aged 18 or over) or on bail.

Miscellaneous

The Secretary of State has published guidance on the use of gang-related injunctions. A chief officer of police for a police area, the chief constable of the British Transport Police Force, or a local authority must have regard to the guidance published.

CLOSURE ORDERS: PREMISES ASSOCIATED WITH PERSISTENT DISORDER OR NUISANCE

These orders are governed by the Anti-social Behaviour Act 2003 (A-sBA 2003), Part 1A.

Part 1A closure notice

A-sBA 2003, s 11A provides that where a superintendent (or above) or the local authority has reasonable grounds for believing that in relation to any premises:

(a) at any time during the relevant period (three months preceding consideration of issue of notice) a person has engaged in anti-social behaviour on the premises; and

(b) the use of the premises is associated with significant and persistent disorder or persistent serious nuisance to members of the public,

the authorising officer may issue a Part 1A closure notice if satisfied that the local authority has been consulted and that reasonable steps have been taken to identify any person who lives on the premises, or who has control of or responsibility for, or an interest in those premises.

A closure notice can also be issued by the local authority where it or a superintendent (or above) has the above reasonable grounds. In such a case, the authority must be satisfied that the relevant chief constable has been consulted and that reasonable steps have been taken to identify any person mentioned above.

An authorisation may be given orally (but must be confirmed in writing as soon as practicable) or in writing.

A closure notice must state that an application will be made under s 11B for closure of the premises; that access to the premises is prohibited other than to those who reside on the premises; give the date upon which the application will be heard; explain the effect of an order under s 11B; state that failure to comply with the notice is an offence; and give information concerning those who will provide advice.

A closure notice must be served by a constable or local authority employee by:

(i)   fixing the notice prominently to the premises;
(ii) fixing it at normal points of access;
(iii) fixing it to outbuildings which appear to be used with the premises;
(iv) giving a copy to at least one person who appears to have control of or responsibility for the premises; or
(v)   giving it to other persons who appear to exercise an element of control or responsibility in respect of the premises.

Reasonable force may be used for the purpose of fixing a copy of the notice to a *prominent place* on the premises. A copy must also be served on any other person who occupies any part of the building if it appears likely that that person's access will be impeded in consequence of the notice.

Closure order

A-sBA 2003, s 11B requires that the above actions must be followed by an application to a magistrates' court, by the issuer of the Part 1A closure notice, for the making of an order. The proceedings are civil in nature; for the implications of this, see pp 745 and 912. Such an application must be heard within 48 hours of the service of the initial notice. The justices may make an order if satisfied of the matters set out at (a) and (b) above and that the making of the order is necessary to prevent the occurrence of such disorder or nuisance for the period specified in the order (not exceeding three months). An order may make provisions relating to access to any part of the building or structure of which the premises forms part. The court may adjourn the hearing for a period of not more than 14 days to enable responsible persons to show why an order should not be made but may order closure during that period.

Enforcement

A-sBA 2003, s 11C provides that where an order is made a relevant person (constable or local authority authorised officer) may enter the premises and secure them against entry. Reasonable force may be used. If required, such a person must offer proof of identity and authority. Relevant persons have similar powers of entry should essential maintenance become necessary during closure.

Offences

By A-sBA 2003, s 11D, it is an offence, without reasonable excuse, to remain on or enter premises in contravention of a closure notice (s 11D(1)); to obstruct a person acting under the authority of the above provisions (s 11D(2)); or, without reasonable excuse, to remain on or enter premises subject to a closure order (s 11D(2)).

POWER TO DISPERSE GROUPS IN AREAS WHERE PERSISTENT ANTI-SOCIAL BEHAVIOUR HAS OCCURRED

Authorisation of dispersal powers

A-sBA 2003, Part 4 provides the police with powers to designate areas where they can disperse groups causing intimidation, direct that groups disperse, and after 9 pm return those under 16 to their homes. Protests are not excluded from the application of Part 4.

The principal provision is A-sBA 2003, s 30. It applies where an officer of above the rank of superintendent has reasonable grounds for believing:

(a) that any members of the public have been intimidated, harassed, alarmed or distressed as a result of the presence or behaviour of groups of two or more persons in public places in any locality in his police area (the 'relevant locality'); and

(b) that anti-social behaviour is a significant and persistent problem in the relevant locality.

In such a case that officer may give an authorisation that the powers to direct dispersal etc and to remove a child under 16 conferred on a constable in uniform by s 30 are to be exercisable for a period specified in the authorisation, which must not exceed six months. Such an authorisation must specify the grounds on which the authorisation was given.

An authorisation under s 30 must be in writing, and signed, and must specify the relevant locality, the grounds for the authorisation, and its duration. It must not be given without the consent of the district council(s) (or equivalent) for the relevant locality.

Publicity must be given to an authorisation by publishing an authorisation notice in a local newspaper and/or posting such a notice in some conspicuous place or places in the locality. An authorisation notice must state that an authorisation has been made, the relevant locality, and the period during which the powers under s 30 are exercisable. The notice should be a single document, including a map, the prohibitions, the area to which it applies, and the other statutory criteria, and must be drafted in the vernacular so that those to whom it relates can understand it.

Power to give directions

By A-sBA 2003, s 30(3), a constable in uniform who has reasonable grounds for believing that the presence or behaviour of a group of two or more persons in any public place in the relevant locality has resulted, or is likely to result, in any members of the public being intimidated, harassed, alarmed or distressed may give one or more of a number of directions under s 30(4). A divisional court has held that whether or not these provisions are satisfied must normally depend, at least in part, on the behaviour of the group, which must indicate in some way or other harassment, intimidation or the causing of alarm or distress. If that is not so, a dispersal order would be an illegitimate intrusion of the rights of people to go as they please in public.

The directions which may be given are:

(a) a direction requiring the persons in the group to disperse (either immediately or by such time as the constable may specify and in such way as he may specify);

(b) a direction requiring any of those persons whose place of residence is not within the relevant locality to leave the relevant locality or any part of the relevant locality (either immediately or by such time as the constable may specify and in such way as he may specify); and

(c) a direction prohibiting any of those persons whose place of residence is not within the relevant locality from returning to the relevant locality or any part of the relevant locality for such period (not exceeding 24 hours) from the giving of the direction as the constable may specify.

Provided a uniformed constable has the necessary grounds for belief, he may give a direction even though the group is of a different type, and their behaviour of a different kind, from that contemplated when the authorisation was given.

In two cases, a constable may not give such a direction: where a group is engaged in conduct which is lawful under the Trade Union and Labour Relations (Consolidation) Act 1992, s 220 (see p 797); or where it is participating in a public procession to which POA 1986, s 11 (see p 761) applies and the requisite advance notice has been given or is not required.

By A-sBA 2003, s 32(1) the directions which may be given by a constable may be given orally and to a person individually or to two or more persons together and may be withdrawn or varied. A person who knowingly contravenes a direction commits an offence (s 32(2)). If it is not admitted by the defendant, the authorisation must be proved in court by the prosecution, both as to the reasons for its making and the publicity given to it. To that end, it will assist the court to have a set of all the relevant documents relating to the authorisation lodged with it.

Power to remove

A-sBA 2003, s 30(6) provides that, if, between 9 pm and 6 am, a constable in uniform finds a person in any public place in the relevant locality who he has reasonable grounds for believing:

(a) is under 16; and

(b) is not under the effective control of a parent or a responsible person aged 18 or over,

he may remove the person to the person's place of residence unless he has reasonable grounds for believing that the person would, if removed to that place, be likely to suffer significant harm. The Court of Appeal has ruled that this power of removal is coercive, so that reasonable force may be used, if necessary, to remove the person.

Where the power to remove has been exercised, the local authority must be notified.

RACIAL OR RELIGIOUS HATRED OR HATRED ON THE GROUNDS OF SEXUAL ORIENTATION

POA 1986, Part III (ss 17 to 29) provides indictable (either way) offences relating to racial hatred. POA 1986, Part IIIA (ss 29A to 29N), added in 2006, introduced indictable (either way) offences relating to religious hatred which were extended to hatred on grounds of sexual orientation in 2008.

To a large extent, the offences of religious hatred and hatred on the grounds of sexual orientation mirror those under ss 17 to 29 which forbid threatening, abusive or insulting words, behaviour or material intended or likely to cause racial hatred, *but they are limited to words, behaviour or material which is 'threatening' and the defendant must intend thereby to stir up religious hatred or hatred on grounds of sexual orientation.* It is convenient to deal with these matters together within the parallel offences.

POA 1986, s 17 provides that '*racial hatred*' means hatred against a group of persons defined by reference to colour, race, nationality (including citizenship) or ethnic or national origins (as to these words see p 687). Hereafter, such a group is described for convenience as a 'racial group'.

POA 1986, s 29A provides that '*religious hatred*' means hatred against a group of persons defined by reference to religious belief or lack of religious belief.

Section 29AB defines '*hatred on the grounds of sexual orientation*' as meaning hatred against a group of persons defined by reference to sexual orientation (whether towards persons of the same sex, the opposite sex or both).

Other introductory points

All offences under POA 1986, Part III require that the material, words or behaviour in question are 'threatening, abusive or insulting'. These words do not bear an unusual legal meaning. Instead, as with offences under ss 4, 4A and 5, the magistrates or jury must decide as a question of fact whether the material, etc was threatening, abusive, or insulting in the ordinary meaning of those terms, and this is judged according to the impact which it would have on a reasonable member of the public.

References to 'abusive' or 'insulting' were excluded from Part IIIA because of concerns about freedom of expression. In addition, POA 1986, s 29J provides that nothing in Part IIIA of the Act should be read or given effect in a way which prohibits or restricts discussion, criticism, or expressions of antipathy, dislike, ridicule, insult or abuse of particular religions or the beliefs or practices of their adherents, or of any other belief system or the beliefs or practices of its adherents, or proselytising or urging adherents of a different religion or belief system to cease practising their religion or belief system. In view of the savings in respect of 'freedom of expression', to offend against Part IIIA the form of 'threat' will have to be very direct such as carrying a banner urging the killing of non-believers in circumstances which make it clear that a particular religion is the only true religion, or the making of a similar threat in some other way. Section 29JA provides that the discussion or criticism of sexual conduct or practices or the urging of persons to refrain from or modify such conduct or practices shall not be taken of itself to be threatening or intended to stir up hatred.

Use of words or behaviour or display of written material

POA 1986, s 18(1) provides that a person who uses threatening, abusive or insulting words or behaviour, or displays any written material which is threatening, abusive or insulting, is guilty of an offence if:

(a) he intends thereby to stir up racial hatred; or
(b) having regard to all the circumstances, racial hatred is likely to be stirred up thereby.

The parallel offence created by s 29B relating to religious hatred or hatred on grounds of sexual orientation requires the use of *threatening* words or behaviour, or the display of written material which is *threatening*, and an *intention* thereby to stir up religious hatred or hatred on the grounds of sexual orientation.

'Written material' includes any sign or other visible representation. POA 1986, ss 18 and 29B do not apply to words or behaviour used, or written material displayed, solely for the purpose of being included in a television or sound broadcasting or cable service. In such a case, however, an offence might be committed under s 22 (or s 29F) when the programme is transmitted.

These offences may be committed in a public place (for example, a football ground) or a private place. There is one limit in relation to private places. An offence is not committed by the use of words or behaviour, or the display of written material, by a person inside a dwelling which is not heard or seen except by other persons in that or another dwelling. Thus, words shouted from a house to people in the street or displayed on a poster on a window visible in the street are caught, but not words shouted inside a house or flat (and only audible within it or another house or flat) or a poster displayed in an inner room of a house.

It is a defence for the defendant (D) to prove that he was inside a dwelling and had no reason to believe that his words, threat or behaviour, or the written material displayed, would be heard or seen by a person outside that or any other dwelling.

As already seen, the prosecution must prove in the case of s 18 offences, that D intended to stir up racial hatred by his threatening, abusive or insulting words, behaviour or display or that such hatred was likely to be stirred up thereby. Where an offence against s 29B is alleged, there must be proof that D intended by his threatening words, behaviour, or display to stir up religious hatred or hatred on grounds of sexual orientation.

POA 1986, s 18(5) provides that a person who is not shown to have intended to stir up racial hatred is not guilty of an offence under s 18 if he did not intend his words or behaviour or the written material to be, and was not aware that it might be, threatening, abusive or insulting. Unlike comparable provisions in other offences in POA 1986, Part III, D does not have the burden of proving this lack of intent or awareness. There is no parallel provision to s 18(5) under s 29B as that section is limited to cases where D intended to stir up religious hatred or hatred on grounds of sexual orientation.

Racial or religious abuse or harassment unaccompanied by the mental element just described might, nevertheless, result in liability for an offence under CDA 1998, ss 31 (p 742) or 32 (p 695).

Publishing or distributing

POA 1986, s 19(1) provides that a person who publishes or distributes written material which is threatening, abusive or insulting is guilty of an offence if:

(a) he intends thereby to stir up racial hatred; or
(b) having regard to all the circumstances, racial hatred is likely to be stirred up thereby.

'Written material' includes any sign or other visible representation. Articles in electronic form are written material.

There must be a publication or distribution to the public or to a section of the public. 'The public' and 'section of the public' are not defined by the Act. In the only reported case which has referred to the point, the Court of Appeal held that a distribution of racist pamphlets to members of a family living together in one house was not a distribution to 'the public at large'. There is no minimum number of persons to whom publication or distribution must be made in order for it to be to 'the public'. Ultimately, the question must be solved by common sense, the question being whether the publication or distribution has been on a scale and on a basis such as to be describable as being to 'the public'.

In the above case, the Court of Appeal held that the family was not a 'section of the public'. This decision was sensible; a family group would not normally be described as a section of the public (and doubtless the same is true of other small, domestic groups). The Court stated that 'section of the public' refers to some identifiable group, 'in other words members of a club or association'.

Although the prosecution must prove that D intended to stir up racial hatred by the publication or distribution or that such hatred was likely to be stirred up thereby, it does not have to prove any knowledge on D's part in relation to the content of the written matter which he has published, or distributed, although he will almost inevitably have had such mens rea if he is proved to have intended to stir up racial hatred. However, under POA 1986, s 19(2), it is a defence for a defendant who is not proved to have intended to stir up racial hatred to prove that he was not aware of the content of the matter and neither suspected nor had reason to suspect it of being threatening, abusive, or insulting. The defence under s 19 is of obvious importance to innocent publishers or distributors, like newsagents.

POA 1986, s 29C provides that a person who publishes or distributes written material which is threatening is guilty of an offence if he intends thereby to stir up religious hatred, or hatred on the grounds of sexual orientation. The publication or distribution of written material must be to the public or a section of the public.

Possession of material

POA 1986, s 23(1) provides that a person who has in his possession written material which is threatening, abusive or insulting, with a view to its being displayed, published, distributed, or included in a television or radio broadcast or in a cable service (whether or not by himself) is guilty of an offence if:

(a) he intends racial hatred to be stirred up thereby; or
(b) having regard to all the circumstances racial hatred is likely to be stirred up thereby.

POA 1986, s 23 makes similar provision in relation to a person who has in his possession a film or sound or video recording.

For the above purposes, regard must be had to such display, publication, distribution, showing, playing, or inclusion in a programme service as the defendant has, or it may reasonably be inferred that he has, in view.

The Act does not define what is required for 'possession' in this context but reference to other areas of the law suggests that actual custody is not necessary provided that there is control over the material. The intended publication or distribution need not be by the person in possession. The result of all this is that, if racially inflammatory pamphlets printed by X are deposited with Y for safekeeping in his warehouse until X wishes to collect and distribute them, the present offence can be committed by X and by Y (as long as the pamphlets are in the warehouse) because, since Y (as well as X) is in control of the pamphlets, Y and X are in possession of them.

As with POA 1986, s 19, the prosecution does not have to prove any mens rea on the part of a person charged with possession contrary to s 23 in relation to the content of the material possessed by him. Likewise, it need not necessarily be proved that the defendant intended racial hatred to be stirred up by the publication or distribution, since it is enough that, if the material were published or distributed, racial hatred would be likely (having regard to all the circumstances) to be stirred up as a result of the publication or distribution. However, under POA 1986, s 23(3), it is a defence for a defendant who is not proved to have intended to stir up racial hatred to prove that he was not aware of the content of the material, and neither suspected nor had reason to suspect it of being threatening, abusive or insulting. This is of obvious importance to 'innocent' possessors of racialist material, such as warehousemen.

The person in possession of the material must have been in possession with a view to its publication or distribution. If there is a dispute about this, the magistrates or jury will have to draw such inferences as seem reasonable from the quantity and nature of the material possessed.

POA 1986, s 29G parallels this offence in relation to religious hatred or hatred on the grounds of sexual orientation. In this case, however, the material must be 'threatening' and intended to stir up religious hatred or hatred on the grounds of sexual orientation.

A justice of the peace, if satisfied by information on oath laid by a constable that there are reasonable grounds to suspect that a person has possession of written material or a recording in contravention of POA 1986, s 23 or s 29G, may issue a warrant authorising the entry and search of premises where it is suspected the material or recording is situated. A constable executing such a warrant may use reasonable force if necessary.

Other offences

POA 1986, ss 20, 21, and 22 respectively provide offences relating to threatening, abusive or insulting words, behaviour or material in public plays, visual or sound recordings, and programmes in radio or television broadcasts or cable services, which are intended or likely to stir up racial hatred. A detailed explanation of these offences is outside the scope of this book.

POA 1986, ss 29D, 29E and 29F respectively provide offences corresponding to those under ss 20, 21, and 22 in relation to threatening words, behaviour or material in public plays, visual or sound recordings, and programmes in broadcasts or cable services. In all these cases the play, recording, programme, or broadcast must be intended to stir up religious hatred or hatred on the grounds of sexual orientation.

General

None of the above offences applies to a fair and accurate report of:

(a) proceedings in Parliament, the Scottish Parliament or the National Assembly of Wales; or

(b) proceedings publicly heard before a court or tribunal exercising judicial authority.

However, in the case of a report of the proceedings of a court or tribunal, the exemption *only* applies if the report is published *contemporaneously* with those proceedings or, if it is not reasonably practicable or would be unlawful to publish a report of them contemporaneously (because of the law of contempt of court), is published *as soon as publication is reasonably practicable and lawful.*

No prosecution for an offence under Part III or Part IIIA of POA 1986 may be instituted except by or with the consent of the Attorney General.

INDECENT, GROSSLY OFFENSIVE, THREATENING OR FALSE COMMUNICATIONS

Two statutes are relevant under this heading.

Malicious Communications Act 1988

The Malicious Communications Act 1988, s 1 makes it an offence for any person to send to another:

(a) a letter, electronic communication or article of any description which conveys:
   (i) a message which is indecent or grossly offensive,
   (ii) a threat, or
   (iii) information which is false and known or believed to be false by the sender; or
(b) any other article or electronic communication which is wholly or partly of an indecent or grossly offensive nature,

if his purpose or one of his purposes in sending it is that the message, threat, or information should cause distress or anxiety to the recipient or to any other person to whom he intends that it, or its content or nature, should be communicated (s 1(1)).

A divisional court has held that the words 'indecent' and 'grossly offensive' in (b) are ordinary English words, and do not bear some special meaning such that communications of a political or educational nature fall outside the ambit of s 1. It said that the fact that a communication is political or educational in nature has no bearing on whether it is indecent or grossly offensive. The court added that it is possible to interpret s 1 in a way that is compatible with the European Convention on Human Rights, arts 9 and 10 (freedom of thought, conscience, and religion and freedom of expression), by giving a heightened meaning to the terms 'grossly offensive' and 'indecent' or by reading into s 1 a provision to the effect that s 1 will not apply where to create an offence would be a breach of a person's Convention rights.

In relation to the sending of a threat, a defence exists if D shows that the threat is to reinforce a demand made by him on reasonable grounds and that he believed and had reasonable grounds for believing that it was a proper means of reinforcing the demand.

For the purposes of the Malicious Communications Act 1988 the term 'electronic communication' includes any oral or other communication by means of an electronic communication system, and any communication (however sent) that is in electronic form.

Communications Act 2003

The Communications Act 2003 (CA 2003), s 127(1) provides that a person commits an offence who:

(a) sends by means of a *public* electronic communications network, a message or other matter which is grossly offensive or of an indecent, obscene or menacing character; or
(b) causes any such message or matter to be so sent.

A divisional court has held that a tweet is a message sent by means of a public electronic communications network because, although the twitter social networking platform is owned by a private company, it operates through the internet, a public electronic network provided for the public and paid for by the public through internet service providers.

The House of Lords has ruled that whether a message or other matter is grossly offensive for the purposes of CA 2003, s 127 must be judged by the standards of an open and just multiracial society; the words must be judged taking account of their context and all other relevant circumstances. To be guilty of an offence under (a) the sender of a grossly offensive message must intend his words to be grossly offensive to those to whom they relate, or be aware that they might be taken to be so. If the sender has such a state of mind he can be convicted under (a) even if a recipient of the message was not offended.

A divisional court has held that a message or other matter which does not create fear or apprehension in those to whom it is communicated, or who may reasonably be expected to see it, is not menacing; thus, if the person or persons who receive or read a message containing a threat would brush it aside as a silly joke, or a joke in bad taste, or empty bombastic banter, it is not menacing. In deciding whether a message is menacing, its precise terms, and inferences to be drawn from it, need to be examined in the context in which (and the means by which) it was sent. The Court added that to be guilty of an offence under (a) the sender of a menacing message must intend that the message should be of a menacing character, or be aware that it may create fear or apprehension in any reasonable member of the public who reads or sees it.

In addition, it is an offence against s 127(2) to send, *for the purpose of causing annoyance, inconvenience or needless anxiety to another*, by means of a *public* electronic communications network, a message which is known to be false, or to cause such a message to be sent, or persistently to make use of such a network for such a purpose.

An offence under CA 2003, s 127 is a 'penalty offence' for the purposes of CJPA 2001 and may be dealt with under a fixed penalty procedure: see p 31.

PUBLIC PROCESSIONS

Advance notice

POA 1986, s 11 requires that, where it applies, written notice specifying the date a procession is intended to be held, the time when it is intended to start, its proposed route, and the name and address of the person (or one of the persons) proposing to organise it, must be given to a police station in the police area in which it is proposed the procession will start. Section 11 applies if the procession is public and it is intended:

(a) to demonstrate support for or opposition to the views or actions of any person or body of persons;

(b) to publicise a cause or campaign; or

(c) to mark or commemorate an event.

If such a procession starts in Scotland, it is the first police area in England along the proposed route which must be given notice. The notice may be given by hand not less than six clear days before the date upon which the procession is intended to be held, or if that is not reasonably practicable, as soon as delivery is reasonably practicable. It will be appreciated that it may be impossible to give six clear days' notice of processions which occur quite spontaneously, following some incident concerning which a group feels inclined to demonstrate.

Section 11 permits delivery of the notice by recorded delivery service, if the notice is delivered not less than six clear days in advance. The provisions of the Interpretation Act 1978 under which a document sent by post is deemed to have been served when posted and to have been delivered in the ordinary course of post do not apply to the service of such notices.

Section 11 does not apply to processions commonly or customarily held (for example, a procession connected with an annual gala, a Remembrance Day parade, or a monthly campaigning mass cycle ride), or to funeral processions organised by funeral directors (as opposed to processions which suddenly appear in protest at a death). The House of Lords has held that a monthly campaigning cycle ride through central London which took a different route each time, although it set off from a fixed starting point, was a commonly or customarily held procession and therefore no prior notice needed to be given to the police.

Each of the persons organising a public procession is guilty of an offence if notice has not been so given, or if the details given in the notice differ from the actuality of the procession. It is a defence for a person to prove that he did not know of, or suspect the failure to give such notice, or that differences in the time, date, or route occurred due to circumstances beyond his control, or with the agreement of a police officer or by his direction.

Conditions

By POA 1986, s 12, the senior police officer may impose conditions in relation to any public procession, having regard to its time, place, or circumstances, including its route, if he reasonably believes that:

(a) it may result in serious public disorder, serious damage to property, or serious disruption to the life of the community; or

(b) the purpose of the persons organising it is the intimidation of others with a view to compelling them not to do an act they have a right to do, or to do an act they have a right not to do.

These conditions may include any measures which appear necessary to prevent such disorder, damage or disruption, or intimidation, including conditions as to the route of the procession or prohibiting it from entering any specified public place.

In the case of a procession which is actually being held, the senior police officer is the police officer most senior in rank present at the scene; in such a case, it is not necessary for the notice to be in writing. In the case where people are assembling for a procession, the senior police officer is the chief officer of police; in such a case the chief officer must give the notice in writing.

Offences are committed by an organiser (s 12(4)) or participant (s 12(5)) who knowingly fails to comply with a condition. It is a defence for a defendant to prove that the failure arose from circumstances beyond his control. A person who incites another to participate in a procession and to fail to comply with a condition also commits an offence (s 12(6)).

Prohibition

A chief officer of police may apply under POA 1986, s 13 to the council of the district for an order prohibiting for a period, not exceeding three months, the holding of all public processions (or any class of procession specified) within that district. The chief officer must reasonably believe that, because of particular circumstances existing, his power to impose conditions will not be sufficient to prevent serious public disorder. Such an order may be made by the council with the consent of the Secretary of State. The Commissioners of the Metropolitan and City of London Police Forces may themselves make such an order in respect of their police areas with the consent of the Secretary of State.

A person who organises (s 13(7)), or takes part in (s 13(8)), a public procession commits an offence if he knows that it has been prohibited. Those who incite others to participate in a prohibited procession are also guilty of an offence (s 13(9)).

Delegation

A chief officer of police may delegate any of his functions under ss 12 or 13 to an assistant chief constable or an assistant commissioner of police (as the case may be).

SQUATTING IN A RESIDENTIAL BUILDING

A person commits an offence under the Legal Aid, Sentencing and Punishment of Offenders Act 2012, s 144(1) if:

(a) he is in a *residential building* as a trespasser having entered it as a trespasser,
(b) he knows or ought to know that he is a trespasser, and
(c) he is living in the building or intends to live there for any period.

The offence is not committed by someone holding over after the end of a lease or licence (even if he leaves and re-enters the building).

For the purposes of s 144:

(a) 'building' includes any structure or part of a structure (including a temporary or movable structure);
(b) a building is 'residential' if it is designed or adapted, before the time of entry, for use as a place to live; and
(c) the fact that a person derives title from a trespasser, or has the permission of a trespasser, does not prevent him from being a trespasser.

ENTERING AND REMAINING ON PROPERTY

The Criminal Law Act 1977 (CLA 1977) provides certain offences relating to entering and remaining on premises. Although these offences are often associated with 'squatters', the relevant provisions extend to situations beyond those involving squatting.

The definitions of the various offences refer to 'premises'. CLA 1977, s 12 defines 'premises' as any building, any part of a building under separate occupation, any land ancillary to a building, and the site comprising any building or buildings together with any land ancillary thereto. Section 12 goes on to say that 'building' includes any immovable structure, and any movable structure, vehicle, or vessel designed or adapted for use for residential purposes. 'Premises' would therefore cover a block of flats, a single flat, the grounds in which the block has been erected, a residential caravan, or a houseboat.

Violence for securing entry

By CLA 1977, s 6(1), it is an offence for any person, without lawful authority, to use or threaten violence for the purpose of securing entry into *any premises* either for himself or for any other person, provided that:

(a) there is someone present on those premises at the time who is opposed to the entry which the violence is intended to secure; and

(b) the person using or threatening the violence knows that this is the case.

Use or threat of violence

The essence of this offence is the use or threat of violence for the purpose of securing entry into premises on which a person opposed to the entry is present: actual entry is not required. It is immaterial whether the entry which the violence is intended to secure is for the purpose of acquiring possession of the premises or for some other purpose. People who use or threaten violence in order to secure entry to a dance are guilty of the present offence if they know that someone inside is opposed to their entry; so are would-be squatters who, with such knowledge, seek to enter a house by such means, and so are protesters who likewise seek to enter a public building or a factory.

The violence used or threatened may be against a person or property (whether he or it is on or off the premises). It is important to recognise that the offence is to use 'violence', not 'force'. Although the difference may seem to be small, it is considerable in certain circumstances. It would no doubt amount to violence against the property to set fire to it to drive out those inside and thereby gain entry, but the degree of force necessary to insert a key and to secure entry does not amount to violence. It would be different if the lock was burst open by using violence against the door.

Someone on the premises opposed to the entry

Someone must be physically present on the premises who is opposed to the entry to them which the violence is intended to secure. One person will suffice and he might equally be the owner of the premises or a trespasser who is opposed to the owner's re-entry. Section 6 does not demand that this person physically opposes entry; it merely requires that the intended entry is against his will. Clearly, the present offence is not committed where someone breaks into an empty house.

Mens rea

In terms of the mens rea required for the offence, D must not only use or threaten violence for the purpose of securing entry into any premises but he must also know that there is someone on the premises at the time who is opposed to the entry in question.

Without lawful authority

An offence is not committed under CLA 1977, s 6(1) if the person using or threatening violence has lawful authority for acting in the prescribed way. This exemption is essential to protect the violent entries which might have to be made by police officers or bailiffs in executing warrants or orders of courts. However, the only entries so protected will be those where the form of violence used to secure entry is authorised by law.

It might be assumed that the owner of the property would always have lawful authority for re-occupying his property which had been unlawfully occupied by those who would exclude him, but this is not so. Section 6(2) states that the fact that a person has any interest or right to possession or occupation of any premises does not give him lawful authority to use or threaten the use of violence for the purpose of securing his entry onto those premises.

This situation is interesting. If the tenant of office accommodation went to enter his premises in the morning and found that the office had been taken over by homeless persons, he would commit the offence under s 6 if he attempted to secure immediate entry by the use or threat of violence, knowing that there was someone on the premises at the time who was opposed to such entry, because he would have no lawful authority for his action. This means that landlords and other non-residential occupiers must seek to recover possession of their premises by an action in the civil courts, unless it is possible for them to effect a peaceful re-entry. If an occupier does succeed in re-entering his premises, he does not commit any offence by proceeding to eject any trespasser, whatever liability he may incur by virtue of his entry.

Displaced residential occupiers and protected intending occupiers

Special provision is made for people falling within the definition of a 'displaced residential occupier' or 'protected intending occupier' of premises or any access to them.

The offence under s 6(1) does not apply to a person who is a *displaced residential occupier* or a *protected intending occupier* of the premises in question or who is acting on behalf of such an occupier. This exemption does not have to be proved by the defendant. Instead, if he adduces sufficient evidence (ie evidence which raises a reasonable doubt) that he was, or was acting on behalf of, such an occupier he is presumed to be, or to be acting on behalf of, such an occupier unless the contrary is proved by the prosecution.

By CLA 1977, s 12, any person who was occupying any premises as a residence immediately before being excluded from occupation by anyone who entered those premises, or any access to those premises, as a trespasser is *a displaced residential occupier* of the premises as long as he continues to be excluded from occupation of the premises by the original trespasser or by any subsequent trespasser. A person who is a displaced residential occupier of premises by virtue of this provision is regarded as such an occupier also of any access to those premises. CLA 1977, s 12 also provides that a person who was himself occupying the premises as a trespasser before being excluded is not a displaced residential occupier. The obvious example of a displaced residential occupier is the householder who discovers squatters in his house when he returns from work or from holiday.

An involved definition of '*protected intending occupier*' is provided by CLA 1977, s 12A.

The first type is an individual who, at the time of the request to leave:

(a) has in the premises in question a freehold interest or leasehold interest with not less than two years still to run;
(b) requires the premises for his own occupation as a residence;
(c) is excluded from occupation of them by a person who entered them, or any access to them, as a trespasser; and
(d) holds, or a person acting on his behalf holds, a written statement, signed by him and witnessed by a magistrate or commissioner for oaths, which:
  (i) specifies his interest in the premises, and
  (ii) states that he requires the premises for occupation as a residence for himself.
  The purpose of the statement is to enable the police to identify the protected intending occupier and thereby prevent abuse of the protection given by the Act.

The second type of protected intending occupier is an individual who, at the time of the request to leave:

(a) has a tenancy of the premises (other than a tenancy falling within the other two definitions) or a licence to occupy them granted by a person with a freehold interest or a leasehold interest with not less than two years still to run in the premises;

(b) requires the premises for his own occupation as a residence;

(c) is excluded from occupation of the premises by a person who entered them, or access to them, as a trespasser; and

(d) holds, or a person acting on his behalf holds, a written statement:
   (i)   which specifies that he has been granted a tenancy of those premises or a licence to occupy them,
   (ii)   which specifies the interest in the premises of the person who granted that tenancy or licence to occupy (the landlord),
   (iii) which states that he requires the premises for occupation as a residence for himself, and
   (iv)   in respect of which there is a statement signed by the landlord and by the tenant or licensee and witnessed by a magistrate or commissioner for oaths.

The third type of protected intending occupier is an individual who, at the time of the request to leave:

(a) has a tenancy of the premises in question (other than a tenancy falling within the other two definitions) or a licence to occupy them granted by a local authority, the Regulator of Social Housing, or a registered housing association or certain other bodies;

(b) requires the premises for his own occupation as a residence;

(c) is excluded from occupation of them by a person who entered them, or any access to them, as a trespasser; and

(d) has been issued by or on behalf of the authority, Regulator or association with a certificate stating that the authority, etc is one to which these provisions apply and that he has been granted a licence or tenancy to occupy the premises as a residence.

Adverse occupation of residential premises

CLA 1977, s 7(1) creates an offence of 'adverse occupation'. It provides that any person who is on any premises (including any access to them whether or not any such access constitutes premises within the meaning of CLA 1977) as a trespasser, after having entered as such, is guilty of an offence if he fails to leave those premises on being required to do so by or on behalf of a *displaced residential occupier*, or *a person who is a protected intending occupier of the premises*.

CLA 1977, s 7 gives a displaced residential occupier or a protected intending residential occupier of premises (eg a buyer or tenant who has not yet taken up occupation) who has been excluded from them by trespassers a swifter remedy for recovering possession of them than the available civil remedy. He may require the trespassers to leave and they commit an offence if they fail to do so.

There is no time set upon departure and it is submitted that this indicates that the requirement is immediate.

Three defences are provided by s 7(3), the burden of proof in each case being on the defendant (D):

(1) It is a defence that D believed that the person requiring him to leave was not a displaced residential occupier or a protected intending occupier of the premises, or someone acting on his behalf (s 7(2)). This plea will rarely succeed, particularly in the light of the requirement in the case of a protected intending occupier of a written statement or certificate to this effect.

(2) It is a defence that the premises in question are or form part of premises used mainly for non-residential purposes and that D was not on any part of the premises used wholly or mainly for residential purposes (s 7(3)). This means, for instance, that people involved in a factory sit-in do not commit the present offence if they fail to leave when required by a resident owner, so long as they are not in his flat or in part of the premises used wholly or mainly for access to, or in connection with, the flat.

(3) Where D was requested to leave by a person claiming to be (or to act on behalf of) a protected intending occupier, it is a defence for D to prove that, although asked to do so by D at the time that he was requested to leave, the person requesting him to leave failed at that time to produce a written statement, or certificate, complying with CLA 1977 (s 12A(9)).

Trespassing with weapon of offence

CLA 1977, s 8(1) provides an offence of trespassing with a weapon of offence, which can be committed whether or not the trespassory entry was secured by the use or threat of violence. Where an armed trespasser commits an offence under s 6 or s 7, discussed above, the effect of the present offence is to impose further liability on him because of the element of aggravation of his being armed.

Section 8(1) states that a person who is on any premises as a trespasser, after having entered as such, is guilty of an offence if, without lawful authority or reasonable excuse, he has with him on the premises any weapon of offence. As to 'has with him' see p 638.

The term 'weapon of offence' means any article made or adapted for use for causing injury to or incapacitating a person, or intended by the person having it with him for such use. An identical definition is discussed on p 942.

INTERIM POSSESSION ORDERS IN RELATION TO PREMISES

Obtaining a final possession order in respect of premises can take rather longer than desirable. As a result an interim possession order, which can be obtained more speedily, has been introduced by rules of court. Breach of such an order was made an offence by the Criminal Justice and Public Order Act 1994 (CJPOA 1994). CJPOA 1994, s 76(2) makes it an offence for a person to be present on premises as a trespasser at any time during the currency of such an order. However, no offence is committed if such a person leaves within 24 hours of the time of service of the order and does not return, or if a copy of the order was not affixed to the premises in accordance with the rules of court. A person in occupation at the time of service, who leaves the premises, commits an offence under s 76(4) if he re-enters the premises as a trespasser or attempts to do so after the expiry of the order but within a period of one year from service of the order.

By CJPOA 1994, s 75(1), a person commits an indictable (either way) offence if, for the purpose of obtaining an interim possession order, he makes a statement which he knows to be false or is misleading in a material particular, or recklessly makes such a statement. Likewise, a person commits an indictable (either way) offence under s 75(2) if he knowingly or recklessly makes such a statement to resist the making of an interim possession order.

POWER TO REMOVE TRESPASSERS

Direction to leave

CJPOA 1994, s 61 provides that if the senior police officer (the most senior in rank of the police officers present at the scene) reasonably believes that two or more persons are trespassing on land, that they are present with the common purpose of residing there for any period, that reasonable steps have been taken by or on behalf of the occupier to ask them to leave and that:

(a) any of those persons has caused damage to property on the land or used threatening, abusive or insulting words or behaviour towards the occupier, a member of his family or an employee or agent of his; or

(b) those persons have between them brought six or more vehicles onto the land,

he may direct those persons, or any of them, to leave the land and to remove any vehicles or other property they have with them on the land. The direction must be to leave immediately or as soon as reasonably practicable, rather than at a future time.

Where the persons in question are reasonably believed by the senior officer present to be persons who were not originally trespassers but have become trespassers on the land, he must reasonably believe that the other conditions above are satisfied after those persons became trespassers before he can exercise these powers.

The senior officer must reasonably believe that two or more persons are present on the land as trespassers with the common purpose of residence, no matter how brief that intended period of residence may be. A person can have a purpose of residing in a place notwithstanding that he has a home elsewhere. 'Land' does not include buildings other than agricultural buildings, nor does it include scheduled monuments or land forming part of a highway unless it is a footpath, bridleway, byway open to all traffic, restricted byway or cycle track. The term includes 'common land', whether public or privately owned common land.

The senior officer must also reasonably believe that reasonable steps have been taken by or on behalf of the occupier (the person entitled to possession of the land by virtue of an estate or interest held by him) to require the trespassers to leave.

The senior police officer, reasonably believing these facts, may require such persons to leave without further reason if he reasonably believes they have brought six or more vehicles onto the land. If they have not, he must reasonably believe that any of those persons has caused damage to the land or to property on the land (eg crops or trees), or has used threatening, abusive or insulting words or behaviour towards the persons specified (the occupier of the land, a member of his family or an employee or agent of his). Thus overnight campers are outside these provisions, provided that they have not caused damage to property on the land or used such words or behaviour. 'Damage' includes the deposit of any substance capable of polluting the land.

Where the land in question is common land, the references in s 61 to trespassing and trespassers include acts and persons doing acts which constitute a trespass as against the occupier or an infringement of the commoners' rights, and references to 'the occupier' include the commoners or any of them or, where the public has access to the common, the local authority as well as any commoner.

For the purposes of s 61, the term 'vehicle' includes any vehicle, whether or not it is in a fit state for use on roads, and includes any chassis or body, with or without wheels, appearing to have formed part of such a vehicle, and any load carried by, and anything attached to, such a vehicle, and a caravan.

The purpose of s 61 is to give the occupier of the land a swifter remedy for recovering possession of it than the available civil remedy.

Offences

If a trespasser directed to leave complies with that direction, he commits no offence. On the other hand, he commits an offence under CJPOA 1994, s 61(4) if, knowing that a direction has been given which applies to him:

(a) he fails to leave the land (with any vehicle or other property he is required to remove), as soon as reasonably practicable; or
(b) having left, he again enters the land as a trespasser within a three-month period beginning on the day on which the direction is given.

(a) and (b) above are separate offences. By s 61(6), it is a defence for the defendant to prove that:

(a) he was not trespassing on the land; or
(b) he had a reasonable excuse for failing to leave the land as soon as reasonably practicable or, as the case may be, for again entering the land as a trespasser.

The defence of 'not trespassing' refers to not trespassing at the time that the senior police officer forms his reasonable belief, and not the time of the prohibited conduct.

Police powers

By CJPOA 1994, s 62, where a direction under s 61 has been given, a constable may seize and remove a vehicle if he reasonably suspects that a person to whom the direction applies has, without reasonable excuse, failed to remove the vehicle which appears to belong to him or be in his possession or control. The same powers apply where such a person has, without reasonable excuse, re-entered the land within a period of three months from the date of the direction.

POWER TO REMOVE TRESPASSERS WHERE AN ALTERNATIVE SITE IS AVAILABLE

Direction to leave

CJPOA 1994, s 62A provides that, where the senior police officer present at the scene reasonably believes that certain conditions are satisfied in relation to a person and land, he may direct the person to leave the land and to remove any vehicle and other property which he has with him on the land. The conditions are:

(a) that the person and one or more others ('the trespassers') are trespassing on land;
(b) that the trespassers have between them at least one vehicle on the land;
(c) that the trespassers are there for the common purpose of residing there for any period;
(d) if it appears to the officer that the person has one or more caravans in his possession or control on the land, that there is a suitable pitch on a relevant caravan site

(ie a site in the same local authority area managed by that authority, a private registered provider of social housing, or a registered social landlord) for the caravan(s); and

(e) that the occupier of the land or someone acting on his behalf has asked the police to remove the trespassers.

Such a direction may be communicated to the person to whom it applies by any constable at the scene. 'Land' does not include buildings other than agricultural buildings or scheduled monuments. A person may be regarded as having a purpose of residing in a place even if he has a home elsewhere, as would be the case where there is a 'sited' residential caravan. 'Occupier', 'trespassing', 'trespassers', and 'vehicle' have the same meaning as in CJPOA 1994, s 61. Section 62D makes the same provision in respect of common land as applies to s 61.

Where a police officer proposes to give such a direction he must consult every local authority within whose area the land is situated as to whether there is a suitable pitch for the caravan or each of the caravans on a relevant caravan site situated in their area.

Offences

By CJPOA 1994, s 62B(1), a person commits an offence if he knows that a direction under s 62A has been given which applies to him and (a) he fails to leave the land as soon as reasonably practicable, or (b) he enters any land within the area of the relevant local authority as a trespasser within a period of three months with the intention of residing there. Section 62B(5) provides defences where a defendant can show:

(a) that he was not trespassing on land in respect of which he is alleged to have committed the offence; or

(b) that he had a reasonable excuse for failing to leave as soon as reasonably practicable, or for entering land in the area of the relevant local authority as a trespasser with the intention of residing there; or

(c) that at the time the direction was given he was under 18 and was residing with his parent or guardian.

Police powers

CJPOA 1994, s 62C provides that, where a constable reasonably suspects that a person subject to such a direction has, without reasonable excuse, failed to remove any vehicle which appears to belong to him or to be under his possession or control, or that such a person has entered any land in the area of the relevant local authority as a trespasser with a vehicle within the period of three months from the day of the direction, he may seize and remove the vehicle.

UNAUTHORISED CAMPING WITH A VEHICLE

CJPOA 1994, s 77 empowers a county council, district council, or London borough council to direct persons residing in a vehicle or vehicles to leave:

(a) any land forming part of a highway;

(b) any other unoccupied land in the open air; or

(c) any occupied land in the open air where they are camping without the consent of the occupier of the land.

Such a direction may be addressed to a particular person or persons or to all of the occupants of vehicles on the land. It is not necessary for the local authority to show that there has been any form of nuisance caused by their presence.

Where such notice of a direction has been served, any person who knows that the direction has been given, and that it applies to him, commits an offence under s 77(3):

(a) if he fails, as soon as practicable, to leave the land or remove from the land any vehicle, or any other property which is a subject of the direction; or

(b) if, having removed any such vehicle or property, he again enters the land with a vehicle within a period of three months from the day upon which the direction was given.

Section 77(5) provides a defence where such failure to leave or remove a vehicle or other property as soon as practicable, or the re-entry with a vehicle, was due to illness, mechanical breakdown, or other immediate emergency. The onus is upon the defendant to show such a defence.

If a direction under s 77 is not complied with, the local authority can make an application to a magistrates' court under s 78 for an order for the removal by local authority officers and employees of persons and vehicles on the land in contravention of the direction. Wilful obstruction of someone acting under such an order is an offence under s 78(4). Although police officers do not actually execute an order under s 78, they will often be in attendance in view of the risk to public order.

AGGRAVATED TRESPASS

Offence of aggravated trespass

CJPOA 1994, s 68(1) states that a person commits the offence of aggravated trespass if he trespasses on land and, in relation to any lawful activity which persons are engaged in, or are about to engage in, on that land or adjoining land, does there anything which is intended by him to have the effect:

(a) of intimidating those persons or any of them so as to deter them or any of them from engaging in that activity;

(b) of obstructing that activity; or

(c) of disrupting that activity.

For this purpose, an activity on the part of a person or persons on land is 'lawful' if he or they may engage in the activity on that land on that occasion without committing an offence against English law or trespassing on the land. Even if proved, the commission of an offence only under international law by a non-trespasser is not enough; there is House of Lords authority to this effect. Nor is an activity rendered unlawful by some fact or event far remote from an activity on the land itself; the unlawfulness must be inherent in the activity in question.

The persons engaged, or about to engage, in the relevant lawful activity must physically be present on the land in question at the time of the alleged trespass.

Some act is required in addition to trespass. It must be specified in the charge and must be shown to be intended to have one of the effects set out at (a)–(c). Thus a trespasser who gives drugged meat to gundogs commits such an act, as does someone who immobilises a bulldozer on a construction site. Indeed, a divisional court has held that a trespasser commits an offence under s 68 if he does an act with intent to commit a further act, which is not committed, and thereby to intimidate, obstruct or disrupt a lawful activity, if the act done is sufficiently closely connected with the intended intimidation, etc as to be more than merely preparatory to it. On this basis, the court upheld the conviction under s 68 of a person who had trespassed on land and run after a hunt with the intention of getting close enough to do something to disrupt it.

The act must be committed on land. By s 68(5), 'land' does not include land forming part of a highway unless it is a footpath, bridleway, etc. A divisional court has held that 'land' in s 68 includes buildings.

A failure to do something is not enough. Trespassers who were already at a particular spot, who refused on an impulse to move to allow other persons to pass, would not commit an offence under s 68; whereas it would be an offence if they deliberately placed themselves there with the intention of disrupting the activity.

The offence is one requiring 'intent' to create one of these specified effects. The trespassing rambler who walks through grouse moors will not commit this offence even though he disrupts a shoot, if that was not his intention. Those who protest at the building of a new road will commit the offence if they deliberately sit down on private land in front of the machines because they intend to obstruct or disrupt the lawful activity of the developers.

Since they are not acting to prevent an unlawful act, protesters who are otherwise guilty under s 68 cannot rely on the common law defence of defence of property as a defence to a charge of aggravated trespass, because that defence is limited to defence against an act which is criminal or tortious (see p 685).

Direction to leave

By CJPOA 1994, s 69 where the senior police officer present at the scene reasonably believes that:

(a) a person is committing, has committed, or intends to commit the offence of aggravated trespass on land; or

(b) two or more persons are trespassing on land and are present there with the common purpose of intimidating persons so as to deter them from engaging in a lawful activity or of obstructing or disrupting a lawful activity,

he may direct that person, or those persons (or any of them), to leave the land. 'Land' has the same meaning as in s 68.

A person who, knowing that such a direction has been given which applies to him, fails to leave the land as soon as practicable or, having left, again enters the land as a trespasser within the period of three months beginning with the day on which the direction was given, commits an offence under s 69(3).

It is a defence to a charge of an offence under s 69(3) for the defendant to prove that he was not trespassing on the land, or that he had a reasonable excuse for failing to leave the land as soon as practicable or, as the case may be, for again entering the land as a trespasser (s 69(4)).

TRESPASSING ON PROTECTED SITE

The Serious Organised Crime and Police Act 2005 (SOCPA 2005), s 128(1) provides that a person commits an offence if he enters, or is on, any protected site in England or Wales as a trespasser.

A 'protected site' is either a nuclear site (ie the outer perimeter (fences, etc) of premises in respect of which a nuclear site licence exists and other premises within that perimeter) or a 'designated site'. A 'designated site' is one specified or described by order by the Secretary of State. A site may only be designated if:

(a) it is comprised in Crown land;
(b) it is comprised in land belonging to Her Majesty in Her private capacity or to the immediate heir to the Throne in his private capacity; or
(c) this is considered appropriate in the interests of national security.

SOCPA 2005 (Designated Sites) Order 2005 designates HM Naval Base, Clyde; Northwood Headquarters; RAF Brize Norton; RAF Croughton; RAF Fairford; RAF Feltwell; RAF Fylingdales; RAF Lakenheath; RAF Menwith Hill; RAF Mildenhall; RAF Welford; Royal Navy Armaments Depot Coulport, and Sea Mounting Centre Marchwood as designated sites. SOCPA 2005 (Designated Sites under s 128) Order 2007 designates 85 Albert Embankment; Buckingham Palace; the Ministry of Defence Main Building, Whitehall; the Old War Office Building, Whitehall; St James's Palace; Thames House, Millbank; Chequers Estate; the Downing Street Site; the GCHQ Harp Hill Site; the GCHQ Hubble Road Site; the GCHQ Scarborough Site; the GCHQ Bude Site; the Highgrove House Site; the Palace of Westminster; the Kensington Palace Site; the Sandringham House Site; and the Windsor Castle Site as designated sites.

It is a defence for a person charged with an offence under s 128 to prove that he did not know, and had no reasonable cause to suspect, that the site was protected (s 128(4)). No proceedings for such an offence may be instituted without the consent of the Attorney General.

CONTROLS ON ACTIVITIES IN PARLIAMENT SQUARE GARDEN AND ADJOINING PAVEMENTS

The Police Reform and Social Responsibility Act 2011 (PRSRA 2011) deals with these matters.

Directions in respect of prohibited activities in controlled area of Parliament Square

PRSRA 2011, s 143 provides that a constable or authorised officer who has reasonable grounds for believing that a person is doing, or is about to do, a prohibited activity may direct the person to cease doing that activity or (as the case may be) not to start doing that activity. A 'prohibited activity' is defined by s 143(2) as any of the following:

(a) operating any amplified noise equipment (eg loudspeakers or loudhailers) in the controlled area of Parliament Square;
(b) erecting or keeping erected in the controlled area of Parliament Square:
    (i)   any tent, or
    (ii) any other structure that is designed, or adapted, (solely or mainly) for the purpose of facilitating sleeping or staying in a place for any period;
(c) using any tent or other such structure in the controlled area of Parliament Square for the purpose of sleeping or staying in that area;
(d) placing or keeping in place in the controlled area of Parliament Square any sleeping equipment with a view to its use (whether or not by the person placing it or keeping it in place) for the purpose of sleeping overnight in that area;
(e) using any sleeping equipment in the controlled area of Parliament Square for the purpose of sleeping overnight in that area.

'Sleeping equipment' means any sleeping bag, mattress, or other similar item designed, or adapted, (solely or mainly) for the purpose of facilitating sleeping in a place. In the case of an activity within (b) or (c) of keeping a tent or similar structure erected or using a tent or similar structure, it is immaterial whether the tent or structure was first erected before or after the coming into force of s 143. In the case of an activity within (d) or (e) of keeping in place or using any sleeping equipment, it is immaterial whether the sleeping equipment was first placed before or after the coming into force of s 143.

The 'controlled area of Parliament Square' means the area of land that is comprised in:

(a) the central garden of Parliament Square, and
(b) the footways that immediately adjoin the central garden of Parliament Square.

An activity is not to be treated as a 'prohibited activity' if it is done:

(a) for police, fire and rescue authority or ambulance purposes,
(b) by or on behalf of a relevant authority (a government minister or department, the Greater London Authority or Westminster City Council),
(c) by a person so far as authorised under s 147 (below) to do it (authorisation for operation of amplified noise equipment).

An 'authorised officer' (see above), in relation to any land in the controlled area of Parliament Square, means:

(a) an employee of the responsible authority for that land who is authorised in writing by the authority for the purposes of the provisions relating to the controlled area of Parliament Square, and
(b) any other person who, under arrangements made with the responsible authority (whether by that or any other person), is so authorised for the purposes of the above provisions.

'Responsible authority', in relation to any land in the controlled area of Parliament Square, means the Greater London Authority, for any land comprised in the central garden of Parliament Square, and Westminster City Council, for any other land.

Section 144 provides that a direction requiring a person to cease doing a prohibited activity may include a direction that the person does not start doing that activity again after having ceased it.

A direction requiring a person not to start doing a prohibited activity continues in force until:

(a) the end of such period (not exceeding 90 days) beginning with the day on which the direction is given as may be specified by the constable or authorised officer giving the direction, or
(b) if no such period is specified, the end of the period of 90 days beginning with the day on which the direction is given.

A direction may be given to a person to cease operating, or not to start operating, any amplified noise equipment only if it appears to the constable or authorised officer giving the direction that the person is operating, or is about to operate, the equipment in such a manner as to produce sound that other persons in or in the vicinity of the controlled area of Parliament Square can hear or are likely to be able to hear.

A direction:

(a) may be given orally,
(b) may be given to any person individually or to two or more persons together, and
(c) may be withdrawn or varied by the person who gave it.

A person who fails without reasonable excuse to comply with a direction commits an offence (s 143(8)), hereafter the 'offence under s 143').

Power to seize property

PRSRA 2011, s 145 provides the following powers.

A constable or authorised officer may seize and retain a prohibited item (or an item of a kind mentioned in s 143(2)) that is on any land in the controlled area of Parliament Square if it appears to that constable or officer that the item is being, or has been, used in connection with the commission of an offence under s 143.

A constable may seize and retain a prohibited item that is on any land outside of the controlled area of Parliament Square if it appears to the constable that the item has been used in connection with the commission of an offence under s 143.

The references above to an item that is 'on' any land includes reference to an item that is in the possession of a person who is on any such land.

A constable may use reasonable force, if necessary, in exercising such a power of seizure. An item seized under s 145 must be returned to the person from whom it was seized:

(a) no later than the end of the period of 28 days beginning with the day on which the item was seized, or
(b) if proceedings are commenced against the person for an offence under s 143 before the return of the item under (a), at the conclusion of those proceedings.

If it is not so possible to return an item because the name or address of the person from whom it was seized is not known:

(i)   the item may be returned to any other person appearing to have rights in the property who has come forward to claim it, or
(ii) if there is no such person, the item may be disposed of or destroyed at any time after the end of the period of 90 days beginning with the day on which the item was seized.

(b) above and this last provision ((i) and (ii)) do not apply if a court makes an order under s 146 (below) for the forfeiture of the item.

Power of court on conviction

By PRSRA 2011, s 146, the court may do either or both of the following on the conviction of a person (D) of an offence under s 143:

(a) make an order providing for the forfeiture of any item of a kind mentioned in s 143(2) (above) that was used in the commission of the offence;
(b) make such other order as the court considers appropriate for the purpose of preventing D from engaging in any prohibited activity in the controlled area of Parliament Square, including (in particular) an order requiring D not to enter the controlled area of Parliament Square for such period as may be specified in the order.

Authorisation for operation of amplified noise equipment

By PRSRA 2011, s 147, the responsible authority (p 774) for any land in the controlled area of Parliament Square may, on application, authorise a person to operate on that land any amplified noise equipment.

PUBLIC ASSEMBLIES

Generally

POA 1986, s 14 authorises the senior police officer, on the basis of the same grounds of reasonable belief as in the case of conditions on public processions (p 762), to impose such conditions in relation to the place at which any public assembly (an assembly of two or more persons in a public place which is wholly or partly open to the air) may be (or continue to be) held, its maximum duration, or the maximum number of persons who may constitute it, as appear to him to be necessary to prevent serious public disorder, serious damage to property, serious disruption to the life of the community, or intimidation. A divisional court has held that conditions may be imposed under this provision requiring those assembled to disperse by a specified route and to stay in a specified place as long as necessary to enable dispersal to take place safely and without disorder.

In the case of an assembly which is actually being held, the senior police officer is the police officer most senior in rank present at the scene; in such a case it is not necessary for the notice to be in writing. In the case of an assembly which is intended to be held, the senior police officer is the chief officer of police; in such a case the chief officer must give the notice in writing. Although extensive detail is not required, the chief officer's notice must provide sufficient detail of the reasons for his belief in the ground (or grounds) for a demonstrator to understand why a direction is being given.

A chief officer of police may delegate any of his functions under ss 14 or 14A (below) to an assistant chief constable or an assistant commissioner of police (as the case may be).

Offences under s 14 are committed by the same classes of persons as in relation to a breach of a public procession condition (s 14(4), (5), and (6)).

Trespassory assemblies

These are dealt with by POA 1986, ss 14A, 14B and 14C.

POA 1986, s 14A is concerned with the prohibition of a trespassory assembly before it has taken place. Where a trespassory assembly has already commenced, police involvement is limited to the prohibition of its continuance if an officer believes that this is necessary to prevent a breach of the peace. Section 14A is, inter alia, aimed at assemblies at such places as Stonehenge at summer solstice time. However, its provisions are more extensive and will cover an assembly which might cause serious disorder, obstruction of the highway, or noise.

Section 14A provides that where a chief officer of police reasonably believes that an assembly of 20 or more people is intended to be held in any district at a place on land in the open air to which the public has no right of access or only a limited right of access and that the assembly:

(a) is likely to be held without the permission of the occupier of the land or to conduct itself in such a way as to exceed the limits of any permission of his or the limits of the public's right of access; and

(b) may result:
  (i)   in serious disruption to the life of the community, or
  (ii) where the land, or a building or monument on it, is of historical, architectural, or
        scientific importance, in significant damage to the land, building or monument,

he may apply to the council of the district for an order prohibiting for a specified period
the holding of all trespassory assemblies in the district, or a part of it as specified. An
order may only be made by a council with the Secretary of State's consent. In London
the relevant Commissioner may make an order with such consent. Where such an
order is made, it will operate to prohibit any assembly of 20 or more which is held on
land in the open air to which the public has no right of access or only a limited right of
access and takes place without the permission of the occupier, or in excess of his permission or the public's right of access. Such an order may not prohibit such an assembly
for a period exceeding four days or in an area exceeding a circle with a radius of five
miles from a specified centre.

It is irrelevant that the anticipated assembly is open to the public or is a private cer-
emony, but it must be held on land in the open air. This can be contrasted with the
power to impose conditions on a public assembly under s 14; there the assembly may
be held wholly or partly in the open air. 'Land' in s 14A includes land forming part of
the highway. It follows, for example, that an intended obstructive assembly of 20 or
more on the highway (which is by definition trespassing, since the public only have a
right to pass and repass on it and make other reasonable use of it) can be the trigger for
an order under s 14A.

It is important to understand that these powers are restricted to assemblies which are
reasonably believed to be trespassory in nature. Assemblies *with permission* are not
covered by the legislation unless there is a reasonable belief that they will be conducted
in such a way as to exceed that permission.

Offences

A person who organises an assembly which he knows to be prohibited under s 14A
commits an offence against s 14B(1). So does a person who takes part (s 14B(2)), or
who incites another to do so (s 14B(3)).

Central to these offences is that the assembly must be prohibited under s 14A, and an
assembly is prohibited only if, within the area and duration of the prohibition order, it:

(a) is held on land in the open air to which the public has no right of access or only a
    limited right of access; and
(b) takes place in the prohibited circumstances, ie without the permission of the occu-
    pier of the land or so as to exceed the limits of any permission of his or the limits
    of the public's right of access.

In the case of assemblies on the highway, the public's right of access to the highway
has been held by the House of Lords to include the right to hold a public assembly
which is peaceful and non-obstructive of the rights of passage of other users of the
highway provided the assembly is a reasonable use of the highway.

Police powers

By s 14C, if a constable in uniform reasonably believes that a person is on his way to an
assembly within the area to which such an order under s 14A applies, which the constable reasonably believes is likely to be an assembly which is prohibited by that order,
he may, within the area specified in the order:

(a) stop that person; and

(b) direct him not to proceed in the direction of the assembly.

A person who fails to comply with such a direction which he knows has been given to him commits an offence under s 14C(3).

Raves

CJPOA 1994, ss 63 to 65 provide the police with certain powers to deal with 'raves'. Section 63 is the main provision. It applies to a gathering *on land in the open air* of 20 or more persons *(whether or not trespassers)* at which amplified music is played during the night (with or without intermissions) and is such as, by reason of its loudness and the duration and the time at which it is played, is likely to cause serious distress to the inhabitants of the locality; and for this purpose:

(a) such a gathering continues during intermissions in the music and, where the gathering extends over several days, throughout the period during which amplified music is played at night (with or without intermissions); and

(b) 'music' includes sounds wholly or predominantly characterised by the emission of a succession of repetitive beats.

'Land in the open air' includes a place partly open to the air. Thus, both an aircraft hangar without doors, or a Dutch barn, would be such a place. The Act does not define the term 'during the night'.

Section 63 also applies to a gathering if:

(a) it is a gathering on *land* of 20 or more persons who are *trespassing* on the land; and

(b) the gathering would be of a kind described above if it took place on land in the open air.

Section 63 does not apply to a gathering which is licensed by a local authority entertainments licence.

Where a superintendent (or above) reasonably believes, in respect of any land, that:

(a) two or more persons are making preparations for the holding there of a gathering to which s 63 applies;

(b) 10 or more are waiting for such a gathering to begin there; or

(c) 10 or more are attending such a gathering which is then in progress,

he may give a direction that those persons and any other persons who come to prepare or wait for or to attend the gathering are to leave the land and remove any vehicles or other property which they have with them on the land. The direction may be conveyed to the gathering by any constable. If reasonable steps have been taken to convey the direction, it is deemed to have been given.

Persons occupying or working on the land and their families are exempt from a direction under s 63.

A person who knows that such a direction has been given which applies to him who:

(a) fails to leave the land as soon as reasonably practicable; or

(b) having left, again enters the land within a period of seven days beginning with the day on which the direction is given, commits an offence under s 63(6). It is a defence for D to show that he had a reasonable excuse for failing to leave the land as soon as reasonably practicable or, as the case may be, for again entering the land (s 63(7)).

A person commits an offence under s 63(7A) if:

(a) he knows that a s 63 direction has been given which applies to him; and
(b) he makes preparations for or attends a gathering to which s 63 applies within the 24-hour period starting when the direction was given.

This means that those who have been given a direction to leave a rave cannot simply move to another site (and carry on raving) with impunity.

Police powers

Section 64 provides that, where a superintendent (or above) reasonably believes that circumstances exist which would justify giving such a direction, he may authorise a constable to enter the land without warrant to ascertain that these circumstances exist and to exercise powers conferred upon him. Where such a direction has been given, and a constable reasonably suspects that any person to whom the direction applies has, without reasonable excuse:

(a) failed to remove any vehicle or sound equipment on the land which appears to the constable to belong to him or to be in his possession or under his control; or
(b) entered the land as a trespasser with a vehicle or sound equipment within the period of seven days beginning with the day on which the direction was given,

the constable may seize and remove that vehicle or sound equipment.

Section 66 permits a court to order the forfeiture of sound equipment but also allows the owner of the equipment (if he is not the person from whom it was seized) to claim it by applying to the court within six months. The Police (Disposal of Sound Equipment) Regulations 1995 provide for the disposal of the equipment where the court has made no such order.

Where a constable in uniform reasonably believes that a person is on his way to such a gathering in respect of which a direction has been given, he may, by s 65, stop that person and direct him not to go in the direction of the gathering. This power may only be exercised within five miles of the boundary of the site of the gathering. It does not apply to occupiers of the land, etc. A person who, knowing that such a direction has been given, fails to comply with such a direction commits an offence under s 65(4).

PUBLIC MEETINGS

It is an offence, contrary to the Public Meeting Act 1908, s 1(1), for any person at a lawful public meeting to act in a disorderly manner for the purpose of preventing the transaction of the business for which the meeting was called together. It is also an offence to incite others to do so (s 1(2)).

'Public meeting' means a meeting open to the public and not restricted to members of a particular organisation or club. Meetings which are open to the public but held on private premises are therefore public meetings. A police officer who reasonably suspects a breach of the peace may enter and/or remain on the private premises.

Section 1 only applies to a lawful public meeting. The fact that a meeting is held on a highway does not render it unlawful merely because it is so held. However, the circumstances in which the meeting is held may make the participants liable for other offences, such as obstructing the highway.

Section 1(3) empowers a constable who reasonably suspects a person of committing an offence under s 1(1) or (2) to require him immediately to give his name and address. However, a constable may only execute this power if requested to do so by the chairman of the meeting. The constable must decide whether or not the person to whom his attention is directed is merely asking questions and making points which the chairman and platform party do not like, or is acting in a disorderly manner for the purpose of preventing the transaction of the business. Refusal or failure to give a name or address, or the giving of a false name and address, is an offence under s 1(3).

PUBLIC ORDER ACT 1936

POA 1936 governs the wearing of political uniforms and participation in quasi-military organisations.

Political uniforms

It is an offence under POA 1936, s 1(1) for any person to wear uniform, in any public place or at any public meeting, which signifies his association with any political organisation or with the promotion of any political object. By way of exception, a chief officer of police, with the consent of the Secretary of State, may by order permit the wearing of such uniforms at a ceremonial, anniversary or other special occasion. The consent of the Attorney General is required for the continuation of the prosecution of a person charged with this offence.

For these purposes, a 'meeting' is a meeting held for the purpose of discussing matters of public interest and a 'public meeting' includes any meeting in a public place and any meeting in a private place if the public (or a section of the public) are permitted to attend (whether on payment or otherwise). There are many organisations (whose objectives are quite harmless) whose members wear some form of identifying clothing within their organisation. This would be within the scope of s 1, but for the fact that it only deals with cases where the uniform signifies association with a political organisation or the promotion of a political object *and* it is worn in a public place or a public meeting. It must be emphasised that even members of a political organisation may wear uniforms in private, even in meetings if these are restricted to their own membership.

The term 'uniform' includes any particular article of clothing which is worn by each member of a group and which is intended to indicate his association with such an organisation or object. The article does not have to cover any major part of the body and it is sufficient to prove that the article has been commonly used by members of a political organisation, eg the berets, dark glasses and dark pullovers which have been used by the IRA.

Quasi-military organisations

POA 1936, s 2 is concerned with the preparation of private quasi-military forces of any description. A person who takes part in the control or management of any association, or in its training, commits an indictable (either way) offence under POA 1936, s 2(1) if its members or adherents are:

(a) organised, trained or equipped for the purpose of enabling them to usurp the functions of the police or armed forces; or

(b) organised and trained or organised and equipped either to promote a political object by the use or display of physical force, or to arouse reasonable apprehension of that purpose.

In relation to the last words in (b), it has been held that the fact that there was no evidence of actual attacks on opponents, or of plans to attack them, did not necessarily remove grounds for 'reasonable apprehension of that purpose'.

Where a person is charged with taking part in the control or management of such an association, as opposed to training, he has a defence if he proves that he neither consented to nor connived at the organisation, training, or equipment in contravention of s 2.

The provision of a reasonable number of stewards to assist in the preservation of order at a public meeting held on private premises is permitted, as is the provision of badges and insignia for them. The instruction of such persons in their lawful duties is also permitted.

The institution of a prosecution for an offence under s 2 requires the Attorney General's consent.

PUBLIC ORDER OFFENCES AND HUMAN RIGHTS

Public order law can interfere with the exercise of Convention rights, particularly those under arts 10 and 11 referred to below.

Article 10 is concerned with freedom of expression. It declares that:

(1) Everyone has the right to freedom of expression. This right shall include freedom to hold opinions and to receive and impart information and ideas without interference by public authority and regardless of frontiers. This Article shall not prevent states from requiring the licensing of broadcasting, television, or cinema enterprises.

(2) The exercise of these freedoms, since it carries with it duties and responsibilities, may be subject to such formalities, conditions, restrictions, or penalties as are prescribed by law and are necessary in a democratic society, in the interests of national security, territorial integrity, or public safety, for the prevention of disorder or crime, for the protection of health or morals, for the protection of the reputation or rights of others, for preventing the disclosure of information received in confidence, or for maintaining the authority or impartiality of the judiciary.

The following provisions of art 11, which are concerned with the freedoms of assembly and association, are likely to lead to challenges. It provides:

(1) Everyone has the right to freedom of peaceful assembly and to freedom of association with others, including the right to form and join trade unions for the protection of his interests.

(2) No restriction shall be placed on the exercise of these rights other than such as are prescribed by law and are necessary in a democratic society in the interests of national security or public safety, for the prevention of disorder or crime, for the protection of health or morals, or for the protection of the rights and freedoms of others. This Article shall not prevent the imposition of lawful restrictions upon the exercise of these rights by members of the armed forces, of the police or the administration of the state.

As can be seen, Articles 10 and 11 begin with a wide declaration concerning an individual's rights in relation to freedom of expression and to freedom of assembly and association and continue with a list of matters which can justify limiting those rights. Where someone is able to show that there has been interference with such a right, that interference will not be in breach of the relevant rights if it was prescribed by law and was necessary in a democratic society in the interests of a specified legitimate aim, and that interference must not be discriminatory. 'Prescribed by law' does not simply mean that an interference must be founded on a legal rule; in addition, a citizen must have access to the information and the law must be formulated with sufficient degree of precision to enable a citizen to regulate his conduct. It will not be sufficient that an interference is reasonable or desirable in the interests of a specified legitimate aim; there must be a pressing social need. An interference within a law must be proportionate to the legitimate aim pursued. While such assessment will initially be made by the state concerned, the 'reasonableness' of that assessment will be subject to scrutiny by the European Court of Human Rights if the individual concerned ultimately takes his case there.

Some of the matters listed as legitimate aims can be described as 'essential', eg matters affecting national security or public safety, where the limitation is necessary in a democratic society for such a purpose. Some of the other limitations, such as the prevention of disorder or the protection of the rights of others, are particularly likely to arise in public order situations. The question will be whether any interference with freedom of expression or of assembly or association is prescribed by law and necessary in a democratic society for such a purpose.

The operation of art 10 in the context of POA 1986, s 5 has been considered by the courts on a number of cases. In a recent decision a divisional court held that the following principles governing the relationship between POA 1986, s 5 and art 10 of the Convention could be distilled from the relevant authorities. The starting point was the importance of the right to freedom of expression. It then had to be recognised that legitimate protest could be offensive at least to some—and on occasions had to be, if it was to have impact. Moreover, the right to freedom of expression had to extend beyond the protection of those holding popular, mainstream views so that minority views could be freely expressed, even if distasteful. Further, while art 10 did not confer an unqualified right to freedom of expression, the restrictions contained in art 10(2) were to be narrowly construed. Furthermore, there was not, and could not be, any universal test for resolving when speech went beyond legitimate protest. The justification for invoking the criminal law was the threat to public order. Inevitably, the context of the particular occasion would be of the first importance. The relevance of the threat to public order should not be taken as meaning that the risk of violence by those reacting to the protest was, without more, determinative; sometimes it might be that protesters were to be protected. That said, in striking the right balance when determining whether speech was 'threatening, abusive or insulting', the focus on minority rights should not result in overlooking the rights of the majority. In addition, even if there was a prima facie case for contending that an offence had been committed under s 5, it was still for the Crown to establish that prosecution was a proportionate response, necessary for the preservation of public order. If the line between legitimate freedom of expression and a threat to public order had indeed been crossed, freedom of speech would not have been impaired by 'ruling out' threatening, abusive or insulting speech. Finally the Divisional Court should not interfere unless, on well-known grounds, the appellants could establish that the decision to which the district judge or justices had come was one that could not properly have been reached.

CHAPTER 27

Public Order Offences Related to Sporting Events and Those Connected with Industrial Disputes

PUBLIC ORDER AND SPORTING EVENTS

Alcohol on coaches, trains, etc

The Sporting Events (Control of Alcohol, etc) Act 1985 (SE(CA)A 1985), ss 1 and 1A provide a number of offences designed to prevent drunken behaviour by football fans en route to or from matches, and to prevent them arriving at grounds drunk. These offences are offences of:

(a) causing or permitting the carriage of alcohol on a specified vehicle;
(b) being in possession of alcohol on such a vehicle; and
(c) being drunk on a specified vehicle.

Specified vehicles

The above offences under SE(CA)A 1985, s 1 apply to public service vehicles (ie coaches, buses, and the like) and passenger trains *which are being used for the principal purpose of carrying passengers for the whole or part of a journey to or from a 'designated sporting event'*. Section 1, therefore, does not apply to a bus or train on a normal scheduled service because it is not being used for the principal purpose of carrying passengers to or from a designated sporting event, even if the majority of the passengers are travelling to or from a match, since the words 'used' and 'principal purpose' must refer to use by, and the principal purpose of, the bus or rail company. On the other hand, s 1 does apply to a 'football special' or to a coach or train chartered by the supporters' club, provided that it is travelling to or from a designated sporting event.

The above offences under SE(CA)A 1985, s 1A apply to a motor vehicle which:

(a) is not a public service vehicle but is adapted to carry more than eight passengers; and
(b) is being used for the principal purpose of carrying *two or more* passengers for the whole or part of a journey to or from a designated sporting event.

It will be noted that vehicles of this type are not limited to minibuses. They therefore include the few types of private car which are adapted to carry more than eight passengers.

Designated sporting event

'Designated sporting event' in SE(CA)A 1985 is defined by s 9(3). It means 'a sporting event or proposed sporting event for the time being designated, or of a class designated, by order made by the Secretary of State'. It also 'includes a designated sporting event within the meaning of the Criminal Justice (Scotland) Act 1980, Part V'.

For the purposes of SE(CA)A 1985, the Sports Grounds and Sporting Events (Designation) Order 2005 designates as sporting events to which the Act applies:

(a) association football matches, at any sports ground in England or Wales, in which one or both of the participating teams represents a club which is for the time being a member (whether a full or associate member) of the Football League, the Football Association Premier League, the Football Conference National Division, the Scottish Football League or Welsh Premier League, or whose home ground is for the time being situated outside England and Wales, or represents a country or territory;

(b) association football matches, at any sports ground in England and Wales, in competition for the Football Association Cup (other than in a preliminary or qualifying round); and

(c) association football matches at a sports ground outside England and Wales in which one or both of the participating teams represents a club which is for the time being a member (whether a full or associate member) of the Football League, the Football Association Premier League, the Football Conference National Division, the Scottish Football League or Welsh Premier League, or represents the Football Association or the Football Association of Wales.

SE(CA)A 1985 does not apply to any sporting event or proposed sporting event where all competitors are to take part otherwise than for reward, and to which all spectators are to be admitted free of charge.

All matches in the Scottish Football League, all matches in the Highland Football League, all Scottish Football League and Association cup matches, all football matches in the three European cups, and soccer internationals, provided in each case that they take place at a designated ground, have been designated by the Sports Grounds and Sporting Events (Designation) (Scotland) Order 1980. The grounds designated by the Order are Hampden Park and the grounds of members of the Scottish Football League or of the Highland League. In addition, the Order designates rugby internationals at Murrayfield as designated sporting events.

Causing or permitting carriage of alcohol on a vehicle

SE(CA)A 1985, s 1(2) provides that a person who knowingly causes or permits alcohol to be carried on a vehicle to which s 1 applies is guilty of an offence:

(a) if the vehicle is a public service vehicle and he is the operator of the vehicle or the employee or agent of the operator; or

(b) if the vehicle is a hired vehicle (eg a chartered train or a football special) and he is the person to whom it is hired or the employee or agent of that person. Thus, an organiser of the supporters' club (or his agent) can be convicted if he permits alcohol to be carried on a chartered train, but a train guard who fails to prevent this cannot because, although he permits it, he is not a person to whom the train is hired (nor the employee or agent of such a person).

SE(CA)A 1985, s 1A(2) provides that a person who knowingly causes or permits alcohol to be carried on a motor vehicle to which s 1A applies is guilty of an offence:

(a) if he is its driver; or
(b) if he is not its driver but its keeper, the servant, or agent of its keeper, a person to whom it is made available (by hire, loan, or otherwise) by its keeper or the keeper's servant or agent, or the servant or agent of a person to whom it is so made available.

The causing or permitting of the carrying of alcohol on the vehicle must be done 'knowingly', which means that D must actually know or be wilfully blind that he is causing or permitting the carrying of alcohol on the vehicle.

Possession of alcohol on a vehicle

SE(CA)A 1985, s 1(3) makes it an offence for a person to have alcohol in his possession while on a vehicle to which s 1 applies. There is a corresponding offence under s 1A(3) in relation to motor vehicles to which s 1A applies.

Being drunk on a vehicle

SE(CA)A 1985, s 1(4) provides that a person who is drunk on a vehicle to which s 1 applies is guilty of an offence. There is a corresponding offence under s 1A(4) in relation to motor vehicles to which s 1A applies.

Police powers

By SE(CA)A 1985, s 7(3), a constable may stop a public service vehicle to which s 1 applies or a motor vehicle to which s 1A applies and may search such a vehicle or a railway passenger vehicle if he has reasonable grounds to suspect that an offence under s 1 or s 1A is being or has been committed in respect of that vehicle.

It will be noted that the power to search under s 7(3) is to search the vehicle, and not a person on board it. As to search of a person see p 787.

Alcohol, containers, fireworks, etc at designated sports grounds

SE(CA)A 1985, ss 2 and 2A provide two offences relating to the possession of alcohol, containers, fireworks, and the like, during the period of a designated sporting event at a designated sports ground.

Period of a designated sporting event

The 'period of a designated sporting event' in SE(CA)A 1985 is defined by s 9(4). Normally, it is the period beginning two hours before the start of the event or (if earlier, as where the start is delayed) two hours before the time at which it is advertised to start and ending one hour after the end of the event. Where a match is postponed to a later day or cancelled, the period ends one hour after the advertised start time. In respect of a room in a designated sports ground from which the designated sporting event may be directly viewed and to which the public are not admitted (eg the directors' box), there is a different period under s 5A in relation only to an offence of possession of alcohol, etc under s 2(1)(a) (below). This is a 'restricted period' beginning 15 minutes before the start of the event (or advertised start) and ending 15 minutes after the end of the event or 15 minutes after the advertised start (if the event is postponed to a later day or cancelled).

Designated sports ground

A 'designated sports ground' in SE(CA)A 1985 is defined by s 9(2) as any place: (a) used (wholly or partly) for sporting events where accommodation is provided for spectators; and (b) for the time being designated, or of a class designated, by order made by the Secretary of State.

The Secretary of State has designated any sports ground in England or Wales as a designated ground.

Possession of alcohol, etc at designated ground

SE(CA)A 1985, s 2(1), which is aimed at preventing drunkenness at matches and at preventing the use of bottles and cans as missiles, provides that a person who has alcohol or an article to which s 2 applies in his possession:

(a) at any time during the period of a designated sporting event when he is in any area of a designated sports ground from which the event may be directly viewed (s 2(1) (a)); or

(b) while entering or trying to enter a designated sports ground at any time during the period of a designated sporting event at that ground (s 2(1)(b)),

is guilty of an offence.

Section 2(3) states that an article to which s 2 applies is any article capable of causing injury to a person struck by it, being:

(a) a bottle, can, or other portable container (including such an article when crushed or broken) which is for holding any drink and is of a kind which, when empty, is normally discarded or returned to, or left to be recovered by, the supplier; or

(b) part of an article falling within (a).

However, the definition expressly does not apply to anything that is for holding any medicinal product.

The container need not be made specifically to hold alcohol, and it is irrelevant that it has never contained alcohol or that it is broken. An empty lemonade bottle is caught, as is a soft drink tin. On the other hand, a re-usable plastic drinks container, a mug, a thermos flask, a decanter, or a hip flask is not (although the latter two are likely to excite suspicion of possession of alcohol), since it is not the kind of container which is normally discarded or returned to, or left to be recovered by, the supplier.

Possession of fireworks, etc

SE(CA)A 1985, s 2A(1), which is essentially aimed at reducing the risk of fire, makes identical provision in relation to the possession of a firework or of distress flares, fog signals, canisters of smoke or visible gas, and similar articles. Matches and cigarette lighters are expressly excluded.

It is a defence for the defendant (D) to prove that he had possession with lawful authority.

Being drunk at a designated sports ground

By SE(CA)A 1985, s 2(2), a person who is drunk in a designated sports ground at any time during the period of a designated sporting event at that ground, or who is drunk while entering or trying to enter such a ground at any time during the period of a designated sporting event at that ground, is guilty of an offence.

Sporting events: general police powers

A constable may, at any time during the period of a designated sporting event at any designated sports ground, enter any part of the ground for the purpose of enforcing SE(CA)A 1985. It will be noted that the constable's power of entry is not limited to the 'public' parts of the ground; if necessary for the purposes of enforcing SE(CA)A 1985, he can enter the directors' suite or the manager's office.

In addition, by SE(CA)A 1985, s 7(2), a constable may search a person he has reasonable grounds to suspect is committing or has committed an offence under that Act. The provisions of PACE, s 2 and Code A, the Stop and Search Code, apply to stop and search under s 7. See pp. 45–9. The need for 'reasonable grounds to suspect' must be emphasised. There must be a sound basis of fact upon which a police officer forms his reasonable suspicion that such an offence is being committed. Searches of supporters entering grounds cannot be carried out on the basis of personal factors; they must be based on intelligence or information, or some behaviour by the person concerned; this is specifically stated in the Code. If a person is seen to be carrying a supermarket bag with the distinctive bulge of a 'four-pack', or the outline of bottles, etc can be seen inside coat pockets, then a reasonable suspicion exists. The suspicion is directed towards an individual and there is reason to suspect him.

The Code provides that its requirement that a person must not be searched, except with his consent, except under a specific power of search does not affect the routine searching of persons entering sports grounds or other premises, *with their consent given as a condition of entry*. It is arguable that a search as a condition of entry to a sports ground is not a search which should be conducted by a police officer, even if he is paid by the proprietor of the ground to do duty there. If a proprietor makes such a condition, it should be enforced by his own stewards as it is no part of a police officer's duty to enforce the rights of such proprietors.

Misbehaviour at a designated football match

The Football (Offences) Act 1991 (F(O)A 1991) creates a number of offences. They can only be committed at a 'regulated football match'. Such matches are designated by the Football (Offences) (Designation of Football Matches) Order 2004. They are association football matches:

(a) in which one or both of the participating teams represents:
 (i) a club which is for the time being a member (whether a full or associate member) of the Football League, the Football Association Premier League, the Football Conference, the Welsh Premier League or the Scottish Football League; or
 (ii) a club whose home ground is for the time being situated outside England and Wales; or
 (iii) a country or territory; or
(b) which is played in the FA Cup, other than a preliminary or qualifying round.

References to things done at a designated football match include anything done there in the period beginning two hours before the start of the match or (if earlier) two hours before the advertised start time and ending one hour after the end of the match. If the match does not take place, the period is two hours before the advertised start time until one hour after that time.

Throwing objects

By F(O)A 1991, s 2, it is an offence to throw anything at or towards:

(a) the playing area or any area adjacent to the playing area to which spectators are not generally admitted; or

(b) any area in which spectators or other persons are or may be present,

without lawful authority or excuse (which it is for D to prove).

Thus, those who throw objects onto the pitch, into the players' tunnel, etc, or into spectator areas will commit offences. Those who may prove 'lawful authority or excuse' would include vendors who throw packets of crisps, etc into the crowd, or spectators who throw money to such persons.

Chanting

F(O)A 1991, s 3(1) makes it an offence to engage or take part in chanting of an indecent or racist nature at a designated football match. 'Chanting' means the repeated uttering of words or sounds (whether alone or in concert with one or more others), and 'racist nature' means consisting of or including matter which is threatening, abusive or insulting to a person by reason of his colour, race, nationality (including citizenship) or ethnic or national origin.

Pitch invasion

By F(O)A 1991, s 4, it is an offence for a person to go on to the playing area, or any area adjacent to the playing area to which spectators are not generally admitted, without lawful authority or lawful excuse (which it is for D to prove).

It is not easy to obtain a conviction where spectators surge forward onto the pitch. Most will contend that they were carried forward unwillingly by the momentum of the crowd. If this is not disproved, a conviction for an offence under s 4 will not be possible, since a person cannot generally be convicted if his conduct was beyond his control. Those who would have lawful excuse for going onto the pitch include trainers and official first aiders.

BANNING ORDERS

The Football Spectators Act 1989 (FSA 1989), Part II deals with these. The relevant provisions only apply in respect of a regulated football match.

Regulated football match

A 'regulated football match' is an association football match (whether in the UK or elsewhere) which is a prescribed match or a match of a prescribed description. The Football Spectators (Prescription) Order 2004 prescribes 'regulated football matches in England and Wales' and 'regulated football matches outside England and Wales'.

Regulated football match in England and Wales

This is an association football match:

(a) in which one or both of the participating teams represents:
   (i)   a club which is for the time being a member (whether a full or associate member) of the Football League, the Football Association Premier League, the

Football Conference, the Welsh Premier League, the Scottish Premier League or the Scottish Football League;

(ii) a club whose home ground is for the time being situated outside England and Wales; or

(iii) a country or territory; or

(b) which is played in the FA Cup, other than a preliminary or qualifying round.

It is no longer a requirement that, to be a regulated match, the match must be played at a specified type of ground.

Regulated football match outside England and Wales

This is an association football match involving:

(a) a national team appointed by the Football Association to represent England or by the Football Association of Wales to represent Wales;

(b) a team representing a club which is for the time being a member (whether a full or associate member) of the Football League, the Football Association Premier League, the Football Conference, the Welsh Premier League, the Scottish Premier League or the Scottish Football League;

(c) a team representing any country or territory whose football association is for the time being a member of FIFA where the match is part of a competition or tournament organised by or under the authority of FIFA or UEFA and the competition is one in which a national team referred to in (a) is eligible to participate, or has participated; or

(d) a team representing a club which is for the time being a member (whether a full or associate member) of, or affiliated to, a national football association which is a member of FIFA, where the match is part of a competition or tournament organised by, or under the authority of, FIFA or UEFA and the competition is such that a club from the Football League, the Football Premier League, the Football Conference or the Welsh Premier League is eligible to participate, or has participated.

When can a banning order be made?

A banning order may be made under FSA 1989, s 14A, s 14B, or s 22.

Banning orders following a conviction for a relevant offence

FSA 1989, s 14A is concerned with a situation in which an offender is convicted of a 'relevant offence'. The relevant offences are set out in FSA 1989, Sch 1. They are:

(a) any offence contrary to FSA 1989, ss 14J(1) or 19(6) or 20(10) or 21C(2), (failure to comply with banning order requirement or requirement under s 14(2B) or (2C), or failure to comply with a requirement made at initial reporting at a police station or, being subject to banning order, knowingly or recklessly providing false or misleading information in support of his application for exemption from requirements imposed under FSA 1989, or non-compliance with a notice under s 21B);

(b) an offence under the Police, Public Order and Criminal Justice (Scotland) Act 2006, s 68(1) or (5) (corresponding offences to those in (a));

(c) any offence contrary to SE(CA)A 1985, ss 2 or 2A (possession of alcohol, containers, or fireworks) committed at a regulated football match or while entering or trying to enter the ground;

(d) any offence involving harassment, alarm or distress contrary to the Public Order Act 1986 (POA 1986), ss 4A or 5, or racial or religious hatred or hatred on the ground of sexual orientation contrary to POA 1986, Part III or IIIA:

    (i) committed during a 'period relevant to a regulated football match' (the period from 24 hours before the start or advertised start of the match (whichever is earlier) to 24 hours after its end, or the period from 24 hours before the advertised start of a cancelled game or one postponed to another day to 24 hours after that time) while at, entering or leaving the ground (or trying to do so), or

    (ii) if the court makes a declaration of relevance (ie declares that the offence related to regulated football matches), while on a journey to or from a regulated football match;

(e) any offence involving the use of violence or threat of violence towards another person or property:

    (i) committed during a period relevant to a regulated football match, while at, entering or leaving the ground (or trying to do so), or

    (ii) if the court makes a 'declaration of relevance', committed while on a journey to or from a regulated football match;

(f) any offence involving harassment, alarm or distress (POA 1986, ss 4A or 5) or racial or religious hatred or hatred on the ground of sexual orientation (POA 1986, Part III or IIIA) which does not fall within (d), or any offence involving the use or threat of violence towards another person or property which does not fall within (e), which was committed during a period relevant to a regulated football match and as respects which the court declares that the offence related to that match or that match and other regulated football matches during that period;

(g) any offence of drunkenness (ie being found drunk, or being drunk and disorderly, in a public place), committed while on such a journey, as to which offence the court makes a declaration of relevance);

(h) any offence contrary to SE(CA)A 1985, s 1 (alcohol on coaches or trains) committed on a journey to or from a regulated match, as to which offence the court makes a declaration of relevance;

(i) any offence contrary to the Road Traffic Act 1988, ss 4 or 5 (drink and driving, etc) committed while the accused was on a journey to or from a regulated football match, as to which offence the court makes a declaration of relevance;

(j) any offence contrary to F(O)A 1991;

(k) any offence involving the use, carrying, or possession of an offensive weapon or firearm:

    (i) committed during a period relevant to a regulated football match while at, or entering or leaving the ground (or trying to do so), or

    (ii) if the court makes a declaration of relevance, committed while on a journey to or from a regulated football match;

(l) any offence involving the use, carrying, or possession of an offensive weapon or firearm which does not fall within (k), which was committed during a period relevant to a regulated football match and as respects which the court declares that the offence related to that match or to that match and any other football offence during that period;

(m) ticket touting in relation to a regulated football match (Criminal Justice and Public Order Act 1994, s 166).

An attempt, conspiracy, encouraging or assisting, or aiding, abetting, counselling or procuring the commission of any such offence is included within these provisions.

A person may be regarded as having been on a journey to or from a football match whether or not he attended or intended to attend the match. A journey includes breaks (including overnight breaks).

If, upon conviction for such an offence, a court is satisfied that there are reasonable grounds to believe that making a banning order would help to prevent violence or disorder at, or in connection with, any regulated football match, it *must* make such an order in respect of the offender. If it is not so satisfied, it must state its reasons in open court. A divisional court has held that a football banning order under s 14A should be made only where there are strong grounds for concluding that the offender has a propensity for taking part in football hooliganism. However, it added that the court is entitled to give weight to deterrence; there are clear benefits in it being widely known that someone who assaults a match official is liable to be made subject to a football banning order even if the incident was, for that person, an isolated one.

A banning order is in addition to a sentence or order of conditional discharge.

Banning orders made on complaint

Under FSA 1989, s 14B, the chief officer of police of an area in which a person resides, or appears to reside, the chief constable of the British Transport Police or the DPP may make a complaint to a magistrates' court that the respondent has at some time contributed to violence or disorder in the UK or elsewhere.

In this respect, the terms 'violence' and 'disorder' carry their usual meanings. 'Violence' means violence against persons and property, threats of violence and endangering life, and 'disorder' includes stirring up racial hatred, threatening, abusive, disorderly or insulting behaviour, or displaying any material which is threatening, abusive or insulting, whether or not committed in connection with football.

If the court is satisfied as to the substance of the complaint and has reasonable grounds for believing that making a banning order would help to prevent violence or disorder at or in connection with any regulated football match it *must* make a banning order. In deciding whether to make an order a court may take into account (among other things):

(a) any decision of a court or tribunal outside the UK;
(b) deportation or exclusion from a country outside the UK;
(c) removal or exclusion from football grounds in the UK or elsewhere; or
(d) conduct recorded by video or by any other means.

However, a court may only take note of matters occurring within the 10 years preceding the application. It must also consider the reasons given by a court when, in relation to a relevant offence, it did not make a banning order.

So far as the standard of proof as to the substance of the complaint is concerned, the Court of Appeal has described it as an exacting one which would be hard in practice to distinguish from the criminal standard of proof beyond reasonable doubt. This high standard is imposed because of the serious restraints on an individual's freedom which a banning order imposes.

Banning order under FSA 1989, s 22

FSA 1989, s 22 governs the making of a banning order as a result of a conviction for a 'corresponding offence' outside England and Wales. A 'corresponding offence' is an offence under the law of a country specified outside England and Wales in an Order in Council. At the time of writing, orders have been made in respect of Italy, Scotland, Sweden, Norway, the Republic of Ireland, France, Belgium, and the Netherlands.

The effect of a banning order

A 'banning order' means an order made by a court under FSA 1989, Part II which:

(a) in relation to regulated football matches in the UK, prohibits the person who is subject to the order from entering premises for the purpose of attending such matches; and

(b) in relation to regulated football matches outside the UK, requires that person to report at a police station in accordance with Part II.

An order will apply to the whole range of matches which are prescribed, whatever the venue and whatever the club. This is sensible. Clearly, a banning order would not be very effective if it barred a person only from the ground at which the offence was committed.

The effect of a banning order must be explained by the court.

A banning order must require the person subject to the order to report to a police station specified in the order, within five days beginning with the day upon which the order is made.

A banning order must require the person subject to the order to notify the enforcing authority of the following events:

(a) a change of any of his names;

(b) the first use by him after the making of the order of a name for himself that was not disclosed by him at the time of the making of the order;

(c) a change of his home address;

(d) his acquisition of a temporary address;

(e) a change of his temporary address or his ceasing to have one;

(f) his becoming aware of the loss of his passport;

(g) receipt by him of a new passport;

(h) an appeal made by him in relation to the order;

(i) an application made by him for termination of the order; and

(j) an appeal made by him against the making of a declaration of relevance in respect of an offence of which he has been convicted.

The notification must be given before the end of the seven-day period beginning with the day on which the event in question occurs and:

(a) in the case of a change of a name or address or the acquisition of a temporary address, must specify the new name or address;

(b) in the case of a first use of a previously undisclosed name, must specify that name; and

(c) in the case of a receipt of a new passport must give details of that.

A banning order must contain a requirement as to the surrender, in accordance with the Act (below), in connection with regulated football matches outside the UK, of the passport of the person subject to the order.

The court may impose additional requirements on a person subject to such an order and may subsequently vary an order so as to impose, replace or omit requirements on the application of the person subject to the order or the person who applied for the order or the prosecutor. In addition, the court has power to require a constable to photograph the person or cause him to be photographed.

Duration of banning order

Where a banning order is made under s 14A (ie following conviction) and is in addition to a sentence of imprisonment (any form of detention) taking immediate effect, the maximum duration is 10 years and the minimum six. In any other case following conviction the maximum is five years and the minimum three. Orders which are made under s 14B or s 22 may be for a maximum of five years and a minimum of three.

Termination of an order

After two-thirds of the period of the ban has passed, the person subject to it may apply to the court by which the order was made to terminate it. The court, in considering whether or not to terminate the ban, must have regard to a person's character; conduct since the order was made; the nature of the offence or conduct concerned; and any other relevant circumstances.

Functions of the enforcing authority and local police forces

FSA 1989, s 19(2) provides that, when a banned person initially reports at a police station, the officer responsible for that station may make such requirements of that person as are determined by the enforcing authority to be necessary or expedient for giving effect to the banning order, so far as matters are related to regulated football matches outside the UK. The 'enforcing authority' is the Football Banning Orders Authority established by the Secretary of State.

If, in connection with any regulated football match outside the UK, that authority considers that a requirement to report is necessary or expedient to reduce the likelihood of violence or disorder at or in connection with the match, the authority is required by s 19(2B) to give the person subject to the order a notice in writing to report as instructed and to surrender his passport as instructed. Under s 19(2B), the notice may also require compliance with additional requirements.

In the case of any regulated football match, the enforcing authority may by notice in writing require the person subject to the order to comply with any additional requirements of the order in the manner specified in the notice (s 19(2C)).

A notice under s 19 may not require the person subject to it to report except in the 'control period' in relation to a regulated football match outside the UK or an external tournament which includes such matches and may not require him to surrender a passport except in such a control period. The 'control period' in relation to such a regulated football match outside the UK is the period commencing five days before the day of the match and ending when the match is finished or cancelled. In relation to an external tournament the 'control period' means any period described in an order made by the Secretary of State beginning five days before the first match outside the UK and ending when the last match outside the UK has been finished or cancelled. However, qualifying matches do not count in determining the start of the tournament.

If the Secretary of State considers it necessary or expedient to do so in order to secure the effective enforcement of these provisions, the 'control period' may be extended by order in relation to any regulated football match to a maximum of not more than 10 days before the day of the match (or the day of the first match in the external tournament, as the case may be).

Failure to comply with a requirement

It is an offence, contrary to FSA 1989, s 19(6), to fail, without reasonable excuse, to comply with a requirement imposed under s 19(2).

It is an offence, contrary to FSA 1989, s 14J(1), for a person subject to a banning order to fail to comply with:

(a) any requirement imposed by the order; or
(b) any requirement imposed by FSA 1989, s 19(2B) or s 19(2C).

Summary measures

FSA 1989, ss 21A and 21B underpin the procedure for the application by way of complaint for a banning order. They provide for a constable in uniform to exercise powers of detention and of reference to a court in specified circumstances. The powers under ss 21A and 21B may be exercised only in relation to a British citizen.

FSA 1989, s 21A provides a constable in uniform with the power to detain a person in his custody if, during any 'control period' in relation to a regulated football match outside the UK or an external tournament:

(a) he has reasonable grounds to suspect that the person has at any time caused or contributed to any violence or disorder in the UK or elsewhere; and
(b) he has reasonable grounds to believe that making a banning order in his case would help to prevent violence or disorder at, or in connection with, any regulated football matches.

Such a person may be detained until the constable has decided whether or not to issue a notice under FSA 1989, s 21B requiring him:

(a) to appear before a magistrates' court at a specified time;
(b) not to leave England and Wales before that time; and
(c) if the control period relates to a regulated football match outside the UK or to an external tournament which includes such matches, to surrender his passport to the constable,

and stating the grounds upon which his decision is based.

Such detention may not exceed four hours or, with the authority of an inspector (or above), six hours. A person so detained may not be further detained within the same control period unless new information becomes available.

The notice referred to above may be issued where the officer is authorised to do so by an inspector (or above). The time at which such a person must appear before a magistrates' court must be within 24 hours of receiving the notice or that person's detention, whichever is the earlier. Such a notice will be treated as an application for a banning order by way of complaint.

Where a person to whom such a notice has been given appears before a magistrates' court, the court may remand him. If he is remanded on bail, he may be required not to leave England and Wales before his appearance before the court and, if the control period relates to a regulated football match outside the UK or to an external tournament which includes such matches, he may be required to surrender his passport to a constable.

It is an offence under s 21C to fail to comply with a notice under s 21B.

Enforcement in England and Wales of the Police, Public Order and Criminal Justice (Scotland) Act 2006, s 68

The following provisions of the Police, Public Order and Criminal Justice (Scotland) Act 2006 extend to England and Wales:

(a) s 68(1) and (2) (offences of failing to comply with a requirement imposed by a football banning order, under s 61(1) or by a notice under s 61(4), and defence of reasonable excuse);

(b) s 68(5) (offence of making a false statement, etc in connection with an application for exemption from a notice under s 61(4)).

TICKET TOUTS

The Criminal Justice and Public Order Act 1994, s 166 makes it an offence for an unauthorised person to sell, or otherwise dispose of to another person, a ticket for a designated football match. The reference to selling includes a reference to offering or exposing a ticket for sale, making it available for sale by another, advertising it as available for purchase, and giving it to a person who pays or agrees to pay for some other goods or services or offers to do so.

The only persons who are 'authorised' are those authorised in writing by the organisers of the match. The term 'ticket' includes anything which purports to be a ticket, so that false tickets are included. However, where a false ticket is involved a charge of fraud would be more appropriate where knowledge of such falsity can be proved. A 'designated football match' has the same meaning as 'regulated football match', described on p 988, except that it does not refer to the Scottish Leagues or the FA Cup.

Section 166 does not apply to internet touting. This is dealt with by special rules under s 166A.

Police powers

The provisions of PACE 1984, s 32 (search of an arrested person and his vehicle) are extended to the case where the vehicle is reasonably believed to have been used for any purpose connected with an offence under s 166.

LABOUR LAWS

The police are inevitably involved in the enforcement of the law concerning trade disputes. Consequently, it is essential that this law is clearly understood by police officers, who are very much in the public eye when dealing with such disputes. The primary piece of legislation dealing with trade disputes is the Trade Union and Labour Relations (Consolidation) Act 1992 (TULR(C)A 1992).

Acts of 'interference' with workers

TULR(C)A 1992, s 241 deals with such acts. It is not directly concerned with picketing. Indeed, it is not confined to the context of trade disputes. However, that is its normal application. It deals with acts which might or might not be committed away from the picket line but which nevertheless amount to attempts to prevent a worker from exercising his own freedom of choice.

An offence is committed under TULR(C)A 1992, s 241(1) by any person who, *with a view to compelling (as opposed simply to persuading) any other person to abstain from doing or to do any act which that other person has a legal right to do or abstain from doing, wrongfully and without legal authority does one of the following things*:

Uses violence to or intimidates such other person or his spouse, civil partner or children, or injures his property

No matter what a mob may represent itself to be, if that mob or any particular person uses violence or intimidates another person an offence is committed against s 241. Acts committed against a person's spouse, civil partner, children or property are also punishable. It is not a form of peaceful persuasion to threaten a worker, his family or his property with violence. Instances have occurred in which the cars of workers who refused to join a strike have been damaged. In addition to the offence of criminal damage, the present offence is also committed.

Persistently follows such other person about from place to place

The word 'persistently' is not meant to convey any form of permanence in this activity and it is sufficient if a person, or part of the mob outside a works, follows a man from the works and through the streets, shouting at him or making hostile gestures. The following of an employer in an attempt to compel him to reinstate an employee is also covered by this provision.

Hides any tools, clothes, or other property owned or used by such other person or deprives him of or hinders him in the use thereof

An effective way of preventing a skilled workman from carrying out his duties would be to prevent him from working by separating him from specialist tools required to carry out his task. If all the miners' lamps for a particular colliery were hidden, this could effectively prevent individual miners, and perhaps the entire workforce, from working.

Watches or besets the house or other place where such other person resides, or works, or carries on business, or happens to be, or the approach to such a house or place

'Watching or besetting' merely describes certain forms of picketing. It must be remembered that all the various types of conduct covered by s 241 are only criminal if they are done wrongfully. As a result, a person engaged in lawful picketing is not guilty under s 241 by virtue of the present provision. What constitutes 'lawful picketing' is described below. There would be little purpose in restricting the nature of picketing at a works to forms of peaceful picketing if pickets could operate outside the houses of individual workers to prevent them from working. This mode of the offence is designed among other things to prevent the removal of picket lines or single persuaders from the works to a dwelling house or its approaches.

Follows such other person with two or more other persons in a disorderly manner in or through any street or road

This offence differs from that of persistently following in that there is no need to prove any form of persistence. The aggravation by being accompanied by two or more persons and the incidence of disorderly conduct are sufficient. This mode of committing the offence can only be committed in a street or road.

Peaceful picketing: Trade Union and Labour Relations (Consolidation) Act 1992

It is extremely important to understand the law concerning peaceful picketing because of the necessity for police officers to ensure that the activities of the pickets are directed towards pursuits which are permitted by law and do not amount to intimidation of other workers, whether they are workers belonging to the same trade union or not.

TULR(C)A 1992, s 220(1) states that it shall be lawful for a person in contemplation or furtherance of a trade dispute to attend:

(a) at or near his own place of work; or
(b) if he is an official of a trade union, at or near the place of work of a member of that union whom he is accompanying and whom he represents,

for the purpose only of peacefully obtaining or communicating information, or peacefully persuading any person to work or abstain from working. These words contain key requirements for lawful picketing. They are concerned with *the place* where a person attends in contemplation or furtherance of a trade dispute and with *the purpose* for which he attends.

The place

TULR(C)A 1992, s 220(1) provides that it is lawful for a person in contemplation or furtherance of a trade dispute to attend at or near *his own place of work*; it does not, of course, authorise access to private premises without the consent of their owner. Except in the case of a trade union official accompanying a member whom he represents at or near the latter's place of work, picketing at some place other than the picket's own place of work is not declared to be lawful. Thus, picketing by 'flying pickets' or by other people who do not work at the place in question (and may not even be members of the trade union engaged in the dispute) is not declared to be lawful by s 220(1); such a picket may be guilty from the outset of an offence against TULR(C)A 1992, s 241 on the ground of 'watching or besetting', however peaceful the picket may be.

It follows that the meaning of 'his own place of work' for the purposes of TULR(C)A 1992, s 220(1) is of crucial importance. In this respect, s 220(2) and (3) make special provision. Section 220(2) deals with the case of a worker who does not work at any one particular place (for example, a service engineer or train driver) or whose place of work is so located that it is impracticable for him to attend there to picket. It provides that the place of work of such a person is *any premises* of his employer *from* which he works or *from* which his work is administered.

Whether or not picketing is *at or near* the picket's place of work depends upon a commonsense approach. In one case the Court of Appeal held that pickets, who stood at the entrance to a trading estate 1,200 yards away from their employer's premises on that estate and would have been trespassing if they had picketed on the estate, were attending (picketing) near their place of work.

There are occasions when the above provisions of TULR(C)A 1992, s 220 would act unfairly against a worker who, having been dismissed from his employment, would be excluded from the right to protest because he would no longer have a place of work at or near which he could attend. Section 220(3) protects such a worker, by stating that where:

(a) his last employment was terminated in connection with a trade dispute; or
(b) the termination of his employment was one of the circumstances giving rise to the dispute,

his former place of work shall be treated as if it was his place of work.

The purpose

Even if the requirement that the picket must be obtaining or communicating information, or peacefully picketing at or near his own place of work is satisfied, his conduct is *only declared to be lawful by TULR(C)A 1992, s 220(1) if his attendance is for the purpose only of peacefully persuading any person to work or abstain from working*. A person who attends for some other purpose, for example forcibly to prevent workers or deliveries entering premises, is not protected by s 220(1) and is liable for any criminal offence which he may commit; he might also, of course, be liable to pay damages under the civil law for any harm which he causes by molesting a worker or interfering with his right to work. Thus, pickets who link arms and form a physical barrier to prevent movement in and out of works are criminally liable, even though they work there, for an offence against TULR(C)A 1992, s 241 and for any other offence which they may commit, as are members of a picket which by weight of numbers seeks to prevent others exercising their right to work since it cannot be said that they are there *only* for fulfilling one of the specified purposes peacefully: intimidation is not peaceful persuasion.

The physical presence of lawful pickets on a highway must represent some form of obstruction and this is permitted to the extent that it is reasonably necessary for such pickets to carry out their task of speaking to their colleagues. However, this right is restricted to those who are lawful pickets in accordance with the provisions of TULR(C)A 1992, s 220. It is a question of fact as to whether or not the degree of obstruction has passed beyond that reasonably required. Mass picketing clearly goes beyond what is reasonably required and is therefore illegal. So is the total obstruction of an entrance, and so are other measures which have the same effect. Where pickets kept moving by walking around in a circle outside the main entrance to a factory and were required to stop doing so by a police officer, they were held to have obstructed him in his duty by their refusal, as they were carrying out an illegal act.

The police have a duty to limit the size of lawful pickets to a number which appears to be reasonable in the circumstances and a refusal by the organisers to comply with reasonable requests made by the police may amount to a wilful obstruction contrary to the Police Act 1996, s 89(2).

The role of the police

The police must not be concerned with the merits of any trade dispute. Their role is the preservation of the peace, and they must impartially enforce and uphold the law where such action becomes necessary. They have a general discretion in relation to their handling of disputes and of pickets to ensure that all remains peaceful and orderly. It is no part of a police officer's duty to assist with civil remedies; if an employer wishes to identify persons on picket lines or outside his works with a view to civil process, that is his responsibility and police officers should not attempt to identify such persons on his behalf. Additionally, the enforcement of any orders made in favour of employers is the responsibility of officers of the court and police participation must be restricted to ensuring the maintenance of the peace.

The code of conduct on picketing issued for the guidance of pickets (which recommends that in general the number of pickets at any entrance to a workplace should not exceed six) is not a part of the criminal law. The number of pickets in particular circumstances is a matter for police discretion bearing in mind their primary purpose of maintaining the peace.

CHAPTER 28

Terrorism Generally

This chapter is concerned with the offences and powers under the Terrorism Acts 2000 and 2006, the Anti-terrorism, Crime and Security Act 2001, Parts 1–4, and the Counter-Terrorism Act 2008, and with the power to impose terrorism prevention and investigation measures under the Terrorism Prevention and Investigation Measures Act 2011 to protect the public from terrorism. These Acts can be described as the 'terrorism legislation'.

All the offences described in this chapter are indictable (either way) offences, unless otherwise indicated.

MEANING OF 'TERRORISM' IN TERRORISM LEGISLATION

For the purposes of this legislation, 'terrorism' is defined by the Terrorism Act 2000 (TA 2000), s 1, as meaning the use or threat of action (inside or outside the UK) which:

- (a) (i) involves serious violence against a person wherever he is,
  - (ii) involves serious damage to property wherever situated,
  - (iii) endangers a person's life, other than that of the person committing the action,
  - (iv) creates a serious risk to the health and safety of the public or a section of the public, or
  - (v) is designed seriously to interfere with or seriously to disrupt an electronic system;
- (b) is designed to influence the UK government, or any other government, or an international governmental organisation, or to intimidate the public or a section of the public anywhere; *and*
- (c) is made for the purpose of advancing a political, religious, racial or ideological cause.

The use or threat of action falling within (a) which includes the use of firearms or explosives is terrorism whether or not (b) is satisfied.

The Court of Appeal has held that the definition of terrorism in TA 2000, s 1 is unambiguous and that the reference to 'any other government' in (b) means the government of any other country and not, as argued before it, a representative or democratic government of another country.

The Court of Appeal has also held that an attack on the military forces of a government or coalition of governments, which satisfies (b) and (c), amounts to terrorism, and that there is no exemption from criminal liability for terrorist activities motivated by the alleged nobility of the terrorist cause.

PROSCRIBED ORGANISATIONS

TA 2000 contains a number of offences which can be committed in relation to a 'proscribed organisation' listed in TA 2000, Sch 2:

(1) Belonging or professing to belong to a proscribed organisation, subject to a defence on 'proof' (interpreted by the House of Lords as only imposing an evidential burden) by the defendant (D) that he joined the proscribed organisation before it was proscribed and he has not taken part in the activities of the organisation since it became proscribed (TA 2000, s 11). The Court of Appeal has held that membership of a proscribed organisation depends on the nature of the organisation in question. Membership of a loose and unstructured organisation may not require an express process, whereas a more structured organisation may have an express process whereby a person becomes a member. The core elements of membership within s 11 will frequently be voluntary and knowing association with others with a view to furthering the aims of the proscribed organisation. Unilateral sympathy with the aims of an organisation, even coupled with acts designed to promote similar objectives, whilst being clear evidence of belonging, will not always be sufficient.

(2) Inviting support for a proscribed organisation, other than support with money or property (s 12(1)).

(3) Arranging, managing, or assisting in arranging or managing a meeting of three or more people (whether or not the public are admitted) which D knows is:
    (a) to support a proscribed organisation,
    (b) to further the activities of a proscribed organisation, or
    (c) to be addressed by a person who belongs or professes to belong to a proscribed organisation, subject to a defence (where the offence relates to a private meeting) if D adduces sufficient evidence that he had no reasonable cause to believe that such an address would support a proscribed organisation or further its activities, whereupon the prosecution must disprove this (s 12(2)).

(4) Addressing a meeting where the purpose is to encourage support for a proscribed organisation or to further its activities (s 12(3)).

(5) Wearing in a public place any item of clothing, or wearing, carrying or displaying any article, in such a way or in such circumstances as to arouse reasonable apprehension of being a member or supporter of a proscribed organisation (s 13). This is a summary offence.

For the purposes of TA 2000, the proscribed organisations associated with terrorism in Northern Ireland are at present:

the Irish Republican Army; Cumann na mBan; Fianna na hEireann; the Red Hand Commando; Saor Eire; the Ulster Freedom Fighters; the Ulster Volunteer Force; the Irish National Liberation Army; the Irish People's Liberation Organisation; the Ulster Defence Association; the Loyalist Volunteer Force; the Continuity Army Council; the Orange Volunteers; and the Red Hand Defenders.

Other proscribed organisations are:

Al-Qa'ida; Egyptian Islamic Jihad; Al-Gama'at al-Islamiya; Armed Islamic Group (Groupe Islamique Armée) (GIA); Salafist Group for Call and Combat (Groupe Salafiste pour la Prédication et le Combat) (GSPC); Babbar Khalsa; International Sikh Youth Federation; Harakat Mujahideen; Jaish e Mohammed; Lashkar e Tayyaba (also known as Jama'at ud Da'wa); Liberation Tigers of Tamil Eelam (LTTE); the military wing of Hizballah, including the Jihad Council and all units reporting to it (including the Hizballah External Security Organisation); Hamas-Izz al-Din al-Qassem Brigades; Palestinian Islamic Jihad—Shaqaqi; Abu Nidal Organisation; Islamic

Army of Aden; Kurdistan Workers' Party (Partiya Karkeren Kurdistan) (PKK) (also known as Kongra Gele Kurdistan, and KADEK); Revolutionary Peoples' Liberation Party—Front (Devrimci Halk Kurtulus Partisi-Cephesi) (DHKP-C); Basque Homeland and Liberty (Euskadi ta Askatasuna) (ETA); 17 November Revolutionary Organisation (N17); Abu Sayyaf Group; Asbat Al-Ansar; Islamic Movement of Uzbekistan; Jemaah Islamiyah; Al Ittihad Al Islamia; Ansar Al Islam; Ansar Al Sunna; Groupe Islamique Combattant Marocain; Harakat-ul-Jihad-ul-Islami; Harakat-ul-Jihad-ul-Islami (Bangladesh); Harakat-ul-Mujahadeen/Alami; Hezb-e Islami Gulbuddin; Islamic Jihad Union; Jamaat ul-Furquan; Jundallah; Khuddam ul-Islam; Lashkar-e Jhangvi; Libyan Islamic Fighting Group; Sipah-e Sahaba Pakistan, Baluchistan Liberation Army; Teyrebaz Azadiye Kurdistan; Jammat-ul Mujahideen Bangladesh; Tehrik Nefaz-e Shari'at Muhammadi; Al-Shabaab; Tehrik-e Taliban Pakistan; Indian Mujahideen; Al-Ghurabaa; The Saved Sect. Al Muhajiroun (ALM); Call to Submission; Islam4UK; Islamic Path; London School of Sharia; and Muslims against Crusades, are treated as alternative names for both Al-Ghurabaa and The Saved Sect.

The Secretary of State has the power to add to, remove or amend a name included in TA 2000, Sch 2. He or she may only add the name of an organisation if he or she believes that it is concerned in terrorism, and for this purpose an organisation is concerned in terrorism if it commits, or participates in, acts of terrorism, prepares for terrorism, promotes or encourages terrorism, or is otherwise concerned in terrorism.

As can be seen, the provisions of TA 2000, ss 11 to 13 create a wide range of offences dealing with membership or professed membership of proscribed organisations, with the promotion of them, and meetings in support of them.

TERRORIST PROPERTY

Fund-raising

TA 2000, s 15 provides that a person is guilty of an offence if he:

(a) invites any other person to provide money or other property, and intends that it should be used, or has reasonable cause to suspect that it may be used, for the purposes of terrorism (s 15(1)); or

(b) receives money or other property, and intends that it should be used, or has reasonable cause to suspect that it may be used, for the purposes of terrorism (s 15(2)); or

(c) provides money or other property, and knows or has reasonable cause to suspect that it will or may be used, for the purposes of terrorism (s 15(3)).

Within s 15, a reference to the 'provision' of money or other property is a reference to its being given, lent or otherwise made available, whether or not for consideration.

A person does not commit an offence under s 15 (on under ss 16 to 18 below) in the circumstances set out in ss 21, 21ZA, 21ZB or 21ZC (pp 803–4).

Use and possession

TA 2000, s 16(1) prohibits as an offence the use of money or property for the purposes of terrorism. Section 16(2) creates a further offence of possessing money or other property intending that it should be used, or having reasonable cause to suspect that it might be used, for the purposes of terrorism.

Funding arrangements

TA 2000, s 17 makes it an offence for a person to enter into, or become concerned in, an arrangement as a result of which money or other property is made (or is to be made) available to another, knowing or having reasonable cause to suspect that it might be used for terrorism.

Money laundering

TA 2000, s 18(1) prohibits as an offence money laundering of terrorist property by concealment, removal from jurisdiction, transfer to nominees, or in any other way. Section 18(2) provides a defence if the defendant proves lack of knowledge or reason to suspect that the arrangement was concerned with terrorist property.

Disclosure of information: duty

TA 2000, s 19(1) and (2) provides that a person commits an offence if he does not disclose to a constable, as soon as reasonably practicable, a belief or suspicion, and the information upon which it is based, where he:

(a) believes or suspects that another person has committed an offence under any of TA 2000, ss 15 to 18; and
(b) bases his belief or suspicion on information which came to his attention in the course of his employment (whether or not in a trade, profession or business).

However, s 19 does not apply if the information came to the person in the course of a business in the regulated sector. A business is in the regulated sector to the extent that it engages in accepting deposits, operating a bureau de change, dealing in, advising in relation to, or managing investments, accountancy business, estate agency or casino, or a range of other financially related activities listed in Sch 3A for the purposes of s 21A (set out below), which provides offences which can be committed in those circumstances.

It is a defence to a charge under s 19 to prove reasonable excuse for non-disclosure. In the case of an employee, where there is an established procedure concerning disclosure, it is a defence for him to prove that disclosure was made within that procedure. The section does not require disclosure by a professional legal adviser of legally privileged information or of a belief or suspicion based on such information.

Co-operation with the police

TA 2000, s 21 makes provision for those who act in co-operation with the police. An offence is not committed against ss 15 to 18 if the person is acting with the express consent of a constable.

Exceptions

In order to implement a Community Directive, TA 2000, ss 21ZA, 21ZB, and 21ZC provide exceptions *which apply to the offences against ss 15 to 18*. Section 21ZA provides an exception if the defendant (D) has made a disclosure to an authorised officer before becoming involved in a transaction or an arrangement and acts with the consent of the authorised officer. 'Authorised officer' means a member of staff of SOCA authorised for the purposes of s 21ZA by the Director General of SOCA. Section 21ZB provides a further exception to cover those who become involved in a transaction or an arrangement and then make a disclosure, so long as there is a reasonable excuse for failure to make a disclosure in advance. Finally, s 21ZC provides a defence if D proves that he intended to make a disclosure under s 21ZA or 21ZB and has a reasonable excuse for failing to do so.

Failure to disclose: regulated sector

TA 2000, s 21A is aimed at preventing money laundering by terrorist organisations. TA 2000, s 21A(1) to (4) creates an offence of failure by D to disclose certain information or other matter to a constable or a nominated officer as soon as is practicable after that information comes into his possession. The offence occurs where:

(a) D knows or suspects or has reasonable grounds for knowing or suspecting that another person (X) has committed or attempted to commit an offence under any of TA 2000, ss 15 to 18; and

(b) that information or other matter, on which D's knowledge or suspicion is based or which gives reasonable grounds for such knowledge or suspicion, came to him in the course of a business in the regulated sector (see p 803).

X will be taken to have committed an offence against ss 15 to 18 for these purposes if:

(a) he has taken action or been in possession of a thing; and

(b) he would have committed the offence if he had been in the UK at the time when he took the action or was in possession of the thing.

D does not commit an offence under s 21A if:

(a) he has a reasonable excuse for not disclosing the information or other matter;

(b) he is a professional legal adviser or relevant professional adviser (a qualified accountant, auditor or tax adviser) and the information or other matter came to him in privileged circumstances; or

(c) (i)   he is employed by, or in partnership with, such an adviser to provide the adviser with assistance or support,

(ii)   the information or other matter comes to him in connection with the provision of such assistance or support, and

(iii)   the information or other matter comes to him in privileged circumstances.

In deciding whether D has committed an offence under s 21A, a court must consider whether D had followed any relevant Treasury approved guidance issued by a supervisory authority and properly brought to the attention of affected persons.

A disclosure to a 'nominated officer' is one made to a person nominated by D's employer to receive such disclosures and is made in the course of D's employment in accordance with established procedures.

Protected disclosures

By TA 2000, s 21B a disclosure will not be taken to have breached any restriction upon the disclosure of information (however imposed) if (a) the information came to the discloser in the course of a business in the regulated sector, (b) the information is such that it causes him to know or suspect, or gives him reasonable grounds for knowing or suspecting, that another person has committed an offence under ss 15 to 18, and (c) the disclosure is made to a constable or nominated officer as soon as is practicable.

Disclosures to SOCA

Where a disclosure is made under the above provisions to a constable, the constable must disclose it in full as soon as practicable to a member of staff of SOCA authorised for this purpose by the Director General of SOCA; where a disclosure is made to a constable under s 21, this duty to disclose is a duty to disclose to SOCA staff specifically authorised to receive TA 2000, s 19 disclosures (s 21C).

TERRORIST INVESTIGATIONS

Police cordons

TA 2000, ss 33 to 36 provide powers to impose a police cordon for the purposes of a 'terrorist investigation'. A 'terrorist investigation' means an investigation of:

(a) the commission, preparation, or instigation of acts of terrorism (see p 800);
(b) an act which appears to have been done for the purposes of terrorism;
(c) the resources of a proscribed organisation (as to which see p 801);
(d) the possibility of making an order proscribing an organisation; or
(e) the commission, preparation, or instigation of an offence under the Act or under the Terrorism Act 2006 (pp 832–5) other than an offence under TA 2006, s 1 or s 2 (encouragement of terrorism and dissemination of terrorist material).

TA 2000, s 34 permits an officer of at least the rank of superintendent, where he considers it expedient for the purpose of a terrorist investigation, to authorise a cordon to be imposed on an area specified by him in that authorisation. (An officer below that rank may do so where there is great urgency. He must, as soon as reasonably practicable, make a written record of the time of the designation of the area and ensure that an officer of at least the rank of superintendent is informed. Such an officer must confirm the designation or cancel it from a specified time, in which case his reason for doing so must be stated.) The area on which a cordon is imposed must, so far as is reasonably practicable, be indicated by means of police tape or in such other manner as appears appropriate to the police officer responsible for carrying out the arrangements for applying the cordon. The period of time initially specified must not exceed 14 days, but may be extended by a superintendent (or above) by one or more written variations; however, the overall period must not exceed 28 days.

Persons must leave the area immediately when ordered to do so by a constable in uniform and persons must also leave premises which are wholly or partly in or adjacent to a cordoned area when so ordered. Drivers or persons in charge of vehicles must move them out of the area when ordered by such a constable (who also has power to remove such vehicles). A constable in uniform may prohibit or restrict vehicular or pedestrian access to a cordoned area. A summary offence is committed under s 36(2) by someone who does not comply with the constable's order, prohibition or restriction. It is a defence to prove a reasonable excuse.

Offences relating to terrorist investigations

Information about acts of terrorism

By TA 2000, s 38B, a person who has information which he knows or believes might be of material assistance:

(a) in preventing the commission by another person of an act of terrorism; or
(b) in securing the apprehension, prosecution or conviction of another person, in the UK, for an offence involving the commission, preparation or instigation of an act of terrorism,

commits an offence if he does not disclose the information as soon as reasonably practicable to a constable.

This offence may be treated as having been committed in any place where the person to be charged is, or has at any time been, since he first knew or believed that the information might be of material assistance, and proceedings may be taken in any such place.

Offences relating to disclosure

TA 2000, s 39(2) is concerned with an offence which is committed by a person who knows or has reasonable cause to suspect that a constable is conducting, or proposes to conduct, a terrorist investigation (as defined on p 805) and who:

(a) discloses to another anything which is likely to prejudice the investigation; or
(b) interferes with material which is likely to be relevant to the investigation.

Where a person knows or has reasonable cause to believe that a disclosure has been or will be made under TA 2000, ss 19 to 21B (pp 803–4) or 38B (above), he commits an offence under s 39(4) if he:

(a) discloses to another anything which is likely to prejudice an investigation resulting from the disclosure under one of these sections; or
(b) interferes with material which is likely to be relevant to an investigation resulting from the disclosure under that section.

It is a defence to a charge under s 39(2) or (4) for a person to adduce evidence that he did not know and had no reasonable cause to suspect that the disclosure was likely to affect a terrorist investigation (whereupon the prosecution must disprove this) or to prove that he had a reasonable excuse for the disclosure or interference.

COUNTER-TERRORIST POWERS

Search of premises

By TA 2000, s 42, a justice of the peace may issue a warrant on the application of a constable in relation to the search of specified premises if satisfied that there are reasonable grounds for suspecting that a person, whom the constable reasonably suspects to be a person who is or has been concerned in the commission, preparation or instigation of acts of terrorism, is to be found there. Such a warrant authorises entry and search for the purpose of the arrest of a person subject to arrest under the provisions of TA 2000, s 41 (p 821). This power of search includes a power to search a container on the premises.

Search warrants may also be granted under TA 2000, Sch 5, described on p 74.

Code of practice relating to searches of persons and vehicles

As required by TA 2000, s 47AA, added by the Protection of Freedoms Act 2012 (PFA 2012), the Secretary of State has issued a Code of Practice for the Exercise of Stop and Search Powers under ss 43 and 43A of TA 2000 and the Authorisation and Exercise of

Stop and Search Powers relating to s 47A of, and Sch 6B to, TA 2000 (hereafter 'the Terrorism Search Powers Code'). These statutory provisions are dealt with below. A constable must have regard to the Terrorism Search Powers Code when exercising any powers to which it relates. A failure on the part of a constable to act in accordance with any provision of the Code does not of itself make him liable to criminal or civil proceedings. However, the Code is admissible in evidence in any such proceedings, and a court or tribunal may, in particular, take into account a failure by a constable to have regard to it in determining a question in any such proceedings. The references to a constable include, in relation to any of the above functions exercisable by a community support officer by virtue of the Police Reform Act 2002, Sch 4 (see p 283), references to that person.

The Code provides that chief officers and 'police authorities' (police and crime commissioners, the Mayor's Office for Policing and Crime and police authorities) must have regard to it when discharging a function to which it relates. The Code must be followed by them unless there is good reason not to do so, in which case the decision not to follow it should be recorded in writing.

Search of persons

A constable is given power by TA 2000, s 43(1) to stop and search *a person* whom he *reasonably suspects* to be a terrorist to discover whether he has in his possession anything which might constitute evidence that he is a terrorist. A 'terrorist' is defined as a person:

(a) who has committed an offence under TA 2000, s 11 (membership of a proscribed organisation); s 12 (support for it); ss 15 to 18 (fund-raising, etc and money laundering); s 54 (weapons training); or ss 56 to 63 (directing terrorist organisation, possession for terrorist purposes, collecting information, inciting terrorism overseas, and foreign terrorist bombing and finance offences); or
(b) who is, or has been, concerned in the commission, preparation, or instigation of acts of terrorism.

This power to stop a person includes the power to stop a vehicle.

By s 43(2), a constable may also search anyone arrested under s 41 to discover whether he has anything in his possession which may constitute such evidence. Reasonable suspicion that such evidence may be found is not required.

The powers to search a person under s 43 include the power to search anything carried by the person, eg a bag. Anything found in a search under s 43(1) or (2) may be seized and retained if the constable reasonably suspects that it is evidence that the person is a terrorist (s 43(4)). The additional powers of seizure under the Criminal Justice and Police Act 2001, s 51 are available: see p 65.

Where a constable exercising the power under s 43(1) to stop a person, stops a vehicle, he may:

(a) search the vehicle and anything in or on it to discover whether there is anything which may constitute evidence that the person concerned is a terrorist (but he may not search someone in the same vehicle as the suspected terrorist solely on the basis that that person is with the suspected terrorist); and
(b) seize and retain anything which he discovers in the course of such a search, and reasonably suspects may constitute evidence that the person is a terrorist (s 43(4A) and (4B), added by the Protection of Freedoms Act (PFA) 2012).

A 'vehicle' includes an aircraft, hovercraft, train or vessel. The additional powers of seizure under the Criminal Justice and Police Act 2001, s 50 are available. A constable stopping a vehicle must be in uniform.

The grounds for stopping and searching a person under s 43 are the same as the grounds for arrest under s 41 (p 821): reasonable suspicion that the person is a terrorist. Stop and search is a less intrusive power than arrest and will be more appropriate in many situations, eg in encounters with individuals where a stop and search may help to allay suspicions. Stop and search should not be used in any situation where it is more appropriate to arrest or where an officer believes it may put him, or members of the public, in danger.

Powers to stop and search must be exercised fairly, responsibly, and in accordance with the Equality Act 2010 (referred to on p 35).

The same provisions apply to the removal of clothing in conducting a search as apply under PACE Code A: Stop and Search Code (see p 47), including the words italicised there. Although there is no longer as statutory requirement for the constable conducting the search to be of the same sex as the person searched, where such a constable is readily available, that constable should carry out the search. Otherwise, searches may be carried out by a constable of the opposite sex unless the removal of clothes other than an outer coat or jacket is required. Particular regard should be paid to the sensitivities of some religious communities in respect of being searched by a member of the opposite sex.

The Counter-Terrorism Act 2008 (C-TA 2008), s 1 prospectively empowers a constable, for the purpose of ascertaining whether a document is one that may be seized under TA 2000, s 43, to remove a document to another place for examination and to retain it there until the examination is complete. By C-TA 2008, s 2(1), it is an offence wilfully to obstruct a constable in the exercise of his powers under s 1. Section 1 does not authorise the removal of a document which the constable has reasonable cause to be, or to contain, an item subject to legal privilege. A record must be made of removals. The period of retention of, access to, and the photographing and copying of, documents which have been removed are controlled by ss 5 to 7 respectively.

Search of vehicles

By TA 2000, s 43A, inserted by PFA 2012, if a constable *reasonably suspects* that a *vehicle* is being used for the purposes of terrorism, he may stop and search:

(a) the vehicle,
(b) the driver of the vehicle,
(c) a passenger in the vehicle,
(d) anything in or on the vehicle or carried by the driver or a passenger,

to discover whether there is anything which may constitute evidence that the vehicle is being used for the purposes of terrorism (s 43A(1) and (2)). An unattended vehicle can be searched under s 43A.

'Driver', in relation to an aircraft, hovercraft, or vessel, means the captain, pilot or other person with control of the aircraft, hovercraft, or vessel or any member of its crew and, in relation to a train, includes any member of its crew. A constable stopping a vehicle must be in uniform.

Searches may be undertaken of anything in or on the vehicle, but care should be taken not to damage a vehicle as part of a search or, in the case of an unattended vehicle, in order to gain entry into it. Vehicles stopped under s 43A and persons in those vehicles may be detained only for so long as is necessary to carry out the searches – at or near the place the vehicle was stopped.

A constable may seize and retain anything which he:

(a) discovers in the course of such a search, and
(b) reasonably suspects may constitute evidence that the vehicle is being used for the purposes of terrorism (s 43A(3)).

A person who has the powers of a constable in one part of the UK may exercise a power under s 43A in any part of the UK.

The additional powers of seizure under the Criminal Justice and Police Act 2001, ss 50 and 51 are available. C-TA 2008, s 1 (referred to on p 808) prospectively applies to a search under TA 2000, s 43A.

Power to give an authorisation to stop and search in specified areas or places: TA 2000, s 47A

By TA 2000, s 47A(1), a senior police officer may give a stop and search authorisation under s 47A(2) or (3) (below) in relation to a specified area or place if the officer:

(a) reasonably suspects that an act of terrorism will take place; and
(b) considers that:
    (i) the authorisation is necessary to prevent such an act;
    (ii) the specified area or place is no greater than is necessary to prevent such an act; and
    (iii) the duration of the authorisation is no longer than is necessary to prevent such an act.

Senior police officer

'Senior police officer' for the purposes of s 47A and Sch 6B means an assistant chief constable (or a commander in the case of the two London police forces) or above. Authorising officers must be either substantive or on temporary promotion to the qualifying rank. Officers who are acting in the rank may not give authorisations.

Specified areas or places

An authorisation given by a senior police officer who is not a member of the British Transport Police Force, the Ministry of Defence Police or the Civil Nuclear Constabulary may specify an area or place in his police area together with the internal waters (ie waters such as a bay, estuary of a large river, or the sea near larger islands) which are not covered in any police area but are adjacent to that area or place, or a specified area of those internal waters. Police force areas do not cover the sea below the low water mark.

An authorisation by an assistant chief constable (or above) of the British Transport Police, the Ministry of Defence Police or the Civil Nuclear Constabulary may only be given in respect of specified areas or places policed by his force. An authorisation given by a senior police officer of the Civil Nuclear Constabulary does not have effect except in relation to times when the specified area or place is a place where members of that Constabulary have the powers and privileges of a constable.

Deciding whether to make an authorisation

Authorising officers should always consider whether giving an authorisation under s 47A is the most appropriate power to use in the circumstances and whether it is appropriate to authorise the powers in the particular circumstances, with regard to the safety of the public; the safety of officers, and the necessity of the powers in relation to the threat.

The Terrorism Search Powers Code states that the following may be taken into account when deciding whether to give an authorisation, but should not form the sole basis of such a decision:

(a) there is a general high threat from terrorism;
(b) a particular site or event is deemed to be 'high risk' or vulnerable.

On the other hand, an authorisation may not be given on the basis that:

(a) the use of the powers provides public reassurance; or
(b) the powers are a useful deterrent or intelligence-gathering tool.

Authorised conduct

An authorisation under TA 2000, s 47A(2) authorises any constable in uniform to stop a vehicle in the area or place specified in the authorisation and to search:

(a) the vehicle;
(b) the driver of the vehicle;
(c) a passenger in the vehicle;
(d) anything in or on the vehicle or carried by the driver or a passenger.

For these purposes, 'vehicle' includes an aircraft, hovercraft, train or vessel, and 'driver', in relation to an aircraft, hovercraft or vessel, means the captain, pilot or other person with control of it or any member of its crew and, in relation to a train, includes any member of its crew.

An authorisation under s 47A(3) authorises any constable in uniform to stop a pedestrian in the area or place specified in the authorisation and to search:

(a) the pedestrian;
(b) anything carried by the pedestrian.

Terms of the authorisation

Authorisations must be as limited as possible and linked to addressing the suspected act of terrorism. In determining the area(s) or place(s) it is necessary to specify in the authorisation, an authorising officer may need to consider the possibility that terrorists may change their method or target of attack, or that there are a number of potential targets. It will be necessary to consider what the appropriate operational response to the intelligence is (eg whether to conduct stop and search around suspected target sites or areas or routes which could allow the police to intercept a terrorist or vehicle). However, any authorisations must be as limited as possible and based on an assessment of the existing intelligence.

One authorisation may be given which encompasses a number of different places or areas within a police force area (whether those are included in response to the same or different threats). The authorisation must set out the necessity for including each of these areas or places and the necessity for the length of time for which the authorisation lasts in respect of each area or place.

The authorisation should also include details of how the exercise of the powers is necessary to prevent the act of terrorism. It must explain how the authorisation will counter the threat, ie why the stopping and searching of individuals and/or vehicles without suspicion is necessary to prevent the suspected act of terrorism. The consideration of necessity will also involve an assessment of why other measures (in particular the stop and search powers in TA 2000, s 43: see p 807) are not sufficient to address the threat.

Change in nature of threat

A new authorisation should be given if there is a significant change in the nature of the particular threat (or the authorising officer's understanding of it) which formed the basis of an existing authorisation. In such circumstances it will be appropriate to cancel the earlier authorisation.

Written authorisation or confirmation

Authorisations should, where practicable, be given in writing. A senior police officer who gives an authorisation under s 47A orally must confirm it in writing as soon as reasonably practicable (TA 2000, Sch 6B).

Where:

(a) a vehicle or pedestrian is stopped by virtue of s 47A(2) or (3), and
(b) the driver of the vehicle or the pedestrian applies for a written statement that the vehicle was stopped, or that the pedestrian was stopped, by virtue of s 47A(2) or (as the case may be) (3),

the written statement must be provided. Such an application must be made within the period of 12 months beginning with the date on which the vehicle or pedestrian was stopped.

Information in support of authorisation

Written authorisations and written confirmation of oral authorisations should include the information set out below and be provided on the form set out in Annex C to the Terrorism Search Powers Code.

Intelligence picture   The authorising officer should provide a detailed account of the intelligence which has given rise to his reasonable suspicion that an act of terrorism will take place. This should include classified material where it exists, which should be provided to the Secretary of State, with the authorisation, by a secure means of communication. References to classified reporting may be used instead of verbatim reports or quotes, but the reporting referenced must have been considered by the authorising officer in making the authorisation, and must be available to the Secretary of State when considering whether to confirm an authorisation.

Geographical extent   Detailed information should be provided to identify the geographical area(s) or place(s) covered by the authorisation. Where possible, maps of the authorised area should be included. The area authorised should be no wider than necessary. Authorisations which cover entire force areas are not justifiable, unless there are exceptional circumstances which support such an authorisation. Force-wide authorisations may be justifiable in respect of City of London Police, purely because of the size of the force area. However, the geographical area should still be no greater than necessary.

If an authorisation is one which covers a similar geographical area to one which immediately preceded it, information should be provided as to how the intelligence has changed since the previous authorisation was given, or if it has not changed, that it has been reassessed in the process of deciding on giving the new authorisation, and that it remains pertinent, and why.

Duration   The time or date of expiry of the authorisation (or times or dates where more than one area is authorised) must be stated. See below as to the duration of an authorisation.

Briefing provided   Information should be provided which demonstrates that all officers involved in exercising s 47A powers receive appropriate briefing in the use of the powers, including the provisions of the Terrorism Search Powers Code, and the reason for the use of the powers on each relevant occasion.

Tactical deployment   The authorising officer should provide information about how the powers will be used and why.

Duration of authorisation

TA 2000, Sch 6B provides that an authorisation under s 47A has effect during the period:

(a) beginning at the time when the authorisation is given, and
(b) ending with the date or at the time specified in the authorisation.

The power under (b) includes power to specify different dates or times for different areas or places.

The specified date or time in (b) must not occur after the end of the period of *14 days* beginning with the day on which the authorisation is given. Where different areas or places are specified within one authorisation, different time periods may be specified in relation to each of these areas or places; indeed the time period necessary for each will need to be considered and justified.

An authorisation should be given for no longer than necessary and should not be made for the maximum period unless it is necessary based on intelligence about the specified threat. Justification should be provided for the length of an authorisation, setting out why the intelligence supports the amount of time authorised. If an authorisation is one which is similar to another immediately preceding it, information should be provided as to why a new authorisation is justified and why the period of the initial authorisation was not sufficient.

If an authorisation is made for the maximum period of 14 days, it must specify an end time no later than 23.59hrs on the 14th day after it was given (or if only the date is given, that date must be the 14th day – and the time will be taken as 23.59hrs on that date). For example, if an authorisation is made at 08.00hrs on 1st November, the specified end time must be no later than 23.59hrs on 14th November.

Confirmation of authorisation

The senior police officer who gives an authorisation must inform the Secretary of State (the relevant Secretary of State is the Home Secretary) of it as soon as reasonably practicable; the police should aim to have provided the written authorisation (or written confirmation of an oral authorisation) within two hours of an authorisation being given. Where practicable, notification of an intention to give an authorisation and (unless the authorisation is for less than 48 hours) a draft of that authorisation should be given before the authorisation is given. If the authorisation is not confirmed within 48 hours of being given it will automatically cease to have effect at the end of that period, but this will not affect the lawfulness of things done in reliance on the authorisation before then.

When confirming an authorisation, the Secretary of State may substitute an earlier date or time for the specified date or time, or substitute a more restricted area or place for the specified area or place, or both. Where an authorisation specifies more than one area or place, the latter power includes a power to remove areas or places from the authorisation.

The Secretary of State may cancel an authorisation which has been confirmed, with effect from a time identified by the Secretary of State.

In the event that an authorisation is given for a period of less than 48 hours the authorising officer must inform the Secretary of State of the authorisation as soon as reasonably practicable. However, there is no requirement for the Secretary of State to confirm the authorisation, although, if it is reasonably practicable to do so, the Secretary of State may confirm or cancel the authorisation before its expiry.

Notification of other police forces and the 'police authority'

A Home Office (ie local) force should notify any non-Home Office force (ie British Transport Police, Ministry of Defence Police or Civil Nuclear Constabulary) when an authorisation covers areas for which both forces have a responsibility, and vice versa. The authorising officer should also notify his 'police authority' (police and crime commissioner, the Mayor's Office for Policing and Crime or police authority). The authorisation provided to the Home Secretary should include confirmation that both such notifications (to other police forces and to the relevant 'police authority') have taken place.

Cancellation or variation of authorisation by senior police officer

By TA 2000, Sch 6B, a senior police officer may cancel an authorisation with effect from a time identified by the officer concerned, or substitute an earlier date or time, or a more restricted area or place, for that specified in the authorisation. Where an authorisation specifies more than one area or place this power of substitution includes a power to remove areas or places from the authorisation. Any cancellation or substitution by a senior officer in relation to an authorisation confirmed by the Secretary of State must be notified to the Secretary of State but does not require confirmation by the Secretary of State. If during the currency of an authorisation, the authorising officer no longer reasonably suspects that an act of terrorism of the description given in the authorisation will take place or no longer considers that the powers are necessary to prevent such an act, the authorising officer must cancel the authorisation immediately. If, during the currency of an authorisation, the authorising officer believes that the duration or geographical extent of the authorisation is no longer necessary for the prevention of such an act of terrorism, he must substitute a shorter period, or more restricted geographical area.

New authorisation

The existence, expiry or cancellation of an authorisation does not prevent the giving of a new authorisation (Sch 6B). An expired or expiring authorisation cannot simply be renewed. A new authorisation covering the same or substantially the same areas or places as a previous authorisation may be given if the intelligence which informed the initial authorisation has been subject to fresh assessment and the officer giving the authorisation is satisfied that the test for authorisation is still met on the basis of that assessment.

Where a new authorisation is given, it may be given before the expiry of the existing authorisation (so as to avoid the need to give the subsequent authorisation at the exact time the existing one expires), but that existing authorisation should be cancelled. However, in the exceptional circumstances where a new authorisation is given in respect of a different threat during the currency of an existing authorisation in that force area, that existing authorisation need not be cancelled if it continues to be necessary.

Exercising the stop and search powers under s 47A

By TA 2000, s 47A(4), a constable in uniform may exercise the power conferred by an authorisation under s 47A(2) or (3) only for the purpose of discovering whether there is anything which may constitute evidence that the vehicle concerned is being used for the purposes of terrorism or (as the case may be) that the person concerned is or has been concerned in the commission, preparation or instigation of acts of terrorism. The search can therefore only be carried out to look for anything that would link the vehicle or the person to terrorism.

The power conferred by such an authorisation may be exercised whether or not the constable reasonably suspects that there is such evidence.

When exercising s 47A powers, officers should have a basis for selecting individuals or vehicles to be stopped and searched. This basis will be set by the tactical briefing referred to above. Constables should still consider whether powers requiring reasonable suspicion are more appropriate and should only use the powers conferred by a s 47A authorisation if they are satisfied that they cannot meet a threshold of reasonable suspicion sufficient to use other police powers.

When selecting individuals to be stopped and searched, officers should consider the following:

Deciding which power to use   If a s 47A authorisation is in place, the powers conferred by that authorisation may be used. However, if there is a reasonable suspicion that a person is a terrorist, then powers requiring reasonable suspicion in TA 2000, s 43 (p 807) or s 43A (p 808) should be used as appropriate instead.

Selecting an individual or vehicle using indicators   What are the *geographical limits* of the authorisation and what are the parameters within which the briefing allows stops and searches to be conducted? *Behaviour*: Is the person to be stopped and searched acting in a manner that gives cause for concern, or is a vehicle being used in such a manner? Could the person's *clothing* conceal an article of concern, which may constitute evidence that a person is a terrorist? Could an *item being carried* conceal an article that could constitute evidence that a person is a terrorist or a vehicle is being used for the purposes of terrorism?

Selecting individuals 'at random'   What are the geographical and other parameters of the operation as set out in the authorisation?

Explanation   Officers should be reminded of the need to explain to people why they or their vehicles are being searched.

Equality   The powers to stop and search must be used fairly, responsibly, and in accordance with the Equality Act 2010: see p 35. Officers should take care to avoid any form of racial or religious profiling when selecting people to search under s 47A powers. Racial or religious profiling is the use of racial, ethnic, religious or other stereotypes, rather than individual behaviour or specific intelligence, as a basis for making operational or investigative decisions about who may be involved in criminal activity. Profiling in this way may amount to an act of unlawful discrimination, as would selecting individuals for a search on the grounds of any of the other protected characteristics. Profiling people from certain ethnicities or religious backgrounds may also lose the confidence of communities.

Great care should be taken to ensure that the selection of people is not based solely on ethnic background, perceived religion, or other protected characteristic. A person's appearance or ethnic background will sometimes form part of a potential suspect's description, but a decision to search a person under powers conferred by s 47A should be made only if such a description is available.

Briefing and tasking

The authorising officer should ensure that officers who will take part in stop and search operations under an authorisation are briefed on the fact of the authorisation, its intended use, and on the provisions of s 47A and Sch 6B and the provisions of the Code. Officers should be briefed on the availability of other powers and the circumstances in which these may be more appropriate. Officers should be fully briefed on and aware of the differences between searches under TA 2000, ss 43, 43A and 47A, and the circumstances in which it is appropriate to use these powers. The stop and search powers under s 47A should only be used by officers who have been briefed about their use.

Officers should be reminded of the grounds for exercising the powers, ie only for the purpose of discovering whether there is anything that may constitute evidence that the vehicle being searched is being used for the purposes of terrorism, or the individual being searched is a terrorist. The purpose of the search must therefore be to look for items which connect the vehicle or individual being searched to terrorism, rather than generally for items which could be used (eg by another individual in different circumstances) in connection with terrorism.

Officers should be reminded of the need to record information and provide anyone who is stopped and searched, or whose vehicle is stopped and searched, with written confirmation that the stop and search took place and details of the power used. Accurate recording of information is essential in order to monitor the use of the powers, safeguard against misuse, and provide individuals with information about the powers which have been used (see below).

The briefing should make officers aware of relevant current information and intelligence including potential threats to locations. Briefings should be as comprehensive as possible in order to ensure officers understand the nature and justification of the operation (which will in turn help officers to understand what evidence they are looking for in the course of a search), while recognising that it may not be possible or appropriate to communicate highly sensitive intelligence to all officers.

Briefings should also provide officers with a form of words that they can use when explaining the use of stop and search powers under s 47A. Officers should be reminded at the briefing of the importance of providing the public with as much information as possible about why the stop and search is being undertaken. The following list can help officers to explain the use of the powers when dealing with the public:

(a) the power that is being used and the fact that an authorisation is in place;
(b) that the powers conferred by s 47A can be exercised without reasonable suspicion;
(c) what the operation is seeking to do, eg, to prevent terrorist activity in response to a specific threat;
(d) why the person or vehicle was selected to be searched;
(e) what entitlements the person has.

In order to demonstrate that the powers are used appropriately and proportionately, the briefing process must be robust and auditable. All officers involved in the process should be reminded that they are fully accountable in law for their own actions.

Officers should be given clear instructions about where, when and how they should use their powers. Officers should be clearly tasked so that their powers are used appropriately and proportionately.

There may be exceptional circumstances where it is impractical to brief officers before they are deployed. Where this occurs, supervisors should provide officers with a briefing as soon as possible after deployment.

Removal of clothing

A constable may not require a person to remove any clothing in public except for headgear, footwear, an outer coat, a jacket or gloves. Officers should be aware of the cultural sensitivities that may be involved in the removal of headgear.

Photography/film

It is important that police officers are aware, in exercising their counter-terrorism powers, that:

(a) members of the public and media do not need a permit to film or photograph in public places;
(b) it is not an offence for a member of the public or journalist to take photographs/film of a public building; and
(c) the police have no power to stop the filming or photographing of incidents or police personnel.

Under s 47A, police officers can stop and search someone taking photographs/film within an authorised area just as they can stop and search any other member of the public in the proper exercise of their discretion in accordance with the legislation and provisions of the Code. However, an authorisation itself does not prohibit the taking of photographs or digital images.

On the rare occasion that an officer reasonably suspects that photographs/film are being taken as part of hostile terrorist reconnaissance, a search under TA 2000, s 43 (p 807) or an arrest should be considered. It is important that police officers do not automatically consider photography/filming as suspicious behaviour. The size of the camera/video equipment should not be considered as a risk indicator.

Health and safety

When undertaking any search, officers should always consider their own safety and the health and safety of others. Officers should have an appropriate level of personal safety training and be in possession of personal protective equipment. Officers carrying out searches should use approved tactics to keep themselves and the public safe.

If, during the course of a stop and search there is a suspicion that a person is in possession of a hazardous device or substance, an officer should immediately request the assistance of officers appropriately trained and equipped to deal with the situation.

Seizure

TA 2000, s 47A(6) provides that a constable may seize and retain anything which he:

(a) discovers in the course of a search under an authorisation under s 47A(2) or (3); and
(b) reasonably suspects may constitute evidence that the vehicle concerned is being used for the purposes of terrorism or (as the case may be) that the person concerned is a person who is or has been concerned in the commission, preparation or instigation of acts of terrorism.

Film and memory cards may be seized as part of the search if the officer reasonably suspects they are evidence that the person is a terrorist, or a vehicle is being used for the purposes of terrorism, but officers do not have a legal power to delete images or destroy film. Cameras and other devices should be left in the state they were found and forwarded to appropriately trained staff for forensic examination. The person being searched should never be asked or allowed to turn the device on or off because of the danger of evidence being lost or damaged.

Seizures of cameras etc may only be made, following a stop and search, where the officer reasonably suspects that they constitute evidence that the person is a terrorist or that the vehicle is being used for the purposes of terrorism as the case may be.

Anything seized may be retained for as long as necessary in all the circumstances. This includes retention for use as evidence at a trial for an offence.

A record should be made of any item seized or retained and made available with a copy of the record of the stop and search. If the reasonable suspicion referred to in (b) above ceases to apply, the item should be returned to the individual from whom it was seized, or the person in charge of the vehicle from which it was seized, unless there are other grounds for retaining it (eg in respect of the investigation of a separate offence). If there appears to be a dispute over the ownership of the article, it may be retained for as long as necessary to determine the lawful owner.

Use of powers by community support officers

Where an authorisation under s 47A is in place, community support officers who are in the company of a constable who is supervising them may stop any pedestrian or vehicle, search anything carried by the pedestrian, the driver or a passenger, the vehicle or anything carried in or on it, and exercise the power of seizure under s 47A(6). They may not, however, search people or people's clothing under the s 47A powers. Authorising officers may consider whether to include community support officers within a stop and search operation authorised by s 47A. If community support officers are to use the powers available, they should be properly briefed on the limitations on their powers, as well as being briefed on the appropriate use of their powers.

Points general to TA 2000, ss 43, 43A, and 47A

Given that they require reasonable suspicion in order to be exercised, the use of powers under ss 43(1) and 43A should be prioritised for the purposes of stopping and searching individuals for the purposes of preventing or detecting terrorism. The authorisation of the no suspicion powers under s 47A should only be considered as a last resort, where reasonable suspicion powers are considered inadequate to respond to the threat. Use of the search powers under s 47A should only be made (in an authorised area) when the powers in ss 43 and 43A are not appropriate.

The Terrorism Search Powers Code provides guidance as to 'reasonable suspicion' which corresponds with that under PACE Code A: the Stop and Search Code (p 38).

Steps to be taken prior to a search

Before any search of a detained person or attended vehicle takes place the officer must take reasonable steps to give his identification number and name of police station (subject to the endangerment exception below) to the person to be searched or to the person in charge of the vehicle to be searched and to give that person the following information:

(a) that he is being detained for the purposes of a search;
(b) the legal search power which is being exercised;
(c) a clear explanation of:
    (i)   the object of the search (ie to search for evidence that the person is a terrorist or that a vehicle is being used for the purposes of terrorism); and
    (ii)   in the case of s 47A, the nature of the powers conferred by s 47A, the fact an authorisation has been given and the reason why he has been selected for a stop and search, or, in the case of ss 43 or 43A, the grounds for suspicion;
(d) that he is entitled to a copy of the search record if he asks within three months of the search;
(e) that if he is not arrested and taken to a police station as a result of the search and it is practicable to make the record on the spot, that immediately after the search is completed he will be given (subject to the officer being called to an incident of higher priority), if he requests, either:
    (i)   a copy of the record, or
    (ii)   a receipt which explains how he can obtain a copy of the full record or access to an electronic copy of the record. A receipt may take the form of a simple business card which includes sufficient information to locate the record should the person ask for a copy, for example, the date and place of the search or a reference number;
(f) that if he is arrested and taken to a police station as a result of the search, that the record will be made at the station as part of his custody record and he will be given, if he requests, a copy of his custody record which includes a record of the search as soon as practicable whilst he is at the station.

A person who is not provided with an immediate copy of a search record may request a copy within three months of being stopped and searched. In addition a person is also entitled, on application, to a written statement that he was stopped by virtue of the powers conferred by s 47A(2) or (3) (p 810), if requested within 12 months of the stop taking place.

If the person to be searched, or person in charge of a vehicle to be searched, does not appear to understand what is being said, or there is any doubt about the person's ability to understand English, the officer must take reasonable steps to bring information regarding that person's rights to his attention. If he is deaf or cannot understand English and is accompanied by someone, then the officer may try to establish whether that person can interpret or otherwise help the officer to give the required information. This does not preclude an officer from conducting a search once he has taken reasonable steps to explain the person's rights.

Conduct of stops and searches

The constable may detain the person or vehicle for such time as is reasonably required to permit the search to be carried out at or near the place where the person or vehicle is stopped. The length of time must be kept to a minimum. A person or vehicle may be detained under the stop and search powers at a place other than where the person or vehicle was first stopped, only if that place, be it a police station or elsewhere, is nearby. Such a place should be located within a reasonable travelling distance using whatever mode of travel (on foot or by vehicle) is appropriate.

All stops and searches must be carried out with courtesy, consideration and respect for the person concerned. Every reasonable effort must be made to minimise the embarrassment that a person being searched may experience. The co-operation of the person to be searched must be sought in every case, even if the person initially objects to the search. A forcible search may be made only if it has been established that the person is unwilling to co-operate or resists. Reasonable force may be used as a last resort if necessary to conduct a search or to detain a person or vehicle for the purposes of a search.

Recording requirements

Searches which do not result in an arrest   When an officer carries out a search under TA 2000, s 43(1) or 43A or in the exercise of powers conferred by s 47A and the search does not result in the person searched, or person in charge of the vehicle searched, being arrested and taken to a police station, a record must be made of it at the time, electronically or on paper, unless there are circumstances which make this wholly impracticable. If a record is not made at the time of the stop and search, the officer must make the record as soon as practicable after the search is completed. There may be situations in which it is not practicable to obtain the information necessary to complete a record, but the officer should make every reasonable effort to do so. If it is not possible to complete a record in full, an officer must make every reasonable effort to at least record details of the date, time and place where the stop and search took place, the power under which it was carried out, and the officer's identification number.

If the record is made at the time, the person who has been searched or who is in charge of the vehicle that has been searched must be asked if he wants a copy of the record and if he does, he must be given immediately, either:

(a) a copy of the record, or
(b) a receipt which explains how he can obtain a copy of the full record or access to an electronic copy of the record.

There is an exception: an officer is not required to provide a copy of the full record or a receipt at the time if he is called to an incident of higher priority.

Where it is not practicable to provide a written copy of the record or immediate access to an electronic copy of the record or a receipt at the time, the officer should give the person details of the police station at which he may request a copy of the record.

Searches which result in an arrest   If a search conducted under s 43, 43A, or 47A results in a person being arrested and taken to a police station, the officer who carried out the search is responsible for ensuring that a record of the search is made as part of that person's custody record. The custody officer must then ensure that the person is asked if he wants a copy of the custody record and if he does, that he is given a copy as soon as practicable.

Record of search

The record of a search must always include the following information:

(a) a note of the self-defined ethnicity, and, if different, the ethnicity as perceived by the officer making the search, of the person searched or of the person in charge of the vehicle searched (as the case may be);

(b) the date, time and place the person or vehicle was searched;

(c) the object of the search;

(d) in the case of:

    (i)   the powers under s 47A, the nature of the powers, the fact an authorisation has been given and the reason the person or vehicle was selected for the search;

    (ii) the powers under s 43 or 43A, the grounds for suspicion;

(e) the officer's warrant number or other identification number (subject to the endangerment exception)

Officers should record the self-defined ethnicity of every person stopped according to the same categories as used in PACE Code A (the Stop and Search Code): see p 48. The procedure is identical to that set out on pp 48–9.

For the purposes of completing the search record, there is no requirement to record the name, address and date of birth of the person searched or the person in charge of a vehicle which is searched and the person is under no obligation to provide this information. An officer may remind a person that providing these details will ensure that the police force is able to provide information about the stop and search in future should the person request that information or if it is otherwise required.

The names of police officers are not required to be shown on the search record in the case of operations linked to the investigation of terrorism or otherwise where an officer reasonably believes that recording names might endanger the officers; this is the 'endangerment exception' referred to above. In such cases the record must show the officers' warrant or other identification number and duty station.

A record is required for each person and each vehicle searched. However, if a person is in a vehicle and both are searched, and the object and grounds of the search are the same, only one record need be completed. If more than one person in a vehicle is searched, separate records for each search of a person must be made. If only a vehicle is searched, the self-defined ethnic background of the person in charge of the vehicle must be recorded, unless the vehicle is unattended.

The record of the grounds for making a search must, briefly but informatively, explain the reason for suspecting the person concerned, by reference to the person's behaviour and/or other circumstances, or, in the case of searches under s 47A, the reason why a particular person or vehicle was selected.

After searching an unattended vehicle, or anything in or on it, an officer must leave a notice in it (or on it, if things on it have been searched without opening it) recording the fact that it has been searched. The notice must include the name of the police station to which the officer concerned is attached and state where a copy of the record of the search may be obtained and how (if applicable) an electronic copy may be accessed and where any application for compensation should be directed. The vehicle must if practicable be left secure.

Monitoring and supervising the use of stop and search powers

The Terrorism Search Powers Code contains provisions in this respect which correspond to those in PACE Code A (the Stop and Search Code): see p 50. Statistical data on the use of powers should be provided quarterly to the Home Office.

Community engagement

Ongoing community engagement is essential in improving relationships with the community. Use may be made, for example, of existing community engagement arrangements. However, where stop and search powers affect sections of the community with whom channels of communication are difficult or non-existent, these should be identified and steps taken to engage. For example, if s 47A authorisations have primarily been made around transport hubs, effort should be made to engage with people using those hubs.

When planning a counter-terrorism search operation, police authorities and the local CONTEST Prevent strategic partnership should be involved at the earliest opportunity to provide advice and assistance in identifying mechanisms for engaging with communities.

If it is not possible to carry out community engagement prior to authorisation, police forces should carry out a retrospective review of the use of the powers, including stakeholders. Police forces should continue to monitor the use of s 47A powers for the duration of an authorisation, both in discussion with community representatives and by explaining how and why the powers are being used to individuals who are stopped and searched. Officers should be ready to explain to individuals why the powers are in place, insofar as this can be communicated without disclosing sensitive intelligence or causing undue alarm. Stop and search operations should form part of wider counter-terrorism policing, and public awareness of the powers should be considered as part of any wider communications strategy associated with an operation.

Prohibitions or restrictions on parking

TA 2000, s 48 permits a police officer of or above the rank of assistant chief constable (or commander), where it appears to him to be expedient in order to prevent acts of terrorism, to give an authorisation to any constable to prohibit or restrict the parking of vehicles on a specified road. This is to be done by the placing of traffic signs. A constable exercising his powers under s 48 may suspend a parking place and this will have the effect of permitting the removal of vehicles. Such an authorisation remains in force for a period, not exceeding 28 days, specified in it. It may be renewed subject to the same rules.

Failing to move a vehicle when ordered to do so by a constable is an offence under s 51(2). Parking in contravention of such a prohibition or restriction is an offence under s 51(1). It is a defence to either offence to prove a reasonable excuse. Current disabled persons' badge-holders are not exempt from these requirements and have no reasonable excuse for failure to comply on those grounds. The powers to impose these restrictions are additional to any other powers available to a constable.

The offences under s 51 are summary offences.

Arrest without warrant

TA 2000, s 41 provides that a constable may arrest without warrant a person whom he reasonably suspects to be a terrorist (as defined on p 807).

A person who has been so detained may be held for 48 hours. Continued detention beyond that period is subject to a warrant of further detention granted in accordance with the procedures prescribed by TA 2000, Sch 8 (described on p 830).

Treatment of persons detained under Terrorism Act 2000, s 41 (or Sch 7)

The following rules relate to those detained under TA 2000, s 41 or Sch 7 (special powers to question at seaports and airports and—relevant only to police in Northern

Ireland—border controls). The relevant statutory provision is TA 2000, Sch 8. The relevant code of practice in relation to those detained under s 41 is not PACE code C (the Detention Code) but is PACE Code H: the Code of Practice in Connection with the Detention, Treatment and Questioning by Police Officers of Persons under s 41 of, and Sch 8 to, the Terrorism Act 2000 and the Treatment and Questioning of Detained Persons in Respect of whom an Authorisation to Question after Charge has been given under C-TA 2008, s 22. In relation to the first part of its subject matter, Code H generally mirrors PACE Code C (see Chapters 4 and 5).

Except in relation to the special powers to question under Sch 7, TA 2000, s 114 empowers a constable to use reasonable force to exercise any power relating to the treatment of those detained under s 41 (or Sch 7).

Place of detention

The Secretary of State is required to designate places at which persons may be detained under s 41 or Sch 7. A reference in Sch 8 to a police station includes a place so designated. A person arrested by a constable under s 41 must be taken, as soon as practicable, to the police station which the constable considers to be the most appropriate. If the person was arrested as a result of a search in which PACE Code A (the Stop and Search Code) or the Terrorism Search Powers Code applies, the officer carrying out the search is responsible for ensuring that the record of that stop and search is made as part of the person's custody record. The custody officer must then ensure that the person is asked if he wants a copy of the search record and if he does, that he is given a copy as soon as practicable. The person's entitlement to a copy of the search record which is made as part of his custody record is in addition to, and does not affect, his entitlement to a copy of his custody record or any other provisions of s 2 of these Codes.

Identification

An 'authorised person' (which term includes a constable) may take any steps which are reasonably necessary for photographing, measuring or identifying the detained person. However, these initial measures do not include the taking of fingerprints, non-intimate samples or intimate samples.

Interviews

Acting under a power in TA 2000, Sch 8, the Secretary of State has made an order requiring the video recording with sound of an interview at a police station by a constable of a person detained under TA 2000. 'Police station' includes any place designated as a place where a person may be detained under TA 2000, s 41. Such an interview must be conducted in accordance with the Code of Practice for the Video Recording with Sound of Interviews with Persons Detained and Post-Charge Questioning of Persons Authorised under C-TA 2008, s 22.

The Code provides in relation to such an interview that it may be necessary to delay an interview to make arrangements to overcome any difficulties that might otherwise prevent the record being made, eg non-availability of suitable recording equipment and interview facilities. If a person refuses to go into or remain in a suitable interview room, and the custody officer considers, on reasonable grounds, that the interview should not be delayed, the interview may, at the custody officer's discretion, be conducted in a cell using portable recording equipment. The reasons must be recorded.

Before any interview starts, the person and any appropriate adult and interpreter must be given a written notice which explains that the interview must be video recorded with sound. At the same time, the person, the appropriate adult and interpreter must be informed verbally of the content of the notice.

If the person interviewed or the appropriate adult raises objections to the interview being recorded, the interviewing officer must explain that the interview is being recorded in order to protect both the person being interviewed and the interviewing officer and that there is no opt-out facility.

The provisions of the Code about the procedure relating to the recording mirror those under PACE Code F, described on p 122.

Rights

A person detained under TA 2000, s 41 (or Sch 7) is entitled, if he so requests, to have a named person who is a friend, relative, or person known to him who is likely to take an interest in his welfare informed, as soon as is reasonably practicable, that he is being detained there. If the detained person is transferred to another police station, he is entitled to exercise that right at the second police station.

In addition, the detained person is entitled, if he so requests, to consult a solicitor as soon as is reasonably practicable, privately and at any time. A record must be made of such a request.

A superintendent (or above) may authorise a delay in informing the person named by the detained person or in permitting the detained person to consult a solicitor, but he must be permitted to exercise these rights within 48 hours. Such an officer may give an authorisation only if he has reasonable grounds for believing that informing the named person or solicitor of the detained person's detention at the time when the person wishes this to be done, will lead to:

(a) interference with or harm to evidence of an indictable offence;
(b) interference with or physical injury to any person;
(c) alerting persons who are suspected of having committed an indictable offence but who have not been arrested for it;
(d) hindering the recovery of property obtained as a result of an indictable offence or in respect of which a forfeiture order in respect of fund raising or money laundering could be made under the Act;
(e) interference with the gathering of information about the commission, preparation or instigation of acts of terrorism;
(f) alerting a person and thereby making it more difficult to prevent an act of terrorism; and
(g) alerting a person and thereby making it more difficult to secure a person's apprehension, prosecution or conviction in connection with the commission, preparation or instigation of an act of terrorism.

In addition, a similar authorisation may be given where a superintendent (or above) has reasonable grounds for believing that the offence concerned is one in which there exist powers of confiscation in respect of the proceeds of an offence, and that the detained person has benefited from the offence and that, by informing the named person, or exercising the right to see a solicitor, the recovery of the value of that benefit will be hindered.

Where any delay is authorised the detained person must be told of the reason for the delay as soon as reasonably practicable and the reason must be recorded.

A direction may be made that a person may only consult a solicitor, under the above right, in the sight and hearing of a qualified officer. Such a direction may only be given by an assistant chief constable (or commander) and only if he has reasonable grounds for believing that:

(a) unless the direction is given, the exercise of the right of the detained person will have any of the consequences specified in (a)–(g) on p 823; or
(b) the detained person has benefited from his criminal conduct and that, unless the direction is given, the exercise of the right by the detained person will hinder the recovery of the value of the property constituting the benefit.

A 'qualified officer' must be a uniformed inspector (or above) who has no connection with the case. Such a direction will cease to exist when the reason for it ceases to exist.

Fingerprinting, non-intimate, and intimate samples

Fingerprints   may be taken from the detained person by a constable with the written consent of the detainee, or without such consent:

(a) where he is detained at a police station and a superintendent (or above) gives an authorisation, or
(b) where the detainee has been convicted of a recordable offence.

The same provisions apply to *non-intimate samples* (p 194) provided that the detained person was convicted of the recordable offence on or after 10 April 1995. As to 'recordable offence', see p 198.

A superintendent (or above) may make an authorisation under (a) *if a person is detained under TA 2000, s 41, where the officer reasonably suspects that the person has been involved in an offence specified under TA 2000, ss 11 and 12* (see p 801), ss 15–18, (see pp 802–3), *s 54* (see p 834, *s 56* (directing terrorist operations), *s 57* (see p 830), *s 58* (see p 831), *s 58A* (see p 832), *s 59* (inciting terrorism overseas), *ss 62 or 63* (terrorist bombing or finance offences outside the UK), *and the officer reasonably believes that the fingerprints or sample will tend to confirm or disprove his involvement, or, in any other case, the officer is satisfied that taking the fingerprints or sample is necessary to assist in determining whether the person has been concerned in the preparation, commission or instigation of acts of terrorism.*

A superintendent (or above) may also authorise the taking under (a) of fingerprints from a person detained at a police station if he is satisfied that this person's fingerprints will facilitate the ascertainment of his identity, and that person has refused to identify himself or the officer has reasonable grounds for suspecting that that person is not who he claims to be. References to ascertaining a person's identity include references to showing that he is not a particular person.

If non-intimate samples of hair are taken, they may be taken by cutting or plucking provided that no more are plucked than is reasonably necessary to provide a sufficient sample.

An *intimate sample* (p 193) may be taken by a constable from a detained person at a police station with the written appropriate consent and the authorisation of a superintendent (or above). However, an intimate sample other than a sample of urine or a dental impression may be taken only by a registered medical practitioner acting on the authority of a constable. A dental impression may be taken only by a registered dentist acting on the authority of a constable. An authorisation for the consensual taking of an intimate sample may only be given in the above two cases if the conditions italicised *above* are satisfied.

Where two or more non-intimate samples suitable for the same means of analysis have been taken from a person and these samples have proved insufficient, and the person concerned has been released from detention, an intimate sample may be taken with written appropriate consent and the authorisation of a superintendent (or above). Where appropriate, if written consent to the taking of an intimate sample is refused without good cause, in any proceedings for an offence, either during committal or at trial, the court may draw such inferences from the refusal as appear proper.

Before fingerprints or samples are taken, the person must be informed that they may be used for the purpose of checking against other fingerprints or samples held on behalf of police forces (speculative search) and, where taken with consent or in consequence of having been convicted of a recordable offence, of the reason for the fingerprints or samples being taken. All such matters must be recorded.

Destruction of fingerprints and samples   *Until a day to be appointed*, fingerprints and samples taken under TA 2000, Sch 8 may be retained but must not be used by any person except for the purposes of a terrorist investigation (as defined on p 805) or for purposes related to the prevention or detection of crime, the investigation of an offence, or the conduct of a prosecution (or, prospectively, identification purposes in respect of a deceased person or the source of the material, or in the interests of national security).

The above provisions are prospectively replaced by the following provisions inserted into TA 2000, Sch 8 by the Protection of Freedoms Act 2012, Sch 1.

Destruction and retention of fingerprints and DNA profiles, etc   TA 2000, Sch 8, para 20A prospectively provides that paragraph 20A material, ie:

(a) fingerprints taken under Sch 8;
(b) a DNA profile derived from a DNA sample taken under Sch 8;
(c) relevant physical data taken or provided by virtue of provisions (as prospectively amended) which deal with the retention, destruction and use of biometric material taken in Scotland;
(d) a DNA profile derived from a DNA sample taken by virtue of specified Scottish provision,

must be destroyed if it appears to the responsible chief officer of police that:

(a) the taking or providing of the material or, in the case of a DNA profile, the taking of the sample from which the DNA profile was derived, was unlawful, or
(b) the material was taken or provided, or (in the case of a DNA profile) was derived from a sample taken, from a person in connection with that person's arrest under TA 2000, s 41 and the arrest was unlawful or based on mistaken identity.

'Responsible chief officer of police' means, in relation to fingerprints or samples taken in England or Wales, or a DNA profile derived from a sample so taken, the chief officer of police for the police area in which the material concerned was taken, or, in the case of a DNA profile, in which the sample from which the DNA profile was derived was taken.

In any other case, para 20A material must be destroyed unless it is retained under any power conferred by paras 20B to 20E (below).

Para 20A material which ceases to be retained under a power mentioned below may continue to be retained under any other such power which applies to it.

Nothing in para 20A prevents a relevant search, in relation to para 20A material, from being carried out within such time as may reasonably be required for the search if the responsible chief officer of police considers the search to be desirable. A 'relevant search' is a search carried out for the purpose of checking the material against:

(a) other fingerprints or samples taken under the above provisions (pp 824–5) or a DNA profile derived from such a sample;

(b) any of the relevant physical data (as defined by the Criminal Procedure (Scotland) Act 1995, s 18(7A)), samples or information mentioned or held by virtue of specified corresponding Scottish legislation;

(c) material to which the Counter-Terrorism Act 2008, s 18 applies (see p 212);

(d) any of the fingerprints, data or samples obtained under the Terrorism Prevention and Investigation Measures Act 2011, Sch 6 or the corresponding Scottish legislation or information derived therefrom;

(e) any of the fingerprints, samples and information mentioned in PACE, s 63A(1)(a) and (b) (see p 202); and

(f) any of the fingerprints, samples and information mentioned in the corresponding Northern Irish legislation about checking of fingerprints and samples.

Any copies of the fingerprints or relevant physical data required to be destroyed by para 20A which are held by a police force must also be destroyed. No copy of a DNA profile required by para 20A to be destroyed may be retained by a police force except in a form which does not identify the person to whom the profile relates.

Retention of para 20A material   By TA 2000, Sch 8 para 20B, the following provisions prospectively apply.

Para 20A material relating to a person who is detained under TA 2000, s 41:

(a) in the case of a person previously convicted of a recordable offence (see p 198) (other than a single exempt conviction), or an imprisonable offence in Scotland, or a person so convicted before the end of the period within which the material may be retained by virtue of para 20B, may be retained indefinitely;

(b) in the case of a person who has no previous convictions, or only one exempt conviction, the material may be retained until the end of the relevant retention period. The retention period is:

    (i) in the case of fingerprints or relevant physical data, the period of *three years* beginning with the date on which the fingerprints or relevant physical data were taken or provided, and

    (ii) in the case of a DNA profile, the period of *three years* beginning with the date on which the DNA sample from which the profile was derived was taken (or, if the profile was derived from more than one DNA sample, the date on which the first of those samples was taken).

Para 20C makes identical provision to that under (a) and (b) above in relation to para 20A material relating to a person detained under Sch 7, except that 'six months' is substituted for 'three years' in both places italicised.

For the above purposes, para 20D(1) provides that a person is to be treated as having been convicted of an offence if:

(a) in relation to a recordable offence in England and Wales or Northern Ireland:

    (i) he has been given a caution in respect of the offence, (or has been warned or reprimanded under the Crime and Disorder Act 1998, s 65),

    (ii) he has been found not guilty by reason of insanity or to be under a disability and to have done the act charged,

(b) in relation to an imprisonable offence in Scotland:

    (i) he has accepted or has been deemed to accept a conditional offer, a compensation offer, a combined offer, or a work offer,

(ii)   he has been acquitted on account of insanity or committed to hospital for inquiry into his mental condition,

(iii)   having been given a fixed penalty notice, he has paid the fixed penalty, or the sum which he is liable to pay, or

(iv)   he has been discharged absolutely.

For the above purposes, 'spent convictions' count as convictions but a conviction in respect of the repealed offences of buggery and gross indecency with a man is not to be treated as a conviction if it is to be disregarded by virtue of a 'disregard decision' by the Secretary of State. In addition:

(a)   a person has no previous convictions if he has not previously been convicted in England and Wales or Northern Ireland of a recordable offence, or, in Scotland, of an imprisonable offence, and

(b)   a conviction for a recordable offence is exempt if it is in respect of a such offence, other than a qualifying offence, committed when the person was under 18.

'Qualifying offence' has the meaning given on p 192 and a corresponding meaning in Northern Ireland.

If a person is convicted of more than one offence arising out of a single course of action, those convictions are treated as a single conviction for the purposes of calculating under para 20B or 20C whether the person has been convicted of only one offence.

The responsible chief officer of police or a specified chief officer of police may apply to a District Judge (Magistrates' Court) for an order extending the retention period for two years. Such an application must be made within a three-month period ending on the last day of the retention period. The responsible chief officer of police, a specified chief officer of police, or the person from whom the material was taken may appeal to the Crown Court against an order, or a refusal to make such an order. A 'specified chief officer of police' means the chief officer of the police force of the area in which the person from whom the material was taken resides, or a chief officer of police who believes that the person is in, or is intending to come to, the chief officer's police area. Nothing in para 20B or 20C prevents the start of a new retention period in relation to para 20A material if a person is detained again under TA 2000, s 41 or (as the case may be) Sch 7 when an existing retention period (whether or not extended) is still in force in relation to that material.

Retention of para 20A material: national security determination   Paragraph 20A material may be retained for as long as a national security determination made by the responsible chief officer of police has effect in relation to it. A national security determination is made if the responsible chief officer of police determines that it is necessary for any para 20A material to be retained for the purposes of national security.

A national security determination:

(a)   must be made in writing,

(b)   has effect for a maximum of two years beginning with the date on which it is made, and

(c)   may be renewed.

Destruction of samples   Paragraph 20G deals with para 20G material, ie samples taken under the provisions of TA 2000, Sch 8 referred to on pp 824–5, or by virtue of corresponding Scottish provisions. Such samples must be destroyed if it appears to the responsible chief officer of police (p 825) that:

(a) the taking of the sample was unlawful, or
(b) the sample was taken from a person in connection with that person's arrest under TA 2000, s 41 and the arrest was unlawful or based on mistaken identity.

Subject to this, the following rules apply to a sample so taken.
A DNA sample must be destroyed:

(a) as soon as a DNA profile has been derived from the sample, or
(b) if sooner, before the end of the period of six months beginning with the date on which the sample was taken.

Any other sample must be destroyed before the end of the period of six months beginning with the date on which it was taken.

The responsible chief officer of police may apply to a District Judge (Magistrates' Courts) for an order to retain a sample beyond the date on which it would otherwise be required to be destroyed by the above two paragraphs if the sample was taken from a person detained under s 41 in connection with the investigation of a qualifying offence, and the responsible chief officer considers that, *having regard to the nature and complexity of other material that is evidence in relation to the offence, the sample is likely to be needed in any proceedings for the offence for the purposes of*:

(a) *disclosure to, or use by, a defendant, or.*
(b) *responding to any challenge by a defendant in respect of the admissibility of material that is evidence on which the prosecution proposes to rely.*

'Qualifying offence has the meaning given on p 192. Such an application must be made before the date on which the sample would otherwise be required to be destroyed by virtue of the above two paragraphs.

If the District Judge is satisfied that the italicised condition is met, he may make an order which:

(a) allows the sample to be retained for a period of 12 months beginning with the date on which the sample would otherwise be required to be destroyed, and
(b) may be renewed (on one or more occasions) for a further period of not more than 12 months from the end of the period when the order would otherwise cease to have effect.

An application for such an order (other than an application for renewal):

(a) may be made without notice of the application having been given to the person from whom the sample was taken, and
(b) may be heard and determined in private in his absence.

A sample retained by virtue of such an order may only be used for the purposes of proceedings for the offence in connection with which it was taken. A sample that ceases to be retained by virtue of such an order must be destroyed. Nothing in para 20G prevents a relevant search (as defined above in relation to para 20A) in relation to the above types of samples from being carried out within such time as may reasonably be required for the search if the responsible chief officer of police considers the search to be desirable.

Use of para 20A or 20G material   Any para 20A or 20G material must not be used other than:

(a) in the interests of national security,
(b) for the purposes of a terrorist investigation (as defined on p 805),
(c) for purposes related to the prevention or detection of crime, the investigation of an offence, or the conduct of a prosecution, or
(d) for purposes related to the identification of a deceased person or of the person to whom the material relates.

The reference to crime includes a reference to any conduct which:

(a) constitutes one or more criminal offences (whether under the law of a part of the UK or of a country or territory outside the UK), or
(b) is, or corresponds to, any conduct which, if it all took place in any one part of the UK, would constitute one or more criminal offences.

Subject to the above paragraph, a relevant search (as defined above) may be carried out in relation to material to which para 20A or 20G applies if the responsible chief officer of police considers the search to be desirable.

Material which is required by para 20A or 20G to be destroyed must not at any time after it is required to be destroyed be used:

(a) in evidence against the person to whom the material relates, or
(b) for the purposes of the investigation of any offence.

The references above to using material include a reference to allowing any check to be made against it and to disclosing it to any person. The references to an investigation and to a prosecution include references, respectively, to any investigation outside the UK of any crime or suspected crime and to a prosecution brought in respect of any crime in a country or territory outside the UK.

Limit The above provisions about the destruction, use and retention of fingerprints and DNA profiles do not apply to para 20A material relating to a person detained under s 41 which is, or may become, disclosable under the Criminal Procedure and Investigations Act 1996 (CPIA 1996) or the CPIA 1996: Code of Practice under Part II (p 266).

Reviews and extensions of detention

The detention of a person arrested under s 41 must be periodically reviewed by a review officer. The first review must be as soon as reasonably practicable after the arrest; thereafter reviews must be carried out at intervals of no more than 12 hours. A review officer may authorise continued detention only if he does so:

(a) to obtain relevant evidence whether by questioning the detainee or otherwise;
(b) to preserve relevant evidence;
(c) while awaiting the result of an examination or analysis of relevant evidence;
(d) for the examination or analysis of anything with a view to obtaining relevant evidence;
(e) pending a decision to apply to the Secretary of State for a deportation notice to be served on the detainee, the making of any such application, or the consideration of any such application by the Secretary of State; and
(f) pending a decision to charge the detainee with an offence.

The review officer may not authorise continued detention unless satisfied that the relevant matter is being dealt with diligently and expeditiously. The detainee may not be held for more than 48 hours unless a warrant of further detention is granted.

Under Sch 8, as amended, a Crown Prosecutor or a superintendent (or above) may apply to a designated District Judge (Magistrates' Court) for a warrant of further detention for a period of seven days from the time of the arrest under s 41, unless the person was being detained by an examining officer under Sch 7 (port and border controls) at the time of arrest (in which case time runs from the start of his examination under Sch 7). The judge may issue a warrant for a shorter period where the application is for a shorter period or he is satisfied that there are circumstances that would make it inappropriate for the specified period to be as long as seven days. This may be extended or further extended, on application to a designated District Judge (Magistrates' Court), if the extension would not extend the period for more than 14 days after the person's arrest (or examination commencement) or a shorter period. Thus, the maximum period of detention of a person arrested under s 41 is 14 days. The grounds for a warrant of further detention or an extension are that there are reasonable grounds for believing that the further detention of the person concerned is necessary to obtain relevant evidence and the investigation is being conducted diligently and expeditiously. However, the Secretary of State has an emergency power to make an order temporarily extending the maximum period of detention of a person arrested under s 41 when Parliament is dissolved or when Parliament has met after a dissolution but before the first Queen's Speech. Such an order would extend the maximum period of detention to 28 days for a period of three months.

An application for a warrant of further detention or an extension may be made orally or in writing depending upon the circumstances of the case and fairness to the detainee. It may not be heard unless notice of it has been given to the detainee. Applications may make use of video conferencing facilities. A judge may require the physical presence of the detainee.

MISCELLANEOUS OFFENCES UNDER TA 2000

Possession of articles for terrorist purposes

Under TA 2000, s 57(1), a person commits an offence if he possesses an article in circumstances giving rise to a reasonable suspicion that the article is in his possession for a purpose connected with the commission, preparation or instigation of acts of terrorism. Section 57(3) provides that, where it is proved that at the time of the commission of such an alleged offence, the person and the article were both present in any premises, or the article was in the premises of which he was the occupier, or which he habitually used other than as a member of the public, the court may assume that the person possessed the article, unless he adduces sufficient evidence to raise the issue that he did not know of the presence on the premises or that he had no control over it, whereupon the prosecution must disprove this.

The Court of Appeal has held that the offence can only be committed if there is a direct connection between the article possessed and an intended act of terrorism. It also held that s 57 should be interpreted so as to read 'a person commits an offence if he possesses an article in circumstances which give rise to a reasonable suspicion that he intends it to be used for the purpose of the commission, preparation or instigation of an act of terrorism'. It added that 'instigation' in this context included 'incitement'.

It is a defence to a charge under s 57 to prove that possession of an article was not for a purpose connected with the commission, preparation or instigation of an act of terrorism.

A document or record in electronic or printed form is an article for the purposes of s 57.

Unlawful collection, recording or possession of information

TA 2000, s 58 provides that a person commits an offence if he collects or makes a record of information of a kind likely to be useful to a person committing or preparing an act of terrorism, or possesses a document or record containing information of that kind. The term 'record' includes a photographic or electronic record. It has been held by the Court of Appeal that 'information of a kind likely to be useful to a person committing or preparing an act of terrorism' is broad enough to potentially include a series of suggestions as to the avoidance of detection or surveillance. On the other hand, the House of Lords has held, if a document containing information is one in everyday use (eg a published timetable or map) it cannot be treated as falling within s 58; the aim of s 58 is to catch information which would typically be of use to terrorists, as opposed to ordinary members of the public. The information collected or possessed must, of its very nature, be designed to provide practical assistance to someone committing or preparing an act of terrorism. It is a defence under s 58 for D to adduce sufficient evidence to raise the issue that he had a reasonable excuse for his action or possession, whereupon the prosecution must disprove this. The House of Lords has held that, if D adduces such evidence of something which would be a reasonable excuse, the defence succeeds unless the prosecution disproves the explanation advanced or proves that, even if D's explanation is true, it does not amount to a reasonable excuse beyond reasonable doubt. If it does disprove that thing, the defence fails and D is guilty under s 58. The prosecution does not have to prove that D did not have a reasonable excuse at all.

The House of Lords has also held as follows in this paragraph. In order for D to be convicted of an offence of possession contrary to TA 2000, s 58, the prosecution must prove beyond reasonable doubt that:

(a) he had control of a record which contained information that was likely to provide practical assistance to a person committing or preparing an act of terrorism;
(b) he knew he had the record;
(c) he knew the kind of information which it contained.

If those elements are established, D falls to be convicted subject to the defence of reasonable excuse. While s 57 focuses on the circumstances of D's possession of the article, s 58 focuses on the nature of the information which D collected, recorded or possessed in a document or record. There is nothing in s 58 which requires the prosecution to show that D had a terrorist purpose for doing what he did. Unless it amounts to a reasonable excuse, D's purpose in doing what he did is irrelevant. There is an overlap between the two sections. The possession of a document can, in an appropriate case, fall within ss 57 and 58.

The provisions of TA 2000, s 58 are wide enough to embrace the failure of close relatives of terrorists to disclose information in their possession as soon as reasonably practicable. It is recommended that relatives of a terrorist, who are not themselves involved in terrorism, should not be investigated with a view to obtaining evidence of offences by them against this section, unless particular extreme circumstances make this desirable. An example of such circumstances would be where the withholding of information could lead to death, serious injury or the escape of a terrorist offender.

The courts have provided the following guidance about 'reasonable excuse' in s 58. For these purposes 'reasonable excuse' means an objectively reasonable excuse; possessing a document for purposes of carrying out a bank raid is a purpose not connected with terrorism, but it is not a reasonable excuse. The Court of Appeal has held that it cannot be a reasonable excuse to a charge of possessing documents, etc contrary to TA 2000, s 58 that the documents, etc originated as part of an effort to change an illegal and undemocratic regime.

Eliciting, publishing or communicating information about members of the armed forces, etc

A person commits an offence under TA 2000, s 58A who:
(a) elicits or attempts to elicit information about an individual who is or has been:
    (i)   a member of Her Majesty's forces,
    (ii) a member of any of the intelligence services, or
    (iii) a constable,
    which is of a kind likely to be useful to a person committing or preparing an act of terrorism; or
(b) publishes or communicates any such information.

It is a defence for a person charged with an offence under s 58A to prove that he had a reasonable excuse for his action. If D adduces evidence sufficient to raise an issue with respect to the defence it is assumed that the defence is satisfied unless the prosecution prove beyond reasonable doubt that it is not.

To ensure compatibility with the EU's E-Commerce Directive, TA 2000, Sch 8A deals with the application of the s 58A offence with regard to information society services providers.

ENCOURAGEMENT, ETC OF TERRORISM

Encouragement of terrorism

TA 2006, s 1(1) provides that a person (D) commits an offence if:

(a) D publishes a statement to which s 1 applies or causes another to publish such a statement; and
(b) at that time, D intends members of the public to be directly or indirectly encouraged or otherwise induced by the statement to commit, prepare or instigate acts of terrorism or Convention offences, or is reckless as to whether they will be.

In TA 2006, an 'act of terrorism' includes anything constituting an action taken for the purposes of terrorism, within the meaning of TA 2000 (see p 800) (including a reference to action taken for the benefit of a proscribed organisation); and 'article' includes anything for storing data. A 'Convention offence' means an offence listed in TA 2006, Sch 1 (eg specified explosives offences, biological, chemical or nuclear weapons offences, hijacking, hostage taking, offences relating to terrorist funds or directing terrorist organisations, and offences directed at a nuclear facility or interference with the operation of such a facility) or an equivalent offence under the law of a country or territory outside the UK.

For the purposes of s 1, the statements that are likely to be understood by members of the public as indirectly encouraging the commission of acts of terrorism or Convention offences include every statement which glorifies the commission or preparation (whether in the past, future or generally) of such acts or offences (whether or not in particular), and is a statement from which those members of the public could reasonably be expected to infer that what is being glorified is conduct that should be emulated by them. 'Glorification' includes any form of praise or celebration.

Where it is not proved that the defendant intended the statement directly or indirectly to bring about the commission, preparation or instigation of acts of terrorism or Convention offences, he has a defence if he proves that the statement neither expressed his view nor had his actual endorsement, and that it was clear that this was so.

Dissemination of terrorist publications

TA 2006, s 2(1) makes it an offence to sell or otherwise disseminate terrorist publications, including information on the internet, if (a) D intends his conduct to encourage or induce people to engage in the commission, preparation or instigation of acts of terrorism, (b) D intends it to assist in the commission or preparation of such acts, or (c) D is reckless as to whether his conduct will have either effect.

By s 2(2), the offence can be committed by distributing or circulating a terrorist publication; giving, selling or lending a terrorist publication; offering such for sale or loan; providing a service which enables a person to obtain, read, listen to or look at such material; transmitting it by electronic means, or possessing it with a view to it being dealt with in one of these ways. Where D within the UK possesses terrorist material with the relevant mens rea, it is irrelevant that the dissemination of the material is to take place abroad.

A publication is a terrorist publication if it contains matter (a) likely to be understood by some or all of the persons to whom it might become available as an encouragement or inducement to them to the commission, preparation or instigation of acts of terrorism, or (b) likely to be useful in the commission or preparation of such acts or offences and likely to be understood (by some or all of such persons) as contained in the publication, or made available, for the purpose of being so useful.

Where the publication is a terrorist publication by virtue of (a) and it is not proved that D acted with the intention of encouraging or inducing the commission, preparation or instigation of acts of terrorism, it is a defence for D to show that the material which encourages terrorism did not express his views, nor had his actual endorsement, and that it was clear, in all of the circumstances, that this was so. The defence will not be available where there has been a failure to comply with a notice under s3 (p 834).

TA 2006, s 28 gives a justice of the peace power to issue a warrant authorising a constable to enter and search premises and seize any article on those premises if it is likely to be subject of conduct falling within s 2(2) and it would be treated as a terrorist publication, where he is satisfied that there are reasonable grounds for suspecting that such an article is on the premises. Reasonable force may be used in effecting entry.

Bulk material may be removed in such circumstances under CJPA 2001, s 50 for later examination. Notice must be given by the constable responsible for the seizure to every person whom he believes to be the owner of any material. In the event of there being no such person, notice must be given to the person believed to be the occupier of the premises.

C-TA 2008, s 1 prospectively provides that, for the purpose of ascertaining whether a document may be seized, it may be removed for examination. See further p 808.

Internet activity

TA 2006, s 3 applies for the purposes of ss 1 and 2 in relation to cases where a statement is published or caused to be published in the course of, or in connection with, the provision or use of a service provided electronically, or where conduct falling within s 2(2) was in the course of, or in connection with, the provision or use of such a service. Section 3 provides that the cases where a statement, or the article or record to which the conduct is related, is to be regarded as having the endorsement of a person at any time, include a case where:

(a) that person has been given a notice by a constable which
  (i) declares that in the constable's opinion the statement, article or record concerned is unlawfully terrorism-related,
  (ii) requires him to secure that the statement, etc (so far as so related) is not available to the public,
  (iii) warns him that a failure to comply with the notice within two working days will result in the statement, etc being regarded as having his endorsement, and
  (iv) explains how he may become liable by virtue of the notice if the statement, etc becomes available to the public after he has complied with the notice;
(b) that time falls more than two working days after the notice was given; and
(c) that person has failed without reasonable excuse to comply with the notice.

The procedures relating to the giving of such notices are set out in s 4.

PREPARATION OF TERRORIST ACTS AND TERRORIST TRAINING

Preparation of terrorist acts

TA 2006, s 5 bites at an earlier stage than the offences of conspiracy or attempt by prohibiting anyone intentionally preparing to commit, or assist others to commit, one or more acts of terrorism, wherever it is to take place. The offence is triable only on indictment.

It is not essential that it is proved that a specific act or acts of terrorism was intended; an intention to carry out such acts generally will suffice.

Training for terrorism

TA 2006, s 6(1) prohibits knowingly giving training to a would-be terrorist in the making or handling of noxious substances or the use of terrorist methods or techniques (including design or adaptation of methods or techniques for the purposes of terrorism). Section 6(2) makes it an offence for a would-be terrorist to receive such training.

For these purposes, a 'noxious substance' means a pathogen or toxin or any other substance which is hazardous or noxious or which may be or become hazardous or noxious only in certain circumstances.

Unless he proves that his purpose was not assisting, preparing for or participating in terrorism, a person who gives or receives weapons training commits an offence under TA 2000, s 54(1) or (2).

Attendance at a place used for terrorist training

TA 2006, s 8 prohibits attending any place in the UK or elsewhere at which terrorist training is taking place. It must be proved that D knew or believed that training for those purposes was taking place, or that D could not reasonably have failed to understand that this was so.

OFFENCES INVOLVING RADIOACTIVE DEVICES AND MATERIALS AND NUCLEAR FACILITIES AND SITES

TA 2006, s 9(1) creates offences related to the making or possession of radioactive devices or the possession of radioactive material, for use in the commission or preparation of an act of terrorism or for purposes of terrorism.

Section 10(1) prohibits the use of such items in the course of or in connection with the commission of an act of terrorism, or for the purposes of terrorism. Section 10(2) creates an offence of using or damaging a nuclear facility in the course of or in connection with acts of terrorism, in such a manner that radioactive material is released, or that the risk that such material will be released is created or increased.

Section 11(1) provides that it is an offence, in the course of or in connection with the commission of an act of terrorism or for the purposes of terrorism, to demand the supply of a radioactive device or radioactive material, or that a nuclear facility, or access to a nuclear facility, be made available, if such a demand is supported by a threat of action if the demand is not met. The threat must be a credible one.

Section 11(2) makes it an offence to make a credible threat to use a radioactive device or material, or to use or damage a radioactive facility, in the course of or in connection with the commission of an act of terrorism or for the purposes of terrorism.

The offences under ss 9 to 11 are triable only on indictment.

OFFENCES INVOLVING THE USE OF NOXIOUS SUBSTANCES OR THINGS TO CAUSE HARM AND INTIMIDATE

The Anti-terrorism, Crime and Security Act 2001, s 113(1) creates the offence committed by any person who takes any action which:

(a) involves the use of a noxious substance or other noxious thing;
(b) has or is likely to have an effect which:
    (i) causes serious violence against a person, or serious damage to property, anywhere in the world,
    (ii) endangers human life or creates a serious risk to the health or safety of the public or a section of the public, or
    (iii) induces in members of the public the fear that the action is likely to have the effect in (ii); and
(c) is designed to influence the government or an international governmental organisation or to intimidate the public or a section of the public.

By s 113(3), an offence is committed by someone who:

(a) threatens that he or another will take any action constituting an offence under s 113(1); and
(b) intends thereby to induce anyone anywhere in the world to fear that the threat is likely to be carried out.

Under s 114(1), a person commits an offence if he:

(a) places any substance or other thing in any place; or
(b) sends any substance or other thing from one place to another,

with the intention of inducing in a person anywhere in the world a belief that it is likely to be (or contain) a noxious substance or other noxious thing and thereby endanger human life or create a serious risk to human health.

A person is guilty of an offence under s 114(2) if he communicates any information which he knows or believes to be false with the intention of inducing in a person anywhere in the world a belief that a noxious substance or other noxious thing is likely to be present in any place and thereby endanger human life or create a serious risk to human health.

For these purposes, 'substance' includes any biological agent and any other natural or artificial substance (whatever its form, origin or method of production). In the case of ss 113(3) or 114 the person concerned need not have any particular person in mind as the person in whom he intends to induce the belief in question.

GENERAL
Consent of DPP

The consent of the DPP is required for any proceedings in relation to any of the above offences under the Terrorism Acts 2000 and 2006. Where an offence appears to have been committed outside the UK or for a purpose wholly or partly connected with the affairs of a country other than the UK, the DPP's consent may only be given with the consent of the Attorney General. Proceedings for an offence committed under the Anti-terrorism, Crime and Security Act 2001, s 113 outside the UK require the Attorney General's consent.

Post-charge questioning

The Counter-Terrorism Act 2008 (C-TA 2008), s 22 permits a judge of the Crown Court to authorise questioning of a person concerning an offence with which he has been charged or informed that he may be prosecuted, where that offence is a 'terrorism offence' or where the judge:

(a) considers the offence to have a terrorist connection, and
(b) is satisfied that:
  (i) further questioning is necessary in the interests of justice;
  (ii) the investigation for the purposes of which the further questioning is being proposed is being conducted diligently and expeditiously; and
  (iii) the questioning would not interfere unduly with the preparation of the person's defence to the charge or any other criminal charge that he may be facing.

'Terrorism offence' includes specified offences, mainly against TA 2000 (eg ss 11 to 13, 15 to 19, 21A, 21D, 38B, 39, 54, and 56 to 58A) and TA 2006 (ss 1, 2, 5, 6, and 8 to 11) and the Anti-Terrorism, Crime and Security Act 2001, s 113. An offence has a 'terrorist connection' if the offence is, or takes place in the course of, an act of terrorism, or is committed for the purpose of terrorism.

PACE Code H applies to the treatment and questioning of the detainee.

Access to a solicitor may not be delayed, nor may the person be required to consult a solicitor within the sight and hearing of a police officer.

Unless the restriction on drawing adverse inferences from silence applies (see Chapter 4), before post-charge questioning begins the caution must be given in the terms set out in Chapter 4. The only restriction on drawing adverse inferences from silence applies where a person has asked for legal advice and is questioned before receiving such advice on grounds of urgency.

An interview by virtue of C-TA 2008, s 22 must be video recorded with sound in accordance with the Code of Practice for the Video Recording with Sound of Interviews with Persons Detained and Post-Charge Questioning of Persons Authorised under C-TA 2008, s 22.

NOTIFICATION REQUIREMENTS

C-TA 2008, Part 4 and associated Schedules:

(a) set out a system of notification requirements (initial notification, notification of change, periodic re-notification, and notification of return after absence from UK) for persons convicted of a terrorism offence or of a non-terrorism offence with a terrorist connection;

(b) make provision to apply notification requirements to persons convicted of equivalent offences outside the UK; and

(c) make provision for the making of foreign travel restriction orders against persons subject to the above notification requirements.

IMPOSITION OF TERRORISM PREVENTION AND INVESTIGATION MEASURES

The Prevention of Terrorism Act 2005, which provided for the making of control orders against individuals suspected of being involved in terrorism-related activity, was repealed by the Terrorism Prevention and Investigation Measures Act 2011 (TPIMA 2011). TPIMA 2011 provides for the making of terrorism prevention and investigation measures against such individuals.

Terrorism prevention and investigation measures notice

The Secretary of State (SoS) may by a TPIM notice impose on an individual terrorism prevention and investigation measures specified in the notice if conditions A to E in s 3 are met. An individual is not bound by a TPIM notice, unless the notice is served personally on the individual (s 28).

'Terrorism prevention and investigation measures' (TPIM) means a range of requirements, restrictions and other provision made in relation to an individual such as:

(a) *overnight residence measure* (restrictions on where the individual resides);

(b) *travel measure* (restrictions on leaving or travelling outside the UK or outside Great Britain (if the individual resides there) or Northern Ireland (if he resides there));

(c) *exclusion measure* (restrictions on entering a specified area or place);

(d) *movement directions measure* (a requirement to comply with directions given by a constable in respect of the individual's movements for the purpose of securing compliance with other specified measures, or with a condition requiring the individual to be escorted by a constable. The maximum period of such a direction is 24 hours);

(e) *electronic communication device measure* (restrictions on possession or use of electronic communication devices and/or requirements on the individual in relation to such possession or use by other persons in the individual's residence);

(f) *association measure* (restrictions on association or communication with others);
(g) *reporting measure* (a requirement to report to such a police station as SoS may by notice require, and to comply with a constable's directions in relation to such reporting);
(h) *monitoring measure* (requirements to co-operate with specified monitoring arrangements).

Conditions A to E are:

(a) Condition A is that SoS reasonably believes that the individual is, or has been, involved in terrorism-related activity (the 'relevant activity').
(b) Condition B is that some or all of the relevant activity is 'new terrorism-related activity'.
(c) Condition C is that SoS reasonably considers that it is necessary, for purposes connected with protecting members of the public from a risk of terrorism, for TPIM to be imposed on the individual.
(d) Condition D is that SoS reasonably considers that it is necessary, for purposes connected with preventing or restricting the individual's involvement in terrorism-related activity, for the specified TPIM to be imposed on the individual.
(e) Condition E is that:
    (i)   the High Court gives SoS permission under s 6, or
    (ii) SoS reasonably considers that the urgency of the case requires TPIM to be imposed without obtaining such permission.

For the purposes of TPIMA 2011, involvement in terrorism-related activity means any one or more of the following:

(a) the commission, preparation or instigation of acts of terrorism;
(b) conduct facilitating the commission, preparation or instigation of such acts, or which is intended to do so;
(c) conduct encouraging (or intended to encourage) the commission, preparation or instigation of such acts;
(d) conduct supporting or assisting individuals who are known or believed by the individual concerned to be involved in conduct falling within (a) to (c).

'Terrorism' has the same meaning as in TA 2000 (see p 800).
    'New terrorism-related activity' means:

(a) if no TPIM notice relating to the individual has ever been in force, terrorism-related activity occurring at any time;
(b) if only one TPIM notice relating to the individual has ever been in force, terrorism-related activity occurring after that notice came into force; or
(c) if two or more TPIM notices relating to the individual have been in force, terrorism-related activity occurring after such a notice came into force most recently.

Two-year limit for TPIM notices

A TPIM notice comes into force when the notice is served on the individual or, if later, at the time specified in the notice. A notice is in force for one year. SoS may extend it for one year on one occasion only, but only if conditions A, C, and D are met.

Court scrutiny of imposition of measures

Prior permission of court

Except in urgent cases, SoS must apply for permission of the High Court to impose measures.

If SoS:

(a) decides that conditions A to D are met in relation to an individual, and
(b) makes an application to the court for permission to impose measures on the individual,

the court must determine whether those decisions are obviously flawed, and determine whether to give permission to impose TPIM on the individual and (where applicable) whether to exercise 'the power of direction'.

The court may consider the application in the individual's absence, and without notification to him.

If the court determines that a decision of SoS that condition A, condition B or condition C is met is obviously flawed, the court may not give permission.

In any other case, the court may give permission. If the court determines that SoS's decision that condition D is met is obviously flawed, the court may (in addition to giving permission) give directions to SoS in relation to the measures to be imposed on the individual. This is 'the power of direction' referred to above.

Urgent cases: reference to the court etc

If SoS decides that conditions A, B, C, D, and E(ii) are met in relation to an individual, and imposes measures on him, the TPIM notice must include a statement that SoS reasonably considers that the urgency of the case requires measures to be imposed without obtaining the permission of the court.

Immediately after serving the TPIM notice, SoS must refer the imposition of the measures to the court.

If the court determines that a decision of SoS that condition A, condition B or condition C is met is obviously flawed, the court must quash the TPIM notice. Otherwise, it must confirm the notice, although where the court determines that a decision of SoS that condition D is met is obviously flawed, the court must quash those of the measures to which that decision relates.

If the court determines that SoS's decision that the urgency condition (ie condition E(ii)) is met is obviously flawed, the court must make a declaration of that determination (whether it quashes or confirms the TPIM notice).

Directions hearing

If the court gives permission or confirms a TPIM notice, it must give directions for a further hearing (a 'directions hearing'). Unless the court otherwise directs, that hearing must be held within seven days of service of the notice or confirmation. The individual has the opportunity to attend the hearing. At the directions hearing, the court must give directions for a review hearing in relation to the imposition of measures.

Review hearing

On a review hearing, the court must review SoS's decisions that conditions A, B, C, and D were met and continue to be met.

It may:

(a) quash the TPIM notice or measures specified in it;
(b) give directions to SoS for, or in relation to, the revocation of the TPIM notice, or the variation of measures specified in it.

If the court does not exercise either power, it must decide that the TPIM notice is to continue in force.

Consultation requirements

Before making an application for permission to impose measures, or before imposing measures in a case to which the urgency condition (E(ii)) applies, SoS must consult the chief officer of the appropriate local police force or the Director General of the Serious Organised Crime Agency about whether there is evidence available that could realistically be used for the purposes of prosecuting the individual for an offence relating to terrorism. The chief officer must consult the DPP before responding to such consultation.

If SoS serves a TPIM notice, SoS must inform the chief officer of the appropriate police force and the chief officer must:

(a) secure that the investigation of the individual's conduct, with a view to his prosecution for an offence relating to terrorism, is kept under review throughout the period of the TPIM notice, and
(b) report to SoS on that review.

Offence

By TPIMA 2011, s 23(1), an individual is guilty of an offence if a TPIM notice is in force in relation to him, and he contravenes, without reasonable excuse, any measure specified in the TPIM notice. If the individual has SoS's permission for an act which would, without that permission, contravene a measure, the individual contravenes that measure by acting otherwise than in accordance with the permission

Powers of entry, search, etc

TPIMA 2011, Sch 5 provides as follows.

To serve TPIM

For the purpose of serving a relevant notice (ie a TPIM notice or a notice extending, varying, or reviving it) on an individual, a constable may enter any premises where he reasonably believes the individual to be, and search those premises for him.

At time of service

Where a TPIM notice is being, or has just been, served on an individual, a constable may (without a warrant):

(a) search the individual;
(b) enter and search his place of residence or other premises to which he has power to grant access,

to ascertain whether there is anything on the individual, or in the premises, that contravenes the TPIM notice.

A constable may seize anything found in the course of such a search:

(a) for the purpose of ascertaining whether the TPIM notice is being or is about to be contravened by the individual;
(b) for the purpose of securing compliance by the individual with the TPIM notice;
(c) if the constable reasonably suspects that the thing is or contains evidence in relation to an offence, and that it must be seized to prevent it being concealed, lost, damaged, altered or destroyed.

Suspicion of absconding

Where a constable reasonably suspects that an individual subject to a TPIM notice has absconded, he may (without a warrant) enter and search the individual's place of residence, other premises to which the individual has power to grant access and any premises to which he had such power and to which he is recently connected:

(a) to determine whether the individual has absconded;
(b) if it appears that the individual has absconded, for anything that may assist in the pursuit and arrest of the individual.

A constable may seize anything that he finds in the course of such a search:

(a) if he reasonably believes that the thing will assist in the pursuit or arrest of the individual;
(b) if he reasonably suspects that it is or contains evidence in relation to an offence, and that it must be seized to prevent it being concealed, lost, damaged, altered or destroyed.

Determination of compliance

A constable may apply to a justice of the peace for a search warrant for the purpose of determining whether an individual is complying with a TPIM notice. Such a warrant may authorise a constable:

(a) to search the individual;
(b) to enter and search his place of residence and/or any other premises that are specified in the warrant.

The application for the warrant must be made without notice and supported by an information in writing. In so far as a warrant authorises a constable to search premises, see PACE, ss 15 and 16 (pp 81–4). A constable may seize anything that he finds in the course of such a search on the same grounds as where a search is conducted without a warrant at the time of serving a TPIM notice. The warrant authorises a search of the individual on one occasion only. The search must be carried out within 28 days and must be carried out at a reasonable hour unless it appears that the purposes of the search may be frustrated if carried out then.

The constable seeking to execute the warrant must, before carrying out a search:

(a) identify himself to the individual,
(b) if not in uniform, produce documentary evidence that he is a constable to the individual,
(c) produce the warrant to the individual, and
(d) supply the individual with a copy of the warrant.

For public safety purposes

A constable may (without a warrant) search an individual subject to a TPIM notice to ascertain whether he is in possession of anything that could be used to threaten or harm anyone. This power may be exercised at any time when the constable is in the presence of the individual. A constable may seize anything found if he reasonably suspects that the thing:

(a) may be used to threaten or harm anyone; or
(b) is or contains evidence in relation to an offence, and that it must be seized to prevent it being concealed, lost, damaged, altered or destroyed.

Retention

Anything seized under a power conferred by virtue of TPIMA 2011, Sch 5 may be subjected to tests and retained for as long as is necessary in all the circumstances. If a constable has reasonable grounds for believing that the thing is or contains evidence in relation to an offence, it may be retained for use as evidence at a criminal trial, or for forensic examination or for investigation in connection with an offence, unless a photograph or copy would be sufficient for that purpose. If a constable has reasonable grounds for believing that the thing has been obtained in consequence of the commission of an offence, it may be retained in order to establish its lawful owner.

General

A constable may detain an individual for the purpose of searching him under one of the above powers, and may use reasonable force, if necessary, for the purpose of exercising any of the above powers.

The C-TA 2008, s 1 (power to remove documents for examination: p 808) prospectively applies to searches at the time of serving a TPIM notice, on suspicion of absconding, to determine compliance or for public safety purposes.

Fingerprints and samples

TPIMA 2011, Sch 6 contains the relevant provisions.

When a TPIM notice is in force in respect of an individual, a constable may take fingerprints or a non-intimate sample from him with his written consent, or without that consent (with reasonable force, if necessary). Before any fingerprints or a non-intimate sample are taken the individual must be informed:

(a) of the reason,
(b) of the fact that the fingerprints or sample are taken under the above power, and
(c) that they may be the subject of a speculative search.

These matters must be recorded as soon as practicable after the fingerprints or sample are taken. The taking of hair is subject to identical rules to those on p 824.

A constable may exercise the above power only if:

(a) in the case of fingerprints:
    (i) the individual has not previously had fingerprints taken under it after the present TPIM notice came into force, or

(ii) fingerprints so taken after that time do not constitute a complete set of the individual's fingerprints, or some or all of the fingerprints taken are not of sufficient quality to allow satisfactory analysis, comparison or matching,

(b) in the case of a sample:

(i) the individual has not previously had a sample of the same type and from the same part of the body taken under it after the present TPIM notice came into force, or

(ii) a sample so taken after that time proved insufficient.

The provisions relating to a requirement to attend a police station for the taking of fingerprints or a sample, and to arrest for non-compliance, are the same as the general provision which apply under PACE. See heading 'General' on p 201.

Checking

Any fingerprints, data or samples obtained under the above provisions, or information derived from such samples, may be checked against:

(a) other such fingerprints, data or samples or any information derived from such a sample,

(b) any fingerprints or samples taken under TA 2000, Sch 8 (p 824) or any information derived from such a sample,

(c) any relevant physical data taken or provided in Scotland by virtue of similar provisions, any samples so taken or any information derived from such material,

(d) material to which the Counter-Terrorism Act 2008, s 18 (p 212) applies,

(e) any fingerprints, sample, or information mentioned in PACE, s 63A(1)(a) or (b) (see pp 201–2),

(f) any fingerprints, relevant physical data, samples, or information mentioned in corresponding Scottish or Northern Irish legislation.

Destruction of paragraph 6 material

'Paragraph 6 material', ie fingerprints taken under the above provisions, and a DNA profile derived from a DNA sample taken under them, must be destroyed if it appears to the responsible chief officer of police that the taking or providing of the material or, in the case of a DNA profile, the taking of the sample from which the DNA profile was derived, was unlawful.

In any other case, such material must be destroyed unless it is retained under a power conferred by para 9 or 11 (below) or it can be retained under any other power.

These provisions do not prevent a speculative search from being carried out, in relation to paragraph 6 material, within such time as may reasonably be required for the search if the responsible chief officer of police considers the search to be desirable.

If fingerprints or a DNA profile are required to be destroyed, any copies of the fingerprints or data held by a police force must also be destroyed, and no copy of a DNA profile may be retained by a police force except in a form which does not include information which identifies the individual to whom it relates.

Retention of paragraph 6 material

By para 8, paragraph 6 material taken from, or provided by, an individual who has no previous convictions in England, Wales or Northern Ireland for a recordable offence (see p 198) (in Scotland, imprisonable offence) or (except in the case of Scotland) only one exempt conviction or caution may generally be retained until the end of the six-month period beginning with the expiry date of the TPIM notice in force when the material was taken. A 'spent conviction' counts as a conviction for current purposes. An exempt 'conviction' is one in respect of a recordable offence, other than 'qualifying offence' (see p 192), committed when the individual was under 18. Convictions of more than one offence committed on the same occasion are deemed to be a single conviction.

By para 9, paragraph 6 material taken from, or provided by, an individual who has been convicted of a recordable offence (other than a single exempt conviction) or of an offence in Scotland which is punishable by imprisonment, or who is so convicted before the end of the period within which the material may be retained by virtue of para 8, may be retained indefinitely.

By para 11, paragraph 6 material may be retained for as long as a national security determination made by the responsible chief officer of police has effect in relation to it. Such a determination is made if the responsible chief officer of police determines that it is necessary for any paragraph 6 material to be retained for the purposes of national security. It must be written, has effect for a maximum of two years, and may be renewed.

Destruction of non-intimate samples

Non-intimate samples must be destroyed if it appears to the responsible chief officer of police that the taking of the sample was unlawful. Subject to this:

(a) a DNA sample must be destroyed as soon as a DNA profile has been derived from the sample, or, if sooner, within six months,

(b) any other sample must be destroyed within six months.

However, the above provisions do not prevent a speculative search from being carried out within such time as may reasonably be required for the search if the responsible chief officer of police considers the search to be desirable.

Use of retained material

Any paragraph 6 material or non-intimate sample which is retained must not be used other than:

(a) in the interests of national security,

(b) for purposes:

(i) of a terrorist investigation (as defined on p 805),

(ii) related to the prevention or detection of crime, the investigation of an offence or the conduct of a prosecution, or

(iii) related to the identification of someone deceased or of someone to whom the material relates.

Material required to be destroyed must not thereafter be used in evidence against the individual to whom the material relates, or for the purposes of the investigation of any offence.

CHAPTER 29

Sexual Offences

SEXUAL OFFENCES: INTRODUCTION

The law in relation to sexual offences was thoroughly overhauled and modernised by the Sexual Offences Act 2003 (SOA 2003). The only part of the previous principal Act, the Sexual Offences Act 1956, which survives is a handful of sections concerned with brothels, dealt with in the next chapter.

Sexual

For the purposes of the various offences in SOA 2003, s 78 provides that, except in relation to sexual activity in a public lavatory, penetration, touching or any other activity is sexual if a reasonable person would consider that:

(a) whatever its circumstances or any person's purpose in relation to it, it is because of its nature sexual; or

(b) because of its nature it *may* be sexual and because of its circumstances or the purpose of any person in relation to it (or both) it *is* sexual.

The Court of Appeal has held that (b) contains two requirements. The first is whether a reasonable person would consider that because of its nature the actual act could be sexual. In relation to this requirement, the circumstances before or after the act took place, or any evidence as to the purpose of any person in relation to it are irrelevant. If the answer to the question posed by this requirement is 'No', the act is not sexual. If the answer to the question is 'Yes', the second requirement comes into play, and requires the jury or magistrates to ask themselves whether because of the circumstances of the activity and/or the purpose of *any* person in relation to it (not just the person who does the act, but—eg—someone who encourages the act to be done), the activity *is* sexual.

Consent

For the purposes of the offences under SOA 2003 involving the absence of consent, 'consent' is defined by SOA 2003, s 74 as follows: a person consents if he agrees by choice, and has the freedom and capacity to make that choice.

Capacity to choose

A person may, for example, lack the capacity to make a choice about whether or not to agree because of mental disorder, because he is drugged or intoxicated or because he is semi-comatose. The courts have held that a person will lack capacity to consent if he or she has no real understanding of what is involved, or has such limited knowledge, awareness, or understanding as to be in no position to decide whether to agree, and that capacity is not only 'issue-specific' in relation to different types of transaction (so that someone may have capacity for one purpose but not for another), but it is also issue-specific in relation to different transactions of the same type (so that a vulnerable adult (B) may have the capacity to consent to one type of sexual activity whilst lacking the capacity to consent to some other (and to B unfamiliar) type of sexual activity). In addition, the House of Lords has held, capacity to choose can be 'person-specific' or 'situation-specific' as well as 'issue-specific'. Thus, for example, B can have capacity vis-à-vis C but not vis-à-vis A.

Speaking in the context of rape, the Court of Appeal has held that if through drink (or for any other reason) the complainant (B) has temporarily lost capacity to choose whether to have intercourse on the relevant occasion, B is not consenting and, subject to questions about whether the defendant had mens rea, if intercourse takes place, this will be rape. However, it said, where B has voluntarily consumed even substantial quantities of alcohol, but nevertheless remains capable of choosing whether or not to have intercourse, and in drink agrees to do so, this will not be rape.

Freedom to choose

A person might not have a freedom to make a choice whether or not to agree if violence is being used or threatened against him or another at the material time or immediately beforehand. A person may also lack freedom of choice for other reasons, as where someone agrees because he is unlawfully detained or where there was the use, or threat, of violence to destroy property which was of special value, financially or emotionally, or threat of dismissal by an employer to an employee, or a threat to remove children. It would all depend on the nature of the threat and the other circumstances, the perception of the complainant, and whether in the light of these factors the complainant was not in reality free to agree or disagree.

Deception and mistake

Some mistakes may vitiate an apparent agreement, especially if induced by deception.

Two kinds of deception are specifically addressed in SOA 2003, s 76, by means of irrebuttable presumptions, but only in the context of alleged offences under SOA 2003, ss 1 to 4 (rape, sexual assault etc).

Section 76 provides that if in proceedings for an offence under s 1 to 4 it is proved that the defendant did the '*relevant act*' and that either of the *specified circumstances* existed, it is to be conclusively (ie irrebuttably) presumed:

(a) that the complainant did not consent to the relevant act; and
(b) that the defendant did not believe that the complainant consented to the relevant act.

The *specified circumstances* are: that the defendant intentionally deceived the complainant as to the nature or purpose of the relevant act; and that the defendant intentionally induced the complainant to consent to the relevant act by impersonating a person known personally to B.

By the SOA 2003, s 77, in relation to an offence to which ss 75 (below) and 76 apply, references to the *relevant act* and to the complainant are to be read as follows:

Offence	Relevant act
Under s 1 (rape)	The defendant intentionally penetrating, with his penis, the vagina, anus, or mouth of the complainant

Under s 2 (assault by penetration)	The defendant intentionally penetrating, with a part of his body or anything else, the vagina or anus of the complainant where the penetration is sexual
Under s 3 (sexual assault)	The defendant intentionally touching the complainant, where the touching is sexual
Under s 4 (causing person to engage in sexual activity without consent)	The defendant intentionally causing the complainant to engage in an activity, where the activity is sexual

Deception or mistake not covered by s 76

Whether or not there is an effective consent in cases of deception falling outside SOA 2003, s 76, or in cases of self-induced mistake, must be determined by the jury by applying the terms of s 74. The statement in s 74 that a person consents if he agrees by choice and has the freedom to make that choice requires an informed choice. A deception about the use of a condom or about the intent to pay for sex, for example, are factors which can be considered by a jury when assessing whether the complainant (B) freely agreed to the act.

Where one party to sexual activity has a sexually transmissible disease which is not disclosed to the other party any consent that may have been given to that activity by the other party is not thereby vitiated. The sexual act remains a consensual act. However, the party suffering from the sexually transmissible disease will not have any defence to any charge of an offence against the person which may result from harm created by that sexual activity, merely by virtue of that consent, because such consent does not include consent to infection by the disease.

Rebuttable presumptions as to the absence of consent

Section 75 provides that if in proceedings for an offence to which s 75 applies (those under ss 1–4) it is proved:

(a) that A did the *relevant act* (see table above);
(b) that any of the *specified circumstances* below existed; and
(c) that A *knew* that those circumstances existed,

B is to be taken (ie presumed) not to have consented to the relevant act unless sufficient evidence is adduced to raise an issue as to whether B consented, and A is to be taken not to have reasonably believed that B consented *unless* sufficient evidence is adduced to raise an issue as to whether he *reasonably* believed it. Evidence is not sufficient if it is fanciful or speculative.

The *specified circumstances* are that:

(a) any person was, at the time of the relevant act or immediately before it began, using violence against B or causing B to fear that immediate violence would be used against him;
(b) any person was, at the time of the relevant act or immediately before it began, causing B to fear that violence was being used, or that immediate violence would be used, against another person;

(c) B was, and A was not, unlawfully detained at the time of the relevant act;

(d) B was asleep or otherwise unconscious at the time of the relevant act;

(e) because of B's physical disability, B would not have been able at the time of the relevant act to communicate to A whether B consented;

(f) any person had administered to or caused to be taken by B, without B's consent, a substance which, having regard to when it was administered or taken, was capable of causing or enabling B to be stupefied or overpowered at the time of the relevant act.

If sufficient evidence is adduced to raise an issue as to one (or both) of the two matters, the matter must be determined in the normal way.

Penetration, touching and parts of the body

By SOA 2003, s 79, 'penetration' is a continuing act from entry to withdrawal. It has long been established by the courts that the slightest degree of penetration is enough. SOA 2003, s 79 also provides that references to a part of the body include references to a part surgically constructed (in particular through gender re-assignment surgery); that 'vagina' includes vulva (external female genital organs); and that 'touching' includes touching with any part of the body, or with anything else, or through anything, and in particular includes touching through penetration. The Court of Appeal has held that 'touching' includes touching a person's clothing without applying any force to his body.

NON-CONSENSUAL SEXUAL OFFENCES

Rape

By SOA 2003, s 1(1), a person (A) commits an offence triable only on indictment if:

(a) he intentionally penetrates the vagina, anus or mouth of another person (B) with his penis;

(b) B does not consent to the penetration; and

(c) A does not reasonably believe that B consents.

The absence of consent does not have to be demonstrated by offering resistance or by communicating it to the defendant. A divisional court has held that if a woman has made it clear that she would only consent to sexual intercourse if the man uses a condom, there would be no consent to the sexual intercourse if, without her consent, he does not use a condom, or removes or tears the condom without her consent.

SOA 2003, s 1(2) provides that whether a belief in consent is reasonable is to be determined having regard to all the circumstances, including any steps A has taken to ascertain whether B consents. The words 'all the circumstances' must refer to those which might be relevant to the issue, including any characteristic of the defendant, permanent or transient, which might affect his ability to perceive or understand whether or not the victim is consenting. Examples would be a learning disability, mental illness, deafness, blindness, extreme youth, and sexual inexperience. Evidence of voluntary intoxication cannot, however, be taken into account under the general principles relating to it.

Proof of lack of consent and of the absence of reasonable belief is assisted by the rebuttable and irrebuttable presumptions in SOA 2003, ss 75 and 76.

Rape of a child under 13

By SOA 2003, s 5(1), a person (A) commits an offence triable only on indictment if:

(a) he intentionally penetrates the vagina, anus or mouth of another person (B) with his penis; and

(b) B is under 13.

Whether or not the other person consents to the penetration is irrelevant; a child under 13 is legally incapable of giving a legally significant consent.

The House of Lords has confirmed that the need for a mental element is negatived by necessary implication, as evidenced by the express references to reasonable belief of age in other sections of the Act. Thus, not even a reasonable belief that B was 13 or over will excuse A.

The offence is one of the offences in respect of which there are exceptions from criminal liability under SOA 2003, s 73, on the basis of aiding, abetting or counselling the commission of the offence if a person acts for the purpose of:

(a) protecting the child from sexually transmitted infection;

(b) protecting the physical safety of the child;

(c) preventing the child from becoming pregnant; or

(d) promoting the child's emotional well-being by the giving of advice,

and not for the purpose of obtaining sexual gratification or for the purpose of causing or encouraging the activity constituting the offence or the child's participation in it.

Assault by penetration

By SOA 2003, s 2(1), a person (A) commits an offence triable only on indictment if:

(a) he intentionally penetrates the vagina or anus of another person (B) with a part of his body (eg a finger or tongue) or anything else;

(b) the penetration is sexual;

(c) B does not consent to the penetration; and

(d) A does not reasonably believe that B consents.

Section 2(2) provides that whether a belief is reasonable must be determined having regard to all the circumstances, including whether A has taken reasonable steps to ascertain whether B consents.

Proof of lack of consent and of the absence of reasonable belief is assisted by the rebuttable and irrebuttable presumptions in SOA 2003, ss 75 and 76.

Assault of a child under 13 by penetration

By SOA 2003, s 6(1), a person commits an offence triable only on indictment if:

(a) he intentionally penetrates the vagina or anus of another person with a part of his body or anything else;

(b) the penetration is sexual; and

(c) the other person is under 13.

The absence of consent by the other person is not an element of this offence. The above exceptions under s 73 from liability for aiding, abetting or counselling apply to this offence.

Sexual assault

By SOA 2003, s 3(1), a person (A) commits an indictable (either way) offence if:

(a) he intentionally touches another person (B);
(b) the touching is sexual;
(c) B does not consent to the touching; and
(d) A does not reasonably believe that B consents.

Section 3(2) provides that whether a belief is reasonable must be determined with regard to all the circumstances, including any steps A has taken to ascertain whether B consents.

The Court of Appeal has held that the 'intentional touching' element of this offence simply requires a deliberate touching. It has also held that this intent is a basic intent, with the result that evidence of voluntary intoxication cannot be relied upon to negate it. These points are equally applicable to other offences under SOA 2003 involving intentional penetration or touching.

Proof of lack of consent and of the absence of reasonable belief is assisted by the rebuttable and irrebuttable presumptions in SOA 2003, ss 75 and 76.

Sexual assault of a child under 13

By SOA 2003, s 7(1), a person commits an indictable (either way) offence if:

(a) he intentionally touches another person;
(b) the touching is sexual; and
(c) the other person is under 13.

The absence of the other person's consent is not an element of the offence. The exceptions under s 73 (p 849) from liability for aiding, abetting or counselling apply to this offence.

Causing a person to engage in sexual activity without consent

By SOA 2003, s 4(1), a person (A) commits an indictable (either way) offence if:

(a) he intentionally causes another person (B) to engage in an activity;
(b) the activity is sexual;
(c) B does not consent to engaging in the activity; and
(d) A does not reasonably believe that B consents.

A more serious offence triable only on indictment is committed under s 4(1) and (4) if the activity caused involves one of four circumstances:

(a) penetration of B's anus or vagina;
(b) penetration of B's mouth with a person's penis;
(c) penetration of a person's anus or vagina with a part of B's body or by B with anything else; or
(d) penetration of a person's mouth with B's penis.

Section 4(2) provides that whether a belief is reasonable must be determined with regard to all the circumstances, including any steps A has taken to ascertain whether B consents.

Proof of lack of consent and of the absence of reasonable belief is assisted by the rebuttable and irrebuttable presumptions in SOA 2003, ss 75 and 76.

Causing or inciting a child under 13 to engage in sexual activity

By SOA 2003, s 8(1), a person commits an indictable (either way) offence if:

(a) he intentionally causes or incites another person (B) to engage in an activity;
(b) the activity is sexual; and
(c) B is under 13.

A more serious offence triable only on indictment is committed under s 8(1) and (2) if the activity caused or incited involved one of the four circumstances set out above in relation to s 4.

The absence of B's consent is not an element of an offence under s 8.

An offence of intentionally inciting a child under 13 to engage in sexual activity can be committed even though it is not possible to identify any specific or identifiable child to whom the incitement was addressed. It matters not whether the incitement was directed at a particular child or a very large group of children, or whether the child or children could be identified or not. This decision is equally applicable to the other offences of incitement to sexual activity in SOA 2003.

The Court of Appeal has held that 'intentional' causing or inciting for the purposes of s 8 means deliberate causing or inciting; recklessness will not do. This is equally applicable to other offences of intentionally causing or inciting under SOA 2003.

CHILD SEX OFFENCES

In these offences, it is irrelevant that the child may have consented.

Sexual activity with a child

By SOA 2003, s 9(1), a person aged 18 or over (A) commits an indictable (either way) offence if:

(a) he intentionally touches another person (B);
(b) the touching is sexual; and
(c) either:
    (i) B is under 16 and A does not reasonably believe that B is 16 or over; or
    (ii) B is under 13.

A more serious offence triable only on indictment is committed under s 9(1) and (2) if the touching involves one of the following four circumstances:

(a) penetration of B's anus or vagina with a part of A's body or anything else;
(b) penetration of B's mouth with A's penis;
(c) penetration of A's anus or vagina with a part of B's body; or
(d) penetration of A's mouth with B's penis.

The exceptions from liability for aiding, abetting or counselling, under s 73, described on p 849 apply to such an offence.

Causing or inciting a child to engage in sexual activity

By SOA 2003, s 10(1), a person aged 18 or over (A) commits an indictable (either way) offence if:

(a) he intentionally causes or incites another person (B) to engage in an activity;
(b) the activity is sexual; and
(c) either:
   (i)   B is under 16 and A does not reasonably believe that B is 16 or over; or
   (ii) B is under 13.

A more serious offence triable only on indictment is committed under s 10(1) and (2) if the activity caused or incited involves:

(a) penetration of B's anus or vagina;
(b) penetration of B's mouth with a person's penis;
(c) penetration of a person's anus or vagina with a part of B's body or by B with anything else; or
(d) penetration of a person's mouth with B's penis.

Engaging in sexual activity in the presence of a child

By SOA 2003, s 11(1), a person aged 18 or over (A) commits an indictable (either way) offence if:

(a) he intentionally engages in an activity;
(b) the activity is sexual;
(c) for the purpose of obtaining sexual gratification, he engages in it:
   (i)   when another person (B) is present or is in a place from which A can be observed; and
   (ii) knowing or believing that B is aware, or intending that B should be aware, that he is engaging in it; and
(d) either:
   (i)   B is under 16 and A does not reasonably believe that B is 16 or over; or
   (ii) B is under 13.

'Observed' in (c) and elsewhere in SOA 2003 means observation whether direct or by looking at an image produced by any means.

Causing a child to watch a sexual act

By SOA 2003, s 12(1), a person aged 18 or over (A) commits an indictable (either way) offence if:

(a) for the purpose of obtaining sexual gratification, he intentionally causes another person (B) to watch a third person engaging in an activity, or to look at an image of any person engaging in an activity;
(b) the activity is sexual; and
(c) either:
   (i)   B is under 16 and A does not reasonably believe that B is 16 or over, or
   (ii) B is under 13.

'Image' in (a), and elsewhere in the Act, includes a moving or still image, however produced, and, where—as here—the context permits, a three-dimensional image. It does not include written material. References to an image of a person include references to an image of an imaginary person.

The purpose of obtaining sexual gratification need not relate to immediate gratification (eg from seeing the victim watch the images). The Court of Appeal has held that the offence under s 12 can be committed where A's purpose involves immediate, or deferred, or immediate and deferred gratification. Thus, the offence can be committed, for example, where A causes a child to watch a sexual act to put the child in the mood for future sexual abuse, as well as where he does so because he derives enjoyment at the time from seeing the child watch the sexual act. This decision is equally applicable to other offences under SOA 2003 in which the phrase 'for the purpose of obtaining sexual gratification' appears.

Child sex offences committed by children or young persons

By SOA 2003, s 13(1), a person under 18 commits an indictable (either way) offence if he does anything which would be an offence under SOA 2003, ss 9 to 12 if he were aged 18. It is, however, a less serious offence than those offences. The exceptions from liability for aiding, abetting or counselling under s 73 (referred to on p 849) apply to this offence if what is done would be an offence under s 9 if the offender were aged 18 or over.

Arranging or facilitating the commission of a child sex offence

By SOA 2003, s 14(1), a person commits an indictable (either way) offence if:

(a) he intentionally arranges or facilitates something that he intends to do, intends another person to do, or believes that another person will do, in any part of the world; and
(b) doing it will involve the commission of an offence under ss 9 to 13.

Section 14(2) and (3) provides exceptions for people who seek to protect a child from pregnancy or sexually transmitted disease, to protect a child's physical safety or to give it advice, where they do not intend an offence under ss 9 to 13 to be committed but believe that it will. They provide that a person does not commit an offence under s 14 if:

(a) he arranges or facilitates something that he believes another person will do, but that he does not intend to do or intend another person to do; and
(b) any offence within ss 9 to 13 which the doing of that thing would involve would be an offence against a child for whose protection he acts.

In this context, a person acts for the protection of a child if he acts for the purpose of:

(a) protecting the child from sexually transmitted infection;
(b) protecting the child's physical safety;
(c) preventing the child from becoming pregnant; or
(d) promoting the child's emotional well-being by the giving of advice,

and not for the purpose of obtaining sexual gratification or for the purpose of causing or encouraging the activity constituting an offence within ss 9 to 13 or the child's participation in it.

Examples of conduct falling within these exceptions would be giving an under-age boy a condom (if done for the purpose of protecting the boy against a sexually transmitted infection, but not if done to protect the boy against the risk of his 16-year-old girlfriend becoming pregnant); giving an under-age girl a condom (if done for the purpose of protecting her against a sexually transmitted infection or pregnancy); giving advice to an under-age child about protected sex (if done for the purpose of protection against sexually transmitted infection, or, where the advice is given to a girl, pregnancy, or to promote the child's emotional well-being).

The Court of Appeal has stated that s 14 covers taking preparatory steps (with the necessary intent) to commit an offence under ss 9 to 13. It also stated that an arrangement may be made without the agreement or acquiescence of anyone else.

Meeting a child following sexual grooming etc with a view to engaging in sexual activity with it

Paedophiles have not been slow to make use of the internet to gain the trust and confidence of children in 'chatroom conversations' and thereby to befriend them. Typically, the paedophile pretends that he is a teenager sharing the same interests and then arranges a meeting with the child.

SOA 2003, s 15(1) deals with grooming (whether or not it involves the internet) by providing that a person aged 18 or over (A) commits an indictable (either way) offence if:

(a) having met or communicated with another person (B) anywhere in the world on at least two earlier occasions:
   (i)   A subsequently intentionally meets B, or
   (ii) A subsequently travels with the intention of meeting B in any part of the world or arranges to meet B in any part of the world, or
   (iii) B travels with the intention of meeting A in any part of the world;
(b) A intends to do anything to or in respect of B, during or after the meeting mentioned in (a)(i)–(iii) above, and in any part of the world, which if done will involve the commission by A of a relevant offence;
(c) B is under 16; and
(d) A does not reasonably believe that B is 16 or over.

ABUSE OF POSITION OF TRUST

All the offences under this heading are indictable (either way) offences.

Abuse of position of trust: sexual activity with a child

Provided that he has any necessary mens rea, a person aged 18 or over (A) commits an offence under SOA 2003, s 16(1) if:

(a) he intentionally touches another person (B);
(b) the touching is sexual;
(c) A is in a position of trust in relation to B; and
(d) B is under 18.

B's consent is, of course, irrelevant in offences involving abuse of a position of trust. The exceptions from liability for aiding, abetting or counselling this offence under s 73 (see p 849) apply to this offence if B is under 16.

Abuse of position of trust: causing or inciting a child to engage in sexual activity

Provided that he has any necessary mens rea, a person aged 18 or over (A) commits an offence under s 17(1) if:

(a) he intentionally causes or incites another person (B) to engage in an activity;
(b) the activity is sexual;
(c) A is in a position of trust in relation to B; and
(d) B is under 18.

Abuse of position of trust: sexual activity in the presence of a child

Provided that he has any necessary mens rea, a person aged 18 or over (A) commits an offence under SOA 2003, s 18(1) if:

(a) he intentionally engages in an activity;
(b) the activity is sexual;
(c) for the purpose of obtaining sexual gratification, he engages in it:
    (i) when another person (B) is present or is in a place from which A can be observed, and
    (ii) knowing or believing that B is aware, or intending that B should be aware, that he is engaging in it;
(d) A is in a position of trust in relation to B; and
(e) B is under 18.

Abuse of position of trust: causing a child to watch a sexual act

Provided that he has any necessary mens rea, a person aged 18 or over (A) commits an offence under SOA 2003, s 19(1) if:

(a) for the purpose of obtaining sexual gratification, he intentionally causes another person (B) to watch a third person engaging in an activity, or to look at an image of any person engaging in an activity;
(b) the activity is sexual;
(c) A is in a position of trust in relation to B; and
(d) B is under 18.

Position of trust

For the purposes of the above offences, a person (A) is, by SOA 2003, s 21, in a position of trust in relation to another person (B) if:

(a) any of paras (1)–(11) below apply; or
(b) any condition specified in an order made by the Secretary of State is met. No order has yet been made.

(1) If A looks after persons under 18 who are detained in an institution by virtue of a court order or under an enactment, and B is so detained in that institution.
(2) If A looks after persons under 18 who are resident in a home or other place for children in residential care, and B is in residential care there.
(3) If A looks after persons under 18 who are accommodated and cared for in a hospital, an independent clinic (in Wales), a care home, residential care home or private hospital, a community home, voluntary home or children's home, or the like, and B is accommodated and cared for in that institution.
(4) If A looks after persons under 18 who are receiving education at an educational institution and B is receiving, and A is not receiving, education at that institution.

(5)   If A is engaged in the provision of a careers service or similar service and, in that capacity, looks after B on an individual basis.

(6)   If A regularly has unsupervised contact with B (whether face to face or by any other means) in the provision of accommodation for children in need thereof, or in police protection or detention, or on remand.

(7)   If A, as a person who is to report to the court on matters relating to the welfare of B, regularly has unsupervised contact with B (whether face to face or by any other means).

(8)   If A is a personal adviser appointed for B under the Children Act 1989, and, in that capacity, looks after B on an individual basis.

(9)   If:
   (a)   B is subject to a care order, a supervision order or an education supervision order, and
   (b)   in the exercise of functions conferred by virtue of the order on an authorised person or the authority designated by the order, A looks after B on an individual basis.

(10)   If A is an officer of the Children and Family Court Advisory Support Service (CAFCASS) appointed for B, or is appointed a children's guardian of B under the Adoption Rules 1968, or is appointed the children's guardian of B under the Family Procedure (Adoption) Rules 2005 or the Family Procedure Rules 2010, and, in that capacity, regularly has unsupervised contact with B (whether face to face or by any other means).

(11)   If:
   (a)   B is subject to requirements imposed by or under an enactment on his release from detention for a criminal offence, or is subject to requirements imposed by a court order made in criminal proceedings, and
   (b)   A looks after B on an individual basis in pursuance of the requirements.

For the purposes of paras (1), (2), (3), and (4), a person looks after persons under 18 at an institution or the like if he is regularly involved in caring for, training, supervising or being in sole charge of such persons there, not necessarily the child abused.

Paragraphs (5), (8), (9), and (11) refer to a person looking after another on an individual basis. A person (A) looks after another (B) on such a basis if:

(a)   A is regularly involved in caring for, training or supervising B; and
(b)   in the course of his involvement, A regularly has unsupervised contact with B (whether face to face or by any other means).

Mens rea

In addition to requiring A intentionally to do the thing specified by each individual section, ss 16 to 19 make further provision as to the mens rea required in respect of the child's age and the existence of a position of trust.

In terms of the mens rea as to the age of the child (B), A must not reasonably believe that B is 18 or over. However, this provision does not apply if B is under 13 at the material time; in such a case the offences are undoubtedly ones of strict liability as to age. Although the prosecution ultimately has the persuasive burden of proof of the absence of reasonable belief that B is 18 or over where B is aged 13 to 17, the prosecution is assisted by the provision that, where in proceedings for an offence under ss 16 to 19 it is proved that B was under 18, A is to be taken not to have reasonably believed that B was 18 or over unless sufficient evidence is adduced to raise an issue as to whether A reasonably believed it.

Where A is in a position of trust in relation to B by virtue of circumstances within paras (1), (2), (3), or (4) above, and, in each case, A is not also in a position of trust by virtue of other circumstances, it must be proved that A knew or could reasonably be expected to know of the circumstances by virtue of which he is in a position of trust in relation to B. Proof of this is aided by the provision that, where it is proved that A was in a position of trust in relation to B by virtue of the four circumstances just referred to, and it is not proved that he was in such a position of trust by virtue of other circumstances, it is to be presumed that A knew or could reasonably have been expected to know of the circumstances by virtue of which he was in such a position of trust unless sufficient evidence is adduced to raise an issue as to whether A knew or could reasonably have been expected to know of those circumstances.

Where a position of trust arises wholly or partly by virtue of the other categories of circumstance referred to above, the Act does not require proof of any mens rea as to the position of trust where such a position of trust is involved.

Exceptions: marriage, civil partnership and existing sexual relationships

Conduct by a person (A) which would otherwise be one of the offences under SOA 2003, ss 16 to 19 against another person (B) is not such an offence if:

(a) B was 16 or over, and the defendant proves that A and B were lawfully married (or civil partners) at the time of the conduct; or

(b) the defendant proves that, immediately before the position of trust arose, a sexual relationship existed between A and B, but this exception does not apply if at that time sexual intercourse between A and B would have been unlawful, eg because B was under 16.

FAMILIAL SEXUAL OFFENCES

Offences involving a child family member

Sexual activity with a child family member

A person (A) commits an indictable (either way) offence under SOA 2003, s 25(1) if:

(a) he intentionally touches another person (B);

(b) the touching is sexual;

(c) the relation of A to B is within the specified relationships;

(d) A knows or could reasonably be expected to know that his relation to B is of a description falling within those relationships; and

(e) either:

(i) B is under 18 and A does not reasonably believe that B is 18 or over; or

(ii) B is under 13.

SOA 2003 has the effect of distinguishing between two offences. The more serious is committed where A is 18 or over at the time of the offence. If the touching involves:

(f) penetration of B's anus or vagina with a part of A's body or anything else;

(g) penetration of B's mouth with A's penis;

(h) penetration of A's anus or vagina with part of B's body (but not with anything else); or

(i) penetration of A's mouth by B's penis,

the offence is triable only on indictment; otherwise it is an indictable (either way) offence.

The less serious offence is where A was not 18 or over at the material time, whatever type of activity was involved. It is an indictable (either way) offence.

Where it is proved that the relation of A to B was of a description falling within the specified relationships, it is to be taken that A knew or could reasonably have been expected to know that his relation to B was of that description unless sufficient evidence is adduced to raise an issue as to whether A knew or could reasonably have been expected to know that it was.

In respect of the mens rea in (e)(i) (no reasonable belief (where B is not under 13) that B is 18 or over), where it is proved that B was under 18, A is to be taken not to have reasonably believed that B was 18 or over unless sufficient evidence is adduced to raise an issue as to whether A reasonably believed it.

The exceptions under s 73 from liability for aiding, abetting or counselling (see p 849) apply to an offence under s 25 if B is under 16.

Inciting a child family member to engage in sexual activity

A person (A) commits an offence under SOA 2003, s 26 if:

(a) he intentionally incites another person (B) to touch, or allow himself to be touched by, A;

(b) the touching is sexual;

(c) the relation of A to B is within the specified relationships;

(d) A knows or could reasonably be expected to know that his relation to B is of a description falling within those relationships; and

(e) either:

  (i) B is under 18 and A does not reasonably believe that B is 18 or over; or

  (ii) B is under 13.

There are two offences under s 26, distinguished (and triable) in a similar way as in s 25.

The mens rea in respect of the fact that the relation of A to B is within the specified relationships is the same as that in the offences described in relation to s 25. Thus, where it is proved that the relation of A to B was of a description falling within the specified relationships, it is to be taken that A knew or could reasonably have been expected to know that his relation to B was of that description unless sufficient evidence is adduced to raise an issue as to whether A knew or could reasonably have been expected to know that it was.

Likewise, in respect of the mens rea in para (e)(i) (no reasonable belief (where B is not under 13) that B is 18 or over), where it is proved that B was under 18, A is to be taken not to have reasonably believed that B was 18 or over unless sufficient evidence is adduced to raise an issue as to whether A reasonably believed it.

Family relationships

For the purposes of SOA 2003, ss 25 and 26, the relation of A and B must be within s 27. The relation of A to B is within the specified relationships if it is within paras (a)–(c) below, including an adoptive relationship (as well as a biological one).

The relation of A and B is within the specified relationships if:

(a) one of them is the other's parent, grandparent, brother, sister, half-brother, half-sister, aunt or uncle, or A is or has been B's foster parent;
(b) A and B live or have lived in the same household, or A is or has been regularly involved in caring for, training, supervising or being in sole charge of B, and:
    (i) one of them is or has been the other's step-parent,
    (ii) A and B are cousins,
    (iii) one of them is or has been the other's stepbrother or stepsister, or
    (iv) the parent or present or former foster parent of one of them is or has been the other's foster parent;
(c) A and B live in the same household, and A is regularly involved in caring for, training, supervising or being in sole charge of B, eg a nanny or au pair. It will be noted that (c) only applies while A is living in the same household.

A 'step-parent' includes someone who is neither married to, nor the civil partner of, a parent, if that person is a parent's 'partner'. In (b)(iii), the reference to a stepbrother or stepsister is to be read as follows: X's stepbrother or stepsister includes someone who is the son/daughter of the civil partner of X's parent (but not the son/daughter of either of X's parents).

Exceptions: marriage, civil partnership and existing sexual relationships

By SOA 2003, ss 28 and 29, conduct by A which would otherwise be an offence under s 25 or s 26 against B is not an offence thereunder if:

(a) B is 16 or over, and A and B are lawfully married (or civil partners); or
(b) (i) the relation of A to B is not within (a) *of the specified relationships above*, either biologically or adoptively; and
    (ii) immediately before the relation of A to B first became such as to fall within the specified relationships, a sexual relationship existed between A and B (as where, when A's mother marries B's father, A and B were already in a sexual relationship).

The defence in (b) does not apply if at the time referred to in (b)(ii) sexual intercourse between A and B would have been unlawful, eg because one of them was under 16.
    It is for the defendant to prove the relationship mentioned in (a) or (b).

Sex with an adult relative

A person aged 16 or over (A) (subject to s 64(3A)—see below) commits an indictable (either way) offence under SOA 2003, s 64(1) if:

(a) he intentionally penetrates another person's vagina or anus with a part of his body or anything else, or penetrates another person's mouth with his penis;
(b) the penetration is sexual;
(c) the other person (B) is aged 18 or over;
(d) A is related to B in a specified way; and
(e) A knows or could reasonably be expected to know that he is related to B in that way.

A person aged 16 or over (A) (subject to s 65(3A)—see below) commits an indictable (either way) offence under SOA 2003, s 65(1) if:

(a) another person (B) penetrates A's vagina or anus with a part of B's body or anything else, or penetrates A's mouth with B's penis;
(b) A consents to the penetration;

(c) the penetration is sexual;

(d) B is aged 18 or over;

(e) A is related to B in a specified way; and

(f) A knows or could reasonably be expected to know that he is related to B in that way.

The specified ways that A may be related to B are as a parent, grandparent, child, grandchild, brother, sister, half-brother, half-sister, uncle, aunt, nephew or niece.

Where a child has been adopted, not only are the biological parent and child related to each other for the purposes of SOA 2003, ss 64 and 65, whenever the child was adopted, but 'parent' also includes an adoptive parent and 'child' includes an adopted person. However where ss 64(1) or 65(1) apply in a case where A is related to B as B's child by virtue of being B's adopted child, A does not commit an offence under ss 64(1) or 65(1), as the case may be, unless A is 18 or over. This is provided by ss 64(3A) and 65(3A). It remains the case that other adoptive relationships, eg that of adoptive brother and sister, are excluded from the application of SOA 2003, ss 64 or 65.

These references to an adoptive relationship are to be read as including a corresponding relationship arising by virtue of a parental order under the Human Fertilisation and Embryology Act 2008 (the 'test tube babies' Act).

In terms of the requirement that the prosecution must prove that A knew or could reasonably be expected to know that he is related to B in a specified way, it is to be taken that A knew or could reasonably have been expected to know that he was related in that way unless sufficient evidence is adduced to raise an issue as to whether A knew or could reasonably have been expected to know that he was.

OFFENCES AGAINST PEOPLE WITH A MENTAL DISORDER

Meaning of mental disorder

For the purposes of these offences, 'mental disorder' means any disorder or disability of the mind. A person with a learning disability falls within this definition.

Offences against persons with a mental disorder impeding choice

Sexual activity with a person with a mental disorder impeding choice

A person (A) commits an indictable (either way) offence under SOA 2003, s 30(1) if:

(a) he intentionally touches another person (B);

(b) the touching is sexual;

(c) B is unable to refuse because of or for a reason related to a mental disorder; and

(d) A knows or could reasonably be expected to know that B has a mental disorder and that because of it or for a reason related to it B is likely to be unable to refuse.

Under s 30(1) and (3), A commits a more serious offence triable only on indictment if the touching involves:

(i)   penetration of B's anus or vagina with a part of A's body or anything else;

(ii)   penetration of B's mouth with A's penis;

(iii) penetration of A's anus or vagina with a part of B's body (but not with anything else); or

(iv) penetration of A's mouth with B's penis.

B is unable to refuse if:

(a) he lacks the capacity to choose (see p 845) whether to agree to the touching (whether because he lacks sufficient understanding of the nature or reasonably foreseeable consequences of what is being done, or for any other reason); or
(b) he is unable to communicate such a choice to A.

In relation to the first type of inability, the House of Lords has held that the words 'for a reason related to mental disorder' in the definition of the offences were clearly capable of encompassing a wide range of circumstances in which a person's mental disorder might rob him or her of the ability to make an autonomous choice, even though he or she might have sufficient understanding of the information relevant to making it. Those circumstances could include the kind of compulsion which drove a person with anorexia to refuse food, the delusions which drove a person with schizophrenia to believe that she had to do something, or the phobia or irrational fear which drove a person to refuse a life-saving injection. Irrational fear plainly was capable of depriving a person of capacity; the question was whether it did in a particular case.

The second type of inability to refuse covers people who might be able to make a choice but are unable to communicate it. The House of Lords has held that it is not limited to cases where B was *physically* unable to communicate because of his mental disorder. It stated that it was quite clear that in SOA 2003 Parliament had had in mind an inability to communicate which was the result of or associated with a disorder of the mind. Inability to communicate had to include a person with such a degree of learning difficulty that he or she had never acquired the gift of speech, so that it was impossible to discover whether or not he or she could understand or make a choice.

The exceptions under SOA 2003, s 73 from liability for aiding, abetting or counselling apply to an offence under s 30 if B is under 16 (see p 849).

Causing or inciting a person with a mental disorder impeding choice to engage in sexual activity

A person (A) commits an indictable (either way) offence under SOA 2003, s 31(1) if:

(a) he intentionally causes or incites another person (B) to engage in an activity;
(b) the activity is sexual;
(c) B is unable to refuse because of or for a reason related to a mental disorder; and
(d) A knows or could reasonably be expected to know that B has a mental disorder and that because of it or for a reason related to it B is likely to be unable to refuse.

Under s 31(1) and (3), A commits a more serious offence triable only on indictment if the activity caused or incited involves:

(a) penetration of B's anus or vagina;
(b) penetration of B's mouth with a person's penis;
(c) penetration of a person's anus or vagina with a part of B's body or by B with anything else; or
(d) penetration of a person's mouth with B's penis.

B is unable to refuse if:

(a) he lacks the capacity to choose whether to agree to engaging in the activity caused or incited (whether because he lacks sufficient understanding of the nature or reasonably foreseeable consequences of the activity, or for any other reason); or
(b) he is unable to communicate such a choice to A.

Engaging in sexual activity in the presence of a person with a mental disorder impeding choice

A person (A) commits an indictable (either way) offence under SOA 2003, s 32(1) if:

(a) he intentionally engages in an activity;
(b) the activity is sexual;
(c) for the purpose of obtaining sexual gratification, he engages in it:
    (i) when another person (B) is present or is in a place from which A can be observed, and
    (ii) knowing or believing that B is aware, or intending that B should be aware, that he is engaging in it;
(d) B is unable to refuse because of or for a reason related to a mental disorder; and
(e) A knows or could reasonably be expected to know that B has a mental disorder and that because of it or for a reason related to it B is likely to be unable to refuse.

  B is unable to refuse if:

(a) he lacks the capacity to choose whether to agree to being present (whether because he lacks sufficient understanding of the nature of the activity, or for any other reason); or
(b) he is unable to communicate such a choice to A.

Causing a person with a mental disorder impeding choice to watch a sexual act

A person (A) commits an indictable (either way) offence under SOA 2003, s 33(1) if:

(a) for the purpose of obtaining sexual gratification, he intentionally causes another person (B) to watch a third person engaging in an activity, or to look at an image of any person engaging in an activity;
(b) the activity is sexual;
(c) B is unable to refuse because of or for a reason related to a mental disorder; and
(d) A knows or could reasonably be expected to know that B has a mental disorder and that because of it or for a reason related to it B is likely to be unable to refuse.

  B is unable to refuse if:

(a) he lacks the capacity to choose whether to agree to watching or looking (whether because he lacks sufficient understanding of the nature of the activity, or for any other reason); or
(b) he is unable to communicate such a choice to A.

Inducements, etc to persons with a mental disorder

Inducement, threat or deception to procure sexual activity with a person with a mental disorder

A person (A) commits an indictable (either way) offence under SOA 2003, s 34(1) if:

(a) with the agreement of another person (B) he intentionally touches that person;
(b) the touching is sexual;
(c) A obtains B's agreement by means of an inducement offered or given, a threat made or a deception practised by A for that purpose;
(d) B has a mental disorder; and
(e) A knows or could reasonably be expected to know that B has a mental disorder.

Under s 34(1) and (2), A commits a more serious offence triable only on indictment if the touching involves:

(a) penetration of B's anus or vagina with a part of A's body or anything else;
(b) penetration of B's mouth with A's penis;
(c) penetration of A's anus or vagina with a part of B's body; or
(d) penetration of A's mouth with B's penis.

It is not necessary in either of these offences or in the case of the related offences under SOA 2003, ss 35 to 37 that B's mental disorder made B unable to refuse. These offences are concerned with gaining the consent of a mentally vulnerable person by inducement (eg a reward), a threat (eg 'I won't tell on you if you agree') or a deception (eg 'This is what everyone does').

The exceptions under s 73 from liability for aiding, abetting or counselling apply to an offence under s 34 if B is under 16 (see p 849).

Causing a person with a mental disorder to engage in, or agree to engage in, sexual activity by inducement, threat or deception

A person (A) commits an indictable (either way) offence under SOA 2003, s 35(1) if:

(a) by means of an inducement offered or given, a threat made or a deception practised by him for this purpose, he intentionally causes another person (B) to engage in, or to agree to engage in, an activity;
(b) the activity is sexual;
(c) B has a mental disorder; and
(d) A knows or could reasonably be expected to know that B has a mental disorder.

A more serious offence triable only on indictment is committed under s 35(1) and (2) if the activity caused or agreed involves:

(a) penetration of B's anus or vagina;
(b) penetration of B's mouth with a person's penis;
(c) penetration of a person's anus or vagina with a part of B's body or by B with anything else; or
(d) penetration of a person's mouth with B's penis.

Engaging in sexual activity in the presence, procured by inducement, threat or deception, of a person with a mental disorder

A person (A) commits an indictable (either way) offence under SOA 2003, s 36(1) if:

(a) he intentionally engages in an activity;
(b) the activity is sexual;
(c) for the purpose of obtaining sexual gratification, he engages in it:
   (i) when another person (B) is present or is in a place from which A can be observed, and
   (ii) knowing or believing that B is aware, or intending that B should be aware, that he is engaging in it;
(d) B agrees to be present or in the place referred to in (c)(i) because of an inducement offered or given, a threat made or a deception practised by A for the purpose of obtaining that agreement;
(e) B has a mental disorder; and
(f) A knows or could reasonably be expected to know that B has a mental disorder.

Causing a person with a mental disorder to watch a sexual act by inducement, threat or deception

A person (A) commits an indictable (either way) offence under SOA 2003, s 37(1) if:

(a) for the purpose of obtaining sexual gratification, he intentionally causes another person (B) to watch a third person engaging in an activity, or to look at an image of any person engaging in an activity;
(b) the activity is sexual;
(c) B agrees to watch or look because of an inducement offered or given, a threat made or a deception practised by A for the purpose of obtaining that agreement;
(d) B has a mental disorder; and
(e) A knows or could reasonably be expected to know that B has a mental disorder.

Offences by care workers with persons with mental disorder

Sexual activity by a care worker with a person with mental disorder

A person (A) commits an indictable (either way) offence under SOA 2003, s 38(1) if:

(a) he intentionally touches another person (B);
(b) the touching is sexual;
(c) B has a mental disorder;
(d) A knows or could reasonably be expected to know that B has a mental disorder; and
(e) A is involved in B's care in a way that falls within the provisions described on pp 865–6.

A more serious offence triable only on indictment is committed under s 38(1) and (3) if the touching involves:

(a) penetration of B's anus or vagina with a part of A's body or anything else;
(b) penetration of B's mouth with A's penis;
(c) penetration of A's anus or vagina with a part of B's body; or
(d) penetration of A's mouth with B's penis.

The exceptions under s 73 from liability for aiding, abetting or counselling apply to an offence under s 38 if B is under 16 (see p 849).

Offences under s 38, and the other 'care worker offences' referred to below, are designed to protect a mentally disordered person with the capacity to refuse consent from exploitation by a care worker of his or her relationship with that person.

Care worker causing or inciting a person with mental disorder to engage in sexual activity

A person (A) commits an indictable (either way) offence under SOA 2003, s 39(1) if:

(a) he intentionally causes or incites another person (B) to engage in an activity;
(b) the activity is sexual;
(c) B has a mental disorder;
(d) A knows or could reasonably be expected to know that B has a mental disorder; and
(e) A is involved in B's care in a way that falls within the provisions described on pp 865–6.

A more serious offence triable only on indictment is committed under s 39(1) and (3) if the sexual activity caused or incited involves:

(a) penetration of B's anus or vagina;
(b) penetration of B's mouth with a person's penis;
(c) penetration of a person's anus or vagina with a part of B's body or by B with anything else; or
(d) penetration of a person's mouth with B's penis.

Sexual activity by care worker in presence of person with mental disorder

A person (A) commits an indictable (either way) offence under SOA 2003, s 40(1) if:

(a) he intentionally engages in an activity;
(b) the activity is sexual;
(c) for the purpose of obtaining sexual gratification, he engages in it:
   (i) when another person (B) is present or is in a place from which A can be observed, and
   (ii) knowing or believing that B is aware, or intending that B should be aware, that he is engaging in it;
(d) B has a mental disorder;
(e) A knows or could reasonably be expected to know that B has a mental disorder; and
(f) A is involved in B's care in a way that falls within the provisions described below.

Care worker causing person with mental disorder to watch a sexual act

A person (A) commits an indictable (either way) offence under SOA 2003, s 41(1) if:

(a) for the purpose of obtaining sexual gratification, he intentionally causes another person (B) to watch a third person engaging in an activity, or to look at an image of any person engaging in an activity;
(b) the activity is sexual;
(c) B has a mental disorder;
(d) A knows or could reasonably be expected to know that B has a mental disorder; and
(e) A is involved in B's care in a way that falls within the provisions described below.

Rebuttable presumption of mens rea as to mental disorder

If it is proved at a trial for an offence under ss 38 to 41 that B had a mental disorder, it is to be taken that A knew or could reasonably have been expected to know that B had a mental disorder unless sufficient evidence is adduced to raise an issue as to whether A knew or could reasonably have been expected to know it (ss 38(2), 39(2), 40(2), and 41(2)).

Definition of care worker

For the purposes of the offences described in SOA 2003, ss 38 to 41, a person (A) is involved in the care of another (B) ('care worker' for short) if para (a), (b) or (c) below applies, that is:

(a) if:
   (i) B is accommodated and cared for in a care home, community home, voluntary home or children's home, and

(ii) A has functions to perform in the home in the course of employment which have brought him or are likely to bring him into regular face-to-face contact with B;

(b) if B is a patient for whom services are provided:
   (i) by a National Health Service body or an independent medical agency, or
   (ii) in an independent clinic (in Wales) or an independent hospital,
   and A has functions to perform for the body or agency or in the clinic or hospital in the course of employment which have brought him or are likely to bring him into regular face-to-face contact with B;

(c) if:
   (i) A is, whether or not in the course of employment, a provider of care, assistance or services to B in connection with B's mental disorder, and
   (ii) as such, has had or is likely to have regular face-to-face contact with B.

Exceptions: marriage, civil partnership and existing sexual relationships

By SOA 2003, ss 43 and 44, conduct by a person (A) which would otherwise be an offence under ss 38 to 41 against another person (B) is not such an offence if respectively:

(a) B was 16 or over at the time of the conduct and the defendant proves that A and B were lawfully married (or civil partners) at that time; or
(b) the defendant proves that immediately before A became involved in B's care in a way described above, a sexual relationship existed between A and B. This exception does not apply if at that time—ie the 'immediately before' time—sexual intercourse between A and B would have been unlawful, eg because B was under 16.

PREPARATORY OFFENCES

Administering a substance with intent

A person (A) commits an indictable (either way) offence under SOA 2003, s 61(1) if he intentionally administers a substance to, or causes a substance to be taken by, another person (B):

(a) knowing that B does not consent; and
(b) with the intention of stupefying or overpowering B, so as to enable any person to engage in a sexual activity that involves B.

Although the nature of the substance administered is not restricted provided that it is intended to have the specified effect, this offence is aimed at the activity which has become known as 'date rape' which is frequently carried out following the 'spiking' of a drink with a stupefying drug. However, it would also include circumstances where a person's drink was spiked with strong alcohol if that person believed that he or she was drinking a non-alcoholic drink or where a person was given an injection or caused to inhale chloroform. It would not, of course, cover circumstances in which a person was merely encouraged to drink alcoholic drinks where that person was aware that he or she was drinking alcohol.

A need not carry out the act so that *he* may thereby be enabled to engage in sexual activity; it will be sufficient if he does so to enable some other person to so engage in that activity. The nature of the sexual activity envisaged by s 61 would include sexual intercourse, masturbation, oral sex and any other associated activity. It does not matter whether sexual activity actually takes place; it is sufficient that A administered the substance, knowing that there was no consent and with the appropriate intention.

Committing an offence with intent to commit a sexual offence

A person commits an offence under SOA 2003, s 62(1) if he commits any offence with the intention of committing a relevant sexual offence. A 'relevant sexual offence' is any offence under SOA 2003, Part 1 (ss 1 to 79), as described in this chapter and, in terms of child prostitution, prostitution and sex trafficking, Chapter 30, including an offence of aiding, abetting, counselling or procuring such an offence. Generally, an offence under s 62 is an indictable (either way) offence. A person who commits an offence under s 62 by kidnapping or false imprisonment is guilty of a more serious offence triable only on indictment (s 62(1) and (3)).

Trespass with intent to commit a sexual offence

A person commits an indictable (either way) offence under SOA 2003, s 63(1) if:

(a) he is a trespasser on any premises;
(b) he intends to commit a relevant sexual offence (as defined in the last paragraph) on the premises; and
(c) he knows that, or is reckless as to whether, he is a trespasser.

MISCELLANEOUS SEXUAL OFFENCES

All the offences under this heading besides the last are indictable (either way) offences.

Exposure

A person commits an offence under SOA 2003, s 66(1) if:

(a) he intentionally exposes his genitals; and
(b) he intends that someone will see them and be caused alarm or distress.

The indecent exposure of any part of the body in a place to which the public has access though not necessarily as of right, or a place where what is done is capable of public view, can constitute the common law offence of outraging public decency, if it is capable of being seen by at least two people who are actually present (even if they do not actually see it). This offence is rarely charged and should not be invoked in a case covered by s 66 unless there is good reason for doing so.

Voyeurism: observing

A person commits an offence under SOA 2003, s 67(1) if:

(a) for the purpose of obtaining sexual gratification, he observes another person doing a private act; and
(b) he knows that the other person does not consent to being observed for his sexual gratification.

For the purposes of s 67, a person is doing a private act if the person is in a place which, in the circumstances, would reasonably be expected to provide privacy, and:

(a) the person's genitals, buttocks, or breasts are exposed or covered only with underwear;

(b) the person is using a lavatory; or

(c) the person is doing a sexual act of a kind not ordinarily done in public.

The Court of Appeal has held that the reference to breasts in (a) is limited to female breasts. The Court has also held that in the context of communal showers or changing rooms there is no reasonable expectation of privacy from casual observation by other users of the communal showers or changing rooms, whereas there is a reasonable expectation of privacy from being spied on in such places by someone who has drilled a hole in the wall for this purpose. Thus, casual observation of other users of communal showers or changing rooms does not amount to the offence of voyeurism, even if the observer gains sexual gratification from what he sees.

A person commits an offence under SOA 2003, s 67(4) if he instals equipment, or constructs or adapts a structure or part of a structure, with the intention of enabling himself or another person to commit the above offence. 'Structure' includes a tent, vehicle or vessel or other temporary or movable structure.

Voyeurism: operating equipment

A person commits an offence under SOA 2003, s 67(2) if:

(a) he operates equipment with the intention of enabling another person to observe, for the purpose of obtaining sexual gratification, a third person (B) doing a private act (as defined above); and

(b) he knows that B does not consent to his operating equipment with that intention.

'Observation' means any observation, whether direct or by looking at a moving or still image (eg by installing a webcam).

Voyeurism: recording

A person commits an offence under SOA 2003, s 67(3), if:

(a) he records another person (B) doing a private act (as defined above); ·

(b) he does so with the intention that he or a third person will, for the purpose of obtaining sexual gratification, look at a moving or still image of B doing the act; and

(c) he knows that B does not consent to his recording the act with that intention.

Intercourse with an animal

A person commits an offence under SOA 2003, s 69(1) if:

(a) he intentionally performs an act of penetration with his penis;

(b) what is penetrated is the vagina or anus of a living animal; and

(c) he knows that, or is reckless as to whether, that is what is penetrated.

In relation to an animal, references to the vagina or anus include references to any similar part.

A person (A) commits an offence under SOA 2003, 69(2) if:

(a) A intentionally causes, or allows, A's vagina or anus to be penetrated;
(b) the penetration is by the penis of a living animal; and
(c) A knows that, or is reckless as to whether, that is what A is being penetrated by.

Sexual penetration of a corpse

A person commits an offence under SOA 2003, s 70 if:

(a) he intentionally performs an act of penetration with a part of his body or anything else;
(b) what is penetrated is a part of the body of a dead person;
(c) he knows that, or is reckless as to whether, that is what is penetrated;
(d) the penetration is sexual.

Sexual activity in a public lavatory

A person commits an offence under SOA 2003, s 71 if:

(a) he is in a lavatory to which the public or a section of the public has, or is permitted to have access, whether on payment or otherwise;
(b) he intentionally engages in an activity; and
(c) the activity is sexual.

The definition of 'sexual' provided by SOA 2003, s 78 (referred to on p 845) does not apply to this offence. Instead, for the purposes of s 71, an activity is sexual if a reasonable person would, in all the circumstances but regardless of any person's purpose, consider it to be sexual.

This offence is not indictable.

RESTRICTIONS ON EVIDENCE OR QUESTIONS ABOUT COMPLAINANT'S SEXUAL HISTORY

The Youth Justice and Criminal Evidence Act 1999 (YJCEA 1999), s 41 imposes such restrictions where a person is charged with any sexual offence under SOA 2003, Part 1 (ss 1 to 79), ie all the offences discussed so far in this chapter, as well as those under SOA 2003 relating to child prostitution, prostitution and sex trafficking referred to in the next chapter, or aiding, abetting, counselling or procuring the commission of such an offence, conspiracy or attempt to commit such an offence, or encouraging or assisting the commission of such an offence.

YJCEA 1999, s 41 requires that, where someone is charged with a sexual offence then, except with the leave of the court, no evidence may be adduced, and no questions may be asked in cross-examination, by or on behalf of any defendant about the 'sexual behaviour' of the complainant. 'Sexual behaviour' means any sexual behaviour or other sexual experience, whether or not involving any defendant or other persons. The Court of Appeal has held that doing sexual quizzes on the internet amounts to 'sexual behaviour' within this definition.

If the defence wishes to introduce evidence or ask questions about such matters, it must apply to the court for leave to do so. The court will decide the application in private and in the absence of the complainant, after the prosecution has had the chance to oppose the application. The court can only grant leave when two conditions are satisfied.

The first is that a refusal of leave might have the result of rendering unsafe a conclusion of the jury or (as the case may be) of the court on any relevant issue in the case. The second condition is that:

(a) the evidence in question relates to a relevant issue in the case and either:

(i) that issue is not an issue of consent (for example, as the Court of Appeal has held, if the defence is that the defendant *believed* the complainant was consenting, evidence of recent consensual activity between them is admissible in relation to the issue of the defendant's *belief*, but not as to whether the complainant had consented), or

(ii) it is an issue of consent and the complainant's sexual behaviour to which the evidence or question relates is alleged to have occurred at or about the same time as the event which is the subject matter of the charge against the defendant (for example, that the complainant had consented to intercourse with the defendant a couple of hours earlier, but not the fact that the complainant was a prostitute), or

(iii) it is an issue of consent and the complainant's sexual behaviour to which the evidence or question relates is so similar either to any sexual behaviour of the complainant which (according to the defence's version) took place as part of the event which is the subject matter of the charge, or to any other sexual behaviour of the complainant which (according to the defence's version) took place at or about the same time as that event, that the similarity cannot reasonably be explained as a coincidence; or

(b) the evidence or question relates to any evidence adduced by the prosecution about any sexual behaviour of the complainant, and would go no further than necessary to enable the evidence adduced by the prosecution to be rebutted or explained by the defendant.

To be admitted under the above provisions, the evidence must relate to a specific instance, or instances, of sexual behaviour. If the court considers that the purpose (or main purpose) of the evidence which the defence seeks to have admitted is to undermine or diminish the complainant's credibility, it will not allow the evidence to be given.

The House of Lords has held that (a)(iii) above must be construed, like any other statutory provision impinging on a Convention right, so as to give effect to that right so far as is possible. It held, therefore, that under (a)(iii) the test of admissibility was whether the evidence, and questioning relating to it, was so relevant to the issue of consent that to exclude it would endanger the fairness of the trial, contrary to the defendant's right to a fair trial under the European Convention on Human Rights, art 6. If that test was satisfied, the sexual behaviour evidence should not be excluded.

ANONYMITY OF COMPLAINANTS

The Sexual Offences (Amendment) Act 1992 provides for the anonymity of complainants in the case of any offence under the provisions of SOA 2003, Part 1, except ss 64 and 65 (sex with an adult relative), 69 (intercourse with an animal) and 71 (sexual activity in a public lavatory). The same restrictions apply to similar offences against legislation which existed before SOA 2003.

Where an *allegation* is made that one of these offences has been committed against a person, no matter relating to that person may, during that person's lifetime, be included in any publication if it is likely to lead members of the public to identify that person as the person against whom the offence was committed. These matters include particularly (if their inclusion in any publication is likely to have such a result):

(a) the person's name or address;
(b) the identity of any educational establishment attended by the person or of any place of work; and
(c) any still or moving picture of the person.

For the purpose of the anonymity provisions, 'publication' is widely defined. It includes any communication, for example, a radio programme, a film, a written communication, or a speech, addressed to the public at large or a section of the public.

This prohibition ceases to apply once a person has been accused of one of the above offences. Thereafter, a corresponding provision applies whereby, where a person has been accused of one of the above offences, no matter whatsoever (including (a)–(c) above) which is likely to lead to the identification of the complainant may be included in any publication during the complainant's lifetime. Provision is made for this prohibition to be set aside or relaxed on application being made to the trial judge where it is considered necessary to induce persons to come forward as witnesses and that the applicant's defence will be substantially prejudiced if the direction is not given. The judge also has a 'public interest' discretion to set aside the prohibition.

If any matter is published in breach of the above rules, an offence is committed:

(a) in the case of a newspaper or periodical, by any proprietor, editor or publisher of it;
(b) in the case of any other publication, by its publisher; or
(c) in the case of a programme, by any body corporate engaged in providing the service and by anyone involved in the programme corresponding to an editor of a newspaper.

NOTIFICATION REQUIREMENTS

SOA 2003, Part 2 requires a 'relevant offender' (a person subject to the notification requirements under the Act) to make an initial notification to the police of his date of birth, his National Insurance number, his name and home address (and any other name and any other address which he uses), and any other information which has been prescribed. The Sexual Offences Act 2003 (Notification Requirements) (England and Wales) Regulations 2012 prescribe the following additional information:

(a) where a relevant offender resides, or stays for a period of at least 12 hours, at a relevant household (a private place where a child resides or stays), he must notify:
    (i)   the date on which he begins to reside or stay at a relevant household,
    (ii) the address of the relevant household, and
    (iii) where he holds such information, the period or periods for which he intends to reside or stay at the relevant household;
(b) where a relevant offender solely or jointly holds an account with a banking institution (defined as a bank, building society or any other institution providing banking services), a debit card in relation to such an account, a credit card account, or a credit card, he must notify specified details relating to it;
(c) where a relevant offender holds any passport, other identity document or (in a case where he does not hold any passport or other identity document) any other document in which his full name appears, he must notify the number and his full name

as it appears in the document and (except in the case of a passport) describe the document. If he holds a passport the information must be given in relation to it. If he does not, the information must be given in relation to another identity document if he holds one. If he does not, it must be given in relation to any other document.

Notification by the relevant offender must be made within three days of the relevant date and must be made by attending at any prescribed police station in his local police area, and giving an oral notification to any police officer, or to any person authorised for the purpose by the officer in charge of the station. The relevant date is the date of conviction, finding or caution (including, until a day to be appointed, a reprimand or warning) but the three-day period does not include any time when the offender is in custody by a court order or in prison, detained in hospital, or outside the UK. On giving notification, the person may be required by the police officer or authorised person to have his fingerprints and a photograph taken.

After such an original notification, a person subject to the procedure must give notice, within a three-day period of the change, of a new (ie unnotified) name; of a change of home address; of a new (ie unnotified) place of residence in the UK where he has resided for a qualifying period of seven days, or periods amounting to seven days in a 12-month period; of his release from custody, imprisonment or detention in hospital; or of any prescribed change of circumstances. The 2012 Regulations prescribe the following changes of circumstance:

(a) where the relevant offender resides, or stays for a period of at least 12 hours, at a relevant household in relation to which there has been no initial notification, or ceases to reside or stay at a relevant household in relation to which there has been an initial notification, a notification of such a change must disclose the date from which he resides or stays, or the date on which he ceases to reside or stay, at a relevant household;

(b) where the relevant offender's account is opened or closed, a debit or credit card is obtained, no longer held, or has expired and information previously notified by him has altered or become inaccurate or incomplete. A notification of such a change must give the same specified details about the account or card as an initial notification;

(c) where the relevant offender obtains a passport, other identity document or other document in relation to which there has been no initial notification, or ceases to hold a passport, other identity document or other document in relation to which there has been an initial notification.

Although notification is permitted before use of the new name or the change of address, if the change subsequently takes place more than two days before the date notified that notification is invalid. Moreover, if the event to which an advance notification relates has not occurred within three days of the date notified, the offender must within six days of the notified date notify the police that it did not occur within that period.

A person subject to the procedure must notify the police of his intention to leave the UK, and of his return, in accordance with the Sexual Offences Act 2003 (Travel Notification Requirements) Regulations 2004, as amended in 2012.

A person subject to the procedure must also annually re-notify the police of the information required to be given on initial notification. By way of exception, by an amendment in 2012, where the home address initially notified, or notified as a change, was a location where the offender can regularly be found in the absence of his having a fixed abode in the UK, the duty to re-notify is not an annual one but is to re-notify every seven days. Where a person is in custody by a court order, in prison, detained in hospital, or outside the UK at the relevant time, the re-notification period is three days from release, or return to the UK.

The persons subject to the notification requirements under SOA 2003, Part 2 are those convicted of an offence listed in SOA 2003, Sch 3; those found not guilty of such an offence by reason of insanity; those found to be under a disability (ie unfit to plead) and to have done the act charged in respect of the offence; or cautioned (or, until a day to be appointed, reprimanded or warned in the case of a child) in respect of such an offence. Persons previously convicted of offences which made them subject to the Sex Offenders Act 1997, Part 1 remain subject to the notification requirements then imposed, until the completion of the period for which notification was required.

Schedule 3 offences

The schedule includes offences under SOA 2003 of rape, assault by penetration, most sexual assaults, child sex offences, sexual grooming, offences involving an abuse of trust in relation to children, familial child sexual offences, offences against persons with a mental disorder including offences by care workers, paying for the sexual services of a child, causing or inciting child prostitution or pornography, controlling a child prostitute or a child in pornography, arranging or facilitating child prostitution or pornography, administering substances with intent, trespassing with intent to commit a sexual offence, sex with an adult relative, exposure, voyeurism, intercourse with an animal, and sexual penetration with a corpse. In brief, this list includes every offence under SOA 2003, Part 1 (ss 1 to 79) besides those relating to prostitution (other than child prostitution), to trafficking for sex, or to sexual activity in a public lavatory. The listed offences also include offences relating to indecent photographs or pseudo-photographs of children, possession of extreme pornographic images, and possession of prohibited images of children. Encouraging or assisting, attempting, conspiring to commit, and aiding and abetting, such offences are also Sch 3 offences. Reference should be made to the Schedule as the offences often only give rise to the notification requirements in particular circumstances or in the case of particular sentences.

Duration of notification requirement

Relevant offenders sentenced to life imprisonment, or to 30 months' imprisonment or more, or persons sentenced to imprisonment for public protection under the Criminal Justice Act 2003, s 225, or persons admitted to hospital under a restriction order, are indefinitely subject to the notification requirement; offenders sentenced to more than six months but less than 30 months are subject for a period of 10 years; offenders sentenced to less than six months or admitted to a hospital without a restriction order are subject for a period of seven years; and persons of any other description, for a period of five years. However, where the offender is under 18, the periods of 10, seven, and five years are halved. Persons who are cautioned are subject to the requirements for two years (one year in the case of a reprimand or warning to an under-18-year-old). Those who are conditionally discharged are subject to the requirements during the period of conditional discharge.

A divisional court has held that the whole of the term of an extended sentence (ie the aggregate of the appropriate custodial term and the extension period for which the offender is to be subject to a licence) constitutes the term for which a person is 'sentenced to imprisonment' for the purposes of determining the notification period.

In the case of a young offender the court may direct a person with parental responsibility for the offender to comply with the notification requirements until the offender reaches the age of 18 or until an earlier date specified in the order.

In 2010, the Supreme Court held that the indefinite notification requirement without review referred to above was incompatible with the European Convention on Human Rights, art 8 (right to private and family life). To cure this defect, the Sexual Offences Act 2003 (Remedial) Order 2012 provides that a relevant offender who is subject to an indefinite notification requirement, and is not subject to a sexual offences prevention order (or an interim order), may apply in writing to the relevant chief officer of police for the area in which he is residing or staying (according to his latest notification) for a determination that he is no longer subject to the indefinite notification requirements. Such an application for review must be made on or after the qualifying date or, as the case may be, the further qualifying date. Where the qualifying relevant offender was 18 or over when the notification requirement began, the qualifying date is the day after the end of the 15-year period beginning with the day on which the relevant offender gives the first notification after release from prison or other detention in relation to the conviction giving rise to the indefinite requirement. Where he was under 18 when the requirement began, it is the day after the end of the eight-year period beginning with that day. As to the further qualifying date, see below.

For the purposes of the determination of an application for review, the relevant offender must satisfy the chief officer of police that it is not necessary for the purpose of protecting the public or any particular members of the public from sexual harm for him to remain subject to the indefinite notification requirements. In determining an application for review, the chief officer must:

(a) have regard to information (if any) received from a probation body, the Prisons Minister and certain other 'responsible bodies';
(b) consider the risk of sexual harm posed by the qualifying relevant offender and the effect of a continuation of the indefinite notification requirements on him; and
(c) take into account a range of specified matters.

If the chief officer determines that the relevant offender should not remain subject to the indefinite notification requirements, he ceases to be subject to them on the date of receipt of the notice of determination.

If the chief officer determines that the relevant offender should remain subject to the indefinite notification requirements, the notice of the determination must:

(a) contain a statement of reasons for the determination; and
(b) inform the offender that he may appeal within 21 days to a magistrates' court against the determination.

In the event of such a determination, the further qualifying date (ie for another review) will be eight years from the determination, or up to 15 years (as determined by the chief officer) if he considers that the risk of sexual harm posed by the offender is sufficient to justify a continuation of those requirements after the end of the eight-year period beginning with the day on which the determination is made.

Offences relating to notification requirements

It is an indictable (either way) offence under SOA 2003, s 91(1) for a person:

(a) to fail without reasonable excuse to comply with the notification requirements;

(b) to notify to the police, in purported compliance with these requirements, any information which he knows to be false.

The offence of failure to notify is a continuing one so that proceedings may be taken at any time after such a failure. It may be dealt with at any place where the offender resides or where he is found.

PREVENTIVE ORDERS

Notification orders

SOA 2003, s 97 provides that a chief officer of police may apply to a magistrates' court for a civil order (a notification order) in respect of a defendant who resides in his police area, or whom he believes is in, or is intending to come to, his police area, where it appears to him that the following conditions are satisfied with respect to the defendant:

(a) under the law in force in a country outside the UK:
  (i) he has been convicted of a relevant offence (whether or not he has been pun-ished for it),
  (ii) a court exercising jurisdiction under that law has made in respect of a relevant offence a finding equivalent to a finding that he is not guilty by reason of insanity,
  (iii) such a court has made in respect of a relevant offence a finding equivalent to a finding that he is under a disability and did the act charged against him in respect of that offence, or
  (iv) he has been cautioned in respect of the relevant offence;
(b) condition (a) above is met because of a conviction, finding or caution which occurred on or after 1 September 1997 (or although a person was convicted before that date he was dealt with after it) or because, although there was a conviction before that date, the person concerned was detained in the foreign country, or subject to supervision or a community sentence; and
(c) the notification requirement period specified in respect of the relevant offence has not expired.

If it is proved that these conditions exist the court must make a notification order. A 'relevant offence' means an act which constituted an offence under the law in force in the country concerned and would have constituted an offence listed in SOA 2003, Sch 3 if it had been done in any part of the UK.

The effect of a notification order is to subject the defendant to the notification requirements under SOA 2003, Part 2 for a period corresponding to that which would apply if he had been convicted in the UK. The notification period runs from the date of the foreign conviction, etc. The initial notification must be made within three days of the service of the order.

Provision is made for an 'interim notification order' pending determination of an application for a notification order. Where a relevant offence has been committed abroad it may take some time to obtain the necessary documentation to put before the court. A person subject to an interim order is subject to the notification requirements while the order is in force and must make that notification within three days of service of the order.

Sexual offences prevention orders

A sexual offences prevention order (SOPO) prohibits the person concerned from doing any act specified in the order. The order will remain in force for a period specified in the order (not less than five years). A person subject to the order is subject to the notification requirements of SOA 2003, Part 2 for the duration of the order.

On conviction

By SOA 2003, s 104 a SOPO may be made when a court deals with a person convicted in respect of the offences listed in SOA 2003, Sch 3 or Sch 5, or when a court deals with a person after a finding of not guilty by reason of insanity, or a finding of disability and to have done the act charged, in respect of such an offence, if it is *necessary for the purpose of protecting the public or any particular members of it from serious sexual harm from that person* (ie protecting the public in the UK or any particular members of the public from serious physical or psychological harm caused by him committing a Sch 3 offence or offences). Schedule 3 offences have been described above, but it should be noted that any restrictions referred to in Sch 3 in terms of particular circumstances or penalties do not apply where a Sch 3 offence is in issue for the purpose of a SOPO. Schedule 5 offences include offences relating to child abuse, to adult prostitution, to trafficking for sex, and to outraging public decency, as well as murder and other offences of serious violence, harassment, and stalking.

On application

SOPOs may also be made under s 104 in civil proceedings in magistrates' courts on application by the chief officer of police for the police area. If, on a police application, it is proved that the defendant is a qualifying offender, the magistrates' court may make an order in respect of him if satisfied that his behaviour since the 'appropriate date' makes it *necessary to make such an order, for the purpose of protecting the public or any particular members of the public from serious sexual harm from him* (as defined in the preceding paragraph). The Administrative Court has held that whether his behaviour was as alleged by the applicant must be proved beyond reasonable doubt; on the other hand, whether it is necessary to make an order does not involve a standard of proof, since it involves an exercise of judgment. As the proceedings are civil, the rules of the civil law of evidence apply (see p 745).

A person is a qualifying offender if he has:

(a) been convicted of a Sch 3 or 5 offence;
(b) been found not guilty of such an offence by reason of insanity, or to be under a disability and to have done the act charged against him in respect of such an offence; or
(c) in England and Wales or Northern Ireland, been cautioned, reprimanded or warned in respect of such an offence.

A person is also a qualifying offender if, under the law of a country outside the UK:

(a) he has been convicted of a relevant offence;
(b) a foreign court has made, in respect of a relevant offence, a finding equivalent to a finding of not guilty by reason of insanity, or a finding that he is under a disability and did the act charged against him in respect of such an offence; or
(c) he has been cautioned in respect of a relevant offence.

A 'relevant' offence means an act which constituted an offence under the law of the country concerned, *and would have constituted a Sch 3 or 5 offence if it had been done in any part of the UK.*

The 'appropriate date', in relation to a qualifying offender, means the date (or first date) on which he was convicted, found or cautioned as mentioned above.

A SOPO may be varied or discharged but it may not be discharged without the consent of both parties before the end of a period of five years.

Interim SOPOs may also be obtained in appropriate circumstances in civil proceedings in a magistrates' court pending determination of an application.

Breach

Breach of a SOPO or interim SOPO without reasonable excuse is an indictable (either way) offence under SOA 2003, s 113(1). In this offence, and those which follow in this chapter, the defendant only has an evidential burden in respect of the defence of reasonable excuse.

Foreign travel orders

SOA 2003, ss 114 to 122 make provision for the foreign travel order, a civil order which enables a court to prohibit for a period not exceeding five years persons who are 'qualifying offenders' (generally persons convicted of sexual offences against children under 18 either in this country or abroad) from travelling abroad, where it is considered necessary to do so to protect children under 18 from serious sexual harm outside the UK. The order may be made by a magistrates' court on the application of a chief officer of police and it may refer to a named country or countries outside the UK, or it may prohibit travel to any country outside the UK other than a named one, or to any country outside the UK. A person becomes a 'qualifying offender' if he is convicted of a relevant sexual offence in respect of a child under 18 or a corresponding foreign offence (or there is a 'finding' or 'caution' in this respect). It does not matter when such a person was dealt with for the relevant offence. It is an indictable (either way) offence under s 122(1) to breach without reasonable excuse any prohibition contained in such an order. An order may be varied or discharged.

Section 117A provides that, where a foreign travel order prohibits foreign travel to any country outside the UK, it must require the surrender of the defendant's passport(s) or travel authorisation at a police station on or before the date when the prohibition takes effect, or within a specified period; failure without reasonable excuse to comply with this requirement is an indictable (either way) offence under s 122(1A).

Risk of sexual harm orders

SOA 2003, s 123 makes provision for another type of civil order, the risk of sexual harm order, which enables a court to prohibit a defendant aged 18 or over from doing anything described in the order for a fixed period (not less than two years) specified in the order or until further order. Such an order may only be made where:

(a) the defendant has on at least two occasions done an act of the following types:
  (i) engaging in sexual activity involving a child under 16 or in the presence of such a child,
  (ii) causing or inciting such a child to watch a person engaging in sexual activity or to look at a moving or still image that is sexual,
  (iii) giving such a child anything that relates to sexual activity or contains a reference to such an activity (eg giving a child a condom or a pornographic DVD), or

    (iv) communicating with such a child, where any part of the communication is sexual; and

(b) as a result, there is reasonable cause to believe that it is necessary for such an order to be made for the protection of children (or any child) under 16 from harm from the defendant.

A divisional court has held that condition (a) must be proved beyond reasonable doubt.

The order may be made by a magistrates' court on the application of a chief officer of police.

A risk of sexual harm order may be varied or discharged but it may not be discharged without the consent of both parties before the end of a period of two years.

Interim orders may also be obtained in appropriate circumstances in civil proceedings in a magistrates' court.

Breach of an order or interim order without reasonable excuse is an indictable (either way) offence under SOA 2003, s 128(1).

CHAPTER 30

Offences Relating to Prostitution, Obscenity, and Indecent Photographs

PROSTITUTION

Prostitute

Various statutes deal with prostitutes. Except in the case of the Sexual Offences Act 2003 (SOA 2003), they do not define that term.

For the purpose of statutes other than SOA 2003, reference must therefore be made to case law for the definition of 'prostitute'. This establishes that a *prostitute* is a woman (or a man) who offers her (or his) body commonly for sexual intercourse or acts of a sexual nature, in return for payment, and it has been held by the Court of Appeal that it is immaterial that the woman (or man) is dishonest and intends simply to pocket advance payment and not to provide sexual services. The reference to other acts of a sexual nature extends the definition of 'prostitute'. Masseuses, for example, who carry out acts of masturbation on request are engaging in such acts. So are women who engage in sado-masochistic sessions for the sexual pleasure of their partner. Since sexual intercourse is not required, even a virgin can be a prostitute. If a person offers intercourse for payment regularly to one person, the offeror is not a prostitute as services are restricted to one person. If the offer is made to a number of persons because of the promiscuous nature of the offeror and no payment is required for the services, that person is not a prostitute as no payment is received in return.

For the purposes of SOA 2003, 'prostitute' is defined as a person (A) who, on at least one occasion and whether or not compelled to do so, offers or provides sexual services to another person in return for payment or a promise of payment to A or a third person; 'prostitution' in SOA 2003 is interpreted accordingly. 'Payment' for the purposes of SOA 2003 means any financial advantage, including the discharge of an obligation to pay or the provision of goods or services (including sexual services) gratuitously or at a discount. Thus, any form of financial arrangement will be classified as payment. The settlement of a debt by the provision of sexual services, or the supply of drugs, or their provision at a discounted price will be sufficient. There is no doubt that a similar approach will be followed in relation to other statutes.

It is not an offence in itself to be a prostitute, but there are a number of offences which can only be committed by, or in respect of, prostitutes.

Persistent loitering or soliciting by a prostitute

The Street Offences Act 1959 (StOA 1959), s 1(1) creates the offence committed by a prostitute (whether male or female) who persistently loiters or solicits in a street or public place for the purposes of prostitution.

Persistently loitering or soliciting for the purposes of prostitution

For these purposes, conduct is persistent if it takes place on two or more occasions in any period of three months.

Loitering by a prostitute does not need to be for the purpose of making approaches to others; it is sufficient that there is loitering for the purpose of being approached by others. Many streets are noted as the haunts of prostitutes and people go there to look for them. The prostitutes are loitering for such a purpose. In the same way a prostitute may loiter in a slowly moving vehicle but it must be shown that the purpose was to solicit others, or to be solicited by them.

Soliciting need not be by words and can be carried out by all of the accepted forms of non-verbal communication. Movements of the body, arms, hands, as well as facial expressions and gestures can be equally compelling forms of solicitation. A deaf and dumb prostitute solicited by making grunting noises accompanied by a gesture with a folded right arm, being bent and straightened. The meaning was never in doubt! Tapping on window panes, leaning out of windows with signals to indicate price, signalling the position of the entry door with the fingers are all forms of solicitation. The test to be applied should be, 'Is it clear to the reasonable man that he is being offered sex for money?'

Street or public place

'Street' for the purpose of StOA 1959 includes any bridge, road, lane, footway, subway, square, court, alley or passage, whether a thoroughfare or not, which is for the time being open to the public. In addition, the doorways and entrances to premises abutting on a street and the ground adjoining and open to a street are treated as forming part of the street.

The definition is quite wide; in effect, it prohibits loitering or soliciting by prostitutes in places which are upon private property if they are open to a street, and the courts have interpreted the legislation in this way. For example, prostitutes who solicited from balconies or from behind windows have been convicted of this offence.

The term 'public place' is not defined but generally the courts have accepted that a public place is one where the public go, no matter whether they have a right to go or not. What is a public place may vary from time to time; the question is whether the place was public at the material time. The point has not been tested whether places such as public houses, restaurants, dance halls or similar places can be public places for the purpose of the Act.

Child prostitutes

Although those under 18 who engage in prostitution are subject to StOA 1959, a Home Office Circular issued in 2000 states that they are almost invariably victims and should be treated as such. Criminal justice action should only be taken against them (as opposed to those who abuse them or seek to exploit them) if all the relevant local agencies are satisfied that the child is involved in prostitution of his or her own free will, and attempts to divert the child out of prostitution have failed.

Orders requiring attendance at meetings

Such orders may be made under the StOA 1959, ss 1(2A)–(2D), 1A and Sch. Under these provisions, the court may deal with a person convicted of an offence of loitering or soliciting for the purposes of prostitution, contrary to the StOA 1959, s 1, by making an order requiring the offender to attend three meetings with the person for the time being specified in the order ('the supervisor') or with such other person as the supervisor may direct. If the court makes such an order it may not impose any other penalty in respect of the offence.

Failure to comply with such an order without reasonable excuse can result in a magistrates' court revoking the order and dealing with the offender, for the offence in respect of which the order was made, in any way in which the court could deal with the offender if the offender had just been convicted by it of the offence.

Soliciting to obtain a prostitute's sexual services

Under SOA 2003, s 51A(1), it is an offence for a person in a street (as defined by the StOA 1959) or public place to solicit another (B) for the purpose of obtaining B's sexual services as a prostitute. The reference to a person in a street or public place includes a person in a vehicle in a street or public place.

Placing of advertisements relating to prostitution

The Criminal Justice and Police Act 2001 (CJPA 2001), s 46(1) creates an offence of placing on, or in the immediate vicinity of, a public telephone, an advertisement relating to prostitution, with intent that the advertisement should come to the attention of any other person. An advertisement is covered by s 46 if it is for the services of a prostitute, whether male or female, or indicates that premises are premises in which such services are offered. Any advertisement which a reasonable person would consider to be an advertisement relating to prostitution is presumed to be so, unless shown not to be.

For the purposes of this section 'public telephone' means any telephone which is located in a public place for use by the public (or a section of the public) together with any structure in which it is housed. A 'public place' means any place to which the public have, or are permitted to have, access, whether on payment or otherwise, other than (a) any place to which children under the age of 16 are not permitted to have access, whether by law or otherwise, and (b) any premises which are wholly or mainly used for residential purposes.

CJPA 2001, s 47 permits the Secretary of State by order to extend these provisions to any public structure specified in the order.

Exploitation of prostitution

The offences under this heading are indictable (either way) offences.

SOA 2003, s 52(1) provides that it is an offence for a person intentionally to cause or incite another person to become a prostitute in any part of the world if he does so for or in the expectation of gain for himself or for a third person. Section 53(1) makes it an offence for a person intentionally to control any of the activities of another person relating to that person's prostitution in any part of the world for or in the expectation of gain for himself or a third person. 'Control' is not limited to conduct which forces another to carry out the relevant activity; it can be exercised in various ways. It is enough if a defendant instructed or directed a prostitute to carry out the relevant activity or do it in a particular way.

For the purposes of these offences the term 'gain' means:

(a) any financial advantage, including the discharge of an obligation to pay or the provision of goods or services (including sexual services) gratuitously or at a discount; or
(b) the goodwill of any person which is or appears likely, in time, to bring financial advantage.

The definition of 'gain' makes it clear that there is no requirement that money is intended to change hands from the prostitute to the defendant. It may be that the defendant wants no more than an occasional 'freebee' for himself or another, or intends that the prostitute should pay for his drug habit out of her earnings.

These sections are not specifically aimed at protecting persons aged 18 or over, but SOA 2003, ss 47 to 50 (pp 884–5) specifically protect those under 18.

Paying for sexual services of a prostitute subjected to force, etc

By SOA 2003, s 53A, a person (A) commits an offence if:

(a) A makes or promises payment for the sexual services of a prostitute (B),
(b) a third person (C) has engaged in exploitative conduct of a kind likely to induce or encourage B to provide the sexual services for which A has made or promised payment, and
(c) C engaged in that conduct for or in the expectation of gain for C or another person (apart from A or B).

It is irrelevant where in the world the sexual services are to be provided or whether those services are provided. It is also irrelevant whether A is, or ought to be, aware that C has engaged in exploitative conduct.

For the purposes of s 53A:

(a) C engages in exploitative conduct if C uses force, threats (whether or not relating to violence) or any other form of coercion, or C practises any form of deception;
(b) 'payment' has the meaning given on p 879; and
(c) 'gain' has the same meaning as in ss 52 and 53 (see p 881).

Trafficking for sexual exploitation

SOA 2003, ss 57 to 59 deal with this. Offences under these sections are indictable (either way) offences. Section 57 explicitly deals with those involved in 'trafficking' a person into the UK for the purpose of sexual activities. It is an offence for a person intentionally to arrange or facilitate the arrival in, or the entry into, the UK of another person (B), either intending to do anything to or in respect of B, after B's arrival, but in any part of the world, which, if done, will amount to a relevant offence, or believing that another person will do something to or in relation to B, after B's arrival but in any part of the world, which if done will amount to a relevant offence. A 'relevant offence' is:

(a) an offence under SOA 2003, Part 1 (ss 1 to 79) (see Chapter 29 and parts of this chapter) or a corresponding Northern Irish offence; or
(b) an offence under the Protection of Children Act 1978, s 1(1)(a) (below) or the corresponding Northern Irish offence; or
(c) activity outside England, Wales, or Northern Ireland which would be an offence under (a) or (b) if done in England, Wales or Northern Ireland.

Section 58 makes similar provision to deal with trafficking within the UK; and s 59 with trafficking out of the UK.

As from a day to be appointed, SOA 2003, ss 57 to 59 are substituted by SOA 2003, s 59A. Section 59A(1) provides that a person (A) commits an indictable (either way) offence if A intentionally arranges or facilitates:

(a) the arrival in, or entry into, the UK *or another country or territory* or other part of the world of another person (B),
(b) the travel of B within the UK *or another country etc*, or
(c) the departure of B from the UK *or another country etc*,

with a view to the sexual exploitation of B.

For the purposes of s 59(A)(1)(a) and (c) A's arranging or facilitating is with a view to the sexual exploitation of B if, and only if:

(a) A intends to do anything to or in respect of B, after B's arrival, entry or (as the case may be) departure but in any part of the world, which if done will involve the commission of a 'relevant offence', or
(b) A believes that another person is likely to do something to or in respect of B, after B's arrival, entry or (as the case may be) departure but in any part of the world, which if done will involve the commission of a 'relevant offence'.

For the purposes of s 59A(1)(b), A's arranging or facilitating is with a view to the sexual exploitation of B if, and only if:

(a) A intends to do anything to or in respect of B, during or after the journey and in any part of the world, which if done will involve the commission of a 'relevant offence', or
(b) A believes that another person is likely to do something to or in respect of B, during or after the journey and in any part of the world, which if done will involve the commission of a 'relevant offence'.

'Relevant offence' means:

(a) any offence under the law of England and Wales which is an offence under SOA 2003, Part 1 (ss 1 to 79) or under the Protection of Children Act 1978, s 1(1)(a), or
(b) anything done outside England and Wales which is not an offence within (a) but would be if done in England and Wales.

Police powers

SOA 2003, s 60B provides that if a person has been arrested for an offence under SOA 2003, ss 57 to 59 (prospectively replaced by s 59A), a constable or a senior immigration officer may detain a relevant vehicle, ship or aircraft:

(a) until a decision is taken as to whether or not to charge the arrested person with that offence;
(b) if the arrested person has been charged, until he is acquitted, the charge against him is dismissed or the proceedings are discontinued; or
(c) if he has been charged and convicted, until the court decides whether or not to order forfeiture of the vehicle, ship or aircraft.

A vehicle, ship or aircraft is a relevant vehicle, ship or aircraft in relation to an arrested person if it is a land vehicle, ship or aircraft which the constable or officer concerned has reasonable grounds for believing could, on conviction of the arrested person for the offence for which he was arrested, be the subject of an order for forfeiture made by a court under s 60A.

A person (other than the arrested person) may apply to the court hearing proceedings against the arrested person (or if proceedings have not commenced, a magistrates' court) for the release of a land vehicle, ship or aircraft on the grounds that:

(a) he owns the vehicle, ship or aircraft;
(b) he was, immediately before the detention of the vehicle, ship or aircraft, in possession of it under a hire-purchase agreement; or
(c) he is a charterer of the ship or aircraft.

Involvement of children in prostitution and pornography

All the offences under this heading are indictable (either way) offences, besides that under s 47(1) and (3) (which is triable only on indictment).

Paying for the sexual services of a child

SOA 2003, s 47(1) makes it an offence for a person (A) intentionally to obtain for himself the sexual services of another person (B) under 18 where, in advance, such services have been paid for or where payment has been promised.

A more serious offence is committed under s 47(1) and (4) if B is under 16.

An even more serious offence is committed under s 47(1) and (3) if B is under 13 and the offence involved:

(a) penetration of B's anus or vagina with a part of A's body or anything else,
(b) penetration of B's mouth with A's penis,
(c) penetration of A's anus or vagina with a part of B's body or by B with anything else, or
(d) penetration of A's mouth with B's penis.

The payment or promise may be made to B or to someone else. Where B is under 13 an offence will be committed regardless of any belief which A might have concerning age. However, where B is 13 or over A is only guilty if he did not reasonably believe that the victim was 18 or over; it will be for the prosecution to prove that such a belief did not exist.

A person is involved in pornography for the purposes of ss 48, 49, and 50 (below) if an indecent image of that person is recorded.

Causing or inciting child prostitution or pornography

SOA 2003, s 48(1) makes it an offence for a person (A) intentionally to cause or incite another person (B) under 18 to become a prostitute or to be involved in pornography in any part of the world. Where B is under 13, it is irrelevant what belief A (however reasonably) might have had as to B's age. If B was 13 or over, the prosecution must prove that A did not reasonably believe that the B was under 18. This offence will be committed by those who recruit young persons into prostitution or pornography. It would be sufficient if a man caused his 17-year-old girlfriend to offer her services to others, either as a prostitute or as an actor in a pornographic film, so that they could afford a holiday. Section 48 provides that the acts concerned can be intended to take place anywhere in the world; the offence lies in 'recruitment' for such purposes. Section 48 does not require proof that A acted for gain. Nor do ss 49 and 50 below.

Controlling a child prostitute or a child in pornography

SOA 2003, s 49(1) makes it an offence if a person (A) intentionally controls any of the activities of another person (B) relating to B's prostitution or B's involvement in pornography in any part of the world, and either B is under 18 and A does not reasonably believe that B is 18 or over, or B is under 13. As to 'control' see p 881.

Arranging or facilitating child prostitution or pornography

SOA 2003, s 50(1) makes it an offence for a person (A) intentionally to arrange or facilitate the prostitution or involvement in pornography in any part of the world of another person (B), where either B is under 18 and A does not reasonably believe that B is 18 or over, or B is under 13.

This offence is intended to punish those who are involved in child prostitution and pornography in other ways. It will cover those who 'convey' young persons to places or premises where such activities are intended to take place and those who merely make the administrative arrangements for such activities.

CLOSURE ORDERS

SOA 2003, Part 2A gives the courts the power to make premises closure orders where there is evidence of the premises being used for activities relating to certain prostitution and pornography offences.

Issue of closure notice

This is dealt with by SOA 2003, s 136B. A superintendent (or above) ('the authorising officer') may authorise the issue of a closure notice in respect of any premises if three conditions are met:

(a) that the officer has reasonable grounds for believing that, within the previous three months
   (i) the premises were used for activities related to one or more specified prostitution offences, unless only one person obtained all of the sexual services in question (whether or not on a single occasion), or
   (ii) the premises were used for activities related to one or more specified pornography offences, or both;
(b) that the officer has reasonable grounds for believing that the making of a closure order under SOA 2003, s 136D is necessary to prevent the premises being used for activities related to one or more specified prostitution or pornography offences;
(c) that the officer is satisfied:
   (i) that the local authority for the area has been consulted, and
   (ii) that reasonable steps have been taken to establish the identity of any person who resides on the premises or who has control of or responsibility for or an interest in the premises.

Such an authorisation may be given orally or in writing, but if it is given orally the authorising officer must confirm it in writing as soon as it is practicable. The issue of a closure notice may be authorised whether or not a person has been convicted of any specified prostitution or pornography offence that the authorising officer believes has been committed.

'Specified prostitution offence' means an offence under SOA 2003, s 47, 52, or 53, or (if committed in relation to a child prostitute/prostitution) ss 48, 49, or 50; and 'specified pornography offence' means an offence under ss 48, 49, or 50 (if, in each case, committed in relation to child pornography). The reference to any such offence includes a reference to the corresponding offence under service law.

The closure notice must give appropriate details and state when and where an application for a magistrates' closure order will be considered.

Such a notice must be served by a constable. When it is served (by fixing notices to the building and serving copies upon relevant persons) it closes the premises to members of the public except the owner or those who habitually reside there, until such time as a magistrates' court decides in civil proceedings whether to issue a closure order.

By s 136G(1) and (3), a person who remains on or enters premises in contravention of a closure notice commits an offence unless he has a reasonable excuse for remaining on or entering the premises.

Closure orders

The rules relating to the making of a closure order are laid down by ss 136D and 136E. If a closure notice has been issued, a constable must apply to a magistrates' court for a closure order. A closure order is an order that the premises in respect of which the order is made are closed to all persons for such period not exceeding three months as is specified in the order. A closure order may be made in respect of the whole or any part of the premises in respect of which the closure notice was issued. The application must be heard by the magistrates' court not later than 48 hours after the notice was served, subject to the justices' power to adjourn the hearing for up to 14 days in specified circumstances.

The magistrates' court may make a closure order if it is satisfied on the balance of probabilities that three conditions are met:

(a) that, during the relevant period (three months ending with the day on which the issue of the closure notice was authorised):
  (i) the premises were used for activities related to one or more specified prostitution offences (but this provision does not apply if only one person obtained all of the sexual services in question (whether or not on a single occasion)); or
  (ii) the premises were used for activities related to one or more specified pornography offences,
  or both;
(b) that the making of the closure order is necessary to prevent the premises being used for activities related to one or more specified prostitution or pornography offences during the period to be specified in the order;
(c) that:
  (i) before the issue of the closure notice was authorised, reasonable steps were taken to establish the identity of any person who resides on the premises or who has control of or responsibility for or an interest in the premises; and
  (ii) a constable gave a copy of the closure notice to the persons so identified.

A magistrates' court is much more likely to be so satisfied where the application is supported by direct evidence of witnesses available for cross-examination and, where there is hearsay evidence, if what is served and adduced is first-hand and complete. As the proceedings are civil in nature, the civil law of evidence applies, as to which see pp 745 and 912.

By s 136G(2) and (3), a person who remains on or enters premises in contravention of a closure order commits an offence unless he has a reasonable excuse for remaining on or entering the premises.

Securing premises

By s 136F, a constable or an authorised person may enter the premises in respect of which a closure order is made and do anything reasonably necessary to secure the premises against entry by any person. An 'authorised person' means a person authorised by the relevant chief officer of police.

A constable or an authorised person acting under the above power may use reasonable force.

A person who obstructs a constable or authorised person acting under the above power commits an offence under s 136G(4).

OFFENCES RELATING TO BROTHELS

Keeping a brothel

By the Sexual Offences Act 1956 (SOA 1956), s 33, it is an offence for a person to keep a brothel, or to manage it, or to act or assist in its management. Premises are a brothel if they are used by persons for illicit heterosexual or homosexual intercourse or other indecent behaviour. It is not necessary to show that some of the people resorting to the premises are prostitutes or that they received payment for their services, but there must be at least three people who use the premises in this way. It does not matter that one of them is the occupier, and it does not matter that only two people at a time ever use the premises for sexual activities.

Keeping a brothel for prostitution

By SOA 1956, s 33A(1), it is an indictable (either way) offence for a person to keep, or to manage, or to act or assist in the management of, a brothel *to which people resort for practices involving prostitution* (whether or not also for other practices).

If separate and self-contained flats are separately let, each to one prostitute, it is likely that the building in its entirety will not be classed as a brothel as there is only one prostitute in each of the flats. However, if single rooms are let to prostitutes in one building, it may be sufficient if the rooms are sufficiently close to constitute what might be described as a nest of prostitutes.

In considering the charges to be preferred when it is established that a building is a brothel used for prostitution, we must look at the offence created by SOA 1956, s 33A. The keeper of the premises, who is most likely to be the residential landlord, a manager, who looks after the maintenance and day-to-day needs of the building and its tenants, the 'madame' of the trade and those who act or assist in the management of the brothel are all guilty of offences. 'Assisting in the management of a brothel' covers any conduct which contributes to the management of the brothel. Assistance in the management of a brothel does not require proof that the person actively exercised some control over the brothel or carried out some specific act of management. A person who takes advertisements to a post office and pays for them assists in the management of the brothel. So does a person who discusses with a potential customer the nature of the sexual activities on offer, or who negotiates the price. On the other hand, it has been held that a cleaner at a brothel does not assist in its management.

Related offences

SOA 1956, ss 34, 35(1) and 36 go further and add offences to cover other possibilities in relation to responsibility for the brothel. First, a lessor or landlord of premises (or his agent) who has knowledge of their intended or actual use as a brothel is guilty of an offence (s 34). In addition, the tenant or occupier, or person in charge, of premises who knowingly permits the whole or part of them to be so used is also guilty of an offence (s 35). Lastly, by s 36, it is an offence for the tenant or occupier of any premises knowingly to permit the whole or part of the premises to be used for the purposes of habitual prostitution (whether any prostitute involved is male or female). It will frequently be found that the same person might fit more than one description. For example, the occupier may frequently be the man whom you would consider to be the keeper of the brothel and it is of advantage to consider all possibilities.

OBSCENE PUBLICATIONS

These are governed in general by the Obscene Publications Act 1959 (OPA 1959).

Under OPA 1959, s 2 an indictable (either way) offence is committed by a person who:

(a) publishes an obscene article, whether for gain or not; or
(b) has an obscene article for publication for gain, whether for himself or another.

Writing or otherwise creating an obscene article is not an offence under OPA 1959, nor is simply possessing it or possessing it to give as a gift.

Obscene publication via a broadcast or cable service is a rather specialised type of obscene publication, and is not dealt with further in this book.

What is an 'obscene article'?

An 'article' for present purposes means any article containing or embodying matter to be read or looked at or both, any sound record, and any film or other record of a picture or pictures (such as a photograph, video cassette or computer disk). OPA 1959 also applies to things like negatives from which an article may be reproduced or manufactured.

An article is deemed to be obscene if its effect, or (where the article comprises two or more distinct items) the effect of any of its items is, taken as a whole, such as to tend to deprave and corrupt a significant proportion of persons who are likely, having regard to all the circumstances, to read, see or hear the matter contained in it.

Though a novel may be considered as a whole, a magazine must be considered item by item and, if any one of the items is obscene, this suffices. 'Deprave and corrupt' are strong words; to lead morally astray is not necessarily to deprave and corrupt. Obscenity is not confined to that which has a tendency to corrupt sexual morals; a book depicting the career of a drug addict has been held to be obscene because of its likely effect. On occasions, articles may be directed at persons who may already be considered to have become depraved and corrupted but this might still amount to an offence if the object is to maintain that state of depravity and corruption and to prevent escape from it. Whether an article is obscene because it is likely to deprave and corrupt is essentially a matter for the jury or magistrates. They are as able as anyone to decide the effect upon people, whilst keeping in mind the current standards of ordinary, decent people.

Police officers should take cognisance of current trends in society in coming to a decision regarding the effect of such articles; the reader, viewer or listener must also be considered. If the article is liable to deprave and corrupt a significant proportion of those likely to read etc it is obscene for the purposes of the Act. It would probably be insufficient if it was likely to affect only a few who were not representative of the 'ordinary man'.

Publication, etc

To 'publish' means to distribute, circulate, sell, let on hire, give, or lend, or to offer it for sale or hire. 'Publishing' also includes 'making available', as where X gives Y a key to a library containing obscene articles. Additionally, in the case of a record, a film, etc 'publish' includes showing, playing, or projecting it. A person who enables another to access electronically stored obscene matter on a computer 'shows' the other that matter, and therefore 'publishes' it. Where the matter is data stored electronically, a person publishes it if he transmits that data.

As implied above, there can be a publication for the purposes of OPA 1959 even if the obscene material has been communicated only to one person.

Defences

Under OPA 1959, s 2(5), it is a defence for a person to prove he had not examined the article and had no reasonable cause to suspect that it was such that his publication of it, or possession, as the case may be, would make him liable under OPA 1959. He must prove both points. If he has examined it, it is no defence to allege that he had not realised its nature.

Section 4 provides a defence of 'public good'. If it is proved that publication was justified as being for the public good on the grounds that it is in the interests of science, literature, art or learning, or of other objects of general concern, a person must not be convicted of the above offences. Expert evidence may be given to establish or negative such a defence.

Police powers

By OPA 1959, s 3, if an information on oath is laid before a justice that there are reasonable grounds for suspecting that obscene articles are kept on any premises, stall or vehicle for publication for gain, he may issue a warrant authorising a constable to search for and seize any articles which he has reason to believe to be obscene and to be kept for publication for gain. The additional powers of seizure provided by the Criminal Justice and Police Act 2001, s 50 apply where such a search warrant is executed. If the justice considers that any articles seized are obscene the justice may issue a summons to the occupier of the premises, etc to appear before a magistrates' court and show cause why the articles should not be forfeited. If the court is satisfied that the articles seized are obscene and kept for publication for gain, it must order their forfeiture.

INDECENT PHOTOGRAPHS OR PSEUDO-PHOTOGRAPHS OF CHILDREN

The Protection of Children Act 1978 (PCA 1978), s 1 and the Criminal Justice Act 1988 (CJA 1988), s 160 provide a range of indictable (either way) offences relating to such photographs or pseudo-photographs.

General definitions

Photographs or pseudo-photographs

References in the offences to an indecent photograph include an indecent film, a copy of an indecent photograph or film, and an indecent photograph comprised in a film. References to photographs also include the negative as well as the positive version, and data stored on a computer disk or by other electronic means which is capable of conversion into a photograph. References to a photograph also include (a) a tracing or other image whether made by electronic or other means (of whatever nature) which is not itself a photograph or pseudo-photograph, but which is derived from the whole or part of a photograph or pseudo-photograph (or a combination of either or both); and (b) data stored on a computer disk or by other electronic means which is capable of conversion into an image within (a). Such items could be described as 'derivative photographs'. Such derivatives will include line-traced and computer-traced images such as might be taken on a mobile telephone.

A 'pseudo-photograph' is an image, whether made by computer graphics or otherwise howsoever, which appears to be a photograph. The term includes:

(a) a copy of an indecent pseudo-photograph; and
(b) data stored on a computer disk or by other electronic means which is capable of conversion into an indecent pseudo-photograph.

An exhibit obviously consisting of parts of two different photographs taped together cannot be said to 'appear to be a photograph' and is therefore not a pseudo-photograph, although, if it was itself photocopied, it could be.

Indecent

The term 'indecent' is an objective one. The test is whether the image was indecent according to recognised standards of propriety, as judged by the ordinary person. A photograph or pseudo-photograph can be indecent even though it is not obscene. The child's age (or in the case of a pseudo-photograph apparent age) is a relevant factor as to whether or not the photograph or pseudo-photograph is indecent, but the circumstances in which it was taken or made, or the motivation of the photographer (or the maker of a pseudo-photograph), is not. Something abstracted from a decent set of images is capable of being indecent if the abstracted matter satisfies the test of indecency. This was held by the Court of Appeal in a case where a man copied a television programme of a medical examination of the genitals of a naked boy and subsequently removed the commentary and slowed down the filming of the manipulation of the penis. The Court of Appeal held that the jury were entitled to look at the images independently of the original decent television programme in order to decide whether they were indecent.

Child

A photograph or pseudo-photograph must be of a child. In the case of a photograph, a child is someone under 18. A person in a photograph is taken to have been a child at the material time if it appears from the evidence as a whole that he was then under 18. It is for a jury or magistrates to decide whether an unknown person in an indecent photograph was under 18 without the assistance of expert evidence. Since a pseudo-photograph will not be an image of a real person with a real age, it is provided that, if the impression conveyed by the pseudo-photograph is that the person shown is a child under 18, the pseudo-photograph is to be treated for all purposes as showing such a child, and so is a pseudo-photograph where the predominant impression conveyed is that the person shown is a child under 18 notwithstanding that some of the physical characteristics shown are those of an adult.

Taking or making

PCA 1978, s 1(1)(a) provides that, subject to ss 1A and 1B, it is an offence for a person to take, or permit to be taken, or to make any indecent photograph or pseudo-photograph of a child.

A person who deliberately downloads an indecent image of a child from a web page on to a computer screen 'makes' a photograph or pseudo-photograph. If he does this knowing that the image was, or was likely to be, an indecent photograph or pseudo-photograph of a child, he commits an offence. It is irrelevant whether or not his motive is sexual gratification.

Even if the images originated outside England and Wales, the downloading or printing of them in England and Wales creates new material which has been *made* inside England and Wales.

Defences

PCA 1978, s 1A provides a defence (to a charge of *taking or making an indecent photograph or pseudo-photograph*) of consent by the child or reasonable belief in consent. It states that, where in such proceedings, the defendant (D) proves that the photograph or pseudo-photograph was of the child *aged 16 or over*, and that at the time of the offence charged the child and he were married or civil partners of each other, or lived together as partners in an enduring family relationship, and sufficient evidence is adduced to raise an issue as to whether the child consented to the photograph or pseudo-photograph being taken or made, or as to whether D reasonably believed that the child so consented, D is not guilty of the offence unless it is proved that the child did not so consent and that D did not reasonably believe that the child so consented. This defence applies whether the photograph or pseudo-photograph showed the child alone or with D, but not if it showed any other person.

In addition, s 1B provides that in respect of a charge of *making an indecent photograph or pseudo-photograph*, for example downloading of an image from the internet, or copying a photograph from a computer hard drive, a person will not be guilty of an offence if he proves that it was done for the purpose of the prevention, detection or investigation of crime, or for the purpose of criminal proceedings. A similar defence also applies to a member of the Security Service, the Secret Intelligence Service or GCHQ who is able to prove that it was necessary to make the photograph or pseudo-photograph for the exercise of any functions of that Service or GCHQ.

Distributing or showing or possession with a view to distribution or showing

By PCA 1978, s 1(1)(b) it is an offence to distribute or show indecent photographs or pseudo-photographs of a child. Section 1(1)(c) provides that it is an offence for a person to have in his possession such a photograph or pseudo-photograph with a view to its distribution or showing by himself or others.

'Showing' includes 'making available', as where a person gives another a key to a cupboard containing indecent photographs. The same would be so where a person makes available a password which enables someone to download a 'photograph' stored on a computer to his own computer. For an offence of 'possession with intent to show' to be committed under s 1(1)(c), a person must be in possession with a view to showing the indecent photographs to a third party; it is not sufficient that he intends to show them to himself.

A person possesses indecent photographs, etc with a view to their being distributed or shown by him to others only if one reason (not necessarily the primary reason) for possessing them is that they would be distributed or shown to others. Thus, a person who allows files containing indecent photographs, etc to remain in his shared electronic folder, where they can be accessed and downloaded into the shared folders of other members of a file-sharing system, possesses those files with a view to their being shown or distributed only if one of his reasons, but not necessarily the primary reason, for doing so was to enable others to use them or download them.

Defences

PCA 1978, s 1(4) provides a defence to charges *of distributing or showing or possession with a view to distribution or showing* if D proves either that:

(a) he had a legitimate reason for distributing or showing the photographs or pseudo-photographs or (as the case may be) having them in his possession; or

(b) he had not seen the photographs or pseudo-photographs and did not know, nor had any reason to suspect, them to be indecent.

In respect of proceedings for *distributing or showing an indecent photograph or pseudo-photograph*, PCA 1978, s 1A provides an additional defence for the case where D proves that the photograph or pseudo-photograph was of the child *aged 16 or over*, and that at the time of the offence charged (ie the distributing or showing), or at the time when he obtained the photograph or pseudo-photograph, the child and he were married or civil partners of each other, or lived together as partners in an enduring family relationship, D is not guilty of the offence unless it is proved that the showing or distributing was to someone other than the child.

In respect of proceedings for *possessing an indecent photograph or pseudo-photograph of a child with a view to its being distributed or shown*, s 1A provides a defence where the child consents to D's possession of the photograph or pseudo-photograph (or that D reasonably believed in such consent) and D intended to distribute or show the photograph or pseudo-photograph only to the child. It states that, where in such proceedings, D proves the photograph or pseudo-photograph was of the child *aged 16 or over*, and that at the time of the offence (ie the possession) charged, or at the time when he obtained the photograph or pseudo-photograph, the child and he were married or civil partners of each other, or lived together as partners in an enduring family relationship, and sufficient evidence is adduced to raise an issue both:

(a) as to whether the child consented to the photograph or pseudo-photograph being in D's possession, or as to whether D reasonably believed that the child so consented; and

(b) as to whether D had the photograph or pseudo-photograph in his possession with a view to its being distributed or shown to anyone other than the child,

D is not guilty of the offence unless it is proved either that the child did not so consent and that D did not reasonably believe that the child so consented, or that D had the photograph or pseudo-photograph in his possession with a view to its being distributed or shown to a person other than the child.

The above defences under s 1A apply whether the photograph or pseudo-photograph showed the child alone or with D, but not if it showed any other person.

Publishing, or causing to be published, advertisements

PCA 1978, s 1(1)(d) provides that it is an offence for a person to publish or cause to be published any advertisement likely to be understood as conveying that the advertiser distributes or shows indecent photographs or pseudo-photographs, or intends to do so.

Simple possession

CJA 1988, s 160 makes it an offence for a person to have any indecent photograph or pseudo-photograph of a child in his possession.

For the purposes of an offence under PCA 1978 or under CJA 1988, s 160, 'possession' means custody or control. It follows, for example, that an assistant in a sex shop containing indecent photographs of children is, like his employer, in possession of them. Where the image concerned is a computer file, the defendant is in possession of it at the relevant time if it is within his control (as where, for example, he can produce it on his screen, make a hard copy of it or send it to someone else). Thus, images which have been emptied from the computer's recycle bin may be considered to be within the control of a defendant who is skilled in the use of computers and owns the software necessary to retrieve the images; whereas the images may not be considered to be within the control of a defendant who does not possess the requisite skill, and does not own the necessary software.

The offence is not committed unless D knew that he had, or once had, the photograph or pseudo-photograph in his possession.

Defences

By CJA 1988, s 160(2), a person charged under s 160 has a defence if he proves:

(a) that he had a legitimate reason for having the photograph or pseudo-photograph in his possession; or
(b) that he had not himself seen the photograph or pseudo-photograph and did not know, nor had any reason to suspect, it to be indecent; or
(c) that the photograph or pseudo-photograph was sent to him without any previous request made by him or on his behalf and that he did not keep it for an unreasonable time.

The Court of Appeal has held that it is implicit in (b) that a defendant who had not seen the photograph or pseudo-photograph but had cause to suspect that it was indecent has a defence if he proves that he had no reason to suspect that it was an indecent photograph or pseudo-photograph *of a child*.

By s 160A, if D proves that the photograph or pseudo-photograph was of the child *aged 16 or over*, and that at the time of the offence charged, or at the time when he obtained the photograph or pseudo-photograph, the child and he were married or civil partners of each other, or lived together as partners in an enduring family relationship, and sufficient evidence is adduced to raise an issue as to whether the child consented to the photograph or pseudo-photograph being in D's possession, or as to whether D reasonably believed that the child so consented, D is not guilty of the offence unless it is proved either that the child did not so consent or that D did not reasonably believe that the child so consented. The exception applies whether the photograph or pseudo-photograph showed the child alone or with D, but not if it showed any other person.

Prosecution

Proceedings for the above offences may only be instituted by or with the consent of the DPP.

The Court of Appeal has stated that, where photographs are contained in books available from reputable outlets, the proper course (if it is claimed that they are indecent) is to prosecute the publisher or retailer under PCA 1978, and not an individual purchaser under CJA 1988, s 160.

Police powers

Under PCA 1978, s 4, on information laid on oath by a constable or by or on behalf of the DPP, a justice may issue a warrant to authorise entry, search for, and seizure of indecent photographs or pseudo-photographs of a child. The additional powers of seizure provided by CJPA 2001, s 50 apply where a search warrant under PCA 1978, s 4 is executed.

PCA 1978, Sch permits forfeiture of indecent photographs or pseudo-photographs of children, and the devices that hold them. Forfeiture is automatic (ie without the involvement of a court) unless the owner or some other person with an interest in the material objects. Computer hard drives which contain indecent photographs or pseudo-photographs of children may be forfeited where it is not technically possible to separate them. PCA 1978, Sch applies irrespective of the power under which material was seized. Thus, a computer seized during an investigation into fraud and found to contain indecent photographs of children may be forfeited.

POSSESSION OF PROHIBITED IMAGES OF CHILDREN

The Coroners and Justice Act 2009, s 62(1) provides that it is an offence for a person to be in possession of a prohibited image of a child, other than an excluded image. An offence under s 62(1) is an indictable (either way) offence. The institution of proceedings requires the DPP's consent.

Prohibited image

A prohibited image is an image which:

(a) is pornographic;
(b) is an image which focuses solely or principally on a child's genitals or anal region, or portrays any of the following acts:
   (i) the performance by a person of an act of intercourse or oral sex with or in the presence of a child;
   (ii) an act of masturbation by, of, involving or in the presence of a child;
   (iii) an act which involves penetration of the vagina or anus of a child with a part of a person's body or with anything else;
   (iv) an act of penetration, in the presence of a child, of the vagina or anus of a person with a part of a person's body or with anything else;
   (v) the performance by a child of an act of intercourse or oral sex with an animal (whether dead or alive or imaginary);

(vi) the performance by a person of an act of intercourse or oral sex with an animal (whether dead or alive or imaginary) in the presence of a child; and

(c) is grossly offensive, disgusting or otherwise of an obscene character.

An 'image' includes (a) a moving or still image (produced by any means), or (b) data (stored by any means) which is capable of conversion into an image within (a), but it does not include an indecent photograph, or indecent pseudo-photograph, of a child within the meaning of PCA 1978. References to an image of a person (or child) include references to an image of an imaginary person (or child).

'Child' means a person under 18. An image of a person is treated as an image of a child if the impression conveyed by the image is that the person shown is a child, or the predominant impression conveyed is that the person shown is a child.

Exclusion of classified film

Section 63 provides that the offence under s 62 does not apply to an 'excluded image', ie an image which forms part of a series of images contained in a recording of the whole or part of a classified work. But such an image is not an 'excluded image' if it is contained in a recording (including a device for storing data electronically and from which images may be produced) of an extract from a classified work and it is of *such a nature that it must reasonably be assumed to have been extracted (whether with or without other images) solely or principally for the purpose of sexual arousal.* 'Classified work' means a video work in respect of which a classification certificate has been issued under the Video Recordings Act 1984 by a designated authority.

Where an extracted image is one of a series of images contained in the recording, the question whether the image is of the nature italicised above is to be determined in the same way as the determination of whether an image which forms part of a series of images is pornographic (see below).

Pornographic

An image is 'pornographic' if it is of such a nature that it must reasonably be assumed to have been produced solely or principally for the purpose of sexual arousal.

Where (as found in the person's possession) an image forms part of a series of images, the question whether the image is of such a nature is determined by reference to the image itself and (if the series of images is capable of providing a context for the image) the context in which it occurs in the series of images.

Defences

Section 64 provides three defences to an offence under s 62. The terms of s 64 are identical to those of CJA 1988, s 160(2) (p 893), with the substitution of 'image' for 'photograph or pseudo-photograph' and 'prohibited' for 'indecent'.

General

By s 67, the provisions of PCA 1978 relating to entry, search and seizure, and to forfeiture apply in relation to prohibited images of children as they apply in relation to indecent photographs of children.

Special rules relating to information society services providers

Schedule 13 makes special provision in connection with the operation of the offence under s 62 in relation to information society services providers in order to ensure compatibility with the EU's E-Commerce Directive where an offence has an international element relating to an EEA member state.

POSSESSION OF EXTREME PORNOGRAPHIC IMAGES

The Criminal Justice and Immigration Act (CJIA) 2008, s 63 created the indictable (either way) offence of possession of an extreme pornographic image. 'Image' means a moving or still image (produced by any means) or data (stored by any means) which is capable of conversion into an image of such a nature.

An image is 'pornographic' if it is of such a nature that it must reasonably be assumed to have been produced solely or principally for sexual arousal. Where an image forms part of a series of images, the question whether it is pornographic is to be determined by reference to:

(a) the image itself; and
(b) (if the series of images is such as to be capable of providing a context for the image) the context in which it occurs in the series of images.

So, for example, where:

(a) an image forms an integral part of a narrative constituted by a series of images; and
(b) having regard to those images as a whole, they are not of such a nature that they must reasonably be assumed to have been produced solely or principally for the purpose of sexual arousal,

the image may, by virtue of being part of that narrative, be found not to be pornographic, even though it might have been found to be pornographic if taken by itself.

An image is 'extreme' if:

(a) it portrays, in an explicit and realistic way:
    (i)   an act which threatens a person's life,
    (ii) an act which results, or is likely to result, in serious injury to a person's anus, breast or genitals,
    (iii) an act which involves sexual interference with a human corpse, or
    (iv) a person performing an act of intercourse or oral sex with an animal (whether dead or alive),
    and a reasonable person looking at the image would think that any such person or animal was real; and
(b) it is grossly offensive, disgusting or otherwise of an obscene character.

These references to parts of the body include references to any part which is surgically reconstructed (in particular through gender reassignment surgery).

The consent of the DPP is required for a prosecution for this offence.

Exclusion of classified films, etc

Section 64 excludes from s 63 an image forming part of a series of images contained in films which have been classified by a designated authority under the Video Recordings Act 1984. The terms of s 64 are identical to those under C&JA 2009, s 63 (p 895).

Defences

Section 65 provides three offences which are identical to those under CJA 1988, s 160(2) (p 893), with the substitution of 'image' for 'photograph or pseudo-photograph' and 'extreme pornographic' for 'indecent'.

In addition, it is a defence under s 66 for a person charged with an offence under s 63 to prove that he directly participated in the acts portrayed; that the act or acts did not involve the infliction of any non-consensual harm on any person; and, if the image portrayed an act of interference with a human corpse, that what is portrayed as a human corpse was not a human corpse. This defence does not apply where the image portrays a person performing intercourse or oral sex with an animal.

Special rules relating to information society services providers

Schedule 14 makes special provision in connection with the operation of the offence under s 63 in relation to information society services providers in order to ensure compatibility with the EU's E-Commerce Directive where an offence has an international element relating to an EEA member state.

MISCELLANEOUS OFFENCES

Harmful publications—children and young persons

A person who prints, publishes, sells, lets on hire or has in his possession for the purpose of selling or letting on hire a work to which the Children and Young Persons (Harmful Publications) Act 1955 (CYP(HP)A 1955) applies commits an offence under CYP(HP)A 1955, s 2(1). CYP(HP)A 1955 applies to any book, magazine or similar work of a kind likely to fall into the hands of children or young persons and consisting wholly or mainly of stories *told in pictures* (with or without the addition of written matter), where those stories portray the commission of crimes, acts of violence or cruelty, or incidents of a repulsive or horrible nature, in such a way that the work as a whole would tend to corrupt a child or young person into whose hands it might fall. A 'child' is someone under 14 years of age, and a 'young person' someone under 18.

Unless the defendant is charged with printing or publishing such a work, it is a defence for him that he had not examined the contents of the publication and had no reason to suspect that it was one to which CYP(HP)A 1955 applies.

A prosecution for an offence under CYP(HP)A 1955 may only be instituted with the Attorney General's consent.

Police powers

The power of a justice to issue a search warrant is peculiar in relation to the CYP(HP)A 1955 because a justice can only issue a search warrant at the time of, or after, the receipt of an information alleging an offence which leads him to authorise the issue of a summons or a warrant to arrest. In effect, therefore, proceedings for the present type of offence must have commenced in one of these two ways in respect of a person allegedly involved in it. The additional powers of seizure provided by CJPA 2001, s 50 apply where a search warrant under CYP(HP)A 1955 is executed.

CYP(HP)A 1955 and other Acts similar to it tend to cause difficulties for police officers considering charges to be preferred against those involved. The correct approach is to examine the evidence at hand (or the information given) and from this to establish everyone who had been involved in the process from the outset. The responsibility of the printer, publisher, wholesaler, retailer or hirer must be considered; in other words, all those who handle the material.

Sending indecent, etc matter through post

Under the Postal Services Act 2000, s 85(1) it is an indictable (either way) offence to send a postal packet which encloses any indecent or obscene matter, or which has on the packet indecent or obscene words, marks or designs. So far as this offence is concerned the words 'indecent' and 'obscene' are directed at offending against the recognised standards of propriety. It is for a court or jury to decide, applying these standards, whether words are indecent or obscene.

Indecent displays, etc

The Indecent Displays (Control) Act 1981 (ID(C)A 1981), s 1(1) provides that it is an indictable (either way) offence to make a public display of indecent matter, or cause or permit such a display.

Matter is deemed to be publicly displayed if displayed in, or visible from, a public place. For these purposes, 'public place' means any place to which the public have access (whether on payment or otherwise) while that matter is displayed, except:

(a) a place to which the public are permitted to have access only on payment which is for, or includes payment for, that display, or
(b) a shop, or any part of a shop, to which public access can only be gained by passing beyond an adequate warning notice,

but the exclusions in (a) and (b) only apply where persons under 18 are not allowed to enter while any such display is actually taking place. The 'adequate warning notice' should read as set out below and this notice should be looked for in premises where it is known that such displays are held:

'WARNING

Persons passing beyond this notice will find material on display which they may consider indecent. No admittance to persons under 18 years of age.'

'Matter', for the purposes of ID(C)A 1981, includes anything capable of being displayed, but does not include the actual human body or a part of it. Thus ID(C)A 1981 is not concerned with strippers. This is a useful Act to police officers as it can be applied to everything from the display of obscene graffiti scrawled on a wall to indecent film shows, etc which are open to the public.

Official TV programmes, art galleries, museums, Crown buildings, local authority buildings, theatres, and arenas controlled by other legislation are totally outside the provisions of the Act.

Police powers

Under ID(C)A 1981, s 2, a constable may seize articles which he has reasonable grounds for believing to be indecent, or to contain indecent matter, or to have been used in the commission of an offence under the Act.

In addition, a justice may grant a search warrant, on information on oath, authorising entry within 14 days and seizure of material reasonably suspected to have been used in an offence under the Act. The additional powers of seizure provided by CJPA 2001, s 50 apply where a search warrant under ID(C)A 1981 is executed.

CHAPTER 31

Drugs

CONTROLLED DRUGS

The Misuse of Drugs Act 1971 (MDA 1971) provides a number of offences intended to control the misuse of drugs. *All the offences under MDA 1971 described below, with the exception of an offence under s 9A, are indictable (either way) offences.* Drugs which are subject to the Act are designated as 'controlled drugs'.

A 'controlled drug' is any substance or product for the time being specified:

(a) in MDA 1971, Sch 2, Part I, II, or III; or
(b) in a temporary class drug order as a drug subject to temporary control.

Part 1 of Sch 2 lists 'Class A drugs'; Part II, 'Class B drugs'; and Part III, 'Class C drugs'. Drugs can be added to the lists contained in Sch 2 by Order in Council, or moved from one class to another. One of the points of the classification of controlled drugs is that it affects the punishment of some of the offences under MDA 1971. As a result of a House of Lords decision, what may appear to be one offence (eg unlawful supply) is in law divisible into distinct offences depending on the maximum penalty for the drug in question.

Class A drugs can be divided into two groups; first, narcotic drugs, such as cocaine, morphine, opium, pethidine and heroin; and, second, hallucinogenic drugs, such as mescaline, LSD and MDMA (ecstasy), however the MDMA is produced, or fungus of any kind which contains psilocin or an ester of psilocin. Narcotic drugs are particularly dangerous because of their addictive qualities, and hallucinogenic ones because of the violent conduct which the hallucinated taker may engage in. Class B drugs include cannabis, cannabis resin and cannabis derivatives, and amphetamines (although methylamphetamine has been reclassified as a Class A drug) (which are stimulant drugs). Class C drugs include benzyphetamine, mephentermine, phendimetrazine, pipradrol and temazepam.

There are more than 100 drugs listed in Class C and a similar number are listed in Class A. There are fewer Class B drugs. Only an analysis of the substance will prove its nature, but the forms of drug in popular usage on the street are almost invariably Classes A and B.

Because of its particular significance and the ease with which the plant can be grown, the expressions 'cannabis' and 'cannabis resin' are defined by MDA 1971. 'Cannabis' (except in the expression 'cannabis resin') means any part of the genus *cannabis* or any part of any such plant (by whatever name designated) except that it does not include cannabis resin, or any of the following products, after separation from the rest of the plant, namely:

(a) mature stalk of any such plant;
(b) fibre produced from mature stalk of any such plant; and
(c) seed of any such plant.

'Cannabis resin' means the separated resin, whether crude or purified, obtained from any plant of the genus *cannabis*.

As indicated above a 'controlled drug' is a specified substance or *product*. In addition 'controlled drug' includes any 'preparation or other product' containing a specified substance or product. Some growing things, such as certain types of mushroom, contain a specified substance. In their natural state such things are not a specified substance or product, but if they are picked and subjected to some process to enable them to be used as a drug, they become a 'preparation' containing a specified substance and become a controlled drug. If they are picked, packed and frozen they become a 'product' containing a specified substance and become a controlled drug.

'*Temporary class drug*' means any substance or product which is for the time being a controlled drug by virtue of a temporary class drug order. Where the punishment depends on the class of the controlled drug a temporary class drug is treated in the same way as a Class B drug. The Secretary of State may make a temporary class drug order specifying any substance or product (other than one specified in Sch 2, Parts I, II, or III) as a drug subject to temporary control. A temporary class drug order must be made by statutory instrument and ceases to have effect unless approved by a resolution of each House of Parliament within a specified time. A substance or product specified in a temporary class drug order as a drug subject to temporary control ceases to be a controlled drug by virtue of the order:

(a) at the end of one year beginning with the day on which the order comes into force; or
(b) if earlier, upon the coming into force of an Order in Council by virtue of which the substance or product is specified as a controlled drug in Sch 2, Parts I, II, or III.

This is without prejudice to the power of the Secretary of State to vary or revoke a temporary class drug order by a further order.

A temporary class drug order may provide for the exception of a temporary class drug from the prohibitions on the import, export, production, or supply of controlled drugs, and for circumstances in which a person's possession of the drug is to be treated as excepted possession for the purposes of MDA 1971.

The provisions about temporary class drug orders were added by the Police Reform and Social Responsibility Act 201 (PRSRA 2011).

UNLAWFUL IMPORT AND EXPORT

MDA 1971, s 3 (as amended by PRSRA 2011) prohibits the import or export of a Class A, B, or C controlled drug, otherwise than as authorised by regulations made under the Act or by a licence issued by the Secretary of State. MDA 1971, s 3 also prohibits the import or export of a temporary class drug unless the drug has been excepted in the circumstances from s 3 by a provision in the temporary class drug order.

Breach of MDA 1971, s 3 is not an offence under the Act but it is an indictable (either way) offence under the Customs and Excise Management Act 1979, ss 50 and 68.

UNLAWFUL PRODUCTION

MDA 1971, s 4(2) states that it is an offence for any person unlawfully to produce a controlled drug or to be concerned in the production of a controlled drug. An offence under s 4(2) is subject to the defence provided by MDA 1971, s 28 (see p 907).

Unlawful

The production of any Class A, B, or C controlled drug, otherwise than as authorised by regulations, is an unlawful production. The Misuse of Drugs Regulations 2001 authorise production by drug companies, by research establishments for experimental purposes, and by chemists in the course of their business. The production of a temporary class drug is an unlawful production unless a provision of a temporary class drug order excepts the drug from the provisions of s 4 or authorises its production in the circumstances in question.

Produce

'Produce' means to produce a controlled drug by manufacture, cultivation or any other means, and 'production' has a corresponding meaning. A substance will pass through a number of processes in its production and a person charged must be clearly shown to have taken some identifiable part in the process of production before he can be convicted of an offence of production. It has been held that the conversion of cocaine hydrochloride into freebase cocaine, in which form it would vaporise and be capable of being inhaled, by dissolving cocaine hydrochloride in water and either baking powder or household ammonia, amounts to production of a Class A drug 'by other means' since the drug, in these two forms, is chemically different. It does not matter that the cocaine hydrochloride was already a Class A drug before the process began. By way of further example, where cannabis plants have been harvested and the plants are then stripped to take out those parts which could be used for smoking, it has been held that this amounts to production of a Class B drug (cannabis) as a controlled drug is produced by some 'other method' than cultivation or manufacture. However, the offence is to produce a controlled drug and it is therefore essential that a controlled drug is actually produced before the offence can be committed. If the process to produce a substance has not been completed, there can be a conviction for attempting to commit the offence of production. Where a person tries to produce a controlled drug but, because of insufficient knowledge, produces a substance which is not in fact a controlled drug, he may nevertheless be convicted of an attempt to produce a controlled drug.

Concerned in the production

The effect of these words is that criminal liability is not limited to those who actually participate in the production of a controlled drug, since those who arrange for the delivery of ingredients to the place of manufacture of such a drug, knowing the purpose for which they are required, are concerned in its production, as is someone who knowingly allows his premises to be used. Not all types of activity covered by 'being concerned in' can properly be described as aiding, abetting, counselling or procuring the actual production of the drug. Consequently, the phrase 'being concerned' widens the ambit of the law beyond that which it would otherwise have been in respect of controlled drug production.

UNLAWFUL SUPPLY

If a controlled drug is unlawfully imported or produced it must then have a distribution network. MDA 1971, s 4(3) states that it is an offence for a person unlawfully to supply a controlled drug to another or to be concerned in the supplying of such a drug to another, or to offer to supply a controlled drug to another, or to be concerned in the making to another of an offer to supply such a drug.

The defence provided by MDA 1971, s 28 (see p 907) applies to an offence under s 4(3).

Unlawful

The supply of a Class A, B or C controlled drug is unlawful unless authorised by regulations. The circumstances in which a Class A, B or C controlled drug may be supplied lawfully are set out in the Misuse of Drugs Regulations 2001 made under the Act. They are not difficult to imagine. For example, doctors may issue drugs direct from their own dispensaries; pharmacists may supply them upon prescription; nurses may supply patients in hospital; laboratory analysts, inspectors and quality controllers may also handle drugs and pass them from one to another. The inclusion of the term 'unlawfully' ensures that all circumstances in which Class A, B or C controlled drugs are supplied to a person outside any exception amount to offences under MDA 1971.

A 'supply' of a temporary class drug is not unlawful if a provision of a temporary class drug order excepts the drug from s 4 or authorises its supply in the circumstances in question.

To supply to another

'Supply' means more than the mere transfer of physical control from one person to another; it means furnishing to another the drug in order to enable the other to use it for his own purposes. At one extreme there is the person who supplies the drug addict. He is the one who is usually described as a 'pusher', forming a rung in the distribution ladder between those who illegally import or produce drugs and those who use them. The person who distributes drugs at a party supplies the drugs to another and is guilty of an offence under MDA 1971, s 4(3). So is someone who returns a drug to a person who already owns it so that he can use it, or who hands a 'joint' to someone so that he can take a puff. On the other hand, a person who hands a drug to another for safe-keeping or to an employee of a professional courier service does not supply it to him. Nor does a person who injects another if that drug is already in the other's control.

Although a person who makes a joint purchase of drugs for consumption by himself and another, paying with their joint funds, supplies the other when he hands over the latter's share of the drugs, the Court of Appeal has stated that a charge of supplying the latter is undesirable.

Before an offence of supplying can be committed the substance supplied must be a controlled drug. It is not sufficient that the supplier believed that the substance was a drug, when in fact it was not, although he could be convicted of an attempt to supply in such a case or, depending on the circumstances, of an offer to supply.

To be concerned in the supply

The wide meaning given to the term 'concerned' when discussed in its application to offences of production should be applied.

To offer to supply or to be concerned in the offer

It is the making of an offer which is the important factor here; the extension of the offence to those who may be concerned in the making of such an offer gives it considerable width. Whereas one must supply an actual controlled drug before committing the offence of supplying, this is not necessary in relation to the making of an offer and this will be appreciated if it is borne in mind that the offence lies in the making of the offer. Therefore, if an offer is made to supply a controlled drug, an offence is committed even though the substance is not in fact a controlled drug, and even though the offeror knows this. Likewise, the offence of offering to supply a controlled drug is even committed if the offeror does not intend to supply anything. Many persons might be involved in the making of the offer. Those who approach people and seek to induce them to purchase drugs or merely receive them are offering to supply; those who send them out into the streets to canvass sale or distribution are concerned in the offer which is subsequently made.

SUPPLY OR OFFER TO SUPPLY ARTICLE

MDA 1971, s 9A(1) makes it an offence to supply or offer to supply an article which may be used or adapted to be used (whether by itself or in combination with another article) in the administration by a person of a controlled drug, or which may be used to prepare a controlled drug for administration, believing it would be so used in circumstances which would be unlawful.

It is not an offence under s 9A(1) to supply a hypodermic syringe. The offence under s 9A(1) is the only offence under MDA 1971 described in this book which is not indictable.

UNLAWFUL POSSESSION

The offences of unlawful possession of controlled drugs are those with which police officers are most commonly involved. MDA 1971, s 5(2) states that it is an offence for a person unlawfully to have a controlled drug in his possession. The defence under MDA 1971, s 28 (p 907) applies to these offences.

The offences under MDA 1971, s 5(2) do not apply in relation to a temporary class drug (s 5(2A) added by PRSRA 2011).

Unlawful

The Misuse of Drugs Regulations 2001 specify when possession of a controlled drug is lawful. They provide that such possession is lawful if it is under the authority of a licence issued by the Secretary of State or under a doctor's, first level nurse's, nurse independent prescriber's, pharmacist's, pharmacist independent prescriber's, or registered midwife's prescription. In addition, a constable who comes into possession of controlled drugs in the course of his duties is in lawful possession of them, and so are carriers, postal workers, despatchers, workers in forensic laboratories who examine drugs on behalf of the police, medical personnel, ship's masters, etc, in circumstances properly connected with their duties.

Possession

Physical custody of the drug is not necessary for possession but physical control over it is. It follows that a person who has bought a controlled drug is not in possession of it if it is still hidden in the seller's car or stored at the seller's home. On the other hand, a person who leaves a drug in his car or at home while he is away remains in possession of the drug since he retains physical control over it.

Possession can be joint: for example, if two people share a car which they know contains cannabis, they are both in possession of the cannabis if each shares with the other the right to control what is done with it. Moreover, MDA 1971, s 37(3) states that for the purposes of the Act the things which a person has in his possession shall be taken to include anything subject to his control which is in the custody of another. Therefore there may be a number of persons in possession of a particular controlled drug. If a man imports cannabis and hands it to his business manager to store pending distribution, both are in possession as the drug is subject to their control. If the business manager then passes it on to the warehouseman to keep until either he or the importer send for the drug, all three are in possession of it for the purpose of MDA 1971.

Possession cannot begin until the person with control is aware that the thing is under his control; if a drug is slipped into a person's pocket, unknown to him, he is not in possession of it. (As an exception, a person is in possession of a drug delivered to his home, even if he is unaware that it has arrived, provided it is delivered in response to a request by him.)

Knowledge of a thing's quality is not required. It follows that a mere mistake by D as to the quality of the thing under his control is not enough to prevent him being in possession. For example, if D knows that he is in control of some tablets which he believes to be aspirin (or, even sweets) but which are, in fact, heroin, D is in possession of the heroin tablets. Likewise, a divisional court has held that if D picks up a cigarette containing cannabis and puts it in his pocket, believing that it only contains tobacco, D is in possession of the cannabis.

In the case of drugs in a parcel, packet or other container in D's physical control, D is in possession of those drugs if he knows that he is in control of that container and that it contains something, even though he thinks that the thing is something different in kind from a drug and even though he has no right to open the container to check its contents.

Possession, once begun, continues as long as the thing is in the person's control, even though he has forgotten about it or mistakenly believes it has been destroyed or disposed of.

Although it is not necessary to prove that a minimum or usable quantity of a controlled drug was unlawfully in D's possession, D must have been in possession of a quantity of it which was visible, tangible and measurable. Persons who are found under the influence of a drug are not then in possession of it for the purposes of this offence, even though traces of it are found in a blood or urine sample. This is because, once consumed, the thing changes its character and can no longer be considered a controlled drug. However, evidence of the presence of a drug in a blood or urine sample can be given to support an allegation of possession of the drug in its true state at some earlier time, ie before it was taken into the body.

Defence

A person is not criminally liable for the unlawful possession of a controlled drug contrary to MDA 1971, s 5(2) in the circumstances outlined by s 5(4).

Section 5(4) provides that if it is proved that D had a controlled drug in his possession it is a defence for D to prove that:

(a) knowing or suspecting it to be a controlled drug, he took possession of it for the purpose of preventing another from committing or continuing to commit an offence in connection with that drug and that as soon as possible after taking possession he took all such steps as were reasonably open to him to destroy the drug or to deliver it into the custody of a person lawfully entitled to take custody of it; or

(b) knowing or suspecting it to be a controlled drug, he took possession of it for the purpose of delivering it into the custody of a person lawfully entitled to the custody of it and that as soon as possible after taking possession of it he took all such steps as were reasonably open to him to deliver it into the custody of such a person.

The circumstances outlined at (a) would therefore cover the situation in which a mother found her child in possession of controlled drugs and took them from the child. Provided that she destroyed the drugs or handed them over to lawful custody as soon as possible, or took reasonable steps to do so, she would commit no offence. The Court of Appeal has held that concealing a controlled drug in the ground is not sufficient even though that drug might be destroyed in the course of time by the forces of nature. There must be an act of destruction. The situation outlined at (b) would cover the circumstances where D found a bottle of amphetamine tablets in a park and took possession of the bottle to prevent the drugs from falling into the wrong hands. Once again, if reasonable steps were taken as soon as possible to hand over the drugs to lawful custody, the finder's possession would not be unlawful.

Despite the fact that MDA 1971, s 5(4) requires a defendant to 'prove' a defence under it, it would seem likely from a House of Lords decision in 2001 that all D has to do is to adduce sufficient evidence to raise the defence, whereupon it will be for the prosecution to prove beyond reasonable doubt that the defence is not made out.

POSSESSION WITH INTENT TO SUPPLY

MDA 1971, s 5(3) provides offences of having a controlled drug in one's possession, whether lawfully or not, with intent to supply it unlawfully to another. The defence under s 28 (p 907) applies to such an offence. This type of offence fills a gap in the process of traffic in drugs. In the beginning, drugs are illegally imported or produced. They will then be possessed by any number of persons if they are stored within an organisation with knowledge on the part of a number of persons who have control over them. All will possess the drugs with intent to supply. Those who go out to peddle the drugs, the 'pushers', possess them with intent to supply them to others. Immediately they supply, or offer to supply, they commit an offence under s 4(3). The persons who are supplied represent the end of the chain. They possess the drugs unlawfully contrary to s 5(2) for their own use.

The Court of Appeal has held that the intended supply must be a supply in the UK.

The Court of Appeal has also held that, to come within s 5(3), the intention to supply (of someone in possession of a controlled drug) has to be an intention to supply *the* thing of which he was then in possession. Thus, it held that where D intended to supply cannabis plants then in his possession when they reached maturity in a few months' time there was no offence under s 5(3).

An offence of possession with intent to supply may be committed by persons who are lawfully in possession in the first instance. For example, it can be committed by a doctor who is in possession of drugs lawfully, but forms an intention to supply them unlawfully (eg merely for profit, as opposed to bona fide treatment). However, the offence is usually committed by drug pushers and the like.

A person can be convicted under s 5(3) if it is proved that he was in possession of a controlled drug and that he intended to supply that substance unlawfully to another. It need not be proved that he knew the identity of the substance.

In terms of proving that possession was with intent unlawfully to supply, evidence of drug-related paraphernalia, evidence of an extravagant lifestyle and evidence of the possession of large amounts of cash *which are prima facie explicable only if derived from drug dealing* are relevant—but not conclusive—to the issue of *intent to supply* but not normally to the issue of possession. A case where such evidence might be relevant to possession, as well as to intent to supply, is where there is evidence of frequent brief visits by different young men, who then leave carrying small packages, and when the premises (whose occupant is long-term unemployed) are searched large sums of money and some drugs are found. Such evidence may be admitted as evidence that the occupant knew of the drugs and was in control of them (ie in possession) as well as of an intent to supply them.

Whilst evidence in the form of documents relating to transactions and cash in the defendant's possession is relevant, the relevance of the cash in the defendant's possession must be related to evidence of ongoing (and not merely previous) drug transactions in order for it to be admissible. By way of qualification, the Court of Appeal has held that, where D explained that a large quantity of money had come into his possession recently, there was no requirement to direct the jury that, if they rejected D's explanation, they also had to be satisfied that the money did not relate only to past drug dealings. The court also stated that evidence which showed that D had supplied drugs in the past was now potentially admissible under the 'bad character' provision in the Criminal Justice Act 2003, s 101(1)(d) (see condition (d) on p 255).

CULTIVATION OF CANNABIS

MDA 1971, s 6(2) states that it is an offence unlawfully to cultivate any plant of the genus *cannabis*. The only lawful cultivation of cannabis is that authorised by a licence issued by the Secretary of State. The defence under MDA 1971, s 28 applies to an offence under s 6(2).

'Cultivate' indicates some form of attention to the plant during the process of its growth. A person who puts seeds in the ground cultivates, as does he who hoes, waters, prunes, or generally cares for a plant during the process of its growth. It is doubtful if a person could be held to have cultivated plants merely because he failed to remove those which were growing wild but this would depend upon the circumstances. If they were deliberately preserved, by caring for the ground in which they were growing, this would amount to the type of care which could be described as cultivation.

MEDICAL NECESSITY

The defence of duress of circumstances is not available to a defendant in relation to offences of cultivation, production, possession or possession with intent to supply cannabis or resin, where his purpose is to alleviate pain arising from an existing illness.

SMOKING OF OPIUM

MDA 1971, s 9 prohibits a person from:

(a) smoking or otherwise using prepared opium; or
(b) frequenting a place used for the purpose of opium smoking; or
(c) having in his possession:
    (i)   any pipes or other utensils made or adapted for use in connection with the smoking of opium, being pipes or utensils which have been used by him or with his knowledge and permission in that connection or which he intends to use or permit others to use in that connection; or
    (ii) any utensils which have been used by him or with his knowledge or permission in connection with the preparation of opium for smoking.

Offences under s 9 are not common. The defence under MDA 1971, s 28 (below) applies to an offence under s 9.

'Prepared opium' is opium prepared for smoking and includes dross and any other residue remaining after opium has been smoked.

The term 'frequenting' means to go there often. The more often a person visits a place at which opium is being smoked, the greater the presumption that he is attending that place for that purpose, in the absence of any other reasonable explanation. There is no requirement that a person who frequents a place used for opium smoking must have been shown to have been involved in opium smoking. Significant factors will be the duration and frequency of visits; the nature of the place (if it is a cafe the possibility of frequent visits being innocent increases); things which actually occurred while the defendant was there; and his own behaviour when at or near that place. The offence is concerned with events which occur at a 'place'. That place does not need to be a building. Proof that the place is used as an opium den will be necessary.

STATUTORY DEFENCE

MDA 1971, s 28 provides a defence in relation to charges contrary to MDA 1971, s 4(2) (unlawful production), s 4(3) (unlawful supply), s 5(2) (unlawful possession), s 5(3) (possession with intent to supply), s 6(2) (unlawful cultivation of cannabis), and s 9 (smoking opium, etc). For convenience, the defence will be explained in relation to the offence of unlawful possession but what is said will be equally applicable (with the appropriate changes of words) to the other offences just mentioned.

Assuming that the prosecution has proved that D was in unlawful possession of a controlled drug, he can be convicted of that offence, even though it is not proved that he knew that what was in possession was a controlled drug. However, s 28 provides D with a defence in the circumstances outlined below. Although s 28 says that D has to prove the defence, the House of Lords has held that s 28 should be read as simply imposing an evidential burden on D so as to make it compatible with the presumption of innocence under the European Convention on Human Rights, art 6(2). The result is that, provided that sufficient evidence is adduced to raise a defence under s 28, the defence will succeed unless the prosecution proves beyond reasonable doubt that the terms of the defence are not satisfied.

The basic definition of the defence is contained in s 28(2), which states that it is a defence for D to 'prove' that *he neither knew of, nor suspected, nor had reason to suspect* the existence of some fact alleged by the prosecution which it is necessary for the prosecution to prove if he is to be convicted of the offence charged. (This does not affect the need for the prosecution to prove the element of knowledge required to establish 'possession'.)

This provision is subject to a qualification, provided by s 28(3), where D alleges, and 'proves', that he did not know, suspect, or have reason to suspect that the thing in question was the controlled drug alleged, and proved, by the prosecution to have been involved. In this case, such 'proof' by D is not enough to give him a defence. In order to be acquitted D must also 'prove' one of two things:

(a) that he neither believed nor suspected, nor had reason to suspect, that the thing in question was a controlled drug at all; or
(b) that he believed that the thing in question was a controlled drug which he was, in fact, legally entitled to possess (or supply or produce, etc as the case may be).

Head (a) can be illustrated as follows: if X gives D for safe-keeping a bottle of tablets which X alleges are aspirin tablets but which are in fact heroin, D will be in possession of the tablets because he is, to his knowledge, in control of the bottle (container) and knows that it contains something but D will have a defence to a charge of unlawful possession if he adduces sufficient evidence that he did not believe, suspect, or have reason to suspect that the tablets were a controlled drug, and the prosecution does not disprove this. Had D been told or had reason to suspect that the bottle contained amphetamines whereas it in fact contained heroin, this would not be a defence as both are controlled drugs.

The following example demonstrates the operation of (b): if an addict is lawfully prescribed methadone and is given cocaine by mistake, he is technically in unlawful possession of the cocaine (since it has not been prescribed). If he adduces sufficient evidence that he neither knew, suspected, nor had reason to suspect that the thing was cocaine, and that he believed he was in possession of methadone, he will have a defence unless the prosecution disproves one or both parts of the defence.

CONTROLLED DRUGS ON PREMISES

A person commits an offence under MDA 1971, s 8 if, being the occupier or concerned in the management of any premises, he knowingly permits or suffers any of the following activities to take place on those premises:

(a) unlawfully producing or attempting to produce a controlled drug;
(b) unlawfully supplying or attempting to supply a controlled drug to another, or offering to supply a controlled drug unlawfully to another;
(c) preparing opium for smoking; or
(d) smoking cannabis, cannabis resin or prepared opium.

There must be proof that the conduct in (a), (b), (c) or (d) actually occurred; merely giving tacit approval in advance is insufficient.

The occupier

To be 'the occupier' a person does not have to be a tenant or have an estate in the premises. A person is the occupier of premises if he is entitled to exclusive possession of them, in the sense that he has the requisite degree of control over them to exclude from them those who might otherwise carry on one of the forbidden activities there. Thus, a student who had a room in a college hostel was held to be the occupier of it because his contractual licence gave him such exclusivity of possession, whether or not he was entitled to exclude the college authorities. If there is drug-taking in a house, and it is knowingly permitted by the householder (ie 'the occupier'), he commits an offence under s 8. However, he would not commit that offence if, in his absence and unknown to him, his teenage son knowingly permitted drug-taking on the premises. Nor would the son be guilty of an offence under s 8 on the basis of being 'the occupier' of the premises since he would not have that status. Nevertheless, depending on the circumstances, the son might be guilty of an offence under s 8 on the basis of 'being concerned in the management of the premises', to which phrase we now turn.

Concerned in management

A person 'concerned in the management of premises' is anyone who is concerned in exercising control over the premises or in running or organising them on a day-to-day basis. It is possible that such a person will have some control over who shall be permitted to enter the premises and who shall not, but this is not a prerequisite for a person to be concerned in their management. If drug-taking was generally permitted on the premises of a club, it is possible that only the general manager would have the right to permit entry but other officials of the club might control activities in different rooms. If drug use is generally and knowingly permitted, then all who are concerned in any way in the management of the premises (ie the general manager and other officials) would be guilty of this offence.

Persons who occupy premises as trespassers (and are therefore not 'occupiers' for the purpose of the offence) might nevertheless be concerned in the management of those premises. For example, if drug-taking activities are organised upon premises by squatters, all concerned in that organisation are guilty of the present offence.

Premises

MDA 1971 does not define the term 'premises'. The term should be given its normal, everyday meaning, and in this sense 'premises' includes any form of building and the grounds in which a building stands and also land without any building on it. Therefore, the organiser of an open-air pop festival who knowingly permitted one of the activities described above would (as a person concerned in the management of the premises) be guilty of the present offence, as would the occupier of the site if he knowingly permitted one of these activities.

Knowingly permits or suffers

'Permit' and 'suffer' are synonymous. In law, a person only permits or suffers something to occur if, physically and legally, he could prevent it but does not do so. The Court of Appeal has held that 'permit' (and presumably 'suffer') require proof of unwillingness to prevent the prohibited activity, which can be inferred from failure to take reasonable steps readily available to prevent it. The fact that a defendant believed that he had taken reasonable steps to prevent the prohibited activity is irrelevant.

The inclusion of the word 'knowingly' does not mean that actual knowledge that the premises were being used in the particular prohibited way must be proved since 'knowingly' also embraces wilful blindness, ie suspecting what is going on but deliberately refraining from making inquiries.

On a charge of permitting the premises to be used for producing or supplying a controlled drug, it is not necessary for the prosecution to prove more than that D 'knew' of the production or supply of a controlled drug; it need not be proved that D knew that it was the particular type of controlled drug supplied. It remains to be seen whether, on a charge of permitting the smoking of cannabis, D could be convicted even if he thought that cannabis resin or opium was being smoked, and so on.

POWERS

Search, seize, and detain

MDA 1971, s 23(2) provides that, if a constable has reasonable grounds to suspect that any person (P) is in *possession of a controlled drug in contravention of MDA 1971 or of any regulations or temporary class drug orders thereunder*, the constable may:

(a) search P, and detain him for the purpose of searching him;
(b) search any vehicle or vessel in which the constable suspects that the drug may be found, and for that purpose require the person in control to stop it;
(c) seize and detain, for the purpose of proceedings under MDA 1971, anything found in the course of the search which appears to the constable to be evidence of an offence under MDA 1971.

It must be emphasised that the exercise of these powers to search, seize, and detain depends upon there being reasonable grounds to suspect possession of a controlled drug in contravention of MDA 1971 or regulations or orders. As to this requirement of reasonable suspicion, see p 40.

MDA 1971, s 23A, added by PRSRA 2011, Sch 17, provides a further power to search, seize, and detain in relation to temporary class drugs which applies where a constable has reasonable grounds to suspect that a person (P) is in *possession of a temporary class drug*, and it does not appear to the constable that a power under s 23(2) applies to the case. Section 23A provides that in such a case the constable may exercise the powers under (a) and (b) above and may seize and detain anything found in the course of the search *which appears to the constable to be a temporary class drug* or to be evidence of an offence under MDA 1971. If a constable reasonably believes that anything so detained is a temporary class drug but is not evidence of any offence under MDA 1971, the constable may dispose of the drug in such manner as he thinks appropriate.

The reason for the addition of s 23A is this. The power of search under s 23(2) applies to a temporary class drug only if a constable has reasonable grounds to suspect that P is in possession of the drug in contravention of MDA 1971. Because the restriction on possession (the offence under s 5(2)) does not apply to temporary class drugs, the power under s 23(2) will apply to a temporary class drug only if the constable has reason to suspect that P's possession is in contravention of other provisions (eg ss 3, 4, or 5(3)). Section 23A ensures that a constable can search for, and seize, a temporary class drug where there is no reason to suspect a contravention of any other provision.

A temporary class drug order may provide for circumstances where a person's possession of a temporary class drug is to be treated as 'excepted possession' for the purposes of MDA 1971. If any provision has been made about excepted possession by a temporary class drug order that applies to the temporary class drug in question, the powers in s 23A apply only if the constable has no reason to believe that P's possession of the drug is to be treated as excepted possession.

The above powers to search a person must extend to searching things in his immediate possession, for example a suitcase or a holdall. If this was not so the power to search persons would be totally ineffective.

In a case where there had been forcible use of emetics to induce vomiting by a man suspected of swallowing 'bubble wraps' of cocaine, the European Court of Human Rights held that forcible medical intervention to obtain evidence had to be *necessary* otherwise the European Convention on Human Rights, art 3 (prohibition of inhuman or degrading treatment) will be contravened. The court considered that in the circumstances it would have been possible to wait for the natural discharge of the 'bubbles'.

Search warrant

MDA 1971, s 23(3) authorises a justice to grant a search warrant if satisfied by information on oath that there is a reasonable ground for suspecting that controlled drugs are, in contravention of MDA 1971 or any regulations or temporary class drug orders thereunder, in the possession of a person on any premises, or that a document directly or indirectly relating to drug dealing is in the possession of persons on any premises. The warrant will name the particular premises, and it is only those premises (and persons in them) which may be searched on its authority. If necessary, force may be used to enter the premises.

If there is reasonable ground for suspecting that an offence has been committed in relation to any controlled drugs found on the premises or in the possession of anyone there, or that a document so found directly or indirectly relates to drug dealings, the drugs or document may be seized and detained.

A divisional court has held that, where a search warrant has been issued under both MDA 1971 and PACE, the warrant refers to both persons and premises. MDA, s 23 provides the power to detain persons for the purpose of a search and PACE, s 117 provides the power to use reasonable force for the purpose of executing the warrant, including moving persons to one room while another was searched.

Additional powers of seizure

The additional powers of seizure provided by the Criminal Justice and Police Act 2001, ss 50 and 51 apply where a search is made under the power in MDA 1971, s 23(2) or where a search warrant under s 23(3) is executed.

Obstruction

It is an indictable (either way) offence intentionally to obstruct a constable in the execution of his powers to search under MDA 1971, s 23 or s 23A (s 23(4), s 23A(6)).

Closure of premises where drugs used unlawfully

The Anti-social Behaviour Act 2003, Part 1 (ss 1 to 11) provides that where a superintendent (or above) has reasonable grounds for believing that, within the previous three months, premises have been used in connection with the unlawful use, production, or supply of a *Class A controlled drug* and that the use of the premises is associated with the occurrence of disorder or serious nuisance to members of the public, the officer, if satisfied that the local authority has been consulted, and that reasonable steps have been taken to identify any person who lives on the premises or who has control or responsibility for or an interest in the premises, may issue a closure notice. The closure notice must give appropriate details and state when and where an application for a magistrates' closure order will be considered.

Such a notice must be served by a constable (by fixing notices to the building and serving copies upon relevant persons); it closes the premises to all members of the public except the owner or those who habitually reside there, until such time as a magistrates' court decides in civil proceedings whether to issue a closure order.

The court must hear an application for a closure order within 48 hours, although it may adjourn the hearing for no more than 14 days to enable the occupier or other person with control or responsibility or an interest in respect of the premises to show cause why the order should not be made. In the event of an adjournment, the magistrates may order the closure notice to remain in force during it. Applications for closure orders should be dealt with speedily and adjournments should not normally be granted beyond the 14 days permitted by the Act.

The magistrates' court may make a closure order only if satisfied on a balance of probabilities that the premises in question have been used in connection with the unlawful use, production or supply of a Class A drug, that this use of the premises is associated with the occurrence of disorder or serious nuisance to members of the public, and that the making of a closure order is necessary to prevent the occurrence of such disorder or serious nuisance for the period of the order. A divisional court has held that a magistrates' court is much more likely to be satisfied, where the application is supported by direct evidence of witnesses available for cross-examination, and, where there is hearsay evidence, if what is served and adduced is first-hand and complete. As the proceedings are civil in nature, the civil law of evidence applies, as to which see p 745. If what is relied on are oral statements to a police officer, the officer should give direct evidence of what was said and the circumstances in which it was said. The Magistrates' Courts (Hearsay Evidence in Civil Proceedings) Rules 1999 require a party who desires to give hearsay evidence to serve a hearsay notice not less than 21 days before the date fixed for the hearing. Where the 21-day rule does not fit with the shorter expected statutory timetable for the hearing of applications for closure orders, the 1999 Rules provide that the court may make a direction substituting a different period. The 1999 Rules cannot be complied with before the first 48-hour hearing of the application for a closure order. If the police intend to rely on hearsay evidence they will have to seek an adjournment and make an application for a direction to reduce the 21-day period. If the court accedes to the application the period for serving the hearsay notice will need to be sufficiently in advance of the adjourned hearing to enable the defendant to deal with it fairly, including making an application to call and cross-examine the maker of a statement whom it is not proposed to call.

It has been held by a judge in the Administrative Court that, where the premises are someone's home, the European Convention on Human Rights, art 8 (right to private and family life) is engaged and the making of a closure order must be necessary and proportionate. However, the judge held, there is no statutory requirement to demonstrate that other, less draconian, measures have been tried; although alternative measures may be taken into account, they are not additional requirements before a closure order can be made.

If an order is made it prohibits entry to the premises *by anyone* for the period of the order.

The maximum period for a closure order is three months, with a possibility of extension to a maximum of six months.

It is an offence contrary to s 4 for a person:

(a) to remain on or enter premises subject to a closure notice without reasonable excuse (s 4(1)), or

(b) (i) to obstruct a constable serving a closure notice or enforcing an order, or

(ii) to remain on or enter premises subject to a closure order without reasonable excuse (s 4(2)).

In the offences where there is a defence of reasonable excuse, D does not bear the burden of proving such excuse but unless he adduces evidence of a reasonable excuse the prosecution does not have the burden of proving that he did not have a reasonable excuse.

TRAVEL RESTRICTIONS ON DRUG TRAFFICKING OFFENDERS

The Criminal Justice and Police Act 2001, s 33 empowers a court to make a 'travel restriction order' where a person has been convicted of a drug-trafficking offence and he is sentenced to four years' or more imprisonment. The reference to a sentence of four years' or more imprisonment is to a single sentence of imprisonment, and does not include consecutive sentences of imprisonment totalling four years or more. Such an order prohibits the offender from leaving the UK at any time after his release from prison until such date as is set out in the order (not less than two years). An order may contain a direction that his passport must be surrendered and it is an offence to fail to comply with a direction to do so. It is an indictable (either way) offence, contrary to s 36(1), to leave the UK while subject to a travel restriction. A person subject to such an order may apply for a suspension (which can only be granted in exceptional circumstances based on compassionate grounds). It is an indictable (either way) offence, contrary to s 36(2), not to be in the UK at a time when such a suspension ends.

The person affected by the travel restriction order may apply for its revocation at any time after the 'minimum period'. The 'minimum period' is two years, where the restriction was for a period of four years or less; four years for a restriction between four years and ten years; and five years in any other case.

For the purposes of the Criminal Justice and Police Act 2001, s 33 a 'drug-trafficking offence' means any of the following offences (including one committed by aiding, abetting, counselling or procuring):

(a) production and supply of controlled drugs: MDA 1971, s 4(2) or (3);

(b) assisting in or inducing commission outside the UK of an offence punishable under a corresponding law: MDA 1971, s 20;

(c) any offence designated by order of the Secretary of State;

(d) improper import, export or fraudulent evasion contrary to Customs and Excise Management Act 1979 in connection with any prohibition or restriction on importation or exportation of a controlled drug;

(e) conspiracy to commit any of the offences in (a) to (d): Criminal Law Act 1977, s 1;

(f) attempting to commit any of the offences in (a) to (d): Criminal Attempts Act 1981, s 1;

(g) inciting another person to commit any offence under MDA 1971: MDA 1971, s 19; and

(h) encouraging or assisting another person to commit any offence in (a) to (d) contrary to the Serious Crime Act 2007, Pt 2.

GLUE SNIFFING

It is an offence, contrary to the Intoxicating Substances (Supply) Act 1985, s 1(1), for a person to supply, or offer to supply, a substance other than a controlled drug:

(a) to a person under 18 whom he knows, or has reasonable cause to believe, to be under that age; or

(b) to a person who is acting on behalf of someone under 18, and whom he knows, or has reasonable cause to believe, to be so acting,

if he knows or has reasonable cause to believe that the substance is, or its fumes are, likely to be inhaled by the person under 18 for the purpose of causing intoxication. Cigarette lighter fuel is such a substance.

It is a defence for a defendant to show that at the material time he was under 18 and was not acting in the course or furtherance of a business.

CHAPTER 32

Theft and Related Offences, Robbery, and Blackmail

THEFT

The Theft Act 1968 (TA 1968), s 1(1) provides that a person is guilty of theft, an indictable (either way) offence, if he dishonestly appropriates property belonging to another with the intention of permanently depriving the other of it.

By TA 1968, s 30, the leave of the DPP is required for the institution of proceedings for the theft by one spouse or civil partner of the other's property, unless, by virtue of any judicial decree or order, the spouses were not obliged to cohabit at the material time or an order is in force providing for the separation of the civil partners, as the case may be.

Theft is a 'penalty offence' for the purposes of the Criminal Justice and Police Act 2001 and may be dealt with by a police officer under a fixed penalty procedure: see p 31. This may be an appropriate course of action in cases of low-level shoplifting.

It is immaterial whether the appropriation is made with a view to gain, or is made for the thief's own benefit. Thus, a postman who flushes postal packets down the lavatory to avoid delivering them, or who takes them to give to his son, is as guilty of theft as if he had taken them for his own benefit. The terms of the definition of theft in TA 1968, s 1(1) are defined, in whole or part, by ss 2 to 6.

For the purposes of exposition, it is best to start by noting that to be guilty of theft D must be proved:

(a) to have appropriated property belonging to another; and
(b) to have done so dishonestly and with the intention of permanently depriving the other of it.

Appropriation

TA 1968, s 3(1) describes appropriation as any assumption by a person of the rights of an owner, and this includes, where he has come by the property (innocently or not) without stealing it, any later assumption of a right to it by keeping or dealing with it as owner.

The essence of this definition is an 'assumption of the rights of an owner'. An owner of property has many rights in relation to it, including the rights to use it, to destroy it, to give it away, to sell it, and so on. The House of Lords has held that, despite the use of the words 'the rights' at the beginning of s 3(1), s 3 as a whole indicates that an appropriation does not require an assumption of all the rights of an owner and that it is enough that there has been an assumption of any of the rights of the owner.

The House of Lords has ruled that an act amounting to an assumption of a right of the owner done with the authority or consent of the owner can amount to an appropriation of goods for the purposes of TA 1968.

A pickpocket who takes someone's wallet clearly appropriates it. An appropriation can occur even though the assumption is only momentary. It has been held, for example, that there was an appropriation where a man wrested a bag from a woman's grasp, even though he then dropped it on the ground and did not make off with it.

A shopper who removes goods from a shelf in a supermarket and conceals them in his shopping bag thereby appropriates them (because this amounts to an assumption of one of the rights of the owner of the goods), and so does someone who simply puts goods in a supermarket basket without concealing them. In both cases, however, the person concerned would not be guilty of theft if he intended to pay at the checkout because he would not appropriate the goods dishonestly.

A fairly common practice among the dishonest is to switch the price labels on articles in a shop or supermarket, so that a lesser price than the true price is paid at the cash desk. This amounts to an assumption of the rights of the owner, and therefore to an appropriation.

Someone can appropriate property even though he never possesses it, as where, pretending to be the owner, he points to another's car and offers to sell it (because the right to sell is one of the rights of the owner and he has assumed that right). On the other hand, the Court of Appeal has held, a person who has never had possession or control of property but who deceives his victim into transferring it to a third party does not thereby appropriate it.

There may also be an appropriation through an innocent agent. If a person in authority signs a false invoice, intending that innocent people take further steps which result in money being debited and thus appropriated from a bank account, he is guilty of theft.

Appropriation by those already in possession

A person can appropriate property even though he is already in possession or control of it. This is made clear by the latter part of TA 1968, s 3(1), which provides that 'appropriation' includes, where the defendant (D) 'has come by the property (innocently or not) without stealing it, any later assumption of a right to it by keeping or dealing with it as owner'. It follows that a shop assistant who knowingly sells goods at less than the marked price thereby appropriates them because he has assumed the owner's right to fix the price. Another example would be where a person hires a car and later decides to sell it. When he sells, or—even—offers to sell, it to another, he thereby appropriates the car because he assumes the right of the owner to sell it.

An important aspect of the latter part of s 3(1) is that it can lead to the conviction of a person who originally came by the property dishonestly without stealing it. Suppose that D helps himself to V's umbrella in order to go out during a shower but intending to return it. D does not steal the umbrella at that stage because, although he has appropriated it, he did not then intend permanently to deprive V. However, if D subsequently decides to keep the umbrella or to sell it, and does so, he is then guilty of theft because his later assumption of a right to it by keeping or dealing with it as owner constitutes an appropriation which is accompanied by an intent permanently to deprive V.

Where D obtains property by a false representation, he is guilty of an offence of fraud, contrary to the Fraud Act 2006, s 1 as soon as he makes his false representation. However, someone who so obtains property thereby appropriates it and can be convicted of theft if he has the necessary mens rea. A charge of fraud will be more appropriate than theft where both offences have been committed.

An express exception

TA 1968, s 3(2) excludes a particular type of case, which falls within the definition in s 3(1), from being an appropriation. It provides that, where property or a right or interest in property is or purports to be *transferred for value* to a person *acting in good faith*, no later assumption by him of rights which he believed himself to be acquiring shall, by reason of any defect in the transferor's title, amount to theft of the property. The effect of s 3(2) is that, if X steals goods from V and sells them to D who neither knows nor suspects that they are stolen, a refusal by D to restore the goods (or his actual disposal of them) after his discovery of the theft by X is not theft by him from V.

Property

'Property' is defined by TA 1968, s 4(1) as including money and all other property, real or personal, including things in action and other intangible property.

'Real property' means land and things forming part of the land, such as plants and buildings. Although land and things forming part of the land are 'property' for the purposes of theft, there are special provisions restricting the theft of them, which are dealt with later.

'Personal property', in its tangible sense, means movable things which can be owned, such as cars, computers, and television sets.

A 'thing in action' is intangible property. It is a right to sue, and its inclusion in the definition of 'property' means that someone who dishonestly assumes rights (or a right) of ownership over a thing in action, such as a debt, copyright or trade mark, with the intention of permanently depriving the person entitled to it, is guilty of theft. Thus, if D dishonestly assigns to X a debt owed to D and his partner, V, in order to defeat V's rights, D is guilty of the theft of a thing in action belonging to V. Where a bank account is in credit the bank owes a debt to its customer for the amount of that credit. Consequently, if D dishonestly draws cheques on V's account and uses the proceeds for his own purposes, D can be convicted of the theft of property belonging to V because he will have appropriated a thing in action (the debt) owned by V when he presents the cheque.

'Other intangible property' covers such things as gas stored in pipes, which is undoubtedly capable of being stolen, and patents.

Despite the wide terms of s 4(1), there are some things which do not, or may not, come within the definition and hence cannot be stolen. A live human body is not property because it can never be owned. The same is true in relation to a human corpse. However, where a body (or part of a body) has undergone the application of human skill (such as embalming or dissecting) it becomes property. Thus, for example, an anatomical or pathological specimen which has been embalmed or dissected for exhibition or teaching purposes is property for the purposes of s 4.

It has been held that confidential information, such as a trade secret or the contents of an examination paper, is not property for the purposes of theft, so that the mere abstraction of the information is not theft, and it has also been held that electricity is not property for such purposes and cannot be stolen. There is, however, a separate offence of abstracting electricity (see p 927).

Land and things forming part of the land

TA 1968, s 4(2) provides that a person cannot steal land, or things forming part of land and severed from it by him or by his directions, except in the following cases:

(a) when he is a trustee or personal representative, or is authorised by power of attorney, or as liquidator of a company, or otherwise, to sell or dispose of land belonging to another, and he appropriates the land or anything forming part of it by dealing with it in breach of the confidence reposed in him; or

(b) when he is not in possession of the land and appropriates anything forming part of the land by severing it or causing it to be severed, or after it has been severed; or

(c) when, being in possession of the land under a tenancy, he appropriates the whole or any part of any fixture or structure let to be used with the land.

TA 1968, s 4(3) goes on to provide that a person who picks mushrooms growing wild on any land, or who picks flowers, fruit or foliage from a plant growing wild on any land, does not (although not in possession of the land) steal what he picks, unless he does it for reward or for sale or other commercial purposes. For these purposes, 'mushroom' includes any fungus, and 'plant' includes any shrub or tree.

These complex provisions can be explained as follows:

(1) Land as a whole cannot be stolen except where the appropriator is of a defined class and acts in a defined way. The class of appropriators comprises a trustee or personal representative, or a person authorised by power of attorney, or as a liquidator of a company, or otherwise, to sell or dispose of land belonging to another. The defined mode of appropriation is dealing with the land in breach of the confidence reposed in the appropriator. The essence of the offence lies in the dishonest breach of a confidence placed in a person who enjoys a position of trust in relation to the land. The result of the rule that land as a whole cannot be stolen except by a trustee, etc is that a person cannot steal land as a whole by moving a boundary fence or by occupying it as a squatter. The appropriation of land in this way must be dealt with by civil process, or in the case of a residential building by a prosecution for the offence of squatting in such a building (see p 763).

(2) Things forming part of the land, such as soil, houses, bricks in a wall, and fixtures, can only be stolen in the following cases:

(a) As for land as a whole, by the defined persons in the defined way.

(b) Where a person not in possession of the land appropriates the thing by severing it or causing it to be severed. If a trespasser digs up turves or gravel, removes bricks from a building, digs up growing things, picks flowers from a cultivated plant, cuts hay, or cuts down trees or saws off their branches, or causes such severance to be done, he may be convicted of theft (although in many cases it may be more appropriate to charge him with, and convict him of, criminal damage).

The present provision (s 4(2)(b)) does not apply to the picking of *wild* mushrooms or fungi nor to picking *from wild* plants and the like. Such conduct is dealt with by s 4(3), as follows. First, the picking of wild mushrooms or other fungi by a person not in possession of the land cannot amount to theft (although clearly there has been a severance) unless it is done for reward or for sale or other commercial purpose. Second, where a person not in possession of the land picks flowers, fruit or foliage from a plant, shrub or tree growing wild, this cannot amount to theft (although, again, there has been a severance) unless the picking is done for reward or for sale or other commercial purpose.

Thus, wild mushroom gathering cannot amount to theft if it is done by a person who picks the mushrooms for his own use, but it can if done for sale. The same considerations apply to flowers, fruit or foliage. Picking a few sprigs of holly for use at home cannot be theft, but it can if done for reward (eg payment by a florist). The term 'pick from' does not include uprooting or sawing off the top of a Christmas tree; both are clear cases of severance covered by s 4(2)(b) and unaffected by s 4(3).

As Christmas approaches, police officers become increasingly involved in the protection of growing things which are a traditional part of Christmas decorations. Vehicles carrying Christmas trees should be accompanied by delivery notes issued by the Forestry Commission or the landowner in question. If they are not, there is reason to suspect that the trees have been stolen.

Before leaving this area, it should be noted that a person who gathers or plucks any part of a 'protected' wild plant without uprooting thereby commits an offence under the Wildlife and Countryside Act 1981, s 13. These matters are referred to in Appendix 4 contained in the companion website to this book. See http://<www.oup.com/>.

(3) Generally, a person in possession of land under a tenancy cannot steal things forming part of the land. Thus, he cannot be convicted of theft if he digs up a plant on the land, or uproots a plant, or picks blackberries from wild plants on the land in order to sell them. The only exception relates to the whole or part of any structure or fixture let to be used with the land; such is stealable by the tenant. The obvious example of a 'structure' is a building but the term also includes a wall or bridge. A 'fixture' is an article, such as a washbasin or fireplace, which is attached to the land or to a building so as to make a permanent improvement to the land or building; by law it becomes part of the land.

The result of all this is that a tenant may be convicted of theft if he demolishes the garage on the land of which he is a tenant, or if he removes a fireplace there in order to sell it.

For the purposes of the above, a person is in possession under a tenancy regardless of whether the tenancy is a lease for 999 years or a weekly tenancy, and also if he is in possession merely under an agreement for such a tenancy. In addition, he must be treated as being in possession under a tenancy if he remains as a statutory tenant after the end of his tenancy.

Of course, once a thing has been severed from the land it ceases to be part of the land and may thereafter be the subject of theft in the same way as any other piece of personal property, which it has become. In other words, the special provisions of TA 1968, s 4(2) and (3) no longer apply to it.

Wild creatures

TA 1968, s 4(4) states that wild creatures, whether tamed or untamed, are to be regarded as property, but that a person cannot steal a wild creature, not tamed or ordinarily kept in captivity, or the carcase of any such creature, unless either it has been reduced into possession by or on behalf of another person and possession of it has not since been lost or abandoned or another person is in course of reducing it into possession.

This appears to be complex at first but it is more easily understood if it is borne in mind that, while they are alive, wild creatures which are neither tamed nor ordinarily kept in captivity are not owned by anyone, but on being killed or taken they become the property of the owner of the land on which they are killed or taken or, if he has granted the sporting rights to someone else, the grantee of those rights. Section 4(4) distinguishes two groups of wild creatures:

Wild creatures which have been tamed or are ordinarily kept in captivity   Such a creature can be stolen in the same ways as any other property. Thus a person may be guilty of theft by dishonestly appropriating a tamed fox or a bear from a zoo.

Wild creatures neither tamed nor ordinarily kept in captivity   Such a creature or its carcase cannot normally be stolen but becomes 'stealable':

(a) if reduced into possession by or on behalf of another (in which case it remains 'stealable' so long as possession has not subsequently been lost or abandoned); or
(b) if another person is in course of reducing it into possession.

Thus, it is not theft to poach game on another's land, unless for instance the game is taken from a sack into which another, even another poacher, has put the product of his own shooting (because there has been a reduction into possession by another) or is picked up from the ground where it is lying after it has been shot by another but not yet picked up by him (because another is in the course of reducing it into his possession). For the above purposes, possession of a live wild creature is abandoned if the possessor allows it to escape from his possession; it is lost if a wild creature not ordinarily kept in captivity escapes of its own volition. Possession of the carcase of a wild creature is not lost by a person who mislays it. Although s 4(4) means that poachers are not normally thieves, there are other offences which they commit, mentioned in Appendix 5 contained in the companion website to this book. See http://<www.oup.com/>.

Belonging to another

The offence of theft requires that the property appropriated should belong to another when appropriated.

The basic rule

TA 1968, s 5(1) states that property is regarded as belonging to any person having possession or control of it, or having in it any proprietary right or interest (not being an equitable interest arising only from an agreement to transfer or grant an interest). Possession or control need not be lawful. Thus, the appropriation of a drug in the unlawful possession of V can amount to theft.

The question whether the property appropriated belonged to some other person causes no problems in the vast majority of cases. If a wallet is taken from V's pocket it quite clearly belongs to V, since he will almost certainly be its owner (and complete ownership is the clearest example of a proprietary right) and, anyway, it will be in his possession. If goods are taken from a shop they clearly belong to the proprietor of the shop for the same reasons. When there are joint owners of property, one of them will steal from the other if he dishonestly assumes one of the rights of the owner, because the property will also belong to the other co-owner under TA 1968, s 5(1).

Someone who leaves his clock to be repaired still owns it and therefore it still belongs to him. The repairer now has possession of the clock, and, if it is then handed to one of his assistants to effect the repair, that assistant has control of it. The clock can now be stolen from either the owner, the repairer, or his assistant, and it can be stolen by one of these from the other. For example, if the assistant takes the clock to the pub at lunchtime and sells it, he thereby appropriates property belonging to another (to the owner and to the repairer, since the clock is technically still in the repairer's possession). Likewise, if the owner sneaks into the repairer's shop and takes away the clock without paying for the repair he appropriates property belonging to another. The same would be true if the property is a hired motor car and its owner drives it away from the hirer's parking space during the hire period.

A person who mislays property nevertheless still retains ownership of it, and he also retains possession until the property comes into the possession of another. Thus, 'lost property' is still capable of being stolen. This must be contrasted with the situation where the property has been abandoned. When a person throws away his old bicycle, not caring what happens to it (ie he abandons it), he loses ownership and possession of it. Since the property has no owner or possessor, it cannot thereafter be stolen unless and until it comes into the possession or control of another. It would be different if the owner placed his cycle behind a hedge because the tyre had punctured and travelled the remainder of his journey by bus. In these circumstances the property is not abandoned because the owner cares about what may happen to the bicycle, and it therefore still belongs to him.

Property subject to a trust

Where property is subject to a trust, it is regarded as belonging to the beneficiaries (who have a proprietary interest in it) as well as to the trustees, with the result that trustees who appropriate trust property can be convicted of stealing it from the beneficiaries. There are two exceptions to this.

First, the beneficial interest of a beneficiary under one type of trust, a constructive trust, may not always be a sufficient proprietary interest under s 5(1). Consequently, there cannot always be a theft of the trust property, as against him.

Second, charitable trusts and certain other types of trust do not, in law, have beneficiaries, with the result that under s 5(1) the trust property belongs only to the trustees. To prevent trust property being unprotected in such a case against appropriations by the trustees, s 5(2) provides that, where property is subject to a trust, the persons to whom it belongs shall be regarded as including any person having a right to enforce the trust, and that an intention to defeat the trust shall be regarded accordingly as an intention to deprive of the property any person having that right. In the case of a charitable trust, the Attorney General, although not a beneficiary, has the right to enforce the trust, so that appropriation of a charitable trust fund by the trustees is capable of amounting to theft since the fund belongs to the Attorney General under s 5(2).

Property received under an obligation to retain and deal with it in a particular way

TA 1968, s 5(3) provides that, where a person receives property from or on account of another and is under an *obligation* (ie a legal obligation) to the other to *retain* and *deal* with that property, or *its* proceeds (ie things into which it has been converted), *in a particular way*, the property or proceeds shall be regarded (*as against him*) as belonging to the other. This is important where ownership, possession and control of the property have been transferred to the recipient.

The essence of s 5(3) is that property (usually money) or its proceeds is regarded (as against the defendant (D)) as belonging to another from or on whose account D has received the property if D is under a *legal obligation* to that person *to retain and deal* with the property or its proceeds *in a particular way*. Section 5(3) is clearly satisfied where D receives money from V which he is legally obliged to V to use in a particular way (eg to pay it into a Christmas Club which D runs), or where D is legally obliged to V to use in a particular way the proceeds of money received from V (eg to use the money to get some goods for V). In the latter case, both the money and the goods (its proceeds) will belong to another under s 5(3). Section 5(3) is also satisfied if a shop assistant receives money from a customer for some of his employer's goods, since he has received the money on account of another (the employer) and is under a legal obligation to deal with it in a particular way (to put it in the till). If D or the shop assistant dishonestly appropriates the property in question with intent permanently to deprive, theft is committed. On the other hand, s 5(3) is not satisfied where D, a decorator, is given a down-payment on a job by a customer. D is obliged to the customer to do the job, but not to retain and deal with the money in a particular way. Nor is s 5(3) satisfied where an employee receives money from a customer for goods which (contrary to his employer's instructions) he is selling on his own account since the money is not received from or on account of another person to whom the employee is legally obliged to retain and deal with it in a particular way. In such a case, however, the employee could be convicted of fraud contrary to the Fraud Act 2006, s 1, by virtue of s 4 of that Act.

Property got by another's mistake

TA 1968, s 5(4) states that where a person gets property by another's mistake, and is under an obligation to make restoration (in whole or in part) of the property or its proceeds or of the value thereof, then to the extent of that obligation the property or proceeds shall be regarded (as against him) as belonging to the person entitled to restoration, and an intention not to make restoration shall be regarded accordingly as an intention to deprive that person of the property or proceeds.

The important point about this provision is that it only applies where the recipient of property transferred under a mistake is thereby under an immediate *legal obligation* to restore it (or its proceeds or value). For practical purposes, this provision is only of importance where the recipient was ignorant of the mistake when he got the property and he has acquired ownership, possession and control of the property to the exclusion of anyone else. If he was aware of the mistake when he got the property he could be convicted of theft on the basis that his appropriation at that time was accompanied by mens rea. On the other hand, if the recipient only discovers the mistake later, but decides not to return the property his appropriation with mens rea will be of property which is then in his ownership, possession and control. Section 5(4) provides that if the recipient is under a legal obligation to restore the property, its proceeds or value, the property is regarded (as against him) as belonging to the person entitled to restoration.

The best example of a case of a legal obligation to make restoration, where a person has received ownership, possession and control of property under a mistake, is where there is a transfer of money under a mistake which leads the transferor to believe that the transferee is legally entitled to the money. Thus, if V, by a mistake as to the number of hours of overtime worked, overpays his employee, D, and D, realising the mistake, appropriates the excess amount, D has appropriated money which by s 5(4) belongs to another. If D in such a case is paid by cheque and cashes the cheque and appropriates the cash received, he will appropriate property belonging to another under s 5(4) because the cash will be the proceeds of the cheque and D would be obliged to make restoration of it to V. On the other hand, if V is induced to give D some money as a gift by a self-induced mistaken belief that D is collecting for charity, D cannot be convicted of theft if he appropriates the money on discovering V's mistake because, the requirements of s 5(4) not having been met (since D is not legally obliged to make restoration of the money), the money will not belong to another (ie other than D) when D appropriates it.

Property of a corporation sole

TA 1968, s 5 contains one other provision, s 5(5), which can be disposed of briefly. Section 5(5) provides that the property of a 'corporation sole', such as a bishop or a police and crime commissioner in his official capacity, shall be regarded as belonging to the corporation notwithstanding a vacancy in the corporation. Thus, the property of a police and crime commissioner 'belongs to another', and is therefore capable of being stolen, even though the commissioner has just died and not yet been replaced by a successor.

Dishonesty

The appropriation of property belonging to another must be committed dishonestly.

TA 1968, s 2(1)

Section 2(1) expressly and as a matter of law excludes appropriations carried out with certain states of mind from being dishonest. Section 2(1) provides that a person's appropriation of property belonging to another is *not* to be regarded as dishonest:

(a) if he appropriates the property in the belief that he has in law the right to deprive the other of it, on behalf of himself or a third person; or

(b) if he appropriates the property in the belief that he would have had the other's consent if the other knew of the appropriation and the circumstances of it; or

(c) (except where the property came to him as a trustee or personal representative) if he appropriates the property in the belief that the person to whom the property belongs cannot be discovered by taking reasonable steps.

These provisions are concerned with the defendant's belief. *It is legally irrelevant that a belief in this context is unreasonable*, although, of course, magistrates or a jury are less inclined to accept an alleged belief as truly held if it is an unreasonable one.

Belief in legal right to deprive By s 2(1)(a), the element of dishonesty is excluded if a person appropriating property belonging to another *believes* that he has a *right in law* to deprive the other of it, whether on behalf of himself or a third person. A husband who genuinely believes that he has a legal right to sell his wife's car on the grounds that he considered that her property became his on marriage does not act dishonestly. If a person is owed money and in order to recover that money he threatens his debtor with a knife, this will not be theft if he believes that he has a legal right to deprive the other of property, even though he recognises that he should not use a knife.

Where a person acts under a belief in a *moral* right to deprive, the question of his dishonesty depends on the two-stage test described on the next page.

Belief that the 'owner' would have consented if he had known Section s 2(1)(b) (belief that the person to whom the property belongs would have consented if he had known of the appropriation and its circumstances) clearly covers the case, for example, of someone who takes a bottle of lager from a flatmate's room, leaving the price behind him and believing that his flatmate would have consented had he known all the circumstances.

Belief that the 'owner' cannot be discovered by taking reasonable steps Section 2(1)(c) is primarily, although not exclusively, concerned with those who find property belonging to another. It exempts the defendant (D) from dishonesty if he appropriates another's property under a *belief* that the person to whom the property belongs cannot be discovered by taking reasonable steps. The question is not whether the 'owner' could not be found by taking reasonable steps, but whether D believed this.

If D finds a £5 note in the street and appropriates it, it will be almost impossible to disprove a claim by him that he believed the owner could not be found by taking reasonable steps. It will be different if the note is contained in a purse bearing the owner's name and address (or containing other material identifying the owner); in that case it will be much easier to disprove a claimed belief that the owner could not be found by taking reasonable steps.

The exemption is not restricted to things which are found. Suppose that D's friend, on emigrating, left property under D's care until he should return to this country. If, after many years, during which D has not heard from his friend, D sells the property, honestly believing that he will not return and that he cannot be traced by taking reasonable steps, D will not be guilty of theft.

Section 2(1)(c) expressly does not apply to a person who received the property as a trustee of property or a personal representative. This is sensible in view of the special obligations of such a person.

Dishonesty in cases outside s 2(1)

The negative definition of dishonesty in TA 1968, s 2(1) is only a partial definition; consequently, a defendant's appropriation may not have been made dishonestly even though the case falls outside s 2(1). Whether or not a defendant who appropriated property with some alleged state of mind other than one of the three referred to in s 2(1) did so dishonestly is a question of fact for the jury. This means that, unlike the situation in which a belief of the type referred to in s 2(1) is pleaded (where the judge must tell the jury that in law an appropriation with such a belief is not dishonest), it is not for the judge to tell the jury whether or not an appropriation with the alleged state of mind is dishonest but for the jury to decide this according to the following two-stage test.

In deciding this, the jury must first see whether, given his state of mind, D's actions were dishonest according to the ordinary standards of reasonable and honest people. If his actions were not dishonest according to those standards, the matter ends there and the prosecution fails. However, if his actions were dishonest by those standards, the jury must go on to decide whether D must have realised that what he was doing would be considered dishonest according to the standards of reasonable and honest people. If D did not realise this, his appropriation will not have been dishonest; if he did it will have been.

Where a theft charge is tried in a magistrates' court the above tests are, of course, applicable and are applied by the justices.

Summary on dishonesty

What has been said about dishonesty so far can be brought together as follows. D is charged with the theft of £10 taken from the till of the shop in which he is employed. If, at his trial, D pleads that his employer owed him £10 and he (D) believed that he was legally entitled to deprive the employer of the £10 taken in order to recoup his debt, the trial judge (assuming a Crown Court trial) must tell the jury that—as a matter of law (s 2(1))—D's alleged belief prevents his appropriation being dishonest and that they must acquit D unless the alleged belief is disproved. The same would be the case if D pleaded that he believed the employer would have consented to the taking if he had known of it and its circumstances.

Suppose, on the other hand, that D admits that he knew he had no legal right to the £10 and that he knew the employer would not have consented to his taking it, but claims instead that he took the money to tide him over to pay day, intending to put in £10 from his pay packet, and claims that what he did was a common practice in the shop. Here, D is not pleading one of the beliefs in s 2(1) and the trial judge must tell the jury that, if they do not find that D's claim that he intended to repay has been disproved by the prosecution, they must decide whether or not—given that intention—

his appropriation was dishonest and must do so by applying the two-fold test referred to above.

For the sake of completeness, it should be mentioned that TA 1968, s 2(2) says what has already been implied, by providing that an appropriation *may* be dishonest notwithstanding that the person concerned intends to pay for what he took. If a collector fails to purchase a valuable antique at an auction, his appropriation would almost certainly be found to be dishonest if he took the antique from the home of the successful bidder and left money in payment, even if that money represented a reasonable purchase price. It has been held that an appropriation can be dishonest even though the original owner of goods or money is not the poorer because of the defendant's conduct.

Intention permanently to deprive

The dishonest appropriation of property belonging to another must be accompanied by an intention permanently to deprive the other of that property. Unless it can be shown that this intention existed at the time of appropriation there can be no theft.

The presence of an intent permanently to deprive will usually be proved by evidence of what D did with the property appropriated. If D takes V's £5 note and spends it on drink this clearly indicates an intent permanently to deprive V of the note as D has passed the note into circulation. It is no use D alleging that he intended to pay it back. Although this may prevent him being found to have been dishonest, and lead to an acquittal on that ground, D will nevertheless have intended permanently to deprive V of the thing (the actual £5 note) which he has appropriated. If a car is appropriated and a false registration book is produced, the engine and chassis numbers are altered, and the colour of the car is changed, this is clear evidence of an intent permanently to deprive.

Where the victim of an appropriation only has a limited interest in the property, a person can intend permanently to deprive even though he intends only a purely temporary borrowing. For example, if V hires a power tool from X for a period of one week, and this is 'unlawfully' borrowed by D who is aware of the circumstances and who intends to retain it throughout that period and then to return it to X, D intends wholly to deprive V of the whole of his interest in the property, and that intended deprivation is therefore permanent in the circumstances.

In certain limited cases a person can be convicted of theft even though he did not mean permanently to deprive, and even though he positively intended to return the property at some future date (or did actually return it). A conviction in such a case is possible if the case falls within TA 1968, s 6, which extends the meaning of 'intention of permanently depriving'.

Section 6(1) provides that a person appropriating property belonging to another without meaning the other permanently to lose the thing itself is nevertheless to be regarded as having the intention of permanently depriving the other of it if his *intention is to treat the thing as his own to dispose of regardless of the other's rights;* and a borrowing or lending of it may amount to so treating it if, but only if, the borrowing or lending is for a period and in circumstances making it equivalent to an outright taking or disposal.

Treating as one's own to dispose of regardless of other's rights

The first part of s 6(1) is the key part. It operates to 'deem' a person to have intended permanent deprivation if he intended to treat the thing as his own to dispose of regardless of the other's rights. If D takes a valuable painting belonging to V, intending to return it to V only if V pays a ransom for it, D clearly intends to treat the thing as his own to dispose of regardless of V's rights, because he intends that V should only get it back by paying for it.

Section 6(1) also catches the rogue who purports to sell property belonging to another in circumstances where it is unlikely that the property will be removed, as where an employee purports to sell a grand piano belonging to his employer which he knows his employer is going to dispose of in a few minutes time. The reason is that the rogue intends to treat the property 'sold' as his own to dispose of regardless of the rights of the other and it is irrelevant that such a disposal is unlikely to occur. A charge for fraud would, however, be more appropriate.

Another type of case falling within s 6(1) is where D abandons the property and is indifferent as to whether it is recovered by the person to whom it belongs. If, by the circumstances of the abandonment and/or the nature of the property, it is (to D's knowledge) extremely unlikely that the property will be recovered, D can be said to intend to dispose of it regardless of the rights of the other. If V's car is taken and driven a distance of 200 miles by D then abandoned, the justices or jury are most unlikely to find that there was an intention to treat it as D's own to dispose of regardless of V's rights, as a car is easily identifiable and will certainly be returned to V. It would be different if what was taken and so abandoned was a watch.

Borrowing or lending

The second part of s 6(1) goes on to provide that a borrowing or lending may amount to treating property as one's own to dispose of regardless of the other's rights, if the borrowing or lending is for a period and in circumstances which make it equivalent to an outright taking or disposal. The Court of Appeal has ruled that this provision is only satisfied by a borrower if his intention is to return the thing only when 'all its goodness or virtue has gone'. This covers the following types of case.

D takes V's monthly season ticket, intending to return it at the end of the month. D's borrowing is clearly for a period and in circumstances making it equivalent to an outright taking since, when it is returned, the season ticket will be a virtually worthless piece of paper.

D takes V's rare plant and its pot, intending to return it and its pot once it has died. D's borrowing of the plant is for a period and in circumstances making it equivalent to an outright taking.

Because the borrowing in both cases is equivalent to an outright taking or disposal, D's intention so to act is regarded by s 6(1) as an intent to treat as his own to dispose of regardless of the V's rights and, hence, as an intent permanently to deprive.

On the other hand, a cinema projectionist who borrows a film in order to make pirate copies does not intend to treat the film as his own to dispose of regardless of the owner's rights because on its return the film would not have lost all of its goodness or virtue.

An example of a case where a lending would satisfy the present provision would be where D, an assistant in a florists', lends some cut flowers to X for a week for a flower display, knowing that they will have died by the time of their return. D intends to treat the flowers as his own to dispose of because, as he knows, the lending is for a period and in circumstances making it equivalent to an outright disposal.

Parting with property subject to a condition

TA 1968, s 6(2) provides a further explanation of 'treating as one's own to dispose of regardless of the other's rights'. It states that, where a person having possession or control (lawfully or not) of property belonging to another, parts with the property under a condition as to its return which he may not be able to perform, this (if done for purposes of his own and without the other's authority) amounts to treating the property as his own to dispose of regardless of the other's rights. Thus, where D, who is in possession or control of V's property, pawns it, intending to redeem it and return it if he wins a bet, this amounts to treating as his own to dispose of regardless of the rights of the other (V) and his intention to do so is deemed by s 6(1) to be an intention permanently to deprive V of it.

ABSTRACTING ELECTRICITY

As already indicated, it has been held that electricity is not property and therefore cannot be stolen. However, a special indictable (either way) offence is provided by TA 1968, s 13, which states that a person who dishonestly uses without due authority, or dishonestly causes to be wasted or diverted, any electricity is guilty of an offence.

The offence will usually be encountered when a person, who has had his electricity supply disconnected, reconnects it, and thus uses electricity without authority; or when evidence is found that a consumer has by-passed his meter, since his authority to use electricity supplied by the electricity company is conditional upon that electricity having passed through the meter before use. No doubt the primary purpose of s 13 was to deal with these matters but the effect of s 13 is more widespread. If a trespasser enters property and switches on the lights he undoubtedly uses electricity, and if this use in the circumstances is considered to be dishonest, he will commit this offence.

Section 13 covers wasting or diverting in addition to using, as where D diverts electricity for use by another. It seems that the person who by-passes his meter could be charged with either dishonest usage or dishonest diversion, as he does not have authority to use in that way and he has certainly caused electricity to be diverted.

Section 13 is not restricted to mains electricity. Thus, a person who dishonestly used the power stored in a radio battery could be guilty of this offence.

It is important not to forget that the element of dishonesty must be proved. The provisions of TA 1968, s 2(1) are limited to theft, and therefore do not apply to an offence under s 13, but the rest of the above explanation of dishonesty for the purposes of theft applies equally to an offence under s 13.

DISHONESTLY OBTAINING ELECTRONIC COMMUNICATIONS SERVICE, AND POSSESSION OR SUPPLY OF APPARATUS FOR DOING SO

It is an offence under the Communications Act 2003 (CA 2003), s 125 dishonestly to obtain an electronic communications service with the intention of avoiding payment of a charge in respect of that service. However, s 125 exempts the dishonest obtaining of a broadcasting or cable programme service provided from a place in the UK.

It is an offence under CA 2003, s 126(1) to possess or have under one's control anything that may be used for obtaining an electronic communications service, or in connection with obtaining such a service, with certain specified intentions. The specified intentions are an intent: to use the thing to obtain such a service dishonestly; to use it for a purpose connected with the dishonest obtaining of such a service; dishonestly to allow it to be so used; or to allow it to be so used for a connected purpose. Once again, s 126 exempts dishonestly obtaining a broadcasting or cable programme service provided from a place in the UK. Section 126(2) also prohibits the supply, or offer to supply, of anything which may be used to commit the above offence where the supplier knows or believes that the person supplied, etc has one of the above intentions.

These offences are indictable (either way) offences.

ROBBERY

TA 1968, s 8(1) provides that a person is guilty of robbery (an offence triable only on indictment) if he steals, and immediately before or at the time of doing so, and in order to do so, he uses force on any person, or puts or seeks to put any person in fear of being then and there subjected to force.

No theft: no robbery

Robbery is an aggravated form of theft, the theft being aggravated by the use of force or threat of force. If there is no theft, there is no robbery. Where a person uses or threatens force in order to steal but has not achieved the appropriation of any property, and is therefore not guilty of robbery, he can be convicted of the offence of assault with intent to rob, which is triable only on indictment. There can be no conviction for robbery if it is found that the person who used or threatened force in order to appropriate the property believed that he had a legal right to it, even though he did not believe he was entitled to use force to obtain it, because the essential ingredient for theft, 'dishonesty', is missing. Of course, there can be a conviction for some offence of assault (other than assault with intent to rob).

Use or threat of force immediately before or at time of theft

To constitute robbery, the force must be used or threatened 'immediately before or at the time of' the theft. There can be no robbery if force is only used or threatened after 'the time' of the theft. A person who pushes an old lady to the ground in order to steal her handbag, and does so, commits robbery; so does someone who approaches her and steals her handbag by threatening to punch her in the face unless she hands it over. The first uses force at the time of the theft and the other threatens force immediately before the theft. However, a person, who approaches a woman and steals her handbag without force but, being discovered by her in possession of the bag shortly afterwards, assaults her, cannot be convicted of robbery. This is because the time of the theft will have elapsed when the force is used. Such a person could, of course, be convicted of theft and assault. The 'time' of the theft is not limited to the split second during which the initial appropriation with mens rea occurs, since an act of appropriation may be a continuing one, in which case the 'time' of the theft lasts as long as the theft can be said still to be in progress in commonsense terms. Thus, there can be a robbery where a person takes property in a shop and, when approached by the owner, uses violence. The act of 'appropriation' would still be continuing at that time.

Use of force on a person or threat then and there to subject to force

Where force is used, it must be used 'on' a person, but it has been held that the force need not be used directly against the person. Consequently, it is enough to use force to obtain possession of property in the physical possession of another. For example, the use of force to wrest a handbag from a woman's grasp is robbery.

Minimal force, such as that used to snatch a cigarette from another's fingers, will not suffice.

In the case of a threat of force, a threat of future force is insufficient; the threat must be 'then and there' to subject another to force. A threat of force to property will not suffice, nor will the actual use of force against it.

The references above to threats of force are a shorthand way of referring to the requirement that D 'puts or seeks to put any person in fear of being then and there subjected to force'. These words must not be forgotten. If D threatens violence to a month-old baby in a pram unless the mother parts with her money, this is not robbery because D cannot be said to have put or sought to put the mother in fear of immediate force to herself. A charge of a less serious offence would be appropriate in such a case.

Even where the victim did not feel threatened or put in fear there may still be a robbery as it is the intention of the perpetrator rather than the fortitude of the victim which has to be considered.

Although the force must be used or threatened on a person, it is not essential that the theft is carried out in his presence, provided that it is used or threatened for the purpose of stealing. It is robbery, for example, where a security guard is tied up so that property may be removed from some other part of the warehouse in which he is on duty.

The theft need not be from the person against whom the force is used or threatened. Thus, if D threatens a married couple that he will stab the wife unless the husband hands over his wallet, D can be convicted of robbery.

Use or threat of force in order to steal

The force used or threatened must be used in order to steal. If a man during an argument with another, threatens to give him a beating and the man threatened gives money to him not to do so, this cannot be robbery as the threat of force was not made with the intention of stealing. Likewise, a man who knocks a woman to the ground to rape her, but who then changes his mind and instead takes the handbag which she has dropped, is not guilty of robbery or of assault with intent to rob, although he might, of course, be convicted of theft and attempted rape.

REMOVAL OF ARTICLES FROM PLACES OPEN TO THE PUBLIC

Because an essential element of theft is an intention permanently to deprive the owner of his property, a charge of theft would not succeed against an art lover who takes a painting from a public gallery, intending to enjoy its presence in his home for a year and thereafter to return it to the gallery. It is for this reason that TA 1968, s 11 creates a specific indictable (either way) offence to cover cases such as this. Section 11(1) provides that, where the public have access to a building in order to view the building or part of it, or a collection or part of a collection housed in it, any person who without lawful authority removes from the building or its grounds the whole or part of any article displayed or kept for display to the public in the building, or that part of it, or in its grounds, is guilty of an offence.

The removal of an article must be either from a building to which the public have access in order to view the building or part of it, or a collection or part of a collection housed in it, or from the grounds of such a building. We are therefore concerned with removals of articles from stately homes, national galleries, historic buildings, etc, provided they are open to the public in the above sense, or from their grounds. A person who removes the portrait of an Edwardian mayor from the entrance of the town hall does not commit the present offence because, although the public have access to the town hall, it is only for the purpose of paying council tax, making inquiries or seeing their councillors; they do not have access in order to view the building, or any collection in it, or any part of the building or collection. If someone removes a painting from a collection in a stately home, access to which is limited to members of the Women's Institute, he does not commit the present offence because the public do not have access to the building in question but only a particular section of the public.

The offence is not committed if the collection has been made or exhibited for the purposes of effecting sales or other commercial dealings. Thus, removals of paintings from commercial art galleries are not caught by s 11. Subject to this, it does not matter that the collection in question is one got together for a temporary purpose. The annual art exhibition in the village hall is therefore caught by s 11.

Generally, an offence under s 11 can be committed whether or not the building is open to the public at the time of the removal. There is one exception: if the thing removed is there otherwise than as forming part of, or being on loan for exhibition with, a collection intended for permanent exhibition to the public, it must be removed on a day when the public has access to the building or grounds. Thus, if a painting is removed from the collection at the National Gallery it is irrelevant that the Gallery is then closed over the Christmas period, whereas it is not an offence to remove a painting from the annual art exhibition in the village hall on a day when the hall is closed.

The offence under s 11 only applies where the thing removed is the whole or part of any article displayed or kept for display to the public in the building, or part of it, to which the public have access or in its grounds. The purpose of this is to separate those things which are there for display and those which are not. If a visitor takes an old vase which forms a part of the display, he commits this offence. If he takes the attendant's coat on the way out he does not, as the coat is not a part of the display.

There must be a removal from the building or its grounds. A visitor who moves the vase from one room to another does not commit the offence, but one who takes it out of the building does.

Section 11(1) makes it clear that no offence is committed where the person removing an article covered by it has lawful authority for doing so.

There is no need to prove dishonesty in respect of the act of removal but s 11(3) exempts someone who believes that he has lawful authority, or that he would have it if the person entitled to give it knew of the removal and its circumstances. Therefore, a furniture remover who was removing articles on behalf of their owner would not commit an offence if he took one of the exhibited articles, believing that it was one of the items to remove. Likewise, a restorer of oil paintings who carried out work for the owner from time to time would not commit an offence if in the owner's absence he took a painting for its five-yearly restoration, believing that, had the owner been present, he would have consented.

TAKING VEHICLES OR OTHER CONVEYANCES

TA 1968, s 12(1) provides that a person is guilty of an offence if, without having the consent of the owner or other lawful authority, he takes any conveyance for his own or another's use, or, knowing that any conveyance has been taken without such authority, drives it or allows himself to be carried in or on it.

There are two offences under TA 1968, s 12(1), that of taking a conveyance without authority and that of driving or allowing oneself to be carried in or on a conveyance which one knows has been so taken. An offence under s 12 does not require proof of an intent permanently to deprive. The section is aimed at 'joy-riders'.

The term 'conveyance' is defined to include any conveyance constructed or adapted for the carriage of a person or persons whether by land, water or air, but it does not include a conveyance constructed or adapted for use only under the control of a person not carried in or on it, and 'drive' is construed accordingly. The term 'conveyance' is therefore wide in meaning and covers almost all motor vehicles, as well as aeroplanes, hovercraft, boats, and ships, but it does not cover pedestrian-controlled vehicles, such as some milk floats and electric trolleys which are drawn by hand. Nor does it cover pedal cycles. Pedal cycles are covered by a separate offence (described on p 932).

Taking without authority

Taking

The mere unauthorised assumption of possession or control is not enough to constitute a 'taking' of a conveyance; *there must be some movement of it, however small.* The result is that a person who gets into the driving seat of a car and drives it a few feet takes a conveyance, as does a person who climbs into a boat on a boating lake and rows it to the other bank. On the other hand, people who unlawfully occupy a conveyance, either to shelter or to make love in it, do not take it. Of course, someone who gets into another's car and starts it is attempting to take a conveyance, but as the taking would amount to a summary offence, there can be no charge of attempting to take it. In such a case there may be a conviction for the offence of interfering with vehicles (discussed on p 933).

Unauthorised use of a conveyance by a person already in lawful possession or control of a conveyance may amount to a 'taking'. A lorry driver who uses his employer's lorry for his own purposes 'out of hours', or who appropriates it to his own use during the working day in a manner which is inconsistent with the rights of the employer and shows that he has assumed control for his own purposes, thereby 'takes' it. Thus, for example, a lorry driver who makes a serious deviation from his proper route for some private purpose can be convicted of the present offence. A similar principle applies to a person who has borrowed a conveyance if he uses it for a purpose other than that for which he has been given permission or after the time he is permitted to have the conveyance. By so using the conveyance, he takes it.

For the defendant's or another's use

Section 12(1) also requires that the taking be for the defendant's own or another's use, and this means that either the conveyance must be used as a conveyance or it must be taken for later use as a conveyance. It follows that a person who cuts the mooring rope of a boat and allows it to drift away empty does not commit this offence, whereas he would if he was aboard or if he towed it away for later use as a boat.

Without consent or other authority

The taking must be without the consent of the owner or other lawful authority. An apparent consent to a taking obtained by intimidation (as where D stops a car, grabs the driver by his lapels, and successfully demands the loan of the car) is not a true consent, so that the taking will be without consent. On the other hand, a consent which has been obtained by fraud is nevertheless valid and prevents the offence being committed, however fundamental (eg as to the identity of the deceiver) the mistake which is induced.

In relation to a conveyance subject to a hiring or hire-purchase agreement, 'owner' means the person in possession of it under that agreement. It follows that, during the currency of the agreement, such a person cannot commit the present offence in relation to that conveyance since he can hardly be said to take it without the consent of the owner.

The addition of the words 'or other lawful authority' excuses lawful takings, such as the removal by a constable of a vehicle which is causing an obstruction. Finance companies on occasion reclaim vehicles which are on hire-purchase from them when the terms of the agreement have been broken by the hirer, and they will usually have lawful authority to do so under the terms of the agreement.

Not only is the consent of the owner or other lawful authority a defence, but so also is a mistaken belief in the existence of such lawful authority or a mistaken belief that the owner would, if asked, have consented.

Driving or allowing self to be driven

In relation to the taking of motor vehicles in particular, but not exclusively, it is frequently the case that, after a vehicle has been taken by one person, it is used to convey a number of persons, each of whom may take a turn at driving. The second offence in s 12(1) deals with this situation, by providing that an offence is committed by anyone who, *knowing* that a conveyance has been taken without the consent of the owner or other lawful authority, drives it or allows himself to be carried in or on it. In circumstances where a vehicle, known to have been 'taken' contrary to s 12(1), is seen to be moving (for it is essential that there is movement in order that a person can be said to be 'carried'), and all the occupants are seen to step out of the vehicle but all deny driving it, the issue of who was driving is unimportant because all have allowed themselves to be 'carried' in the vehicle (since that expression covers a person who was driving).

Where a person takes a vehicle without consent and later picks up a friend and takes him for a drive, his friend commits no offence unless he knows that the vehicle has been so taken. Should the driver disclose that the vehicle has been unlawfully taken in the course of the journey, the passenger is guilty if he continues to allow himself to be carried.

Pedal cycles

Pedal cycles are not conveyances for the purposes of TA 1968, s 12(1) but are separately dealt with by s 12(5). Section 12(5) provides that a person commits an offence if, without having the consent of the owner or other lawful authority, he takes a pedal cycle for his own or another's use, or rides a pedal cycle knowing it to have been taken without such authority. What was said earlier about the various elements of the offence under s 12(1) is equally applicable to the present offences.

Aggravated vehicle-taking

TA 1968, s 12A provides indictable (either way) offences of aggravated vehicle-taking. An offence is committed under s 12A(1) where a person has committed *either of the offences under TA 1968, s 12(1)* (the basic offence) in any way in relation to a *mechanically propelled vehicle* and it is proved that, at any time after the vehicle was unlawfully taken (whether by himself or another) and before it was recovered, the vehicle was driven, or injury or damage was caused, in one or more of the following circumstances:

(a) the vehicle was driven in a dangerous manner on a road or other public place; the same test of such driving applies as in the offence of dangerous driving (see p 512);
(b) owing to the driving of the vehicle, an accident occurred by which injury was caused to any person;
(c) owing to the driving of the vehicle, an accident occurred by which damage was caused to any property other than the vehicle; or
(d) damage was caused to the vehicle.

The prosecution does not have to prove that the dangerous driving was by D, or that the injury, damage or accident was caused by D's driving or by D at all. Nor, under (b) or (c), need it be proved that there was any fault in the driving of the vehicle. 'Accident' in (b) and (c) includes a situation where a person has deliberately caused injury or damage. Once it is proved that the driving, injury or damage was caused during the period between the taking of the vehicle contrary to s 12(1) and its recovery, D is fixed with liability for an offence contrary to s 12A, unless he has one of the defences referred to in the next paragraph. A vehicle is 'recovered' when it is returned to its owner or other lawful possession or custody. The importance of the fact that the aggravating circumstances can occur at any time up to the recovery of the vehicle is shown by a case where a man, who was in the course of taking a vehicle, was 'locked in' the vehicle by an anti-theft device and he then damaged the vehicle in an attempt to escape before the police arrived. An aggravated vehicle-taking offence was committed as damage was caused to the vehicle before it was recovered.

It is a defence for D to prove that the relevant driving, accident or damage occurred before he committed the basic offence, or that he was neither in, nor on, nor in the immediate vicinity of the vehicle when such driving, accident or damage occurred.

Since the maximum penalty is greater where death is caused, s 12A(1) creates two offences: one where death is caused, and the other for other situations. It has been held that there is nothing to prevent both aggravated vehicle-taking (involving an allegation that the vehicle was driven dangerously) and dangerous driving being charged.

INTERFERENCE WITH VEHICLES

The Criminal Attempts Act 1981 (CAA 1981), s 9(1) provides that a person is guilty of the offence of vehicle interference if he interferes with a motor vehicle (p 342) or trailer or with anything carried in or on a motor vehicle or trailer with the intention that an offence:

(a) of theft of the motor vehicle or trailer or part of it;
(b) of theft of anything carried in or on the motor vehicle or trailer; or
(c) under TA 1968, s 12(1) (taking without authority),

shall be committed by himself or some other person.

CAA 1981, s 9 states that, if D can be proved to have intended that one of these offences should be committed, it is immaterial that it cannot be shown which offence it was.

If a group of rowdy youths rock a vehicle in order to set off its intruder alarm, they do not commit an offence under s 9. They certainly interfere with the vehicle but they lack the intention to commit any of the specified offences. On the other hand, if they start to unscrew the aerial or a wing mirror with the intention of stealing it, they commit an offence under s 9. The removal of tarpaulins from goods vehicles carrying loads indicates an interference with the intention to steal part of the load.

If someone is seen trying to open the door of someone else's motor vehicle this is certainly an interference with that vehicle. However, it is unlikely to satisfy a court that he intends to steal or take the vehicle, or to steal anything contained in it, unless there are further circumstances which point to an intention to commit one of those offences. The intention of the person interfering with vehicles becomes more apparent as attention is paid by him to more than one vehicle, or he is seen to examine the interior of the vehicle through its windows to check its contents, or even to try a number of doors on the same vehicle. The further the interference extends, the more likely it becomes that there is an appropriate criminal intent.

GOING EQUIPPED TO STEAL

Under TA 1968, s 25(1), a person commits an indictable (either way) offence if, when not at his place of abode, he has with him any article for use in the course of or in connection with any burglary or theft.

The offence can be committed anywhere besides D's place of abode. It has been decided that, where a person lives in a motor vehicle, it is his place of abode whilst on the site where he intends to abide, but that as soon as the vehicle leaves the site he is no longer at his place of abode.

Although the offence is described in the marginal note to s 25 as 'going equipped for stealing, etc', and is commonly so described, it is not limited to conduct which could be described as 'going equipped'. The term 'has with him' has the same meaning as in the Prevention of Crime Act 1953 (PCA 1953) (p 643).

The specified purposes are that D must intend to use the article in the course of or in connection with any burglary or theft; it is not necessary to prove that the articles are to be used in connection with any particular burglary or theft. 'Possession' to enable someone else to use the article is sufficient for the purposes of s 25. For the purposes of the present offence, an offence under TA 1968, s 12 of taking a conveyance is treated as theft.

If D is found with an article made or adapted for use in committing burglary or theft, proof of the offence under s 25 is assisted by s 25(3), which states that where there is proof that D had with him such an article that is evidence that he had it with him for such use. Of course, this can be rebutted by evidence of a contrary intention. The result of s 25(3) is that, if D is found trespassing in the grounds of a dwelling house with a bunch of skeleton keys in his pocket, this is evidence that he had those articles with him for use in committing burglary.

BLACKMAIL

The offence of blackmail, which is triable only on indictment, is dealt with by TA 1968, s 21(1) which provides that a person is guilty of blackmail if, with a view to gain for himself or another or with intent to cause loss to another, he makes any unwarranted demand with menaces; and for this purpose a demand with menaces is unwarranted unless the person making it does so in the belief:

(a) that he has reasonable grounds for making the demand; and
(b) that the use of the menaces is a proper means of reinforcing the demand.

Demand with menaces

To be guilty of blackmail, D must have made an unwarranted demand with menaces (with the appropriate mens rea). It is irrelevant that D obtained nothing as a result of his demand.

The nature of the act or omission demanded is immaterial. An oral demand is made when the words are said; if it is made by letter, it is made when that letter is posted. A demand need not be made in terms of an express demand or requirement, since (taken together with the menaces) it may be implied by a suggestion or other conduct which is by no means aggressive or forceful.

'Menaces' are not limited to threats of violence, since they include 'threats of action detrimental to or unpleasant to the person addressed'. It is immaterial whether the menaces do or do not relate to action to be taken by the person making the demand. The man who says, 'Pay me £5,000 or my daughter will tell the world that you seduced her', is as guilty of blackmail as the man who reinforces his demand with threats of action by himself.

Trivial threats will not suffice. The threat must be of 'such a nature and extent that the mind of an ordinary person of normal stability and courage might be influenced or made apprehensive so as to accede unwillingly to the demand'.

If, on the facts known to D, his threats might have affected the mind of a person of ordinary stability, they will amount to menaces, even though they did not affect the person to whom they were addressed. If, although they would not have affected the mind of an ordinary person of normal stability, the threats affected the addressee's mind, they will amount to menaces if D was aware of the likely effect of his actions on the victim, eg because D knew of an unusual susceptibility on the victim's part.

It is irrelevant whether the person making the demand intends to carry out the menaces or is in any position to effect them.

With a view to gain or intent to cause loss

D must make his demand with menaces with a view to gain for himself or another, or with an intent to cause loss to another. The terms 'gain' and 'loss' are defined by TA 1968, s 34 as extending only to gain or loss in money or other property, whether temporary or permanent. Section 34 also provides that:

(a) 'gain' includes a gain by keeping what one has, as well as a gain by getting what one has not; and
(b) 'loss' includes not getting what one might get, as well as a loss by parting with what one has.

The definition of these terms limits blackmail offences to cases with which one would expect a Theft Act to deal, namely, those concerned with intended or foreseen economic advantage or prejudice. If menaces are used with a view to sexual gratification, then (as one would expect) they are dealt with by the Sexual Offences Act 2003.

Unwarranted

As already mentioned, the demand with menaces must be unwarranted; for this purpose s 21 provides that a demand with menaces *is unwarranted unless* the person making it does so in the *belief* that he has reasonable grounds for making the demand *and* that the use of the menaces is a proper means of reinforcing the demand. If a man has sex with a girl after promising payment of £500 and then refuses to pay, a demand by her for the money supported by a threat to inform the man's wife will not be blackmail by the girl if she *believes* that she has reasonable grounds for making such a demand *and* that her threat is a proper means of reinforcing the demand.

D does not have to prove these beliefs, but this does not mean that the prosecution must negative the existence of a belief for which there is no evidence, since the prosecution need only negative the existence of one of the specified beliefs if there is evidence before the court in support of both types of belief; otherwise the jury is obliged to find that the demand with menaces was unwarranted.

CHAPTER 33

Burglary

The Theft Act 1968 (TA 1968), s 9(1) states that a person is guilty of burglary if:

(a) he enters any building or part of a building as a trespasser and with intent to commit any such offence as is mentioned in s 9(2); or

(b) having entered any building or part of a building as a trespasser he steals or attempts to steal anything in the building or that part of it or inflicts or attempts to inflict upon any person therein any grievous bodily harm.

It has been held that TA 1968, s 9(1) creates two types of offence, the first being set out by s 9(1)(a) and the second by s 9(1)(b). Because in each type of offence there is a higher maximum penalty if the building entered as a trespasser is a dwelling, each of the two types of offence has in it two offences, one relating to dwellings and the second to other buildings. The definitions of the offences under s 9(1)(a) and (b) include many common terms which require explanation. These are given as s 9(1)(a) is described but what is said will be equally applicable to s 9(1)(b). Burglary offences are triable only on indictment where an offence triable only on indictment is committed or intended, or where the burglary is in a dwelling and either a person there is subjected to, or threatened with, violence or the defendant is 18 or over and has two previous convictions for domestic burglary at the time of the burglary; otherwise, they are triable either way.

BURGLARY CONTRARY TO THEFT ACT 1968, s 9(1)(a): ENTRY WITH INTENT

The effect of s 9(1)(a) is that a person is guilty of burglary if he enters any building or part of a building as a trespasser and with intent to commit one of the offences listed in s 9(2), namely to steal anything in the building or part of a building in question, or to inflict on any person therein grievous bodily harm, or to do unlawful damage to the building or anything therein.

Enters

The Court of Appeal has adopted the test of an 'effective entry'. This test excludes minimal intrusions, as where D's fingers are inserted through a gap between a window and its frame in order to open the window. However, where D was found stuck in a downstairs window of a house with his head and right arm inside but trapped by the window itself, which rested on his neck, the Court of Appeal held that there had been an entry. The issue of whether D was able, from that position, to steal anything was irrelevant.

Under pre-TA 1968 law, an entry could be effected merely by the insertion of an instrument without the intrusion of any part of the body *provided it was inserted to commit a relevant further offence*, but not if it was inserted merely to facilitate access by a person's body. Assuming that this remains the law, a person who, whilst remaining outside a building at all times in a physical sense, inserts his walking stick in an endeavour to remove goods from the building enters the building for the purposes of burglary. On the other hand, a person who inserts a jemmy behind a window which has been left ajar does not enter the building because the insertion of the instrument is merely to facilitate access by his body, not to commit an offence inside.

A person can enter by means of an innocent agent. Thus, a person who uses a child under the age of criminal responsibility to enter a building and steal is regarded as himself entering the building.

As a trespasser

A person enters a building or part of a building as a trespasser if it is in the possession of another and he enters without a right by law or permission to do so; the entry need not involve any force at all.

Rights of entry are granted by statute to certain people, such as the police and public health inspectors, for certain purposes. For instance, a public health inspector has power to enter a building to check whether there has been a breach of the public health law; he is not a trespasser if he enters for this purpose. However, he enters as a trespasser if he enters premises for an unauthorised purpose, eg to steal something inside.

Likewise, a permission to enter will be given for a particular purpose or purposes. A person who enters for a purpose other than one for which he has permission enters as a trespasser. For example, the Court of Appeal has held that a man, who had permission to enter his father's house, entered it as a trespasser when he entered to steal his father's television set because he entered in excess of his permission.

Permission to enter for a particular purpose or purposes may be given by the occupier or by someone with the express or implied authority of the occupier. For example, a member of the family has authority to invite someone into her parents' house for a cup of tea but does not have authority to invite that person in in order to steal her parents' property.

Permission to enter may be implied, instead of express. For instance, in the case of a shop there is an implied permission for members of the public to enter the public parts of the shop for the purposes of inspecting goods on display or making purchases, and a person who enters for such a purpose is not a trespasser.

A permission to enter might not necessarily extend to every part of the building. Thus a person might lawfully enter a building such as a hotel or shop, but trespass in the manager's office or the stockroom; equally, he might be a lawful guest at a meal in a private house, but enter a bedroom as a trespasser. In both of these cases the entry as a trespasser will be into a 'part of a building'. On the other hand, if a person enters a building (or part of a building) with a right by law or permission to do so and then stays on after the expiry of his entitlement (as where D, who has entered a shop for a lawful purpose, decides to hide and stay on after the shop closes, and does so in order to steal) he cannot be convicted of burglary because, although he becomes a trespasser by staying after hours, he has not entered the building (or part) as a trespasser. If, however, he then moves into another part of the building to carry out the theft, he will then commit burglary because he will have entered that part as a trespasser with the requisite intent.

As a final point, it should be noted that the 'owner' of a building may trespass in part of it if that part is in the exclusive possession of someone else. For example, if a householder rents out the rooms in his attic to a student, on terms whereby the student obtains exclusive possession of them, the householder will enter them as a trespasser if he enters without the student's permission.

Building or part of a building

'Building' should be given its everyday meaning of a structure with walls and a roof and of a permanent or semi-permanent nature. Dwelling houses, warehouses, shops, office premises and the like are all buildings; so are outhouses and greenhouses (provided they are at least semi-permanent) and substantial portable structures with most of the attributes normally found in buildings, provided that there is an element of permanence in their site. On the other hand, tents, partially-built but unroofed houses, and open-sided barns, are not.

Section 9(4) states that references to a building also apply to an inhabited vehicle or vessel, and this is so whether or not the person having a habitation in it is there at the time. Clearly, a caravan or houseboat which is someone's permanent home is an 'inhabited vehicle or vessel', even though he is not there at the time but, say, abroad on a holiday; so is a caravan or boat which is used as a holiday home in the summer during those weeks or weekends in which it is being so used, but not at other times in the summer and not at all in the rest of the year when it is closed up.

The term 'part of a building' refers to a particular area of a building. An obvious example of 'part of a building' is a separate room but the term is not limited to this. It also includes a physically marked-out area in a room, such as the area behind a counter in a shop, from which the defendant is plainly excluded, whether expressly or impliedly.

Mens rea

The mens rea required for burglary contrary to s 9(1)(a) is that, when entering the building or part of a building, the defendant (D) must satisfy two requirements.

First, D must know he is entering the building, or part, as a trespasser (ie he must know the facts which make him a trespasser), or at least be reckless as to whether he is so entering. In most circumstances the issue will be straightforward and it will be a relatively simple task to prove that D knew that he had entered as a trespasser; if, for example, a glass patio door is smashed to pieces then it is reasonable to assume that the person who entered through the gap realised that he had no permission to enter.

Second, D must enter with intent to commit one of the offences listed in TA 1968, s 9(2):

(a) to 'steal' anything in the building or, as the case may be, the part trespassed in;
(b) to inflict grievous bodily harm on any person in the building or, as the case may be, the part trespassed in; or
(c) to do unlawful damage to the building or anything therein (whether or not D has trespassed in the part in which the damage is intended to occur).

It is, of course, irrelevant that it might be impossible for D to carry out his intent.

Intent to steal

When entering the building, or part, as a trespasser, D must have intended dishonestly to appropriate therein property (such as money or valuables) belonging to another with intent permanently to deprive the other of it. In this context, the reader is reminded that obtaining goods by a false representation can amount to theft, and that it is irrelevant that what has occurred might also constitute an offence of fraud.

Intent to inflict grievous bodily harm

When entering the building, or part, as a trespasser, D must have intended to inflict serious harm on a person therein.

Intent to do unlawful damage

On entering the building, or part, as a trespasser, D must have intended to destroy or damage the building or property in the building belonging to another without lawful excuse (ie to commit an offence contrary to the Criminal Damage Act 1971, s 1(1)). Someone who enters the flat of his ex-lover as a trespasser with the intention of breaking up pieces of her furniture, as a punishment for rejecting him, commits burglary. If he enters as a trespasser but only intending to plead with her to take him back, he does not commit burglary if he then loses his temper in consequence of her insistence that the affair is over, and breaks up furniture before leaving.

General point

In most instances, unless there is an admission by D, the only way in which one of the requisite intentions will be apparent is if there has been some act almost amounting to an attempt to commit the intended offence.

BURGLARY CONTRARY TO THEFT ACT 1968, s 9(1)(b): HAVING ENTERED AS A TRESPASSER, STEALING OR INFLICTING GRIEVOUS BODILY HARM, OR ATTEMPTING ONE OF THESE CRIMES

Section 9(1)(b) provides that a person is guilty of burglary if having entered a building or part of a building as a trespasser he steals or attempts to steal anything in the building or that part of it or inflicts or attempts to inflict on any person therein any grievous bodily harm.

What was said in relation to s 9(1)(a) applies equally to the corresponding terms in this definition.

TA 1968, s 9(1)(a) distinguished

An important distinction between an offence of burglary under TA 1968, s 9(1)(a) and that under TA 1968, s 9(1)(b) is that the latter requires D, having entered a building or part of a building as a trespasser, actually to have committed or attempted to commit in the building or part trespassed in:

(a) the offence of theft (contrary to TA 1968, s 1); or
(b) an offence involving the infliction of grievous bodily harm contrary to the Offences Against the Person Act 1861 (OAPA 1861), ss 18, 20, or 23.

Another important distinction is that, unlike the offence under s 9(1)(a), the offence under s 9(1)(b) does not require D to have intended to commit one of the above offences when he entered as a trespasser. Consequently if D enters a building as a trespasser, but without one of the intents specified in s 9(2) (so that he is not guilty under s 9(1)(a)), he can only be guilty of burglary (under s 9(1)(b)) if he then steals or inflicts grievous bodily harm in the building or attempts to do either.

Mens rea

Apart, of course, from having the mens rea required for theft, or an offence involving the infliction of grievous bodily harm, or an attempt to commit such, as the case may be, D must know or be reckless that he has entered as a trespasser when he commits one of these offences. It is irrelevant whether or not he realised at the time of entry that he was entering as a trespasser. Thus, if a person enters a building, thinking that he has permission, and later realises that he has not and then steals something inside or inflicts grievous bodily harm on someone inside (eg the occupier who is trying to eject him) he is guilty of burglary of the present type.

Examples of TA 1968, s 9(1)(b) offence

The boundaries of burglary contrary to s 9(1)(b) can be illustrated by the following examples. Theft requires the dishonest appropriation of property belonging to another with intent permanently to deprive the other of it. A person who enters an empty house as a trespasser to sleep in it for the night does not commit burglary contrary to s 9(1)(b), nor does he if he switches on the electric fire (because electricity is not property and cannot be stolen). But if he turns on a gas fire, he commits burglary contrary to s 9(1)(b) because gas is property and can be stolen. Likewise, he would be guilty of burglary contrary to s 9(1)(b) if, being discovered there by a security guard, he then deliberately strikes the guard with a piece of wood lying nearby and inflicts grievous bodily harm, whether he intended to or not, since he will have committed the offence of unlawfully and maliciously inflicting grievous bodily harm, contrary to OAPA 1861, s 20.

Of course, there is some overlap between the two types of offence of burglary. Where a person enters a building (or part) as a trespasser with intent to steal or to inflict grievous bodily harm therein, and he commits the intended offence or attempts to do so, he can be charged with either offence. In practice, it is normally preferable to charge burglary contrary to s 9(1)(b) in such a case since it is easier to prove.

AGGRAVATED BURGLARY

The element of aggravation lies in the possession of weapons or explosives at the time of the burglary, which creates a risk of death or injury to someone inside the building.

TA 1968, s 10(1) states that a person is guilty of aggravated burglary if he commits any burglary and at the time has with him any firearm or imitation firearm, any weapon of offence, or any explosive. Offences of aggravated burglary are triable only on indictment.

Firearm, imitation firearm, weapon of offence, or explosive

By s 10(1), 'firearm' includes an air gun or an air pistol, but 'firearm' is not otherwise defined. There is no doubt that this omission is deliberate so that courts may apply the term in a realistic sense and apply it to anything which can be fired and can kill or wound. It is clear that the definition of a firearm given in the Firearms Act 1968 was not included in TA 1968 because it includes component parts. There is very little threat of bodily injury posed by the possession of a magazine case for a rifle.

Things which have the appearance of being a 'firearm' but cannot be fired are covered by the term 'imitation firearm'.

'Weapon of offence' in this context means any article made or adapted for use for causing injury to or incapacitating a person, or intended by the person having it with him for such use. Thus, 'weapon of offence' covers not only articles which would be offensive weapons for the purposes of the Prevention of Crime Act 1953, such as coshes, knuckledusters, caps with razor blades in the peak, or even pickaxe handles, but also articles made, adapted or intended to be used for incapacitating a person. Articles made for incapacitation, that is articles having no other real purpose, will include handcuffs, leg irons or a straitjacket; those adapted could include a scarf or a pair of tights knotted at intervals for use for strangulation; and those intended for such use might include drugs to induce sleep or handkerchiefs or pads for use with chloroform.

If the article in question is made or adapted for causing injury to, or incapacitating, a person, it will be necessary to prove no more than that a burglary was committed by D and that he was in possession of such a weapon of offence at the time. If it is alleged he was in possession of an article which he intended to use to cause injury or to incapacitate, it would be necessary to prove D's intention so to use it. In the absence of an admission, this is only likely to occur where D threatens someone in the building in such a way that he indicates an intention to use that weapon. For the purposes of aggravated burglary, an article not made or adapted to injure or incapacitate can be a weapon of offence, even if the necessary intent is only formed an instant before it is used to injure or incapacitate (which makes an interesting contrast to the different rule which applies to other offences (see, eg, pp 638 and 643). Thus, a trespasser who, hearing an occupant of the building coming downstairs, picks up a poker from the fireplace (or takes a screwdriver from his bag), having decided to use it to injure the occupant, commits aggravated burglary.

'Explosive' in this context means any article manufactured for the purpose of producing a practical effect by explosion, or intended by the person having it with him for that purpose. This definition makes clear that a thing which simply causes a 'pyrotechnic effect' (and is therefore an 'explosive substance' under the Explosives Act 1883) is not an 'explosive substance' for present purposes.

In most cases, an offender under s 10 intends to use one of the above articles in the course of the burglary. However, this is not essential; it suffices that he had it with him for such use on another occasion (as, for example, where the burglary is in an empty house and the offender intends to use a cosh to enable him to hijack a get-away car).

Has with him at time of burglary

In order to 'have with him' a firearm, etc, D must be armed with it; it is not enough that it is readily accessible to D. Thus, if the firearm, etc is carried not by the burglar but by an accomplice waiting outside the building, aggravated burglary is not committed. This is a stricter approach than is taken to the phrase 'has with him' in other offences where the term appears. In addition, D must know that he has it with him: a burglar does not have with him a cosh which somebody has slipped into his swag bag, unknown to him, for example.

D must be shown to have had with him a relevant article *at the time of committing* the offence of burglary. This is important.

Where the burglary is alleged to have been committed by committing or attempting theft or the infliction of grievous bodily harm after entry as a trespasser, then the possession must be proved at the time at which the theft, etc was committed or attempted, because that is the time at which the offence of burglary will have been committed. Where the burglary is alleged to have been committed by an entry with intent to commit one of the offences specified for s 9(1)(a), D must be proved to have been in possession at the time of entry, because that is the time at which the offence of burglary will have been committed. Thus, if D enters a building as a trespasser intending to steal and he has with him a cosh at the time of entry, D is guilty of aggravated burglary. The time of commission of the burglary is when D entered and a cosh is a weapon of offence because it is made for use for causing injury. If D then only has with him a pocket knife, it would be very difficult on that evidence to secure a conviction for aggravated burglary *at that point of time*, because—since a pocket knife is not made or adapted for use for causing injury—it would have to be proved that at that point of time D intended to use that knife as a weapon of offence. However, if, confronted by the householder, he pulls out the knife and threatens him, this would be very strong evidence that when D entered he intended to use the knife as a weapon of offence and a conviction for aggravated burglary would be far more likely. By way of further example, if someone enters a motor workshop without a weapon, merely intending to trespass there, he is not guilty of an offence of burglary at that stage; but if, when confronted by a security guard, he arms himself with a tyre lever stored in the workshop and uses it to strike the guard, causing him grievous bodily harm, he would be guilty not only of burglary at that stage but also of aggravated burglary. This is because he had the lever with him at the time of committing burglary and the lever was clearly intended by him for use for causing injury (and was therefore a weapon of offence).

CHAPTER 34

Offences of Fraud and Bribery

THE OFFENCE OF 'FRAUD'

The Fraud Act 2006 (FA 2006), s 1(1) and (2) provides that a person is guilty of the offence of fraud if he is in breach of ss 2, 3 or 4 (which provide different ways of committing the offence). Section 2 is concerned with fraud by false representation; s 3 with fraud by failing to disclose information; and s 4 with fraud by abuse of position.

The offence of fraud is an indictable (either way) offence.

Fraud by false representation

Under FA 2006, s 2, a person is in breach of s 1 if he:

(a) dishonestly makes a false representation; and
(b) intends by making the representation to make a gain for himself or another, or to cause loss to another, or to expose another to a risk of loss.

This is the widest of the three ways of committing fraud.

Making false representation

No gain or loss or risk of loss is required to result from the false representation. No one is required to have been deceived by it or to have acted on it.

Representation   FA 2006, s 2(3) provides that 'representation' means any representation as to fact or law, including a representation as to the state of mind of:

(a) the person making the representation, or
(b) any other person.

By s 2(4), a representation may be express or implied.

An obvious example of a representation of fact would be a statement that a worthless ring was a diamond ring. A statement as to the meaning of a statute is clearly a representation of law.

Because 'representation' includes a representation as to the state of mind of the representor or another, the making of a false statement of the present intentions of the person making the statement or another person (eg a false promise) can amount to a false representation. The intention may, of course, be implied from the nature of the transaction in which the defendant engages. A request for a loan of money implies an intention to repay, and the ordering of a meal in a restaurant implies a representation that the representor (or, possibly, another) intends to pay for it.

The requirement that the representation must be as to fact (ie a past or present verifiable thing) or law, or as to a state of mind, means that a statement which merely expresses an opinion does not in itself constitute a false representation if the opinion turns out to be unjustified. By way of example, if a statement that a picture is worth £1,000 turns out to be unjustified there is no false representation. However, if the person making the statement is aware that the opinion is unjustified, he will at the same time by his conduct make a false representation as to his state of mind, because he will impliedly represent that he believes the opinion is justified when in fact he does not so believe.

There is no limit on how an express representation may be made. Thus, it can be stated by words, whether oral or written. It can be communicated by conduct (as where a rogue dresses up in a security guard's uniform in order to convey the impression that he is a security guard).

An implied representation may be made by words or by conduct, such as the implied representation by conduct, referred to above, made by someone who orders a meal in a restaurant that he intends to pay for it, or such as that made by someone who sells property that he has a right to do so.

A common example of an implied false representation by conduct concerns 'bouncing cheques'. The giver of a cheque impliedly represents that the state of facts existing at the date of delivery of the cheque is such that the cheque will be honoured in the ordinary course of events on presentation for payment on or after the date specified on the cheque. If the facts are not as represented, a false representation is made.

If a credit card or debit card is used then, provided any conditions referred to by the card are complied with, the card company is legally obliged to honour the transaction, because a contract to this effect is brought into being between the payee and the card company. It is irrelevant that the user has no authority to use the card because his authority to use it has been withdrawn or because he has stolen it. In such a case, there will not be a false representation about payment. However, a person who uses a credit card or debit card impliedly represents by his conduct that he has actual authority from the card company to use the card to make a contract with the payee on behalf of the card company. If he has no such authority the representation as to it is false.

By s 2(5), a representation may be regarded for the purposes of s 2 as made if it (or anything implying it) is submitted in any form to any system or device designed to receive, convey or respond to communications (with or without human intervention). Thus, s 2 can be breached where the false representation is submitted to a computer or other machine rather than being addressed to a human being, as where a person unauthorisedly enters someone else's number into a 'CHIP and PIN' machine.

False representation   By s 2(2), a representation is false if:

(a) it is untrue or misleading; and
(b) the person making it knows that it is, or might be, untrue or misleading.

A false representation may involve a half-truth. A representation is a half-truth where, although it is literally true, it omits a material matter, as where an applicant for a job correctly states that he does not have a criminal record but fails to state that he has been charged with theft to which he intends to plead guilty.

Mens rea

In addition to knowing that his representation is, or might be, untrue or misleading:

(a) D must make the false representation dishonestly. 'Dishonesty' in ss 2 to 4 involves a two-stage test: whether D's behaviour would be regarded as dishonest by the ordinary standards of reasonable and honest people; and, where this is so, whether D was aware that his conduct would be regarded as dishonest by reasonable and honest people. The answer to both tests must be 'yes';

(b) D must intend, by making the representation to make a gain for himself or another, or to cause loss to another or to expose another to a risk of loss. 'Gain' and 'loss' have the same meaning as in blackmail (p 935).

Fraud by failing to disclose information

FA 2006, s 3 provides that a person is in breach of s 1 if he:

(a) dishonestly fails to disclose to another person information which he is under a legal duty to disclose; and

(b) intends, by failing to disclose the information to make a gain for himself or another, or to cause loss to another or to expose another to a risk of loss.

A 'legal duty to disclose' means one in civil law. It may be one prescribed by statute; from the fact that the transaction is one of good faith (such as a contract of insurance); from the express or implied terms of a contract; from the custom of a trade or market; or from the existence of a relationship (such as that of a solicitor and client, trustee and beneficiary, agent and principal). By way of example, a person in a position of trust has a duty to disclose material information when entering into a contract with a beneficiary.

Fraud by abuse of position

By FA 2006, s 4 a person is in breach of s 1 if he:

(a) occupies a position in which he is expected to safeguard, or not to act against, the financial interests of another person;

(b) dishonestly abuses that position; and

(c) intends, by means of the abuse of that position, to make a gain for himself or another, or to cause loss to another or to expose another to the risk of loss.

A person may be regarded as having abused his position even though his conduct consisted of an omission rather than an act.

The offence is aimed at those who are in a position to safeguard another's financial interests and have authority to exercise discretion and act on that person's behalf. Such persons may have access to assets, premises or equipment and need no further co-operation from that person to commit fraud against him. If such a person dishonestly acts against his client's interests for gain, he commits an offence of fraud. The term 'abuse' is not defined by FA 2006 and it may cover a wide range of conduct.

ARTICLES FOR USE IN FRAUD

Possession of articles for use in fraud

By FA 2006, s 6, a person commits an indictable (either way) offence if he has in his possession or under his control any article for use in the course of or in connection with any fraud.

A general intention to commit fraud is sufficient for this offence.

The term 'articles' in this and s 7 below includes any program or data held in electronic form. Computer programs can generate credit card numbers; computer templates can be used for producing blank bills; and computer files may contain credit card details of persons.

Making or supplying articles for use in fraud

A person commits an indictable (either way) offence against FA 2006, s 7 if he makes, adapts, supplies or offers to supply any article:

(a) knowing that it is designed or adapted for use in the course of or in connection with fraud; or

(b) intending it to be used to commit, or assist in the commission of, fraud.

Where payment is made based upon energy consumed by a customer and consumption is measured by a meter, a person who makes or supplies a device intended to interfere with the record made by the device will intend it to be used to commit fraud.

OBTAINING SERVICES DISHONESTLY

A person commits an indictable (either way) offence against FA 2006, s 11(1) if he obtains services for himself or another:

(a) by a dishonest act; and

(b) in breach of the provisions of s 11(2).

By s 11(2), a person obtains services in breach of s 11 if:

(a) they are made available on the basis that payment has been, is being or will be made for or in respect of them;

(b) he obtains them without any payment having been made for or in respect of them or without payment having been made in full; and

(c) when he obtains them he knows:

    (i) that they are being made available on the basis described in (a), or

    (ii) that they might be,

but intends that payment will not be made, or will not be made in full.

The offence does not require a false representation. There must be an 'obtaining' of a service. An example would be where a film is exhibited in a cinema and D sneaks in to watch it. Obtaining services by the dishonest use of false credit card details or personal information would similarly amount to an offence against s 11. Trespassory entry into premises to view a free event is not an offence against s 11 as the service provided is not one for which a person is expected to pay.

Dishonesty bears the same meaning as described on pp 945–6.

MAKING OFF WITHOUT PAYMENT

The Theft Act 1978, s 3(1) provides that a person who, knowing that payment on the spot for any goods supplied or service done is required or expected from him, dishonestly makes off without having paid as required or expected and with intent to avoid payment of the amount due is guilty of an offence. The offence is an indictable (either way) offence. These provisions are useful in that they cover opportunist offences in which it will often be difficult to prove that any particular intention existed at the time that the goods were supplied or the service was done.

Because D must make off 'without having paid as required or expected', an offence is not committed if the creditor (or his agent) has agreed that payment would be postponed, even if that postponement has been procured by a dishonest deception.

Police officers are frequently called to incidents involving 'making off'. It is common in respect of restaurants where late-night revellers eat well and look for opportunities to escape from the restaurant without paying. Restaurants demand payment on the spot from casual customers and this is well known by all. Officers called to such incidents need only be concerned with whether or not the persons concerned dishonestly made off without paying and with intent to avoid payment. If they ran through the door and into the street that intention is quite obvious. In circumstances in which they discovered that they did not have sufficient money to pay, but gave their correct names and addresses to the proprietor and insisted upon leaving, they will certainly have made off without paying but their conduct does not indicate that they did so dishonestly nor with an intention to avoid payment. Those who make off without paying, with the consent of the creditor, do not commit the offence because it cannot be said that they have not paid as required or expected, even if they obtained that consent by fraud.

The other common incident involves the self-service petrol station. These stations make it quite clear that payment is demanded on the spot, by posting notices which declare that self-service is in operation and that payment should be made at the kiosk. A motorist who drives out of such a station without paying will experience considerable difficulty in persuading a jury that his actions were not dishonest and not done with intent to avoid payment (although, of course, the onus of proving the offence is on the prosecution). Once again, it would be different if he left his name and address, together with the registration number of his car, with the attendant in the kiosk.

The words 'make off without payment' involve a departure without paying from the place where payment would normally be made. For example, in the case of a taxi, payment may be made while sitting in it or standing at the window and it can therefore be an offence to make off from either place without paying. Section 3 distinguishes between transactions which are on-the-spot cash transactions and those which involve trade credit. If an employee of a garage proprietor goes to his employer's wholesaler, collects spare parts and leaves without signing the invoice, he does not commit an offence. The wholesaler will send an account to the employer; payment was not expected on the spot. However, if such an employee went to an auto discount store at which all transactions were cash transactions and was sold goods and then saw the opportunity to leave without paying, he would be guilty of this offence if he left with the intention of avoiding payment.

'Payment on the spot' includes payment at the time of collecting goods on which work has been done or in respect of which a service has been provided.

Section 3 does not apply if the payment required or expected is not legally due (eg because the person demanding it is seriously in breach of contract). Nor does the section apply to the supplying of goods or the doing of services which is contrary to the law, nor where the service done is such that payment is not enforceable (s 3(3)). Consequently, for example, the offence is not committed by the man who makes off without paying a prostitute for services rendered.

The term 'knowing that payment on the spot is required or expected' relates to the knowledge D must have of when payment must be made (s 3(2)).

Dishonesty needs to be shown to have existed at the time of 'making off'. Dishonesty is a question of fact for the jury or justices and is approached in the same way as in the offence of fraud.

It has been held by the House of Lords that an intention to evade payment permanently is part of the mental element to be proved by the prosecution.

FALSE ACCOUNTING

The indictable (either way) offences of false accounting contrary to the Theft Act 1968 (TA 1968), s 17 are not restricted to clerks and other people who are employed in the traditional sense for the purpose of bookkeeping. The falsity need not necessarily be with a view to gain since it is sufficient that the falsity is accompanied by an intent to cause loss to another.

TA 1968, s 17(1) states that a person is guilty of an offence where he dishonestly, with a view to gain for himself or another or with intent to cause loss to another:

(a) destroys, defaces, conceals or falsifies any account or any record or document made or required for any accounting purpose, or
(b) in furnishing information for any purpose produces or makes use of any account, or any such record or document as aforesaid, which to his knowledge is or may be misleading, false or deceptive in a material particular.

Section 17(1) creates two quite separate and distinct offences which might be described as the falsification of accounts (s 17(1)(a)) and the use of false or deceptive accounts (s 17(1)(b)). Before examining these offences separately a number of points can be made which apply to both of them.

Mens rea

For the purposes of either type of offence, D's conduct must be carried out dishonestly and with a view to gain for himself or another or with intent to cause loss to another. 'Dishonesty' in this context is understood in the same way as in the offences of fraud (p 945–6). 'With a view to gain... or with intent to cause loss ...' bears the same meaning as in blackmail (p 935). There is no need for any gain or loss actually to be caused.

Account, record, or document made or required for any accounting purpose

The acts specified by s 17(1)(a) and (b) must be done in relation to 'any account, record or document made or required for any accounting purpose'. These terms should be given their ordinary meaning. An accounts book, balance sheet or a payroll record is made for an accounting purpose. That is the reason for its existence; it has no other real purpose as it can be used for little other than the keeping of accounts. Documents may be required for an accounting purpose, even though they have other purposes as well as an accounting purpose. For example, a delivery note is for the purpose of allowing the recipient of goods to check that all of the goods ordered have been delivered, but a firm may use that delivery note as an accounting document to be retained in the storeroom to account for stock in excess of that recorded on inventories or stock sheets. Until the additional stock is recorded on an inventory or stock sheet, the delivery note will provide the only account for its presence should an audit take place. It will therefore be used for an accounting purpose at that time. As a further example, a housing benefit claim form which contained the only information used to calculate housing benefit has been held by a divisional court to be a document required for an accounting purpose, despite the fact that it is also used to determine entitlement to benefit.

The terms 'account' or 'record' are wide enough to cover an account or record produced by a mechanical device, such as a taxi meter or the turnstile at a soccer ground which records the number of persons admitted so that the entries may be related to the money collected.

The separate requirements of the two offences are as follows.

Falsification of accounts (s 17(1)(a))

What is required here is the destruction, defacement, concealment or falsification of any account, etc. If entry to a cinema is recorded by the issue of a ticket by a process which produces a duplicate copy on a roll, the destruction of any part of that record, if carried out with the necessary intent, would be an offence. If some of the duplicate copies were not handed over to the manager so that a false total figure could be shown to cover deficiencies, those copies would be 'concealed' for the purposes of s 17(1)(a). If, to cover deficiencies in the accounts, a corrosive liquid, or other damaging agent, was applied to the duplicate records, this would amount to a defacement. However, the most common offence is always likely to be the falsification of figures in an account, record or document. 'Falsification' covers the preparation of false accounts, as well as the falsification of existing ones.

Section 17(2) states that a person who makes or concurs in making in an account or other document an entry which is or may be misleading, false or deceptive in a material particular, or who omits or concurs in omitting a material particular from an account or other document, is to be treated as falsifying the account or document. However, this is not an exclusive definition of falsification. In one case, it has been held that a turnstile operator, who allowed two people through the turnstile while only recording one of them, falsified the record. It might be that the falsification was within s 17(2) (by omitting a material particular) but if not there was a 'falsification' within the ordinary meaning of that term.

A person can falsify an accounting document by completely failing to fill in a blank form required for an accounting purpose, and even though the particular document so falsified cannot be identified. This surprising ruling was made by the Court of Appeal in a case where it upheld the conviction of an international telephone operator who had failed to log calls on the forms provided for this purpose. The court held that, as soon as a call was made, it was the operator's duty to fill in one of the forms in a pile in front of him and that thereby one of them became a document required for an accounting purpose and the fact that the particular form could not be identified (since the operator might not have chosen to use the first form) did not matter.

Use of false or deceptive account (s 17(1)(b))

Whereas TA 1968, s 17(1)(a) is concerned with those who falsify or destroy, etc any account, etc, s 17(1)(b) deals with those who, in furnishing information for any purpose, produce or make use of any account or any record or document made or required for any accounting purpose, *knowing* it is or might be misleading, false or deceptive in a material particular (ie liable to mislead in a significant way).

Of course, a person who has falsified an account contrary to TA 1968, s 17(1)(a) might go on to use it contrary to s 17(1)(b), in which case he will have committed both offences. However, an offence under s 17(1)(b) may also be committed by a person who has not falsified the document in question, for it is not uncommon for persons with a view to gain to use in a dishonest way documents which have been made out erroneously by someone else. If a person, who is entitled to receive payment for money which he has spent on petrol for use in his firm's car, receives a receipt which he knows has been wrongly made out for a higher amount, he commits an offence against s 17(1)(b) if, when making out his claim (furnishing information), he makes use of that receipt since, to his *knowledge*, it is or may be misleading, false or deceptive in a material particular.

BRIBERY

The common law offence, and the legislation (notably of 1889 and 1906), relating to bribery were abolished and repealed by the Bribery Act 2010 (BA 2010). All the offences under BA 2010 are indictable; most are either way offences but that under BA 2010, s 7 (below) is triable only on indictment. BA 2010 provides as follows.

General bribery offences

Offences of bribing another person

BA 2010, s 1(1) provides that a person (P) is guilty of an offence if either of the following cases applies.

Case 1 is where:

(a) P offers, promises or gives a financial or other advantage to another person; and
(b) P intends the advantage to induce a person to perform improperly a relevant function or activity, or to reward a person for the improper performance of such a function or activity.

It does not matter whether the person to whom the advantage is offered, promised or given is the same person as the person who is to perform, or has performed, the function or activity concerned.

Case 2 is where P offers, promises or gives a financial or other advantage to another person, and P knows or believes that the acceptance of the advantage would itself constitute the improper performance of a relevant function or activity.

It does not matter in either case whether the advantage is offered, promised or given by P directly or through a third party.

Offences relating to being bribed

By BA 2010, s 2(1), person (R) is guilty of an offence if any of the following four cases applies.

Case 3 is where R requests, agrees to receive or accepts a financial or other advantage intending that, in consequence, a relevant function or activity should be performed improperly (whether by R or another person).

Case 4 is where R requests, agrees to receive or accepts a financial or other advantage, and the request, agreement or acceptance itself constitutes the improper performance by R of a relevant function or activity.

Case 5 is where R requests, agrees to receive or accepts a financial or other advantage as a reward for the improper performance (whether by R or another person) of a relevant function or activity.

Case 6 is where, in anticipation of or in consequence of R requesting, agreeing to receive or accepting a financial or other advantage, a relevant function or activity is performed improperly by R, or by another person at R's request or with R's assent or acquiescence.

In Cases 3 to 6 it does not matter:

(a) whether R requests, agrees to receive or accepts (or is to request, agree to receive or accept) the advantage directly or through a third party,
(b) whether the advantage is (or is to be) for the benefit of R or another person.

In Cases 4 to 6 it does not matter whether R knows or believes that the performance of the function or activity is improper.

In Case 6, where a person other than R is performing the function or activity, it also does not matter whether that person knows or believes that the performance of the function or activity is improper.

General

Relevant function or activity   BA 2010, s 3 provides that a function or activity is a relevant function or activity if it is:

(a) any function of a public nature;
(b) any activity connected with a business, trade or profession;
(c) any activity performed in the course of a person's employment; or
(d) any activity performed by or on behalf of a body of persons (whether corporate or unincorporate); and

it meets one or more of conditions A to C.

Condition A is that a person performing the function or activity is expected to perform it in good faith.

Condition B is that a person performing the function or activity is expected to perform it impartially.

Condition C is that a person performing the function or activity is in a position of trust by virtue of performing it.

A function or activity is a relevant function or activity even if it has no connection with the UK, and is performed in a country outside the UK.

Improper performance to which bribe relates   By BA 2010, s 4, a relevant function or activity is performed improperly if it is performed in breach of a relevant expectation, and is to be treated as being performed improperly if there is a failure to perform the function or activity and that failure is itself a breach of a relevant expectation.

A 'relevant expectation':

(a) in relation to a function or activity which meets Condition A or B, means the expectation mentioned in the condition concerned; and
(b) in relation to a function or activity which meets Condition C, means any expectation as to the manner in which, or the reasons for which, the function or activity will be performed that arises from the position of trust mentioned in that condition.

Anything that a person does (or omits to do) arising from or in connection with that person's past performance of a relevant function or activity is to be treated as being done (or omitted) by that person in the performance of that function or activity.

Expectation test   BA 2010, s 5 provides that, for the purposes of ss 3 and 4, the test of what is expected is a test of what a reasonable person in the UK would expect in relation to the performance of the type of function or activity concerned.

In deciding what such a person would expect in relation to the performance of a function or activity where the performance is not subject to the law of any part of the UK, any local custom or practice is to be disregarded unless it is permitted or required by legislation or a reported judicial decision applicable to the country concerned.

Defence   It is a defence under BA 2010, s 13 for a person charged with:

(a) an offence under s 1 which would not also be an offence under s 6 (below);
(b) an offence under s 2;
(c) an offence of aiding, abetting, counselling or procuring, attempting or conspiring, or encouraging or assisting, the commission of such an offence,

to prove that the person's conduct was necessary for the proper exercise of any function of an intelligence service, or the proper exercise of any function of the armed forces when engaged on active service.

Bribery of foreign public officials

This is dealt with by BA 2010, s 6(1) and (2), which provides that a person (P) who bribes a foreign public official (F) is guilty of an offence if P's intention is:

(a) to influence F in F's capacity as a foreign public official; and
(b) to obtain or retain business, or an advantage in the conduct of business.

In this context, a trade or profession is a business.

For the purposes of s 6, P bribes F if, and only if:

(a) directly or through a third party, P offers, promises or gives any financial or other advantage to F, or to another person at F's request or with F's assent or acquiescence, and
(b) F is neither permitted nor required by the legislation or a reported judicial decision applicable to F to be influenced in F's capacity as a foreign public official by the offer, promise or gift.

Failure of commercial organisations to prevent bribery

BA 2010, s 7 provides that (C), a body corporate partnership carrying on a business, trade or profession, is guilty of an offence if a person (A) associated with C bribes another person intending:

(a) to obtain or retain business for C; or
(b) to obtain or retain an advantage in the conduct of business for C.

For the purposes of s 7, A bribes another person if, and only if, A is, or would be, guilty of an offence under s 1 or 6 (whether or not A has been prosecuted for such an offence).

It is a defence for C to prove that C had in place adequate procedures designed to prevent persons associated with C from undertaking such conduct. The Secretary of State has published guidance about procedures that relevant commercial organisations can put in place to prevent persons associated with them from bribing.

Prosecution

The personal consent of the Director of Public Prosecutions, the Director of the Serious Fraud Office, or the Director of Revenue and Customs Prosecutions is required before proceedings may be instituted under BA 2010. The Director of the Serious Fraud Office and the Director of Public Prosecutions have published joint guidance on the approach to prosecutorial decision-making in respect of offences under BA 2010, s 1, 2, 6, or 7, which is to be read in conjunction with the guidance above issued by the Secretary of State.

CHAPTER 35

Handling Stolen Goods and Related Offences

HANDLING STOLEN GOODS

If goods which had been stolen had no sales outlet then the incidence of theft would undoubtedly diminish significantly. Many thefts, especially where the appropriator engages in widespread offences of burglary, are committed in the knowledge that there is a ready market for certain types of article: jewellery, computers, television sets and DVD recorders. The law concerning the indictable (either way) offence of handling of stolen goods is concerned with punishing not only the ultimate receiver, in the sense that he is the buyer of the property, but also others who are involved with the goods after they have been stolen.

The Theft Act 1968 (TA 1968), s 22(1) states that a person handles stolen goods if (otherwise than in the course of the stealing) knowing or believing them to be stolen goods he dishonestly receives the goods, or dishonestly undertakes or assists in their retention, removal, disposal or realisation by or for the benefit of another person, or if he arranges to do so.

In order to establish the nature of the offence it is necessary to consider the meaning of the words 'goods', 'stolen' and 'handling'.

Goods

'Goods' are defined by TA 1968, s 34(2)(b), as including money and every other description of property except land, and includes things severed from the land by stealing.

Stolen

For the offence to be committed, the goods handled must be 'stolen goods' at that point of time. TA 1968, s 24 states that 'stolen goods' are goods which have been:

(a) stolen, contrary to TA 1968, s 1;
(b) obtained as a result of blackmail, contrary to TA 1968, s 21;
(c) obtained by fraud, contrary to the Fraud Act 2006 (FA 2006), s 1; and
(d) 'stolen' abroad contrary to the law of that land, provided that had the 'stealing' occurred in England or Wales an offence contrary to TA 1968, ss 1 or 21 or FA 2006, s 1 would have been committed.

In addition, references to stolen goods also include money which is dishonestly withdrawn from an account to which a 'wrongful credit' has been made, but only to the extent that the money derives from the credit. 'Wrongful credit' is defined on p 963.

If a child who is below the age of criminal responsibility appropriates property in circumstances which would amount to theft by someone over that age, a person who dishonestly handles that property is not guilty of this offence as the goods are not 'stolen goods'. However, that person would normally be guilty of theft.

The fact that goods were stolen goods at the time of the handling can be proved by evidence of the conviction of the thief. The acquittal of an alleged thief does not prevent the goods being found to be stolen goods. Another way of proving the status of the property is by offering evidence of ownership, the owner identifying the property and describing the circumstances of its loss. It is not necessary to prove that goods were stolen by any particular person; merely that they were stolen by someone and were dishonestly handled by the defendant.

When goods cease to be stolen

TA 1968, s 24(3) provides that no goods shall be regarded as having continued to be stolen goods after they have been restored to the person from whom they were stolen or to other lawful possession or custody. Clearly, this goes further than repossession by the owner, since it includes cases in which goods have been restored to other lawful possession or custody. When a police officer in the course of his duties takes possession of stolen goods, they are thereby restored to 'other lawful possession or custody' and are no longer stolen; consequently, it is not an offence to 'handle' them thereafter. If an officer interviews a thief at his home, and the thief admits stealing a watch and hands it over to the officer, it is now in the officer's lawful custody and is no longer stolen goods. If the thief then tells the officer that a man (D) is to call at any moment to examine the watch, which he knows to be stolen, with a view to buying it, there can be no successful charge of dishonest handling against D if the officer returns the watch to the thief in order to allow D to receive it and D does receive it. However, had the thief merely reached the stage at which he had admitted to the officer that he had stolen the watch but had not handed it over, the watch would remain stolen and D could be convicted of handling if he arrived a few minutes later and received the watch.

The issue is in reality whether or not the stolen goods have been taken into possession or custody on the owner's account so that they may be returned to him. Where a security guard marked cartons of stolen cigarettes so that they would more easily be identified in the hands of a handler, they were not restored to lawful possession or custody. If a police officer sees property inside a parked car which he suspects might be stolen and immobilises the car to ensure that he will have an opportunity of questioning the driver, he does not take possession of the stolen goods unless he immobilises the car with the intention of taking charge of those goods so that they cannot be removed. If he has retained an open mind as to whether he should take possession, and merely immobilises the car to prevent the driver getting away without questioning, he does not reduce the goods into his possession or custody. It is the state of mind of the officer which is the deciding factor in each case.

TA 1968, s 24(3) also provides that goods cease to be stolen goods where the person from whom they were stolen and any other person claiming through him have ceased to have rights of restitution in respect of the theft. The right to restitution of property is a matter of civil law. There are various ways in which the right to restitution might have been lost. An example is where X obtains goods from Y by fraud. If Y, on discovering the fraud, nevertheless affirms the transaction he thereby ceases to have any right to restitution of the goods, which therefore cease to be stolen goods at that point of time.

Goods representing those originally stolen

TA 1968, s 24(2) provides that references to stolen goods include, in addition to the goods originally stolen and parts of them (whether in their original state or not):

(a) any other goods which directly or indirectly represent or have at any time represented the stolen goods in the hands of the thief as being the proceeds of any disposal or realisation of the whole or part of the goods stolen or of goods so representing the stolen goods; and

(b) any other goods which directly or indirectly represent or have at any time represented the stolen goods in the hands of a handler of the stolen goods or any part of them as being the proceeds of any disposal or realisation of the whole or part of the stolen goods handled by him or of goods so representing them.

'The thief' means the person by whose conduct the goods were originally stolen. 'A handler' means any person who has committed the actus reus of handling with the appropriate mens rea. The Court of Appeal has held that goods are in the hands of the thief or of a handler if they are in his possession or under his control; physical custody is not required.

The 'proceeds rule' provided by TA 1968, s 24(2) is essentially as follows: goods which directly or indirectly represent or have represented the originally stolen goods *in the hands of the thief or a handler as the proceeds* of the disposal or realisation of those stolen goods, or goods so representing those stolen goods, are themselves deemed to be stolen goods. Consequently, once goods have been deemed to be stolen goods by this rule, an offence is committed if they are 'handled' thereafter with the appropriate mens rea.

The rule can be illustrated as follows. A steals a car. He sells it to B for £1,000 and receives that sum in cash. The car and the cash are now both stolen goods, the latter because it directly represents the original goods (the car) in the hands of the thief—as the proceeds of the car's disposal or realisation. Therefore, if A then gives the £1,000 (or part of it) to C, who receives it knowing it has represented the original stolen goods in A's hands and C buys a camera with the £1,000, the camera becomes stolen goods once it is in C's hands because it indirectly represents the original stolen goods in the hands of a handler as the proceeds of the disposal or realisation of goods representing the original stolen goods. Consequently if D receives the camera from C, knowing it has represented the stolen goods in C's hands, D can be convicted of handling stolen goods. However, if E receives the camera from D, unaware that it represents the original stolen goods, and then sells it for cash, the cash which he receives will not become stolen goods because, lacking mens rea, he is not a handler and therefore *that* cash does not *represent the original stolen goods in the hands of a handler* as the proceeds of their disposal or realisation.

Various forms of handling

TA 1968, s 22 defines 'handling' as receiving stolen goods, or undertaking or assisting in their retention, removal, disposal or realisation by or for the benefit of another person, or arranging to do one of these things. The offence of handling therefore covers the passage or handling of the goods through as many pairs of hands as may be involved, on their passage to the receiver, and also dealings with them thereafter. An examination of the definition of 'handling' shows that there are 18 different ways of doing so.

It must not be forgotten that s 22 excludes from its provisions those who handle in one of these ways in the course of the original stealing. This is a commonsense approach to offences of handling. We are not concerned with thieves (and their accomplices) who handle stolen goods in the course of the original theft as they are punishable in respect of the theft, whatever form that theft may take.

The charge

Although there are 18 different ways in which handling can be committed, it is unnecessary to make exclusive selections of a particular variant of the offence. Section 22 provides a single offence of handling stolen goods, which can be committed by receiving or by any of the other ways specified. Consequently, an information or written charge or indictment, which simply alleges handling of stolen goods, is unlikely to fail for duplicity.

Nevertheless, in order to be fair and clear to the defendant (D), the better practice is to particularise the form of handling relied on, and, if there is any uncertainty about the form of handling in question, it is advisable to have more than one information or written charge (or more than one count in the indictment). But only two informations or written charges (or counts) should generally be used in such a case: one charging receiving, and the other charging the various forms of 'undertaking or assisting in' by or for the benefit of another (or such forms of these as are clearly the only ones relevant).

The forms of handling can be explained as follows.

Receiving

This requires proof that D obtained possession or control of stolen goods from someone else; a finder of goods does not receive them. The presence of stolen goods on the premises of another does not necessarily mean that they are in the possession or control of the owner of the premises. If a thief calls at the home of a friend and his pockets contain a number of items of stolen property, that stolen property is in the possession of the thief, not the householder. To be a 'receiver' a person need not have contact with the goods in any physical sense, since a person can have control of goods without any physical contact with them, as where an employee or agent acting on his orders received them (in which case the employee or agent is also a receiver).

Often, a receiver is acting solely for his own benefit, but it is unnecessary that a receiver should act to gain any profit or even advantage from his possession of stolen goods.

Arranging to receive

This requires preparation by D, or a concluded agreement between D and another (eg the thief), for the receiving of stolen goods by D. It is essential that the goods are stolen goods at the time the arrangement to receive is made. Thus, D does not commit handling where he commissions others to steal a certain type of property which D agrees to receive from them if they succeed in the theft, because at the time of his arrangement to receive there are no stolen goods to which it can relate. (D would, of course, be guilty with the others of a conspiracy to steal and of a conspiracy to handle stolen goods; if the theft was actually committed, D would also be guilty of theft as an accomplice.)

The other forms of handling set out below differ in a vital respect from receiving, or arranging to receive, in that they must be done 'by or for the benefit of' a person other than the alleged handler (or, the Court of Appeal has held, a co-defendant on the same charge of handling).

Undertaking the retention, removal, disposal or realisation of stolen goods for the benefit of another

These four forms of handling cover the case where D, either alone or with another, retains, removes, disposes or realises the stolen goods for the benefit of another.

The four activities can be explained as follows. 'Retention' means 'keeping possession of, not losing, continuing to have'. 'Removal' refers to the movement of stolen goods from one place to another, eg transporting stolen goods to a hideout for the benefit of the thief or another. 'Disposal' covers dumping, giving away or destroying stolen goods, eg melting down candlesticks for the thief. 'Realisation' means the exchange of stolen goods for money or some other property. A person who sells stolen goods as agent for a third party (eg the thief) undertakes their realisation for the benefit of another. However, the House of Lords has held that a person who sells stolen goods on his own behalf does not undertake their realisation for the benefit of another because the buyer benefits from the purchase and not from the realisation (which benefits only the seller).

Of course, a person who undertakes one of these four activities will often be in possession or control of the stolen goods. If he knew or believed they were stolen when he acquired possession or control, he is guilty of handling anyway on the basis of receiving. However, if he lacked such a state of mind at that point of time but realised the goods were stolen when he undertook one of the four activities, he can be convicted of handling on that basis, provided that his 'undertaking' was for the *benefit of another*.

Assisting in the retention, removal, disposal or realisation of stolen goods by another

These four forms of handling are appropriate to cover cases where D provides assistance to another person, the thief or another handler, who is going to undertake the retention, removal, disposal or realisation of stolen goods.

For there to be 'assistance', D must do something for the purpose of enabling the goods to be retained, etc, whether or not he succeeds.

There is some overlap with cases of 'undertaking'. For example, a person who joins with another in removing stolen goods not only undertakes their removal for the benefit of another but also assists in their removal by another.

A person *assists in the retention* of stolen goods by another if he puts the thief in touch with a warehouse-keeper, or provides tarpaulins to conceal stolen goods in the possession of the thief or a handler, or tells lies so as to make it more difficult for the police to find or identify stolen goods retained by the thief or a handler. On the other hand, the Court of Appeal has held, a refusal to answer questions put by the police as to the whereabouts of stolen goods does not amount to handling, although it might well assist in their retention by another. A person, who innocently allows goods to be left on his premises but later discovers that they are stolen, assists in their retention by another if he nevertheless permits them to continue to remain on the premises. Merely to use stolen goods does not suffice, since it does not in itself amount to assistance in their retention.

A person *assists in the removal* of stolen goods by another if he lends a lorry for their removal. He *assists in their disposal* by another if he advises the thief as to how to get rid of the goods. He *assists in their realisation* by another if he puts a 'fence' in touch with the thief.

Arranging to undertake or assist in the retention, removal, disposal or realisation of stolen goods by or for the benefit of another

The effect of the section is further extended by the addition of the words 'or arranging to do so'. Any arrangement to undertake or assist in one of the activities described above can suffice; it is irrelevant that nothing further is done. However, as mentioned in relation to the offence of 'arranging to receive', it must be proved that the arrangements in respect of these other forms of handling relate to goods which were stolen goods at the time of the arrangements.

By or for the benefit of another person

As indicated, in all cases of handling (other than those of receiving and arranging to receive), it must be shown that the acts which were undertaken to retain, etc were carried out for the benefit of another or were carried out to assist in retention, etc by another, and that person should be named in the charge if his identity is known. If it is not, the charge should indicate that the acts were done, as appropriate 'by or for the benefit of' some person unknown and such a charge will have to be supported by strong evidence that that other person existed.

Mens rea

It must be proved that, when he handled the stolen goods, D knew or believed that they were stolen, and acted dishonestly.

Knowledge or belief

Wilful blindness, ie deliberately turning a blind eye to the question of whether or not goods are stolen, does not suffice for 'knowledge' or 'belief', but it has been held that, if wilful blindness as to the goods being stolen is proved, knowledge or belief *may* be inferred from it. This is important since, in the absence of an admission by the handler, knowledge or belief (at the time of the handling) that the goods were stolen can be difficult to prove, particularly in the common case of sales at bargain prices in public houses and other places where people assemble, of goods which 'fell off a lorry' and which turn out to have been stolen. Unless the buyer was of below average intelligence or there were other special circumstances, wilful blindness on his part as to the fact that the goods were stolen *may* be capable of proof. If it is, the jury *may* (not must) infer knowledge or belief therefrom.

D need not be aware of the precise nature of the goods. If D receives boxes believing them to contain stolen whisky, it is immaterial that the boxes actually contained stolen wine.

Proof   Frequently, knowledge or belief is proved by reference to the surrounding circumstances. If stolen goods have been carefully concealed on private premises, this suggests not only that the occupier of the premises did not wish to be found in possession of them but also that he knew that the goods were stolen. Knowledge or belief that goods were stolen is also very likely to be inferred where D denied that stolen goods, subsequently found on his premises, were on the premises.

In general, where D is found in possession of property which has been recently stolen, a judge may direct a jury that they may infer knowledge or belief if D fails to offer an explanation for his possession, or if they are satisfied beyond reasonable doubt that any explanation which is offered is false. This rule is merely an application of the ordinary rules of circumstantial evidence. In addition, TA 1968, s 27, which applies where D is being prosecuted at the trial in question only for handling stolen goods, recognises the difficulties which may exist in proving knowledge in handling offences by allowing special evidence to be offered in certain circumstances. It provides that, if evidence has been given of an act of handling by D in relation to the goods in question, the following evidence may be given to assist proof of knowledge or belief that the property was stolen:

(a) evidence that D has had in his possession, or has undertaken or assisted in the retention, removal, disposal or realisation of, stolen goods from any theft taking place not earlier than 12 months before the offence charged; and

(b) provided that seven days' notice in writing have been given to D of the intention to prove the conviction, evidence that he has, within the five years preceding the date of the offence charged, been convicted of theft or of handling stolen goods.

These provisions of s 27 supplement the general rule about admissibility of 'bad character' evidence (see p 255). It must be emphasised that they only permit the evidence described in (a) and (b) to be given to prove knowledge or belief that the goods were stolen. They do not enable such evidence to be used for any other purpose, for example to prove dishonesty on D's part or an act of handling by him.

The provisions in (b) must be read with PACE, s 73(2) which provides that where evidence of a previous conviction on indictment is admissible by means of a certificate of conviction the certificate must give 'the substance and effect of the indictment and conviction'. The House of Lords has held that, when (b) is read together with PACE, s 73, a certificate of previous conviction should:

(a) where the conviction for theft or handling was on indictment, state the substance and effect of the indictment and conviction, including the nature of the property concerned; and

(b) where the conviction for theft or handling was in summary proceedings, record the nature of the property concerned.

The whole of such a certificate is admissible.

Dishonestly

Dishonesty is always a question of fact for the jury or justices, and the same approach is to be taken by them, as it is in relation to the offence of fraud (pp 945–6). It follows, for example, that if a person knowingly receives stolen goods, but does so in order to restore them to their owner, or to hand them over to the police, his handling is not likely to be found to be dishonest by the jury or justices.

MONEY LAUNDERING OFFENCES

The offence of handling stolen goods is, strictly, no longer necessary in virtually every case covered by it because of the wider money laundering provisions of the Proceeds of Crime Act 2002 (PCA 2002), Part 7 (ss 327–340). Stolen goods in all their forms fall within the definition of 'criminal property' within PCA 2002, s 340(3) which provides that property is criminal property if:

(a) it constitutes a person's benefit from criminal conduct or it represents such a benefit (in whole or part and whether directly or indirectly), and

(b) the alleged offender knows or suspects that it constitutes or represents such a benefit.

PCA 2002, s 327(1) makes it an offence to conceal, disguise, convert or transfer criminal property, or to remove it from England and Wales. Section 328(1) provides that it is an offence for a person to enter into or become concerned in an arrangement which he knows or suspects facilitates (by whatever means) the acquisition, retention, use or control of criminal property by or on behalf of another person. By s 329(1), it is an offence for a person to acquire, use or possess criminal property, unless he did so for adequate consideration or certain other exceptions apply. Although many instances of handling fall outside the popular conception of money laundering, the offences in ss 327–329 are, between them, capable of covering virtually anything which constitutes handling stolen goods. In addition, the mens rea requirement for these offences is less demanding since D is not required to know or believe that the property constitutes or represents the benefit from criminal conduct, but is simply required to know or suspect this. In addition, there is no requirement of 'dishonesty'. The offences, all of which are indictable (either way) offences, clearly have the potential to be more attractive to a prosecutor than that of handling stolen goods.

A divisional court has cautioned against charging offences under PCA 2002, s 329 as opposed to charging the offence of handling stolen goods. It held that, when the offence under s 329 was created it was in the context of legislation directed primarily at money laundering and matters of serious criminality, and that it should be resorted to only in serious cases, as is clear from the Crown Prosecution Service's guidance. This is equally applicable to ss 327 and 328.

ADVERTISING REWARDS FOR RETURN OF STOLEN OR LOST GOODS

TA 1968, s 23 punishes the public advertisement of a reward for the return of any lost or stolen goods which uses any words to the effect that no questions will be asked, or that the person producing the goods will be safe from apprehension or inquiry, or that any money paid for the purchase of the goods or advanced by way of loan on them will be repaid. The printer and publisher of such an advertisement are liable, as well as the advertiser.

SEARCH WARRANTS

By TA 1968, s 26, a justice may grant a warrant, upon information being received on oath that there is reasonable cause to believe that any person has in his custody or possession or on his premises any stolen goods, to search for and seize those goods.

A Crown Court judge has power to make a search and seizure warrant under PCA 2002, s 352 where someone is subject to a money laundering investigation.

The additional powers of seizure provided by the Criminal Justice and Police Act 2001, s 50 apply where a search warrant under one of these two provisions is executed.

DISHONESTLY RETAINING A WRONGFUL CREDIT

The offence of handling is not committed by someone into whose bank account a 'wrongful credit', as defined below, has been received because that credit itself is not stolen goods.

This gap is filled by TA 1968, s 24A which provides that a person (D) is guilty of an offence if:

(a) a wrongful credit has been made to an account kept by him or in respect of which he has any right or interest;

(b) he knows or believes that the credit is wrongful; and

(c) he dishonestly fails to take such steps as are reasonable in the circumstances to secure that the credit is cancelled.

The offence is an indictable (either way) offence.

What is required is a failure by D to take such steps as are reasonable in the circumstances to secure the cancellation of a wrongful credit made to an account kept by D or in respect of which D has any right or interest. Nothing need be done by D. The mere omission to take reasonable steps suffices.

A 'credit' refers to a credit of an amount of money in an account. 'Money' includes currencies other than sterling. A credit to an account is wrongful to the extent that it derives from theft, blackmail, fraud (contrary to FA 2006, s 1) or stolen goods. An 'account' is an account kept with:

(a) a bank;
(b) a person carrying on a business:
 (i) in the course of which money is received by way of deposit which is lent to others; or
 (ii) any other activity is financed, wholly or to any material extent, out of the capital of, or the interest on, money received by way of a deposit; or
(c) an issuer of electronic money (as defined for the purposes of the Financial Services and Markets Act 2000, Part 2).

In determining whether a credit to an account is wrongful, it is immaterial whether the account is overdrawn before or after the credit is made.

D must know or believe that the credit is wrongful; he must know or believe the facts which make the credit 'wrongful' in law, although he need not know that they have this effect (since ignorance of the criminal law is no defence).

D must dishonestly fail to take such steps which are reasonable in the circumstances to secure that the wrongful credit is cancelled. The approach to this question is the same as in offences of fraud and of handling.

Section 24A covers a range of situations. Suppose that X commits an offence of fraud and thereby causes a money transfer to be made to D's account, unknown to D. If D dishonestly fails to take reasonable steps to cancel the credit on discovering the truth, D commits an offence under s 24A because the credit is wrongful. Another example is where Y pays money which he has stolen into his bank account, and then transfers the credit thereby created to D's bank account. If D dishonestly fails to take reasonable steps to cancel that credit he can be convicted of an offence under s 24A, because the credit is wrongful.

CHAPTER 36

Forgery and Counterfeiting

The law relating to forgery and counterfeiting is governed by the Forgery and Counterfeiting Act 1981 (FCA 1981). Part I of the Act is concerned with forgery and related offences, and Part II with counterfeiting and related offences.

All the offences under FCA 1981 described in this chapter are indictable (either way) offences.

Offences under the Identity Documents Act 2010 are also dealt with in this chapter.

FORGERY

This offence is defined by FCA 1981, s 1(1) which states that a person is guilty of forgery if he makes a false instrument, with the intention that he or another shall use it to induce somebody to accept it as genuine, and by reason of so accepting it to do or not to do some act to his own or any other person's prejudice.

False instrument

'Instrument'

For the purpose of forgery and other offences involving false instruments under FCA 1981, an 'instrument' is:

(a) any document, whether of a formal or informal character (other than a currency note);
(b) any stamp issued or sold by a postal operator (or a metered postage mark);
(c) any Inland Revenue stamp denoting any duty or fee; and
(d) any disc, tape, soundtrack or other device on or in which information is *recorded or stored* by mechanical, electronic, or other means. To be 'recorded' or 'stored' the information must be preserved for an appreciable time with the object of subsequent retrieval. Examples of items covered are microfilm records and information on computer tapes or discs and tachograph record sheets, but not electronic impulses in a computer or its 'user segment' (which stores information momentarily while the computer searches its memory, eg to check a password). Thus, computer hacking is not forgery although it is an offence under the Computer Misuse Act 1990, s 1.

The only part of this list which calls for further definition is 'document' in (a). The Court of Appeal has held that a thing is only a document if it conveys two messages: a message about the thing itself (eg that it is a cheque) and a message to be found in the words or other symbols that is to be accepted and acted on (eg the message in a cheque to the banker to pay a specified sum). Thus, cheques, wills, and building society passbooks are examples of documents (and are therefore instruments) but paintings (even if falsely signed), false autographs, and any writing on manufactured articles or their wrappings indicating the name of the manufacturer or country of origin, are not.

'False'

FCA 1981, s 9(1) states that an instrument is false for the purposes of forgery and other offences involving false instruments if it purports to have been:

(a) *made in the form* in which it is made by *a person who did not in fact make it* in that form; or

(b) *made in the form* in which it is made *on the authority of a person who did not in fact authorise its making* in that form; or

(c) *made in the terms* in which it is made *by a person who did not in fact make it* in those terms; or

(d) *made in the terms* in which it is made *on the authority of a person who did not in fact authorise its making* in those terms; or

(e) *altered* in any respect *by a person who did not in fact alter it* in that respect; or

(f) *altered* in any respect *on the authority of a person who did not in fact authorise the alteration* in that respect; or

(g) *made* or *altered* on a *date* on which, or at a *place* at which, or *otherwise in circumstances* in which, it was *not in fact made or altered*; or

(h) *made* or *altered* by an *existing person* but he did *not in fact exist*.

This definition of the falsity of an instrument is quite complex and needs to be simplified to assist understanding. The key point is that it is not enough that the document tells a lie (ie contains a false statement); what is required is that it should tell a lie about itself in relation to the person who made the instrument, or authorised its making, or altered it, or if it purports to have been made or altered on a date, or in a place, or otherwise in circumstances, in which it was not in fact made or altered, or if it represents itself as having been made or altered by an existing person who in fact did not exist. If D writes an application for a job as an economist and falsely alleges that he is studying for a postgraduate degree in that field, that instrument is not a forgery although its contents are untrue. It was made by the applicant, it has not been altered in any way or falsely dated and it is made by an existing person. Should D make out a reference which is allegedly from his tutor that would be a false instrument, as it alleges that it was made by a person who did not make it or authorise its making.

If D finds a cheque book and signs the name of the person who holds the account, the cheque is a false instrument as it lies about itself by alleging that it was signed by another who did not make the instrument or authorise its making. On the other hand, someone who opens an account in a false name in order to pay in a stolen cheque, does not make a false instrument when he completes a withdrawal form in that name. The drawer's name is the same as the depositor's (although false) and the withdrawal form does not purport to be made by a person who did not make it. The term 'authorise its making' is important. A person may draw up a document on behalf of another (and even sign it on his behalf) without creating a false instrument, provided that he was authorised to do so. A cheque, made out quite properly by the holder of the bank account for the sum of £100 becomes a false instrument when another person alters that cheque to show a sum of £1,000 by adding another zero to the figure shown on the face of the cheque and writing alongside it the initials of the account holder without that person's authority. It would be different if the person making the alteration was authorised to do so.

Mens rea

D must make the false instrument with the intention that he or another person shall use it to induce somebody to accept it as genuine, and with the intention to induce that person by reason of so accepting it to do or not to do some act to his own or any other person's prejudice. Consequently, it is not enough simply to intend to induce someone to believe that an instrument is genuine. For example, making a false birth certificate solely to induce a belief that one comes from a noble family is not forgery. If D acts with the necessary double intent, it is irrelevant whether the instrument is communicated to anyone, whether anyone is induced to accept the instrument as genuine or whether prejudice (within the meaning set out below) is caused. D need not intend to induce another human being, it suffices that he intends to induce a machine to respond to the instrument as if it were genuine.

The act or omission intended to be induced must be to the prejudice of the person induced or of someone else (besides D). FCA 1981, s 10(1) provides that, for the purposes of forgery and related offences, an act or omission intended to be induced is only to a person's prejudice if it is one which, if it occurs:

(a) will result:
  (i) in his temporary or permanent loss of property (including a loss by not getting what he might get as well as a loss by parting with what he has);
  (ii) in his being deprived of an opportunity to earn remuneration or greater remuneration or to gain a financial advantage otherwise than by way of remuneration; or
(b) will result in somebody being given an opportunity:
  (i) to earn remuneration or greater remuneration from him (the person induced); or
  (ii) to gain a financial advantage from him otherwise than by way of remuneration; or
(c) will be the result of his having accepted a false instrument as genuine (or—and this is only relevant to offences under FCA 1981, ss 2 and 4 below—a copy of a false instrument as a copy of a genuine one) in connection with his performance of a duty.

Where the intended inducement is of a machine (eg a cash dispenser), the act or omission intended to be induced by the machine responding to the instrument is treated as an act or omission to a person's prejudice.

Section 10(1) can be illustrated as follows. If D signs a cheque in B's name, intending to give it to C as payment for a car which C is to hire to D for a day, D has made a false instrument and he intends to use it to induce C to accept it as genuine, and by reason of so accepting it to do some act to his own prejudice, because C's handing over of the car will result in his temporary loss of it (see (a)(i), above). D is therefore guilty of forgery.

If D learns that his rival, C, is about to be promoted and, to prevent this, D writes to C's employer, F, a letter purportedly written by X, a clergyman, which alleges that C is dishonest, D is guilty of forgery because he has made a false instrument with intent to induce F to accept it as genuine, and by reason of so accepting it not to do an act to the prejudice of some other person (C), because F's non-promotion of C will result in C being deprived of an opportunity to earn greater remuneration (see (a)(ii), above).

If, instead, the letter referred to above had said that C was highly efficient, in an effort to secure the promotion for him, D would still be guilty of forgery because he has made a false instrument with intent to induce F to accept it as genuine, and by reason of so accepting it to do an act to his own prejudice, because it will result in C being given greater remuneration (see (b)(i), above).

If D learns that his trading rival, C, is tendering to supply goods to F and, to prevent this, D writes a letter to F which purports to have been written by someone who does not in fact exist and alleges that C produces shoddy goods, D is guilty of forgery. The reason is that he has made a false instrument and intends to use it to induce F to accept it as genuine, and by reason of so accepting it to do some act to the prejudice of some other person (C), because the award of the tender to someone else will result in C being deprived of an opportunity to gain a financial advantage (see (a)(ii), above).

If D makes a false airline ticket in order to get a free flight, D is guilty of forgery because he intends to use the ticket to induce an airline employee to accept it as genuine, and by reason of so accepting it to do some act to the prejudice of the airline by giving a financial advantage (ie the free flight) to D (see (b)(ii), above).

It is clear from (c), above, that the intended prejudice need not be financial in any sense at all, since (c) provides that it is enough that the act or omission intended to be induced will be to a person's prejudice if it will be the result of his having accepted a false instrument as genuine in connection with the performance of any duty, as where a false pass is made to induce a doorkeeper to admit an unauthorised person to premises. The duty referred to here means a legal duty, as opposed simply to a moral one.

By virtue of s 10(2), it is not forgery where the maker of a false instrument intends to induce someone to do something which he is under an enforceable legal duty to do (or to induce someone not to do something he is not legally entitled to do).

Provided that the requirements of s 10(1) are satisfied, an honest and reasonable belief in a legal or moral claim to the gain which D intended to make as a result of falsifying the instrument is no defence (unless s 10(2) applies). A worker might genuinely believe that he is entitled to the salary increase which he seeks to gain by use of a false instrument, but such a belief can never amount to a defence to a charge under FCA 1981. Indeed, it is not a defence in itself that D might actually have been entitled to have property transferred to him if he had made a true claim (but not if he made a false instrument).

COPYING A FALSE INSTRUMENT

FCA 1981, s 2 is concerned with the separate offence of copying a false instrument. It provides that it is an offence for a person to make a copy of an instrument which is, and which he knows or believes to be, a false instrument, with the intention that he or another will use it to induce somebody to accept it as a copy of a genuine instrument, and with the intention to induce that person by reason of so accepting it to do some act to the prejudice of himself or some other person.

The essence of the offence under s 2 lies in the intention to induce a belief that the copy is a copy of a genuine instrument, whilst in reality it is a copy of a false instrument. Section 2 is meant to close loopholes which might otherwise exist. The essential points to prove are that the original instrument is a false instrument; that the person who made the copy knew or believed this to be so; and that the copy was made to induce someone to act, etc. If someone wished to avoid paying his gas bill, he could allege that he had already paid and in support of this he might falsify a receipt for the money made out to appear as if it had been issued by the gas supplier. Clearly, if he did that he would be guilty of forgery as he would have made a false instrument with the requisite intents. Section 2 ensures that it is equally an offence then to photocopy that false receipt with intent to use that copy in an attempt to avoid payment.

USING A FALSE INSTRUMENT OR COPY OF IT

FCA 1981, s 3 makes it an offence for a person to use an instrument which is false, and which he knows or believes to be false, with the intention of inducing somebody to accept it as genuine, and with the intention of inducing that person by reason of so accepting it to do or not to do some act to his own or any other person's prejudice.

Section 4 provides a similarly worded offence of using a copy of a false instrument which is, and which he knows or believes to be, a false instrument, with the intention of inducing somebody to accept it as a copy of a genuine instrument, and by reason of so accepting it to do or not to do some act to his own or any other person's prejudice.

Any use of a false instrument (or, as the case may be, a copy of a false instrument) with the necessary intent suffices. The verb 'use' is wide in meaning and covers, for example, a person who offers, delivers, tenders in payment or exchange, or exposes for sale, a false instrument (or a copy of one).

CUSTODY OR CONTROL OF MONEY ORDERS, SHARE CERTIFICATES, ETC

FCA 1981, s 5 provides a number of offences under this heading, which are concerned with the following instruments:

(a) money orders or postal orders;
(b) UK postage stamps;
(c) Inland Revenue stamps;
(d) share certificates;
(e) cheques or other bills of exchange;
(f) travellers' cheques;
(g) bankers' drafts;
(h) promissory notes;
(i) credit cards or debit cards;
(k) certified copies relating to an entry in a register of births, adoptions, marriages, civil partnerships or deaths and issued by the Registrar General, the Registrar General for Northern Ireland, a registration officer or a person lawfully authorised to issue such certified copies; and
(l) certificates relating to entries in such registers.

Any such instrument is hereafter referred to as a 'specified instrument'.

Custody or control of such instruments

By s 5(1), it is an offence for a person to have in his custody or under his control a specified instrument which is, and which he knows or believes to be, false, with the intention that he or another shall use it to induce somebody to accept it as genuine, and by reason of so accepting it to do or not to do some act to his own or any other person's prejudice.

This 'possession' offence completes the cycle of offences which are likely to be committed if a false instrument is made for the purposes previously described. If D makes out a false cheque with intent to induce someone to accept it as genuine, and by reason of so accepting it to do something to his prejudice, D commits forgery contrary to FCA

1981, s 1. If D walks through the streets to a bank, with the false cheque, in order to cash it, he commits the present offence under FCA 1981, s 5(1). If D then passes the cheque to a bank official in order to induce him to part with money, D commits the offence of 'using' contrary to FCA 1981, s 3. Of course, it might be that different people will commit different offences in the cycle, as where the person who makes the false instrument gets other people to engage in the use of such false instruments.

If the intent required for an offence under s 5(1) cannot be proved, one can fall back on FCA 1981, s 5(2). This makes it an offence for a person merely to have in his custody or control, without lawful authority or excuse, a specified instrument which is, and which he knows or believes to be, false. 'Lawful authority or excuse' is likely to be limited to such matters as possession by a police officer after seizure of a specified instrument or possession by some other person who is in the course of handing over to the police such an instrument.

Making, custody or control of equipment or materials

FCA 1981, s 5(3) and (4) is aimed at the tools of a forger's trade. Section 5(3) provides that it is an offence for a person to make or to have in his custody or under his control a machine or implement, or paper or any other material, which to his knowledge is or has been specially designed or adapted for the making of a specified instrument, with the intention that he or another shall make a specified instrument which is false and that he or another shall induce somebody to accept it as genuine, and by reason of so accepting it to do or not to do some act to his own or another's prejudice. In this way the Act strikes at a would-be forger even before he starts to make a false instrument. Whether or not the necessary intent for an offence under s 5(3) can be proved will often depend, in part, on the amount of forging equipment, etc in D's custody or control.

If the intent required under FCA 1981, s 5(3) cannot be proved, one can fall back on s 5(4), which makes it an offence for a person to make or to have in his custody or control any such machine, implement, paper or material, without lawful authority or excuse.

Defence for refugees

It is a defence under the Immigration and Asylum Act 1999, s 31, for a refugee charged with an offence under FCA 1981, Part I or the Identity Documents Act 2010, s 4 or 6 (below) to show that, having come to the UK directly from a country where his life or freedom was threatened (within the meaning of the Refugee Convention), he:

(a) presented himself to the authorities in the UK without delay;
(b) showed good cause for his illegal entry or presence; and
(c) made a claim for asylum as soon as was reasonably practicable after his arrival in the UK.

If, in coming from the country where his life or freedom was threatened, the refugee stopped in another country outside the UK, the defence applies only if he shows that he could not reasonably have expected to be given protection under the Refugee Convention in that other country.

Police powers

See p 975.

MAKING OR POSSESSION OF FALSE IDENTITY DOCUMENTS, ETC

Possessing false identity documents, etc with improper intent

It is an offence, triable only on indictment, against the Identity Documents Act 2010 (IDA 2010), s 4(1) for a person (D) with the improper intention to have in his possession or under his control:

(a) a false identity document he knows or believes to be false;
(b) an improperly obtained identity document which he knows or believes to have been improperly obtained; or
(c) an identity document relating to someone else.

The improper intention is:

(a) the intention of using the document for establishing personal information about D; or
(b) the intention of allowing or inducing another to use it for establishing, ascertaining or verifying personal information about D or about any other person (with the exception, in the case of an identity document that relates to someone else, of the individual to whom it relates).

Possession of apparatus with prohibited intention

Under IDA 2010, s 5(1), it is an offence triable only on indictment for D with the prohibited intention to make or to have in his possession or under his control:

(a) any apparatus which, to his knowledge, is or has been specially designed or adapted for use in making false identity documents; or
(b) any article or material which, to D's knowledge, is or has been specially designed or adapted for use in making false identity documents.

The prohibited intention is the intention:

(a) that D or another will make a false identity document; and
(b) that the document will be used by somebody for establishing, ascertaining or verifying personal information about a person.

Possession without reasonable excuse

It is an indictable (either way) offence against s 6(1) for D to have in his possession or under his control, without reasonable excuse:

(a) a false identity document;
(b) an improperly obtained identity document;
(c) an identity document relating to someone else; or
(d) any apparatus, article, or material which, to his knowledge, is or has been specially designed or adapted to make false identity documents or to be used to make such documents.

The Court of Appeal has held that the mere fact that D did not know or believe that the document was false cannot of itself and without more amount to a reasonable excuse, but (it held) lack of such knowledge or belief can be relevant to a defence of reasonable excuse by way of explanation of D's possession— it might explain why the document had not been thrown away or handed to the police. Possession of a document for an innocent purpose cannot in itself amount to 'reasonable excuse'. Subject to these limits, 'reasonable excuse' is a matter for the jury or magistrates.

Meaning of terms

Identity document

'Identity document' means any document that is, or purports to be:

(a) an immigration document;
(b) a UK passport;
(c) a passport issued by or on behalf of the authorities of a country or territory outside the UK or by or on behalf of an international organisation;
(d) a document that can be used (in some or all circumstances) instead of a passport;
(e) a UK driving licence; or
(f) a driving licence issued by or on behalf of the authorities of a country or territory outside the UK.

For the above purposes, immigration document means a document used for confirming the right of a person under the EU Treaties in respect of entry or residence in the UK, or a document which is given in exercise of immigration functions and records information about leave granted to a person to enter or to remain in the UK, or a registration card (within the meaning of the Immigration Act 1971, s 26A).

False identity document

For the purposes of IDA 2010, a document includes a stamp or label. An identity document is false only if it is false within the meaning of FCA 1981, Part I (see p 965).

Improperly obtained identity document

An identity document is improperly obtained if false information was provided, in or in connection with, the application for its issue or an application for its modification, to the person who issued it or (as the case may be) to a person entitled to modify it. For these purposes:

(a) 'false' information includes information containing any inaccuracy or omission that results in a tendency to mislead;
(b) 'information' includes documents (including stamps and labels) and records; and
(c) the 'issue' of a document includes its renewal, replacement or re-issue (with or without modifications).

Making a false identity document

References to the making of a false identity document include references to the modification of an identity document so that it becomes false.

Personal information

For the purposes of ss 4 and 5, 'personal information', in relation to an individual, means:

(a) his full name;
(b) other names by which he is or has previously been known;

(c) his gender;

(d) his date and place of birth;

(e) his external characteristics that are capable of being used for identifying him;

(f) the address of his principal place of residence in the UK;

(g) the address of every other place in the UK or elsewhere where he has a place of residence;

(h) where in the UK and elsewhere he has previously been resident;

(i) the times at which he was resident at different places in the UK or elsewhere;

(j) his current residential status;

(k) residential statuses previously held by him; and

(l) information about numbers allocated to him for identification purposes and about the documents (including stamps or labels) to which they relate.

'Residential status' means:

(i) an individual's nationality;

(ii) an individual's entitlement to remain in the UK; and

(iii) if that entitlement derives from a grant of leave to enter or remain in the UK, the terms and conditions of that leave.

Defence for refugees

See p 969.

COUNTERFEITING OFFENCES: GENERAL POINTS

Definition of counterfeit

By FCA 1981, s 28(1), a thing is a counterfeit of a currency note or of a protected coin:

(a) if it is not a currency note or a protected coin, but *resembles a currency note or protected coin* (whether on one side only or on both) *to such an extent that it is reasonably capable of passing for a currency note or protected coin of that description*; or

(b) if it is a currency note or protected coin which has been *so altered that it is reasonably capable of passing for a currency note or protected coin of some other description.*

For the avoidance of any doubt on the matter, s 28(2) goes on to provide that a thing consisting of one side only of a currency note, with or without the addition of other material, is a counterfeit of such a note, and that a thing consisting of parts of two or more currency notes (or of parts of such note(s) and other material) is capable of being a counterfeit of a currency note. Thus, for example, a supposed currency note composed of parts of true currency notes and other materials is a counterfeit, as is a thing which consists of one side only of a currency note as a result of that note being 'split'.

For the purposes of FCA 1981, 'currency note' means:

(a) any note which has been lawfully issued in the UK, the Channel Islands, the Isle of Man or the Irish Republic, *is or has been* customarily used as money in the country of issue, and is payable on demand; or

(b) any note which has been lawfully issued in some other country, and *is* customarily used as money in that country.

Thus, a £20 note a €20 note and a 100 dinar note are all 'currency notes'; so is an old style £5 note, which is no longer legal tender, but not a note which is no longer valid currency in the foreign country where it was issued.

A 'protected coin' is defined as any coin which is customarily used as money in any country, ie any coin which *is still* valid tender at the time. It also includes a sovereign, half-sovereign, krugerrand (or a coin denominated as a fraction thereof), a Maria-Theresia thaler dated 1780, and any euro coin.

Passing or tendering

In the offences below, references to 'passing or tendering' a note or coin are not confined to passing or tendering it as legal tender, so that (for example) passing or tendering a note or coin to a coin dealer or as a collector's item is a 'passing or tendering' for the purpose of these offences. A person 'passes' a note or coin to somebody when the latter actually accepts it from him; a person 'tenders' a note or coin when he offers to pass it to somebody. On the other hand, simply to produce a bundle of counterfeit notes to impress a lady friend does not constitute a tender of them, since it does not involve any offer to pass them to her or anyone else.

Mode of trial

As noted on p 964, all the offences described below are indictable (either way) offences.

COUNTERFEITING

FCA 1981, s 14(1) states that it is an offence for a person to make a counterfeit of a currency note or protected coin, intending that he or another shall pass or tender it as genuine. Section 14(2) makes it an offence for a person to make a counterfeit of a currency note or protected coin without lawful authority or excuse.

Both offences punish those who make a counterfeit currency note or protected coin; the difference between them is this. If the maker's intention is that he or another shall pass it into circulation, he commits an offence under s 14(1). If he did not so intend, or that intent cannot be proved, he can be convicted of the lesser offence under s 14(2) unless he had a lawful authority or excuse for making the thing (which will be rare).

PASSING OR TENDERING COUNTERFEIT CURRENCY

Passing or tendering counterfeit as genuine

By FCA 1981, s 15(1)(a), it is an offence for a person to pass or tender as genuine anything which is, and which he knows or believes to be, a counterfeit of a currency note or of a protected coin.

Someone who sells to another counterfeit notes or coins, having declared them to be such, does not pass or tender them as genuine.

Delivering counterfeit

FCA 1981, s 15(1)(b) makes it an offence for someone to deliver to another anything which is, and which he knows or believes to be, a counterfeit of a currency note or protected coin, intending that the person to whom it is delivered or another shall pass or tender it as genuine. Section 15(1)(b) deals, for example, with the person who knowingly takes counterfeits from the maker and delivers them to a second person, intending that the second person should pass or tender them as genuine. It is irrelevant whether or not the second person is an innocent recipient.

Where it cannot be proved that the person who delivered the counterfeit intended that the recipient or another should pass or tender it as genuine, he may be convicted of the offence of delivery without lawful authority or excuse, which is dealt with by s 15(2).

CUSTODY OR CONTROL OF COUNTERFEIT CURRENCY AND COUNTERFEITING IMPLEMENTS

The offences of 'possession' under FCA 1981, s 5 of false instruments and of materials and implements for their making dealt with above have their counterparts in ss 16 and 17 in relation to people who have counterfeit currency or counterfeiting materials or implements in their custody or under their control.

Custody or control of counterfeit currency

By FCA 1981, s 16(1), it is an offence for a person to have in his custody or control a counterfeit of a currency note or of a protected coin, knowing or believing it to be so and intending either to pass or tender it as genuine or to deliver it to another with the intention that he or another shall pass or tender it as genuine. Section 16(2) makes it an offence for a person to have such custody or control, with such knowledge or belief, without lawful authority or excuse. On a charge under s 16(2) D's intention is irrelevant. Whilst a settled intention to hand in counterfeit currency may amount to a lawful excuse, the fact that a person has not yet decided what to do with it cannot amount to such an excuse.

The offences of 'possession' in respect of currency may be committed even though the coin or note is not in a fit state to be passed or tendered or even though its making or counterfeiting has not been finished or perfected. Consequently, these offences may be committed, for example, in relation to the part-finished efforts of a counterfeiter.

Making, custody or control of counterfeiting materials and implements

FCA 1981, s 17(1) makes it an offence for a person to make, or to have in his custody or under his control, anything *which he intends to use, or to permit any other person to use, for the purpose of making a counterfeit of a currency note or of a protected coin with the intention that it be passed or tendered as genuine*. The words 'anything which he intends to use' include *anything used as a part of the process of counterfeiting*. This includes chromolins (printers' proofs used to check the quality of an aluminium plate produced from a film) of a currency note, special papers and inks, and reprographic equipment.

Section 17(2) provides that it is an offence for a person without lawful authority or excuse to make or to have in his custody or under his control any thing which, to his knowledge, is or has been specially designed or adapted for the making of a counterfeit of a currency note. The intentions italicised above are not required.

By s 17(3), it is an offence for a person to make or have in his custody or under his control, any implement which, to his knowledge, is capable of imparting to anything a resemblance to the whole or part of either side of a protected coin, or of the reverse of the image on either side of a protected coin. A person charged with this offence has a defence if he proves that he had the written consent of the Treasury or some other lawful authority or excuse. This is the only offence in the Act where the defendant has the burden of proving a lawful authority or excuse.

REPRODUCING BRITISH CURRENCY

FCA 1981, ss 18 and 19 deal respectively with the reproduction of British currency notes without written consent to do so from the relevant authority, and with the making, sale or distribution of imitation British coins in connection with a scheme intended to promote the sale of any product or service.

These offences are neither serious (since, although triable either way, they are punishable only by way of a fine) nor do they require any counterfeiting in its strict sense (ie notes and coins reasonably capable of passing as currency notes or protected coins), but set out to prevent the use of reproductions in any form, even though the copy reproduced would not fool any reasonable person. If there was no legislation to prevent the production of good quality 'stage money', this could lead to abuse. Colour supplement magazines could print a reproduction of one side of a currency note as a voucher entitling the holder to a reduction on the price of an article in certain stores. This would no doubt be done innocently, but the reproduction might be used falsely by some other person. Many modern copiers can produce good quality copies of colour documents and there is no reason to suppose that machines could not be produced which could reproduce reasonable copies. Section 18, which deals with notes, goes to the extent of prohibiting copies which are not reproduced on the correct scale, in order to prevent 'blow-ups' being produced which may be of assistance to a counterfeiter.

If the reproductive processes led to the production of a copy which is reasonably capable of passing for a currency note, the more serious offences under s 14 of counterfeiting with intent to pass or tender, or of counterfeiting without lawful authority or excuse, should be considered.

POLICE POWERS

FCA 1981, ss 7 and 24 authorise a justice who is satisfied upon information on oath that there is reasonable cause to believe that a person has in his *custody* or under his *control*:

(a) anything which has been used, or is intended to be used, for the making of a false instrument or copy of a false instrument, contrary to ss 1 or 2;

(b) any false instrument or copy which has been used, or is intended to be used, contrary to ss 3 or 4;

(c) anything which it is unlawful to possess without authority, etc, under s 5 (false money orders, stamps, etc);

(d) anything which is a counterfeit currency note or protected coin, or a reproduction made in breach of ss 18 or 19; or

(e) anything which has been used, or is intended to be used, for the making of such counterfeit or reproductions,

to issue a warrant authorising a constable to enter premises, search for and seize such objects. The additional powers of seizure provided by the Criminal Justice and Police Act 2001, s 50 apply where a search warrant under FCA 1981 is executed.

A constable may, at any time after seizure, apply to a magistrates' court for an order for the forfeiture and destruction or disposal of objects seized.

CHAPTER 37

Criminal Damage and Computer Misuse

CRIMINAL DAMAGE: INTRODUCTION

The Criminal Damage Act 1971 (CDA 1971) deals with most offences concerned with damage to property but other legislation still exists in this area. The Malicious Damage Act 1861 still deals with offences of obstructing railways or interfering with them (see Chapter 21) and of concealing or removing navigation marks or buoys. If damage is caused by an explosion the offence under the Explosive Substances Act 1883, s 2 (p 653) should be considered.

All the offences under CDA 1971 described in this chapter are indictable (either way) offences, except the offences under CDA 1971, s 1(2) or s 1(2) and (3), which are triable only on indictment.

CRIMINAL DAMAGE

CDA 1971, s 1(1) provides what is known as the simple offence of criminal damage. It states that a person who without lawful excuse destroys or damages any property belonging to another intending to destroy or damage any such property, or being reckless as to whether any such property would be destroyed or damaged, is guilty of an offence.

If the destruction or damage is by fire, there is a separate offence under s 1(1) and (3), required to be charged as arson, which carries a higher maximum punishment. As a result there are technically two offences: criminal damage otherwise than by fire contrary to s 1(1) and criminal damage committed by fire, contrary to CDA 1971, s 1(1) and (3).

By the Theft Act 1968 (TA 1968), s 30 the leave of the DPP is required for the institution of proceedings for criminal damage by one spouse or civil partner to the other's property, unless, by virtue of any judicial decree or order, the spouses were not obliged to cohabit at the material time or an order is in force providing for the separation of the civil partners.

Criminal damage contrary to CDA 1971, s 1(1) (but not s 1(1) and (3)) is a 'penalty offence' for the purposes of the Criminal Justice and Police Act 2001, and may be dealt with under a fixed penalty procedure: see p 31. This may be an appropriate course of action in minor cases.

What is said below about the elements of an offence of criminal damage is equally applicable to the other offences under the Act, unless the contrary is indicated.

Destroy or damage

Property may be damaged if it suffers physical harm which involves permanent or temporary impairment of the property's use or value. If a motor car is scratched when a coin is scraped along its side it is damaged thereby, because its value is impaired; like-wise a wall is damaged if slogans are painted on it, as is beer if water is poured into it. If part of a machine is removed, without which it cannot work, the machine may be dam-aged, even though neither it nor the part suffers actual physical injury, because its use is impaired. Consequently, a car may be damaged if the rotor arm is removed from its engine.

The fact that what is done is rectifiable does not prevent the property being dam-aged but the amount and cost of rectification are relevant factors in determining whether there has been damage; if they are minimal it may be found that the property has not been damaged. The Crown Court has held on appeal, for example, that there was no damage where D spat on V's coat and the spittle could be removed with a damp cloth.

In each case the circumstances must be considered, together with the nature of the article alleged to have been damaged, what has happened to it, and the above factors.

By s 10(5), any modification of the contents of a computer is not to be regarded as damaging any computer or computer storage medium (eg a hard disk), unless its effect on the computer or medium impairs its *physical* condition. Unauthorised acts with intent to impair the operation of a computer are dealt with by the Computer Misuse Act 1990, s 3, see p 985.

The destruction of property involves something which goes beyond damage, such as the demolition of a machine, the pulling down of a wall or other structure, or the killing of an animal.

If arson is charged, it must also be proved that the destruction or damage was caused by fire.

Property

CDA 1971, s 10(1) defines property as being property of a tangible nature, whether real or personal, including money and:

(a) including wild creatures which have been tamed or are ordinarily kept in captivity, and any other wild creatures or their carcasses *if,* but only if, they have been reduced into possession which has not been lost or abandoned, or are in the course of being reduced into possession; but

(b) *not* including mushrooms growing wild on any land or flowers, fruit or foliage of a plant growing wild on any land.

The term 'mushroom' includes any fungus and 'plant' includes shrubs and trees.

Thus, 'property' is defined by CDA 1971, s 10 in a similar way to the definition of that term in TA 1968 for the purposes of theft. One difference is that land itself, which gen-erally cannot be stolen, is not subjected to any limits on when it can be the subject of criminal damage. A man who moves his fence to capture a little of his neighbour's lawn cannot be convicted of theft of that piece of lawn, but he would be guilty of criminal damage if he damaged it. Another difference is that intangible things, such as copy-right, cannot be the subject of criminal damage although they may be stolen. A third difference is that wild mushrooms and wild flowers, etc can never be the subject of *criminal* damage, although they can be stolen in certain circumstances. The provisions of the Wildlife and Countryside Act 1981 (see Appendix 4 contained in the companion website to this book <http://www.oup.com/>) offer protection to some wild creatures and plants in circumstances which would include forms of damage.

Belonging to another

The class of persons to whom property is treated for the purposes of CDA 1971 as belonging by s 10(2) to (4) is by no means limited to the owners of property, but includes a range of other people with a connection with it.

Section 10(2) provides that property is to be treated as belonging to any person:

(a) having the custody or control of it;

(b) having in it any proprietary right or interest (not being an equitable interest arising only from an agreement to transfer or grant an interest); or

(c) having a charge on it.

If D hires his boat to X for a week, X thereby obtains the custody or control of it. If D intentionally or recklessly destroys or damages the boat without lawful excuse while it is in X's custody or control, D can be convicted of criminal damage against X. If A damaged the boat during the week, A would commit criminal damage against D and X,

Co-owners of property each have a proprietary right or interest in the property and if one damages the property he may be convicted of criminal damage since the property 'belongs to another'. The adjective 'proprietary' excludes those with what might be described as a second-generation interest, such as insurance companies which, although they have an interest in the property, do not have a proprietary interest.

Finally, persons having a charge on property have a proprietary interest in it. The best example of a charge is where, to buy his house, a house owner mortgages it by way of charge to a building society. As a result of the present provision, the house will belong to the building society, as well as to the house owner, and if the house owner intentionally or recklessly damages it without lawful excuse he can be convicted of criminal damage, since the house will 'belong to another'.

CDA 1971, s 10(3) and (4) provides that, as in the case of theft, where property is subject to a trust, the person to whom it belongs shall include any person having the right to enforce the trust; and that property belonging to a corporation sole (see p 922) is to be treated as belonging to the corporation notwithstanding a vacancy in the corporation.

Mens rea

To do an act deliberately, eg deliberately throwing a stone, is not enough; D must have intended his conduct to result in property belonging to another being destroyed or damaged, or been reckless as to the risk of such destruction or damage resulting from his conduct.

A person acts recklessly as to whether or not any property belonging to another would be destroyed or damaged when he is aware that a risk will occur, and it is (in the circumstances known to him) unreasonable to take the risk.

Without lawful excuse

In order to commit an offence under CDA 1971, s 1(1) or s 1(1) and (3), D must destroy or damage another's property 'without lawful excuse'. D does not have the burden of proof in respect of a lawful excuse, only an evidential burden. For these purposes, s 5(2) provides that a person is to be treated as having a lawful excuse if he acted with one of two types of belief.

Belief in consent

Section 5(2)(a) provides that a person has a lawful excuse if, at the time of the act or acts alleged to constitute the offence, he believed that the person or persons whom he believed to be entitled to consent to the destruction of or damage to the property had so consented, or would have so consented if he or they had known of the destruction or damage and its circumstances.

If a business firm was altering its premises and, in the course of doing so, was clearing some old buildings from a yard at the rear, an employee who demolished a valuable building on the site would have a lawful excuse for doing so if he believed that he had been given permission by the foreman when given the general direction, 'Clear that yard at the back'. The test is whether his belief was honest, although the more reasonable the belief was the more likely it is that the justices or jury would find that it was honestly held. If no such direction had been given, but the worker honestly believed that he would have been given permission by the foreman had he asked, this would still amount to lawful excuse.

Belief in defence of property

Section 5(2)(b) provides that a person is to be treated as having a lawful excuse if he destroyed or damaged the property in question in order to protect his own property or that of some other person, or a right or interest (such as a right of way) in property which was or which he believed to be vested in himself or another, *and* at the time of the act he believed that the property, right or interest was in immediate need of protection, and at that time he believed that the means of protection adopted or proposed to be adopted were reasonable having regard to all the circumstances. It is immaterial whether or not the threatened harm which the defendant sought to prevent was unlawful or lawful.

The property intended to be protected, unlike that damaged, need not be tangible; it can also consist of a right or privilege in or over land, whether created by grant, licence or otherwise. Just as a person is entitled in appropriate circumstances to shoot a dog attacking his sheep, so he is entitled to demolish a wall barring a right of way which he has (or believes he has). Because a person is not 'property', breaking down a door to recover a child who is being unlawfully detained does not fall within the defence of 'lawful excuse' under s 5(2).

The defence under s 5(2)(b) involves the following four elements:

(1) *D must have destroyed or damaged the property in question in order to protect property or a right or interest in it.* Whether or not he did so depends on an objective test: 'Whatever D's state of mind and assumption on honest belief, can it be said that what D did was done in order to protect particular property?' This was stated by the House of Lords in a case where D had set fire to bedding in an isolated part of a sheltered accommodation in order, D said, to demonstrate that the fire alarm was not working and thereby to protect the building from the risk posed to it. Applying the above test, the House of Lords held that it admitted of only one answer: D's act was not done to protect the building; it was not an act which in itself protected or was capable of protecting property.

(2) *The property must belong to D or another.* D cannot rely successfully on s 5(2)(b) if what he seeks to protect is neither property belonging to himself or another nor a right or interest in property which is (or which he believes is) vested in himself or another. This was the crucial point in a case where D went onto farmland and destroyed badger traps in order to protect wild badgers. A divisional court held

that D could not rely on s 5(2)(b) because the badgers, being wild and not reduced into possession, did not belong to anyone.

(3) *D must believe that the property or right or interest is in need of immediate protection.* The Court of Appeal has held that whether D believes that the property, etc is in need of protection is a subjective question. On the other hand, it has been held that whether the property, etc is in need of 'immediate' protection is an objective question, to be determined by the court or jury in the light of all the circumstances as D believed them to be.

(4) *D must believe that the means adopted were reasonable.* A divisional court has held that this is a purely subjective question. The question is not whether the means adopted by D were objectively reasonable having regard to the circumstances, but whether D believed them to be so.

Lawful excuse in a general sense

Quite apart from the statutory instances of lawful excuse provided by CDA 1971, s 5, any other defence recognised by law amounts to a lawful excuse. A police officer, in executing a search warrant, may, if denied entry, break a lock, thereby committing damage. He would fall outside s 5(2)(a) or (b), but nevertheless he would have a lawful excuse for his actions because the statutes under which search warrants may be granted authorise entry by force, if necessary. Other examples of lawful excuses besides those provided s 5 are self-defence and the defence of another.

On the other hand, a belief in a moral entitlement is not a lawful excuse, nor is a belief that the destruction or damage was reasonable in pursuit of some political objective, nor is a belief that in damaging property one is carrying out God's instructions.

RACIALLY OR RELIGIOUSLY AGGRAVATED CRIMINAL DAMAGE

A person commits an offence under the Crime and Disorder Act 1998, s 30(1) if he commits an offence under CDA 1971, s 1(1) which is racially or religiously aggravated.

An offence of criminal damage is racially or religiously aggravated if:

(a) at the time of committing it, or immediately before or after doing so, the offender demonstrates towards the person to whom the property belongs or is treated as belonging for the purposes of CDA 1971 hostility based on that person's membership (or presumed membership) of a racial or religious group; or

(b) the offence is motivated (wholly or partly) by hostility towards members of a racial or religious group based on their membership of that group.

For this purpose, in (a) 'membership of a racial or religious group' includes association with members of that group, and 'presumed' means presumed by the offender. A 'racial group' means a group of persons defined by reference to race, colour, nationality (including citizenship) or ethnic or national origins. A 'religious group' is a group of persons defined by reference to religious belief or lack of religious belief.

Although (a) requires proof of what D did at the time of committing the offence, (b) can be established by evidence relating to what D may have said or done on other occasions (since such evidence may be relevant to D's motivation at the time of the offence).

See pp 687–9 for further explanation of racial or religious aggravation.

DESTROYING OR DAMAGING PROPERTY WITH INTENT TO ENDANGER LIFE OR RECKLESSNESS AS TO LIFE BEING ENDANGERED

CDA 1971, s 1(2) declares that it is an offence for a person without lawful excuse to destroy or damage any property, whether belonging to himself or another:

(a) intending to destroy or damage any property or being reckless as to whether any property would be destroyed or damaged; *and*

(b) intending the destruction or damage to endanger the life of another or being reckless as to whether the life of another would thereby be endangered.

An offence under s 1(2) is generally described as aggravated criminal damage.

By s 1(3), an offence committed under s 1(2) by destroying or damaging property by fire is required to be charged as arson and is charged as contrary to s 1(2) and (3).

There are four separate offences under s 1(2):

(a) criminal damage with intent to endanger life;

(b) criminal damage reckless as to whether life would be endangered;

(c) arson with intent to endanger life; and

(d) arson reckless as to whether life would be endangered.

It is, of course, open to the prosecution to charge more than one count, alleging different offences in the above list, for example one alleging an offence committed with intent to endanger life and another an offence committed recklessly as to such endangerment.

An offence under CDA 1971, s 1(2) (or s 1(2) and (3)) can be committed in respect of property which 'belongs' only to the defendant (D), and the reason for this can easily be appreciated. The essence of the offence is the endangering of life and life can as easily be endangered in D's own dwelling house as in other property. If D sets fire to his house which 'belongs' only to him with his wife asleep inside it, D can be charged under s 1(2) and (3).

Except for the fact that the property need not belong to another, the actus reus of an offence under s 1(2) is the same as under s 1(1).

In terms of mens rea, D must either have intended to destroy or damage the property or been reckless in that respect. D must additionally have intended that the destruction or damage would endanger someone's life, or been reckless as to whether human life would be endangered by the destruction or damage, depending on the terms of the indictment.

'Recklessness' is used in the same sense as in CDA 1971, s 1(1) and this is not just in relation to the risk of property being destroyed or damaged but also in relation to the risk that another's life may thereby be endangered. Thus, as far as recklessness is concerned, the question is whether D was aware that such a risk existed and it was, in the circumstances known to him, unreasonable to take that risk.

D must have intended to endanger life, or been reckless as to whether life would be endangered, *by the destruction or damaging* of property which he intentionally or recklessly caused; it is not enough that he merely intended to endanger life, or was reckless as to whether life would be endangered, by the act which caused the destruction or damage. Consequently, a person who fires a gun from outside a house at a person standing behind a window in it cannot be convicted under s 1(2), even though he intended to endanger that person's life, if he did not intend the damaging of the window to endanger life (and was not reckless as to that damage doing so).

An offence under s 1(2), or s 1(2) and (3), is close to the offence of attempted murder in many respects. The difference lies in the distinction between the intention to kill required for attempted murder and the intention to endanger life or recklessness as to whether life is endangered required for the present offences.

The provisions in s 5(2) about lawful excuse do not apply to the present offences. 'Lawful excuse' for an offence under s 1(2), or s 1(2) and (3), is therefore restricted to those defences recognised under the general law, such as self-defence and defence of another.

THREATS TO DESTROY OR DAMAGE PROPERTY

Threats to destroy or damage property are dealt with under CDA 1971, s 2 which states that a person who without lawful excuse makes to another a threat, intending that that other would fear it would be carried out:

(a) to destroy or damage any property belonging to that other or a third person; or

(b) to destroy or damage his own property in a way which he knows is likely to endanger the life of that other or a third person,

is guilty of an offence.

The threat must be to do something which would be an offence against CDA 1971, s 1. It must be carried out with the intention of inducing a fear in the mind of the recipient that it would be carried out. It does not matter how the threat is communicated; a letter, a telephone call, or threat in person or by any other means of communication suffices. It does not matter that the person who offers the threat does not intend to carry it out, provided that he intends to create the fear that he would do so in the mind of the recipient. Nor does it matter that the recipient is not actually put in fear by the threat.

Someone who communicates the threat of an explosion to another person, intending that the recipient will fear that the threat will be carried out, commits the present offence if the threat is concerned with destruction or damage to property, etc. There is often confusion with the bomb hoax offences created by the Criminal Law Act 1977, s 51(2) (see p 656) which deals with the offence of communicating false information to induce such a fear. That offence is distinguished from the one under CDA 1971, s 2 by its limitations to false information whereas the offence under s 2 can be committed whether or not the threat involves false information.

The provisions of CDA 1971, s 5(2) relating to 'lawful excuse' apply (with a minor modification) to threats to destroy or damage another's property but do not apply to threats to destroy or damage the threatener's own property in a way likely to endanger the life of some person.

POSSESSING WITH INTENT

The possession of things to be used for the purpose of causing damage is dealt with by CDA 1971, s 3 which states that a person who has anything in his custody or under his control intending without lawful excuse to use or cause or permit another to use it:

(a) to destroy or damage any property belonging to some other person; or

(b) to destroy or damage his own or the user's property in a way which he knows is likely to endanger the life of some other person,

is guilty of an offence.

As can be seen, the possession of the 'thing' must be for the purpose of doing something (or causing or permitting something to be done) which would be an offence under CDA 1971, s 1. There must be a clear intention to use the thing in such a way or to cause or permit another to do so; it is not sufficient to prove that D realised that it 'might' be so used. Provided that such an intention does exist it is immaterial that there is no immediate intention to use it but only a conditional one. A terrorist group which possesses explosives in a warehouse, intending to use them to destroy or damage property if, and when, the opportunity arises can therefore be convicted of the present offence.

'Possession' is covered in s 3 by the use of 'in his custody or under his control'. These precise terms cover the same situations as possession but their use avoids the technicalities of the concept of 'possession'. The explosives contained in a warehouse might be in the custody of the keeper of that warehouse but they might also be under the control of the leaders of the terrorist group, who can order their removal and use at any time.

The offence as described is sufficient to include instances of possession of a terrorist arsenal, the possession of pickaxe handles by protection racketeers, or even the possession of paint or sprays by those who intend to endorse graffiti on the walls of buildings.

Where the offence involves an intent falling within (a), ie to destroy or damage another's property, 'without lawful excuse' is subject to CDA 1971, s 5(2) (with a minor modification), but where the intent falls within (b), ie to destroy or damage property in a way known to be likely to endanger life, it is not.

POLICE POWERS

CDA 1971, s 6 empowers a justice, following information given on oath, to grant a search warrant if there is reasonable cause to believe that a person has in his custody or under his control or on his premises anything which there is reasonable cause to believe *has been* used, or is *intended for use*, without lawful excuse to destroy or damage property belonging to another or to destroy or damage property in a way likely to endanger the life of another.

If such a search warrant is granted, a constable may enter (if need be by force) any premises and search for the thing in question. He may seize anything which he believes to have been used or to be intended to be used as aforesaid.

SALE OF AEROSOL PAINT TO A CHILD

Although this is not an offence against CDA 1971 it is most conveniently dealt with here. The Anti-social Behaviour Act 2003, s 54(1) makes it an offence for a person to sell an aerosol paint container to a person under the age of 16.

It is a defence for a person to show that he took all reasonable steps to determine the purchaser's age and that he reasonably believed that the purchaser was not under 16. Where the sale was effected by another person it is a defence to prove that the defendant took all reasonable steps to avoid the commission of the offence.

COMPUTER MISUSE

The misuse of computer hardware or software may involve one or more of the offences described elsewhere in this book.

In addition, the misuse of computer hardware or software may involve one or more of three indictable (either way) offences under the Computer Misuse Act 1990 (CMA 1990):

(a) unauthorised access to computer material;
(b) unauthorised access with intent to commit or facilitate further offence; or
(c) unauthorised access with intent to impair, or with recklessness as to impairing, the operation of a computer, etc.

Unauthorised access to computer material

By CMA 1990, s 1(1), a person commits an offence if:

(a) he causes a computer to perform any function with intent to secure access to any program or data held in any computer;
(b) the access he intends to secure or to enable to be secured is unauthorised; and
(c) he knows at the time when he causes the computer to perform the function that this is the case.

The scope of this offence is wide, since it covers all forms of computer hacking. On the other hand, the offence does not cover computer eavesdropping; mere surveillance of data displayed on a VDU screen does not trigger it, since D must cause the computer to perform a function if he is to be guilty.

Actual access to any program or data held in a computer is not required, since it is enough that D simply causes a computer to perform a function with intent to secure access to a program or data held in it, such intended access being unauthorised to his knowledge.

A person intends to secure access to a program or data if he intends, by causing a computer to perform any function, to:

(a) alter or erase the program or data;
(b) copy or move it to any storage medium other than that in which it is held or to a different location in the storage medium in which it is held;
(c) use it; or
(d) have it output from the computer in which it is held (whether by having it displayed or in any other manner).

The intended access need not relate to any particular program or data, nor any particular type of program or data, nor to a program or data held in any particular computer. It is immaterial whether the program or data is unauthorisedly accessed directly from the computer containing it or indirectly via another computer. Intent to secure access to a program or data is to be understood accordingly.

The requirement in s 1 that the intended access be unauthorised means that all computer hackers are caught, including those 'computer enthusiasts' who seek access merely because of the challenge of breaking through a security system designed to restrict access.

Access of any kind by any person to a program or data held in a computer is unauthorised if:

(a) he is not himself entitled to control access of the kind in question to the program or data; and
(b) he does not have consent to access by him of the kind in question to the program or data from any person who is so entitled.

Because the definition refers to 'access of the kind' in question, a person who has authority to view data may nevertheless unauthorisedly access it if he accesses it to alter or copy it if he has no authority to access for such a purpose.

Unauthorised access with intent to commit or facilitate further offence

By CMA 1990, s 2(1), a person commits an offence if he commits the unauthorised access offence under s 1 with intent:

(a) to commit an offence to which s 2 applies; or
(b) to facilitate the commission of such an offence (whether by himself or by any other person).

CMA 1990, s 2 applies to murder, and to any offence whose sentence is fixed by law or for which an offender of 21 or over may be sentenced to imprisonment for five years (eg fraud, theft, forgery and criminal damage).

It is immaterial whether the further offence is to be committed on the same occasion as the unauthorised access offence or on any future occasion, and it is also immaterial that the facts are such that the commission of the further offence is impossible.

Unauthorised acts with intent to impair, or with recklessness as to impairing, operation of computer, etc

By CMA 1990, s 3(1), a person is guilty of an offence if:

(a) he does any unauthorised act in relation to a computer;
(b) at the time when he does the act he knows that it is unauthorised; and
(c) either s 3(2) or 3(3) (below) applies.

For the purposes of s 3:

(a) a reference to doing an act includes a reference to causing an act to be done;
(b) 'act' includes a series of acts.

An act is unauthorised if the person doing the act (or causing it):

(a) is not himself a person who has responsibility for the computer and is entitled to determine whether the act should be done; and
(b) does not have consent to the act from any such person.

Although the owner of a computer which is able to receive email is ordinarily to be taken to consent to the sending of emails to the computer, such implied consent is not without limits. For example, a divisional court has held, it does not extend to emails which are not sent for the purpose of communicating with the owner, but are sent as a 'mail bombing campaign' for the purpose of interrupting the proper operation and use of the system.

Section 3(2) applies if the person intends by doing the act:

(a) *to impair the operation of any computer;*
(b) *to prevent or hinder access to any program or data held in the computer; or*
(c) *to impair the operation of any such program or the reliability of any such data.*

'Impairing, preventing or hindering' something includes doing so temporarily.

An example of s 3(2) would be where someone, by misusing or bypassing a password, places in the files of a computer a bogus email pretending that the password holder was the author; such an addition would result in an unauthorised alteration of the contents of the computer and would clearly be done with intent to cause an alteration of the contents, and by so doing to impair the reliability of the data on the computer.

Section 3(3) applies if the person is reckless as to whether the act will do any of the things italicised above. A person will be reckless as to one of these resulting from his act if he foresees the risk that it might result but carries on with his act, thereby taking an unjustified risk of the thing occurring.

The intention or recklessness referred to in s 3(2) or (3) above need not relate to any particular computer or any particular program or data, or a program or data of any particular kind.

Section 3 criminalises the intentional or reckless impairment of a computer system by unauthorised inputting, transmitting, damaging, deleting, deteriorating, altering, suppressing or rendering inaccessible computer data. Thus, inter alia, programs which generate denial of service (eg by intentionally overloading the Internet Service Provider of a website with emails), or malicious codes such as viruses, are prohibited.

Making, supplying or obtaining articles for use in an offence against CMA 1990, ss 1 or 3

CMA 1990, s 3A provides indictable (either way) offences preparatory to an offence under ss 1 or 3. It states that a person commits an offence in the following three cases if:

(a) he makes, adapts, supplies or offers to supply any article intending it to be used to commit, or to assist in the commission of, an offence against ss 1 or 3;
(b) he supplies or offers to supply any article believing that it is likely to be so used; or
(c) he obtains any article with a view to it being supplied for such use.

'Article' includes any program or data held in electronic form, and therefore includes a computer password or other means by which a computer system may be accessed.

These offences are aimed at 'hacker tools' which are increasingly being used in connection with organised crime.

Where a charge alleges supplying or offering to supply a quantity of articles it will be necessary to prove that charge in relation to a particular article or a particular number of articles. It will not suffice to prove that a person believed that a proportion of the articles was likely to be used in connection with an offence against s 1 or 3.

CHAPTER 38

Offences Against Administration of Justice

With two exceptions indicated at the appropriate points, the offences described in this chapter are indictable. Besides perjury and perverting the course of justice, all these indictable offences are triable either way.

ASSISTING OFFENDERS

The Criminal Law Act 1967 (CLA 1967), s 4(1) provides that, where a person has committed a relevant offence, another person is guilty of an offence if (knowing or believing him to be guilty of the offence, or of some other relevant offence) without lawful authority or reasonable excuse that person does any act with intent to impede his apprehension or prosecution. A 'relevant offence' is (a) an offence for which the sentence is fixed by law (murder is the prime example); (b) an offence for which a person of 18 years or over (not previously convicted) may or might be sentenced to a term of imprisonment for a term of five years. Such a person is not guilty, as an accomplice, of the relevant offence which has been committed, because this conduct occurs after its commission; the offence under s 4(1) is a separate offence. By way of example, if D knows that his friend, E, has committed an offence of murder and, with intent to impede the arrest or prosecution of E, disposes of the gun used by E to commit the murder, D is guilty of the offence under s 4.

Although the *commission* of the 'relevant offence' by the principal offender (E) must be proved, it is not necessary that E should have been convicted of it. Indeed, the acquittal of E does not prevent a conviction of D for assisting that person; the commission of the relevant offence by E may be established in the case of D, even though it is not established against E himself, eg because evidence admissible against D was not admissible against E, or because, after E's acquittal, but before D's trial, the discovery of further evidence puts the commission of the offence by E beyond doubt.

CONCEALING OFFENCES

This offence is governed by CLA 1967, s 5(1), which provides that, where a person has committed a relevant offence (as defined above), another person is guilty of an offence if he, knowing or believing that the offence or some other relevant offence has been committed, and that he has information which might be of assistance in securing the prosecution or conviction of an offender for it, accepts or agrees to accept for not disclosing it any consideration other than the making good of loss or injury caused by the offence, or the making of reasonable compensation for it.

Prosecutions for offences contrary to CLA 1967, ss 4 or 5 may only be instituted by or with the consent of the DPP.

WASTEFUL EMPLOYMENT OF POLICE

The CLA 1967, s 5(2) states that it is an offence for a person to cause any wasteful employment of the police by knowingly making to any person a false report tending to show that an offence has been committed or that the informant has any information material to any police inquiry, or giving rise to apprehension for the safety of any persons or property. The offence is not indictable.

The Criminal Justice and Police Act 2001 provides that this is a 'penalty offence' in respect of which a 'penalty notice' may be given: see p 31.

PERJURY

The Perjury Act 1911 (PA 1911), s 1(1) provides that it is an offence for any person, lawfully sworn as a witness or interpreter in a judicial proceeding, to wilfully make a statement material in that proceeding which he knows to be false or does not believe to be true.

A 'person lawfully sworn' includes a person who has made an affirmation or declaration that he will tell the truth. A 'judicial proceeding' is a proceeding before any court, tribunal or person having by law power to hear, receive and examine evidence on oath. The presence of the word 'wilfully' means that it must be proved that the person concerned made that statement deliberately. A 'material statement' is one which might affect the decision of the court.

By the Youth Justice and Criminal Evidence Act 1999, s 29, this offence applies to an intermediary (see p 229) as it applies to an interpreter lawfully sworn in a judicial proceeding.

PA 1911, s 13 states that a person shall not be convicted of perjury or any other offence under PA 1911 solely on the evidence of one witness as to the falsity of any statement alleged to be false, so that there is a requirement of corroboration in this respect.

Subornation of perjury

PA 1911, s 7(1) provides that a person who aids, abets, counsels, procures or suborns (ie procures by bribery or other corrupt means another to commit perjury) is liable for perjury 'as if he were a principal offender'. This provision is redundant since it adds nothing to the criminal liability which would otherwise be imposed under the principles of aiding, abetting, counselling or procuring an offence.

OFFENCES AKIN TO PERJURY

False unsworn statement

The Youth Justice and Criminal Evidence Act 1999, s 57(1) and (2) provides that an unsworn witness commits an offence if he wilfully gives false evidence in such circumstances that, had the evidence been given on oath, he would have been guilty of perjury. The offence is not indictable.

False written statements tendered in evidence in criminal proceedings

By the Criminal Justice Act 1967, s 89(1), a person is guilty of an offence if in criminal proceedings, by virtue of s 9 of that Act (p 241), he wilfully makes a written statement material in those proceedings which he knows to be false or does not believe to be true.

False statements on oath made otherwise than in a judicial proceeding

If any person:

(a) being required or authorised by law to make any statement on oath for any purpose, and being lawfully sworn (otherwise than in a judicial proceeding), wilfully makes a statement which is material for that purpose and which he knows to be false or does not believe to be true; or
(b) wilfully uses any false affidavit for the purposes of the Bills of Sale Act 1878,

he is guilty of an offence under PA 1911, s 2.

False statutory declaration and other false statements without oath

Under PA 1911, s 5, a person commits an offence if he knowingly and wilfully makes, otherwise than on oath, a statement false in a material particular, and the statement is made:

(a) in a statutory declaration; or
(b) in an abstract, account, balance sheet, book, certificate, declaration, entry, estimate, inventory, notice, report, return, or other document which he is authorised or required to make, attest, or verify by any statute for the time being in force; or
(c) in any oral declaration or oral answer which he is required to make by, under, or in pursuance of any statute for the time being in force.

PERVERTING THE COURSE OF JUSTICE

The common law offence of perverting the course of justice may be committed by any act or series of acts which has a tendency to pervert the course of justice and is intended to do so. Police officers may be prosecuted for this offence if they carry out such acts which are intended to defeat or pervert the due course of justice.

The course of justice may be perverted, for example, by discontinuing a criminal prosecution in return for payment; making false statements to police officers investigating an offence; making a false complaint to the police capable of being taken seriously, whether or not it identifies particular individuals; retracting a truthful allegation of an offence, or truthful evidence; interfering with a witness or a juror; producing fabricated evidence; and destroying evidence of an offence to hamper an investigation (actual or potential).

INTIMIDATION OF WITNESSES, JURORS, AND OTHERS
Intimidation, etc before or during a criminal trial

The Criminal Justice and Public Order Act 1994 (CJPOA 1994), s 51(1) provides that a person commits an offence if:

(a) he does an act which intimidates, and is intended to intimidate, another person (the victim);

(b) he does the act knowing or believing that the victim is assisting in the investigation of an offence or is a witness or potential witness, or a juror or potential juror, in proceedings for an offence; and

(c) he does it thereby intending to cause the investigation or the course of justice to be obstructed, perverted or interfered with.

In respect of the requirement of the doing of an act which intentionally results in another person being intimidated, it is immaterial that the act is done otherwise than in the presence of the victim, or to a person other than the victim.

The Court of Appeal has held that 'intimidation' includes not only putting a person in fear by threat or violence, whether to persons or property, but also seeking to deter someone from some relevant action by an improper threat or violence which did not cause fear or deter that person. A threat need not necessarily be a threat of violence, because it can be of a financial nature, but mere pressure is insufficient.

Section 51(1) does not require that the person who is intimidated be actually assisting in the investigation of an offence at the time, or be a witness or potential witness, or a juror or potential juror, in proceedings for an offence. It is sufficient that D believes that the person so intimidated is involved in that way. There must, however, be an investigation in progress; it is insufficient that D believed that such an investigation was taking place. An 'investigation into an offence' means an investigation by the police or other persons charged with the duty of investigating offences or charging offenders.

D must intend, by the intimidating act done to the other person, to cause the investigation or the course of justice to be perverted, obstructed or interfered with. However, in this respect, CJPOA 1994, s 51(7) provides that if it is proved that such an act was done with the required knowledge or belief, it must be presumed, unless the contrary is proved, that D did the act with the required intention. Thus, in such circumstances, the onus is upon D to show that he did not have such an intention.

Reprisals against witnesses, jurors and others in criminal cases

CJPOA 1994, s 51(2) provides that a person commits an offence if:

(a) he does an act which harms, and is intended to harm, another person or, intending to cause another person to fear harm, he threatens to do an act which would harm that other person;

(b) he does or threatens to do the act knowing or believing that the person harmed or threatened to be harmed (the victim), or some other person, has assisted in the investigation into an offence or has given evidence or particular evidence in proceedings for an offence, or has acted as a juror or concurred in a particular verdict in proceedings for an offence; and

(c) he does or threatens to do it because of that knowledge or belief.

It must be shown that D did (or threatened to do) something to another person, which results in harm (or would result in harm) to that other person. It is immaterial that the act is or would be done, or that the threat is made, otherwise than in the presence of the victim, or to a person other than the victim. There is no requirement that the other person is actually intimidated thereby. The remaining points which have to be proved are similar to those already discussed in relation to s 51(1). The act carried out or threatened must be intended to harm that person.

The harm which may be done or threatened may be financial as well as physical (whether to the person or a person's property). The Court of Appeal has held that, financial harm aside, 'harm' means physical harm, and not, eg, simply spitting at someone.

Proof of knowledge or belief that the other person, or some other person, has assisted in an investigation or has given evidence, etc is also required.

Lastly, it must be proved that D did, or threatened to do, the act because of what he knows or believes about the assisting in an investigation or the giving of evidence, etc. In this respect, s 51(8) provides that if it is proved that within the 'relevant period':

(a) D did an act which harmed, and was intended to harm, another person; or
(b) intending to cause another person fear of harm, he threatened to do an act which would harm that other person,

and that he did the act, or (as the case may be) threatened to do the act, with the knowledge or belief required by s 51(2)(b), then D is presumed, unless the contrary is proved, to have done the act, or (as the case may be) threatened to do the act, because of that knowledge or belief.

For the purposes of this presumption, the 'relevant period' in relation to:

(a) *a witness or juror*, begins with the institution of proceedings and ends with the first anniversary of the conclusion of the trial, or of any appeal;
(b) *a person who has assisted in the investigation of an offence (or is believed by D to have done so) but who was not a witness in proceedings for an offence*, is the period of one year beginning with the act (or believed act) which assisted the investigation; and
(c) *a person who has assisted in the investigation of an offence (or is believed by D to have done so) and was also a witness in proceedings for an offence*, is the period beginning with the act (or believed act) which assisted in the investigation and ending with the first anniversary of the conclusion of the trial, or of any appeal.

General

CJPOA 1994, s 51(5) provides that the intention/motive required (in either case) need not be the only or predominating intention/motive with which the act is done or threatened. This should exclude defences based upon the fact that the primary intention of the perpetrator was to avoid a miscarriage of justice.

CORRESPONDING PROVISIONS IN RESPECT OF CIVIL PROCEEDINGS

The Criminal Justice and Police Act 2001 (CJPA 2001), ss 39 and 40 provide for the protection of witnesses in proceedings, other than those in respect of an offence, which take place before the Court of Appeal, the High Court, the Crown Court, a county court or a magistrates' court. The offences provided by ss 39 and 40 shadow those set out in this chapter with the exception that they refer to 'relevant proceedings', a term which means proceedings which are not proceedings for an offence.

Intimidation

A person commits an offence against s 39(1) if he commits similar acts to those set out in CJPOA 1994, s 51(1), but those acts are related to actual or potential witnesses in 'relevant proceedings' but not to actual or potential members of juries (which are extremely rare in civil cases). In such a case, the act must be done knowing or believing that the victim is, or may be, a witness in such proceedings and with the intention to cause the course of justice to be obstructed, perverted or interfered with. Proof that D intended the course of justice to be obstructed, perverted or interfered with is aided by a rebuttable presumption corresponding to that under CJPOA 1994, s 51(7).

Harming witnesses

A person commits an offence against s 40(1) and (2) if he commits similar acts to those set out in CJPOA 1994, s 51(2), but those acts are related to witnesses in 'relevant proceedings'. In such a case, the act must be done knowing or believing that some person (whether or not the person harmed or threatened or the person against whom harm is threatened) has been a witness in such proceedings and D must do or threaten to do the act because of that knowledge or belief. Proof that D did, or threatened, the act because of that belief is aided by a rebuttable presumption corresponding to that under CJPOA 1994, s 51(8).

CHAPTER 39

Preventive Justice

The preceding chapters have referred to various specific statutory offences of inciting, or arranging to do, something, which are specifically aimed at nipping crime in the bud. In addition, legislation provides general statutory offences of encouraging or assisting crime, conspiracy to commit an offence, and attempt to commit an offence. The common law offence of conspiracy also survives.

ENCOURAGING OR ASSISTING CRIME

The Serious Crimes Act 2007 (SCA 2007), s 59 abolished the common law offence of incitement and SCA 2007, Part 2 (ss 44 to 67) introduced three offences of encouraging or assisting crime which are committed by persons who do an act capable of encouraging or assisting the commission of an offence with certain intentions or beliefs.

The three offences are:

Intentionally encouraging or assisting an offence

A person commits an offence against SCA 2007, s 44 if:

(a) he does an act capable of encouraging or assisting the commission of an offence other than encouraging or assisting suicide; and
(b) he intends to encourage or assist its commission.

The reference to the doing of an act includes a reference to a failure to act, the continuation of an act already begun and an attempt to do an act (except an act amounting to the commission of the offence of attempting to commit another offence).

Encouraging or assisting an offence believing it will be committed

A person commits an offence against SCA 2007, s 45 if:

(a) he does an act capable of encouraging or assisting the commission of an offence; and
(b) he believes that the offence will be committed and that his act will encourage or assist its commission.

For this offence, it need not be proved that the defendant (D) intended to encourage or assist the commission of the offence which his act is capable of assisting or encouraging. Instead, it is sufficient to prove that D believed that an act would be done which would amount to the commission of that offence and that his act would encourage or assist the doing of that act.

In reckoning whether (for the purposes of s 45) an act is capable of encouraging or assisting the commission of an offence, specified offences are to be disregarded. As a result, a person cannot be guilty under s 45 of encouraging a specified offence. The offences specified are:

(a) an offence under SCA 2007, ss 44, 45 or 46, and
(b) an offence listed in SCA 2007, Sch 3, Parts 1, 2, or 3 (mainly various statutory offences of incitement already referred to in this book). They also include the following offences:
   (i) solicitation of murder (Offences Against the Person Act 1861, s 4);
   (ii) encouraging or assisting suicide (Suicide Act 1961, s 2(1));
   (iii) assisting an offender (Criminal Law Act 1967, s 4(1));
   (iv) concealing an offence for reward (Criminal Law Act 1967, s 5(1));
   (v) statutory conspiracy (Criminal Law Act 1977, s 1(1));
   (vi) common law conspiracy; and
   (vii) criminal attempt (Criminal Attempts Act 1981, s 1(1)).

It is sufficient if D believes that the offence will be committed once certain conditions are met. Thus, if D encourages E to beg some money from V and tells him that, if V refuses, E should take some money from V by force, D can be convicted under s 45 of encouraging or assisting robbery because D believes that the offence (of robbery) will be committed if certain conditions are met (ie V refuses to hand over money).

If it is alleged under s 45 that D believed that an offence would be committed and that his act would encourage or assist its commission, it is sufficient to prove that D believed:

- that an act would be done which would amount to the commission of that offence; and
- that his act would encourage or assist the doing of that act.

The reference to the doing of an act includes a reference to a failure to act, the continuation of an act already begun and an attempt to do an act (except an act amounting to the commission of the offence of attempting to commit another offence).

Encouraging or assisting an offence believing one or more will be committed

By SCA 2007, s 46, a person commits an offence if:

(a) he does an act capable of encouraging or assisting the commission *of one or more of a number of offences*; and
(b) he believes:
   (i) that one or more of those offences will be committed (but has no belief as to which), and
   (ii) that his act will encourage or assist the commission of one or more of them.

It is immaterial for the purposes of (b)(ii) whether the person has any belief as to which offence will be encouraged or assisted. The Court of Appeal has held that s 46 should only be used when it may be that D, at the time of doing the act, believes that one or more of, for example, *either* offence X, *or* offence Y, *or* offence Z will be committed, but has no belief as to which one or ones of the three will be committed.

An offence under ss 44, 45 or 46, or an offence under Sch 3, Parts 1, 2, or 3 (above), is to be disregarded in reckoning whether an act is capable of encouraging or assisting the commission of one or more of a number of offences.

If it is alleged under (b) that D believed that one or more of a number of offences would be committed and that his act would encourage or assist the commission of one or more of them, it is sufficient to prove that D believed that one or more of a number of acts would be done which would amount to the commission of one or more of those offences; and that his act would encourage or assist the doing of one or more of those acts. The reference to the doing of an act includes a reference to a failure to act, the continuation of an act already begun and an attempt to do an act (except an act amounting to the commission of the offence of attempting to commit an offence).

Points relating to ss 44 to 46 in general

Act capable of encouraging or assisting

SCA 2007, s 65 provides that the reference to a person's doing an act that is capable of encouraging the commission of an offence includes a reference to his doing so by:

(a) threatening another person or otherwise putting pressure on another person to commit the offence;

(b) taking steps to reduce the possibility of criminal proceedings being brought in respect of that offence; or

(c) failing to take reasonable steps to discharge a duty.

However, it also provides that a person is not to be regarded as doing an act that is capable of encouraging or assisting the commission of an offence merely because he fails to respond to a constable's request for assistance in preventing a breach of the peace.

Further provisions about mens rea

SCA 2007, s 47(5) sets out the mens rea that must be proved under ss 44, 45 or 46 if an offence that it is alleged D intended or believed would be committed requires proof of mens rea as to circumstances or consequences. It provides that, in proving whether an act or omission is one which, if done, would amount to the commission of an offence:

(a) if the offence is one requiring proof of fault, it must be proved that:
    (i)   D believed that, were the act to be done, it would be done with that fault,
    (ii) D was reckless as to whether or not it would be done with that fault, or
    (iii) D's state of mind was such that, were he to do it, it would be done with that fault; and

(b) if the offence is one requiring proof of particular circumstances or consequences, it must be proved that:
    (i)   D believed that, were the act to be done, it would be done in those circumstances or with those consequences, or
    (ii) D was reckless as to whether or not it would be done in those circumstances or with those consequences.

In the case of an offence under s 44, (b)(i) is to be read as if the reference to 'D believed' were a reference to 'D intended or believed'.

It follows from (a) that, if an offence that D is alleged to have intended or believed would be encouraged or assisted requires mens rea, D must believe or be reckless to the possible consequence that, if the act encouraged or assisted is done, it would be done with the necessary mens rea by the person encouraged or assisted, or (by (a)(iii)) D must have the necessary mens rea for that offence. The latter point is important where

D thinks that the other person will lack the mens rea. Thus, the offences under ss 44, 45 or 46 apply to the encouragement or assistance of an innocent agent. Section 47(6) provides that, for the purposes of (a)(iii), D is assumed to be able to do the act in question. Thus, D cannot escape liability in respect of (a)(iii) simply because it is impossible for him to commit the offence encouraged or assisted. Suppose that D (a woman) encourages E to penetrate V with his penis, believing that if E were to do so it would be without V's consent. D knows that E will reasonably believe that V is consenting if E acts on D's encouragement. Although a woman cannot perpetrate rape, D can be convicted of encouraging or assisting rape.

It follows from (b) that a requirement to prove mens rea on D's part applies in respect of any circumstances or consequences of the actus reus of the offence that D is alleged to have intended or believed would be encouraged or assisted, and that this is so even though that offence is one of strict liability as to that particular element. For example, the offence of driving a motor vehicle on a road or other public place with excess alcohol, contrary to the Road Traffic Act 1988, s 5, is one of strict liability, for which no mens rea is required. If D asks E to drive him to the station, in ignorance that E has been drinking and is 'over the limit', D cannot be convicted of an offence of encouraging or assisting crime (the only relevant one would be that under s 44) because he neither believes that E is over the limit, nor is he reckless of the consequence that if E complies with his request he would prove to be over the limit, despite the fact that if E did drive D as requested E would commit the substantive offence.

In the case of an offence under s 46 it is sufficient to prove the matters referred to in s 47(5) by reference to one offence only.

Commission of offence encouraged or assisted not required

SCA 2007, s 49 provides that D may be guilty of offences under ss 44, 45 or 46 whether or not any offence capable of being encouraged or assisted is in fact committed. Thus, an offence under ss 44, 45 or 46 is complete on the giving of the encouragement or assistance.

Where, however, the offence encouraged or assisted by D is *committed*, an offence under ss 44, 45 or 46 exists alongside D's liability for that offence as a party to it, referred to in Chapter 1.

Defence of acting reasonably

SCA 2007, s 50 provides that D is not guilty of an offence under ss 44, 45 or 46 if he proves that (a) he knew certain circumstances existed, and that it was reasonable for him to act as he did in those circumstances; or (b) he reasonably believed certain circumstances to exist, and it was reasonable for him to act as he did in the circumstances as he believed them to be.

The factors which might be considered include, in determining whether it was reasonable for a person to act as he did: the seriousness of the anticipated offence; any purpose for which he claims to have been acting; and any authority by which he claims to be acting. However, there might be other factors which would be equally relevant.

Protective offences: victims not liable

In the case of 'protective offences' D does not commit an offence under SCA 2007, ss 44, 45, or 46 if he falls within the category of a 'protected person' and he is the person in respect of whom the offence is committed or would have been committed. A 'protective offence' is one that exists (wholly or partly) for the protection of a particular category of persons. Many of the offences included in the Sexual Offences Act 2003 exist to protect a child. Thus, where a child encourages a man to commit a sexual offence against her, that child is not guilty of an offence of encouraging or assisting that offence, as she would be considered to be a victim of that offence should it take place and the legislation was fashioned to protect her. Nor could she be convicted as an accomplice to the sex offence itself if it was committed.

Mode of trial

An offence under ss 44 or 45 is triable in the same way as the anticipated offence. An offence under s 46 is only triable on indictment.

Application of other provisions

By SCA 2007, s 54 any provision in other legislation which:

(a) requires the consent to a prosecution of the DPP or some other person;
(b) confers a power to prosecute;
(c) confers a power of seizure;
(d) confers a power of forfeiture of property,

in relation to a substantive offence, also applies to the offence of encouraging or assisting that offence.

CONSPIRACY: INTRODUCTION

There are two offences of conspiracy:

(1) It is a *statutory* offence to agree with any other person or persons to commit an offence. Statutory conspiracy is governed by the Criminal Law Act 1977 (CLA 1977).
(2) It is a *common law* offence to agree to defraud or, to the extent that the conduct agreed on would not amount to or involve an offence if carried out by a single person, to engage in conduct which tends to corrupt public morals or outrages public decency. Prior to CLA 1977, an agreement to commit an offence or an agreement to do certain other things was a common law conspiracy but that Act abolished common law conspiracy except to the extent just stated.

Both types of conspiracy are only triable on indictment. They require a concluded agreement between two or more people. It is not sufficient for one person to have spoken in the presence of another of his intention to commit a crime, for example; that other person must agree with him that the crime be committed. Immediately such an agreement has been reached, the offence of conspiracy is complete; no steps need be taken in furtherance of it, although it will usually be most unlikely that the conspiracy will be discovered or capable of proof if no further steps are taken. A party cannot escape liability for conspiracy by withdrawing from the agreement.

STATUTORY CONSPIRACY

CLA 1977, s 1(1) provides that if a person agrees with any other person or persons that a course of conduct shall be pursued which, if the agreement is carried out in accordance with their intentions, either:

(a) will necessarily amount to or involve the commission of any offence or offences by one or more of the parties to the agreement (s 1(1)(a)); or

(b) would do so but for the existence of facts which render the commission of the offence or any of the offences impossible (s 1(1)(b)),

he is guilty of conspiracy to commit the offence or offences in question.

The effect of s 1(1)(a) is that a person commits statutory conspiracy if he agrees with any other person or persons *that a course of conduct shall be pursued which, if the agreement is carried out in accordance with their intentions, will necessarily amount to or involve the commission of an offence or offences by one or more of the parties to the agreement.* Special provision is made by CLA 1977, s 1(1)(b) for the case where the criminal objective is impossible, and this is dealt with shortly.

The key issue under s 1(1)(a) is whether, when the agreement is made, the course of conduct agreed on by the parties will necessarily amount to or involve the commission of an offence by one or more of them if it is carried out in accordance with their intentions. Thus, if D1 and D2 agree to have intercourse with a woman without her consent, there is a statutory conspiracy to rape because the course of conduct agreed on—penile penetration—will necessarily amount to the commission of rape if it was carried out in accordance with their intentions, namely to have penile penetration with a woman without her consent.

The offence which the agreed course of conduct will necessarily amount to or involve may be of any type, including (with one exception) a summary offence. By CLA 1977, s 1A, s 1(1) applies in certain cases to an agreement to pursue a course of conduct outside England and Wales which would amount to an offence under the law of the country concerned.

The exceptional case referred to above is provided by the Trade Union and Labour Relations (Consolidation) Act 1992, s 242. It is that where, in pursuance of any agreement, the acts constituting the offence are to be done in contemplation or furtherance of a trade dispute, that offence is not an 'offence' for the purposes of conspiracy if it is triable only summarily and *not* punishable with imprisonment. This exemption is provided to remove the potential danger of conspiracy charges in relation to the many minor offences which might be committed by union members in the course of a dispute, for example, simple obstructions of highways.

Impossibility

CLA 1977, s 1(1)(b) deals with agreements which are impossible of fulfilment. It provides that an agreement on a course of conduct which, if the agreement is carried out in accordance with the parties' intentions, would necessarily amount to or involve the commission of an offence or any offences by one or more of the parties *but for the existence of facts which render the commission of the offence or any of the offences impossible* is a statutory conspiracy. This is a sensible provision; the essence of the offence is hatching a plot to commit a crime and this is not made less blameworthy because the actual commission of that crime is rendered impossible because of some fact.

As a result of s 1(1)(b), it is clear, for example, that D1 and D2 can be convicted of conspiracy to murder even though their intended victim was already dead when they agreed to kill him.

Mens rea

At least two parties to the agreement must share the mens rea set out below.

If the actus reus of the substantive offence (ie the agreed offence) requires the existence of a fact or circumstance, a defendant and at least one other party to the agreement (X) must intend or know that it shall or will exist.

There cannot be a statutory conspiracy unless there are at least two parties to an agreement who intend that the agreement be carried out and that the offence they are alleged to have conspired to commit be committed. Surprisingly, because it does violence to the wording of CLA 1977, s 1(1), the House of Lords has held that an individual party to an agreement can be convicted of conspiracy, even though he did not intend that it be carried out and the offence intended by the other parties be committed. In practice this ruling has been ignored and the courts require an intention that the agreement be carried out and that the offence be committed to be proved against an individual defendant.

A defendant and at least one other party (X) must have any additional mens rea (eg dishonesty and an intent permanently to deprive on a charge of conspiracy to steal) required for the substantive offence.

If these requirements are satisfied, it is no defence to allege ignorance that the course of conduct agreed on was a criminal offence.

Exemptions from liability for statutory conspiracy

CLA 1977, s 2 provides the following exemptions:

(a) a person cannot be guilty of a conspiracy to commit any offence if he or she is the intended victim of that offence;
(b) a person is not guilty of a conspiracy to commit any offence if the *only* other person or persons with whom he or she agrees (both initially and at all times during the currency of the agreement) is or are:
  (i)   his or her spouse or civil partner,
  (ii) under the age of criminal responsibility (ie under 10), or
  (iii) an intended victim or victims of the substantive offence.

COMMON LAW CONSPIRACY

As already explained, the only types of common law conspiracy which now exist are conspiracy to defraud and, to the extent that the conduct agreed on would not amount to or involve an offence if carried out by a single person, conspiracy to engage in conduct which tends to corrupt public morals or outrages public decency. A husband and wife (but not civil partners) are not guilty of common law conspiracy if they are the only parties to the agreement.

Conspiracy to defraud requires further explanation. There can be a conspiracy to defraud without any element of deception since it is sufficient to prove an agreement by dishonesty to deprive a person of something which is his (or to which he is or would be or might be entitled) or an agreement by dishonesty to injure some proprietary right of his. Where the intended victim of an agreement is a person performing public duties, as distinct from a private individual, there can also be a conspiracy to defraud if the agreement is dishonestly to deceive such a person into acting contrary to his duty (eg in granting a licence or giving information). The causing of economic loss or prejudice, or (as the case may be) the deceiving of a public official into acting contrary to his duty, need not be the purpose of the parties to the agreement, since it suffices if they have dishonestly agreed to bring about a state of affairs which they realised would or might have such a result.

Clearly, the definition of conspiracy to defraud is wide enough to cover cases where the object of the agreement would itself be an offence as well as those where the object would not be criminal. Agreements to steal, or to forge, and so on, may, of course, be prosecuted as statutory conspiracies to steal, etc but, by virtue of the Criminal Justice Act 1987, s 12, they may instead be charged as common law conspiracies to defraud, since they satisfy the definition of conspiracy to defraud.

ATTEMPT

The Criminal Attempts Act 1981 (CAA 1981) abolished the common law offence of attempt and replaced it by a statutory, indictable offence of attempt (which is triable either way). CAA 1981, s 1(1) provides that if, with intent to commit an offence to which CAA 1981, s 1 applies, a person does an act which is more than merely preparatory to the commission of the offence, he is guilty of attempting to commit the offence.

The offences to which CAA 1981, s 1 applies are described by s 1(4) which provides that s 1 applies to any offence which, if completed, would be triable in England and Wales as an indictable offence, except:

(a) conspiracy (whether common law or statutory);
(b) aiding, abetting, counselling, procuring or suborning the commission of an offence;
(c) offences under the Criminal Law Act 1967, s 4(1) (assisting offenders) or s 5(1) (concealing offences); and
(d) encouraging or assisting suicide under the Suicide Act 1961, s 2(1).

It follows that all attempts to commit indictable offences, other than those specified above, are offences contrary to s 1 but attempts to commit summary offences are not. However, it should be noted that a number of statutes providing summary offences also provide specific offences of attempt in relation to them.

Mens rea

The requirement of mens rea plays a particularly important role in the crime of attempt because whether or not a particular act amounts to an attempt might well hinge on the intent with which it is done. For example, to strike a match near a haystack might or might not be attempted arson of a haystack, depending on whether there is an intent to set fire to the haystack or to light a cigarette: the intent colours the act.

The mens rea specified by CAA 1981, s 1(1) is an 'intent to commit an offence to which this section [ie s 1] applies' and which the defendant (D) is alleged to have attempted. This apparently straightforward statement needs further explanation since 'an intent to commit the offence attempted' may involve a number of mental states.

D must, of course, intend to commit an act or to continue with a series of acts which, when successfully completed, will amount to or lead to an offence. In addition, if the crime attempted requires some consequence to result from his conduct, D must *intend* to cause that consequence. This is so even though some other type of mens rea (eg recklessness) is required or suffices for the full offence. This requirement of mens rea in attempt can be illustrated as follows:

(1) On a charge of attempted murder, it must be proved that D intended the unlawful death of another human being. By way of comparison, if D had actually killed someone he could be convicted of murder merely because he intended his act unlawfully to cause grievous bodily harm to another person.

(2) On a charge of attempted criminal damage, it must be proved that D intended the destruction or damaging of property belonging to another, even though if D had actually destroyed or damaged that property he could have been convicted of criminal damage if he was reckless as to the risk that his act might possibly have this effect.

Where the actus reus of the crime attempted includes some circumstance, such as the fact that the goods handled are stolen in handling stolen goods, D will have sufficient mens rea as to that circumstance on a charge of attempt if he knew or believed that that circumstance existed. Moreover, where some lesser mental state as to a circumstance suffices for the full offence or no mental state as to it is required at all, recklessness as to it suffices on a charge of attempt. This rule can mean that the requirements on an attempt charge are greater than on a charge for the full offence. For example, on a charge of attempting to commit the offence of rape of a child under 13, which offence does not require mens rea as to age, it must be proved not only that D had decided to have intercourse with the girl concerned but also that he knew or was reckless as to the fact that she was under 13.

The requirement that D must intend to commit the offence attempted means that D must have any other mental element, additional to mens rea as to the elements of the actus reus of the crime attempted, required for that crime. Thus, to be convicted of attempted theft D must not only have intended to appropriate the property belonging to another but have acted dishonestly and with intent permanently to deprive the 'owner' of it.

Actus reus

CAA 1981, s 1(1) requires 'an act that is *more than merely preparatory* to the commission of the offence', ie the full offence which D intends to commit.

The 'more than merely preparatory' formula is not limited to 'last act' cases, ie cases where D has done the last act towards the commission of the full offence which, to his knowledge, it was necessary for him to do in order to commit the full offence, even though something more remains to be done by another, innocent, person, since it *can* be satisfied where D still has to take some further step or steps himself before the full offence can be committed by him. In this context it must be emphasised that the question is not whether D has done an act which was more than preparatory but whether D has done an act which was *more than merely* preparatory. Appeal courts have held that if D has got as far as having embarked on the commission of the offence (ie 'on the job'), there is sufficient evidence to leave to the jury of an act *more than merely* preparatory to the commission of the intended crime.

Examples of cases where a judge has held that there is or is not sufficient evidence of a more than merely preparatory act are as follows.

A case where there was sufficient evidence was where D had got into V's car and pointed a loaded firearm at him. V managed to disarm him. D was charged with attempted murder. The trial judge rejected a submission that there was insufficient evidence to leave to the jury the question of whether D had done a more than merely preparatory act. That submission had been based on the argument that at least three more preparatory acts would have had to be carried out by D before the substantive offence was committed, ie remove the safety catch, put his finger on the trigger and pull it. D appealed unsuccessfully against conviction for attempted murder. The Court of Appeal held that, although D's earlier acts prior to entering V's car could only be regarded as preparatory, once D had got into V's car, taken out the loaded firearm and pointed it at V there was sufficient evidence to leave to the jury of a more than merely preparatory act.

In another case, the evidence was that the defendants had equipped themselves with oxyacetylene equipment, driven to the scene, concealed the oxyacetylene equipment in a hedge, approached a barn door and bent down to examine a heavy padlock. The Court of Appeal said that there had been sufficient evidence to leave to the jury the question of whether the defendants had done an act which was more than merely preparatory to committing burglary.

In contrast, the Court of Appeal thought that there was not sufficient evidence of a more than merely preparatory act to committing robbery where D had been arrested, armed with an imitation firearm, as he approached within a yard of the door of a post office where he intended to commit a robbery.

The same conclusion was reached in a case where D was seen in the boys' lavatory block in a school. He was in possession of a rucksack which contained a large kitchen knife, lengths of rope and a roll of masking tape. He was charged with attempted false imprisonment. The Court of Appeal said that there was not much room for doubt about D's intention and there was clear evidence of preparation, but there was no evidence that he had even put himself in a position to commit an offence and he had had no contact or communication with, nor had confronted, any pupil. There was therefore no evidence of an act which was more than merely preparatory to an act of false imprisonment. The Court said that the question was whether a defendant had actually tried to commit the offence in question or whether he had merely got ready to do so. 'Trying to commit the offence' seems to be a stricter test than 'having embarked on the commission of the offence'.

More recently, a divisional court has held that opening a car door with the intent to drive home did not amount to evidence capable of amounting to a more than merely preparatory act of driving while under the influence of drink. The court said that on such facts D could not be said to have embarked on the offence of drink-driving; that stage would only have been reached if D had done something that was part of putting the car in motion, eg turning on the engine.

Impossibility

CAA 1981, s 1(2) provides that a person may be guilty of attempting to commit an offence to which s 1 applies, even though the facts are such that the commission of the offence is impossible. Therefore, a person who attempts to murder by an inadequate dosage of poison is guilty of attempted murder.

Section 1(3) purports to reinforce the rule in s 1(2), by declaring that where:

(a) apart from s 1(3) a person's intention would not be regarded as having amounted to an intent to commit an offence; but

(b) if the facts of the case had been as that person believed them to be, his intention would have been so regarded,

he is to be regarded as having an intent to commit that offence.

By virtue of s 1(2) and (3), a person who intends to kill another by shooting him in a bed, but who discovers after he has fired the shot that the assumed and intended victim was a pillow, can be convicted of attempted murder. The application of s 1(2) and (3) is also illustrated by a case where the House of Lords held that there was an attempt where D had been arrested carrying a package which he believed to contain either heroin or cannabis. In fact, the package did not contain a controlled drug but a harmless substance. The House of Lords held that D had properly been convicted of attempting to commit the offence of knowingly being concerned in dealing with a drug the importing of which was prohibited. He had had an intent to commit the offence in question and, with that intent, he had done an act which was more than merely preparatory to the commission of that intended offence (since he had to be judged on the facts as he believed them to be).

Other statutory offences of attempt

CAA 1981, s 3 applies the provisions of the Act to other existing statutory attempts to commit offences, by stating that the same provisions apply to those attempts. Section 3 therefore ensures a common approach to all offences of attempted crime, even where the specific offence of attempt is created by a particular statute and even where that specific offence relates to a summary offence.

Online Supplements

As a result of the large amount of legislation which continues to be made, the increasing size of *Police Law* edition by edition has become a concern. A further increase in size is not sustainable. It has been necessary to exclude from the body of the book a few topics of marginal importance to police officers. However, those excluded topics, revised as necessary, will be dealt with on the companion website to *Police Law* <http://www.oup.com/>.

The online supplements available for *Police Law* are:

Appendix 1 Public Service Vehicles
Appendix 2 Goods Vehicles
Appendix 3 Aliens
Appendix 4 Animals, Birds, and Plants
Appendix 5 Game, Deer, and Fish

Please visit the companion website to sign up for access to these supplements, as well as any legislative updates available during the course of the 13th edition.

Index